Lecture Notes in Artificial Intelligence   2711

Edited by J. G. Carbonell and J. Siekmann

Subseries of Lecture Notes in Computer Science

Springer
Berlin
Heidelberg
New York
Barcelona
Hong Kong
London
Milan
Paris
Tokyo

Thomas Dyhre Nielsen
Nevin Lianwen Zhang (Eds.)

Symbolic and Quantitative Approaches to Reasoning with Uncertainty

7th European Conference, ECSQARU 2003
Aalborg, Denmark, July 2-5, 2003
Proceedings

Springer

Series Editors

Jaime G. Carbonell, Carnegie Mellon University, Pittsburgh, PA, USA
Jörg Siekmann, University of Saarland, Saarbrücken, Germany

Volume Editors

Thomas Dyhre Nielsen
Aalborg University, Department of Computer Science
Fredrik Bajersvej 7E, 9220 Aalborg, Denmark
E-mail: tdn@cs.auc.dk

Nevin Lianwen Zhang
Hong Kong University of Science and Technology
Department of Computer Science
Clear Water Bay Road, Kowloon, Hong Kong, China
E-mail: lzhang@cs.ust.hk

Cataloging-in-Publication Data applied for

A catalog record for this book is available from the Library of Congress

Bibliographic information published by Die Deutsche Bibliothek
Die Deutsche Bibliothek lists this publication in the Deutsche Nationalbibliographie;
detailed bibliographic data is available in the Internet at <http://dnd.ddb.de>.

CR Subject Classification (1998): I.2, F.4.1

ISSN 0302-9743
ISBN 3-540-40494-5 Springer-Verlag Berlin Heidelberg New York

Springer-Verlag Berlin Heidelberg New York,
a member of BertelsmannSpringer Science+Business Media GmbH

http://www.springer.de

© Springer-Verlag Berlin Heidelberg 2003
Printed in Germany

Typesetting: Camera-ready by author, data conversion by PTP-Berlin GmbH
Printed on acid-free paper   SPIN: 10928769   06/3142   5 4 3 2 1 0

Preface

Since 1991, the European Conference on Symbolic and Quantitative Approaches to Reasoning with Uncertainty (ECSQARU) has been a major forum for advances in the theory and practice of reasoning and decision making under uncertainty. The scope of ECSQARU is wide and includes, but is not limited to, fundamental issues, representation, inference, learning, and decision making in qualitative and numeric paradigms. The first ECSQARU conference (1991) was held in Marseilles, and since then it has been held in Granada (1993), Fribourg (1995), Bonn (1997), London (1999) and Toulouse (2001).

This volume contains the papers that were presented at ECSQARU 2003, held at Aalborg University, Denmark, from July 2 to July 5, 2003. The papers went through a rigorous reviewing process: three program committee members reviewed each paper monitored by an area chair, who made a final recommendation to the program co-chairs. In addition to the regular presentations, the technical program for ECSQARU 2003 also included talks by three distinguished invited speakers: Didier Dubois, Philippe Smets and Jeroen Vermunt. Didier Dubois and Jeroen Vermunt also contributed to this volume with papers on the subjects of their talks.

As a continuation of tradition, an affiliated workshop was held prior to the conference itself. The workshop was entitled "Uncertainty, Incompleteness, Imprecision and Conflict in Multiple Data Sources" and it was organized by Weiru Liu (UK), Laurence Cholvy (France), Salem Benferhat (France) and Anthony Hunter (UK). ECSQARU 2003 also included a special software demo session which was intended to promote software development activities in the area of tools supporting symbolic and quantitative approaches to reasoning with uncertainty. This volume contains two special papers that describe two of the presentations.

Finally, we would like to thank the area chairs, the members of the program committee and all the additional referees for their work. We would also like to thank Regitze Larsen and Lene Mogensen for their help with the organization of the conference.

April 2003

Thomas D. Nielsen
Nevin L. Zhang

Organization

ECSQARU 2003 was organized by the Decision Support Systems group at the Department of Computer Science, Aalborg University, Denmark.

Executive Committee

General Conference Chair:	Finn V. Jensen (Aalborg University, Denmark)
Program Co-chairs:	Thomas D. Nielsen (Aalborg University, Denmark)
	Nevin L. Zhang (Hong Kong University of Science and Technology, China)
Organizing Chair:	Kristian G. Olesen (Aalborg University, Denmark)
Demo Chair:	Anders L. Madsen (Hugin Expert A/S, Denmark)

Area Chairs

Gerd Brewka (Germany)
Luis M. de Campos (Spain)
Khaled Mellouli (Tunisia)
Serafín Moral (Spain)

Simon Parsons (UK)
Henri Prade (France)
Prakash P. Shenoy (USA)

Program Committee

Mokhtari Aïcha (Algeria)
Alain Appriou (France)
Ofer Arieli (Israel)
John Bell (UK)
Salem Benferhat (France)
Philippe Besnard (France)
Claudette Cayrol (France)
Giulianella Coletti (Italy)
Fabio Gagliardi Cozman (Brazil)
Adnan Darwiche (USA)
James P. Delgrande (Canada)
Thierry Denœux (France)
Patrick Doherty (Sweden)
Peter A. Flach (UK)
Angelo Gilio (Italy)
Lluís Godo (Spain)

Jean-Louis Golmard (France)
Michel Grabisch (France)
Andreas Herzig (France)
Anthony Hunter (UK)
Jean-Yves Jaffray (France)
Katsumi Inoue (Japan)
Tomáš Kočka (Denmark)
Jürg Kohlas (Switzerland)
Rudolf Kruse (Germany)
Jérôme Lang (France)
Helge Langseth (Norway)
Laurence Cholvy (France)
Daniel Lehmann (Israel)
Paolo Liberatore (Italy)
Weiru Liu (UK)
Thomas Lukasiewicz (Italy)

Christophe Marsala (France)
Robert E. Mercer (Canada)
Serafín Moral (Spain)
Rui Da Silva Neves (France)
Ilkka Niemelä (Finland)
Ewa Orlowska (Poland)
Odile Papini (France)
José M. Peña (Denmark)
Luís Moniz Pereira (Portugal)
Ramón Pino Pérez (Venezuela)

David Poole (Canada)
Alessandro Saffiotti (Sweden)
Torsten Schaub (Germany)
Romano Scozzafava (Italy)
Milan Studený (Czech Republic)
Marco Valtorta (USA)
Leon van der Torre (The Netherlands)
Jiří Vomlel (Czech Republic)
Mary-Anne Williams (Australia)
Cees Witteveen (The Netherlands)

Additional Referees

Christian Anger
Christian Borgelt
Sylvie Galichet
Joerg Gebhardt
Elias Gyftodimos
Jaakko Hollmen
Eyke Hüllermeier
Joris Hulstijn
Gabriele Kern Isberner

Tomi Janhunen
Reinhard Kahle
Gytis Karciauskas
Kathrin Konczak
Jonathan Lawry
Marie-Hélène Masson
Gilles Mauris
Jeff Paris
Chiaki Sakama

Philippe Smets
Laurent Ughetto
Carlos Uzcátegui
Barbara Vantaggi
Ivan Jose Varzinczak
Marta Vomlelová
Thomas Whalen
Gregory R. Wheeler

Table of Contents

Fuzzy Sets

Possibility Theory

Default Reasoning

Belief Revision and Inconsistency Handling

Logics

Demo Papers

Author Index

Qualitative Decision Rules under Uncertainty

Didier Dubois[1], Hélène Fargier[1], and Régis Sabbadin[2]

[1] IRIT, Université Paul Sabatier
31062 Toulouse Cedex 4, France
{dubois,fargier}@irit.fr
[2] INRA-BIA, Chemin de Borde Rouge, B.P37
31326 Castanet-Tolosan cedex
sabbadin@toulouse.inra.fr

Abstract. This paper is a survey of qualitative decision theory focused on the available decision rules under uncertainty, and their properties. It is pointed out that two main approaches exist according to whether degrees of uncertainty and degrees of utility are commensurate (that is, belong to a unique scale) or not. Savage-like axiomatics for both approaches are surveyed. In such a framework, acts are functions from states to results, and decision rules are used to characterize a preference relation on acts. It is shown that the emerging uncertainty theory in qualitative settings is possibility theory rather than probability theory. However these approaches lead to criteria that are either little decisive due to incomparabilities, or too adventurous because focusing on the most plausible states, or yet lacking discrimination because or the coarseness of the value scale. Some new results overcoming these defects are reviewed. Interestingly, they lead to genuine qualitative counterparts to expected utility.

1 Introduction

Traditionally, decision making under uncertainty (DMU) relies on a probabilistic framework. The ranking of acts is done according to the expected utility of the consequences of these acts. This proposal was made by economists in the 1950's, and justified on an axiomatic basis by Savage [36] and colleagues. More recently, in Artificial Intelligence, this setting has been applied to problems of planning under uncertainty, and is at the root of the influence diagram methodology for multiple stage decision problems. However, in parallel to these developments, Artificial Intelligence has witnessed the emergence of a new decision paradigm called qualitative decision theory, where the rationale for choosing among decisions no longer relies on probability theory nor numerical utility functions [7]. Motivations for this new proposal are twofold. On the one hand, there exists a tradition of symbolic processing of information in Artificial Intelligence, and it is not surprising that this tradition should try and stick to symbolic approaches when dealing with decision problems. Formulating decision problems in a symbolic setting may be more compatible with a declarative expression

T.D. Nielsen and N.L. Zhang (Eds.): ECSQARU 2003, LNAI 2711, pp. 1–21, 2003.
© Springer-Verlag Berlin Heidelberg 2003

of uncertainty and preferences in some logic-based language [3, 39]. On the other hand, the emergence of new technologies like information systems or autonomous robots has generated many new decision problems involving intelligent agents [4] where quantifying preference and belief is neither imperative nor easy.

There is a need for qualitative decision rules. However there is no real agreement on what "qualitative" means. Some authors assume incomplete knowledge about classical additive utility models, whereby the utility function is specified via symbolic constraints ([31, 1] for instance). Others use sets of integers and the like to describe rough probabilities or utilities [38]. Lehmann [33] injects some qualitative concepts of negligibility in the classical expected utility framework. However some approaches are genuinely qualitative in the sense that they do not involve any form of quantification. We take it for granted that a qualitative decision theory is one that does not resort to the full expressive power of numbers for the modeling of uncertainty, nor for the representation of utility.

2   Quantitative and Qualitative Decision Rules

A decision problem is often cast in the following framework [36]: consider set S of states (of the world) and a set X of potential consequences of decisions. States encode possible situations, states of affairs, etc. An act is viewed as a mapping f from the state space to the consequence set, namely, in each state $s \in S$, an act f produces a well-defined result $f(s) \in X$. The decision maker must choose acts without knowing what is the current state of the world in a precise way. The consequences of an act can often be ranked in terms of their relative appeal: some consequences are judged to be better than others. This is often modeled by means of a numerical utility function u which assigns to each consequence $x \in X$ a utility value $u(x) \in r$. Besides, there are two usual approaches to modeling the lack of knowledge of the decision maker about the state. The most widely found assumption is that there is a probability distribution p on S. It is either obtained from statistics (this is called decision under risk) or it is a subjective probability supplied by the agent via suitable elicitation methods. Then the most usual decision rule is based on the expected utility criterion:

$$EU(f) = \Sigma_{s \in S} \, p(s)u(f(s)). \tag{1}$$

An act f is strictly preferred to act g if and only if $EU(f) > EU(g)$. This is by far the most commonly used criterion. It makes sense especially for repeated decisions whose results accumulate. It also clearly presupposes subjective notions like belief and preference to be precisely quantified. It means that, in the expected utility model, the way in which the preference on consequences is numerically encoded will affect the induced preference relation on acts. The model exploits some extra information not contained solely in a preference relation on X, namely, the absolute order of magnitude of utility grades. Moreover the same numerical scale is used for utilities and degrees of probability. This is based on the idea that a lottery (involving uncertainty) can be compared to a sure gain or a sure loss (involving utility only) in terms of preference.

Another proposal is the Wald criterion. It applies when no information about the current state is available, and it ranks acts according to its worst consequence:

$$W^-(f) = \min_{s \in S} u(f(s)). \tag{2}$$

This is a well-known pessimistic criterion. An optimistic counterpart $W^+(f)$ of $W^-(f)$ is obtained by turning minimum into maximum. These criteria do not need numerical utility values. Only a total ordering on consequences is needed. No knowledge about the state of the world is necessary. Clearly this criterion has the major defect of being extremely pessimistic. In practice, it is never used for this reason. Hurwicz has proposed to use a weighted average of $W^-(f)$ and its optimistic counterpart, where the weight bearing on $W^-(f)$ is viewed as a degree of pessimism of the decision maker. Other decision rules have been proposed, especially some that generalize both EU(f) and $W^-(f)$, based on Choquet Integral [29]. However, all these extensions again require the quantification of preferences and/or uncertainty.

Qualitative variants of the Wald criterion nevertheless exist. Boutilier [3] is inspired by preferential inference of nonmonotonic reasoning whereby a proposition p entails another one q by default if q is true in the most normal situations where p is true. He assumes that states of nature are ordered in terms of their relative plausibilities using a complete preordering $\geq$ on S. He proposes to choose decisions on the basis of the most plausible states of nature in accordance with additional information, neglecting other states. If the additional information is that $s \in A$, a subset of states, and if A* is the set of maximal elements in A according to the plausibility ordering $\geq$, then the criterion is defined by

$$W_{\geq}^-(f) = \min_{s \in A*} u(f(s)). \tag{3}$$

This approach has been axiomatized by Brafman and Tennenholtz [5] in terms of conditional policies (rather than acts). Lehmann [33] axiomatizes a refinement of the Wald criterion whereby ties between equivalent worst states are broken by considering their respective likelihood. This decision rule takes the form of an expected utility criterion with qualitative (infinitesimal) utility levels. An axiomatization is carried out in the Von Neumann-Morgenstern style.

Another refinement of Wald criterion, the possibilistic qualitative criterion [18, 17] is based on a utility function u on X and a possibility distribution[19, 42] π on S, both mapping to the same totally ordered scale L, with top **1** and bottom **0**. The ordinal value $\pi(s)$ represents the relative plausibility of state s. A pessimistic criterion $W^-_\pi(f)$ is proposed of the form:

$$W^-_\pi(f) = \min_{s \in S} \max(n(\pi(s)), u(f(s))) \tag{4}$$

Here, L is equipped with its involutive order-reversing map n; in particular $n(\mathbf{1}) = \mathbf{0}$, $n(\mathbf{0}) = \mathbf{1}$. So, $n(\pi(s))$ represents the degree of potential surprise caused by realizing that the state of the world is s. In particular, $n(\pi(s)) = 1$ for impossible states. The value of $W^-_\pi(f)$ is small as soon as there exists a highly plausible state $(n(\pi(s)) = 0)$ with low utility value. This criterion is actually a *prioritized* extension of the Wald criterion $W^-(f)$. The latter is recovered if $\pi(s) = 1$ for all $s \in S$. The decisions are again made according to the merits of acts in their worst consequences, now restricted to the most plausible states. But the set of most plausible states $(S^* = \{s, \pi(s) \geq n(W^-_\pi(f))\})$ now depends on the act itself. It is defined by the compromise between belief and utility expressed in the min-max expression. The possibilistic qualitative criterion presupposes that degrees of utility $u(f(s))$ and possibility $\pi(s)$ share the same scale and can be compared.

The optimistic counterpart of this criterion is [18]:

$$W^+_\pi(f) = \max_{s \in S} \min(\pi(s)), u(f(s)))$$ (5)

This optimistic criterion has been first proposed by Yager [41] and the pessimistic criterion by Whalen [40]. These optimistic and pessimistic possibilistic criteria are actually particular cases of a more general criterion based on the Sugeno integral (a qualitative counterpart of the Choquet integral [29]) one expression of which can be written as follows:

$$S_\gamma(f) = \max_{A \subseteq S} \min(\gamma(A), \min_{s \in A} u(f(s))),$$ (6)

where $\gamma(A)$ is the degree of confidence in event A, and γ is a set-function which reflects the decision-maker attitude in front of uncertainty. If the set of states is rearranged in decreasing order via f in such a way that $u(f(s_1)) \geq \ldots \geq u(f(s_n))$, then denoting $A_i = \{s_1, \ldots, s_i\}$, it turns out that $S_\gamma(f)$ is the median of the set $\{u(f(s_1)), \ldots, u(f(s_n))\} \cup \{\gamma(A_1), \ldots, \gamma(A_{n-1})\}$.

The restriction to the most plausible states, as implemented by the above criteria, makes them more realistic than the Wald criterion, but they still yield coarse rankings of acts (there are no more classes than the number of elements in the finite scale L). The above qualitative criteria do not use all the available information to discriminate among acts. Especially an act f can be ranked equally with another act g even if f is at least as good as g in all states and better in some states (including most plausible ones). This defect cannot be found with the expected utility model. Yet it sounds natural that the following constraint be respected by decision rules :

Pareto-dominance: if $\forall s, u(f(s)) \geq u(g(s))$, and $\exists s, u(f(s)) > u(g(s))$, then f is preferred to g.

The lack of discrimination of the Wald criterion was actually addressed a long time ago by Cohen and Jaffray [6] who improved it by comparing acts on the basis of their worst consequences of *distinct* merits, i.e. one considers only the set $D(f, g) = \{s, u(f(s)) \neq u(g(s))\}$ when performing a minimization. Denoting by $f >_D g$ the strict preference between acts,

$$f >_D g \text{ iff } \min {}_{s \in D(f, g)} u(f(s)) > \min {}_{s \in D(f, g)} u(f(s)) \tag{7}$$

This refined rule always rates an act f better than another act g whenever f Pareto-dominates g. However, only a partial ordering of acts is then obtained. This last decision rule is actually no longer based on a preference functional. It has been independently proposed and used in fuzzy constraint satisfaction problems under the name "discrimin ordering" (see references in [16]).

3 An Ordinal Decision Rule without Commensurateness

Many of the above decision rules presuppose that utility functions and uncertainty functions share the same range, so that it makes sense to write $\min(\pi(s)), u(f(s)))$, for instance. In contrast, one may look for a natural decision rule that computes a preference relation on acts from a purely symbolic perspective, no longer assuming that utility and partial belief are commensurate, that is, share the same totally ordered scale [10]. The decision-maker only supplies a confidence relation between events and a preference ordering on consequences.

In the most realistic model, a confidence relation on the set of events is an irreflexive and transitive relation $>_L$ on 2^S, and a non-trivial one ($S >_L \varnothing$), faithful to deductive inference. $A >_L B$ means that event A is more likely than B. Moreover, if $A \subseteq B$ and $C \subseteq D$, then $A >_L D$ should imply $B >_L C$ [27]. This so-called *orderly property* implies that if $A \subseteq B$, then A cannot be more likely than B. Define the weak likelihood relation $\geq_L$ induced from $>_L$ via complementation, and the indifference relation $\sim_L$ as usual: $A \geq_L B$ iff not ($B >_L A$); and $A \sim_L B$ iff $A \geq_L B$ and $B \geq_L A$.

The preference relation on the set of consequences X is supposed to be a complete preordering. Namely, $\geq_P$ is a reflexive and transitive relation, and completeness means $x \geq_P y$ or $y \geq_P x$. So, $\forall x, y \in X$, $x \geq_P y$ means that consequence x is not worse than y. The induced strict preference relation is derived as usual: $x >_P y$ if and only if $x \geq_P y$ and not $y \geq_P x$. It is assumed that X has at least two elements x and y s.t. $x >_P y$. The assumptions pertaining to $\geq_P$ are natural in the scope of numerical representations of utility, however we do not require that the weak likelihood relation be a complete preordering.

If the likelihood relation on events and the preference relation on consequences are not comparable, a natural way of lifting the pair $(>_L, \geq_P)$ to X^S is as follows: an act f is more promising than an act g if and only if the event formed by the disjunction of states in which f gives better results than g, is more likely than the event formed by the disjunction of states in which g gives results better than f. A state s is more promising for act f than for act g if and only if $f(s) >_P g(s)$. Let $[f >_P g]$ be an event made of all states where f outperforms g, that is $[f >_p g] = \{s \in S, f(s) >_p g(s)\}$. Accordingly, we define the strict preference between acts (>) as follows:

$$f > g \quad \text{if and only if} \quad [f >_p g] >_L [g >_p f];$$

This is the *Likely Dominance Rule* [10]. $f \geq g$ (complete preordering) and $f \sim g$ (incomparability or indifference) stand for not(g > f), and $f \geq g$ and $g \geq f$, respectively. It is the first one that comes to mind when information is only available under the form of an ordering of events and an ordering of consequences and *when the preference and uncertainty scales are not comparable*. Events are only compared to events, and consequences to consequences. The properties of the relations $\geq$, $\sim$, and $>$ on X^S will depend on the properties of $\geq_L$ with respect to Boolean connectives. Note that if $\geq_L$ is a comparative probability ordering then the strict preference relation $>$ in X^S is not necessarily transitive.

Example 1:
A very classical and simple example of undesirable lack of transitivity is when $S = \{s_1, s_2, s_3\}$ and $X = \{x_1, x_2, x_3\}$ with $x_1 >_p x_2 >_p x_3$, and the comparative probability ordering is generated by a uniform probability on S. Suppose three acts f, g, h with $f(s_1) = x_1 >_p f(s_2) = x_2 >_p f(s_3) = x_3$, $g(s_3) = x_1 >_p g(s_1) = x_2 >_p g(s_2) = x_3$, $h(s_2) = x_1 >_p h(s_3) = x_2 >_p h(s_1) = x_3$. Then $[f >_p g] = \{s_1, s_2\}$; $[g >_p f] = \{s_3\}$; $[g >_p h] = \{s_1, s_3\}$; $[h >_p g] = \{s_2\}$; $[f >_p h] = \{s_1\}$; $[h >_p f] = \{s_2, s_3\}$.

The likely dominance rule yields f > g, g > h, h > f. Note that the presence of this cycle does not depend on figures of utility that could be attached to consequences insofar as the ordering of utility values is respected for each state. The undesirable cycle remains if probabilities $p(s_1) > p(s_2) > p(s_3)$ are attached to states, and the degrees of probability remain close to each other (so that $p(s_2) + p(s_3) > p(s_1)$). In contrast the ranking of acts induced by expected utility completely depends on the choice of utility values, even if we keep the constraint $u(x_1) > u(x_2) > u(x_3)$. The reader can check that, by symmetry, any of the three linear orders f > g > h, g > h > f, h > f > g can be obtained by suitably quantifying the utility values of states without changing their preference ranking.

This situation can be viewed as a form of the Condorcet paradox in social choice, here in the setting of DMU. Indeed the problem of ranking acts can be cast in the context of voting. The likely dominance rule is a generalization of the so-called pairwise majority rule, whereby states are identified to voters and acts to candidates to be voted for. It is well-known that the social preference relation is often not transitive and may contain cycles. And that the transitivity of R is impossible under natural requirements on the voting procedure, such as independence of irrelevant alternatives, unanimity, and non-dictatorship. Variants of the pairwise majority rule are commonly found in multicriteria decision-making. However, the likely dominance rule makes sense for any inclusion-monotonic likelihood relation between events and is much more general than the pairwise majority rule even in its weighted version.

Assume now that a decision maker supplies a complete preordering of states in the form of a possibility distribution π on S and a complete preordering of consequences $\geq_P$ on X. Let $>_\Pi$ be the induced possibility relations on events [34, 8]. Namely, denoting max(A) any (most plausible) state $s \in A$ such that $s \geq_\pi s'$ for any $s' \in A$ $A \geq_\Pi B$ if and only if max(A) $\geq_\pi$ max(B). Define the preference on acts in accordance with the likely dominance rule, that is, for acts f and g: $f > g$ iff $[f >_P g] >_\Pi [g >_P f]$; $f \geq g$ iff $\neg(g > f)$. Then, the undesirable intransitivity of the strict preference vanishes.

Example 1 (continued)
Consider again the 3-state/3-consequence example of Section 3. If a uniform probability is changed into a uniform possibility distribution, then it is easy to check that the likely dominance rule yields $f \sim g \sim h$. However, if $s_1 >_\pi s_2 >_\pi s_3$ then

$[f >_P g] = \{s_1, s_2\} >_\Pi [g >_P f] = \{s_3\}$; $[g >_P h] = \{s_1, s_3\} >_\Pi [h >_P g] = \{s_2\}$;

$[f >_P h] = \{s_1\} >_\Pi [h >_P f] = \{s_2, s_3\}$.

So $f > g > h$ follows. It contrasts with the cycles obtained with a probabilistic approach. However the indifference relation between acts is not transitive.

Let us describe the likely dominance rule induced by a single possibility distribution (and the possibilistic likelihood relation it induces). If the decision maker is ignorant about the state of the world, all states are equipossible, and all events but $\emptyset$ are equally possible as well. So, if f and g are such that $[g >_P f] \neq \emptyset$ and $[f >_P g] \neq \emptyset$ hold, then none of $f > g$ and $g > f$ hold as per the likely dominance rule. The case when $[f >_P g] \neq \emptyset$ and $[g >_P f] = \emptyset$ holds is when f Pareto-dominates g. Then, the relation on acts induced by the likely dominance rule reduces to Pareto-dominance. This method, although totally sound, is not decisive at all (it corresponds to the unanimity rule in voting theory).

Conversely, if there is an ordering $s_1, ..., s_n$ of S such that $\pi(s_1) > \pi(s_2) > ... > \pi(s_n)$, then for any A, B such that $A \cap B = \emptyset$, either $A >_\Pi B$ or $B >_\Pi A$. Hence $\forall f \neq g$, either $f > g$ or $g > f$. Moreover this is a lexicographic ranking of vectors $(f(s_1), ..., f(s_n))$ and $(g(s_1), ..., g(s_n))$: $f > g$ iff $\exists k$ such that $f(s_k) >_P g(s_k)$ and $f(s_i) \sim_P g(s_i)$, $\forall i < k$. It corresponds to the procedure: check if f is better than g in the most normal state; if yes prefer f; if f and g give equally preferred results in s_1, check in the second most normal state, and so on recursively. It is a form of dictatorship by most plausible states, in voting theory terms. It also coincides with Boutilier's criterion (3), except that ties can be broken by less normal states.

More generally any complete preordering splits S into a well-ordered partition $S_1 \cup S_2 \cup ... \cup S_k = S$, $S_i \cap S_j = \emptyset$ $(i \neq j)$, such that states in each S_i are equally plausible and states in S_i are more plausible than states in S_j, $\forall j > i$. In that case, the ordering of events is defined as follows: $A >_{\Pi L} B$ if and only if $\min\{i:$ $S_i \cap A \cap B^c\} < \min\{i: S_i \cap B \cap A^c\}$, and the decision criterion is a blending of lexicographic ranking and unanimity among states. Informally, the decision maker proceeds as follows: f and g are compared on the set of most normal states (S_1): if f Pareto-dominates g in S_1, then f is preferred to g; if there is a disagreement in S_1 about the relative performance of f and g then f and g are not comparable. If f and g have equally preferred consequences in each most normal state then the decision maker considers the set of second most normal states S_2, etc. In a nutshell, it is a prioritized Pareto-dominance relation. Preferred acts are selected by focusing on the most plausible states of the world, and a unanimity rule is used on these maximally plausible states. Ties are broken by lower level oligarchies. So this procedure is similar to Boutilier's decision rule in that it focuses on the most plausible states, except that Pareto-dominance is required instead of the Wald criterion, and ties can be broken by subsets of lower plausibility. This decision rule is cognitively appealing, but it has a limited expressive and decisive power. One may refine Boutilier's rule using Wald criterion instead of Pareto-dominance inside the oligarchies of states. It is also easy to imagine a counterpart of the likely dominance rule where expected utility applies inside the oligarchies of states [32]. However reasonable these refined decision rules may look, they need to be formally justified.

4   Axiomatics of Qualitative Decision Theory

A natural question is then whether it is possible to found rational decision making in a purely qualitative setting, under an act-driven framework a la Savage. The Savage framework is adapted to our purpose of devising a purely ordinal approach because its starting point is indeed based on relations and their representation on an interval scale. Suppose a decision maker supplies a preference relation $\geq$ over acts f: $S \to X$. X^S usually denotes the set of all such mappings. In Savage's approach, any mapping in the set X^S is considered as a possible act (even if it is an imaginary one rather than a feasible one). The idea of the approach is to extract the decision maker's confidence relation and the decision maker's preference on consequences from the decision maker's preference pattern on acts. Enforcing "rationality" conditions on the way the decision maker should rank acts then determines the kind of uncertainty theory implicitly "used" by the decision maker for representing the available knowledge on states. It also prescribes a decision rule. Moreover, this framework is operationally testable, since choices made by individuals can be observed, and the uncertainty theory at work is determined by these choices.

As seen in Sects. 2 and 3, two research lines can be followed in agreement with this definition: the relational approach and the absolute approach. Following the relational approach, the decision maker uncertainty is represented by a partial ordering relation among events (expressing relative likelihood), and the utility function is just encoded as another ordering relation between potential consequences of decisions.

The advantage is that it is faithful to the kind of elementary information users can directly provide. The other approach, which can be dubbed the absolute approach [20, 21] presupposes the existence of a totally ordered scale (typically a finite one) for grading both likelihood and utility. Both approaches lead to an act-driven axiomatization of the qualitative variant of possibility theory [19].

4.1   The Relational Approach to Decision Theory

Under the relational approach [10, 12] we try to lay bare the formal consequences of adopting a purely ordinal point of view on DMU, while retaining as much as possible from Savage's axioms, and especially the sure thing principle which is the cornerstone of the theory. However, an axiom of *ordinal invariance* [22], originally due to Fishburn [26] in another context, is added. This axiom stipulates that what matters for determining the preference between two acts is the relative positions of consequences of acts for each state, not the consequences themselves, nor the positions of these acts relative to other acts. More rigorously, two pairs of acts (f, g) and (f', g') such that $\forall s \in S$, $f(s) \geq_P g(s)$ if and only if $f'(s) \geq_P g'(s)$ are called *statewise order-equivalent*. This is denoted (f, g) $\equiv$ (f', g'). It means that in each state consequences of f, g, and of f', g', are rank-ordered likewise. The *Ordinal Invariance* axiom [22] is:

OI: $\forall f, f'$ g, g' $\in X^S$, if (f, g) $\equiv$ (f', g') then (f $\geq$ g iff f' $\geq$ g').

where "iff" is shorthand for "if and only if". It expresses the purely ordinal nature of the decision criterion. It is easy to check that the likely dominance rule obeys axiom OI. This is obvious noticing that if (f, g) $\equiv$ (f', g') then by definition, [f >p g] = {s, f(s) >p g(s)} = [f' >p g'] . More specifically, under OI, if the weak preference on acts is reflexive and the induced weak preference on consequences is complete, the only possible decision rule is likely dominance.

Let A $\subseteq$ S be an event, f and g two acts, and denote by fAg the act such that fAg(s) = f(s) if s $\in$ A, and g(s) if s $\notin$ A. The set of acts is closed under this combination involving acts and events. Under the same assumptions, OI ensures the validity of basic Savage axioms:

S2 (Sure-Tthing Principle): $\forall A$, f, g, h, h', fAh $\geq$ gAh iff fAh' $\geq$ gAh'

Axiom S2 claims that the relative preference between two acts does not depend on states where the acts have the same consequences. In other words, the preference between fAh and gAh does not depend on the choice of h. Conditional preference on a set A, denoted $(f \geq g)_A$, is when $\forall h$, fAh $\geq$ gAh holds (which under S2 is equivalent to $\exists h$, fAh $\geq$ gAh). An event A is said to be null if and only if $\forall f$, g, $(f \geq g)_A$. Any non-empty set of states A on which all acts make no difference is then like the empty set: the reason why all acts make no difference is because this event is considered impossible by the decision maker.

Among acts in X^S are *constant acts* such that: $\exists\, x \in X$, $\forall\, s \in S$, $f(s) = x$. They are denoted fx. It seems reasonable to identify the set of constant acts {fx, $x \in X$} and X. The preference $\geq_p$ on X can be induced from $(X^S, \geq)$ as follows:

$$\forall x, y \in X, x \geq_p y \text{ if and only if } fx \geq fy. \tag{8}$$

This definition is self-consistent provided that the preference between constant acts is not altered by conditioning. This is the third Savage's postulate

S3: $\forall\, A \subseteq S$, A not null, fxAh $\geq$ fyAh, $\forall$ h, if and only if $x \geq_p y$.

The preference on acts also induces a likelihood relation among events. For this purpose, it is enough to consider the set of binary acts, of the form fxAfy, which due to (S3) can be denoted xAy, where $x \in X$, $y \in X$, and $x >_p y$. Clearly for fixed $x >_p$ y, the set of acts {x, y}^{S} is isomorphic to the set of events 2^S. However the restriction of $(X^S, \geq)$ to {x, y}^{S} may be inconsistent with the restriction to {x', y'}^{S} for other choices of consequences $x' >_p y'$. A relative likelihood $\geq_L$ among events can however be recovered, as suggested by Lehmann [32]:

$\forall A, B \subseteq S$, A $\geq_L$ B if and only if xAy $\geq$ xBy, $\forall x, y \in X$ such that $x >_p y$.

In order to get a complete preordering of events, Savage added another postulate:

S4: $\forall x, y, x', y' \in X$ s.t. $x >_p y$, $x' >_p y'$, then xAy $\geq$ xBy iff x'Ay' $\geq$ x'By'.

Under this property, the choice of $x, y \in X$ with $x >_p y$ does not affect the ordering between events in terms of binary acts, namely: A $\geq_L$ B is short for $\exists\, x >_p y$, xAy$\geq$ xBy.

Adopting axiom OI and sticking to a complete and transitive weak preference on acts (axiom **S1** of Savage) leads to problems met in the previous section by the probabilistic variant of the likely dominance rule. The following result was proved [12]:

Theorem: If $(X^S, \geq)$ is a complete preordering satisfying axiom OI, and S and X have at least three non-equally preferred elements, let $>_L$ be the likelihood relation (induced by S4). Then, there is a permutation of elements of S, such that $s_1 >_L s_2 >_L \cdots >_L s_{n-1} \geq_L s_n >_L \varnothing$ and $\forall\, i = 1, \ldots n - 2$, $s_i >_L \{s_{i+1}, \ldots, s_n\}$. Other states s_i such that $i > n$ are impossible ($s_i \sim_L \varnothing$).

If X only has two consequences of distinct values, then such a trivialization is avoided. Nevertheless in the general case where X has more than two non-equally preferred elements, the Ordinal invariance axiom forbids a Savagean decision maker to believe that there are two equally likely states of the world, each of which being more likely than a third state. This is clearly not acceptable in practice. If we analyze the reason why this phenomenon occurs, it is easy to see that the transitivity of $(X^S,$

$\geq$) plays a crucial role, in so far as we wish to keep the sure-thing principle. It implies the full transitivity of the likelihood relation $\geq_L$. Giving up the transitivity of $\geq_L$ suppresses the unnatural restriction of an almost total ordering of states: we are led to a weaker condition:

WS1: $(X^S, >)$ is a partially ordered set equipped with a transitive, irreflexive relation.

As a consequence, if one insists on sticking to a purely ordinal view of DMU, we come up to the framework defined by axioms WS1, S3, and OI, plus a non-triviality axiom (**S5** : $f > g$ for at least two acts). The likelihood relation $>_L$ induced by S4 is then orderly (coherence with set inclusion). Moreover, if X has more than two non equally preferred elements, $>_L$ satisfies the following strongly non-probabilistic property: for any three pairwise disjoint non-null events A, B, C,

$$B \cup C >_L A \text{ and } A \cup C >_L B \text{ imply } C >_L A \cup B. \tag{9}$$

Dropping the transitivity of $\geq$ cancels some useful consequences of the sure-thing principle under S1, which are nevertheless consistent with the likely dominance rule, especially the following unanimity axiom [32]:

U: $(f \geq g)_A$ and $(f \geq g)_{A^c}$ implies $f \geq g$.

If this property is added, null events are then all subsets of a subset N of null states. The likelihood relation can then always be represented by a family of possibility relations. Namely, there is a family $\mathscr{F}$ of possibility relations on S and a complete preordering $\geq_P$ on X such that the preference relation on acts is defined by

$$f > g \text{ iff } \forall >_\Pi \in \mathscr{F}, \ [f >_P g] >_\Pi [g >_P f]. \tag{10}$$

This ordinal Savagean framework actually leads to a representation of uncertainty that is at work in the nonmonotonic logic system of Kraus, Lehmann and Magidor [30], as also shown by Friedman and Halpern [27] who study property (9).

A more general setting starting from a reflexive weak preference relation on acts is used in Dubois et al. [13, 14]. In this framework S3 is replaced by a monotonicity axiom on both sides, that is implied by Savage's framework, namely for any event A:

If $[h >_P f] = S$ and $f \geq g$ then $fAh \geq g$;   If $[g >_P h] = S$ and $f \geq g$ then $f \geq gAh$.

The weak likelihood relation $\geq_L$ can be represented by a single possibility relation if the unanimity property is extended to the disjunction of any two subsets of states, and an axiom of anonymity, stating that exchanging the consequences of two equally plausible states does not alter the decision maker's preference pattern, is added. Then the decision rule described at the end of section 3 is recovered exactly.

The restricted family of decison rules induced by the purely relational approach to the decision problem under uncertainty reflects the situation faced in voting theories where natural axioms lead to impossibility theorems. These results question the very possibility of a purely ordinal solution to this problem, in the framework of transitive and complete preference relations on acts. The likely dominance rule lacks discrimination, not because of indifference between acts, but because of incomparabilities. Actually, it may be possible to weaken axiom OI while avoiding the notion of certainty equivalent of an uncertain act. It must be stressed that OI requires more than the simple ordinal nature of preference and uncertainty (i.e. more than separate ordinal scales for each of them). Condition OI also involves a condition of independence with respect to irrelevant alternatives. It says that the preference $f > g$ only depends on the relative positions of quantities $f(s)$ and $g(s)$ on the preference scale. This unnecessary part of the condition could be cancelled within the proposed framework, thus leaving room for a new family of rules not considered in this paper, for instance involving a third act or some prescribed consequence considered as an aspiration level.

4.2   Qualitative Decision Rules under Commensurateness

Let us now consider the absolute qualitative criteria (4), (5), (6), based on Sugeno integral in the scope of Savage theory. Clearly, they satisfy S1. However the sure thing principle can be severely violated by Sugeno integral. It is easy to show that there may exist f, g, h, h' such that $fAh > gAh$ while $gAh' > fAh'$. It is enough to consider binary acts (events) and notice that, generally if A is disjoint from $B \cup C$, nothing forbids, for a fuzzy measure γ, to satisfy $\gamma(B) > \gamma(C)$ along with $\gamma(A \cup C) > \gamma(A \cup B)$ (for instance, belief functions are such). The possibilistic criteria (4), (5) violate the sure-thing principle to a lesser extent since:

$$\forall A \subseteq S, \forall f, g, h, h', W^-_\pi(fAh) > W^-_\pi(gAh) \text{ implies } W^-_\pi(fAh') \geq W^-_\pi(gAh')$$

And likewise for W^+_π. Moreover, only one part of S3 holds, for Sugeno integrals. The obtained ranking of acts satisfies the following axiom:

WS3: $\forall A \subseteq S, \forall f, x \geq_p y$ implies $xAf \geq yAfy$.

Besides, axiom S4 is violated by Sugeno integrals, but to some extent only. Namely, $\forall x, y, x', y' \in X$ s.t. $x >_p y, x' >_p y'$: $S_\gamma(xAy) > S_\gamma(xBy)$ implies $S_\gamma(x'Ay') \geq S_\gamma(x'By')$, which forbids preference reversals when changing the pair of consequences used to model events A and B. Moreover the strict preference is maintained if the pair of consequences is changed into more extreme ones: If $x' >_p x >_p y >_p y'$ then $S_\gamma(xAy) > S_\gamma(xBy)$ implies $S_\gamma(x'Ay') > S_\gamma(x'By')$. Sugeno integral and its possibilistic specializations are weakly Pareto-monotonic since $\forall f, f \geq_p g$ implies $S_\gamma(f) \geq S_\gamma(g)$, but one may have $f(s) >_p g(s)$ for some state s, while $S_\gamma(f) = S_\gamma(g)$. This is the so-called drowning effect, which also appears in the violations of S4. This is because some states are neglected when comparing acts. The basic properties of Sugeno integrals exploit disjunctive and conjunctive combinations of acts. Namely, given a preference relation $(X^S, \geq)$, and two acts f and g, define $f \wedge g$ and $f \vee g$ as follows

$$f \wedge g \ (s) = f(s) \text{ if } g(s) \geq_P f(s), \text{ and } g(s) \text{ otherwise}$$

$$f \vee g \ (s) = f(s) \text{ if } f(s) \geq_P g(s), \text{ and } f(s) \text{ otherwise}$$

Act $f \wedge g$ always produces the worst consequences of f and g in eact state, while $f \vee g$ always makes the best of them. They are union and intersection of acts viewed as fuzzy sets. Obviously $S_\gamma(f \wedge g) \leq \min(S_\gamma(f), S_\gamma(g))$ and $S_\gamma(f \vee g) \geq \max(S_\gamma(f), S_\gamma(g))$ from weak Pareto monotonicity. These properties hold with equality whenever f or g is a constant act (or when they are comonotonic). These properties are in fact characteristic of Sugeno integrals for monotonic aggregation operators [29]. These properties can be expressed by means of axioms, called restricted conjunctive and disjunctive dominance (RCD and RDD) on the preference structure $(X^S, \geq)$:

Axiom RCD: if f is a constant act, $f > h$ and $g > h$ imply $f \wedge g > h$

Axiom RDD: if f is a constant act, $h > f$ and $h > g$ imply $h > f \vee g$

For instance, RCD means that upper-bounding the potential utility values of an act g that is better than another one h by a constant value that is better than the utility of act h still yields an act better than h. This is in contradiction with expected utility theory. Indeed, suppose g is a lottery where you win 1000 euros against nothing with equal chances. Suppose the certainty equivalent of this lottery is 400 euros, received for sure, and h is the fact of receiving 390 euros for sure. Now, it is likely that, if f represents the certainty-equivalent of g, $f \wedge g$ will be felt strictly less attractive than h as the former means you win 400 euros against nothing with equal chances. Axiom RCD implies that such a lottery should ever be preferred to receiving $400 - \varepsilon$ euros for sure, for arbitrary small values of ε. This axiom is thus strongly counterintuitive in the context of economic theory, with a continuous consequence set X. However the range of validity of qualitative decision theory is precisely when both X and S are finite. Two presuppositions actually underlie axiom RCD (and similar ones for RDD)

1) There is no compensation effect in the decision process: in case of equal chances, winning 1000 euros cannot compensate the possibility of not getting anything. It fits with the case of one-shot decisions where the notion of certainty equivalent can never materialize: you can only get 1000 euros or get nothing if you just play once. You cannot get 400 euros. The latter can only be obtained in the average, by playing several times.

2) There is a big step between one level $\lambda_i \in L$ in the qualitative value scale and the next one λ_{i+1} with $L = \{1 = \lambda_1 > ... > \lambda_n = 0\}$. The preference pattern $f > h$ always means that f is *significantly* preferred to h so that the preference level of $f \wedge g$ can never get very close to that of h when $g > h$. The counterexample above is obtained by precisely moving these two preference levels very close to each other so that $f \wedge g$ can become less attractive than the sure gain h. Level λ_{i+1} is in some sense negligible in front of λ_i.

Sugeno integral and can be axiomatized in the style of Savage [20, 21]. Namely, if the preference structure $(X^S, \geq)$ satisfies S1, WS3, S5, RCD and RDD, then there a finite chain of preference levels L, an L-valued possibility monotonic set-function γ, and an L-valued utility function on the set of consequences X, such that the preference relation on acts is defined by : $f \geq g$ iff $S_\gamma(f) \geq S_\gamma(g)$. Namely, S1, WS3, and S5 imply Pareto-monotonicity. In the representation method, L is the quotient set $X^S/\sim$, the utility value u(x) is the equivalence class of the constant act fx, the degree of likelihood $\gamma(A)$ is the equivalence class of the binary act **1A0**, having extreme consequences.

It is easy to check that the equalities $W^-_\pi(f \wedge g) = \min(W^-_\pi(f), W^-_\pi(g))$ and $W^+_\pi(f \vee g) = \max(W^+_\pi(f), W^+_\pi(g))$ hold with any two acts f and g, for the pessimistic and the optimistic possibilistic preference functionals respectively. The criterion $W^-_\pi(f)$ can thus be axiomatized by strengthening the axioms RCD as follows:

Axiom CD: $\forall f, g, h, f > h$ and $g > h$ imply $f \wedge g > h$ (conjunctive dominance)

Together with S1, WS3, RDD and S5, CD implies that the set-function γ is a necessity measure and so, $S_\gamma(f) = W^-_\pi(f)$ for some possibility distribution π. Similarly, the criterion $W^+_\pi(f)$ can be axiomatized by strengthening the axioms RDD as follows

Axiom DD: $\forall f, g, h, f > h$ and $g > h$ imply $f \wedge g > h$ (disjunctive dominance)

Together with S1, WS3, RCD and S5, DD implies that the set-function γ is a possibility measure and so, $S_\gamma(f) = W^+_\pi(f)$ for some possibility distribution π.

In order to figure out why axiom CD leads to a pessimistic criterion, Dubois Prade and Sabbadin [21] have noticed that it can be replaced by the following property:

$$\forall A \subseteq S, \forall f, g, fAg > g \text{ implies } g \geq gAf \qquad (11)$$

This property can be explained as follows: if changing g into f when A occurs results in a better act, the decision maker has enough confidence in event A to consider that improving the results on A is worth trying. But in this case there is less confidence on the complement A^c than in A, and any possible improvement of g when A^c occurs is neglected. Alternatively, the reason why fAg > g holds may be that the consequences of g when A occurs are very bad and the occurrence of A is not unlikely enough to neglect them, while the consequences of g when A^c occurs are acceptable. Then suppose that consequences of f when A occurs are acceptable as well. Then fAg > g. But act gAf remains undesirable because, even if the consequences of f when A^c occurs are acceptable, act gAf still possesses plausibly bad consequences when A occurs. So, $g \geq gAf$. For instance, g means losing (A) or winning (A^c) 10,000 euros with equal chances according to whether A occurs or not, and f means winning either nothing (A) or 20,000 euros (A^c) conditioned on the same event. Then fAg is clearly safer than g as there is no risk of losing money. However, if (11) holds, then the chance of winning much more money (20,000 euros) by choosing act gAf is neglected because there is still a good chance to lose 10,000 euros with this lottery. This behavior is clearly cautious. An optimistic counterpart to (11) can serve as a substitute to axiom CD for the representation of W^+_π:

$$\forall A \subseteq S, \forall f, g, g > fAg \text{ implies } gAf \geq g \tag{12}$$

5   Toward More Efficient Qualitative Decision Rules

The absolute approach to qualitative decision criteria is simple (especially in the case of possibility theory). It looks more realistic and flexible than the likely dominance rule, but it has some shortcomings. First one has to accept the commensurateness between utility and degrees of likelihood. It assumes the existence of a common scale for grading uncertainty and preference. It can be questioned, although it is already taken for granted in classical decision theory (via the notion of certainty equivalent of an uncertain event). It is already implicit in Savage approach, and looks acceptable for decision under uncertainty (but more debatable in social choice). Of course, the acts are then totally preordered.

But absolute qualitative criteria lack discrimination due to many indifferent acts. They are consistent with Pareto-dominance only in the wide sense. Two acts can be considered as indifferent even if one Pareto-dominates the other. The Sure Thing principle is violated (even if not drastically for possibilistic criteria). The obtained ranking of decisions is bound to be coarse since there cannot be more classes of preference-equivalent decisions than levels in the finite scale used.

Giang and Shenoi [28] have tried to obviate the need for making assumptions on the pessimistic or optimistic attitude of the decision-maker and improve the discrimination power in the absolute qualitative setting by using, as a finite bipolar utility scale, a totally ordered set of possibility measures on a two element set $\{0, 1\}$ containing the values of the best and the worst consequences. This setting leads to simple very natural axioms on possibilistic lotteries. Yet, this criterion has a major drawback: whenever there are two acts with contrasted consequences (respectively a bad or neutral one, and a good or neutral one) that have maximal possibility, then these acts are indifferent.

The drowning effect of the possibilistic criteria can be fixed, in the face of total ignorance as done in eq. (7) on the Wald criterion. This criterion can be further refined by the so-called leximin ordering: The idea is to reorder utility vectors $(u(f(s_1)), \ldots u(f(s_n)))$ by non-decreasing values as $(u(f(s_{\sigma(1)})), \ldots u(f(s_{\sigma(n)})))$, where σ is a permutation such that $u(f(s_{\sigma(1)})) \leq u(f(s_{\sigma(2)})) \leq \ldots \leq u(f(s_{\sigma(1)}))$. Let τ be the corresponding permutation for an act g. Define the leximin criterion $>_{Leximin}$ as follows: f $>_{Leximin}$ g iff $\exists$ k $\leq$ n such that $\forall$ i < k, $u(f(s_{\sigma(i)})) = u(g(s_{\tau(i)}))$ and $u(f(s_{\sigma(k)})) > u(g(s_{\tau(k)}))$.

The two possible decisions are indifferent if and only if the corresponding reordered vectors are the same. The leximin-ordering is a refinement of the discrimin ordering, hence of both the Pareto-ordering and the maximin-ordering [9]: $f >_D g$ implies $f >_{Leximin} g$. Leximin optimal decisions are always discrimin maximal decisions, and thus indeed min-optimal and Pareto-maximal: $>_{Leximin}$ is the most selective among these preference relations. Converse implications are not verified. The Leximin ordering can discriminate more than any symmetric aggregation function, since when, e.g. the sum of $u(f(s_{\sigma(i)}))$'s equals the sum of $u(g(s_{\tau(i)}))$'s, it does not mean that the reordered vectors are the same.

5.1   Additive Refinements of Possibilistic Preference Functionals

Interestingly, the qualitative leximin rule can be simulated by means of a sum of utilities provided that the levels in the qualitative utility scale are mapped to values sufficiently far away from one another on a numerical scale. Consider a finite utility scale $L = \{\lambda_0 < ... < \lambda_m\}$. Let $\alpha_i = u(f(s_i))$, and $\beta_i = u(g(s_i))$ in L. Consider an increasing mapping ψ from L to the reals whereby $a_i = \psi(\alpha_i)$ and $b_i = \psi(\beta_i)$. It is possible to define this mapping in such a way that

$$\min_{i=1,...n} \alpha_i > \min_{i=1,...n} \beta_i \text{ implies } \Sigma_{i=1,...n} a_i > \Sigma_{i=1,...n} b_i \qquad (12)$$

Moreover it can be checked that the leximin ordering comes down to applying the Bernoulli criterion with respect to a *concave* utility function $\psi \circ u$

$$f >_{leximin} g \text{ iff } \Sigma_{i=1,...n} \psi(u(f(s_i))) > \Sigma_{i=1,...n} \psi(u(g(s_i))).$$

The optimistic maximax criterion can be refined similarly by a leximax ordering which can also be simulated by the Bernoulli criterion with respect to a *convex* utility function $\phi \circ u$, using an increasing mapping ϕ from L to the reals

$$f >_{leximax} g \text{ iff } \Sigma_{i=1,...n} \phi(u(f(s_i))) > \Sigma_{i=1,...n} \phi(u(g(s_i))). \qquad (13)$$

The qualitative pessimistic and optimistic criteria under ignorance are thus refined by means of a classical criterion with respect to a risk-averse and risk-prone utility function respectively, as can be seen by plotting L against numerical values $\psi(L)$ and $\phi(L)$. These results have been recently extended to possibilistic qualitative criteria $W^-_\pi(f)$ and $W^+_\pi(f)$ by Fargier and Sabbadin [25]. They refine possibilistic utilities by means of weighted averages, thus recovering Savage five first axioms.

Consider first the optimistic possibilistic criterion $W^+_\pi(f)$ under a possibility distribution π. Let $\alpha_i = u(f(s_i))$, and $\beta_i = u(g(s_i))$. We can again define an increasing mapping ψ from L to the reals such that $\psi(\lambda_m) = 1$ and $\psi(\lambda_0) = 0$, and $\max_i \min(\pi_i, \alpha_i) > \max_i \min(\pi_i, \beta_i)$ *implies* $\Sigma_{i=1,...n} \psi(\pi_i) \cdot \psi(\alpha_i) > \Sigma_{i=1,...n} \psi(\pi_i) \cdot \psi(\beta_i)$

A sufficient condition is that if $\lambda_j \geq \lambda_i$, $\psi(\lambda_i) \cdot \psi(\lambda_j) > \psi(\lambda_{i-1}) \cdot (\psi(\lambda_j) + m \cdot \psi(\lambda_m))$. The following mapping ψ can be chosen , K being a normalization factor:

$$\psi(\lambda_i) = 1/Kn2^{m-i}, i = 1 \dots m.$$

Moreover, let $\{S_1, \dots, S_k\}$ be the well-ordered partition of S induced by π, S_1 containing the most plausible states $n_i = |S_i|$. Suppose $K = \Sigma_{i=1 \dots k} n_i /n^{2^{m-i}}$. Then:

• $\psi O \pi$ is a probability assignment p respectful of the possibilistic ordering of states: p is uniform on equipossible states (the sets S_i). Moreover, if $s \in S_i$ then p(s) is greater than the sum of the probabilities of all less probable states, that is, $p(s) > P(S_{i+1} \cup \dots \cup S_k)$. Such probabilities generalize the so-called "big-stepped" probabilities (when the S_i are singletons [2, 37]).

• $\psi O \mu$ is a big-stepped numerical utility function that can be encoded by a convex real mapping.

• $EU^+(f) = \Sigma_{i=1, \dots n} \psi(\pi_i) \cdot \psi(u(f(s_i)))$ is an expected (big-stepped) utility for a risk-seeking decision-maker, and $W^+_\pi(f) > W^+_\pi(g)$ implies $EU^+(f) > EU^+(g)$.

The pessimistic criterion can be similarly refined. Notice that $W^-_\pi(f ; u, \pi) = n(W^+_\pi (f ; nOu, \pi))$ using the order-reversing map of L. Then, choosing the same mapping ψ as above, one may have $min_i max(\pi_i, \alpha_i) > min_i max(\pi_i, \beta_i)$ *implies* $\Sigma_{i=1, \dots n} \psi(\pi_i) \cdot \phi(u_i) > \Sigma_{i=1, \dots n} \psi(\pi_i) \cdot \phi(v_i)$ where $\phi^*(\lambda_i) = \psi(\lambda_m) - \psi On(\lambda_i)$. $\phi O \mu$ is a big-stepped numerical utility function that can be encoded by a concave real mapping, $EU^-(f) = \Sigma_{i=1, \dots n} \psi(\pi_i) \cdot \phi(u(f(s_i)))$ is an expected (big-stepped) utility for a risk-averse decision-maker, and $W^-_\pi(f) > W^-_\pi(g)$ implies $EU^-(f) > EU^-(g)$.

5.2   Weighted Lexicographic Criteria

The orderings induced by $EU^+(f)$ and $EU^-(f)$ actually correspond to generalizations of leximin and leximax to prioritized minimum and maximum aggregations, thus bridging the gap between possibilistic criteria and classical decision theory. These generalizations are nested lexicographic structures. Note that leximin and leximax orderings are defined on sets of tuples whose components belong to a totally ordered set $(\Omega, \geq)$, say Leximin($\geq$) and Leximax($\geq$). Suppose $\Omega = (L^p, \text{Leximin})$ or $(L^p, \text{Leximax})$. Then, nested lexicographic ordering relations (Leximin(Leximin($\geq$)), Leximax(Leximin($\geq$)), Leximin(Leximax($\geq$)), Leximax(Leximax($\geq$))), can be recursively defined, in order to compare L-valued matrices.

Consider for instance the relation Leximax(Leximin($\geq$)), denoted $\geq_{Lexmaxmin}$, on set M of n×p matrices [a] with coefficients a_{ij} in (L, $\geq$). M can be totally ordered in a very refined way by this relation. Denote by $a_{i\bullet}$ row i of [a]. Let [a*] and [b*] be rearranged matrices [a] and [b] such that terms in each row are reordered increasingly and rows are arranged lexicographically top-down in decreasing order. $[a] \geq_{Lexmaxmin}$ [b] is defined by : $\exists\, k \leq n$ s.t. $\forall\, i < k$, $a^*_{i\bullet} =_{Leximin} b^*_{i\bullet}$ and $a^*_{k\bullet} >_{Leximin} b^*_{k\bullet}$.

Relation $\geq_{Lexmaxmin}$ is a complete preorder on M. $[a] =_{Lexmaxmin} [b]$ iff both matrices have the same coefficients up to a rearrangement. Moreover, $\geq_{Lexmaxmin}$ refines the optimistic criterion: $\max_i \min_j a_{ij} \geq \max_i \min_j b_{ij}$ implies $[a] >_{Lexmaxmin} [b]$. Moreover, if [a] Pareto-dominates [b], then $[a] >_{Lexmaxmin} [b]$

The same consideration applies when refining the minmax ordering by means of Leximin(Leximax($\geq$)). Comparing acts f and g in the context of a possibility distribution π can be done using relations $\geq_{Lexmaxmin}$ and $\geq_{Lexminmax}$ applied to $n \times 2$ matrices [f] and [g] on (L, $\geq$) with coefficients $f_{i1} = \pi_i$ (resp. $n(\pi_i)$) and $f_{i2} = u_i = \mu(f(s_i))$, $g_{i1} = \pi_i$ (resp. $n(\pi_i)$) and $g_{i2} = v_i = \mu(g(s_i))$. If ψ is the transformation from $W^+_\pi(f)$ to $EU^+_\pi(f)$ such that $\psi o \pi$ is a big-stepped probability assignment, $\psi o \mu$ and $\phi o \mu$ are big-stepped utility assignments defined earlier, then it is possible to show that $EU^+(f)$ and $EU^-(f)$ just encode the $\geq_{Lexmaxmin}$ and $\geq_{Lexminmax}$ relations [25] :

Theorem: $[f] \geq_{Lexmaxmin} [g]$ iff $EU^+(f) \geq EU^+(f)$; $[f] \geq_{Lexminmax} [g]$ iff $EU^-(f) \geq EU^-(f)$.

As a consequence, the additive preference functionals $EU^+(f)$ and $EU^-(f)$ refining the possibilistic criteria are qualitative despite their numerical encoding. Moreover, the two orderings $\geq_{Lexmaxmin}$ and $\geq_{Lexminmax}$ of acts obey the Savage axioms of rational decision. These orderings can be viewed as weighted generalizations of leximin and leximax relations (recovered if $\pi_i = 1$ for all i in case of total ignorance on states).

They are also generalizations of possibility and necessity orderings on events. Relations $\geq_{Lexmaxmin}$ and $\geq_{Lexminmax}$ between acts coincide if the utility functions are Boolean. This uncertainty representation is probabilistic, although qualitative, and is a lexicographic refinement of both possibility and necessity orderings. Suppose $\exists$ A, B, $f = \chi_A$, $g = \chi_B$ (indicator functions). Then define $A \geq_{\Pi Lex} B \Leftrightarrow v_A \geq_{leximax} v_B$ where v_A is the vector $(a_1, ..., a_n)$ such that $a_i = \pi(s_i)$ if $s_i \in A$; $a_i = 0$ otherwise, This relation is called "leximax" likelihood. The leximax likelihood relation can be generated from the well-ordered partition $\{S_1, ..., S_k\}$ of S induced by π: $A >_{\Pi Lex} B$ iff there is an S_j such that $|B \cap (S_1 \cup ... \cup S_j)| < |A \cap (S_1 \cup ... \cup S_j)|$ and $|A \cap (S_1 \cup ... \cup S_p)| = |B \cap (S_1 \cup ... \cup S_p)|$ for all $p < j$.

The relation $\geq_{\Pi Lex}$ is a complete preordering of events whose strict part refines the possibilistic likelihood $>_{\Pi L}$ of section 3. In fact, $\geq_{\Pi Lex}$ coincides with $\geq_{\Pi L}$ for linear possibility distributions. For a uniform possibility distribution $\geq_{\Pi Lex}$ coincides with the comparative probability relation that is induced by a uniform probability (the cardinality-based definition gives $A >_{\Pi Lex} B$ iff $|B| < |A|$). This is not surprising in view of the fact that the leximax likelihood relation is really a comparative probability relation in the usual sense.

An open problem is to provide a similar lexicographic refinement of Sugeno integral. Some preliminary discussions [24] provide some insight on the discrimin extension of this criterion. There is no hope of refining Sugeno integral by means of an expected utility since the former strongly violates the sure-thing principle. More recent results [15] and the form of equation (6) suggest that it makes sense to refine a Sugeno integral by means of a Choquet integral with respect to a special kind belief function which is a generalization of big-stepped probabilities.

6 Conclusion

This paper has provided an account of qualitative decision rules under uncertainty. They can be useful for solving discrete decision problems involving finite state spaces when it is not natural or very difficult to quantify utility functions or probabilities. For instance, there is no time granted to do it because a quick advice must be given (recommender systems). Or the problem takes place in a dynamic environment with a large state space, a non-quantifiable goal to be pursued, and there is only partial information on the current state (autonomous vehicles). Or yet a very high level description of a decision problem is available, where states and consequences are roughly described (strategic decisions). The possibilistic criteria are compatible with dynamic programming algorithms for multiple-stage decision problems [23, 35]. This topic, with minor adaptation, is also relevant to multicriteria decision making, where the various objectives play the role of the states and the likelihood relation is used to compare the relative importance of groups of objectives [11, 13].

Two kinds of qualitative decision rules have been found. Some are consistent with the Pareto ordering and satisfy the sure thing principle, but leave room to incomparable decisions, and overfocus on most plausible states. The other ones do rank decisions, but lack discrimination. It seems that there is a conflict between fine-grained discrimination and the requirement of a total ordering in the qualitative setting. Future works should strive towards exploiting the complementary features of prioritized Pareto-efficient decision methods as the likely dominance rule, and of the pessimistic decision rules related to the Wald criterion. Putting these two requirements together seems to lead us back to a very special case of expected utility, as very recent results described in the previous section show. The lexicographic criteria so-obtained meet requirements for a good qualitative decision theory: no numbers are requested as inputs, only a few levels of preference are needed (cognitive relevance), decisiveness is ensured (no incomparability), as well as optimal discrimination in accordance with Pareto-dominance.

References

1. Bacchus F. and Grove A. (1996). Utility independence in a qualitative decision theory. In *Proc. of the 5th Inter. Conf. on Princ. Of Know. Repres. and Reas. (KR'96)*, Cambridge, Mass., 542–552.

2. Benferhat, S. Dubois, D. Prade H. (1999). Possibilistic and standard probabilistic semantics of conditional knowledge. *J. Logic and Computation*, 9, 873–895, 1999.

3. Boutilier C. (1994). Towards a logic for qualitative decision theory. In *Proc. of the 4rd Inter. Conf. on Princ. of Knowl. Repres. and Reason. (KR'94)*, Bonn, Germany, 75–86.

4. Brafman R.I., Tennenholtz M. (1997). Modeling agents as qualitative decision makers. *Artificial Intelligence*, 94, 217–268.

5. Brafman R.I., Tennenholtz M. (2000). On the Axiomatization of Qualitative Decision Criteria, *J. ACM*, 47, 452–482

6. Cohen M. Jaffray J. (1980) Rational behavior under complete ignorance. *Econometrica*, 48, 1280–1299.

7. Doyle J., Thomason R. (1999). Background to qualitative decision theory. *The AI Magazine*, 20 (2), Summer 1999, 55–68

8. Dubois D. (1986). Belief structures, possibility theory and decomposable confidence measures on finite sets. *Computers and AI* (Bratislava), 5(5), 403–416.

9. Dubois D., Fargier H., and Prade H. (1996). Refinements of the maximin approach to decision-making in fuzzy environment. *Fuzzy Sets and Systems*, 81, 103–122.

10. Dubois D., Fargier H., and Prade H. (1997). Decision making under ordinal preferences and uncertainty. *Proc. of the 13th Conf. on Uncertainty in AI*, Providence, RI, Morgan & Kaufmann, San Francisco, CA, 157–164.

11. Dubois D., Fargier H., and Perny P. (2001). Towards a qualitative multicriteria decision theory. To appear in Int. J. Intelligent Systems.

12. Dubois D., Fargier H., Perny P. and Prade H. (2002). Qualitative Decision Theory: from Savage's Axioms to Non-Monotonic Reasoning. *Journal of the ACM*, 49, 455–495.

13. Dubois D., Fargier H., and Perny P. (2002). On the limitations of ordinal approaches to decision-making. *Proc.of the 8th Int. Conf., Principles of Knowledge Repres. and Reasoning* (KR2002), Toulouse, France. Morgan Kaufmann, San Francisco, Ca., 133–144.

14. Dubois D., Fargier H., and Perny P. (2003). Qualitative Decision Theory with preference relations and comparative uncertainty: an axiomatic aproach. *Artificial Intelligence,* to appear.

15. Dubois D., Fargier H., Sabbadin R. (2003) Additive refinements of qualitative decision criteria. 24th Int. Seminar on Fuzzy Set Theory, Linz.

16. Dubois D., Fortemps P. (1999). Computing improved optimal solutions to max-min flexible constraint satisfaction problems. *Eur. J. of Oper. Res,* 118, p. 95–126, 1999.

17. Dubois D., Godo L., Prade H., Zapico A. (1999) On the possibilistic decision model: from decision under uncertainty to case-based decision. *Int. J. Uncertainty, Fuzziness and Knowledge-Based Systems*, 7, p. 631—670.

18. D. Dubois, H. Prade (1995) Possibility theory as a basis for qualitative decision theory. *Proc. IJCAI'95*, Montréal, Canada, 1924–1930

19. Dubois D., Prade H. (1998). Possibility theory: qualitative and quantitative aspects. P. Smets, editor, *Handbook on Defeasible Reasoning and Uncertainty Management Systems, Volume 1,* Kluwer Academic Publ., Dordrecht, The Netherlands, 169–226

20. Dubois D., Prade H., and Sabbadin R. (1998). Qualitative decision theory with Sugeno integrals. *Proc. of 14th Conf. on Uncertainty in AI* (UAI'98), Madison, WI, USA. Morgan Kaufmann, San Francisco, CA, p. 121–128.

21. Dubois D., Prade H., and Sabbadin R. (2001). Decision-theoretic foundations of possibilty theory. *European Journal of Operational Research*, 128, 459–478.

22. Fargier H., Perny P. (1999). Qualitative models for decision under uncertainty without the commensurability assumption. *Proc. of the 15th Conf. on Uncertainty in AI*, Providence, RI, Morgan & Kaufmann, San Francisco, CA, 157–164.

23. Fargier H., Lang J., Sabbadin R. (1998). Towards qualitative approaches to multi-stage decision making. *International Journal of Approximate Reasoning*, 19, 441–471.

24. Fargier H., Sabbadin R., (2000) Can qualitative utility criteria obey the surething principle? *Proceedings IPMU2000*, Madrid, 821–826.

25. Fargier H. Sabbadin R. (2003) Qualitative decion under uncertainty: back to expected utility, *Proc. IJCAI'03*, Acapulco, Mexico.

26. Fishburn P. (1975). Axioms for lexicographic preferences. *Rev. Econ. Stud.*, 42, 415–419

27. Friedman N., Halpern J. (1996). Plausibility measures and default reasoning. *Proc of the 13th National Conf. on AI (AAAI'96)*, Portland, 1297–1304.

28. Giang P., Shenoy P. (2001). A comparison of axiomatic approaches to qualitative decision-making using possibility theory. *Proc. 17th Int. Conf. on Uncertainty in AI*, Morgan Kaufmann, San Francisco, Ca. pp 162–170.

29. Grabisch M. Murofushi T. Sugeno M. (2000) Eds. *Fuzzy Measures and Integrals* Physica-Verlag, Heidelberg, Germany,

30. Kraus K., Lehmann D., Magidor M. (1990). Nonmonotonic reasoning, preferential models and cumulative logics. *Artificial Intelligence*, 44, 167–207.

31. Lang J. (1996). Conditional desires and utilities: an alternative logical approach to qualitative decision theory. *Proc. 12th Eur. Conf. on AI (ECAI96)*, Budapest, 318–322.

32. Lehmann D. (1996). Generalized qualitative probability: Savage revisited. *Proc. 12th Conf. on Uncertainty in AI*, Portland, Morgan & Kaufman, San Mateo, CA, 381–388.

33. Lehmann D. (2001). Expected Qualitative Utility Maximization, *J. Games and Economic Behavior*. 35, 54–79

34. Lewis D. (1973). *Counterfactuals*. Basil Blackwell, London.

35. Sabbadin R. (2000), Empirical comparison of probabilistic and possibilistic Markov decision processes algorithms. *Proc. 14th Eur. Conf. on AI (ECAI'00)*, Berlin, Germany, 586–590.

36. Savage L.J. (1972). *The Foundations of Statistics*. Dover, New York.

37. Snow P. (1999) Diverse confidence levels in a probabilistic semantics for conditional logics. *Artificial Intelligence*, 113, 269–279

38. Tan S. W., Pearl. J. (1994). Qualitative decision theory. *Proc. 11th National Conf. on AI (AAAI-94)*, Seattle, WA, pp. 70–75.

39. Thomason R. (2000), Desires and defaults: a framework for planning with inferred goals. *Proc. of the Inter. Conf. on Principles of Knowledge Representation and Reasoning (KR'00)*, Breckenridge, Col., Morgan & Kaufmann, San Francisco, 702–713.

40. Whalen T. (1984). Decision making under uncertainty with various assumptions about available information. *IEEE Trans. on Systems, Man and Cybernetics*, 14:888–900.

41. Yager.R.R. (1979). Possibilistic decision making. *IEEE Trans. on Systems, Man and Cybernetics*, 9:388–392.

42. Zadeh L.A. (1978). Fuzzy sets as a basis for a theory of possibility. *Fuzzy Sets and Systems*, 1, 3–28.

Applications of Latent Class Analysis in Social Science Research

Jeroen K. Vermunt

Department of Methodology and Statistics, Tilburg University, PO Box 90153
5000 LE Tilburg, The Netherlands

Abstract. An overview is provided of recent developments in the use of latent class (LC) models in social science research. Special attention is paid to the application of LC analysis as a factor-analytic tool and as a tool for random-effects modeling. Furthermore, an extension of the LC model to deal with nested data structures is presented.

1 Introduction

Latent class (LC) analysis was introduced by Lazarsfeld in 1950 as a way of formulating latent attitudinal variables from dichotomous survey items (see [11]). During the 1970s, LC methodology was formalized and extended to nominal variables by Goodman [6] who also developed the maximum likelihood algorithm that has served as the basis for most LC programs. It has, however, taken many years till the method became a generally accepted tool for statistical analysis. The history and state-of-art of LC analysis in social science research is described in the recent volume "Applied Latent Class Analysis" edited by Hagenaars and McCutcheon [8].

Traditionally, LC models were used as clustering and scaling tools for dichotomous indicators. Scaling models, such as the probabilistic Guttman scales, involved specification of simple equality constraints on the item conditional probabilities in order to guarantee that the latent variable would capture a single underlying dimension. A more recent development is to parametrize the item conditional by means of logit models, yielding restricted variants of LC analysis which are similar to latent trait models (see [4], [9], and [19]). The log-linear modeling framework with latent variables implemented in the LEM software package yields are general class of probability models (graphical models) for categorical observed and latent variables in which each of the model probabilities can be restricted by logit constraints (see [7] and [17]). The LEM framework contains most types of LC models for categorical observed variables as special cases, including models with several latent variables, models with covariates, models for ordinal variables, models with local dependencies, causal models with latent variables, and latent Markov models.

A very much related field is the field of finite mixture (FM) modelling (see[15]). Traditionally, finite mixture models dealt with continuous outcome variables. The underlying idea of LC and FM models is, however, the same: the

T.D. Nielsen and N.L. Zhang (Eds.): ECSQARU 2003, LNAI 2711, pp. 22–36, 2003.

population consists of a number of subgroups which differ with respect to the parameters of the statistical model of interest. It is, therefore, not surprising that in recent years, the fields of LC and FM modeling have come together and that the terms LC model and FM model have become interchangeable with each other. For example, mixture model clustering and mixture regression analysis are now also known as LC clustering and LC regression analysis.

The software package Latent GOLD (see [20] and [21]) implements the most important social science application types of LC and FM models – clustering, scaling, and random-effects modeling – in three modules: LC cluster, LC factor, and LC regression. What is very important for applied researchers is that the models are implemented in a SPSS-like graphical user interface. The use of LC analysis for clustering purposes is also well-known outside the social science field. LC factor is a factor-analytic tool for discrete or mixed outcome variables (see [12]). LC regression makes it possible to take into account unobserved population heterogeneity with respect to the coefficients of a regression model (see [23] and [24]). In this paper, I will explain the basic ideas underlying the LC factor and LC regression models and present several empirical examples.

LC models are models for two-level data structures. The data consists of a set of indicators or a set of repeated responses which are nested within individuals. Recently, models have been proposed for nested data structures consisting of more than two levels, such as repeated measures nested within persons and persons nested with groups – teams, countries, or organizations (see [18]). At the end of this paper, I will pay attention to this hierarchical or multilevel extension of the LC model and present a procedure called upward-downward algorithm that can be used to solve the maximum likelihood estimation problem.

2   The LC Factor Model

Let us start introducing some notation. Let y_{ik} denote the realized value of person i on the kth indicator, item, or response variable. The total number of response variables is denoted by K. A category of the ℓth latent class variable will be denoted as x_ℓ, its total number of categories as T_ℓ, and the total number of latent variables by L.

The standard LC model that I will refer to as the LC cluster model assumes that responses are independent of each other given a single latent variable with T_1 unordered categories. The density of $\mathbf{y}_i$ is defined as

$$f(\mathbf{y}_i) = \sum_{x_1=1}^{T_1} P(x_1) \prod_{k=1}^{K} f(y_{ik}|x_1),$$

where the exact form of the class-specific densities $f(y_{ik}|x_1)$ depends on the scale type of the response variable concerned. The $f(y_{ik}|x_1)$ are taken from the exponential family.

The main difference between the LC factor and the LC cluster model is that the former may contain more than one latent variable. Another difference is that in the factor model the categories of the latent variables are assumed to be ordered. Thus, rather than working with a single nominal latent variable, here we work with one or more dichotomous or ordered polytomous latent variables (Magidson and Vermunt in [12]). The advantage of this approach is that it guarantees that each of the factors capture no more than one dimension.

The primary difference between our LC factor and the traditional factor analysis model is that the latent variables (factors) are assumed to be dichotomous or ordinal as opposed to continuous and normally distributed. Because of the strong similarity with traditional factor analysis, this approach is called LC factor analysis. There is also a strong connection between LC factor models and item response or latent trait models. Actually, LC factor models are discretized variants of well-known latent trait models for dichotomous and polytomous items (see [9], [19], and [22]).

As in maximum likelihood factor analysis, modeling under the LC factor approach can proceed by increasing the number of factors until a good fitting model is achieved. This approach to LC modeling provides a general alternative to the traditional method of obtaining a good fitting model by increasing the number of latent classes. In particular, when working with dichotomous uncorrelated factors, there is an exact equivalence in the number of parameters of the two models. A LC factor model with 1 factor has the same number of parameters as a 2-class LC cluster model, a model with 2 factors as a 3-class model, a model with 3 factors as a 4-class model, etc. Thus, in an exploratory analysis, rather than increasing the number of classes one may instead increase the number of factors until an acceptable fit is obtained.

2.1   A Two-Factor Model for Nominal Indicators

To illustrate the LC factor model, let us assume that we have a two-factor model for four nominal categorical indicators. The corresponding probability structure is of the form

$$P(y_{i1}, y_{i2}, y_{i3}, y_{i4}) = \sum_{x_1=1}^{T_1} \sum_{x_2=1}^{T_2} P(x_1, x_2) \prod_{k=1}^{4} P(y_{ik}|x_1, x_2).$$

The conditional response probabilities $P(y_{ik}|x_1, x_2)$ are restricted by means of multinomial logit models with linear terms

$$\pi(y_{ik}|x_1, x_2) = \pi_{0y_k} + \pi_{1y_k} \cdot v_{x_1} + \pi_{2y_k} \cdot v_{x_2}.$$

Because the factors are assumed to be ordinal (or discrete interval) variables, the two-variable terms are restricted by using fixed category scores for the levels of the factors. Note that the factors are treated as metric variables, which are, however, not continuous but discrete. The scores v_{x_ℓ} for the categories of the ℓth factor are equidistant scores ranging from 0 to 1. The first level of a factor gets the score 0 and the last level the score 1. The parameters describing the strength of relationships between the factors and the indicators – here, π_{1y_k} and π_{2y_k} – can be interpreted as factor loadings.

Note that the above logit model does not include the three-variable inter-action term of the two factors and the indicator. These higher-order terms are excluded from the model in order to be able to distinguish the various dimensions. If we would include the three-variable interaction term, our two-factor model would be equivalent to an unrestricted 4-cluster model. By excluding this term, we obtain a restricted 4-cluster model in which each of the four clusters can be conceived as being a combination of two factors.

In the standard LC factor model, the factors are specified to be dichotomous, which means that the scoring of the factor levels does not imply a constraint. An important extension of this standard model is, however, increasing the number of levels of a factor, which makes it possible to describe more precisely the distribution of the factor concerned. Note that the levels of the factors remain ordered by the use of fixed equal-interval category scores in their relationships with the indicators. Therefore, each additional level costs only one degree of freedom; that is, there is one additional class size to be estimated.

In the default setting, the factors are assumed to be independent of one another. This is specified by the appropriate logit constraints on the latent probabilities. In the two-factor case, this involves restricting the linear term in the logit model for $P(x_1, x_2)$ by

$$\square_{x_1 x_2} = \square_{x_1} + \square_{x_2}.$$

Working with correlated factors is comparable to performing an oblique rotation. The association between each pair of factors is described by a single uniform association parameter:

$$\square_{x_1 x_2} = \square_{x_1} + \square_{x_2} + \square_{12} \cdot v_{x_1} \cdot v_{x_2}.$$

It should be noted that contrary to traditional factor analysis, the LC factor model is identified without additional constraints, such as setting certain factor loadings equal to zero. Nevertheless, it is possible to specify models in which factor loadings are fixed to zero. Together with the possibility to include factor correlation in the model, this option can be used for a confirmatory factor analysis. Other extensions are the use of indicators which are ordinal, continuous, or counts, the inclusion of local dependencies, and the inclusion of covariates affecting the factors.

Zhang [25] proposed a LC model with several latent variables called hierarchical LC model that is similar to our LC factor model presented. Three important differences are that his factors are nominal instead of ordinal, that indicators are allowed to be related to only one factor, and that factor correlations are induced by higher-order factors.

2.2 Graphical Displays

Magidson and Vermunt [12] proposed a graphical display similar to the one obtained in correspondence analysis to depict the results of a LC factor analysis.

These displays help in detecting which indicators are related to which factors. The measures that are display are derived from the posterior factor means.

Case i's posterior mean on factor $\blacksquare$ equals

$$E\left(v_{i\ell}\right) = \sum_{x_\ell=1}^{\blacksquare^{T_\ell}} v_{x_\ell} P\left(x_\ell | y_i\right).$$

The basic idea is to aggregate these posterior means (factor scores) and plot the resulting numbers in a two-dimensional display. Note that these numbers will be in the 0-1 range because the category score v_{x_ℓ} is 0 for the lowest factor level and 1 for the highest level. The most important aggregation is within categories of the indicators; that is,

$$E\left(v_\ell | y_k\right) = \frac{\sum_{i=1}^{\blacksquare^{N}} E\left(v_{i\ell}\right) I(y_{ik} = y_k)}{\sum_{i=1}^{\blacksquare^{N}} I(y_{ik} = y_k)},$$

where $I(y_{ik} = y_k)$ equals 1 if person i's value on indicator k is y_k, and 0 otherwise. This yields the mean of factor $\blacksquare$ for persons who give response y_k on indicator k. These category-specific factor means will be very different if an indicator is strongly related to a factor.

Aggregation can be done for any relevant subgroup and not just for categories of the indicators. Often it is useful to depict the position of groups formed on the basis of socio-demographic characteristics. It is also possible to depict the posterior means of individual cases in the plot, yielding what is sometimes referred to as a bi-plot.

2.3   Application: Types of Survey Respondents

We will now consider an example that illustrates how the LC factor model can be used with nominal variables. It is based on the analysis of 4 variables from the 1982 General Social Survey given by McCutcheon [13] to illustrate how standard LC modeling can be used to identify different types of survey respondents. Two of the variables ascertain the respondent's opinion regarding the purpose of surveys (Purpose) and how accurate they are (Accuracy), and the others are evaluations made by the interviewer of the respondent's levels of understanding of the survey questions (Understanding) and cooperation shown in answering the questions (Cooperation). McCutcheon initially assumed the existence of 2 latent classes corresponding to 'ideal' and 'less than ideal' types. The study included separate samples of white and black respondents. Here, I use the data of the white respondents only.

The two-class LC model – or, equivalently, the 1-factor LC model – does not provide a satisfactory description of this data set ($L^2 = 75.5$; $df = 22$; $p < .001$). Two options for proceeding are to increase the number of classes or to increase the number of factors. The 2-factor LC model fits very well ($L^2 = 11.1$; $df = 15$; $p = .75$), and also much better than the unrestricted 3-class model ($L^2 = 22.1$; $df = 15$; $p = .11$) that was selected as final model by McCutcheon.

Table 1. Logit parameter estimates for the 2-factor LC model as applied to the GSS'82 respondent-type items

Item	Category	x_1	x_2
Purpose	good	-1.12	2.86
	depends	0.26	-0.82
	waste	0.86	3.68
Accuracy	mostly true	-0.52	-1.32
	not true	0.52	1.32
Understanding	good	-1.61	0.58
	fair/poor	1.61	-0.58
Cooperation	interested	-2.96	-0.57
	cooperative	-0.60	-0.12
	impatient/hostile	3.56	0.69

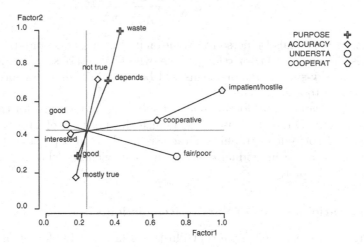

Fig. 1. Graphical display of category-specific posterior factor means for the 2-factor LC model as applied to the GSS'82 respondent-type items

The logit parameter estimates obtained from the 2-factor LC model are given in Table 1. These show the magnitude of the relationship between the observed variables and the two factors. As can be seen, the interviewers' evaluations of respondents and the respondents' evaluations of surveys are clearly different factors: Understanding and Cooperation are more strongly affected by the first factor and Purpose and Accuracy by the second factor.

Figure 1 depicts the bi-plot containing the category-specific factor means of the four indicators. The plot shows even more clearly than the logit coefficients that the first dimension differentiates between the categories of Understanding and Cooperation and the second between the categories of Purpose and Accuracy.

3   LC Regression Analysis

One of the differences between LC regression analysis and the other forms of LC analysis discussed so far is that it concerns a model for a single response variable. This response variable is explained by a set of predictors, where the predictor effects may take on different values for each latent class (see [10,23,24] and Sect. 13.2 in [1]).

An important feature of LC regression models is that for each case we may have more than one observation. These multiple observations may be experimental replications, repeated measurements at different time points or occasions, clustered observations, or other types of dependent observations. Here, I will use the term replications, where the replication number will be denoted by k. The value of the response variable for case i at replication k is denoted by y_{ik}. The number of replications, which is not necessarily the same for all cases, is denoted by K_i. Because we are dealing with models with a single latent variable, we drop the index ∎ from x_ℓ.

Note that I am describing a two-level data structure in which a predictor may either have the same value or change its value across replications. The former are the higher-level or level-2 predictors and the latter are lower-level or level-1 predictors. Here, k indexes the (dependent) lower-level observations within a certain higher-level observation. Level-1 predictors will be denoted as z_{ikp} and level-2 predictors as w_{iq}. The LC regression model can be used to define (non-parametric) two-level or random-coefficient models. Using k as an index for time points or time intervals, one obtains models for longitudinal data, such as growth or event-history models with non-parametric random coefficients (see [17] and [23]).

Using the same notation as above, the probability structure underlying the LC regression model can be defined as

$$f(\mathbf{y}_i | \mathbf{w}_i, \mathbf{z}_i) = \prod_{x=1}^{T_1} P(x) \prod_{k=1}^{K_i} f(y_{ik} | x, \mathbf{w}_i, \mathbf{z}_{ik}) .$$

Similarly to other LC models, replications are assumed to be independent given class membership. For nominal or ordinal dependent variables, the probability density $f(y_{ik} | x, \mathbf{w}_i, \mathbf{z}_{ik})$ will usually be assumed to be multinomial, for continuous variables, univariate normal, and for counts, Poisson or binomial.

The linear predictor in $f(y_{ik} | x, \mathbf{w}_i, \mathbf{z}_{ik})$ equals

$$\blacksquare(y_{ik} | x, \mathbf{w}_i, \mathbf{z}_{ik}) = \blacksquare_{0x} + \sum_{p=1}^{P} \blacksquare_{px} z_{ikp} + \sum_{q=1}^{Q} \blacksquare_{P+q} w_{iq}$$

where P and Q denote the number of level-1 and level-2 predictors. This regression model contains a class-specific intercept, P class-specific regression coefficients, and Q class-independent regression coefficients. The P + 1 coefficient that are class dependent are random coefficients.

The conceptual equivalence between the LC regression model and a two-level random-coefficient model becomes even clearer if one realizes that it is possible to compute the means, variances, and covariances of the class-specific coefficients from the standard LC class output. These are obtained by elementary statistics calculus:

$$\mu_p = \sum_{x=1}^{\square^T} \square_{px} P(x)$$

$$\square_{pp'} = \sum_{x=1}^{\square^T} (\square_{px} - \mu_p)(\square_{p'x} - \mu_{p'}) P(x),$$

This shows that LC regression analysis results can be summarized to yield information that is equivalent to the one obtained in regression models with random coefficients coming from a normal distribution; that is, it possible to obtain the mean vector and the covariance matrix of the random coefficients.

3.1   Application: Longitudinal Study on Attitudes towards Abortion

In order to demonstrate the non-parametric random-coefficient model, I used a data set obtained from the data library of the Multilevel Models Project, at the Institute of Education, University of London. The data consist of 264 participants in 1983 to 1986 yearly waves from the British Social Attitudes Survey (see [14]). It is a three-level data set: individuals are nested within constituencies and time-points are nested within individuals. I will only make use of the latter nesting, which means that we are dealing with a standard repeated measures model. As was shown by Goldstein [5], the highest level variance – between constituencies – is so small that it can reasonably be ignored. Below, I will show how to extend the LC model to deal with higher-level data structures.

The dependent variable is the number of yes responses on seven yes/no questions as to whether it is woman's right to have an abortion under a specific circumstance. Because this variable is a count with a fixed total, it most natural to work with a logit link and binomial error function. Individual level predictors in the data set are religion, political preference, gender, age, and self-assessed social class. In accordance with the results of Goldstein, I found no significant effects of gender, age, self-assessed social class, and political preference. Therefore, I did not used these predictors in the further analysis. The predictors that were used are the level-1 predictor year of measurement (1=1983; 2=1984; 3=1985; 4=1986) and the level-2 predictor religion (1=Roman Catholic, 2=Protestant; 3=Other; 4=No religion). Effect coding is used for nominal predictors.

The LC regression models were estimated by means of version 3.0 of the Latent GOLD program (see [21]), which also provides the multilevel type parameters μ and $\sqrt{\square^2}$. I started with three models without random effects: an intercept-only model (Ia), a model with a linear effect of year (Ib), and a model with year dummies (Ic). Models Ib and Ic also contained the nominal level-2 predictor religion. The test results reported in the first part of Table 2 show

Table 2. Test results for the estimated models with the attitudes towards abortion data

Model	Log-likelihood	# parameters	BIC
No random effects			
Ia. empty model	-2309	1	4623
Ib. time linear + religion	-2215	5	4458
Ic. time dummies + religion	-2188	7	4416
Ic + Random intercept			
IIa. 2 classes	-1755	9	3560
IIb. 3 classes	-1697	11	3456
IIc. 4 classes	-1689	13	3451
IId. 5 classes	-1689	15	3461
Ic + Random intercept and slope			
IIIa. 2 classes	-1745	12	3558
IIIb. 3 classes	-1683	17	3460
IIIc. 4 classes	-1657	22	3436
IIId. 5 classes	-1645	27	3441

Table 3. Parameters estimates obtained with Model IIIc for the attitudes towards abortion data

Parameter	Class 1	Class 2	Class 3	Class 4	Mean	Std.Dev.
Class size	0.30	0.28	0.24	0.19		
Intercept	-0.34	0.60	3.33	1.59	1.16	1.38
Time						
1983	0.14	0.26	0.47	-0.58	0.12	0.35
1984	-0.11	-0.46	-0.35	-1.11	-0.45	0.34
1985	-0.04	-0.44	-0.26	1.43	-0.10	0.66
1986	-0.06	0.64	0.14	0.26	0.24	0.27
Religion						
Catholic	-0.53	-0.53	-0.53	-0.53	-0.53	0.00
Protestant	0.20	0.20	0.20	0.20	0.20	0.00
Other	-0.10	-0.10	-0.10	-0.10	-0.10	0.00
No Religion	0.42	0.42	0.42	0.42	0.42	0.00

that year and religion have significant effects on the outcome variable and that it is better to treat year as non-linear. I proceeded by adding a random intercept. The test results show that the model with 4 classes is the best one in terms of BIC value. Subsequently, I allowed the time effect to be class specific. Again, the 4-class model turned out to be the best according to the BIC criterion.

Table 3 reports the parameter estimates for Model IIIc. The means indicate that the attitudes are most positive at the last time point and most negative at the second time point. Furthermore, the effects of religion show that people without religion are most in favor and Roman Catholics and Others are most against abortion. Protestants have a position that is close to the no-religion group.

Table 4. Estimates of the parameters for 3-class choice model

Parameter	Class 1	Class 2	Class 3	Mean	Std.Dev.
Class size	0.51	0.26	0.24		
Fashion	3.03	-0.17	1.20	1.77	1.37
Quality	-0.09	2.72	1.12	0.92	1.16
Price	-0.39	-0.36	-0.56	-0.42	0.08
None	1.29	0.19	-0.43	0.60	0.73

As can be seen, the 4 latent classes have very different intercepts and time patterns. The largest class 1 is most against abortion and class 3 is most in favor of abortion. Both latent classes are very stable over time. The overall level of latent class 2 is somewhat higher than of class 1, and it shows somewhat more change of the attitude over time. People belonging to latent class 4 are very instable: at the first two time points they are similar to class 2, at the third time point to class 4, and at the last time point again to class 2 (this can be seen by combining the intercepts with the time effects). Class 4 could therefore be labelled as random responders. It is interesting to note that in a three-class solution the random-responder class and class two are combined. Thus, by going from a three- to a four-class solution one identifies the interesting group with less stable attitudes.

3.2   Application: Choice-Based Conjoint Study

The LC regression model is a popular tool for the analysis of data from conjoint experiments in which individuals rate separate product or choose between sets of products having different attributes (see [10]). The objective is to determine the effect of product characteristics on the rating or the choice probabilities or, more technically, to estimated the utilities of product attributes. LC analysis is used to identify market segments for which these utilities differ. The class-specific utilities can be used to estimate the market share of possible new products; that is, to simulate future markets.

For illustration of LC analysis of data obtained from choice-based conjoint experiments, I will use a generated data set. The products are 12 pairs of shoes that differ on 3 attributes: Fashion (0=traditional, 1= modern), Quality (0=low, 1=high), and Price (ranging from 1 to 5). Eights choice sets offer 3 of the 12 possible alternative products to 400 individuals. Each choice task consists of indicating which of the three alternatives they would purchase, with the response "none of the above" allowed as a fourth choice option.

The regression model that is used is a multinomial logit model with choice-specific predictors, also referred to as the conditional logit model. The BIC values indicated that the three-class model is the model that should be preferred. The parameter estimates obtained with the 3-class model are reported in Table 4. As can be seen, Fashion has a major influence on choice for class 1, Quality for class 2, and both Fashion and Quality affect the choice for class 3. The small differences in price effect across the three classes turned out to be insignificant.

In addition to the conditional logit model which shows how the attributes affect the likelihood of choosing one alternative over another, differentially for each class, I specified a second logit model to describe the latent class variable as a function of the covariates sex and age. Females turn out to belong more often to class 1 and males to class 3. Younger persons have a higher probability of belonging to class 1 (emphasize Fashion in choices) and older persons are most likely to belong to class 2 (emphasize Quality in choices).

4   LC Models for Nested Data Structures

As explained in the context of the LC regression model, LC analysis is a technique for analyzing two-level data structures. In most cases, this will be repeated measures or item responses that are nested within individuals. Here, I will present a three-level extension of the LC model and discuss the complications in parameter estimation, as well as indicate how these complications can be resolved.

Before proceeding, some additional notation has to introduced. Let y_{ijk} denote the response of individual j within group i on indicator or item k. The number of groups is denoted by N, the number of individuals within group i by n_i, and the number of items by K. The latent class variable at the individual level is denoted as x_j. For reasons that will be clear below, I will use the index j in x when referring to the latent class membership of a certain individual within a group.

The standard method for analyzing such grouped data structures is the multiple-group LC model (see [3]). A multiple-group LC model with group-specific class sizes would be of the form

$$P(y_i) = \prod_{j=1}^{n_i} \sum_{x=1}^{T} \prod_{k=1}^{K} P(y_{ijk}|x) \; P(x_j|i).$$

As can be seen, observations within a group are assumed to be independent of each other given the group-specific latent distribution $P(x_j|i)$.

A disadvantage of this "fixed-effects" approach is that the number of unknown parameters increases rapidly as the number of groups increases. An alternative is to assumed that groups belong to latent classes of groups, denoted by w, that differ with respect to the latent distribution of individuals. This yields a LC model of the form

$$P(y_i) = \sum_{w=1}^{M} \prod_{j=1}^{n_i} \sum_{x_j=1}^{T} \prod_{k=1}^{K} P(y_{ijk}|x_j) \; P(x_j|w) \; P(w).$$

This model can be represented as a graphical model containing one latent variable at the group level and one latent variable for each individual within a group. The fact that the model contains so many latent variables makes the use of a standard EM algorithm for maximum likelihood estimation impractical.

The contribution of group i to the completed data log-likelihood that has to be solved in the M step of the EM algorithm has the form

$$\log L_i = \sum_{w=1}^{M} \sum_{x=1}^{T} \sum_{j=1}^{n_i} \sum_{k=1}^{K} P(x_j, w | \mathbf{y}_i) \log P(y_{ijk} | x_j)$$

$$+ \sum_{w=1}^{M} \sum_{x=1}^{T} \sum_{j=1}^{n_i} P(x_j, w | \mathbf{y}_i) \log P(x_j | w)$$

$$+ \sum_{w=1}^{M} P(w | \mathbf{y}_i) \log P(w).$$

This shows that the "only" thing that has to be obtained in the E step of the EM algorithm are the $T \cdot M$ marginal posteriors $P(x_j, w | \mathbf{y}_i)$ for each individual within a group. It turns out that these can be obtained in an efficient manner by making use of the conditional independence assumptions implied by underlying graphical model. More precisely, the new algorithm makes use of the fact that lower-level observations are independent of each other given the higher-level class memberships. The underlying idea of using the structure of the model of interest for the implementation of the EM algorithm is similar to what is done in hidden Markov models. For these models, Baum et al. in [2] developed an efficient EM algorithm which is known as the forward-backward algorithm because it moves forward and backward through the Markov chain. Vermunt in [18] called the version of EM for the new LC model the upward-downward algorithm because it moves upward and downward through the hierarchical structure: First, one marginalizes over class memberships going from the lower to the higher levels. Subsequently, the relevant marginal posterior probabilities are computed going from the higher to the lower levels. The method can easily be generalized to data structures consisting of more than three levels. Moreover, it cannot only be used in LC cluster-like applications, but also in the context of LC regression analysis.

The upward-downward algorithm makes use of the fact that

$$P(x_j, w | \mathbf{y}_i) = P(w | \mathbf{y}_i) P(x_j | \mathbf{y}_i, w) = P(w | \mathbf{y}_i) P(x_j | \mathbf{y}_{ij}, w);$$

that is, that given class membership of the group (w), class membership of the individuals (x_j) is independent of the information of the other group members. The terms $P(w | \mathbf{y}_i)$ and $P(x_j | \mathbf{y}_{ij}, w)$ are obtained with the model parameters:

$$P(x_j | \mathbf{y}_{ij}, w) = \frac{P(x_j, \mathbf{y}_{ij} | w)}{P(\mathbf{y}_{ij} | w)} = \frac{P(x_j | w) \prod_{k=1}^{K} P(y_{ijk} | x_j)}{P(\mathbf{y}_{ij} | w)}$$

$$P(w | \mathbf{y}_i) = \frac{P(w) \prod_{j=1}^{n_i} P(\mathbf{y}_{ij} | w)}{\sum_{w=1}^{M} P(w) \prod_{j=1}^{n_i} P(\mathbf{y}_{ij} | w)},$$

where $P(\mathbf{y}_{ij} | w) = \sum_{x=1}^{T} P(x_j | w) \prod_{k=1}^{K} P(y_{ijk} | x_j)$. In the upward part, we compute $P(x_j, \mathbf{y}_{ij} | w)$ for each individual, collapse these over x_j to obtain $P(\mathbf{y}_{ij} | w)$, and use these to obtain $P(w|\mathbf{y}_i)$ for each group. The downward part involves computing $P(x_j,w|\mathbf{y}_i)$ for each individual using $P(w|\mathbf{y}_i)$ and $P(x_j|\mathbf{y}_{ij},w)$.

In the upward-downward algorithm computation time increases linearly with the number of individuals within groups instead of exponentially, as would be the case in a standard E step. Computation time can be decreased somewhat more by grouping records with the same values for the observed variables within groups. A practical problem in the implementation of the upward-downward method is that underflows may occur in the computation of $P(w|\mathbf{y}_i)$. More precisely, because it may involve multiplication of a large number $(1+n_i \cdot K)$ of probabilities, the term $P(w) \prod_{j=1}^{n_i} P(\mathbf{y}_{ij}|w)$ may become equal to zero for each w. Such underflows can, however, easily be prevented by working on a log scale. Letting $a_{iw} = \log[P(w)] + \sum_j^{n_i} \log[P(\mathbf{y}_{ij}|w)]$ and $b_i = \max(a_{iw})$, $P(w|\mathbf{y}_i)$ can be obtained as follows:

$$P(w|\mathbf{y}_i) = \frac{\exp[a_{iw} - b_i]}{\sum_w^M \exp[a_{iw} - b_i)]}.$$

4.1 Application: Team Differences in Perceived Task Variety

In a Dutch study on the effect of autonomous teams on individual work conditions, data were collected from 41 teams of two organizations, a nursing home and a domiciliary care organization. These teams contained 886 employees. For the example, I took five dichotomized items of a scale measuring perceived task variety (see [16]). The item wording is as follows (translated from Dutch):

1. Do you always do the same things in your work?
2. Does your work require creativity?
3. Is your work diverse?
4. Does your work make enough usage of your skills and capacities?
5. Is there enough variation in your work?

The original items contained four answer categories. In order simplify the analysis, I collapsed the first two and the last two categories. Because some respondents had missing values on one or more of the indicators, the estimation procedure was adapted to deal with such partially observed indicators.

The fact that this data set is analyzed by means of LC analysis means that it is assumed that the researcher is interested in building a typology of employees based on their perceived task variety. On other hand, if one would be interested in constructing a continuous scale, a latent trait analysis would be more appropriate. Of course, also in that situation the multilevel structure should be taken into account.

Table 5 reports the log-likelihood value, the number of parameters, and the BIC value for the models that were estimated. I first estimated models without taking the group structure into account. The BIC values for the one to three class model (Models I-III) without a random latent class distribution show that a solution with two classes suffices. Subsequently, I introduced group-specific

Table 5. Test results for the estimated models with the task variety data

Model	Individuals	Groups	Log-likelihood	# parameters	BIC
I	1 class	1 class	-2685	5	5405
II	2 classes	1 class	-2385	11	4844
III	3 classes	1 classes	-2375	16	4859
IV	2 classes	2 classes	-2367	13	4822
V	2 classes	3 classes	-2366	15	4835

latent distributions in the two-class model (Models IV and V). From the results obtained with these two models, it can be seen that there is clear evidence for between-team variation in the latent distribution: These models have much lower BIC values than the two-class model without group-specific class sizes. The model with three classes of groups (Model V) has almost the same log-likelihood value as Model IV, which indicates that no more than two latent classes of teams can be identified.

The conditional response probabilities obtained with Model IV indicated that the first class has a much lower probability of giving the high task-variety response than class two on each of the five indicators. The two classes of team members can therefore be named "low task-variety" and "high task-variety". The two classes of teams contained 37 and 63 percent of the teams. The proportion of team members belonging to the high task-variety class are .41 and .78, respectively. This means, for instance, that in the majority of teams (63%) the majority of individuals (78%) belong to the high task-variety group. The substantive conclusion based on Model IV would be that there are two types of employees and two types of teams. The two types of teams differ considerably with respect to the distribution of the team members over the two types of employees.

References

1. Agresti, A.: Categorical Data Analysis. Second Edition, New York: Wiley (2002)
2. Baum, L.E., Petrie, T., Soules, G., Weiss, N.: A maximization technique occurring in the statistical analysis of probabilistic functions of Markov chains. Annals of Mathematical Statistics **41** (1970) 164–171
3. Clogg, C.C., Goodman, L.A.: Latent structure analysis of a set of multidimensional contingency tables. Journal of the American Statistical Association **79** (1984) 762–771.
4. Formann, A.K.: Linear logistic latent class analysis for polytomous data. Journal of the American Statistical Association **87** (1992) 476–486
5. Goldstein, H.: Multilevel statistical models. New York: Halsted Press (1995)
6. Goodman, L.A.: The analysis of systems of qualitative variables when some of the variables are unobservable: Part I – A modified latent structure approach. American Journal of Sociology **79** (1974) 1179–1259
7. Hagenaars, J.A.: Loglinear Models with Latent Variables, Sage University Paper. Newbury Park: Sage Publications (1993)

8. Hagenaars. J.A., McCutcheon., A.L.: Applied Latent Class Analysis, Cambridge: Cambridge University Press (2002)
9. Heinen, T.: Latent Class and Discrete Latent Trait Models: Similarities and Differences. Thousand Oakes: Sage Publications (1996)
10. Kamakura, W.A., Wedel, M., Agrawal, J.: Concomitant variable latent class models for the external analysis of choice data. International Journal of Marketing Research **11** (1994) 541–464
11. Lazarsfeld, P.F., Henry, N.W.: Latent Structure Analysis. Boston: Houghton Mill (1968)
12. Magidson, J., Vermunt, J.K.: Latent class factor and cluster models, bi-plots and related graphical displays, Sociological Methodology **31** (2001) 223–264
13. McCutcheon, A.L.: Latent Class Analysis, Sage University Paper. Newbury Park: Sage Publications (1987)
14. McGrath, K., Waterton, J.: British social attitudes, 1983–1986 panel survey. London: Social and Community Planning Research, Technical Report (1986)
15. McLachlan, G.J., Peel, D.: Finite Mixture models. New York: John Wiley & Sons, Inc. (2000)
16. Van Mierlo, H., Vermunt, J.K., Rutte, C.: Using individual level survey data to measure group constructs: A comparison of items with reference to the individual and to the group in a job design context (submitted for publication)
17. Vermunt, J.K.: Log-linear Models for Event Histories. Thousand Oakes: Series QASS, vol. 8. Sage Publications (1997)
18. Vermunt, J.K.: Multilevel latent class models, Sociological Methodology, 33, (to appear)
19. Vermunt, J.K.: The use restricted latent class models for defining and testing nonparametric and parametric IRT models: Applied Psychological Measurement **25** (2001) 283–294
20. Vermunt, J.K., Magidson, J.: Latent GOLD 2.0 User's Guide. Belmont, MA: Statistical Innovations Inc. (2000)
21. Vermunt, J.K., Magidson, J.: Addendum to the Latent GOLD User's Guide: Upgrade Manual for Version 3.0. Belmont, MA: Statistical Innovations Inc. (2003)
22. Vermunt J.K., Magidson, J.: Factor Analysis with Categorical Indicators: A Comparison Between Traditional and Latent Class Approaches. A. Van der Ark, M. Croon, and K. Sijstma. Advancements in Categorical Data Analysis. Erlbaum, (to appear)
23. Vermunt, J.K., Van Dijk. L.: A nonparametric random-coefficients approach: the latent class regression model. Multilevel Modelling Newsletter **13** (2001) 6–13
24. Wedel, M. and DeSarbo, W.: Mixture regression models. J. Hagenaars and A. McCutcheon (eds.), Applied Latent Class Analysis, 366–382. Cambridge University Press (2002)
25. Zhang, N.L.: Hierarchical latent class models for cluster analysis. Journal of Machine Learning Research (to appear)

Transformations from Imprecise to Precise Probabilities

Pietro Baroni[1] and Paolo Vicig[2]

[1] Dip. di Elettronica per l'Automazione, Univ. of Brescia, Via Branze 38
I-25123 Brescia, Italy
`baroni@ing.unibs.it`
[2] Dip. di Matematica Applicata 'B. de Finetti', Univ. of Trieste, Piazzale Europa 1
I-34127 Trieste, Italy
`paolo.vicig@econ.units.it`

Abstract. Several known procedures transforming an imprecise probability into a precise one focus on special classes of imprecise probabilities, like belief functions and 2–monotone capacities, while not addressing the more general case of coherent imprecise probabilities, as defined by Walley. In this paper we first analyze some of these transformations, exploring the possibility of applying them to more general families of uncertainty measures and evidencing their limitations. In particular, the pignistic probability transformation is investigated from this perspective. We then propose a transformation that can be applied to coherent imprecise probabilities, discussing its properties and the way it can be used in the case of partial assessments.

1   Introduction

The study of transformation procedures between uncertainty representation formalisms attracts the interest of researchers for several reasons. Firstly, transforming a more complex representation into a simpler one is often computationally advantageous. Further, these procedures are a key issue for enabling interoperability among heterogeneous uncertain reasoning systems, adopting different approaches to uncertainty, as is the case in *multi-agent systems* [1].

In this paper we focus on procedures for transforming an imprecise probability, defined on a finite set of events, into a precise one. Among the main choices underlying the definition of such a procedure we mention the *class* of imprecise probabilities to which the procedure is applicable and the *criteria* that define desirable transformation properties. As to the former point, we are aware of transformation proposals regarding some classes of imprecise probabilities, namely *possibilities*, *belief functions* and *2–monotone* capacities. As to the latter, several criteria have been considered in literature proposals, as we will discuss in Sect. 3.

As to our knowledge, no existing proposal addresses the problem of defining a transformation procedure from a coherent imprecise probability [2] into a precise one. This problem is more general in two main respects:

T.D. Nielsen and N.L. Zhang (Eds.): ECSQARU 2003, LNAI 2711, pp. 37–49, 2003.

- on one hand, coherent imprecise probabilities cover a larger set of uncertainty assignments and include as special cases the subclasses mentioned above [3];
- on the other hand, a coherent imprecise probability can be assigned on an arbitrary set of events, while other formalisms require an algebraic structure.

In this paper, after recalling some basic concepts in Sect. 2, we first discuss several transformation procedures in Sect. 3, investigating to which extent they can be generalized to coherent imprecise probabilities. In particular we discuss Voorbraak's transformation in Sect. 3.1, the pignistic probability transformation in Sect. 3.2, uncertainty invariant transformations in Sect. 3.3. In Sect. 4 we provide some empirical results about the relevance of specific subclasses within coherent imprecise probabilities and evidence the necessity of introducing a new procedure, which is then defined and discussed, considering also the case of partial assessments. Section 5 concludes the paper.

2   Basic Concepts

We use the symbol Ω to denote both the certain event and a *finite* set - also called *universal set* or *partition* - of pairwise disjoint (non-impossible) events whose union is the certain event: $\Omega = \{\omega_1, \ldots, \omega_N\}$. Then $\omega_1, \ldots, \omega_N$ are called *atoms*, 2^Ω is the powerset of Ω, $|A|$ is the cardinality of $A \in 2^\Omega$, i.e. the number of distinct atoms of Ω whose union is A.

A mapping $C : 2^\Omega \to [0,1]$ is a (normalized) *capacity* [4] whenever:

$C(\emptyset) = 0$; $C(\Omega) = 1$; $C(A_1) \le C(A_2), \forall A_1, A_2 \in 2^\Omega$ such that $A_1 \subset A_2$.

A capacity is *2-monotone* iff $\forall A, B \in 2^\Omega, C(A \cup B) \ge C(A) + C(B) - C(A \cap B)$. Belief functions [5], and in particular necessity measures [6] and, when defined on 2^Ω, finitely additive probabilities, are special cases of 2–monotone capacities. Their definitions are well known; we shall recall in Proposition 1 their characterizations in terms of their Möbius inverses [4].

For any $f : 2^\Omega \to \mathbb{R}$, there is a one-to-one correspondence between f and its *Möbius inverse* or *mass function* $m : 2^\Omega \to \mathbb{R}$, given $\forall A \in 2^\Omega$ by ([4], [7]):

$$m(A) = \sum_{B \subseteq A} (-1)^{|A \setminus B|} f(B), \qquad f(A) = \sum_{B \subseteq A} m(B) \qquad (1)$$

The events $A \in 2^\Omega$ such that $m(A) \neq 0$ are called *focal elements*.

Proposition 1. *Given* $f : 2^\Omega \to \mathbb{R}$, *let* m *be its Möbius inverse. Then*
(a) f *is a capacity iff* m *is such that:* $m(\emptyset) = 0$; $\sum_{B \in 2^\Omega} m(B) = 1$;
$\sum_{\omega \in B \subseteq A} m(B) \ge 0, \forall A \in 2^\Omega, \forall \omega \in A$.
Further, if f *is a capacity and* F *the set of its focal elements, then*
(b) f *is a 2–monotone capacity iff* $\forall A, B \in 2^\Omega$, $\sum_{C \subset A \cup B, C \not\subseteq A, C \not\subseteq B} m(C) \ge 0$;
(c) f *is a belief function iff* m *is non-negative;*
(d) f *is a necessity measure iff* F *is totally ordered by relation* '$\subset$';
(e) f *is a (precise) probability iff* $(A \in F) \Rightarrow (A$ *atom of* $\Omega)$.

Note that if f is a capacity, $f(\omega) = m(\omega) \geq 0$, $\forall \omega \in \Omega$.

The *conjugate* C' of a capacity C is defined by $C'(A) = 1 - C(A^c)$, $\forall A \in 2^\Omega$. The conjugate of a 2–monotone capacity (a belief function, a necessity measure) is termed 2-alternating capacity (plausibility function, possibility). A precise probability is self-conjugate.

The notion of *coherent lower probability*[1] specializes that of (coherent) lower prevision and is defined in [2], sec. 2.5, referring to an *arbitrary* (finite or not, structured or not) set of events S. We assume here that $S \subseteq 2^\Omega$.

Coherent lower probabilities are indirectly characterized as lower envelopes on S of precise probabilities. Denoting with $\mathcal{M}$ the set of all precise probabilities dominating $\underline{P}$ on S (i.e. $P \in \mathcal{M}$ iff $P(A) \geq \underline{P}(A), \forall A \in S$), the following *lower envelope theorem* holds [2]:

Proposition 2. $\underline{P}$ *is a coherent lower probability on S iff there exists a (non-empty) set $D \subseteq \mathcal{M}$ such that $\underline{P}(A) = \inf_{P \in D}\{P(A)\}$, $\forall A \in S$ (inf is attained).*

One may refer to either lower ($\underline{P}$) or upper ($\overline{P}$) probabilities only, exploiting conjugacy. In particular, assessing both $\underline{P}(A)$ and $\overline{P}(A)$ is equivalent to assessing $\underline{P}(A)$ and $\underline{P}(A^c) = 1 - \overline{P}(A)$. When $\underline{P}(A) = \overline{P}(A) = P(A), \forall A \in S$, P is a coherent precise probability on S (a finitely additive probability if $S = 2^\Omega$).

Later, we shall use the following necessary condition for coherence:

$$\underline{P}(A \cup B) \geq \underline{P}(A) + \underline{P}(B), \forall A, B : A \cap B = \emptyset \quad (A, B, A \cup B \in S) \qquad (2)$$

When $S = 2^\Omega$, lower (upper) probabilities are formally capacities, and include as special cases 2–monotone (2–alternating) capacities, therefore also belief functions and necessity measures (their conjugates).

Later in this paper we shall be concerned with transforming an imprecise (lower or upper) probability assessment on S into a precise probability. Since S will be finite but arbitrary, coherent imprecise and precise probabilities will be used. A relevant question will be what does a given lower probability assessment $\underline{P}$ on S entail on other events, not belonging to S. Concerning this problem, it is known that coherent lower probabilities can *always* be coherently extended on any $S' \supset S$. In particular, when considering one additional event A, the set of all coherent extensions of $\underline{P}$ to A is a closed (non-empty) interval $[\underline{P}_E(A), \underline{P}_U(A)]$, where $\underline{P}_E(A)$ is the *natural extension* [2] of $\underline{P}$ to A. That is $\underline{P}_E(A)$ is the *least committal* or vaguest admissible coherent extension of $\underline{P}$ on A. It may be obtained as the infimum value on A of all precise probabilities dominating $\underline{P}$ on S, which requires solving a linear programming (LP) problem. In principle, other coherent extensions may be interesting, especially the *upper extension* $\underline{P}_U(A)$ which has the opposite meaning of least vague coherent extension of $\underline{P}$. However, as shown in [8], sec. 5, computing $\underline{P}_U(A)$ may require solving $|S|$ distinct LP problems. The natural extension has also another advantage: if we compute separately $\underline{P}_E(A_i)$ for $i = 1, \ldots, m$ (i.e. we find separately the natural extension of $\underline{P}$ on $S_i = S \cup \{A_i\}$), then $\{\underline{P}_E(A_1), \ldots, \underline{P}_E(A_m)\}$ is the natural extension of $\underline{P}$

---

[1] We shall often omit the term coherent in the sequel.

on $S \cup \{A_1, \ldots, A_m\}$. This is generally not true for any other coherent extension: for instance, if we compute $\underline{P}_U(A_1)$ and put $\underline{P}(A_1) = \underline{P}_U(A_1)$, then the upper extension $\overline{P}_U^*(A_2)$ of $\underline{P}$ from $S \cup \{A_1\}$ to $S \cup \{A_1, A_2\}$ will be generally less than the value $\overline{P}_U(A_2)$ representing the upper extension of $\underline{P}$ from S to $S \cup \{A_2\}$.

3   An Analysis of Previously Proposed Transformations

Firstly, we briefly recall different transformation criteria considered in the past.

Consistency criteria impose some logical relation between the transformed uncertainty assignment U_2 and the original assignment U_1. In particular, when transforming a lower probability $\underline{P}$ into a precise probability P the commonly adopted consistency criterion [9] is applied requiring that

$$P(A) \geq \underline{P}(A), \forall A \in 2^\Omega \tag{3}$$

Similarity criteria aim at minimizing some difference between U_2 and U_1; in particular two kinds of similarity can be considered:

- *ordinal similarity*: some credibility order induced on events by U_1 should be preserved by U_2, an example is the *(strict) preference preservation* principle: $U_1(A) > U_1(B) \Leftrightarrow U_2(A) > U_2(B), \forall A, B \in 2^\Omega$;
- *quantitative similarity*: some distance between U_1 and U_2 should be minimized.

Selection criteria determine the selection of a particular U_2 when there are multiple results compatible with other transformation criteria.

3.1   Voorbraak's Bayesian Transformation

Voorbraak's Bayesian transformation takes as input the mass function m of a given belief function and outputs a mass function m_V which, in [10], is defined to be zero for all non-atomic events of 2^Ω, while for every atom $\omega \in \Omega$ it is:

$$m_V(\omega) = \frac{\sum_{B \supseteq \omega} m(B)}{\sum_{C \subseteq \Omega} m(C) \cdot |C|} \tag{4}$$

Such a mass assignment corresponds to a precise probability $P_V(\omega) = m_V(\omega)$, $\forall \omega \in \Omega$ (cf. Sect. 2). We note that this still holds if m is the mass function of a capacity, since again m_V is non-negative, by Proposition 1(a). The transformation can be equivalently rewritten in terms of the initial plausibility values of atoms: $P_V(\omega) = m_V(\omega) = Pl(\omega)/\sum_{\omega \in \Omega} Pl(\omega)$.

In other words, Voorbraak's proposal is a normalization of the plausibility values of atoms of Ω (more generally, when applied to a capacity C, it normalizes the values on the atoms of its conjugate C'). As such, it clearly respects an ordinal similarity criterion *restricted* to the plausibility values of the atoms of Ω. This is a relatively weak property, in particular the transformation does not match with the consistency criterion (3), as pointed out e.g. in [11].

In [12] a method for approximating belief functions based on the concept of fuzzy T-preorder is proposed. A detailed review of this approach can not be carried out here due to space limitations. However this work is mainly focused on possibility distributions approximating a belief function, while the existence and uniqueness of a probability which approximates the belief function is guaranteed only for a specific choice of the T-norm to be used in the transformation. In this case, as shown in [12], the probability obtained coincides with Voorbraak's, therefore the same considerations can be applied.

3.2 Pignistic Probability

The pignistic probability transformation (PPT) has been considered in a variety of publications mainly concerning belief functions (e.g. [11], [13]). It takes in input a mass function m and produces a probability P_{pign} on the atoms of Ω:

$$P_{pign}(\omega) = m_{pign}(\omega) = \sum_{\Omega \supseteq A \ni \omega} \frac{m(A)}{|A|}, \forall \omega \in \Omega \tag{5}$$

This transformation is based on the principle of insufficient reason applied to the focal events: it distributes uniformly their masses over their atoms.

Assuming now that m is the Möbius inverse of a capacity C, it is easy to see (using (1), (5) and additivity of P_{pign}) that

$$P_{pign}(B) = C(B) + \sum_{A \not\subseteq B} \frac{|A \cap B|}{|A|} m(A), \forall B \in 2^{\Omega} \tag{6}$$

It is clear from (6) and Proposition 1(c) that PPT preserves the consistency criterion when C is a belief function. Now the point is: what if C is not a belief function? It is not even immediate that P_{pign} is then a probability, since negative masses appear in (5). The question was first addressed in [13], where P_{pign} was also derived from axioms for combining *credibility functions*, i.e. capacities with some additional axiomatical properties. We extend this result by proving in Proposition 4 that PPT returns a precise probability from any capacity. Preliminarily we summarize some results stated in [4].

Proposition 3. *Given a capacity $C : 2^{\Omega} \to \mathbb{R}$, an associated set of precise probabilities V can be defined as follows. Let Σ be the set of all permutations of the atoms of Ω, with $|\Omega| = N$. Given $S \in \Sigma$, $S = (\omega_{i_1}, \ldots, \omega_{i_N})$, define $S_0 = \emptyset$ and, for $n = 1, \ldots, N$, $S_n = \omega_{i_1} \cup \ldots \cup \omega_{i_n}$, $P_S(\omega_{i_n}) = C(S_n) - C(S_{n-1})$. Let $V = \{P_S : S \in \Sigma\}$. Then*
(a) Every P_S is a (precise) probability, and it is, $\forall \omega \in \Omega$,

$$P_S(\omega) = \sum_{\Omega \supseteq A \ni \omega} \lambda(A, \omega) m(A) \tag{7}$$

where $\lambda(A, \omega_S(A)) = 1$, $\omega_S(A)$ being the last element of A in permutation S, and $\lambda(A, \omega) = 0$, $\forall \omega \neq \omega_S(A)$.

(b) *The set* V *coincides with the set of the vertices of the set* $\mathcal{M}$ *of all precise probabilities dominating* C *if and only if* C *is 2–monotone.*

Proposition 4. *Let* m *be the mass function corresponding to a capacity* C. *Then* P_{pign} *as defined in (5) is a precise probability.*

Proof. Using (7), we have that $P_S(\omega)$, and consequently $\sum_{S\in\Sigma} P_S(\omega)$, are a weighted sum of the masses of events A such that $A \ni \omega$. The weight of a generic $m(A)$ in $\sum_{S\in\Sigma} P_S(\omega)$ is equal to the cardinality of the set $\{S' \mid S' \in \Sigma, \omega = \omega_{S'}(A)\}$, i.e. to the number of times $\lambda(A,\omega) = 1$. The cardinality of this set is actually $\frac{N!}{|A|}$, since any $\omega \in A$ has the same chance of being the last element of A in a given permutation S. Therefore

$$\frac{1}{N!} \sum_{S\in\Sigma} P_S(\omega) = \frac{1}{N!} \sum_{\Omega\supseteq A\ni\omega} \frac{N!}{|A|} m(A) = P_{pign}(\omega), \forall \omega \in \Omega \tag{8}$$

From (8) and Proposition 3(a), P_{pign} is a convex combination of precise probabilities, and is therefore itself a precise probability. $\square$

We answer now a further question concerning how PPT relates to the consistency criterion.

Proposition 5. *Let* $C : 2^\Omega \to \mathbb{R}$ *be a given capacity with mass function* m, *and* P_{pign} *be defined by (5).*
(a) If C *is 2–monotone,* $P_{pign}(A) \geq C(A), \forall A \in 2^\Omega$.
(b) If C *is not 2–monotone,* P_{pign} *may or may not dominate* C. *If* $\underline{P}$ *is a coherent lower probability,* P_{pign} *dominates* $\underline{P}$ *on the atoms of* Ω, *i.e.* $P_{pign}(\omega) \geq \underline{P}(\omega)$, $\forall \omega \in \Omega$, *but not necessarily elsewhere.*

Proof. To prove (a), observe that if C is 2–monotone the probabilities P_S are vertices of $\mathcal{M}$ by Proposition 3(b), and as such dominate C; then also their convex combination P_{pign} dominates C (see (8)).

If C is not 2–monotone, examples may be found where P_{pign} does not dominate C. Consider for instance the coherent lower probability $\underline{P}$ on 2^Ω, with $\Omega = \{a,b,c,d,e\}$, which is the lower envelope of the three precise probabilities P_1, P_2, P_3, determined by orderly assigning the following values on the atoms a,b,c,d,e: P_1 - values $[0.49, 0.35, 0.12, 0.01, 0.03]$, P_2 - values $[0.14, 0.03, 0.07, 0.36, 0.40]$, P_3 - values $[0.36, 0.05, 0.29, 0.14, 0.16]$. Then P_{pign} is given by the following values on the atoms a,b,c,d,e: $[0.319\overline{83}, 0.163\overline{16}, 0.142\overline{3}, 0.172\overline{3}, 0.202\overline{3}]$. We have that $\underline{P}(a \cup d) = 0.5 > P_{pign}(a \cup d) = 0.4921\overline{6}$.

To prove the second part of (b), let $\omega \in \Omega$. Considering a permutation S (Proposition 3), let r be the position of ω in S, i.e. $\omega_{i_r} = \omega$. Then $P_S(\omega) = P_S(\omega_{i_r}) = \underline{P}(\omega_{i_1} \cup \ldots \cup \omega_{i_r}) - \underline{P}(\omega_{i_1} \cup \ldots \cup \omega_{i_{r-1}}) \geq \underline{P}(\omega_{i_r}) = \underline{P}(\omega)$, using (2) in the inequality. Since S is arbitrary, $P_S(\omega) \geq \underline{P}(\omega), \forall S$. Hence also the convex combination P_{pign} of the probabilities P_S is such that $P_{pign}(\omega) \geq \underline{P}(\omega)$. $\square$

We may conclude from Proposition 5 that PPT preserves the consistency criterion as far as it is applied to 2–monotone capacities. It may not preserve it outside 2–monotonicity, even though consistency may at least partially hold, as demonstrated in (b). To get some empirical insight of the behaviour of PPT outside 2–monotonicity, we randomly generated a large number of coherent lower probabilities which were not 2–monotone (see Sect. 4), computing also their corresponding P_{pign}: it has to be reported that the percentage of non-dominating P_{pign} was relatively low, and dominance violation numerically rather small. One of the examples we found is used in the proof of Proposition 5.

The pignistic probability has also been interpreted (e.g. in [9], which focuses on possibility measures) as center of gravity of the vertices of $\mathcal{M}$. This interpretation is clearly supported by Proposition 3(b) and (8), from which it is also patent that its validity is limited to 2–monotone probabilities. However the interpretation seems to us debatable even in the context of 2–monotonicity. In fact, from (8), P_{pign} is the average of $N!$ probabilities P_S, which are *not* necessarily all distinct: distinct permutations in Proposition 3 may well originate the same probability (examples are easily found). This means that P_{pign} is actually a *weighted* average of the *distinct* P_S, and the weight of any P_S is given by the number of distinct permutations S which give rise to it (analogously, the vertices obtained in [9] by means of 'selection functions' are also not necessarily distinct).

A point which seems therefore difficult to justify in the center of gravity interpretation is the real meaning of the weights in terms of the initially assigned 2–monotone capacity. More generally, it is also questionable, when transforming a given uncertainty measure μ, to use a criterion which is based on properties of different uncertainty measures, that only indirectly relate to μ.

3.3   Uncertainty Invariant Transformations

In [14] the uncertainty invariance principle is proposed, which states that uncertainty transformations should not modify the information contents of a given assignment. To apply this principle a measure of information has to be defined for the uncertainty measures involved in the transformation process. Several proposals to extend the classical Hartley measure for crisp sets and Shannon entropy for precise probabilities to fuzzy sets and belief functions are considered in [14]. Those based on mass values, interpreted as 'degrees of evidence', can not be extended to the case of imprecise probabilities, where masses can be negative and have no clear intuitive interpretation [15]. On the other hand, the definition of the *aggregate uncertainty measure* (AU), namely the maximum value of the Shannon entropy among all probability distributions dominating a given belief function, could be directly extended to coherent imprecise probabilities. Some limitations of AU are pointed out in [16]. In particular, AU does not distinguish among all imprecise probabilities which are consistent with the uniform probability, including the case of total ignorance.

A transformation based on the uncertainty invariance principle and using the AU measure consists in determining the maximum entropy precise probability among those in $\mathcal{M}$. This is equivalent to adopting the consistency criterion with maximum entropy as a selection criterion, but is intrinsically in contrast with similarity and in particular with preference preservation, tending to equate all probability values of atoms, as far as allowed by consistency. In our opinion, this is a drawback of the criterion in transformations devoted to uncertainty interchange. A discussion of pros and cons of maximum entropy methods may be found in [2], sec. 5.12, where it appears that these methods may be appropriate in certain specific decision problems.

Apart from theoretical issues, as to our knowledge no algorithm has been devised for computing the maximum entropy probability P_{ME} consistent with an imprecise probability assessment. In the case of 2–monotone capacities, it is shown in [17] that the solution is unique and an algorithm is provided. We checked that the procedure does not ensure the consistency condition (3) outside 2–monotonicity. Consider for this the lower probability assignment $\underline{P}$ in the proof of Proposition 5(b). The resulting P_{ME}, determined by the values $[0.26, 0.16, 0.16, 0.16, 0.26]$ on the atoms of Ω, is such that $P_{ME}(a \cup d) = 0.42 < \underline{P}(a \cup d) = 0.5$.

4   An Imprecise to Precise Probability Transformation

Even though there are important situations which cannot be adequately described by 2–monotonicity ([2], sec. 5.13.4), it is also known that 2–monotonicity arises in certain contexts, for instance when using pari-mutuel models (at racetracks or in life insurance) [2], or more generally convex transformations of precise probabilities [18]. As shown in the previous section, some transformation procedures preserve their applicability or some important properties only in the context of 2–monotone capacities. One may then wonder whether these procedures should be applied to imprecise probabilities too, assuming that a 'large' part of them is 2–monotone. To give an empirical answer to this question, we wrote a computer program in Java language whose main loop randomly generates a coherent imprecise probability and verifies whether it is a belief function and, if not, whether it is 2–monotone. All random selections are carried out using the standard Java function $Math.random$ which generates pseudorandom numbers in $[0, 1]$, with an approximately uniform distribution (see documentation at http://java.sun.com/j2se/1.4.1/docs/api/java/util/Random.html for details).

The program was run for $|\Omega| = 3, \ldots, 10$ and generated 100000 imprecise probabilities for each cardinality. The results are shown in Table 1.

As can be noted, the relevance of 2–monotone capacities rapidly decreases as $|\Omega|$ increases. Moreover, for $|\Omega| > 5$, the number of 2–monotone capacities which are not belief functions is extremely small (11 over 874 for $|\Omega| = 10$). These results suggest that, in general, 2–monotone capacities can not be considered a numerically adequate representative of coherent lower probabilities. Another point from Sect. 3 is that known transformations often make use of the mass function m. This might suggest seeking for a transformation based on m in our context too. However the interpretation of m for imprecise probabilities

Table 1. Percentage of belief functions and 2–monotone capacities within randomly generated coherent lower probabilities

Cardinality of Ω	belief functions	2–monotone capacities
3	90.58	100
4	9.46	13.08
5	2.80	2.99
6	1.71	1.77
7	1.27	1.31
8	1.12	1.14
9	1.02	1.04
10	0.863	0.874

is unclear (see [15] for a discussion). Also we are aware of no characterization of imprecise probabilities in terms of m (like those in Proposition 1).[2]

Further, we shall be interested in transforming assessments on a generic (finite) set of events. For instance, in the case of a multi-agent system, agents are not necessarily interested in exchanging information about the whole 2^Ω but may focus on a more restricted set S_{INT} of interesting events. Although the mass function exists also in the partial case [7], it is easy to see that it does not preserve the properties it has in a complete assignment.

We shall now illustrate another transformation procedure, which extends a proposal initially presented in [1]. Defining $S^* = 2^\Omega \setminus \{\emptyset, \Omega\}$, we suppose at first $S_{INT} = S^*$: the case $S_{INT} \subset S^*$ will be considered later. We require the transformation to meet the consistency principle, which in terms of upper and lower probabilities imposes for the resulting precise probability P^* that

$$\underline{P}(A) \leq P^*(A) \leq \overline{P}(A), \forall A \in S^* \tag{9}$$

When $|\Omega| = 2$ (hence $S^* = \{A, A^c\}$), P^* may be fully determined from $P^*(A) = \frac{\overline{P}(A) + \underline{P}(A)}{2}$. This seems reasonable, since P^* reduces then the imprecision of both $\underline{P}$ and $\overline{P}$ by the same amount, and there is no reason for P^* to be closer to either of $\underline{P}$ or $\overline{P}$. A straightforward generalization for $|\Omega| > 2$ of the idea of eliminating imprecision in a symmetric way for each event in S^* leads to considering $P_m = \frac{\overline{P}(A) + \underline{P}(A)}{2}$, $\forall A \in S^*$.

In general P_m is not a precise probability, but we may choose a probability P^* close to it in some way. Obviously there are several approximation choices; selecting in particular the common *least-squares* approximation of P_m leads to the following *transformation problem* (TP):

$$min \; \varphi = \sum_{A \in S^*} (P^*(A) - P_m(A))^2 \tag{10}$$

---

[2] Several necessary conditions for coherence may be found. For instance, rewriting (2) using (1) leads to condition $\sum_{C \subseteq A \cup B, C \not\subseteq A, C \not\subseteq B} m(C) \geq 0, \forall A, B : A \cap B = \emptyset$, which is a special case of the 2–monotonicity characterization in Proposition 1(a) and also implies (putting $A = \omega_i$, $B = \omega_j \neq \omega_i$) $m(A) \geq 0$ if $|A| = 2$.

with the constraints (9) and

$$P^*(A) = \sum_{\omega \in A} P^*(\omega), \ \forall A \in S^*; \ P^*(\omega_i) \geq 0, i = 1, \ldots, N; \ \sum_{i=1}^{N} P^*(\omega_i) = 1 \quad (11)$$

The variables in TP are $P^*(\omega_1), \ldots, P^*(\omega_N)$. Since φ is convex on $\mathbb{R}^{|\Omega|}$ and the set of constraints S_C is a (non-empty)[3] polyhedral set, TP is a convex quadratic programming problem, for which polynomial-time solving algorithms are known (see e.g. [19], sec. 11.2). TP has some desirable properties, which we derived using well-known results in calculus and convex programming:

(a) problem TP always returns a unique P^*. In particular, TP detects whether P_m is a precise probability, since in such a case it gives $P^* = P_m$.
(b) It may be useful to solve the linear system which equates to zero the gradient vector of φ. In fact, if its (unique) solution is an interior point in S_C then it is the required P^*; otherwise we get to know that P^* will be equal to either $\overline{P}(A)$ or $\underline{P}(A)$ for at least one $A \in S^*$.
(c) If $\overline{P}(A) = 1, \underline{P}(A) = 0, \forall A \in S^*$ (vague statement), TP returns the uniform probability as P^* (that may be seen applying (b)).

Let us now suppose that $S_{INT} \subsetneq S^*$, which is the *partial assignment* case.

Most known transformations can not be *directly* applied to partial assignments, because they are based on quantities which are typically defined on the whole 2^Ω. They might anyway be applied *indirectly*, extending the coherent lower probability to 2^Ω. As discussed in Sect. 2, the natural extension $\underline{P}_E$ appears to be the most appropriate extension both theoretically and computationally. A transformation requiring a complete assignment could then be applied to $\underline{P}_E$ on 2^Ω, with the same limitations discussed, for each case, in Sect. 3.

The transformation we are proposing may be applied *directly* to partial assessments, as far as both lower and upper probability values are assigned for each $A \in S_{INT}$.

If this condition holds, it suffices to replace S^* with S_{INT} in TP; otherwise the natural extension (of either $\underline{P}$ or $\overline{P}$) on $S^*_{INT} = S_{INT} \cup \{A : A^c \in S_{INT}\}$ should be computed before replacing S^* with S^*_{INT}. In both cases the transformation problem still returns a unique coherent precise probability $P^*(A), \forall A \ (A \in S_{INT}$ or $A \in S^*_{INT}$, respectively). Note that $P^*(\omega_1), \ldots, P^*(\omega_N)$ are generally not uniquely determined in the partial assessment case.

The direct way appears more appealing at a first glance. However, the choice between direct and indirect way is not straightforward, and this does not uniquely depend on the specific transformation we are applying here.

On one hand, the direct way avoids or reduces the computations required to determine the natural extension. Moreover, in the case of information exchange between agents adopting different uncertainty formalisms, no non-requested information is introduced. On the other hand, a partial assignment contains some

---

[3] Non-emptiness is implied by coherence, which ensures that $\mathcal{M} \neq \emptyset$ in the lower envelope theorem.

implicit information which is actually ignored by the direct way, but could affect transformation results if considered. Therefore ignoring *all* implications of a given partial assessment might be expected to originate an unsatisfactory transformation result. For instance, there may sometimes be a unique coherent extension to some event(s) in S^*. Should this piece of information be ignored? The following example illustrates this situation.

Example. Given $\Omega = \{\omega_1, \omega_2, \omega_3\}$ and $S_{INT} = \{\omega_1, \omega_1 \cup \omega_2\}$, the assignment $\underline{P}(\omega_1) = \underline{P}(\omega_1 \cup \omega_2) = a$, $\overline{P}(\omega_1) = \overline{P}(\omega_1 \cup \omega_2) = 1 - a$, $(a \in [0, \frac{1}{3}])$ on S_{INT} is equivalent to the lower probability assignment $\underline{P}(\omega_1) = \underline{P}(\omega_1 \cup \omega_2) = \underline{P}(\omega_3) = \underline{P}(\omega_2 \cup \omega_3) = a$ on the set $S^L = \{\omega_1, \omega_1 \cup \omega_2, \omega_3, \omega_2 \cup \omega_3\}$, which is easily seen to be coherent (for instance, using the envelope theorem). Since upper and lower probabilities are given for every event in S_{INT}, we may consider finding P^* in a direct way. Here $P_m(\omega_1) = P_m(\omega_1 \cup \omega_2) = \frac{1}{2}$ is a coherent probability on S_{INT} (being the restriction on S_{INT} of a probability on 2^Ω obtained from $P_m(\omega_1) = P_m(\omega_3) = \frac{1}{2}$, $P_m(\omega_2) = 0$), hence $P^* = P_m$.

However, using (2) to obtain $\underline{P}(\omega_1 \cup \omega_2) \geq \underline{P}(\omega_1) + \underline{P}(\omega_2)$ and since $\underline{P}(\omega_1 \cup \omega_2) = \underline{P}(\omega_1) = a$, we note that the given $\underline{P}$ has a unique coherent extension on ω_2, $\underline{P}(\omega_2) = \underline{P}_E(\omega_2) = \underline{P}_U(\omega_2) = 0$. Since $\underline{P}(\omega_2)$ is determined by the assessment on S_{INT}, we consider computing P^* starting from $S_{INT}^+ = S_{INT} \cup \{\omega_2\}$. We therefore add $\underline{P}(\omega_2) = 0$ and, to be able to apply the transformation to the new assignment, $\overline{P}_E(\omega_2) = 1 - 2a$ to the initial assessment (note that the initial assignment does not entail a unique $\overline{P}(\omega_2)$). The new P_m is no longer a coherent probability ($P_m(\omega_1) = P_m(\omega_1 \cup \omega_2) = \frac{1}{2}$, $P_m(\omega_2) = \frac{1}{2} - a$, hence P_m is not additive), and we may compute P^* noting that the global minimum of $\varphi = (P^*(\omega_1) - \frac{1}{2})^2 + (P^*(\omega_2) - \frac{1}{2} + a)^2 + (P^*(\omega_1) + P^*(\omega_2) - \frac{1}{2})^2$ satisfies (9), (11) and therefore gives the required P^*, which is such that $P^*(\omega_1) = \frac{1+a}{3}$, $P^*(\omega_2) = \frac{1-2a}{3}$. Summoning up, we obtain:

$P^*(\omega_1) = P^*(\omega_1 \cup \omega_2) = \frac{1}{2}$, operating on S_{INT};

$P^*(\omega_1) = \frac{1+a}{3}$, $P^*(\omega_1 \cup \omega_2) = \frac{2-a}{3}$, operating on S_{INT}^+.

To get an idea of the difference, let $a = 0$. $\underline{P}$ is then vague, and its most intuitive transformation appears to be the (restriction on S_{INT}) of the uniform probability P_{unif}. However P^* is equal to P_{unif} when working on S_{INT}^+, not when using S_{INT}. $\square$

Clearly, the example above is not sufficient to infer what implications of a given assessment should be necessarily considered before running the transformation. For instance, it is not even simple in general to detect a priori (i.e. without computing upper and lower extensions) those events, if any, which allow a unique extension of $\underline{P}$, and this task may be not necessarily simpler than just computing $\underline{P}_E$ for all $A \notin S_{INT}$, $A \in S^*$.

5   Conclusions

The contribution of this paper is twofold. On one hand, we have discussed several existing transformations and obtained new results about their properties and limitations when applied to the case of coherent imprecise probabilities; this kind of analysis had not been previously considered in the literature. On the other hand, we have proposed an alternative transformation, applicable also to partial assignments, showing that it features some desirable properties: it preserves the consistency criterion and tends to remove imprecision in a symmetric way, gives a unique solution, returns the uniform probability from a vague assignment on 2^{Ω}, is computable in polynomial time. We then discussed basic problems concerning the alternative between direct vs. indirect application of transformations on partial assignments: this question deserves further investigation, as well as some aspects of the use of uncertainty invariant transformations with imprecise probabilities.

Acknowledgments. We thank one of the referees for helpful comments.

References

1. Baroni, P., Vicig, P.: An uncertainty interchange format for multi-agent systems based on imprecise probabilities. Proc. of IPMU 2000, Madrid, E, (2000) 1027–1034
2. Walley, P.: Statistical reasoning with imprecise probabilities. Chapman and Hall, London, UK, (1991)
3. Walley, P.: Measures of uncertainty in expert systems. Artificial Intelligence **83** (1996) 1–58
4. Chateauneuf, A., Jaffray, J.-Y.: Some characterizations of lower probabilities and other monotone capacities through the use of Möbius inversion. Mathematical Social Sciences **17** (1989) 263–283
5. Shafer, G.: A mathematical theory of evidence. Princeton University Press, Princeton, NJ, (1976)
6. Dubois, D., Prade, H.: Possibility theory. Plenum Press, New York, NY, (1988)
7. Rota, G.C.: On the foundations of combinatorial theory. I. Theory of Möbius functions. Z. für Wahrscheinlichkeitstheorie und Verwandte Gebiete **2** (1964) 340–368
8. Vicig, P.: An algorithm for imprecise conditional probability assessments in expert systems. Proc. of IPMU 1996, Granada, E, (1996) 61–66
9. Dubois, D., Prade, H., Sandri, S.: On possibility/probability transformations. In: Lowen, R., Roubens, M. (eds.): Fuzzy Logic - State of the art. Kluwer, Dordrecht, NL, (1993) 103–112
10. Voorbraak, F.: A computationally efficient approximation of Dempster-Shafer theory. Int. J. Man-Machine Studies **30** (1989) 525–536
11. Dubois, D., Prade, H.: Consonant approximations of belief functions. International Journal of Approximate Reasoning **4** (1990) 419–449
12. Hernandez, R., Recasens, J.: On possibilistic and probabilistic approximations of unrestricted belief functions based on the concept of fuzzy T-preorder. Int. J. of Uncertainty, Fuzziness and Knowledge-Based Systems **10** (2002) 185–200
13. Smets, P.: Constructing the pignistic probability function in a context of uncertainty. In: Henrion, M., Shachter, R.D., Kanal, L.N., Lemmer, J.F.(eds.): Uncertainty in Artificial Intelligence 5 North Holland, Amsterdam, NL, (1990) 29–39
14. Klir, G. J., Wierman, M. J.: Uncertainty-based information. Elements of generalized information theory. Physica-Verlag, Heidelberg, D, (1998)
15. Baroni, P., Vicig, P.: On the conceptual status of belief functions with respect to coherent lower probabilities. Proc. of ECSQARU 2001, Toulouse, F, (2001) 328–339

16. Klir, G.: Uncertainty and information measures for imprecise probabilities: an overview. Proc. of ISIPTA'99, Ghent, B, (1999)
17. Jaffray, J.-Y.: On the maximum-entropy probability which is consistent with a convex capacity. Int. J. of Uncertainty, Fuzziness and Knowledge-Based Systems **3** (1995) 27–33
18. Denneberg, D.: Non-additive measure and integral. Kluwer, Dordrecht, NL, (1994)
19. Bazaraa, M. S., Sherali, H. D., Shetty, C. M.: Nonlinear programming. Wiley, NY, USA, 2nd ed. (1993)

A Representation Theorem and Applications

Manfred Jaeger

Max-Planck-Institut für Informatik
Stuhlsatzenhausweg 85, 66123 Saarbrücken
jaeger@mpi-sb.mpg.de

Abstract. We introduce a set of transformations on the set of all probability distributions over a finite state space, and show that these transformations are the only ones that preserve certain elementary probabilistic relationships. This result provides a new perspective on a variety of probabilistic inference problems in which invariance considerations play a role. Two particular applications we consider in this paper are the development of an equivariance-based approach to the problem of measure selection, and a new justification for Haldane's prior as the distribution that encodes prior ignorance about the parameter of a multinomial distribution.

1 Introduction

Many rationality principles for probabilistic and statistical inference are based on considerations of indifference and symmetry. An early expression of such a principle is Laplace's principle of insufficient reason: *"One regards two events as equally probable when one can see no reason that would make one more probable than the other, because, even though there is an unequal possibility between them, we know not which way, and this uncertainty makes us look on each as if it were as probable as the other"* (Laplace, Collected Works vol. VIII, cited after [3]). Principles of indifference only lead to straightforward rules for probability assessments when the task is to assign probabilities to a finite number of different alternatives, none of which is distinguished from the others by any information we have. In this case all alternatives will have to be assigned equal probabilities. Such a formalization of indifference by equiprobability becomes notoriously problematic when from state spaces of finitely many alternatives we turn to infinite state spaces: on countably infinite sets no uniform probability distributions exist, and on uncountably infinite sets the concept of uniformity becomes ambiguous (as evidenced by the famous Bertrand's paradox [6,19]).

On (uncountably) infinite state spaces concepts of uniformity or indifference have to be formalized on the basis of certain transformations of the state space: two sets of states are to be considered equiprobable, if one can be transformed into the other using some natural transformation t. This, of course, raises the sticky question what transformations are to be considered as natural and probability-preserving. However, for a given state space, and a given class of probabilistic inference tasks, it often is possible to identify natural transformation, so that the solution to the inference tasks (which, in particular, can be probability assessments) should be invariant under the transformations. The widely accepted resolution of Bertrand's paradox, for example, is based on such considerations of invariance under certain transformations.

T.D. Nielsen and N.L. Zhang (Eds.): ECSQARU 2003, LNAI 2711, pp. 50–61, 2003.

In this paper we are concerned with probabilistic inference problems that pertain to probability distributions on finite state spaces, which are by far the most widely used type of distributions used for probabilistic modelling in artificial intelligence. As indicated above, when dealing with finite state spaces there does not seem to be any problem of capturing indifference principles with equiprobability. However, even though the underlying space of alternatives may be finite, the object of our study very often is the infinite set of probability distributions on that space, i.e. for the state space $S = \{s_1, \ldots, s_n\}$ the $(n-1)$-dimensional probability polytope

$$\Delta^n = \{(p_1, \ldots, p_n) \in \mathbb{R}^n \mid p_i \in [0,1], \quad \sum_i p_i = 1\}.$$

The objective of this paper now can be formulated as follows: we investigate what natural transformations there exist of Δ^n, such that inference problems that pertain to Δ^n should be solved in a way that is invariant under these transformations. In Sect. 2 we identify a unique class of transformations that can be regarded as most natural in that they alone preserve certain relevant relationships between points of Δ^n. In Sects. 3 and 4 we apply this result to the problems of measure selection and choice of Bayesian priors, respectively.

An extended version of this paper containing the proofs of theorems is available as [9].

2 Representation Theorem

The nature of the result we present in this section can best be explained by an analogy: suppose, for the sake of the argument, that the set of probability distributions we are concerned with is parameterized by the whole Euclidean space $\mathbb{R}^n$, rather than the subset Δ^n. Suppose, too, that all inputs and outputs for a given type of inference problem consist of objects (e.g. points, convex subsets, ...) in $\mathbb{R}^n$. In most cases, one would then probably require of a rational solution to the inference problem that it does not depend on the choice of the coordinate system; specifically, if all inputs are transformed by a translation, i.e. by adding some constant offset $r \in \mathbb{R}^n$, then the outputs computed for the transformed inputs should be just the outputs computed for the original inputs, also translated by r:

$$sol(i + r) = sol(i) + r, \tag{1}$$

where i stands for the inputs and sol for the solution of an inference problem. Condition (1) expresses an *equivariance principle*: when the problem is transformed in a certain way, then so should be its solution (not to be confused with *invariance principles* according to which certain things should be unaffected by a transformation).

The question we now address is the following: what simple, canonical transformations of the set Δ^n exist, so that for inference problems whose inputs and outputs are objects in Δ^n one would require an equivariance property analogous to (1)? Intuitively, we are looking for transformations of Δ^n that can be seen as merely a change of co-ordinate system, and that leave all relevant geometric structures intact. The following definition collects some key concepts we will use.

Definition 1. A transformation *of a set S is any bijective mapping t of S onto itself. We often write ts rather than t(s). For a probability distribution* $p = (p_1, \ldots, p_n) \in \Delta^n$ *the set* $\{i \in \{1, \ldots, n\} \mid p_i > 0\}$ *is called the* set of support *of p, denoted* support(p). *A transformation t of* Δ^n *is said to*

- preserve cardinalities of support *if for all p:* $|\text{support}(p)| = |\text{support}(tp)|$
- preserve sets of support *if for all p:* $\text{support}(p) = \text{support}(tp)$.

A distribution p is called a mixture *of p' and p'' if there exists* $\lambda \in [0, 1]$ *such that* $p = \lambda p' + (1 - \lambda)p''$ *(in other words, p is a convex combination of p' and p''). A transformation t is said to*

- preserve mixtures *if for all* p, p', p'': *if p is a mixture of p' and p'', then tp is a mixture of tp' and tp''.*

The set of support of a distribution $p \in \Delta^n$ can be seen as its most fundamental feature: it identifies the subset of states that are to be considered as possible at all, and thus identifies the relevant state space (as opposed to the formal state space S, which may contain states s_i that are effectively ruled out by p with $p_i = 0$). When the association of the components of a distribution p with the elements of the state space $S = \{s_1, \ldots, s_n\}$ is fixed, then p and p' with different sets of support represent completely incompatible probabilistic models that would not be transformed into one another by a natural transformation. In this case, therefore, one would require a transformation to preserve sets of support.

A *permutation* of Δ^n is a transformation that maps $(p_1, \ldots, p_n)$ to $(p_{\pi(1)}, \ldots, p_{\pi(n)})$, where π is a permutation of $\{1, \ldots, n\}$. Permutations preserve cardinalities of support, but not sets of support. Permutations of Δ^n are transformations that are required to preserve the semantics of the elements of Δ^n after a reordering of the state space S: if S is reordered according to a permutation π, then p and πp are the same probability distribution on S. Apart from this particular need for permutations, they do not seem to have any role as a meaningful transformation of Δ^n.

That a distribution p is a mixture of p' and p'' is an elementary probabilistic relation between the three distributions. It expresses the fact that the probabilistic model p can arise as an approximation to a finer model that would distinguish the two distinct distributions p' and p'' on S, each of which is appropriate in a separate context. For instance, p' and p'' might be the distributions on $S = \{jam, heavy \ traffic, light \ traffic\}$ that represent the travel conditions on weekdays and weekends, respectively. A mixture of the two then will represent the probabilities of travel conditions when no distinction is made between the different days of the week.

That a transformation preserves mixtures, thus, is a natural requirement that it does not destroy elementary probabilistic relationships. Obviously, preservation of mixtures immediately implies preservation of convexity, i.e. if t preserves mixtures and A is a convex subset of Δ^n, then tA also is convex.

We now introduce the class of transformations that we will be concerned with in the rest of this paper. We denote with $\mathbb{R}^+$ the set of positive real numbers.

Definition 2. *Let* $r = (r_1, \ldots, r_n) \in (\mathbb{R}^+)^n$. *Define for* $p = (p_1, \ldots, p_n) \in \Delta^n$

$$t_r(p) := (r_1 p_1, \ldots, r_n p_n) / \sum_{i=1}^{n} r_i p_i.$$

Also let $T_n := \{t_r \mid r \in (\mathbb{R}^+)^n\}$.

Note that we have $t_r = t_{r'}$ if r' is obtained from r by multiplying each component with a constant $a > 0$. We can now formulate our main result.

Theorem 1. *Let* $n \geq 3$ *and* t *be a transformation of* Δ^n.

(i) *t preserves sets of support and mixtures iff $t \in T_n$.*
(ii) *t preserves cardinalities of support and mixtures iff $t = t' \circ \pi$ for some permutation π and some $t' \in T_n$.*

The statements (i) and (ii) do not hold for $n = 2$: Δ^2 is just the interval $[0, 1]$, and every monotone bijection of $[0, 1]$ satisfies (i) and (ii). A weaker form of this theorem was already reported in [8]. The proof of the theorem closely follows the proof of the related representation theorem for collineations in projective geometry. The following example illustrates how transformations $t \in T_n$ can arise in practice.

Example 1. In a study of commuter habits it is undertaken to estimate the relative use of buses, private cars and bicycles as a means of transportation. To this end, a group of research assistants is sent out one day to perform a traffic count on a number of main roads into the city. They are given count sheets and short written instructions. Two different sets of instructions were produced in the preparation phase of the study: the first set advised the assistants to make one mark for every bus, car, and bicycle, respectively, in the appropriate column of the count sheet. The second (more challenging) set of instructions specified to make as many marks as there are actually people travelling in (respectively on) the observed vehicles. By accident, some of the assistants were handed instructions of the first kind, others those of the second kind.

Assume that on all roads being watched in the study, the average number of people travelling in a bus, car, or on a bicycle is the same, e.g. 10, 1.5, and 1.01, respectively. Also assume that the number of vehicles observed on each road is so large, that the actually observed numbers are very close to these averages.

Suppose, now, that we are more interested in the relative frequency of bus, car and bicycle use, rather than in absolute counts. Suppose, too, that we prefer the numbers that would have been produced by the use of the second set of instructions. If, then, an assistant hands in counts that were produced using the first set of instructions, and that show frequencies $f = (f_1, f_2, f_3) \in \Delta^3$ for the three modes of transportation, then we obtain the frequencies we really want by applying the transformation t_r with $r = (10, 1.5, 1.01)$. Conversely, if we prefer the first set of instructions, and are given frequencies generated by the second, we can transform them using $r' = (1/10, 1/1.5, 1/1.01)$.

This example gives rise to a more general interpretation of transformations in T_n as analogues in discrete settings to rescalings, or changes of units of measurements, in a domain of continuous observables.

3 E uivariant Measure Selection

A fundamental probabilistic inference problem is the problem of *measure selection*: given some incomplete information about the true distribution p on S, what is the best rational hypothesis for the precise value of p? This question takes on somewhat different aspects, depending on whether p is a statistical, observable probability, or a subjective degree of belief. In the first case, the "true" p describes actual long-run frequencies, which, in principle, given sufficient time and experimental resources, one could determine exactly. In the case of subjective probability, the "true" p is a rational belief state that an ideal intelligent agent would arrive at by properly taking into account all its actual, incomplete knowledge.

For statistical probabilities the process of measure selection can be seen as a prediction on the outcome of experiments that, for some reason, one is unable to actually conduct. For subjective probabilities measure selection can be seen as an introspective process of refining one's belief state. A first question then is whether the formal rules for measure selection should be the same in these two different contexts, and to which of the two scenarios our subsequent considerations pertain.

Following earlier suggestions of a frequentist basis for subjective probability [16, 1], this author holds that subjective probability is ultimately grounded in empirical observation, hence statistical probability [7]. In particular, in [7] the process of subjective measure selection is interpreted as a process very similar to statistical measure selection, namely a prediction on the outcome of hypothetical experiments (which, however, here even unlimited experimental resources may not permit us to carry out in practice). From this point of view, then, formal principles of measure selection will have to be the same for subjective and statistical probabilities, and our subsequent considerations apply to both cases. We note, however, that Paris [12] holds an opposing view, and sees no reason why his rationality principles for measure selection, which were developed for subjective probability, should also apply to statistical probability. On the other hand, in support of our own position, it may be remarked that the measure selection principles Shore and Johnson [18] postulate are very similar to those of Paris and Vencovská [15], but they were formulated with statistical probabilities in mind.

There are several ways how incomplete information about p can be represented. One common way is to identify incomplete information with some subset A of Δ^n: A is then regarded as the set of probability distributions p that are to be considered possible candidates for being the true distribution. Often A is assumed to be a closed and convex subset of Δ^n. This, in particular, will be the case when the incomplete information is given by a set of linear constraints on p. In that case, A is the solution set of linear constraints, i.e. a polytope.

Example 2. (continuation of example 1) One of the research assistants has lost his count sheet on his way home. Unwilling to discard the data from the road watched by this assistant, the project leader tries to extract some information about the counts that the assistant might remember. The assistant is able to say that he observed at least 10 times as many cars as buses, and at least 5 times as many cars as buses and bicycles combined. The only way to enter the observation from this particular road into the study, however, is in the form of accurate relative frequencies of bus, car, and bicycle use. To this end, the project leader has to make a best guess of the actual frequencies based on the linear constraints given to him by the assistant.

Common formulations of the measure selection problem now are: define a selection function *sel* that maps closed and convex subsets A of Δ^n (or, alternatively: polytopes in Δ^n; or: sets of linear constraints on p) to distributions $sel(A) \in A$.

The most widely favored solution to the measure selection problem is the *entropy maximization* rule: define $sel_{me}(A)$ to be the distribution p in A that has maximal entropy (for closed and convex A this is well-defined). Axiomatic justifications for this selection rule are given in [18,15]. Both these works postulate a number of formal principles that a selection rule should obey, and then proceed to show that entropy maximization is the only rule satisfying all the principles. Paris [13] argues that all these principles in essence are just expressions of one more general underlying principle, which is expressed by an informal statement (or slogan) by van Fraassen [19]: *Essentially similar problems should have essentially similar solutions*.

In spite of its mathematical sound derivation, entropy maximization does exhibit some behaviors that appear counterintuitive to many (see [8] for two illustrative examples). Often this counterintuitive behavior is due to the fact that the maximum entropy rule has a strong bias towards the uniform distribution $u = (1/n, \ldots, 1/n)$. As u is the element in Δ^n with globally maximal entropy, u will be selected whenever $u \in A$. Consider, for example, Fig. 1(i) and (ii). Shown are two different subsets A and A' of Δ^3. Both contain u, and therefore $sel_{me}(A) = sel_{me}(A') = u$. While none of Paris' rationality principles explicitly demands that u should be selected whenever possible, there is one principle that directly implies the following for the sets depicted in Fig. 1: assuming that $sel(A) = u$, and realizing that A' is a subset of A, one should also have $sel(A') = u$. This is an instance of what Paris [14] calls the *obstinacy principle*: for any A, A' with $A' \subseteq A$ and $sel(A) \in A'$ it is required that $sel(A') = sel(A)$. The intuitive justification for this is that additional information (i.e. information that limits the previously considered distribution A to A') that is consistent with the previous default selection (i.e. $sel(A) \in A'$) should not lead us to revise this default selection. While quite convincing from a default reasoning perspective (in fact, it is a version of Gabbay's [2] *restricted monotonicity* principle), it is not entirely clear that this principle is an expression of the van Fraassen slogan. Indeed, at least from a geometric point of view, there does seem to exist little similarity between the two problems given by A and A', and thus the requirement that they should have similar solutions (or even the same solution) hardly seems a necessary consequence of the van Fraassen slogan.

An alternative selection rule that avoids some of the shortcomings of sel_{me} is the *center of mass* selection rule sel_{cm}: $sel_{cm}(A)$ is defined as the center of mass of A. With sel_{cm} one avoids the bias towards u, and, more generally, the bias of sel_{me} towards points on the boundary of the input set A is reversed towards an exclusive preference for points in the interior of A. A great part of the intuitive appeal of sel_{cm} is probably owed to the fact that it satisfies (1), i.e. it is translation-equivariant.

Arguing that translations are not the right transformations to consider for Δ^n, however, we would prefer selection rules that are T_n-equivariant, i.e. for all A for which *sel* is to be defined, and all $t_r \in T_n$:

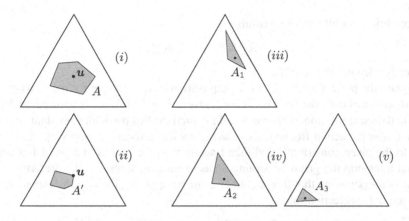

Fig. 1. Maximum Entropy and T_n- equivariant selection

$$sel(t_r A) = t_r sel(A). \tag{2}$$

This, we would claim, is the pertinent (and succinct) formalization of the van Fraassen slogan for the measure selection problem. In fact, van Fraassen [19], after giving the informal slogan, proceeds to explain it further as a general equivariance principle of the form (1) and (2). The question, thus, is not so much whether this slogan is best captured as an equivariance requirement, but with which class of transformations the equivariance principle is to be instantiated. Interpreting theorem 1 as an identification of the transformations in T_n as the most "similarity preserving" transformations of Δ^n, we arrive at our answer that T_n-equivariance is the principle we require.

Figure 1(iii)–(v) illustrates the T_n-equivariance principle: shown are three different transformations A_1, A_2, A_3 of a polytope defined by three linear constraints, and the corresponding transformations p_1, p_2, p_3 of one distinguished element inside the A_i. T_n-equivariance now demands that $sel(A_1) = p_1 \Leftrightarrow sel(A_2) = p_2 \Leftrightarrow sel(A_3) = p_3$.

Example 3. (continuation of example 2) Assume that the unlucky assistant in example 2 was given instructions of the first type, and that he collected his data accordingly. If, instead, he had been given instructions of the second type, then the frequencies on the lost count sheet would have been frequencies $f' = t_r f$, where f are the actual frequencies on the lost sheet, and t_r is as in example 1. The partial information he would then have been able to give also would have taken a different form. For instance, he might then have stated that he observed at least 6 times as many cars as buses, and at least 4.5 times as many cars as buses and bicycles combined.

One can show [8] that under very natural modelling assumptions, there corresponds to the transformation t_r on Δ^n a dual transformation $\bar{t}_r$ on the space of linear constraints, such that stating a constraint c for p corresponds to stating the constraint $\bar{t}_r c$ for $t_r p$. The crucial assumption is *consistency preservation*, which, in our example, means that a constraint c the research assistant will state when the frequencies on the lost count sheet are f is consistent for f (i.e. satisfied by f) iff the constraint c' he would give for frequencies f' is consistent for f'. The transformation $\bar{t}_r$ can also be characterized by the condition: for all sets of constraints c

$$Sol(\bar{t}_r c) = t_r Sol(c),$$

where *Sol* denotes the solution set.

When the project leader uses a T_n-equivariant selection rule for reconstructing the true frequencies from the information he is given, then the following two approaches will lead to the same solution, whatever set of instructions this particular assistant was using: 1: first infer the actual frequencies observed by the assistant by applying the selection rule to the given constraints, and then transform to the preferred type of frequencies. 2: first transform the given constraints so as to have them refer to the preferred type of frequencies (knowing that this should be done by applying the $\bar{t}_r$ transformation), and then apply the selection rule.

T_n-equivariance imposes no restriction on what $sel(A_i)$ should be for any single A_i in Fig. 1. It only determines how the selections for the different A_i should be related. It thus is far from providing a unique selection rule, like the rationality principles of Paris and Vencovská [15]. On the other hand, we have not yet shown that T_n-equivariant selection rules even exist. In the remainder of this section we investigate the feasibility of defining T_n-equivariant selection rules, without making any attempts to find the best or most rational ones.

From (2) one immediately derives a limitation of possible T_n-equivariant selection rules: let $A = \Delta^n$ in (2). Then $t_r A = A$ for every $t_r \in T_n$, and equivariance demands that $t_r sel(A) = sel(A)$ for all t_r, i.e. $sel(A)$ has to be a fixpoint under all transformations. The only elements of Δ^n that have this property are the n vertices $v_1, \ldots, v_n$, where v_i is the distribution that assigns unit probability to $s_i \in S$. Clearly a rule with $sel(\Delta^n) = v_i$ for any particular i would be completely arbitrary, and could not be argued to follow any rationality principles (more technically, such a rule would not be *permutation equivariant*, which is another equivariance property one would demand in order to deal appropriately with reorderings of the state space, as discussed in Sect. 2).

Similar problems arise whenever *sel* is to be applied to some $A \subseteq \Delta^n$ that is invariant under some transformations of T_n. To evade these difficulties, we focus in the following on sets that are not fixpoints under any transformations t_r (this restriction can be lifted by allowing selection rules that may also return subsets of A, rather than unique points in A). Let $\mathcal{A}$ denote the class of all $A \subseteq \Delta^n$ with $t_r A \neq A$ for all $t_r \in T_n$. One can show that $\mathcal{A}$ contains (among many others) all closed sets A that lie in the interior of Δ^n, i.e. $support(p) = \{1, \ldots, n\}$ for all $p \in A$. In the following example a T_n-equivariant selection rule is constructed for all convex $A \in \mathcal{A}$. This particular rule may not be a serious candidate for a best or most rational equivariant selection rule. However, it does have some intuitive appeal, and the method by which it is constructed illustrates a general strategy by which T_n-equivariant selection rules can be constructed.

Example 4. Let $\mathcal{A}^c$ denote the set of all convex $A \in \mathcal{A}$. On $\mathcal{A}^c$ an equivalence relation $\sim$ is defined by

$$A \sim A' \quad \Leftrightarrow \quad \exists t_r \in T_n : A' = t_r A.$$

The equivalence class $orb(A) := \{A' \mid A' \sim A\} \ (= \{t_r A \mid t_r \in T_n\})$ is called the *orbit* of A (these are standard definitions). It is easy to verify that for $A \in \mathcal{A}$ also

$orb(A) \subseteq \mathcal{A}$, and that for every $A' \in orb(A)$ there is a unique $t_r \in T_n$ with $A' = t_r A$ (here transformations are unique, but as observed above, this does not imply that the parameter r representing the transformation is unique).

Suppose that $sel(A) = p = (p_1, \ldots, p_n)$. With $r = (1/p_1, \ldots, 1/p_n)$ then $t_r p = u$, and by equivariance $sel(t_r A) = u$. It follows that in every orbit there must be some set A' with $sel(A') = u$. On the other hand, if $sel(A') = u$, then this uniquely defines $sel(A)$ for all A in the orbit of A': $sel(A) = p$, where $p = t_r u$ with t_r the unique transformation with $t_r A' = A$. One thus sees that the definition of an equivariant selection rule is equivalent to choosing for each orbit in $\mathcal{A}^c$ a representative A' for which $sel(A') = u$ shall hold.

One can show that for each $A \in \mathcal{A}^c$ there exists exactly one $A' \in orb(A)$ for which u is the center of mass of A'. Combining the intuitive center-of-mass selection rule with the principle of T_n-equivariance, we thus arrive at the T_n-equivariant center-of-mass selection rule: $sel_{equiv\text{-}cm}(A) = p$ iff $A = t_r A'$, u is the center of mass of A', and $p = t_r u$.

4   oninformative Priors

Bayesian statistical inference requires that a prior probability distribution is specified on the set of parameters that determines a particular probability model. Herein lies the advantage of Bayesian methods, because this prior can encode domain knowledge that one has obtained before any data was observed. Often, however, one would like to choose a prior distribution that represents the absence of any knowledge: an ignorant or noninformative prior. The set Δ^n is the parameter set for the multinomial probability model (assuming some sample size N to be given). The question of what distribution on Δ^n represents a state of ignorance about this model has received much attention, but no conclusive answer seems to exist.

Three possible solutions that most often are considered are: the uniform distribution, i.e. the distribution that has a constant density c with respect to Lebesgue measure, Jeffreys' prior, which is given by the density $c \prod_i p_i^{-1/2}$ (where c is a suitable normalizing constant), and Haldane's prior, given by density $\prod_i p_i^{-1}$. Haldane's prior (so named because it seems to have first been suggested in [4]) is an improper prior, i.e. it has an infinite integral over Δ^n. All three distributions are Dirichlet distributions with parameters $(1, \ldots, 1), (1/2, \ldots, 1/2)$, and $(0, \ldots, 0)$, respectively (in the case of Haldane's distribution, the usual definition of a Dirichlet distribution has to be extended so as to allow the parameters $(0, \ldots, 0)$). Schafer [17] considers all Dirichlet distributions with parameters $(\alpha, \ldots, \alpha)$ for $0 \le \alpha \le 1$ as possible candidates for a noninformative prior.

The justifications for identifying any particular distribution as the appropriate noninformative prior are typically based on invariance arguments: generally speaking, ignorance is argued to be invariant under certain problem transformations, and so the noninformative prior should be invariant under such problem transformations. There are different types of problem transformations one can consider, each leading to a different concept of invariance, and often leading to different results as to what constitutes a noninformative prior (see [5] for a systematic overview). In particular, there exist strong invariance-based arguments both for Jeffreys' prior [11], and for Haldane's prior [10, 20]. In the following, we present additional arguments in support of Haldane's prior.

Example 5. (continuation of example 3) Assume that the true, long-term relative frequencies of bus, car, and bicycle use are the same on all roads at which the traffic count is conducted (under both counting methods). Then the counts obtained in the study are multinomial samples determined by a parameter $f_1^* \in \Delta^3$ if the first set of instructions is used, and $f_2^* \in \Delta^3$ if the second set of instructions is used. Suppose the project leader, before seeing any counts, feels completely unable to make any predictions on the results of the counts, i.e. he is completely ignorant about the parameters f_i^*.

When the samples are large (i.e. a great number of vehicles are observed on every road), then the observed frequencies f obtained using instructions of type i are expected to be very close to the true parameter f_i^*. The prior probability Pr assigned to a subset $A \subseteq \Delta^n$ then can be identified with a prior expectation of finding in the actual counts relative frequencies $f \in A$. If this prior expectation is to express complete ignorance, then it must be the same for both sampling methods: being told by the first assistant returning with his counts that he had been using instructions of type 2 will have no influence on the project leader's expectations regarding the frequencies on this assistant's count sheet. In particular, merely seeing the counts handed in by this assistant will give the project leader no clue as to which instructions were used by this assistant.

The parameters f_i^* are related by $f_2^* = t_r f_1^*$, where t_r is as in example 1. Having the same prior belief about f_2^* as about f_1^* means that for every $A \subseteq \Delta^3$ one has $Pr(A) = Pr(t_r A)$. A noninformative prior, thus, should be invariant under the transformation t_r. As the relation between f_1^* and f_2^* might also be given by some other transformation in T_n, this invariance should actually hold for all these transformations.

This example shows that invariance under T_n-transformations is a natural requirement for a noninformative prior. The next theorem states that this invariance property only holds for Haldane's prior. In the formulation of the theorem a little care has to be taken in dealing with the boundary of Δ^n, where the density of Haldane's prior is not defined. We therefore restrict the statement of the theorem to the prior on the interior of Δ^n, denoted $int\Delta^n$.

Theorem 2. Let Pr be a measure on $int\Delta^n$ with $Pr(int\Delta^n) > 0$ and $Pr(A) < \infty$ for all compact subsets A of $int\Delta^n$. Pr is invariant under all transformations $t_r \in T_n$ iff Pr has a density with respect to Lebesgue measure of the form $c \prod_i p_i^{-1}$ with some constant $c > 0$.

It is instructive to compare the justification given to Haldane's prior by this theorem with the justification given by Jaynes [10]. Jaynes gives an intuitive interpretation of a noninformative prior as a distribution of beliefs about the true value of p that one would find in "a population in a state of total confusion": an individual i in the population believes the true value of p to be $p_i \in \Delta^n$. The mixture of beliefs one finds in a population whose individuals base their beliefs on "different and conflicting information" corresponds to a noninformative prior on Δ^n. Supposing, now, that to all members of this population a new piece of evidence is given, and each individual changes its belief about p by conditioning on this new evidence, then a new distribution of beliefs is obtained.

By a suitable formalization of this scenario, Jaynes shows that a single individual's transition from an original belief θ to the new belief θ' is given by $\theta' = a\theta/(1 - \theta + a\theta)$ (Jaynes only considers the binary case, where $\theta \in [0, 1]$ takes the role of our $p \in \Delta^n$). This can easily be seen as a transformation from our group T_2. Jaynes' argument now is that a collective state of total confusion will remain to be one of total confusion even after the new evidence has been assimilated by everyone, and so the belief distribution about θ in the population must be invariant under the transformation $\theta \mapsto \theta'$.

This justification, thus, derives a transformation of Δ^2 in a concrete scenario in which it seems intuitively reasonable to argue that a noninformative prior should be invariant under these transformations. This is similar to our argument for the invariance of a noninformative prior under the transformation t_r in example 5. Justifications of Haldane's (or any other) prior that are based on such specific scenarios, however, always leave the possibility open that similarly intuitive scenarios can be constructed which lead to other types of transformations, and hence to invariance-based justifications for other priors as noninformative. Theorems 1 and 2 together provide a perhaps more robust justification of Haldane's prior: any justification for a different prior which is based on invariance arguments under transformations of Δ^n must use transformations that do not have the conservation properties of definition 1, and therefore will tend to be less natural than the transformations on which the justification of Haldane's prior is based.

5 Conclusions

Many probabilistic inference problems that are characterized by a lack of information have to be solved on the basis of considerations of symmetries and invariances. These symmetries and invariances, in turn, can be defined in terms of transformations of the mathematical objects one encounters in the given type of inference problem.

The representation theorem we have derived provides a strong argument that in inference problems whose objects are elements and subsets of Δ^n, one should pay particular attention to invariances (and equivariances) under the transformations T_n. These transformations can be seen as the analogue in the space Δ^n of translations in the space $\mathbb{R}^n$.

One should be particularly aware of the fact that it usually does not make sense to simply restrict symmetry and invariance concepts that are appropriate in the space $\mathbb{R}^n$ to the subset Δ^n. A case in point is the problem of noninformative priors. In $\mathbb{R}^n$ Lebesgue measure is the canonical choice for an (improper) noninformative prior, because its invariance under translations makes it the unique (up to a constant) "uniform" distribution. Restricted to Δ^n, however, this distinction of Lebesgue measure does not carry much weight, as translations are not a meaningful transformation of Δ^n. Our results indicate that the choice of Haldane's prior for Δ^n is much more in line with the choice of Lebesgue measure on $\mathbb{R}^n$, than the choice of the "uniform" distribution, i.e. Lebesgue measure restricted to Δ^n.

In a similar vein, we have conjectured in Sect. 3 that some of the intuitive appeal of the center-of-mass selection rule is its equivariance under translations. Again, however, translations are not the right transformations to consider in this context, and one therefore should aim to construct T_n-equivariant selection rules, as, for example, the T_n-equivariant modification of center-of-mass.

An interesting open question is how many of Paris and Vencovská's [15] rationality principles can be reconciled with T_n-equivariance. As the combination of all uniquely identifies maximum entropy selection, there must always be some that are violated by T_n-equivariant selection rules. Clearly the obstinacy principle is rather at odds with T_n-equivariance (though it is not immediately obvious that the two really are inconsistent). Can one find selection rules that satisfy most (or all) principles except obstinacy?

References

1. R. Carnap. *Logical Foundations of Probability*. The University of Chicago Press, 1950.
2. D. Gabbay. Theoretical foundations for nonmonotonic reasoning in expert systems. In K. Apt, editor, *Logics and Models of Cuncurrent Systems*. Springer-Verlag, Berlin, 1985.
3. I. Hacking. *The Emergence of Probability: a Philosophical Study of Early Ideas About Probability, Induction and Statistical Inference*. Cambridge University Press, 1975.
4. J.B.S. Haldane. A note on inverse probability. *Proceedings of the Cambridge Philosophical Society*, 28:55–61, 1932.
5. J. Hartigan. Invariant prior distributions. *Annals of Mathematical Statistics*, 35(2):836–845, 1964.
6. J. Holbrook and S.S. Kim. Bertrand's paradox revisited. *The Mathematical Intelligencer*, pages 16–19, 2000.
7. M. Jaeger. Minimum cross-entropy reasoning: A statistical justification. In Chris S. Mellish, editor, *Proceedings of the Fourteenth International Joint Conference on Artificial Intelligence (IJCAI-95)*, pages 1847–1852, Montréal, Canada, 1995. Morgan Kaufmann.
8. M. Jaeger. Constraints as data: A new perspective on inferring probabilities. In B. Nebel, editor, *Proceedings of the Seventeenth International Joint Conference on Artificial Intelligence (IJCAI-01)*, pages 755–760, 2001.
9. M. Jaeger. A representation theorem and applications to measure selection and noninformative priors. Technical Report MPI-I-2003-2-002, Max-Planck-Institut für Informatik, 2003. in preparation.
10. E.T. Jaynes. Prior probabilities. *IEEE Transactions on Systems Science and Cybernetics*, 4(3):227–241, 1968.
11. H. Jeffreys. *Theory of Probability*. Oxford University Press, third edition edition, 1961.
12. J. Paris. On filling-in missing information in causal networks. Submitted to *Knowledge-based Systems*.
13. J. Paris. Common sense and maximum entropy. *Synthese*, 117:75–93, 1999.
14. J.B. Paris. *The Uncertain Reasoner's Companion*. Cambridge University Press, 1994.
15. J.B. Paris and A. Vencovská. A note on the inevitability of maximum entropy. *International Journal of Approximate Reasoning*, 4:183–223, 1990.
16. H. Reichenbach. *The Theory of Probability*. University of California Press, 1949.
17. J.L. Schafer. *Analysis of Incomplete Multivariate Data*. Chapman & Hall/CRC, 1997.
18. J.E. Shore and R.W. Johnson. Axiomatic derivation of the principle of maximum entropy and the principle of minimum cross-entropy. *IEEE Transactions on Information Theory*, IT-26(1):26–37, 1980.
19. B.C. van Fraassen. *Laws and Symmetry*. Clarendon, 1989.
20. C. Villegas. On the representation of ignorance. *Journal of the American Statistical Association*, 72:651–654, 1977.

On Modal Probability and Belief

Andreas Herzig and Dominique Longin

Institut de Recherche en Informatique de Toulouse (CNRS – UMR 5505)
118 route de Narbonne, F-31062 Toulouse cedex 04, France
{herzig,longin}@irit.fr
http://www.irit.fr/~Andreas.Herzig
http://www.irit.fr/~Dominique.Longin

Abstract. We investigate a simple modal logic of probability with a unary modal operator expressing that a proposition is more probable than its negation. Such an operator is not closed under conjunction, and its modal logic is therefore non-normal. Within this framework we study the relation of probability with other modal concepts: belief and action.

1 Introduction

Several researchers have investigated modal logics of probability. Some have added probability measures to possible worlds semantics, most prominently Fagin, Halpern and colleagues. [1]. They use modal operators of knowledge, $\mathcal{K}\phi$ expressing that the agent knows that ϕ, and they introduce modal operators of the kind $w(\phi) \geq b$ expressing that "according to the agent, formula ϕ holds with probability at least b".

Others have studied the properties of comparative probability, following Kraft, Pratt, and Seidenberg, and Segerberg. They use a relation $\phi > \psi$ (that can also be viewed as a binary modal construction) expressing "ϕ is more probable than ψ".

Only few have studied a still more qualitative notion, viz. the modal logic of constructions of the kind $\mathcal{P}\phi$ expressing that ϕ is more probable than $\neg\phi$ (or at least as probable as $\neg\phi$). Among those are Hamblin [2], Burgess [3], and T. Fine [4]. Halpern and colleagues have studied the similar notion of likelihood [5,6]. Also related is research on modal logics allowing to count the accessible worlds [7,8]. One can also read $\mathcal{P}\phi$ as "probability of ϕ is high", and interpret "high" as "greater than b", for $1 > b \geq 0.5$. We then basically get the same account as for $b = 0.5$.[1]

---

[1] As suggested by one of the reviewers, another option is to interpret $\mathcal{P}\phi$ not as a two-valued modal proposition but as a many-valued modal proposition, as it is done in [9, Chapter 8] and [10]. There, the truth degree of $\mathcal{P}\phi$ is taken as $Prob(\phi)$, so the bigger is the probability of ϕ, the 'more true' is the proposition $\mathcal{P}\phi$. One can then express that ϕ is more probable for the agent than $\neg\phi$ by a non-classical implication $\mathcal{P}\neg\phi \to \mathcal{P}\phi$.

T.D. Nielsen and N.L. Zhang (Eds.): ECSQARU 2003, LNAI 2711, pp. 62–73, 2003.
© Springer-Verlag Berlin Heidelberg 2003

Probably one of the reasons for the lack of interest in such approaches is that the corresponding logical systems are very poor, and do not allow to obtain completeness results w.r.t. the underlying probability measures.[2]

We here investigate the logic of the modal operator $\mathcal{P}$. We start by analyzing its properties, in particular in what concerns the interplay with the notion of belief. Contrarily to comparative possibility, such an operator is not closed under conjunction, and therefore its modal logic is non-normal [14].

We then turn to semantics. While probability distributions over sets of accessible worlds are helpful to explain modal constructions such as $\mathcal{P}\phi$, it is known that they do not allow complete axiomatizations. We here study a semantics that is closer to the set of properties that we have put forward. Our models are minimal models in the sense of [14], that are based on neighborhood functions instead of probability distributions. The logic is a non-normal, monotonic modal logic.[3]

Within this framework our aim is to study the relation of probability with other modal concepts such as belief and action. We propose principles for the interplay between action, belief, and probability, and formulate successor state axioms for both belief and probability. While there is a lot of work on probabilistic accounts of belief and action, as far as we are aware there is no similar work relating modal probability to belief and action.

2   Preliminaries

For the time being we do not consider interactions between several agents, and therefore we only consider a single agent.

2.1   Atomic Formulas, Atomic Actions

We have a set of atomic formulas $Atm = \{p, q, \dots\}$. Our running example will be in terms of playing dice; we thus consider atomic formulas $d_1, d_2, \dots$, respectively expressing "the dice shows 1", etc.

We have set of atomic actions $Act = \{\alpha, \beta, \dots\}$. In our example we have the *throw* action of throwing the dice, and the actions $observe_1, observe_2, \dots$ of the agent observing that the dice shows 1, etc.

Actions are not necessarily executed by the agent under concern, but may be executed by other agents or by nature. (So we might as well speak about events instead of actions.)

We could have considered complex actions, but for the sake of simplicity we shall not do so here.

---

[2] Note that things are simpler if we do not take probability theory but possibility theory: As shown in [11,12], Lewis' operator of comparative possibility [13] provides a complete axiomatization of qualitative possibility relations.

[3] Hence our semantics is rather far away from probabilities. This might be felt to be at odds with intuitions, but as a matter of fact what we have done is to exactly capture all that can be formally said about the property $\mathcal{P}$ of being probable.

From these ingredients complex formulas will be built together with modal operators in the standard way.

2.2   Modal Operators

We have a standard doxastic modal operator $\mathcal{B}$, and the formula $\mathcal{B}\phi$ is read "the agent believes that ϕ", or "ϕ is true for the agent". For example $\neg\mathcal{B}d_6$ expresses that the agent does not believe that some dice shows "6". The formula $\mathcal{B}(d_1 \vee d_2 \vee d_3 \vee d_4 \vee d_5 \vee d_6)$ expresses that the agent believes the dice shows one of 1, 2, 3, 4, 5, or 6.

Moreover we have a modal operator $\mathcal{P}$ where $\mathcal{P}\phi$ is read "ϕ is probable for the agent". The dual $\neg\mathcal{P}\neg\phi$ expresses that ϕ is not improbable. (This operator has been considered primitive in some papers in the literature.) For example, $\mathcal{P}(d_1 \vee d_2 \vee d_3 \vee d_4)$ expresses that it is probable for the agent that the dice shows one of 1, 2, 3, or 4. $\neg\mathcal{P}d_6$ expresses that it is improbable for the agent that the dice shows "6".

Finally, for every action $\alpha \in Act$ we have a dynamic logic operator $[\alpha]$. The formula $[\alpha]\phi$ is read "ϕ holds after every execution of α". For example $\neg[throw]\neg d_6$ expresses that the dice may show 6 after the throwing action. $\neg\mathcal{P}[throw]d_6$ expresses that this is improbable for the agent. $[throw]\mathcal{P}\neg d_6$ expresses that after throwing the dice it is probable for the agent that it did not fall 6. $[throw][observe_6]\mathcal{B}d_6$ expresses that after throwing the dice and observing that it fell 6 the agent believes that it fell 6.

2.3   Relations Agreeing with a Probability Measure

$\mathcal{P}$ can also be viewed as a relation on formulas. Let *Prob* be any subjective probability measure defined on formulas that is associated to the agent. When it holds that

$$\mathcal{P}\phi \text{ iff } Prob(\phi) > Prob(\neg\phi)$$

we say that $\mathcal{P}$ *agrees with Prob*.

2.4   Hypotheses about Action

We make some hypotheses about actions and their perception by the agent. They permit to simplify the theory.

Public Action Occurrences. We suppose that the agent perceives action occurrences completely and correctly. For example whenever a dice is thrown the agent is aware of that, and whenever the agent believes a dice is thrown then indeed such an action has occurred. (One might imagine that action occurrences are publicly announced to all agents.)

Public Action Laws. We suppose that the agent knows the laws governing the actions. Hence the agent knows that after throwing a dice the effect always is that 1, 2, 3, 4, 5, or 6 show up, and that 1 and 2 cannot show up simultaneously, etc.

Non-informativity. We suppose that all actions are non-informative. *Non-informative actions* are actions which are not observed by the agent beyond their mere occurrence. In particular the agent does not observe the outcome of nondeterministic actions such as that of throwing a dice. Upon learning that such an action has occurred the agent updates his belief state: he computes the new belief state from the previous belief state and his knowledge about the action laws. Hence the new belief state neither depends on the state of the world before the action occurrence, nor on the state of the world after the action occurrence.

In our example we suppose that the *throw* action is non informative: the agent throws the dice without observing the outcome. If the agent learns that the action of throwing a dice has been executed then he does not learn which side shows up.

Clearly, the action *observe* of observing the outcome of the *throw* action is informative: the new belief state depends on the position of the dice in the real world. Other examples of informative actions are that of looking up a phone number, *testing if* a proposition is true, *telling whether* a proposition is true, etc.

Nevertheless, the agent is not disconnected from the world: he may learn that some proposition is true (i.e. that some action of observing that some proposition has some value has occurred). For example, when he learns that it has been observed that the dice fell 6 (i.e. he learns that the action of observing 6 has been executed) then he is able to update his belief state accordingly. Indeed, the $observe_i$ actions are non-informative according to our definition: when the agent learns that $observe_i$ has occurred then he is able to update his belief state accordingly, and there is no need to further observation of the world. Other examples of noninformative actions are that of *learning that* the phone number of another agent is N, *testing that* a proposition is true (in the sense of Dynamic Logic tests), *telling that* a proposition is true, etc.

3   Axioms for Probability

In this section we give an axiomatization for $\mathcal{P}$.

The inference rule for $\mathcal{P}$ is

$$\text{if } \phi \rightarrow \psi \text{ then } \mathcal{P}\phi \rightarrow \mathcal{P}\psi \qquad (\text{RM}_\mathcal{P})$$

and the axioms are as follows:

$$\mathcal{P}\top \qquad (\text{N}_\mathcal{P})$$
$$\mathcal{P}\phi \rightarrow \neg\mathcal{P}\neg\phi \qquad (\text{D}_\mathcal{P})$$

These axioms match those that have been put forward in the literature, e.g. those in [4]. As stated there, it seems that there are no other principles of probability that could be formulated using $\mathcal{P}$.

Clearly such an axiomatization is sound w.r.t. the intended reading:

Theorem 1. *Let Prob be any probability measure, and suppose the property $\mathcal{P}$ agrees with $\mathcal{P}$, i.e. $\mathcal{P}\phi$ iff $Prob(\phi) > Prob(\neg\phi)$. Then $\mathcal{P}$ satisfies (RM$_{\mathcal{P}}$), (N$_{\mathcal{P}}$), (D$_{\mathcal{P}}$).*

Another way of expressing this is that whenever we define $\mathcal{P}\phi$ by $Prob(\phi) > 0.5$ then $\mathcal{P}$ satisfies (RM$_{\mathcal{P}}$), (N$_{\mathcal{P}}$), (D$_{\mathcal{P}}$).[4]

Nevertheless, such an axiomatics is not complete w.r.t. probability measures. This will be illustrated in Section 9.

4   Axioms for Belief

Following [15] we suppose a standard KD45 axiomatics for $\mathcal{B}$: we have the inference rule

$$\text{if } \phi \to \psi \text{ then } \mathcal{B}\phi \to \mathcal{B}\psi \qquad \text{(RM}_{\mathcal{B}})$$

and the following axioms:

$$\mathcal{B}\top \qquad \text{(N}_{\mathcal{B}})$$
$$\mathcal{B}\phi \to \neg\mathcal{B}\neg\phi \qquad \text{(D}_{\mathcal{B}})$$
$$(\mathcal{B}\phi \land \mathcal{B}\psi) \to \mathcal{B}(\phi \land \psi) \qquad \text{(C}_{\mathcal{B}})$$
$$\mathcal{B}\phi \to \mathcal{B}\mathcal{B}\phi \qquad \text{(4}_{\mathcal{B}})$$
$$\neg\mathcal{B}\phi \to \mathcal{B}\neg\mathcal{B}\phi \qquad \text{(5}_{\mathcal{B}})$$

Hence the set of beliefs is closed under logical consequences, and we suppose agents are aware of their beliefs and disbeliefs, i.e. we suppose introspection.

5   Axioms Relating Belief and Probability

What is the relation between $\mathcal{P}$ and $\mathcal{B}$? According to our reading we should have that things that are believed are also probable for an agent, i.e. we expect $\mathcal{B}\phi \to \mathcal{P}\phi$ to hold. The following main axiom will allow us to derive that:

$$(\mathcal{B}\phi \land \mathcal{P}\psi) \to \mathcal{P}(\phi \land \psi) \qquad \text{(C-MIX)}$$

Just as for the case of beliefs and disbeliefs, agents are aware of probabilities. This is expressed by the following two axioms:

$$\mathcal{P}\phi \to \mathcal{B}\mathcal{P}\phi \qquad \text{(4-MIX)}$$
$$\neg\mathcal{P}\phi \to \mathcal{B}\neg\mathcal{P}\phi \qquad \text{(5-MIX)}$$

Other principles of introspection for $\mathcal{P}$ will be derived from them in the sequel.

---

[4] This can be strengthened: if for some $b > 0.5$, $\mathcal{P}\phi$ is defined as $Prob(\phi) > b$ then $\mathcal{P}$ satisfies (RM$_{\mathcal{P}}$), (N$_{\mathcal{P}}$), (D$_{\mathcal{P}}$). Note that thus our axioms do not conflict with the view of $\mathcal{P}\phi$ as "probability of ϕ is high".

5.1   Some Provable Formulas

1. if $\vdash \phi \equiv \psi$ then $\vdash \mathcal{P}\phi \equiv \mathcal{P}\psi$
   This can be derived from $(RM_{\mathcal{P}})$.
2. $\vdash \neg(\mathcal{P}\phi \wedge \mathcal{P}\neg\phi)$
   This is an equivalent formulation of $(D_{\mathcal{P}})$.
3. $\vdash \neg\mathcal{P}\bot$
   By $(D_{\mathcal{P}})$, $\mathcal{P}\bot \to \neg\mathcal{P}\neg\bot$. Then $\mathcal{P}\bot \to \bot$ by $(N_{\mathcal{P}})$.
4. $\vdash \mathcal{B}\phi \to \mathcal{P}\phi$
   This follows from $(N_{\mathcal{P}})$ and (C-MIX), putting $\psi = \top$.
5. $\vdash (\mathcal{B}\phi \wedge \neg\mathcal{P}\neg\psi) \to \neg\mathcal{P}\neg(\phi \wedge \psi)$
   From (C-MIX) together with $(RM_{\mathcal{P}})$ it follows $\vdash (\mathcal{B}\phi \wedge \mathcal{P}\neg(\phi \wedge \psi)) \to \mathcal{P}\neg\psi$.
6. $\vdash \mathcal{P}\phi \to \neg\mathcal{B}\neg\phi$
   This follows from the next formula.
7. $\vdash (\mathcal{P}\phi \wedge \mathcal{P}\psi) \to \neg\mathcal{B}\neg(\phi \wedge \psi)$
   This can be proved as follows: first, (C-MIX) together with $(RM_{\mathcal{P}})$ entails $\vdash (\mathcal{P}\phi \wedge \mathcal{B}\neg(\phi \wedge \psi)) \to \mathcal{P}\neg\psi$. Then with (D) we get $\vdash (\mathcal{P}\phi \wedge \mathcal{B}\neg(\phi \wedge \psi)) \to \neg\mathcal{P}\psi$, from which the theorem follows by classical logic.
8. $\vdash (\mathcal{B}(\phi \to \psi) \wedge \mathcal{P}\phi) \to \mathcal{P}\psi$
   This follows from (C-MIX) together with $(RM_{\mathcal{P}})$.
9. $\vdash \mathcal{P}\phi \equiv \mathcal{B}\mathcal{P}\phi$
   The "$\to$" direction follows from (4-MIX). The other direction follows from (5-MIX) and $(D_{\mathcal{P}})$.
10. $\vdash \neg\mathcal{P}\phi \equiv \mathcal{B}\neg\mathcal{P}\phi$
    The "$\to$" direction follows from (5-MIX). The other direction follows from (4-MIX) and $(D_{\mathcal{P}})$.
11. $\vdash \mathcal{P}\phi \equiv \mathcal{P}\mathcal{P}\phi$
    The "$\to$" direction follows from (4-MIX). The other direction follows from (5-MIX) and $(D_{\mathcal{P}})$.
12. $\vdash \neg\mathcal{P}\phi \equiv \mathcal{P}\neg\mathcal{P}\phi$
    The "$\to$" direction follows from (5-MIX) and $\vdash \mathcal{B}\phi \to \mathcal{P}\phi$. The other direction follows from (4-MIX) and $(D_{\mathcal{P}})$.
13. $\mathcal{P}\mathcal{B}\phi \to \mathcal{P}\phi$
    From $\vdash \mathcal{B}\phi \to \mathcal{P}\phi$ it follows that $\mathcal{P}\mathcal{B}\phi \to \mathcal{P}\mathcal{P}\phi$. And as we have seen, $\mathcal{P}\mathcal{P}\phi \to \mathcal{P}\phi$.

5.2   Some Formulas That Cannot Be Proved

The following formulas will not be valid in our semantics. Non-deducibility will follow from soundness.

1. $\mathcal{P}\phi \to \mathcal{B}\phi$
   This would in fact identify $\mathcal{P}$ and $\mathcal{B}$.
2. $\mathcal{P}\phi \to \mathcal{P}\mathcal{B}\phi$
   Indeed, given that we expect $\mathcal{P}\phi \wedge \neg\mathcal{B}\phi$ to be consistent, such a formula would even lead to inconsistency (due to axioms $(5_{\mathcal{B}})$ and (C-MIX)).

3. $(\mathcal{P}\phi \wedge \mathcal{P}\psi) \to \mathcal{P}(\phi \wedge \psi)$
    This would clash with the probabilistic intuitions: $Prob(\phi) > Prob(\neg\phi)$ and $Prob(\psi) > Prob(\neg\psi)$ does not imply $Prob(\phi \wedge \psi) > Prob(\neg(\phi \wedge \psi))$.
4. $(\mathcal{P}\phi \wedge \mathcal{P}(\phi \to \psi)) \to \mathcal{P}\psi$
    The reasons are the same as for the preceding formula.

6   Axioms for Action

We suppose the logic of action is just K. We therefore have the inference rule

$$\text{if } \phi \to \psi \text{ then } [\alpha]\phi \to [\alpha]\psi \qquad\qquad (\text{RM}_\alpha)$$

and the following axioms:

$$[\alpha]\top \qquad\qquad (\text{N}_\alpha)$$
$$([\alpha]\phi \wedge [\alpha]\psi) \to [\alpha](\phi \wedge \psi) \qquad\qquad (\text{C}_\alpha)$$

Hence our logic of action is a simple version of dynamic logic [16].

7   Axioms Relating Belief and Action

We recall that we have stated in Section 2.4

-   that the agent perceives action occurrences completely and correctly,
-   that he knows the laws governing the actions, and
-   that actions are non-informative, i.e. the agent does not learn about particular effects of actions beyond what is stipulated in the action laws.

As action effects are not observed, when the agent learns that the action of throwing a dice has been executed then he does not learn whether it fell 6 or not.

In [17,18] we have argued that under these hypotheses the following axioms of "no forgetting" (NF) and "no learning" (NL) are plausible. They express that the agent's new belief state only depends on the previous belief state and the action whose occurrence he has learned.

$$(\neg[\alpha]\bot \wedge [\alpha]\mathcal{B}\phi) \to \mathcal{B}[\alpha]\phi \qquad\qquad (\text{NL}_\mathcal{B})$$
$$(\neg\mathcal{B}[\alpha]\bot \wedge \mathcal{B}[\alpha]\phi) \to [\alpha]\mathcal{B}\phi \qquad\qquad (\text{NF}_\mathcal{B})$$

For the "no learning" axiom, we must suppose that the action α is executable (else from $[\alpha]\mathcal{B}\phi$) we could not deduce anything relevant). Similarly, for the "no forgetting" axiom we must suppose that the agent does not believe α to be inexecutable (else from $\mathcal{B}[\alpha]\phi$ we could not deduce anything relevant). When the agent believes α to be inexecutable and nevertheless learns that it has occurred then he must revise his beliefs. In [19,18] it has been studied how AGM style belief revision operations [20] can be integrated. We do not go into details here, and just note that both solutions can be added in a modular way.

(NF$_{\mathcal{B}}$) and (NL$_{\mathcal{B}}$) together are equivalent to

$$(\neg[\alpha]\bot \wedge \neg\mathcal{B}[\alpha]\bot) \to ([\alpha]\mathcal{B}\phi \equiv \mathcal{B}[\alpha]\phi)$$

Axioms having this form have been called successor state axioms in cognitive robotics, and it has been shown that (at least in the case of deterministic actions) they enable a proof technique called regression [21,22].

8   Axioms Relating Probability and Action

Suppose before you learn that a dice has been thrown it is probable for the agent that the dice will not fall 6: $\mathcal{P}[throw]\neg d_6$. When the agent learns that the dice-throwing action has been executed (without learning the outcome, cf. our hypotheses) then it is probable for him that the dice does not show 6. Therefore the following no-learning axiom for $\mathcal{P}$ is plausible for non-informative actions:

$$(\neg[\alpha]\bot \wedge [\alpha]\mathcal{P}\phi) \to \mathcal{P}[\alpha]\phi \tag{NL$_{\mathcal{P}}$}$$

The other way round, when it is probable for the agent that 6 shows up after *throw* then (as we have supposed that he does not observe the outcome of throwing) it was already probable for the agent that 6 would show up *before* learning that the action has been executed. This is expressed by the following no-forgetting axiom.

$$(\neg\mathcal{P}[\alpha]\bot \wedge \mathcal{P}[\alpha]\phi) \to [\alpha]\mathcal{P}\phi \tag{NF$_{\mathcal{P}}$}$$

Again, both axioms are conditioned by executability of α (respectively belief of executability of α).

9   Semantics

Actions are interpreted as transition systems: truth of a formula $[alpha]\phi$ in a state (alias possible world) means truth of ϕ in all states possibly resulting from the execution of α.

Truth of the formula $\mathcal{B}\phi$ means truth of ϕ in all worlds that are possible for the agent.

In what concerns the formula $\mathcal{P}\phi$, the intuition is that to every possible world there is associated a probability measure over the set of epistemically accessible worlds, and that $Prob(\phi) > Prob(\neg\phi)$. Sometimes the intuition is put forward that among the set of accessible worlds there are more worlds where ϕ is true than worlds where ϕ is false. We shall show in the sequel that such an explanation is misleading.

A *frame* is a tuple $\langle W, B, P, \{R_\alpha : \alpha \in Act\}\rangle$ such that

- W is a nonempty set of possible worlds
- $B : W \longrightarrow 2^W$ maps worlds to sets of worlds
- $P : W \longrightarrow 2^{2^W}$ maps worlds to sets of sets of worlds
- $R_\alpha : W \longrightarrow 2^W$ maps worlds to sets of worlds, for every $\alpha \in Act$

Thus for every possible world $w \in W$, $B(w)$ and $R_\alpha(w)$ are sets of accessible worlds as usual.

By convention, for a set of possible worlds $V \subseteq W$ we suppose $R_\alpha(V) = \bigcup_{v \in V} R_\alpha(v)$, etc.

$P(w)$ is a *set of sets* possible worlds. Although intuitively P collects 'big' subsets of B (in the sense that for $V \in P$, V contains more elements than its complement w.r.t. W, $W \setminus V$), there is no formal requirement reflecting this.

Every frame must satisfy some *constraints*: for every $w \in W$,

(d$_\mathcal{B}$) $B(w) \neq \emptyset$
(45$_\mathcal{B}$)   if $w' \in B(w)$ then $B(w') = B(w)$
(n$_\mathcal{P}$) $P(w) \neq \emptyset$
(d$_\mathcal{P}$)   if $V_1, V_2 \in P(w)$, $V_1 \cap V_2 \neq \emptyset$
(c-mix)   if $V \in P(w)$ then $V \subseteq B(w)$
(45-mix)   if $w \in B(w)$ then $P(w') = P(w)$
(nf-nl$_\mathcal{B}$)   if $w' \in R_\alpha(w)$ and $R_\alpha(B(w)) \neq \emptyset$ then $B(w') = R_\alpha(B(w))$.
(nf-nl$_\mathcal{P}$)   if $w' \in R_\alpha(w)$ then $P(w') = \{R_\alpha(V) : V \in P(w)$ and $R_\alpha(V) \neq \emptyset\}$

As usual a *model* is a frame together with a valuation: $\mathcal{M} = \langle \mathcal{F}, V \rangle$, where $V : Atm \longrightarrow 2^W$ maps every atom to the set of worlds where it is true. To formulate the *truth conditions* we use the following abbreviation:

$$\|\phi\|_\mathcal{M} = \{w \in W : \mathcal{M}, w \models \phi\}$$

Then given a model $\mathcal{M}$, the truth conditions are as usual for the operators of classical logic, plus:

- $\mathcal{M}, w \models \phi$ if $\phi \in Atm$ and $w \in V(\phi)$
- $\mathcal{M}, w \models \mathcal{B}\phi$ if $B(w) \subseteq \|\phi\|_\mathcal{M}$
- $\mathcal{M}, w \models \mathcal{P}\phi$ if there is $V \in P(w)$ such that $V \subseteq \|\phi\|_\mathcal{M}$
- $\mathcal{M}, w \models [\alpha]\phi$ if $R_\alpha(w) \subseteq \|\phi\|_\mathcal{M}$

9.1   An Example

Let us give an example. It will at the same time illustrate that the intuition of $P(w)$ 'collecting more than 50% of the accessible worlds' is misleading.

Let the agent learn in w_0 that a dice has been thrown. Then we might suppose that after *throw* the situation is described by a possible world w where $B(w) = \{v_1, \ldots, v_6\}$ such that $v_i \in V(d_j)$ iff $i = j$, and where $P(w)$ is the set of all subsets of $B(w)$ containing more than half of the worlds in $B(w)$, i.e. $P(w) = \{V \subseteq B(w) : card(V) > 3\}$.

Now suppose we are in a game where a player is entitled to throw his dice a second time if (and only if) his first throw was a 6. Let *throwif6* describe that deterministic conditional action. We have thus $R_{throwif6}(v_6) = \{v'_{6_1}, \ldots, v'_{6_6}\}$ with $v'_{6_i} \in V(d_j)$ iff $i = j$. For $i \leq 5$, we have $R_{throwif6}(v_i) = \{v'_i\}$ with $v'_i \in V(d_j)$ iff $v_i \in V(d_j)$. According to our semantics, the situation after a completed turn can be described by a possible world w' where

- $R_{throwif6}(w) = \{w'\}$ □
- $B(w') = R_{throwif6}(v_6) \cup {}_{i\leq 5} R_{throwif6}(v_i)$.
- The neighborhood $P(w')$ of w' contains in particular $\{v'_1, v'_2, v'_3, v'_4\}$, although this set contains much less than half of the worlds in $B(w')$.

9.2   Soundness and Completeness

Our axiomatization is sound w.r.t. the present neighborhood semantics:

Theorem 2. *If ϕ is provable from our axioms and inference rules, then ϕ is valid in neighborhood semantics.*

We conjecture that we have completeness, too. The only nonstandard part of the Henkin proof concerns the neighborhood semantics: In principle, for all $w \in W$ and $V \in P(w)$ our axiom (C-MIX) only enforces that *there is* some $V' \in P(w)$ such that $V' \subseteq V \cap B(w)$. What we would like our model to satisfy is that $V \in B(w)$. In order to guarantee that frames must be transformed in the following way:

Lemma 1. *Let $\langle \mathcal{F}, V \rangle$ be any model satisfying all the constraints except (c-mix). If $\mathcal{F} \models$ (C-MIX) and $\langle \mathcal{F}, V \rangle, w \models \phi$ then there is a model $\langle \mathcal{F}', V' \rangle$ such that $\langle \mathcal{F}', V' \rangle$ satisfies the constraints and such that $\langle \mathcal{F}', V' \rangle, w \models \phi$.*

Proof. We define $W' = W$, $V' = V$, $B' = B$, $R'_\alpha = R_\alpha$, and $P'(w) = \{V \in P(w) : V \subseteq B(w) \}$ As for every $V \in P(w)$ there is some $V' \in P(w)$ such that $V' \subseteq V \cap B(w)$, $P(w)$ is nonempty. Moreover, we can prove by induction that for every $w \in W$ and every formula ψ, we have $\langle \mathcal{F}, V \rangle, w \models \psi$ iff $\langle \mathcal{F}', V' \rangle, w \models \psi$.

9.3   The Relation with Probability Measures

In any case, our neighborhood semantics differs from the standard semantics in terms of probability measures. The latter is not complete w.r.t. probability measures, as announced in Section 3.

Theorem 3 ([4]). : *Let $Atm = \{a, b, c, d, e, f, g\}$. Take a model $\mathcal{M}$ where*

- $W = 2^{Atm}$
- *for every $w \in W$, $N(w) = \{efg, abg, adf, bde, ace, cdg, bcf\}$, where efg is used to denote $\{e, f, g\}$, etc.*
- $V(p) = \{w \in W : p \in W\}$

Then $\mathcal{M}$ satisfies the above constraints on neighborhood frames, but their is no agreeing probability measure.

10 Conclusion

We have investigated a 'very qualitative' notion of probability, that of a formula
being more probable than its negation. We have presented the axioms governing
its relation with belief, and we have proposed principles for the interplay between
action, belief, and probability.

While there is a lot of work on probabilistic accounts of belief and action, as
far as we are aware there is no similar work relating modal probability to belief
and action.

While we provide a probabilistic account of belief, we do not consider probabilistic action here. Therefore (and just as in the logics of belief and action)
uncertainty can only diminish as actions occur, and on the long run probabilities will converge towards belief, in the sense that we will have $P(w) = \{B(w)\}$.
Just as in the case of shrinking belief states, this is unsatisfactory. In future
work we shall introduce misperception (as already done for beliefs in [18]) and
probabilistic actions in order to improve the account.

Acknowledgements. Thanks to the three reviewers, all of which have provided
comments that hopefully enabled us to improve our exposition.

References

1. Fagin, R., Halpern, J.Y.: Reasoning about knowledge and probability. Journal of
   the ACM **41** (1994) 340–367
2. Hamblin, C.: The modal 'probably'. Mind **68** (1959) 234–240
3. Burgess, J.P.: Probability logic. J. of Symbolic Logic **34** (1969) 264–274
4. Walley, P., Fine, T.L.: Varieties of modal (classificatory) and comparative probability. Synthese **41** (1979) 321–374
5. Halpern, J., Rabin, M.: A logic to reason about likelihood. Artificial Intelligence
   J. **32** (1987) 379–405
6. Halpern, J., McAllester, D.: Likelihood, probability, and knowledge. Computational Intelligence **5** (1989) 151–160
7. Fattorosi-Barnaba, M., de Caro, F.: Graded modalities I. Studia Logica **44** (1985)
   197–221
8. van der Hoek, W.: On the semantics of graded modalities. J. of Applied Non-
   classical Logics (JANCL) **2** (1992)
9. Hajek, P.: Metamathematics of fuzzy logic. Kluwer (1998)
10. Godo, L., Hajek, P., Esteva, F.: A fuzzy modal logic for belief functions. In: Proc.
    17th Int. Joint Conf. on Artificial Intelligence (IJCAI'01). (2001) 723–732
11. Fariñas del Cerro, L., Herzig, A.: A modal analysis of possibility theory. In:
    Proc. European Conf. on Symbolic and Quantitative Approaches to Uncertainty
    (ECSQAU'91). Number 548 in LNCS, Springer Verlag (1991) 58–62 (short version;
    long version published in FAIR'91).
12. Fariñas del Cerro, L., Herzig, A.: A modal analysis of possibility theory (invited
    paper). In Jorrand, P., Kelemen, J., eds.: Proc. of the Int. Workshop on Foun-
    dations of AI Research (FAIR 91). Number 535 in LNAI, Springer Verlag (1991)
    11–18 (short version published in ECSQAU'91).

13. Lewis, D.: Counterfactuals. Basil Blackwell, Oxford (1973)
14. Chellas, B.: Modal logic: An introduction. Cambridge University Press (1980)
15. Hintikka, J.K.K.: Knowledge and belief. Cornell University Press, Ithaca, N.Y. (1962)
16. Harel, D.: Dynamic logic. In Gabbay, D.M., Günthner, F., eds.: Handbook of Philosophical Logic. Volume II. D. Reidel, Dordrecht (1984) 497–604
17. Herzig, A., Lang, J., Longin, D., Polacsek, T.: A logic for planning under partial observability. In: Proc. Nat. (US) Conf. on Artificial Intelligence (AAAI'2000), Austin, Texas (2000)
18. Herzig, A., Longin, D.: Sensing and revision in a modal logic of belief and action. In van Harmelen, F., ed.: Proc. ECAI2002, IOS Press (2002) 307–311
19. Shapiro, S., Pagnucco, M., Lespérance, Y., Levesque, H.J.: Iterated belief change in the situation calculus. In: Proc. KR2000. (2000) 527–538
20. Gärdenfors, P.: Knowledge in Flux: Modeling the Dynamics of Epistemic States. MIT Press (1988)
21. Reiter, R.: The frame problem in the situation calculus: A simple solution (sometimes) and a completeness result for goal regression. In Lifschitz, V., ed.: Artificial Intelligence and Mathematical Theory of Computation: Papers in Honor of John McCarthy. Academic Press, San Diego, CA (1991) 359–380
22. Levesque, H.J., Reiter, R., Lespérance, Y., Lin, F., Scherl, R.: GOLOG: A logic programming language for dynamic domains. J. of Logic Programming (1997) special issue on reasoning about action and change.

A Multi-layered Bayesian Network Model for Structured Document Retrieval

Fabio Crestani[1], Luis M. de Campos[2], Juan M. Fernández-Luna[2], and Juan F. Huete[2]

[1] Department of Computer and Information Sciences
University of Strathclyde, Glasgow, Scotland, UK
Fabio.Crestani@cis.strath.ac.uk
[2] Departamento de Ciencias de la Computación e Inteligencia Artificial
E.T.S.I. Informática. Universidad de Granada, 18071 – Granada, Spain
{lci,jmfluna,jhg}@decsai.ugr.es

Abstract. New standards in document representation, like for example SGML, XML, and MPEG-7, compel Information Retrieval to design and implement models and tools to index, retrieve and present documents according to the given document structure. The paper presents the design of an Information Retrieval system for multimedia structured documents, like for example journal articles, e-books, and MPEG-7 videos. The system is based on Bayesian Networks, since this class of mathematical models enable to represent and quantify the relations between the structural components of the document. Some preliminary results on the system implementation are also presented.

1 Introduction

Information Retrieval (IR) systems are powerful and effective tools for accessing documents by content. A user specifies the required content using a query, often consisting of a natural language expression. Documents estimated to be relevant to the user query are presented to the user through an interface. New standards in multimedia document representation compel IR to design and implement models and tools to index, retrieve and present documents according to the given document structure. In fact, while standard IR treats documents as if they were atomic entities, modern IR needs to be able to deal with more elaborate document representations, like for example documents written in SGML, HTML, XML or MPEG-7. These document representation formalisms enable to represent and describe documents said to be *structured*, that is documents whose content is organised around a well defined structure. Examples of these documents are books and textbooks, scientific articles, technical manuals, educational videos, etc. This means that documents should no longer be considered as atomic entities, but as aggregates of interrelated objects that need to be indexed, retrieved, and presented both as a whole and separately, in relation to the user's needs. In other words, given a query, an IR system must retrieve the

T.D. Nielsen and N.L. Zhang (Eds.): ECSQARU 2003, LNAI 2711, pp. 74–86, 2003.

set of document components that are most relevant to this query, not just entire documents.

In order to enable querying both content and structure an IR system needs to possess the necessary primitives to model effectively the document's content and structure. Taking into account that Bayesian Networks (BNs) have been already successfully applied to build standard IR systems, we believe that they are also an appropriate tool to model both in a qualitative and quantitative way the content and structural relations of multimedia structured documents.

In this paper we propose a BN model for structured document retrieval, which can be considered as an extension of a previously developed model to manage standard (non-structured) documents [1,6]. The rest of the paper is organized as follows: we begin in Sect. 2 with the preliminaries. In Sect. 3 we introduce the Bayesian network model for structured document retrieval, the assumptions that determine the network topology being considered, the details about probability distributions stored in the network, and the way in which we can efficiently use the network model for retrieval, by performing probabilistic inference. Section 4 shows preliminary experimental results obtained with the model, using a structured document test collection [9]. Finally, Sect. 5 contains the concluding remarks and some proposals for future research.

2   Preliminaries

Probabilistic models constitute an important kind of IR models, which have been widely used for a long time [5], because they offer a principled way to manage the uncertainty that naturally appears in many elements within this field. These models (and others, as the Vector Space model [15]) usually represent documents and queries by means of vectors of *terms* or *keywords*, which try to characterize their information content. Because these terms are not equally important, they are usually weighted to highlight their importance in the documents they belong to, as well as in the whole collection. The most common weighting schemes are [15] the *term frequency*, $tf_{i,j}$, i.e., the number of times that the ith term appears in the jth document, and the *inverse document frequency*, idf_i, of the ith term in the collection, $idf_i = \lg(N/n_i) + 1$, where N is the number of documents in the collection, and n_i is the number of documents that contain the ith term. The combination of both weights, $tf_{i,j} \cdot idf_i$, is also a common weighting scheme.

2.1   Information Retrieval and Bayesian Networks: The Bayesian Network Model with Two Layers

Bayesian networks have also been successfully applied in a variety of ways within the IR environment, as an extension/modification of probabilistic IR models [6, 13,16]. We shall focus on a specific BN-based retrieval model, the Bayesian Network Retrieval Model with two layers (BNR-2) [1,6], because it will be the starting point of our proposal to deal with structured documents.

The set of variables V in the BNR-2 model is composed of two different sets, $V = \mathcal{T} \cup \mathcal{D}$: the set $\mathcal{T} = \{T_1, \dots, T_M\}$, containing binary random variables

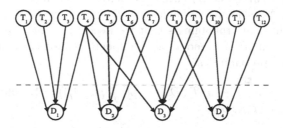

Fig. 1. Two-layered Bayesian network for the BNR-2 model

representing the M terms in the glossary from a given collection, and the set $\mathcal{D} = \{D_1, \ldots, D_N\}$, corresponding also to binary random variables, representing the N documents that compose the collection. We will use the notation T_i (D_j, respectively) to refer to the term (document, respectively) and also to its associated variable and node. A variable D_j has its domain in the set $\{d_j^-, d_j^+\}$, where d_j^- and d_j^+ respectively mean 'the document D_j is not relevant', and 'the document D_j is relevant' for a given query[1]. A variable T_i takes its values from the set $\{t_i^-, t_i^+\}$, where in this case t_i^- stands for 'the term T_i is not relevant', and t_i^+ represents 'the term T_i is relevant'[2]. To denote a generic, unspecified value of a term variable T_i or a document variable D_j, we will use lower-case letters, t_i and d_j.

With respect to the topology of the network (see Fig. 1), there are arcs going from term nodes to those document nodes where these terms appear, and there are not arcs connecting pairs of either document nodes or term nodes. This means that terms are marginally independent among each other, and documents are conditionally independent given the terms that they contain. In this way, we get a network composed of two simple layers, the term and document subnetworks, with arcs only going from nodes in the first subnetwork to nodes in the second one.

The probability distributions stored in each node of the BNR-2 model are computed as follows: For each term node we need a marginal probability distribution, $p(t_i)$; we use $p(t_i^+) = \frac{1}{M}$ and $p(t_i^-) = \frac{M-1}{M}$ (M being the number of terms in the collection)[3]. For the document nodes we have to estimate the conditional probability distribution $p(d_j|pa(D_j))$ for any configuration $pa(D_j)$

---

[1] A document is relevant for a given query if it satisfies the user's information need expressed by means of this query.

[2] A term is relevant in the sense that the user believes that this term will appear in relevant documents.

[3] Although these probabilities could also be estimated from the dataset, the uninformed estimate proposed produces better results.

of $Pa(D_j)$ (i.e., any assignment of values to all the variables in $Pa(D_j)$), where $Pa(D_j)$ is the parent set of D_j (which coincides with the set of terms indexing document D_j). As a document node may have a high number of parents, the number of conditional probabilities that we need to estimate and store may be huge. Therefore, the BNR-2 model uses a specific canonical model to represent these conditional probabilities:

$$p(d_j^+|pa(D_j)) = \sum_{T_i \in R(pa(D_j))} w(T_i, D_j), \quad p(d_j^-|pa(D_j)) = 1 - p(d_j^+|pa(D_j)), \quad (1)$$

where $R(pa(D_j)) = \{T_i \in Pa(D_j) \,|\, t_i^+ \in pa(D_j)\}$, i.e., the set of terms in $Pa(D_j)$ that are instantiated as relevant in the configuration $pa(D_j)$; $w(T_i, D_j)$ are weights verifying $w(T_i, D_j) \geq 0$ and $\sum_{T_i \in Pa(D_j)} w(T_i, D_j) \leq 1$. So, the more terms are relevant in $pa(D_j)$, the greater the probability of relevance of D_j.

The BNR-2 model can be used to obtain a relevance value for each document given a query Q. Each term T_i in the query Q is considered as an evidence for the propagation process, and its value is fixed to t_i^+. Then, the propagation process is run, thus obtaining the posterior probability of relevance of each document given that the terms in the query are also relevant, $p(d_j^+|Q)$. Later, the documents are sorted according to their corresponding probability and shown to the user. Taking into account the number of nodes in the network $(N + M)$ and the fact that, although its topology seems relatively simple, there are multiple pathways connecting nodes as well as nodes with a great number of parents, general purpose inference algorithms cannot be applied due to efficiency considerations, even for small document collections. So, the BNR-2 model uses a tailored inference process, that computes the required probabilities very efficiently and ensures that the results are the same that those obtained using exact propagation in the entire network. The key result is stated in the following proposition [7]:

Proposition 1. *Let D_j be a binary variable in a Bayesian network having only binary variables as its parents. Assume an evidence Q d-separated from D_j by its parents. If $p(d_j^+|pa(D_j))$ is defined as in eq. (1), then*

$$p(d_j^+|Q) = \sum_{T_i \in Pa(D_j)} w(T_i, D_j) \cdot p(t_i^+|Q). \quad (2)$$

Taking into account the topology of the term subnetwork, $p(t_i^+|Q) = 1$ if $T_i \in Q$ and $p(t_i^+|Q) = \frac{1}{M}$ if $T_i \notin Q$, hence Eq. (2) becomes

$$p(d_j^+|Q) = \sum_{T_i \in Pa(D_j) \cap Q} w(T_i, D_j) + \frac{1}{M} \sum_{T_i \in Pa(D_j) \setminus Q} w(T_i, D_j). \quad (3)$$

Observe that eq. (3) also includes those terms in $Pa(D_j)$ that are not in the query. This is due to the fact that the user has not established that terms outside the query are irrelevant, and therefore they contribute to the relevance of the document with their prior probability.

2.2   Structured Document Retrieval

In IR the area of research dealing with structured documents is known as *structured document retrieval*. A good survey of the state of the art of structured document retrieval can be found in [4]. The inclusion of the structure of a document in the indexing and retrieval process affects the design and implementation of the IR system in many ways. First of all, the indexing process must consider the structure in the appropriate way, so that users can search the collection both by content and structure. Secondly, the retrieval process should use both structure and content in the estimate of the relevance of documents. Finally, the interface and the whole interaction has to enable the user to make full use of the document structure. In fact, querying by content and structure can only be achieved if the user can specify in the query *what* he/she is looking for, and *where* this should be located in the required documents. The "what" involves the specification of the content, while the "where" is related to the structure of the documents.

It has been recognised that the best approach to querying structured documents is to let the user specify in the most natural way both the content and the structural requirements of the desired documents [4]. This can be achieved by letting the user specify the content requirement in a natural language query, while enabling the user to qualify the structural requirements through a graphical user interface. A GUI is well suited to show and let the user indicate structural elements of documents in the collection [17].

This paper addresses the issues related to the modelling of the retrieval of structured documents when the user does not explicitly specifies the structural requirements. In standard IR retrievable units are fixed, so only the entire document, or, sometimes, some pre-defined parts such as chapters or paragraphs constitute retrievable units. The structure of documents, often quite complex and consisting of a varying numbers of chapters, sections, tables, formulae, bibliographic items, etc., is therefore "flattened" and not exploited. Classical retrieval methods lack the possibility to interactively determine the size and the type of retrievable units that best suit an actual retrieval task or user preferences. Some IR researchers are aiming at developing retrieval models that dynamically return document components of varying complexity. A retrieval result may then consist of several entry points to a same document, corresponding to structural elements, whereby each entry point is weighted according to how it satisfies the query. Models proposed so far exploit the content and the structure of documents to estimate the relevance of document components to queries, based on the aggregation of the estimated relevance of their related components. These models have been based on various theories, like for example fuzzy logic [3], Dempster-Shafer's theory of evidence [10], probabilistic logic [2], and Bayesian inference [11]. What these models have in common is that the basic components of their retrieval function are variants of the standard IR term weighting schema, which combines term frequency with inverse document frequency, often normalised keeping into account document length. Evidence associated with the document structure is often encoded into one or both of these term weighting functions. A somewhat different approach has been presented in [14], where evidence associated with the document structure is made explicit by introducing an "accessibility" dimension. This dimension measures the strength of the structural relationship between document components: the stronger the relationship, the more impact has the content of a component in describing the content of its related components. Our approach is based on a similar view of structured document retrieval, where a quantitative model is used to compute the strength of the relations between structural elements. In fact, we use a BN to model these relations. A BN is a very powerful tool to capture these relations, with particular regards to hierarchically structured document. The next section contains a detailed presentation of our approach. Other approaches to structured document retrieval also based on BNs can be found in [8,11,12].

3 From Two-Layered to Multi-layered Bayesian Networks for Structured Document Retrieval

To deal with structured document retrieval, we are going to assume that each document is composed of a hierarchical structure of l abstraction *levels* $\mathcal{L}_1, \ldots, \mathcal{L}_l$, each one representing a structural association of elements in the text. For instance, chapters, sections, subsections and paragraphs in the context of a general structured document collection, or scenes, shots, and frames in MPEG-7 videos. The level in which the document itself is included will be noted as level 1 ($\mathcal{L}_1$), and the more specific level as $\mathcal{L}_l$.

Each level contains *structural units*, i.e., single elements as Chapter 4, Subsection 4.5, Shot 54, and so on. Each one of these structural units will be noted as $U_{i,j}$, where i is the identifier of that unit in the level j. The number of structural units contained in each level $\mathcal{L}_j$ is represented by $|\mathcal{L}_j|$. Therefore, $\mathcal{L}_j = \{U_{1,j}, \ldots, U_{|\mathcal{L}_j|,j}\}$. The units are organised according to the actual structure of the document: Every unit $U_{i,j}$ at level j, except the unit at level $j = 1$ (i.e., the complete document $D_i = U_{i,1}$), is contained in only one unit $U_{z(i,j),j-1}$ of the lower level $j - 1^4$, $U_{i,j} \subseteq U_{z(i,j),j-1}$. Therefore, each structured document may be represented as a tree (an example is displayed in Fig. 2).

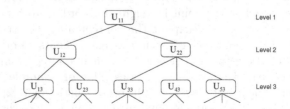

Fig. 2. A structured document

---

4 $z(i, j)$ is a function that returns the index of the unit in level $j - 1$ where the unit with index i in level j belongs to.

Now, we shall describe the Bayesian network used by our Bayesian Network Retrieval model for Structured Documents (BNR-SD).

3.1   Network Topology

Taking into account the topology of the BNR-2 model for standard retrieval (see Fig. 1), it seems to us that the natural extension to deal with structured documents is to connect the term nodes with the structural units $U_{1,l}, \ldots, U_{|\mathcal{L}_l|,l}$ of the upper level $\mathcal{L}_l$. Therefore, only the units in level $\mathcal{L}_l$ will be indexed, having associated several terms describing their content (see Fig. 3).

From a graphical point of view, our Bayesian network will contain two different types of nodes, those associated to structural units, and those related to terms, so that $V = \mathcal{T} \cup \mathcal{U}$, where $\mathcal{U} = \cup_{j=1}^{l} \mathcal{L}_j$. As in the BNR-2 model, each node represents a binary random variable: $U_{i,j}$ takes its values in the set $\{u_{i,j}^-, u_{i,j}^+\}$, representing that the unit is not relevant and is relevant, respectively; a term variable T_i is treated exactly as in the BNR-2 model. The independence relationships that we assume in this case are of the same nature that those considered in the BNR-2 model: terms are marginally independent among each other, and the structural units are conditionally independent given the terms that they contain.

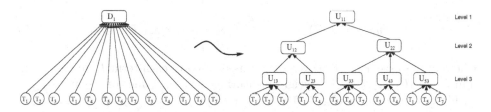

Fig. 3. From an indexed document to an indexed structured document

These assumptions, together with the hierarchical structure of the documents, completely determine the topology of the Bayesian network with $l + 1$ layers, where the arcs go from term nodes to structural units in level l, and from units in level j to units in level $j-1$, $j = 2, \ldots, l$. So, the network is characterized by the following parent sets for each type of node:

- $\forall T_k \in \mathcal{T},\ Pa(T_k) = \emptyset.$
- $\forall U_{i,l} \in \mathcal{L}_l,\ Pa(U_{i,l}) = \{T_k \in \mathcal{T} \mid U_{i,l} \text{ is indexed by } T_k\}.$
- $\forall j = 1, \ldots, l-1,\ \forall U_{i,j} \in \mathcal{L}_j,\ Pa(U_{i,j}) = \{U_{k,j+1} \in \mathcal{L}_{j+1} \mid U_{k,j+1} \subseteq U_{i,j}\}.$

An example of this multi-layer BN is depicted in Fig. 4, for $l = 3$.

3.2   Conditional Probabilities

The following task is the assessment of the (conditional) probability distributions:

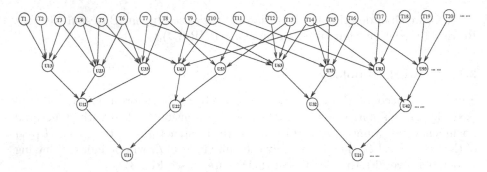

Fig. 4. Multi-layered Bayesian network for the BNR-SD model

• Term nodes T_k: they store the same marginal probabilities $p(t_k)$ as in the BNR-2 model.

• Structural units $U_{i,j}$: to compute $p(u_{i,l}|pa(U_{i,l}))$ and $p(u_{i,j}|pa(U_{i,j}))$, $j \neq l$, we use the same kind of canonical model considered for the relationships between terms and documents in the BNR-2 model (see Eq. (1)):

$$p(u_{i,l}^+|pa(U_{i,l})) = \sum_{T_k \in R(pa(U_{i,l}))} w(T_k, U_{i,l}), \qquad (4)$$

$$p(u_{i,j}^+|pa(U_{i,j})) = \sum_{U_{h,j+1} \in R(pa(U_{i,j}))} w(U_{h,j+1}, U_{i,j}), \qquad (5)$$

where in this case $w(T_k, U_{i,l})$ is a weight associated to each term T_k indexing the unit $U_{i,l}$, $w(U_{h,j+1}, U_{i,j})$ is a weight measuring the importance of the unit $U_{h,j+1}$ within $U_{i,j}$, with $w(T_k, U_{i,l}) \geq 0$, $w(U_{h,j+1}, U_{i,j}) \geq 0$, $\sum_{T_k \in Pa(U_{i,l})} w(T_k, U_{i,l}) = 1$ and $\sum_{U_{h,j+1} \in Pa(U_{i,j})} w(U_{h,j+1}, U_{i,j}) = 1$[5]. In either case $R(pa(U_{i,j}))$ is the subset of parents of $U_{i,j}$ (terms for $j = l$, units in level $j + 1$ for $j \neq l$) that are instantiated as relevant in the configuration $pa(U_{i,j})$.

To conclude the specification of the conditional probabilites in the network, we have to give values to the weights $w(T_k, U_{i,l})$ and $w(U_{h,j+1}, U_{i,j})$. Let us introduce some additional notation: for any unit $U_{i,j} \in \mathcal{U}$, let $A(U_{i,j}) = \{T_k \in \mathcal{T} \mid T_k$ is an ancestor of $U_{i,j}\}$, i.e., $A(U_{i,j})$ is the set of terms that are included in the unit $U_{i,j}$[6]. Let $tf_{k,C}$ be the *frequency* of the term T_k (number of times that T_k occurs) in the set of terms C and idf_k be the *inverse document frequency* of T_k in the whole collection. We shall use the weighting scheme $\rho(T_k, C) = tf_{k,C} \cdot idf_k$. We define

$$\forall U_{i,l} \in \mathcal{L}_l, \ \forall T_k \in Pa(U_{i,l}), \ w(T_k, U_{i,l}) = \frac{\rho(T_k, A(U_{i,l}))}{\sum_{T_h \in A(U_{i,l})} \rho(T_h, A(U_{i,l}))}. \qquad (6)$$

---

[5] Notice that we use here the symbol = instead of ≤. The only reason for this restriction is to ease some implementation details of the model.

[6] Notice that, although a unit $U_{i,j}$ in level $j \neq l$ is not connected directly to any term, it contains all the terms indexing structural units in level l that are included in $U_{i,j}$. Notice also that $A(U_{i,l}) = Pa(U_{i,l})$.

$\forall j = 1, \ldots, l - 1, \ \forall U_{i,j} \in \mathcal{L}_j, \ \forall U_{h,j+1} \in Pa(U_{i,j}),$

$$w(U_{h,j+1}, U_{i,j}) = \frac{\sum_{T_k \in A(U_{h,j+1})} \rho(T_k, A(U_{h,j+1}))}{\sum_{T_k \in A(U_{i,j})} \rho(T_k, A(U_{i,j}))} \qquad (7)$$

Observe that the weights in eq. (6) verify that $\sum_{T_k \in Pa(U_{i,l})} w(T_k, U_{i,l}) = 1$. In fact, they are only the classical tfidf weights, normalized to sum up one. It is also important to notice that, as $tf_{k,B \cup C} = tf_{k,B} + tf_{k,C}$, then $\rho(T_k, B \cup C) = \rho(T_k, B) + \rho(T_k, C)$. Moreover, $A(U_{i,j}) = \sum_{U_{h,j+1} \in Pa(U_{i,j})} A(U_{h,j+1})$. Taking into account these facts, it is also clear that the weights in eq. (7) verify that $\sum_{U_{h,j+1} \in Pa(U_{i,j})} w(U_{h,j+1}, U_{i,j}) = 1$. The weights $w(U_{h,j+1}, U_{i,j})$ measure, in some sense, the proportion of the content of the unit $U_{i,j}$ which can be attributed to each one of its components.

3.3 Inference

The inference process that we have to carry out in order to use the BNR-SD model is, given a query Q, to compute the posterior probabilities of relevance of all the structural units, $p(u_{i,j}^+|Q)$. Although this computation may be difficult in a general case, in our case all the conditional probabilities have been assessed using the canonical model in eq. (1) and only terms nodes are instantiated (so that only a top-down inference is required). In this context, having in mind the result in Proposition 1, the inference process can be carried out very efficiently, in the following way:

- For the structural units in level $\mathcal{L}_l$, the posterior probabilities are (as in the BNR-2 model):

$$P(u_{i,l}^+|Q) = \sum_{T_k \in Pa(U_{i,l}) \cap Q} w(T_k, U_{i,l}) + \frac{1}{M} \sum_{T_k \in Pa(U_{i,l}) \backslash Q} w(T_k, U_{i,l}). \qquad (8)$$

- For the structural units in level $\mathcal{L}_j$, $j \neq l$:

$$P(u_{i,j}^+|Q) = \sum_{U_{h,j+1} \in Pa(U_{i,j})} w(U_{h,j+1}, U_{i,j}) \cdot p(u_{h,j+1}^+|Q). \qquad (9)$$

Therefore, we can compute the required probabilities on a level-by-level basis, starting from level l and going down to level 1.

It can be easily proven that, using the proposed tfidf weighting scheme, the BNR-SD model is equivalent to multiple BNR-2 models, one per level $\mathcal{L}_j$. In other words, if we consider each unit $U_{i,j}$ in $\mathcal{L}_j$ as a single document (indexed by all the terms in $A(U_{i,j})$) and build a BNR-2 model, then the posterior probabilities of relevance are the same as in the BNR-SD model. The advantage of BNR-SD is that it can manage all the levels simultaneously, and is much more efficient in terms of storage requirements and running time than multiple BNR-2 models.

3.4   Model Implementation

The BNR-SD model has been implemented using the *Lemur Toolkit*, a software written in C++ designed to develop new applications on Information Retrieval and Language Modelling. This package (available at http://www-2.cs.cmu.edu/~lemur/) offers a wide range of classes that cover almost all the tasks required in IR.

Our implementation uses an inverted file, i.e., a data structure containing, for each term in the collection, the structural units in level l where it occurs (the term's children in the network). The evaluation of units in level l is carried out by accumulating, for each unit $U_{i,l}$, the weights $w(T_k, U_{i,l})$ of those terms belonging to the query by which they have been indexed. To speed up the retrieval, all the weights $w(T_k, U_{i,l})$ (eq. 6) have been precomputed at indexing time and stored in a binary random access file. When the accumulation process is finished, for each unit $U_{i,l}$ sharing terms with the query (i.e., $Pa(U_{i,l}) \cap Q \neq \emptyset$) we have an accumulator $S_{i,l} = \sum_{T_k \in Pa(U_{i,l}) \cap Q} w(T_k, U_{i,l})$; then we can compute the value $P(u_{i,l}^+|Q)$ in eq. (8) as $P(u_{i,l}^+|Q) = S_{i,l} + \frac{1}{M}(1 - S_{i,l})$. Notice that the units containing no query term do not need to be evaluated, and their posterior probability is the same as their prior, $P(u_{i,l}^+|Q) = \frac{1}{M}$.

With respect to the structural units from the rest of layers, the only information needed is also stored in a binary random access file, containing, for each unit $U_{h,j+1}$, that one where it is contained (its unique child in the network), $U_{i,j}$, and the corresponding weight $w(U_{h,j+1}, U_{i,j})$ (eq. 7), which are also precomputed at indexing time. In order to evaluate the units in level $j \neq l$, those units in level $j+1$ evaluated in a previous stage will play the same role as query terms do in the evaluation of units in level l: for each unit $U_{i,j}$ containing units $U_{h,j+1}$ previously evaluated (this happens if $A(U_{h,j+1}) \cap Q \neq \emptyset$), we use two accumulators, one for the weights $w(U_{h,j+1}, U_{i,j})$ and the other for the products $w(U_{h,j+1}, U_{i,j}) \cdot p(u_{h,j+1}^+|Q)$. At the end of the accumulation process, for each one of these units $U_{i,j}$ we have two accumulators, $S_{i,j} = \sum_{U_{h,j+1} \in Q_{i,j}} w(U_{h,j+1}, U_{i,j})$ and $SP_{i,j} = \sum_{U_{h,j+1} \in Q_{i,j}} w(U_{h,j+1}, U_{i,j}) \cdot p(u_{h,j+1}^+|Q)$, where $Q_{i,j} = \{U_{h,j+1} \in Pa(U_{i,j}) \mid A(U_{h,j+1}) \cap Q \neq \emptyset\}$. Then we can compute the value $P(u_{i,j}^+|Q)$ in eq. (9) as $P(u_{i,j}^+|Q) = SP_{i,j} + \frac{1}{M}(1 - S_{i,j})$.

4   Preliminary Experiments

Our BNR-SD model has been tested using a collection of structured documents, marked up in XML, containing 37 William Shakespeare's plays [9]. A play has been considered structured in acts, scenes and speeches (so that $l = 4$), and may contain also epilogues and prologues. Speeches have been the only structural units indexed using Lemur. The total number of unique terms contained in these units is 14019, and the total number of structural units taken into account is 32022. With respect to the queries, the collection is distributed with 43 queries, with their corresponding relevance judgements. From these 43 queries, the 35 which are content-only queries were selected for our experiments.

Table 1. Average precision values for the experiments with the BNR-SD model

Recall	AP-PLAY	AP-ACT	AP-SCENE	AP-SPEECH	AP-All
0	0.9207	0.7797	0.5092	0.1957	0.2019
0.1	0.9207	0.7797	0.5065	0.1368	0.1346
0.2	0.9207	0.7797	0.4600	0.1100	0.1008
0.3	0.9207	0.7738	0.4279	0.0846	0.0719
0.4	0.9207	0.7518	0.4088	0.0721	0.0632
0.5	0.9207	0.7318	0.3982	0.0434	0.0437
0.6	0.9207	0.6755	0.3663	0.0362	0.0380
0.7	0.9207	0.6512	0.3220	0.0201	0.0288
0.8	0.9207	0.6453	0.3054	0.0138	0.0189
0.9	0.9207	0.6253	0.2580	0.0079	0.0107
1	0.9207	0.6253	0.2484	0.0025	0.0059
AVP-11p	0.9207	0.7108	0.3828	0.0657	0.0653

As a way of showing the new potential of retrieving structured documents, several experiments have been designed. Let us suppose that a user is interested in the structural units of a specific type that are relevant for each query (i.e., s/he selects a given granularity level). Therefore, four retrievals have been run for the set of queries: only retrieving plays, only acts, only scenes, prologues and epilogues, and finally, speeches. A last experiment tries to return to the user, in only one ranking, all the structural units ranked according to their relevance. Table 1 shows the average recall-precision values (using the 11 standard recall values) for the five experiments. The row *AVP-11p* shows the average precision for the 11 values of recall. The maximum number of units retrieved for each experiment has been fixed to 1000.

An important fact to notice is that when the system offers a ranking with all the structural units, the performance is not very good. This behaviour is due to the fact that, according to the expressions used to compute the relevance of the units, the posterior probability of a play, for instance, is very small compared to that assigned to a speech. This implies that the lower level units, like plays or acts, for example, are located in the furthest positions in the ranking and therefore, never retrieved. After observing the ranking produced in the last two experiments, we noticed that there are a number of units, in this case speeches, that have a posterior probability equal to 1.0. The reason is that they are very short, perhaps one or two terms, occurring all of them in the query. As the weights are normalised to 1.0, the final relevance is very high and these units are placed on the top of the ranking but introducing some noise. This is other cause of the poor behaviour of the retrieval considering only speeches and all types of units as well. These facts suggests the convenience of including in our model a decision procedure to select the appropriate units to be retrieved.

On the other hand, the effectiveness of the system is quite good for the first three experiments, where the objective is to retrieve larger units, containing more terms, as acts and scenes. However, it should be noticed that the effectiveness decreases as the number of units involved in the retrieval increases and the number of terms per unit decreases.

5   Concluding Remarks

In this paper a Bayesian network-based model for structured document retrieval, BNR-SD, has been presented, together with some promising preliminary experiments with the structured test collection of Shakespeare's plays. Our model can be extended/improved in several ways, and we plan to pursue some of them in the near future:

- To incorporate to our network model a decision module, in order to select the appropriate structural units (the *best entry points*) that will be shown to the users, depending on their own preferences.
- To allow that structural units in levels different from l have associated specific textual information (for example the title of a chapter or a section); to allow also direct relationships between units in non-consecutive levels of the hierarchy (e.g. paragraphs and chapters). These questions do not bring any technical complications, is only a matter of implementation.
- To include in our network model specific term relationships (as those in [7]) and/or document relationships (as those in [1]). Alternatively, we could also use *Ontologies* to model concepts and their relationships in a given domain of knowledge.
- To permit our model to deal, not only with content-only queries, but also with structure-only and content-and-structure queries; to let the queries to include, in addition to terms, also structural units.
- To apply our model, in combination with techniques for image analysis, to multimedia retrieval, particularly MPEG-7 videos.

Acknowledgments. This work has been supported by the Spanish CICYT and FIS, under Projects TIC2000-1351 and PI021147 respectively, and by the European Commission under the IST Project MIND (IST-2000-26061). We are grateful to Mounia Lalmas and Gabriella Kazai, who provided us with the relevance judgements of the Shakespeare collection in TREC format.

References

1. S. Acid, L.M. de Campos, J.M. Fernández-Luna, and J.F. Huete. An information retrieval model based on simple Bayesian networks. *International Journal of Intelligent Systems*, 18:251–265, 2003.
2. C. Baumgarten. A probabilistic model for distributed information retrieval. In *Proceedings of the 20th ACM SIGIR Conference*, 258–266, 1997.
3. G. Bordogna and G. Pasi. Flexible representation and querying of heterogeneous structured documents. *Kibernetika*, 36(6):617–633, 2000.
4. Y. Chiaramella. Information retrieval and structured documents. *Lectures Notes in Computer Science*, 1980:291–314, 2001.

5. F. Crestani, M. Lalmas, C.J. van Rijsbergen, and L. Campbell. Is this document relevant?... probably. A survey of probabilistic models in information retrieval. *ACM Computing Survey*, 30(4):528–552, 1998.
6. L.M. de Campos, J.M. Fernández-Luna, and J.F. Huete. A layered Bayesian network model for document retrieval. *Lecture Notes in Computer Science*, 2291:169–182, 2002.
7. L.M. de Campos, J.M. Fernández-Luna, and J.F. Huete. The Bayesian network retrieval model: Foundations and performance. Submitted to the *International Journal of Approximate Reasoning*.
8. A. Graves and M. Lalmas. Video retrieval using an MPEG-7 based inference network. In *Proceedings of the 25th ACM–SIGIR Conference*, 339–346, 2002.
9. G. Kazai, M. Lalmas, and J. Reid. The Shakespeare test collection. Available at http://qmir.dcs.qmul.ac.uk/Focus/resources2.htm
10. M. Lalmas and I. Ruthven. Representing and retrieving structured documents with Dempster-Shafer's theory of evidence: Modelling and evaluation. *Journal of Documentation*, 54(5):529–565, 1998.
11. S.H. Myaeng, D.H. Jang, M.S. Kim, and Z.C. Zhoo. A flexible model for retrieval of SGML documents. In *Proceedings of the 21th ACM–SIGIR Conference*, 138–145, 1998.
12. B. Piwowarski, G.E. Faure, and P. Gallinari. Bayesian networks and INEX. In *Proceedings of the INEX Workshop*, 7–12, 2002.
13. B.A. Ribeiro-Neto and R.R. Muntz. A belief network model for IR. In *Proceedings of the 19th ACM–SIGIR Conference*, 253–260, 1996.
14. T. Roelleke, M. Lalmas, G. Kazai, I. Ruthven, and S. Quicker. The accessibility dimension for structured document retrieval. *Lecture Notes in Computer Science*, 2291:284–302, 2002.
15. G. Salton and M.J. McGill. *Introduction to Modern Information Retrieval*. McGraw-Hill, Inc., 1983.
16. H. R. Turtle and W. B. Croft. Evaluation of an inference network-based retrieval model. *Information Systems*, 9(3):187–222, 1991.
17. J. Vegas, P. de la Fuente, and F. Crestani. A graphical user interface for structured document retrieval. *Lecture Notes in Computer Science*, 2291:268–283, 2002.

Using Kappas as Indicators of Strength in Qualitative Probabilistic Networks

Silja Renooij[1], Simon Parsons[2], and Pauline Pardieck[1]

[1] Institute of Information and Computing Sciences, Utrecht University
P.O. Box 80.089, 3508 TB Utrecht, The Netherlands
silja@cs.uu.nl
[2] Department of Computer and Information Science
Brooklyn College, City University of New York
2900 Bedford Avenue, Brooklyn, New York 11210
parsons@sci.brooklyn.cuny.edu

Abstract. Qualitative probabilistic networks are designed for probabilistic inference in a qualitative way. They capture qualitative influences between variables, but do not provide for indicating the strengths of these influences. As a result, trade-offs between conflicting influences remain unresolved upon inference. In this paper, we investigate the use of order-of-magnitude kappa values to capture strengths of influences in a qualitative network. We detail the use of these kappas upon inference, thereby providing for trade-off resolution.

1 Introduction

Qualitative probabilistic networks [1] and the kappa calculus [2] both provide for probabilistic reasoning in a qualitative way. A qualitative probabilistic network is basically a qualitative abstraction of a probabilistic network and similarly encodes variables and the probabilistic relationships between them in a directed acyclic graph. The encoded relationships represent influences on the probability distributions of variables and are summarised by a sign indicating the direction of *change* or shift (positive, negative, zero, or unknown) in the distribution of one variable occasioned by another. The kappa calculus offers a framework for reasoning with defeasible beliefs, where belief states are given by a ranking function that maps propositions into non-negative integers called kappa values. Kappa values, by means of a probabilistic interpretation [3], were previously used to abstract probabilistic network into so-called Kappa networks, where a network's probabilities are abstracted into kappa values, which are easier to assess than precise probabilities and lead to more robust inference results [4,5].

Inference in Kappa networks is based on the use of kappa calculus and is in general of the same order of complexity as inference in probabilistic networks (NP-hard). In contrast, inference with a qualitative probabilistic network can be done efficiently by propagating and combining signs [6]. However, qualitative probabilistic networks, due to the high level of abstraction, do not provide for weighing influences with conflicting signs and, hence, do not provide for resolving

T.D. Nielsen and N.L. Zhang (Eds.): ECSQARU 2003, LNAI 2711, pp. 87–99, 2003.

such *trade-offs*. Inference with a qualitative probabilistic network therefore often results in ambiguous signs that will spread throughout most of the network.

Preventing ambiguous inference results is essential as qualitative networks can play an important role in the construction of quantitative probabilistic networks for realistic applications [7]. Assessing the numerous required point probabilities for a probabilistic network is a hard task and typically performed only when the network's digraph is considered robust. By first assessing signs for the modelled relationships, a qualitative network is obtained that allows for studying the inference behaviour of the projected quantitative network, prior to probability assessment. Ambiguous inference results in a qualitative network can to some extent be averted by, for example, introducing a notion of strength of influences. To this end, previous work partitions the set of qualitative influences into strong and weak influences [8]. In this paper, we investigate the combination of qualitative probabilistic networks and kappa values. A novel approach to using kappa values allows us to distinguish *several* levels of strength of qualitative influences, thereby enabling the resolution of more trade-offs.

This paper is organised as follows. Section 2 provides preliminaries concerning qualitative probabilistic networks; Sect. 3 details our use of kappa values to indicate strengths of influences. Section 4 presents an inference procedure for our kappa enhanced networks. The paper ends with some conclusions in Sect. 5.

2   Qualitative Probabilistic Networks

A probabilistic network, or Bayesian network, uniquely encodes a joint probability distribution Pr over a set of statistical variables. A *qualitative probabilistic network* (QPN) can be viewed as a qualitative abstraction of such a network, similarly encoding statistical variables and probabilistic relationships between them in an acyclic directed graph $G = (V(G), A(G))$ [1]. Each node $A \in V(G)$ represents a variable, which, for ease of exposition, we assume to be binary, writing a for $A = true$ and $\bar{a}$ for $A = false$. The set $A(G)$ of arcs captures probabilistic independence between the variables. Where a quantitative probabilistic network associates conditional probability distributions with its digraph, a qualitative probabilistic network specifies qualitative influences and synergies that capture shifts in the existing, but as of yet unknown (conditional) probability distributions. A *qualitative influence* between two nodes expresses how the values of one node influence the probabilities of the values of the other node. For example, a *positive qualitative influence along arc* $A \to B$ of node A on node B, denoted $S^+(A, B)$, expresses that observing a high value for A makes the higher value for B more likely, regardless of any other direct influences on B, that is, for $a > \bar{a}$ and any combination of values x for the set $\pi(B) \setminus \{A\}$ of (direct) predecessors of B other than A:

$$\Pr(b \mid ax) - \Pr(b \mid \bar{a}x) \geq 0.$$

A negative qualitative influence S^- and a zero qualitative influence S^0 are defined analogously; if an influence is not monotonic or if it is unknown, it is called

Table 1. The ⊗- and ⊕-operators for combining signs

⊗	+	−	0	?
+	+	−	0	?
−	−	+	0	?
0	0	0	0	0
?	?	?	0	?

⊕	+	−	0	?
+	+	?	+	?
−	?	−	−	?
0	+	−	0	?
?	?	?	?	?

ambiguous, denoted $S^?$. The definition of qualitative influence can be straightforwardly generalised to an influence along a *chain* of nodes in G.

A qualitative probabilistic network also includes *product synergies* [6], that capture the sign of the (*intercausal*) qualitative influence induced between the predecessors A and B of a node C upon its observation; an induced intercausal influence behaves as a regular qualitative influence.

The set of qualitative influences exhibits various properties. The property of *symmetry* states that, if the network includes the influence $S^\delta(A, B)$, then it also includes $S^\delta(B, A)$, $\delta \in \{+, -, 0, ?\}$. The *transitivity* property asserts that the signs of qualitative influences along a chain with no head-to-head nodes combine into a sign for a net influence with the ⊗-operator from Table 1. The property of *composition* asserts that the signs of multiple influences between nodes along parallel chains combine into a sign for a net influence with the ⊕-operator. Note that composition of two influences with conflicting signs, modelling a *trade-off*, results in an ambiguous sign, indicating that the trade-off cannot be *resolved*.

For inference with a qualitative network an efficient algorithm, that builds on the properties of symmetry, transitivity, and composition of influences, is available [6] and summarised in Fig. 1. The algorithm traces the effect of observing a value for one node on the other nodes by message-passing between neighbours. For each node, a *node sign* is determined, indicating the direction of change in its probability distribution occasioned by the new observation. Initial node signs equal '0', and observations are entered as a '+' for the observed value *true* or a '−' for the value *false*. Each node receiving a message updates its sign with the ⊕-operator and subsequently sends a message to each (induced) neighbour that is not independent of the observed node. The sign of this message is the ⊗-product of the node's (new) sign and the sign of the influence it traverses.

procedure PropagateSign(*from*,*to*,*messagesign*):

    sign[*to*] ← sign[*to*] ⊕ *messagesign*;
    for each (induced) neighbour V_i of *to*
    do *linksign* ← sign of (induced) influence between *to* and V_i;
        messagesign ← sign[*to*] ⊗ *linksign*;
        if $V_i \neq$ *from* **and** $V_i \notin$ *Observed* **and** sign[V_i] $\neq$ sign[V_i] ⊕ *messagesign*
        then PropagateSign(*to*,V_i,*messagesign*)

Fig. 1. The sign-propagation algorithm

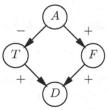

Fig. 2. The qualitative *Antibiotics* network

This process is repeated throughout the network, until each node has changed its sign at most twice (once from '0' to '+', '−', or '?', then only to '?').

Example 1. Consider the qualitative network from Fig. 2, representing a fragment of fictitious medical knowledge which pertains to the effects of taking antibiotics on a patient. Node A represents whether or not the patient takes antibiotics. Node T models whether or not the patient has typhoid fever and node D represents presence or absence of diarrhoea in the patient. Node F describes whether or not the patient's bacterial flora composition has changed. Typhoid fever and bacterial flora change can both cause diarrhoea: $S^+(T, D)$ and $S^+(F, D)$. Antibiotics can cure typhoid fever, $S^-(A, T)$, but may also change the bacterial flora composition, $S^+(A, F)$.

We observe that a patient has taken antibiotics and enter the sign '+' for node A. Node A propagates this sign to T, which receives '$+ \otimes − = −$' and sends this to node D. Node D in turn receives '$− \otimes + = −$' and does not pass on any sign. Node A also sends its sign to F, which receives '$+ \otimes + = +$' and passes this on to node D. Node D then receives the additional sign '$+ \otimes + = +$'. The two signs for D are combined, resulting in the ambiguous '$− \oplus + = ?$'; the modelled trade-off thus remains unresolved. □

3   Introducing a Notion of Strength into QPNs

To provide for trade-off resolution in qualitative probabilistic networks, we introduce a notion of strength of qualitative influences using kappa values.

3.1   Kappa Rankings and Their Interpretations

The *kappa calculus* provides for a semi-qualitative approach to reasoning with uncertainty [2][3]. In the kappa calculus, degrees of (un)certainty are expressed by a ranking κ that maps propositions into non-negative integers such that $\kappa(true) = 0$ and $\kappa(a \vee b) = \min\{\kappa(a), \kappa(b)\}$. For reasoning within the kappa calculus simple combination rules for manipulation of κ-values exist.

Kappa rankings can be interpreted as order-of-magnitude approximations of probabilities [3], allowing, for example, to compute posterior probabilities using kappa calculus. A probability $\Pr(x)$ can be approximated by a polynomial written in terms of a (infinitesimal) *base* number $0 < \epsilon < 1$. $\kappa(x)$ now represents the order of magnitude of this polynomial. More formally,

$$\kappa(x) = n \quad \text{iff} \quad \epsilon^{n+1} < \Pr(x) \leq \epsilon^n . \tag{1}$$

Note that higher probabilities are associated with lower κ-values; for example, $\kappa(x) = 0$ if $\Pr(x) = 1$, and $\kappa(x) = \infty$ iff $\Pr(x) = 0$.

3.2 Using Kappas as Indicators of Strength

We consider a qualitative probabilistic network with nodes A, B and X such that $\pi(B) = X \cup \{A\}$. Let $I_x(A, B)$ denote the influence of A on B for a certain combination of values x for the set X. We recall that the sign δ of the qualitative influence of A on B is defined as the sign of $\Pr(b \mid ax) - \Pr(b \mid \bar{a}x)$, for all x; the absolute values of these differences lie in the interval $[0, 1]$. Analogous to equivalence (1), we define the κ-value of an influence of A on B for a certain x:

$$\kappa(I_x(A, B)) = n \quad \text{iff} \quad \epsilon^{n+1} < |\Pr(b \mid ax) - \Pr(b \mid \bar{a}x)| \leq \epsilon^n.$$

We then define the *strength factor* associated with the influence of A on B to be an *interval* $[p, q]$ such that

$$p \geq \max_x \kappa(I_x(A, B)) \quad \text{and} \quad 0 \leq q \leq \min_x \kappa(I_x(A, B)),$$

and each κ expresses an order of magnitude in terms of the same base. We associate strength factors with positive and negative influences; zero and ambiguous influences are treated as in regular qualitative probabilistic networks. The above definitions extend to chains of influences as well. The resulting network will be termed a *kappa-enhanced* qualitative probabilistic network and we write $S^{\delta[p,q]}(A, B)$ to denote a qualitative influence of node A on node B with sign δ and strength factor $[p, q]$ in such a network.

Note that for a strength factor $[p, q]$ we always have that $p \geq q$, where p is greater than or equal to the kappa value of the *weakest* possible influence and q is less than or equal to the kappa value of the *strongest* possible influence. The reason for allowing influences to pretend to be stronger or weaker than they are will become apparent. Note that for each influence $[\infty, 0]$ is a valid strength factor, but not a very informative one.

We can now express strength of influences in a kappa-enhanced network in terms of the base ϵ chosen for the network: the influence of node A on node B has strength factor $[p, q]$ iff for all x

$$\epsilon^{p+1} < |\Pr(b \mid ax) - \Pr(b \mid \bar{a}x)| \leq \epsilon^q .$$

Instead of capturing the influences between variables by using kappa values for probabilities, as is done in Kappa networks, we capture influences by associating kappa values with the arcs. A Kappa network requires a number of kappa values that is exponential in the number of parents for each node; our kappa-enhanced networks require only a number of kappa values that is linear in the number of parents for each node.

4   Inference in Kappa-Enhanced Networks

Probabilistic inference in qualitative probabilistic networks builds on the properties of symmetry, transitivity and composition of influences. In order to exploit the strength of influences upon inference in a kappa-enhanced network, we define new $\otimes$- and $\oplus$-operators.

4.1   Kappa-Enhanced Transitive Combination

To address the effect of multiplying two signs with strength factors in a kappa-enhanced network, we consider the *left* network fragment from Fig. 4. The fragment includes the chain of nodes A, B, C, with two qualitative influences between them; in addition, we take $X = \pi(B) \setminus \{A\}$, and $Y = \pi(C) \setminus \{B\}$. For the net influence of A on C, we now find by conditioning on B that

$$\Pr(c \mid axy) - \Pr(c \mid \bar{a}xy) = (\Pr(c \mid by) - \Pr(c \mid \bar{b}y)) \cdot (\Pr(b \mid ax) - \Pr(b \mid \bar{a}x)) \quad (2)$$

for any combination of values x for the set X and y for Y. Similar equations are found given other arc directions, as long as node B has at least one outgoing arc. Other influences of A on C than those shown are taken into account by the $\oplus$-operator.

$\otimes$	$+[r, s]$	$-[r, s]$	0	?
$+[p, q]$	$+[p + r + 1, q + s]$	$-[p + r + 1, q + s]$	0	?
$-[p, q]$	$-[p + r + 1, q + s]$	$+[p + r + 1, q + s]$	0	?
0	0	0	0	0
?	?	?	0	?

Fig. 3. The new $\otimes$-operator for combining signs and strength factors

Transitively combining influences amounts to multiplying differences in probability, resulting in differences that are smaller than those multiplied; transitive combination therefore causes weakening of influences. This is also apparent from Fig. 3 which shows the table for the new $\otimes$-operator: upon transitive combination, the strength factor shifts to higher kappa values, corresponding to weaker influences. From the table it is also readily seen that signs combine as in a regular qualitative probabilistic network; the difference is just in the handling of the strength factors. We illustrate the combination of two positive influences; similar observations apply to other combinations.

Proposition 1. *Let A, B and C be as in the left fragment of Fig. 4, then*

$$S^{+[p,q]}(A, B) \ \wedge \ S^{+[r,s]}(B, C) \ \Rightarrow \ S^{+[p+r+1,q+s]}(A, C) \ .$$

Proof: Let X and Y be as in the left fragment of Fig. 4. Suppose $S^{+[p,q]}(A, B)$ and $S^{+[r,s]}(B, C)$. We now have for the network-associated base ϵ that

$$\epsilon^{p+1} < \Pr(b \mid ax) - \Pr(b \mid \bar{a}x) \leq \epsilon^q \text{ and}$$
$$\epsilon^{r+1} < \Pr(c \mid by) - \Pr(c \mid \bar{b}y) \leq \epsilon^s .$$

From Equation (2) for the net influences of node A on node C, we now find that

$$\epsilon^{(p+r+1)+1} = \epsilon^{p+1} \cdot \epsilon^{r+1} < \Pr(c \mid axy) - \Pr(c \mid \bar{a}xy) \leq \epsilon^q \cdot \epsilon^s = \epsilon^{q+s}$$

for any combination of values xy for the set $X \cup Y$. As $\epsilon \geq 0$, we find that the resulting net influence of A on C is positive with strength $[p + r + 1, q + s]$. $\square$

4.2 Kappa-Enhanced Parallel Composition

For combining multiple qualitative influences between nodes along parallel chains, we provide the new $\oplus$-operator in Fig. 5, which takes strength factors into account. In addressing parallel composition we first assume that ϵ is infinitesimal; the effect of a non-infinitesimal ϵ on the $\oplus$-operator is discussed at the end of this section. We consider the *right* network fragment from Fig. 4, which includes the parallel chains A, C, and A, B, C, respectively, between the nodes A and C, and various qualitative influences; in addition, we take $X = \pi(B) \setminus \{A\}$ and $Y = \pi(C) \setminus \{A, B\}$. For the net influence of A on C along the two parallel chains, conditioning on B gives the following equation for any combination of values x for X and y for Y

$$
\begin{aligned}
\Pr(c \mid axy) - \Pr(c \mid \bar{a}xy) = \quad & (\Pr(c \mid aby) - \Pr(c \mid a\bar{b}y)) \cdot \Pr(b \mid ax) \\
& - (\Pr(c \mid \bar{a}by) - \Pr(c \mid \bar{a}\bar{b}y)) \cdot \Pr(b \mid \bar{a}x) \quad (3) \\
& + \Pr(c \mid a\bar{b}y) - \Pr(c \mid \bar{a}\bar{b}y) .
\end{aligned}
$$

Similar equations are found if arc directions are changed, as long as the fragment remains acyclic and B has at least one outgoing arc.

Parallel composition of influences may result in a net influence of larger magnitude: the result of adding two positive or two negative influences is at least as strong as the strongest of the influences added. This observation is also apparent from Fig. 5: the minimum of kappa values represents a stronger net influence. On the other hand, adding conflicting influences may result in a net influence of smaller magnitude, which is also apparent from Fig. 5.

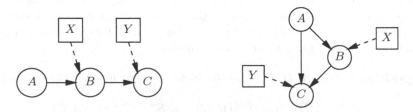

Fig. 4. Two illustrative network fragments

As examples, we now illustrate the parallel composition of two positive influences, and — more interesting in the light of resolving trade-offs — the composition of a positive and a negative influence. Similar observations with respect to the sign and strength factor of a net influence apply to situations in which the signs of the influences are different from those discussed.

Proposition 2. *Let A and C be as in the right fragment of Fig. 4, then*

$$S_1^{+[p,q]}(A,C) \wedge S_2^{+[r,s]}(A,C) \Rightarrow S_{net}^{+[\min\{p,r\},\min\{q,s\}]}(A,C) \ .$$

Proof: Let B, X and Y be as in the right fragment of Fig. 4. Suppose that $S_1^{+[p,q]}(A,C)$ and $S_2^{+[r,s]}(A,C)$, and that the positive influence $S_2^{+[r,s]}(A,C)$ is composed of the influences $S^{+[r',s']}(A,B)$ and $S^{+[r'',s'']}(B,C)$ such that $r = r' + r'' + 1$ and $s = s' + s''$. Similar observations apply when these latter two influences are negative. We now have for the network-associated base ϵ that

$$\epsilon^{p+1} < \Pr(c \mid ab_iy) - \Pr(c \mid \bar{a}b_ix) \le \epsilon^q, \text{ for all values } b_i \text{ of } B,$$
$$\epsilon^{r'+1} < \Pr(b \mid ax) - \Pr(b \mid \bar{a}x) \le \epsilon^{s'}, \text{ and}$$
$$\epsilon^{r''+1} < \Pr(c \mid a_iby) - \Pr(c \mid a_i\bar{b}y) \le \epsilon^{s''}, \text{ for all values } a_i \text{ of } A.$$

From Equation (3) for the net influence of node A on node C, we now find that

$$\Pr(c \mid axy) - \Pr(c \mid \bar{a}xy) > \epsilon^{r'+r''+2} + \epsilon^{p+1} = \epsilon^{r+1} + \epsilon^{p+1} \ge \epsilon^{\min\{r,p\}+1}, \text{ and}$$
$$\Pr(c \mid axy) - \Pr(c \mid \bar{a}xy) \le \epsilon^q + \epsilon^{s'+s''} = \epsilon^q + \epsilon^s,$$

for any combination of values xy for the set $X \cup Y$. The lower-bound for this difference is, for example, attained for $\Pr(b \mid \bar{a}x) = 0$ and $\Pr(b \mid ax) = \epsilon^{r'+1}$. The upper-bound is attained, for example, for $\Pr(b \mid ax) = 1$ and $\Pr(b \mid \bar{a}x) = 1 - \epsilon^{s'}$. In computing these bounds, we have exploited the available information with regard to the signs and strengths of the influences involved.

For infinitesimal ϵ the upper-bound $\epsilon^q + \epsilon^s$ is approximated by $\epsilon^{\min\{q,s\}}$; the net influence is thus positive with strength factor $[\min\{p,r\},\min\{q,s\}]$. $\square$

If two influences have conflicting signs, then one 'outweighs' the other if its weakest effect is stronger than the other influence's strongest effect. We adapt the

$\oplus$	$+[r,s]$	$-[r,s]$	0	?
$+[p,q]$	$+[u,v]$	a)	$+[p,q]$	?
$-[p,q]$	b)	$-[u,v]$	$-[p,q]$	?
0	$+[r,s]$	$-[r,s]$	0	?
?	?	?	?	?

$[u,v] = [\min\{p,r\}, \min\{q,s\}]$
a) $+[p,q]$, if $p+1 < s$;
    $+[\infty,q]$, if $p < s$;
    $-[r,s]$, if $r+1 < q$;
    $-[\infty,s]$, if $r < q$;
    ?, otherwise
b) see a) with $+$ and $-$ reversed

Fig. 5. The new $\oplus$-operator for combining signs and strength factors (ϵ infinitesimal)

safest and most conservative approach to combining conflicting influences, that is, by comparing the lower bound of the one influence with the upper bound of the other. Other interval comparison methods are however possible (see e.g. [9]).

Proposition 3. *Let A and C be as in the right fragment of Fig. 4, then*

$$S_1^{+[p,q]}(A,C) \ \wedge \ S_2^{-[r,s]}(A,C) \Rightarrow S_{net}^{+[p,q]}(A,C) \ \text{ if } p+1 < s;$$
$$S_{net}^{+[\infty,q]}(A,C) \ \text{ if } p < s;$$
$$S_{net}^{-[r,s]}(A,C) \ \text{ if } r+1 < q;$$
$$S_{net}^{-[\infty,s]}(A,C) \ \text{ if } r < q;$$
$$S_{net}^{\ ?}(A,C) \ \text{ otherwise.}$$

Proof: Let B, X and Y be as in the right fragment of Fig. 4. Suppose $S_1^{+[p,q]}(A,C)$ and $S_2^{-[r,s]}(A,C)$, and let the negative influence $S_2^{-[r,s]}(A,C)$ be composed of $S^{-[r',s']}(A,B)$ and $S^{+[r'',s'']}(B,C)$ such that $r = r' + r'' + 1$ and $s = s' + s''$. Similar observations apply when these latter signs are switched. From Equation (3), we now have for the network-associated base ϵ that

$$\Pr(c \mid axy) - \Pr(c \mid \bar{a}xy) > \epsilon^{p+1} - \epsilon^{s''} \cdot \epsilon^{s'} = \epsilon^{p+1} - \epsilon^s, \text{ and}$$
$$\Pr(c \mid axy) - \Pr(c \mid \bar{a}xy) < \epsilon^q - \epsilon^{r''+1} \cdot \epsilon^{r'+1} = \epsilon^q - \epsilon^{r+1},$$

for any combination of values xy for $X \cup Y$. The lower-bound for the difference (not distance!) is attained, for example, for $\Pr(b \mid ax) = 0$ and $\Pr(b \mid \bar{a}x) = \epsilon^{s'}$; the upper-bound for the difference is attained, for example, for $\Pr(b \mid \bar{a}x) = 1$ which enforces $\Pr(b \mid ax) < 1 - \epsilon^{r'+1}$. In computing these bounds, we have once again exploited the available information with regard to the signs and strengths of the influences involved.

Now, if $\epsilon^{p+1} \geq \epsilon^s$ then $\Pr(c \mid axy) - \Pr(c \mid \bar{a}xy) > 0 = \epsilon^\infty$. Given infinitesimal ϵ the lower-bound $\epsilon^{p+1} - \epsilon^s$ is approximated by ϵ^{p+1} under the tighter constraint $p + 1 < s$. The constraint $p + 1 \leq s$ also implies $q < r + 1$, giving an upper-bound of $\epsilon^q - \epsilon^{r+1} \leq \epsilon^q$. We conclude that the resulting influence is positive with strength factor $[p,q]$ if $p + 1 < s$ and strength factor $[\infty, q]$ if $p < s$.

On the other hand, if $\epsilon^{r+1} \geq \epsilon^q$ then $\Pr(c \mid axy) - \Pr(c \mid \bar{a}xy) < 0 = \epsilon^\infty$. Given infinitesimal ϵ the (negative!) upper-bound $-\epsilon^{r+1} + \epsilon^q$ is approximated by $-\epsilon^{r+1}$ under the tighter constraint $r + 1 < q$. The constraint $r + 1 \leq q$ also implies $p + 1 > s$, so we find a (negative) lower-bound of $-\epsilon^s + \epsilon^{p+1} \geq -\epsilon^s$. We conclude that the resulting influence is negative. Taking the absolute values of the given bounds, we find a strength factor $[r,s]$ if $r+1 < q$ and $[\infty, s]$ if $r < q$. $\square$

The Non-infinitesimal Case. The $\oplus$-operator defined above explicitly uses the fact that our kappa values are order of magnitude *approximations* of differences in probability by just taking into account the most significant ϵ-term in determining the strength factor of the net influence. Such approximations are valid as long as ϵ indeed adheres to the assumption that it is infinitesimal. In a realistic problem domain, however, probabilities and even differences in probability are hardly ever all very close to zero or one, and a non-infinitesimal ϵ is required to distinguish different levels of strength.

Although the inference algorithm sums only two signs with strength factors at a time, ultimately a sign and strength factor can be the result of a larger summation. If $1/\epsilon$ parallel chains to a single node are combined upon inference, the approximation used by the $\oplus$-operator will be an order of magnitude off, affecting not only the strength factor of the net influence (the interval becomes too 'tight': the influence can be stronger or weaker than captured by the interval), but possibly its sign as well. For inference in a kappa-enhanced network in which the assumption of an infinitesimal ϵ is violated, therefore, we have to perform an additional operation. We have a choice between two types of operation, depending on whether or not the actual value of ϵ is known. If ϵ is unknown, this operation consists of 'broadening' the interval an extra order of magnitude upon each sign addition: when composing two influences with the same sign, the occurrences of $\min\{q, s\}$ in Fig. 5 should be replaced by $\max\{0, \min\{q, s\} - 1\}$ to obtain a true upper-bound, assuming that $\epsilon \leq 0.5$. Under this same assumption, when adding a positive and a negative influence, we find true lower-bounds by replacing in Fig. 5 each p and r in a) and b) by $p + 1$ and $r + 1$, respectively. If the actual value of ϵ is known, the additional operation consists of performing the discussed correction only when necessary, that is, if a sign is composed (a multiple of) $1/\epsilon$ times. For this option, each sign needs to record how often it is summed during sign-propagation.

The adaption of parallel composition for non-infinitesimal ϵ leads to weaker, but at least correct, results. In correcting the upper- and lower-bounds of the strength factor, we have assumed that $\epsilon \leq 0.5$. This assumption seems reasonable, as each probability distribution has at most one probability larger than 0.5, and differences between probabilities are therefore likely to be less than 0.5.

4.3   Applying the Inference Algorithm

The properties of transitivity and parallel composition of influences can, as argued, be applied in a kappa-enhanced network. The property of symmetry holds for qualitative influences with respect to their sign, but not with respect to their strength. For an influence against the direction of an arc, we must therefore either use the default interval $[\infty, 0]$, or an explicitly specified strength factor.

Using the new $\otimes$- and $\oplus$-operators, the sign-propagation algorithm for regular qualitative probabilistic networks can now be applied to kappa-enhanced networks. Node-signs are again initialised to '0'; observations are once again entered as a '+' or '−'. The strength factor associated with an observation is either a *dummy* interval $[-1, 0]$ (so as to cause no loss of information upon the first operations), or an actual interval of kappa values to capture the strength of the observation. We illustrate the application of the algorithm.

Example 2. Consider the network from Fig. 6, with strength factors provided by domain experts. We again observe that a patient has taken antibiotics and enter this observation as '$+[-1,0]$' for node A. Node A propagates this 'sign' to T, which receives '$+[-1,0] \otimes - [1,0] = -[1,0]$' and sends this to D. Node D in turn receives '$-[1,0] \otimes + [2,0] = -[4,0]$' and does not pass on any sign. Node A also sends its sign to F, which receives '$+[-1,0] \otimes + [4,3] = +[4,3]$' and passes this on to D. Node D receives the additional sign '$+[4,3] \otimes + [5,3] = +[10,6]$'. The net influence of node A on D therefore is '$-[4,0] \oplus + [10,6]$' which equals '$-[4,0]$' if ϵ is infinitesimal, and '$-[5,0]$' otherwise. Taking antibiotics thus decreases the chance of suffering from diarrhoea. Note that we are now able to resolve the represented trade-off. $\square$

Inference in a kappa-enhanced network may become less efficient than in a regular qualitative network, because strength factors change more often than signs. In theory, a strength factor could change upon each sign-addition enforcing propagation to take time polynomial in the number of *chains* to a single node in the digraph. Kappa-enhanced networks, however, allow for resolving trade-offs which qualitative networks do not. A polynomial bound on inference in kappa-enhanced networks can be ensured by limiting the number of sign-additions performed and reverting to the use of default intervals once this limit is reached. The use of default intervals may again lead to weaker results, but never to incorrect ones. Another option is to isolate the area in which trade-offs occur, use kappa-enhanced inference in that area and regular qualitative inference in the remaining network [10].

5 Conclusions and Further Research

A drawback of qualitative probabilistic networks is their coarse level of detail. Although sufficient for some problem domains, this coarseness may lead to unresolved trade-offs during inference in other domains. In this paper, we combined and extended qualitative probabilistic networks and kappa values. We introduced the use of kappa values to provide for levels of strength within the qualitative probabilistic network framework, thereby allowing for trade-off resolution. The kappa-enhanced networks are very suitable for domains in which all differences in probability are close to zero. Previous research has shown that Kappa networks can give good results even for non-infinitesimal ϵ [5,11]. For our purpose, however, we feel that the little information we are depending on better be reli-

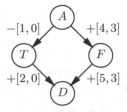

Fig. 6. The kappa-enhanced *Antibiotics* network.

able. If ϵ is not infinitesimal, a minor adaption upon sign-addition ensures that inference still leads to correct, though possibly weaker, results.

This paper presents a possible way of combining qualitative probabilistic networks with elements from the kappa calculus. Other combinations may of course be possible. We adapted the basic sign-propagation algorithm for regular qualitative probabilistic networks, with new operators for propagating signs and strength factors in kappa-enhanced networks; the resulting algorithm may, however, become less efficient. We already mentioned two possible solutions to this problem. Another possibility may be to exploit more elements from the kappa calculus: although NP-hard in general, under certain conditions, reasoning with kappa values can be tractable [12]; further research should indicate if strength factors may and can be propagated more efficiently using combination rules from the kappa calculus.

Acknowledgements. We thank Linda van der Gaag for her useful comments and the fruitful discussions on the use of kappas within the qualitative probabilistic network framework. This research was (partly) supported by the Netherlands Organisation for Scientific Research (NWO).

References

1. M.P. Wellman (1990). Fundamental concepts of qualitative probabilistic networks. *Artificial Intelligence*, vol. 44, pp. 257–303.
2. W. Spohn (1990). A general non-probabilistic theory of inductive reasoning. In R.D. Shachter, T.S. Levitt, L.N. Kanal, and J.F. Lemmer, eds., *Uncertainty in Artificial Intelligence 4*, Elsevier Science Publishers, Amsterdam, pp. 149–158.
3. W. Spohn (1988). Ordinal conditional functions: a dynamic theory of epistemic states. In W.L. Harper and B. Skyrms, eds., *Causation in Decision, Belief Change, and Statistics*, Reidel, Dordrecht, pp. 105–134.
4. A. Darwiche (1992). *A Symbolic Generalization of Probability Theory*. Ph.D. dissertation, Computer Science Department, Stanford University, Palo Alto.
5. A. Darwiche and M. Goldszmidt (1994). On the relation between kappa calculus and probabilistic reasoning. In R. Lopez de Mantaras and D. Poole, eds., *Proceedings of the 10th Conference on Uncertainty in Artificial Intelligence*, Morgan Kaufmann Publishers, San Francisco, pp. 145–153.
6. M.J. Druzdzel and M. Henrion (1993). Efficient reasoning in qualitative probabilistic networks. *Proceedings of the 11th National Conference on Artificial Intelligence*, AAAI Press, Menlo Park, pp. 548–553.
7. S. Renooij and L.C. van der Gaag (2002). From qualitative to quantitative probabilistic networks. In A. Darwiche and N. Friedman, eds., *Proceedings of the 18th Conference on Uncertainty in Artificial Intelligence*, Morgan Kaufmann Publishers, San Francisco, pp. 422–429.
8. S. Renooij and L.C. van der Gaag (1999). Enhancing QPNs for trade-off resolution. In K.B. Laskey and H. Prade, eds., *Proceedings of the 15th Conference on Uncertainty in Artificial Intelligence*, Morgan Kaufmann Publishers, San Francisco, pp. 559–566.

9. S. Parsons (2001). *Qualitative Methods for Reasoning under Uncertainty*, MIT Press.

10. S. Renooij, L.C. van der Gaag, S. Parsons and S. Green (2000). Pivotal pruning of trade-offs in QPNs. In G. Boutilier and M. Goldszmidt, eds., *Proceedings of the 16th Conference on Uncertainty in Artificial Intelligence*, Morgan Kaufmann Publishers, San Francisco, pp. 515–522.

11. M. Henrion, G. Provan, B. Del Favero and G. Sanders (1994). An experimental comparison of numerical and qualitative probabilistic reasoning. In R. Lopez de Mantaras and D. Poole, eds., *Proceedings of the 10th Conference on Uncertainty in Artificial Intelligence*, Morgan Kaufmann Publishers, San Francisco, pp. 319–326.

12. M. Goldszmidt and J. Pearl (1992). Reasoning with qualitative probabilities can be tractable. In D. Dubois, M.P. Wellman, B. D'Ambrosio, and Ph. Smets, eds., *Proceedings of the 8th Conference on Uncertainty in Artificial Intelligence*, Morgan Kaufmann Publishers, San Francisco, pp. 112–120.

Qualitative Bayesian Networks with Logical Constraints

Barbara Vantaggi

Dip. Metodi e Modelli Matematici, University "La Sapienza"
via Scarpa 16, 00161 Roma, Italy
vantaggi@dmmm.uniroma1.it

Abstract. An important feature of Qualitative Bayesian Networks is that they describe conditional independence models. However, they are not able to handle models involving logical constraints among the given variables. The aim of this paper is to show how this theory can be extended in such a way to represent also the logical constraints in the graph through an enhanced version of Qualitative Bayesian Networks. The relative algorithm for building these graphs (which is a generalization of the well-known algorithm based on D-separation criterion) is given.
This theory is particularly fit for conditional probabilistic independence models based on the notion of cs-independence. This notion avoids the usual critical situations shown by the classic definition when logical constraints are present.

1 Introduction

The important feature of Qualitative Bayesian Networks, and more in general of graphical models, is that they describe conditional independence models induced by a given probability. However, the graphical representation is apt to describe only the conditional independence statements and *not* the (possible) logical constraints among the variables. Actually, a first attempt in this direction has been done by Pearl in [1] proposing an enhanced version of d-separation criterion (called D-separation), which encodes also the functional dependencies among the variables of the domain. But the functional dependencies are actually only a particular case of logical constraints (see Section 2), which cannot be ignored; in fact, they have a crucial role from a practical point of view (see e.g. [2], [3]) and from a theoretic one: e.g. in the independence notion and in the inference processes [4], [5], [6].

In this paper we present an enhanced version of Qualitative Bayesian Networks, which is able to describe both conditional independence statements and logical constraints among the variables.

We show that this theory is particularly fit for the independence models induced by conditional probabilities, which cover more general situations and they avoid the well-known critical situations related to logical dependence relations and probability values 0 and 1 on *possible* (i.e. different to the impossible and certain event, respectively) events.

T.D. Nielsen and N.L. Zhang (Eds.): ECSQARU 2003, LNAI 2711, pp. 100–112, 2003.

These models do not necessarily satisfy the symmetric property [9], and the representation problem of *asymmetric structures* has been studied in [7] and [8].

In this paper we focus on a subclass of these conditional independence models (those closed under symmetric property), which obey graphoid properties (see [9]); in Section 3 some further relevant results concerning conditional independence have been proved. These results are deeply used in the next section.

In Section 4 we deal with the representation problem of these independence model, showing how to describe both conditional independence statements and logical constraints. As in the classic independence models, obviously, also in our setting, there are some models not completely representable by a graph (even if the models obey graphoid properties, see Example 1), so, for a given independence model $\mathcal{M}$, the notion of minimal I-map (i.e. a directed acyclic graph such that every statement represented by it is also in $\mathcal{M}$, while the graph obtained by removing any arrow from it would represent a statement not in $\mathcal{M}$) can be redefined - taking in account logical constraints - along the same lines of the classic case (see, e.g. [1], [10]).

Moreover, we generalize the procedure for building such minimal I-maps proving that any ordering on the variables gives rise to a minimal I-map for $\mathcal{M}$.

2   Logical Constraints

A *possible* event denotes an event different from $\emptyset$ and Ω. Two distinct non-trivial partitions $\mathcal{E}_1$ and $\mathcal{E}_2$ of Ω are *logically independent* if the "finer" partition $\mathcal{E}$ (called also *set of atoms*) generated by them, coincides with the set of all possible conjunctions between the events of $\mathcal{E}_1$ and $\mathcal{E}_2$, i.e.

$$\mathcal{E} = \mathcal{E}_1 \times \mathcal{E}_2 = \{C = C_1 \wedge C_2 \neq \emptyset \, : \, C_1 \in \mathcal{E}_1 \, ; \, C_2 \in \mathcal{E}_2\}.$$

Note that for simplicity we denote any atom of $\mathcal{E}_i$ by C_i ($i = 1, 2$). So, in such case the cardinality $|\mathcal{E}|$ of $\mathcal{E}$ is equal to $|\mathcal{E}_1| \cdot |\mathcal{E}_2|$. In particular, the events A and B are logically independent if the partitions $\mathcal{E}_1 = \{A, A^c\}$ and $\mathcal{E}_2 = \{B, B^c\}$ are logically independent, so the set of atoms is $\{A \wedge B, A \wedge B^c, A^c \wedge B, A^c \wedge B^c\}$.

A logical constraint exists between two partitions if they are not logical independent, i.e. some conjunction of the kind $C_1 \wedge C_2$ is not possible (they are said also semi-dependent in [11]).

Analogously, the partitions $\mathcal{E}_1, \ldots, \mathcal{E}_n$ are *logically independent* if $C_1 \wedge \ldots \wedge C_n \neq \emptyset$ for any $C_i \in \mathcal{E}_i$ (with $i = 1, \ldots, n$). Obviously, if n partitions are logically independent, then any k partitions ($1 < k < n$) are logically independent too. On the other hand, n partitions $\mathcal{E}_1, \ldots, \mathcal{E}_n$ are not necessarily logically independent, even if for every choice of $n-1$ partitions $\mathcal{E}_{i_1}, \ldots, \mathcal{E}_{i_{n-1}}$, they are logically independent; it follows that there is some logical constraint of the kind $C_1 \wedge \ldots \wedge C_n = \emptyset$, with $C_i \in \mathcal{E}_i$ (while for any $i_1, \ldots, i_{n-1}$ one has $C_{i_1} \wedge \ldots \wedge C_{i_{n-1}} \neq \emptyset$).

For example, consider $\mathcal{E}_1 = \{A, A^c\}$, $\mathcal{E}_2 = \{B, B^c\}$ and $\mathcal{E}_3 = \{C, C^c\}$ three distinct partitions of Ω such that $A \wedge B \wedge C = \emptyset$. All the pairs of these partitions are logically independent, but the partition, for example $\mathcal{E}_1$, is not logically independent of the partition generated by $\{\mathcal{E}_2, \mathcal{E}_3\}$.

Given n partitions and a logical constraint among them, it is possible to find the minimal subset $\{\mathcal{E}_1, \ldots, \mathcal{E}_k\}$ of partitions generating such constraint: there exists at least one combination of atoms, with $C_i \in \mathcal{E}_i$, such that $C_1 \wedge \ldots \wedge C_k = \emptyset$, while $C_1 \wedge \ldots C_{j-1} \wedge C_{j+1} \wedge \ldots \wedge C_k \neq \emptyset$ for all $j = 1, \ldots, k$. Note that this does not imply that all the subsets of the k partitions are logically independent, because there could be another different logical constraint involving some subset.

We say that such set of partitions $\{\mathcal{E}_1, \ldots, \mathcal{E}_k\}$ is the *minimal set* generating the given logical constraint.

Remark 1. The fact that $\{\mathcal{E}_1, \ldots, \mathcal{E}_k\}$ is the minimal set for a given logical constraint does not imply that a partition, e.g. $\mathcal{E}_k$, is logically dependent on the others. In fact, $\mathcal{E}_k$ is logically dependent on the other partitions (or better on the set of atoms generated by the other partitions) if for any $C_k \in \mathcal{E}_k$ and any atom C, generated by $\mathcal{E}_1, \ldots, \mathcal{E}_{k-1}$, one has either $C \subseteq C_k$ or $C \wedge C_k = \emptyset$. Thus, the partition generated by $\mathcal{E}_1, \ldots, \mathcal{E}_{k-1}$ refines $\mathcal{E}_k$. Therefore, the presence of some logical constraints is a situation more general than logical dependence.

Analogously we say that a vector of random variables $(X_1, \ldots, X_n)$ is linked by a logical constraint, if there is a logical constraint among the partitions $\mathcal{E}_1, \ldots, \mathcal{E}_n$ generated, respectively, by $X_1, \ldots, X_n$. Moreover, for a given logical constraint we say that the sub-vector $(X_1, \ldots, X_k)$ is the *minimal set* for it, if $\mathcal{E}_1, \ldots, \mathcal{E}_k$ is the minimal set generating it.

On the other hand, X_n is functionally dependent on $(X_1, \ldots, X_{n-1})$ if its value is completely determined by the values assumed by the variables $X_1, \ldots, X_{n-1}$, i.e. the partition $\mathcal{E}_n$ is logical dependent on $\mathcal{E}_1, \ldots, \mathcal{E}_{n-1}$.

3   Conditional Independence Models

Conditional independence models have been developed for a variety of different uncertainty formalism (see e.g. [12]), here we recall that one based on conditional probability as defined by de Finetti [11], Krauss [13], Dubins [14].

Definition 1. *Given a finite Boolean algebra $\mathcal{B}$ and an additive set $\mathcal{H}$ (i.e. closed w.r.t. finite disjunctions) such that $\emptyset \notin \mathcal{H}$, a conditional probability on $\mathcal{B} \times \mathcal{H}$ is a function $P(\cdot|\cdot)$ into $[0, 1]$, which satisfies the following conditions:*
(i) $P(\cdot|H)$ is a finitely additive probability on $\mathcal{B}$ for any $H \in \mathcal{H}$;
(ii) $P(H|H) = 1$ for every $H \in \mathcal{H}$;
(iii) $P(E \wedge A|H) = P(E|H)P(A|E \wedge H)$, whenever $E, A \in \mathcal{B}$ and $H, E \wedge H \in \mathcal{H}$;

Note that (iii) reduces, when $H = \Omega$, to the classic "chain rule" for probability $P(E \wedge A) = P(E)P(A|E)$. In the case $P_0(\cdot) = P(\cdot|\Omega)$ is strictly positive on $\mathcal{B}^0$, any conditional probability can be derived as a ratio (Kolmogorov's definition) by this unique "unconditional" probability P_0.

As proved in [6], in all other cases to get a similar representation we need to resort to a finite family $\mathcal{P} = \{P_0, \ldots, P_k\}$ of unconditional probabilities: every

P_α is defined on a proper set (taking $\mathcal{A}_0 = \mathcal{B}$)

$$\mathcal{A}_\alpha = \{E \in \mathcal{A}_{\alpha-1} \, : \, P_{\alpha-1}(E) = 0\};$$

and for each event $B \in \mathcal{B}^0$ (with $\mathcal{B}^0 = \mathcal{B} \setminus \emptyset$) there exists a unique α such that $P_\alpha(B) > 0$ and for every conditional event $A|B$ one has

$$P(A|B) = \frac{P_\alpha(A \wedge B)}{P_\alpha(B)}. \tag{1}$$

The class $\mathcal{P} = \{P_0, \ldots, P_k\}$ of probabilities, with P_α defined on $\mathcal{A}_\alpha$ (for $\alpha = 0, \ldots, k$), is said to *agree* with the conditional probability $P(\cdot|\cdot)$. This class is unique if the conditional probability is defined on $\mathcal{B} \times \mathcal{B}^0$.

Let us recall one of the main feature of this approach: to assess an evaluation P directly on an arbitrary set of conditional events:

Definition 2. *The assessment P on an arbitrary family $\mathcal{F} = \{E_1|H_1, \ldots, E_n|H_n\}$ of conditional events is coherent if there exists $\mathcal{K} \supseteq \mathcal{F}$, with $\mathcal{K} = \mathcal{B} \times \mathcal{H}$ with $\mathcal{H} \subset \mathcal{B}$ ($\mathcal{B}$ Boolean algebra, $\mathcal{H}$ an additive set), such that P can be extended from $\mathcal{F}$ to $\mathcal{K}$ as a conditional probability.*

For the checking of coherence and to find the agreeing class we refer to [6].

Definition 3. *Let P be a coherent conditional probability on $\mathcal{F}$ and consider an agreeing class $\mathcal{P} = \{P_0, \ldots, P_k\}$. For any event E belonging to $\mathcal{B}^0$ we call zero-layer of E, with respect to $\mathcal{P}$, the (non-negative) number α such that $P_\alpha(E) > 0$ (in symbols $\circ(E) = \alpha$). Moreover, we define $\circ(\emptyset) = +\infty$.*
While for any $E|H \in \mathcal{B} \times \mathcal{B}^0$ we define $\circ(E|H) = \circ(E \wedge H) - \circ(H)$.

Note that the zero-layers depend on the chosen agreeing class $\mathcal{P}$.
In this framework the following definition of independence has been given in [4]:

Definition 4. *Given a coherent conditional probability P, defined on a family $\mathcal{F}$ containing $\mathcal{D} = \{A^*|B^* \wedge C, B^*|A^* \wedge C\}$ (with A^* - analogously B^* - stands for either A or its contrary A^c), A is conditionally cs-independent of B given C with respect to P if both the following conditions hold:*
(i) $P(A|B \wedge C) = P(A|B^c \wedge C)$;
(ii) there exists a class $\{P_\alpha\}$ of probabilities agreeing with the restriction of P to the family $\mathcal{D}$, such that

$$\circ(A|B \wedge C) = \circ(A|B^c \wedge C) \quad \text{and} \quad \circ(A^c|B \wedge C) = \circ(A^c|B^c \wedge C).$$

Note that if $0 < P(A|B \wedge C) = P(A|B^c \wedge C) < 1$ (so $0 < P(A^c|B \wedge C) = P(A^c|B^c \wedge C) < 1$), then both equalities in condition (ii) are trivially satisfied

$$\circ(A|B \wedge C) = 0 = \circ(A|B^c \wedge C) \quad \text{and} \quad \circ(A^c|B \wedge C) = 0 = \circ(A^c|B^c \wedge C).$$

Hence, in this case condition (i) completely characterizes conditional cs-independence, and, in addition, also B is cs-independent of A given C, so this definition coincides with the classic formulations when also $P(B|C)$ and $P(C)$ are in $(0, 1)$.

However, in the other cases (when $P(A|B \wedge C)$ is 0 or 1) condition (i) needs to be "reinforced" by the requirement that also their zero-layers must be equal, otherwise we can meet critical situations (see, e.g. [6]).

Remark 2. Even if *different* classes agreeing with $P_{|\mathcal{D}}$ may give rise to *different* zero-layers, nevertheless it has been proved in [6] that condition *(ii)* of Definition 4 either holds for all the agreeing classes of P or for none of them.

Notice that for every event A the notion of cs-independence is always irreflexive (also when the probability of A is 0 or 1) because $\circ(A|A) = 0$, while $\circ(A|A^c) = \infty$. Actually, the following result holds (see [4], [9]):

Theorem 1. *Let A and B two possible events such that $A \wedge C \neq \emptyset$ and $A \neq C$. If $A\perp\!\!\!\perp_{cs}B|C$ under a conditional probability P, then A and B are logically independent with respect to C (i.e. all the events $A^* \wedge B^* \wedge C$ are possible).*

Note that

$$A\perp\!\!\!\perp_{cs}B|C \implies P(A|B \wedge C) = P(A|C), \tag{2}$$

it means that cs-independence implies classic independence notion, but the converse implication does not hold (as shown above, for more details see [4]).

In [4] also a theorem characterizing cs-independence of two logically independent events A and B in terms of probabilities $P(B|C), P(B|A \wedge C)$ and $P(B|A^c \wedge C)$ is given, giving up any direct reference to the zero-layers.

Theorem 2. *Let A, B be two events logically independent with respect to the event C. If P is a coherent conditional probability such that $P(A|B \wedge C) = P(A|B^c \wedge C)$, then $A\perp\!\!\!\perp_{cs}B \mid C$ if and only if one (and only one) of the following conditions holds:*

(a) $0 < P(A|B \wedge C) < 1$;
(b) $P(A|B \wedge C) = 0$ *and the extension of P to $B|C$ and $B|A \wedge C$ satisfies one of the following conditions*
    1. $P(B|C) = 0, P(B|A \wedge C) = 0,$
    2. $P(B|C) = 1, P(B|A \wedge C) = 1,$
    3. $0 < P(B|C) < 1, 0 < P(B|A \wedge C) < 1$;
(c) $P(A|B \wedge C) = 1$ *and the extension of P to $B|C$ and $B|A^c \wedge C$ satisfies one of the following conditions*
    1. $P(B|C) = 0, P(B|A^c \wedge C) = 0,$
    2. $P(B|C) = 1, P(B|A^c \wedge C) = 1,$
    3. $0 < P(B|C) < 1, 0 < P(B|A^c \wedge C) < 1.$

The probability assessments satisfying the symmetric property (when it makes sense), are characterized by the next result (proved in [9]).

Proposition 1. *Let A, B be two events logically independent with respect to C. If P is a coherent probability, then $A\perp\!\!\!\perp_{cs}B|C$ [P] and $B\perp\!\!\!\perp_{cs}A|C$ [P] iff*

$$P(A|B \wedge C) = P(A|B^c \wedge C) \quad and \quad P(B|A \wedge C) = P(B|A^c \wedge C) \tag{3}$$

Remark 3. The validity of $A \perp\!\!\!\perp_{cs} B|C$ and its symmetric statement under P is again more general than that described in the classic kolmogorovian context: in fact the two conditions coincide only if $P(A|C)$ and $P(B|C)$ are in $(0,1)$; while the conditional probabilities $P(B|A \wedge C)$ and $P(A|B \wedge C)$ are not defined when $P(A|C)$ or $P(B|C)$ is 0. In conclusion, Proposition 1 points out that requiring the symmetry only condition (3) must be checked and the different cases considered by Theorem 2 are absorbed.

Indeed, in the quoted paper the definition of cs-independence has been extended to the case of finite sets of events and to finite random variables.

Definition 5. *Let $\mathcal{E}_1, \mathcal{E}_2, \mathcal{E}_3$ be three different finite partitions such that $\mathcal{E}_2$ is not trivial. The partition $\mathcal{E}_1$ is independent of $\mathcal{E}_2$ given $\mathcal{E}_3$ under the coherent conditional probability P (in symbols $\mathcal{E}_1 \perp\!\!\!\perp_{cs} \mathcal{E}_2 | \mathcal{E}_3$ [P]) iff $C_{i_1} \perp\!\!\!\perp_{cs} C_{i_2} | C_{i_3}$ [P] for every $C_{i_1} \in \mathcal{E}_1, C_{i_2} \in \mathcal{E}_2, C_{i_3} \in \mathcal{E}_3$ such that $C_{i_2} \wedge C_{i_3} \neq \emptyset$, and $C_{i_2} \neq C_{i_3}$.*

Let $X = (X_1, \ldots, X_n)$ be a finite random vector with values in $R_X \subseteq \mathbb{R}^n$. The partition generated by X is denoted by $\mathcal{E}_X = \{X = x : x \in R_X\}$.

Definition 6. *Let (X, Y, Z) be a finite discrete random vector with values in $R \subseteq R_X \times R_Y \times R_Z$ and $\mathcal{E}_X, \mathcal{E}_Y, \mathcal{E}_Z$ the partitions generated, respectively, by X, Y and Z. Let P be a conditional probability on $\mathcal{F} \supseteq \{A|BC : A \in \mathcal{E}_X, B \in \mathcal{E}_Y, C \in \mathcal{E}_Z\}$: then X is cs-independent of Y given Z with respect to P (in symbol $X \perp\!\!\!\perp_{cs} Y|Z$ [P]) iff $\mathcal{E}_X \perp\!\!\!\perp_{cs} \mathcal{E}_Y | \mathcal{E}_Z$ [P].*

The following result is a generalization of Proposition 1.

Theorem 3. *Let $\mathcal{E}_1, \mathcal{E}_2$ be two logical independent partitions, given a conditional probability P, the statement $\mathcal{E}_1 \perp\!\!\!\perp_{cs} \mathcal{E}_2$ and its symmetric hold under P iff for any $A_i \in \mathcal{E}_1$ and $B_j \in \mathcal{E}_2$ one has*

$$P(A_i|B_j) = P(A_i) \quad \text{and} \quad P(B_j|A_i) = P(B_j). \tag{4}$$

Proof: From implication (2) it follows that if $\mathcal{E}_1 \perp\!\!\!\perp_{cs} \mathcal{E}_2$, then for $A_i \in \mathcal{E}_1$ one has $P(A_i|B_j) = P(A_i)$ for any $B_j \in \mathcal{E}_2$.
Conversely, if $P(A_i|B_j) = P(A_i)$ holds for any $B_j \in \mathcal{E}_2$, then one has from disintegration property and equation (1), being $\circ(B_j^c) = \alpha$ (with α equal to 0 if $P(B_j^c) > 0$ and 1 when $P(B_j) = 1$), that

$$P(A_i|B_j^c) = \frac{\overset{\square}{\underset{k \neq j}{\sum}} P_\alpha(A_i \wedge B_k)}{P_\alpha(B_j^c)} = \frac{\overset{\square}{\underset{k \neq j}{\sum}} P(A_i|B_k) P_\alpha(B_k)}{P_\alpha(B_j^c)} = P(A_i).$$

Therefore, for any A_i the first equality of condition (3) holds for any $B_j \in \mathcal{E}_2$. Analogously, the second equality of the condition (3) can be proved from the second equality of condition (4). So, the conclusion follows from Proposition 1.

Theorem 3 can be generalized as follows (the proof goes along the same line):

Theorem 4. *Let (X, Y, Z) be a random vector such that any $A_i \in \mathcal{E}_X, B_j \in \mathcal{E}_Y$ are logically independent with respect to any $C_k \in \mathcal{E}_Z$ if $B_j \wedge C_k \neq \{\emptyset, C_k\}$. Given*

*a conditional probability P, the statement $X_1 \perp\!\!\!\perp_{cs} X_2 | X_3$ and its symmetric hold
under P iff for any $x_i \in \mathcal{R}_X$, $y_j \in \mathcal{R}_Y$ and $z_k \in \mathcal{R}_Z$ one has*

$$P(X = x_i | Y = y_j, Z = z_k) = P(X = x_i | Z = z_k) \tag{5}$$
$$P(Y = y_j | X = x_i, Z = z_k) = P(Y = y_j | Z = z_k). \tag{6}$$

Remark 4. From Theorem 4 it comes out the crucial role of logical constraints. Actually, it can happen that equations (5) and (6) hold even if the cs-independence statement is not valid because of a logical constraint involving both X and Y.

The set $\mathcal{M}_P$ of cs-independence statements induced by a coherent conditional probability P of the form $X_I \perp\!\!\!\perp_{cs} X_J | X_K$, with I, J, K three disjoint subsets, is called *cs-independence model*. Every cs-independence model induced by P is closed with respect to the following properties (for the proof see [9]):

Decomposition property

$X_I \perp\!\!\!\perp_{cs} [X_J, X_K] | X_W \, [P] \Longrightarrow X_I \perp\!\!\!\perp_{cs} X_J | X_W \, [P]$;

Reverse decomposition property

$[X_I, X_J] \perp\!\!\!\perp_{cs} X_W | X_K \, [P] \Rightarrow X_I \perp\!\!\!\perp_{cs} X_W | X_K \, [P]$;

Weak union property

$X_I \perp\!\!\!\perp_{cs} [X_J, X_K] | X_W \, [P] \Rightarrow X_I \perp\!\!\!\perp_{cs} X_J | [X_W, X_K] \, [P]$;

Contraction property

$X_I \perp\!\!\!\perp_{cs} X_W | [X_J, X_K] \, [P] \, \& \, X_I \perp\!\!\!\perp_{cs} X_J | X_K \, [P] \Rightarrow X_I \perp\!\!\!\perp_{cs} [X_J, X_W] | [X_K] \, [P]$;

Reverse contraction property

$X_I \perp\!\!\!\perp_{cs} X_W | [X_J, X_K] \, [P] \, \& \, X_J \perp\!\!\!\perp_{cs} X_W | X_K \, [P] \Rightarrow [X_I, X_J] \perp\!\!\!\perp_{cs} X_W | [X_K] \, [P]$;

Intersection property

$X_I \perp\!\!\!\perp_{cs} X_J | [X_W, X_K] \, [P] \, \& \, X_I \perp\!\!\!\perp_{cs} X_W | [X_J, X_K] \, [P] \Rightarrow$
$X_I \perp\!\!\!\perp_{cs} [X_J, X_W] | [X_K] \, [P]$;

Reverse intersection property

$X_I \perp\!\!\!\perp_{cs} X_W | [X_J, X_K] \, [P] \, \& \, X_J \perp\!\!\!\perp_{cs} X_W | [X_I, X_K] \, [P] \Rightarrow$
$[X_I, X_J] \perp\!\!\!\perp_{cs} X_W | [X_K] \, [P]$.

Hence, these models satisfy all graphoid properties (see [1]) except the symmetry property $X_I \perp\!\!\!\perp_{cs} X_J | X_K \Rightarrow X_J \perp\!\!\!\perp_{cs} X_I | X_K$ and reverse weak union property $[X_J, X_W] \perp\!\!\!\perp_{cs} X_I | [X_K] \Rightarrow X_J \perp\!\!\!\perp_{cs} X_I | [X_W, X_K]$.

However, the conditional independence models closed under symmetric property, obey graphoid properties [9].

In the sequel we deal only with such class of independence models. As noted in Remark 3 this class is larger than the class of probability distributions inducing a graphoid structure according to classic independence notion.

4   Qualitative Bayesian Network with Logical Component

In this section we focus our attention on the representation problem of the conditional independence models and logical constraints.

A *l-graph* is a triplet $G = (V, E, \mathcal{B})$, where V is a finite set of *vertices*, E is a set of *edges* defined as a subset of $V \times V$ (i.e. set of all ordered pairs of distinct vertices), and $\mathcal{B} = \{B : B \subseteq V\}$ is a family of subsets of vertices (called logical components).

The vertices are represented by circles, and each $B \in \mathcal{B}$ by a box enclosing those circles corresponding to vertices in B.

Definition of l-graph differs from that of graph (see [15],[1]), since our interest for $\mathcal{B}$ is to cluster the sets of variables linked by some logical constraint. More precisely, every vertex $v \in V$ or subset $I \subseteq V$ is associated to a variable X_v or to a random vector X_I, respectively, and a *box* $B = \{v : v \in J\}$ *visualizes the minimal set of random variables* $\{X_v : v \in J\}$ *whose partitions generate the given logical relation* (see Section 3).

For example, in the l-graph in Figure 1 (which has no edges) the box $B = \{1, 2, 3\}$ is a logical component and represents a logical relation among the variables X_1, X_2, X_3: it could be, e.g. that the event $(X_1 = 1, X_2 = 1, X_3 = 1)$ is not possible.

Fig. 1. Graphical representation of variables linked by a logical constraint

More precisely, each box is used to emphasize where the logical constraint is localized, so which variables are involved.

An edge $(u, v) \in E$ such that its "opposite" (v, u) is not in E is called *directed*. A directed edge (u, v) is represented by $u \to v$ and u is said to be a *parent* of v and v a *child* of u. If a l-graph has only directed edges, it is called *directed* l-graph.

A *path* of length n from u to v is a sequence of distinct vertices $u = u_0, \ldots, u_n = v$ ($n \geq 1$) such that either $(u_i, u_{i+1}) \in E$ and $(u_{i+1}, u_i) \notin E$ or $(u_{i+1}, u_i) \in E$ and $(u_i, u_{i+1}) \notin E$ for $i = 0, \ldots, n - 1$. A path from u to v is *directed* if $u_i \to u_{i+1}$ for all $i = 0, \ldots, n - 1$.

If there is a directed path from u to v, we say that u *leads to* v, and we denote it as $u \mapsto v$.

An *n-cycle* is a directed path of length n with $u_n \to u_0$. A directed l-graph is *acyclic* if it contains no cycles.

The vertices u such that $u \mapsto v$ and there is no path from v to u, are the *ancestors* $an(v)$ of v; the *descendants* $ds(u)$ of u are the vertices v such that $u \mapsto v$ and there is no path from v to u.

Note that, according to our definition, a sequence consisting of one vertex is a directed path of length 0, and therefore every vertex is its own descendent and ancestor, i.e. $u \in an(u), u \in ds(u)$.

4.1 Separation Criteria for Directed Acyclic l-Graph

Before introducing the new separation criterion, we recall the classical definition of blocked path (see, e.g. [1]).

Definition 7. *Let G be an acyclic directed graph. A path $u_1, \ldots, u_m$ in G is blocked by a set of vertices $S \subseteq V$, whenever there exists a triplet of connected vertices u, v, w on the path such that of the following condition holds:*

1. *either $u \to v$, $v \to w$ or $w \to v$, $v \to u$, and $v \in S$*
2. *$v \to u$, $v \to w$ and $v \in S$*
3. *$u \to v$, $w \to v$ and $ds(v) \notin S$*

The conditions can be illustrated by Figure 2 where the grey vertices are those belonging to S.

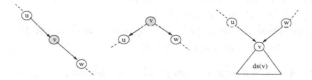

Fig. 2. Blocked paths

Vertex d-separation criterion [1] requires that every path going from one set to the other is blocked. The following generalization of this criterion is obtained using the notion of logical components.

Definition 8. *Let $G = (V, E, \mathcal{B})$ be an acyclic directed l-graph and let V_1, V_2 and S be three disjoint sets of vertices of V. The set of vertices V_1 is dl-separated from V_2 through S in the directed acyclic l-graph G (in symbol $(V_1, V_2|S)_G^{dl}$) if the following conditions hold:*

1. *every path in G from V_1 to V_2 is blocked by S;*
2. *there is no $B_i \in \mathcal{B}$ such that $B_i \subseteq V_1 \cup V_2 \cup S$, and both sets $B_i \cap V_1$ and $B_i \cap V_2$ are not empty.*

Obviously when the set of logical components $\mathcal{B}$ is empty, dl-separation criterion coincides with d-separation. It is easy to check that the possible boxes B_i in the three situations of Figure 2 can be formed only by $\{u, v\}$ and $\{v, w\}$. Actually, putting a logical component, e.g. $B = \{u, v, w\}$ in the left-side of Figure 2, the vertexes u and w are not dl-separated given v, even if u, v, w is a blocked path.

The statement "the set of vertices V_1 is dl-separated by V_2 given S" in a l-graph $G = (V, E, \mathcal{B})$ is denoted as $(V_1, V_2 | S)_G^{dl}$. The difference between dl-separation criterion and the classical one [1] is established by the condition 2. of Definition 8. Therefore, to detect the properties of dl-separation criterion, we must check the graphoid properties verified by the relation $X \perp\!\!\!\perp_\mathcal{B} Y | Z$:

$$\forall B \in \mathcal{B} \ \ B \subseteq X \cup Y \cup Z \implies B \subseteq X \cup Z \text{ or } B \subseteq Y \cup Z.$$

The following result has been proved in [7]:

Theorem 5. *The relation $X \perp\!\!\!\perp_\mathcal{B} Y | Z$ is a graphoid.*

It is well known that d-separation criterion for Bayesian Networks satisfies graphoid properties [1], so by the previous result we get the following result:

Corollary 1. *The vertex dl-separation criterion verifies graphoid properties.*

4.2 Representation Problem through Directed Acyclic l-Graphs

Given an independence model $\mathcal{M}$, we look for a directed acyclic l-graph G able to visualize the logical constraints by means of the boxes, and to describing all the statements T in $\mathcal{M}$. If such G describing all $T \in \mathcal{M}$ exists, then we say that G is a perfect map for the model $\mathcal{M}$. Generally, it is not always feasible to have a perfect I-map G for $\mathcal{M}$ (see Example 1).

Therefore, we need to introduce, analogously as done in [1], the notion of I-map and the related algorithm to build it.

Definition 9. *A directed acyclic l-graph G is an I-map for a given independence model $\mathcal{M}$ iff every independence statement represented by means of dl-separation criterion in G is also in $\mathcal{M}$.*

Thus an I-map G for $\mathcal{M}$ may not represent every statement of $\mathcal{M}$, but the ones it represents are actually in $\mathcal{M}$, it means that the set $\mathcal{M}_G$ of statements described by G is contained in $\mathcal{M}$.

An I-map G for $\mathcal{M}$ is said *minimal* if removing any arrow from the l-graph G, the obtained l-graph will no longer be an I-map for $\mathcal{M}$.

Given an independence model $\mathcal{M}$ over the random vector $(X_1, ..., X_n)$ possibly linked by some logical constraints, let $\mathcal{B}$ the set of logical components and for any ordering $\pi = (\pi_1, ..., \pi_n)$ on the variables, consider the graph G obtained according to the following procedure (which is an enhanced version of that given by Pearl): draw the vertices according the ordering π and the boxes $B \in \mathcal{B}$; for each vertex π_j, let $U_{\pi_j} = \{\pi_1, ..., \pi_{j-1}\}$ be the set of vertices before π_j, and draw an arrow pointing to π_j from each vertex in $D_{\pi_j} \subseteq U_{\pi_j}$, which satisfies the following rules: if $\pi_j \in B$, then $B \cap R_{\pi_j}$ is empty, with $R_{\pi_j} = U_{\pi_j} \setminus D_{\pi_j}$; moreover $X_{\pi_j} \perp\!\!\!\perp_{cs} X_{R_{\pi_j}} | X_{D_{\pi_j}} \in \mathcal{M}$; remove from the boxes B the superfluous arrows (if there are).

In other words, D_{π_j} is the set of parents of π_j.

Given the ordering π, a suitable basic list of independence statements Θ_π arises from $\mathcal{M}$, and it allows us to build a directed acyclic l-graph. Actually,

110   B. Vantaggi

such graph is an I-map for $\mathcal{M}$; the proof is analogous to that given in [10]. In fact, the main difference consists in the set of logical components, which *does not depend on the chosen ordering*.

Theorem 6. *Let $\mathcal{M}$ be an independence model induced by a conditional probability, and π an ordering on the random variables. Then the directed acyclic l-graph G generated by Θ_π is an I-map for $\mathcal{M}$.*

Now, we give an example to show how to build the I-maps for a given conditional independence model.

Example 1. Let X_1, X_2, X_3 be three random variables: the codomain of X_1 is $\{0,1,2\}$, while the other two variables take values in $\{0,1\}$ and they are linked by the logical constraint $(X_1 = 0) \wedge (X_3 = 1) = \emptyset$. Consider the following assessment P (the sub-vector (X_i, X_j) is denoted as $X_{i,j}$)

	$X_{2,3}=(1,1)$	$X_{2,3}=(1,0)$	$X_{2,3}=(0,1)$	$X_{2,3}=(0,0)$
$X_{1,4}=(0,0)$	0	$\alpha\beta\gamma$	0	$\alpha(1-\beta)\gamma$
$X_{1,4}=(1,0)$	$b_1\beta-c$	$c\gamma$	$b_1(1-\beta)-(\frac{1-\beta}{\beta})c$	$(1-\beta)\frac{c}{\beta}\gamma$
$X_{1,4}=(2,0)$	$b_2\beta-d$	$d\gamma$	$b_2(1-\beta)-(\frac{1-\beta}{\beta})d$	$(1-\beta)\frac{d}{\beta}\gamma$
$X_{1,4}=(0,1)$	0	$\alpha\beta(1-\gamma)$	0	$\alpha(1-\beta)(1-\gamma)$
$X_{1,4}=(1,1)$	0	$c(1-\gamma)$	0	$(1-\beta)\frac{c}{\beta}(1-\gamma)$
$X_{1,4}=(2,1)$	0	$d(1-\gamma)$	0	$(1-\beta)\frac{d}{\beta}(1-\gamma)$

and suppose that $P(X_2 = 1|X_1 = 1, X_3 = 1) = \beta = P(X_2 = 1|X_1 = 2, X_3 = 1)$, while $P(\cdot|X_3 = 1, X_4 = 1)$ over $X_{1,2}$ is defined as follows

	$X_2 = 1$	$X_2 = 0$
$X_1 = 0$	0	0
$X_1 = 1$	$\frac{(b_1\beta-c)\beta}{(b_1+b_2)\beta-c-d}$	$\frac{(b_1\beta-c)(1-\beta)}{(b_1+b_2)\beta-c-d}$
$X_1 = 2$	$\frac{(b_2\beta-d)\beta}{(b_1+b_2)\beta-c-d}$	$\frac{(b_1\beta-d)(1-\beta)}{(b_1+b_2)\beta-c-d}$

where $\alpha, \beta, \gamma b_1, b_2, c, d$ parameters in $(0,1)$ with $\alpha+b_1+b_2 = 1$ and $\alpha+c+d = 1$.

Obviously, if $b_1 \neq \frac{c}{\beta}$ and $b_2 \neq \frac{d}{\beta}$, then the values of conditional probability $P(X_2 = 1|X_1 = 1, X_3 = 1)$ and $P(X_2 = 1|X_1 = 2, X_3 = 1)$ can be easily computed by the joint probability. Note that, if $b_1 = \frac{c}{\beta}$ (or $b_2 = \frac{d}{\beta}$), then $P(X_1 = 1|X_2 = 1, X_3 = 1) = 0 = P(X_1 = 1|X_2 = 0, X_3 = 1)$ (or $P(X_1 = 2|X_2 = 1, X_3 = 1) = 0 = P(X_1 = 2|X_2 = 0, X_3 = 1)$).

However, for any value of the parameters (also $b_1 = \frac{c}{\beta}$ and/or $b_2 = \frac{d}{\beta}$) it is easy to verify using Theorem 4 that the conditional independence model $\mathcal{M}$ induced by P is composed by the statements $X_1 \perp\!\!\!\perp_{cs} X_2|X_3$, $X_1 \perp\!\!\!\perp_{cs} X_2$, $(X_1, X_2) \perp\!\!\!\perp_{cs} X_4|X_3$, (so $X_1 \perp\!\!\!\perp_{cs} X_4|(X_2, X_3)$, $X_2 \perp\!\!\!\perp_{cs} X_4|(X_1, X_3)$) and their symmetric ones.

Therefore there is not a unique minimal I-map, in Fig. 3 two possible ones are shown: that in the left-side is related to, e.g., the ordering $\pi_1 = (1,2,3,4)$, while that in the right-side is related to, e.g $\pi_2 = (4,3,1,2)$.

Fig. 3. Minimal I-maps for $\mathcal{M}$

Actually, the picture in the left-side represents the following independence statements $X_1 \perp\!\!\!\perp_{cs} X_2, X_4 \perp\!\!\!\perp_{cs} (X_1, X_2) | X_3$ and their symmetric ones, while that one on the right-side describes the statements $X_1 \perp\!\!\!\perp_{cs} X_2 | X_3, (X_1, X_2) \perp\!\!\!\perp_{cs} X_4 | X_3$ and their symmetric ones. Note that these two graphs are minimal I-maps; in fact removing any arrow from them, we may read independence statements not in $\mathcal{M}_P$. The block $B = \{1, 3\}$ localizes the given logical constraint such that $(X_1 = 0) \wedge (X_3 = 1) = \emptyset$.

Actually, a perfect map G for a given independence model over n variables (if it exists) can be found detecting the (possible) $n!$ I-maps. More precisely, such orderings, which give rise to G, are all the orderings compatible with the partial order induced by G.

5   Conclusions

An enhanced version of Qualitative Bayesian Networks has been presented and its main properties have been shown. This is particularly useful for effective description of independence models and logical constraints among the given variables. We have generalized the procedure (given through d-separation) for finding, for any independence model $\mathcal{M}$, given an ordering on the variables, a minimal I-map for $\mathcal{M}$.

Along the same lines, we can generalize the well-known classic separation criterion for undirected graphs [15]; this can be done by introducing the notion of logical components in undirected graphs and by redefining the separation criterion.

In this paper we have shown that this theory is particularly fit for conditional probabilistic independence models, but we want to stress that it can be used also for independence models induced by other uncertainty measures.

References

1. Pearl, J.: Probabilistic Reasoning in Intelligent Systems: Networks of Plausible Inference. Morgan Kaufmann (1988)

2. Coletti, G., Scozzafava, R.: The Role of Coherence in Eliciting and Handling Imprecise Probabilities and its Application to Medical Diagnosis. Information Sciences **130** (2000) 41–65
3. Hill, J.R.: Comment on "Graphical models". Statistical Science **8** (1993) 258–261.
4. Coletti, G., Scozzafava, R.: Zero Probabilities in Stochastical Independence. In: Bouchon-Meunier, B., Yager, R.R., Zadeh, L.A. (eds.): Information, Uncertainty, Fusion. Kluwer, Dordrecht (2000) 185–196 (Selected papers from IPMU '98)
5. Coletti, G., Scozzafava, R.: Stochastic Independence in a Coherent Setting. Annals of Mathematics and Artificial Intelligence **35** (2002) 151–176
6. Coletti, G., Scozzafava, R.: Probabilistic logic in a coherent setting. Trends in logic n. 15, Kluwer, Dordrecht/Boston/London (2002)
7. Vantaggi, B.: The L-separation criterion for description of cs-independence models. International Journal of Approximate Reasoning **29** (2002) 291–316
8. Vantaggi, B.: Graphical representation of asymmetric graphoid structures. Submitted to ISIPTA'03, Lugano (2003)
9. Vantaggi, B.: Conditional Independence in a Coherent Finite Setting. Annals of Mathematic and Artificial Intelligence **32** (2001) 287–314
10. Geiger, D., Verma, T., Pearl, J.: Identifying Independence in Bayesian Networks. Networks **20** (1990) 507–534
11. de Finetti, B.: Sull'Impostazione Assiomatica del Calcolo delle Probabilità. Annali dell'Università di Trieste **19** (1949) 3-55 (Eng. transl.: Ch. 5 in Probability, Induction, Statistics, London: Wiley, 1972)
12. Dawid, P.: Separoids: A mathematical framework for conditional independence and irrelevance. Annals of Mathematic and Artificial Intelligence **32** (2001) 335–372
13. Krauss, P.H.: Representation of Conditional Probability Measures on Boolean Algebras. Acta Math. Acad. Sci. Hungar **19** (1968) 229–241
14. Dubins, L.E.: Finitely Additive Conditional Probabilities, Conglomerability and Disintegration. Annals of Probability **3** (1975) 89–99
15. Lauritzen, S.L.: Graphical Models. Clarendon Press, Oxford (1996)

Introducing Situational Influences in QPNs

Janneke H. Bolt, Linda C. van der Gaag, and Silja Renooij

Institute of Information and Computing Sciences, Utrecht University
P.O. Box 80.089, 3508 TB Utrecht, The Netherlands
{janneke,linda,silja}@cs.uu.nl

Abstract. A qualitative probabilistic network models the probabilistic relationships between its variables by means of signs. Non-monotonic influences are modelled by the ambiguous sign '?', which indicates that the actual sign of the influence depends on the current state of the network. The presence of influences with such ambiguous signs tends to lead to ambiguous results upon inference. In this paper we introduce the concept of situational influence into qualitative networks. A situational influence is a non-monotonic influence supplemented with a sign that indicates its effect in the current state of the network. We show that reasoning with such situational influences may forestall ambiguous results upon inference; we further show how these influences change as the current state of the network changes.

1   Introduction

The formalism of Bayesian networks [1] is generally considered an intuitively appealing and powerful formalism for capturing the knowledge of a complex problem domain along with its uncertainties. The usually large number of probabilities required for a Bayesian network, however, tends to pose a major obstacle to the construction [2]. *Qualitative probabilistic networks* (QPNs), introduced as qualitative abstractions of Bayesian networks [3], do not suffer from this quantification obstacle. Like a Bayesian network, a qualitative network encodes variables and the probabilistic relationships between them in a directed graph; the relationships between the variables are not quantified by conditional probabilities as in a Bayesian network, however, but are summarised by qualitative signs instead. For inference with a qualitative probabilistic network an efficient algorithm is available, based on the idea of propagating and combining signs [4].

Although qualitative probabilistic networks do not suffer from the obstacle of requiring a large number of probabilities, their high level of abstraction causes some lack of representation detail. As a consequence, for example, qualitative networks do not provide for modelling *non-monotonic* influences in an informative way. An influence of a variable A on a variable B is called non-monotonic if it is positive in one state and negative in another state of the network. Such a non-monotonic influence is modelled by the ambiguous sign '?'. The presence of influences with such ambiguous signs typically leads to ambiguous, and thereby uninformative, results upon inference.

T.D. Nielsen and N.L. Zhang (Eds.): ECSQARU 2003, LNAI 2711, pp. 113–124, 2003.

Non-monotonicity of an influence in essence indicates that the influence cannot be captured by an unambiguous sign of general validity. In each particular state of the network, however, the influence is unambiguous. In this paper we extend the framework of qualitative probabilistic networks with *situational influences* that capture information about the current effect of non-monotonic influences. We show that these situational influences can be used upon inference and may effectively forestall ambiguous results. Because the sign of a situational influence depends on the current state of the network, we investigate how it changes as the state of the network changes. We then adapt the standard propagation algorithm to inference with networks including situational influences.

The remainder of this paper is organised as follows. Section 2 provides some preliminaries on qualitative probabilistic networks. Section 3 introduces the concept of situational influence. Its dynamics are described in Sect. 4, which also gives an adapted propagation algorithm. The paper ends with some conclusions and directions for further research in Sect. 5.

2   Preliminaries

Qualitative probabilistic networks were introduced as qualitative abstractions of Bayesian networks. Before reviewing qualitative networks, therefore, we briefly address their quantitative counterparts.

A Bayesian network is a concise representation of a joint probability distribution Pr on a set of statistical variables. In the sequel, (sets of) variables are denoted by upper-case letters. For ease of exposition, we assume all variables to be binary, writing a for $A = true$ and $\bar{a}$ for $A = false$. We further assume that $true > false$. Each variable is now represented by a node in an acyclic directed graph. The probabilistic relationships between the variables are captured by the digraph's set of arcs. Associated with each variable A is a set of (conditional) probability distributions $\Pr(A \mid \pi(A))$ describing the influence of the parents $\pi(A)$ of A on the probability distribution for A itself.

Example 1. We consider the small Bayesian network shown in Fig. 1. The network represents a fragment of fictitious knowledge about the effect of training and fitness on one's feeling of well-being. Node T models whether or not one has undergone a training session, node F captures one's fitness, and node W models whether or not one has a feeling of well-being. □

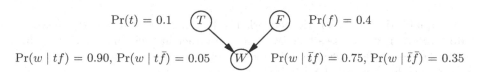

$$\Pr(t) = 0.1 \quad \fbox{T} \qquad \fbox{F} \quad \Pr(f) = 0.4$$

$$\Pr(w \mid tf) = 0.90,\ \Pr(w \mid t\bar{f}) = 0.05 \quad \fbox{W} \quad \Pr(w \mid \bar{t}f) = 0.75,\ \Pr(w \mid \bar{t}\bar{f}) = 0.35$$

Fig. 1. An example Bayesian network, modelling the influences of training (T) and fitness (F) on a feeling of well-being (W)

In its initial state where no observations for variables have been entered, a Bayesian network captures a prior probability distribution. As such evidence becomes available, the network converts to another state and then serves to represent the posterior distribution given the evidence.

Qualitative probabilistic networks bear a strong resemblance to Bayesian networks. A qualitative network also comprises an acyclic digraph modelling variables and the probabilistic relationships between them. Instead of conditional probability distributions, however, a qualitative probabilistic network associates with its digraph *qualitative influences* and *qualitative synergies*, capturing features of the existing, albeit unknown, joint distribution Pr [3].

A *qualitative influence* between two nodes expresses how the values of one node influence the probabilities of the values of the other node. For example, a *positive qualitative influence* of a node A on a node B along an arc $A \to B$, denoted $S^+(A, B)$, expresses that observing a high value for A makes the higher value for B more likely, regardless of any other direct influences on B, that is

$$\Pr(b \mid ax) - \Pr(b \mid \bar{a}x) \geq 0,$$

for any combination of values x for the set $\pi(B) \setminus \{A\}$ of parents of B other than A. A negative qualitative influence, denoted S^-, and a zero qualitative influence, denoted S^0, are defined analogously. A non-monotonic or unknown influence of node A on node B is denoted by $S^?(A, B)$.

The set of all influences of a qualitative network exhibits various important properties [3]. The property of *symmetry* states that, if the network includes the influence $S^\delta(A, B)$, then it also includes $S^\delta(B, A)$, $\delta \in \{+, -, 0, ?\}$. The *transitivity* property asserts that the signs of qualitative influences along a trail without head-to-head nodes combine into a sign for the net influence with the $\otimes$-operator from Table 1. The property of *composition* asserts that the signs of multiple influences between two nodes along parallel trails combine into a sign for the net influence with the $\oplus$-operator.

Table 1. The $\otimes$- and $\oplus$-operators for combining signs

$\otimes$	+	−	0	?	$\oplus$	+	−	0	?
+	+	−	0	?	+	+	?	+	?
−	−	+	0	?	−	?	−	−	?
0	0	0	0	0	0	+	−	0	?
?	?	?	0	?	?	?	?	?	?

A qualitative probabilistic network further includes *additive synergies*. An additive synergy expresses how two nodes interact in their influence on a third node. For example, a *positive additive synergy* of a node A and a node B on a common child C, denoted $Y^+(\{A, B\}, C)$, expresses that the joint influence of A and B on C exceeds the sum of their separate influences regardless of any other direct influences on C, that is

$$\Pr(c \mid abx) + \Pr(c \mid \bar{a}\bar{b}x) \geq \Pr(c \mid a\bar{b}x) + \Pr(c \mid \bar{a}bx),$$

for any combination of values x for the set $\pi(C) \setminus \{A, B\}$ of parents of C other than A and B. A negative additive synergy, denoted Y^-, and a zero additive synergy, denoted Y^0, are defined analogously. A non-monotonic or unknown additive synergy of nodes A and B on a common child C is denoted by $Y^?(\{A, B\}, C)$.

Example 2. We consider the qualitative abstraction of the Bayesian network from Fig. 1. From the conditional probability distributions specified for node W, we have that $\Pr(w \mid tf) - \Pr(w \mid t\bar{f}) \geq 0$ and $\Pr(w \mid \bar{t}f) - \Pr(w \mid \bar{t}\bar{f}) \geq 0$, and therefore that $S^+(F, W)$: fitness favours well-being regardless of training. We further have that $\Pr(w \mid tf) - \Pr(w \mid \bar{t}f) > 0$ and $\Pr(w \mid t\bar{f}) - \Pr(w \mid \bar{t}\bar{f}) < 0$, and therefore that $S^?(T, W)$: the effect of training on well-being depends on one's fitness. From $\Pr(w \mid tf) + \Pr(w \mid \bar{t}\bar{f}) \geq \Pr(w \mid t\bar{f}) + \Pr(w \mid \bar{t}f)$, to conclude, we find that $Y^+(\{T, F\}, W)$. The resulting qualitative network is shown in Fig. 2; the signs of the qualitative influences are shown along the arcs, and the sign of the additive synergy is indicated over the curve over variable W. $\square$

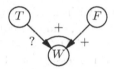

Fig. 2. The qualitative abstraction of the Bayesian network from Fig. 1

We would like to note that, although in the previous example the qualitative relationships between the variables are computed from the conditional probabilities of the corresponding quantitative network, in realistic applications these relationships are elicited directly from domain experts.

For inference with a qualitative probabilistic network, an efficient algorithm based on the idea of propagating and combining signs is available [4]. This algorithm traces the effect of observing a value for a node upon the other nodes in a network by message passing between neighbouring nodes. The algorithm is summarised in pseudo-code in Fig. 3. For each node V, a *node sign* 'sign[V]' is determined, indicating the direction of change in its probability distribution occasioned by the new observation; initial node signs equal '0'. Observations are entered as a '+' for the observed value *true*, or a '−' for the value *false*. Each node receiving a message updates its sign using the $\oplus$-operator and subsequently sends a message to each neighbour that is not independent of the observed node. The sign of this message is the $\otimes$-product of the node's (new) sign and the sign of the influence it traverses. This process of message passing between neighbours is repeated throughout the network, building on the properties of symmetry, transitivity, and composition of influences. Since each node can change its sign at most twice (once from '0' to '+', '−' or '?', and then only to '?'), the process visits each node at most twice and therefore halts in polynomial time.

Example 3. We consider the qualitative network shown in Fig. 4. Suppose that we are interested in the effect of observing the value *false* for node A upon the other nodes in the network. Prior to the inference, the node signs for all nodes

procedure Process-Observation($Q,O,sign$):
    for all $V_i \in V(G)$ in Q
    do sign$[V_i] \leftarrow$ '0';
    Propagate-Sign($Q,\varnothing,O,sign$).

procedure Propagate-Sign($Q,trail,to,message$):
    sign$[to] \leftarrow$ sign$[to] \oplus message$;
    $trail \leftarrow trail \cup \{to\}$;
    for each neighbour V_i of to in Q
    do $linksign \leftarrow$ sign of influence between to and V_i;
        $message \leftarrow$ sign$[to] \otimes linksign$;
        if $V_i \notin trail$ and sign$[V_i] \neq$ sign$[V_i] \oplus message$
        then Propagate-Sign($Q,trail,V_i,message$).

Fig. 3. The sign-propagation algorithm

are set to '0'. Inference now starts with node A receiving the message '$-$'. Node A updates its node sign to $0 \oplus - = -$, and subsequently computes the messages to be sent to its neighbours E, B and D. To node E, node A sends the message $- \otimes - = +$. Upon receiving this message, node E updates its node sign to $0 \oplus + = +$. Node E does not propagate the message it has received from A to node B because A and B are independent on the trail $A \to E \leftarrow B$. To node B, node A sends the message $- \otimes ? = ?$. Upon receiving this message, node B updates its node sign to $0 \oplus ? = ?$. Node B subsequently computes the message $? \otimes + = ?$ for E. Upon receiving this message, node E updates its node sign to $+ \oplus ? = ?$. Node B does not propagate the message it has received from A to node C because A and C are independent on the trail $A \to B \leftarrow C$. Exploiting the property of symmetry, node A sends the message $- \otimes + = -$ to node D. Upon receiving this message, node D updates its node sign to $0 \oplus - = -$. Node D subsequently computes the message $- \otimes + = -$ for C. Upon receiving this message, node C updates its node sign to $0 \oplus - = -$. Node C then sends the message $- \otimes - = +$ to B, upon which node B should update its node sign to $? \oplus + = ?$. Since this update would not change the node sign of B, the propagation of messages halts. The node signs resulting from the inference are shown in the network's nodes in Fig. 4. □

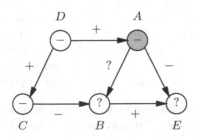

Fig. 4. A qualitative network and its node signs after the observation $A = false$

3   Situational Influences

The presence of influences with ambiguous signs in a qualitative network is likely to give rise to uninformative ambiguous results upon inference, as illustrated in Example 3. We take a closer look at the origin of these ambiguous signs. We observe that a qualitative influence of a node A on a node B along an arc $A \to B$ is only unambiguous if the difference $\Pr(b \mid ax) - \Pr(b \mid \bar{a}x)$ has the same sign for *all* combinations of values x for the set $X = \pi(B) \backslash \{A\}$. As soon as the difference $\Pr(b \mid ax) - \Pr(b \mid \bar{a}x)$ yields contradictory signs for different combinations x, the influence is non-monotonic and is assigned the ambiguous sign '?'. In each specific state of the network, associated with a specific probability distribution $\Pr(X)$ over all combinations x, however, the influence of A on B is unambiguous, that is, either positive, negative or zero. To capture the current sign of a non-monotonic influence in a specific state, we introduce the concept of *situational influence* into the formalism of qualitative probabilistic networks.

We consider a qualitative network as before and consider the evidence e entered so far. A *positive situational influence* of a node A on a node B given e, denoted $S_e^{?(+)}(A, B)$, is a non-monotonic influence of A on B for which

$$\Pr(b \mid ae) - \Pr(b \mid \bar{a}e) \geq 0.$$

In the sequel we omit the subscript e from $S_e^{?(+)}$ as long as ambiguity cannot occur. A negative situational influence, denoted $S^{?(-)}$, and a zero situational influence, denoted $S^{?(0)}$, are defined analogously. An unknown situational influence of node A on node B is denoted by $S^{?(?)}(A, B)$. The sign between the brackets will be called *the sign of the situational influence*. A qualitative network extended with situational influences will be called a *situational qualitative network*. Note that while the signs of qualitative influences and additive synergies have general validity, the signs of situational influences pertain to a specific state of the network and depend on $\Pr(X)$.

Example 4. We consider once again the network fragment from Fig. 1 and its qualitative abstraction shown in Fig. 2. The qualitative influence of node T on node W was found to be non-monotonic. Its sign therefore depends on the state of the network. In the prior state of the network where no evidence has been entered, we have that $\Pr(f) = 0.4$. Given this probability, we find $\Pr(w \mid t) = 0.39$ and $\Pr(w \mid \bar{t}) = 0.51$. From the difference $\Pr(w \mid t) - \Pr(w \mid \bar{t}) = -0.12$ being negative, we conclude that the influence of node T on node W is negative in this particular state. The current sign of the influence is therefore '$-$'. The situational qualitative network for the prior state is shown in Fig. 5. The dynamic nature of the sign of the situational influence is illustrated by a change from '$-$' to '$+$' after, for example, the observation $F = true$ is entered into the network, in which case $\Pr(w \mid tf) - \Pr(w \mid \bar{t}f) = 0.90 - 0.75 = 0.15$. $\square$

Once again we note that, although in the previous example the sign of the situational influence is computed from the quantitative network, in a realistic application it would be elicited directly from a domain expert. In the remainder

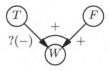

Fig. 5. The network from Fig. 2, now with the prior situational influence of T on W

of the paper, we assume that the expert has given the signs of the situational influences for the prior state of the network.

4   Inference with a Situational Qualitative Network

For inference with a regular qualitative probabilistic network, an efficient algorithm is available that is based on the idea of propagating and combining signs of qualitative influences, as reviewed in Sect. 2. For inference with a situational qualitative network, we observe that the sign of a situational influence indicates the sign of the original qualitative influence in the current state of the network. After an observation has been entered into a situational network, therefore, the signs of the situational influences can in essence be propagated as in regular qualitative networks, *provided* that these signs are still valid in the new state of the network. In this section we discuss how to verify the validity of the sign of a situational influence as observations become available that cause the network to convert to another state. In addition, we show how to incorporate this verification into the sign propagation algorithm.

4.1   Dynamics of the Signs of Situational Influences

We begin by investigating the simplest network fragment in which a non-monotonic qualitative influence can occur, consisting of a single node with two independent parents. We show for this fragment how the validity of the sign of the situational influence can be verified during inference by exploiting the associated additive synergy. We then extend the main idea to more general situational networks.

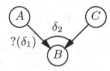

Fig. 6. A fragment of a situational network, consisting of node B and its parents A and C, with $S^{?(\delta_1)}(A, B)$ and $Y^{\delta_2}(\{A, C\}, B)$

We consider the network fragment from Fig. 6, consisting of node B and its mutually independent parents A and C. We assume for now that the nodes A and C remain independent as observations are being entered into the network. By conditioning on A and C, we find for the probability of b:

$$\Pr(b) = \Pr(a) \cdot [\Pr(c) \cdot (\Pr(b \mid ac) - \Pr(b \mid a\bar{c}) - \Pr(b \mid \bar{a}c) + \Pr(b \mid \bar{a}\bar{c})) +$$
$$\Pr(b \mid a\bar{c}) - \Pr(b \mid \bar{a}\bar{c})] + \Pr(c) \cdot (\Pr(b \mid \bar{a}c) - \Pr(b \mid \bar{a}\bar{c})) + \Pr(b \mid \bar{a}\bar{c}) \,.$$

We observe that $\Pr(b)$ is a function of $\Pr(a)$ and $\Pr(c)$, and that for a fixed $\Pr(c)$, $\Pr(b)$ is a linear function of $\Pr(a)$. For $\Pr(a) = 1$, the function yields $\Pr(b \mid a)$; for $\Pr(a) = 0$, it yields $\Pr(b \mid \bar{a})$. Moreover, the gradient of the function at a particular $\Pr(c)$ matches the sign of the situational influence of node A on node B for that $\Pr(c)$. In essence, we have two different, so-called, *manifestations* of the non-monotonic influence of A on B: either the sign of the situational influence is negative for low values of $\Pr(c)$ and positive for high values of $\Pr(c)$, as shown in Fig. 7, or vice versa, as shown in Fig. 8.

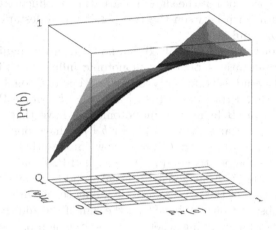

Fig. 7. An example $\Pr(b)$ as a function of $\Pr(a)$ and $\Pr(c)$, with $S^?(A,B), S^+(C,B)$ and $Y^+(\{A,C\},B)$

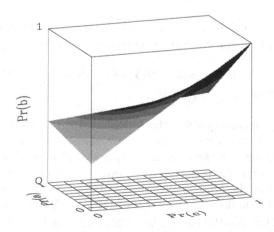

Fig. 8. An example $\Pr(b)$ as a function of $\Pr(a)$ and $\Pr(c)$, with $S^?(A,B), S^+(C,B)$ and $Y^-(\{A,C\},B)$

As a result of observations being entered into the network, the probability of c may change. The sign of the situational influence of node A on node B may then change as well. For some changes of the probability of c, however, the sign will definitely stay the same. Whether or not it will do so depends on the manifestation of the non-monotonic influence, on the current sign, and on the direction of change of the probability of c. In the graph depicted in Fig. 7, for example, the sign of the situational influence will definitely persist if it is negative and the probability of c decreases, or if it is positive and the probability of c increases. The reverse holds for the graph depicted in Fig. 8. A method for verifying whether or not the sign of a situational influence retains its validity thus has to distinguish between the two possible manifestations of the underlying non-monotonic influence.

The sign of the additive synergy involved can now aid in distinguishing between the possible manifestations of a non-monotonic influence under study. We recall that a positive additive synergy of nodes A and C on their common child B indicates that $\Pr(b \mid ac) - \Pr(b \mid \bar{a}c) \geq \Pr(b \mid a\bar{c}) - \Pr(b \mid \bar{a}\bar{c})$. From the influence of A on B being non-monotonic, we have that the differences $\Pr(b \mid ac) - \Pr(b \mid \bar{a}c)$ and $\Pr(b \mid a\bar{c}) - \Pr(b \mid \bar{a}\bar{c})$ have opposite signs. A positive additive synergy of A and C on B now implies that the sign of $\Pr(b \mid ac) - \Pr(b \mid \bar{a}c)$ must be positive and that the sign of $\Pr(b \mid a\bar{c}) - \Pr(b \mid \bar{a}\bar{c})$ must be negative, as in Fig. 7. Analogously, a negative additive synergy corresponds to the manifestation of the non-monotonic influence shown in Fig. 8.

From the previous observations, we have that the sign of the additive synergy involved can be exploited for verifying whether or not the sign of a situational influence retains its validity during inference. Suppose that, as in Fig. 6, we have $S^{?(\delta_1)}(A, B)$ and $Y^{\delta_2}(\{A, C\}, B)$. Further suppose that new evidence causes a change in the probability of c, the direction of which is reflected in sign$[C]$. Then, we can be certain that δ_1 will remain valid if

$$\delta_1 = \text{sign}[C] \otimes \delta_2 .$$

Otherwise, δ_1 has to be changed into '?'. We can substantiate our statement as follows. Abstracting from previously entered evidence, we have that

$$\Pr(b \mid a) - \Pr(b \mid \bar{a}) = \Pr(c) \cdot (\Pr(b \mid ac) - \Pr(b \mid a\bar{c}) - \Pr(b \mid \bar{a}c) + \Pr(b \mid \bar{a}\bar{c})) + \Pr(b \mid a\bar{c}) - \Pr(b \mid \bar{a}\bar{c}) .$$

We observe that the equation expresses the difference $\Pr(b \mid a) - \Pr(b \mid \bar{a})$ as a linear function of $\Pr(c)$. We further observe that the sign of the gradient of this function equals the sign of the additive synergy of A and C on B. Now suppose that the probability of c increases as a result of the new evidence, and that $Y^+(\{A, C\}, B)$. Since the gradient then is positive, a positive sign for the situational influence will remain valid. If, on the other hand, the probability of c increases and $Y^-(\{A, C\}, B)$, then a negative sign for the situational influence will remain valid. We conclude that upon an increase of $\Pr(c)$, δ_1 persists if $\delta_1 = + \otimes \delta_2$. Otherwise, we cannot be certain of the sign of the situational influence and δ_1 is changed to '?'. Similar observations hold for a decreasing probability of c.

In our analysis so far, we have assumed that the two parents A and C of a node B are mutually independent and remain to be so as evidence is entered into the network. In general, however, A and C can be (conditionally) dependent. Node A then not only influences B directly, but also indirectly through C. The situational influence of A on B, however, pertains to the direct influence in isolation even though a change in the probability of c may affect its sign. When a change in the probability of a causes a change in the probability of c which in turn influences the probability of b, the indirect influence on b is processed by the sign-propagation algorithm building upon the composition of signs.

4.2   The Adapted Sign-Propagation Algorithm

The sign-propagation algorithm for inference with a qualitative network has to be adapted to render it applicable to situational qualitative networks. In essence, two modifications are required. First, in case of non-monotonicities, the algorithm must use the signs of the situational influences involved. Furthermore, because the sign of a situational influence of a node A on a node B is dynamic, its validity has to be verified as soon as an observation causes a change in the probability distribution of another parent of B. Due to the nature of sign propagation, it may occur that a sign is propagated along a situational influence between A and B, while the fact that the probability distribution of another parent of B changes does not become apparent until later in the propagation. It may then turn out that the sign of the situational influence should have been adapted and that incorrect signs were propagated. A solution to this problem is to verify the validity of the sign of the situational influence as soon as information to this end becomes available; if the sign requires updating, inference is restarted with the updated network. Since the sign of a situational influence can change only once, the number of restarts is limited. The adapted part of the sign-propagation algorithm is summarised in pseudo-code in Fig. 9.

Example 5. We consider the situational qualitative network from Fig. 10. The network is identical to the one shown in Fig. 4, except that it is supplemented with a situational sign for the non-monotonic influence of node A on node B. Suppose that we are again interested in the effect of observing the value *false* for node A upon the other nodes in the network. Inference starts with node A receiving the message '$-$' and updating its node sign to $0 \oplus - = -$. Node A subsequently determines the messages to be sent to its neighbours E, B and D. To node E, it sends $- \otimes - = +$. Upon receiving this message, node E updates its node sign to $0 \oplus + = +$ as before; node E does not propagate the message to B. To node B, node A sends the message $- \otimes - = +$, using the sign of the situational influence. Node B updates its node sign to $0 \oplus + = +$. It subsequently computes the message $+ \otimes + = +$ for E. Upon receiving this message, node E does not need to change its node sign. Node B does not propagate the message it has received from A to node C. To node D, node A

procedure Propagate-Sign($Q,trail,to,message$):

$sign[to] \leftarrow sign[to] \oplus message$;
$trail \leftarrow trail \cup \{to\}$;
Determine-Effect-On(Q,to);
for each neighbour V_i of to in Q
do $linksign \leftarrow$ sign of influence between to and V_i;
   $message \leftarrow sign[to] \otimes linksign$;
   if $V_i \notin trail$ and $sign[V_i] \neq sign[V_i] \oplus message$
   then Propagate-Sign($Q,trail,V_i,message$).

procedure Determine-Effect-On(Q,V_i):

$N_{V_i} \leftarrow \{V_j \to V_k \mid V_j \in \pi(V_k) \setminus \{V_i\}, V_k \in \sigma(V_i), S^{?(\delta)}(V_j, V_k), \delta \neq ?\}$;
for all $V_j \to V_k \in N_{V_i}$
do Verify-Update($S^{?(\delta)}(V_j, V_k)$);
if a δ changes
then $Q \leftarrow Q$ with adapted signs;
   return Process-Observation($Q,O,sign$).

Fig. 9. The adapted part of the sign-propagation algorithm

sends $- \otimes + = -$. Node D updates its node sign to $0 \oplus - = -$. It subsequently
determines the message $- \otimes + = -$ for node C. Upon receiving this message,
C updates its node sign to $0 \oplus - = -$. The algorithm now establishes that
node C is a parent of node B which has node A for its other parent, and that
the influence of node A on B is non-monotonic. Because the node sign of C has
changed, the validity of the sign of the situational influence of A on B needs to
be verified. Since $- = - \otimes +$, the algorithm finds that the sign of the situational
influence of A on B remains valid. The inference therefore continues. Node C
sends the message $- \otimes - = +$ to B. Since node B need not change its node
sign, the inference halts. The node signs resulting from the inference are shown
in the network's nodes in Fig. 10. □

Examples 3 and 5 demonstrate that inference with a situational network can
yield more informative results when compared to a regular qualitative network.

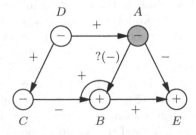

Fig. 10. A situational network and its node signs after the observation $A = false$

5 Conclusions and Further Research

Qualitative probabilistic networks model the probabilistic relationships between their variables by means of signs. If such a relationship is non-monotonic, it has associated the ambiguous sign '?', even though the influence is always unambiguous in the current state of the network. The presence of influences with ambiguous signs typically leads to ambiguous, and thus uninformative, results upon inference. In this paper we extended qualitative networks with situational influences that capture qualitative information about the current effect of non-monotonic influences. We showed that these situational influences can be used upon inference and may then effectively forestall ambiguous inference results. Because the signs of situational influences are dynamic in nature, we identified conditions under which these signs retain their validity. We studied the dynamics of the signs of situational influences in cases where the non-monotonicity involved originates from a single variable. The presented ideas and methods, however, are readily generalised to cases where the non-monotonicity is caused by more than one variable. To conclude, we adapted the existing sign-propagation algorithm to situational qualitative networks.

By introducing situational influences we have, in essence, strengthened the expressiveness of a qualitative network. Recently, other research has also focused on enhancing the formalism of qualitative networks, for example by introducing a notion of strength of influences [5]. In the future we will investigate how these different enhancements can be integrated to arrive at an even more powerful framework for qualitative probabilistic reasoning.

Acknowledgement. This research has been supported by the Netherlands Organisation for Scientific Research (NWO).

References

1. J. Pearl. *Probabilistic Reasoning in Intelligent Systems: Networks of Plausible Inference*. Morgan Kaufmann Publishers, Palo Alto, 1988.
2. M.J. Druzdzel and L.C. van der Gaag. Elicitation of probabilities for belief networks: combining qualitative and quantitative information. In Ph. Besnard and S. Hank, editors, *Proceedings of the Eleventh Conference on Uncertainty in Artificial Intelligence*, pages 141–148, Morgan Kaufmann Publishers, San Francisco, 1995.
3. M.P. Wellman. Fundamental concepts of qualitative probabilistic networks. *Artificial Intelligence*, 44:257–303, 1990.
4. M.J. Druzdzel and M. Henrion. Efficient reasoning in qualitative probabilistic networks. In *Proceedings of the Eleventh National Conference on Artificial Intelligence*, pages 548–553, AAAI Press, Menlo Park, California, 1993.
5. S. Renooij and L.C. van der Gaag. Enhancing QPNs for trade-off resolution. In K. Laskey and H. Prade, editors, *Proceedings of the Fifteenth Conference on Uncertainty in Artificial Intelligence*, pages 480–487, Morgan Kaufmann Publishers, San Francisco, 1999.

Classification of Aerial Missions Using Hidden Markov Models

Maria Andersson

Division of Command and Control Systems
Swedish Defence Research Agency FOI
SE-581 11 Linkoping, Sweden
`maria.andersson@foi.se`

Abstract. This paper describes classification of aerial missions using first-order discrete Hidden Markov Models based on kinematic data. Civil and military aerial missions imply different motion patterns as described by the altitude, speed and direction of the aircraft. The missions are transport, private flying, reconnaissance, protection from intruders in the national airspace as well as on the ground or the sea. A procedure for creating a classification model based on HMMs for this application is discussed. An example is presented showing how the results can be used and interpreted. The analysis indicates that this model can be used for classification of aerial missions, since there are enough differences between the missions and the kinematic data can be seen as observations from unknown elements, or states, that form a specific mission.

1 Introduction

An important matter in surveillance and tracking systems is target classification, which aims at recognising or even identifying the targets.

Classification and tracking are fundamental for obtaining situation awareness, i.e. understanding what situation that has given rise to the observed data. For example, in a military surveillance and tracking system it is of interest to understand how threatful a certain situation is. Once situation awareness has been obtained different types of decision can be made for the coming time period, for exemple concerning sensor management.

In a multitarget environment an algorithm for automated classification will support the operator in the work of handling and prioritising a large number of targets. Furthermore, with the help of automated classification, decisions can be taken in a shorter time.

Classification of aerial missions can be performed using different types of sensor data such as kinematic data, ESM (Electronic Support Measures) data and RCS (Radar Cross Section) signature data. An ESM sensor detects emissions from radar sensors and communication systems carried by the targets. RCS signatures indicate the shape of the targets. The signatures are obtained from analysing the intensity of reflected radar signals. Many targets have unique RCS signatures.

T.D. Nielsen and N.L. Zhang (Eds.): ECSQARU 2003, LNAI 2711, pp. 125–136, 2003.

Classification models based on ESM or RCS data consist of sensor measurements of specific aircraft and their sensors. On the other hand, military aircraft are interested in hiding the identity. Therefore there are numerous of methods for misleading an opponent. Since new variants of equipment and new methods for misleading are developed continuously the classification libraries need to be updated to meet the development. Kinematic data are somewhat more robust in this respect. However, misleading with kinematic data can be performed, for example, by flying a small military aircraft as in a transport mission or by emitting false targets.

This paper describes a model for automated classification of civil and military aerial missions. The purpose is not first of all to classify the aircraft itself, but its mission. Therefore, different missions could be performed by the same type of aircraft. The missions analysed are transport, private flying, reconnaissance, protection from intruders in the national airspace as well as on the ground or the sea. The missions imply different motion patterns in the airspace described by kinematic data such as flight altitude, speed and direction. The motion patterns are reflected in first-order discrete Hidden Markov Models (HMMs), where each mission is represented by a specific HMM.

A first-order discrete HMM is a stochastic model used for time series analysis. The system is observed through observation symbols. Meanwhile the system passes through a random walk between states, which can not be observed. In the case of aerial-mission classification the observation symbols reflect the aircraft behavior via kinematic data. The states are related to different elements of the missions, characterised by different motion patterns.

The theory of HMM was presented in the 1960s and has, since then, been used for analysing various types of system to recognise certain patterns. Such systems include for example speech [15], word [10] and gesture recognition [9].

HMMs have also been used for image analysis. In [12] target classification using images from a SAR (Synthetic Aperture Radar) is discussed.

In [4] the application of HMM to the recognition problem of military columns is discussed. The purpose is to recognise ground troop organisations using different types of data such as human observations and radar sensors data.

Different statistical methods have been investigated for the problem of aircraft classification. For example, in [3] HMMs are used to represent ESM data in the form of multiaspect electromagnetic scattering data. In [6] discrete Markov models are used to represent different sensor observables such as ESM data, IFF (Identification, friend or foe) data and aircraft speed and trajectory profiles. In [1] the theory of evidence is used to handle different types of sensor data, ambiguities and uncertainties. In [16] Bayes rule is used to update the classification based on different sensor observables. The model distinguishes between different military aircraft and is based on flight envelopes and ESM data. In [7] an algorithm is developed that incorporates target classification into the target tracking process. The integration is accomplished using Bayesian network techniques. In doing so the process for associating new observations to existing tracks is improved.

2   Hidden Markov Models

In this section some of the basic equations are presented. For a more close description of the different steps towards the final equations, the reader is referred to [13].

A discrete HMM, λ, is described by a number of states N and a number of discrete observation symbols M. The individual states are denoted $S = \{S_1, S_2, ..., S_N\}$ and the individual discrete observation symbols are denoted $V = \{v_1, v_2, ..., v_M\}$. The model λ is also described by the following parameter set:

$$\lambda = (A, B, \pi) \tag{1}$$

$$A = \{a_{ij}\} = \{P[q_{t+1} = S_j | q_t = S_i]\} \tag{2}$$

$$B = \{b_j(k)\} = \{P[O_t = v_k | q_t = S_j]\} \tag{3}$$

$$\pi = \{\pi_i\} = \{P[q_1 = S_i]\} \tag{4}$$

where A represents the state transition probabilities, B represents the probability distributions of the discrete observation symbols and π represents the probability distribution of the states initially. Moreover, a_{ij} denotes the probability for the system to change from state i to state j and $b_j(k)$ denotes the probability distribution of the symbols for a certain state j. The current state is denoted q_t, the current observation is denoted O_t and $1 \leq i, j \leq N$, $1 \leq k \leq M$.

The parameters A, B and π can be estimated by HMM learning. In this work, HMM learning is performed using the Baum-Welch method [13].

Once λ is defined, it can be used to calculate the likelihood L of an observation sequence O, given a specific model λ, i.e.

$$L = P(O|\lambda) \tag{5}$$

where O consists of observations registered at T points of time, i.e. $O = (O_1 O_2 ... O_T)$. In a classification problem the purpose is to compare O to an HMM library and to find out what λ that gives the highest L value.

To calculate L the forward algorithm is introduced as follows:

$$\alpha_t(i) = P(O_1 O_2 ... O_t, q_t = S_i | \lambda) \ . \tag{6}$$

The forward algorithm describes the probability of observing the partial observation sequence $O_1 O_2 ... O_t$ in state S_i at time t, given the model λ.

For the first observation O_1, α is calculated as follows:

$$\alpha_1(i) = \pi_i b_i(O_1) \ . \tag{7}$$

For the following observations, α is calculated according to:

$$\alpha_{t+1}(j) = \left[\sum_{i=1}^{N} \alpha_t(i) a_{ij} \right] b_j(O_{t+1}) \tag{8}$$

where $1 \le t \le T - 1$. The equation illustrates how S_j can be reached at time $t + 1$ from the N possible states at time t. The calculation is performed for all states j at time t. The calculation is then iterated for $t = 1, 2, ..., T - 1$. The final result is given by the sum of the terminal forward variables $\alpha_T(i)$, i.e.

$$P(O|\lambda) = \sum_{i=1}^{N} \alpha_T(i) . \tag{9}$$

During the calculation procedure there are several multiplications with probabilities well below 1.0, leading to a final result which is close to 0. Problems arise when the result is less than the smallest number that the computer can represent. In [13] the problem is solved by introducing the scaling factor c_t:

$$c_t = \frac{1}{\left(\sum_{i=1}^{N} \alpha_t(i) \right)} . \tag{10}$$

The final equation, useful for this kind of problem, becomes

$$\log[P(O|\lambda)] = - \sum_{t=1}^{T} \log c_t . \tag{11}$$

The procedure for the introduction of the scaling and for coming to Eq. 11 can be studied in [13].

3   Application on Aerial Missions

In [2], [8] and [11] some characteristics of aerial missions can be studied. The characteristics that were assumed useful for classification are presented below.

Aircraft performing transport missions fly mainly in straight lines. They follow so-called standard flight paths. The turns are wide compared to small military aircraft. The cruising speed for bigger passenger aircraft ranges from 500 to 950 km/h. The cruising level for long distance flights is around 10 km.

The private aircraft fly mainly at low altitude and with low speed. They have probably a greater inclination to deviate from a straight line than the transport aircraft have. Smaller private aircraft have a maximum speed of 200 to 300 km/h and fly at an altitude of a few hundred meters up to 3 to 5 km at the most.

Aircraft performing reconnaissance missions fly either at very low or very high altitudes. Which altitude that is used depends on type of reconnaissance mission. At high altitude a large area will be surveyed. At low altitude a detailed part of the area will be surveyed. The aircraft fly mainly in straight lines and with low or high speed.

Small military aircraft have a maximum speed well above 950 km/h. They perform missions directed towards different military targets such as targets in the air (air target mission), on the ground or the sea (ground/sea target missions). There are different ways in performing the missions, depending on the type of target as well as weather and geographical conditions. However, the missions are characterised by a fast course of events, high speed, sharp turns and rapid ascents. One major difference between the air target mission and the ground/sea target missions is that the ground/sea target missions are performed at very low altitude.

For military as well as non-military missions sharp turns may also be observed close to airports indicating landing and take-off processes.

3.1   Multiple Target Tracking Model

When using kinematic data for classification a first step is to process sensor data in a Multiple Target Tracking (MTT) model. The MTT model transforms the sensor data into target tracks. Once tracks are formed quantities such as target altitude, velocity and direction can be computed.

The quality of the classification results is dependent not only on the HMMs but also on the MTT model. If the target can not be tracked good enough the classification results will be poor and unreliable.

To this stage this classification model has been investigated outside the MTT model, using Matlab. However, the next step is to fully integrate it with the MTT model. Input data to the classification model from the MTT model will be a vector containing target speed in x, y and z directions, flight altitude and information on straight line or sharp turn. Output data from the classification model back to the MTT model will be a vector containing the likelihood distribution of the five possible aerial missions. The MTT model is also provided with a presentation part that will include the classification results for presentation to the operator.

The MTT model that will serve the classification model with kinematic data is described in [14]. Some of its basic functions will be described below. For a more close description on the different methods associated with target tracking se also [5]. The target tracking in based on Kalman filtering, where sensor and environment are modelled statistically. The sensor is represented by a measurement equation and the movement of the target is represented by a state equation. For each target there is an estimated state vector and an estimated covariance matrix. The estimated state vector consists of information on target position, speed and acceleration calculated from radar data. The covariance matrix is used to describe the uncertainty of the state vector estimation. The purpose of the Kalman filter is to minimise the mean squared error of model and measurement data.

Data association is an important but complicated procedure in a multi-target environment. Data association deals with the problem of pairing the observations with the existing tracks maintained by the MTT model. The method used is the GNN method (Global Nearest Neighbour). The observation that is closest to the predicted position of the track (according to the Kalman filter) is connected to the track. In the GNN method, each observation is only connected to one track. Observations that are not connected to any tracks can be seen as possible new targets for which new tracks are to be constructed.

The ability of the MTT model to track maneuvering targets is of vital importance for what motion patterns that can be described by the classification model. The method Interacting Multiple Models (IMM) is used to represent maneuverability. The IMM consist of different potential motion models, that are combined according to a Markov model for transitions between the motion models. In the MTT model the IMM consist of two motion models. One of them describes a motion in a straight line (or almost a straight line). The other describes a sharp turn. Consequently, the classification model is in the representation of motion patterns restricted to a straight line and a sharp turn.

An observation in the classification model consists of a combination of speed, altitude and direction. The output data from the MTT model must therefore be translated into observation sequences suitable for the classification model. This is, among other things, discussed in the following section.

3.2   The Choice of HMM Model and Model Parameters

The HMM library in the classification model consists of λ_{tr} (transport), λ_{pr} (private flying), λ_{re} (reconnaissance), λ_{tar1} (air target), and λ_{tar2} (ground/sea target).

A flight is here seen as consisting of two states $(N = 2)$. Each state consists of a specific collection of straight lines and sharp turns at different speeds and altitudes. The states should not be mixed up with the two motion models in the IMM. The motion models reflect only the direction and say nothing about speed and altitude.

State S_1 represents flying the aircraft in predominantly straight lines and with very few sharp turns. It is more frequently observed at the higher altitude intervals. This is of course the dominating state in the transport or reconnaissance missions but it also appears, for example, before and after a military attack. State S_1 can be said to reflect regular motion patterns. State S_2 represents flying the aircraft more frequently in sharp turns but also periodically in straight lines. It is typical during the attack and includes sharp turns, rapid ascents at high speed. The behaviour can also be observed for military as well as non-military aircraft close to airports indicating landing and take-off processes, at somewhat lower speed. This behaviour is probably more frequent at the lower altitudes. In contrast to S_1, S_2 can be said to reflect irregular motion patterns.

The discrete symbol v_k is a combination of speed, altitude and direction according to Table 1. For this application $M = 10$, i.e. $V = \{v_1, v_2, ..., v_{10}\}$. In the table h represents altitude intervals, vel represents speed intervals and m represents directions. The altitude is divided into three intervals to distinguish between low and high flying aircraft. The interval h_1 ranges from 0 to 0.7 km, h_2 ranges from 0.7 to 15 km and h_3 starts from 15 km and with no specific end specified.

The speed intervals are used to distinguish between military aircraft with high speed performance from other aircraft. The interval vel_1 ranges from 0 to 950 km/h and vel_2 starts from 950 km/h and with no specific end specified.

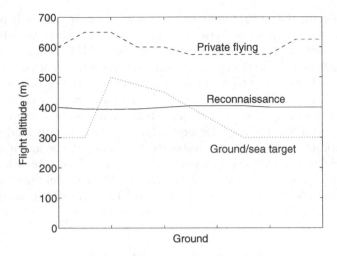

Fig. 1. Characteristic motion patterns in two dimensions for the private aircraft, reconnaissance and ground/sea target missions

Aircraft that fly at very high altitude have no division in speed intervals. The speed at very high altitude is denoted vel_3.

Finally m_1 and m_2 are associated with the motion models in the IMM. The direction m_1 represents a straight line (or almost a straight line) and m_2 represents a sharp turn.

For example, v_1 implies an aircraft flying in a straight line, at an altitude somewhere between 0 and 0.7 km and with a speed somewhere between 0 and 950 km/h.

Since we do not have real measurement data from different missions, the HMM learning is based on artificial data that have been created using information from [2], [8] and [11]. The learning process needs initial values for a_{ij}, $b_j(k)$ and π_i. Initial values for a_{ij} and π_i were created using uniform distributions. Initial values for $b_j(k)$ were estimated using a priori information about the missions, as described above.

Totally around 100 artificial observations per mission were used as input data to the HMM learning. The greater part of the training data are selected to reflect specific characteristics of each mission. However, those parts of the missions that represent more normal motion patterns are also represented. Figure 1 illustrates some characteristic motion patterns in two dimensions for the private flying, reconnaissance and ground/sea target missions. Table 2 presents $b_1(k)$ and $b_2(k)$ obtained from HMM learning.

Table 3 presents a_{ij} obtained from HMM learning. For example, the probability for an aircraft performing a transport mission to continue to fly in regular motion patterns is 0.72. The probability for changing to irregular motion patterns is 0.28.

Table 1. Definition of the discrete symbols V

Observation / V	v_1	v_2	v_3	v_4	v_5	v_6	v_7	v_8	v_9	v_{10}
$h_1 = (0, 0.7)$ km	X	X							X	X
$h_2 = (0.7, 15)$ km			X	X			X	X		
$h_3 = (15, -)$ km					X	X				
$vel_1 = (0, 950)$ km/h	X	X	X	X						
$vel_2 = (950, -)$ km/h							X	X	X	X
$vel_3 = (0, -)$ km/h					X	X				
$m_7 = $ straight line	X		X		X		X		X	
$m_8 = $ sharp turn		X		X		X		X		X

Table 2. Observation probabilities obtained from HMM learning

$(b_j(k))_n$ / k	1	2	3	4	5	6	7	8	9	10
$(b_1(k))_{tr}$	0.01	0.04	0.72	0.02	0.03	0.03	0.03	0.04	0.03	0.04
$(b_2(k))_{tr}$	0.11	0.07	0.32	0.09	0.07	0.07	0.07	0.07	0.07	0.06
$(b_1(k))_{pr}$	0.47	0.15	0.05	0.05	0.05	0.05	0.05	0.05	0.05	0.05
$(b_2(k))_{pr}$	0.16	0.46	0.05	0.05	0.05	0.05	0.05	0.05	0.05	0.05
$(b_1(k))_{re}$	0.37	0.03	0.04	0.04	0.34	0.03	0.04	0.04	0.04	0.04
$(b_2(k))_{re}$	0.21	0.08	0.07	0.07	0.24	0.08	0.07	0.06	0.06	0.06
$(b_1(k))_{tar1}$	0.07	0.07	0.16	0.13	0.07	0.07	0.14	0.14	0.07	0.07
$(b_2(k))_{tar1}$	0.07	0.07	0.16	0.13	0.07	0.07	0.14	0.14	0.07	0.07
$(b_1(k))_{tar2}$	0.22	0.11	0.06	0.06	0.06	0.06	0.06	0.06	0.22	0.11
$(b_2(k))_{tar2}$	0.11	0.23	0.05	0.05	0.05	0.05	0.05	0.06	0.11	0.22

Table 3. State transition probabilities obtained from HMM learning

A_n	a_{11}	a_{12}	a_{21}	a_{22}
A_{tr}	0.72	0.28	0.53	0.47
A_{pr}	0.53	0.47	0.48	0.52
A_{re}	0.62	0.38	0.50	0.50
A_{tar1}	0.50	0.50	0.50	0.50
A_{tar2}	0.45	0.55	0.55	0.45

The time aspect of the system is reflected by the A matrix. If the time period between observations is short, the probability for the system to change states will be small. On the other hand, if the time period is longer, the probability of changing states will be higher. In the MTT model the tracking information is updated once per second and consequently the classification information can also be updated once per second. It is however possible to vary the measurement time period in the MTT model. If that is utilised, it must be possible to change the values of A in order to correctly reflect possible changes of the states.

4   Some Reflections on the Classification Procedure

In the following classification example some reflections on the classification procedure will be discussed.

In this example the target tracking system is assumed to track an aircraft whose mission is to protect the national airspace from intruders (air target mission). To start with the target gives rise to the following observations recorded during 5 seconds: altitude 8 km, speed < 950 km/h and a straight line. These observations correspond to v_3 in Table 1. During the next 9 seconds the speed is increased so that it exceeds 950 km/h (v_7). The target then deviates from the straight line (v_8) and performs a sharp turn during 3 seconds. At the end of the observation period (3 seconds) it returns to the straight line (v_7). The motion pattern is illustrated by Eqs. 12 - 15.

$$O_a = O_1\ O_2\ O_3\ O_4\ O_5 \Rightarrow (v_3\ v_3\ v_3\ v_3\ v_3) \tag{12}$$

$$O_b = O_6\ O_7\ O_8\ O_9\ O_{10} \Rightarrow (v_7\ v_7\ v_7\ v_7\ v_7) \tag{13}$$

$$O_c = O_{11}\ O_{12}\ O_{13}\ O_{14}\ O_{15} \Rightarrow (v_7\ v_7\ v_7\ v_7\ v_8) \tag{14}$$

$$O_d = O_{16}\ O_{17}\ O_{18}\ O_{19}\ O_{20} \Rightarrow (v_8\ v_8\ v_7\ v_7\ v_7)\ . \tag{15}$$

A new likelihood calculation is performed every fifth second according to Eqs. 16 - 19. This is to illustrate how the target unveils its characteristic features as time goes. The results are presented in Table 4.

$$O_{1st} = O_a \tag{16}$$

$$O_{2nd} = O_a + O_b \tag{17}$$

$$O_{3rd} = O_a + O_b + O_c \tag{18}$$

$$O_{4th} = O_a + O_b + O_c + O_d\ . \tag{19}$$

Table 4. Classification results for $O_{1st} - O_{4th}$

O	$\log[P(O|\lambda_{tr})]$	$\log[P(O|\lambda_{pr})]$	$\log[P(O|\lambda_{re})]$	$\log[P(O|\lambda_{tar1})]$	$\log[P(O|\lambda_{tar2})]$
O_{1st}	-4.8	-15.2	-15.7	-9.2	-14.5
O_{2nd}	-18.6	-30.4	-31.3	-19.0	-28.9
O_{3rd}	-32.4	-45.7	-46.9	-28.7	-43.4
O_{4th}	-46.3	-60.9	-62.6	-38.4	-57.8

After the first short sequence O_{1st}, the model suggests that the target performs a transport mission, since $\log[P(O_{1st}|\lambda_{tr})]$ has the highest value. If the number of observations is increased to O_{2nd} the likelihood for a transport mission is reduced. At this stage $\log[P(O_{2nd}|\lambda_{tr})] \approx \log[P(O_{2nd}|\lambda_{tar1})]$. When a sharp turn at high speed is observed (O_{3rd} and O_{4th}) the most likely mission is instead the air target mission.

Table 5. Classification results for O_{5th}

O	$\log[P(O|\lambda_{tr})]$	$\log[P(O|\lambda_{pr})]$	$\log[P(O|\lambda_{re})]$	$\log[P(O|\lambda_{tar1})]$	$\log[P(O|\lambda_{tar2})]$
O_{5th}	-47.7	-72.3	-78.3	-51.1	-76.2

Assume that the tracking of the target is continued and that the following is registered for 5 seconds: altitude 8 km, speed < 950 km/h and a straight line (v_3). The motion pattern according to O_e is added to the analysis and the likelihood of O_{5th} is calculated. The result is presented in Table 5.

$$O_e = O_{21}\, O_{22}\, O_{23}\, O_{24}\, O_{25} \Rightarrow (v_3\ v_3\ v_3\ v_3\ v_3) \tag{20}$$

$$O_{5th} = O_a + O_b + O_c + O_d + O_e\ . \tag{21}$$

As can be seen the classification model suggests again that the most likely mission is the transport mission.

According to this example there are important motion patterns that may be hidden if O includes too many observations. These motion patterns last for relatively short time periods and they represent, for example, the attacks in the air and ground/sea target missions. To be able to observe these specific motion patterns the likelihood calculations should be based on relatively few observations, perhaps < 5 observations at a time. The optimal length of O will presumably vary depending on the prevailing situation.

5   Discussion and Further Work

As mentioned earlier the classification model will be integrated into the MTT model. To run the classification model together with the MTT model will most certainly help in bringing suggestions for improvements of the classification model. For example, is the model too rough, should there be more states and observations to be able to classify the aerial missions in a satisfying way.

Another problem to deal with is the risks for misclassifications, i.e. to classify a non-military mission as a military mission and vice versa. At present the model consists of only five missions and their representations in the HMMs are probably not complete.

It should be investigated more closely the behaviour of the aircraft at different parts of the missions so that no important parts are omitted in the HMMs. This is also associated with the HMM learning and the problem of getting input data of good quality for the learning process. It is for example difficult to get real radar data on the different missions and especially the characteristic parts of each mission.

Since this type of classification is closely related to the target tracking process, problems associated with target tracking will also be associated with classification. Problems in target tracking appear, for example, in environments that include a large number of targets. In such environments it is difficult to associate the correct observations with the correct tracks. If the association is incorrectly performed, strange tracks will appear and misleading classification will be performed.

When classifying aerial missions there is, except for the information based on kinematic data, another kind of characteristic associated with the missions, namely the number of aircraft performing the same mission. For example, the air and ground/sea target missions are usually performed by a group of aircraft. The group performing the air target mission usually consists of a smaller number of aircraft compared to the group performing the ground/sea target missions. The transport and reconnaissance missions are usually performed by a single aircraft. By fusing the information about the number of aircraft with the information given from the HMMs based on kinematic data, the classification of aerial missions could be improved further.

Acknowledgement. The author would like to thank people from the project group at the Division of Command and Control Systems as well as the conference reviewers for valuable comments and viewpoints on the work and this paper.

References

1. Appriou, A.: Multisensor Data Fusion in Situation Assessment Processes. European Conf. on Symbolic and Qualitative Approaches to Reasoning with Uncertainty (ECSQARU), Germany, 9–12 June (1997)
2. Aircraft (In Swedish). ISBN 91-973255-8-9, Gummessons, Falkoping, Sweden (1999)
3. Bharadwaj, P., Runkle, P., Carin, L., Berrie, J.A., Hughes, J.A.: Multiaspect Classification of Airborne Targets via Physics-Based HMMs and Matching Pursuits. IEEE Transactions on Aerospace and Electronic Systems, Vol. 37. No. 2. April (2001) 595–606
4. Bjornfot, J., Svensson, P.: Modeling the Column Recognition Problem in Tactical Information Fusion. Proc. 3rd Int. Conf. on Information Fusion, Paris, 10–13 July (2000) 24–30
5. Blackman, S., Popoli, R.: Design and Analysis of Modern Tracking Systems. ISBN 1-58053-006-0, Artech House, Norwood, MA (1999)
6. Caromicoli, A., Kurien, T.: Multitarget Identification in Airborne Surveillance. SPIE, Aerospace Pattern Recognition, Vol. 1098 (1989) 161–176
7. Chang, K-C., Fung, R.: Target Identification with Bayesian Networks in a Multiple Hypothesis Tracking System. Optical Engineering, Vol. 36. No. 3. March (1997) 684–691
8. Chant, C., Taylor, M.J.H. (ed): The Worlds Greatest Aircraft: Specialized Aircraft. ISBN: 1 84013 467 4, Grange Books, Kent, UK (2002)
9. Choi, H.-I., Rhee, P.-K.: Head Gesture Recognition using HMMs. Expert Systems with Application, Vol 17 (1999) 213–221
10. Cho, W., Lee, S.-W., Kim, J.H.: Modeling and Recognition of Cursive Words with Hidden Markov Models. Pattern Recognition, Vol. 28. No. 12 (1995) 1941–1953
11. Liander, P.: Flying Defenders – Swedish Fighters of Today (In Swedish). ISBN 91-85496-59-6, Gummessons, Falkoping, Sweden (1993)

12. Nilubol, C., Mersereau, R.M., Smith, M.J.T.: A SAR Target Classifier Using Radon Transforms and Hidden Markov Models. Digital Signal Processing, Vol. 12 (2002) 274–283
13. Rabiner, L.R.: A Tutorial on Hidden Markov Models and Selected Applications in Speech Recognition. Proc. of the IEEE, Vol. 77. No. 2. February (1989) 257–286
14. Stromberg, D., Andersson, M., Lantz, F.: On Platform-Based Sensor Management. Proc. of the 5th Int. Conf. on Information Fusion, Vol. Annapolis, USA, July (2002) 600–607
15. de la Torre, A., Peinado, A.M., Rubio, A.J.: Discriminative Feature Weighting for HMM-Based Continuous Speech Recognizers. Speech Communications, Vol. 38 (2002) 267–286
16. Wigren, T.: Noncooperative Target Type Identification in Multi-sensor Tracking. Proc. of the IRCTR Colloquium on Surveillance Sensor Tracking, Delft, 26 June (1997) 1–12

Dynamic Importance Sampling Computation in Bayesian Networks*

Serafín Moral[1] and Antonio Salmerón[2]

[1] Dpt. Computer Science and Artificial Intelligence
University of Granada
Avda. Andalucía 38
18071 Granada, Spain
smc@decsai.ugr.es

[2] Dpt. Statistics and Applied Mathematics
University of Almería
La Cañada de San Urbano s/n
04120 Almería, Spain
Antonio.Salmeron@ual.es

Abstract. This paper proposes a new version of importance sampling propagation algorithms: dynamic importance sampling. Importance sampling is based on using an auxiliary sampling distribution. The performance of the algorithm depends on the variance of the weights associated with the simulated configurations. The basic idea of dynamic importance sampling is to use the simulation of a configuration to modify the sampling distribution in order to improve its quality and so reducing the variance of the future weights. The paper shows that this can be done with little computational effort. The experiments carried out show that the final results can be very good even in the case that the initial sampling distribution is far away from the optimum.

Keywords: Bayesian networks, probability propagation, approximate algorithms, importance sampling

1   Introduction

This paper proposes a new propagation algorithm for computing marginal conditional probabilities in Bayesian networks. It is well known that this is an NP-hard problem even if we only require approximate values [7]. So, we can always find examples in which polynomial approximate algorithms provide poor results, mainly if we have extreme probabilities: There is a polynomial approximate algorithm if all the probabilities are strictly greater than zero [8].

There are deterministic approximate algorithms [1,2,3,4,5,13,16,20,21] and algorithms based on Monte Carlo simulation with two main approaches: Gibbs sampling [12,15] and importance sampling [8,10,11,18,19,22].

* This work has been supported by the Spanish Ministry of Science and Technology, project Elvira II (TIC2001-2973-C05-01 and 02)

T.D. Nielsen and N.L. Zhang (Eds.): ECSQARU 2003, LNAI 2711, pp. 137–148, 2003.

A class of these heuristic procedures is composed by the importance sampling algorithms based on approximate pre-computation [11,18,19]. These methods perform first a fast but non exact propagation, following a node removal process [23]. In this way, an approximate 'a posteriori' distribution is obtained. In a second stage a sample is drawn using the approximate distribution and the probabilities are estimated according to the importance sampling methodology.

In this paper we start off with the algorithm based on approximate pre-computation developed in [18]. One of the particularities of that algorithm is the use of *probability trees* to represent and approximate probabilistic potentials. Probability trees have the possibility of approximating in an asymmetrical way, concentrating more resources (more branching) where they are more necessary: higher values with more variability (see [18] for a deeper discussion on these issues). However, as pointed out in [5], one of the problems of the approximate algorithms in Bayesian networks is that sometimes the final quality of an approximate potential will depend on all the potentials, including those which are not necessary to remove a variable. Imagine that we find that after deleting variable Z, the result is a potential that depends on variable X, and we find that this dependence is meaningful (i.e. the values of the potential are high and different for the different cases of X). If there is another potential not considered at this stage, in which all the cases of X except one have assigned a probability equal to zero, then the discrimination on X we have done when deleting Z is completely useless: finally only one value of X will be possible. This is an extreme situation, but illustrates that even if the approximation is carried out in a local way, the quality of the final result will depend on the global factors. There are algorithms that take into account this fact, as Markov Chain Monte Carlo, the Penniless propagation method presented in [5], and the Adaptive Importance Sampling (AIS-BN) given in [6].

In this work, we improve the algorithm proposed in [18] allowing to modify the approximate potentials (the sampling distribution) taking as basis the samples we are obtaining during the simulation. If samples with very small weights are drawn, the algorithm detects the part of the sampling distribution (which is represented as an approximate probability tree) which is responsible of this fact, and it is updated in such a way that the same problem will not appear in the next simulations. Actually, this is a way of using the samples to obtain the necessary information to improve the quality of the approximations taking into account other potentials in the problem. Trees are very appropriate for this as they allow to concentrate more efforts in the most necessary parts: the configurations that were more frequently obtained in past simulations and for which the approximation was not good.

The paper is organised as follows: in Sect. 2 it is described how probability propagation can be carried out using the importance sampling technique. The new algorithm called *dynamic importance sampling* is described in Sect. 3. In Sect. 4 the performance of the new algorithm is evaluated according to the results of some experiments carried out in large networks with very poor initial approximations. The paper ends with conclusions in Sect. 5.

2 Importance Sampling in Bayesian Networks

Throughout this paper, we will consider a Bayesian network in which $\mathbf{X} = \{X_1, \dots, X_n\}$ is the set of variables and each variable X_i takes values on a finite set Ω_i. If I is a set of indices, we will write $\mathbf{X}_I$ for the set $\{X_i | i \in I\}$, and Ω_I will denote the Cartesian product $\times_{i \in I} \Omega_i$. Given $\mathbf{x} \in \Omega_I$ and $J \subseteq I$, $\mathbf{x}_J$ is the element of Ω_J obtained from $\mathbf{x}$ by dropping the coordinates not in J.

A potential f defined on Ω_I is a mapping $f : \Omega_I \to \mathbb{R}_0^+$, where $\mathbb{R}_0^+$ is the set of non-negative real numbers. Probabilistic information will always be represented by means of potentials, as in [14]. The set of indices of the variables on which a potential f is defined will be denoted as $\mathrm{dom}(f)$.

The conditional distribution of each variable X_i, $i = 1, \dots, n$, given its parents in the network, $\mathbf{X}_{pa(i)}$, is denoted by a potential $p_i(x_i | \mathbf{x}_{pa(i)})$ where p_i is defined over $\Omega_{\{i\} \cup pa(i)}$. If $N = \{1, \dots, n\}$, the joint probability distribution for the n-dimensional random variable $\mathbf{X}$ can be expressed as

$$p(\mathbf{x}) = \prod_{i \in N} p_i(x_i | \mathbf{x}_{pa(i)}) \quad \forall \mathbf{x} \in \Omega_N . \tag{1}$$

An *observation* is the knowledge about the exact value $X_i = e_i$ of a variable. The set of observations will be denoted by $\mathbf{e}$, and called the *evidence set*. E will be the set of indices of the variables observed.

The goal of probability propagation is to calculate the 'a posteriori' probability function $p(x_k' | \mathbf{e})$, $x_k' \in \Omega_k$, for every non-observed variable X_k, $k \in N \setminus E$. Notice that $p(x_k' | \mathbf{e})$ is equal to $p(x_k', \mathbf{e}) / p(\mathbf{e})$, and, since $p(\mathbf{e}) = \sum_{x_k' \in \Omega_k} p(x_k', \mathbf{e})$, we can calculate the *posterior* probability if we compute the value $p(x_k', \mathbf{e})$ for every $x_k' \in \Omega_k$ and normalise afterwards.

Let $H = \{p_i(x_i | \mathbf{x}_{pa(i)}) | i = 1, \dots, n\}$ be the set of conditional potentials. Then, $p(x_k', \mathbf{e})$ can be expressed as

$$p(x_k', \mathbf{e}) = \sum_{\substack{\mathbf{x} \in \Omega_N \\ \mathbf{x}_E = \mathbf{e} \\ \mathbf{x}_k = x_k'}} \prod_{i \in N} p_i(x_i | \mathbf{x}_{pa(i)}) = \sum_{\substack{\mathbf{x} \in \Omega_N \\ \mathbf{x}_E = \mathbf{e} \\ \mathbf{x}_k = x_k'}} \prod_{f \in H} f(\mathbf{x}_{\mathrm{dom}(f)}) \tag{2}$$

If the observations are incorporated by restricting potentials in H to the observed values, i.e. by transforming each potential $f \in H$ into a potential $f_\mathbf{e}$ defined on $\mathrm{dom}(f) \setminus E$ as $f_\mathbf{e}(\mathbf{x}) = f(\mathbf{y})$, where $y_{\mathrm{dom}(f) \setminus E} = \mathbf{x}$, and $y_i = e_i$, for all $i \in E$, then we have,

$$p(x_k', \mathbf{e}) = \sum_{\substack{\mathbf{x} \in \Omega_N \\ \mathbf{x}_k = x_k'}} \prod_{f_e \in H} f_e(\mathbf{x}_{\mathrm{dom}(f_e)}) = \sum_{\mathbf{x} \in \Omega_N} g(\mathbf{x}), \tag{3}$$

where $g(\mathbf{x}) = \prod_{f_e \in H} f_e(\mathbf{x}_{\mathrm{dom}(f_e)})$.

Thus, probability propagation consists of estimating the value of the sum in (3), and here is where the *importance sampling* technique is used. Importance sampling is well known as a variance reduction technique for estimating integrals by means of Monte Carlo methods (see, for instance, [17]), consisting of transforming the sum in (3) into an expected value that can be estimated as a sample mean. To achieve this, consider a probability function $p^* : \Omega_N \to [0,1]$, verifying that $p^*(\mathbf{x}) > 0$ for every point $\mathbf{x} \in \Omega_N$ such that $g(\mathbf{x}) > 0$. Then formula (3) can be written as

$$p(x_k', \mathbf{e}) = \sum_{\substack{\mathbf{x} \in \Omega_N, \\ g(\mathbf{x}) > 0}} \frac{g(\mathbf{x})}{p^*(\mathbf{x})} p^*(\mathbf{x}) = \mathrm{E}\left[\frac{g(\mathbf{X}^*)}{p^*(\mathbf{X}^*)}\right] ,$$

where $\mathbf{X}^*$ is a random variable with distribution p^* (from now on, p^* will be called the *sampling distribution*). Then, if $\{\mathbf{x}^{(j)}\}_{j=1}^m$ is a sample of size m taken from p^*,

$$\hat{p}(x_k', \mathbf{e}) = \frac{1}{m} \sum_{j=1}^m \frac{g(\mathbf{x}^{(j)})}{p^*(\mathbf{x}^{(j)})} \tag{4}$$

is an unbiased estimator of $p(x_k', \mathbf{e})$ with variance

$$\mathrm{Var}(\hat{p}(x_k', \mathbf{e})) = \frac{1}{m}\left(\left(\sum_{\mathbf{x} \in \Omega_N} \frac{g^2(\mathbf{x})}{p^*(\mathbf{x})}\right) - p^2(x_k', \mathbf{e})\right) .$$

The value $w_j = g(\mathbf{x}^{(j)})/p^*(\mathbf{x}^{(j)})$ is called the weight of configuration $\mathbf{x}^{(j)}$.

Minimising the error in unbiased estimation is equivalent to minimising the variance. As formulated above, importance sampling requires a different sample to estimate each one of the values x_k' of X_k. However, in [18] it was shown that it is possible to use a unique sample to estimate all the values x_k'. In such case, the minimum variance is reached when the sampling distribution $p^*(\mathbf{x})$ is proportional to $g(\mathbf{x})$, and is equal to:

$$\mathrm{Var}(\hat{p}(x_k'|\mathbf{e})) = \frac{1}{m}(p(x_k'|\mathbf{e})(1 - p(x_k'|\mathbf{e})) .$$

This provides very good estimations depending on the value of m (analogously to the estimation of binomial probabilities from a sample), but it has the difficulty that it is necessary to handle $p(x|\mathbf{e})$, the distribution for which we want to compute the marginals. Thus, in practical situations the best we can do is to obtain a sampling distribution as close as possible to the optimal one.

Once p^* is selected, $p(x_k', \mathbf{e})$ for each value x_k' of each variable X_k, $k \in N \setminus E$ can be estimated with the following algorithm:

Importance Sampling

1. For $j := 1$ to m (sample size)
   a) Generate a configuration $\mathbf{x}^{(j)} \in \Omega_N$ using p^*.
   b) Calculate the weight:

$$w_j := \frac{\prod_{f \in H} f_e(\mathbf{x}_{dom(f_e)}^{(j)})}{p^*(\mathbf{x}^{(j)})} . \tag{5}$$

2. For each $x'_k \in \Omega_k$, $k \in N \setminus E$, estimate $p(x'_k, \mathbf{e})$ as the average of the weights in formula (5) corresponding to configurations containing x'_k.
3. Normalise the values $p(x'_k, \mathbf{e})$ in order to obtain $p(x'_k | \mathbf{e})$.

The sampling distribution for each variable can be obtained through a process of eliminating variables in the set of potentials H. An elimination order σ is considered and variables are deleted according to such order: $X_{\sigma(1)}, \ldots, X_{\sigma(n)}$.

The deletion of a variable $X_{\sigma(i)}$ consists of marginalising it out from the combination of all the functions in H which are defined for that variable. More precisely, the steps are as follows:

- Let $H_{\sigma(i)} = \{f \in H | \sigma(i) \in \mathrm{dom}(f)\}$.
- Calculate $f_{\sigma(i)} = \prod_{f \in H_{\sigma(i)}} f$ and $f'_{\sigma(i)}$ defined on $\mathrm{dom}(f_{\sigma(i)}) \setminus \{\sigma(i)\}$, by $f'_{\sigma(i)}(\mathbf{x}) = \sum_{x_{\sigma(i)}} f_{\sigma(i)}(\mathbf{x}, x_{\sigma(i)})$.
- Transform H into $H \setminus H_{\sigma(i)} \cup \{f'_{\sigma(i)}\}$.

Simulation is carried out in order contrary to the order in which variables are deleted. To obtain a value for $X_{\sigma(i)}$, we will use the function $f_{\sigma(i)}$ obtained in the deletion of this variable. This potential is defined for the values of variable $X_{\sigma(i)}$ and other variables already sampled. Potential $f_{\sigma(i)}$ is restricted to the already obtained values of variables in $\mathrm{dom}(f_{\sigma(i)}) \setminus \{\sigma(i)\}$ giving rise to a function which depends only on $X_{\sigma(i)}$. Finally, a value for this variable is obtained with probability proportional to the values of this potential. If all the computations are exact, it was proved in [11] that we are really sampling with the optimal probability $p^*(\mathbf{x}) = p(\mathbf{x} | \mathbf{e})$. But the result of the combinations in the process of obtaining the sampling distributions may require a large amount of space to be stored, and therefore approximations are usually employed, either using probability tables [11] or probability trees [18] to represent the distributions. Instead of computing the exact potentials we calculate approximate ones but with much fewer values. Then the deletion algorithm is faster and the potentials need less space. But sampling distribution is not the optimal one and the quality of estimations will depend on the quality of approximations.

In [11] an alternative procedure to compute the sampling distribution was used. Instead of restricting $f_{\sigma(i)}$ to the values of the variables already sampled, all the functions in $H_{\sigma(i)}$ are restricted, resulting in a set of functions depending only on $X_{\sigma(i)}$. The sampling distribution is then computed by multiplying all these vectors. If computations are exact, then both distributions are the same, as restriction and combination commute. When the combinations are not exact, generally the option of restricting $f_{\sigma(i)}$ is faster and the restriction of functions in $H_{\sigma(i)}$ is more accurate, as there is no need to approximate in the combination of functions depending only on one variable $X_{\sigma(i)}$.

3 Dynamic Importance Sampling

Dynamic importance sampling follows the same general structure as our previous importance sampling algorithms but with the difference that sampling distributions can change each time that a configuration $\mathbf{x}^{(j)}$ is simulated. The algorithm follows the option of restricting the functions in $H_{\sigma(i)}$ before combining the functions to obtain the distribution for $X_{\sigma(i)}$.

Assume that we have already simulated the values $c_i^j = (x_{\sigma(n)}^{(j)}, \ldots, x_{\sigma(i+1)}^{(j)})$ and that we are going to simulate a value $x_{\sigma(i)}^{(j)}$ for $X_{\sigma(i)}$. Let us denote by $f_{c_i^j}$ the result of restricting the potential f to the values of c_i^j, and let $f'_{\sigma(i)}$ be the function that was computed when removing variable $X_{\sigma(i)}$ in the elimination algorithm. Note that this function is contained in H. For the simulation of value $x_{\sigma(i)}^{(j)}$ we compute the following elements:

- $(H_{\sigma(i)})_{c_i^j} = \{f_{c_i^j} | f \in H_{\sigma(i)}\}$, the result of restricting all the functions in $H_{\sigma(i)}$ to the values already simulated.
- $q_{\sigma(i)}$, the result of the the combination of all the functions in $(H_{\sigma(i)})_{c_i^j}$. This is a vector depending only on variable $X_{\sigma(i)}$. A case for this variable is obtained by simulation with probability proportional to the values of this vector.
- $b_{\sigma(i)} = \sum_{x_{\sigma(i)}} q_{\sigma(i)}(x_{\sigma(i)})$ (the normalisation value of vector $q_{\sigma(i)}$).
- $a_{\sigma(i)}$, equal to the value of potential $f'_{\sigma(i)}$ when instantiated for the cases in vector c_i^j.

If all the computations are exact (i.e. the trees representing the potentials have not been pruned during the variable elimination phase), then $b_{\sigma(i)}$ must be equal to $a_{\sigma(i)}$. $b_{\sigma(i)}$ is obtained by restricting to $c_i^j = (x_{\sigma(n)}^{(j)}, \ldots, x_{\sigma(i+1)}^{(j)})$ the potentials in $H_{\sigma(i)}$, combining them, and summing out variable $X_{\sigma(i)}$; while $a_{\sigma(i)}$ is the result of combining potentials in $H_{\sigma(i)}$, summing out $X_{\sigma(i)}$ and restricting the result to c_i^j. This is clear if we notice that $f'_{\sigma(i)}$ is the result of combination of potentials in $H_{\sigma(i)}$ and then summing out $X_{\sigma(i)}$. In other words, we do the same operations but with the difference that restriction to configuration c_i^j is done at the beginning for $b_{\sigma(i)}$ and at the end for $a_{\sigma(i)}$. If the computation had been exact the results should be the same, but these operations do not commute if the potentials involved have been previously pruned. $b_{\sigma(i)}$ is the correct value and $a_{\sigma(i)}$ the value that can be found in potential $f'_{\sigma(i)}$. This potential is the one that has been used to compute the sampling probabilities of variables $(X_{\sigma(n)}^{(j)}, \ldots, X_{\sigma(i+1)}^{(j)})$. Therefore, if $b_{\sigma(i)}$ and $a_{\sigma(i)}$ are very different, it means that configuration c_i^j is being drawn with a probability of occurrence far away from its actual value. The worst case is when $a_{\sigma(i)}$ is much greater than $b_{\sigma(i)}$. For example, imagine in an extreme situation that $b_{\sigma(i)}$ is equal to zero and $a_{\sigma(i)}$ is a large value. Then we would be obtaining, with high probability, a configuration that should never be drawn (its real probability is zero)[1]. This is very bad, because the weights of all these configurations will be zero and will be completely useless. If instead of zero values the real probability had been very

---

[1] If we had stored in $f'_{\sigma(i)}$ the exact value (zero), then, as this value is used to simulate the values of $(X_{\sigma(n)}, \ldots, X_{\sigma(i+1)})$, the probability of this configuration should have been zero.

small, we would have a similar situation, but now the weights would be very small, and the real impact of these configurations in the final estimation would be very small as well. Summing up, we would be doing a lot of work with very little reward.

Dynamic importance sampling computes the minimum of the values $a_{\sigma(i)}/b_{\sigma(i)}$ and $b_{\sigma(i)}/a_{\sigma(i)}$, considering that this minimum is one if $a_{\sigma(i)} = 0$. If this value is less than a given threshold, then potential $f'_{\sigma(i)}$ is updated to the exact value $b_{\sigma(i)}$ for the given configuration $c_i^j = (x_{\sigma(n)}^{(j)}, \ldots, x_{\sigma(i+1)}^{(j)})$. This potential will be used in the next simulations, and thus c_i^j will be drawn with a more accurate probability in the future.

The updating of the potential is not simply to change the value $a_{\sigma(i)}$ by the new value $b_{\sigma(i)}$. The reason is that a single value on a tree affects to more than one configuration (if the branch corresponding to that configuration has been pruned) and then we may be changing the values of other configurations different to c_i^j. If $b_{\sigma(i)} = 0$, we could even introduce zeros where the real exact value is positive, thus violating the basic property of importance sampling which says that any possible configuration must have a chance to be drawn. In order to keep this property, we must branch the tree representing $f'_{\sigma(i)}$ in such a way that we do not change its value for configurations for which $b_{\sigma(i)}$ is not necessarily the actual value. Therefore, the basic problem is to determine a subset of variables $\{X_{\sigma(n)}, \ldots, X_{\sigma(i+1)}\}$, for which we have to branch the node of the tree associated to $f'_{\sigma(i)}$ so that only those leaves corresponding to the values of these variables in c_i^j are changed to the new value.

The first step is to consider the subset of active variables, $A_{\sigma(i)}$ associated with the potential $f'_{\sigma(i)}$. This set is computed during the variable elimination phase. Initially, $A_{\sigma(i)}$ is the union of all the domains of potentials in $H_{\sigma(i)}$ minus $X_{\sigma(i)}$. But if a variable, X_j, can be pruned without error from $f'_{\sigma(i)}$ (i.e. for every configuration of the other variables, $f'_{\sigma(i)}$ is constant on the values of $X_{\sigma(i)}$) and all the potentials in $H_{\sigma(i)}$ containing this variable have been calculated in an exact way (all the previous computations have only involved pruning without error) then X_j can be removed from $A_{\sigma(i)}$. Though this may seem at first glance a situation difficult to appear in real examples, it happens for all the variables for which there are not observed descendants [18]. All these variables can be deleted in an exact way by pruning the result to the constant tree with value 1.0 and this provides an important initial simplification.

Taking $A_{\sigma(i)}$ as basis, we consider the tree representing $f'_{\sigma(i)}$ and follow the path corresponding to configuration c_i^j (selecting for each variable in a node the child corresponding to the value in the configuration) until we reach for a leaf. Let $B_{\sigma(i)}$ be the set of all the variables in $A_{\sigma(i)}$ which are not in the branch of the tree leading to the leaf node, L, that we have reached. The updating is carried out according to the following recursive procedure:

Procedure Update $(L, a_{\sigma(i)}, b_{\sigma(i)}, B_{\sigma(i)})$
1. If $B_{\sigma(i)} = \emptyset$,
    2. Assign the value $b_{\sigma(i)}$ to leaf L

3. Else
    4. Select a variable $Y \in B_{\sigma(i)}$
    5. Remove Y from $B_{\sigma(i)}$
    6. Branch L by Y
    7. For each possible value y of Y
        8. If y is not the value of Y in c_i^j
           9. Make the child corresponding to y be a leaf with value $a_{\sigma(i)}$
        10. Else
           11. Let L_y the child corresponding to value y
           12. **Update(**$L_y, a_{\sigma(i)}, b_{\sigma(i)}, B_{\sigma(i)}$**)**

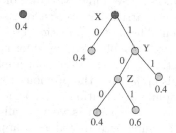

Fig. 1. Example of tree updating

In this algorithm, branching a node by a variable Y consists of transforming it into an interior node with a child for each one of the values of the variable. Imagine the case of Fig. 1. In which we have arrived to the leaf in the left with a value of $a_{\sigma(i)} = 0.4$ and that the variables in $B_{\sigma(i)}$ are X, Y and Z, each one of the them taking values in $\{0, 1\}$ and that the values of these variables in the current configuration are $1, 0$ and 1 respectively, and that we have to update the value of this configuration in the tree to the new value $b_{\sigma(i)} = 0.6$. The result is the tree in the right side of the figure.

Though, with this algorithm different configurations in the sample are dependent, as all the simulations are unbiased (we never introduce a zero value when the true probability is different from zero) and the expectation is always additive, we have that the resulting estimator $\hat{p}(x_k', \mathbf{e})$ is unbiased.

4   Experimental Evaluation of the New Algorithm

The performance of the new algorithm has been evaluated by means of several experiments carried out over two large real-world Bayesian networks. The two networks are called pedigree4 (441 variables) and munin2 (1003 variables). The networks have been borrowed from the Decision Support Systems group at Aalborg University (Denmark) (www.cs.auc.dk/research/DSS/misc.html).

The dynamic importance sampling algorithm, denoted by (dynamic is) has been compared with importance sampling without this feature (is), using the same implementation as in [18]. The new algorithm has been implemented in Java, and included in the Elvira shell (leo.ugr.es/~elvira) [9].

Our purpose is to show that dynamic is can have a good performance even in the case that initial approximations are very poor. Thus, in the computation of the sampling distributions we have carried out a very rough approximation: In all of the experiments the maximum potential size has been set to 20 values, and the threshold for pruning the probability trees has been set to $\epsilon = 0.4$. This value of ϵ indicates that the numbers in a set of leaves of the tree whose difference (in terms of entropy) with respect to a uniform distribution is less than a 40% are replaced by their average (see [18]). This is a very poor approximation and implies that it is possible to obtain configurations with very low weights with high probability which will give rise a high variance of the estimator.

The experiments we have carried out consist of 20 consecutive applications of the dynamic is algorithm. The first application uses the approximate potentials computed when deleting variables. We consider a threshold to update the potentials of 0.95 (see Sect. 3). In each subsequent application of the algorithm we start with the potentials updated in the previous application. In this way, we expect to have better sampling distributions each time.

The sample size in each application is very small (50 configurations). We have chosen such a small sample size in order to appreciate the evolution of the accuracy of the sampling distributions in each of the 20 applications of the algorithm. The behaviour of the dynamic algorithm is so good that choosing a larger sample (for instance, with 2000 individuals) the difference among the 20 runs of the algorithm would not be significant, because in the first sample, the algorithm is able to find sampling distributions very close to the optimal.

The accuracy of the estimated probability values is measured as the mean squared error (denoted by MSE in Fig. 2). Due to the small sample size the variance of the errors is high and therefore we have repeated the series of applications a high number of times, computing the average of the errors in all of them to reduce the differences due to randomness.

The experiments have been carried out on a Pentium 4, 2.4 GHz computer, with 1.5 GB of RAM and operating system Suse Linux 8.1. The Java virtual machine used was Java 2 version 1.4.1. The results of the experiments are reported in Fig. 2 where the error (MSE) is represented as a function of the number of applications of the dynamic is algorithm (from 1 to 20). The horizontal line is the optimum error: the error that is obtained when the optimum sampling distribution is used (the variable elimination phase is carried out without approximations) and with the same parameters as dynamic is, i.e. sample size 50, maximum potential size 20.

The accuracy of the iis algorithm described in [18] is far away from the accuracy of dynamic is. With similar computing times, the MSE for is are 0.22 with the pedigree4 network and 0.14 with the munin2 network, whilst the worst errors reached by dynamic is are 0.045 and 0.034 respectively.

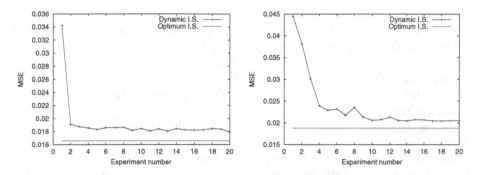

Fig. 2. Evolution of the error in networks munin2 network (left) and pedigree4 (right)

4.1   Results Discussion

The experiments show that even with a very bad initial sampling distribution, dynamic is updates the approximate potentials towards potentials with a performance close to the exact ones, just after simulating a few configurations. The updating is very fast at the beginning, but afterwards the improvement is very slow. This fact agrees with the results of experiments reported in [20], in which it is shown that in general the mass of probability is concentrated in some few configurations. When the sampling probability is updated for these configurations, then the performance is good. To achieve the accuracy of the exact distribution we need to update a lot of configurations with little mass of probability. This is a slow process. We have observed that initially the updating of a potential is very frequent, but after a few iterations, then updating of a potential seldom occurs. Another important fact is that updating is propagated: If we update a potential, this new potential will be the one that will appear associated with the variables that are deleted afterwards. Then, the new potential will be the one considered when the condition for updating is evaluated. This usually gives rise to new updates.

The updating of potentials does not convey an important increase in time. The dynamic algorithm is slower that is during the first iterations, but very quickly it becomes faster as the sampling distributions are more accurate and the updating procedure is rarely called. In fact, the only important additional step is the restriction of potentials in $H_{\sigma(i)}$ and the combination of them. The restriction of each one of the potentials has a complexity proportional to the number of variables in it. As the resulting potentials depend only on variable $X_{\sigma(i)}$, the complexity of combination is proportional to the number of cases of this variable.

5   Conclusions

We have introduced a modification over importance sampling algorithms for probabilistic propagation in Bayesian networks, consisting of the updating of the sampling distribution taking as basis the configurations we are obtaining during the simulation. This allows, with little additional time, to obtain good quality sampling distributions even if the initial ones are bad. Dynamic (or adaptive) sampling algorithms are not new within the context of Bayesian networks. Perhaps the most known case is AIS-BN [6]. However, the use of probability trees makes the convergence much faster (in experiments in [6] thousands of configurations are considered).

In the future, we plan to modify the dynamic is algorithm to carry out the updating in a first stage, changing to is afterwards. For this, we should determine a point in which updating no longer provides benefit because it occurs very rarely, for configurations of little probability which therefore will appear in very few occasions afterwards. But perhaps, the most important study will be to evaluate until which point it is worthy to make more effort in the initial approximation or it is better to make a very bad approximation at the beginning leaving to the updating phase the responsibility of computing better sampling distributions. The results of our experiments indicate that surely the second option will be better, but more extensive experiments comparing both options will be necessary to give a more founded answer.

Acknowledgements. We are very grateful to Finn V. Jensen, Kristian G. Olesen and Claus Skaaning, from the Decision Support Systems group at Aalborg University for providing us with the networks used in the experiments reported in this paper. We are also very grateful to the anonymous referees for their valuable comments and suggestions.

References

1. R.R. Bouckaert, E. Castillo, and J.M. Gutiérrez. A modified simulation scheme for inference in Bayesian networks. *Int. Jnl. of Approximate Reasoning*, 14:55–80, 1996.
2. A. Cano and S. Moral. Propagación exacta y aproximada con árboles de probabilidad. In *Actas de la VII Conferencia de la Asociación Española para la Inteligencia Artificial*, pages 635–644, 1997.
3. A. Cano, S. Moral, and A. Salmerón. Penniless propagation in join trees. *Int. Jnl. of Intelligent Systems*, 15:1027–1059, 2000.
4. A. Cano, S. Moral, and A. Salmerón. Lazy evaluation in penniless propagation over join trees. *Networks*, 39:175–185, 2002.
5. A. Cano, S. Moral, and A. Salmerón. Novel strategies to approximate probability trees in penniless propagation. *Int. Jnl. of Intelligent Systems*, 18:193–203, 2003.
6. J. Cheng, and M.J. Druzdzel. AIS-BN: An adaptive importance sampling algorithm for evidential reasoning in large Bayesian networks. *Jnl of Artificial Intelligence Research*, 13:155–188, 2000.
7. P. Dagum and M. Luby. Approximating probabilistic inference in Bayesian belief networks is NP-hard. *Artificial Intelligence*, 60:141–153, 1993.
8. P. Dagum and M. Luby. An optimal approximation algorithm for Bayesian inference. *Artificial Intelligence*, 93:1–27, 1997.

9. Elvira Consortium. Elvira: An environment for creating and using probabilistic graphical models. In J.A. Gámez and A. Salmerón, editors, *Proceedings of the First European Workshop on Probabilistic Graphical Models*, pages 222–230, 2002.
10. R. Fung and K.C. Chang. Weighting and integrating evidence for stochastic simulation in Bayesian networks. In M. Henrion, R.D. Shachter, L.N. Kanal, and J.F. Lemmer, editors, *Uncertainty in Artificial Intelligence*, volume 5, pages 209–220. North-Holland (Amsterdam), 1990.
11. L.D. Hernández, S. Moral, and A. Salmerón. A Monte Carlo algorithm for probabilistic propagation in belief networks based on importance sampling and stratified simulation techniques. *Int. Jnl. of Approximate Reasoning*, 18:53–91, 1998.
12. C.S. Jensen, A. Kong, and U. Kjærulff. Blocking Gibbs sampling in very large probabilistic expert systems. *Int. Jnl. of Human-Computer Studies*, 42:647–666, 1995.
13. U. Kjærulff. Reduction of computational complexity in Bayesian networks through removal of weak dependencies. In *Proc. of the 10th Conference on Uncertainty in Artificial Intelligence*, pages 374–382. Morgan Kaufmann, San Francisco, 1994.
14. S.L. Lauritzen and D.J. Spiegelhalter. Local computations with probabilities on graphical structures and their application to expert systems. *Jnl. of the Royal Statistical Society, Series B*, 50:157–224, 1988.
15. J. Pearl. Evidential reasoning using stochastic simulation of causal models. *Artificial Intelligence*, 32:247–257, 1987.
16. D. Poole. Probabilistic conflicts in a search algorithm for estimating posterior probabilities in bayesian networks. *Artificial Intelligence*, 88:69–100, 1996.
17. R.Y. Rubinstein. *Simulation and the Monte Carlo Method*. Wiley (New York), 1981.
18. A. Salmerón, A. Cano, and S. Moral. Importance sampling in Bayesian networks using probability trees. *Comput. Statistics and Data Analysis*, 34:387–413, 2000.
19. A. Salmerón and S. Moral. Importance sampling in Bayesian networks using antithetic variables. In S. Benferhat and P. Besnard, editors, *Symbolic and Quantitative Approaches to Reasoning with Uncertainty*, pages 168–179. Springer Verlag, 2001.
20. E. Santos and S.E. Shimony. Belief updating by enumerating high-probability independence-based assignments. In *Proceedings of the 10th Conference on Uncertainty in Artificial Intelligence*, pages 506–513, 1994.
21. E. Santos, S.E. Shimony, and E. Williams. Hybrid algorithms for approximate belief updating in Bayes nets. *Int. Jnl. of Approximate Reasoning*, 17:191–216, 1997.
22. R.D. Shachter and M.A. Peot. Simulation approaches to general probabilistic inference on belief networks. In M. Henrion, R.D. Shachter, L.N. Kanal, and J.F. Lemmer, editors, *Uncertainty in Artificial Intelligence*, volume 5, pages 221–231. North Holland (Amsterdam), 1990.
23. N.L. Zhang and D. Poole. Exploiting causal independence in Bayesian network inference. *Jnl. of Artificial Intelligence Research*, 5:301–328, 1996.

Morphing the Hugin and Shenoy–Shafer Architectures

James D. Park and Adnan Darwiche

UCLA, Los Angeles CA 90095, USA
{jd,darwiche}@cs.ucla.edu

Abstract. The Hugin and Shenoy–Shafer architectures are two variations on the jointree algorithm, which exhibit different tradeoffs with
respect to efficiency and query answering power. The Hugin architecture
is more time–efficient on arbitrary jointrees, avoiding some redundant
computations performed by the Shenoy–Shafer architecture. This efficiency, however, comes at the price of limiting the number of queries the
Hugin architecture is capable of answering. In this paper, we present a
simple algorithm which retains the efficiency of the Hugin architecture
and enjoys the query answering power of the Shenoy–Shafer architecture.

1   Introduction

There are a number of algorithms for answering queries with respect to Bayesian
networks. Among the most popular of these are the algorithms based on jointrees,
of which the Shenoy–Shafer [10] and Hugin [4,3] architectures represent two
prominent variations. While superficially similar, these architectures differ in
both efficiency and query answering power. Specifically, the Hugin architecture is
faster on arbitrary jointrees, but the Shenoy–Shafer architecture results in more
information and can answer more queries. This paper presents an architecture
that combines the best of both algorithms. In particular, we show that a simple
modification to the Hugin architecture which does not alter its time and space
efficiency, allows it to attain the same query answering power exhibited by the
Shenoy–Shafer.

This paper is structured as follows. Section 2 reviews the definition of jointrees, and details the Shenoy–Shafer and Hugin architectures. Section 3 introduces the main idea of the paper, and provides a corresponding algorithm which
can be thought of as either a more efficient Shenoy–Shafer architecture or a more
expressive Hugin architecture. It also details the semantics of messages and data
maintained by the new algorithm. Section 4 closes the paper with some concluding remarks. Proofs of all theorems are delegated to the appendix.

2   Jointree Algorithms

We review the basics of jointrees and jointree algorithms in this section. Let $\mathcal{B}$
be a belief network. A jointree for $\mathcal{B}$ is a pair $(\mathcal{T}, \mathbf{C})$, where $\mathcal{T}$ is a tree and $\mathbf{C}$ is a

T.D. Nielsen and N.L. Zhang (Eds.): ECSQARU 2003, LNAI 2711, pp. 149–160, 2003.

function that assigns a label C_i to each node i in tree $\mathcal{T}$. A jointree must satisfy three properties: (1) each label C_i is a set of variables in the belief network; (2) each network variable X and its parents U (a family) must appear together in some label C_i; (3) if a variable appears in the labels of nodes i and j in the jointree, it must also appear in the label of each node k on the path connecting them. The label of edge ij in tree $\mathcal{T}$ is defined as $S_{ij} = C_i \cap C_j$. The nodes of a jointree and their labels are called *clusters.* Moreover, the edges of a jointree and their labels are called *separators.* The *width* of a jointree is defined as the number of variables in its largest cluster minus 1.

Jointree algorithms start by constructing a jointree for a given belief network [10,4,3]. They associate *tables* (also called *potentials*) with clusters and separators.[1] The *conditional probability table* (CPT) of each variable X with parents U, denoted $\theta_{X|U}$, is assigned to a cluster that contains X and U. In addition, a table over each variable X, denoted λ_X and called an *evidence table,* is assigned to a cluster that contains X. Evidence e is entered into a jointree by initializing evidence tables as follows: we set $\lambda_X(x)$ to 1 if x is consistent with evidence e, and we set $\lambda_X(x)$ to 0 otherwise.

Given some evidence e, a jointree algorithm propagates messages between clusters. After passing two message per edge in the jointree, one can compute the marginals $\Pr(C, e)$ for every cluster C. There are two main methods for propagating messages in a jointree, known as the Shenoy–Shafer [10] and the Hugin [4] architectures, which we review next (see [5,6] for a thorough introduction to each architecture).

2.1 The Shenoy–Shafer Architecture

Shenoy–Shafer propagation proceeds as follows. First, evidence e is entered into the jointree through evidence indicators. A cluster is then selected as the root and message propagation proceeds in two phases, inward and outward. In the *inward phase,* messages are passed toward the root. In the *outward phase,* messages are passed away from the root. Cluster i sends a message to cluster j only when it has received messages from all its other neighbors k. A message from cluster i to cluster j is a table M_{ij} defined as follows:

$$M_{ij} = \sum_{C_i \setminus S_{ij}} \Phi_i \prod_{k \neq j} M_{ki}, \tag{1}$$

where Φ_i is the product of CPTs and evidence tables assigned to cluster i.

Once message propagation is finished in the Shenoy–Shafer architecture, we have the following for each cluster i in the jointree:

$$\Pr(C_i, e) = \Phi_i \prod_k M_{ki}. \tag{2}$$

---

[1] A table is an array which is indexed by variable instantiations. Specifically, a table ϕ over variables X is indexed by the instantiations x of X. Its entries $\phi(x)$ are in $[0, 1]$. We assume familiarity with table operations, such as multiplication, division and marginalization [3].

Let us now look at the time and space requirements of the Shenoy–Shafer architecture. The space requirements are simply those needed to store the messages computed by Equation 1. That is, we need two tables for each separator $\mathbf{S}_{ij}$, one table stores the message from cluster i to cluster j, and the other stores the message from j to i. We will assume in our time analysis below the availability of the table Φ_i, which represents the product of all CPT and evidence tables assigned to cluster i. This is meant to simplify our time analysis, but we stress that one of the attractive aspects of the Shenoy–Shafer architecture is that one can afford to keep this table in factored form, therefore, avoiding the need to allocate space for this table which may be significant.

As for time requirements, suppose that we have a jointree with n clusters and width w. Suppose further that the table Φ_i is already available for each cluster i, and let us bound the amount of work performed by the inward and outward passes of the Shenoy–Shafer architecture, i.e., the work needed to evaluate Equations 1 and 2. We first note that for each cluster i, Equation 1 has to be evaluated n_i times and Equation 2 has to be evaluated once, where n_i is the number of neighbors for cluster i. Each evaluation of Equation 1 leads to multiplying n_i tables, whose variables are all in cluster $\mathbf{C}_i$. Moreover, each evaluation of Equation 2 leads to multiplying $n_i + 1$ tables, whose variables are also all in cluster $\mathbf{C}_i$. The total complexity is then:

$$\sum_i O(n_i(n_i - 1) \exp(|\mathbf{C}_i|) + n_i \exp(|\mathbf{C}_i|)),$$

(since multiplying n elements requires $n - 1$ multiplications) which reduces to $\sum_i O(n_i^2 \exp(w))$ where w is the jointree width. This further reduces to $O(\alpha \exp(w))$, where $\alpha = \sum_i n_i^2$ is a term that ranges from $O(n)$ to $O(n^2)$ depending on the jointree struture. For example, we may have what is known as a *binary jointree* in which each cluster has at most three neighbors, leading to $\alpha \leq 6(n - 1)$. Or we may have a jointree with one cluster having the other $n - 1$ clusters as its neighbors, leading to $\alpha = n^2 - n$.

Given a Bayesian network with n variables, and an elimination order of width w, we can construct a binary jointree for the network with the following properties: the jointree has width $\leq w$, and no more than $2n - 1$ clusters. Hence, we can avoid the quadratic complexity suggested above by a careful construction of the jointree, although this can dramatically increase the space requirements.

2.2 The Hugin Architecture

We now discuss the Hugin architecture, which tends to take less time but uses more space. We first consider Fig. 1 which provides an abstraction of the difference between the Hugin and Shenoy–Shafer architectures. Here, node r has neighbors $1, \ldots, n$, where each edge between r and its neighbor i is labeled with a number x_i. Node r is also labeled with a number x_r. Suppose now that node r wants to send a message m_i to each of its neighbors i, where the content of this message is: $m_i = x_r \prod_{j \neq i} x_j$. One way to do this is to compute the above

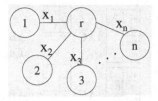

Fig. 1. A simplified jointree message example

product for each neighbor i. This is the approach taken by the Shenoy–Shafer architecture and leads to a quadratic complexity in the number of neighbors n. Alternatively, we can compute the product $p = x_r \prod_{j=1}^n x_j$ only once, and then use it to compute the message to each neighbor i as $m_i = p/x_i$. This is the approach taken by the Hugin architecture. It is clearly more efficient as it only requires one division for each message, while the first method requires n multiplications per message. However, it requires that $x_i \neq 0$, otherwise, p/x_i is not defined. But if the message is going to be later multiplied by an expression of the form $x_i \alpha$, then we can define $p/0$ to be 0, or any other number for that matter, and our computations will be correct since $(x_r \prod_{j \neq i} x_j) x_i \alpha = 0$ regardless of the message value. This is exactly what happens in the Hugin architecture when computing joint marginals and, hence, the division by zero does not pose a problem. Yet, for some other queries which we discuss later, the quantity $\prod_{i=1}^n x_i$ is needed when $x_r = 0$, in which case it cannot be recovered by dividing p by x_r. Moreover, as we see next, since the Hugin architecture does not save the numbers x_i, it cannot compute the product $\prod_{i=1}^n x_i$ through an explicit multiplication of the terms appearing in this product. This is basically the main difference between the Hugin and Shenoy–Shafer architectures except that the above analysis is applied to tables instead of numbers.

Hugin propagation proceeds similarly to Shenoy–Shafer by entering evidence **e** using evidence tables; selecting a cluster as root; and propagating messages in two phases, inward and outward. The Hugin method, however, differs in some major ways. First, it maintains a table Φ_{ij} with each separator, whose entries are initialized to 1s. It also maintains a table Φ_i with each cluster i, initialized to the product of all CPTs and evidence tables assigned to cluster i; see Fig. 2.

Cluster i passes a message to neighboring cluster j only when i has received messages from all its other neighbors k. When cluster i is ready to send a message to cluster j, it does the following:

- it saves the separator table Φ_{ij} into Φ_{ij}^{old}
- it computes a new separator table $\Phi_{ij} = \sum_{\mathbf{C}_i \setminus \mathbf{S}_{ij}} \Phi_i$
- it computes a message to cluster j: $M_{ij} = \Phi_{ij}/\Phi_{ij}^{old}$
- it multiplies the computed message into the table of cluster j: $\Phi_j = \Phi_j M_{ij}$

After the inward and outward–passes of Hugin propagation are completed, we have the following for each cluster i in the jointree: $\Pr(\mathbf{C}_i, \mathbf{e}) = \Phi_i$. The space requirements for the Hugin architecture are those needed to store cluster and

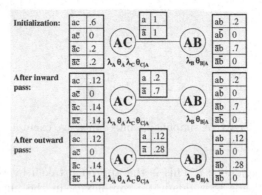

Fig. 2. Hugin propagation on a jointree under evidence b. The jointree is for network $A \rightarrow B$, where $\theta_a = .6$, $\theta_{b|a} = .2$, $\theta_{b|\bar{a}} = .7$, $\theta_{c|a} = 1$, and $\theta_{c|\bar{a}} = .5$

separator tables: one table for each cluster and one table for each separator. Note that the Hugin architecture *does not save* the message $M_{ij} = \Phi_{ij}/\Phi_{ij}^{old}$ sent from cluster i to cluster j.

As for time requirements, suppose that we have a jointree with n clusters and width w. Suppose further that the initial tables Φ_i and Φ_{ij} are already available for each cluster i and separator ij. Let us now bound the amount of work performed by the inward and outward passes of the Hugin architecture, i.e., the work needed to pass a message from each cluster i to each of its neighbors j. Saving the old separator table takes $O(\exp(|\mathbf{S}_{ij}|))$; computing the message takes $O(\exp(|\mathbf{C}_i|) + \exp(|\mathbf{S}_{ij}|))$, and multiplying the message into the table of cluster j takes $O(\exp(|\mathbf{C}_j|))$. Hence, if each cluster i has n_i neighbors, the total complexity is:

$$\sum_i \sum_j O(\exp(|\mathbf{C}_i|) + 2\exp(|\mathbf{S}_{ij}|) + \exp(|\mathbf{C}_j|)),$$

which reduces to $O(n \exp(w))$, where w is the jointree width. Note that this result holds regardless of the jointree structure. Hence, the linear complexity in n is obtained for any jointree, without a need to use a special jointree as in the Shenoy–Shafer architecture.

2.3   Beyond Joint Marginals

The Hugin architecture gains efficiency over the Shenoy–Shafer architecture on arbitrary jointrees by employing division. Moreover, although the use of division does not prevent the architecture from producing joint marginals, it does prevent it from producing answers to some other queries which are useful for a variety of applications including sensitivity analysis [1], local optimization problems like parameter learning [9], and MAP approximation [7].

To explain these additional queries, suppose that we just finished jointree propagation using evidence **e**. This gives us the probability of evidence **e**, since for any cluster $\mathbf{C}$, we have $\Pr(\mathbf{e}) = \sum_{\mathbf{c}} \Pr(\mathbf{c}, \mathbf{e})$. Suppose now that we need the probability of some new evidence which results from erasing the value of variable X from $\mathbf{e}$, denoted $\mathbf{e} - X$. More generally, suppose that we need the probability of evidence $\mathbf{e} - X, x$, where x is a value of variable X which is different from the one appearing in evidence $\mathbf{e}$. Both of these probabilities can be obtained locally using the Shenoy–Shafer architecture without further propagation, but cannot in general be computed locally using the Hugin architecture (see [2] for some special cases). The other type of query which falls in this category is that of computing the derivative $\partial \Pr(\mathbf{e})/\partial \theta_{x|u}$ of the likelihood $\Pr(\mathbf{e})$ with respect to a network parameter $\theta_{x|u} = 0$. We will now show how these queries can be answered locally using the Shenoy–Shafer architecture. We later show how they can be computed using the modification we suggest to the Hugin architecture.

To compute the probabilities $\Pr(\mathbf{e} - X, x)$ for a variable X using the Shenoy–Shafer architecture, we first need to identify the cluster i which contains the evidence table λ_X. The probabilities $\Pr(\mathbf{e} - X, x)$, for each value x, are then available in the following table which is defined over variable X:

$$\sum_{\mathbf{C}_i \setminus X} \prod_k \phi_k \prod_j M_{ji}.$$

Here, ϕ_k ranges over all CPTs and evidence tables assigned to cluster i, excluding the evidence table λ_X [2,8].

Similarly, to compute the derivatives $\partial \Pr(\mathbf{e})/\partial \theta_{x|u}$, we need to identify the cluster i which is assigned the CPT of variable X. The derivatives for all instantiations $x\mathbf{u}$ of variable X and its parents $\mathbf{U}$ are then available in the following table, which is defined over family $X\mathbf{U}$:

$$\sum_{\mathbf{C}_i \setminus X \cup \mathbf{U}} \prod_k \phi_k \prod_j M_{ji}.$$

Here, ϕ_k ranges over all CPTs and evidence tables assigned to cluster i, excluding the CPT $\theta_{X|\mathbf{U}}$ [8].

Hugin is not able to handle these queries in general because it does not save messages that are exchanged between clusters, and because table division may lead to a division by zero (see [2] for a special case where Hugin can handle some of these queries).

3   Getting the Best of Both Worlds

We now present a jointree propagation algorithm that combines the query answering power of Shenoy–Shafer propagation with the efficiency of Hugin propagation. The messages sent between clusters are the same as Shenoy–Shafer messages, but the tables stored at each cluster represent the product of assigned tables and incoming messages in a manner similar to the Hugin approach.

As discussed earlier, division is a key to Hugin efficiency, but it also produces a loss of information. The problem is that multiplication by zero is noninvertible. In Sect. 3.1 we discuss the problem in detail and introduce a simple and efficient technique to circumvent it. In Sect. 3.2 we describe the new propagation algorithm. Section 3.3 details the semantics of messages in the new architecture, as well as the content of cluster and separator tables.

3.1 Handling Zeros

This section introduces the notion of a *zero conscious number:* a pair (z, b), where z is a scalar and b is a bit. It also defines various operations on these numbers. We then show in the following section that by employing such numbers in a variation on the Hugin architecture, we can attain the same query answering power exhibited by the Shenoy–Shafer architecture.

To motivate zero conscious numbers, consider a set of numbers $x_1, \ldots, x_n$ and suppose that for each $i = 1, \ldots, n$, our goal is to compute the product $m_i = \prod_{j \neq i} x_j$. We distinguish between three cases:

Case 1: $x_1, \ldots, x_n$ contain no zeros. Then $m_i = p/x_i$, where $p = \prod_j x_j$.
Case 2: $x_1, \ldots, x_n$ contain a single zero x_k. Then $m_k = \prod_{j \neq k} x_j$ and $m_i = 0$ for all $i \neq k$.
Case 3: $x_1, \ldots, x_n$ contain more than one zero. Then $m_i = 0$ for all i.

Note that in Case 3, we have $m_i = 0 = \prod_{j \neq k} x_j$ for any k since we have more than one zero. Hence, Case 2 and Case 3 can be merged together. Using these cases, the messages m_i can be computed efficiently by first computing a pair (z, b) such that:

– b is a bit which indicates whether any of the elements x_i is a zero (Cases 2,3).
– z is the product of all elements x_i, excluding the single zero if one exists.

For example, if the elements x_i are $1, 2, 3, 4, 5$, we would compute $(1 * 2 * 3 * 4 * 5, f) = (120, f)$ since no zero was withheld. For elements $1, 2, 0, 4, 5$, we would compute $(40, t)$. Finally, for elements $1, 2, 0, 4, 0$, we would compute $(0, t)$.

Then each message m_i can be computed from the pair (z, b) as follows:

$$m_i = \begin{cases} z/x_i \text{ if } b = f \\ 0 \quad \text{ if } b = t \text{ and } x_i \neq 0 \\ z \quad \text{ if } b = t \text{ and } x_i = 0 \end{cases}$$

This can be thought of as dividing the pair (z, b) by x_i. In fact, we will call the pair (z, b) a *zero conscious number* and define division by a scalar as given above. Two more operations on zero conscious numbers will be needed. In particular, multiplying a zero conscious number (z, b) by a scalar c is defined as:

$$(z, b) * c = \begin{cases} (z, t) & \text{if } b = f \text{ and } c = 0 \\ (c * z, b) & \text{otherwise.} \end{cases}$$

Moreover, the addition of two zero conscious numbers is defined as:

$$(z_1, b_1) + (z_2, b_2) = \begin{cases} (z_1, b_1) & \text{if } b_1 = f \text{ and } b_2 = t \\ (z_2, b_2) & \text{if } b_1 = t \text{ and } b_2 = f \\ (z_1 + z_2, b_1) & \text{otherwise.} \end{cases}$$

Finally, we define

$$real(z, b) = \begin{cases} z \text{ if } b = f \\ 0 \text{ otherwise.} \end{cases}$$

Note that if the zero conscious number (z, b) was computed for elements $x_1, \ldots, x_n$, then $real(z, b)$ recovers the product $\prod_j x_j$ of these elements.

We can also defined *zero conscious tables* which map variable instantiations to zero conscious numbers. Now let Ψ be a zero conscious table and Φ be a standard table. The marginal $\sum_{\mathbf{X}} \Psi$, product $\Psi\Phi$, and division Ψ/Φ can then be defined in the obvious way. Moreover, $real(\Psi)$ is defined as a standard table which results from applying the $real$ operation to each entry of Ψ.

3.2 Algorithmic Description

The algorithm we propose is very similar to Hugin propagation. Like the Hugin architecture, it maintains a table Φ_{ij} for each separator ij. A table is also maintained for each cluster. Unlike for Hugin, the table Ψ_i associated with cluster i is a zero conscious table. From here on, we will use Ψ to denote a zero conscious table and Φ to denote a standard table.

Initialization. The separator table entries are initialized to 1, and the cluster table entries are initialized to $(1, f)$. The CPTs and evidence tables assigned to a cluster are multiplied into the corresponding cluster table.

Message Propagation. This algorithm requires the same obedience to message ordering that the other jointree algorithms do. That is, messages are sent from the leaves, toward some root, then back from the root to the leaves. A message from cluster i to cluster j is computed as follows:

- $\Psi_{temp} \leftarrow \sum_{\mathbf{C}_i \backslash \mathbf{S}_{ij}} \Psi_i$
- $\Psi_j \leftarrow \Psi_j(\Psi_{temp}/\Phi_{ij})$
- $\Phi_{ij} \leftarrow real(\Psi_{temp})$

Figure 3 illustrates an example of this propagation scheme. This algorithm basically mirrors Hugin propagation, but with zero conscious tables for clusters. It has some minor time and space overhead over what the Hugin algorithm requires. The time overhead consists of an additional logical test per operation. The storage requirement is also fairly insignificant. Single precision floating point numbers require 32 bits and double precision numbers require 64 bits, so an extra bit (or even byte, if the processor can't efficiently manipulate bits) per number will increase the space requirements only slightly.

3.3 The Semantics

The message passing semantics is the same as for Shenoy–Shafer.

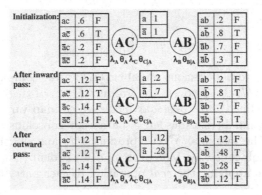

Fig. 3. Zero conscious propagation illustrated on a simple jointree under evidence b, where the left cluster is root. The jointree is for network $C \leftarrow A \rightarrow B$, where $\theta_a = .6$, $\theta_{b|a} = .2$, $\theta_{b|\bar{a}} = .7$, $\theta_{c|a} = 1$, and $\theta_{c|\bar{a}} = .5$

Theorem 1. *The message passed from cluster i to cluster j is the same as the message passed using Shenoy–Shafer propagation. That is, if Φ_{ij} is the product of all tables assigned to clusters on the i–side of edge ij, and if $\mathbf{X}$ are the variables appearing in these tables, then the message $M_{ij} = \sum_{\mathbf{X} \backslash \mathbf{S}_{ij}} \Phi_{ij}$.*

The cluster and separator table semantics closely resemble the corresponding Hugin semantics.

Theorem 2. *After all the messages have been passed, $real(\Psi_i) = \Pr(\mathbf{C}_i, \mathbf{e})$ and $\Phi_{ij} = \Pr(\mathbf{S}_{ij}, \mathbf{e})$ for all neighboring clusters i and j.*

Although very similar to the Hugin semantics, the difference in the cluster table makes these semantics significantly more powerful.

Theorem 3. *Let $\phi_{i1}...\phi_{in}$ be the CPTs and evidence tables assigned to cluster i, and let $\mathbf{X}_m$ be the set of variables of ϕ_{im}. Then after message passing is complete,*

$$\sum_{\mathbf{C}_i \backslash \mathbf{X}_k} \prod_{m \neq k} \phi_{im} \prod_j M_{ji} = \left(\sum_{\mathbf{C}_i \backslash \mathbf{X}_k} \Psi_i \right) / \phi_{ik}.$$

This theorem shows that we can use zero conscious division to perform the same local computations permitted by the Shenoy–Shafer architecture. Consider Fig. 3 for an example, which depicts an example of zero conscious propagation under evidence $\mathbf{e} = b$. Given the table associated with the left cluster, we have $\Pr(\mathbf{e}) = .12+.14+.14 = .4$. Suppose now that we want to compute the probability of $(\mathbf{e} - B, \bar{b}) = \bar{b}$. We can do this by identifying the cluster AB which contains the evidence table λ_B and then computing: $(\sum_A \Psi_{AB})/\lambda_B$. This leads to the first division shown in Fig. 4, showing that the probability of $\bar{b} = .6$.

Similarly, to compute the partial derivatives of $\Pr(\mathbf{e})$ with respect to parameters $\theta_{C|A}$, we need $\Psi_{AC}/\theta_{C|A}$ which is also shown in Fig. 4. According to

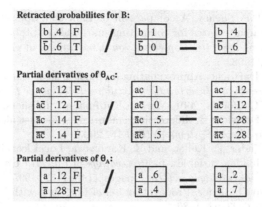

Fig. 4. Evidence retraction and partial derivative operations for the jointree in Fig. 3

this computation, for example, we have $\partial \Pr(e)/\partial\theta_{c|\bar{a}} = .28$. Finally, the partial derivatives $\partial \Pr(e)/\partial\theta_a$ are obtained from $(\sum_C \Psi_{AC})/\theta_A$, which is also shown in Fig. 4. According to this computation, $\partial \Pr(e)/\partial\theta_{\bar{a}} = .7$.

4   Conclusion

We proposed a combination of the Shenoy–Shafer and Hugin architectures, in which we use zero conscious tables/potentials. The use of these tables provide a simple way to exploit the efficiency of the Hugin method, while extending the set of queries that can be answered efficiently. For the price of a single bit per cluster entry, and some minimal logic operations, all queries answerable using Shenoy–Shafer propagation can now be answered using Hugin type operations. For applications that require more than just marginal probabilities, such as local search methods for MAP and sensitivity analysis, this can produce a significant speed up over the use of Shenoy–Shafer architecture.

References

1. H. Chan and A. Darwiche. When do numbers really matter? In *Proceedings of the 17th Conference on Uncertainty in Artificial Intelligence (UAI)*, pages 65–74, San Francisco, California, 2001. Morgan Kaufmann Publishers, Inc.
2. R. Cowell, A. Dawid, S. Lauritzen, and D. Spiegelhalter. *Probabilistic Networks and Expert Systems*. Springer, 1999.
3. C. Huang and A. Darwiche. Inference in belief networks: A procedural guide. *International Journal of Approximate Reasoning*, 15(3):225–263, 1996.
4. F.V. Jensen, S. Lauritzen, and K. Olesen. Bayesian updating in recursive graphical models by local computation. *Computational Statistics Quarterly*, 4:269–282, 1990.
5. S.L. Lauritzen and F.V. Jensen. Local computation with valuations from a commutative semigroup. *Annals of Mathematics and Artificial Intelligence*, 21(1):51–69, 1997.

6. V. Lepar and P.P. Shenoy. A comparison of Lauritzen-Spiegelhalter, Hugin and Shenoy-Shafer architectures for computing marginals of probability distributions. In *Proceedings of the 14th Conference on Uncertainty in Artificial Intelligence*, pages 328–337, 1998.
7. J. Park and A. Darwiche. Approximating map using local search. In *Proceedings of the 17th Conference on Uncertainty in Artificial Intelligence (UAI)*, pages 403–410, San Francisco, California, 2001. Morgan Kaufmann Publishers, Inc.
8. J. Park and A. Darwiche. A differential semantics for jointree algorithms. In *Neural Information Processing Systems (NIPS)* 15, 2003.
9. S. Russell, J. Binder, D. Koller, and K. Kanazawa. Local learning in probabilistic networks with hidden variables. In *Proceedings of the 11th Conference on Uncertainty in Artificial Intelligence (UAI)*, pages 1146–1152, 1995.
10. P.P. Shenoy and G. Shafer. Propagating belief functions with local computations. *IEEE Expert*, 1(3):43–52, 1986.

A   Proof of Theorems

We first introduce a few lemmas about zero conscious potentials that we will need to prove the theorems.

Lemma 1. *Let Ψ be the zero conscious product of potentials $\Phi_1, ..., \Phi_n$. Then $\Psi/\Phi_i = \prod_{j \neq i} \Phi_j$.*

Proof. Consider an entry ψ of Ψ, and the unique compatible entry ϕ_i in from each table. Then, based on the division property of zero conscious numbers, $\psi/\phi_i = \prod_{j \neq i} \phi_j$. This is true for all entries ψ, thus proving the result.

Lemma 2. *Let c be a factor of zero conscious numbers $a = (n_a, z_a)$ and $b = (n_b, z_b)$. Then $(a + b)/c = a/c + b/c$*

Proof. We simply break it into cases and show that the definitions of the operations require that they agree.

Case 1 $(c = 0)$ Then $z_a = z_b = t$. Thus $(a + b)/c = (n_a + n_b, t)/c = n_a + n_b = a/c + b/c$ since $a/c = n_a$ and $b/c = n_b$.
Case 2 $(c \neq 0, z_a = f, z_b = f)$ Then $(a+b)/c = (n_a + n_b, f)/c = (n_a + n_b)/c = n_a/c + n_b/c = a/c + b/c$.
Case 3 $(c \neq 0, z_a = f, z_b = t)$ Then $(a + b)/c = a/c = a/c + b/c$ since $b/c = 0$.
Case 4 $(c \neq 0, z_a = t, z_b = f)$ Then $(a + b)/c = b/c = a/c + b/c$ since $a/c = 0$.
Case 5 $(c \neq 0, z_a = t, z_b = t)$ Then $(a + b)/c = 0 = a/c + b/c$.

Lemma 3. *Let Ψ be the zero conscious product of potentials $\Phi_1, ..., \Phi_n$. Then $(\sum_{\mathbf{C} \backslash \mathbf{S}} \Psi)/\Phi_i = \sum_{\mathbf{C} \backslash \mathbf{S}} (\Psi/\Phi_i)$ where $\mathbf{C}$ are the variables of Ψ, and $\mathbf{S}$ are the variables of Φ_i.*

Proof. Consider the instances $\mathbf{c}$ of $\mathbf{C}$ compatible with instance $\mathbf{s}$ of $\mathbf{S}$. Repeated application of Lemma 2 implies that summing them, then dividing is the same as dividing them summing. This is true for each element, and so for the table as a whole.

Proof of Theorem 1

We will first prove the theorem for messages sent towards the root. We will then prove it for messages away from the root.

Consider a leaf node i sending a message to its neighbor j. The cluster potential Ψ_i consists of the product of all tables $\phi_{i1}...\phi_{in}$ assigned to it. The message sent is $(\sum_{\mathbf{C}\backslash\mathbf{S}} \Psi_i)/1 = \sum_{\mathbf{C}\backslash\mathbf{S}} \prod_k \phi_{ik} = \sum_{\mathbf{C}\backslash\mathbf{S}} \Phi_i$ which is the Shenoy–Shafer message from a leaf node.

Now, assume by way of induction that all messages toward the root have been received for cluster i. The cluster Ψ_i contains the product of the assigned tables $\phi_{i1}, ..., \phi_{in}$ and the incoming upward messages M_{ki} from neighbors k. Then the upward message is $(\sum_{\mathbf{C}\backslash\mathbf{S}} \Psi_i)/1 = \sum_{\mathbf{C}\backslash\mathbf{S}} \prod_m \phi_{im} \prod_k M_{ki} = \sum_{\mathbf{C}\backslash\mathbf{S}} \Phi_i \prod_k M_{ki}$ which again is the Shenoy–Shafer message.

So, for the upward pass the messages sent equal the corresponding Shenoy–Shafer messages.

Now, consider a message sent from the root r. The cluster potential Ψ_r consists of the product of the assigned tables, and the incoming messages of all neighbors. The message sent to neighbor j is $(\sum_{\mathbf{C}\backslash\mathbf{S}} \Psi_r)/M_{jr}$ which by application of Lemma 3 followed by Lemma 1 yields $\sum_{\mathbf{C}\backslash\mathbf{S}} \Phi_r \prod_{i\neq j} M_{ir}$ which is again the appropriate Shenoy–Shafer message.

Now, assume by way of induction that a cluster i has received messages which equal the corresponding Shenoy–Shafer messages from each of its neighbors. Then, the message sent to neighbor j away from the root is $(\sum_{\mathbf{C}\backslash\mathbf{S}} \Psi_i)/M_{ji}$ which again appealing to Lemmas 3 and 1 equals $\sum_{\mathbf{C}\backslash\mathbf{S}} \Phi_i \prod_{k\neq j} M_{ki}$ which is the same as the Shenoy–Shafer message.

Proof of Theorem 2

After propagation completes, Ψ_i contains the product of the locally assigned tables $\phi_{i1}...\phi_{in}$, and the incoming messages. Thus $real(\Psi_i) = \prod_k \phi_{ik} \prod_j M_{ji} = \Phi_i \prod_j M_{ji}$. Since the messages are the same as the Shenoy–Shafer messages, and in the Shenoy–Shafer architecture $\Pr(\mathbf{C}_i, \mathbf{e}) = \Phi_i \prod_j M_{ji}$, $real(\Psi_i) = \Pr(\mathbf{C}_i, \mathbf{e})$. For separator ij, where i is closer to the root, after propagation completes, $\Phi_{ij} = real(\sum_{\mathbf{C}_i\backslash\mathbf{S}_{ij}} \Psi_i) = \sum_{\mathbf{C}_i\backslash\mathbf{S}_{ij}} real(\Psi_i) = \sum_{\mathbf{C}_i\backslash\mathbf{S}_{ij}} \Pr(\mathbf{C}_i, \mathbf{e}) = \Pr(\mathbf{S}_{ij}, \mathbf{e})$.

Proof of Theorem 3

After propagation completes, Ψ_i consists of the product of the tables $\phi_{i1}...\phi_{in}$ assigned to cluster i, and the incoming messages M_{ji}. Then $(\sum_{\mathbf{C}_i\backslash\mathbf{X}_k} \Psi_i)/\phi_{ik} = \sum_{\mathbf{C}_i\backslash\mathbf{X}_k} \prod_{m\neq k} \phi_{im} \prod_j M_{ji}$, which contains the partial derivatives of $\Pr(\mathbf{e})$ with respect to the parameters of ϕ_{ik} [8].

Characterization of Inclusion Neighbourhood in Terms of the Essential Graph: Upper Neighbours

Milan Studený*

Institute of Information Theory and Automation
Academy of Sciences of the Czech Republic
Pod vodárenskou věží 4, 18208 Prague, Czech Republic
studeny@utia.cas.cz

Abstract. The problem of efficient characterization of inclusion neighbourhood is crucial for some methods of learning (equivalence classes of) Bayesian networks. In this paper, neighbouring equivalence classes of a given equivalence class of Bayesian networks are characterized efficiently by means of the respective essential graph. The characterization reveals hidded internal structure of the inclusion neighbourhood. More exactly, upper neighbours, that is, those neighbouring equivalence classes which describe more independencies, are completely characterized here. First, every upper neighbour is characterized by a pair $([a, b], C)$ where $[a, b]$ is an edge in the essential graph and $C \subseteq N \setminus \{a, b\}$ a disjoint set of nodes. Second, if $[a, b]$ is fixed, the class of sets C which characterize the respective neighbours is a *tuft* of sets determined by its least set and the list of its maximal sets. These sets can be read directly from the essential graph. An analogous characterization of lower neighbours, which is more complex, is mentioned.

1 Motivation

1.1 Learning Bayesian Networks

Several approaches to learning Bayesian networks use the method of maximization of a *quality criterion*, named also 'quality measure' [3] and 'score metric' [4]. Quality criterion is a function, designed by a statistician, which ascribes to data and a network a real number which 'evaluates' how the statistical model determined by the network is suitable to explain the occurence of data. Since the actual aim of the learning procedure is to get a statistical model (defined by a network) reasonable quality criteria do not distinguish between equivalent Bayesian networks, that is, between networks which define the same statistical model. Therefore, from operational point of view, the goal is to learn an equivalence class of Bayesian networks, that is, a class of acyclic directed graphs (over a fixed set of nodes N).

As direct maximization of a quality criterion is typically infeasible the *method of local search* is often used. The main idea of this approach is that suitable

---

* This research has been supported by the grant GA ČR n. 201/01/1482.

T.D. Nielsen and N.L. Zhang (Eds.): ECSQARU 2003, LNAI 2711, pp. 161–172, 2003.

concept of neighbourhood is introduced for acyclic directed graphs over N. The point is that the change in the value of a (reasonable) quality criterion is easy to compute for neighbouring graphs. Thus, instead of global maximization of a quality criterion one searches for a local maximum of the criterion with respect to the considered neighbourhood structure and this task is usually computationally feasible. Typical neighbourhood structures used in practice are defined by means of simple graphical operations with considered graphs - for details see [5,7].

The algorithms of this kind can also be classified according to the method of representation of equivalence classes of networks. In some algorithms, an equivalence class is represented by any of its members which may, however, result in computational complications. In other algorithms, a special representative of each equivalence class is used. The most popular representative of an equivalence class of Bayesian networks is the *essential graph* which is a certain chain graph describing some common features of acyclic directed graphs from the class. The term 'essential graph' was proposed by Andersson, Madigan and Perlman [1]; altenative names 'completed pattern', 'maximally oriented graph for a pattern' and 'completed pdag' have also appeared in the literature.

1.2   Inclusion Neighbourhood

There exists a neighbourhood structure (for equivalence classes of Bayesian networks) which has a good theoretical basis. The inclusion of statistical models defined by the networks, which corresponds to the inclusion of conditional independence structures defined by the network, induces a natural *inclusion ordering* on the collection of equivalence classes. This ordering induces a neighbourhood concept then. More specifically, two different types of neighbouring equivalence classes are assigned to every equivalence class of networks: the *upper* neighbours and *lower* neighbours. Thus, the *inclusion neighbourhood*, sometimes also named 'inclusion boundary neighbourhood' [7], consists of these two parts. There are also some practical reasons for using the inclusion neighbourhood - for details see [4]. Note that Chickering [5] has recently confirmed Meek's conjecture [9] about transformational characterization of the inclusion ordering. A consequence of this result is a graphical description of the inclusion neighbourhood in terms of the collection of members of the considered equivalence class (see Sect. 2.4).

The topic of this contribution is to characterize the inclusion neighbourhood of a given equivalence class of Bayesian networks in terms of the respective essential graph in such a way that it can be used efficiently in a method of local search for maximization of a quality criterion. Two recent papers were devoted to this problem, but, in author's view, none of them brought a satisfactory solution to the problem.

Chickering, in Sect. 5 of [5], gave a method which is able to generate tentatively all neighbouring equivalence classes (of a given equivalence class described by the respective essential graph). More specifically, two (composite) graphical operations applicable to an essential graph and respective legality tests which are able to decide whether the respective graphical operation leads to a neighbouring equivalence class are designed in that paper. One of the operations and the respective legality test are aimed to generate upper neighbours, the other operation and test correspond to lower neighbours. Although the graphical description of the inclusion neighbourhood in terms of individual networks from Sect. 2.4 implies that every inclusion neighbour can be reached in this way the method has two drawbacks.

- The first drawback of the method is that it is tentative: different graphical operations may lead to the same equivalence class. Therefore, additional checking must be done to cure this imperfection.
- The second drawback of this mechanistic approach is that it does not allow one to discern possible internal structure of the inclusion neighbourhood.

Auvray and Wehenkel [2] made an attempt at direct characterization of the inclusion neighbourhood. Their characterization of the upper inclusion neighbourhood, that is, of those neighbouring equivalence classes which describe more independencies, removes the first drawback. They uniquely characterized and classified neighbouring equivalence classes of a given equivalence class (described in terms of the respective essential graph) by means of certain mathematical objects. However, these object are still unnecessarily complicated which means that their characterization of upper inclusion neighbourhood is too awkward. In particular, the second drawback is not removed by their approach since their approach does not allow one to make out the internal structure of the inclusion neighbourhood. Moreover, their characterization is incomplete: only partial direct characterization of lower neighbours is given there.

1.3   Compact Characterization of Inclusion Neighbours

In this paper an elegant characterization of the inclusion neighbourhood of a given equivalence class in terms of the respective essential graph is presented. Each inclusion neighbour is uniquely described by a pair $([a, b], C)$ where $[a, b]$ is an unordered pair of distinct nodes and $C \subseteq N \setminus \{a, b\}$ a disjoint set of nodes. More specifically, $[a, b]$ is an edge of the essential graph in case of the upper neighbourhood while $[a, b]$ is a pair of nodes which is not an edge in the essential graph in case of the lower neigbourhood.

The first new observation made in this paper is that every inclusion neighbour is uniquely characterized by a pair $([a, b], C)$ of this kind. The second observation is that, for given $[a, b]$, the collection of those sets C which correspond to inclusion neighbours has a special form.

In this contribution, a complete analysis of the upper inclusion neighbourhood is given. In this case, the collection of sets C for a given edge $[a, b]$ has the form of a *tuft*. This means that it is a collection of sets with the least set ($=$ the unique minimal set) and with possibly several maximal sets such that every set which contains the least set and which is contained in one of the maximal sets belongs to the collection. In particular, a tuft is completely described by its least set and by the list of its maximal sets. Given an essential graph G^* and an edge $[a, b]$ in G^* the least and maximal sets of the respective tuft of sets are characterized directly in terms of G^*.

The structure of the lower inclusion neighbourhood is similar but more complex. In that case, given a pair of nodes which is not an edge in the essential graph, the respective collection of sets C is the union of (at most) two tufts. The least and maximal sets of these two tufts can also be read from the essential graph. However, because of page limitation the case of lower neighbourhood will be completely analyzed in a future paper [15].

Note that the characterization of inclusion neighbours by means of pairs $([a, b], C)$ where $C \subseteq N \setminus \{a, b\}$ and the way how it is done in this paper is not incidental. An interesting fact is that, from a certain perspective which is explained in details in Chapter 8 of [13], the pair $([a, b], C)$ has close relation to conditional independence interpretation of the 'move' from the considered equivalence class to its respective inclusion neighbour.

The proofs are omitted because of strict limit 12 pages for contributions to Proceedings of ECSQARU 2003. The reader interested in the proofs can download an extended version of this paper at

http://www.utia.cas.cz/user_data/studeny/aalb03.html.

The proofs combine the ideas motivated by an arithmetic approach to the description of Bayesian network models from [13] with certain graphical procedures which were already used in [2].

2   Basic Concepts

2.1   Graphical Notions

Graphs considered here have a finite non-empty set N as the set of *nodes* and two possible types of edges. An undirected edge or a *line* over N is a subset of N of cardinality two, that is, an unordered pair $\{a, b\}$ where $a, b \in N$, $a \neq b$. The respective notation is $a - b$. A directed edge or an *arrow* over N is an ordered pair (a, b) where $a, b \in N$, $a \neq b$. The notation $a \rightarrow b$ reflects its pictorial representation. A *hybrid graph* over N is a graph without multiple edges, that is, a triplet $H = (N, \mathcal{L}(H), \mathcal{A}(H))$ where N is a set of nodes, $\mathcal{L}(H)$ a set of lines over N and $\mathcal{A}(H)$ a set of arrows over N such that whenever $(a, b) \in \mathcal{A}(H)$ then $(b, a) \notin \mathcal{A}(H)$ and $\{a, b\} = \{b, a\} \notin \mathcal{L}(H)$. A pair $[a, b]$ of distinct elements of N will be called an *edge in* H (between a and b) if one of the following cases occurs: $a - b$ in H, $a \rightarrow b$ in H and $b \rightarrow a$ in H. If $\emptyset \neq A \subseteq N$ then the *induced subgraph* H_A of H is the triplet $(A, \mathcal{L}(H) \cap \mathcal{P}(A), \mathcal{A}(H) \cap (A \times A))$ where $\mathcal{P}(A)$ denotes the power set of A (= the collection of subsets of A).

A set $K \subseteq N$ is *complete* in a hybrid graph H over N if $\forall a, b \in N$ $a \neq b$ one has $a - b$ in H. By a *clique* of H will be understood a maximal complete set in H (with respect to set inclusion). The collection of cliques of H will be denoted by *cliques(H)*. A set $C \subseteq N$ is *connected* in H if, for every $a, b \in N$, there exists an undirected path connecting them, that is, a sequence of distinct nodes $a = c_1, \ldots, c_n = b$, $n \geq 1$ such that $c_i - c_{i+1}$ in H for $i = 1, \ldots, n - 1$. Connectivity *components* of H are maximal connected sets in H.

An *undirected graph* is a hybrid graph without arrows, that is, $\mathcal{A}(H) = \emptyset$. A *directed graph* is a hybrid graph having arrows only, that is, $\mathcal{L}(H) = \emptyset$. An *acyclic directed graph* is a directed graph without directed cycles, that is, without any sequence $d_1, \ldots, d_n, d_{n+1} = d_1$, $n \geq 3$ such that $d_1, \ldots, d_n$ are distinct and $d_i \to d_{i+1}$ in H for $i = 1, \ldots, n$.

A *chain graph* is a hybrid graph H for which there exists a *chain*, that is, an ordered partitioning of N into non-empty sets, called *blocks*, $B_1, \ldots, B_m$, $m \geq 1$ such that

- if $a - b$ in H then $a, b \in B_i$ for some $1 \leq i \leq m$,
- if $a \to b$ in H then $a \in B_i, b \in B_j$ with $1 \leq i < j \leq m$.

An equivalent definition of a chain graph is that it is a hybrid graph H without *semi-directed cycles*, that is, without any sequence $d_1, \ldots, d_n, d_{n+1} = d_1$, $n \geq 3$ such that $d_1, \ldots, d_n$ are distinct, $d_1 \to d_2$ in H and $\forall i = 2, \ldots, n$ either $d_i \to d_{i+1}$ or $d_i - d_{i+1}$ in H - see Lemma 2.1 in [12]. Clearly, every undirected graph and every acyclic directed graph is a chain graph. Moreover, there is no arrow in a chain graph between nodes of a connected set $C \subseteq N$; in other words, the induced subgraph H_C is undirected. Thus, the set of *parents* of C, that is,

$$pa_H(C) = \{a \in N\,;\, \exists\, b \in C \;\; a \to b \text{ in } H\,\}$$

is disjoint with C. The set

$$ne_H(C) = \{a \in N \setminus C\,;\, \exists\, b \in C \;\; a - b \text{ in } H\,\}$$

will be named the set of *neighbours* of C.

2.2 Bayesian Networks and Their Equivalence

A *Bayesian network* is a certain statistical model, that is, a class of (multidimensional probability) distributions, appended to an acyclic directed graph. It could be introduced as the class of distributions (on a fixed sample space) which factorize according to the graph in a certain way. An alternative definition of that class can be given terms of conditional independence restrictions, using the *d*-separation criterion from [10] or using the moralization criterion from [8] which are known to be equivalent. Since exact definitions of these concepts are not needed in this paper they are omitted. Nevertheless, given an acyclic directed graph G over N, the symbol $\mathcal{I}(G)$ will be used to denote the collection of conditional independence restrictions determined by G. Moreover, the phrase "Bayesian network" will be used as a synonym for an acyclic directed graph throughout the rest of the paper.

An important concept is the concept of *equivalence of Bayesian networks*. Two Bayesian networks G_1 and G_2 are considered to be equivalent if they represent the same statistical model, which requirement is typically equivalent to the condition $\mathcal{I}(G_1) = \mathcal{I}(G_2)$. Given an equivalence class $\mathcal{G}$ of Bayesian networks over N the symbol $\mathcal{I}(\mathcal{G})$ will denote the shared collection of conditional independence restrictions $\mathcal{I}(G)$ for $G \in \mathcal{G}$. Verma and Pearl [16] gave a direct graphical characterization of equivalent Bayesian networks which can be used as its formal definition here. The *underlying graph* of a hybrid graph H over N is an undirected graph H^u over N such that $a - b$ in H^u iff $[a, b]$ is an edge in H. An *immorality* in H is a special induced subgraph of H, namely the configuration $a \to c \leftarrow b$ where a, b, c are distinct nodes and the pair $[a, b]$ is not an edge in H. Two Bayesian networks G_1, G_2 over N are (graphically) *equivalent* iff they have the same underlying graph and the same collection of immoralities. The equivalence characterization makes the following definition consistent: given an equivalence class $\mathcal{G}$ of Bayesian networks, a pair $[a, b]$ of distinct nodes is called an *edge in* $\mathcal{G}$ if $[a, b]$ is an edge in some $G \in \mathcal{G}$, which means, it is an edge in every $G \in \mathcal{G}$.

2.3   Essential Graphs

An equivalence class $\mathcal{G}$ of Bayesian networks (over N) can be described by its *essential graph* which is a hybrid graph G^* (over N) such that

- $a \to b$ in G^* if and only if $a \to b$ in G for every $G \in \mathcal{G}$,
- $a - b$ in G^* if and only if there exist $G_1, G_2 \in \mathcal{G}$ such that $a \to b$ in G_1 and $b \to a$ in G_2.

A graphical characterization of essential graphs was given by Andersson, Madigan and Perlman as Theorem 4.1 in [1]. Recently, a simpler alternative characterization has been found in [14] and, independently, in [11]. As complete characterization of essential graphs is not needed in this paper, it is omitted. However, what is needed is the following observation. It follows from Theorem 4.1 of [1] that every essential graph H (of an equivalence class of Bayesian networks) is a chain graph without flags. Recall that by a *flag* in a hybrid graph H is meant a special induced subgraph of H, namely the configuration $a \to c - b$ where a, b, c are distinct nodes and the pair $[a, b]$ is not an edge in H. Note that every chain graph without flags has the following property: for every component C of H and $a, b \in C$ one has $pa_H(a) = pa_H(b)$; in particular, $pa_H(a) = pa_H(C)$ for any $a \in C$.

Remark 1. Note that there are other possible ways of representing an equivalence class $\mathcal{G}$ of Bayesian networks. One of them is the concept of *largest chain graph* [6] of the collection of chain graphs which are equivalent to (any) $G \in \mathcal{G}$. Another alternative is brought by the arithmetic approach presented in Sect. 8.4 of [13] which offers the concept of *standard imset*.

2.4   Inclusion Ordering and Neighbourhood

The *inclusion ordering* on the set of equivalence classes of Bayesian networks (over N) is defined by the binary relation $\mathcal{I}(\mathcal{K}) \subseteq \mathcal{I}(\mathcal{L})$ for equivalence classes $\mathcal{K}$ and $\mathcal{L}$. The symbol $\mathcal{I}(\mathcal{K}) \subset \mathcal{I}(\mathcal{L})$ will denote the *strict ordering*, that is, the situation when $\mathcal{I}(\mathcal{K}) \subseteq \mathcal{I}(\mathcal{L})$ and $\mathcal{I}(\mathcal{K}) \neq \mathcal{I}(\mathcal{L})$. Finally, the symbol $\mathcal{I}(\mathcal{K}) \sqsubset \mathcal{I}(\mathcal{L})$ will mean that $\mathcal{I}(\mathcal{K}) \subset \mathcal{I}(\mathcal{L})$ but there is no equivalence class $\mathcal{G}$ of Bayesian networks (over N) such that $\mathcal{I}(\mathcal{K}) \subset \mathcal{I}(\mathcal{G}) \subset \mathcal{I}(\mathcal{L})$. If this is the case then $\mathcal{L}$ is called the *upper neighbour* of $\mathcal{K}$ and $\mathcal{K}$ is called the *lower neighbour* of $\mathcal{L}$. By the *inclusion neighbourhood* of an equivalence class is understood the collection its upper and lower neigbours.

Transformational characterization of the inclusion ordering from [5] allows one to derive a simple graphical description of the relation $\mathcal{I}(\mathcal{K}) \sqsubset \mathcal{I}(\mathcal{L})$ as a consequence - see Lemma 8.5 in [13].

Lemma 1. *If $\mathcal{K}$ and $\mathcal{L}$ are equivalence classes of Bayesian networks over N then one has $\mathcal{I}(\mathcal{K}) \sqsubset \mathcal{I}(\mathcal{L})$ iff there exists $K \in \mathcal{K}$ and $L \in \mathcal{L}$ such that L is made of K by the removal of (exactly) one edge.*

Remark 2. The relation $\mathcal{I}(\mathcal{K}) \subseteq \mathcal{I}(\mathcal{L})$ corresponds to the situation when the statistical model given by $K \in \mathcal{K}$ contains the statistical model given by $L \in \mathcal{L}$. The networks in $\mathcal{K}$ have more edges than networks in $\mathcal{L}$ then. The reader may ask why $\mathcal{L}$ is supposed to be 'above' $\mathcal{K}$ in this paper (and not conversely). The terminology used in this paper simply emphasizes the conditional independence interpretation of considered statistical models which is in the center of author's interests - for more detailed justification see Remark 8.10 in [13].

2.5   Tuft of Sets

Let $\mathcal{T}$ be a non-empty collection of subsets of N, that is, $\emptyset \neq \mathcal{T} \subseteq \mathcal{P}(N)$, and $\mathcal{T}_{max}$ denotes the collection of maximal sets in $\mathcal{T}$ (with respect to set inclusion). The collection $\mathcal{T}$ will be called a *tuft* of sets if

- $\mathcal{T}$ has the least set T_{min}, that is, $T_{min} \in \mathcal{T}$ with $T_{min} \subseteq T$ for $T \in \mathcal{T}$,
- every set $T \subseteq N$ such that $T_{min} \subseteq T \subseteq T'$ for some $T' \in \mathcal{T}_{max}$ belongs to $\mathcal{T}$.

Thus, a tuft of sets $\mathcal{T}$ is determined by its unique least set T_{min} and by the class of its maximal sets $\mathcal{T}_{max}$. Alternatively, it can be described by T_{min} and the class $\{T' \setminus T_{min} ; T' \in \mathcal{T}_{max}\}$. More specifically, assume that $A \subseteq N$ and $\mathcal{B}$ is a non-empty class of incomparable subsets of $N \setminus A$, that is, there are no $B, B' \in \mathcal{B}$ with $B \subset B'$. Introduce a special notation:

$$\mathsf{TUFT}(A|\mathcal{B}) = \{T = A \cup C ; \exists B \in \mathcal{B} \ C \subseteq B\}.$$

Evidently, $\mathcal{T} = \mathsf{TUFT}(A|\mathcal{B})$ is a tuft such that $\mathcal{T}_{max} = \{A \cup B; B \in \mathcal{B}\}$ and $T_{min} = A$. Of course, every tuft of subsets of N can be described in this way.

Example 1. Suppose $N = \{a, b, c, d\}$ and put $A = \{a\}$. Consider the class $\mathcal{B} = \{\{b\}, \{c\}, \{d\}\}$ which is a class of incomparable subsets of $N \setminus A$ (actually, the sets in $\mathcal{B}$ are disjoint). Then $\mathsf{TUFT}(A|\mathcal{B})$ consists of four sets: $\{a\}, \{a, b\}, \{a, c\}$ and $\{a, d\}$. The tuft is shown in Fig. 1.

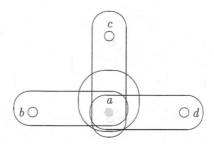

Fig. 1. A tuft of sets $\mathsf{TUFT}(\{a\}|\{b\},\{c\},\{d\})$

3 Upper Inclusion Neigbourhood

3.1 Description of Upper Neighbours

By the *upper neigbouhood* of an equivalence class $\mathcal{K}$ of Bayesian networks is understood the collection $o^\uparrow(\mathcal{K})$ of equivalence classes $\mathcal{L}$ such that $\mathcal{I}(\mathcal{K}) \sqsubset \mathcal{I}(\mathcal{L})$. It follows from Lemma 1 that each $K \in \mathcal{K}$ and each edge in K define together an element of $o^\uparrow(\mathcal{K})$ and every element of $o^\uparrow(\mathcal{K})$ is obtained in this way. Thus, the upper neigbourhood $o^\uparrow(\mathcal{K})$ is, in fact, described in terms of elements of $\mathcal{K}$. Nevertheless, the above described correspondence is not a one-to-one mapping because different elements of $\mathcal{K}$ may yield the same neighbouring class $\mathcal{L}$.

One the other hand, every neighbouring class is uniquely characterized by a certain pair $([a, b], C)$ where $a, b \in N$, $a \neq b$ and $C \subseteq N \setminus \{a, b\}$. The pair $([a, b], C)$ can be introduced in graphical terms as follows.

Let $\mathcal{K}$ be an equivalence class of Bayesian networks over N, $\mathcal{L} \in o^\uparrow(\mathcal{K})$. Choose $K \in \mathcal{K}$ and $L \in \mathcal{L}$ such that L is obtained from K by the removal of an arrow $a \to b$ in K. Then $\mathcal{L}$ will be described by the pair $([a, b], C)$ where $C = pa_K(b) \setminus \{a\}$.

To show that the definition above is consistent one has to show that the pair $([a, b], C)$ does not depend on the choice of K and L and that distinct pairs are ascribed to distinct upper neighbours.

Proposition 1. *Let $\mathcal{K}$ be an equivalence class of Bayesian networks, $\mathcal{L}_1, \mathcal{L}_2 \in o^\uparrow(\mathcal{K})$. Suppose, for $i = 1, 2$, that graphs $K_i \in \mathcal{K}$ and $L_i \in \mathcal{L}_i$ are given such that L_i is made of K_i by the removal of an arrow $a_i \to b_i$ in K_i and $C_i = pa_{K_i}(b_i) \setminus \{a_i\}$. Then $\mathcal{L}_1 = \mathcal{L}_2$ iff $[\{a_1, b_1\} = \{a_2, b_2\}$ and $C_1 = C_2]$.*

The proof of Proposition 1, which can be found in the exteded version of this paper, is based on a special arithmetic characterization of equivalence of Bayesian networks. Note that one can perhaps also prove this result using purely graphical tools, but the given proof is more elegant.

Example 2. To illustrate concepts introduced above let us consider an equivalence class $\mathcal{K}$ of Bayesian networks over $N = \{a, b, c, d, e\}$ shown in the lower

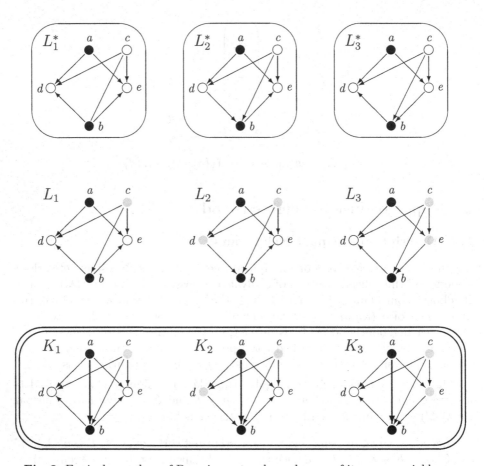

Fig. 2. Equivalence class of Bayesian networks and some of its upper neighbours

layer of Fig. 2. For every $i = 1, 2, 3$, an acyclic directed graph L_i is obtained from $K_i \in \mathcal{K}$ by the removal of the arrow $a \to b$ (see the medium layer of the figure). In this example, each of K_i, $i = 1, 2, 3$ establishes a different neighbouring class $\mathcal{L}_i \in o^{\uparrow}(\mathcal{K})$ - the respective essential graphs are in the upper layer of Fig. 2. Since $pa_{K_2}(b) \setminus \{a\} = \{c, d\}$, the equivalence class containing L_2 is characterized by the pair $([a, b], \{c, d\})$.

Remark 3. The pair $([a, b], C)$ describing uniquely an upper neighbour $\mathcal{L} \in o^{\uparrow}(\mathcal{K})$ was introduced in terms of individual networks from $\mathcal{K}$ and $\mathcal{L}$. If $\mathcal{K}$ and $\mathcal{L}$ are represented by the respective essential graphs K^* and L^* then $[a, b]$ is simply the edge of K^* which is not an edge in L^*. The question of how to define C in terms of K^* and L^* have not been examined so far by the author. On the other hand, the pair $([a, b], C)$ is obtained immediately if $\mathcal{K}$ and $\mathcal{L}$ are represented by means of their standard imsets - see [13].

3.2 Characterization of Upper Neighbourhood

Given an equivalence class $\mathcal{K}$ the next step is to characterize those pairs $([a, b], C)$ which define elements $L \in o^{\uparrow}(\mathcal{K})$. In this section, this task is answered for a fixed unordered pair of distinct nodes $[a, b]$. For this purpose, put

$$\mathcal{C}_{\mathcal{K}}^{-}(a \to b) = \{ C; \ \exists K \in \mathcal{K} \text{ such that } a \to b \text{ in } K \text{ and } C = pa_K(b) \setminus \{a\} \}$$

for every ordered pair of distinct nodes (a, b). It follows from what it says in Sect. 3.1 that $\mathcal{C}_{\mathcal{K}}^{-}(a \to b) \cup \mathcal{C}_{\mathcal{K}}^{-}(b \to a)$ is the class of sets which has to be characterized. Therefore, given (a, b), one needs to find out when $\mathcal{C}_{\mathcal{K}}^{-}(a \to b)$ is non-empty and describe that collection if it is non-empty.

Proposition 2. *Let $\mathcal{K}$ be an equivalence class of Bayesian networks, K^* the essential graph of $\mathcal{K}$ and (a, b) an ordered pair of distinct nodes of K^*. Put $P = pa_{K^*}(b) \setminus \{a\}$ and $M = \{c \in ne_{K^*}(b) \setminus \{a\}; \ [a, c] \text{ is an edge in } K^*\}$. Then*

(i) $\mathcal{C}_{\mathcal{K}}^{-}(a \to b) \neq \emptyset$ *iff $[a, b]$ is an edge in K^* and $b \notin pa_{K^*}(a)$, that is, either $a \to b$ in K^* or $a - b$ in K^*.*
(ii) *If $a \to b$ in K^* or $a - b$ in K^* then $\mathcal{C}_{\mathcal{K}}^{-}(a \to b) = \mathsf{TUFT}(P | cliques(K_M^*))$ where $cliques(K_\emptyset^*) = \{\emptyset\}$ by convention.*

The proof is given in the extended version of this paper.

Corollary 1. *Let $\mathcal{K}$ be an equivalence class of Bayesian networks over N, K^* the essential graph of $\mathcal{K}$ and $[a, b]$ an edge in K^*. Then the collection of those sets $C \subseteq N \setminus \{a, b\}$ such that $([a, b], C)$ describes an upper neighbour $L \in o^{\uparrow}(\mathcal{K})$ is a tuft $\mathsf{TUFT}(P | cliques(K_M^*))$ where*

(a) *if $a \to b$ in K^* then $P = pa_{K^*}(b) \setminus \{a\}$ and $M = ne_{K^*}(b)$,*
(b) *if $a \leftarrow b$ in K^* then $P = pa_{K^*}(a) \setminus \{b\}$ and $M = ne_{K^*}(a)$,*
(c) *if $a - b$ in K^* then $M = \{c \in N; a - c - b \text{ in } K^*\}$ and $P = pa_{K^*}(b) = pa_{K^*}(a)$.*

Proof. Recall that one needs to characterize $\mathcal{C}_{\mathcal{K}}^{-}(a \to b) \cup \mathcal{C}_{\mathcal{K}}^{-}(b \to a)$ using Proposition 2. In case (a) observe that $\mathcal{C}_{\mathcal{K}}^{-}(b \to a) = \emptyset$. As concerns $\mathcal{C}_{\mathcal{K}}^{-}(a \to b)$, the fact that K^* has no flags implies $M = ne_{K^*}(b)$. The case (b) is symmetric. In case (c) realize that the fact that K^* has no flags implies $pa_{K^*}(b) = pa_{K^*}(a)$. This observation and the fact that K^* is a chain graph allow one to show that $\mathcal{C}_{\mathcal{K}}^{-}(a \to b) = \mathcal{C}_{\mathcal{K}}^{-}(b \to a) \neq \emptyset$.

Example 3. To illustrate the previous result consider the essential graphs shown in Fig. 3. The case (a) from Corollary 1 occurs for the graph K^* in the left-hand picture of the figure. More specifically, one has $P = \{c\}$, $M = \{d, e\}$ and $cliques(K_M^*) = \{ \{d\}, \{e\} \}$. Thus, the class of sets $C \subseteq N \setminus \{a, b\}$ such that $([a, b], C)$ describes an upper neighbour of the respective equivalence class is $\mathsf{TUFT}(\{c\} | \{d\}, \{e\})$, that is, the class which involves three sets: $\{c\}$, $\{c, d\}$ and $\{c, e\}$. Indeed, it was shown in Example 2 that those upper neighbours of the

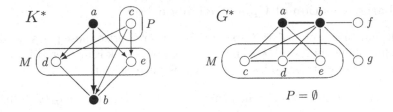

Fig. 3. Two essential graphs

respective equivalence class which "correspond" to the "removal" of $a \to b$ are characterized by pairs $([a,b],\{c\})$, $([a,b],\{c,d\})$ and $([a,b],\{c,e\})$.

If the graph G^* in the right-hand picture of Fig. 3 is considered then the case (c) from Corollary 1 occurs. One has $P = \emptyset$, $M = \{c,d,e\}$ and $cliques(G_M^*) = \{\{c,d\},\{d,e\}\}$. The respective class $\mathsf{TUFT}(\emptyset|\{c,d\},\{d,e\})$ has five sets: $\emptyset$, $\{c\}$, $\{d\}$, $\{e\}$, $\{c,d\}$ and $\{d,e\}$.

4   Conclusions

In this contribution a characterization of the upper inclusion neighbourhood was presented. Analogous results for the lower inclusion neighbourhood have also been achieved and they will be presented in a later paper [15]. Note that lower neighbours of a given equivalence class of Bayesian networks over N can also be described uniquely by pairs $([a,b],C)$ where $a,b \in N$, $a \neq b$ and $C \subseteq N \setminus \{a,b\}$ and that, given $[a,b]$, the class of sets C which correspond to lower neighbours is the union of two tufts which can be characterized in terms of the respective essential graph. An important fact is that if $\mathcal{I}(\mathcal{K}) \sqsubset \mathcal{I}(\mathcal{L})$ then the pair $([a,b],C)$ describing $\mathcal{L}$ as one of the upper neighbours of $\mathcal{K}$ coincides with the pair $([a,b],C)$ which describes $\mathcal{K}$ as one of the lower neighbours of $\mathcal{L}$. Thus, there is internal consistency of both characterizations and the pair $([a,b],C)$ can be viewed as a natural characteristic of the 'move' between $\mathcal{K}$ and $\mathcal{L}$.

As explained in Sect. 1 the presented characterization is more elegant than the previous ones. Indeed, Chickering [5] only gave a tentative algorithmic method and Auvrey and Wehenkel [2] characterized every inclusion neighbour by an unordered pair of nodes and by an opaque collection of immoralities, namely those which are either created or cancelled if an equivalence class is replaced by its inclusion neighbour. Finally, the characterization presented in this paper has a close connection to an arithmetic method of description of equivalence clases of Bayesian networks (from Chapter 8 of [13]) and leads to conditional independence interpretation of 'moves' in the method of local search.

References

1. Andersson, S.A., Madigan, D. and Perlman, M.D.: A characterization of Markov equivalence classes for acyclic digraphs. *Annals of Statistics* 25 (1997) 505–541.

2. Auvray, V. and Wehenkel, L.: On the construction of the inclusion boundary neighbourhood for Markov equivalence clases of Bayesian network structures. In: Darwiche, A. and Friedman, N. (eds.): Uncertainty in Artificial Intelligence 18. Morgan Kaufmann, San Francisco (2002) 26–35.
3. Bouckaert, R.R.: Bayesian belief networks: from construction to inference. PhD thesis, University of Utrecht (1995).
4. Castelo, R.: The discrete acyclic digraph Markov model in data mining. PhD thesis, University of Utrecht (2002).
5. Chickering, D.M.: Optimal structure identification with greedy search. To appear in *Journal of Machine Learning Research* (2003).
6. Frydenberg, M.: The chain graph Markov property. *Scandinavian Journal of Statistics* 17 (1990) 333–353.
7. Kočka, T. and Castello, R.: Improved learning of Bayesian networks. In: Breese, J. and Koller, D. (eds.): Uncertainty in Artificial Intelligence 17. Morgan Kaufmann, San Francisco (2001) 269–276.
8. Lauritzen, S.L.: Graphical Models. Clarendon Press, Oxford (1996).
9. Meek, C.: Graphical models, selectin causal and statistical models. PhD thesis, Carnegie Mellon University (1997).
10. Pearl, J.: Probabilistic Reasoning in Intelligent Systems: Networks of Plausible Inference. Morgan Kaufmann, San Mateo (1988).
11. Rovenato, A.: A unified approach to the characterisation of equivalence classes of DAGs, chain graphs with no flags and chain graphs. Technical report, Dipartimento di Scienze Sociali Cognitive e Quantitative, University of Modena and Reggio Emilia (2003), submitted to *Annals of Statistics*.
12. Studený, M.: A recovery algorithm for chain graphs. *International Journal of Approximate Reasoning* 17 (1997) 265–293.
13. Studený, M.: On probabilistic conditional independence structures. A research monograph, Institute of Information Theory and Automation, Prague, Czech Republic (2003), offered to *Springer Verlag*.
14. Studený, M.: Characterization of essential graphs by means of an operation of legal merging of components. Submitted to *International Journal of Uncertainty, Fuzziness and Knowledge-based Systems*.
15. Studený, M.: Characterization of inclusion neighbourhood in terms of the essential graph: lower neighbours. In preparation, to be submitted to Proceedings of WUPES 2003.
16. Verma, T. and Pearl, J.: Equivalence and synthesis of causal models. In: Bonissone, P.P., Henrion, M., Kanal L.N. and Lemmer, J.F. (eds.): Uncertainty in Artificial Intelligence 6. Elsevier, New York (1991) 220–227.

Approximating Conditional MTE Distributions by Means of Mixed Trees[*]

Serafín Moral[1], Rafael Rumí[2], and Antonio Salmerón[2]

[1] Dept. Ciencias de la Computación e Inteligencia Artificial
Universidad de Granada, 18071 Granada, Spain
smc@decsai.ugr.es
[2] Dept. Estadística y Matemática Aplicada
Universidad de Almería, 04120 Almería, Spain
{rrumi,Antonio.Salmeron}@ual.es

Abstract. Mixtures of truncated exponential (MTE) distributions have been shown to be a powerful alternative to discretisation within the framework of Bayesian networks. One of the features of the MTE model is that standard propagation algorithms as Shenoy-Shafer and Lazy propagation can be used. Estimating conditional MTE densities from data is a rather difficult problem since, as far as we know, such densities cannot be expressed in parametric form in the general case. In the univariate case, regression-based estimators have been successfully employed. In this paper, we propose a method to estimate conditional MTE densities using mixed trees, which are graphical structures similar to classification trees. Criteria for selecting the variables during the construction of the tree and for pruning the leaves are defined in terms of the mean square error and entropy-like measures.

1 Introduction

Bayesian networks have been widely employed to reason under uncertainty in systems involving many variables where the uncertainty is represented in terms of a multivariate probability distribution. The structure of the network encodes the independence relationships amongst the variables, so that the network actually induces a factorisation of the joint distribution which allow the definition of efficient algorithms for probabilistic inference [2,5,6,10,13].

The algorithms mentioned above are, in principle, designed for discrete variables. However, in many practical applications, it is common to find problems in which discrete and continuous variables appear simultaneously. Some methods approach this kind of problems for special models as, for instance, the conditional Gaussian distribution [4,9], but the most general solution was to discretise the continuous variables and then proceed using algorithms for discrete variables [3].

Recently, an alternative to discretisation has been proposed, based on the use of MTE distributions. The usefulness of MTE models can be understood

---

[*] This work has been supported by the Spanish Ministry of Science and Technology, project Elvira II (TIC2001-2973-C05-01 and 02)

T.D. Nielsen and N.L. Zhang (Eds.): ECSQARU 2003, LNAI 2711, pp. 173–183, 2003.
© Springer-Verlag Berlin Heidelberg 2003

if we realise that discretising a variable or a set of variables can be regarded as approximating its distribution by a mixture of uniforms, and that standard propagation algorithms in fact are able to work with mixtures of uniforms. If we could use, instead of uniforms, other distributions with higher fitting power and verifying that standard propagation algorithms remain valid, then discretisation would not necessarily be the best choice. This is the motivation of MTE models. Propagation in Bayesian networks with MTE distributions was shown to be correct for the Shenoy-Shafer architecture and for MCMC simulation algorithms in [7], and a method for estimating univariate MTE distributions from data was proposed in [8].

However, a complete specification of a Bayesian network requires not only univariate distributions for the root nodes but conditional distributions for the others as well. In this paper, we propose a method to estimate conditional MTE densities using mixed trees [7], which are graphical structures similar to classification trees [11].

This article continues with a description of the MTE model in Sect. 2. The representation based on mixed trees can be found in Sect. 3. Section 4 contains the formulation of the method proposed here for constructing mixed trees, which is illustrated with some experiments reported in Sect. 5. The paper ends with conclusions in Sect. 6.

2   The MTE Model

Throughout this paper, random variables will be denoted by capital letters, and their values by lowercase letters. In the multi-dimensional case, boldfaced characters will be used. The domain of the variable $\mathbf{X}$ is denoted by $\Omega_{\mathbf{X}}$. The MTE model is defined by its corresponding potential and density as follows [7]:

Definition 1. (MTE potential) *Let $\mathbf{X}$ be a mixed n-dimensional random variable. Let $\mathbf{Y} = (Y_1, \ldots, Y_d)$ and $\mathbf{Z} = (Z_1, \ldots, Z_c)$ be the discrete and continuous parts of $\mathbf{X}$ respectively, with $c + d = n$. We say that a function $f : \Omega_{\mathbf{X}} \mapsto \mathbb{R}_0^+$ is a mixture of truncated exponentials potential (MTE potential) if one of the next two conditions holds:*

i. *f can be written as*

$$f(\mathbf{x}) = f(\mathbf{y}, \mathbf{z}) = a_0 + \sum_{i=1}^{m} a_i \exp \left\{ \sum_{j=1}^{d} b_i^{(j)} y_j + \sum_{k=1}^{c} b_i^{(d+k)} z_k \right\} \quad (1)$$

for all $\mathbf{x} \in \Omega_{\mathbf{X}}$, where a_i, $i = 0, \ldots, m$ and $b_i^{(j)}$, $i = 1, \ldots, m$, $j = 1, \ldots, n$ are real numbers.

ii. *There is a partition $\Omega_1, \ldots, \Omega_k$ of $\Omega_{\mathbf{X}}$ verifying that the domain of the continuous variables, $\Omega_{\mathbf{Z}}$, is divided into hypercubes and such that f is defined as*

$$f(\mathbf{x}) = f_i(\mathbf{x}) \quad \text{if} \quad \mathbf{x} \in \Omega_i ,$$

where each f_i, $i = 1, \ldots, k$ can be written in the form of equation (1).

Example 1. The function ϕ defined as

$$\phi(z_1, z_2) = \begin{cases} 2 + e^{3z_1 + z_2} + e^{z_1 + z_2} & \text{if } 0 < z_1 \le 1,\ 0 < z_2 < 2 \\ 1 + e^{z_1 + z_2} & \text{if } 0 < z_1 \le 1,\ 2 \le z_2 < 3 \\ \dfrac{1}{4} + e^{2z_1 + z_2} & \text{if } 1 < z_1 < 2,\ 0 < z_2 < 2 \\ \dfrac{1}{2} + 5e^{z_1 + 2z_2} & \text{if } 1 < z_1 < 2,\ 2 \le z_2 < 3 \end{cases}$$

is an MTE potential since each of its parts are MTE potentials.

Definition 2. (MTE density) *An MTE potential f is an MTE density if*

$$\sum_{y \in \Omega_Y} \int_{\Omega_z} f(\mathbf{y}, \mathbf{z}) d\mathbf{z} = 1 \ .$$

In a Bayesian network, we find two types of densities:

1. For each variable X which is a root of the network, a density $f(x)$ is given.
2. For each variable X with parents $\mathbf{Y}$, a conditional density $f(x|\mathbf{y})$ is given.

A *conditional MTE density* $f(x|\mathbf{y})$ is an MTE potential $f(x, \mathbf{y})$ such that fixing $\mathbf{y}$ to each of its possible values, the resulting function is a density for X.

3   Mixed Trees

In [7] a data structure was proposed to represent MTE potentials: the so-called *mixed probability trees* or mixed trees for short. The formal definition is as follows:

Definition 3. (Mixed tree) *We say that a tree $\mathcal{T}$ is a mixed tree if it meets the following conditions:*

i. *Every internal node represents a random variable (either discrete or continuous).*
ii. *Every arc outgoing from a continuous variable Z is labeled with an interval of values of Z, so that the domain of Z is the union of the intervals corresponding to the arcs Z-outgoing.*
iii. *Every discrete variable has a number of outgoing arcs equal to its number of states.*
iv. *Each leaf node contains an MTE potential defined on variables in the path from the root to that leaf.*

Mixed trees can represent MTE potentials defined by parts. Each entire branch in the tree determines one sub-region of the space where the potential is defined, and the function stored in the leaf of a branch is the definition of the potential in the corresponding sub-region.

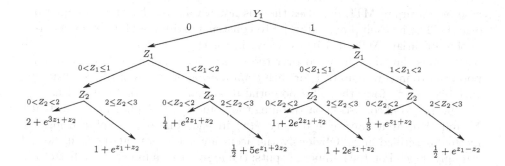

Fig. 1. A mixed probability tree representing the potential ϕ in example 2

Example 2. Consider the following MTE potential, defined for a discrete variable (Y_1) and two continuous variables (Z_1 and Z_2).

$$\phi(y_1, z_1, z_2) = \begin{cases} 2 + e^{3z_1+z_2} & \text{if } y_1 = 0, \ 0 < z_1 \leq 1, \ 0 < z_2 < 2 \\[2mm] 1 + e^{z_1+z_2} & \text{if } y_1 = 0, \ 0 < z_1 \leq 1, \ 2 \leq z_2 < 3 \\[2mm] \dfrac{1}{4} + e^{2z_1+z_2} & \text{if } y_1 = 0, \ 1 < z_1 < 2, \ 0 < z_2 < 2 \\[2mm] \dfrac{1}{2} + 5e^{z_1+2z_2} & \text{if } y_1 = 0, \ 1 < z_1 < 2, \ 2 \leq z_2 < 3 \\[2mm] 1 + 2e^{2z_1+z_2} & \text{if } y_1 = 1, \ 0 < z_1 \leq 1, \ 0 < z_2 < 2 \\[2mm] 1 + 2e^{z_1+z_2} & \text{if } y_1 = 1, \ 0 < z_1 \leq 1, \ 2 \leq z_2 < 3 \\[2mm] \dfrac{1}{3} + e^{z_1+z_2} & \text{if } y_1 = 1, \ 1 < z_1 < 2, \ 0 < z_2 < 2 \\[2mm] \dfrac{1}{2} + e^{z_1-z_2} & \text{if } y_1 = 1, \ 1 < z_1 < 2, \ 2 \leq z_2 < 3 \end{cases}$$

A possible representation of this potential by means of a mixed probability tree is displayed in Fig. 1.

The operations required for probability propagation in Bayesian networks (restriction, marginalisation and combination) can be carried out by means of algorithms very similar to those described, for instance in [3,12].

4   Constructing Mixed Trees from Data

The aim of this paper is to describe a method to construct, from a database, a conditional MTE density $f(x|\mathbf{y})$ for each family in the network, where X denotes the child variable and $\mathbf{Y}$ its parents. A first approach to estimate conditional MTE densities from data could be the application of a standard estimation procedure as, for instance, maximum likelihood (ML). However, even in the case of univariate MTE densities there is not a way to solve the ML equations exactly. The method proposed in [8] to construct estimators for the parameters of the univariate MTE density is not valid for the conditional case, since more restrictions should be imposed over the parameters in order to force the MTE potential to integrate up to 1 for each combination of values of the conditioning variables, i.e. to force the MTE potential to actually be a conditional density.

Our proposal consists of partitioning the domain of the conditioning variables Y and then fit a univariate density $f(x)$ in each one of the splits using the method described in [8]. Obviously, the accuracy of the estimated density would strongly depend on the number of splits: the higher this number is the better the fitting power becomes. Nevertheless, another factor that always determines the goodness of fit is the sample size. If the number of splits is too high, the subset of the sample that would be used to estimate the density in each region may be too small or even of size zero. This argument must be taken into account when deciding where to partition the domain.

The process of splitting the domain of the variables in Y can be seen as constructing a mixed tree where each internal node is a variable $Y_j \in Y$ and finally each leaf will contain an MTE density for the variable X in the split determined by the branch of the tree that leads to it. In order to design an algorithm to construct the tree, the following issues must be addressed:

1. *Selection of the variable to expand.* Similarly to the case of probability trees [12], it can help to construct smaller trees without loss of accuracy.
2. *Determination of the splits of the selected variable.* The ideal is to select the cut-points of the domain in such a way that the data best fits to an MTE density in each split. Trying to evaluate this is not an easy task and, furthermore, may be too costly, since we think that an optimal partitioning strategy should consider aspects like the remaining sample size in each part and the accuracy of the models fitted with respect to different partitions, in order to choose the best. This can be regarded as an optimisation problem in which each movement through the search space requires the estimation of new MTE densities and the evaluation of their accuracy. That is why we have decided to partition the domain in equal width intervals, being the number of splits a parameter given by the user according to the available resources.
3. *Definition of a criterion to stop branching the tree.* Again, following the guidelines in [12], we propose to expand the tree until the number of leaves does not surpass a threshold which is given by the user, again taking into account the available resources.
4. *Pruning the tree.* Once the tree has been constructed, it is useful to have a method to reduce its size by pruning branches which are equal or very similar. In fact this is not very useful during the learning stage, but when the learnt network is used for probability propagation, the combination operation can produce very large trees, which might lead the computer to run out of memory.

In the next section we shall study some of the issues above in more detail.

4.1   Selection of the Variable to Expand

The initial step in the construction of the tree we are looking for is to build a tree consisting of only a leaf, which is an MTE density fitted to the entire database, i.e. the conditional distribution $f(x|\mathbf{y})$ is considered to be the same for every value $\mathbf{y}$. Then, the variable selected to expand the tree is that one which divides the domain of $\mathbf{Y}$ into more different sub-regions, understanding the difference among the sub-regions as the goodness of fit of the current conditional density $f(x|\mathbf{y})$ in each of them. The idea behind this criterion is to avoid expanding the tree when no gain in accuracy is achieved.

In order to determine how different the goodness of fit among the different splits is, we use the following measure, called *splitting gain*.

Definition 4. (Splitting gain) *Let $f(x)$ be the MTE density for the target variable X in a leaf of a mixed tree which is to be expanded. Let $W \in \mathbf{Y}$ be a variable not already expanded in the current branch of the tree, and $D_1, \ldots, D_j$ the splits into which the domain of $\mathbf{Y}$ would be partitioned if we expanded by W. Let $e_1, \ldots, e_j$ denote the normalised mean squared error between $f(x)$ and the empirical histogram of variable X in $D_1, \ldots, D_j$ respectively. We define the splitting gain of variable W in a function $f(x)$ as*

$$SG(f, W) = \sum_{i=1}^{j} e_i \log e_i \; . \tag{2}$$

This measure, which is similar to the entropy of a probability distribution, is equal to $-\log j$ if the normalised errors are uniform, and equal to 0 if all the normalised errors are 0 but one, which is equal to 1. Our proposal is to expand by the variable maximising the splitting gain. If the gain is vary low, it means that the error in the different splits is the same, i.e., a single MTE desity fits the data in the different splits with the same accuracy. It suggests that there is no need to split that variable, since the fitted models in each region would be the same. On the contrary, a high value of SG (close to zero) means that the function fits badly at least in one of the splits, while in the others the performance is good. In this case it is worthy to expand that variable, since the new functions will be more accurate.

4.2   The Learning Algorithm

In order to sum up what we have presented in this section, we describe the algorithm to construct a mixed tree with at most M leaves for the conditional density of a variable X given its parents $\mathbf{Y}$, from a database D, and splitting the domain of each variable into j parts.

LEARN_MIXED_TREE(D,X,Y,M,j)

1. Fit an MTE density $f(x)$ for variable X to the data in D using the method described in [8].
2. If the number of leaves in the tree is lower than M,
   a) Choose the variable $W \in Y$ such that

$$W = \text{argmax}_{W \in Y} SG(W) \ .$$

   b) Split the domain of W into j parts.
   c) Split D into j parts $D_1, \dots, D_j$ according to the partition of W.
   d) For $i = 1$ to j
      LEARN_MIXED_TREE(D_i,X,$Y \setminus \{W\}$,M,j).

4.3 Pruning the Tree

Pruning a mixed tree consists of choosing a variable whose children are leaves (i.e. functions) and replace it and its children by a single function which is fitted again to joined resulting domain. We define the error of pruning in the following way:

Definition 5. (Error of pruning) *Let W be a variable in a mixed tree with children $f_1(x), \dots, f_j(x)$. Let D_W be the subset of the database corresponding to values compatible with the branch that leads to W, and D_{W_i}, $i = 1 \dots, j$ the partition of D_W induced by the split of W. Let e_i, $i = 1 \dots, j$ be the mean squared errors of f_i with respect to the empirical histograms for the variable X in D_{W_i}, $i = 1, \dots, j$. Let $f(x)$ be an MTE density fitted to the data in D_W and e the mean squared error for $f(x)$ in D_W. We define the error of pruning the variable W as*

$$EP(W) = e - \sum_{i=1}^{j} e_i \ . \tag{3}$$

There are two ways of carrying out the pruning:

1. Sequentially select a variable W minimising $EP(W)$ and prune it until the size of the tree (its number of leaves) is reduced to a given threshold (specified by the user).
2. Prune all the leaves W for which $EP(W) < \epsilon$, where $\epsilon > 0$ is an error threshold given by the user.

5 Experiments

In order to illustrate how the algorithm works we shall describe in this section the results of fitting a mixed tree to a conditional normal distribution. The experiment was conducted as follows.

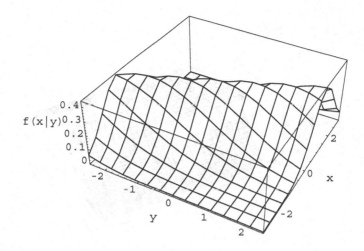

Fig. 2. The density function of a $\mathcal{N}(0.5y, \sqrt{0.75})$ distribution

We consider a pair of random variables X and Y following a bivariate normal distribution with means vector $\vec{\mu} = (0,0)$ and covariance matrix

$$\mathrm{Cov}(X,Y) = \begin{pmatrix} 1 & 0.5 \\ 0.5 & 1 \end{pmatrix} ,$$

which means that the covariance is $\sigma_{XY} = 0.5$, the marginal of Y is $\mathcal{N}(0,1)$ and the conditional distribution of X given Y is $\mathcal{N}(0.5y, \sqrt{0.75})$. The conditional density corresponding to this distribution is displayed in Fig. 2.

Then we generated a sample of 500 values of X from the conditional distribution. In order to simulate a value for X, first a value for Y is drawn from the $\mathcal{N}(0,1)$ distribution and then a value for X is drawn from $\mathcal{N}(0.5y, \sqrt{0.75})$, replacing y by the simulated value. We have run the algorithm with 2, 3, 4 and 5 number of splits when branching a variable. The fitted conditional densities are displayed in Figs. 3, 4, 5, and 6.

It can be seen how the accuracy of the estimated density increases as the number of splits grows.

6   Conclusions

We have proposed a method for estimating conditional MTE densities from data. This work, together with [8] allows to learn the distributions in a Bayesian network, either marginal or conditional. The model has shown to be adequate for fitting some well known conditional models as the conditional normal distribution.

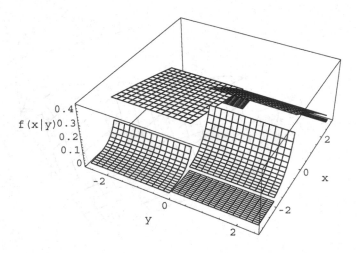

Fig. 3. Fitted density taking two splits per variable

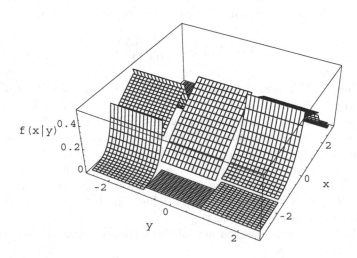

Fig. 4. Fitted density taking three splits per variable

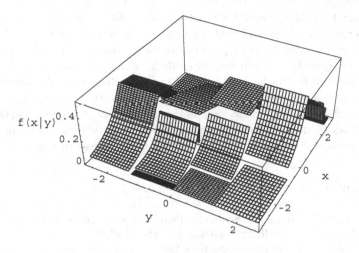

Fig. 5. Fitted density taking four splits per variable

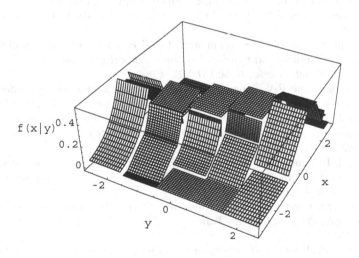

Fig. 6. Fitted density taking five splits per variable

However, some work yet remains to be done. A thorough experimental testing is necessary to actually check the practical value of the algorithm. The problem is that experiments with models which involve many variables are difficult to report (plots are not possible). So we plan to randomly generate mixed trees and then generate samples from them and estimate new mixed trees from the samples. The goodness of fit can be measured using the Kullback-Leibler divergence.

Furthermore, the performance of mixed trees during the propagation is another open field. An important issue in this framework is the pruning of the tree, which allows to define approximate propagation algorithms, perhaps based on importance sampling [12] or in ideas related to Penniless propagation [1].

References

1. A. Cano, S. Moral, and A. Salmerón. Penniless propagation in join trees. *International Journal of Intelligent Systems*, 15:1027–1059, 2000.
2. F.V. Jensen, S.L. Lauritzen, and K.G. Olesen. Bayesian updating in causal probabilistic networks by local computation. *Computational Statistics Quarterly*, 4:269–282, 1990.
3. D. Kozlov and D. Koller. Nonuniform dynamic discretization in hybrid networks. In D. Geiger and P.P. Shenoy, editors, *Proceedings of the 13th Conference on Uncertainty in Artificial Intelligence*, pages 302–313. Morgan & Kaufmann, 1997.
4. S.L. Lauritzen. Propagation of probabilities, means and variances in mixed graphical association models. *Journal of the American Statistical Association*, 87:1098–1108, 1992.
5. S.L. Lauritzen and D.J. Spiegelhalter. Local computations with probabilities on graphical structures and their application to expert systems. *Journal of the Royal Statistical Society, Series B*, 50:157–224, 1988.
6. A.L. Madsen and F.V. Jensen. Lazy propagation: a junction tree inference algorithm based on lazy evaluation. *Artificial Intelligence*, 113:203–245, 1999.
7. S. Moral, R. Rumí, and A. Salmerón. Mixtures of truncated exponentials in hybrid Bayesian networks. In *Lecture Notes in Artificial Intelligence*, volume 2143, pages 135–143, 2001.
8. S. Moral, R. Rumí, and A. Salmerón. Estimating mixtures of truncated exponentials from data. In *Proceedings of the First European Workshop on Probabilistic Graphical Models*, pages 156–167, 2002.
9. K.G. Olesen. Causal probabilistic networks with both discrete and continuous variables. *IEEE Transactions on Pattern Analysis and Machine Intelligence*, 15:275–279, 1993.
10. J. Pearl. *Probabilistic reasoning in intelligent systems*. Morgan-Kaufmann (San Mateo), 1988.
11. J.R. Quinlan. Induction of decision trees. *Machine Learning*, 1:81–106, 1986.
12. A. Salmerón, A. Cano, and S. Moral. Importance sampling in Bayesian networks using probability trees. *Computational Statistics and Data Analysis*, 34:387–413, 2000.
13. P.P. Shenoy and G. Shafer. Axioms for probability and belief function propagation. In R.D. Shachter, T.S. Levitt, J.F. Lemmer, and L.N. Kanal, editors, *Uncertainty in Artificial Intelligence 4*, pages 169–198. North Holland, Amsterdam, 1990.

Effective Dimensions of Partially Observed Polytrees

Tomáš Kočka[1] and Nevin L. Zhang[2]

[1] Aalborg University, Denmark
kocka@cs.auc.dk
[2] Hong Kong University of Science and Technology, Hong Kong, China
lzhang@cs.ust.hk

Abstract. Model complexity is an important factor to consider when selecting among graphical models. When all variables are observed, the complexity of a model can be measured by its standard dimension, i.e. the number of independent parameters. When latent variables are present, however, the standard dimension might no longer be appropriate. Instead, an effective dimension should be used [5]. Zhang & Kočka [13] showed how to compute the effective dimensions of partially observed trees. In this paper we solve the same problem for partially observed polytrees.

1 Introduction

Learning graphical models from data has been widely studied in recent years. Two approaches have been developed. One approach builds models based on statistical independence tests. The other approach searches, in a space of models, the model that maximizes a certain scoring function.

From the Bayesian perspective, a natural scoring function is the marginal likelihood of model given data. In [4], Cooper and Herskovits gave a formula for computing the Bayesian score in the case of complete data. At the same time, they showed that exact computation of the score is intractable when latent variables are present. In such cases asymptotic approximations of the marginal likelihood such as the Bayesian Information Criterion (BIC) [10] and the Cheeseman-Stutz Criterion (CS) [3] are usually employed.

The BIC score has two parts: one evaluates the fit of the model to the data and the other penalizes the model according to its complexity. The complexity of a model is measured by use of the standard dimension, i.e. the number of independent parameters. However, the standard dimension might prove incorrect when latent variables are present. Consider the model $O \rightarrow H$ with two variables - observed variable O and latent variable H. All the parameters in $P(H|O)$ are irrelevant as they do not influence the fit of the model to the (observed) data. Thus, there is no reason to penalize the model for such parameters.

Reexamining the derivation of the BIC score, Geiger *et al.* [5] concluded that the standard dimension should be replaced by the *effective dimension*. They also showed that the effective dimension of a model is the rank of the Jacobian matrix

T.D. Nielsen and N.L. Zhang (Eds.): ECSQARU 2003, LNAI 2711, pp. 184–195, 2003.

of the transformation between the parameters of the model and the parameters of the distribution over the observed variables.

Effective dimension is useful for several reasons. First, BIC with effective dimension was in [5] shown to be an asymptotic approximation of the marginal likelihood at regular points, although it was later shown not to be so at singular points [9]. Second, the BIC and CS scores, when used together with standard dimension, can easily be shown to be inconsistent model selection criteria. When used with effective dimension, however, they are likely to be consistent mainly because of the close relationship between effective dimension and model inclusion (see Lemma 1).[1] Third, effective dimension fits perfectly into the penalization scheme in the AIC score [1]. Note that the AIC score has a quite different objective than the marginal likelihood. Fourth, effective dimension can be used to judge upon the identifiability of a model and its parameters. This approach is used, for example, in mark-recovery and capture-recapture studies [2].

The straightforward method of computing effective dimension has an exponential complexity in the number of observed nodes. The main concern of this paper is how to compute effective dimensions efficiently. For partially observed trees, this problem was solved in [13], where a theorem allowing a decomposition of the problem into the same problem for a set of latent class models was proved. The effective dimensions of latent class models can be computed either using the tight upper bound developed in [6] or by the direct computation of the rank of the Jacobian matrix. See also [11] and [12] for interesting special cases.

In this paper we present a solution for partially observed polytrees. In Sect. 2 we introduce our notations, definitions, special classes of models and known results concerning effective dimension. In Sect. 3 we show how to compute the effective dimension of a polytree consisting of a single latent node and its observed Markov boundary. We call such a polytree a primitive polytree and relate its effective dimension to some latent class model. We utilize a very special parameterization to obtain this result. Section 4 utilizes a result by Zhang & Kočka [13] to decompose polytrees using some of their observed nodes. Moreover it shows how to decompose polytrees further using their latent nodes. Thus we decompose any polytree into a set of primitive polytrees. We end by concluding in Sect. 5.

2   Basic Concepts

In this section we review basic concepts of graphs, graphical models and results concerning effective dimension of models with latent variables.

2.1   Graphs

A *graph* G is a pair (N, E), where N is a set of nodes and E is a set of edges, i.e. a subset of $N \times N$ of ordered pairs of distinct nodes. Each node $X \in N$, denoted

---

[1] The marginal likelihood has not been shown to be consistent for models with latent variables yet, either.

by an upper-case letter, represents a discrete random variable. We denote the number of states of a variable X by $|X|$ and a particular state of a variable X by a lower-case letter x. We often use a set of variables $R \subseteq N$ to represent a joint variable over its elements which has number of states $|R| = \prod_{X \in R} |X|$.

An *Acyclic Directed Graph* (DAG) is a graph where all edges are directed and there are no directed cycles. If a graph has a directed edge $A \to B$, then node A is *parent* of node B, i.e. $A \in Pa(B)$, and B is *child* of A, i.e. $B \in Ch(A)$. The union of a node's children and parents is called *neighbors*, i.e. $Ne(A) = Pa(A) \cup Ch(A)$. The union of parents, children and parents of children of a node is called the *Markov boundary*, i.e. $Mb(A) = Pa(A) \cup Ch(A) \cup_{Z \in Ch(A)} Pa(Z)$. A node A in a DAG is d-separated by its Markov boundary $Mb(A)$ from all other nodes (see [7] for the definition of d-separation).

2.2   Graphical Models

A *Bayesian network* is a pair (G, θ_G) where G is a DAG and θ_G are parameters. The parameters describe the conditional probability distribution $P(X|Pa(X))$ for each variable X given its parents $Pa(X)$. The standard dimension of a Bayesian network model is $ds(G) = \sum_{X \in N} (|X| - 1) * \prod_{Y \in Pa(X)} |Y|$, where N is the set of all nodes.

A Bayesian network represents a joint probability distribution $P(N|G, \theta_G)$ via the factorization formula $P(N|G, \theta_G) = \prod_{X \in N} P(X|pa(X))$. D-separation in G implies a conditional independence w.r.t the joint probability P. In particular, any node A is independent of all other nodes given its Markov boundary.

A model is *completely observed* if all its nodes are observed. Otherwise it is *partially observed*. The unobserved nodes are called *latent nodes*. A *Bayesian network model* $M(G)$ is the set of all joint probability distributions over the observed nodes that can be represented by any Bayesian network (G, θ_G).

We say that model M_1 *includes* model M_2 if for every parameterization θ_2 of M_2 there exists a parameterization θ_1 of M_1 such that M_1 and M_2 represent the same joint probability distribution over observed variables. Two models M_1 and M_2 are said to be *equivalent* if M_1 includes M_2 and M_2 includes M_1. Note that these definitions extend the standard ones by considering the possibility of having both latent and observed variables.

A Bayesian network model whose DAG is a rooted tree is in this paper referred to as a *tree model* or simply a *tree*. A *latent class* (LC) model is a special tree model that consists of one latent node and a number of observed nodes. In a tree model, each latent node and its neighbors form an LC model.

In a rooted tree, each node has at most one parent. In a polytree, a node may have multiple parents and there are no cycles. A *polytree model* or simply a *polytree* is a Bayesian network model whose DAG is a polytree. A *primitive polytree* (PP) is a polytree with one latent node H and a number of observed nodes consisting of the parents of H, the children of H, and the parents of the children of H. In a polytree, each latent node together with its Markov boundary forms a primitive polytree. A *compact polytree* (CP) model is a polytree where each observed node has either no children or just one child and no parents. Each

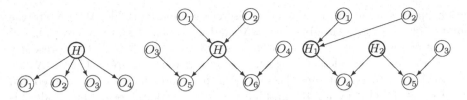

Fig. 1. Example of a) latent class, b) primitive polytree and c) compact polytree models

latent node in a CP model induces, together with its Markov boundary, a PP model. Examples of LC, PP, and CP models are shown in Fig. 1.

Note that all LC models are PP models and all PP models are CP models. This hierarchy of classes of models plays an important role in this paper.

A tree model is *regular* if for each latent node H holds $|H| \leq \frac{|Ne(H)|}{max_{Z \in Ne(H)}|Z|}$. Each irregular tree is equivalent to some regular tree, which can be obtained via a simple regularization process reducing the cardinality of the latent nodes concerned [6]. Thus, by computing the effective dimension for all regular trees one solves the problem for all trees.

2.3   Effective Dimension

In a (partially observed) graphical model G, the joint probability distribution $P(O)$ over the observed variables O depends on the parameters θ_G of the model. It can be viewed as a transformation from the parameters to the vector $(P(O_1), P(O_2), \ldots)$, where O_j is a combination of the values of the observed variables. As the parameters vary, the vector spans a subspace of an Euclidean space. The dimension of this subspace is defined to be the *effective dimension* of the model G [5]. We denote it by $de(G)$. The following lemma is obvious.

Lemma 1. *Let M_1 and M_2 be two graphical models having the same set of observed variables. If M_1 includes M_2 then $de(M_1) \geq de(M_2)$.*

We denote by $J_O(\theta_G) = [J_{jk}] = [\frac{\partial p(o_j)}{\partial \theta_k}]$ the Jacobian matrix of the aforementioned transformation. Rows of $J_O(\theta_G)$ correspond to states in the observed space O of the model G, columns to the parameters θ_G. Geiger *et al.* [5] showed that the *effective dimension* $de(G)$ of a model G is the rank of $J_O(\theta_G)$.

The *rank* of a matrix is the number of (row or column) vectors in a basis of the matrix. A *basis* is a set of linearly independent vectors such that all other vectors can be expressed as a linear combination of the vectors in the basis. Note that for any set of independent vectors there is always a basis which includes this set.

The rank of $J_O(\theta_G)$ is in general a function of θ_G but Geiger *et al.* [5] showed that it is constant almost everywhere, except a set of singular points having a zero measure, under the assumption that the model is parameterized in such a way that the joint probability distribution it represents is a polynomial function of the parameters. Therefore, two models M and M^* having the same parameters and model equation, where the parameters of M are subject to some additional inequality constraints compared to M^*, have the same effective dimension if the constrained parameters of M form a set of a positive measure in the space of parameters of M^*.

Geiger *et al.* [5] suggest the following numerical approach to compute the effective dimension of a model: generate a random θ, compute the Jacobian and its rank with sufficient numerical precision. We used this algorithm implemented in Matlab by Rusakov [8] to study the effective dimensions of some polytrees empirically.

Settimi & Smith [11] solved the effective dimension of latent class models with two observed nodes. Kočka & Zhang [6] derived a tight upper bound on the effective dimension of any latent class model.

The following theorem takes advantage of the above solution(s) for LC models and solves the problem of the effective dimension of a tree with latent variables.

Theorem 1. *[13] Let M be a regular partially observed tree model. Let M_i be the local LC model induced by a latent node H_i. Then the difference between the standard and effective dimensions of M equals the sum of the same differences over all the local models, i.e. $ds(M) - de(M) = \sum_{H_i} ds(M_i) - de(M_i)$, where the summation is over all latent nodes in the model.*

Moreover the following straightforward theorem proves essential in the next two sections.

Theorem 2. *[13] Let M be a graphical model over observed variables O and latent variables H. Let $S \subseteq O$ be a subset of the observed nodes such that there exist two nonempty sets of variables V_1 and V_2 where $V_1 \cap S = \emptyset$, $V_2 \cap S = \emptyset$, $V_1 \cup V_2 \cup S = O \cup H$ and $V_1 \perp\!\!\!\perp V_2 | S$ is true for any distribution encoded by the model M. Let M_0, M_1 and M_2 be the sub models induced in M by the sets S, $V_1 \cup S$ and $V_2 \cup S$. Then $de(M) = de(M_1) + de(M_2) - ds(M_0)$.*

3   Effective Dimension of Primitive Polytrees

In this section, we prove a theorem that relates the effective dimension of a PP model to that of an LC model. Consider the PP model in Fig. 2 (a). Denote it by M. Construct an LC model with a structure as shown in Fig. 2 (c) and where the number of states of variable Y is the product $|P_1||P_2|$ of those of variables P_1 and P_2, that of X_1 is $1 + (|C_1| - 1)||O_1|)$, and that of X_2 is $1 + (|C_2| - 1)||O_2|)$. Denote the LC model M_{LC}. According to the theorem, $de(M) = de(M_{LC}) + \sum_{i=1}^{2}(|O_i| - 1) + \sum_{i=1}^{2}(|P_i| - 1) + 1 - \prod_{i=1}^{2}|P_i|$.

Theorem 3. *Let M be a primitive polytree model. Let H be the unique latent node; P_i ($i = 1, \ldots, I$) be the parents of H; T_r ($r = 1, \ldots, R$) be those children of H that have only one parent, namely H; and C_j ($j = 1, \ldots, J$) be those children of H that have more than one parent. For each j, let $O_{k,j}$ ($k = 1, \ldots, K_j$) be the*

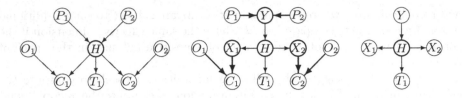

Fig. 2. a) primitive polytree model M, b) model M_X with the deterministic nodes X and Y introduced and c) latent class model M_{LC}

observed parents of C_j. Let M_{LC} be a latent class model with one latent variable H and observed variables Y, T_r $(r = 1, \ldots, R)$, and X_j $(j = 1, \ldots, J)$ where

$$|Y| = \prod_{i=1}^{I} |P_i|, \quad |X_j| = 1 + (|C_j| - 1) \prod_{k=1}^{K_j} |O_{k,j}| \ (j = 1, \ldots, J).$$

Then $de(M) = de(M_{LC}) + \sum_{j,k}(|O_{k,j}| - 1) + \sum_i(|P_i| - 1) + 1 - \prod_i |P_i|$.

Proof. We prove the theorem in two steps. First, we introduce a graphical model M_X with a special parameterization and show that $de(M) = de(M_X)$. Second, we use the latent class model M_{LC} and show that $de(M_X) = de(M_{LC}) + 1 + \sum_{j,k}(|O_{k,j}| - 1) + \sum_i(|P_i| - 1) - \prod_i |P_i|$. We sometimes denote by O_j the Cartesian product over all $O_{k,j}$ and similarly by P the same over all P_i.

The model M_X is obtained from the model M by the introduction of a new latent variable Y and new latent variables X_j for each node C_j. The parameters $P(Y|P)$ are fixed in such a deterministic way that there is a one-to-one correspondence between the values of Y and the values of the Cartesian product of all P_i. The parameters of each $P(C_j|X_j, O_j)$ are fixed in a deterministic way, too. Thus, these "parameters" are in fact not parameters of the model M_X. We denote each state of X_j (except one state) by a pair of numbers (c^*, o^*) where $c^* \in\, < 1, |C_j| - 1 >$ and $o^* \in\, < 1, |O_j| >$. The last state of X_j is denoted by a number $c' = |C_j|$. The four states of the node X_j in the example in Table 1 are $\{(1,1), (1,2), (1,3), 2\}$ in this notation. We set the $P(C_j|X_j, O_j)$ in this way: $p(C_j = c|X_j = c', O_j) = 1$ if $c = c'$; and $p(C_j = c|X_j = (c^*, o^*), O_j = o) = 1$ if $((c = c^*$ and $o = o^*)$ or $(c = c'$ and $o \neq o^*))$. All other probabilities in $P(C_j|X_j, O_j)$ are zero. An example of such a distribution is in Table 1.

Table 1. Example of the deterministic distribution $P(C_j|X_j, O_j)$ in the model M_X for $|O_j| = 3$, $|C_j| = 2$ and thus $|X_j| = 4$

$X_j =$	(1,1)			(1,2)			(1,3)			(2)		
$O_j =$	1	2	3	1	2	3	1	2	3	1	2	3
$C_j = 1$	1	0	0	0	1	0	0	0	1	0	0	0
$C_j = 2$	0	1	1	1	0	1	1	1	0	1	1	1

Consider a joint probability distribution over observed variables represented by the model M. If we try to represent the same distribution by the model M_X we find out that a transformation from the parameters describing $P(C_j|H, O_j)$ to parameters describing $P(X_j|H)$ always exists however it can yield $P(X_j|H)$ which is not a probability distribution (some values are lower than zero or even higher than one but note that any parameterization makes always sure the sum given any condition is equal to one). Thus, the model M_X doesn't include the model M. But let us consider a model M_X^* having the same parameters and model equation as the model M_X but relaxing all the constraints which the model M_X puts on its parameters, except the constraint that the model M_X^* represents a joint probability distribution over the observed variables. Note that M_X^* is not a graphical model and $P(X_j|H)$ is not necessarily a probability distribution. Obviously, M_X^* includes M, M_X^* includes M_X and moreover the parameters of the model M_X form a set with a positive measure in the space of the parameters of the model M_X^*. Thus, the effective dimension of the two models M_X^* and M_X is the same.

Because by marginalizing the variables X and Y out of the graphical model M_X one obtains the graphical model M, it follows that the model M includes the model M_X. From the facts that M_X^* includes M, M includes M_X and $de(M_X) = de(M_X^*)$ and from Lemma 1 follows that $de(M) = de(M_X)$. Thus, the first claim is proved.

Note that the nodes X and Y can be introduced in any polytree for any latent variable and all the arguments above apply to such a case, too.

Back to the model M_X. The fixed deterministic distribution $P(C_j|X_j, O_j)$ has the property that as long as the marginal probability $P(O)$ is positive then for every state (c^*, o^*) of X_j there exists a state c^* of C_j and a state o^* of O_j such that $p(X_j = (c^*, o^*)|C_j = c^*, O_j = o^*) = 1$, i.e. $p(X_j = (c^*, o^*), C_j = c^*, O_j = o^*) = p(C_j = c^*, O_j = o^*)$. We have defined the distribution $P(C_j|X_j, O_j)$ including the condition $p(C_j = c^*|X_j = (c^*, o^*), O_j = o^*) = 1$, i.e. $p(C_j = c^*, X_j = (c^*, o^*), O_j = o^*) = p(X_j = (c^*, o^*), O_j = o^*)$. Moreover note that X_j and O_j are marginally independent and thus $p(X_j = (c^*, o^*), O_j = o^*) = p(X_j = (c^*, o^*)) * p(O_j = o^*)$. All these equations together imply that $p(X_j = (c^*, o^*)) = p(C_j = c^*, O_j = o^*)/p(O_j = o^*)$. We denote by B_j any set of nodes in the model M_X except the nodes X_j, C_j and O_j. Note that B_j can be for example the set of all such observed nodes. Then, from the distribution $P(C_j, O_j, B_j)$ one can easily compute the distribution $P(X_j, B_j)$ and $P(X_j, C_j, O_j, B_j) = P(X_j, B_j) * P(O_j) * P(C_j|X_j, O_j)$ as well. Thus, the special fixed distribution $P(C_j|X_j, O_j)$ of M_X defined above causes the nodes X to be de facto observed, too.

Because the nodes X are observed, we can apply Theorem 2 and we obtain $de(M_X) = de(M_{LC}^*) + \sum_{j,k}(|O_{j,k}| - 1)$ where M_{LC}^* is the sub model induced from the model M_X by the latent nodes H and Y and observed nodes X and T. Because of the special parameterization of $P(Y|P)$, this model is equivalent to the latent class model M_{LC} with the special requirement that the marginal distribution $P(Y)$ has to correspond to the mutually marginally independent nodes P_i. The question is if all these $|Y| - 1 - \sum_i(|P_i| - 1)$ independent equality

Fig. 3. Examples a) W structure in [5] with $|O_i| = 2$, b) Compact polytree model with $|O_1| = |O_2| = |O_3| = |O_4| = |O_5| = |H_3| = 2$ and $|O_6| = |H_1| = |H_2| = 3$

constraints decrease the effective dimension of the model M_{LC}^* compared to the model M_{LC}. Because all the parameters characterizing the observed marginal $P(Y)$ in M_{LC} are independent and one can choose a basis of the Jacobian matrix of model M_{LC} to contain all the corresponding vectors, each of the independent constrains reduces the basis by one vector. Thus, we have shown that $de(M_X) = de(M_{LC}) + \sum_{j,k}(|O_{j,k}| - 1) - (\prod_i |P_i| - 1) + \sum_i(|P_i| - 1)$. Q.E.D

We say that a polytree M is *reduced* if for every latent node H_i in M after the addition of the X and Y nodes around H_i (as in the proof above) the latent class model induced by the Markov boundary of H_i is regular. If some polytree model is not reduced, we can reduce it by decreasing the cardinality of the appropriate node H_i to satisfy the regularity constraint.

Suppose having a non-reduced polytree model M and denote by M_R the model obtained by the reduction process described above. Then the two models M and M_R have the same effective dimension. We show this by showing that it holds for a single step of the reduction process decreasing the cardinality of H_i. Thus, assume that only one step was needed to reduce M. Denote by M^* and M_R^* the models obtained from M and M_R by adding the nodes X and Y. The first part of the proof of Theorem 3 applies to any polytree because the node H_i is d-separated from all other nodes by its Markov boundary and it is exactly this boundary to which the proof applies. Thus $de(M^*) = de(M)$ and $de(M_R^*) = de(M_R)$. And now in the two models M^* and M_R^* the node H_i has different cardinality but the same Markov boundary, which forms a latent class model. Again, using the d-separation of H_i from all other nodes given its Markov boundary and the fact that the two latent class models are equivalent, it follows that the two models M^* and M_R^* are equivalent, too. Thus, using Lemma 1 they have the same effective dimension, too.

We can demonstrate the use of Theorem 3 on the W structure reported in [5]. The W structure consists of one latent node H, two binary observed children, each of them having one extra binary observed parent (see Fig. 3). It was reported in [5] that this structure has $de = 9$ for $|H| = 2$, $de = 10$ for $|H| = 3$, $de = 10$ for $|H| = 4$ and $de = 11$ for $|H| = 5$. This was later on corrected to $de = 10$ for $|H| = 5$. However, no explanation of these results was available up to now. We can apply Theorem 3 that converts the problem into an LC problem with one latent variable H and two observed variables with three states. For these, we can use the exact solution from [11]. The result is $de = 9$ for $|H| = 2$ and $de = 10$ for $|H| \geq 3$ as all the LC models with $|H| \geq 3$ are equivalent.

4   Decomposition of Polytrees

It is easy to realize that by applying Theorem 2 to any polytree, one decomposes it into a set of compact polytrees. The sets S used for this decomposition correspond to single observed nodes that have either more than one child or some parents as well as a child.

In this section, we show how to compute the effective dimension of any reduced compact polytree by decomposing it into a set of reduced primitive polytrees. It was explained in the previous section that we can limit ourselves to reduced polytrees because any non-reduced polytree can be easily converted into a reduced one with the same effective dimension. The following theorem states the main result of this section, which we prove in the rest of this section.

Theorem 4. *Let M be a reduced compact polytree with observed nodes O and latent nodes H. Let M_i denote the reduced primitive polytree model induced in M by any latent node $H_i \in H$ and its Markov boundary $Mb(H_i)$ in M. Then $de(M) = ds(M) - \sum_{H_i \in H}(ds(M_i) - de(M_i))$.*

Proof. We prove this theorem by showing three things. First, we prove a lemma characterizing what a compact polytree having more than a single latent node looks like. Second, we prove a lemma describing a special parametrization of parts of reduced compact polytrees and its properties. Third, we prove a lemma enabling a decomposition of any reduced compact polytree into two reduced compact polytrees, each having less latent nodes than the original one. This lemma builds upon the two previous ones and directly proves the theorem above because it ends with a set of reduced primitive polytrees. Q.E.D

Lemma 2. *Let M be a compact polytree model having more than a single latent node. For any latent node H_1 there is a latent node H_2 in M such that H_1 and H_2 are either neighbors or both parents of an observed node O in M.*

Proof. M is a polytree, thus there is a unique path between any two nodes. Choose H_2 to be such a latent node in M that the path from H_1 to H_2 in M doesn't contain any other latent node. The path can thus contain only observed nodes or no node at all (except H_1 and H_2). Every observed node in the path has at least two neighbors. This is possible in a compact polytree only if all its neighbors are its parents. Thus, there can not be more than a single observed node in the path and the lemma is proved. Q.E.D

We define a *sub polytree* at a node A away from nodes B in a polytree M with nodes N as the subgraph of M induced by all nodes $C \in N$ such that the path from A to C doesn't contain any node from the set B.

Lemma 3. *Let M be a reduced compact polytree model having nodes $N = H \cup O$, where H are latent nodes and O are observed. Let M_U be a sub polytree of M at a latent node $H_i \in H$ away from a node $C \in Ch(H_i)$ consisting of nodes U. Let M_W be a sub polytree of M at a latent node $H_i \in H$ away from the nodes*

$Pa(H_i)$ consisting of nodes W. Then the sub model M_U can be parameterized in such a way that $P(O)$ determines $P(O, H_i)$ and $P(H_i)$ can be chosen a positive distribution. Moreover the sub model M_W can be parameterized in such a way that $P(O)$ determines $P(O, H_i)$ and $P(H_i|(O\backslash W))$ can be any distribution.

Proof. We present a sketch of the proof only. The proof is done by induction over the number of latent nodes in model M. First for a single latent node. We can introduce the X and Y nodes from the proof of Theorem 3. Because M is reduced, the induced latent class model is regular and M_W can be parameterized to encode a bijection between the states of H_i and the Cartesian product of all X nodes. For M_U one can encode a similar bijection to all X nodes but one and the states of Y which are restricted to distributions satisfying the marginal independence among $Pa(H_i)$. We have already seen that the rest of the polytree can be parameterized to make the X and Y nodes de facto observed and we note that a positive distribution satisfying the marginal independence is always possible. The nodes X and Y can be marginalized out and we obtain the parameterization needed for the model M and thus prove the first induction hypothesis. The induction step again uses a latent node H_i and the nodes X and Y around it. But the $Pa(H_i)$, $Ch(H_i)$ and $Pa(Ch(H_i))\backslash H_i$ in M can be latent nodes now. For $Pa(H_i)$ we use the induction hypothesis of sub polytrees away from the node H_i, for $Ch(H_i)$ we use the sub polytrees away from their parents and for $Pa(Ch(H_i))\backslash H_i$ we use the sub polytree away from $Ch(H_i)$, resp. the C nodes. Note that for both $Pa(H_i)$ and $Pa(Ch(H_i))\backslash H_i$ any positive marginal distribution is sufficient, while for $Ch(H_i)$ one needs to be able to encode any distribution as needed which is possible by the induction hypothesis. This finishes the induction step and thus the whole proof. Q.E.D

Lemma 4. *Let M be a reduced compact polytree model having nodes $N = H \cup O$, where H are latent nodes and O are observed. Then there is a latent node $S \in H$, its child $T \in Ch(S)$, observed parents of the child $O_0 \in O \cap Pa(T)$ and other latent parents of the child $R \in H \cap (Pa(T)\backslash\{S\})$ in M where $H \cap (\{T\} \cup R) \neq \emptyset$. The nodes S, T, R and O_0 induce in M a sub model M_0 with all nodes observed. The sub polytree of M at the node S away from T consists of nodes N_S. The nodes $N_S \cup S$, T, R and O_0 induce in M a sub model M_1 with the nodes T and R observed. The nodes $(N\backslash N_S) \cup \{S\}$ induce in M a sub model M_2 with the node S observed. For the effective dimensions of these models holds $de(M) = de(M_1) + de(M_2) - ds(M_0)$.*

Proof. We present a sketch of the proof only due to page limit. From Lemma 2 follows either the existence of the latent nodes S and T or the latent nodes S and $R_i \in R$ having a common observed child T. We consider the first case only, which may contain latent nodes R, too. The same proof applies to the second case, it is just simpler because node T is observed. Moreover, for simplicity we consider only a single node R, all $R_i \in R$ can be dealt with in the same way.

The situation is depicted in Fig. 4. We denote by J the Jacobian matrix of the polytree model M and similarly use J_1 and J_2 for M_1 and M_2. Moreover,

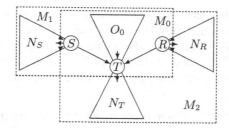

Fig. 4. Compact polytree model M and its induced sub-models

we denote by θ_O, θ_t, θ_r and θ_s the marginal parameters of O_0, T, R and S and by θ_{tt}, θ_{rr} and θ_{ss} the parameters of the sub polytrees at T, R and S except for θ_t, θ_r and θ_s.

The columns of J_2 corresponding to the parameters $\theta_{o,t,s}$ are independent because the variables are either observed or can be observed and encode any distribution if the special parameterization of θ_{tt} from Lemma 3 is used. Thus, there is a basis B_2 of J_2 which contains these and as many columns corresponding to θ_r as possible. Similarly, we denote by B_1 the basis of J_1 which contains all the columns $\theta_{o,t,r}$ and as many θ_s as possible. Obviously, B_0 contains all the columns $\theta_{o,t,s}$. Let $B = (B_1\backslash B_0) \cup (B_2\backslash B_0) \cup (B_1 \cap B_2)$.

All vectors in J depend on the vectors in B because $\theta_{ss,s}$ depend on $B_1\backslash\theta_r$ in M_1, $\theta_{rr,r,tt,o,t}$ on $B_2\backslash\theta_s$ in M_2 and these dependencies imply dependence in B because of the d-separations. The fact that all vectors in B are independent is proved by contradiction. If there is a dependence then it has to hold even with the special parameterization of $\theta_{ss,rr,tt}$ using Lemma 3 and this leads to a dependence in B_0 what contradicts the fact of B_0 being basis. Thus, B is a basis of J. From $B = (B_1\backslash B_0) \cup (B_2\backslash B_0) \cup (B_1 \cap B_2)$, $\theta_{o,t,r} \subseteq B_1$, $\theta_{o,t,s} \subseteq B_2$ and $B_0 = \theta_{o,t,r,s}$ follows $|B| = |B_1| + |B_2| - |B_0|$. Q.E.D

We can demonstrate the use of Theorem 4 on the reduced compact polytree in Fig. 3. This model has $ds = 41$. It has three latent nodes and they induce three reduced primitive polytree models with $ds = 23$, $ds = 28$ and $ds = 20$. These primitive polytree models have $de = 17$, $de = 22$ and $de = 18$. Thus the compact polytree model in Fig. 3 has $de = 27$.

As mentioned in the introduction, effective dimensions can, in theory, be computed from some Jacobian matrices whose sizes are exponential in the number of observed variables. This straightforward method nonetheless turned out viable in this example due to its small size. It lasted 34 seconds on a PC. In contrast, the use of Theorem 4 enabled us to complete the computation in 1.5 seconds.

5   Conclusion

In this paper, we present two important results concerning the computation of effective dimensions of graphical models with latent variables. The first result enables us to compute the effective dimension of primitive polytrees. It transforms the problem into the same problem for some latent class model. The second result enables us to decompose a polytree model into primitive sub models and obtain the effective dimension of the model from those of the sub models. This makes it feasible to compute the effective dimension of large polytree models.

Acknowledgment. This research was partially supported by Hong Kong Research Grants Council under grant HKUST6088/01E. We would like to thank Marta Vomlelová, Finn Verner Jensen and the whole BSS group for helpful inputs.

References

1. Akaike, H. (1974). A new look at the statistical model identification. In *IEEE Transactions on Automatic Control*, AC-19, pp. 716–723.
2. Catchpole, E.A. and Morgan, B.J.T. (2001). Deficiency of parameter-redundant models. In *Biometrika*, 88, 2, pp. 593–598.
3. Cheeseman, P. and Stutz, J. (1995). Bayesian classification (AutoClass): Theory and results. In Fayyad, U., Paitesky-Shapiro, G., Smyth, P., Uthurusamy, R. (Eds.), *Advances in knowledge discovery and data mining*, pp. 153–180.
4. Cooper, G. and Herskovits, E. (1992). A Bayesian method for the induction of probabilistic networks from data, *Machine Learning*, 9, pp. 309–347.
5. Geiger, D., Heckerman, D. and Meek, C. (1996). Asymptotic model selection for directed networks with hidden variables. In *Proc. of the 12th Conference on Uncertainty in Artificial Intelligence*, pp. 283–290.
6. Kočka, T. and Zhang, N. L. (2002). Dimension correction for hierarchical latent class models. In *Proc. of the 18th Conference on Uncertainty in Artificial Intelligence (UAI-02)*, pp. 267–274.
7. Lauritzen, S. L. (1996). Graphical models. Clarendon Press, Oxford.
8. Rusakov, D. (2002). Effective dimension calculations for Bayesian networks, code in Matlab,
   http://www.cs.technion.ac.il/~rusakov/archive/bn_dimension/bn_dimension.m.
9. Rusakov, D. and Geiger, D. (2002). Asymptotic model Selection for naive Bayesian networks. In *Proc. of the 18th Conference on Uncertainty in Artificial Intelligence (UAI-02)*, pp. 438–445.
10. Schwarz, G. (1978). Estimating the dimension of a model. In *Annals of Statistics*, 6, pp. 461–464.
11. Settimi, R. and Smith, J.Q. (1998). On the geometry of Bayesian graphical models with hidden variables. In *Proc. of the 14th Conference on Uncertainty in Artificial Intelligence*, pp. 472–479.
12. Settimi, R. and Smith, J.Q. (1999). Geometry, moments and Bayesian networks with hidden variables. In *Proc. of the 7th International Workshop on Artificial Intelligence and Statistics*, Fort Lauderdale, Florida (3–6 January 1999), Morgan Kaufmann Publishers, S. Francisco, CA.
13. Zhang, N. L. and Kočka, T. (2003). Effective dimensions of hierarchical latent class models, Technical Report HKUST-CS03-03, Department of Computer Science, Hong Kong University of Science and Technology.

Applying Numerical Trees to Evaluate Asymmetric Decision Problems

Manuel Gómez and Andrés Cano

Dpt. Computer Science and Artificial Intelligence, E.T.S. Ingeniería Informática
University of Granada, C/ Periodista Daniel Saucedo Aranda s/n
18071 Granada Spain
{mgomez,acu}@decsai.ugr.es

Abstract. This paper describes some ideas for applying *numerical trees* in order to represent and solve asymmetric decision problems with influence diagrams (IDs). Constraint rules are used to represent the asymmetries between the variables of the ID. These rules will be transformed into numerical trees during the evaluation of the ID. The application of numerical trees can reduce the number of operations required to evaluate the ID. The paper also presents how numerical trees may be approximated, thereby enabling complex decision problems to be evaluated.

Keywords: Influence diagrams, asymmetric decision problems, numerical trees, probability trees

1 Introduction

Asymmetric decision problems under uncertainty have traditionally been represented and solved using *Decision Trees*. This tool is easy to understand and solve, and it encodes the asymmetries without introducing dummy states for the variables. Its main problem is the exponential growth of the representation. Influence diagrams (IDs) have been also applied to represent and solve decision problems. The power of an influence diagram, both as an analysis tool and as a communication tool, lies in its ability to concisely and precisely describe the structure of decision problems [20]. An ID encodes the independence relations between variables, thereby avoiding the exponential growth of Decision Tree representation. The ID representation has weaknesses, the most serious being the difficulty to deal with highly asymmetric decision problems, where particular acts or events lead to different possibilities [1]. In order to represent an asymmetric decision problem as an ID, the problem must be symmetrized by adding artificial states and assuming degenerated probability distributions and/or value functions. These adaptations obscure the structure of the problem and, most importantly, increase the time and space required for solution. Several attempts have been made to solve this drawback. Call and Miller [13], Fung and Shachter [9], Smith et al. [20], Qi et al. [16], Covaliu and Oliver [7], Shenoy [19], Nielsen and Jensen [14], Demirer and Shenoy [8] have proposed

T.D. Nielsen and N.L. Zhang (Eds.): ECSQARU 2003, LNAI 2711, pp. 196–207, 2003.

modifications to the influence diagram technique in order to deal with asymmetric decision problems. In this paper, we follow a similar technique to Smith's *distribution trees* [20], to represent the asymmetries between the variables. We use an only tool (numerical trees) to encode all the knowledge about the decision problem: asymmetries, probability distributions and utility functions. The main difference between Smith's technique and ours is that we are able to carry out approximated operations with numerical trees.

In any case, for complex decision problems, the evaluation of an ID becomes impossible due to its computational cost: the set of information states exceeds the storage capacity of personal computers or the optimal policy must be obtained in a short period of time. So if computational cost is prohibitive, the decision maker may be better off with a policy that it is not optimal. This is the main objective of this work: to make possible the evaluation of asymmetric and complex decision problems.

Here, we combine two different lines: use of qualitative information about the problem (constraints, due to asymmetries) and approximation. Both of these can be easily used thanks to the use of numerical trees to represent conditional probabilities and utilities. Constraints explicitly state asymmetries and reduce the number of scenarios to consider. Approximation simplifies the problem and may be the sole solution when exact evaluation is impossible, giving a policy to the decision maker even though it is not optimal.

We can find other approximated methods to evaluate IDs. For example, Lauritzen and Nilsson [12] introduce *Limited Memory Influence Diagrams* (LIMIDs) to describe multi-stage decision problems where the no-forgetting assumption is relaxed. This method can be seen as a way of approximate inference. Charnes and Shenoy [6] use a sampling technique to solve complex IDs.

The remainder of the paper is organized in the following way: Sect. 2 introduces some concepts and notation about IDs and asymmetries, as well as computational issues faced when solving complex decision problems; Sect. 3 presents key issues about numerical trees and how they are used to evaluate IDs; Sect. 4 describes the algorithms used to put our ideas into practice and the way they must be changed to do so; Sect. 5 includes the experimental results; and finally Sect. 6 details sets out our conclusions and lines for future work.

2   Influence Diagrams and Asymmetries

IDs are directed acyclic graphs with three types of nodes: *decision nodes* (mutually exclusive actions which the decision maker must choose from), *chance nodes* (events which the decision maker cannot control), and *utility nodes* (representing decision maker preferences). Links represent dependencies: probabilistic for links into chance nodes, informational for links into decision nodes (states for decision parents are known before the decision is taken), and functional for links into value nodes. The semantic of IDs usually assumes that the decision maker remembers past observations and decisions (*no-forgetting assumption*), although some authors (Lauritzen and Nilsson [12]) relax this assumption.

Direct predecessors of chance or value nodes are called *conditional* predecessors; direct predecessors of decision nodes are designated *informational* predecessors. Decision maker preferences are expressed as *utility functions*, indicating the local utility for the configurations of the variables in their domain.

The set of chance nodes is denoted V_C, the set of decision nodes is denoted V_D, and the set of utility nodes is denoted V_U. The set of all possible combinations of values for the direct predecessors of decision node D is called the *information set* for D. The elements of this set are denoted *information states for D*. The *universe* of the ID is $V = V_C \cup V_D = \{X_1, \ldots, X_n\}$. Let us suppose that each variable X_i takes values on a finite set U_i containing $|U_i|$ elements. If I is a set of indices, we shall write $\mathbf{X}_I$ for the set of variables $\{X_i | i \in I\}$, defined on $U_I = \times_{i \in I} U_i$. A *potential* ϕ defined on U_I will be a mapping $\phi : U_I \to I\!\!R$, where $I\!\!R$ is the set of real numbers. Potentials are used to refer to both probability distributions and utility functions. For probability distributions, a potential will be a mapping $\phi : U_I \to [0, 1]$; for utility functions, it is a mapping $\phi : U_I \to I\!\!R$. The sets of utility potentials and probability potentials are denoted Ψ and Φ, respectively. A *policy* for an ID prescribes an action (or a sequence of actions, if there are several decision nodes) for each possible combination of outcomes of its informational predecessors. An *optimal policy* is a policy which maximizes the decision maker's expected value. This will be the objective for ID evaluation algorithms.

The drawback of using IDs to model asymmetric decision problems is well known. It is sometimes possible to identify the source of asymmetry and to point out this qualitative knowledge with relations between variables. In our solution, we try to keep qualitative and quantitative knowledge separate, merely because (as will be explained later) qualitative knowledge may affect several distributions, with some of them not being present in the model (i.e. distributions managed during the evaluation process and derived from initial ones). On the other hand, we attempt to store both kinds of knowledge in similar structures, making their joint application easier. In order to represent the qualitative knowledge about a decision problem, we therefore propose that *constraint rules* be used.

A constraint rule is an expression *antecedent* $\Rightarrow$ *consequent*. An *atomic sentence* is a pair (variable, set of values): $X_i \in \{x_i, \ldots, x_j\}$. Atomic sentences can be connected with logical operators to form *logical sentences*. Valid logical operators are $\wedge$ (and), $\vee$ (or), and $\neg$ (not). For constraint rules, both antecedents and consequents are expressed using logical sentences.

By way of example, let us suppose that X_1, X_2, and X_3 take values respectively on the sets $U_1 = \{x_1^1, x_1^2, x_1^3\}$, $U_2 = \{x_2^1, x_2^2\}$, $U_3 = \{x_3^1, x_3^2\}$, then the constraint rule

$$X_1 \in \{x_1^1, x_1^3\} \wedge X_2 \in \{x_2^2\} \Rightarrow X_3 \in \{x_3^2\} \tag{1}$$

states that if X_1 is equal to x_1^1, or x_1^3 and X_2 is equal to x_2^2 then X_3 must be equal to x_3^2. Considering this constraint rule and the conditional probability distribution $P(X_3|X_1, X_2)$, we can state that $P(X_3 = x_3^1|X_1 = x_1^1, X_2 = x_2^2) = 0$. An atomic sentence could have an empty set of values for the consequent. For example, the constraint rule $X_1 \in \{x_1^1\} \wedge X_2 \in \{x_2^1\} \Rightarrow X_3 \in \{\}$ means that

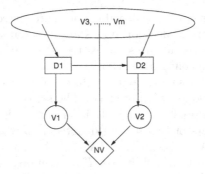

Fig. 1. Example of constraint between decision variables

$X_1 = x_1^1, X_2 = x_2^1$ is an impossible scenario and should not be considered for computations.

Sometimes the qualitative knowledge is not directly linked to any distribution of the model. For example, we could have the following situation: a constraint links the values of D_1 and D_2, but there is no distribution where these variables take part together in the model (see Figure 1). However, during the evaluation process the value node will depend on D_1 and D_2 and this will be the moment to *activate* the constraint.

We can therefore distinguish two general situations: qualitative knowledge related to initial distributions, and qualitative knowledge related to distributions derived from the initial ones and used during the evaluation of the model. In the first case, there is some redundancy between qualitative and quantitative knowledge, but we consider it is very useful to use the rules even so. Firstly, constraint rules make the elicitation process easier (reducing the number of scenarios and therefore the number of parameters to assess); secondly, they help to make both qualitative and quantitative knowledge consistent; and thirdly, they clearly state invalid scenarios, making the contingent nature of the decision problem clear.

3   Numerical Trees

Probability trees ([2,3,17,4,5]) have previously been used to represent probability distributions (probability potentials). These papers show how probability trees may be used in order to calculate in an exact and approximate way. The main advantage of probability trees is that they allow a large potential to be approximated by another of a smaller size, by collapsing several of its branches into a single leaf which contains the average of the values stored in the removed branches. In this paper, we will also use trees of numbers to represent utility functions and constraints rules. The trees for utility functions will be called *utility trees* and the trees for constraint rules will be called *constraint trees*. We will call *numerical trees* to all of them.

A numerical tree $\mathcal{T}$ on the set of variables X_I is a directed tree, where each internal node is labeled with a variable (random variable or decision node), each

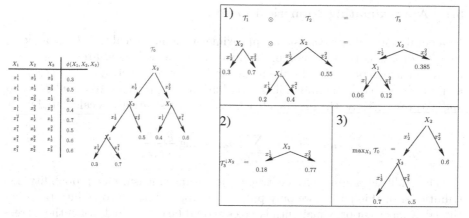

Fig. 2. a) A potential ϕ and a numerical tree representing it. b) Examples of combination, marginalization and maximization in numerical trees

leaf node is labeled with a number (a probability, a utility value or a $0-1$ value for constraints). Each internal node has an outgoing arc for each state of the variable associated with that node. Outgoing arcs from a node X_i are labeled with the name of the associated state $(x_i \in U_i)$ of X_i. The *size* of a tree, denoted $size(\mathcal{T})$, is defined as the number of leaves of $\mathcal{T}$.

It can be said that a numerical tree $\mathcal{T}$ on variables X_I represents a potential $\phi : U_I \to \mathbb{R}$ if for each $\mathbf{x}_I \in U_I$ the value $\phi(\mathbf{x}_I)$ is the number stored in the leaf node, which is reached starting in the root node and selecting the child corresponding to coordinate x_i for each internal node labeled with X_i. The potential represented by tree $\mathcal{T}$ is denoted by $\phi_{\mathcal{T}}(\mathbf{X}_I)$. Given a potential ϕ, a numerical tree for ϕ is denoted by $\mathcal{T}_\phi$. Figure 2.a shows an example of a numerical tree for the potential $\phi(X_1, X_2, X_3)$. This is a probability tree for the conditional distribution $P(X_1|X_2, X_3)$.

Three basic operations are necessary to evaluate IDs: combination (denoted with $\phi_1 \otimes \phi_2$), marginalization (denoted with $\phi^{\downarrow X_I}$), and maximization (denoted with $\max_{X_i} \phi$). The three operations can be carried out directly on the numerical tree representation. In [4] and [17], the authors show how to perform the first two operations, and how to build a numerical tree from a potential in detail. Maximization is used when a decision node is going to be removed. This operation is completely analogous to marginalization because it also deletes a variable from the numerical tree, but now instead of adding up values, we take the maximum. Figure 2.b shows examples for the combination, marginalization and maximization in numerical trees. When approximate evaluation of IDs is used, then a way of approximating numerical trees must be specified. In the following section, we shall briefly describe the approximation operation.

3.1   Approximating Numerical Trees

In general, the problem consists in approximating a numerical tree $\mathcal{T}_\phi$ by another tree $\mathcal{T}'_\phi$ of a smaller size. For probability trees, we will measure the *distance* between the two potentials by the Kullback-Leibler cross entropy [11] between ϕ and ϕ'. If we denote the probability distributions proportional to ϕ and ϕ' by p_ϕ and $p_{\phi'}$, respectively, then the Kullback-Leibler cross entropy is calculated with:

$$D(\mathcal{T}, \mathcal{T}') = \sum_{x_I \in U_I} p_\phi(x_I) \log \frac{p_\phi(x_I)}{p_{\phi'}(x_I)}. \tag{2}$$

The Kullback-Leibler cross entropy is a distance measure for probability distributions. In this paper, we only propose to approximate probability trees, although a way to approximate utility trees should be considered, when these trees are large. This aspect is a task for future work.

One way of obtaining $\mathcal{T}'$ is to prune $\mathcal{T}$. In order to prune a numerical tree, we select a *terminal node* (a node such that all its children are leaves) and we replace it with the average of its child nodes. The pruning operation can be applied again to the pruned tree $\mathcal{T}'$, until we get a tree of an acceptable size, or while the *error* (distance) with respect to the original tree ($\mathcal{T}$) is below a given threshold. For probability trees, it can be proved that the pruning operation minimizes the Kullback-Leibler divergence between the original tree and the pruned tree [3,17]. These authors have used approximate probability trees in order to propagate in Bayesian networks.

The main issue when pruning a numerical tree $\mathcal{T}$ is how to select the terminal nodes to prune [3,17]. We consider a threshold $\Delta_p \geq 0$ and we then approximate the children of X_k by their average if the Kullback-Leibler divergence between the original tree and the approximate one is less than Δ_p.

We have also applied the *sort* operation [3,17] to numerical trees. This operation tries to restructure the nodes of the numerical tree in such a way that the more informative variables are in the upper levels of the tree. In this way, if the tree is pruned, then only the less informative variables will be eliminated. The algorithm for this operation is very similar to the algorithm to build a numerical tree. Both operations construct the tree incrementally, by including the most informative variable (the variable minimizing the distance to the exact potential) at every step in the new tree.

3.2   Constraint Trees

From a constraint rule we can obtain a numerical tree (a constraint tree). Leaf nodes in constraint trees contain the values 0 or 1. If $\mathcal{T}^c$ is a constraint tree for a constraint rule with variables $\mathbf{X}_J$, then a value of 0 in a leaf node λ, means that the configuration of its ancestor variables corresponds to an impossible scenario in the ID. A value equal to 1 means that, taking into account only this constraint tree, the configuration is possible. A simple procedure can be implemented in order to build a constraint tree from a constraint rule, but it is not included

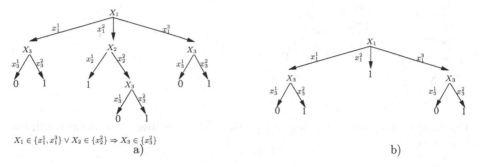

$$X_1 \in \{x_1^1, x_1^3\} \vee X_2 \in \{x_2^2\} \Rightarrow X_3 \in \{x_3^2\}$$

a)

b)

Fig. 3. a) A constraint rule and its associated constraint tree. b) Maximization on X_2 in tree of Fig. a)

here for brevity. Figure 3 part a), shows an example of one constraint rule and its associated constraint tree.

Constraint rules and trees are useful when evaluating the ID in order to reduce the size of the potentials (probability trees and utility trees). This reduction causes that the complexity of operations (combination and marginalization) is also reduced. To decide if a constraint rule for the variables $\mathbf{X}_J$ is applicable to a potential ϕ for the variables $\mathbf{X}_I$, we have to check the *applicability* of the constraint rule. The applicability of the complete constraint rule depends on the logical operator involved with the atomic sentences of the rule. We use the following definitions to decide if the constraint rule is applicable. We say that an atomic sentence in a constraint rule for $\mathbf{X}_J$ is *applicable* to a potential ϕ for $\mathbf{X}_I$ if the variable X_i of the atomic sentence is in $\mathbf{X}_J \cap \mathbf{X}_I$. The negation of a sentence is applicable if and only if the sentence itself is applicable. A conjunction is applicable if and only if the two conjuncts are applicable. A disjunction is applicable if and only if at least one of the disjuncts is applicable. With these definitions, the constraint rule is applicable if and only if both the antecedent and the consequent are applicable.

Suppose $\mathcal{T}^c$ is the constraint tree associated to a constraint rule, and $\mathcal{T}_\phi$ the numerical tree of a potential ϕ. If the constraint rule is applicable to ϕ, then we can combine $\mathcal{T}^c$ and $\mathcal{T}_\phi$ in order to obtain a smaller numerical tree. Before combining $\mathcal{T}^c$ and $\mathcal{T}_\phi$, we must remove the variables not included in ϕ from $\mathcal{T}^c$. If X_i is one of these variables, then X_i is removed from $\mathcal{T}^c$ by maximization in X_i: $\max_{X_i} \mathcal{T}^c$. By way of example, let us suppose that we have a potential (utility) ϕ for variables X_1 and X_3, represented with the utility tree in Fig. 4a, and the constraint rule in Fig. 3a. It is possible to prove that this constraint rule is applicable to ϕ. As the variable X_2 is in $\mathcal{T}^c$ but not in ϕ, we must therefore remove X_2 from $\mathcal{T}^c$ by calculating $\max_{X_2} \mathcal{T}^c$ (see Fig. 3b). This new constraint tree can now be combined with potential ϕ. Figure 4b shows the resulting utility tree.

The combination of numerical trees and constraint trees will be used in the evaluation of the ID, for the initial numerical trees (conditional distributions and

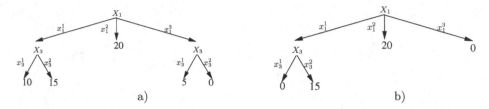

Fig. 4. a) A utility tree for X_1 and X_3. b) The utility tree after applying the constraint rule in Fig. 3

utility functions), and also for the new numerical trees obtained in the evaluation process, after eliminating a decision or chance variable.

4 Evaluating Influence Diagrams

In order to show how constraints and approximation can be applied to evaluate IDs, we have decided to work with two algorithms: *arc reversal* [18] and *variable elimination* [10]. This selection is based on the different nature of the operations they require to compute the optimal policy.

Arc reversal (AR) uses the structure of the ID to decide the next operation to be done (chance node removal, decision node removal or arc reversal). Each operation modifies the quantitative knowledge and the structure of the ID. These operations are combined sequentially until all the chance and decision nodes have been removed. The detailed explanation for these operations can be found in [18]. The general schema for this algorithm is shown below: an initialization phase (1) is added, and also an additional step for applying constraints and pruning after computations (2.b).

1. Initialization phase
   a) Build initial trees: $\forall \phi \in \Phi \cup \Psi$ obtain $\mathcal{T}_\phi$
   b) Apply constraints: $\forall \mathcal{T}^c$, if $\mathcal{T}^c$ is applicable to $\mathcal{T}_\phi$ (and has not yet been applied) then $\mathcal{T}'_\phi = \mathcal{T}_\phi \otimes \mathcal{T}^c$, else $\mathcal{T}'_\phi = \mathcal{T}_\phi$
   c) Sort variables in utility and probability trees
   d) Prune all the trees with $\Delta = 0$ as the threshold (without approximation): $\forall \phi \in \Phi \cup \Psi$, prune($\mathcal{T}'_\phi, 0$)
2. Set a new Δ for approximation operations
3. While there are conditional predecessors for utility nodes
   a) Decide next operation to do and compute
   b) Apply constraints to modified potentials, as explained in the initialization phase (1.b). If chance or decision node was removed, sort variables in utility and probability trees. If arc reversal was the operation selected, normalize the modified distributions
   c) Prune modified trees with Δ as threshold: prune($\mathcal{T}'_\phi, \Delta$)

Variable Elimination (VE) uses the temporal order between the decision nodes to partition the whole set of nodes according to when they are observed. Let us consider an ID with n decision nodes. I_0 is the set of chance nodes observed prior to taking any decision. I_i is the set of chance nodes observed after D_i was taken and before taking D_{i+1}. That is to say, nodes are partially ordered: $I_0 < D_1 < \ldots < D_n < I_n$. If $A \in V_C < D \in V_D$ then there is a directed path from A to D. Once this order has been established, the algorithm eliminates all the variables one by one, with two operations: sum-marginalization and max-marginalization. The detailed explanation for this algorithm can be found in [10]. The final schema is presented below.

1. Initialization phase, as explained for AR algorithm (phase 1)
2. Set a new Δ for approximation operations
3. While there are nodes to remove, from I_n to I_0
   a) Decide next node to remove (N) and combine all potentials (trees) related to it: Ψ_N, Φ_N. New trees are obtained as result: $\mathcal{T}_\psi$ and $\mathcal{T}_\phi$
   b) Apply constraints to modified potentials, as explained in the initialization phase (1.b). Sort variables in $\mathcal{T}_\psi'$ and $\mathcal{T}_\phi'$. If a constraint is applied to $\mathcal{T}_\phi'$, normalize
   c) Prune $\mathcal{T}_\psi'$ and $\mathcal{T}_\phi'$ with Δ as threshold: $\mathrm{prune}(\mathcal{T}_\psi', \Delta)$, $\mathrm{prune}(\mathcal{T}_\phi', \Delta)$

It should be noted that the operations to apply constraints and to prune the trees (exactly or with approximation) do not change the global structure of the algorithms; they merely add pre-processing at their beginning and post-processing after operations which change the potentials. The use of these ideas therefore relies on the use of numerical trees to encode the quantitative knowledge, but not on the algorithm itself.

5   Experimental Results

For testing purposes, we have used an ID with 31 chance nodes, 2 decision nodes and 1 value node. The number of outcomes for variables range between 2 and 9. Nodes are related with 56 different links. The total sum of the sizes of the ID potentials is 951. The temporal order between decisions imposes a constraint between its values. The ID models a short version of a medical problem where the decisions are related to different treatments. So, if Treatment1 decision variable takes the values "do not treat" or "observe and dismiss", then the only valid value for Treatment2 decision is "do not treat".

The tests applied consists of (1) exact evaluation with each algorithm, without trees (AR and VE) and with trees: without constraints (ARWT, VEWT) and with constraints (ARWTC, VEWTC); (2) for both algorithms, evaluations with approximations for probability potentials, without constraints (AARWT, AVEWT) and with constraints (AARWTC, AVEWTC), varying the threshold (Δ_p) for pruning from 0.001 to 0.1, with 10 steps between these two values, applying the criteria explained in Section 3.1.

The graphics included in Fig. 5 show: (**a**) storage requirements for AR algorithms, with tables to store quantitative information, using trees and applying constraints (AR, ARWT, ARWTC). No approximation has been performed. The horizontal axis indicates the number of operations required to complete the evaluation; (**b**) as (a), for VE algorithms. The curve for ARWTC (the most economical storage size) is included in order to compare the performance of both families of algorithms; (**c**) time of computation for the six tests; (**d**) maximum size reached during approximate evaluation, for AARWT, AARWTC, AVEWT, and AVEWTC. The horizontal axis represents the thresholds used for the approximations; (**e**) as (d), with time of computation; (**f**) errors regarding expected utility values computed without approximation, for AARWT, AARWTC, AVEWT, and AVEWTC.

Experiments show that the VE requires less storage space than AR in all the versions of these algorithms (compare the exact methods: VE-AR, VEWT-ARWT, VEWTC-ARWTC in Fig. 5a and 5b; and the approximate ones: AVEWT-AARWT, AVEWTC-AARWTC in Figure 5d). The use of numerical trees reduces storage space in both algorithms (see Figs. 5c, 5b, 5d). Constraints reduce the required space even further (compare VEWT-VEWTC and ARWT-ARWTC in Fig. 5d). Storage requirements can be controlled using a parameter Δ obtaining good approximations to the expected utility (see Figs. 5d and 5e). Approximate evaluation VE requires less time than AR in all versions (see Figs. 5c for exact evaluation and 5e for approximate). Approximate VE obtain fewer errors in the expected utility than AR (see Fig. 5f). These algorithms were implemented in Java with the Elvira tools (`http://leo.ugr.es/~elvira`). The tests were run on a Pentium 4 computer (2GHz) with Linux Red Hat 7.3 operating system.

6   Conclusions and Future Work

In this paper we have presented some ideas for evaluating complex influence diagrams. These ideas include the use of numerical trees to represent and compute with probability distributions and utility functions. We have also specified asymmetries by means of constraint rules and constraint trees, in order to reduce the size of the scenarios to be considered. The paper also shows how to use a deterministic approximate method for very complex problems. This allows us to compute a policy although it will not be optimal.

We conclude that the use of numerical trees for evaluating IDs requires less storage space than traditional methods. If we also use constraint trees, we further reduce the space required to compute the models. When the problem is too complex, we can use pruning operations, obtaining good approximate results.

In future lines of work, we shall study additional pruning methods for utility trees, e.g. pruning terminal nodes with standard deviation (regarding the maximum possible) below a given threshold. We are now considering the application of approximate methods in junction trees, for penniless [4] and lazy penniless [5] algorithms.

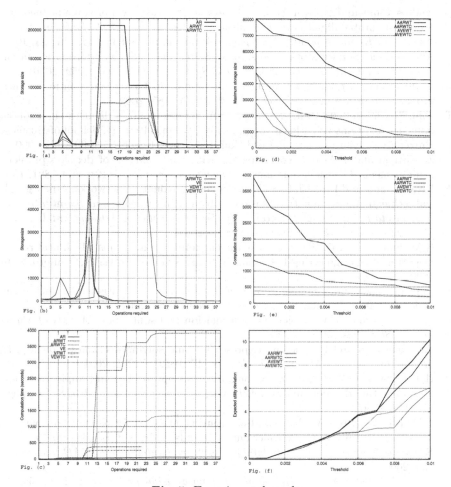

Fig. 5. Experimental results

Acknowledgments. This work has been supported by the Spanish MCYT under project TIC2001-2973-C05-01. We want to thank the anonymous reviewers for their insightful comments which have helped to improve the paper.

References

1. Concha Bielza and Prakash P. Shenoy. A comparison of graphical techniques for asymmetric decision problems. *Management Science*, 45(11):1552–1569, 1999.
2. C. Boutilier, N. Friedman, M. Goldszmidt, and D. Koller. Context-specific independence in Bayesian networks. In *Proceedings of the Twelfth Annual Conference on Uncertainty in Artificial Intelligence (UAI-96)*, pages 115–123, Portland, Oregon, 1996.

3. Andrés Cano and Serafín Moral. Propagación exacta y aproximada mediante árboles de probabilidad en redes causales. In *Actas de la VII Conferencia de la Asociación Española para la Inteligencia Artificial*, pages 635–644, Málaga, 1997.
4. Andrés Cano, Serafín Moral, and Antonio Salmerón. Penniless propagation in join trees. *International Journal of Intelligent Systems*, 15(11):1027–1059, 2000.
5. Andrés Cano, Serafín Moral, and Antonio Salmerón. Lazy evaluation in penniless propagation over join trees. *Networks*, 39(4):175–185, 2002.
6. John M. Charnes and Prakash P. Shenoy. A forward monte carlo method for solving influence diagrams using local computation. Technical report, School of Business. University of Kansas., Summerfield Hall. Lawrence, KS 66045-2003, July 2000.
7. Z. Covaliu and R.M. Oliver. Representation and solution of decision problems using sequential decision diagrams. *Management science*, 41(12):1860–1881, 1995.
8. Riza Demirer and Prakash P. Shenoy. Sequential valuation networks: A new graphical technique for asymmetric decision problems. In *Symbolic and Quantitative Approaches to Reasoning with Uncertainty, Lectures Notes in Artificial Intellingence, Vol. 2143*, pages 252–265. Springer-Verlag, 2001.
9. R.M. Fung and R.D. Shachter. Contingent influence diagrams. Technical report, Department of Engineering-Economic Systems, Stanford Univerity, Stanford, Calif, 1990.
10. Finn V. Jensen. *Bayesian Networks and Decision Graphs*. Statistics for Engineering and Information Science. Springer-Verlag, New York, 2001.
11. S. Kullback and R.A. Leibler. On information and sufficiency. *Annals of Mathematical Statistics*, 22:76–86, 1951.
12. S.L. Lauritzen and D. Nilsson. Representing and solving decision problems with limited information. *Management Science*, 47(9):1235–1251, 2001.
13. H.J. Miller and W.A. Miller. A comparison of approaches and implementations for automating decision analysis. *Reliability Engineering and System Safety*, pages 115–162, 1990.
14. T.D. Nielsen and F.V. Jensen. Representing and solving asymmetric bayesian decision problems. In C. Boutilier and M. Goldszmidt, editors, *Proceedings of the Sixteenth Conference on Uncertainty in Artificial Intelligence (UAI)*, pages 416–425, 2000.
15. S. M. Olmsted. *On representing and solving decision problems*. PhD thesis, Department of Engineering-Economic Systems, Stanford University, Stanford, CA., 1983.
16. R. Qi, N.L. Zhang, and D. Poole. Solving asymmetric decision problems with influence diagrams. In *Proc. of the 10th conference on AI*, pages 491–497, 1994.
17. Antonio Salmerón, Andrés Cano, and Serafín Moral. Importance sampling in Bayesian networks using probability trees. *Computational Statistics and Data Analysis*, 34:387–413, 2000.
18. R.D. Shachter. Evaluating influence diagrams. *Operations Research*, 34:871–882, 1986.
19. P. Shenoy. Valuation network representation and solution of asymmetric decision problems. *European Journal of Operational Research*, 121(3):579–608, 2000.
20. James E. Smith, Samuel Holtzman, and James E. Matheson. Structuring conditional relationships in influence diagrams. *Operations Research*, 41(2):280–297, 1993.

Mixed Influence Diagrams

Anders L. Madsen[1] and Frank Jensen[1]

Hugin Expert A/S
Niels Jernes Vej 10
DK-9220 Aalborg Ø
Denmark
Anders.L.Madsen@hugin.com,Frank.Jensen@hugin.com

Abstract. This paper presents an architecture for exact evaluation of influence diagrams containing a mixture of continuous and discrete variables. The proposed architecture is the first architecture for efficient exact solution of linear-quadratic conditional Gaussian influence diagrams with an additively decomposing utility function. The solution method as presented in this paper is based on the idea of lazy evaluation. The computational aspects of the architecture are illustrated by example.

1   Introduction

The framework of influence diagrams [1] is an effective modeling framework for analysis of Bayesian decision making under uncertainty. The influence diagram is a natural representation for capturing the semantics of decision making with a minimum of clutter and confusion for the decision maker. An influence diagram is essentially a Bayesian network augmented with decision variables, utility nodes, and precedence constraints. Solving a Bayesian decision problem amounts to determining an optimal strategy maximizing the expected utility for the decision maker. Determining an optimal strategy is, unfortunately, a computationally intensive task to solve.

Different architectures for solving discrete Bayesian decision problems have been proposed [12, 15, 2, 7, 5, 9]. Many real-life decision problems do, however, involve reasoning about uncertain entities and decisions, which take on values in continuous ranges. Few architectures for solving continuous Bayesian decision problems exist [3, 14]. Even fewer architectures deal with the mixed case. In [11] an architecture where arbitrary continuous distributions are approximated using (artificial) mixtures of Gaussians is described.

We present a computationally efficient architecture for representing and solving mixed Bayesian decision problems. The architecture is for simplicity of exposition based on formulating Bayesian decision problems as mixed influence diagrams and the solution method is an extension of Lazy propagation [7]. The proposed architecture can be considered as an extension of conditional-Gaussian Bayesian networks and discrete influence diagrams to the case of linear-quadratic conditional Gaussian influence diagrams with decomposing utility functions.

T.D. Nielsen and N.L. Zhang (Eds.): ECSQARU 2003, LNAI 2711 , pp. 208–219, 2003.

Even though we present the solution method of the architecture as a message passing algorithm based on Lazy propagation, the results are applicable to most other algorithms (including variable elimination). A detailed treatment of the general applicability of the results is, however, outside the scope of this paper.

2   Mixed Influence Diagrams

A mixed influence diagram N is defined as a triple $N = (G, \Phi, \Psi)$ where $G = (V, E)$ is a acyclic, directed graph (DAG) with chance, decision, and utility (value) nodes, Φ is a set of probability functions, and Ψ is a set of utility functions.

The nodes V of G are partitioned into the set of continuous nodes Γ, the set of discrete nodes Δ, and the set of utility nodes Υ, i.e. $V = \Gamma \cup \Delta \cup \Upsilon$. The set of decision nodes is denoted as $\mathcal{D}$ and the set of chance nodes as $\mathcal{C}$. We define subsets $\Delta_\mathcal{C} = \{X \in \Delta : X \in \mathcal{C}\}$ and $\Delta_\mathcal{D} = \{Y \in \Delta : Y \in \mathcal{D}\}$. Subsets $\Gamma_\mathcal{C}$ and $\Gamma_\mathcal{D}$ are defined similarly. We will refer to nodes and variables interchangeably.

An arc into a node $X \in \mathcal{C}$ denotes a possible probabilistic dependence relation whereas an arc from a node Y into a node $D \in \mathcal{D}$ indicates that Y is observed prior to decision D. Arcs into decision nodes are referred to as information arcs. The information arcs of N induce a partial precedence order $\prec$ on $\Gamma \cup \Delta$ of N s.t. $\mathcal{I}_0 \prec D_1 \prec \mathcal{I}_1 \prec \cdots \prec D_n \prec \mathcal{I}_n$ where $\mathcal{I}_i$ is the set of chance variables observed after D_i but before D_{i+1}. We assume a total order on the decision variables and a non-forgetting decision maker.

We consider the case of linear-quadratic conditional Gaussian influence diagrams. This implies $pa(X) \subseteq \Delta$ whenever $X \in \Delta$ and $pa(X) \subseteq \Delta \cup \Gamma$ whenever $X \in \Gamma \cup \Upsilon$. Each chance node $X \in \Delta$ has a conditional probability distribution $P(X \mid pa(X))$ whereas each chance node $X \in \Gamma$ is linear Gaussian conditional on $pa(X) \cap \Delta$. Each value node $U \in \Upsilon$ has a local utility function which assigns a value to each configuration of its parents in the discrete case and is a conditional quadratic function of its continuous parents in the mixed case. The set of local utility functions represents an additively decomposing utility function.

Fig. 1 shows an example of a mixed influence diagram N where the continuous nodes are indicated using a wider border.

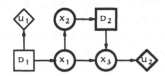

Fig. 1: A mixed influence diagram N

To solve a mixed influence diagram N is to determine an optimal strategy $\hat{S} = \{\delta_1, \ldots, \delta_{|\mathcal{D}|}\}$ consisting of a policy δ for each decision $D \in \mathcal{D}$ and to compute the maximum expected utility of adhering to $\hat{S}$.

The computations involved in solving a mixed influence diagram N can be organized in a strong junction tree representation T of N. We abstain here from describing all details of the compilation process. Instead we refer the reader to [2] for details on the junction tree compilation process. The construction of T consists of four main steps:

Minimalization where information arcs from non-requisite parents of decision nodes and barren variables are removed.

Moralization where all pairs of parents with a common child are *married* by inserting an undirected edge between them. The graph is made undirected and all utility nodes are removed to obtain G^M.

Triangulation where G^M is triangulated to obtain G^T with an elimination order σ such that $\sigma(\Gamma) < \sigma(\Delta)$ and $\sigma(\mathcal{I}_i) > \sigma(D_{i+1}) > \sigma(\mathcal{I}_{i+1})$ for all $i \in [0, n-1]$. That is, G^T is a strong triangulation of G^M.

Junction tree construction where the cliques $\mathcal{C}$ of G^T are organized as a strong junction tree $T = (\mathcal{C}, \mathcal{S})$ with strong root R.

Fig. 2 shows a mixed influence diagram representing a simple game. The first decision is to either accept an immediate award or to play a game where you will receive a payoff determined by how good you are at guessing the height of a person based on knowledge about the sex of the person. The payoff is a constant (higher than the award) minus the distance of your guess from the true height of the person measured as height minus guess squarred.

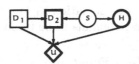

Fig. 2: A mixed influence diagram for a simple game

2.1 Conditional Linear Gaussians

Let X be an n-dimensional continuous variable with discrete parents I and continuous parents Z, then X has a *conditional linear Gaussian distribution* if:

$$\mathcal{L}(X \mid Z = z, I = i) = \mathcal{N}(A(i) + B(i)z, C(i)), \tag{1}$$

The mean vector of X depends linearly on the states of the continuous parent variables Z, while the covariance matrix is independent of Z. In equation 1, X is an $n \times 1$-dimensional vector, $A(i)$ is a table of $n \times 1$-dimensional vectors, $B(i)$ is a table of $n \times |Z|$-dimensional matrices, and $C(i)$ is a table of $n \times n$-dimensional positive semi-definite matrices.

We will use a notation similar to that of [4]. A cg-potential $p(i) \cdot \mathcal{L}(X \mid Z = z, I = i)$ is represented as $p(i)$ and $\lambda = [A, B, C](\{X\} \mid \{Z, I\})$ where $(\{X\}, \{Z, I\})$

is a partitioning of the domain variables $\text{dom}(\lambda)$ of λ into head $H(\lambda) = \{X\}$ and tail $T(\lambda) = \{Z, I\}$, respectively. Notice that we have separated the discrete part $p(i)$ of the cg-potential from the continuous part λ. We define $\mathcal{P} \subseteq \Phi$ as $\mathcal{P} = \{p(X|pa(X)) : X \in \Delta_C\}$ and $\Lambda \subseteq \Phi$ as $\Lambda = \{\mathcal{L}(X|pa(X)) : X \in \Gamma_C\}$.

Consider a cg-potential $\lambda(X_1, X_2 | Z) = [A, B, C]$ and let

$$A = \begin{pmatrix} A_1 \\ A_2 \end{pmatrix}, B = \begin{pmatrix} B_1 \\ B_2 \end{pmatrix}, \text{ and } C = \begin{pmatrix} C_{11} & C_{12} \\ C_{21} & C_{22} \end{pmatrix}$$

be a partitioning of A, B, and C relative to X_1 and X_2, respectively. The strong marginal of λ w.r.t. X_1 is $\lambda(X_1 | Z) = [A_1, B_1, C_{11}]$. Using : to indicate that the matrix is extended with an additional column for each new tail variable, the complement of λ w.r.t. X_1 is:

$$\lambda(X_2 | X_1, Z) = [A_2 - C_{21} C_{11}^{-1} A_1, [C_{21} C_{11}^{-1} : B_2 - C_{21} C_{11}^{-1} B_1], C_{22} - C_{21} C_{11}^{-1} C_{12}].$$

Let $X_1 | Z = z \sim \mathcal{N}(A_1 + B_1 z, C_1)$ and $X_2 | X_1 = x_1, Z = z \sim \mathcal{N}(A_2 + B_{21} x_1 + B_{22} z, C_2)$ have cg-potentials λ_1 and λ_2, respectively. The combination $\lambda(X_1, X_2) = \lambda_1 \dot{\otimes} \lambda_2 = [U, V, W]$ is:

$$U = \begin{pmatrix} A_1 \\ A_2 + B_{21} A_1 \end{pmatrix}, V = \begin{pmatrix} B_1 \\ B_{22} + B_{21} B_1 \end{pmatrix}, W = \begin{pmatrix} C_1 & C_1 B_{21}^{\mathsf{T}} \\ B_{21} C_1 & C_2 + B_{21} C_1 B_{21}^{\mathsf{T}} \end{pmatrix}.$$

The combination $\lambda_1 \dot{\otimes} \lambda_2$ is only defined, when $H(\lambda_2) \cap \text{dom}(\lambda_1) = \emptyset$ or $H(\lambda_1) \cap \text{dom}(\lambda_2) = \emptyset$. *Recursive combination* $\lambda_1 \otimes \lambda_2$ is used to combine λ_1 and λ_2 when direct combination is not possible. The potentials λ_1 and λ_2 are decomposed recursively until direct combination can be applied, see [4] for details. For notational convenience a combination $\lambda_1 \otimes \cdots \otimes \lambda_n$ is written as $\prod_{i=1}^{n} \lambda_i$. We assume the tail of all cg-potentials to be minimal [4].

2.2 The Quadratic Utility Function

In the linear-quadratic conditional Gaussian influence diagram, the utility function $U(\Gamma, \Delta)$ is a second-order polynomial in Γ conditional on Δ. Thus, the utility function has the form $U(X = x, I = i) = x^{\mathsf{T}} Q(i) x + R(i) x + S(i)$, where X is a $|X| \times 1$ vector of continuous variables, $I \subseteq \Delta$, $Q(i)$ is a table of $|X| \times |X|$ symmetric negative semi-definite matrices, $R(i)$ is a table of $1 \times |X|$ vectors, and $S(i)$ is a table of constants.

The utility function $U(X, I)$ may decompose into a set of simpler terms $\Psi = \{\psi_1, \ldots, \psi_m\}$ s.t. $U(X, I) = \sum_{j=1}^{m} \psi_j(X_j, I_j)$, where $X_j \subseteq X$, $I_j \subseteq I$, and each $\psi_j(X_j, I_j)$ has the form $x_j^{\mathsf{T}} Q(i_j) x_j + R(i_j) x_j + S(i_j)$. Each term $\psi(X, I)$ is represented as $[Q, R, S](\{X, I\})$ where $\text{dom}(\psi) = X \cup I$ with $X \subseteq \Gamma$ and $I \subseteq \Delta$. Notice that special care should be taken in the specification of $Q = [q_{ij}]$ since $q_{ij} = \frac{1}{2} Q_{x_i, x_j}$ when $i \neq j$ and $x_i Q_{x_i, x_j} x_j$ is a term of U.

Let ψ_1 and ψ_2 be two utility functions such that $\psi_1 = [Q_1, R_1, S_1](\{X, I\})$ and $\psi_2 = [Q_2, R_2, S_2](\{X, I\})$ after proper domain extensions. The combination $\psi_1 + \psi_2$ is a utility function $[Q_1 + Q_2, R_1 + R_2, S_1 + S_2](\{X, I\})$.

Recall, that a polynomial $Q x^2 + R x + S$ with $Q < 0$ takes on its maximum value at its vertex $v = (x, y)$ where $x = -\frac{R}{2Q}$ and $y = \frac{-R^2}{4Q} + S$.

3   Solving Mixed Influence Diagrams

The maximum expected utility of a mixed influence diagram N can be calculated by eliminating the variables of N in reverse order of the precedence ordering under the constraint that $\sigma(\Gamma) < \sigma(\Delta)$ where σ is the elimination order and the first variable to eliminate Y has $\sigma(Y) = 1$. From $\Phi = \mathcal{P} \cup \Lambda$ and Ψ, the maximum expected utility MEU is computed as:

$$\text{MEU} = \underset{X \in V}{\mathsf{M}} \prod_{\phi \in \Phi} \phi \sum_{\psi \in \Psi} \psi, \qquad (2)$$

where M is a further generalization of the generalized marginalization operator introduced by [2]. Here the operator is generalized such that a continuous chance variable X is eliminated by integration, i.e. $\mathsf{M}_X \, \rho = \int_X \rho \, dx$ whereas discrete chance variables are eliminated by summation and decision variables are eliminated by maximization as usual. The operator is defined precisely below.

Following the approach of [7], we assume that the first variable to eliminate according to the strong elimination order σ is Y, i.e. $\sigma(Y) = 1$. Let Ψ_Y be the subset of Ψ including Y in the domain, i.e. $\Psi_Y = \{\psi \in \Psi : Y \in \text{dom}(\psi)\}$ and let Φ_Y be the subset of Φ including Y in the domain, i.e. $\Phi_Y = \{\phi \in \Phi : Y \in \text{dom}(\phi)\}$. Define ϕ_Y and ψ_Y as follows:

$$\phi_Y = \underset{Y}{\mathsf{M}} \prod_{\phi \in \Phi_Y} \phi, \qquad \psi_Y = \underset{Y}{\mathsf{M}} \left(\frac{\prod_{\phi \in \Phi_Y} \phi}{\phi_Y} \right) \sum_{\psi \in \Psi_Y} \psi. \qquad (3)$$

With these definitions, equation 2 is rewritten as:

$$\text{MEU} = \underset{X \in V}{\mathsf{M}} \left(\prod_{\phi \in \Phi} \phi \sum_{\psi \in \Psi} \psi \right) \qquad (4)$$

$$= \underset{X \in V}{\mathsf{M}} \left[\prod_{\phi \in \Phi \setminus \Phi_Y} \phi \prod_{\phi' \in \Phi_Y} \phi' \left(\sum_{\psi \in \Psi \setminus \Psi_Y} \psi + \sum_{\psi' \in \Psi_Y} \psi' \right) \right]$$

$$= \underset{X \in V \setminus \{Y\}}{\mathsf{M}} \left[\prod_{\phi \in \Phi \setminus \Phi_Y} \phi \underset{Y}{\mathsf{M}} \prod_{\phi' \in \Phi_Y} \phi' \left(\sum_{\psi \in \Psi \setminus \Psi_Y} \psi + \frac{\underset{Y}{\mathsf{M}} \prod_{\phi' \in \Phi_Y} \phi' \sum_{\psi' \in \Psi_Y} \psi'}{\underset{Y}{\mathsf{M}} \prod_{\phi' \in \Phi_Y} \phi'} \right) \right]$$

$$= \underset{X \in V \setminus \{Y\}}{\mathsf{M}} \left[\phi_Y \prod_{\phi \in \Phi \setminus \Phi_Y} \phi \left(\sum_{\psi \in \Psi \setminus \Psi_Y} \psi + \underset{Y}{\mathsf{M}} \left(\frac{\prod_{\phi' \in \Phi_Y} \phi'}{\underset{Y}{\mathsf{M}} \prod_{\phi' \in \Phi_Y} \phi'} \right) \sum_{\psi' \in \Psi_Y} \psi' \right) \right]$$

$$= \underset{X \in V \setminus \{Y\}}{\mathsf{M}} \left[\phi_Y \prod_{\phi \in \Phi \setminus \Phi_Y} \phi \left(\sum_{\psi \in \Psi \setminus \Psi_Y} \psi + \psi_Y \right) \right]. \qquad (5)$$

The sets $\Phi^* = (\Phi \setminus \Phi_Y) \cup \{\phi_Y\}$ and $\Psi^* = (\Psi \setminus \Psi_Y) \cup \{\psi_Y\}$ are the updated sets of probability and utility potentials obtained after the elimination of Y. The evaluation of N proceeds in a similar manner for the remaining variables.

If Y is a continuous variable, then $\sum_{\psi \in \Psi_Y} \psi$ is either a constant, a first order, or second order polynomial in Y. If Y is a discrete variable, then $\sum_{\psi \in \Psi_Y} \psi$ is constant in Y. If Y is a decision variable, then $\prod_{\phi \in \Phi_Y} \phi$ considered as a function of Y alone is a non-negative constant. This implies that the elimination of Y is simple. This observation is due to Lemma 1 of [2].

Consider the division of probability potentials in equation 3. If $Y \in \Gamma_C$, then either Y is probabilistic barren and no division is necessary or the division corresponds to the complement operation described in section 2.1.

During the evaluation of N, we eliminate variables from the combination of probability and cg-potentials, and from the combination of probability, cg, and utility potentials. Notice, however, that if the variable Y to be eliminated next is a continuous variable, then no probability potential is involved in the elimination. Similarly, if Y is a discrete variable, then all (relevant) continuous variables have been eliminated and no cg-potential is involved. This is due to the model structure constraints.

The constraint $\sigma(\Delta) > \sigma(\Gamma)$ on σ can be relaxed. The relaxation can be explained in terms of the topological of $G = (V, E)$. Let $\mathcal{P}(D_i)$ and $\mathcal{F}(D_i)$ denote the past and future of D_i, respectively. That is, $\mathcal{P}(D_i) = \bigcup_{j=0}^{i-1} \mathcal{I}_j \cup \{D_1, \ldots, D_{i-1}\}$ and $\mathcal{F}(D_i) = \bigcup_{j=i}^{n} \mathcal{I}_j \cup \{D_{i+1}, \ldots, D_n\}$. The requisite past $\mathrm{Rq}(D_i)$ and relevant future $\mathrm{Rl}(D_i)$ of D_i are defined as [13, 10]:

$$\mathrm{Rq}(D_i) = \{X \in \mathcal{P}(D_i) : X \not\perp \mathrm{de}(D_i) \cap \Upsilon_{D_i} | \mathrm{pa}(D_i) \setminus \{X\}\},$$
$$\mathrm{Rl}(D_i) = \{X \in \mathcal{F}(D_i) : X \not\perp \mathrm{de}(D_i) \cap \Upsilon_{D_i} | \mathrm{pa}(D_i)\},$$

where $\mathrm{de}(D_i)$ are the descendants of D_i in the graph of the minimalization of N ignoring information arcs.

A discrete variable X is not allowed to be relevant Rl for a continuous decision variable D, but X is allowed to be requisite Rq for $D \in \Gamma$. That is, the condition $\mathrm{Rl}(D) \cap \Delta = \emptyset$ must be satisfied whereas there is no constraint on $\mathrm{Rq}(D)$.

The above derivation is based on the assumption that variables can be eliminated using efficient local operations. Such operations are derived next.

3.1   The Marginalization Operator

As continuous variables are eliminated before discrete variables, the elimination of a discrete variable involves either maximization or summation over a discrete function. Hence, the set of cg-potentials is empty. This implies that elimination of a discrete variable proceeds as in the case of pure discrete influence diagrams, see e.g. [7] for details.

Definition 1. *The operation of marginalization* M *of a discrete variable* X *is defined as* $\mathsf{M}_X = \sum_X$.

Definition 2. *The operation of marginalization* M *of a discrete decision variable* X *from a utility potential* $\psi(X, I)$ *is defined as* $\mathsf{M}_X \psi = \max_X \psi$. *The optimal policy* $\delta_X(i)$ *for* X *is:*

$$\delta_X(i) = \arg \max_X \psi_X(x, i).$$

Consider the elimination of a continuous decision variable X from a utility potential $\psi = \sum_{\psi' \in \Psi_X} \psi'$ such that $\psi = [Q, R, S](\{Y, I\})$. For each i, the $Q(i)$ matrix is partitioned relative to the decision variable X as follows (assuming $Y = (X, Z^T)^T$):

$$Q(i) = \begin{pmatrix} Q_{XX}(i) & Q_{XZ}(i) \\ Q_{ZX}(i) & Q_{ZZ}(i) \end{pmatrix}.$$

where $Q_{XZ} = Q_{ZX}^T$. Similarly, for each i, the vector $R(i)$ is partitioned relative to X into $R_X(i)$ and $R_Z(i)$. With this partitioning, we get:

$$\bigwedge_X \psi(y, i) = \bigwedge_X y^T Q(i) y + R(i) y + S(i)$$

$$= z^T Q_{ZZ}(i) z + R_Z(i) z + S(i)$$

$$+ \bigwedge_X x^T Q_{XX}(i) x + R_X(i) x + 2x^T Q_{XZ}(i) z.$$

Considered as a function of x, $\psi(y, i)$ takes on its maximum value (i.e. $\arg\max_X \psi(y, i)$) at $x = -\frac{R_X(i) + 2Q_{XZ}(i) z}{2Q_{XX}(i)}$ for each i assuming that $Q_{XX}(i) < 0$ (or $\psi(y, i)$ is constant in x in which case ψ is not a function of X). The maximum value of $\psi(y, i)$ at x (i.e. $\max_X \psi(y, i)$) is:

$$\max_X \psi(y, i) = -\frac{(R_X(i) + 2Q_{XZ}(i) z)^2}{4Q_{XX}(i)} + (z^T Q_{ZZ}(i) z + R_Z(i) z + S(i)).$$

The result of $\max_X \psi(y, i)$ is a utility potential $\psi(z, i) = [Q^*, R^*, S^*]$.

Definition 3. *The operation of marginalization of a continuous decision variable X from a utility potential* $\psi(y, i) = [Q, R, S]$ *is defined as* $\bigwedge_X \psi$ *with* $\bigwedge_X \psi = [Q^*, R^*, S^*](\{z, i\})$ *where:*

$$Q^*(i) = -\frac{Q_{ZX}(i) Q_{XZ}(i)}{Q_{XX}(i)} + Q_{ZZ}(i),$$

$$R^*(i) = \frac{R_X(i) Q_{XZ}(i)}{Q_{XX}(i)} + R_Z(i),$$

$$S^*(i) = -\frac{R_X(i)^2}{4Q_{XX}(i)} + S(i).$$

The optimal decision policy $\delta_X(z, i)$ *for X is:*

$$\delta_X(z, i) = -\frac{R_X(i) + 2Q_{XZ}(i) z}{2Q_{XX}(i)}.$$

Notice that the constraint that Q is negative semi-definite can be relaxed. It is sufficient that $Q_{XX}(i) < 0$ for all i when eliminating the continuous decision variable X since this implies that the second order polynomial has a unique maximum with respect to X.

There are two cases to consider when defining the operation of marginalization of a continuous chance variable X. First the simple case where X has to be eliminated from a cg-potential.

Definition 4. *Marginalization of a continuous chance variable* X *from a cg-potential* λ *is strong marginalization* $\mathsf{M}_X \lambda = \int_x \lambda dx$.

In the general case we need to eliminate X from a combination $\phi * \psi$ of a cg-potential $\phi = [A, B, C](\{X\}|\{Z, I\})$ and utility potential $\psi = [Q, R, S](\{Y, I\})$. We assume proper domain extensions have been made such that $\text{dom}(\lambda) = \text{dom}(\psi)$. Let R and Q be partitioned relative to X and Z as described above. The properties $\mathbb{E}(X) = \mu$ and $\mathbb{E}(X^2) = \mu^2 + \sigma^2$ of the normal distribution are exploited when eliminating $X \sim N(\mu, \sigma^2)$. The variable X is eliminated from $(\phi * \psi)(y, i)$ as follows:

$$\mathsf{M}_X \phi * \psi = \mathsf{M}_X \phi * (y^T Q(i)y + R(i)y + S(i)) = z^T Q^*(i)z + R^*(i)z + S^*(i).$$

Definition 5. *Let* ϕ *and* ψ *be a cg-potential and a utility potential, respectively. The operation of marginalization of continuous chance variable* X *from* $(\phi * \psi)(y, i)$ *is defined as* $\mathsf{M}_X \phi * \psi = [Q^*, R^*, S^*](\{Z, I\})$ *where:*

$$Q^*(i) = Q_{zz}(i) + 2Q_{zx}(i)B(i) + Q_{xx}(i)(B(i)^T B(i)),$$
$$R^*(i) = R_z(i) + 2A(i)Q_{xz}(i) + (2Q_{xx}(i)A(i) + R_x(i))B(i),$$
$$S^*(i) = Q_{xx}(i)(A(i)^2 + C(i)) + S(i) + R_x(i)A(i).$$

4 Lazy Propagation

Lazy propagation in an extended version can be used to solve N efficiently by message passing in a strong junction tree representation T of N. In this section we present the extensions of Lazy propagation necessary to solve N. The main idea of Lazy propagation is to maintain decompositions of clique potentials until combination becomes mandatory by a variable elimination. Therefore, the notion of a potential is introduced:

Definition 6 (Potential). *A potential on* $W \subseteq V$ *is a pair* $\pi_W = (\Phi, \Psi)$ *where* Φ *is a set of non-negative real functions on subsets of* W *and* Ψ *is a set of real functions on subsets of* W.

The probability part $\Phi = \{p_i\} \cup \{\lambda_j\}$ of a potential is a set of probability potentials $\{p_i\}$ and cg-potentials $\{\lambda_j\}$ whereas the utility part $\Psi = \{\psi_k\}$ is a set of local utility functions as defined above. We call a potential π_W *vacuous*, if $\pi_W = (\emptyset, \emptyset)$. We define new operations of combination and marginalization.

Definition 7 (Combination). *The combination of potentials* $\pi_{W_1} = (\Phi_1, \Psi_1)$ *and* $\pi_{W_2} = (\Phi_2, \Psi_2)$ *denotes the potential on* $W_1 \cup W_2$ *given by* $\pi_{W_1} \otimes \pi_{W_2}$ *where* $\pi_{W_1} \otimes \pi_{W_2} = (\Phi_1 \cup \Phi_2, \Psi_1 \cup \Psi_2)$.

Definition 8 (Marginalization). *The marginalization of* $\pi_W = (\Phi, \Psi)$ *onto* $W \setminus W_1$ *is defined as:*

$$\pi_W^{\downarrow W \setminus W_1} = (\Phi \setminus \Phi_{W_1} \cup \{\phi_{W_1}\}, \Psi \setminus \Psi_{W_1} \cup \{\psi_{W_1}\}),$$

where:

$$\phi_{W_1} = \bigwedge_{W_1} \prod_{\phi \in \Phi_{W_1}} \phi, \qquad \psi_{W_1} = \bigwedge_{W_1} \left(\frac{\prod_{\phi \in \Phi_{W_1}} \phi}{\phi_{W_1}} \right) \sum_{\psi \in \Psi_{W_1}} \psi,$$

$\Phi_{W_1} = \{\phi \in \Phi : W_1 \cap \mathrm{dom}(\phi) \neq \emptyset\}$, *and* $\Psi_{W_1} = \{\psi \in \Psi : W_1 \cap \mathrm{dom}(\psi) \neq \emptyset\}$.
We use the convention that $0/0 = 0$.

4.1   Initialization

The first step in initialization of $T = (\mathcal{C}, \mathcal{S})$ is to associate a vacuous potential
with each clique $C \in \mathcal{C}$. Then, for each chance variable X, $\phi(X \mid \mathrm{pa}(X))$ is associated with the probability part of π_C for any clique C satisfying $C \supseteq \mathrm{fa}(X)$.
Similarly, for each utility node U, $\psi(\mathrm{pa}(U))$ is associated with the utility part
of π_C for any clique C satisfying $C \supseteq \mathrm{pa}(U)$.

After initialization each clique C holds a potential $\pi_C = (\Phi, \Psi)$ and the joint
potential on T is:

$$\pi_V = (\Phi_V, \Psi_V) = \bigotimes_{C \in \mathcal{C}} \pi_C.$$

Notice, that $\bigcup_{\phi \in \Phi_C} \mathrm{dom}(\phi) \cup \bigcup_{\psi \in \Psi_C} \mathrm{dom}(\psi) \subseteq C$ for $\pi_C = (\Phi_C, \Psi_C)$.

4.2   Message Passing

A mixed influence diagram N is solved by message passing in T via the separators
of T. The separator between two neighboring cliques A and B is $A \cap B$. Messages
are passed from the leaf cliques of T to the strong root R by recursively letting
each clique A pass a message to its parent B whenever A has received a message
from each of its children. The message $\pi_{A \to B}$ is passed from clique A to clique B
by absorption. Absorption from A to B involves eliminating the variables $A \setminus B$
from the combination of the potential associated with A and the messages passed
to A from its neighbors $\mathrm{ne}(A)$ except B. The message $\pi_{A \to B}$ is:

$$\pi_{A \to B} = \left(\pi_A \otimes \left(\otimes_{C \in \mathrm{ne}(A) \setminus \{B\}} \pi_{C \to A} \right) \right)^{\downarrow B},$$

where $\pi_{C \to A}$ is the message passed from C to A.

Theorem 1. *Suppose we start with a joint potential* π_V *on a strong junction tree*
T, *and pass messages toward the root clique* R *as described above. When* R *has
received a message from each of its neighbors, the combination of all messages
with its own potential is equal to the* R-*marginal of* π_V:

$$\pi_V^{\downarrow R} = (\otimes_{C \in \mathcal{C}} \pi_C)^{\downarrow R} = \pi_R \otimes (\otimes_{C \in \mathrm{ne}(R)} \pi_{C \to R}),$$

where $\mathcal{C}$ *is the set of cliques in* T.

4.3   Local Optimization and Local Computation

The maximizing alternatives of the utility potential ψ from which decision variable D is eliminated during evaluation of N are recorded as the optimal decision rule for D, which is either a constant of a linear function in the parents.

A message passed from clique A to clique B is as explained above computed by eliminating all variables of $A \setminus B$. The structure of the strong junction tree T imposes a partial order on the variable elimination order. The structure of T does not impose any constraints on the order in which the variables of $A \setminus B$ have to be eliminated, but the constraint $\sigma(\Delta) > \sigma(\Gamma)$ has to be satisfied. Thus, the variables of $A \setminus B$ can be eliminated in any legal order when computing the message to pass from A to B.

In [8, 7] it is described how independence relations and probabilistic barren variables can be exploited to decrease the computational cost of message passing in Bayesian networks and discrete influence diagrams, respectively. Independence relations and barren variables can be exploited during the solution of mixed influence diagrams in a similar way.

4.4   Example

Consider the mixed influence diagram N of Fig. 3 and its corresponding strong junction tree T shown in Fig. 4. The initialization of T proceeds as explained in section 4.1. The precedence order on the chance variables is: $\{I_2\} \prec D_1 \prec \{X_2\} \prec D_2 \prec \{I_1, X_1, X_3\}$ which does not satisfy $\Delta \prec \Gamma$. Notice, however, that $Rq(D_1) = \{I_2\}$, $Rq(D_2) = \{I_2, D_1, X_2\}$, $Rl(D_1) = \{I_1, X_1, X_2, D_2, X_3\}$, and $Rl(D_2) = \{X_3\}$. Thus, even though $I_1 \in \mathcal{I}_2$ it is possible to solve N since $I_1 \notin Rl(D_2)$.

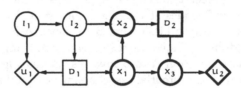

Fig. 3: An extension of the mixed influence diagram N shown in Fig. 1

In order to solve N messages are passed in T from the leaf clique $C_3 = D_1 X_1 X_3$ to the strong root $C_1 = I_2 D_1 I_1$ as follows (where $C_2 = I_2 D_1 X_2 D_2 X_1$ and $S_{23} = C_2 \cap C_3 = \{D_1, X_1\}$):

$$\pi_{S_{23}} = \pi_{C_3}^{\downarrow S_{23}} = (\emptyset, \psi(X_1, D_2)) = (\emptyset, \{\bigwedge_{X_3} U_2(X_3)\lambda(X_3 | X_1, D_2)\}).$$

Notice, that X_3 is probabilistic barren implying that the probability part of $\pi_{S_{23}}$ is the empty set. The second message is computed as:

$$\pi_{S_{12}} = (\pi_{C_2} \otimes \pi_{S_{23}})^{\downarrow S_{12}} = (\emptyset, \{\psi(I_2, D_1)\}).$$

Fig. 4: Strong junction tree representation of N in Fig. 3

To obtain the maximum expected utility and the optimal strategy, we compute $(\pi_V)^{\downarrow\emptyset} = (\pi_{C_1} \otimes \pi_{S_{1_2}})^{\downarrow\emptyset}$. The structure of T induces the elimination order. Due to the simplicity of the example there is no freedom w.r.t. selecting the on-line elimination order.

5 Discussion and Conclusion

The work by [3, 14] on linear-quadratic-Gaussian influence diagrams imposes a number of restrictions on the structure of the influence diagram. All (chance) variables are Gaussian distributed, the interaction between chance variables is linear, and the sources of uncertainty are Gaussian distributed and uncorrelated. These restrictions are similar to the restrictions our architecture puts on the continuous variables.

In the architecture of [14], the utility function is assumed to decompose additively into a set of local utility functions. Prior to evaluating the influence diagram, the local utility functions are combined into a single utility function with a domain equal to the union of the set of chance and the set of decision variables. This more or less corresponds to assuming that all variables in the model condition the utility function. This assumption is made due to difficulty with maintaining minimal conditional predecessors and not letting the utility function be a part of the influence diagram. This implies, for instance, that the architecture is not able to exploit probabilistic barren variables. Barren variables, on the other hand, can be removed from the diagram as a preprocessing step. The solution method is based on arc-reversal. During the evaluation, the expected value of the value function is maintained as the influence diagram is transformed via reduction operations. In this way, the architecture maintains a valid influence diagram representation during the evaluation of the decision problem where the utility function is maintained outside the influence diagram.

The work of [11] on mixed influence diagrams is based on an (artificial) mixture distribution approach. The distribution of a continuous variable is approximated using an mixture of Gaussians. The structure of the influence diagram models are constrained under the same conditions as the architecture we present.

Both of the above architectures are based on the central-moment representation whereas the architecture we propose is based on the raw-moment representation. This gives a few differences with respect to specification of the decision problem. For instance, it is necessary to make additional passes over the structure using the central-moment representation.

We have presented the first junction tree based architecture for solving influence diagrams with a mixture of continuous and discrete variables, i.e. linear-quadratic conditional Gaussian influence diagrams. The architecture which is based on exact computation is also the first architecture to efficiently exploit (additively or multiplicatively) decomposing utility functions. This makes the architecture more efficient than the architecture of [14], for instance.

Returning to the example of the simple game with two decisions, the optimal strategy is, of course, to stay in the game make and a guess on the height, which is the average height of a person with the given sex.

Recently, there has been some development in representation and solution of Bayesian network models containing both discrete and continuous variables, see e.g. [6]. This includes discrete children of continuous variables and arbitrarily distributed continuous variables. Extending these methods to the case of influence diagrams is an interesting topic of future research.

References

1. R. A. Howard and J. E. Matheson. Influence Diagrams. In *The Principles and Applications of Decision Analysis*, volume 2, chapter 37, pages 721–762. 1981.
2. F. Jensen, F. V. Jensen, and S. Dittmer. From Influence Diagrams to Junction Trees. In *Proc. of the 10th UAI*, pages 367–373, 1994.
3. C. R. Kenley. *Influence Diagram Models with Continuous Variables*. PhD thesis, EES Department, Stanford University, 1986.
4. S. L. Lauritzen and F. Jensen. Stable Local Computation with Mixed Gaussian Distributions. *Statistics and Computing*, 11(2):191–203, 2001.
5. S. L. Lauritzen and D. Nilsson. Representing and solving decision problems with limited information. *Management Science*, 47:1238–1251, 2001.
6. U. Lerner, E. Segal, and D. Koller. Exact Inference in Networks with Discrete Children of Continuous Parents. In *Proc. of the 17th UAI*, pages 319–328, 2001.
7. A. L. Madsen and F. V. Jensen. Lazy Evaluation of Symmetric Bayesian Decision Problems. In *Proc. of the 15th UAI*, pages 382–390, 1999.
8. A. L. Madsen and F. V. Jensen. Lazy propagation: A junction tree inference algorithm based on lazy evaluation. *Artificial Intelligence*, 113(1-2):203–245, 1999.
9. A. L. Madsen and D. Nilsson. Solving Influence Diagrams using HUGIN, Shafer-Shenoy and Lazy Propagation. In *Proc. of the 17th UAI*, pages 337–345, 2001.
10. T. D. Nielsen. Decomposition of Influence Diagrams. In *Proc. of the 6th EC-SQARU*, pages 144–155, 2001.
11. W. B. Poland. *Decision Analysis with Continuous and Discrete Variables: A Mixture Distribution Approach*. PhD thesis, Engineering-Economic Systems, Stanford University, Stanford, CA, 1994.
12. R. Shachter. Evaluating influence diagrams. *Operations Research*, 34(6):871–882, 1986.
13. R. Shachter. Bayes-Ball: The Rational Pasttime (for Determining Irrelevance and Requisite Information in Belief Networks and Influence Diagrams). In *Proc. of the 14th UAI*, pages 480–487, 1998.
14. R. D. Shachter and C. R. Kenley. Gaussian influence diagrams. *Management Science*, 35(5):527–549, 1989.
15. P. P. Shenoy. Valuation-Based Systems for Bayesian Decision Analysis. *Operations Research*, 40(3):463–484, 1992.

Decision Making Based on Sampled Disease Occurrence in Animal Herds

Michael Höhle[1,2] and Erik Jørgensen[2]

[1] Department of Animal Science and Animal Health, Royal Veterinary and
Agricultural University, Grønnegårdsvej 3, 1870 Frb. C, Denmark
hoehle@dina.dk
[2] Department of Animal Breeding and Genetics, Danish Institute of Agricultural
Sciences, Research Centre Foulum, PO Box 50, 8830 Tjele, Denmark
Erik.Jorgensen@agrsci.dk

Abstract. To make qualified decisions when extrapolating results from
a survey sample with imprecise tests requires careful handling of uncertainty. Both the imprecise test and uncertainty introduced by the sampling have to be taken into account in order to act optimally. This paper
formulates an influence diagram with discrete and continuous nodes to
handle an example typical for animal production: a veterinarian who –
as part of a biosecurity program – has to decide whether to treat a herd
of animals after inspecting a small fraction of them.
Our aim is to investigate the robustness of the obtained strategy by performing a two-way sensitivity analysis with respect to the proportion of
false positives and false negatives of the test. Output of the analysis is
a treatment map illustrating how the chosen strategy varies according
to variation in these proportions. The map helps to investigate whether
a certain variation is acceptable or if the test procedure has to be stan-
dardized in order to reduce variation. Objective of the paper is to be an
appetizer to work more with the issues raised in obtaining a practical
solution.

1 Introduction

Traditional survey sampling as e.g. in [1] is concerned with establishing the
proportion of individuals having a specific characteristic in a population. This
is done by extrapolating results from a sample to the entire population. In the
traditional case, investigation of each individual in the sample will reveal its true
state, i.e. as either having the property or not. In many practical applications
such precise answers are not available – the test is imprecise thus introducing
both false negatives and false positives. An example from the veterinarian field
is the use of a diagnostic test to determine the disease prevalence of a herd.
The task of establishing the disease status of a herd is typical for biosecurity
programs, e.g. for salmonella in pigs or Johne's disease in cattle [2,3]. Similar
examples are found in clinical decision making or when testing for GM-seeds in
seed lots [4,5]. Estimates on disease prevalence, $0 \leq p \leq 1$, need to take the

T.D. Nielsen and N.L. Zhang (Eds.): ECSQARU 2003, LNAI 2711, pp. 220–229, 2003.

sensitivity and *specificity* of the diagnostic test into account, i.e. respectively the fractions of diseased and non-diseased cases correctly diagnosed by the test. In practical situations these fractions can be hard and resource demanding to establish for a test method. Even worse, they are also open for a great deal of variation. For example when different veterinarians have to determine herd prevalence of e.g. pneumonia or diarrhea in a section of slaughter pigs [4].

If the same test is performed in all cases, an investigation could be performed to establish the sensitivity and specificity (Se, Sp) of the test procedure. With the uncertainty in p due to sampling taken into account a biosecurity program could recommend the following treatment strategy: Treat all animals in the section at cost C_D if p is above some threshold T and do nothing if $p \leq T$. Based on the true prevalence and treatment chosen at the current time stage a reward is given. The aim is to choose the threshold maximizing the expected reward. Even though we find the optimal T, and recommend the strategy to all veterinarians, we would not take into account the variability in (Se, Sp) due to each veterinarian making his own subjective clinical diagnosis for every investigated individual. Assume the specific veterinarian has a true (but unknown) setup of $(Se + \delta, Sp + \epsilon)$. If he follows the threshold based on (Se, Sp) he might not achieve the maximum expected utility because his uncertainty in p is of a different magnitude and shape.

Current biosecurity programs, e.g. the voluntary herd status program against Johne's disease [2], operate with fixed point estimates on sensitivity and specificity of the diagnostic test. To assess the impact of the above variability a proper sensitivity analysis should therefore be an integral part of the modeling. Methods such as one-way and two-way sensitivity analysis, tornado, rainbow diagrams, etc., provide valuable insights about implementational robustness of an optimal strategy [6]. Another approach would be to quantify uncertainty on sensitivity and specificity by distributions [7,8]. Our interest, however, is the decision analytic dimension of the problem: How does variability affect a biosecurity program that assume fixed point estimates on sensitivity and specificity? How large deviations are allowed before the recommended strategy is suboptimal.

The following sections will show how the above considerations boil down to performing a two-way sensitivity analysis for an influence diagram with both discrete and continuous nodes. How to perform analytically sensitivity analysis in Bayesian networks is already well established [9,10] whereas the matter is more complicated in influence diagrams. Here, especially sequential decision problems quickly become intractable to handle [11,10]. As the above treatment considerations only contain a single decision, analytical calculations are tractable up to certain herd sizes, e.g. using Maple [12]. Solution of the diagram can also be done numerically using Gibbs sampling, where sensitivity analysis becomes a matter of performing many point-wise evaluations. For small herds both analytic and numeric solutions can be applied to verify correctness, while the numeric approach is the only tractable method once herd size become large.

The structure of this article is as follows. Section 2 describes how the clinical treatment example can be formulated as an influence diagram. Hereafter,

Sect. 3 describes how to calculate expected utilities in this model in order to select the best decision alternative. Robustness of these decisions to variation of the diagnostic test sensitivity and specificity is illustrated in Sect. 4. Finally, a discussion of the obtained results is given.

2   Influence Diagram Formulation

This section introduces the notation used to describe the decision problem. Let the herd be of size N from which a simple random sample of size n is drawn. The aim of the investigation is to determine the proportion of diseased animals, i.e. $p = d/N$ with d being the number of sick in the population. We assume that the true number of diseased individuals in the sample, D^+, is obtained by drawing a sample of size n without replacement from the population. In this case D^+ follows the *hypergeometric distribution* with parameters N, d, n. If sampling is with replacement or an infinite population can be assumed, D^+ is a sample from the *binomial distribution* with herd prevalence $p \in [0, 1]$. Also, if n is small compared to both d and $N - d$ the binomial distribution is a good approximation to the hypergeometric distribution. Such approximations are necessary because computations with the hypergeometric distribution quickly become intractable [1]. In the following, only binomial sampling is considered. The number of test positives, T^+, is then given as a sum of two binomial distributions with fixed values of the sensitivity, Se, and specificity, Sp, of the diagnostic test as parameters. Note that our interest is in the fixed value Se and Sp situation; otherwise a natural way to quantify uncertainty on the two variables would be by e.g. a beta distribution as in [7,8]. Figure 1 illustrates the above as a graphical model using notation from [13]. By specifying a graphical model we obtain a clear overview of the dependence structure of the variables. Furthermore, the decision part is easily specified using influence diagram notation for which software would exist to solve at least a discretized version of the problem.

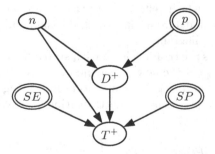

Fig. 1. Graphical model illustrating how the number of test positives, T^+, is obtained by sampling with replacement introducing both false positives and false negatives. Double lined nodes indicate continuous nodes, however, the Se and Sp distributions will be trivial in our application

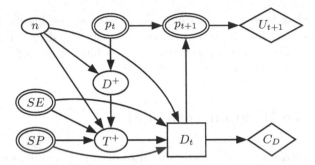

Fig. 2. Influence diagram describing the treatment strategy based on the number of animals tested positive

The above distributional explanations are expressed as

$$D^+ \sim \text{Bin}(n, p),$$
$$T^+ \sim \text{Bin}(D^+, Se) + \text{Bin}(n - D^+, 1 - Sp).$$

Inference for the herd prevalence can be formulated in the Bayesian context as follows. Given $\{n, T^+, Se, Sp\}$, what is the posterior distribution on p? A typical application would be to use this distribution to calculate a posterior mean for p together with a credibility interval. This estimate could then be used by the veterinarian to determine whether a herd should be classified as disease free [7,8].

Classical survey sampling would be concerned with how large to choose n in order to get a certain confidence in p. Our focus is, however, on the application of the prevalence estimate, namely a decision to apply a treatment reducing prevalence. Going back the the herd context, a veterinarian typically has to decide between two decision alternatives: Either treat all animals in the herd, e.g. by adding antibiotics to the water supply, or do nothing. Whether to apply treatment is decided by the observed number of test positives. In order to decide which treatment to use, it is necessary to model how the disease prevalence will develop with time and how treatment influences it. A reward is given based on the disease prevalence which reflects the price of animals being sick. Figure 2 extends the graphical model from Fig. 1 with decision and utility nodes (see [14]) making it an influence diagram.

Here, the D_t node is the treat decision with states *treat all* (ta) and *do nothing* (dn). Furthermore, p_{t+1} is the new prevalence[1], C_D a utility node reflecting the cost of the treatment, and U_{t+1} a utility node indicating the cost of disease as a function of the new prevalence. The transition probability between the two prevalences is given by

$$P(p_{t+1}|p_t, D_t) = \begin{cases} k_3 p_t & \text{if } D_t = \text{ta} \\ p_t & \text{otherwise} \end{cases}$$

---

[1] Basically, the situation could be handled without introducing a p_{t+1} node by simply integrating the disease development into the utility function. But our choice is conceptual clearer.

To illustrate the principle, simple proportional reduction in case of treating, i.e. $0 \leq k_3 \leq 1$ and preservation of status quo in case of not treating, is used. This ignores that an infectious disease would spread within the population if nothing is done. Modeling such a characteristic could although easily be done using e.g. a logistic model.

Economic preference is modeled with the two utility nodes C_D and U_{t+1}. Typically, costs can be established on a per animal basis, which requires knowledge of the the number of animals, N, in the herd to make calculations realistic. A possible specification of the two utility functions could then be as follows.

$$C(D_t) = -k_1 N \, I(D_t = \text{treat all})$$
$$U_{t+1}(p_{t+1}) = -k_2(p_{t+1}N),$$

where I is an indicator function.

To solve the decision scenario of Fig. 2 it is necessary to find the decision alternative for D_t, which given evidence $e = \{n, T^+, Se, Sp\}$, yields the highest expected utility. Because we are using a continuous representation of p, standard Bayesian Network software for solving the influence diagram of Fig. 2 is not directly applicable. Instead both an analytic solution method in Maple [12] and a simulation based using WinBugs [15] are investigated. For small herds the analytic approach is doable and allows us to verify how good an approximation the sampling approach is in this situation. Advantage of the analytic implementation is also that we can use the capabilities of Maple when performing sensitivity analysis.

3 Derivation of the Expected Utility

In order to calculate the required expected utility given $e = \{n, T^+, Se, Sp\}$ we need to calculate the posterior distribution $P(p_{t+1}|e)$, which again requires calculation of $P(p_t|e)$. As already mentioned, only the binomial case is considered. To calculate $P(p_t|e)$ we exploit the standard result, see e.g. [16], that

$$P(T^+ = x | \ldots) = \binom{n}{x} \Big[pSe + (1-p)(1-Sp) \Big]^x \Big[p(1-Se) + (1-p)Sp \Big]^{n-x}.$$

If expert information exist on the prevalence of the herd this is easily integrated using prior distributions. If nothing is known, a uniform prior distribution for p is sufficient. Bayes Rule is exploited to obtain the posterior distribution

$$P(p|T^+, n, Se, Sp) \propto P(T^+|p, n, Se, Sp)P(p|n, Se, Sp).$$

To ensure that the above distribution is proper it is necessary to find an expression for the normalization constant $P(T^+|n, Se, Sp)$. Normally in a Bayesian analysis proportionality of the posterior is sufficient, but, as $P(T^+|n, Se, Sp)$ depends on Se and Sp, calculating it becomes a concern in the latter sensitivity analysis.

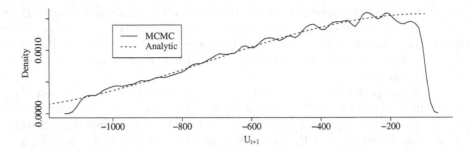

Fig. 3. Comparison of the posterior density $P(U_{t+1}|\dots)$ calculated analytically and numerically; the x-axis is obtained utility while the y-axis is the corresponding density. The MCMC density is obtained by kernel smoothing the posterior samples obtained from WinBugs. The deviations at the end points are partly due to the kernel smoother and partly due to problems of the Gibbs sampler to investigate these areas

Continuing our calculations we observe that p_{t+1} is just a functional transformation of p_t when $D_t = ta$, i.e. we can use the standard rule for transformation of random variables to calculate the posterior $P(p_{t+1}|e, D_t = ta)$. If $D_t = dn$ no transformation is needed. Regarding U_{t+1} as a random variable its distribution can be obtained in the same way as for p_{t+1} by exploiting the above rule. Given an observed number of test positives, $T^+ = x$, the expected utility of the treat and no-treat alternatives can now be calculated as

$$\mathrm{EU}(D_t = ta) = \mathrm{E}\left[U_{t+1}(p_{t+1}, D_t = ta)\right] + C_D(ta),$$
$$\mathrm{EU}(D_t = dn) = \mathrm{E}\left[U_{t+1}(p_{t+1}, D_t = dn))\right] + C_D(dn).$$

The above has been implemented in Maple yielding functions of Se, Sp. To evaluate the approximation of a simulation based approach the model was also formulated in WinBugs [15], which uses Gibbs sampling to calculate the expected utility. Figure 3 shows the posterior distribution of U_{t+1} obtained from Gibbs Sampling (using 10,000 samples after a burn-in of 1,000) and the analytical distribution of $EU(D_t = ta)$ in a pseudo realistic setup of $Se = 0.8, Sp = 0.6, n = 5, T^+ = 2, k_3 = \frac{1}{2}, k_2 = -20, k_1 = -1, N = 100$. In the figure the analytical expected utility (obtained by integrating the density between the worst case -1100 and best case -100) is -475.1. The numeric mean (obtained as empirical mean of the samples) is -481.2. In the case $D_t = dn$ we obtain values of -750.4 and -762.5, respectively. Hence, in the chosen setup we decide to treat all animals. Note that the WinBugs approach is much easier to implement and solve than the analytic approach and appears to be a good approximation. However, it lacks the power of being able to describe the expected utility as function of sensitivity and specificity.

The desired strategy for D_t is now obtained by investigating the expected utility for both the ta and dn alternative for all $0 \le T^+ \le n$, Empirical investigations show that for this strategy there will exist a unique threshold T, s.t.

$$\arg\max_{d_t \in D_t} \mathrm{EU}(D_t = d_t | T^+ = x) = \begin{cases} dn & \text{if } 0 \leq x < T \\ ta & \text{if } T \leq x \leq n \end{cases}$$

That is, with the chosen specification of utilities and transitions, any strategy for D_t can be compactly represented by the minimum number of test positives necessary before all animals will be treated. In the setup used in Fig. 3 we obtain $T = 0$, i.e. we trivially treat no matter the number of observed test-positives.

Assuming n, Sp, and Se to be fixed, the expected value of a strategy s for D_t is given as

$$\mathrm{EU}(s) = \sum_{x=0}^{n} P(T^+ = x | n, Se, Sp) \, \mathrm{EU}(D_t | T^+ = x, n, Se, Sp),$$

where $\mathrm{EU}_s(D_t | \dots)$ denotes the expected utility obtained for D_t when choosing the decision dictated by $s(x)$.

4   Sensitivity Analysis

In realistic situations, the sensitivity and specificity of the test are either unknown or subject to a great deal of variation. If we e.g. recommend a fixed threshold to all veterinarians investigating diarrhea in pig herds, the large variation in the two parameters between veterinarians would be ignored. A way to investigate a strategy's robustness towards variations in sensitivity and specificity is to find out how the best decision alternative changes with variation in Se and Sp. Here, the analytical representation in Maple is of advantage because we immediately have the expected utility as a function of Se and Sp. This is not possible using a simulation approach, instead the influence diagram would have to be solved for a grid of Se and Sp combinations.

Continuing with the values from the veterinarian example, but changing the sample size n to 10 and increasing the price of a treatment to $k_1 = -2$, gives a more interesting example. Figure 4 shows the line of indifference, i.e. the solution of

$$f(Se, Sp) = \mathrm{EU}(D_t = ta | Se, Sp) - \mathrm{EU}(D_t = dn | Se, Sp) = 0.$$

To investigate the robustness of the decision using the sensitivity and specificity configuration $p = (Se', Sp')$ it might be worth to investigate how much p can change before a different decision is made. This is equivalent to finding the distance to the intersection line, i.e.

$$r_c = \mathrm{dist}(p, l), \quad \text{where} \quad l = \{(Se, Sp) \mid f(Se, Sp) = 0\}$$

also known as the *radius of change* or radius of the *safe-ball*, see [11,10]. The higher this radius the more robust the specific policy is against variations. Also,

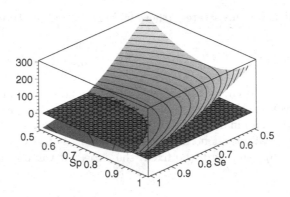

Fig. 4. Indifference between the two decision alternatives occurs on the line $f(Se, Sp) = 0$, The figure shows the intersection of $f(Se, Sp)$ with $z = 0$, i.e. the z-axis is the difference in utility between the two strategies. To the left of the intersection line, dn is selected, to the right ta

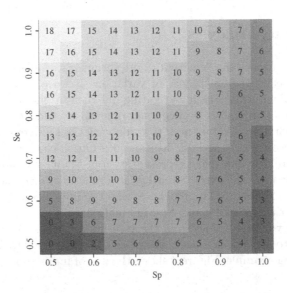

Fig. 5. Threshold T as a function of (Se, Sp) – a so called treatment map. Calculated by evaluating the analytical expression for a grid layout of (Se, Sp) configurations

the difference in expected utility between the two alternatives evaluated at specific points tells us about the benefit of getting the (Se, Sp) correctly estimated.

To get a better overview of the variation in the strategy we can illustrate the obtained T-values as a function of Se and Sp – a two-dimensional analogue of a rainbow diagram. Figure 5 shows this *treatment map* in case 30 of the herd's 100 individuals are investigated.

For a fixed sensitivity above 0.6, T is higher for specificities near 0.5 than those near 1. This might be surprising because a heuristic like "the higher the test quality the higher the number of positive tests before we react" feels natural. But such a heuristic neglects that a good test also results in fewer test-positives, because fewer are erroneously classified as positives. Looking at the figure also reveals that the radius of change for T will be quite low due to the high variation of T values over the parameter space. Again, this underlines the fact that care should be taken when sensitivity and specificity varies.

5   Discussion

Generation of treatment maps illustrating the sensitivity for varying probabilities is a strong tool helping to provide insight into the decision scenario. Calculations, where the expected utility function is given as an analytical function of Se and Sp works until samples sizes of 30-40. Hereafter, Maple is not capable of dealing with the generated polynomials anymore. By fixing (Se, Sp) and calculating its values on a grid much higher n can be achieved — either in Maple or by using Gibbs sampling in WinBugs.

Estimation of the constants k_1, k_2, and k_3 for a specific decision problem is problematic; guesstimates, small scale experiments, and sensitivity analysis could be employed. Once a reasonable single time-slice model is established, extension to the more realistic case with additional time-slices is desirable. Biosecurity programs are often a temporal matter, where diagnosis and treatment are made repetitively. Limited memory strategies as in [17] might be necessary to obtain a tractable solution of the influence diagram. Despite such approximation our approach to sensitivity analysis would not scale up very well in respect to additional decisions; even Gibbs sampling would only be feasible for a small number of decisions.

To establish how large a sample size n to choose in order to make an optimal decision about treatment would require conversion of n in Fig. 2 into a decision node together with a cost of performing the diagnostic test. An analytical computation quickly becomes intractable here because n is part of the exponent of $P(T^+|\ldots)$. Solving the influence diagram with the two sequential decisions would have to be done by numerical methods such as forward Monte Carlo sampling or Markov chain Monte Carlo sampling as described in [18,19].

All these above mentioned problems would arise, in case one tries to evaluate and revise e.g. the current Danish Salmonella treatment strategy [3], which currently is taking neither uncertainty from imprecise tests nor any variability in sensitivity and specificity into account. This paper is merely an appetizer to work more intensively with the issues raised to get a practical solution.

References

1. Barnett, V.: Sample survey : Principles and methods. Edward Arnold (1991)
2. Anonymous: U.S Voluntary Johne's Disease Herd Status Program for Cattle. Technical report, United States Animal Health Association (1998)
3. Alban, L., Stege, H., Dahl, J.: The new classification system for slaughter pig-herds in the danish salmonella surveillance-and-control program. Preventive Veterinary Medicine **1659** (2001) 1–14 Submitted for publication.
4. Baadsgaard, N.P.: Development of Clinical Monitoring Methods in Pig Health Management. PhD thesis, Department of Clinical Studies, The Royal Veterinary and Agricultural University and Department of Animal Health and Welfare, Research Center Foulum (2001)
5. Kristensen, K.: A collection of some statistical issues to consider when testing for GM seeds in conventional seed lots. Technical report, Biometry Research Unit, Danish Institute of Agricultural Sciences (2001)
6. Clement, R.: Making Hard Decisions: An Introduction to Decision Analysis. Duxbury Press (1996)
7. Johnson, W., Su, C.L., Gardner, I.: Sample size calculations for surveys to substantiate freedom of populations from infectious agents. (2002) Submitted to Biometrics.
8. Hanson, T., Johnson, W., Gardner, I., Georgiadis, M.: Determining the infection status of a herd. Journal of Agricultural, Biological, and Environmental Statistics (2003) In press.
9. Coupé, V.M.H., van der Gaag, L.C.: Practicable sensitivity analysis of Bayesian belief networks. Technical Report UU-CS-1998-10, Utrecht University, Department of Computer Science (1998)
10. Nielsen, T.D., Jensen, F.V.: Sensitivity analysis in influence diagrams. IEEE Transactions on Systems Man and Cybernetics (2001) Submitted for publication.
11. Höhle, M., Kristiansen, B.: Sensitivity analysis in Bayesian networks and influence diagrams. http://www.dina.dk/~hoehle/pubs/sensitivity.pdf (1998)
12. Waterloo Maple Inc.: Maple 6.02. (2001)
13. Lauritzen, S.L.: Graphical Models. Oxford University Press (1996)
14. Jensen, F.V.: Bayesian Networks and Decision Graphs. Statistics for Engineering and Information Science. Springer (2001)
15. Spiegelhalter, D., Thomas, A., Best, N.: WinBUGS Version 1.2 User Manual. MRC Biostatistics Unit. (1999)
16. Cameron, A., Baldock, F.: A new probability formula for surveys to substantiate freedom from disease. Prev. Vet. Medicine **34** (1998) 1–17
17. Lauritzen, S.L., Nilsson, D.: Representing and solving decision problems with limited information. Management Science **47** (2001) 1235–51
18. Charnes, J., Shenoy, P.: A forward Monte Carlo method for solving influence diagrams using local computation. Working paper No. 273, School of Business, University of Kansas (2000)
19. Bielza, C., Müller, P., Insua, D.: Decision analysis by augmented probability simulation. Management Science **45** (1999) 995–1007

Decision Network Semantics of Branching Constraint Satisfaction Problems

K. Brown, P. Lucas, and D. Fowler

[1] Cork Constraint Computation Centre, Department of Computer Science
University College, Cork, Ireland
k.brown@cs.ucc.ie
[2] Institute for Computer and Information Sciences, University of Nijmegen
Toernooiveld 1, 6525 ED Nijmegen, The Netherlands
peterl@cs.kun.nl
[3] Department of Computing Science, Meston Building
University of Aberdeen, AB24 3EU, Aberdeen, UK
dfowler@csd.abdn.ac.uk

Abstract. Branching Constraint Satisfaction Problems (BCSPs) have been introduced to model dynamic resource allocation subject to constraints and uncertainty. We give BCSPs a formal probability semantics by showing how they can be mapped to a certain class of Bayesian decision networks. This allows us to describe logical and probabilistic constraints in a uniform fashion. We also discuss extensions to BCSPs and decision networks suggested by the relationship between the two formalisms.

1 Introduction

Resource allocation is the problem of assigning resources to tasks subject to constraints, and has been studied in operations research and computer science for many years [1,2,9]. Recently, the problem has been investigated using constraint satisfaction methods [17], which allow arbitrary combinatorial constraints to be placed on the problem. In its simplest form, tasks can be represented by variables, and resources by values to be assigned to the variables, while constraints restrict the values that can be assigned simultaneously. A solution to a problem is then an assignment of values such that all constraints are satisfied. Initially, such approaches were restricted to deterministic, static problems; more recently it has been extended to problems that change over time, and for which there is some uncertainty about what the changes will be. *Branching Constraint Satisfaction* [6,7] has been proposed to model problems where new variables (or tasks) are added to the problem after some decisions have been made. The uncertainty in the sequence of additions is modelled by a transition tree with arcs labelled with probabilities. Branching CSPs are known to be NP hard [8]. Complete and incomplete optimising algorithms have been developed, using a combination of constraint-based tree search and decision-theoretic computation, and the

T.D. Nielsen and N.L. Zhang (Eds.): ECSQARU 2003, LNAI 2711, pp. 230–242, 2003.
© Springer-Verlag Berlin Heidelberg 2003

methods have been compared to those used in Markov Decision Problems [8]. However, the probability semantics of BCSPs were presented only informally.

Bayesian networks have been introduced as formalisms to represent and reason with joint probability distributions, taking into account conditional independence statements [15]. Given a Bayesian network and a (possibly empty) set of evidence concerning the variables included in the network, the probability distribution on any subset of variables can be computed. For this, efficient algorithms exist with fast, well-engineered computer implementations [10,13], even though the problem of probabilistic reasoning in Bayesian networks is known to be NP hard in general [4]. However, reasoning with Bayesian networks for real-world problems is normally feasible. Formally, Bayesian networks can only be used for probabilistic reasoning, but recent work [14,12] shows how some logical consistencies can be modelled and solved. Finally, we can augment a network with decision theory, to obtain *influence diagrams* or *decision networks*, which can be used for decision-making under uncertainty [10,16].

In this paper, we study the relationship between branching CSPs, Bayesian networks and decision networks. Our aim is to establish the probability semantics by mapping BCSPs to decision networks, providing a uniform representation for probabilistic and logical constraints. We introduce Branching CSPs, giving a precise, formal definition, and we summarise Bayesian networks and decision networks. We then show how BCSPs can be mapped to decision networks, and in particular we show how to represent combinatorial constraints. We prove that optimal solutions to problems in the two different formalisms are equivalent. Finally we consider how the techniques of decision networks may be used to generalise BCSPs, and, similarly, how BCSP methods might allow us to make explicit use of constraints in decision networks.

2   Branching Constraint Satisfaction Problems

2.1   Preliminary Definitions

In the following, we borrow the terminology for graphs from [18]; if $S = (V, A)$ is a directed tree with set of vertices V and set of directed arcs $A \subseteq V \times V$, then the set of children of a vertex $v \in V$ is denoted by $\sigma(v)$; the unique parent of a vertex $v \in V$ is represented by $\pi(v)$. Furthermore, the *level* of a vertex v is defined as the length of the path from the root to v [11]. The set of all vertices in the tree at the same level $n \in \mathbb{N}$ is denoted by $\lambda(n)$. The terminology will be generalised for acyclic directed graphs. Sets of elements will be represented by bold face letters, e.g. $\mathbf{V}$, if confusion may arise otherwise.

2.2   A Motivating Example

We first present a simple motivating example. A company has three workers, x, y and z, and five possible tasks, A, B, C, D and E that it may be asked to carry out. Each worker is qualified to do some of the tasks, as shown in Fig. 1; each task

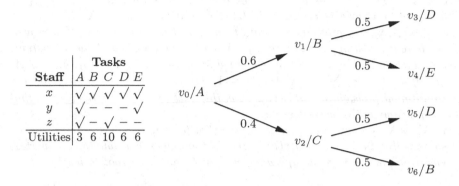

Fig. 1. An example BCSP. *Left:* table of staff skills and tasks, with associated utilities for individual tasks; $\sqrt{}$ means that the task is suitable for the worker, and '$-$' that it is unsuitable. *Right:* probabilistic state transition tree. An entry v/X indicates that variable X arrives in vertex v; numeric labels on the arcs indicate transition probabilities.

is associated with a utility, representing the profit resulting from completing the task successfully. No worker can do more than one task. The company has some uncertain knowledge about the sequence of tasks it will be asked to perform, sketched as a probabilistic state transition tree in Fig. 1. There will definitely be three tasks, and the first task to arrive will be A. Subsequently, either task B or C will arrive, with probabilities 0.6 and 0.4 respectively. If the second task is B, then the last task will be either D (with probability 0.5) or E (probability 0.5). If the second task is C, then the last task will either be D (0.5) or B (0.5). Some sequences of tasks may not be feasible for the company to do, and so it may choose to reject some tasks. The aim is to assign workers to tasks as soon as the tasks arrive, maximising the expected utility, while ensuring all constraints are satisfied.

2.3   Formal Definition

We give the formal definition of branching CSPs below. $\top$, or *null*, is a special value used to represent an explicit decision not to assign a value to a variable. An assignment of $\top$ to a variable will mean that any constraint on that variable will be satisfied by default.

Definition 1. *A binary branching CSP is a tuple* BCSP $= (X, D, \delta, C, U, S, \tau)$:

- X *is a finite set of* variables;
- D *is a finite set of* values, *with function* $\delta : X \to \wp(D \cup \{\top\})$ *associating a* domain *of possible values to each variable* $x \in X$, *such that* $\top \in \delta(x)$ *for each* $x \in X$;
- C *is a finite set of* binary *constraints, where each* $c \in C$ *is a set of triples* (x, y, R), $x, y \in X$, *and* $R \subseteq \delta(x) \times \delta(y)$ *such that* $\forall a \in \delta(x) \forall b \in \delta(y) :$ $(\top, b) \in R$ *and* $(a, \top) \in R$;

- $U : X \times (D \cup \{\top\}) \to \mathbb{R}$ *associates a* utility *to each value* $w \in D \cup \{\top\}$ *assigned to a variable* $x \in X$, *with* $U(x, \top) = 0$ *for each* $x \in X$;
- $S = (V, A, \gamma)$ *is a probabilistic state transition tree with vertices* V *and arcs* A; *there is a distinguished vertex* $v_0 \in V$ *called the* root, *which has no parent; the function* $\gamma : V \times V \to [1, 0]$ *is defined such that* $\gamma(v, v') = 0$ *if* $(v, v') \notin A$, *and if* $\sigma(v) \neq \varnothing$, $\sum_{v' \in \sigma(v)} \gamma(v, v') = 1$, *for each* $v \in V$; γ *represents the conditional probability that vertex* v' *is the next to become active, given that the previous active vertex was* v;
- $\tau : V \to X$ *is a surjective function such that for any two vertices* v, v' *on the same path* p *in* S, $v = v'$ *if* $\tau(v) = \tau(v')$. τ *assigns a variable to each vertex, ensuring that no variable appears twice on a path from root to leaf.*

The probabilistic transitions are defined in terms of the vertices of the tree, and not directly in terms of the variables. Each vertex represents an *event*, and multiple different events may cause the same variable to become active. The probability of an event depends only on its immediate predecessor, and thus the problem obeys the Markov property.

Definition 2. *An* assignment *to a BCSP is a function* $\varphi : V \to D \cup \{\top\}$ *which assigns to each vertex either a value from the domain of its associated variable or the null value* $\top$.

Definition 3. *A* solution *to a BCSP is an assignment* φ *such that if* v *and* w *are vertices on a path in* $S = (V, A, \gamma)$ *and* $(\tau(v), \tau(w), R) \in C$, *then* $(\varphi(v), \varphi(w)) \in R$, *i.e.* φ *satisfies all constraints appearing on a path.*

Definition 4. *The* expected utility *of a vertex* v *in a solution* φ *to a BCSP, denoted by* $\hat{U}_\varphi(v)$, *is defined as*

$$\hat{U}_\varphi(v) = U(\tau(v), \varphi(v)) + \sum_{v' \in \sigma(v)} \gamma(v, v') \hat{U}_\varphi(v')$$

The expected utility of a solution to a BCSP is the expected utility of the root vertex in the solution, i.e. $\hat{U}_\varphi(v_0)$.

Note that a solution φ is a contingent solution, specifying an assignment to a variable dependent on the sequence of arrivals. In fact, the assignments are defined in terms of events (i.e. vertices of the tree), and not directly in terms of the variables. Further, the solution can be executed as the problem unfolds; the assignments are not dependent on subsequent developments of the problem. Thus the solution is a *policy*.

Definition 5. *Let* v_i *be a vertex at level* i *in the tree* $S = (V, A, \gamma)$, *and let* $\mathbf{h} = \{(v_0, x_0), (v_1, x_1), \ldots, (v_{i-1}, x_{i-1})\}$ *be the* history *of assignments made at vertices in the path from* v_0 *to* v_i, *with* $v_{j+1} \in \sigma(v_j)$, *in some solution* φ. *We say that the pair* (v_i, x_i) *is* consistent *with* $\mathbf{h}$, *written* $(v_i, x_i) \propto \mathbf{h}$, *if it satisfies all constraints between* v_i *and assignments in* $\mathbf{h}$.

Definition 6. *The* maximum expected utility *at a vertex v given its history* h *is the maximum, over consistent assignments, of the utility of an assignment plus the weighted sum of the maximum expected utility of the child vertices, given the history* h *extended with the new assignment:*

$$\hat{U}(v \mid h) = \max_{x \in \delta(\tau(v)):(v,x) \propto h} \left[U(\tau(v), x) + \sum_{v' \in \sigma(v)} \gamma(v, v') \hat{U}(v' \mid h \sqcup \{(v,x)\}) \right]$$

The goal of a BCSP is to find a solution with maximal expected utility. The maximal expected utility is thus $\hat{U}(v_0 \mid \varnothing)$. A BCSP is essentially a decision tree, but which separates out the probabilities from the logical constraints on the decisions. It is possible to combine the constraints into the tree, but at the cost of a (worst-case) exponential explosion in the tree size [8].

Reconsider the example introduced above. Formulated as a branching CSP it holds that $X = \{A, B, C, D, E\}$, $D = \{x, y, z\}$, $\delta(A) = \cdots = \delta(E) = \{x, y, z, \top\}$, $U(x, \top) = 0$ for each $x \in X$, and for each $w \in D$: $U(A, w) = 3$, $U(B, w) = 6$, $U(C, w) = 10$, $U(D, w) = 6$, $U(E, w) = 5$, and the constraint set C consists of the following elements:

 - $\langle A, B, \{(x, \top), (y, x), (y, \top), (z, x), (z, \top), (\top, x), (\top, \top)\} \rangle$
 - $\langle A, C, \{(x, z), (x, \top), (y, x), (y, z), (y, \top), (z, x), (z, \top), (\top, x), (\top, z), (\top, \top)\} \rangle$
 - $\langle A, D, \{(x, \top), (y, x), (y, \top), (z, x), (z, \top), (\top, x), (\top, \top)\} \rangle$
 - $\langle A, E, \{(x, y), (x, \top), (y, x), (y, \top), (z, x), (z, y), (z, \top), (\top, x), (\top, y), (\top, \top)\} \rangle$
 - $\langle B, C, \{(x, z), (x, \top), (\top, x), (\top, z), (\top, \top)\} \rangle$
 - $\langle B, D, \{(x, \top), (\top, x), (\top, \top)\} \rangle$
 - $\langle B, E, \{(x, y), (x, \top), (\top, x), (\top, y), (\top, \top)\} \rangle$
 - $\langle C, D, \{(x, \top), (z, x), (z, \top), (\top, x), (\top, \top)\} \rangle$
 - $\langle C, E, \{(x, y), (x, \top), (z, x), (z, y), (z, \top), (\top, x), (\top, y), (\top, \top)\} \rangle$
 - $\langle D, E, \{(x, y), (x, \top), (\top, x), (\top, y), (\top, \top)\} \rangle$

The probabilistic state transition tree $S = (V, A, \gamma)$ with the definition of the function τ is according to Fig. 1. The optimal solution is $\varphi(v_0) = y$, $\varphi(v_1) = x$, $\varphi(v_2) = z$, $\varphi(v_3) = \top$, $\varphi(v_4) = \top$, $\varphi(v_5) = x$, $\varphi(v_6) = x$, with expected utility $\hat{U}_\varphi(v_0) = 13$. Note that the task D is given a different allocation depending on the arrival sequence: it is rejected if it arrives in event v_3 (after B in v_1), but it is allocated worker x if it arrives in event v_5 (after C in v_2).

The definition above is a slightly modified form of the one given in [7]. There it was assumed that the the utility function U did not distinguish between different values for a given variable (with the exception of $\top$); i.e. $U(x, v) = U(x, v')$ for each $v', v \in \delta(x) \backslash \{\top\}$. Also, in the probabilistic state transition tree, the sum of the transition probabilities for the children of a vertex was allowed to be less than 1. The missing probability represented the case where the parent event had no successor. In the definition given here, we could represent this by having a special variable whose domain is restricted to $\top$, and ensuring any vertex which activates this variable has no children.

3   Bayesian Networks and Decision Networks

A *Bayesian network* $\mathcal{B}$ is a pair $\mathcal{B} = (G, P)$, where $G = (\mathbf{N}, A)$ is an acyclic directed graph with set of chance nodes $\mathbf{N}$, representing random variables, and set of arcs $A \subseteq \mathbf{N} \times \mathbf{N}$, representing statistical independence relationships among the variables [15]. Here we assume all random variables to be discrete. A joint probability distribution P is defined on the set of variables as follows:

$$P(N) = \prod_{X \in \mathbf{N}} P(X \mid \pi(X))$$

A Bayesian network allows for computing any a posteriori probability distribution of interest after entering evidence $\mathbf{e}$ into the network. In Bayesian network software packages, a posteriori probability distributions are computed from the marginal probability distribution of an updated probability distribution $P^{\mathbf{e}}$; for every (free) variable $X \in \mathbf{N}$, it holds that

$$P^{\mathbf{e}}(X) = P(X \mid \mathbf{e})$$

A *decision network* $\mathcal{D} = (G, P, \mathbf{N}, \mathbf{D}, \mathbf{W}, \mathbf{u})$, or *influence diagram*, is a Bayesian network with the addition of decision nodes $\mathbf{D}$ and utility nodes $\mathbf{W}$, standing for decision and utility variables, respectively. There is always a unique directed path in a decision network, on which every decision node D in $\mathbf{D}$ occurs, i.e. decision nodes are linearly ordered. Each utility variable $W \in \mathbf{W}$ stands for a utility function $u_W : \delta(\mathbf{Z}) \to \mathbb{R}$, where $\delta(\mathbf{Z})$ is the Cartesian product of the domains of variables in $\mathbf{Z}$, and $\mathbf{Z} = \pi(W)$. The collection of utility functions is indicated by $\mathbf{u}$.

Initial proposals of decision networks only included a single utility node. In more recent descriptions, such as in the book by Jensen [10], a decision network may incorporate more than one utility node W_i, $i = 1, \ldots, n$, and it is assumed that the resulting multi-attribute utility function $u_{\mathbf{W}}$ is additive, i.e. the resulting utility $u_{\mathbf{W}}$ is defined as follows:

$$u_{\mathbf{W}}(\mathbf{Z}) = \sum_{i=1}^{n} u_{W_i}(\mathbf{Z}_i)$$

where $\mathbf{Z}_i = \pi(W_i)$, $\mathbf{W} = \bigcup_{i=1}^{n}\{W_i\}$, $\mathbf{Z} = \bigcup_{i=1}^{n}\mathbf{Z}_i = \pi(\mathbf{W})$. Clearly, defining a utility function in this fashion reduces the amount of utility information that has to be specified; the space-complexity reduction can be as drastic as from exponential to linear.

The aim of evaluating a decision network is to determine the optimal expected utility $\hat{u}$ for each decision d at a given decision node D, given the available evidence $\mathbf{e}$, which includes all previously made decisions. We assume a topological order $\prec$ of the nodes in the network, in which we have combined consecutive nodes of the same type, and we place the utility nodes last. Thus we have $Y_0 \prec D_0 \prec Y_1 \prec D_1 \prec \cdots \prec D_{n-1} \prec Y_n \prec W$. We then define the maximum expected utility at a decision node D_i given some evidence $\mathbf{e}$ to be

$$\hat{u}_{D_i}(\mathbf{e}) = \max_{d_i \in D_i} \hat{u}_{Y_{i+1}}(\mathbf{e} \cup \{D_i = d_i\})$$

and at a chance node Y_i the expected utility is

$$\hat{u}_{Y_i}(\mathbf{e}) = \sum_{y_i \in Y_i} P(Y_i = y_i \mid \mathbf{e})\hat{u}_{D_i}(\mathbf{e} \cup \{Y_i = y_i\})$$

In particular, we have the expected utility over the whole network:

$$\hat{u}_{Y_0}(\varnothing) = \sum_{y_0 \in Y_0} P(Y_0 = y_0)\hat{u}_{D_0}(\{Y_0 = y_0\})$$

and for the terminating case we have:

$$\hat{u}_{Y_n}(\mathbf{e}) = \sum_{y_n \in Y_n} P(Y_n = y_n \mid \mathbf{e})u_W(\mathbf{e} \cup \{Y_n = y_n\})$$

In diagrams of Bayesian networks and decision networks, chance nodes are indicated by circles or ellipses, decision nodes by boxes and utility nodes by diamonds.

4   Relationship of Branching CSPs to Decision Networks

4.1   Mapping Branching CSPs to Decision Networks

Let BCSP $= (X, D, \delta, C, U, S, \tau)$. Below, we define the steps that make up the mapping from this representation to a decision network $\mathcal{D} = (G, P, \mathbf{N}, \mathbf{D}, \mathbf{W}, \mathbf{u})$.

- For each set of vertices $\lambda(n)$ at level $n \in \mathbb{N}$ of the tree S, there is a chance node Y_n. The domain of the associated random variable Y_n is $\delta(Y_n) = \{v \mid v \in \lambda(n)\}$. The associated probability distribution P is defined by: $P(Y_n = u \mid Y_{n-1} = v) = \gamma(v, u)$ for $n > 0$, and $P(Y_0 = v_0) = 1$. Note that for two vertices $v \in \lambda(n-1)$ and $u \in \lambda(n)$ with $(v, u) \notin A_S$ we have that $P(Y_n = u \mid Y_{n-1} = v) = 0$, indicating that this transition cannot take place.
- Corresponding to each random variable Y_n with domain $\delta(Y_n)$, there is a decision node D_n, with domain equal to $\delta(D_n) = \{v.x \mid v \in \delta(Y_n), x \in \delta(\tau(v))\}$. There exists an incoming arc to each decision node from its associated chance node. In addition, the decision nodes are linked in a chain in an order reflecting the order of their associated chance nodes. The nodes will be used to assign values to their associated decision variables, which corresponds to assigning values to variables in the BCSP.
- For each chance node Y_n there is a corresponding utility node U_n. The parents of U_n are Y_n and the decision node D_n. If Y_n takes value v, and the decision node D_n takes any value $v.x$, $x \neq \top$, then the utility value is $U(\tau(v), x)$; otherwise it is 0. The utility nodes give their reward if a vertex (and hence a variable) has become active, and we have assigned a non-null value to that instance of the variable.
- For each pair of chance nodes (Y_i, Y_j) such that there are vertices $v \in \delta(Y_i)$ and $v' \in \delta(Y_j)$ with a constraint $(\tau(v), \tau(v'), R) \in C$, there exists a chance

node $C_{i,j}$ with domain $\{t, f\}$ to represent the constraints on the corresponding decisions. The parents of $C_{i,j}$ are the decision nodes D_i and D_j. The probability distribution is defined as follows:

$$P(C_{i,j} = t \mid D_i = v.x, D_j = w.y) = \begin{cases} 0 \text{ if } (\tau(v), \tau(w), R) \in C, (x, y) \notin R \\ 1 \text{ otherwise} \end{cases}$$

- There is one distinguished utility node U_C, whose parents are all the constraint chance nodes, with utility value 0 if all parents have value t, and utility value equal to $-M$ otherwise, where M is a penalty value larger than the sum of all utilities in the BCSP. This node ensures that the constraints are satisfied.
- Finally, for any given history in the execution of a BCSP solution, there is a corresponding evidence set for the network, defined by the function β below. Let $\mathbf{H}$ be the set of all possible history sets, and $\mathbf{E}$ be the set of all possible evidence sets. Then

$$\beta : \mathbf{H} \to \mathbf{E} : h \mapsto \{Y_i = v, D_i = v.x : (v, x) \in \mathbf{h}, v \in \lambda(i)\}$$

Note that there are particular features of the mapping above, which can be exploited to simplify the utility calculations:

(1) Each variable Y_j is conditionally independent of each variable Y_k, $k = 0, \ldots, j - 2$, and of each decision variable D_l given variable Y_{j-1}.
(2) The utility function u defined above for the utility nodes U_j is additive:

$$u(\tau(y_0), d_0, \ldots, \tau(y_m), d_m) = \sum_{i=0}^{m} U(\tau(y_j), d_j)$$

where y_j is a possible value of random variable Y_j and d_j is a possible value of decision variable D_j.
(3) We can create a topological order $Y_0 \prec D_0 \prec Y_1 \prec D_1 \prec \cdots \prec D_n \prec \mathbf{C} \prec \mathbf{W}$ where $\mathbf{C}$ represents the constraint chance nodes, and $\mathbf{W}$ represents the utility nodes. The initial node Y_0 has domain $\{v_0\}$, so the maximum expected utility of the network $\hat{u}_{Y_0}(\varnothing) = \hat{u}_{D_0}(Y_0 = v_0)$, and the utility function $u_W(\mathbf{e}) = \sum_{i=0}^{n} U(\tau(y_i), d_i) + u_C(\mathbf{e})$.

We can now simplify the utility definitions as follows:

$$\hat{u}_{D_i}(\mathbf{e}) = \max_{d_i \in D_i} \left[U(\tau(y_i), d_i) + \hat{u}_{Y_{i+1}}(\mathbf{e} \cup \{D_i = d_i\}) \right]$$

$$\hat{u}_{D_n}(\mathbf{e}) = \max_{d_n \in D_n} \left[U(\tau(y_n), d_n) + \hat{u}_C(\mathbf{e} \cup \{D_n = d_n\}) \right]$$

The $\hat{u}_C$ term in the second equation is simply the maximum expected utility from the constraint nodes. If any of the constraints evaluate to false, then the utility is $-M$. Otherwise, it is 0.

The highest expected utility at the first decision node is equal to the optimal expected utility of the BCSP, and the optimal decisions of the decision nodes correspond to the optimal plan of the BCSP. We prove this in the next section.

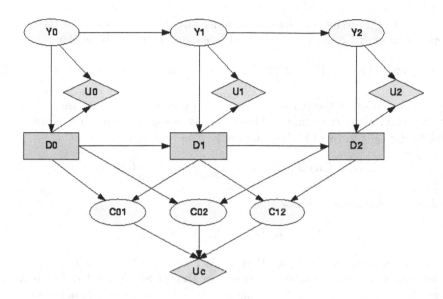

Fig. 2. Decision network resulting from the mapping of the example BCSP.

The result of mapping the example BCSP discussed in Sect. 2 is shown in Fig. 2. From the mapping designed above, it follows that the domain of the variable Y_0 is equal to $\{v_0\}$, for Y_1 it is equal to $\{v_1, v_2\}$; the domain of the decision variable D_0 is $\{v_0.x, v_0.y, v_0.z, v_0.\top\}$, and for D_1 it is equal to $\{v_1.x, v_1.\top, v_2.x, v_2.z, v_2.\top\}$.

4.2   Proof That the Mapping Is Correct

We need to show that the optimal solution to the BCSP (i.e. the maximum expected utility at the root node) has the same value as the maximum expected utility of the first decision node in the network.

We will show that the maximum expected utility from any node in the tree given some history is the same as the maximum expected utility from the corresponding decision node in the decision network, given the corresponding evidence.

Theorem 1. *Let $\mathcal{D} = (G, P, \mathbf{N}, \mathbf{D}, \mathbf{W}, \mathbf{u})$ be the decision network corresponding to the* BCSP $= (X, D, \delta, C, U, S, \tau)$ *obtained by the mapping defined in Sect. 4.1, then for each node at level k it holds that:*

$$\hat{U}(v_k \mid \mathbf{h}) = \hat{u}_D(\beta(\mathbf{h}) \cup \{Y_k = v_k\})$$

Proof. (By backwards induction on the level of the node in the tree.)

Basis Suppose v is a vertex in $\lambda(n)$, with n maximal level. Then v must be a leaf vertex. It holds that

$$\hat{U}(v \mid \mathbf{h}) = \max_{x \in \delta(\tau(v)):(v,x)\propto\mathbf{h}} U(\tau(v), x)$$

and Y_n and D_n are its corresponding chance and decision nodes. For the decision network, v must be the value observed at chance node Y_n, so we have:

$$\hat{u}_{D_n}(\beta(\mathbf{h}) \cup \{Y_n = v\}) = \max_{d_n \in D_n} [U(\tau(v), d_n) + \hat{u}_C(\beta(\mathbf{h}) \cup \{Y_n = v, D_n = d_n\}]$$

By the definition of the penalty value, we only need to consider those d_n which do not violate the constraints. There will always be at least one, namely $v.\top$, and so the $\hat{u}_C$ term will be 0. Thus we have as required

$$\hat{u}_{D_n}(\beta(\mathbf{h}) \cup \{Y_n = v\}) = \max_{x \in \delta(\tau(v)):(v,x) \propto \mathbf{h}} U(\tau(v), x)$$

Induction hypothesis Suppose that

$$\hat{U}(v_j \mid \mathbf{h}) = \hat{u}_{D_j}(\beta(\mathbf{h}) \cup \{Y_j = v_j\})$$

holds for all vertices in the BCSP at levels $j = n, n - 1, \ldots, i + 1$.
Induction step Now consider a vertex v in the BCSP at level i. If v is a leaf, then the result is true by the basis argument. Now, suppose v is not a leaf, then it holds that:

$$\hat{U}(v \mid \mathbf{h}) = \max_{x \in \delta(\tau(v)):(v,x) \propto \mathbf{h}} \left[U(\tau(v), x) + \sum_{v' \in \sigma(v)} \gamma(v, v')\hat{U}(v' \mid \mathbf{h} \cup \{(v, x)\}) \right]$$

but v' must be a node at level $i + 1$, so by the induction hypothesis

$$= \max_{x \in \delta(\tau(v)):(v,x) \propto \mathbf{h}} [U(\tau(v), x)$$
$$+ \sum_{v' \in \sigma(v)} \gamma(v, v')\hat{u}_{D_{i+1}}(\beta(\mathbf{h}) \cup \{Y_i = v, D_i = v.x, Y_{i+1} = v'\})]$$

but since all $v_{i+1} \in Y_{i+1}$ with $v_{i+1} \notin \sigma(v)$ give a zero probability, and the decisions in D_i which give a non-negative utility are exactly those in $\delta(\tau(v))$ which satisfy the constraints in $\mathbf{h}$

$$= \max_{d_i \in D_i} [U(\tau(v), d_i) + \sum_{v' \in Y_{i+1}} P(Y_{i+1} = v' \mid Y_i = v)$$
$$\hat{u}_{D_{i+1}}(\beta(\mathbf{h}) \cup \{Y_i = v, D_i = d_i, Y_{i+1} = v'\})]$$
$$= \max_{d_i \in D_i} [U(\tau(v), d_i) + \hat{u}_{Y_{i+1}}(\beta(\mathbf{h}) \cup \{Y_i = v, D_i = d_i\})]$$
$$= \hat{u}_{D_i}(\beta(\mathbf{h}) \cup \{Y_i = v\})$$

and thus we have proved the result by induction.

As a corollary, we obtain that if the root node of the BCSP has an empty history, we can write $\hat{U}(v_0) = \hat{u}_{D_0}(Y_0 = v_0)$. Thus, we have proved the equivalence of the two representations of the problem.

5   Future Work: Generalised Branching CSPs

The mapping designed in Sect. 4.1 not only offers a decision-theoretic description of a BCSP's components, but also indicates how these components interact. The decision networks that are produced are of a restricted form. Studying these restrictions suggests ways in which BCSPs might be generalised to handle a wider range of problems.

The Bayesian network component of the resulting decision network is a linear chain $Y_0 \rightarrow Y_1 \rightarrow \cdots \rightarrow Y_n$ with a completely certain initial event, whereas general Bayesian networks are directed acyclic graphs. This restriction arises from the BCSP state transition tree, and the fact that the root node of the tree is the known arrival of the first variable. The certain initial event can easily be relaxed by having an empty root vertex with a number of possible children, but relaxing the cause of the linear chain would require replacing the tree with a directed acyclic graph more similar in style to a Bayesian network. This would allow us to represent events which have multiple conditionally independent successors, while maintaining a temporal interpretation of the arcs, instead of mutually exclusive children as at present. Similarly, we could represent mutually independent parents of an event, instead of single parents. We would also be able to make a distinction between temporal (state-transition) and atemporal arcs, thus giving us a structure similar to a dynamic Bayesian network [5].

BCSPs currently assume that the arrival of variables is governed by uncertainty, but actual decisions to assign a value to a variable do not influence the uncertainty. By adding observation nodes to the uncertainty structure, linking these to explicit decision nodes, and taking these observations into account when assessing utilities, we could model situations where decisions may have an effect on the future distribution of tasks.

If we introduce both non-temporal arcs and explicit decision nodes, then we can represent problems where instant decisions are not necessary. Solutions to the problem could wait until more evidence had been received before making a decision (a restricted form of this was proposed in [7]), or the solution method would be required to decide upon the best sequence of decisions.

It should be noted that new algorithms would be required for the BCSP generalisations discussed above, and that these algorithms might be neither easy to develop nor efficient. Further study will be aimed at determining which of the generalisations still allow us to solve BCSPs in reasonable time (in the average case). A different approach might be to add explicit logical constraints into a decision network, and then attempt to produce BCSP-style algorithms for these extended decision networks.

Finally, although we have presented a mapping from BCSPs to decision networks, we have said nothing about the complexity of the mapping, or the ease of constructing representations of problems. One of the advantages of Constraint Programming in general is the ease of modelling, and the simplicity with which complex combinatorial constraints can be expressed. Similarly, constraint algorithms are design to take advantage of the structure of the constraints. We need to establish the complexity of the transformation in Sect. 4.1, and determine what effect the extensional representation of the constraints has on the running time of the decision network algorithms. Results here would help indicate which of our plans for future work would be most profitable.

6   Conclusions

In this paper, we have given a decision-theoretic interpretation to a particular class of constraint-satisfaction problems with uncertainty, viz. branching constraint satisfaction problems. We have done this using decision networks as a representation formalism to which decision-theoretic, probabilistic and logical constraints were mapped, giving rise to a uniform representation. The biggest advantage of this approach is that it allows us to study the interactions between the various components of a BCSP more clearly. In addition, the insight gained this way acted as a suitable foundation for the design of extensions to the original BCSP formalism.

Acknowledgements. This work was carried out while Ken Brown was at the University of Aberdeen.

References

1. R.E. Bellman. Dynamic Programming. Princeton University Press, Princeton, 1957.
2. R.W. Conway, W.L. Maxwell and L.W. Miller. Theory of Scheduling. Addison-Wesley, Reading, Massachusetts, 1967.
3. G.F. Cooper. A method for using belief networks as influence diagrams. In: Proceedings of the 4th Workshop on Uncertainty in Artificial Intelligence 1988: 55–63.
4. G.F. Cooper. The computational complexity of probabilistic inference using Bayesian belief networks. Artificial Intelligence 1990; 42(2-3): 393–348.
5. P. Dagum, A. Galper and E. Horvitz. Dynamic network models for forecasting. In: Proceedings of UAI92, 1992, pp. 41–48.
6. D.W. Fowler and K.N. Brown. Branching constraint satisfaction problems for solutions robust under likely changes. Proceedings CP2000, Springer Verlag, Berlin, 2000, pp. 500–504.
7. D. W. Fowler. Branching Constraint Satisfaction Problems. PhD Thesis, Department of Computing Science, University of Aberdeen, 2002.
8. D.W. Fowler and K.N. Brown. Branching constraint satisfaction problems and Markov decision problems compared. Annals of Operations Research 2003; 118: 85–100.
9. E. Ignall and L. Schrage. Applications of the branch and bound technique to some flow-shop scheduling problems. Operations Research 1965; 13(3): 400–412.
10. F.V. Jensen. Bayesian Networks and Decision Graphs. Springer, New York, 2001.
11. D.E. Knuth. The Art of Computer Programming, Vol. 1: Fundamental Algorithms, 3rd Ed. Addison-Wesley, Reading, MA, 1997.
12. D. Larkin and R. Dechter. Bayesian inference in the presence of determinism. In: C.M. Bishop and B.J. Frey (eds), Proceedings of the 9th International Workshop on Artificial Intelligence and Statistics, Jan 3-6, 2003, Key West, FL.

13. S.L. Lauritzen, D.J. Spiegelhalter. Local computations with probabilities on graphical structures and their application to expert systems. Journal of the Royal Statistical Society (Series B) 1987; 50: 157–224.
14. P.J.F. Lucas. Bayesian model-based diagnosis. International Journal of Approximate Reasoning 2001; 27: 99–119.
15. J. Pearl. Probabilistic Reasoning in Intelligent Systems. Morgan Kaufman, San Mateo, California, 1988.
16. R.D. Shachter. Evaluating influence diagrams. Operation Research 1986; 34(6): 871–882.
17. E. Tsang. Foundations of Constraint Satisfaction. Academic Press, London, 1993.
18. R.J. Wilson. Introduction to Graph Theory. Longman, Burnt Mill, 1979.

Web of Trust: Applying Probabilistic Argumentation to Public-Key Cryptography[*]

Rolf Haenni

University of Konstanz, Center for Junior Research Fellows
D-78457 Konstanz, Germany
rolf.haenni@uni-konstanz.de
http://haenni-shorturl.com

Abstract. The purpose of this paper is to show how probabilistic argumentation is applicable to modern public-key cryptography as an appropriate tool to evaluate webs of trust. This is an interesting application of uncertain reasoning that has not yet received much attention in the corresponding literature.

1   Introduction

In large open networks like the internet an increasing demand for security is observed. In order to establish a confidential channel between two users of the network, classical single-key cryptography requires them to exchange a common secret key over a secure channel. This may work if the network is small and local, but it is infeasible in non-local or large networks. To simplify the key exchange problem, modern *public-key cryptography* provides a mechanism in which the keys to be exchanged are not secret. In such a framework, every user owns a key pair consisting of a (non-secret) *public key* and a (secret) *private key*. Only public keys are exchanged. They are used to encrypt messages to be sent to the owner of the key and to verify digital signatures issued by the owner of the key.

Before using someone else's public key to encrypt a message or verify a signature, one should make sure that the key really belongs to the intended recipient or the indicated issuer of the signature. Achieving authenticity of public keys can be done in several ways. The most popular approach is based on the concept of digital *certificates*. The idea is that different users of a network certify public keys of other network users. This leads to a *certificate graph*. Of course, certificates should only be issued if the key's authenticity is verified. On the basis of a certificate graph, one can then evaluate the authenticity of the keys on the basis of how much trust one assigns to the different issuers of the certificates. Because such an evaluation depends on *trust*, it is common to call such a certificate graph *web of trust*. Section 2 gives a short introduction to public-key cryptography and webs of trust. For more information we refer to the literature [10,18].

[*] Research supported by (1) Alexander von Humboldt Foundation, (2) German Federal Ministry of Education and Research, (3) German Program for the Investment in the Future.

T.D. Nielsen and N.L. Zhang (Eds.): ECSQARU 2003, LNAI 2711, pp. 243–254, 2003.

PGP (Pretty Good Privacy) is a widely used implementation of public-key cryptography for email security [21]. It organizes public keys on the basis of a web of trust [17]. PGP's way of evaluating the web of trust is a simple mechanism based on three pragmatic rules. Some authors have tried to formalize the concepts of *trust* and *confidence* more properly [1,2,3,9,12,13,19], but approaches to look at the problem from the perspective of the uncertain reasoning community are rare. One exception is the idea of applying Dempster-Shafer theory to a distributed reputation management [20].

Among the various formalisms for uncertain reasoning, *probabilistic argumentation* [8] seems to be to most promising candidate. Ordinary Bayesian networks, for example, fail as a possible candidate because they require the underlying graphs to be acyclic [11] (whereas general certificate graphs are cyclic). The basic concepts of probabilistic argumentation are summarized in Sect. 3. As Sect. 4 demonstrates, by modeling trust as the probability of somebody's reliability, translating a web of trust into a corresponding probabilistic argumentation system is straightforward. And it leads to a one-to-one correspondence between the concepts of certificate chains and arguments. Degree of support, which is the probability that at least one argument holds, can then be used to measure quantitatively the overall reliability of all possible certificate chains and to rate the validity of the public keys.

The goal of this paper is twofold. First, it is supposed to increase the awareness of people interested in reasoning under uncertainty for this interesting application in public-key cryptography. Second, the paper intends to demonstrate how to use probabilistic argumentation in real world applications and to underline the value of this elegant formalism.

2   Public-Key Cryptography and the Web of Trust

Modern cryptography consists of two major tasks: *encryption* and *signing*. To transmit a message m securely from sender A to recipient B, both sender and recipient have to be equipped with a corresponding pair of *public* and *private* keys. Private keys are kept secret, whereas public keys are widely available for any recipient. From A's perspective, sending m over an insecure channel (e.g. the internet) to recipient B requires A to encrypt the message with B's public key and to digitally sign it with A's own private key. On the side of recipient B, the message is decrypted with B's private key and the digital signature is verified with A's public key. Provided that A and B have properly exchanged their public keys, this simple scheme realizes the main security goals (secrecy, message integrity, authentication, non-repudiation) for such a two-party communication.

Public keys are usually distributed with the aid of key servers. Before sending encrypted messages to recipients B, A may copy B's public key from a key server. On the other side, B may copy A's public key from a key server in order to verify A's digital signatures. The question is whether the keys copied from the key servers are really owned by B and A, respectively. A possible attacker O could easily generate key pairs and post the corresponding public keys in A's or B's name onto the server. Encrypting a message falsely to O's public key enables O to decrypt and read the message (and at the same time disables B to decrypt the message). Similarly, verifying a digital signature with false public key enables the attacker O to sign messages in the name of A. An important issue is thus the verification of public keys before use. One way to verify a public key is to compare its unique fingerprint (a hash code of fixed length) over a secure channel (e.g. the telephone line). This method may work in small or local networks with few users, but is impractical in large networks like the internet.

The most practical way to solve the public key exchange problem is to use digital *certificates*. A certificate can be seen as a signed public key. For example, to issue a certificate for A, the issuer C digitally signs A's public key with C's own private key. By doing this, C certifies that A is the true owner of the key. Of course, certificates should only be issued when the public key was either obtained or successfully verified over a secure channel. Note that certificates may consist of signatures from different issuers.

If A receives B's certificate issued by C, then A has good reasons to accept the corresponding public key as B's public key, whenever the following three conditions are satisfied:

- A fully trusts C to carefully verify public keys before issuing certificates,
- A has received or verified C's public key over a secure channel,
- A has successfully verified the certificate using C's public key.

A collection of digital certificates is called *public-key infrastructure* (PKI). In practice, there are two approaches to build PKIs.

2.1   Certificate Authorities

The first approach requires the certificates to be issued by trustworthy *certificate authorities* (CA). For example, if C is a trustworthy CA (i.e. before issuing a certificate, C carefully checks if the applicant is the true owner of the public key), then the users of a large network may exchange their public keys by exchanging respective certificates issued by C. Certificates issued by C can be verified using C's public key. From the successful verification follows then the authenticity of the corresponding public key. If more than one CA issues certificates, it is possible that the different CAs mutually issue certificates to each other. This leads to undirected *certificate trees* which are usually organized hierarchically. Figure 1 shows such a tree in which network users are represented by circles and CAs by squares. An arrow from entity X to entity Y (users or CAs) represents X's certificate issued by Y. The formal notation for such a certificate will be $X \Rightarrow Y$.

If A has an authentic copy of Aut_1's public key, then the authenticity of M's certificate $M \Rightarrow Aut_3$ can be verified using Aut_3's certificate $Aut_3 \Rightarrow Aut_2$ and Aut_2's certificate $Aut_2 \Rightarrow Aut_1$. Such a *certificate chain* $M \Rightarrow Aut_3 \Rightarrow Aut_2 \Rightarrow Aut_1 \Rightarrow A$ requires A to fully and unconditionally trust all CAs along the path between M and A. If any CA in the path has incorrectly issued the certificate of

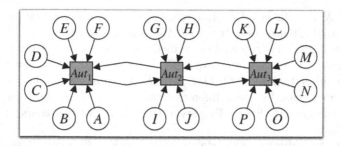

Fig. 1. Example of an undirected certificate tree.

the next CA, then A can be misled regarding the authenticity of M's certificate. Note that there is a unique certificate chain between any two users attached to such a certificate tree.

The major advantage of such a centralized PKI is that every user is required to employ only one secure channel in order to get an authentic copy of its own CA's public key. The major disadvantage is the requirement of unconditional trust in all CAs involved.

2.2   Web of Trust

The second approach does not require certificate authorities. The idea is that every user in the network can issue certificates. This leads to *certificate graphs* rather than trees. In such a decentralized context, one usually speaks about signing public keys rather than issuing certificates. Thus, every user collects signed public keys from different keys servers or other sources. A personal collection of signed public keys is called *key ring*. Note that every individual key ring defines a corresponding certificate graph (which is a sub-graph of the complete certificate graph of all signed public keys). Figure 2 shows the certificate graph that corresponds to A's key ring. An arrow from user X to user Y means that Y

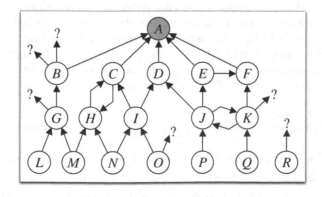

Fig. 2. Example of a certificate graph.

has signed X's public key. Question marks represent users whose public keys are unknown to A. A has directly signed the public keys of B, C, D, E, and F. This means that A has received or verified these keys over a secure channel and accepts them as the authentic keys of B, C, D, E, and F, respectively. In other words, the public keys of B, C, D, E, and F are *valid* for A. Many other keys in the graph are signed by users different from A. User G, for example, has signed the keys of L and M. From A's perspective, G is called *introducer* of L's and M's certificate.

In order to indirectly validate someone else's public key, A must have full confidence in all introducers along the path of at least one certificate chain. This means that A must consider the corresponding introducers to be trustworthy in the sense that they only issue certificates for public keys received or verified over secure channels.

Example 1: There is only one certificate chain $L \Rightarrow G \Rightarrow B \Rightarrow A$ from L to A. In order to validate L's public key, A has to trust both G and B.

Example 2: There are two certificate chains $M \Rightarrow G \Rightarrow B \Rightarrow A$ and $M \Rightarrow H \Rightarrow C \Rightarrow A$ from M to A. In order to validate M's public key, A has to trust either G and B or H and C.

A certificate graph in which the validity of the public keys is evaluated on the basis of trust is called *web of trust*. Note that hierarchical certificate trees with fully trustworthy CAs are particular webs of trust.

A general web of trust allows the owner of the key ring to specify gradual levels of trust for all individuals involved in the web. "Completely trusted" and "untrusted" are the two extreme cases of maximal and minimal trust, respectively. Evaluating the validity of the public keys should then lead to gradual levels of validity. Full validity, for example, only results from full trust along the path of at least one certificate chain (such as in the hierarchical case using CAs). The evaluation of such a general web of trust on the basis of probabilistic argumentation systems is the topic of this paper.

2.3   PGP's Web of Trust

PGP is one of the most popular tools for public-key cryptography. The software can be used to encrypt and digitally sign electronic mail. It is based on a web of trust with some particular characteristics. First of all, PGP allows (only) three levels of trust: "completely trusted", "marginally trusted", and "untrusted". Note that the owner of the key ring automatically receives full trust. In order to rate a public key as "valid", PGP either requires

a) the key to belong to the owner of the key ring,
b) a signature from at least one[1] completely trusted introducer with a "valid" public key,
c) signatures from at least two[2] marginally trusted introducers with "valid" public keys.

---

[1] One is the default value, but a different (higher) value may be chosen by the user.
[2] Two is the default value, but a different (higher) value may be chosen by the user.

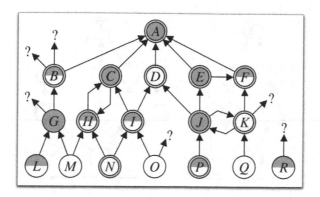

Fig. 3. Example of a PGP's web of trust.

Otherwise, the key is rated as "invalid".[3] Note that all public keys directly signed by the owner of the key ring are "valid". An example to illustrate PGP's trust model is shown in Fig. 3. Gray circles stand for completely trusted, gray semicircles for marginally trusted, and white circles for untrusted public keys. "Valid" public keys are indicated by nested circles. A's public key is "valid" because it is owned by A. The public keys of B, C, D, E, and F are all "valid" because they are directly signed by A. H and I are "valid" because C is "valid" and completely trusted. J is "valid" because E is "valid" and completely trusted. K is "valid" because J is "valid" and completely trusted. N is "valid" because both H and I are "valid" and marginally trusted. Finally, P is "valid" because J is "valid" and completely trusted. All other keys are "invalid".

The PGP trust model is unsatisfactory in many ways. First of all, although trust is a *gradual* quantity that reflects someone's confidence in someone else's reliability, PGP provides only three levels of trust. Similarly, by simply distinguishing between "valid" and "invalid" public keys, PGP is not able to gradually rate the authenticity of the keys. Another problem is the rule that keys signed by at least two marginally trusted introducers are rated as "valid". This rule seems to be the product of a pragmatic way of evaluating webs of trust, but it is certainly not the result of a proper and well-founded trust model. In fact, one can easily construct counter-intuitive examples such as the ones shown in Fig. 4.

On the left hand side of Fig. 4, PGP's trust model rates B's public key as "valid", whereas on the right hand side, it is rated as "invalid". However, because there is any desired number of possible certificate chains in the web of trust on the right hand side, each chain including one marginally trusted and one completely trusted introducer, one would expect to rate the validity of B's key with a much higher degree than in the web of trust shown on the left hand side with only two possible certificate chains.

---

[3] PGP also defines "marginally valid" public keys, but they are considered as "invalid" by default.

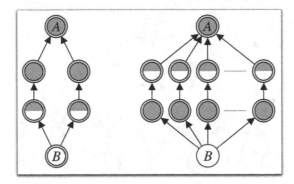

Fig. 4. More examples of PGP's web of trust.

3 Probabilistic Argumentation

The basic idea behind probabilistic argumentation comes goes back to the concept of *assumption-based truth maintenance systems* (ATMS) [5]. The goal is not to describe argumentation as a dialectical process, but rather to serve as a *deductive tool* that helps to judge *hypotheses* in the light of the given uncertain and partial knowledge. Hypotheses represent open questions about the unknown or future world.

From a qualitative point of view, the problem is to derive *arguments* in favor and *counter-arguments* against the hypothesis *h* of interest. An argument is a defeasible proof built on uncertain *assumptions*. In other words, arguments are combinations of true or false assumptions that permit to infer the truth of the hypothesis *h* from the given knowledge base. Every argument provides thus a sufficient reason that proves the hypothesis in the light of the available knowledge. And it finally contributes to the possibility of believing or accepting the hypothesis. In other words, arguments *support* and counter-arguments *defeat* the hypothesis *h*. Note that counter-arguments can be regarded as arguments in favor of the negated hypothesis ¬*h* and vice versa.

A quantitative judgement of the situation is obtained by considering the probabilities that the arguments and counter-arguments are valid. The *credibility* of a hypothesis is measured by the total probabilities that it is supported or defeated by arguments. Conflicts are handled through conditioning. The resulting *degree of support* and *degree of possibility* correspond to *belief* and *plausibility*, respectively, in the Dempster-Shafer theory of evidence [14,16].

For the construction of probabilistic argumentation systems, consider two disjoint sets A and P of propositions. The elements of A are called *assumptions* and represent uncertain events, unknown circumstances, or possible states or outcomes. $\mathcal{L}_{A \cup P}$ denotes the propositional language over $A \cup P$. The available uncertain *knowledge base* is then encoded by a sentence $\xi \in \mathcal{L}_{A \cup P}$. It is often specified by a conjunctively interpreted set $\Sigma = \{\xi_1, \ldots, \xi_r\}$ of sentences $\xi_i \in \mathcal{L}_{A \cup P}$ for which ξ is defined by $\xi = \xi_1 \wedge \cdots \wedge \xi_r$.

3.1   Arguments, Counter-Arguments, Conflicts

Consider the case where a second propositional sentence $h \in \mathcal{L}_{A \cup P}$ represents a *hypothesis* about some of the propositions in $A \cup P$. What can be inferred from ξ about the possible truth of h with respect to the given set of uncertain assumptions? Possibly, if some of the assumptions are set to *true* and others to *false*, then h may be a logical consequence of ξ.

More formally, if $\mathcal{T}_A$ denotes the set of all conjunctions of non-repeating literals over A, then such a term $\alpha \in \mathcal{T}_A$ is an *argument* for h, if $\alpha \wedge \xi \models h$. Similarly, if $\alpha \wedge \xi \models \neg h$, then α is a *counter-argument* against h. Note that counter-arguments are arguments for $\neg h$. An argument α for h is called *minimal*, if there is no shorter argument $\alpha' \subset \alpha$ for h. The sets of all minimal arguments and minimal counter-argument with respect to h and ξ are denoted by $Args(h, \xi)$ and $Args(\neg h, \xi)$, respectively. Note that every $\alpha \in Args(h, \xi)$ increases the support for h, whereas every $\alpha \in Args(\neg h, \xi)$ decreases the possibility of h.

If a term $\alpha \in \mathcal{T}_A$ is both argument and counter-argument of h, then it is called *conflict*. Conflicts are inconsistent with the knowledge base ξ. They represent impossible states of the world which have be excluded. Note that conflicts are arguments for $\bot$. The set of all minimal conflicts is denoted by $Args(\bot, \xi)$.

Consider two sets $A = \{a_1, a_2, a_3\}$, $P = \{X, Y\}$, and a knowledge base ξ given as a set $\Sigma = \{a_1 \rightarrow X, \ \neg a_2 \rightarrow Y, \ a_3 \wedge Y \rightarrow X, \ a_2 \rightarrow \neg X\}$ of material implications. If X is the hypothesis of interest, then there are two arguments, one counter-argument, and one conflict:

$$Args(X, \xi) = \{a_1, \neg a_2 \wedge a_3\}, \ Args(\neg X, \xi) = \{a_2\}, \ Args(\bot, \xi) = \{a_1 \wedge a_2\}.$$

Computing the sets $Args(h, \xi)$, $Args(\neg h, \xi)$, and $Args(\bot, \xi)$ is the main computational problem of probabilistic argumentation [8]. Efficient algorithms are obtained by focussing the search on the most relevant arguments [6,7].

3.2   Degrees of Support and Possibility

In order to judge h quantitatively, let every assumption $a \in A$ be linked to a corresponding *prior probability* $p(a)$. We suppose them to be mutually independent. Then the probability of a term $\alpha \in \mathcal{T}_A$ is

$$p(\alpha) \;\; = \;\; \prod \{p(a) : a \in \alpha\} \cdot \prod \{1 - p(a) : \neg a \in \alpha\}. \tag{1}$$

If $T \subseteq \mathcal{T}_A$ is an arbitrary set of terms, then $p(T)$ denotes the overall probability of all terms included in T. It corresponds to the probability that at least one term of T is true. Note that any such set $T = \{\alpha_1, \ldots, \alpha_n\}$ can be interpreted as a disjunctive normal form $\alpha_1 \vee \cdots \vee \alpha_n$ (DNF for short). The problem of computing $p(T)$ is thus equivalent to the general problem of computing probabilities of DNFs. For further information on this we refer to the corresponding literature, in particular to Darwiche's d-DNNF compiler [4].

Consider now the conditional probability that at least one argument for h is true under the condition that none of the conflicts of ξ is true. This is a quantitative measure of how much h is supported by arguments in the light of the given knowledge. In depends on the two sets $Args(h,\xi)$ and $Args(\perp,\xi)$. If $Args(\perp,\xi)$ is considered as DNF, then $\neg Args(\perp,\xi)$ represents the condition that conflicts are impossible. This allows us to define *degree of support* of h as

$$dsp(h,\xi) = p(Args(h,\xi) \mid \neg Args(\perp,\xi)) = \frac{p(Args(h,\xi)) - p(Args(\perp,\xi))}{1 - p(Args(\perp,\xi))}. \quad (2)$$

For a more detailed derivation of the above formula we refer to [8]. Note that degree of support is equivalent to the notion of (normalized) *belief* in the Dempster-Shafer theory of evidence [14,16]. It can also be interpreted as the probability of provability [11,15].

A second way of judging the hypothesis h is to look at the conditional probability that no counter-argument is true under the condition that none of the conflicts of ξ is true. This is a quantitative measure of how possible h is in the light of the given knowledge. Thus, *degree of possibility* of h is defined as

$$dps(h,\xi) = p(\neg Args(\neg h,\xi) \mid \neg Args(\perp,\xi)) = 1 - dsp(\neg h,\xi). \quad (3)$$

Degree of possibility is equivalent to the notion of *plausibility* in the Dempster-Shafer theory. Note that $dsp(h,\xi) \leq dps(h,\xi)$ for all $h \in \mathcal{L}_{A \cup P}$ and $\xi \in \mathcal{L}_{A \cup P}$. The particular case of $dsp(h,\xi) = 0$ and $dps(h,\xi) = 1$ represents total ignorance over h.

Consider the example at the end of the previous subsection and suppose that $p(a_1) = 0.2$, $p(a_2) = 0.4$, and $p(a_3) = 0.1$ are the probabilities of the assumptions. The probabilities of the DNFs formed by the respective sets of arguments, counter-arguments, and conflicts are then as follows:

$$p(Args(X,\xi)) = p(a_1 \vee \neg a_2 \wedge a_3) = 0.248, \quad p(Args(\neg X,\xi)) = p(a_2) = 0.4,$$
$$p(Args(\perp,\xi)) = p(a_1 \wedge a_2) = 0.08.$$

Finally, according to (2) and (3), degree of support and degree of possibility is computed as follows:

$$dsp(X,\xi) = \frac{0.248 - 0.08}{1 - 0.08} = 0.183, \quad dps(X,\xi) = 1 - \frac{0.4 - 0.08}{1 - 0.08} = 0.652.$$

Although there is only a weak support, the hypothesis X remains quite possible. This is an example where gathering more information should precede any rash decision for or against X.

4   Trust Evaluation Based on Probabilistic Argumentation

We will now see how to encode a web of trust as a probabilistic argumentation system. Because trust can be seen as someone's confidence in someone else's reliability, we denote the reliability of an introducer X by the proposition $rel(X)$. Gradual confidence in X can then be quantified by the probability $p(rel(X))$ of

X being a reliable introducer. The special case where X is a fully trustworthy CA is encoded by $p(rel(X)) = 1$. On the other hand, $p(rel(X)) = 0$ stands for the case where X deserves no trust at all.

In a similar way, we use the proposition $Val(X)$ to represent the case where X's public key is valid. Note that there is usually no prior knowledge about how certain $Val(X)$ is. It is therefore not possible to specify corresponding probabilities.

If $\mathcal{U} = \{X_0, X_1, \ldots, X_n\}$ is the set of all users included in the key ring owned by X_0, then

$$A = \{rel(X_1), \ldots, rel(X_n)\}, \quad P = \{rel(X_0), Val(X_0), \ldots, Val(X_n)\}, \quad (4)$$

are the two sets of propositions needed to build a probabilistic argumentation system. Note that the probabilities $p(rel(X_i))$, $1 \le i \le n$, are specified by X_0, whereas X_0 is implicitly assumed to be fully reliable by default. Similarly, because X_0's own public key is implicitly valid, $Val(X_0)$ is true by default.

Finally, in order to formulate X_0's certificate graph as an assumption-based knowledge base ξ, consider the set $\mathcal{C} = \{c_1, \ldots, c_m\}$ of all certificates contained in X_0's key ring that are issued by known users. A single certificate $c \in \mathcal{C}$ of the form $X_i \Rightarrow X_j$ translates then into the following propositional formula:

$$\xi(c) = rel(X_j) \wedge Val(X_j) \to Val(X_i). \quad (5)$$

The idea of this translation is to consider X_i's public key as valid whenever X_j is a reliable introducer with a valid public key. Note that this corresponds to Rule b) in PGP's trust model. The complete knowledge base ξ is now determined by the following set Σ of propositional formulas:

$$\Sigma = \{rel(X_0), Val(X_0), \xi(c_1), \ldots, \xi(c_m)\}. \quad (6)$$

The certificate graph in Fig. 2, for example, includes 18 users $\mathcal{U} = \{A, B, \ldots, R\}$ who have issued 24 certificates (6 certificates were issued by unknown users). This leads to the following knowledge base ξ consisting of 26 formulas:

$$\Sigma = \left\{ \begin{array}{l} rel(A),\ Val(A), \\ rel(A) \wedge Val(A) \to Val(B),\ rel(A) \wedge Val(A) \to Val(C),\ rel(A) \wedge Val(A) \to Val(D), \\ rel(A) \wedge Val(A) \to Val(E),\ rel(A) \wedge Val(A) \to Val(F),\ rel(B) \wedge Val(B) \to Val(G), \\ rel(C) \wedge Val(C) \to Val(H),\ rel(C) \wedge Val(C) \to Val(I),\ rel(D) \wedge Val(D) \to Val(I), \\ rel(D) \wedge Val(D) \to Val(J),\ rel(E) \wedge Val(E) \to Val(J),\ rel(F) \wedge Val(F) \to Val(E), \\ rel(F) \wedge Val(F) \to Val(K),\ rel(G) \wedge Val(G) \to Val(L),\ rel(G) \wedge Val(G) \to Val(M), \\ rel(H) \wedge Val(H) \to Val(M),\ rel(C) \wedge Val(H) \to Val(M),\ rel(H) \wedge Val(H) \to Val(N), \\ rel(I) \wedge Val(I) \to Val(N),\ rel(I) \wedge Val(I) \to Val(O),\ rel(J) \wedge Val(J) \to Val(P), \\ rel(J) \wedge Val(J) \to Val(K),\ rel(K) \wedge Val(K) \to Val(J),\ rel(K) \wedge Val(K) \to Val(Q) \end{array} \right\}$$

How can such a model be used to evaluate the validity of public keys? First of all, if it is X_i's key to be rated, then $Val(X_i)$ is the hypothesis of interest. Every minimal argument $\alpha \in Args(Val(X_i), \xi)$ corresponds then to a (minimal) certificate chain from X_i to X_0. On the other had, because ξ contains only positive literals, there are no counter-arguments against $Val(X_i)$. This implies $Args(\neg Val(X_i), \xi) = Args(\bot, \xi) = \emptyset$ and therefore $dsp(Val(X_i), \xi) = p(Args(Val(X_i), \xi))$ and $dps(Val(X_i), \xi) = 1$ for all $X_i \in \mathcal{U}$. Therefore, degree of support is the only relevant quantity to rate the validity of X_i's public key. It corresponds to the probability that all introducers of at least one certificate chain are all reliable.

In the example above, if it is P's public key to be rated, there are three minimal arguments supporting the hypothesis $Val(P)$:

$$Args(Val(P), \xi) = \{rel(D) \wedge rel(J), \; rel(E) \wedge rel(J), \; rel(F) \wedge rel(K) \wedge rel(J)\}.$$

The first argument $rel(D) \wedge rel(J)$, for example, corresponds to the certificate chain $P \Rightarrow J \Rightarrow D \Rightarrow A$. Note that non-minimal certificate chains such as $P \Rightarrow J \Rightarrow E \Rightarrow F \Rightarrow A$ correspond to non-minimal arguments and are thus not listed in the set $Args(Val(P), \xi)$.

Suppose now that A has specified the reliability of the introducers B to R according to the second row of the following table. The corresponding degrees of supports are then shown in the third row.

X_i	A	B	C	D	E	F	G	H	I	J	K	L	M	N	O	P	Q	R
$p(rel(X_i))$	$-$	.5	.9	.1	.8	.6	.9	.4	.5	.8	.2	.5	0	.1	0	.3	.1	.6
$dsp(Val(X_i), \xi)$	1	1	1	1	1	1	1	.5	.9	.91	.842	.862	.45	.648	.635	.455	.673	.172	0

A's public key receives automatically maximal support. The keys of B, C, D, E, and F receive maximal support because they are directly signed by A. R's public key receives no support because no certificate has been issued for R. All other keys are rated with values between 0 and 1. For example, consider the case of P's public key. The corresponding degree of support $dsp(Val(P), \xi) = 0.673$ is composed of the probabilities $p(rel(D) \wedge rel(J)) = 0.08$, $p(rel(E) \wedge rel(J)) = 0.64$, and $p(rel(F) \wedge rel(K) \wedge rel(J)) = 0.096$ of the individual minimal certificate chains.

5   Conclusion

This paper investigates trust evaluation in public-key infrastructures based on probabilistic argumentation. It is remarkable how straightforwardly certificate graphs are expressible as assumption-based knowledge bases. Degree of support seems then to be an appropriate quantity to rate the validity of public keys. We propose the results of this paper to be taken as the basis for a more sophisticated trust model in cryptographic applications like PGP.

Future work will focus on how to include *negative evidence* in the form of key revocations, *recommendations* about someone else's trustworthiness, and *dependencies* between the introducers. Due to the clear conflict management of probabilistic argumentation and the expressive power of assumption-based modeling, it should not be too hard to extend the basic model accordingly.

References

1. T. Beth, M. Borcherding, and B. Klein. Valuation of trust in open networks. In *Proceedings of the 3rd European Symposium on Research in Computer Security – ESORICS '94*, LNCS 875, pages 3–18. Springer-Verlag, 1994.
2. A.D. Birrell, B.W. Lampson, R.M. Needham, and M.D. Schoreder. A global authentication service without global trust. In *Proceedings of the IEEE Symposium on Security and Privacy*, pages 223–230, 1986.
3. M. Branstad, W.C. Barker, and P. Cochrane. The role of trust in protected mail. In *IEEE Symposium on Security and Privacy*, pages 210–215, 1990.
4. A. Darwiche. A compiler for deterministic, decomposable negation normal form. In *Proceedings of the 18th National Conference on Artificial Intelligence*, pages 627–634. AAAI Press, 2002.
5. J. de Kleer. An assumption-based TMS. *Artificial Intelligence*, 28:127–162, 1986.
6. R. Haenni. Cost-bounded argumentation. *International Journal of Approximate Reasoning*, 26(2):101–127, 2001.
7. R. Haenni. A query-driven anytime algorithm for argumentative and abductive reasoning. In D. Bustard, W. Liu, and R. Sterrit, editors, *Soft-Ware 2002, 1st International Conference on Computing in an Imperfect World*, LNCS 2311, pages 114–127. Springer-Verlag, 2002.
8. R. Haenni, J. Kohlas, and N. Lehmann. Probabilistic argumentation systems. In J. Kohlas and S. Moral, editors, *Handbook of Defeasible Reasoning and Uncertainty Management Systems, Volume 5: Algorithms for Uncertainty and Defeasible Reasoning*, pages 221–288. Kluwer, Dordrecht, 2000.
9. U. Maurer. Modelling a public-key infrastructure. In E. Bertino, H. Kurth, G. Martella, and E. Montolivo, editors, *ESORICS: European Symposium on Research in Computer Security*, LNCS 1146, pages 324–350. Springer-Verlag, 1996.
10. A.J. Menezes, P.C. van Oorschot, and S.A. Vanstone. *Handbook of Applied Cryptography*. CRC Press, 1997.
11. J. Pearl. *Probabilistic Reasoning in Intelligent Systems*. Morgan Kaufmann, 1988.
12. M.K. Reiter and S.G. Stubblebine. Path independence for authentication in large-scale systems. In *ACM Conference on Computer and Communications Security*, pages 57–66, 1997.
13. M.K. Reiter and S.G. Stubblebine. Authentication metric analysis and design. *ACM Transactions on Information and System Security*, 2(2):138–158, 1999.
14. G. Shafer. *The Mathematical Theory of Evidence*. Princeton Univ. Press, 1976.
15. Ph. Smets. Probability of provability and belief functions. In M. Clarke, R. Kruse R., and S. Moral, editors, *Proceedings of the ECSQARU'93 Conference*, pages 332–340. Springer-Verlag, 1993.
16. Ph. Smets and R. Kennes. The transferable belief model. *Artificial Intelligence*, 66:191–234, 1994.
17. W. Stallings. *Protect Your Privacy, a Guide for PGP Users*. Prentice Hall, 1995.
18. W. Stallings. *Cryptography and Network Security: Principles and Practice*. Prentice Hall, 3rd edition, 2003.
19. R. Yahalom, B. Klein, and Th. Beth. Trust relationships in secure system - a distributed authentication perspective. In *Proceedings of the 1993 IEEE Symposium on Research in Security and Privacy*, pages 150–164, 1993.
20. B. Yu and M.P. Singh. An evidential model of distributed reputation management. In *Proceedings of the First International Joint Conference on Autonomous Agents and Multiagent Systems, AAMAS 2002*, pages 294–301. ACM, 2002.
21. P. Zimmermann. *PGP User's Guide, Volumes I and II*, 1994.

A Comparison of Methods for Transforming Belief Function Models to Probability Models

Barry R. Cobb and Prakash P. Shenoy

University of Kansas School of Business, 1300 Sunnyside Ave., Summerfield Hall
Lawrence, KS 66045-7585, USA
{brcobb,pshenoy}@ku.edu

Abstract. Recently, we proposed a new method called the plausibility transformation method to convert a belief function model to an equivalent probability model. In this paper, we compare the plausibility transformation method with the pignistic transformation method. The two transformation methods yield qualitatively different probability models. We argue that the plausibility transformation method is the correct method for translating a belief function model to an equivalent probability model that maintains belief function semantics.

1 Introduction

Bayesian probability theory and the Dempster-Shafer (D-S) theory of belief functions are two distinct calculi for modeling and reasoning with knowledge about propositions in uncertain domains. In a recent paper [1], we have argued that these two calculi have roughly the same expressive power. Also, in [2,3], we have proposed a new method, called the plausibility transformation method, for transforming a belief function model to an equivalent probability model.

In this paper, we compare two techniques—the pignistic transformation [11] and the plausibility transformation—for transforming a belief function model to a Bayesian probability model. In many cases, these two methods lead to radically different probability models starting from the same belief function model. We argue that the plausibility transformation method is the correct method and that it provides an equivalent probability model that is consistent with belief function semantics.

There are many different semantics of belief functions, including multivalued mapping [5], random codes [9], transferable beliefs [11], and hints [7], that are compatible with Dempster's rule of combination. However, the semantics of belief functions as upper and lower probability bounds on some true but unknown probability function are incompatible with Dempster's rule [12]. In this paper, we are concerned with the D-S theory of belief functions with Dempster's rule of combination as the updating rule, and not with theories of upper and lower probabilities that admit various other rules for updating beliefs. One benefit of studying probability functions derived from D-S belief functions is a more clear understanding of D-S belief function semantics.

T.D. Nielsen and N.L. Zhang (Eds.): ECSQARU 2003, LNAI 2711, pp. 255–266, 2003.

The remainder of this paper is organized as follows. Section 2 contains notation and definitions associated with probability theory and the Dempster–Shafer theory of belief functions. Section 3 defines the pignistic and plausibility transformation methods. Section 4 describes three examples that are studied in great detail. Section 5 contains four theorems that define the properties of the plausibility transformation. In Sect. 6, we summarize and conclude. Proofs of all theorems can be found in [2]. This paper is extracted from a larger unpublished working paper [2].

2   Notation and Definitions

This section establishes notation and definitions that will be used throughout the paper.

2.1   Probability Theory

A probability potential P_s for s is a function $P_s : \Omega_s \rightarrow [0,1]$. We express our knowledge by probability potentials, which are combined to form the joint probability distribution, which is then marginalized to the relevant variables.

Projection of States. If (w, x, y, z) is a state of $\{W, X, Y, Z\}$, for example, then the projection of (w, x, y, z) to $\{W, X\}$ is simply (w, x), which is a state of $\{W, X\}$. If s and t are sets of variables, $s \subseteq t$, and x is a state of t, then $x^{\downarrow s}$ denotes the projection of x to s.

Combination. Combination in probability theory is "pointwise" multiplication of potentials followed by normalization. Suppose P_s is a probability potential for s and P_t is a probability potential for t. Then $P_s \otimes P_t$ is a probability potential for $s \cup t$ defined as follows:

$$(P_s \otimes P_t)(x) = K^{-1} P_s(x^{\downarrow s}) P_t(x^{\downarrow t}), \tag{1}$$

for each $x \in \Omega_{s \cup t}$, where $K = \sum \{P_s(x^{\downarrow s}) P_t(x^{\downarrow t}) \mid x \in \Omega_{s \cup t}\}$ is the normalization constant.

Marginalization. Marginalization in probability theory involves addition over the state space of the variables being eliminated. Suppose P_s is a probability potential for s, and suppose $X \in s$. The marginal of P_s for $s \setminus \{X\}$, denoted by $P_s^{\downarrow(s \setminus \{X\})}$, is the probability potential for $s \setminus \{X\}$ defined as follows:

$$P_s^{\downarrow(s \setminus \{X\})}(y) = \sum \{P_s(y, x) \mid x \in \Omega_X\}, \tag{2}$$

for all $y \in \Omega_{s \setminus \{X\}}$.

2.2   Dempster-Shafer Theory of Belief Functions

A Dempster-Shafer basic probability assignment (bpa) assigns values to subsets of the state space. If Ω_s is the state space of a set of variables s, a function $m : 2^{\Omega_s} \to [0, 1]$ is a bpa for s whenever $m(\emptyset) = 0$ and

$$\sum \{m(\mathbf{a}) \mid \mathbf{a} \in 2^{\Omega_s}\} = 1. \tag{3}$$

A bpa can also be stated in terms of a corresponding plausibility function. The plausibility function Pl_m corresponding to a bpa m for s is defined as $Pl_m : 2^{\Omega_s} \to [0, 1]$ such that for all $\mathbf{a} \in 2^{\Omega_s}$,

$$Pl_m(\mathbf{a}) = \sum \{m(\mathbf{b}) \mid \mathbf{b} \cap \mathbf{a} \neq \emptyset\}. \tag{4}$$

Projection and Extension of Subsets. If r and s are sets of variables, $r \subseteq s$, and $\mathbf{a}$ is a nonempty subset of Ω_s, then the *projection of* $\mathbf{a}$ *to* r, denoted by $\mathbf{a}^{\downarrow r}$, is the subset of Ω_r given by $\mathbf{a}^{\downarrow r} = \{x^{\downarrow r} \mid x \in \mathbf{a}\}$.

By extension of a subset of a state space to a subset of a larger state space, we mean a cylinder set extension. If r and s are sets of variables, $r \subset s$, and $\mathbf{a}$ is a subset of Ω_r, then the *extension of* $\mathbf{a}$ *to* s is $\mathbf{a} \times \Omega_{s \setminus r}$. Let $\mathbf{a}^{\uparrow s}$ denote the extension of $\mathbf{a}$ to s. For example, if $\mathbf{a}$ is a subset of $\Omega_{\{W,X\}}$, then $\mathbf{a}^{\uparrow \{W,X,Y,Z\}} = \mathbf{a} \times \Omega_{\{Y,Z\}}$.

Combination. Calculation of a joint bpa is accomplished by using Dempster's rule of combination [5]. Consider two bpa's m_A and m_B for a and b, respectively. The combination of m_A and m_B, denoted by $m_A \oplus m_B$, is the bpa for $a \cup b$ given by

$$(m_A \oplus m_B)(\mathbf{c}) = K^{-1} \sum \{m_A(\mathbf{x}) m_B(\mathbf{y}) \mid (\mathbf{x}^{\uparrow (a \cup b)}) \cap (\mathbf{y}^{\uparrow (a \cup b)}) = \mathbf{c}\} \tag{5}$$

for all nonempty $\mathbf{c} \subseteq \Omega_{a \cup b}$, where K is a normalization constant given by $K = \sum \{m_A(\mathbf{x}) m_B(\mathbf{y}) \mid (\mathbf{x}^{\uparrow (a \cup b)}) \cap (\mathbf{y}^{\uparrow (a \cup b)}) \neq \emptyset\}$.

Marginalization. Suppose m is a bpa for s, and suppose $t \subset s$. The marginal of m for t, denoted $m^{\downarrow t}$, is the bpa for t defined as follows:

$$m^{\downarrow t}(\mathbf{a}) = \sum \{m(\mathbf{b}) \mid \mathbf{b}^{\downarrow t} = \mathbf{a}\} \tag{6}$$

for each $\mathbf{a} \subset \Omega_t$.

3   Transformation Methods

In this section, we define the pignistic transformation and the plausibility transformation methods for converting belief functions to probability functions.

3.1 Pignistic Transformation

Suppose m is a bpa for s. Let $BetP_m$ denote the corresponding probability function obtained using the pignistic transformation method [10,11]. $BetP_m$ is defined as follows:

$$BetP_m(x) = \sum_{\substack{\mathbf{a} \subseteq \Omega_s \\ x \in \mathbf{a}}} \frac{m(\mathbf{a})}{|\mathbf{a}|} \tag{7}$$

for each $x \in \Omega_s$. To simplify terminology, we will refer to the $BetP_m$ as a pignistic probability function (corresponding to bpa m).

3.2 Plausibility Transformation

Suppose m is a bpa for s. Let Pl_m denote the plausibility function for s corresponding to bpa m. Let Pl_P_m denote the probability function for s corresponding to m obtained using the plausibility transformation method. Pl_P_m is defined as follows:

$$Pl\_P_m(x) = K^{-1}Pl_m(\{x\}) \tag{8}$$

for all $x \in \Omega_s$, where $K = \sum\{Pl_m(\{x\}) \mid x \in \Omega_s\}$ is the normalization constant. To simplify terminology, we will refer to Pl_P_m as the plausibility probability function (corresponding to bpa m).

4   Three Examples

The examples in this section will highlight the differences between the pignistic and plausibility transformation methods.

4.1 Example 1: Peter, Paul, and Mary [11]

A mafia don, the Godfather, has three assassins, Peter, Paul, and Mary. Needing to assassinate an informant, Mr. Jones, the Godfather decides to first toss a fair coin to decide the sex of the assassin. If the toss results in heads, he will pick Mary for the job. If the toss results in tails, he will ask either Peter or Paul to do the job. In the case of tails, we have no knowledge of how the Godfather will select between Peter and Paul. Now suppose we find Mr. Jones assassinated. An informant in the mafia organization has informed the district attorney (DA) about the Godfather's incomplete mechanism for choosing among Peter, Paul, and Mary. The DA would like to indict Peter, Paul, or Mary (in addition to the Godfather). Who should the DA indict?

Let A denote the assassin variable with three states: Peter, Paul, and Mary. Given our knowledge of the incomplete protocol of how the assassin was selected, we can represent it by the bpa m_1 for A as follows: $m_1(\{Mary\}) = 0.5$, $m_1(\{Peter, Paul\}) = 0.5$. The pignistic probability function corresponding to m_1 is as follows: $BetP_{m_1}(Mary) = 0.5$, $BetP_{m_1}(Peter) = BetP_{m_1}(Paul) =$

0.25. The plausibility probability function corresponding to m_1 is as follows: $Pl\_P_{m_1}(Mary) = Pl\_P_{m_1}(Peter) = Pl\_P_{m_1}(Paul) = 1/3$. The pignistic transformation completes the Godfather's incomplete selection protocol by dividing the 0.5 probability equally between Peter and Paul. We refer to this assignment of equal probabilities as a random choice protocol. The plausibility transformation makes no assumption about the mechanism that will be used. The mafia don may always prefer Peter to Paul, or perhaps Paul to Peter. Using standard belief function semantics, there is a 0.5 chance that Mary is not the assassin, a 0.5 chance that Peter is not the assassin, and a 0.5 chance that Paul is not the assassin. This explains the plausibility probability function $Pl\_P_{m_1}$.

Clearly, the two transformation methods yield qualitatively different results starting from the same bpa m_1. Which probability distribution can be considered as equivalent to m_1? In the following paragraphs, we describe one argument (flawed, in our opinion) in favor of the pignistic transformation method and two arguments (compelling, in our opinion) in favor of the plausibility transformation method.

Consider the following argument in favor of the pignistic transformation method[1].

There is exactly one "argument" for Mary and one "counter-argument" each for Mary, Peter and Paul, respectively, as follows [6]:

	Arguments	Counter-arguments		Bel	Pl
Mary	Heads	Tails	⇒	0.5	0.5
Peter	–	Heads	⇒	0	0.5
Paul	–	Heads	⇒	0	0.5

A transformation method should take both arguments and counter-arguments into account. The pignistic transformation method considers both in this example by averaging the weights of arguments and counter-arguments. On the other hand, the plausibility transformation method takes only counter-arguments into account (ignoring arguments).

What this argument fails to notice is that the counter-arguments for Peter and Paul are exactly the same as the argument for Mary. Thus, in averaging the weights of arguments and counter-arguments, we are selectively double-counting information, violating a fundamental tenet of uncertain reasoning. A belief function has exactly the same information as the corresponding plausibility function, $Pl(\mathbf{a}) = 1 - Bel(\Omega_A \setminus \mathbf{a})$. By ignoring arguments, the plausibility transformation method avoids double counting uncertain information.

One way to resolve the conflict between $BetP$ and Pl_P is to appeal to the property of idempotency. Suppose we have two pieces of identical, independent evidence about the assassin, both equal to the bpa m_1. If we use Dempster's rule to combine these two pieces of evidence, we observe that $m_1 \oplus m_1 = m_1$, i.e.,

---

[1] This argument was provided by Rolf Haenni [private communication].

m_1 is idempotent. $Pl\_P_{m_1}$ is also idempotent, i.e., $Pl\_P_{m_1} \otimes Pl\_P_{m_1} = Pl\_P_{m_1}$. However, notice that $BetP_{m_1}$ is not idempotent. Denoting $BetP_{m_1} \otimes BetP_{m_1}$ by $BetP_m$, we have $BetP_m(Mary) = 2/3$ and $BetP_m(Peter) = BetP_m(Paul) = 1/6$. Idempotency is an important qualitative property of uncertain knowledge because double-counting of idempotent information is harmless.

Continuing the Peter, Paul or Mary saga, suppose we subsequently learn that Peter has a cast-iron alibi during the time Mr. Jones was assassinated. This piece of evidence can be represented by the bpa m_2 for A as follows: $m_2(\{Paul, Mary\}) = 1$. If we combine the two independent bpa's m_1 and m_2, we get $(m_1 \oplus m_2)(\{Paul\}) = (m_1 \oplus m_2)(\{Mary\}) = 0.5$. Since the joint bpa has only singleton focal subsets, both the pignistic and plausibility probability functions corresponding to $m_1 \oplus m_2$ agree: $BetP_{m_1 \oplus m_2}(Paul) = Pl\_P_{m_1 \oplus m_2}(Paul) = BetP_{m_1 \oplus m_2}(Mary) = Pl\_P_{m_1 \oplus m_2}(Mary) = 0.5$. However, if we were using the pignistic probability distribution $BetP_{m_1}$, and we update this probability distribution (using Bayes rule) with the evidence of Peter's alibi (represented with a likelihood vector that has 0 for Peter and 1's for Paul and Mary), we end with a probability distribution for A that has probability 2/3 for Mary and 1/3 for Paul, a result that does not coincide with $BetP_{m_1 \oplus m_2}$. On the other hand, if we were using the plausibility probability distribution $Pl\_P_{m_1}$, and we update this distribution with the evidence of Peter's alibi, the result is a probability distribution for A that has probability 1/2 for Paul and 1/2 for Mary, exactly the same probability distribution as $Pl\_P_{m_1 \oplus m_2}$.

4.2   Example 2: Counter-Example [10]

Consider a bpa m for a variable H with state space $\Omega_H = \{h_1, \ldots, h_{70}\}$ as follows: $m(\{h_1\}) = 0.30$, $m(\{h_2\}) = 0.01$, $m(\{h_2, h_3, \ldots, h_{70}\}) = 0.69$. For this bpa m, the pignistic probability function $BetP_m$ is as follows: $BetP_m(h_1) = 0.30$, $BetP_m(h_2) = 0.02$, $BetP_m(h_3) = \ldots = BetP_m(h_{70}) = 0.01$. The unnormalized plausibility probability function $Pl\_P'_m$ is as follows: $Pl\_P'_m(h_1) = 0.30$, $Pl\_P'_m(h_2) = 0.70$, $Pl\_P'_m(h_3) = \ldots = Pl\_P'_m(h_{70}) = 0.69$.

Clearly, the two probability functions are very different. The pignistic probability function has h_1 15 times more likely than h_2 whereas the plausibility probability function has h_2 2.33 times more likely than h_1. Our interpretation is that the pignistic transformation uses a random protocol where the probability of 0.69 is divided equally amongst the 69 states $h_2, \ldots, h_{70}$. Smets [10] argues that the originality of Shafer's model is that—unlike probabilistic models—it does not resort to an argument of symmetry to arbitrarily split belief assigned to non-singleton subsets into equal parts; however, we interpret the pignistic transformation as performing this very allocation.

Shafer [8] states that $m(A)$ should be interpreted as the probability mass that is "confined to A but can move freely to every point of A" (p. 40). In this example, we have belief of 0.70 against h_1, a belief of 0.30 against h_2, and a belief of 0.31 against $h_3, \ldots, h_{70}$. Rather than use a random choice protocol, the plausibility transformation assumes that all mass can move freely to any state in the focal element of the belief function, which is consistent with belief function semantics.

Another compelling argument for the plausibility transformation method is as follows. Consider an hypothetical situation where we have n independent pieces of evidence, all exactly equal to m. Combining these n pieces of evidence by Dempster's rule yields m^n. For $n \geq 500$, we observe that $m^n(\{h_2\}) \approx 1$, so the result is more consistent with Pl_P_m (that has h_2 as the most probable state) than with $BetP_m$ (that has h_1 as the most probable state). Notice that if we combine Pl_P_m n times using Bayes rule (or pointwise multiplication) and denote the result by $(Pl\_P_m)^n$, for large n we get the result that $(Pl\_P_m)^n(h_2) \approx 1$.

4.3   Example 3: Target Identification Problem [4]

A target identification system is composed of 30 sensors, S_i, $i = 1, \ldots, 30$. Each sensor S_i is in one of two states x_i or y_i. The state of the sensors depends on an unknown target that is assumed to be in one of two states: t_1 denoting friend, or t_2 denoting foe. The state of each sensor also depends on whether it is working or not. When in working condition, a sensor reading of x_i correctly identifies a target of type t_1 and a sensor reading of y_i correctly identifies a target of type t_2. When the sensors are not in working condition, nothing is known about what the sensor readings mean. The first 11 sensors $S_1, \ldots, S_{11}$ are high quality sensors, and the remaining 19 sensors $S_{12}, \ldots, S_{30}$ are low quality sensors. A high quality sensor has a 99% probability of being in working condition whereas a low quality sensor has only a 90% probability of being in working condition. Data in the form of sensor readings is collected as follows: $x_1, \ldots, x_{10}, y_{11}, x_{12}, y_{13}, \ldots, y_{30}$. What conclusions can we draw about the actual target type?

First, we will represent the evidence from the 30 sensors by bpa's and compute the joint belief function for T. Subsequently, we will represent the evidence by probability functions using the pignistic transformation and the plausibility transformation, in each case computing the joint probability function for T.

Table 1 shows the data collected from the sensors represented as evidence in bpa's. We can reach a conclusion about the target identity by calculating the joint bpa for the 30 sensors. Using Dempster's rule, the joint bpa m is given by $m = m_1 \oplus \ldots \oplus m_{30}$. The results are presented in Table 2. Thus, as per the belief function model, the target is approximately 10 times more likely to be a friend than a foe.

Table 1. Bpa encoding of sensor readings

Sensor $S_i = x_i$ $i = 1, \ldots, 10$		Sensor $S_{11} = y_{11}$		Sensor $S_{12} = x_{12}$		Sensor $S_i = y_i$ $i = 13, \ldots, 30$	
$\mathbf{a} \subseteq 2^{\Omega_T}$	$m_i(\mathbf{a})$	$\mathbf{a} \subseteq 2^{\Omega_T}$	$m_{11}(\mathbf{a})$	$\mathbf{a} \subseteq 2^{\Omega_T}$	$m_{12}(\mathbf{a})$	$\mathbf{a} \subseteq 2^{\Omega_T}$	$m_i(\mathbf{a})$
$\{t_1\}$	0.99	$\{t_2\}$	0.99	$\{t_1\}$	0.90	$\{t_2\}$	0.90
$\{t_1, t_2\}$	0.01	$\{t_1, t_2\}$	0.01	$\{t_1, t_2\}$	0.10	$\{t_1, t_2\}$	0.10

Table 2. Joint Bpa and Plausibility Functions for 30 Sensors

$a \in 2^{\Omega_T}$	Un-normalized bpa	Normalized bpa (m)	Plausibility (Pl_m)
$\emptyset$	≈ 1	0	0
$\{t_1\}$	$\approx 1.00 \times 10^{-20}$	0.9091	0.9091
$\{t_2\}$	$\approx 1.00 \times 10^{-21}$	0.0909	0.0909
$\{t_1, t_2\}$	$\approx 1.00 \times 10^{-41}$	0.0000	1

Table 3. Pignistic Probability Function Encoding of Sensor Readings

Sensor $S_i = x_i$ $i = 1, \ldots, 10$		Sensor $S_{11} = y_{11}$		Sensor $S_{12} = x_{12}$		Sensor $S_i = y_i$ $i = 13, \ldots, 30$	
$x \in \Omega_T$	$BetP_{m_i}(x)$	$x \in \Omega_T$	$BetP_{m_{11}}(x)$	$x \in \Omega_T$	$BetP_{m_{12}}(x)$	$x \in \Omega_T$	$BetP_{m_i}(x)$
t_1	0.995	t_1	0.005	t_1	0.95	t_1	0.05
t_2	0.005	t_2	0.995	t_2	0.05	t_2	0.95

Table 4. The Joint Pignistic Probability Model for the Target Identification Problem

$x \in \Omega_T$	Un-normalized Probability	Normalized Probability
t_1	$\approx 1.723E - 26$	≈ 0.0820
t_2	$\approx 1.930E - 25$	≈ 0.9180
Sum	$\approx 2.102E - 25$	1

Next, we will model this problem using probabilities from pignistic transformations of the 30 belief functions. The probability functions are shown in Table 3. The results of combining the 30 probability functions using pointwise multiplication and normalizing the resulting probability function are presented in Table 4.

Notice that the pignistic probability model of the target identification problem is qualitatively different from the belief function model. As per the pignistic probability model, the probability that the target is a foe is approximately 11 times more likely than the probability that the target is a friend. In general, if m_1 and m_2 are two bpa's on the same domain, then $(BetP_{m_1} \otimes BetP_{m_2}) \neq BetP_{m_1 \oplus m_2}$.

Next, consider the probability model for the target identification problem obtained from the belief function model using the plausibility transformation. This model is shown in Table 5. If we combine the 30 plausibility probability functions using pointwise multiplication and normalize the resulting probability function, we obtain the results in Table 6.

Notice that the conclusion is similar to the result obtained in the belief function model. In the next section, we will show that this equivalence between the belief function model conclusion and plausibility probability function is always true.

Table 5. Plausibility Probability Function Encoding of Sensor Readings

Sensor $S_i = x_i$ $i = 1, \ldots, 10$		Sensor $S_{11} = y_{11}$		Sensor $S_{12} = x_{12}$		Sensor $S_i = y_i$ $i = 13, \ldots, 30$	
$x \in \Omega_T$	$Pl\_P_{m_i}(x)$	$x \in \Omega_T$	$Pl\_P_{m_{11}}(x)$	$x \in \Omega_T$	$Pl\_P_{m_{12}}(x)$	$x \in \Omega_T$	$Pl\_P_{m_i}(x)$
t_1	0.9901	t_1	0.0099	t_1	0.9091	t_1	0.0909
t_2	0.0099	t_2	0.9901	t_2	0.0909	t_2	0.9091

Table 6. The Joint Plausibility Probability Model

$x \in \Omega_T$	Un-normalized Probability	Normalized Probability
t_1	$\approx 1.4656E - 21$	≈ 0.9091
t_2	$\approx 1.4656E - 22$	≈ 0.0909
Sum	$\approx 1.6121E - 21$	1

5 Justification and Properties of the Plausibility Transformation

In all three examples described in the previous section, there is a discrepancy between the pignistic probability function(s) obtained before and after combining all evidence. Smets [10] resolves this apparent discrepancy of the pignistic transformation by stating that beliefs are held at the credal level and one only descends to the probability space for decision making at the time a decision has to be made. However, we view decision-making as a dynamic activity.

Probability theory and belief function theory are two uncertainty calculi with roughly the same expressive power [1]. One should get roughly the same results regardless of the calculi one is using to represent knowledge if the models built using the calculi are equivalent. An appropriate transformation method can allow a model of an uncertain domain in one calculus to be translated into the other. Thus we can exploit the advantages of both calculi.

The pignistic transformation is justified based on a so-called "rationality" requirement, which implies a mathematical requirement of linearity. Other justifications for the pignistic transformation are given in [10,11]. Some intuitive justifications for the plausibility transformation are given in [2,3]. Here we will state four theorems that demonstrate that the plausibility transformation is consistent with belief functions semantics.

Theorem 1. Suppose $m_1, \ldots, m_k$ are k bpa's. Suppose $Pl_{m_1}, \ldots, Pl_{m_k}$ are the associated plausibility functions, and suppose $Pl\_P_{m_1}, \ldots, Pl\_P_{m_k}$ are the corresponding probability functions. If $m = m_1 \oplus \ldots \oplus m_k$ is the joint bpa, Pl_m is the associated plausibility function, and Pl_P_m is the corresponding plausibility probability function, then $Pl\_P_{m_1} \otimes \ldots \otimes Pl\_P_{m_k} = Pl\_P_m$.

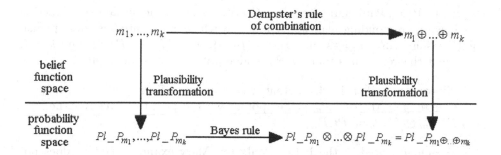

Fig. 1. A pictorial depiction of Theorem 1

Theorem 1 is depicted pictorially in Fig. 1. Notice that from a computational perspective, it is much faster to compute $Pl\_P_{m_1} \otimes \ldots \otimes Pl\_P_{m_k}$ than it is to compute Pl_P_m (since the latter involves Dempster's rule of combination and the former involves Bayes rule).

Given bpa m, we don't view Pl_P_m as an approximation of m. Instead, we view Pl_P_m as an equivalent probability encoding of the information in m. Thus if we have a belief function model consisting of $\{m_1, \ldots, m_k\}$, then we view $\{Pl\_P_{m_1}, \ldots, Pl\_P_{m_k}\}$ as an equivalent probability model. Theorem 1 can be viewed as a regularity condition for any transformation method. As demonstrated in the Peter, Paul, and Mary, and the target identification problems, the pignistic transformation does not satisfy this condition.

If a unique state x exists in a bpa m such that $Lim_{n \to \infty} m^n(\{x\}) = 1$ (where $m^n = m \oplus \ldots \oplus m$, n times), an equivalent probability function should have x as its most probable state. This property is satisfied for the plausibility transformation, as stated in the following theorem.

Theorem 2. Consider a bpa m for s (with corresponding plausibility function Pl_m) such that $x \in \Omega_s$ is the most plausible state, i.e., $Pl_m(\{x\}) > Pl_m(\{y\})$, for all $y \in \Omega_s \setminus \{x\}$. If Pl_{m^∞} denotes the plausibility function corresponding to m^∞, then $Pl_{m^\infty}(\{x\}) = 1$, and $Pl_{m^\infty}(\{y\}) = 0$ for all $y \in \Omega_s \setminus \{x\}$.

In Example 2 presented in Sect. 4, $m^{500}(\{h_2\}) \approx 1$, so the most plausible hypothesis in m is h_2, consistent with Pl_P_m and not $BetP_m$.

If a bpa function has a subset of most plausible states, all with equal plausibility, the following theorem applies.

Theorem 3. Consider a bpa m for s (with corresponding plausibility function Pl_m) such that $\mathbf{t} \subseteq \Omega_s$ is a subset of most plausible states, i.e., $Pl_m(\{x\}) = Pl_m(\{y\})$ for all $x, y \in \mathbf{t}$, and $Pl_m(\{x\}) > Pl_m(\{z\})$ for all $x \in \mathbf{t}$, and $z \in \Omega_s \setminus \mathbf{t}$. Then there exists a partition $\{\mathbf{a}_1, \ldots, \mathbf{a}_k\}$ of $\mathbf{t}$ such that $m^\infty(\mathbf{a}_i) = 1/k$ for $i = 1, \ldots, k$, i.e., $Pl_{m^\infty}(x) = Pl_{m^\infty}(y) = 1/k$ for all $x, y \in \mathbf{t}$, and $Pl_{m^\infty}(z) = 0$ for all $z \in \Omega_s \setminus \mathbf{t}$.

In the Peter, Paul, and Mary saga described earlier, the initial belief function m_1 has a corresponding plausibility function where each state has equal plausibilities. Theorem 3 applies with $a_1 = \{Mary\}$, $a_2 = \{Peter, Paul\}$, and $k = 2$. The next theorem states that Pl_P_m is idempotent if m is idempotent.

Theorem 4. If m is idempotent with respect to Dempster's rule, i.e., $m \oplus m = m$, then Pl_P_m is idempotent with respect to Bayes rule, i.e., $Pl\_P_m \otimes Pl\_P_m = Pl\_P_m$.

As demonstrated in the Peter, Paul, and Mary example, $BetP_m$ does not satisfy this property.

6   Conclusions and Summary

In summary, if T transforms a bpa m in a belief function model to an equivalent probability function $T(m)$, T should satisfy four basic properties:

1). *Invariance with respect to combination*: $T(m_1 \oplus \ldots \oplus m_n) = T(m_1) \otimes \ldots \otimes T(m_n)$, which is satisfied for the plausibility transformation, according to Theorem 1;

2) *Unique most plausible state*: $Lim_{n \to \infty} T^n(m)(h_i) = 1$ if $Lim_{n \to \infty} m^n(h_i) = 1$, which is satisfied for the plausibility transformation according to Theorem 2;

3) *Non-unique most plausible states*: If $Lim_{n \to \infty} Pl_{m^n}(x) = Lim_{n \to \infty} Pl_{m^n}(y)$ for all $x, y \in \mathbf{t} \subseteq \Omega_s$ and $Lim_{n \to \infty} Pl_{m^n}(z) = 0$ for all $z \in \Omega_s \setminus \mathbf{t}$, then $Lim_{n \to \infty} T^n(m)(x) = Lim_{n \to \infty} T^n(m)(y)$ for all $x, y \in \mathbf{t}$, and $Lim_{n \to \infty} T^n(m)(z) = 0$ for all $z \in \Omega_s \setminus \mathbf{t}$; this property is satisfied for the plausibility transformation according to Theorem 3; and

4) *Idempotency*: $T(m)$ is idempotent if m is idempotent, which is satisfied by the plausibility probability transformation according to Theorem 4.

The main goal of this paper is to compare the pignistic and plausibility transformation methods for transforming belief function models to probability models. Until now, most of the literature on belief functions has used the pignistic method. The pignistic transformation method does not satisfy the invariance with respect to combination, most plausible, and idempotency axioms. On the other hand, the plausibility transformation satisfies all intuitively acceptable axioms we have postulated for an acceptable transformation method. We conjecture that the plausibility transformation method is the only method that satisfies these axioms, but we don't have a proof of this claim.

Acknowledgements. The research was partly funded by a contract from Sparta, Inc., to the second author. We are grateful for extensive comments from Philippe Smets, Rolf Haenni, and Yang Chen on earlier drafts of this paper.

References

1. Cobb, B.R., Shenoy, P.P.: A Comparison of Bayesian and Belief Function Reasoning. Working Paper No. 292, University of Kansas School of Business (2002)
2. Cobb, B.R., Shenoy, P.P.: On Transformations of Belief Function Models to Probability Models. Working Paper No. 293, University of Kansas School of Business (2003)
3. Cobb, B.R., Shenoy, P.P.: Converting Belief Function Models to Probability Models Using the Plausibility Transformation. Working Paper, University of Kansas School of Business, submitted to UAI–03 (2003)
4. Delmotte, F., Smets, P.: Target Identification Based on the Transferable Belief Model Interpretation of the Dempster-Shafer Model, Part II: Applications. Working Paper, LAMIH-Université de Valenciennes, IRIDIA-Université Libre de Bruxelles (2001)
5. Dempster, A.P.: New Methods of Reasoning Toward Posterior Distributions Based on Sample Data. Annals of Mathematical Statistics. **37** (1987) 355–374
6. Haenni, R., Lehmann, N.: Probabilistic Argumentation Systems: A New Perspective on Dempster-Shafer Theory. International Journal of Intelligent Systems, in press (2003)
7. Kohlas, J., Monney, P.A.: A Mathematical Theory of Hints. In: Lecture Notes in Economics and Mathematical Systems, vol. 425. Springer-Verlag, Berlin (1995)
8. Shafer, G.: A Mathematical Theory of Evidence. Princeton University Press, Princeton, N.J. (1976)
9. Shafer, G.: Belief Functions and Possibility Measures. In: Bezdek, J. (ed.): The Analysis of Fuzzy Information. CRC Press, Boca Raton, FL (1987) 51–84
10. Smets, P.: Decision Making in a Context Where Uncertainty is Represented by Belief Functions. In: Srivastava, R.P., Mock, T.J. (eds.): Belief Functions in Business Decisions. Physica-Verlag, Heidelberg (2002) 17–61
11. Smets, P., Kennes, R.: The Transferable Belief Model. Artificial Intelligence. **66** (1994) 191–234
12. Walley, P.: Statistical Reasoning with Imprecise Probabilities. Chapman and Hall, London (1991)

Fuzzy Matching and Evidential Reasoning

Martin Folkesson

Swedish Defence Research Agency (FOI)
Division of Command and Control Systems
Department of Data and Information Fusion
Box 1165, 581 11 Linkoping, Sweden
martin.folkesson@foi.se http://www.foi.se

Abstract. In this paper a general framework consisting of fuzzy database matching and evidential reasoning is presented. Data is matched onto a database in a fuzzy, i.e. quantified, way. Pieces of evidence are herefrom constructed. These update belief measures connected to the elements of the database, using a *simple support belief function*. A sorting and grouping of the database elements, and thresholding the beliefs, makes the process stepwise. A qualitative, unambiguous *decision support* is obtained at every step. The threshold and the maximum belief for a piece of evidence are the parameters varied. Some properties of the framework are examplified in a case study of identifying air targets. For a given ratio of the two parameters, the identification performance shows a surprising non-monotonicity with respect to the threshold.

1 Introduction

When matching data onto a database a certain "softness" can be useful. For example, if data in the database is approximative, a soft matching process might prevent a mismatch. On the other hand, a critical decision needs easily interpreted decision support. A quantitative measure which is truly meaningful and unambiguous is hard to provide. Here we investigate some properties of a system where the quantitative measures are thresholded, providing a stepwise process with qualitative output.

In [1] an evidential reasoning identification scheme based on *partial probability models* is shown. Its advantages are concluded as: *It is better to be only partially but correctly informed than to risk being completely but incorrectly informed.* Here the same guiding star is followed, however with no likelihood information at all. It is believed that even partial probabilities are hard to find, especially in military applications as the one in the case study below.

2 The Theory of Evidential Reasoning

For a thorough description of the theory of belief functions, see e.g. [12]-[13]. [10], [11] and [15] deals with both belief functions and Dempster's rule of combination. Below, a somewhat specialised description of the concepts and theories follow.

T.D. Nielsen and N.L. Zhang (Eds.): ECSQARU 2003, LNAI 2711, pp. 267–278, 2003.

2.1   Belief and Belief Functions

A property called *belief*, or *belief mass*, is assigned to different hypotheses. The total belief that has been assigned directly to a hypothesis H_i is here denoted $Bel(H_i)$, and describes to what degree hypothesis H_i is supported by so far gathered evidence. It takes values in $[0, 1]$. The total belief mass spread out among a set of hypotheses sum to unity. Thus, belief resembles probability. Some important distinctions between probability and belief should however be made:

1. belief is not a statistical property, i.e. has no interpretation as the frequency of a certain outcome in a random process, and

2. implications as

$$A = B \cup C \Rightarrow Bel(A) \leq Bel(B) + Bel(C) \tag{1}$$
$$Bel(A) = c \Rightarrow Bel(\neg A) = 1 - c \tag{2}$$

   need *not* hold.

(1)-(2) above indicate that evidential reasoning is in a way more general than probability theory. Whether this is so, in an actual application, is determined by the choice of *belief function* (bf). The bf determines how gathered evidence is used to update the beliefs. A hypotheses to which a bf assignes mass is called a *focal element* of the bf.

A *bayesian* bf distributes the belief of an evidence among a set of exhaustive, disjunct hypotheses. For a bayesian bf (1)-(2) are true.

In the study of this paper a *simple support* bf will be used. Such a bf assigns belief to

1. *one* of the hypotheses, and to
2. the set of *all* hypotheses – the *frame of discernment*.

The belief in the frame of discernment(fd), denoted $Bel(\theta)$, is belief not distributed among the true hypotheses. Instead, it is assigned to the hypotheses as a whole. This is useful when one does not know how to distribute the belief mass. Therefore, it can be seen as a measure of the *ignorance* in the system.

The property $Bel(\neg A)$, see above, can be as interesting as $Bel(A)$ in an application. It is represented through the *plausibility* for A, which is denoted $Pl(A)$ and given by $1 - Bel(\neg A)$.

2.2   Dempster's Rule of Combination

Dempster's rule of combination is a stringent way to combine quantified evidence. Suppose a belief function has assigned belief mass to a set of focal elements indexed with i, according to some evidence. Also, it assigns belief to a set of focal elements indexed with j, according to some other piece of evidence. The belief masses are denoted $\{m(H_i)\}$ and $\{m(H_j)\}$, respectively. Then, the belief mass implicitly assigned directly to some third hypothesis H_k is given by

$$m(H_k) = \frac{1}{1-K} \sum_{i,j;H_i \cap H_j = H_k} m(H_i)m(H_j) \ . \tag{3}$$

K is the *conflict*, given by

$$\sum_{i,j;H_i \cap H_j = \emptyset} m(H_i)Bel(H_j) \ . \tag{4}$$

The conflict is thus a measure of how much the two pieces of evidence contradicts each other. Note in (3) that $m(H_k)$ increases with K. This can be interpreted as en elimination; if there is a a large conflict between $\{H_i\}$ and $\{H_j\}$ many possibilities are eliminated and the belief is concentrated to the intersection(s) of $\{H_i\}$ and $\{H_j\}$.

Dempster's rule is especially applicable in situations where evidence and/or hypotheses are hierarchichally structured, or otherwise non-disjunct. Also, "negative evidence", i.e. $m(\neg H_k)$, can take part in the combination. These properties make evidential reasoning generally applicable. They can however also be a drawback, since the intersection between two hypotheses (see (3)) might form a new, unwanted hypothesis, or even a nonsense hypothesis. Such problems are discussed and addressed in [3] and [11].

In this study Dempster's rule will be used to write down update rules for the beliefs. With the simple support bf only two update rules, or *mappings*, are needed. If H_i is a focal element $Bel(H_i)$ undergoes

$$Bel(H_i) \longmapsto \frac{m(H_i)Bel(H_i)}{1-K} \ , \tag{5}$$

otherwise it follows

$$Bel(H_i) \longmapsto \frac{m(\theta)Bel(H_i)}{1-K} \ . \tag{6}$$

$Bel(\theta)$ can always be computed using the fact that the total belief must sum to unity:

$$Bel(\theta) = 1 - \sum_i Bel(H_i) \ , \tag{7}$$

but an update rule can be formulated as well:

$$Bel(\theta) \longmapsto \frac{m(\theta)Bel(\theta)}{1-K} \ . \tag{8}$$

3 Database Matching with the Simple Support Belief Function

The hypotheses, characterised by some data, are stored as database elements. Incoming data is then compared to, or matched against, the stored data for each

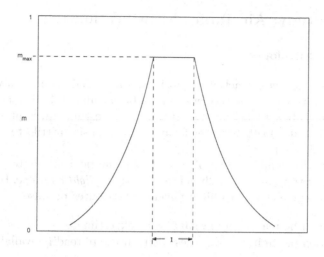

Fig. 1. The matching function: On the horisontal axis is the incoming data sample; a value of some property. On the vertical axis is the belief mass, m, of the resulting piece of evidence. Values in I match the stored data and yield maximum belief, m_{max}. Values outside I yield belief masses that are damped towards zero according to their distance to I

hypotheses, respectively. Each matching results in a piece of evidence. The simple support bf assigns the mass to the hypotheses, and to the fd. If the incoming data matches the stored data for a hypotheses, the amount of belief mass assigned to that hypothesis is m_{max}. If not, the belif mass is smaller, but always non-zero. Figure 1 shows (roughly) this fuzzy matching. In the figure the stored data is an interval and the incoming data is a single value (along the horisontal axis).

Constructing pieces of evidence based on Euclidian distances has earlier been proposed by Denœux;[4]-[5]. The methods of Denœux does however require training data. Here, the data available is just the uncertain estimates of the data characterising each hypotheses.

In order to avoid matching the incoming data against all database elements, the elements are grouped into a tree structure, so that the matching is made hierarchically – coarse-to-fine. The grouping of the elements require that these can be sorted. If data describing the elements is multidimensional, one sorting for every dimension is generally needed.

In the tree of hypotheses *each set of sibling nodes make up their own fd*. Note this difference from [3] and [11], where evidence and/or hypotheses are naturally hierchical. Matching starts at the children of the root. When the belief for one of those nodes becomes greater than some threshold value, *thr*, the matching process proceeds down the subtree of that node. This process is repeated until the belief in a leaf node reaches the threshold value. A data sample that leads to reaching a threshold is immediately used again, in the new fd.

m_{max} and *thr* are *parameters* in the study of this system. Furthermore, m_{max} is kept < 1. Thus, $0 < 1 - m_{max} \leq m(\theta) < 1$.

4 Case Study: Air Target Identification

4.1 Flight Envelopes

As an air target is being tracked, its position and velocity is normally estimated. From this an estimate of the acceleration can be calculated. If also the orientation of the aircraft is being tracked,[1] the g-load can be estimated. Synthetic data for height, speed and g-load, together forming a composite attribute, will be used as input in this study.

Limits in the combinations of in-flight kinematical attribute values, for a certain aircraft type, are generally referred to as its *flight envelope*. Height, speed and g-load are here chosen as flight envelope attributes because

- they should be reasonably feasible to track/estimate
- information on limitations in these attributes are readily available for many air targets
- limitations in these attributes (separately or combined) make up large parts of the actual flight envelope

The actual flight envelope should involve more or less complicated dependencies between the three attributes, as well as others. However, for simplicity, the limitations are here chosen to be independent. Thus, our flight envelopes are boxes in height-speed-g-space, see Fig. 2.

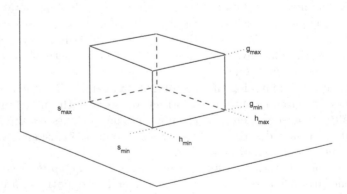

Fig. 2. The flight envelopes are chosen to be the trivial combination of limitations in height(h), speed(s) and g-load(g), respectively

---

[1] a numerical tracking method, such as *particle filtering*[6], is believed to be needed

4.2   The Database

The flight envelope is here considered a single but multidimensional attribute. Therefore, only one sorting is performed. The way to sort the flight envelopes accordingly is not straightforward. Here, a *Bounding Volume Hierarchy* (BVH)[9] is created:

1. find the minimal volume enclosing all multidimensional objects (flight envelopes)
2. divide the objects into two groups by splitting the minimal volume along its longest axis, into two volumes
3. for each volume, go back to 2. and repeat the process until no volume contains more than one object

A few additional conditions are needed:

- If an object is cut into two pieces in the split, it is assigned to the volume in which its largest part resides. This volume must then be enhanced according to the object.
- In 2. we interpret "longest" as "longest relative", so that the extension of the objects along the particular axis matters. Since in this case we deal with boxlike objects, we compute the mean box length along every axis. The length of the bounding volume (see 1.) is then divided by this mean, yielding the number for comparison in 2.

The database for this study was taken to consist of the target hypotheses shown in Table 1.[2]

Table 1. The target types and their flight envelopes

Type	heights (m)	speeds (km/h)	g-loads
Apache	0-4570	0-365	-0.5–3.5
F 16	0-15240	0–2124	-5*–9
Hawk 200	0-13715	0–1065	-4–8
Jaguar S	0-14000	0–1699	-4.6*–8.6
Mig 23 B	0-16800	0–1900	-4*–7
Mig 29	0-17000	0–2445	-5*–9
Mirage 2000 C	0-18000	0–2338	-5*–9
Su-27	0-17700	0–2280	-4*–8
Tornado IDS	0-15240	0–2338	-3.9*–7.5

Most values were taken from [7]. Others, marked with *, have been calculated using the approximative equation $g_{min} = -0.6(g_{max} - 1)$. This was taken from [8]. The BVH of the flight envelopes for the target type hypotheses is seen in Fig. 3.

---

[2] The target types were chosen on an entirely non-political basis.

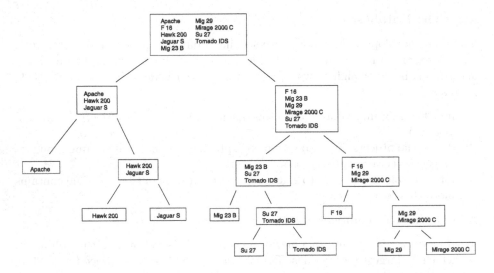

Fig. 3. The Bounding Volume Hierarchy of the aircraft flight envelopes used in this study

4.3   More on Matching with a Simple Support BF

In our case every fd is made up of *two* disjunct hypotheses, H_1 and H_2. Data is matched against *both* hypotheses in a fd, i.e the two hypotheses take turns being the focal element. Each of the two beliefs thus undergo both (5) and (6) for each incoming data sample. Accordingly, $Bel(\theta)$ undergoes (8) twice. Combining (5) and (6) into one mapping, regardless of order(!), gives:

$$Bel(H_1) \longmapsto \frac{(1 - m(H_2))(Bel(H_1) + m(H_1)Bel(\theta))}{1 - m(H_1)Bel(H_2) - m(H_2)Bel(H_1) - m(H_1)m(H_2)Bel(\theta)}. \quad (9)$$

The mapping for H_2 is obtained if '1' and '2' is interchanged in (9).

The only valid *fixed points*[14] for $(Bel(H_1), Bel(H_2))$ are $(Bel(H_1),$ $Bel(H_2)) = (1, 0)$ and $(Bel(H_1), Bel(H_2)) = (0, 1)$. However, for the special case $m(H_1) = m(H_2)$ every pair of values $(Bel(H_1), 1 - Bel(H_1))$ is a fixed point. Either way, $Bel(\theta)$ must approach zero. This is understood from (8).

As a belief threshold *thr* is introduced, its value together with the matching function (Fig. 1) and of course the incoming data, will determine if the threshold is reached. m_{max} and *thr* are the parameters varied. The curved parts of the matching function are chosen to have exponential shape. The exponent is a "relative distance to a match", with an overall minus sign. For example, if a height h is found to exceed the maximum height h_{max} for a certain flight envelope, a penalty factor of $exp(-\frac{|h - h_{max}|}{h_{max} - h_{min}})$ multiplies m_{max}. Each dimension of the database elements possibly contributes with its own penalty factor, independent of the others.

4.4   Results

The scenario consists of an agile aircraft coming in at high altitude and high speed. Maintaining speed and altitude it performs a heavy level turn, then leaves. The data in Table 2 is an attempt to mimic this.

Table 2. The scenario data

Time	height (m)	speed (km/h)	g-load
1	17500	2000	1
2	17500	2000	1
3	17500	2000	1
4	17500	2000	1
5	17500	2000	3
6	17500	2000	6
7	17500	2000	9
8	17500	2000	9
9	17500	2000	6
10	17500	2000	3
11	17500	2000	1
12	17500	2000	1
13	17500	2000	1
14	17500	2000	1

Figures 4–6 show the identification progress when $threshold = m_{max} = 0.5, 0.7$ and 0.9, respectively. (Thresholds below 0.5 are not allowed, since it could result in the identification process proceeding down *both* branches of a node in the BVH.) The plots show the highest belief in the current fd at time t, after including the (two pieces of) evidence governed at that time. Note that passing a threshold – dotted line – means a partial or full identification has been made. All dotted lines except the uppermost thus separates different fd's, and therefore represents $Bel(\cdot) = thr$ in one fd and $Bel(\cdot) = 0$ in the other (see figures). True identification has obviously been reached only for $thr = m_{max} = 0.5$, see Fig. 4.

The other two cases, Figs. 5 and 6, show similar results, where belief seem to have converged two levels beneath true identification.

In order to reach identification also for the higher thresholds, m_{max} was increased to $1.1 \cdot thr$, see Figs. 7–9. The identification performance then changes dramatically for $thr = 0.9$, Fig. 9. This configuration is now the fastest to complete the identification.

Surprisingly the performance is lowest, and has seemingly not changed at all, for the intermediate threshold 0.7, see Fig. 8. Intuitively, there seem to be no reason for such non-monotonicity in identification performance. This is further discussed in the concluding words, Sect. 5.

Increasing m_{max} further eventually led to full identification also for the intermediate threshold.

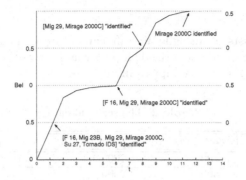

Fig. 4. The highest belief, in the current frame of discernment, after including evidence at time t. Here, with $thr = m_{max} = 0.5$, the Mirage 2000C is identified. Note that each dotted line (except the uppermost) separates two fd's and thus represents two belief values

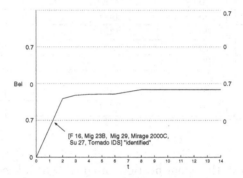

Fig. 5. The highest belief, in the current frame of discernment, after including evidence at time t. Here, with $thr = m_{max} = 0.7$, the belief converges below the {F16, Mig29, Mirage 2000C}-threshold. Note that each dotted line (except the uppermost) separates two fd's and thus represents two belief values

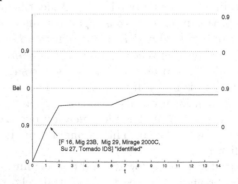

Fig. 6. The highest belief, in the current frame of discernment, after including evidence at time t. Here, with $thr = m_{max} = 0.9$, the belief converges below the {F16, Mig29, Mirage 2000C}-threshold. Note that each dotted line (except the uppermost) separates two fd's and thus represents two belief values

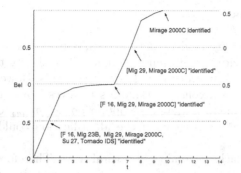

Fig. 7. The highest belief, in the current frame of discernment, after including evidence at time t. Here, with $thr = 0.5$ and $m_{max} = 0.55$, the Mirage 2000C is identified. Note that each dotted line (except the uppermost) separates two fd's and thus represents two belief values

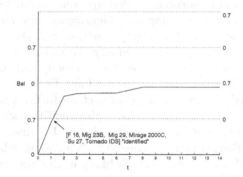

Fig. 8. The highest belief, in the current frame of discernment, after including evidence at time t. Here, with $thr = 0.7$ and $m_{max} = 0.77$, the belief converges below the {F16, Mig29, Mirage 2000C}-threshold. Note that each dotted line (except the uppermost) separates two fd's and thus represents two belief values

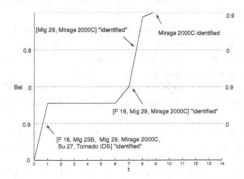

Fig. 9. The highest belief, in the current frame of discernment, after including evidence at time t. Here, with $thr = 0.9$ and $m_{max} = 0.99$, the Mirage 2000C is identified. Note that each dotted line (except the uppermost) separates two fd's and thus represents two belief values

5   Conclusions

Using a fuzzy matching of data onto a database means a balancing between softness and sensitivity to data must be made. Translating the softness into an evidential reasoning framework would not resolve this. However, the framework presented provides two explicit parameters to investigate and control the sensitivity of the system. In a system of operation i.e. m_{max} could be a runtime variable. This way the sensitvity of the identification could be related to the current situation.

The case study lacks generality in several ways. Therefore, it should be considered mostly a way to examplify some of the properties of the proposed framework. The results are summarised below.

For the parameter values tried, it is indicated that a threshold close to 1 provides the largest range of sensitivity. The corresponding smallest range seem to occur for a threshold in the interior of $[0.5, 1]$ rather than at the boundary $thr = 0.5$. This is found surprising. Perhaps the parameter ratio m_{max}/thr, which was kept constant when comparing identification performance for different thresholds, is not the relevant property. Instead, e.g. the square root of that property might bring back the monotonicity. To investigate this the mappings (9) have to be extended with the modulus function, and analysed. As this is complicated by the nonlinearity of the modulus function further simulations might also be needed. All this must be subject for future studies.

As an alternative to the design above, the identification progress could be "stepped back" at some criterion, i.e. when $Bel(\theta)$ becomes too small. Allowing revokable identifications is however considered dangerous when the result is the basis for unrevokable decisions, which is likely in the application above. A less sensitive, more "soft" identification should then be preferred.

References

1. Blackman, S. & Popoli, R: Design and Analysis of Modern Tracking Systems, Artech House, Norwood MA, USA, 1999
2. Bossé, E. & Roy, J: Fusion of identity declarations from dissimilar sources using the Dempster-Shafer Theory, Optical Engineering 36(3), p. 648–657, 1997
3. Bossé, E. & Simard, M-A: Managing evidential reasoning for identity information fusion, Optical Engineering 37(2), p. 391–400, 1998
4. Denœux, T: A k-Nearest Neighbor Classification Rule Based on Dempster-Shafer Theory, IEEE Transactions on Systems, Man and Cybernetics, Vol. 25(5), p. 804–813, 1995
5. Denœux, T: A Neural Network Classifier Rule Based on Dempster-Shafer Theory, IEEE Transactions on Systems, Man and Cybernetics – Part A: Systems and Humans, Vol. 30(2), p. 131–150, 2000
6. Doucet, A, de Freitas, N. & Gordon, N: Sequential Monte Carlo Methods in practice, Springer Verlag, New York, 2001
7. Encyclopedia of World Military Aircraft, Aerospace publishing, London, UK, 1994
8. Eshelby, M.E: Aircraft Performance: Theory and Practice, American Institute of Aeronautics and Astronautics Inc, Reston, VA, USA, 2000

9. Moller, T. & Haines, E: Real-Time Rendering, AK Peters, Natick MA, USA, 1999
10. Shafer, G: A mathematical Theory of Evidence, Princeton University Press, Princeton, NJ, USA, 1976
11. Shafer, G. & Logan, R: Implementing Dempster's Rule for Hierarchical Evidence, Artificial Intelligence 33, p. 271–298, 1987
12. Smets, Ph.: Belief Functions and the Transferable Belief Model, http://ippserv.rug.ac.be/documentation/belief/belief.pdf, 2000
13. Smets, Ph.: Belief Functions, Non standard Logics for Automated reasoning (Smets, Ph., Mamdani, A., Dubois, D. & Prade, H. eds.), Academic Press, London, p .253–286, 1988
14. Strogatz, Steven H: Nonlinear Dynamics and Chaos, Addison-Wesley Publishing Company, Reading MA, USA, 1995
15. Yager, R.R: On the Dempster-Shafer Framework and new Combination Rules, Information Sciences 41, p. 93–137, 1987

Modeling Positive and Negative Pieces of Evidence in Uncertainty

Christophe Labreuche[1] and Michel Grabisch[2]

[1] Thales Research & Technology
Domaine de Corbeville, 91404 Orsay Cedex, France
Christophe.Labreuche@thalesgroup.com
[2] Université Paris I – Panthéon-Sorbonne
LIP6, 8 rue du Capitaine Scott, 75015 Paris, France
Michel.Grabisch@lip6.fr

Abstract. In Dempster-Shafer theory, belief degrees on any subset $A \subseteq \Omega$ of states of nature are computed through a basic belief *mass* $m(A)$, that quantifies the strength of the statement: "the agent has some reason to believe that the true world is in A". We may be interested into representing some *negative belief*, as for example: "the agent has some reason *not* to believe that the true world is in A". However, as remarked by Smets, this is not allowed in the theory of Dempster-Shafer. Attempts to model this situation have been proposed by Smets, and by Dubois, Prade and Smets in the framework of possibility theory. These solutions however, do not seem to be able to handle all the facets of the problem, and have the drawback to come up with an interval or a pair of values. In this paper, we propose an alternative solution consisting in assigning a single number to a pair of events.

1 Introduction

In Dempster-Shafer theory [7], belief degrees on any subset $A \subseteq \Omega$ of states of nature are computed through a basic *mass* (of belief) allocation function $m : 2^{\Omega} \longrightarrow [0,1]$, which assigns values to specific subsets of Ω, called *focal elements*. The mass function is such that $\sum_{A \subseteq \Omega} m(A) = 1$, and $m(A) = 0$ if A is not a focal element. Then the belief function $\text{Bel} : 2^{\Omega} \longrightarrow [0,1]$ is given by $\text{Bel}(A) := \sum_{B \subseteq A} m(A)$.

The mass function m represents the basic knowledge, or belief, of some agent on the true (but unknown) state of nature (or world). The value $m(A)$ quantifies the strength of the statement: "the agent have some reason to believe that the true world is in A", based on some information concerning *solely* A. We may be interested into representing some *negative belief*, as for example: "the agent has some reason *not* to believe that the true world is in A". But, as remarked by Smets [8], this is not allowed in the theory of Dempster-Shafer. The reason is that there is no inverse mass function for the Dempster rule of combination. The following example from Smets [8] shows that in some situation we may need such notion of negative belief.

T.D. Nielsen and N.L. Zhang (Eds.): ECSQARU 2003, LNAI 2711, pp. 279–290, 2003.

The Ukalvia Example. You are told that a newspaper reports that the economic situation in Ukalvia is good. You have never heard about Ukalvia before, so you may start to believe the information. Later, you discover that the newspaper is controlled by the unique authorized party in Ukalvia. So you think that it may be propaganda, and you may have now some reason not to believe that the economic situation is good.

Attempts to model this situation have been given by Smets [8] by means of a pair of functions called *confidence* and *diffidence*, and by Dubois, Prade and Smets [4] in the framework of possibility theory, using also a pair of functions, which represent a guaranteed possibility and a (usual) possibility degree. These solutions however, do not seem to be able to handle all the facets of the problem, and have the drawback to come up with an interval or a pair of values. In this paper, we propose an alternative solution based on bi-capacities [6,5]. As it will be seen, our solution is in some sense the converse of the previous ones: instead of assigning a pair of numbers to an event, we assign a single number to a pair of events.

In the sequel, the finite universal set (states of nature) will be denoted Ω, of cardinality n.

2   Background

Let $\mathcal{Q}(\Omega) := \{(A, B) \in 2^\Omega \times 2^\Omega | A \cap B = \emptyset\}$. It is easy to see that $\mathcal{Q}(\Omega)$ is a lattice, when equipped with the following order: $(A, B) \sqsubseteq (C, D)$ if $A \subseteq C$ and $B \supseteq D$. Supremum and infimum are respectively

$$(A, B) \sqcup (C, D) = (A \cup C, B \cap D)$$
$$(A, B) \sqcap (C, D) = (A \cap C, B \cup D).$$

Top and bottom are respectively $(\Omega, \emptyset)$ and $(\emptyset, \Omega)$. We call *vertices* of $\mathcal{Q}(\Omega)$ any element (A, B) such that $A \cup B = \Omega$, since they coincide with the vertices of $[0, 1]^n$. We give in figure 1 the Hasse diagram of $(\mathcal{Q}(\Omega), \sqsubseteq)$ for $n = 3$.

In [2], Bilbao *et al.* introduced other operations on $\mathcal{Q}(\Omega)$, which are:

$$(A, B) \sqsubseteq' (C, D) \quad \text{if } A \subseteq C \text{ and } B \subseteq D$$
$$(A, B) \sqcup' (C, D) := ((A \cup C) \setminus (B \cup D), (B \cup D) \setminus (A \cup C))$$
$$(A, B) \sqcap' (C, D) := (A \cap C, B \cap D).$$

However, $(\mathcal{Q}(\Omega), \sqcup', \sqcap')$ is not a lattice since e.g. for any $A \subseteq \Omega, (A, A^c) \sqcup'$ $(A^c, A) = (\emptyset, \emptyset)$ but $(A, A^c) \not\sqsubseteq' (\emptyset, \emptyset)$ since $(A, A^C) \sqcup (\emptyset, \emptyset) = (A, A^c) \neq (\emptyset, \emptyset)$. This justifies the choice of operations $\sqsubseteq$, $\sqcup$ and $\sqcap$ instead of $\sqsubseteq'$, $\sqcup'$ and $\sqcap'$.

Following usual conventions, $\mathcal{Q}(\Omega)$ is the lattice called 3^n. For any ordered pair $((A, B), (A \cup D, B \setminus C))$ of $\mathcal{Q}(\Omega)$ with $C \subseteq B$ and $D \subseteq (\Omega \setminus (A \cup B)) \cup C$, the interval $[(A, B), (A \cup D, B \setminus C)]$ is a sub-lattice of type $2^k \times 3^l$, with $k = |C \Delta D|$, and $l = |C \cap D|$.

We recall some definitions and a fundamental result of lattice theory [3].

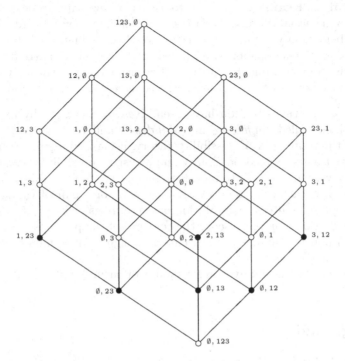

Fig. 1. The lattice $\mathcal{Q}(\Omega)$ for $n = 3$

Definition 1. *Let $(L, \sqsubseteq)$ be a lattice. Its bottom is denoted by $\perp$. An element $x \in L$ is $\sqcup$-irreducible if $x \neq \perp$ and $x = a \sqcup b$ implies $x = a$ or $x = b$, $\forall a, b \in L$.*

In a finite lattice, x is $\sqcup$-irreducible if it has only one predecessor. It is easy to see that the $\sqcup$-irreducible elements of $\mathcal{Q}(\Omega)$ are $(\emptyset, i^c)$ and (i, i^c), for all $i \in \Omega$. On Figure 1, $\sqcup$-irreducible elements are indicated by black circles. The main interest of $\sqcup$-irreducible elements lies in the fact that every element in $\mathcal{Q}(\Omega)$ can be written as supremum over these elements [6,5] :

$$(A, B) = \bigsqcup_{i \in A} (i, i^c) \sqcup \bigsqcup_{j \in B^c} (\emptyset, j^c) . \tag{1}$$

The $\sqcap$-irreducible elements are $(i^c, \emptyset)$ and (i^c, i), for all $i \in \Omega$. Every element in $\mathcal{Q}(\Omega)$ can be written as infimum over these elements [6,5] :

$$(A, B) = \bigsqcap_{i \in A^c} (i^c, \emptyset) \sqcap \bigsqcap_{j \in B} (j^c, j) . \tag{2}$$

It may be more natural to introduce the *dual* structure of $\mathcal{Q}(\Omega)$ by replacing an element $(A, B) \in \mathcal{Q}(\Omega)$ by (A, B^c). We thus obtain $Q^*(\Omega) := \{(A, B) | A \subseteq B\}$.

Bi-capacities in [6,5] were defined as follows. $v : \mathcal{Q}(\Omega) \longrightarrow \mathbb{R}$ is a *bi-capacity* if $v(\emptyset, \emptyset) = 0$, and $A \subseteq B$ implies $v(A, \cdot) \leq v(B, \cdot)$ and $v(\cdot, A) \geq v(\cdot, B)$ (isotonicity). If in addition $v(\Omega, \emptyset) = 1$ and $v(\emptyset, \Omega) = -1$, v is said to be *normalized*.

In terms of ordered sets, v is an order-preserving mapping from $(\mathcal{Q}(\Omega), \sqsubseteq)$ to $([-1, 1], \leq)$, preserving also top and bottom, and with a fixed point $(\emptyset, \emptyset)$. This definition was motivated by multicriteria decision making on bipolar scales, hence the interval centered around 0, and the fixed point. We may have a slightly more general view, by dropping the fixed point restriction and allowing any totally ordered set with top and bottom instead of the interval $[-1, 1]$. Indeed, in the present case, we are dealing with *uncertainty*, where the usual scale is rather $[0, 1]$ (unipolar), and we have no reason to consider some central point $1/2$ or whatsoever. Hence, we adopt the following definition.

Definition 2. *A* unipolar bi-capacity *is a function* $v : \mathcal{Q}(\Omega) \longrightarrow [0, 1]$ *such that* $v(\Omega, \emptyset) = 1$, $v(\emptyset, \Omega) = 0$, *and isotone.*

In the sequel we drop the term "unipolar" as far as no confusion arises.

A fundamental notion for bi-capacities is the Möbius transform. It is shown in [6,5] that its expression is, for any function v on $\mathcal{Q}(\Omega)$:

$$m(A, A') = \sum_{\substack{(B, B') \sqsubseteq (A, A') \\ B' \cap A = \emptyset}} (-1)^{|A \setminus B| + |B' \setminus A'|} v(B, B')$$

and conversely,

$$v(A, A') = \sum_{(B, B') \sqsubseteq (A, A')} m(B, B'). \tag{3}$$

For unipolar bi-capacities, normalization conditions write:

$$\sum_{(A, B) \in \mathcal{Q}(\Omega)} m(A, B) = 1 \tag{4}$$

$$m(\emptyset, \Omega) = 0 \tag{5}$$

By analogy with classical definitions, a bi-capacity is said to be k-*monotone* ($k \geq 2$) if for all families of k elements $(A_1, B_1), \ldots, (A_k, B_k)$ in $\mathcal{Q}(\Omega)$,

$$v\left(\bigsqcup_{i=1}^{k} (A_i, B_i)\right) \geq \sum_{\emptyset \neq I \subset \{1, \ldots, k\}} (-1)^{|I|+1} v\left(\bigsqcap_{i \in I} (A_i, B_i)\right). \tag{6}$$

For $k = 2$, the definition reduces to

$$v((A, B) \sqcup (C, D)) + v((A, B) \sqcap (C, D)) \geq v(A, B) + v(C, D)$$

and v is said to be *supermodular* or convex. A bi-capacity v is said to be k-*alternating* when v satisfies the reversed inequality with $\sqcup$ and $\sqcap$ inverted. 2-alternating bi-capacities are said to be *submodular*. When v is k-monotone (resp.

alternating) for any $k \geq 2$, then v is said to be *totally monotone (resp. alternating)*.

The *conjugate* of a (unipolar) bi-capacity is defined by

$$\overline{v}(A, B) = 1 - v(B, A).$$

3   Bi-belief Functions

3.1   Mathematical Definition

Let v be a function on $\mathcal{Q}(\Omega)$ such that $v(\emptyset, \Omega) = 0$ and $v(\Omega, \emptyset) = 1$, and let m be its Möbius transform. By analogy with the classical case, we say that v is a *bi-belief function* if for any $(A, B) \in \mathcal{Q}(\Omega)$ we have $m(A, B) \geq 0$. Clearly, the non-negativity of m implies that v is isotone, hence v is a unipolar bi-capacity. We denote bi-belief functions by Bel.

If v is a bi-belief function, then the conjugate bi-capacity $\overline{v}$ is called a *bi-plausibility function*, which we will denote by Pl. We have:

$$\text{Pl}(A, B) = 1 - \text{Bel}(B, A), \forall (A, B) \in \mathcal{Q}(\Omega). \tag{7}$$

If we stick to the usual vocabulary of Shafer, elements of $\mathcal{Q}(\Omega)$ where the Möbius transform is strictly positive are called *focal elements*, and m could be called the *mass allocation* or simply *mass*. By (3), (4) and (5), we can express bi-belief and bi-plausibility functions in terms of mass:

$$\text{Bel}(A, B) = \sum_{(C,D) \sqsubseteq (A,B)} m(C, D) = \sum_{\substack{C \subseteq A,\ D \supseteq B \\ C \cap D = \emptyset}} m(C, D) \tag{8}$$

$$\text{Pl}(A, B) = 1 - \sum_{(C,D) \sqsubseteq (B,A)} m(C, D) = \sum_{(C,D) \not\sqsubseteq (B,A)} m(C, D)$$

$$= \sum_{\substack{C \cap B^c \neq \emptyset,\ D \supseteq A \\ C \cap D = \emptyset}} m(C, D) + \sum_{\substack{D \cup A^c \neq \Omega,\ C \subseteq B \\ C \cap D = \emptyset}} m(C, D)$$

$$+ \sum_{\substack{C \cap B^c \neq \emptyset,\ D \cup A^c \neq \Omega \\ C \cap D = \emptyset}} m(C, D) . \tag{9}$$

Note the analogy with classical formulas. The following property shows the similarity with the classical case.

Proposition 1. *A (unipolar) bi-capacity is totally monotone (resp. alternating) if and only if it is a bi-belief (resp. bi-plausibility) function.*

The proof comes from a general result by Barthélemy [1], proving that when the Möbius transform of some function f on a finite lattice is non negative, f is monotone and totally monotone. The case of bi-plausibility is obtained dually.

3.2   Interpretation

After having given a mathematical definition which seems to keep in a more general framework all usual properties of classical belief functions, we focus on interpretation and go back to our main motivation.

Generally speaking, the quantity $\mathrm{Bel}(A, B)$ represents the degree to which the agent believes that A contains the true state of nature (say ω_0) *and* B does not contain it. The remaining part $(A \cup B)^c$ is the "ignorance" part. For classical belief functions, $\mathrm{Bel}(A)$ is the degree to which the agent believes that A contains the true state ω_0, or equivalently that A^c does not contain ω_0, hence corresponding to $\mathrm{Bel}(A, A^c)$. We have here much more flexibility, and the degree of belief about whether A contains ω_0 is expressed by all the quantities $\{\mathrm{Bel}(A, B)\}_{B \subseteq A^c}$. Due to isotonicity, all these quantities are ordered along chains from $(A, \emptyset)$ to (A, A^c):

$$\mathrm{Bel}(A, \emptyset) \geq \mathrm{Bel}(A, \{i\}) \geq \mathrm{Bel}(A, \{i, j\}) \geq \cdots \geq \mathrm{Bel}(A, A^c)$$

for any $i, j, \ldots$ in A^c. Note that $(A, \emptyset)$ is the less "demanding" event since $\emptyset$ cannot contain the true state whatsoever, while (A, A^c) is the most demanding event. In the classical view, all these quantities collapse to a single one (we will properly show this below). Conversely, let us consider for a given B all the quantities $\{\mathrm{Bel}(A, B)\}_{A \subseteq B^c}$. They are also partially ordered along chains from (B^c, B) to $(\emptyset, B)$:

$$\mathrm{Bel}(B^c, B) \geq \mathrm{Bel}(B^c \setminus \{i\}, B) \geq \mathrm{Bel}(B^c \setminus \{i, j\}, B) \geq \cdots \geq \mathrm{Bel}(\emptyset, B)$$

for any $i, j, \ldots$ in B. The event $(\emptyset, B)$ is a situation when there is no evidence that ω_0 could be in some subset of Ω, but we have some evidence that ω_0 is not in B.

With this interpretation in mind, we speak of a *purely positive* or *confidence* belief with events of the form (A, A^c), while *purely negative* or diffidence belief are events of the form $(\emptyset, B)$.

What about mass allocation ? Let us stick first to the view of Smets [8]. We should define a *confidence mass* m^+ and a *diffidence mass* m^- with the meaning explained in the introduction: $m^+(A)$ quantifies the statement "the agent have some reason to believe that the true world is in A", while $m^-(A)$ quantifies "the agent has some reason *not* to believe that the true world is in A". Now, we can merge this together into a single mass function on $\mathcal{Q}(\Omega)$. We put accordingly to the above interpretation $m(A, A^c) := m^+(A)$, and $m(\emptyset, A) := m^-(A)$. We have thus recovered the model sought by Smets, and we are even more general, since in principle we could define m on any element of $\mathcal{Q}(\Omega)$.

Using the dual structure $Q^*(\Omega)$, another interesting interpretation comes up, which will correspond to the view of Dubois *et al.* [4]. To switch from $\mathcal{Q}(\Omega)$ to $\mathcal{Q}^*(\Omega)$, it suffices for an element (A, B) of $\mathcal{Q}(\Omega)$ to turn B into B^c. Then in $Q^*(\Omega)$, an element (A, B) is such that $A \subset B$. In the framework above inspired from Smets, such an event could be interpreted as: B (certainly) contains the true state, while A may contain it (since A^c certainly does not contain it).

3.3   Relation with the Classical Belief Model; The Confidence/Diffidence Model

The classical belief model is embedded into our general framework. According to the interpretation given above, a classical mass allocation corresponds to a confidence mass m^+, without any diffidence component. Hence, the corresponding Möbius transform m is non null only for elements of the form (A, A^c) in $\mathcal{Q}(\Omega)$. The consequence is that, as claimed above, $\text{Bel}(A, B)$ depends no more on B :

$$\text{Bel}(A, B) = \sum_{(C,D) \sqsubseteq (A,B)} m(C, D) = \sum_{C \subseteq A} m(C, C^c) .$$

Consequently, $\text{Pl}(A, B)$ does not depend on A.

Symmetrically, we could imagine a situation where only diffidence mass is given, so that the corresponding Möbius transform is non zero only for elements of the form $(\emptyset, B)$. In this case,

$$\text{Bel}(A, B) = \sum_{C \supseteq B} m(\emptyset, C)$$

so that $\text{Bel}(A, B)$ does not depend on A (and $\text{Pl}(A, B)$ no more on B).

The confidence/diffidence model appears as a particular case of the bi-belief model easier to handle. Let us remark that in general, m^+, m^- are *not* usual mass allocations since:

- $m^+(\emptyset) = 0$, and $m^+(\Omega)$ represents ignorance, but $\sum_{A \subseteq \Omega} m^+(A) \neq 1$ in general.
- $m^-(\Omega) = m^+(\emptyset) = 0$, $m^-(\emptyset)$ represents ignorance (of the diffidence part), and again $\sum_{A \subseteq \Omega} m^-(A) \neq 1$ in general.

However, note that

$$\sum_{A \subseteq \Omega} m^+(A) + \sum_{A \subseteq \Omega} m^-(A) = 1.$$

This allows a free balance of the confidence and diffidence parts (which would have been impossible with bipolar bi-capacities), including the classical belief model, and a symmetric purely diffidence model. The quantities $\sum_{A \subseteq \Omega} m^+(A)$ and $\sum_{A \subseteq \Omega} m^-(A)$ represent the "weights" of the diffidence and confidence parts (if they come from two different sources, they may be simply the confidence degree we have in these sources).

Combining both the confidence and the diffidence, we have

$$m(A, B) = \begin{cases} m^+(A) & \text{if } B = A^c \\ m^-(B) & \text{if } A = \emptyset \\ 0 & \text{otherwise} \end{cases}$$

and

$$\text{Bel}(A, B) = \sum_{C \subseteq A} m^+(C) + \sum_{C \supseteq B} m^-(C) .$$

3.4   The Ukalvia Example Revisited

Let us try to apply the confidence/diffidence model to the Ukalvia case, with different balances between the two parts of the model.

The possible states of nature are: the economic situation is good (G), or it is bad (B), hence $\Omega = \{G, B\}$. The confidence part is given by the statement: "the agent believes to some extent that the economic situation is good", which can be modeled by

$$m^+(G) = \alpha, \quad m^+(B) = 0, \quad m^+(G) + m^+(\{G, B\}) = \alpha^+$$

and $\alpha^+ - \alpha = m^+(\{G, B\})$ represents ignorance of the confidence part. Now the diffidence part is expressed by the statement: "the agent does not trust (to some extent) the journal", hence he/she does not believe to some extent that the situation is good. This can be modeled by

$$m^-(G) = \beta, \quad m^-(B) = 0, \quad m^-(G) + m^-(\emptyset) = \beta^-$$

where again $\beta^- - \beta = m^-(\emptyset)$ represents ignorance. Figure 2 illustrates the situation (masses equal to 0 are not figured). We can compute explicitly all beliefs:

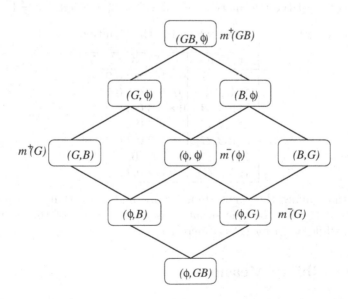

Fig. 2. The Ukalvia example modeled by bi-belief functions

$$\mathrm{Bel}(G, \emptyset) = m^+(G) + m^-(G) + m^-(\emptyset) = \alpha + \beta^-$$
$$\mathrm{Bel}(B, \emptyset) = m^-(G) + m^-(\emptyset) = \beta^-$$
$$\mathrm{Bel}(G, B) = m^+(G) = \alpha$$
$$\mathrm{Bel}(\emptyset, \emptyset) = m^-(\emptyset) + m^-(G) = \beta^-$$
$$\mathrm{Bel}(B, G) = m^-(G) = \beta$$
$$\mathrm{Bel}(\emptyset, B) = 0$$
$$\mathrm{Bel}(\emptyset, G) = m^-(G) = \beta$$

It is interesting to give various values to the masses, so as to model typical situations, e.g.

- situation 1: the agent has not heard about the origin of the journal: $\alpha = 0.8$, $\alpha^+ = 1$, $\beta = 0$, $\beta^- = 0$.
- situation 2: the agent trusts more the journal: $\alpha = 0.6$, $\alpha^+ = 0.7$, $\beta = 0.2$, $\beta^- = 0.3$.
- situation 3: the agent feels confused (equal weight for confidence and diffidence): $\alpha = 0.4$, $\alpha^+ = 0.5$, $\beta = 0.4$, $\beta^- = 0.5$.
- situation 4: the agent does not trust so much the journal: $\alpha = 0.2$, $\alpha^+ = 0.3$, $\beta = 0.6$, $\beta^- = 0.7$.
- situation 5: the agent, knowing from the beginning the origin of the journal, does not trust the information: $\alpha = 0$, $\alpha^+ = 0$, $\beta = 0.8$, $\beta^- = 1$.

We obtain the following results, which fits the intuition.

situation →	1	2	3	4	5
$\mathrm{Bel}(G, \emptyset)$	0.8	0.9	0.9	0.9	1
$\mathrm{Bel}(B, \emptyset)$	0	0.3	0.5	0.7	1
$\mathrm{Bel}(G, B)$	0.8	0.6	0.4	0.2	0
$\mathrm{Bel}(\emptyset, \emptyset)$	0	0.3	0.5	0.7	1
$\mathrm{Bel}(B, G)$	0	0.2	0.4	0.6	0.8
$\mathrm{Bel}(\emptyset, B)$	0	0	0	0	0
$\mathrm{Bel}(\emptyset, G)$	0	0.2	0.4	0.6	0.8

Note that, along the agent thinks more and more that it is propaganda, the belief for (G, B) (the true situation is G, and B is not the true situation) decreases, while belief for (B, G) increases.

4   Bi-possibility Measures

As possibility measures play a particular role in capacity theory, we try to define here the corresponding concept for bi-capacities. It is well known that necessity and possibility measures are particular cases of belief and plausibility functions, when focal elements are nested.

Results are relatively easy to generalize when all is expressed into the language of ordered sets, and in particular lattices. Nested focal elements form in fact a maximal chain from bottom to top of the lattice, so we keep the same notion for $\mathcal{Q}(\Omega)$. A maximal chain in $\mathcal{Q}(\Omega)$ is a sequence of elements starting from $(\emptyset, \Omega)$ and finishing at $(\Omega, \emptyset)$, and between two consecutive elements, either i is deleted from the right argument, or j is added to the left argument, provided j is not present in the right argument.

We say that a bi-belief function is a *bi-necessity measure* if the focal elements form a maximal chain in $\mathcal{Q}(\Omega)$. A *bi-possibility measure* is the conjugate of a bi-necessity measure. We denote by Π and N bi-possibility and bi-necessity measures.

The following result holds.

Proposition 2. *Let Π and N be any bi-possibility and bi-necessity measure. Then for any $(A, B), (C, D)$ in $\mathcal{Q}(\Omega)$,*

$$\Pi((A, B) \sqcup (C, D)) = \Pi(A, B) \vee \Pi(C, D)$$
$$N((A, B) \sqcap (C, D)) = N(A, B) \wedge N(C, D).$$

The proof is based on a general result by Barthélemy [1]. Observe that these properties extend those known for the classical possibility and necessity measures.

Since any element in $\mathcal{Q}(\Omega)$ can be expressed with the help of sup-irreducible or inf-irreducible elements by equations (1) and (2), we can write:

$$\Pi(A, B) = \bigvee_{i \in A} \pi^+(i) \vee \bigvee_{j \in B^c} \pi^-(j) \tag{10}$$

$$N(A, B) = \bigwedge_{i \in B} \left(1 - \pi^+(i)\right) \wedge \bigwedge_{j \in A^c} \left(1 - \pi^-(j)\right) \tag{11}$$

$$= \bigwedge_{i \in A^c} n^+(i) \wedge \bigwedge_{j \in B} n^-(j). \tag{12}$$

putting $\pi^+(i) := \Pi(i, i^c)$, $\pi^-(i) := \Pi(\emptyset, i^c)$, and $n^+(i) := N(i^c, \emptyset)$, $n^-(i) := N(i^c, i)$. These functions could be called *distributions* as in the classical case. More precisely, the pair (π^+, π^-) is the *bi-possibility distribution* (idem for bi-necessity distribution). The name "distribution" is justified since the value of Π or N at any point of $\mathcal{Q}(\Omega)$ can be recovered from the distribution. We call π^+, π^- the *left* and *right* distribution functions respectively (idem for necessity).

Let us express the relation between the distribution and the Möbius transform. We assume first that the Möbius transform is given, i.e. we know the maximal chain $\mathcal{C}$ and values of m on it. Any maximal chain is a sequence of $2n + 1$ elements starting with $(\emptyset, \Omega)$ and finishing with $(\Omega, \emptyset)$. A convenient way of denoting a chain is to write the $2n$ length sequence of elements of Ω which are deleted or added, with a "+" sign if added, and a "−" sign if deleted. For example for $n = 3$, the maximal chain

$$\{(\emptyset, 123), (\emptyset, 12), (\emptyset, 1), (2, 1), (2, \emptyset), (12, \emptyset), (123, \emptyset)\}$$

is denoted $-3, -2, 2, -1, 1, 3$. By construction, each index appears only once, with each sign, and a positive index cannot be before the corresponding negative index. This sequence is denoted σ_C, and is a permutation on $\{-n, -n + 1, \ldots, -1, 1, 2, \ldots, n\}$.

Let us compute the possibility distribution (π^+, π^-) for a given Möbius transform m living on a chain C. Let σ^+, σ^- denote the permutations on Ω defining the ordering of the positive and negative indices in C. With these notations, the following holds.

Proposition 3. *For a given Möbius transform m living on a chain C, the possibility distribution (π^+, π^-) is given by:*

$$\pi^+(\sigma^-(k)) = 1 - \sum_{(C,D) \in \mathcal{C} \cap [(\emptyset, \Omega), (., \Omega \setminus \{\sigma^-(1), \ldots, \sigma^-(k)\})[} m(C, D)$$

$$\pi^-(\sigma^+(k)) = 1 - \sum_{(C,D) \in \mathcal{C} \cap [(\emptyset, \Omega), (\{\sigma^+(1), \ldots, \sigma^+(k)\}, .)[} m(C, D)$$

The sequences π^+ and π^- are ordered w.r.t. σ^- and σ^+ respectively, and moreover the sequence (π^+, π^-) is ordered w.r.t. σ_C, specifically :

$$1 = \pi^+(\sigma_C(-n)) \geq \pi^{-\text{sgn}(\sigma_C(-n+1))}(\sigma_C(-n+1)) \geq \cdots$$

$$\geq \pi^{-\text{sgn}(\sigma_C(1))}(\sigma_C(1)) \geq \cdots \geq \pi^-(\sigma_C(n)) = m(\Omega, \emptyset) \ .$$

Applying Proposition 3 to our example above, we have:

$$\pi^+(3) = 1$$
$$\pi^+(2) = 1 - m(\emptyset, 12)$$
$$\pi^+(1) = 1 - m(\emptyset, 12) - m(\emptyset, 1) - m(2, 1)$$
$$\pi^-(2) = 1 - m(\emptyset, 12) - m(\emptyset, 1)$$
$$\pi^-(1) = 1 - m(\emptyset, 12) - m(\emptyset, 1) - m(2, 1) - m(2, \emptyset)$$
$$\pi^-(3) = 1 - m(\emptyset, 12) - m(\emptyset, 1) - m(2, 1) - m(2, \emptyset) - (12, \emptyset),$$

and $1 = \pi^+(3) \geq \pi^+(2) \geq \pi^-(2) \geq \pi^+(1) \geq \pi^-(1) \geq \pi^-(3)$. Since the equation system is triangular, one easily recovers m from a given distribution, the chain of focal elements being defined by the distribution.

References

1. J.P. Barthélemy. Monotone functions on finite lattices: an ordinal approach to capacities, belief and necessity functions. In J. Fodor, B. De Baets, and P. Perny, editors, Preferences and Decisions under Incomplete Knowledge, pages 195–208. Physica Verlag, 2000.

2. J.M. Bilbao, J.R. Fernandez, A. Jiménez Losada and E. Lebrón. Bicooperative games. In: J.M. Bilbao Eds. Cooperative games on Combinatorial stractures. Kluwer Acad. Publi., 2000.
3. B.A. Davey and H.A. Priestley. Introduction to Lattices and Orders. Cambridge University Press, 1990.
4. D. Dubois, H. Prade, and Ph. Smets. "Not impossible" vs. "guaranteed possible" in fusion and revision. In S. Benferhat and Ph. Besnard, editors, 6th Eur. Conf. on Symbolic and Quantitative Approaches to Reasoning with Uncertainty (ECSQARU'2001), Lecture Notes in Computer Science, pages 522–531, Toulouse, France, September 2001. Springer Verlag.
5. M. Grabisch and Ch. Labreuche. Bi-capacities. In Joint Int. Conf. on Soft Computing and Intelligent Systems and 3d Int. Symp. on Advanced Intelligent Systems, Tsukuba, Japan, October 2002.
6. M. Grabisch and Ch. Labreuche. Bi-capacities for decision making on bipolar scales. In EUROFUSE Workshop on Informations Systems, pages 185–190, Varenna, Italy, September 2002.
7. G. Shafer. A Mathematical Theory of Evidence. Princeton Univ. Press, 1976.
8. Ph. Smets. The canonical decomposition of a weighted belief. In Proc. of the 14th Int. Joint Conf. on Artificial Intelligence (IJCAI'95), pages 1896–1901, Montreal, August 1995.

Directed Evidential Networks with Conditional Belief Functions

Boutheina Ben Yaghlane[1], Philippe Smets[2], and Khaled Mellouli[1]

[1] LARODEC, Université de Tunis
IHEC Carthage Présidence 2016 Tunisia
{boutheina.yaghlane,Khaled.mellouli}@ihec.rnu.tn
[2] IRIDIA, Université Libre de Bruxelles
50, av. F. Roosevelt, CP 194/6 1050 Bruxelles Belgium
psmets@ulb.ac.be

Abstract. The main question addressed in this paper is how to represent belief functions independencies by graphical model. Directed evidential networks (DEVNs) with conditional belief functions are then proposed. These networks are directed acyclic graphs (DAGs) similar to Bayesian networks but instead of using probability functions, we use belief functions. Directed evidential network with conditional belief functions has the advantage of providing an appropriate representation of the knowledge that can be produced as conditional relationships.

Keywords: belief functions, transferable belief model, conditional belief functions, directed evidential networks

1   Introduction

In this paper, we discuss some aspects related to uncertainty[1] representation in directed evidential networks with conditional belief functions. Pearl starts with conditional independence relationships when building his *probabilistic graphical model* where conditional probabilities can be directly manipulated using Bayes' theorem (Pearl, 1988). The graphical model is considered as a picture that provides an intuitive description of the problem. It is also considered as a mathematical structure that specifies the different connections between the variables of a problem transforming a complex problem into an easily and clear representation.

However, in the *networks using belief functions*, the relations among the variables are generally represented by joint belief functions (Shafer et al., 1987) rather than conditional belief functions. Nevertheless, the use of graphs to represent conditional independence relations is useful since an exponential number of conditional independence statements can be represented by a graph with a polynomial number of vertices (Shenoy, 1993). So, we will be interested, in this paper, by showing how to represent independencies by directed evidential networks with conditional belief functions.

---

[1] Uncertainty is expressed by belief functions as understood in the context of the transferable belief model (TBM).

T.D. Nielsen and N.L. Zhang (Eds.): ECSQARU 2003, LNAI 2711, pp. 291–305, 2003.
© Springer-Verlag Berlin Heidelberg 2003

The remainder of this paper is organized as follows. In Sect. 2, we present some useful definitions and notations needed for belief function context. Next, before presenting and discussing the belief function networks, we focus on the study of directed acyclic graph as a general graphical model that displays qualitatively the dependence relationships, under any assignment of numerical values (Sect. 3), and then briefly present some well-known graphical representations (Sect. 4), namely Bayesian networks (BN), valuation networks (VN), and evidential networks with conditional belief functions (ENC), these types of networks seem to be a good start point for our work. Then, Sect. 5 is devoted to present the directed evidential networks (DEVN) with conditional belief functions, we especially discuss the links between the directed evidential networks and the other networks (Bayesian networks and valuation networks).

2   Definitions and Notations of Belief Functions

When we model aspects of the real word, we often deal with multivariate situations where the state space is a product space. Therefore, multivariate belief functions theory turn out to be well suited for modelling real world problems. We present below some definitions necessary when belief functions are used.

2.1   Variables

Let $\mathbf{U} = \{X, Y, Z, ...\}$ be a set of finite variables, $\Theta_X = \{x_1, ..., x_n\}$ be the domain relative to the variable X (with a finite cardinality n), and x represents any instance of X. For simplicity sake, we denote Θ_X by X, Θ_Y by Y... Let Ω be a frame of discernment (Shafer, 1976). It is the Cartesian product of the domains of the variables in $\mathbf{U}$. For a subset of variables $A \subseteq \mathbf{U}$, the *frame for A*, denoted by Θ_A, is the Cartesian product of the frames for the variables in A, and its elements are called the *configurations* of A. For example, $X \times Y$ represents the product space of variables X and Y, and when there is no ambiguity, it is simply denoted by XY. The elements of X (Y ...) are represented by indexed variables like x_i (y_j ...) whereas x (y ...) denote subsets of X (Y ...). For $x \subseteq X$ and $y \subseteq Y$, (x, y) is defined by $(x, y) = \{(x_i, y_j) : x_i \in x, y_j \in y\}$, and similarly for $(x, y, z) \ldots$. Extension and projection of sets of configurations are very important in belief functions theory. Therefore, let's define these two operations:

Definition 1. Cylindrical Extension. *For* $x \subseteq X$, $x^{\uparrow XY}$ *is the* cylindrical extension of x on XY: $x^{\uparrow XY} = (x, Y)$.

Definition 2. Projection. *For* $w \subseteq \Omega$, $w^{\downarrow X}$ *is the* projection of w on X: $w^{\downarrow X} = \{x_i : x_i \in X, x_i^{\uparrow \Omega} \cap w \neq \emptyset\}$.

We give now the definition of independent variables.

Definition 3. Independent Variables. *Two variables X and Y are independent iff* $(x_i, y_j) \neq \emptyset$, $\forall x_i \in X, y_j \in Y$.

2.2 Belief Function Conditioning

Let x denote the background knowledge that holds and that underlies the beliefs. In x, we find the classical conditioning events.

- We use the notation $m^{\Omega}[x]$ to represent the bba (shorthand for basic belief assignment) m defined on the domain Ω given the belief holder knows (accepts) that x is true (i.e. x holds). The term m can be replaced by bel, pl, q in order to denote the *belief function*, the *plausibility function* and the *commonality function*. The values taken by these functions at $w \subseteq \Omega$ are denoted by $m^{\Omega}[x](w)$, $bel^{\Omega}[x](w)$, $pl^{\Omega}[x](w)$, $q^{\Omega}[x](w)$, respectively. $m^{\Omega}[x](w)$ is called a *basic belief mass* (bbm). $bel^{\Omega}[x]$ is called a *conditional belief function*. It can be seen as a vector in a $2^{|\Omega|}$ dimensional space. Classically, it was denoted as $bel^{\Omega}(. \mid x)$, but the bracket notation turns out to be more convenient. The Ω superscript will not be mentioned when there is no risk of confusion.
- Given a belief function bel^{Ω} on Ω, let

$$b^{\Omega}(w) = bel^{\Omega}(w) + m^{\Omega}(\emptyset), \forall w \subseteq \Omega.$$

This function b^{Ω} is called the *implicability function*. In practice, the b function is much more convenient to work with than the bel function.

- $bel^{\Omega}[x](w)$ denotes the value of $bel^{\Omega}[x]$ at $w \subseteq \Omega$. It represents the belief of w given x. When x is the proposition that states that the actual value of Ω belongs to $y \subseteq \Omega$, its value is given by

$$b^{\Omega}[y](w) = b^{\Omega}(w \cup \overline{y}),$$
$$bel^{\Omega}[y](w) = bel^{\Omega}(w \cup \overline{y}) - bel^{\Omega}(\overline{y}),$$
$$pl^{\Omega}[y](w) = pl^{\Omega}(w \cap y),$$
$$q^{\Omega}[y](w) = \begin{cases} q^{\Omega}(w) & \text{if } w \subseteq y, \\ 0 & \text{otherwise.} \end{cases}$$

These are the so called *Dempster's rule of conditioning* (except for the normalization factor).

2.3 Combination

The $\oplus$ symbol represents *Dempster's rule of combination* in its normalized form and $\odot$ represents the *conjunctive combination*, i.e., the same operation as Dempster's rule of combination except that the normalization is not performed.

The conjunctive combination rule (as well as its Dempster' form) are applicable to combine the belief functions produced by distinct pieces of evidence and can be written equivalently as:

$$m_{1 \odot 2}(w) = m_1 \odot m_2(w) = \sum_{w_1, w_2 \subseteq \Omega, w_1 \cap w_2 = w} m_1(w_1) m_2(w_2)$$

$pl_1 \odot pl_2$ is the plausibility function obtained from $m_1 \odot m_2$ where m_1 and m_2 are the bba's related to pl_1 and pl_2, respectively (and similarly with bel and q).

2.4   Marginalization

The belief function $bel^{\Omega\downarrow X}$ is the marginal of bel^{Ω} on X. In particular, we have:

$$bel^{XY\downarrow X}(x) = bel^{XY}(x, Y),$$

$$pl^{XY\downarrow X}(x) = pl^{XY}(x, Y).$$

Note that conditioning and marginalization do not commute, so the order of the symbols is important. $bel^{XY}[y]^{\downarrow X}$ is the belief function obtained by conditioning bel^{XY} on y and the result is then marginalized on X.

2.5   Ballooning Extension

Let X and Y be two independent variables, and let $bel^X[y_i]$ be a conditional belief function defined on X for $y_i \in Y$. The ballooning extension of the conditional belief function, denoted $m^{X\uparrow XY}$, is the belief function defined on XY which bba satisfies (Smets, 1978):

$$m^{X\uparrow XY}(w) = \begin{cases} m^X[y_i](x) & \text{if } w = (x, y_i) \cup (X, \overline{y_i}), \\ 0 & \text{otherwise.} \end{cases} \qquad (1)$$

The belief function obtained by ballooning extension is the least committed belief function among all the belief functions defined on XY which conditioning on (X, y_i) (followed by the trivial marginalization on X in order to be defined on X and not on XY) reproduces $bel^X[y_i]$ (Shafer, 1982).

3   Conditional Independence in Directed Acyclic Graphs

Developing a graphical representation for judgments about independencies facilitates a qualitative organization of knowledge. Geiger *et al.* have investigated the problem of determining exactly what independencies are implied by the structure of the DAG in a causal network[2] (Geiger et al., 1990).

In this section, we give the definition of the graphical criterion identifying conditional independencies in DAGs, called **d-separation**. First, let's look at the preliminary definitions which are useful for further interpretations.

3.1   Dependency Models

The notion of dependency models presented here was originated by (Pearl and Paz, 1987). Formally, a *dependency model* M over a finite set of elements **V** is defined as any subset of triplets (X, Z, Y) where X, Y, and Z are

---

[2] Causal network consists of a set of *variables*, and a set of *directed links* between variables. Mathematically, the structure is a *directed graph* (Jensen and Lauritzen, 2000).

three disjoint subsets of **V**. The triplets in M represent independencies, that is, $(X, Y, Z) \in M$ asserts that "X is independent of Y given Z". This statement is called an *independence statement* and is written as $I(X, Z, Y)$ (Pearl, 1988).

The intended interpretation of $I(X, Z, Y)$ is that when we observe Z, no additional information about X could be obtained by also observing Y, or equivalently X and Y interact only via Z. In a belief network, the independence statements are important because they reduce the complexity of inference.

A graphical representation of a dependency model M is a one-to-one correspondence between the elements in M and the set of vertices in a graph G.

3.2   d-Separation Criterion

The study of the concept of conditional independence in probability theory has resulted in the identification of several properties that may be reasonable to demand of any relationship which attempts to capture the intuitive notion of independence. These properties are called *graphoid axioms* (i.e. *symmetry, decomposition, weak union, contraction,* and *intersection* axioms).

Interestingly, directed acyclic graphs conform to the graphoid axioms if we relate the independence statement $I(X, Z, Y)$ in M with the graphical condition "every chain from X to Y is *blocked* by the set of nodes Z" (Pearl, 1988). From this, we can define the d-separation criterion.

Definition 4. *d-Separation.* *Given a DAG $G = (V, E)$. Two subsets of nodes, X and Y, are said to be **d-separated** by Z, denoted by $< X \mid Z \mid Y >_G$, if all chains between the nodes in X and the nodes in Y are blocked by Z.*

Intuitively, d-separation reflects a basic property of sound human reasoning, and therefore any uncertainty computation in causal networks should satisfy the principle that whenever X and Y are *d-separated* then new information about one of them does not change the certainty of the other when the Z variables are fixed.

4   Graphical Representations

We first consider two well-known frameworks for graphical representation of uncertain knowledge: *Bayesian networks* (Pearl, 1988) and *valuations networks* (Shenoy and Shafer, 1990). Bayesian networks are used for the probabilistic inference, while valuation networks represent several uncertainty formalisms in a unified framework. Then, as in the valuation networks, it is not possible to represent knowledge in conditional form, (Xu, 1995) proposes a new network for the belief function inference called *evidential network with conditional belief function* (ENC).

4.1   Bayesian Networks

We focus on the possibility of using DAGs as graphical representation for probabilistic models. Indeed, Pearl defines a Bayesian network as a *directed acyclic*

graph (DAG) in which the nodes represent (random) variables, the arcs signify
the existence of direct causal influences between the linked variables, and the
strengths of these influences are expressed by conditional probabilities. Formally,
a Bayesian network can be regarded as a triplet **V**, **E**, **P** where:

- **V** = $\{X_1, ..., X_n\}$ is a set of variables, for each variable X_i, we associate a
  frame Θ_{X_i} representing a set of all its possible instances,
- **E** is a set of arcs over **V** such that the pair (**V**,**E**) is a DAG where the nodes
  represent the variables and arcs represent conditional dependency relations
  among the variables,
- **P** = $\{P(X_i \mid X_{i_1}, ..., X_{i_t}) : X_i \in \mathbf{V}, X_{i_j} \in Pa(X_i)\}$ is a set of *assessment
  functions* defining conditional probabilities of the variables given their par-
  ents, stored at node X_i. When X_i has no parents, $P(X_i)$ represents the prior
  probability of X_i.

Probabilistic Chain Rule. A fundamental assumption of a Bayesian network
is that when we multiply the conditionals for each variable, we get a *unique*
joint probability distribution for all variables in the network that agrees with
the independencies represented by the network structure[3]. The *joint probability*
of a Bayesian network is given by the following *chain rule*:

Definition 5. *Probabilistic Chain Rule.* *Let BN be a Bayesian network over*
$V=\{X_1, ..., X_n\}$, *then the joint probability distribution P(V) is the product of all
conditional probabilities specified in BN :*

$$P(X_1, ..., X_n) = \prod_i P(X_i \mid Pa(X_i)) \tag{2}$$

where $Pa(X_i)$ is the parent set of X_i.

4.2   Valuation Networks

Valuation networks are another well-known framework for the graphical representations of uncertain knowledge. They are graphical depiction of valuation-
based systems (VBS) that can represent several uncertainty formalisms (probability theory, possibility theory, belief function theory, ...) in a unified framework.
Valuation networks have been originally proposed by (Shenoy and Shafer, 1990).
Formally, a valuation network can be regarded as a 3-tuple $\{X, \{\Theta_{X_i}\}_{X_i \in X},$
$\{V_1, ..., V_m\}\}$ with operators $\{\oplus, \downarrow\}$ where:

- X is a set of variables representing the universe of discourse,
- $\{\Theta_{X_i}\}$ is the set of frames associated with each variable X_i,
- $\{V_1, ..., V_m\}$ is a collection of valuations defined on the subsets of variables,

---

[3] Due to the independencies, far fewer probabilities need to be specified than with an
exhaustive list of the joint probability distribution (Pearl, 1988).

- ⊕ is the combination operation. Intuitively, combination corresponds to the aggregation of knowledge,
- ↓ is the marginalization operation. Intuitively, marginalization corresponds to the coarsening of knowledge.

Graphically, there are two types of vertices in valuation networks (VNs). One set of vertices represents variables, denoted by *circles*, and the other set represents valuations, denoted by *diamonds*. In VNs, there are *edges* only between variables and valuations. There is an edge between a variable and a valuation if and only if the variable is in the domain of the valuation.

Valuation Networks vs. Bayesian Networks. Valuation networks (VNs) are general graphical representations because they can represent several uncertainty formalisms in a unified framework, while Bayesian networks (BNs) have been proposed as graphical representations of probabilistic models.

Graphically, a valuation network is a hypergraph and a Bayesian network is a directed acyclic graph. In a BN, arcs describe conditional dependence relations among the variables, whereas in a VN, such relations are represented by joint valuations on the product space of the involved variables. Finally, in VNs, two valuations can bear on the same variables, whereas in BNs, it is not allowed that two nodes are directly connected by two arcs. A comparison of the Bayesian network and the valuation network is given in Table 1. Notice that we can obtain a valuation network from a Bayesian network, but the reverse is usually not possible.

Features	Bayesian network	Valuation network
Graphical structure		
1. Type of graph	Directed acyclic graph	Hypergraph
2. Definition of relations	Based on conditional independence	Joint form
3. Nodes	Random variables	Variables and valuations
Inference Procedure		
4. Type of uncertainty	Probabilistic	Several uncertainty formalisms
5. Inference process	Quantitative based on probability propagation	Quantitative based on fusion algorithm

Table 1. A comparison of Bayesian networks and valuation networks

Valuation Networks and Conditional Independence. In this section, we show how to represent conditional independence relations in VNs. Indeed, in VNs, there are edges only between variables and valuations. If a valuation is a conditional for X given Y, then a *directed edge* between the conditional valuation and variables in X is drawn, this edge is pointed toward the variables in X.

For belief function context, (Cano et al., 1993) and (Shenoy, 1994b) have both defined the concept of a *conditional belief function*, but their definition is different from ours definition of conditional belief function. To avoid confusion with our definition, we change the name they use and we call it *joint belief function with a vacuous marginal*:

Definition 6. *(Cano et al., 1993)*[4] *Given two independent variables X and Y. Let bel be a belief function defined on the product space $\Theta_{X \cup Y}$. It is said that bel is a joint belief function with a vacuous marginal over X if and only if $bel^{\downarrow X}$ is a vacuous belief function over X.*

Intuitively, the *joint belief function with a vacuous marginal* means that if *bel* is a belief function on Θ_Y conditioned on Θ_X, then it may gives some information about variable Y and their relationships with variable X, but no information about X. Xu has shown that this property can be easily verified when the belief is represented in normalized conditional form (Xu, 1995).

Following (Shenoy, 1994b), valuation networks explicitly depict a factorization of the joint valuation. Since there is a one-to-one correspondence between a factorization of the joint valuation and the conditional independence relation that holds in it, valuation networks also explicitly represent conditional relations.

Shenoy has also defined conditional independence in valuation networks and shown that it satisfies the graphoid axioms (Shenoy, 1994a). As the valuation-based systems (VBS) is a general framework, thus the graphoid axioms are also satisfied by the conditional independence relations in all uncertainties that fit in the VBS framework including probability theory, belief function theory and possibility theory. For further information, the reader is referred to (Shenoy, 1993; Shenoy, 1994b; Ben Yaghlane et al., 2002; Ben Yaghlane, 2002).

4.3   Evidential Networks with Conditional Belief Functions

Evidential networks[5] *with conditional belief functions*, called ENC, was originally proposed by Smets for the propagation of beliefs (Smets, 1993). Then these networks have been deeply studied in (Xu, 1995). Graphically, the network is a directed acyclic graph. But, conditional beliefs are defined in a different manner from conditional probabilities in the Bayesian network (BN): each edge represents a conditional relation between the two nodes it connects. For example, the edges (X,Z) and (Y,Z) in Fig. 1 mean that we have $\{bel^Z[x_i] : x_i \in \Theta_X\}$ and $\{bel^Z[y_i] : y_i \in \Theta_Y\}$, but not $\{bel^Z[x_i, y_i] : x_i \in \Theta_X, y_i \in \Theta_Y\}$ as in BN.

However, if conditional beliefs such as $\{bel^Z[x_i, y_i] : x_i \in \Theta_X, y_i \in \Theta_Y\}$ are given, Xu' method build an ENC in which nodes X and Y are merged as one

---

[4] In (Cano et al., 1993; Shenoy, 1994b), this belief function is called "conditional belief function" and, in (Xu, 1995), it is called "non-informative belief function".

[5] When the VBS is specialized in belief function theory, it is called an *evidential system*, and the valuation network is the *evidential network*.

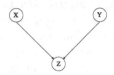

Fig. 1. An evidential network with conditional belief functions

node. For any merged node, the belief function is obtained by combining the ballooning extension[6] of each conditional belief function.

5 DAG Representation of Belief Functions Models: Directed Evidential Networks

In the previous section, we have presented Xu' graphical representation (i.e. ENC) which uses conditional belief functions for the knowledge representation and reasoning. By comparing some relations between the representation by joint belief and by conditional form, Xu and Smets have shown that the conditional form takes less space. Indeed, in ENC, any computations involving two connected variables X and Y are processed on the space Θ_X or Θ_Y, while in the network with joint beliefs, such computations are always done on the product space $\Theta_{X \cup Y}$. Thus the computations in ENC needs fewer set-comparisons and multiplications than that in the latter one.

Nevertheless, the computation in ENC is not quite efficient because the reasoning process is based on the ballooning extension of conditional belief functions. Furthermore, the representation and propagation algorithm proposed by Xu are restricted because they are for the evidential network which only have binary relations between the nodes (Xu, 1995).

Thus, in this section, we generalize ENC to the case where relations are for any number of nodes. In order to distinguish the two kinds of networks, we call ours DEVN which means a *directed evidential network with conditional belief functions*.

5.1 Knowledge Representation Using Conditional Belief Functions

In this section, we discuss the relationships between joint belief functions and conditional belief functions which represent the same knowledge.

Example 1. Suppose that we have two variables X and Y with frames $\Theta_X = \{x_1, x_2\}$ and $\Theta_Y = \{y_1, y_2\}$, respectively. To represent a relation between X and Y such that "if $X = x_1$ then $Y = y_1$ with $m = 0.7$" by a belief function in:

---

[6] See Sect. 2.5.

joint form: the rule is represented by a belief function on the space $\Theta = \Theta_X \times \Theta_Y = \{(x_1, y_1), (x_1, y_2), (x_2, y_1), (x_2, y_2)\}$, with masses: 0.7 on the subset $\{(x_1, y_1), (x_2, y_1), (x_2, y_2)\}$, and 0.3 on Θ.

conditional form: the rule is represented by the conditional bba:

$$m[x_1](\{y_1\}) = 0.7,$$
$$m[x_1](\Theta_Y) = 0.3,$$
$$m[x_2](\Theta_Y) = 1,$$
$$m[\Theta_X](\Theta_Y) = 1.$$

From this example, it can be shown that the conditional representation is more "easy" for the users to provide and to understand. In general, to represent conditional belief functions for Y given X, by a joint form, it needs $2^{|\Theta_X| \times |\Theta_Y|}$ elements in the worst case, while by a conditional form, it only needs $2^{|\Theta_X| + |\Theta_Y|}$ elements in the worst case.

But following (Xu and Smets, 1994), not all belief functions on $\Theta_{X \cup Y}$ admit an equivalent representation by a set of conditional belief functions. Further, they think that the users' knowledge is encoded in the conditional form and that the joint beliefs the users would provide are those based on the known conditional form. In many situations, the users' beliefs can be represented by the conditional belief functions for Y given $x_i \in \Theta_X$. The conditional belief for Y given $x \subseteq \Theta_X$ is then derived from the disjunctive rule of combination (DRC). Example 1 is such a case. In the worst case, it needs only $|\Theta_X| \times 2^{|\Theta_Y|}$ elements.

The Joint bba Generated by the Set of Conditional bba. Let X and Y be two independent variables, and let the set of conditional belief functions $bel^X[y_i]$ be defined on X for each $y_i \in Y$. The conditional belief functions are considered as produced by distinct pieces of evidence. In practice, this means that the knowledge of the value of $bel^X[y_i]$ does not produce constraints on what might be the values of $bel^X[y_j]$ for $j \neq i$.

We want to build a bba on XY such that its conditioning on (X, y_i) reproduces $bel^X[y_i]$ when the conditional belief functions are generated by distinct pieces of evidence. The solution, presented in (Smets, 1978; Smets, 1993) is obtained as follows:

Each $bel^X[y_i]$ is extended by a ballooning extension on the frame XY by relation (1) and the results are conjunctively combined. The value of the resulting belief function is given in the following theorem.

Theorem 1. *Let X and Y be two independent variables, and let the set of conditional belief functions $bel^X[y_i]$ be defined on X for each $y_i \in Y$. Let $w \subseteq XY$. For each $y_i \in Y$, let $x_i^X(w)$ be the projection on X of the elements of w which intersect (X, y_i): $x_i^X(w) = (w \cap (X, y_i))^{\downarrow X}$. Then the conjunctive combination of the ballooning extensions of each conditional belief function on XY, $m^{XY} = \bigcirc_{y_i \in Y} m^X[y_i]^{\uparrow XY}$, admits the following representations:*

$$m^{XY}(w) = \prod_{y_i \in Y} m^X[y_i](x_i^X(w)) \tag{3}$$

$$b^{XY}(w) = \prod_{y_i \in Y} b^X[y_i](x_i^X(w)) \tag{4}$$

$$pl^{XY}(w) = 1 - \prod_{y_i \in Y} (1 - pl^X[y_i](x_i^X(w)) \tag{5}$$

$$q^{XY}(w) = \prod_{y_i \in Y} q^X[y_i](x_i^X(w)) \tag{6}$$

The formulas of theorem 1 are proved in (Smets, 1978; Smets, 1993).

This construction is linked to the concept of a joint belief function with a vacuous marginal by the next lemma. The joint belief function built according to theorem 1 is a joint belief function with a vacuous marginal over Y once all the conditional belief functions are normalized.

Lemma 1. Let $\{bel^X[y] : y \in \Theta_Y\}$ be a family of normalized conditional belief functions for X given Y. Then $bel^{XY} = \bigcirc_{y \in \Theta_Y} bel^X[y]^{\uparrow XY}$ is a joint belief function with a vacuous marginal over Y.

5.2   Directed Evidential Network Model

In the following, we relate belief functions with directed acyclic graphs and introduce the notion of directed evidential network with conditional belief functions (Ben Yaghlane and Mellouli, 2001). The directed evidential network (**DEVN**) model is represented by:

1. **A knowledge base** : we can distinguish two levels: qualitative and quantitative. At *the qualitative level*, we have a **directed acyclic graph** (DAG) in which the nodes represent variables and directed arcs describe the conditional dependence relations embedded in the model (i.e. the link between the variables). At *the quantitative level*, the dependence relations are expressed by **conditional belief functions** for each variable given its parents.
2. **Facts** representing the new observations introduced in the network and that will be represented by belief functions allocated to some nodes.

Directed evidential networks are similar to Bayesian networks but instead of using conditional probability functions, we use conditional belief functions. Notice that directed evidential networks (i.e. belief function models) have a greater expressive power than probabilistic ones (i.e. Bayesian networks); however they are more complex, and often have higher computational cost (Almond, 1995).

– Each variable X in the DEVN has a set of possible values, called *frame of discernment*, that consists of mutually exclusive and exhaustive values of the variable. Parents of X are denoted by Pa_X.

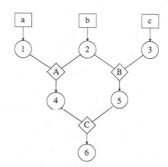

Fig. 2. A Bayesian network drawn as an evidential network

- For each root node X $(Pa_X = \emptyset)$, uncertainty is represented by an *a priori* belief function bel_0^X on X.
- For the other nodes (i.e. $Pa_X \neq \emptyset$), uncertainty is represented by a *conditional belief function* $bel^X[Pa_X]$ on X given the value taken by its parents.

Belief Chain Rule. Given all the a priori and conditional belief functions, the *joint distribution* relative to the set of variable $\{X_1, ..., X_N\}$ is computed using the following *belief chain rule*:

$$bel^{X_1 X_2 ... X_N} = \bigodot_{i=1,...,N}\left(\bigodot_{\omega \in Pa_{X_i}} bel^{X_i}[\omega]^{\uparrow X_i \times Pa_{X_i}}\right)$$

So, corresponding to each variable X_i, in the directed evidential network, we create a belief function $bel^{X_i}[Pa_{X_i}]$ over the frame $\Theta_{X_i \cup Pa_{X_i}}$.

5.3   Links with Bayesian Networks and Valuation Networks

In a Bayesian network, there is only one incoming conditional probability function attached to a node. So a Bayesian Network is an evidential network where we keep first the diamonds, but there is only one arrow that enters into a node (we don't have Dempster's rule of combination.). See Fig. 2 for an example.

Note that the evidential network of Fig. 3 cannot be represented as a Bayesian network, what reflect we lost Dempster's rule of combination.

We can change the meaning of the links and use the Bayesian approach, in which case we obtain Fig. 4. We can profit from the fact that we have conditional belief functions and quite a simplified evidential network.

6   Conclusion

There are two types of graphical models commonly in use: *undirected graphs* and *directed graphs*. Directed graphs are more appropriate for representing conditional relationships (Pearl, 1988), and in particular, conditional belief functions whereas Shafer-Shenoy (Shenoy and Shafer, 1990) used undirected graphs

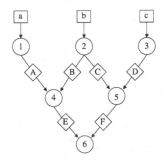

Fig. 3. An evidential network

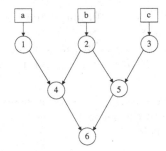

Fig. 4. Directed Evidential Network (DEVN)

as they work with joint belief functions. In many applications, conditional belief functions provide a more natural representations of the knowledge, and are easier to collect, hence the interest of the *directed evidential networks with conditional belief functions*.

Inference algorithms in knowledge-based systems with a directed evidential network (DEVN) obtain their efficiency by making use of the represented independencies in their network. This can be done by using two rules proposed by Smets and called *disjunctive rule of combination* (DRC) and *generalized Bayesian theorem* (GBT) which make possible the use of the conditional belief functions directly for reasoning in the directed evidential networks, avoiding the computations of joint belief function on the product space (Ben Yaghlane, 2002).

Acknowledgments. The authors are grateful to the anonymous reviewers for their helpful comments and suggestions.

References

Almond, R.G. (1995). *Graphical Belief Modeling*. Chapman & Hall.

Ben Yaghlane, B. (2002). *Uncertainty Representation and Reasoning in Directed Evidential Networks*. PhD thesis, University of Tunisia, Institut Supérieur de Gestion.

Ben Yaghlane, B. and Mellouli, K. (2001). Directed belief networks. In *Proceedings of International NAISO Congress on Information Science Innovations ISI'2001*, American University in Dubai, U.A.E.

Ben Yaghlane, B., Smets, P., and Mellouli, K. (2002). Belief function independence: II. the conditional case. *International Journal of Approximate Reasoning*, 31/1-2:31–75.

Cano, J., Delgado, M., and Moral, S. (1993). An axiomatic framework for propagating uncertainty in directed acyclic networks. *Int.J.Approximate Reasoning.*, 8:253–280.

Geiger, D., Verma, T., and Pearl, J. (1990). Identifying independence in Baycsian networks. *Networks*, 20:507–533.

Jensen, F. and Lauritzen, S. (2000). Probabilistic networks. In *Handbook of Defeasible Reasoning and Uncertainty Management Systems. Algorithms for Uncertainty and Defeasible Reasoning*, volume 5, pages 289–320. Kluwer Academic Publishers, Doordrecht, The Netherlands.

Pearl, J. (1988). *Probabilistic Reasoning in Intelligent Systems: Networks of Plausible Inference*. Morgan Kaufmann Pub. San Mateo, Ca, USA.

Pearl, J. and Paz, A. (1987). Graphoids: A graph based logic for reasoning about relevance relations. In B.D. Boulay et al., editor, *Advances in Artificial Intelligence 2*, pages 357–363. North-Holland, Amsterdam.

Shafer, G. (1976). *A Mathematical Theory of Evidence*. Princeton Univ. Press. Princeton, NJ.

Shafer, G. (1982). Belief functions and parametric models. *J. Roy. Statist. Soc. B.*, 44:322–352.

Shafer, G., Shenoy, P.P., and Mellouli, K. (1987). Propagating belief functions in qualitative markov trees. *Int. J. Approx. Reasoning*, 1:349–400.

Shenoy, P.P. (1993). Valuation networks and conditional independence. In Heckerman, D. and Mamdani, A., editors, *Uncertainty in Artificial Intelligence 93*, pages 191–199. Morgan Kaufmann, San Mateo, Ca, USA.

Shenoy, P.P. (1994a). Conditional independence in valuation-based systems. *Int. J. Approx. reasoning*, 10:203–234.

Shenoy, P.P. (1994b). Representing conditional independence relations in valuation networks. *Int. J. of Uncertainty, Fuzziness and Knowledge-Based Systems*, 2(2):143–165.

Shenoy, P.P. and Shafer, G. (1990). Axioms for probability and belief functions propagation. In Shachter, R.D., Levitt, T.S., Kanal, L.N., and Lemmer, J.F., editors, *Uncertainty in Artificial Intelligence 4*, pages 159–198. North Holland, Amsterdam.

Smets, P. (1978). *Un modèle mathématico-statistique simulant le processus du diagnostic médical*. PhD thesis, Université Libre de Bruxelles, (available through University Microfilm International, 30-32 Mortimer street, London W1N 7RA, thesis 80-70,003).

Smets, P. (1993). Belief functions: the disjunctive rule of combination and the generalized Bayesian theorem. *International Journal of Approximate Reasoning*, 9:1–35.

Xu, H. (1995). *Uncertainty reasoning and decision analysis using belief functions in the valuation-based systems*. PhD thesis, Université Libre de Bruxelles.

Xu, H. and Smets, P. (1994). Evidential reasoning with conditional belief functions. In Heckerman, D., Poole, D., and Lopez De Mantaras, R., editors, *Uncertainty in Artificial Intelligence 94*, pages 598–606. Morgan Kaufmann, San Mateo, Ca.

Computational-Workload Based Binarization and Partition of Qualitative Markov Trees for Belief Combination

Weiru Liu, Xin Hong, and Kenny Adamson

School of Computing and Mathematics, University of Ulster at Jordanstown, UK
w.liu@ulster.ac.uk

Abstract. Binary join trees have been a popular structure to compute the impact of multiple belief functions initially assigned to nodes of trees or networks. Shenoy has proposed two alternative methods to transform a qualitative Markov tree into a binary tree. In this paper, we present an alternative algorithm of transforming a qualitative Markov tree into a binary tree based on the computational workload in nodes for an exact implementation of evidence combination. A binary tree is then partitioned into clusters with each cluster being assigned to a processor in a parallel environment. These three types of binary trees are examined to reveal the structural and computational differences.

1 Introduction

Expensive computational cost of Dempster's rule in DS theory led to a stream of study on efficient implementations of the rule over the last two decades. The proposed approaches have emphasized either exact implementations of the rule (e.g., [1, 6, 10, 11, 13, 17], etc.) or its approximations (e.g., [2, 3, 4, 15, 16], etc.), under the assumption that evidence distributions follow certain structures.

Among all these approaches, the method on belief propagation in qualitative Markov trees has been popular. As proved in [11], with this method, the exponential computational complexity in the size of total variables is reduced to the size of the largest node in a tree, a node with the largest number of variables. The major technique supporting the method is *local computation* [14], which was initiated for propagating probabilities in Bayesian causal trees by Pearl [8]. Local computation refers to computation that involves only a small number of nodes in a large tree (or network). The basic idea of local computation is message passing among neighboring nodes in a qualitative Markov tree to compute marginals of the joint belief distribution without actually calculating the joint belief distribution. The sizes of nodes in a qualitative Markov tree determine how efficient the local computation can be. If a node has a large number of neighbors, even local computation can be very inefficient. To solve this problem, concept *binary join trees* (or simply *binary trees*) was proposed by Shenoy in [12], in which every non-leaf node performs *at most one combination*, and the corresponding algorithm was introduced. Using this algorithm, any qualitative Markov tree can be first transformed into a binary join tree on which local computation can be carried out. Subsequently, Shenoy improved this transformation

T.D. Nielsen and N.L. Zhang (Eds.): ECSQARU 2003, LNAI 2711, pp. 306–318, 2003.

algorithm in [13]. The improved algorithm constructs a binary tree based on a *one-step lookahead* technique which looks for an optimal order of variables being deleted. Given a qualitative Markov tree, these two algorithms construct rather different join trees, with the second tree bearing little resemblance to the original Markov tree. Furthermore, the *one-step lookahead* algorithm adds many more nodes in the transformation procedure than the first algorithm. These extra nodes will increase the computational costs in terms of calculating marginals for them.

In this paper, we propose a different method to transform a qualitative Markov tree into a binary tree, based on the amount of combinations at each sub-tree. A binary tree derived in this way is almost balanced in respect to the workload of combining evidence. We then partition a binary tree into a set of clusters with the intention that each cluster will be assigned to a processor in a parallel processing environment. The appearance of our binary tree is similar to the tree obtained from Shenoy's first approach, except that Shenoy's tree may have more added nodes because this tree permits only one combination in each node. However, our study on these two similar types of binary trees shows that Shenoy's tree requires less amount of computation than ours since it eliminates some duplicate combinations. Our study on Shenoy's second approach reveals that a binary tree obtained in this way (it permits one combination per node as well) is very complex and adds much extra computation due to a large number of added nodes, comparing to his first approach.

Other algorithms that binarizing a qualitative Markov tree into a binary tree include a straight-forward binarization procedure for approximate computation in Bayesian networks [2] and a computational workload based algorithm for executing a parallel program using multiple processors [7]. Our algorithm is similar to the procedure in [2] in respect to the structure of the tree, that is, each node has maximum two children. However, our algorithm is more comprehensive because it assesses the amount of computation at each sub-tree before merging two sub-trees together. As a result, our binary tree is a balanced one while a tree from [2] can be extremely unbalanced (see the example in Section 3). If there are many processors available to process some nodes (sub-trees) in parallel [5], a balanced tree provides a good structure to partition it into clusters so as to assign workloads to processors evenly. Our algorithm is also similar to the binarization procedure in [7] in the sense that the latter considers workloads on sub-trees as well when merging two sub-trees (units of a parallel program). The difference between them is that our algorithm needs to consider the amount of computation being carried out in added nodes (which may affect the total workload of a sub-tree with this added node as the root). While the algorithm in [7] does not involve computation in added nodes (only message passing).

The rest of the paper is organized as follows. Section 2 introduces the basics of DS theory and the terminology for belief propagation in qualitative Markov trees. Section 3 provides the algorithm that transforms a qualitative Markov tree into a binary join tree and partitions a binary tree into clusters for parallel processing. Section 4 reviews the two algorithms on binarization proposed by Shenoy, with examples. Section 5 provides a detailed analysis and comparison of our algorithm with that of Shenoy's and concludes the paper.

2 DS Theory and Qualitative Markov Trees

2.1 Basics of DS Theory

In the Dempster-Shafer theory of evidence (DS theory) [9], a piece of information is described as a *mass function* on a set of mutually exclusive and exhaustive elements, known as a *frame of discernment* (or simply a *frame*), denoted as Θ. A mass function $m: 2^\Theta \rightarrow [0,1]$, represents the distribution of a unit of belief over a frame, Θ, satisfying the following two conditions: $m(\Phi) = 0$ and $\Sigma_{A \subseteq \Theta} m(A)=1$. A *belief function* over Θ is a function $Bel: 2^\Theta \rightarrow [0,1]$, satisfying $Bel(A)= \Sigma_{B \subseteq A} m(B)$. When several belief functions are obtained through distinct sources based on the same frame of discernment, a new belief function representing the consensus of them can be produced. Assume that Bel_1 and Bel_2 are two such obtained belief functions on the same frame Θ, the combined impact of them is calculated using the *Dempster's rule of combination*, $Bel = Bel_1 \oplus Bel_2$. The computational complexity of combining two belief functions over a frame is exponential to the size of the initial frame.

2.2 Qualitative Markov Trees

Qualitative Markov Trees: We use graph-oriented terminology and notation for qualitative Markov trees here. Let a pair $\{V, E\}$ be a graph, with V a finite set of nodes (or variables) and E a set of unordered pairs of distinct nodes in V. A qualitative Markov tree is a graph which has no cycles, and any variable in two nodes should be in any node in the path linking them. Elements in V are denoted using capital letters, such as A, B, S, and subsets of V are denoted with lower cases, such as, x, y, z. A qualitative Markov tree can either be derived from a Bayesian network [2, 13] or from a diagnostic tree [11, 14] as shown in Fig. 1a and Fig. 1b respectively.

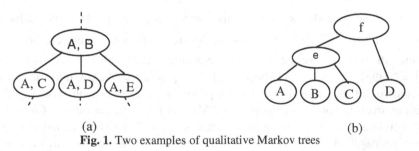

(a)   (b)

Fig. 1. Two examples of qualitative Markov trees

When a qualitative Markov tree is constructed from a diagnostic tree, the collection of all leaf nodes defines the overall frame of discernment represented by the root. Any non-leaf node, such as e, contains all the leaf nodes in the sub-tree with this node as the root. The corresponding frame for belief combination is $\{e, \neg e\}=\{A, B, C, \neg e\}$. While the frame for a node in Fig. 1a is the Cartesian product of its variable frames. In the rest of the paper, we use a qualitative Markov tree in the form of Fig. 1b. Our algorithm and discussions are equally applicable to a tree in the form of Fig. 1a.

Variables and Configurations: Let x be a node in a qualitative Markov tree representing a set of *variables* and Θ_x be the frame corresponding to x. Elements of Θ_x are referred to as *configurations* of x, denoted by bold-faced lower cases, such as, *g, f, h*.

Projection and Extension: Let g and h be two sets of variables, $h \subseteq g$, and *g* is a configuration of g. The *projection* of *g* to Θ_h, denoted by $g^{\downarrow h}$ is a configuration of h. Let G be a non-empty subset of Θ_g, the projection of G to h, denoted by $G^{\downarrow h}$, is obtained by $G^{\downarrow h} = \{g^{\downarrow h} \mid g \in G\}$. If g and h are two sets of variables, $h \subset g$, and H is a subset of Θ_h, then the *extension* of H to g, denoted by $H^{\uparrow g}$, is $H \times \Theta_{g-h}$.

Marginalization: If m is a mass function on g, and $h \subseteq g$, $h \neq \Phi$, the marginal of m on h, denoted by $m^{\downarrow h}$, is a mass function on h defined by

$$m^{\downarrow h}(H) = \sum_{H \subseteq \Theta_h} \{m(G) \mid G \subseteq \Theta_g, G^{\downarrow h} = H\}.$$

On the other hand, if m is a mass function on h, and $h \subseteq g$, $h \neq \Phi$, the marginal of m on g, denoted by $m^{\uparrow g}$, is a mass function on g defined by

$$m^{\uparrow g}(G) = \sum_{G \subseteq \Theta_g} \{m(H) \mid H \subseteq \Theta_h, H^{\uparrow g} = G\}.$$

Belief Propagation: Let $\{V, E\}$ be a qualitative Markov tree on which a set of belief functions are assigned to its nodes. Given a node x, $V_x = \{i \mid (i,x) \in E\}$ denotes the set of neighbours of x, a set of nodes that are directly linked with x. Bel_x represents the initial belief function assigned to node x. To propagate initial belief functions to obtain the final marginal on a designated node (containing a set of variables), the propagation scheme starts with the leaves of a qualitative Markov tree and moves step by step towards the targeted node. Each time a node x sends a message $M^{x \to i}$, referring to the belief function sent by x to i, to each of its neighbors,

$$M^{x \to i} = ((Bel_x \oplus (\oplus \{M^{k \to x} \mid k \in (V_x - \{i\})\}))^{\downarrow(x \cap i)})^{\uparrow i}. \tag{1}$$

For a leaf node x with only one neighbor i, $M^{x \to i}$ is reduced to $M^{x \to i} = ((Bel_x)^{\downarrow(x \cap i)})^{\uparrow i}$. After the designated node y has received the messages from all of its neighbors, the marginal $Bel^{\downarrow y}$ for y is obtained as $Bel^{\downarrow y} = Bel_y \oplus (\oplus \{M^{i \to y} \mid i \in V_y\})$. As stated in [13], a qualitative Markov tree can always be re-constructed as a rooted one. In this paper, we concentrate on rooted qualitative Markov trees. Let node r be the root of a Markov tree, x be a node. Let $Ch_x = \{k \mid k \in V_x, k \text{ is a child node of } x\}$ be the set of children of x, and $P_x = \{p\}$ be the parent of x. The belief propagation scheme can be carried out in two phases to calculate the combined beliefs on any node [11]:

Phase I. Propagate Messages up the Tree: starting at leaf nodes, messages are sent up step by step. $M^{x \to p} = ((Bel_x \oplus (\oplus \{M^{k \to x} \mid k \in Ch_x\}))^{\downarrow(x \cap p)})^{\uparrow p}$.

The maximum number of belief functions accumulated in a non-leaf, non-root node in this phase is $1 + |Ch_x|$, if this node has an initial belief function and every of its child node sends a message to it. Therefore the number of combinations is $(1 + |Ch_x|)$ -1, *i.e.* $|Ch_x|$. For a leaf node, no combinations are involved. For the root node, there are maximum $1 + |Ch_r|$ belief functions accumulated. Since the root will not send any messages up, Phase I stops here. After computing the marginal of the root, messages are then sent back down the tree. Therefore, we will count the total number of combinations in the root in the next phase.

Phase II. Propagate Messages down the Tree: starting at the root node, messages are sent back down step by step.

$$M^{x \to k} = ((Bel_x \oplus M^{p \to x} \oplus (\oplus\{M^{j \to x} \mid j \in Ch_x, j \neq k\}))^{\downarrow(x \cap k)})^{\uparrow k}. \qquad (2)$$

For a non-root, non-leaf node x, the maximum number of belief functions accumulated for propagating down to its child node k is $1 + |P_x| + (|Ch_x|-1)$, so the number of combinations is $|Ch_x|$ (with $|P_x|=1$), if we have stored every $M^{i \to x}$ in Phase I. The maximum total number of combinations in x is $|Ch_x| \times |Ch_x|$. Its final marginal is

$$Bel^{\downarrow x} = Bel_x \oplus M^{p \to x} \oplus (\oplus\{M^{i \to x} \mid i \in Ch_x\}). \qquad (3)$$

If the marginal of the joint for x from Equation (2) is reserved before it is projected to node k, then it can be incorporated into Equation (3) to replace all the messages except $M^{k \to x}$. Equation (3) can be rewritten as $Bel^{\downarrow x} = (M^{x \to k})^{\uparrow x} \oplus M^{k \to x}$. Therefore, there is only one extra combination to obtain the final marginal for a node.

Because a root has maximum $1 + |Ch_r|$ belief functions, the maximum number of combinations for propagating a message down a branch is $|Ch_r|-1$ (the message from a branch to which the message is being sent will not be combined with the rest). The maximum total number of combinations is $(|Ch_r|-1) \times |Ch_r|$. The root needs one combination for its final marginal. A leaf node also needs one combination for its final marginal. The total number of combinations in a qualitative Markov tree is the sum of numbers of combinations of all the nodes.

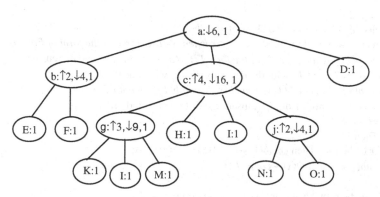

Fig. 2. A rooted qualitative Markov tree with maximum number of combinations in each node when an initial belief function is assigned to each node and a final marginal is required for every node

$(x: \uparrow t_1, \downarrow t_2, 1)$ indicates that in node x, there are t_1 combinations when x sends a message to its parent, there are t_2 combinations when it sends messages to all of its children, and there is one extra combination to obtain the final marginal for x. When t_1 or t_2 is zero, we have omitted it from the above graph.

3 A Weight-Based Binarization Algorithm

When binarizing a qualitative Markov tree, for each non-leaf node x with more than two children, we repeatedly merge two of its children to get a new one with these two children carrying the least amount of computation, until x has only two children left. Such a binary tree should have almost balanced workloads among its branches.

Although a new affiliated node is added whenever two branches are merged, these newly created nodes will only calculate and store some intermediate results of combinations and no computation is required to calculate their own marginals. In the algorithm below, $comb(x)$ represents the total number of combinations in node x, and $comb(T_x)$ is the total number of combinations in sub-tree T_x with x as the root.

Algorithm: Binarization of a Qualitative Markov Tree (BQMT)
Input: a qualitative Markov tree with a designated root r.
$x \leftarrow r$.
Procedure Binarization (x):
1. If x is a leaf node and $x = r$ Then $comb(x) \leftarrow 0$, $comb(T_x) \leftarrow 0$. Terminate the Procedure. (The tree has only one level, the root is also a leaf.)
2. If x is a leaf node and $x \neq r$ Then $comb(x) \leftarrow 1$, $comb(T_x) \leftarrow 1$. Terminate the Procedure. (The tree has more than one level.)
3. For each child node $c_i \in Ch_x$ do **Binarization** (c_i).
4. Sort Ch_x in ascending order, where $Ch_x = \{c_1, ..., c_k\}$ satisfying
   $comb(T_{ci}) \leq comb(T_{cj})$ if c_j is after c_i in the ordered set Ch_x.
5. $l \leftarrow 1$.
6. While $|Ch_x| > 2$ do
   6.1 Select c_1, c_2, the first two elements in Ch_x;
   6.2 Create a new node x_l ($x_l = (c_1 \cup c_2) \cap x$ when we use a tree in the form of Fig. 1a;
       $x_l = (c_1 \cup c_2)$ when a tree is of the form Fig. 1b) to connect c_1 and c_2, replace
       sub-trees T_{c1} and T_{c2} with the new sub-tree T_{xl} with x_l as the root;
   6.3. $comb(x_l) \leftarrow 3$, $comb(T_{xl}) \leftarrow comb(x_l) + comb(T_{c1}) + comb(T_{c2})$;
   6.4. Remove c_1 and c_2 from Ch_x, insert x_l into Ch_x in sorted order;
   6.5. $l = l + 1$.
7. If $|Ch_x| = 1$ Then
   7.1 If x is the root Then $comb(x) \leftarrow 1$ Else $comb(x) \leftarrow 3$;
   7.2 $comb(T_x) \leftarrow comb(x) + comb(T_{c1})$.
   Else
   7.3 If x is the root Then $comb(x) \leftarrow 3$ Else $comb(x) \leftarrow 7$;
   7.4 $comb(T_x) \leftarrow comb(x) + comb(T_{c1}) + comb(T_{c2})$.
Return (T_r): A binary tree with the same root

For each newly added node, the maximum number of belief functions accumulated in it is $|Ch_{xl}|$ (it has no initial belief function) instead of $1 + |Ch_{xl}|$, so, the maximum number of combinations is $(\uparrow 1, \downarrow 2, 0) = 3$. Applying this algorithm to the tree in Fig. 2, we get a balanced binarised tree as in Fig. 3 where bold-faced nodes are added nodes.

However, if we do not merge the two branches with the lightest workloads each time during the binarization procedure, we could end up with a tree that is totally unbalanced. For example, an alternative binary tree from the qualitative Markov tree in Fig. 2 can be in the form as shown in Fig. 4. This unbalanced tree will make the parallel processing much less efficient if we were to use multiple processors to process each part simultaneously [5]. Given a multiple processor environment, it is in general not possible to assign each node to a processor, due to the fact that either there are less processors available than the total number of nodes or the communication cost between processors are too expensive comparing to the calculation.

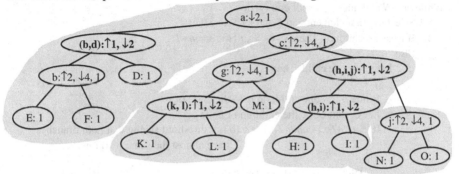

Fig. 3. A binary tree constructed from a qualitative Markov tree in Fig. 2

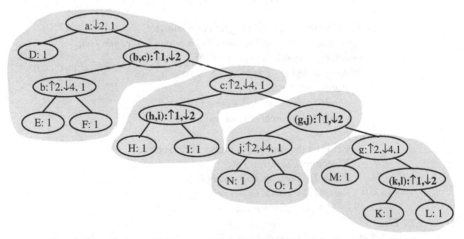

Fig. 4. An unbalanced binary tree from the qualitative Markow tree in Fig. 2

Below is a clustering algorithm that partitions a binary tree into clusters and assigns each cluster to a processor. In [5], we have been testing the algorithm in a four-processor environment where a tree in Fig. 3 is partitioned into four clusters as illustrated with shade. These four processors perform combinations simultaneously starting from leaves. Each sends its results to the processor that contains its parent for further combination before it calculates final marginals for its nodes. This algorithm also partitions the tree in Fig. 4 into four clusters as shown. However, the processor that contains node (b,c) has to wait for the result of other three processors which deal with clusters from its right branch before it can go further. Therefore, the intended parallel process is reduced to almost a linear one, in addition to the extra cost of communication between processors.

Algorithm: Clustering a Binary Tree

Input: r – the binary tree with the root r, N – the number of processors provided

1. Create two empty queues S and S_t (S is the working queue, S_t is the temporary queue);
2. $S \leftarrow \{r\}$, counter $m \leftarrow 1$;
3. While $m < N$ and queue S is not empty, do

    3.1 Select the first element v in S and let $S \leftarrow S/\{v\}$;

    3.2 If v has no children, Then $S_t \leftarrow S_t \cup \{v\}$; $m = m + 1$;

        Else

            3.2.1 If v has one child, Then

                $p \leftarrow v$

                While p has one child, do $p \leftarrow$ the child of p

                Let C_L and C_R be the children of node p;

                If $|comb(Tc_L) - comb(Tc_R)| < \delta$ (δ is a threshold saying that both branches

                                    have almost the same workload)

            Then

                Disconnect Tc_R from Tp;

                $comb(Tp) = comb(Tp) - comb(Tc_R)$, $comb(Tv) = comb(Tv) - comb(Tc_R)$;

                $S \leftarrow S \cup \{v, C_R\}$, $m = m + 1$;

            Else

                Let w be the root of p's bigger child subtree;

                Disconnect Tw from Tp, $comb(Tv) = comb(Tv) - comb(Tw)$;

                $comb(Tp) = comb(Tp) - comb(Tw)$;

                While $|comb(Tv) - comb(Tw)| > \delta$, do

                    Reconnect Tw to Tp;

                    $comb(Tp) = comb(Tp) + comb(Tw)$;

                    $comb(Tv) = comb(Tv) + comb(Tw)$;

                    $p \leftarrow w$;

                    Let w be the root of p's bigger child subtree;

                    Disconnect Tw from Tp;

                    $comb(Tp) = comb(Tp) - comb(Tw)$;

                    $comb(Tv) = comb(Tv) - comb(Tw)$;

                $S \leftarrow S \cup \{v, w\}$, $m = m + 1$;

        3.2.2 Else

            Let C_L and C_R be the children of node v;

            If $|comb(Tc_L) - comb(Tc_R)| < \delta$, Then

                Disconnect Tc_R from Tv;

                $comb(Tv) = comb(Tv) - comb(Tc_R)$;

                $S \leftarrow S \cup \{v, C_R\}$, $m = m + 1$;

            Else

                Let w be the root of v's bigger child subtree;

                Disconnect Tw from Tv, $comb(Tv) = comb(Tv) - comb(Tw)$;

                While $|comb(Tv) - comb(Tw)| > \delta$, do

If v was w's parent node, Then
  Reconnect Tw to Tv, $comb(Tv) = comb(Tv) + comb(Tw)$;
Else
  $p \leftarrow w$'s parent node, reconnect Tw to Tp;
  $comb(Tp) = comb(Tp) + comb(Tw)$;
  $comb(Tv) = comb(Tv) + comb(Tw)$;
  $p \leftarrow w$;
  Let w be the root of p's bigger child subtree;
  Disconnect Tw from Tp;
  $comb(Tp)=comb(Tp)-comb(Tw)$, $comb(Tv)=comb(Tv)-comb(Tw)$;
  $S \leftarrow S \cup \{v, w\}$, $m=m+1$;

4. $S \leftarrow S \cup S_i$;
5. Each element of S leads a cluster; assign each cluster to a processor.

---

4   Shenoy's Binary Trees

Shenoy described an approach to constructing a binary join tree in [12] where each node accumulates at most two pieces of evidence. This approach was further developed based on a one-step lookahead heuristic search to construct binary trees [13].

Approach in [12]: For a given qualitative Markov tree (that could be derived from a valuation network), a designated node is chosen as the root. Starting from the root, the total number of belief functions that are to be combined in the root is counted, in order to obtain the marginal for the root. If the root has n children, each sending it a belief function, in addition to its own, there will be $(n+1)-1=n$ combinations. When $n>2$, multiple replicates ($n-1$ replicates) of the root are created. These multiple copies and the children of the root are re-organized so that there is only *one combination* in each replicate node and in the root. For each tree in the forest obtained by ignoring the root and all its multiple copies (and the links from them), repeat the above procedure until every node has only one combination. It should be pointed out that this *one combination* in a node only contributes to the final marginal of the joint for the root. That is, this *one* combination happens in Phase I in Sect. 2. If the marginals for some non-root nodes are required, there will be *at least another (and at most two)* combination in such a node when messages are propagated down the tree, depending on whether the node has one child or two. The total number of combinations in each node is shown in Fig. 5, if we assume that a marginal for every node is of interest.

One-Step Lookahead Heuristic Approach in [13]: Given a qualitative Markov tree, to compute the marginal for a node, alternative sequences of combinations of belief functions with different amount of computation, can be carried out. The heuristics in the one-step lookahead approach schedules combinations by sequencing deletion of variables from a qualitative Markov tree. The variable to be deleted next is the one that leads to a combination over the smallest set of configurations [13]. Starting from the nodes containing variables that should be deleted first, this method constructs a binary tree with these nodes as initial leaves, and build the binary tree as more variables to be deleted. Let Ω be the set containing all the nodes in a Markov tree (network), we summarize Shenoy's algorithm as follows.

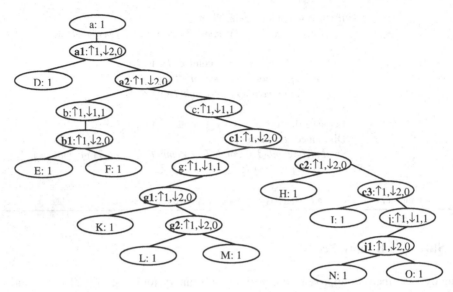

Fig. 5. A binary join tree created using Shenoy's first method based on the original Markov tree in Fig. 2. Bold-faced nodes are added ones. The multiple replicates of a node are numbered following the name of the original node

Step 1. Selecting the variable(s) that should be deleted first, a subset Φ of Ω is formed with each element in Φ containing this (or these) variable(s). Let $\Omega=\Omega\backslash\Phi$.

Step 2. A pair of elements in Φ is chosen with the union set of the pair containing the minimum number of variables among all possible unions of pairs in set Φ. The elements in the pair are two leaves and removed from Φ. The union set of the pair is created and inserted into Φ. This new node acts as the parent of the two leaves.

Step 3. The above step is repeated until Φ has only one node, m, left. Create a new node, n, containing the remaining variables after deleting the chosen variable(s) from m and let n be its parent. Let $\Omega=\Omega\cup\{n\}$.

Step 4. Repeating Steps 1 to 3 for the next chosen variable(s) that should be deleted, until Ω has one element left which will be the root of the created binary tree.

When using Shenoy's second approach to transforming the qualitative Markov tree in Fig. 2, we assume that each leaf node contains one variable, such as $e=\{E\}$, and every non-leaf node contains the collection of variables in the leaves below it, such as $b=\{E,F\}$. Based on the deleting sequence $\{E\}, \{F\}, \{K\}, \{L\}, \{M\}, \{H\}, \{I\}, \{N\}, \{O\}$, and with $\{D\}$ as the final remaining variable, the binary tree is built as shown in Fig. 6. All the leaf nodes are the initial subsets of variables with original belief functions. All the other nodes are inserted later in order to either merge two subsets or to delete a variable(s) from a merged node, with latter being denoted with bold-faced font. If the final marginal is required for every original subset, the total number of combinations in each node is shown in Fig. 6. In summary, the total numbers of combinations in the original Markov tree (Fig. 2), in the binary tree in Fig. 3, and in the binary trees in Fig. 5 and Fig. 6 are 64, 53, 50 and 55 respectively.

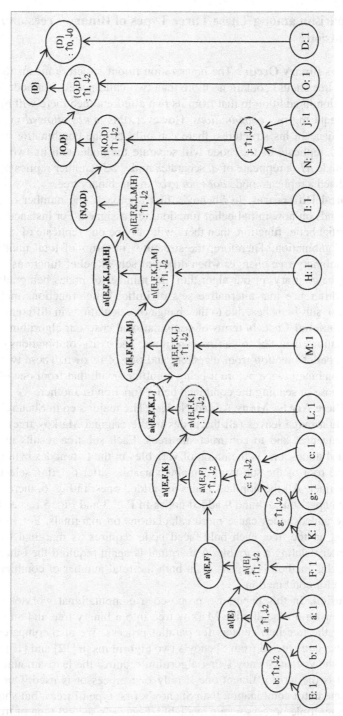

Fig. 6. A binary tree created from Shenoy's second approach based on Fig. 2

5 Comparison among These Three Types of Binary Trees and Conclusion

Where Does Binary Occur? The binarization in our structure means that each node in the final tree should contain no more than two child nodes. If a node has its initial belief function in addition to that from its two children, then there will be three belief functions requiring *two combinations*. However, this is *not allowed* in Shenoy's approaches. Since in his structures, there can only be one combination in each node. Therefore, a replicate of this node will separate the node with its two children. For example, node *a1,* a replicate of *a,* separates nodes *a2* (another replicate of *a*) and *D,* in Fig. 5. Such a replicate node *does not exist* in our binary tree.

Structural Differences. In Shenoy's first approach, the number of nodes being added depends on how initial belief functions are assigned. For instance, if *a* does not have its initial belief function, then there will only be one replicate of *a,* since there is only one combination. Therefore, the structure (in terms of total number of added nodes) of a binary tree changes when different sets of belief functions are given initially. On the contrary, in our algorithm, the number of nodes being added is fixed. The only difference that alternative sets of initial belief functions make is the arrangement of sub-branches, due to the change of calculations in different branches.

Computational Cost. In terms of computational cost, our algorithm has some extra combinations than Shenoy's first algorithm. The extra combinations occur when a node has a belief function from its parent and one of its own. These two belief functions are combined twice before it being combined with that from one of its children for the purpose of sending the combined belief function to another.

Why There Are So Many Added Nodes? The major step in Shenoy's second approach is to arrange leaves (all the nodes in the original Markov tree) based on the deletion sequence, and to construct sub-trees. Each sub-tree results in at least two newly added nodes, one is the union of variables in the two nodes being merged and another (the root of the sub-tree) contains variables after deleting selected variables from the former. All the non-leaf nodes are added ones. In Fig. 6, there are 23 added nodes in comparison to 4 and 9 added nodes in Fig. 3 and Fig. 5 respectively. Moreover, these added nodes cause more calculations on marginals. For example, when propagating up the tree, each bold-faced node requires its marginal from the node below it after deleting a variable. A marginal is again required the other way round. Therefore, this method is expensive in both the total number of combinations and in preparation for combinations.

Conclusion. In this paper, we proposed a computational workload-based algorithm to transform a qualitative Markov tree into a binary tree and an algorithm for partitioning the tree into clusters for parallel process. We also compared our binary tree with that constructed from Shenoy's two algorithms in [12] and [13] respectively. The study shows that Shenoy's first algorithm requires the least amount of combination and it is the most efficient one if only one processor is used. Our binary trees require some extra combination than Shenoy's first type of trees, but should perform well when multiple processors are available. Shenoy's second type of trees is expensive both in a single or a multiple processor environment due to large number of added nodes and additional calculations on marginals for added nodes.

References

1. Barnett, J.A.: Computational methods for a mathematical theory of evidence. *Proc. of IJCAI'81*, Vancouver, BC, 868–875
2. Cano, A., Moral, S., and Salmeron, A.: Penniless propagation in join trees. *International Journal of Intelligent Systems*, Vol. 15, 2000, 1027–1059
3. Dubois, D. and Prade, H.: Inference in possibilistic hypergraphs. *Proc. of IPMU'90*, 228–30
4. Gordon, J. and Shortliffe, E.H.: A method for managing evidential reasoning in a hierarchical hypothesis space. *Artificial Intelligence*, Vol. 26, 1985, 323–357
5. Liu, W., Hong, X., and Adamson, K.: Parallel implementation of evidence combination in qualitative Markov tress. Technical Report, University of Ulster
6. Madsen, A. and Jensen, F.: LAZY propagation: A junction tree inference algorithm based on lazy propagation. *Artificial Intelligence*, Vol. 113, 1999, 203–245
7. Maheshwari, P. and Shen, H.: An efficient clustering algorithm for partitioning parallel programs. *Parallel Computing*, Vol. 24, 1998, 893–909
8. Pearl J.: *Probabilistic reasoning in intelligent systems: networks of plausible inference.* Morgan Kaufmann, San Mateo, 1988
9. Shafer, G.: *A mathematical theory of evidence.* Princeton University Press, 1976
10. Shafer, G. and Logan, R.: Implementing Dempster's rule for hierarchical evidence. *Artificial Intelligence*, Vol. 33, 1987, 271–298
11. Shafer, G., Shenoy, P. and Mellouli, K.: Propagating belief functions in qualitative Markov trees. *Int. J. of Approx. Reasoning.* Vol. 1, 1987, 349–400
12. Shenoy, P.: Binary join trees. *Proc. of UAI'96*, 492–499
13. Shenoy, P.: Binary join trees for computing marginals in the Shenoy-Shafer architecture. *Int. J. of Approx. Reasoning*, Vol. 17, 1997, 239–263
14. Shenoy, P. and Shafer, G.: Propagating belief functions with local computations. *IEEE Expert*, Vol. 1, 1986, 43–52
15. Tessem, B.: Approximations for efficient computation in the theory of evidence. *Artificial Intelligence*, Vol. 61, 1993, 315–329
16. Voorbraak, F.: A computationally efficient approximation of Dempster-Shafer theory. *International Journal of Man-Machine Studies*, Vol. 30, 1989, 525–536
17. Wilson, N.: A Monte-Carlo algorithm for Dempster-Shafer belief. *Proc. of UAI'91*, 414

Risk Assessment in Drinking Water Production Using Belief Functions

Sabrina Démotier[1,2], Thierry Denœux[2], and Walter Schön[2]

[1] Ondeo Services, Information Technology Division
38, rue du Président Wilson
78230 Le Pecq, France
sabrina.demotier@ondeo.com
[2] Université de Technologie de Compiègne, UMR CNRS 6599 Heudiasyc
BP 20529, 60205 Compiègne, France
{tdenoeux,wschon}@hds.utc.fr

Abstract. This paper presents an original method for risk assessment in water treatment, based on belief functions. The risk of producing non-compliant drinking water (i.e., such that one of the quality parameter exceeds the regulation standards), is estimated taking into account the quality parameters of raw water and the process line of the treatment plant (technology, different failure modes and corresponding failure rates). Uncertainty on available data (treatment steps efficiency, failure rates, times to repair and raw water quality) is modeled using belief functions that are combined to compute a degree of confidence that the produced water will meet quality standards. The methodology recovers the classical results (obtained by fault tree analysis) as a limit case when uncertainties on input data are modeled by probabilities, and still provides informative results when only weaker forms of knowledge are available.

1 Problem Description

The production and distribution of good quality water to consumers is a fundamental issue, given the medical and financial consequences that could result from the delivery of insufficient quality water. It is therefore necessary to set up a treatment process adapted to the raw water to be treated, and to estimate the residual risk of producing water that does not comply with the regulation (in most cases the problem is detected by real time monitoring and the production is stopped, but this induces heavy financial penalties).

In the classical approach, this risk assessment process is performed by determining the probability of the undesirable event "production of non-compliant water", taking into account the quality of the resource to be treated (i.e., the estimated probability to find a given concentration of an undesirable component), characteristics of the treatment unit (efficiency of the treatment steps), as well as different failure modes that can occur in the process line (failure rates and repair times of each mode). Such a process was developed and described in detail in previous papers [5,1].

T.D. Nielsen and N.L. Zhang (Eds.): ECSQARU 2003, LNAI 2711, pp. 319–331, 2003.

One major difficulty in applying risk assessment methods in the environmental engineering domain is that basic data are not perfectly known and are often determined by expert judgement with a high level of uncertainty. In this paper, it is proposed to model the uncertainty on raw water quality, process line efficiency and state of the treatment plant (nominal or failure mode) in the belief function framework. Each source of information will be modeled by a belief function and combined to obtain an assessment of the plausibility to produce non compliant water.

In the limit case where the basic belief functions are probabilities, the proposed methodology recovers the results obtained by the classical approach: in that case, the belief function obtained for the variable representing the non compliance of produced water is also a probability measure. In the general case, however, the belief function obtained is no more a probability and it is possible to compute the belief, the plausibility and the pignistic probability to produce non compliant water. These results can be used to estimate a level of confidence to meet contractual requirements with a given treatment plant technology, and therefore to help treatment plant designers to choose the optimal architecture, given an objective level of residual risk.

The rest of the paper is organized as follows. The classical methodology is first recalled in Sect. 2. Our approach is then described in Sect. 3, and compared to the classical approach in Sect. 4. Simulations are presented in Sect. 5, and Sect. 6 concludes the paper.

2   Classical Approach

The following is just a brief reminder of the major concepts described in [5,1]. The current regulation on potable water takes into account 62 quality parameters of various types (turbidity, colour, concentration of mineral or organic components, physicochemical properties...). To meet these requirements, the treatment process must be adapted, on the one hand, to the general quality of water, and on the other hand to exceptional pollution peaks. To take into account this resource variability, a treatment plant is composed of the succession of various treatment processes (preoxydation, clarification, polishing, disinfection...).

For each quality parameter, the efficiency of each treatment step is represented by a transfer function, giving the output concentration C_{out} as a function of the input concentration C_{in} for the considered parameter. In most cases, this transfer function is linear and can be expressed using a single parameter α, called the abatement rate or reduction factor: $C_{out} = (1 - \alpha)C_{in}$. It is also possible to account for nonlinear transfer functions by defining different abatement rates according to the input concentration, but we will not consider that case in this paper.

By combining these local transfer functions (established for each treatment step), it is possible to define a global transfer function, which represents the global efficiency of the treatment line for a given parameter. This global transfer function must be determined for the nominal mode of the treatment plant

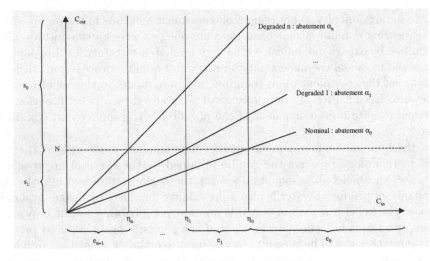

Fig. 1. Transfer function (output concentration of an undesirable water characteristics, as a function of the input concentration) in nominal mode and for n degraded mode of the treatment plant. In this linear approximation, the transfer function for mode i only depends on an abatement rate α_i, such as $C_{out} = (1 - \alpha_i)C_{in}$

(abatement rate α_0) and also for all possible failure modes. The "Failure Modes Effects and Criticality Analysis" (FMECA) methodology allows to determine, for each of the n possible failure modes, the corresponding degraded abatement rate α_i, the failure rate λ_i and the repair time T_i. The probability to be in failure mode i is then

$$p_i = \lambda_i T_i, \tag{1}$$

and the probability of being in the nominal state is given by

$$p_0 = 1 - \sum_{i=1}^{n} p_i. \tag{2}$$

Based on previously defined transfer functions, it is possible to define acceptable water quality thresholds for raw water in each operating mode (nominal and degraded) of the treatment plant, by inverting all global transfer functions and by applying these inverse functions to the normalized threshold N imposed for produced water. This step is illustrated in Fig. 1: $n + 1$ thresholds concerning raw water are obtained as: $\eta_i = N/(1 - \alpha_i)$, $(0 \leq i \leq n)$, and $n + 2$ possible raw water states are defined as: $e_i = [\eta_i, \eta_{i-1}]$, $(0 \leq i \leq n + 1)$, with $\eta_{n+1} = 0$ and $\eta_{-1} = \infty$. Two possible states for the produced water are also defined: s_0 (corresponding to non compliance with the norm: $C_{out} > N$) and s_1 ($C_{out} \leq N$). The last step of classical methodology is performed via Fault Tree Analysis (FTA), as illustrated in Fig. 2. For the considered parameter, the top level event of the fault tree is "Produced water in state s_0 (non compliant with norm N)".

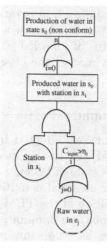

Fig. 2. Fault tree analysis of event "Production of water in state s_0" (non conform to the norm)

The first level of the fault tree is a decomposition between the different possible modes (nominal and failure modes) of the treatment plant by the top level OR gate. The plant being in a given mode i will not accept input concentrations exceeding η_i for the considered parameter: second level AND gate. The raw water states whose concentration is more than η_i are states $e_j (0 \leq j \leq i)$: third level OR gate. The minimal cutset is easily obtained and the probability of non compliance (unavailability concerning the considered parameter) is given by:

$$p(s_0) = \sum_{i=0}^{n} \sum_{j=0}^{i} p_i q_j , \qquad (3)$$

where q_j is the probability that the raw water is in state e_j. The global unavailability is simply obtained by adding the contribution of each quality parameter.

3   Belief Function Approach

3.1   Rationale

The classical solution described above assumes the availability of precise and complete prior knowledge of transfer functions, failure rates and repair times, as well as enough historical data to estimate the distribution of water quality parameters. However, such knowledge and data are usually not available, in particular in the case of call for bids, where a proposal must be submitted based on partial information. Moreover, transfer functions, repair time and failure rates can only be obtained by tests laboratories, expert knowledge or feedback from operational sites, which generally does not allow to obtain reliable estimates for a specific site. That is why an approach integrating these various uncertainties was developed. The belief function framework was chosen because of its flexibility for representing weak forms of knowledge [7], and because it generalizes Probability Theory, allowing to recover the classical results when all required data are available.

3.2   Notations and Background

The interpretation of belief functions adopted in this paper is that of Smets' Transferable Belief Model (TBM) [9]. In this model, a belief function is understood as representing an agent's state of belief, without resorting to an underlying probability model. Only the essential definitions and specific notations will be given here. A detailed exposition of the TBM may be found in [9].

A basic belief assignment (bba) on domain (or frame of discernment) X is noted m^X (for convenience, we use the same notation X for a variable and its domain). It is defined as a function from the powerset 2^X of X to $[0,1]$ verifying $\sum_{A \subseteq X} m^X(A) = 1$. The corresponding belief and plausibility functions are defined, respectively, as:

$$bel^X(A) = \sum_{\emptyset \neq B \subseteq A} m^X(B), \tag{4}$$

$$pl^X(A) = \sum_{B \cap A \neq \emptyset} m^X(B). \tag{5}$$

Given a bba $m^{X \times Y}$ defined on the Cartesian product of two domains X and Y, the marginal bba $m^{X \times Y \downarrow X}$ on X is defined, for all $A \subseteq X$, as

$$m^{X \times Y \downarrow X}(A) = \sum_{\{B \subseteq X \times Y \mid \mathrm{Proj}(B \downarrow X) = A\}} m^{X \times Y}(B) , \tag{6}$$

where $\mathrm{Proj}(B \downarrow X)$ denotes the projection of B onto X, defined as

$$\mathrm{Proj}(B \downarrow X) = \{x \in X \mid \exists y \in Y, (x,y) \in B\} . \tag{7}$$

Conversely, let m^X be a bba on X. Its *vacuous extension* on $X \times Y$ is defined as:

$$m^{X \uparrow X \times Y}(B) = \begin{cases} m^X(A) & \text{if } B = A \times Y \text{ for some } A \subseteq X, \\ 0 & \text{otherwise.} \end{cases} \tag{8}$$

Another useful notion is that of *ballooning extension* [8]. Let $m^X[y]$ denote the conditional bba on X, given that $Y = y$. The ballooning extension of $m^X[y]$ on $X \times Y$ is the least committed bba, whose conditioning on y yields $m^X[y]$ (see [8] for detailed justification). It is obtained for all $B \subseteq X \times Y$ as:

$$m^X[y]^{\uparrow X \times Y}(B) = \begin{cases} m^X[y](A) & \text{if } B = (A \times \{y\}) \cup (X \times (Y \setminus \{y\})) \text{ for some } A \subseteq X, \\ 0 & \text{otherwise.} \end{cases} \tag{9}$$

Let us now consider two bba's m_1^X and m_2^X induced by two distinct sources of information. If both sources are known to be reliable, they can be combined using the (unnormalized) Dempster's rule of combination, leading to a new bba $m_{1 \cap 2}^X = m_1^X \cap m_2^X$, defined as:

$$m_{1 \cap 2}^X(A) = \sum_{B \cap C = A} m_1^X(B) m_2^X(C). \tag{10}$$

Finally, the TBM is based on a two level mental modals: the *credal level* where beliefs are entertained and represented by belief functions, and the *pignistic level* where decisions are made. The *pignistic transformation* maps a bba m^X to a probability measure $BetP^X$ on X, defined as:

$$BetP^X(A) = \sum_{B \subseteq X} \frac{m^X(B)}{1 - m^X(\emptyset)} \frac{|A \cap B|}{|B|}, \quad \forall A \subseteq X. \tag{11}$$

3.3 Application

Available Data. Let us go back to the problem presented in Sect. 2, but let us now assume that, for each failure mode x_i ($i = 1, \dots, n$), the abatement rate α_i, the failure rate λ_i and the repair time T_i are not known precisely. Let $\tilde{\alpha}_i = (\alpha_i^-, \alpha_i^0, \alpha_i^+)$ be a triangular fuzzy number defining a flexible constraint on α_i, and let $[\lambda_i^-, \lambda_i^+]$ and $[T_i^-, T_i^+]$ denote interval-valued assessments of λ_i and T_i, respectively. Furthermore, the probability distribution (q_j) of input concentrations is no longer assumed to be known. Instead, we more realistically assume that a finite sample $C_{in,1}, \dots, C_{in,K}$ has been observed.

Discretization of Input and Output Spaces. To translate this information in the TBM framework, we first have to define the underlying variables expressed on suitable finite domains. In the classical approach, the output concentration was discretized in two categories: water either meets or does not meet a fixed quality limit. However, this approach is too restrictive and results in a loss of information. To refine this discretization, we now define $\ell + 1$ thresholds σ_k, $k = 0, \dots, \ell$, which induce $\ell + 2$ possible states s_k, $k = 0, \dots, \ell + 1$ for the output water (see Fig. 3). In practical cases, tool can manage values of ℓ up to about 10, which is sufficiently accurate for real cases. For a given mode x_i of the treatment plant, the output threshold σ_k defines an input threshold $\theta_{k,i}$ (the input concentration must be less than $\theta_{k,i}$ for the output concentration to be less than σ_k when the treatment plant is in mode x_i). In order to recover the classical limit, one of the output thresholds must be the norm ($N = \sigma_k$ for some k) and the input thresholds must at least contain the $n + 1$ values $\theta_{k,i}$ obtained with that k and all functioning modes i of the treatment plant. However, the discretization can take into account more values than this minimal set. We note η_j ($0 \leq j \leq m$) the input thresholds arranged in decreasing order and e_j ($0 \leq j \leq m + 1$) the corresponding input states. Note that we define $\ell + 1$ thresholds for each of the $n + 1$ modes, so that $m + 1 \leq (n + 1)(l + 1)$ (the upper bound may not be strict because some of the thresholds may be equal).

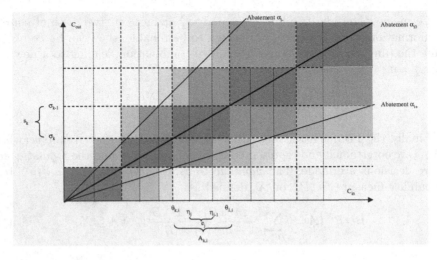

Fig. 3. Discretization of input and output concentrations, and fuzzy transfer function

Frames of Discernment. We thus have three underlying variables: the discretized input concentration taking values in $E = \{e_0, \dots, e_{m+1}\}$, the discretized output concentration taking values in $S = \{s_0, \dots, s_{\ell+1}\}$, and the plant state in $X = \{x_0, \dots, x_n\}$. We now have to translate the available pieces of information into belief functions on the joint space $X \times E \times S$, combine this evidence, and marginalize on S to obtain our belief concerning the output concentration values.

Representation of Transfer Functions. The fuzzy abatement rate $\widetilde{\alpha}_i$ for operating mode i may be seen as defining a fuzzy relation between input and output concentrations. This fuzzy relation may be expressed as a possibility distribution π_i on variables C_{in} and C_{out} defined as a function of the ratio $\rho = C_{out}/C_{in}$ as:

$$\pi_i(C_{in}, C_{out}) = \begin{cases} 0 & \text{if } \rho \leq \alpha_i^- \text{ or } \rho \geq \alpha_i^+ \\ \dfrac{\rho - \alpha_i^-}{\alpha_i^0 - \alpha_i^-} & \text{if } \alpha_i^- < \rho \leq \alpha_i^0 \\ \dfrac{\alpha_i^+ - \rho}{\alpha_i^+ - \alpha_i^0} & \text{if } \alpha_i^0 < \rho < \alpha_i^+ \end{cases} \tag{12}$$

After discretization of input and output concentrations, π_i induces possibility distribution $\pi_i^{E \times S}$ on the product space $E \times S$ (see Fig. 3), defined as:

$$\pi_i^{E \times S}(e_j, s_k) = \sup_{C_{in} \in e_j, C_{out} \in s_k} \pi_i(C_{in}, C_{out}) \tag{13}$$

Such a possibility distribution is known to be equivalent to a consonant bba $m^{E \times S}[x_i]$ (see [2]).

Belief on X. In the classical case, knowledge of failure rates λ_i and repair times T_i induced a probability function on X using (1) and (2). Since λ_i and T_i are now only known to lie in given intervals, we have a family $\mathcal{P}^X$ of probability distributions on X, defined by the contraints $p_i^- \leq p_i \leq p_i^+$ $(i = 0, \ldots, n)$, with $p_i^- = \lambda_i^- T_i^-$, $p_i^+ = \lambda_i^+ T_i^+$ $(i = 1, \ldots, n)$, $p_0^- = 1 - \sum_{i=1}^{n} \lambda_i^+ T_i^+$ and $p_0^+ = 1 - \sum_{i=1}^{n} \lambda_i^- T_i^-$. The lower and upper probability of an event $A \subseteq X$ are given by:

$$P^-(A) = \max \left(\sum_{x_i \in A} p_i^-, 1 - \sum_{x_i \notin A} p_i^+ \right) \qquad (14)$$

$$P^+(A) = \min \left(\sum_{x_i \in A} p_i^+, 1 - \sum_{x_i \notin A} p_i^- \right) \qquad (15)$$

These lower and upper probabilities do not, in general, verify the axioms of belief and plausibility measures. However, we may represent this information in the belief function framework by the most specific bba m^X (according, e.g., to the nonspecificity uncertainty measure [4]), whose set of compatible probability functions includes $\mathcal{P}^X$. This may be obtained by solving the following linear program:

$$\min_{m^X} \sum_{\emptyset \neq A \subseteq X} m^X(A) \log |A|$$

under the constraints:

$$bel^X(A) \leq P^-(A) \leq P^+(A) \leq pl^X(A), \quad \forall A \subseteq X.$$

Belief on E. The available information on E is of a different nature: it consists of a finite sample $C_{in,1}, \ldots, C_{in,K}$ of sample values. A simple approach to build a belief function on E might be to consider the histogram, i.e. to define $m^E(e_j)$ as the relative frequency of observations falling in class e_j. This approach, however, is not satisfactory in the small sample case because it does not take into account the sample size. Ideally, the inferred belief function should reflect the amount of available information, and hence the sample size. One way to achieve this goal is to generate B bootstrap replicates of the data [3]. Let $p_b(e_j)$ be the relative frequency of class e_j in bootstrap sample b, and define $p^-(e_j)$ and $p^+(e_j)$ as, say, the 1st and 9th deciles of the distribution $p_b(e_j), b = 1, \ldots, B$. We then obtain lower and upper probabilities on E, which define a family $\mathcal{P}^E$ of probability distributions. As before, we may translate this information in the belief function format by considering the most specific bba m^E, whose set of compatible probability distributions includes $\mathcal{P}^E$. However, as E may be much larger than X, the complexity of this solution might become too high. A simpler approach is to restrict the number of focal elements of m^E. For instance, if m^E is constrained to be quasi-Bayesian (i.e., to have only singletons and E as focal elements), the solution can be shown to be:

$$m^E(\{e_j\}) = p^{*-}(e_j) \quad j = 0, \ldots, m+1 \tag{16}$$

$$m^E(E) = \max_j(p^{*+}(e_j) - p^{*-}(e_j)) \tag{17}$$

$$m^E(A) = 0 \quad \forall A \subseteq E, A \neq E, |A| \neq 1 \tag{18}$$

with

$$p^{*-}(e_j) = \max\left(p^-(e_j), 1 - \sum_{\substack{j' \neq j}}^{m+1} p^+(e_{j'})\right) \quad j = 0, \ldots, m+1 \tag{19}$$

$$p^{*+}(e_j) = \min\left(p^+(e_j), 1 - \sum_{\substack{j' \neq j}}^{m+1} p^-(e_{j'})\right) \quad j = 0, \ldots, m+1 \tag{20}$$

Combination and Marginalization. The final step is to combine all the available evidence, and marginalize on S. For that purpose, all belief functions must first be extended to the product space $X \times E \times S$ using the ballooning extension for $m^{E \times S}[x_i]$ $(i = 0, \ldots, n)$, and using the vacuous extension for m^X and m^E. The resulting belief functions are combined using Dempster's rule, and the result is marginalized on S. Formally, the final bba on S is thus defined as:

$$\left(\left(\bigcirc_{i=0}^n m^{E \times S}[x_i]^{\Uparrow X \times E \times S}\right) \bigcirc m^{X \uparrow X \times E \times S} \bigcirc m^{E \uparrow X \times E \times S}\right)^{\downarrow S}. \tag{21}$$

Note that these operations may be performed very efficiently using local computation algorithms such as the one described in [6].

4   Comparison with the Classical Solution

In this section, we will show that our method yields the same results as the classical method where all necessary data are precisely known. When α_i is known, $m^{E \times S}[x_i]$ has a unique focal element: we have

$$m^{E \times S}[x_i](B_i) = 1, \tag{22}$$

where B_i is defined as $B_i = \bigcup_{k=0}^{\ell+1} A_{k,i} \times \{s_k\}$, with

$$A_{k,i} = \{e_j | e_j \subseteq [\theta_{k,i}, \theta_{k-1,i}]\}$$

The ballooning extension of $m^{E \times S}[x_i]$ yields:

$$m^{E \times S \Uparrow X \times E \times S}[x_i](\{x_i\} \times B_i \cup \{\overline{x_i}\} \times E \times S) = 1. \tag{23}$$

It can be shown by induction that

$$\bigcap_{i=0}^n (\{x_i\} \times B_i \cup \{\overline{x_i}\} \times E \times S) = \bigcup_{i=0}^n (\{x_i\} \times B_i). \tag{24}$$

Hence, if we note $m_1^{X \times E \times S} = \bigcap_{i=0}^{n} m^{E \times S}[x_i]^{\Uparrow X \times E \times S}$, we obtain:

$$m_1^{X \times E \times S} \left(\bigcup_{i=0}^{n} \{x_i\} \times B_i \right) = 1. \tag{25}$$

In a second step, we have to express our beliefs concerning the raw water and plant states. In the classical case, m^X and m^S are probability functions defined by $m^X(\{x_i\}) = p_i$ ($i = 0, \dots, n$) and $m^S(\{e_j\}) = q_j$ ($j = 0, \dots, m+1$). The vacuous extension of these bba's on the joint space yields:

$$m^{X \uparrow X \times E \times S}(\{x_i\} \times E \times S) = p_i \quad i = 0, \dots, n \tag{26}$$

$$m^{E \uparrow X \times E \times S}(X \times \{e_j\} \times S) = q_j \quad j = 0, \dots, m+1. \tag{27}$$

Let $m_2^{X \times E \times S}$ denote the combination of $m_1^{X \times E \times S}$ with m^X. We have

$$m_2^{X \times E \times S}(\{x_i\} \times B_i) = p_i \quad i = 0, \dots, n. \tag{28}$$

Finally, let $m_3^{X \times E \times S}$ denote the combination of $m_2^{X \times E \times S}$ with m^E. By construction, there is only one k such that $e_j \in A_{k,i}$, considering a fixed state i of the plant. Consequently, the resulting focal sets are all of the form:

$$\left(\{x_i\} \times \bigcup_{k=0}^{\ell+1} (A_{k,i} \times \{s_k\}) \right) \cap (X \times \{e_j\} \times S) = \{x_i\} \times \{e_j\} \times \{s_k\} \tag{29}$$

with $e_j \in A_{k,i}$. Hence, $m_3^{X \times E \times S}$ is a probability function.

In order to conclude this demonstration and to show the equality between our approach and the classical one, we will now study the particular case developed in the classical method presentation, which consists in considering only one threshold for treated water, which must be the norm N. We then only have two states for treated water s_0 and s_1 and, consequently, two states for raw water $A_{0,i}$ and $A_{1,i}$. In this case, we have

$$m_3^{X \times E \times S}(D_{i,j}) = p_i q_j \tag{30}$$

with

$$D_{i,j} = \begin{cases} \{x_i\} \times \{e_j\} \times \{s_0\} & \text{if } j \leq i \\ \{x_i\} \times \{e_j\} \times \{s_1\} & \text{if } j > i. \end{cases} \tag{31}$$

We then finally obtain, after marginalization:

$$m^{X \times E \times S \downarrow S}(\{s_0\}) = \sum_{i=0}^{n} \sum_{j=0}^{i} p_i q_j, \tag{32}$$

which completes the proof.

5   Simulations

Figure 4 shows simulation results, for one normal mode x_0, one failure mode x_1, and seven output concentration thresholds $s_k, k = 0, \ldots, 6$. The three graphs correspond to three states of knowledge:

1. In the first case (upper left), the abatement rates, failure rate and latency time are known:

$$\alpha_0 = 0.8 \quad \alpha_1 = 0.4$$

$$\lambda_1 = 2 \times 10^{-3} \text{ h}^{-1} \quad T_1 = 4 \times 24 \text{ h}.$$

2. In the second case (upper right), the abatement rates are still known, but the failure rate and latency time are only bounded by:

$$\lambda_1^- = 10^{-3} \text{ h}^{-1}, \quad \lambda_1^+ = 2 \times 10^{-3} \text{ h}^{-1}$$

$$T_1^- = 4 \times 24 \text{ h}, \quad T_1^+ = 8 \times 24 \text{ h}.$$

3. In the third case (lower graph), the same knowledge of λ_1 and T_1 is assumed, and the abatement rates are constrained by fuzzy numbers:

$$\tilde{\alpha}_0 = (0.79, 0.8, 0.81), \quad \tilde{\alpha}_1 = (0.39, 0.4, 0.41).$$

As expected, the induced belief measure on S is a probability measure when all necessary data are available. In that case, the solution is identical to that of the classical fault tree approach. In contrast, results with the TBM approach degrade gracefully when the imprecision in input data increases, the pignistic probability getting closer to the uniform distribution.

6   Conclusion

In this paper, an original method allowing to take into account data uncertainties in risk assessment for drinking water production process has been described. In order to evaluate compliant water unavailability, this method takes into account resource quality, characteristics of treatment plant, and different operating modes of the treatment plant. Belief functions are used to describe expert knowledge of treatment steps efficiency, failure rates, times to repair and raw water quality. By combination of these belief functions, it is possible to define the belief to produce compliant water. In the case where all data are precisely known, this approach was shown to be equivalent to the classical fault tree analysis.

Preliminary validation showed that this approach fits well the experts needs, by allowing to simulate various process line scenarios to propose the best technical option, based on available partial information.

330   S. Démotier, T. Denœux, and W. Schön

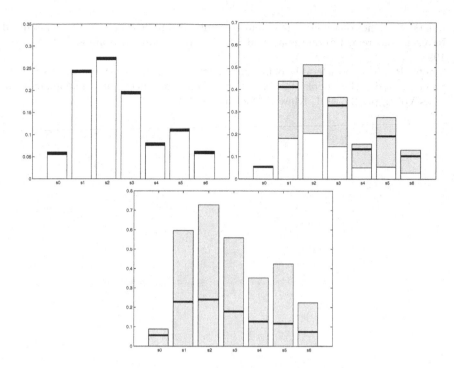

Fig. 4. Results obtained in case 1 (upper left), case 2 (upper right) and case 3 (down). The white bars correspond to the belief given to each singleton of S. The black lines indicate the pignistic probabilities, and the full bars (white and grey parts) show the plausibities

References

1. Démotier, S., Odeh, K., Schön, W., Charles, P., Footohi, F., Allioux, J.-F.: Risk assessment for drinking water production process. In proceedings of European Conference on System Dependability and Safety, pp. 544–550. Lyon, France, 2002.
2. Dubois, D., Prade, H.: Possibility theory, An approach to computerized processing of uncertainty. Ed. Plenum, 59–66, 1988.
3. Efron, B., Tibshirani, R.: An introduction to the bootstrap. Chapman and Hall, New York, 199).
4. Klir, G.J., Wierman, M.J.: Uncertainty-Based Information. Elements of Generalized Information Theory. Springer-Verlag, New-York, 1998.
5. Lainé, J.-M., Démotier, S., Odeh, K., Schön, W., Charles, P.: Risk assessment for drinking water production. Assessing the potential risk due to the presence of cryptosporidium oocysts in water. In proceedings of IWA. Berlin, Germany, 2001.
6. Shenoy, P.P.: Binary joint trees for computing marginals in the Shenoy-Shafer architecture. International Journal of Approximate Reasoning, Vol. 17, 239–263, 1997.
7. Smets, P.: The transferable belief model for expert judgments and reliability problems. Reliability Engineering and Systems Safety, 59–66, 1992.

8. Smets, P.: Belief functions: the disjunctive rule of combination and the generalized bayesian theorem. International Journal of Approximate Reasoning, Vol. 9, 1–35, 1993.
9. Smets, P. : The transferable belief model for quantified belief representation. In Smets, P. (ed.), Handbook of defeasible reasoning and uncertainty managment systems Vol.1., pp. 267–301, Kluwer, Doordrecht, 1998.

Algebraic Structures Related to the Consensus Operator for Combining of Beliefs*

Milan Daniel

Institute of Computer Science, Academy of Sciences of the Czech Republic
Pod vodárenskou věží 2, CZ – 182 07 Prague 8, Czech Republic
milan.daniel@cs.cas.cz, milan.daniel@becherovka.cz

Abstract. To overcome the frequent criticism of Dempster's rule for combination of belief functions several alternatives were defined, the consensus operator among them. Algebraic analysis of the consensus operator is presented using the methodology introduced by Hájek-Valdés for Dempster's semigroup. The methodology and Dempster's semigroup is recalled. Jøsang's semigroup and related structures are introduced, analysed, and compared with those related to the Dempster's case.

Keywords: belief functions, Dempster-Shafer theory, combination of belief functions, Dempster's rule, Dempster's semigroup, consensus operator, Jøsang's semigroup, expert systems

1   Introduction

Ever since the publication of Shafer's book *A Mathematical Theory of Evidence* [12] there has been continuous controversy around the so-called *Dempster's rule*. The purpose of Dempster's rule is to combine two beliefs into a single belief that reflects the two beliefs in a fair and equal way.

Dempster's rule has been criticised mainly because highly conflicting beliefs tend to produce counterintuitive results. This has been formulated in the form of examples by Zadeh [15], Cohen [1], and Daniel [2] among others. The problem with Dempster's rule is due to its normalisation which redistributes conflicting belief masses to non-conflicting ones, and thereby tends to eliminate any conflicting characteristics in the resulting belief mass distribution. Some people criticize the rule also for the fact that it is not defined for combining of 'totally' conflicting pieces of evidence. An alternative called the non-normalised Dempster's rule proposed by Smets [13] avoids this particular problem by allocating all conflicting belief masses to the empty set. The idea is that conflicting belief masses should be allocated to this missing (empty) event.

Unfortunately even the non-normalised version does not solve all the disadvantages of Dempster's rule. Thus several other alternatives were suggested later. Among the newest ones belongs the *consensus operator* [10,11], which is

---

* Partial support by the COST action 274 TARSKI is acknowledged.

T.D. Nielsen and N.L. Zhang (Eds.): ECSQARU 2003, LNAI 2711, pp. 332–344, 2003.
© Springer-Verlag Berlin Heidelberg 2003

developed with the intention to combine highly conflicting beliefs better. The consensus operator forms part of subjective logic described by Jøsang in [10].

An algebraic structure of binary belief functions with Dempster's rule $\oplus$, called *Dempster's semigroup*, has been in detail studied in a series of publications, e.g. [8,9]. The appearance of the consensus operator $\copyright$, which is recently developped to overcome the disadvantages of the Dempster's rule, is a motivation for studying of algebraic structures of belief functions with $\copyright$ to obtain a better theoretical comparison of both approaches.

The next section briefly recalls the basic definitions. The algebraic analysis of Dempster's semigroup, which is used as a methodology for the presented investigation, is overviewed in the third section.

Section 4 brings basic ideas and facts about the opinion space to prepare us for introduction of the consensus operator in the consecutive section.

In Sect. 6, a new algebraic structure – the algebraic structure of binary belief functions with the consensus operator $\copyright$ – is defined. The new structure called *Jøsang's semigroup* is analysed there. The results are discussed and compared with those of Dempster's semigroup in Sect. 7.

In the end, some ideas for future research are outlined as well.

2   Preliminaries

Let us recall some basic algebraic notions and some basic notions from the Dempster-Shafer theory before we begin a description of its algebra.

A *commutative semigroup* (called also an *Abelian semigroup*) is a structure $\mathbf{X} = (X, \oplus)$ formed by the set X and a binary operation $\oplus$ on X which is commutative and associative ($x \oplus y = y \oplus x$ and $x \oplus (y \oplus z) = (x \oplus y) \oplus z$ holds for all $x, y, z \in X$). A *commutative group* is a structure $\mathbf{X} = (X, \oplus, -, o)$ such that $(X, \oplus)$ is a commutative semigroup, o is a neutral element ($x \oplus o = x$) and $-$ is a unary operation of the inverse ($x \oplus -x = o$). An *ordered Abelian (semi)group* consists of a commutative (semi)group $\mathbf{X}$ as above and a linear ordering $\leq$ of its elements satisfying monotonicity ($x \leq y$ implies $x \oplus z \leq y \oplus z$ for all $x, y, z \in X$). A subset of X which is a (semi)group itself is called a *sub(semi)group*. A subsemigroup ($\{x | x \geq o, x \in X\}, \oplus, o$) is called *the positive cone* of the ordered Abelian group (OAG) X, similarly *a negative cone* for $x \leq o$. An ordered semigroup $\mathbf{X} = (X, \oplus, \leq)$ is *Archimedean* if for any $x, y \in X$ there exists a natural number n such that $y < nx$, where $nx = x \oplus ... \oplus x$ (n summands).

For uncertainty processing, we extend an OAG with *extremal elements* $\top$ and $\bot$ representing *True* and *False*, $\top \oplus x = \top$, $\bot \oplus x = \bot$, $\top \oplus \bot$ not defined.[1]

---

[1] Some examples are OAG^+ **PP** $= ([0,1], \oplus_{PP}, 1 - x, \frac{1}{2}, \leq)$ and **MC** $= ([-1,1], \oplus_{MC}, -, 0, \leq)$ corresponding to the combining structures of the classical expert systems PROSPECTOR and EMYCIN, see [8], where $x \oplus_{PP} y = \frac{xy}{xy + (1-x)(1-y)}$ and $x \oplus_{MC} y = x + y - xy$ for $x, y \geq 0$, $x + y + xy$ for $x, y \leq 0$ and $\frac{x+y}{1 - min(|x|, |y|)}$ for $xy \leq 0$.

A *homomorphism* $p : (X, \oplus_1) \longrightarrow (Y, \oplus_2)$ is a mapping which preserves structure, i.e. $p(x \oplus_1 y) = p(x) \oplus_2 p(y)$ for each $x, y \in X$. Morphisms which also preserve ordering of elements are called *ordered morphisms*, see [7].

Ordered structures and ordered morphisms are very important for a comparative approach to uncertainty management and decision making.

Let us consider a two-element *frame of discernment* $\Theta = \{0, 1\}$. A *basic belief assignment* is a mapping $m : \mathcal{P}(\Theta) \longrightarrow [0, 1]$, such that $\sum_{A \subseteq \Theta} m(\Lambda) = 1$, $m(\emptyset) = 0$. Each subset $A \subseteq \Theta$ such as $m(A) > 0$ is called a *focal element* of m. A *belief function* is a mapping $bel : \mathcal{P}(\Theta) \longrightarrow [0, 1]$, $bel(A) = \sum_{\emptyset \neq X \subseteq A} m(X)$. In our special case $bel(1) = m(1)$, $bel(0) = m(0)$, $bel(\{0, 1\}) = m(1) + m(0) + m(\{0, 1\}) = 1$. Each basic belief assignment determines a *d*-pair $(m(1), m(0))$ and conversely, each *d*-pair determines a basic belief assignment.

The Dempster's (conjunctive) rule of combination is given as $(bel_1 \textcircled{\tiny O} bel_2)(A) = \sum_{X \cap Y = A} \frac{1}{K} m_1(X) m_2(Y)$, where $K = \sum_{X \cap Y \neq \emptyset} m_1(X) m_2(Y)$. Specially for $(m_1(1), m_1(0)) = (a, b)$, $(m_2(1), m_2(0)) = (c, d)$ we have $(a, b) \oplus (c, d) = (1 - \frac{(1-a)(1-c)}{1-(ad+bc)}, 1 - \frac{(1-b)(1-d)}{1-(ad+bc)})$.

If all the focal elements are singletons (i.e. one-element subsets of Ω) then we speak about *a Bayesian belief function*. A *dogmatic belief function* is defined by Smets as a belief function for which $m(\Omega = 0)$. Let us note that trivially every Bayesian belief function is dogmatic.

A *Bayesian transformation* is a mapping $t : Bel_{\Omega} \longrightarrow Prob_{\Omega}$, such that $bel(x) \leq t(bel)(x) \leq 1 - bel(\overline{x})$. Thus a Bayesian transformation assigns a Bayesian belief function (i.e. probability function) to every general one. The fundamental example of Bayesian transformation is the pignistic transformation introduced by Smets.

3   On the Dempster's Semigroup

Definition 1. *A Dempster's pair (or d-pair) is a pair of reals such that* $a, b \geq 0$ *and* $a + b \leq 1$. *A d-pair* (a, b) *is Bayesian if* $a + b = 1$, (a, b) *is simple if* $a = 0$ *or* $b = 0$, *in particular, extremal d-pairs are pairs (1,0) and (0,1). (Definitions of Bayesian and simple d-pairs correspond evidently to the usual definitions of Bayesian and simple belief assignments [8,12]).*

Definition 2. *Dempster's semigroup[2]* $\mathbf{D_0} = (D_0, \oplus)$ *is the set of all non-extremal Dempster's pairs, endowed with the operation* $\oplus$ *and two distinguished elements* $0 = (0, 0)$ *and* $0' = (\frac{1}{2}, \frac{1}{2})$, *where the operation* $\oplus$ *is defined by*

$$(a, b) \oplus (c, d) = (1 - \frac{(1-a)(1-c)}{1 - (ad + bc)}, 1 - \frac{(1-b)(1-d)}{1 - (ad + bc)}).$$

---

[2] A generalization of a notion of the Dempster's semigroup is described in [9], see also [8]. The resulting algebraic structure is called *a dempsteroid*. It has a similar relation to the Dempster's semigroup as OAG has to **PP** or **MC**.

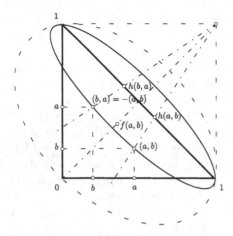 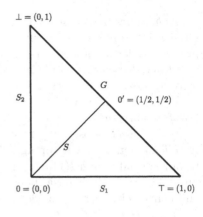

Fig. 1. Dempster's semigroup. Homomorphism h is in this representation a projection to group G along the straight lines running through the point $(1,1)$. All the Dempster's pairs lying on the same ellipse are mapped by homomorphism f to the same d-pair in semigroup S

Definition 3. *For* $(a,b) \in \mathbf{D}_0$ *we define*
$-(a,b) = (b,a)$,
$h(a,b) = (a,b) \oplus 0' = (\frac{1-b}{2-a-b}, \frac{1-a}{2-a-b})$, $\quad h_1(a,b) = \frac{1-b}{2-a-b}$,
$f(a,b) = (a,b) \oplus (b,a) = (\frac{a+b-a^2-b^2-ab}{1-a^2-b^2}, \frac{a+b-a^2-b^2-ab}{1-a^2-b^2})$.
For $(a,b), (c,d) \in \mathbf{D}_0$ *we further define*
$(a,b) \leq_\oplus (c,d)$ *iff* $h_1(a,b) < h_1(c,d)$ *or if* $h_1(a,b) = h_1(c,d)$ *and* $a \leq c$.
Let G *denote the set of all Bayesian non-extremal d-pairs. Let us denote the set of all simple d-pairs such that* $b = 0$ $(a = 0)$ *as* S_1 (S_2). *Furthermore, put* $S = \{(a,a) : 0 \leq a \leq 0.5\}$. *(Note:* $h(a,b)$ *is an abbreviation for* $h((a,b))$, *etc.)*

Theorem 1.

(i) *The Dempster's semigroup with the relation* $\leq_\oplus$ *is an ordered commutative semigroup with neutral element* 0; $0'$ *is the only nonzero idempotent of it.*

(ii) *The set* G *with the ordering* $\leq_\oplus$ *is an ordered Abelian group* $(G, \oplus, -, 0', \leq_\oplus)$ *which is isomorphic to the PROSPECTOR group* **PP** *(cf. [8]) and consequently isomorphic to the additive group of reals with usual ordering.*

(iii) *The sets* S, S_1 *and* S_2 *with the operation* $\oplus$ *and the ordering* $\leq_\oplus$ *form ordered commutative semigroups with neutral element* 0, *and are all isomorphic to the positive cone of the MYCIN group* **MC**.

(iv) *The mapping* h *is an ordered homomorphism of the ordered Dempster's semigroup onto its subgroup* G *(i.e. onto* **PP**).

(v) *The mapping* f *is a homomorphism of the Dempster's semigroup onto its subsemigroup* S *(but it is not an ordered homomorphism).*

Using the theorem, see (iv) and (v), we can express[3]

$$(a \oplus b) = h^{-1}(h(a) \oplus h(b)) \cap f^{-1}(f(a) \oplus f(b)).$$

4   The Opinion Space

Let us briefly recall some notions from [10,11] before the definition of the consensus operator. Let us consider a binary frame of discernment Θ again[4]. Let $\Theta = \{x, \overline{x}\}$, where x (resp. $\overline{x}$) could be a simple element from an application domain or a subset of an original multidimensional frame of discernment Θ_0 and $\overline{x} = \Theta_0 - x$. In the later case, let the belief function on Θ be constructed by the method of focusing, see [10,11]. Let us assume a basic belief assignment m such that $m(x) = b, m(\overline{x}) = d, m(\Theta) = u$. Hence $bel(x) = b, bel(\overline{x}) = d$, and we can consider b as a belief about the truth of x, d as a disbelief about x (a belief about the complement of x), and $u = 1 - b - d$ as an uncertainty[5] about x. Let us further recall a 3-dimensional metric[6] called *opinion*[7].

Definition 4. *Let Θ be a binary frame of discernment containing x and $\overline{x}$ as its elements, let m be a basic belief assignment which defines observer's belief b about x, disbelief d about x (a belief of the complement of x), and uncertainty u about x. Let a represent the relative atomicity of x in Θ_0 if Θ is focused Θ_0 (or simply in Θ if $\Theta = \Theta_0$); $a = \frac{|x|}{|\Theta_0|}$ (it is $\frac{|x|}{|\Theta|} = \frac{1}{2}$ if $\Theta = \Theta_0$). Then the observer's opinion about x is the tuple:*

$$\omega = (b, d, u, a).$$

Thus an opinion ω_x represents an observer's belief, disbelief and uncertainty about the truth of x and a *relative atomicity* a_x of x in the original frame of discernment Θ_0 in the case of focusing. The opinion contains a redundant parameter $u = 1 - b - d$ which allows a simple definition of the consensus operator, see the next section. Because we consider the only x, we can omit indexing of b, d, u, a by x, which is used in the case where focusing given by different subsets of Θ is considered.

The opinion space can be graphically represented by a triangle as shown in Fig. 2.

---

[3] Note that in fact. $h(x)$ expresses *certainty / uncertainty* of belief x, while $f^{-1}(f(x)) \cap S$ expresses *vagueness / preciseness* of x.

[4] In [10] and [11] there is described a method of focusing of belief functions on a general Θ_0 to belief functions on a focused binary Θ such that probabilistic expectations remain the same.

[5] We use Jøsang's terminology here. Note that $bel(\overline{x}) = dou(x)$ is called (degree of) doubt of x by Shafer in [12]. $u = 1 - b - d$ corresponds rather to vagueness than to uncertainty in Hájek-Valdés.

[6] From the mathematical point of view, it is not any metric. It is just an extended representation of a binary belief function (belief).

[7] Note that there are used upper indices $A, B, C, ...$ for opinions differing in [10,11].

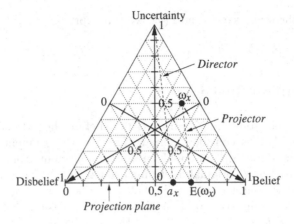

Fig. 2. Opinion triangle. ω_x is an example of an opinion about $x \in \Theta$

As an example the position of the opinion $\omega_x = (0.4, 0.1, 0.5, 0.6)$ is indicated as a point in the triangle. The horizontal base line between the Belief and Disbelief corners is called *the probability axis*. As shown in the figure, the probability expectation value $E(x) = 0.7$ and the relative atomicity $a(x) = 0.6$ can be graphically represented as points on the probability axis. The line joining the top corner of the triangle and the relative atomicity point is called *the director*. *The projector* is parallel to the director and passes through the opinion point ω_x. Opinions situated on the probability axis are called *dogmatic opinions*, representing traditional probability. The distance between an opinion point and the probability axis can be interpreted as a degree of uncertainty. Opinions situated in the left of right corner, i.e. with either $b = 1$ or $d = 1$ are called *the absolute opinions*, corresponding to TRUE or FALSE values in two-valued logic.

Because the relative atomicity does not play any role in the consensus operator (it is used for computing of the probability expectation and by another operator of Jøsang's subjective logic), we can omit it as redundant from our point of interest[8].

4.1   Analogy of Opinions and d-Pairs

Trivially, any opinion (b, d, u) gives the unique d-pair (b, d), and analogically any d-pair (v, w) gives the opinion $(v, w, 1 - v - w)$ which is unique if relative atomicity is omitted or fixed. We can observe that the absolute opinion $(1, 0, 0)$ in the right corner of the opinion triangle (Belief) corresponds to $\top = (1, 0)$ in the notation of the Dempster's semigroup, while Disbelief $(0, 1, 0)$ in the left corner

---

[8] Especially in the case of two simple elements x and $\bar{x}$ of a domain ($\Theta = \Theta_0$, i.e. $|\Theta_0| = 2$), or in the case where $|x| = |\bar{x}| \in \Theta_0$ for $|\Theta_0| > 2$, there is the fix relative atomicity $a_x = \frac{1}{2}$, and all the projectors are perpendicular to the probability axis, and the probability expectation is equal to the pignistic probability defined in the Transferable Belief Model [13,14].

corresponds to $\perp = (0,1)$, and Uncertainty $(0,0,1)$ in the top corner corresponds to $0 = (0,0)$ which is interpreted as *total ignorance* in the Dempster's semigroup. Analogically the probability axis corresponds to the set G of all the Bayesian d-pairs, and the right (or left) arm of the opinion space triangle corresponds to S_1, i.e. to the set of all simple d-pairs $(b,0)$ (or to S_2 respectively). And the vertical median of the opinion triangle connecting $(0,0,1)$ and $(\frac{1}{2},\frac{1}{2},0)$ corresponds to the set S. Using the analogies we will use denotations G, S, S_1, and S_2 also in the context of the opinion space.

5   The Consensus Operator

The consensus of two opinions is an opinion that reflects both argument opinions in a fair and equal way, i.e. when two observers have beliefs about the truth of x resulting from distinct pieces of evidence about x, the consensus operator produces a consensus belief that combines the two separate beliefs into one.

Definition 5. *Let* $\omega_A = (b_A, d_A, u_A)$ *and* $\omega_B = (b_B, d_B, u_B)$ *be opinions[9] respectively held by agents A and B about the same element x of $\Theta = \{x, \bar{x}\}$, and let* $\kappa = u_A + u_B - u_A u_B$. *When* u_A, $u_B \to 0$, *the relative dogmatism between* ω_A *and* ω_B *is defined by γ so that $\gamma = u_A/u_B$. Let $\omega_{AB} = (b_{AB}, d_{AB}, u_{AB})$ be the opinion such that:*

for $\kappa \neq 0$:	*for* $\kappa = 0$:
1. $b_{AB} = (b_A u_B + b_B u_A)/\kappa$	$b_{AB} = \frac{\gamma b_A + b_B}{\gamma + 1}$
2. $d_{AB} = (d_A u_B + d_B u_A)/\kappa$	$d_{AB} = \frac{\gamma d_A + d_B}{\gamma + 1}$
3. $u_{AB} = (u_A u_B)/\kappa$	$u_{AB} = 0$.

Then ω_{AB} is called the consensus opinion between ω_A and ω_B, representing an imaginary agent [A,B]'s opinion about x, as if that agent represented both A and B. By using the symbol © to designate this operator[10] we define $\omega_{AB} = \omega_A © \omega_B$.

6   Jøsang's Semigroup

Let us turn our attention to an algebra of belief functions on a binary frame of discernment (i.e. to an algebra of d-pairs – opinions) with the binary consensus operator ©. As is already stated in [10], the consensus operator © is a commutative and associative operation on the set of all non-dogmatic binary belief functions (opinions), hence we can speak about an Abelian semigroup again. Associativity of consensus of several dogmatic beliefs is more complicated, thus we still postpone its discussion and a formal definition of the Jøsang's semigroup.

---

[9] Let us note that (from our point of view) redundant relative atomicity and indexing by x is omitted in this definition, originally from [11], further upper indices A, B are substituted by the lower ones.

[10] ⊕ is used in [10,11]. Let us use © here to distinguish the consensus operator © from the Dempster's rule ⊕.

6.1   An Algebraization of the Consensus Operator

Because we have no more information than beliefs, i.e. opinion and we do not
expect any additional ones, we have to consider the same approximation of u
to 0 for all dogmatic opinions. Hence $\gamma = 1$ and we can express the consensus
operator as follows:

$(b_A, d_A, u_A) \copyright (b_B, d_B, u_B) = (\frac{b_A u_B + b_B u_A}{u_A + u_B - u_A u_B}, \frac{d_A u_B + d_B u_A}{u_A + u_B - u_A u_B}, \frac{u_A u_B}{u_A + u_B - u_A u_B})$ for
$u_A u_B \neq 0$

$(b_A, d_A, 0) \copyright (b_B, d_B, 0) = (\frac{b_A + b_B}{2}, \frac{d_A + d_B}{2}, 0)$ for two dogmatic opinions, a consensus of several dogmatic opinions we will discuss later.

Lemma 1. *(i) Both the* $0 = (0, 0, 1)$ *and* $0' = (\frac{1}{2}, \frac{1}{2}, 0)$ *are idempotents of the
consensus operator.*

(ii) All the Bayesian d-pairs (dogmatic opinions)[11] *are idempotents with respect
to the consensus operator.*

(iii) All the Bayesian d-pairs (dogmatic opinions)[12] *are absorbing elements with
respect to the consensus with non-Bayesian ones.*

(iv) $0 = (0, 0, 1)$ *is the only non-Bayesian idempotent.*

(v) $0 = (0, 0, 1)$ *is the neutral element for non-Bayesian d-pairs (opinions).*

Lemma 2. *(i) All the subsets* $G, S, S_1,$ *and* S_2 *of the opinion space are closed
with respect to the consensus operator.*

*(ii) Consensus of two opinions is Bayesian iff at least one of the opinions
consensed (i.e. combined by the consensus operator) is Bayesian.*

(iii) All the subsets $S_{(k)} = \{(b, kb, 1 - (1 + k)b) \mid (b, kb, 1 - (1 + k)b) \text{ is opinion}\}$
of the opinion space are closed with respect to the consensus operator.

For proofs of these and the following lemmata see [5].

Definition 6. *Let us define for* (b, d, u) *from the opinion space the following:*
$-(b, d, u) = (d, b, u)$,
$q(b, d, u) = (b, d, u) \copyright 0' = 0'$,
$q_0(b, d, u) = q^{-1}(q(b, d, u)) \cap (S_1 \cup S_2)$, *where*
$q_0(b, d, u) = (\frac{d-b}{2d-1}, 0, \frac{b+d-1}{2d-1})$ *for* $b \geq d$, $q_0(b, d, u) = (\frac{b-d}{2b-1}, 0, \frac{b+d-1}{2b-1})$ *for* $b \leq d$,
$r(b, d, u) = (b, d, u) \copyright - (b, d, u) = (\frac{1-u}{2-u}, \frac{1-u}{2-u}, \frac{u}{2-u})$ *for* $u \neq 0$,
$r(b, d, 0) = (b, d, 0) \copyright (d, b, 0) = (\frac{b+d}{2}, \frac{b+d}{2}, 0) = (\frac{1}{2}, \frac{1}{2}, 0) = 0'$.
For $(b, d, u), (b', d', u') \in \mathbf{D}_0$ *we further define*
$(b, d, u) \leq_\copyright (b', d', u')$ *iff* $(q_0)_2(b, d, u) < (q_0)_2(b', d', u')$ *or if* $(q_0)_2(b, d, u) =$
$(q_0)_2(b', d', u')$ *and* $(q_0)_1(b, d, u) < (q_0)_1(b', d', u')$ *or if* $q_0(b, d, u) = q_0(b', d', u')$
and $b \leq b'$, *where* $q_0(b, d, u) = ((q_0)_1(b, d, u), (q_0)_2(b, d, u), (q_0)_3(b, d, u))$.

Lemma 3. *(i)* $-(-x) = x$ *(i.e.* $-(-(b, d, u)) = (b, d, u))$,
(ii) $-(x \copyright y) = -x \copyright - y$ *(i.e.* $-((b_1, d_1, u_1) \copyright (b_2, d_2, u_2)) = -(b_1, d_1, u_1) \copyright -
(b_2, d_2, u_2))$,

---

[11] Including extremal d-pairs (absolute opinions) TRUE and FALSE.

[12] Including extremal d-pairs (absolute opinions) TRUE and FALSE.

(iii) $-x$ *is not an inverse to* x, *i.e. the equation* $(b_1, d_1, u_1) \copyright (b_2, d_2, u_2) =$
     $(0, 0, 1)$ *has no solution in the opinion space for* $(b_1, d_1, u_1) \neq (0, 0, 1)$.

(iv)   *The mapping* q *is a trivial ordered homomorphism of the set of all non-Bayesian opinions to* $\{0'\}$.

(v)   *The mapping* q_0 *is an ordered homomorphism of* $(D_1 - G)$ *onto* S_1 *and of* $(D_2 - G)$ *onto* S_2, *where* $D_1 = \{(b, d, u) \in D_0 | b \geq d\}$, $D_2 = \{(b, d, u) \in D_0 | b \leq d\}$, *but it is not a homomorphism of* $(D_0 - G)$ *onto* $S_1 \cup S_2$.

(vi)   *The mapping* r *is a homomorphism of all the opinion space onto its subalgebra* S *(but it is not an ordered homomorphism).*

(vii)   *The sets* S, S_1, S_2, *and* $S_{(k)}$ *with the consensus operator and with ordering* $\leq_\copyright$ *form Archimedean OAGs with neutral element* $(0, 0, 1)$. *They are all isomorphic to the positive cone of the MYCIN group* MC.

(viii)   *There is no neutral element in* G, *there is no inverse on* G, *i.e. there is no relation of* G *to any group.*

(ix)   *The set* $S_0 = S_1 \cup S_2$ *with operator* $\copyright_{S_0} = \copyright \circ q_0$, *with operator* $-$, *with distinguished element* $0 = (0, 0, 1)$ *and with ordering* $\leq_\copyright$ *forms Archimedean OAG* $S_0 = (S_0, \copyright_{S_0}, -, 0, \leq_\copyright)$. S_0 *is isomorphic to the MYCIN group* MC.

6.2   Associativity of Computing of the Consensus of Bayesian Opinions

The consensus operator of non-Bayesian opinions is computed as an increased weighted mean. Both belief and disbelief components are weighted by u of the other opinion and the resulting mean is increased by a factor $\frac{u_1 + u_2}{u_1 + u_2 - u_1 u_2} > 1$, i.e. we can express the consensus of non-Bayesian opinions as

$$(b_1, d_1, u_1) \copyright (b_2, d_2, u_2) =$$
$$\left(\frac{b_1 u_2 + b_2 u_1}{u_1 + u_2} \frac{u_1 + u_2}{u_1 + u_2 - u_1 u_2}, \frac{d_1 u_2 + d_2 u_1}{u_1 + u_2} \frac{u_1 + u_2}{u_1 + u_2 - u_1 u_2}, \frac{u_1 u_2}{u_1 + u_2 - u_1 u_2} \right)$$

for $u_1 u_2 \neq 0$. While the consensus of Bayesian opinions without any additional information corresponds just to non-associative arithmetical mean. To overcome it additional tools requiring additional information are used to obtain $\gamma \neq 1$, see Definition 5. If there is no additional information we have to distinguish whether the opinions to be combined are 'single', i.e. not results of any previous applications of the consensus operator, or how many times the consensus has been already used. We use $\gamma = 1$ for two 'single' opinions, $\gamma = n$ in the case where $(b_1, d_1, 0)$ is a result of just n applications of the consensus operator and $(b_2, d_2, 0)$ is a 'single' one. In the case where the first argument $(b_1, d_1, 0)$ is a 'single' and the second one is already consensed we use $\gamma = \frac{1}{n}$. Hence, the computation of the consensus corresponds to stepwise computation of n-ary arithmetic mean. For an example of an associative combination of three Bayesian opinions see [6].

    Using the above procedure, we are able to compute the consensus of several Bayesian opinions in an associative way. But this method is not general. We have to always remember and handle the history of the opinions (how many times the consensus has been used). And it is not always easy. In the case of subjective opinions it is often even for an opinion agent himself quite difficult to decide whether his opinion is 'single' or is already implicitly consensed (i.e. implicitly combined by the consensus operator) from two or several opinions.

6.3   A Formal Definition of Jøsang's Semigroup

From the algebraical point of view we have obtained, instead of the operator on opinions, a new one defined on the Cartesian product of the set of opinions with the set of positive integers or reals if we admit non-integer γ based on different additional information. Because even this method is not completely general, we do not include it into formal definition of Jøsang's semigroup, and we keep limited to non-Bayesian opinions.

Definition 7. *Jøsang's semigroup* $\mathbf{J_0} = (J_0, \copyright)$ *is the set of all non-Bayesian Dempster's pairs (opinions), endowed with the operation $\copyright$ and with a distinguished element* $0 = (0, 0, 1)$, *where the operation $\copyright$ is defined by*

$$(b_A, d_A, u_A) \copyright (b_B, d_B, u_B) = (\tfrac{b_A u_B + b_B u_A}{u_A + u_B - u_A u_B}, \tfrac{d_A u_B + d_B u_A}{u_A + u_B - u_A u_B}, \tfrac{u_A u_B}{u_A + u_B - u_A u_B}).$$

Theorem 2.

  (i) *z The Jøsang's semigroup with the relation $\leq_\copyright$ is an ordered commutative semigroup with neutral element* $0 = (0, 0, 1)$; 0 *is the only idempotent of it.*

 (ii) *The sets S, S_1, S_2 and $S_{(k)}$ with the operation $\copyright$ and the ordering $\leq_\copyright$ form Archimedean ordered commutative semigroups with neutral element 0, and they are all isomorphic to the semigroup of nonnegative elements (positive cone) of the MYCIN group* **MC**.

(iii) *The set $S_0 = S_1 \cup S_2$ with the operations $\copyright_{S_0} = \copyright \circ q_0$ and $-$, and with the ordering $\leq_\copyright$ form an Archimedean OAG with neutral element 0: $S_0 = (S_0, \copyright_{S_0}, -, 0, \leq_\copyright)$. S_0 is isomorphic to the MYCIN group* **MC**.

 (iv) *The mapping q_0 is an ordered homomorphism of the Jø 's semigroup onto group S_0, it preserves the ordering $\leq_\copyright$ (S_0 is a subset of J_0 but not a subalgebra of J_0).*

  (v) *The mapping r is a homomorphism of the Jøsang's semigroup onto its subsemigroup S (but it is not an ordered homomorphism). For any $k \geq 0$, r is an ordered isomorphism of $S_{(k)}$ onto S.*

 (vi) *The mapping q is a trivial homomorphic Bayesian transformation of J_0. No non-trivial homomorhic Bayesian transformation of J_0 exists. No homomorhic Bayesian transformation of the whole opinion space which is homomorphic with respect to the consensus operator exists.*

For proofs see [5].

Using the theorem, see (iv) and (v), we can express the consensus $\copyright$ for every couple of non-Bayesian opinions x, y as:

$$(x \copyright y) = q_0^{-1}(q_0(x) \copyright q_0(y)) \cap r^{-1}(r(x) \copyright r(y)).$$

7 A Comparison of the Jøsang's Semigroup with the Dempster's One

Both the algebraic structures have the following **similarities:**
Both of them are ordered Abelian semigroups with neutral element $(0,0,1)$.
They have the same unary operation minus $-$ which is not inverse in both the
cases. Both the structures have subsemigroups S, S_1, S_2 with neutral elements.
Both of them have a surjective (i.e. onto) homomorphism $D_0 \longrightarrow S$. We can
define group S_0 on subsets $S_0 = S_1 \cup S_2$ of both the structures (with $\oplus \circ h_0$, -,
and $\leq_\oplus$, in the case of D_0, while with $\copyright \circ q_0$, -, and $\leq_\copyright$ in the case of J_0). In
both the cases there exists a surjective ordered homomorphism onto group S_0.
Both the operations $\oplus$ and $\copyright$ are expressible using the pair of homomorphisms.

Differences:
The Demspter's semigroup is defined on all non-extremal d-pairs, $\oplus$ is not defined
for $\top \oplus \bot$, while the Jøsang's semigroup is defined on non-Bayesian d-pairs only,
i.e. on $D_0 - G$. On the other hand, the consensus operator $\copyright$ is defined on the
whole extended D_0^+ but it is necessary to use additional information to obtain
its associativity. $S_0^\oplus = (S_0, \oplus_{S_0}, -, 0, \leq_\oplus)$ is isomorphic to $G = (G, \oplus, -, 0', \leq_\oplus)$
while $S_0^\copyright = (S_0, \copyright_{S_0}, -, 0, \leq_\copyright)$ collapses to $\{0'\}$.

$\oplus$ forms an Archimedean OAG on G, while the behaviour of $\copyright$ is completely
different on G: $\copyright$ is not associative on the set G, $0' = (\frac{1}{2}, \frac{1}{2})$ is not a neutral element, all Bayesian opinions are idempotent and they are absorbing with respect
to non-Bayesian ones, extremal elements (absolute opinions) are not absorbing
with respect to Bayesian ones.

We have to remember a different interpretation of uncertainty here. In the
Dempster's semigroup certainty / uncertainty of d-pair x is defined as $h(x)$,
especially for Bayesian d-pair $y = (b, d, 0)$ the value b is just the certainty /
uncertainty of y. Value $f(x)$ corresponds to the vagueness / impreciseness of x.
The Bayesian d-pairs are precise, while $0 = (0, 0, 1)$ is the vaguest d-pair. This
corresponds also to general consideration of probability as a tool for uncertainty
processing.

In the opinion space interpretation, Bayesian opinions have no uncertainty,
they are considered to be certain. And uncertainty increases with the distance
from the set of Bayesian opinions.

The principal is the following:
$\oplus$ combination of any two elements (d-pairs / opinions) is on an ellipse further
from 0 (closer to G), and similarly, $\copyright$ combination of any two elements is on a
straight line (r-line) further from 0. I.e. the measure $u = 1 - b - d$ is decreased
by the combination, regardless of its interpretation (vagueness / uncertainty).
Both combinations $\oplus$ and $\copyright$ of two elements $\geq_\oplus 0'$ ($\geq_\copyright 0'$ respectively) or of two
ones $\leq_\oplus 0$ ($\leq_\copyright 0$) are on homomorphic straight lines (h-lines, q-lines) further
from S. In the case of the Dempster's semigroup, we can interpret it so that the
big values (close to $(1, 0, 0)$, d-pairs $\geq_\oplus 0'$) are increased (closer to $(1, 0, 0)$), while

the small values are decreased (closer to $(0, 1, 0)$). It is caused by the cumulative nature of the Dempster's rule $\oplus$. There is no such an interpretation in the case of the Jøsang's semigroup. It is caused by an averaging nature of the consensus operator $\copyright$.

8   Conclusions and Perspectives

A new algebraic structure – Jøsang's semigroup – is defined on a binary frame of discernment. The Jøsang's semigroup and related structures are analysed in this text. It is compared with the analogically constructed Dempster's semigroup.

The analysis of the algebraic nature of the consensus operator moves us on to better and deeper understanding of this operator and also deeper understanding of combining several beliefs in general.

The main theoretical disadvantage of the present state of the consensus operator is its non-associativity on dogmatic beliefs. This problem has been already partially solved by using additive information, see an example of associative consensus of three dogmatic beliefs in [6]. On the other hand, a theoretically clean associative consensus of several dogmatic beliefs is still an interesting open problem.

Another interesting topic for future research is a comparison of the focusing of a frame of discernment introduced by Jøsang, see [10,11], with the approach of refinement / coarsening of a frame of discernment which has been suggested in [3] and used in [4].

References

1. Cohen, M.S.: An expert system framework for non-monotonic reasoning about probabilistic assumptions, In Kanal, L.N., Lemmer, J.F. (eds.): *Uncertainty in Artificial Intelligence 1*. North-Holland (1986)
2. Daniel, M.: Distribution of Contradictive Belief Masses in Combination of Belief Functions. In: Bouchon-Meunier, B., Yager, R.R., Zadeh, L.A. (eds.): *Information, Uncertainty and Fusion*. Kluwer Academic Publishers (2000) 431–446
3. Daniel., M.: Composition and Decomposition of Belief Functions. In: Jiroušek, R., Vejnarová, J. (eds.): *Proc. of 4th Czech-Japan Sem. on Data Analysis and Decision Making under Uncertainty*. Jindřichův Hradec (2001) 21–32
4. Daniel., M.: Combination of Belief Functions and Coarsening/Refinement. In: Proceedings Ninth International conference IPMU, Université de Savoie, Annecy, Vol. I. (2002) 587–594
5. Daniel., M.: *Algebraic structures related to Combinations of Belief Functions. The Consensus operator and Jøsang's semigroup*. Technical Report V-890, Inst. of Comp. Sci., Academy of Sciences of the Czech Republic, Prague, 2003.
6. Daniel., M., Jøsang, A., Vannoorenberghe, P.: Strategies for Combining Conflicting Dogmatic Beliefs. In: Proceedings Fusion 2003, in preparation (2003)
7. Fuchs, L.: *Partially ordered algebraic systems*. Pergamon Press (1963)
8. Hájek, P., Havránek, T., Jiroušek, R.: *Uncertain Information Processing in Expert Systems*. CRC Press, Boca Raton, Florida (1992)

344   M. Daniel

9. Hájek, P., Valdés, J.J.: Generalized algebraic foundations of uncertainty processing in rule-based expert systems (dempsteroids). *Computers and Artificial Intelligence* **10** (1991) 29–42
10. Jøsang., A.: A Logic for Uncertain Probabilities. *International Journal of Uncertainty, Fuzziness and Knowledge-Based Systems* **9** (2001) 279–311
11. Jøsang., A.: The Consensus Operator for Combining Beliefs. *Artificaial Intelligence Journal* **141/1–2** (2002) 157–170
12. Shafer, G.: *A Mathematical Theory of Evidence.* Princeton University Press, Princeton, New Jersey (1976)
13. Smets, Ph.: The combination of evidence in the transferable belief model. *IEEE-Pattern analysis and Machine Intelligence* **12** (1990) 447–458
14. Smets, Ph., Kennes, R.: The transferable belief model. *Artificial Intelligence* **66** (1994) 191–234
15. Zadeh, L.A.: Review of Shafer's A Mathematical Theory of Evidence, *AI Magazine* **5** (1984) 81–83

Inclusion Measures in Intuitionistic Fuzzy Set Theory

Chris Cornelis and Etienne Kerre

Department of Mathematics and Computer Science
Fuzziness and Uncertainty Modelling Research Unit, Ghent University
Krijgslaan 281 (S9), B-9000 Gent, Belgium
{chris.cornelis,etienne.kerre}@rug.ac.be
http://fuzzy.rug.ac.be

Abstract. Twenty years after their inception, intuitionistic fuzzy sets are on the rise towards making their "claim to fame". Competing alongside various other, often closely related, formalisms, they are catering to the needs of a more demanding and rapidly expanding knowledge-based systems industry. In this paper, we develop the notion of a graded inclusion indicator within this setting, drawing inspiration from related concepts in fuzzy set theory, yet keeping a keen eye on those particular challenges raised specifically by intuitionistic fuzzy set theory. The use of our work is demonstrated by its applications in approximate reasoning and non-probabilistic entropy calculation.

1 Introduction and Problem Definition

1.1 Putting Intuitionistic Fuzzy Set Theory on the Map

IFS theory basically enriches Zadeh's fuzzy set theory with a notion of indeterminacy expressing hesitation or abstention. While in the latter, membership degrees, identifying the degree to which an object satisfies a given property (generally speaking), are taken to be exact, in the former extra information in the guise of a non-membership degree is permitted to address a commonplace feature of uncertainty. Imagine, for instance, a voting procedure in which delegates have to express their feelings w.r.t. a number of proposals. It is obvious that while one can be in favour or in disfavour of a proposal to a certain extent, one can also abstain from the vote; an attitude inspired by, e.g., a lack of background or interest, or simply because no obvious arguments for or against the cause at stake have been raised. In such a situation, using only a $[0,1]$-valued degree α expressing support for the proposal is arguably too committing. A similar argument can be set up when the opinion of a given voter is not (fully) known, and we should be duly hesitant to classify him as a supporter or an opponent of the proposal.

IFS theory allows for an easy, yet elegant, way out of such problems by not insisting that membership and non-membership to a set be strictly complementary properties. In an IFS A defined in a universe[1] X, alongside a **membership**

---

[1] For simplicity, throughout this paper X is assumed to be finite.

T.D. Nielsen and N.L. Zhang (Eds.): ECSQARU 2003, LNAI 2711, pp. 345–356, 2003.

degree $\mu_A(x)$ of x to A, we also distinguish a non-membership degree $\nu_A(x)$, such that $\mu_A(x) + \nu_A(x) \leq 1$. Note that a fuzzy set in X is then just an IFS for which $\mu_A(x) + \nu_A(x) = 1$ holds for every x. The degree $\pi_A(x) = 1 - \mu_A(x) - \nu_A(x)$ quantifies the degree of indeterminacy associated with x and A.

Just like the relationship between classical logic and set theory was exploited in fuzzy set theory to define "fuzzy logics" (in a narrow sense), so we may also introduce a notion of "intuitionistic fuzzy (IF) logics"; with a proposition P a degree of truth μ_P and one of falsity ν_P may be associated, such that $\mu_P + \nu_P \leq 1$. This idea is elaborated in e.g. [1].

As it turns out, IFSs pop up quite naturally. Attempts to embed IFS theory within more "familiar" frameworks have shown that they fit in with, and enrich, a well-established tradition of modeling imprecision rather than setting off on an entirely new course, which marks their relevance. It can easily be seen, for instance, that IFSs are formally equivalent to interval-valued fuzzy sets: indeed, a couple $(\mu_A(x), \nu_A(x))$ may be mapped bijectively onto an interval $[\mu_A(u), 1 - \nu_A(u)]$. Some would consider this syntactical equivalence sufficient evidence to dismiss IFS theory as superfluous and giving cause to unnecessary confusion. We raise two arguments against such allegations:

1. Interval-valued fuzzy set theory is currently associated, *de facto*, with the work of Mendel and others on type-2 fuzzy logic systems (see e.g. [13]). That setting is characterized by a probability-like treatment of uncertainty on the membership degrees in a fuzzy set; an interval-valued fuzzy set is designated as a special type-2 fuzzy set[2] that exhibits a uniform spread of uncertainty on the membership degrees. IFS theory, however, does not make any assumptions on the nature of its indeterminacy – it merely gives a quantitative representation of "missing information".

2. We consider IFS theory as a stepping stone in a larger context that is specifically tuned to the concept of positive and negative constituents, rather than lower and upper approximations. Indeed, if we relax the constraint that $\mu_A(x)$ and $\nu_A(x)$ sum up to at most 1, letting either degree range freely in $[0,1]$, we arrive in the realm of fuzzy four-valued logics first suggested by Stickel [15] and given a nice practical application by Fortemps and Slowinski [9], who used degrees $(\alpha, \beta) \in [0,1]^2$ whose respective components express positive and negative evidence in a preference setting. It is clear that as soon as $\alpha + \beta > 1$, evidence is inconsistent to some extent. In that sense, IFS theory can be seen as the consistent restriction of the fuzzy four-valued framework.

Unfortunately, also a lot of misunderstandings concerning terminology have sprung up. The term "intuitionistic" is to be read in a "broad" sense here, alluding loosely to the denial of the law of the excluded middle on element level (since $\mu_A(x) + \nu_A(x) < 1$ is possible). A "narrow", graded extension of intuitionistic logic proper has also been proposed and is due to Takeuti and Titani [17] – it bears no relationship to our notion of IFS theory.

---

[2] i.e. a fuzzy set whose membership degrees are themselves fuzzy sets in $[0,1]$

1.2   An Introduction to Graded Inclusion Measures

In fuzzy set theory, inclusion is, by default, defined as follows: for A and B fuzzy sets[3] in a universe X, $A \subseteq B \iff (\forall x \in X)(A(x) \leq B(x))$, i.e. $A \subseteq B$ if and only if the graph of A fits beneath the graph of B. A natural extension of this definition to IFS theory reads, for A and B IFSs in X: $A \subseteq B \iff \mu_A \subseteq \mu_B$ and $\nu_B \subseteq \nu_A$.

While in many theoretical and practical settings this two-valued character-ization of subsethood suffices, it could be argued that the definition is overly restrictive: just as an element can belong to a fuzzy set to varying degrees, so we may also want to talk about a fuzzy set being "more or less" a subset of another one. Many researchers [2,7,8,11,12,14,18] have tried to capture this intuition by proposing concrete operators Inc that take a couple of fuzzy sets (A, B) as their input and return a value $Inc(A, B)$ in $[0, 1]$ indicating the degree of subsethood of A to B.

Typically, to define fuzzy subsethood one takes a definition of classical set inclusion and tries to extend ("fuzzify") it to apply to fuzzy sets. Below we quote three distinct, but essentially equivalent[4], definitions of the inclusion of A into B, where $A, B \in \mathcal{P}(X)$:

$$A \subseteq B \iff (\forall x \in X)(x \in A \Rightarrow x \in B), \tag{1}$$

$$\iff A = \emptyset \text{ or } \frac{|A \cap B|}{|A|} = 1, \tag{2}$$

$$\iff \frac{|co(A) \cup B|}{|X|} = 1 \tag{3}$$

While (1) is stated in strictly logical terms, the other two are based on count-ing the elements of a set, i.e. on cardinality, and have a probabilistic (i.e. fre-quentist) touch about them. It is therefore not surprising that their respective generalizations to fuzzy set theory cease to be equivalent. Without going into the details at this point, we might roughly state that adepts of the different crisp definitions have put fuzzy subsethood on two separate tracks, one logic-based, the other frequency-based. One situation where this distinction comes to light is when one tries to mould fuzzy inclusion measures into axiomatic characteriza-tions by listing desirable properties for them, as several authors have attempted. The most strident dissonance (see e.g. Young [18] on this) seems to concern the condition

$$A, B \in \mathcal{P}(X) \Rightarrow Inc(A, B) \in \{0, 1\} \tag{4}$$

called heritage by Kitainik [11]. As will be revealed later on, choosing to impose it pretty much forces us into the logic-based approach, although useful trade-offs are possible.

---

[3] For simplicity, we identify a fuzzy set A with its membership function μ_A and write $A(x)$ to denote $\mu_A(x)$.

[4] Arguably, (1) is more general since it can also deal with infinite sets.

In this paper, we are going to pursue this discussion to the framework of IFS theory. Our aim is twofold: first we are going to try and convey as complete and uniform as possible a picture of IF inclusion by contrasting and generalizing corresponding fuzzy approaches; and secondly, we will highlight a few distinguishing features that are specific only to the extension, and which are meant to refute the criticism that IF subsethood assessment merely amounts to applying fuzzy inclusion measures twice.

The paper is organized as follows: in Sect. 2, we recall the necessary mathematical background on IFS theory. Section 3 starts by investigating what an IF inclusion measure should look like, and what properties it should ideally satisfy. This results in the development of logic- and frequency-based approaches. In Sect. 4, we briefly sketch the application of these measures in two concrete domains: approximate reasoning and entropy measurement. Finally, Sect. 5 offers a brief conclusion.

2   Preliminaries of Intuitionistic Fuzzy Set Theory

Atanassov [1] gives the following definition of an IFS A in X:

$$A = \{(x, \mu_A(x), \nu_A(x)) \mid x \subset X\} \tag{5}$$

where μ_A and ν_A are called membership and non-membership function of A respectively. They satisfy $\mu_A(x) + \nu_A(x) \leq 1$ for every $x \in X$. The class of all IFSs in X is denoted $\mathcal{IF}(X)$.

This definition is easy to absorb for humans but lacks mathematical conciseness. Just as a fuzzy set in X can be interpreted as a mapping from X to $[0,1]$, so we may define an IFS A in X as a mapping from X to the set $L^* = \{(x_1, x_2) \in [0,1]^2 \mid x_1 + x_2 \leq 1\}$. Moreover, equiping L^* with an ordering $\leq_{L^*}$ defined as $(x_1, x_2) \leq_{L^*} (y_1, y_2) \Leftrightarrow x_1 \leq y_1$ and $x_2 \geq y_2$, $(L^*, \leq_{L^*})$ assumes the structure of a complete, bounded lattice with greatest element $1_{L^*} = (1, 0)$ and smallest element $0_{L^*} = (0, 1)$. The sup and inf operations on this lattice are derived from $\leq_{L^*}$ as:

$$\sup((x_1, y_1), (x_2, y_2)) = (\max(x_1, x_2), \min(y_1, y_2)) \tag{6}$$

$$\inf((x_1, y_1), (x_2, y_2)) = (\min(x_1, x_2), \max(y_1, y_2)) \tag{7}$$

The intersection, union and complement of IFSs A and B in $\mathcal{IF}(X)$ are defined by, for $x = (x_1, x_2) \in L^*$, $A \cap B(x) = \inf(A(x), B(x))$, $A \cup B(x) = \sup(A(x), B(x))$, $co(A)(x) = A(x_2, x_1)$. Thus, IFSs are a special case of L-fuzzy sets in the sense of Goguen [10], with $L = L^*$. As a shorthand notation, for $x \in L^*$, we denote its first, resp. second component by x_1 and x_2. A special subset D of "fuzzy values" of L^* is defined by $D = \{(x_1, x_2) \in L^* \mid x_1 = 1 - x_2\}$.

Since $\leq_{L^*}$ is a partial order, an order-theoretic extension of classical negation, conjunction, disjunction and implication on L^*, as negators, triangular norms and conorms, and implicators, respectively, arises quite naturally: a negator on L^* is any decreasing $L^* \to L^*$ mapping $\mathcal{N}$ that satisfies $\mathcal{N}(0_{L^*}) = 1_{L^*}$ and

$\mathcal{N}(1_{L^*}) = 0_{L^*}$. The mapping $\mathcal{N}_s$, defined as $\mathcal{N}_s(x_1, x_2) = (x_2, x_1), \forall(x_1, x_2) \in L^*$, will be called the *standard negator*.

A t-norm on L^* is any increasing, commutative, associative $(L^*)^2 \to L^*$ mapping $\mathcal{T}$ that satisfies $\mathcal{T}(1_{L^*}, x) = x$, for all $x \in L^*$; a t-conorm on L^* is any increasing, commutative, associative $(L^*)^2 \to L^*$ mapping $\mathcal{S}$ satisfying $\mathcal{S}(0_{L^*}, x) = x$, for all $x \in L^*$. Obviously, the greatest t-norm with respect to the ordering $\leq_{L^*}$ is inf, while the smallest t-conorm w.r.t. $\leq_{L^*}$ is sup. Note that it does not hold that for all $x, y \in L^*$, either $\inf(x, y) = x$ or $\inf(x, y) = y$. For instance, $\inf((0.1, 0.3), (0.2, 0.4)) = (0.1, 0.4)$. t-norms and t-conorms can be partitioned into two classes by the following definition: a t-norm $\mathcal{T}$ on L^* (resp. t-conorm $\mathcal{S}$) is called t-representable if there exists a t-norm T and a t-conorm S on $[0, 1]$ (resp. a t-conorm S' and a t-norm T' on $[0, 1]$) such that, for $x = (x_1, x_2), y = (y_1, y_2) \in L^*$, $\mathcal{T}(x, y) = (T(x_1, y_1), S(x_2, y_2)), \mathcal{S}(x, y) = (S'(x_1, y_1), T'(x_2, y_2))$; T and S (resp. S' and T') are called the representants of $\mathcal{T}$ (resp. $\mathcal{S}$). Clearly, inf and sup are t-representable. The following mappings $\mathcal{T}_W$ and $\mathcal{S}_W$, called IF Łukasiewicz t-norm and t-conorm, are not [4]:

$$\mathcal{T}_W(x, y) = (\max(0, x_1 + y_1 - 1), \min(1, x_2 + 1 - y_1, y_2 + 1 - x_1)) \qquad (8)$$

$$\mathcal{S}_W(x, y) = (\min(1, x_1 + 1 - y_2, y_1 + 1 - x_2), \max(0, x_2 + y_2 - 1)) \qquad (9)$$

It can be verified that $\mathcal{T}_W$ is a t-norm on L^* and $\mathcal{S}_W$ a t-conorm on L^*; their existence rules out the conjecture, implicit in most of the existing literature that t-norms and t-conorms on L^* are necessarily characterized by a pair of fuzzy connectives.

Negators, t-norms and t-conorms on L^* may be used to define generalized versions of complementation, intersection and union of IFSs. Specifically, we may define $co_{\mathcal{N}}(A)$, $A \cap_{\mathcal{T}} B$ and $A \cup_{\mathcal{T}} B$ by $co_{\mathcal{N}}(A)(x) = \mathcal{N}(A(x))$, $A \cap_{\mathcal{T}} B(x) = \mathcal{T}(A(x), B(x))$, $A \cup_{\mathcal{S}} B(x) = \mathcal{S}(A(x), B(x))$, where $x \in X$.

The final and for our purposes most important construct is that of an implicator on L^*: an $(L^*)^2 \to L^*$-mapping $\mathcal{I}$ satisfying $\mathcal{I}(0_{L^*}, 0_{L^*}) = 1_{L^*}, \mathcal{I}(1_{L^*}, 0_{L^*}) = 0_{L^*}, \mathcal{I}(0_{L^*}, 1_{L^*}) = 1_{L^*}, \mathcal{I}(1_{L^*}, 1_{L^*}) = 1_{L^*}$. Moreover we require $\mathcal{I}$ to be decreasing in its first, and increasing in its second component. This definition is very general; as in fuzzy set theory, we may distinguish implicators on L^* w.r.t. their construction. Explicitly, an S-implicator $\mathcal{I}_{\mathcal{S}, \mathcal{N}}$ is defined as, for $x, y \in L^*$:

$$\mathcal{I}_{\mathcal{S}, \mathcal{N}}(x, y) = \mathcal{S}(\mathcal{N}(x), y) \qquad (10)$$

with $\mathcal{S}$ a t-conorm and $\mathcal{N}$ a negator on L^*. An R-implicator $\mathcal{I}_{\mathcal{T}}$, generated by a t-norm $\mathcal{T}$ on L^* is defined as, for $x, y \in L^*$, by

$$\mathcal{I}_{\mathcal{T}}(x, y) = \sup\{\gamma \in L^* \mid \mathcal{T}(x, \gamma) \leq_{L^*} y\} \qquad (11)$$

These two classes contain most of the prominent implicators. For example, the S-implicator of $\mathcal{S}_W$ and $\mathcal{N}_s$, equal to the R-implicator of $\mathcal{T}_W$ is given by

$$\mathcal{I}_{\mathcal{S}_W, \mathcal{N}_s} = \mathcal{I}_{\mathcal{T}_W}(x, y) = (\min(1, y_1 + 1 - x_1, x_2 + 1 - y_2), \max(0, y_2 + x_1 - 1)) \quad (12)$$

Other than by their construction, implicators on L^* may also be classified by the properties they satisfy. The following important theorem is based on [4].

Theorem 1. *A continuous implicator $\mathcal{I}$ on L^* satisfies*

$$(\forall x, y, z \in L^*)(\mathcal{I}(x, \inf(y, z)) = \inf(\mathcal{I}(x, y), \mathcal{I}(x, z)))) \tag{13}$$

$$(\forall x \in L^*)(\mathcal{I}(1, x) = x) \tag{14}$$

$$(\forall x, y \in L^*)(\mathcal{I}(\mathcal{N}_s(y), \mathcal{N}_s(x)) = \mathcal{I}(x, y)) \tag{15}$$

$$(\forall x, y, z \in L^*)(\mathcal{I}(x, \mathcal{I}(y, z)) = \mathcal{I}(y, \mathcal{I}(x, z))) \tag{16}$$

$$(\forall x, y \in L^*)(x \leq_{L^*} y \iff \mathcal{I}(x, y) = 1_{L^*}) \tag{17}$$

$$(\forall x, y \in L^*)(x = 1_{L^*} \text{ and } y = 0_{L^*} \iff \mathcal{I}(x, y) = 0_{L^*}) \tag{18}$$

$$\mathcal{I}(D, D) \subseteq D \tag{19}$$

iff there exists a continuous increasing permutation[5] ϕ of $[0, 1]$ s. t., for $x, y \in L^*$,

$$\mathcal{I}(x, y) = (\varphi^{-1} \min(1, 1 + \varphi(y_1) - \varphi(x_1), 1 + \varphi(1 - y_2) - \varphi(1 - x_2)),$$
$$1 - \varphi^{-1} \min(1, 1 - \varphi(x_1) + \varphi(1 - y_2))) \tag{20}$$

To conclude this section, the cardinality of an IFS A in X was defined by Szmidt and Kacprzyk [16] as the couple $(\min \Sigma Count(A), \max \Sigma Count(A))$, where

$$\min \Sigma Count(A) = \sum_{x \in X} \mu_A(x) \tag{21}$$

$$\max \Sigma Count(A) = \sum_{x \in X} \mu_A(x) + \pi_A(x) = \sum_{x \in X} (1 - \nu_A(x)) \tag{22}$$

3   Construction of IF Inclusion Measures

In this section, we study different strategies to come up with reasonable subset-hood indicators $\mathcal{I}nc$ for IFSs. A first question that needs to be answered is what kind of a mapping $\mathcal{I}nc$ should be: evidently, its inputs are IFSs in X, but what kind of object should its output be? Since we have been speaking about graded inclusion indicators, the natural option seems to be just a number in $[0, 1]$; the following example, however, shows that this strategy can lead to anomalies.

Example 1. *Let A, B be IFSs in $X = \{x_1, x_2\}$, such that $A(x_1) = 1_{L^*}$, $B(x_1) = (0, 0)$, $A(x_2) = (0, 0)$, $B(x_2) = 0_{L^*}$. Obviously, $A \nsubseteq B$. Yet, due to the indeterminacy w.r.t. B and x_1, and w.r.t. A and x_2, there is no indication that A is not a subset of B at all, nor can it be argued that A is a subset of B to a given extent $\alpha \in [0, 1]$: in fact, it could be a subset, to a certain extent, of B, but the presence of maximal indeterminacy does not allow to cut the knot! In this sense, forcing $\mathcal{I}nc(A, B)$ to be in $[0, 1]$ is too committing, and a more natural way to express A's inclusion into B is by the element $(0, 0) \in L^*$, exploiting it to express the same kind of indeterminacy as it does for partial membership to a set: we simply cannot tell.*

---

[5] It can be verified that this is equivalent to the existence of a permutation Φ of L^*, where $\Phi(x) = (\phi(x_1), 1 - \phi(1 - x_2))$, such that $\mathcal{I} = \Phi^{-1} \circ \mathcal{I}_{T_W} \circ (\Phi, \Phi)$. For this reason, $\mathcal{I}$ is also called a Φ-transform of the R-implicator of the IF Łukasiewicz t-norm.

This example suggests that $\mathcal{I}nc$ be an $\mathcal{IF}(X) \times \mathcal{IF}(X) \to L^*$ mapping. It also presents a criterion for IF inclusion measures without an analog in fuzzy set theory, namely that $\mathcal{I}nc(A, B) = (0, 0)$ when A and B are as in the above test case. On the other hand, we can borrow substantially from the available literature on fuzzy inclusion measures, as we will see shortly.

A convenient way to derive IF inclusion measures is to list a number of criteria for them, and then find out which operations satisfy these conditions. In fuzzy set theory, such an approach was taken by Sinha and Dougherty [14], and independently also by Kitainik [11]. Although neither linked their results explicitly to one of the formulas (1–3) defining crisp subsethood, subsequent research [7] pointed out that they implicitly invoked (1), and thus the use of an implicator on [0, 1], by their insistence on the heritage property (4). For now, we will take this property for granted; a convenient working set of criteria is then given as:

(I1) Contrapositivity $\mathcal{I}nc(A, B) = \mathcal{I}nc(coB, coA)$
(I2) Distributivity $\quad \mathcal{I}nc(A, B \cap C) = \inf(\mathcal{I}nc(A, B), \mathcal{I}nc(A, C))$
(I3) Symmetry $\quad\quad \mathcal{I}nc(A, B) = \mathcal{I}nc(S(A), S(B))$
$\quad\quad\quad\quad\quad\quad$ a) $\mathcal{I}nc(A, B) = 1_{L^*} \iff A \subseteq B$
$\quad\quad\quad\quad\quad\quad$ b) $\mathcal{I}nc(A, B) = 0_{L^*} \iff$
(I4) Faithfulness $\quad\quad\quad\quad (\exists x \in X)(A(x) = 1_{L^*}$ and $B(x) = 0_{L^*})$
$\quad\quad\quad\quad\quad\quad$ c) $A, B \in \mathcal{F}(X) \Rightarrow \mathcal{I}nc(A, B) \in D$

where $A, B, C \in \mathcal{IF}(X)$ and S an $\mathcal{IF}(X) \to \mathcal{IF}(X)$ mapping defined by, for $x \in X$, $S(A)(x) = A(s(x))$, with s a permutation of X.

Historically, these conditions go back to different sources[6]: the first three requirements were adopted from Kitainik's work on fuzzy inclusion measures [11], while the two faithfulness conditions (I4a–b) are due to Sinha and Dougherty. [14] The heritage property is a consequence of (I4a–b). Finally, we added another faithfulness condition to ensure that $\mathcal{I}nc$, when applied to fuzzy information, acts like a fuzzy inclusion measure. It can be verified that a mapping satisfying (I1–I4) is decreasing in its first, and increasing in its second component. The following theorem gives an explicit characterization. Its proof draws its inspiration from [7],[8] and [11].

Theorem 2. *An $\mathcal{IF}(X) \times \mathcal{IF}(X) \to L^*$ mapping $\mathcal{I}nc$ satisfies (I1)–(I4) iff*

$$\mathcal{I}nc(A, B) = \inf_{x \in X} \mathcal{I}(A(x), B(x)), \tag{23}$$

with $\mathcal{I}$ an IF implicator satisfying properties (13),(15), (17), (18) and (19).

It is interesting that in order to be compliant with the test case of example 1, $\mathcal{I}$ should also satisfy (14). Few candidates $\mathcal{I}$ fulfill all requirements; theorem 5

---

[6] For a detailed account of the various links between Kitainik's and Sinha and Dougherty's approach, and their unification, we refer the interested reader to [7].

characterized all continuous mappings complying with these stringent conditions, i.e. the Φ-transforms of the R-implicator of the Łukasiewicz t-norm $\mathcal{T}_W$. The simplest of these uses $\Phi(x) = x$ for all $x \in L^*$ and will be called $\mathcal{I}nc_{\mathcal{T}_W}$:

$$\mathcal{I}nc_{\mathcal{T}_W}(A, B) = \inf_{x \in X} \mathcal{I}_{\mathcal{T}_W}(A(x), B(x)) \tag{24}$$

A byproduct of this result is that it forces us to reject the argument that a graded subsethood assessment for IFSs could be reduced trivially to assessing e.g. $\mathcal{I}nc_{\mathcal{T}_W}(\mu_A, \mu_B)$ and $\mathcal{I}nc_{\mathcal{T}_W}(\nu_B, \nu_A)$, which are both in D by (14c). Indeed, for the test case in example 1, both of these are equal to 0_{L^*}, whereas $\mathcal{I}nc_{\mathcal{T}_W}(A, B) = (0, 0)$. In other words, determining subsethood for IFSs does not amount to a mere double application of a fuzzy inclusion measure, as some IFS critics suggest!

Let us focus again on the heritage condition (4). In her paper on fuzzy subsethood, Young [18] raises skepticism about it: she reasons that much of the relative structure of fuzzy sets, and by extension IFSs, is lost when imposing it; indeed, if two fuzzy sets A and B are equal everywhere, except in the point x for which $A(x) = 1$ and $B(x) = 0$, (4) forces $Inc(A, B) = 0$. One can think of very concrete instances in which this indeed makes no sense. Imagine for instance that we are to evaluate to what extent the young people in a company are also rich. Testing subsethood of the fuzzy set of young workers into that of rich workers should then be based on the relative fraction (i.e. the *frequency*) of good earners among the youngsters, and not on whether there exists or does not exist one poor, young employee. This observation has led researchers to consider extensions to definition (2) of crisp subsethood, which works well for fuzzy inclusion measures. Indeed, if A and B are fuzzy sets, then e.g. $\min \Sigma Count(A) = \max \Sigma Count(A)$; putting $|A| = \min \Sigma Count(A)$, one can define the subsethood of A into B as the ratio of $|A \cap B|$ and $|A|$ if $A \neq \emptyset$, and 0 otherwise (see e.g. [12]). Unfortunately, there is no straightforward extension to IFS theory, since IF cardinalities are intervals of positive real values; resorting to interval calculus is not a viable option, either, as the following example shows.

Example 2. *Given two strictly positive real intervals $[a, b]$ and $[c, d]$, interval calculus defines their ratio as*

$$\frac{[a, b]}{[c, d]} = \left[\frac{a}{d}, \frac{b}{c}\right] \tag{25}$$

Define f, for IFSs A and B in X, as

$$f(A, B) = \frac{[\min \Sigma Count(A \cap B), \min \Sigma Count(A \cap B)]}{[\min \Sigma Count(A), \max \Sigma Count(A)]} \tag{26}$$

Let $X = \{x\}$, $A(x) = (0.5, 0.3)$, $B(x) = (0.6, 0.2)$. Then $A \subseteq B$, but $f(A, B) = \frac{[0.5, 0.7]}{[0.5, 0.7]} = [\frac{5}{7}, \frac{7}{5}] \neq [1, 1]$. It is also unclear how to associate $f(A, B)$ with an element of L^*.

Evidently, the extension of (2) by interval calculus is problematic and appears to be due to definition (25). If however in (25) we put $c = d$, the result *will* be an interval in $[0, 1]$. This property is particularly useful when one considers the alternative definition (3) of crisp inclusion. Indeed, using the definition of generalized IF union and complement, we can compute

$$f_{\mathcal{S},\mathcal{N}}(A, B) = \frac{[\min \Sigma Count(co_{\mathcal{N}}(A) \cup_{\mathcal{S}} B), \max \Sigma Count(co_{\mathcal{N}}(A) \cup_{\mathcal{S}} B)]}{[\min \Sigma Count(X), \max \Sigma Count(X)]} \quad (27)$$

Let $f_{\mathcal{S},\mathcal{N}}(A, B) = [c_1, c_2]$. Since $\min \Sigma Count(X) = \max \Sigma Count(X) = |X|$, $(c_1, 1 - c_2) \in L^*$. Recalling definition (10) of an S-implicator on L^*, we may therefore introduce the following class of inclusion measures $Inc_{\mathcal{S},\mathcal{N}}$:

$$Inc_{\mathcal{S},\mathcal{N}}(A, B) = \left(\frac{1}{|X|} \sum_{x \in X} (\mathcal{I}_{\mathcal{S},\mathcal{N}}(A(x), B(x)))_1, \frac{1}{|X|} \sum_{x \in X} (\mathcal{I}_{\mathcal{S},\mathcal{N}}(A(x), B(x)))_2 \right)$$

$$= \frac{1}{|X|} \sum_{x \in X} \mathcal{I}_{\mathcal{S},\mathcal{N}}(A(x), B(x)) \quad (28)$$

The second equality introduces a convenient shorthand notation.

An example at hand is $Inc_{\mathcal{S}_W, \mathcal{N}_s}$. It satisfies all of (I1–I3), (I4a) and (I4c), but not (I4b). In that sense, it has a much more lenient behaviour w.r.t. the young and rich employee problem. In fact, it can be seen that it bears a close relationship to $Inc_{\mathcal{T}_W}$: instead of taking the infimum of all values $\mathcal{I}_{\mathcal{T}_W}(A(x), B(x))$, it computes their "average", which allows for a much greater deal of compensation.

4   Applications of IF Inclusion Measures

4.1   Inclusion-Based Approximate Reasoning

Roughly, approximate reasoning is concerned with the deduction of imprecise conclusions from imprecise premises. In the context of IFS theory, an IF if–then rule is a construct with the generic form "If $\mathcal{V}_1$ is A then $\mathcal{V}_2$ is B" where $\mathcal{V}_1$ and $\mathcal{V}_2$ represent an input and an output variable, respectively, and A and B are normalized[7] IFSs in the universes X of $\mathcal{V}_1$ and Y of $\mathcal{V}_2$. Typically, then, the system is presented with an observation on the input variable of the form "$\mathcal{V}_1$ is A'" with A' not necessarily equalling A, and asked to derive a suitable IFS B' such that "$\mathcal{V}_2$ is B'". One way of obtaining B' is by applying the Compositional Rule of Inference [6]: the if–then rule is paraphrased by an IF relation[8] R from X to Y, i.e. an IFS in $X \times Y$, and B' is computed by taking the $\circ_{\mathcal{T}}$-composition of R and A', defined by, for $y \in Y$

$$B'(y) = R \circ_{\mathcal{T}} A'(y) = \sup_{x \in X} \mathcal{T}(A'(x), R(x, y))) \quad (29)$$

---

[7] An IFS A in X is called normalized if there exists at least one $x \in X$ such that $A(x) = 1_{L^*}$.

[8] Typically, $R(x, y) = \mathcal{I}(A(x), B(x))$ for some implicator $\mathcal{I}$ on L^* or $R(x, y) = \mathcal{T}(A(x), B(x))$ for some t-norm $\mathcal{T}$ on L^*.

This calculation is computationally costly. In [6], a procedure called inclusion-based approximate reasoning was shown to approximate $B'(y)$ in particular cases.

Theorem 3. *If* $B'(y) = \sup\limits_{x \in X} \mathcal{T}_W(A'(x), \mathcal{I}_{\mathcal{T}_W}(A(x), B(y)))$, *then*
$\mathcal{I}_{\mathcal{T}_W}(\mathcal{I}nc_{\mathcal{T}_W}(A', A), B(y)) \geq_{L^*} B'(y)$, *and* $\mathcal{I}nc_{\mathcal{T}_W}(B', B) \geq_{L^*} \mathcal{I}nc_{\mathcal{T}_W}(A', A)$.
Additionally, if the range of B *is* L^*, *then* $\mathcal{I}nc_{\mathcal{T}_W}(B', B) = \mathcal{I}nc_{\mathcal{T}_W}(A', A)$.

The approximation is much easier to calculate, since it bypasses the expensive supremum operation. Some promising examples (so far only in fuzzy set theory) have demonstrated the practical use of inclusion-based approximate reasoning. [5]

Note also that the theorem uses $\mathcal{I}nc_{\mathcal{T}_W}$, which satisfies the controversial property (I4b). Another setting in which this measure appears is in the calculation of lower approximations in IF rough set theory as developed in [3].

4.2 Entropy of IFSs

In fuzzy set theory, a common task is to determine the amount of fuzziness in a given fuzzy set (see e.g. [12,18]). A measure of fuzziness, also called entropy measure, is taken to express the extent to which a crisp distinction between the elements belonging and not belonging to a fuzzy set is lacking, i.e. the extent to which all the elements' membership degrees are close to 0.5. In IFS theory, first steps were taken to define a measure of entropy by Szmidt and Kacprzyk in [16].

To Szmidt and Kacprzyk, an IF entropy measure on X is an $\mathcal{IF}(X) \to [0,1]$ mapping $\mathcal{E}$ satisfying

1. $\mathcal{E}(A) = 0 \iff A \in \mathcal{P}(X)$
2. $\mathcal{E}(A) = 1 \iff \mu_A = \nu_A$
3. $(\forall x \in X)(\mu_A(x) \leq \mu_B(x) \leq \nu_B(x) \leq \nu_A(x)$ or $\mu_A(x) \geq \mu_B(x) \geq \nu_B(x) \geq \nu_A(x)) \Rightarrow \mathcal{E}(A) \leq \mathcal{E}(B))$
4. $\mathcal{E}(co(A)) = \mathcal{E}(A)$.

These conditions are faithful extensions to those imposed on fuzzy entropy measures[9]. Still, we wish to adjust these requirements in the following respects. First, in a similar vein as for IF inclusion measures, it can be argued that entropy of IFSs cannot be reasonably captured by just one number and is better expressed by elements of L^*. For instance, if $(\forall x \in X)(A(x) = (0,0))$, then $\mathcal{E}(A)$ should be equal to $(0,0)$, since no information is available on the fuzziness of A. This also explains our feeling that requirements 2. and 3. are too strong, and should be replaced by $\mathcal{E}(A) = 1_{L^*} \iff (\forall x \in X)(\mu_A(x) = \nu_A(x) = 0.5)$ and $(\forall x \in X)(\mu_A(x) \leq \mu_B(x) \leq 0.5 \leq \nu_B(x) \leq \nu_A(x)$ or $\mu_A(x) \geq \mu_B(x) \geq 0.5 \geq \nu_B(x) \geq \nu_A(x)) \Rightarrow \mathcal{E}(A) \leq_{L^*} \mathcal{E}(B))$.

In fact, we feel that IF entropy should reflect the range of situations that *could* occur if the indeterminacy in A were to disappear, that is: if $\pi_A(x)$ were distributed between $\mu_A(x)$ and $\nu_A(x)$. This idea is illustrated by an example.

---

[9] Replacing ν_A by $co(\mu_A)$ in the above definition, we can obtain them.

Example 3. *Let A be the IFS in $X = \{x_1, x_2\}$ defined by $A(x_1) = (0.2, 0.3)$, $A(x_2) = (0.1, 0.1)$. Then $\pi_A(x_1) = 0.5$ and $\pi_A(x_2) = 0.8$. The "least fuzzy" fuzzy set obtainable by distributing π_A among μ_A and ν_A is A' defined by $A'(x_1) = (0.2, 0.8)$, $A'(x_2) = (0.9, 0.1)$. The "most fuzzy" fuzzy set derived in this way is A'' defined by $A''(x_1) = (0.5, 0.5)$, $A''(x_2) = (0.5, 0.5)$. Applying an arbitrary fuzzy entropy measure E on X to A' and A'', we have $E(A') \le E(A'')$. The "real" fuzziness of A is therefore somewhere in the interval $[E(A'), E(A'')]$, and hence could be represented equivalently by $(E(A'), 1 - E(A'')) \in L^*$.*

Kosko [12] was the first to link the entropy of a fuzzy set A to the degree to which $A \cup co(A)$ is included into $A \cap co(A)$, using specific definitions for E and Inc. It is therefore interesting to investigate whether IF entropy measures like the one suggested in the above example can be obtained at all using IF inclusion measures. The following theorem is a very nice affirmation of this conjecture, showing at once the use of frequency-based IF inclusion measures and of t-representable connectives on L^*.

Theorem 4. *Let $\mathcal{E}(A)$, for $A \in \mathcal{IF}(X)$, be defined as*

$$\mathcal{E}(A) = Inc_{\mathcal{S}, \mathcal{N}_s}(A \cup co(A), A \cap co(A)) \tag{30}$$

where $\mathcal{S}(x, y) = (\min(1, x_1 + y_1), \max(0, x_2 + y_2 - 1))$. Then $\mathcal{E}$ satisfies the modified conditions of Szmidt and Kacprzyk, and

$$\mathcal{E}(A) = (E(A'), 1 - E(A'')) \tag{31}$$

where A' and A'' are fuzzy sets in X such that for $x \in X$, $A'(x) = \max(1 - \mu_A(x), 1 - \nu_A(x))$, and $A''(x) = \max(0.5, \mu_A(x), \nu_A(x))$, and E is a fuzzy entropy measure, defined for a fuzzy set B in X by

$$E(B) = \frac{2}{|X|} \sum_{x \in X} B \cap co(B)(x) \tag{32}$$

It can be verified that defining e.g. $\mathcal{E}(A) = Inc_{\mathcal{S}_W, \mathcal{N}_s}(A \cup co(A), A \cap co(A))$, a similar decomposition is not possible.

5   Conclusion

This paper has studied various approaches to the definition of intuitionistic fuzzy inclusion measures. We have attempted to reconcile various requirements posed by fuzzy set theory with the specific indeterministic nature of IFSs. This has resulted in two essentially different types of IF inclusion measures, although both are dependent on an implicator on the evaluation set L^*. Future work should focus on the particular meaning of the individual degrees of the result. The example on IF entropy has already shown that under specific conditions on the operations involved a very attractive interpretation can be endowed to the result.

Acknowledgements. The authors would like to thank the anonymous referees for their critical analysis of the paper. Chris Cornelis would like to thank the Fund for Scientific Research-Flanders for funding the research elaborated on in this paper.

References

1. Atanassov, K.T.: Intuitionistic Fuzzy Sets. Physica-Verlag, Heidelberg, New York (1999)
2. Bandler, W., Kohout, L. Fuzzy power sets and fuzzy implication operators. Fuzzy Sets and Systems, **4** (1980) 13–30
3. Cornelis, C., De Cock, M., Kerre, E.: Intuitionistic fuzzy rough sets: on the crossroads of imperfect knowledge. Accepted to: Expert Systems (2003)
4. Cornelis, C., Deschrijver, G., Kerre, E.E.: Implication in intuitionistic and interval–Valued fuzzy set theory: construction, classification, application. Submitted to: International Journal of Approximate Reasoning (2002)
5. Cornelis, C., Kerre, E.E.: A Fuzzy Inference Methodology Based on the Fuzzification of Set Inclusion. Recent Advances in Intelligent Paradigms and Applications, (A. Abraham, L. Jain, J. Kacprzyk, eds.), Physica-Verlag (2002) 71–89.
6. Cornelis, C., Kerre, E.E.: On the structure and interpretation of an intuitionistic fuzzy expert system. In: Proceedings of EUROFUSE 2002 (B. De Baets, J. Fodor, G. Pasi, eds.) (2002) 173–178.
7. Cornelis, C., Van Der Donck, C., Kerre, E.E.: Sinha–Dougherty approach to the fuzzification of set inclusion revisited. Fuzzy Sets and Systems, **134(2)** (2003) 283–295.
8. Fodor, J., Yager, R.: Fuzzy set theoretic operators and quantifiers. Fundamentals of Fuzzy Sets (D. Dubois, H. Prade, eds.), Kluwer, Boston, Mass. (2000) 125–193
9. Fortemps, P., Slowinski, R.: A graded quadrivalent logic for ordinal preference modelling: Loyola–like approach. Fuzzy Optimization and Decision Making **1** (2002) 93–111
10. Goguen, J.: L–fuzzy Sets. J. Math. Anal. Appl. **18** (1967) 145–174.
11. Kitainik, L.: Fuzzy decision procedures with binary relations. Kluwer, Dordrecht, The Netherlands (1993)
12. Kosko, B.: Fuzzy entropy and conditioning. Kluwer, Dordrecht, the Netherlands (1993)
13. Mendel, J.M.: Uncertain rule–based fuzzy logic systems. Prentice Hall PTR, Upper Saddle River, New Jersey (2001)
14. Sinha, D., Dougherty, E.R.: Fuzzification of set inclusion: theory and applications. Fuzzy Sets and Systems, **55(1)** (1993) 15–42.
15. Stickel, M.E.: Fuzzy four–valued logic for inconsistency and uncertainty. Proceedings of the Eighth International Symposium on Multiple–Valued Logic (1978)
16. Szmidt, E., Kacprzyk, J., Entropy for intuitionistic fuzzy sets. Fuzzy Sets and Systems, **118(3)** (2001), 467–477.
17. Takeuti, G., Titani S.: Intuitionistic fuzzy logic and intuitionistic fuzzy set theory. Journal of Symbolic Logic, **49(3)** (1984) 851–866.
18. Young, V.: Fuzzy subsethood. Fuzzy Sets and Systems, **77(3)** (1996) 371–384.

A Random Set Model for Fuzzy Labels

Jonathan Lawry[1] and Jordi Recasens[2]

[1] Department of Engineering Mathematics
University of Bristol
Bristol, UK
j.lawry@bris.ac.uk
[2] Secció Matemàtiques i Informàtica – ETSAV
Univ. Politècnica de Catalunya
Pere Serra 1-15. Sant Cugat del Vallès, Barcelona, Spain
recasens@ea.upc.es

Abstract. A random set semantics for fuzzy labels is proposed in which we model the vagueness of fuzzy concepts in terms of their level of appropriateness as descriptions for values. This random set model is then shown to be characterised by a certain axiom system for appropriateness measures. It is then shown how some t-norms can generate appropriateness measures and an attempt is made to identify a family of t-norms that can be used consistently for this purpose. The calculus that is introduced is functional but not truth-functional.

1 Introduction

The use of fuzzy labels to describe system variables and parameters has proved to be a highly effective modelling tool applied in a wide range of applications. Despite this there remain a number of unresolved fundamental issues associated with fuzzy methods in general and truth-functional fuzzy logic in particular. Central to these is the problem that fuzzy logic lacks an agreed operational semantics providing a clear interpretation of membership functions and justifying the truth-functionality assumption. Indeed, it is interesting to observe that many of the most contoversial aspects of fuzzy logic are a direct consequence of truth-functionality, including the failure to satisy the law of excluded middle and the fact that (classically) equivalent expressions may have different membership degrees (see Elkan [2] and associated replies for an interesting discussion of these two properties). Intuitively, however, we expect the meaning of compound fuzzy expressions to be captured entirely by the meaning of the basic fuzzy labels from which they are generated. This suggests that some form of functionality should be a feature of any calculus for fuzzy labels. In addition, there are, of course, good practical arguments for functionality in terms of efficiency of both representation and reasoning. We claim, however, that these requirements can be met by a type of functionality much weaker than truth-functionality.

In the sequel we propose a model for fuzzy labels based on random sets. This differs from previous random set interpetation such as those proposed by Goodman and Nguyen (see [4], [5]) in that the random sets are defined on subsets of

T.D. Nielsen and N.L. Zhang (Eds.): ECSQARU 2003, LNAI 2711, pp. 357–369, 2003.

labels rather than subsets of parameter values. Within this framework we define
a measure of appropriateness of a label to a value and show how this can be
extended to compound logical expressions. A type of functionality is then introduced by means of a mass selection function. This random set model is then
shown to be characterised by a certain axiom system for appropriateness measures. We then show how some t-norms can generate appropriateness measures
and we attempt to identify a family of t-norms that can be used consistently for
this purpose.

2   Label Semantics

For a variable x into a domain of discourse Ω we identify a finite set of words
$LA = \{L_1, \ldots, L_n\}$ with which to label the values of x. Then for a specific value
$x \in \Omega$ an individual I identifies a subset of LA, denoted $\mathcal{D}_x^I$ to stand for the
description of x given by I, as the set of words with which it is appropriate to
label x. Within this framework then, an expression such as 'the diastolic blood
pressure is $high$', as asserted by I, is interpreted to mean $high \in \mathcal{D}_{bp}^I$ where bp
denotes the value of the variable blood pressure. If we allow I to vary across a
population of individuals V then we naturally obtain a random set $\mathcal{D}_x$ from V
into the power set of LA where $\mathcal{D}_x(I) = \mathcal{D}_x^I$. A probability distribution (or mass
assignment) associated with this random set can be defined and is dependent on
the prior distribution over the population V. We can view the random set $\mathcal{D}_x$
as a description of the variable x in terms of the labels in LA.

Definition 1. *(Label Description) For $x \in \Omega$ the label description of x is a
random set from V into the power set of LA, denoted $\mathcal{D}_x$, with associated distribution m_x, given by*

$$\forall S \subseteq LA \; m_x(S) = P_V(\{I \in V : \mathcal{D}_x^I = S\})$$

where P_V is the underlying distribution on V.

Another high level measure associated with m_x is the following quantification
of the degree of appropriateness of a particular word $L \in LA$ as a label of x.

Definition 2. *(Appropriateness Degrees)*

$$\forall x \in \Omega, \; \forall L \in LA \; \mu_L(x) = \sum_{S \subseteq LA : L \in S} m_x(S)$$

We now extend the notion of appropriateness degrees from labels to compound descriptions generated as logical combinations of labels.

Definition 3. *Label Expressions*
The set of label expressions of LA,LE, is defined recursively as follows:

(i) $L_i \in LE$ for $i = 1, \ldots, n$
(ii) If $\theta, \varphi \in LE$ then $\neg\theta, \theta \wedge \varphi, \theta \vee \varphi, \theta \rightarrow \varphi \in LE$

In the context of this assertion-based framework we interpret the main logical connectives in the following manner: $L_1 \wedge L_2$ means that both L_1 and L_2 are appropriate labels, $L_1 \vee L_2$ means that either L_1 or L_2 are appropriate labels and $\neg L$ means that L is not an appropriate label. More generally, a label expression θ identifies a set of possible label sets $\lambda(\theta)$ as follows:

Definition 4. *For $L \in LA$ $\lambda(L) = \{S \subseteq LA : L \in S\}$ and for label expressions θ and φ*

(i) $\forall L_i \in LA$ $\lambda(L_i) = \{S \subseteq LA | L_i \in S\}$
(ii) $\lambda(\theta \wedge \varphi) = \lambda(\theta) \cap \lambda(\varphi)$
(iii) $\lambda(\theta \vee \varphi) = \lambda(\theta) \cup \lambda(\varphi)$
(iv) $\lambda(\neg\theta) = \overline{\lambda(\theta)}$
(v) $\lambda(\theta \to \varphi) = \lambda(\neg\theta) \cup \lambda(\varphi)$

Intuitively, $\lambda(\theta)$ corresponds to those subsets of LA identified as being possible values of $\mathcal{D}_x$ by expression θ. In this sense the imprecise linguistic restriction 'x is θ' on x corresponds to the strict constraint $\mathcal{D}_x \in \lambda(\theta)$ on $\mathcal{D}_x$. Hence, we can view label descriptions as an alternative to linguistic variables [9] as a means of encoding linguistic constraints.

The notion of appropriateness degree given above can now be extended so that it applies to compound label expressions. The idea here is that $\mu_\theta(x)$ quantifies the degree to which expression θ is appropriate to describe x.

Definition 5. *Compound Appropriateness Degrees*
For θ a label expression and $x \in \Omega$ the appropriateness of θ to x is given by:

$$\mu_\theta(x) = \sum_{S \in \lambda(\theta)} m_x(S)$$

3 Mass Assignments and Appropriateness Degrees

In general, for $LA = \{L_1, \ldots, L_n\}$ the values $\mu_{L_1}(x), \ldots, \mu_{L_n}(x)$ determine an infinite set of possible mass assignments for $\mathcal{D}_x$ satisfying the constraints $\sum_{S \subseteq LA : L_i \in S} m_{\mathcal{D}_x}(S) = \mu_{L_i}(x)$ for $i = 1, \ldots, n$. In terms of random set theory this means that the appropriateness values correspond to the fixed point coverage of the random set $\mathcal{D}_x$ [4]. Now clearly this property will be problematic for the practical application of a label semantics based calculus. To determine m_x directly we must have total knowledge of V and P_V which is unlikely to be the case and even if such information is available then general inference on appropriateness degrees would require the storage of $2^n - 1$ pieces of information. Clearly, this is not feasible even for moderately large values of n. However, we now argue that there is a case for assuming a functional relationship between $\mu_{L_1}(x), \ldots, \mu_{L_n}(x)$ and m_x.

Given that $\mathcal{D}_x$ encodes the use of labels across a population of individuals who are able to communicate and use these labels to convey information then we would expect the variation of $\mathcal{D}_x$ between individuals to be strictly limited. This in turn suggests that we should only consider candidates for m_x with a somewhat restricted structure. Indeed, if the nature of the variation of $\mathcal{D}_x$ is sufficiently restricted we might expect that a unique solution to the above constraints would be identified. This would mean a functional relationship between $\mu_{L_1}(x), \ldots, \mu_{L_n}(x)$ and m_x. Such a functional relationship is formalised by the following notion of a mass selection function:

Definition 6. *Mass Selection Function*
A mass selection function is a function $\Delta : [0,1]^n \to \mathcal{M}^{(n)}$, *where* $\mathcal{M}^{(n)}$ *is the set of all possible mass assignments on* 2^{LA}, *satisfying*

$$\sum_{S:L_i \in S} \Delta(\langle \mu_{L_1}(x), \ldots, \mu_{L_n}(x) \rangle)(S) = \mu_{L_i}(x) \text{ for } i = 1, \ldots, n$$

In effect then a mass selection function provides sufficient information regarding the nature of the variation of $\mathcal{D}_x$ to uniquely determine the mass assignment m_x from the values of the appropriateness degrees on LA. Furthermore, since the value of $\mu_\theta(x)$ for any expression θ can be evaluated directly from m_x then given an appropriate mass selection function we need no longer have any knowledge of the underlying population V but rather we need only define appropriateness degrees μ_L for $L \in LA$ corresponding to the fuzzy definition of each label.

Example 1. Examples of Mass Selection Functions

The Consonant Mass Selection Function
Given appropriateness degrees $\mu_{L_1}(x), \ldots, \mu_{L_n}(x)$ ordered such that $\mu_{L_i}(x) \geq \mu_{L_{i+1}}(x)$ for $i = 1, \ldots, n-1$ then the consonant mass selection function identifies the mass assignment,

$\{L_1, \ldots, L_n\} : \mu_{L_n}(x), \{L_1, \ldots, L_i\} : \mu_{L_i}(x) - \mu_{L_{i+1}}(x) \quad i = 1, \ldots, n-1$ and $\emptyset : 1 - \mu_{L_1}(x)$

The Independent Mass Selection Function
Given appropriateness degrees $\mu_{L_1}(x), \ldots, \mu_{L_n}(x)$ then the independent mass selection function identifies the mass assignment:

$$\forall S \subseteq LA \; m_{\mathcal{D}_x}(S) = \prod_{L \in S} \mu_L(x) \times \prod_{L \notin S} (1 - \mu_L(x))$$

4   A Calculus for Appropriateness Measures

In this section we propose an axiomatic foundation for measures of appropriateness and investigate its relationship to the random set model proposed above. In particular, we investigate the role of t-norms as generators of measures of appropriateness. The following definition proposes a system of axioms for appropriateness measures on $LE \times \Omega$:

Definition 7. *Appropriateness Measures*
An appropriateness measure on $LE \times \Omega$ *is a function* $\mu : LE \times \Omega \to [0,1]$ *such that* $\forall x \in \Omega, \theta \in LE$ $\mu_\theta(x)$ *quantifies the appropriateness of label expression* θ *as a description of value* x *and satisfies:*

AM1 $\forall \theta \in LE$ if $\models \theta$ then $\forall x \in \Omega\ \mu_\theta(x) = 1$

AM2 $\forall \theta, \varphi \in LE$ if $\theta \equiv \varphi$ then $\forall x \in \Omega\ \mu_\theta(x) = \mu_\varphi(x)$

AM3 $\forall \theta, \varphi \in LE$ if $\models \neg(\theta \wedge \varphi)$ then $\forall x \in \Omega\ \mu_{\theta \vee \varphi}(x) = \mu_\theta(x) + \mu_\varphi(x)$

AM4 $\forall \theta \in LE$ there exists a function $f_\theta : [0,1]^n \to [0,1]$ such that
$$\forall x \in \Omega\ \mu_\theta(x) = f_\theta(\mu_{L_1}(x), \ldots, \mu_{L_n}(x))$$

A possible justification for these axioms is as follows: AM1 can be justified on the basis that a tautology can be applied as a description to any value. AM2 states that the level of appropriateness is invariant under logical equivalence. In other words, if two expressions have the same meaning then they should be equally appropriate to describe any value. We can argue for AM3 on the basis that if two expression can never both be appropriate descriptions then the appropriateness of their disjunction should be the sum of their respective appropriateness degrees. Taken together AM1-AM3 ensure that for a fixed x an appropriateness measure defines a probability measure over LE. AM4 captures the intuition that the meaning of compound expressions should be completely determined by the meaning of the fuzzy labels in LA as represented by their appropriateness degrees. We now show that this system of axioms can be characterised by the random set model introduced in Sects. 2 and 3 taken in conjunction with a mass selection function.

Definition 8. *Logical Atoms*

(i)   Let ATT denote the set of logical atoms of LE (i.e. all expressions of the form $\alpha = \bigwedge_{i=1}^{n} \pm L_i$)

(ii) Let $ATT_\theta = \{\alpha \in ATT | \alpha \models \theta\}$

(iii) $\forall S \subseteq LA\ \alpha_S = \left(\bigwedge_{L_i \in S} L_i\right) \wedge \left(\bigwedge_{L_i \notin S} \neg L_i\right)$

Lemma 1. *Let Val denote the set of valuations on LA and let $\tau : Val \to 2^{LA}$ such that $\forall v \in Val\ \tau(v) = \{L_i : v(L_i) = true\}$ then*

$$\forall \theta \in LE\ \lambda(\theta) = \{\tau(v) : v(\theta) = true\}$$

Lemma 2.
$$\forall \theta \in LE\ ATT_\theta = \{\alpha_S : S \in \lambda(\theta)\}$$

Proof

($\Rightarrow$)

Let $v_\alpha \in Val$ be defined such that $\forall L \in LA\ v_\alpha(L) = true$ if and only if $\alpha \models L$

Suppose $\alpha \in ATT_\theta$ then $v_\alpha(\theta) = true \Rightarrow \tau(v_\alpha) \in \{\tau(v) : v(\theta) = true\}$

$\Rightarrow \tau(v_\alpha) \in \lambda(\theta)$ by Lemma 1

Now letting $S = \tau(v_\alpha)$ then $\alpha = \alpha_S$ and therefore, $\alpha \in \{\alpha_S : S \in \lambda(\theta)\}$

($\Leftarrow$)

Suppose $\alpha = \alpha_S$ for some $S \in \lambda(\theta)$ then

$\exists v \in Val : v(\theta) = true$ and $S = \tau(v)$ by Lemma 1

$\Rightarrow \alpha \in ATT_\theta$ since $v(\theta) = true$ if and only if $\alpha_{\tau(v)} \in ATT_\theta$

Lemma 3. $\forall \theta, \varphi \in LE \ \theta \equiv \varphi$ *if and only if* $\lambda(\theta) = \lambda(\varphi)$

Lemma 4. *If* $\theta \in LE$ *is a tautology then* $\lambda(\theta) = 2^{LA}$

Proofs of Lemmas 1, 3 and 4 are given in [6]

Theorem 1. *Characterization Theorem*
μ *is an appropriateness measure on* $LE \times \Omega$ *iff* $\forall x \in \Omega$ *there exists a mass assignment* m_x *on* 2^{LA} *such that*

$$m_x = \Delta(\mu_{L_1}(x) \ldots \mu_{L_n}(x))$$

for some mass selection function Δ *and*

$$\forall \theta \in LE \ \mu_\theta(x) = \sum_{S \in \lambda(\theta)} m_x(S)$$

Proof
$(\Leftarrow)$
By Lemma 4 if $\models \theta$ then $\mu_\theta(x) = \sum_{S \subseteq LA} m_x(S) = 1$ and hence AM1 holds.
$\forall \theta, \varphi \in LE : \theta \equiv \varphi$ we have by Lemma 3 that

$$\forall x \in \Omega \ \mu_\theta(x) = \sum_{S \in \lambda(\theta)} m_x(S) = \sum_{S \in \lambda(\varphi)} m_x(S) = \mu_\varphi(x)$$

Hence, AM2 holds.
If $\models \neg(\theta \wedge \varphi)$ then by Lemma 4 and Definition 4 $\lambda(\theta \wedge \varphi) = \emptyset \Rightarrow \lambda(\theta) \cap \lambda(\varphi) = \emptyset$
hence $\forall x \in \Omega$

$$\mu_{\theta \vee \varphi}(x) = \sum_{S \in \lambda(\theta) \cup \lambda(\varphi)} m_x(S) = \sum_{S \in \lambda(\theta)} m_x(S) + \sum_{S \in \lambda(\varphi)} m_x(S) = \mu_\theta(x) + \mu_\varphi(x)$$

Hence AM3 holds.
$\forall \theta \in LE \ \mu_\theta(x) = f_\theta(\mu_{L_1}(x), \ldots, \mu_{L_n}(x))$ where

$$f_\theta(\mu_{L_1}(x), \ldots, \mu_{L_n}(x)) = \sum_{S \in \lambda(\theta)} \Delta(\mu_{L_1}(x), \ldots, \mu_{L_n}(x))(S)$$

Hence AM4 holds.
$(\Rightarrow)$
By the disjunctive normal form theorem for propositional logic it follows that
$\forall \theta \in LE \ \theta \equiv \bigvee_{\alpha \in ATT_\theta} \alpha$ therefore by AM2 and AM3 we have that:

$$\forall x \in \Omega \ \mu_\theta(x) = \mu \left(\bigvee_{\alpha \in ATT_\theta} \alpha \right)(x) = \sum_{\alpha \in ATT_\theta} \mu_\alpha(x)$$

Now $\forall x \in \Omega$, $\forall S \subseteq LA$ let

$$m_x(S) = \mu_{\alpha_S}(x)$$

then clearly m_x defines a mass assignment on 2^{LA}. Also m_x can be determined uniquely from $\mu_{L_1}(x), \ldots, \mu_{L_n}(x)$ according to the mass selection function

$$\Delta(\mu_{L_1}(x), \ldots, \mu_{L_n}(x))(S) = f_{\alpha_S}(\mu_{L_1}(x), \ldots, \mu_{L_n}(x))$$

where $f_{\alpha_S} : [0,1]^n \to [0,1]$ is the function identified for α_S by AM4. Finally, by Lemma 2

$$\forall \theta \in LE \ \mu_\theta(x) = \sum_{\alpha \in ATT_\theta} \mu_\alpha(x) = \sum_{S \in \lambda(\theta)} \mu_{\alpha_S}(x) = \sum_{S \in \lambda(\theta)} m_x(S)$$

as required

The above theorem shows that appropriateness measures (Definition 7) correspond to compound appropriateness degrees (Definition 5) where the mass assignment m_x is determined using some mass selection function. It is important to realize that while appropriateness measures are functional, no non-trivial appropriateness measures are truth-functional. To see this note that by AM1 appropriateness degrees satisfy the laws of excluded middle. However, from a theorem due to Dubois and Prade [1] it is know that any truth-functional logic satisfying the law of excluded middle can only be binary. Hence, non-binary appropriateness measures cannot be truth-functional.

There are a number of clear connections between appropriateness measures and Shafer-Dempster theory [8]. Suppose we simply view m_x as a conditional mass assignment on 2^{LA} given value x. In this case, for any $k \leq n$ labels $L_1, \ldots, L_k$ the appropriateness of the disjunction $L_1 \vee \cdots \vee L_k$ as a description of x is given by:

$$\mu_{L_1 \vee \cdots \vee L_k}(x) = \sum_{S : \{L_1, \ldots, L_k\} \cap S \neq \emptyset} m_x(S) = Pl(\{L_1, \ldots, L_k\}|x)$$

Similarly the appropriateness of the conjunction $L_1 \wedge \cdots \wedge L_k$ as a description of x is given by:

$$\mu_{L_1 \wedge \cdots \wedge L_k}(x) = \sum_{S : \{L_1, \ldots, L_k\} \subseteq S} m_x(S) = Q(\{L_1, \ldots, L_k\}|x)$$

Here Q denotes the commonality function for m_x where for subset S, $Q(S)$ represents the total mass that can be moved freely to every element of S [8]. This latter relationship is used in the following proposition to show how appropriateness measures can be charaterized by t-norms.

Proposition 1. *If μ is an appropriateness measure on $LE \times \Omega$ then there exists a t-norm $\wedge_t$ such that*

$$\forall x \in \Omega \ \forall R \subseteq LA \ \mu_{\left(\bigwedge_{L \in R} L\right)}(x) = \wedge_t(\mu_L(x) : L \in R)^1$$

---

[1] For notational elegance we take $\wedge_t(\mu_L(x)) = \mu_L(x)$

if and only if there exists a valid mass assignment m_x satisfying $\forall x \in \Omega$,
$\forall \theta \in LE$ $\mu_\theta(x) = \sum_{S \in \lambda(\theta)} m_x(S)$ where

$$\forall S \subseteq LA \ m_x(S) = \sum_{T:T \supseteq S} (-1)^{|T-S|} \wedge_t (\mu_L(x) : L \in T)$$

Proof
Since μ is an appropriateness measure then by Theorem 1 it follows that there exists a valid mass assignment m_x satisfying

$$\mu_{\left(\bigwedge_{L \in R} L\right)}(x) = \sum_{S:S \supseteq R} m_x(S) = Q(R|x)$$

Then $\forall R \subseteq LA$ $Q(R|x) = \wedge_t(\mu_L(x) : L \in R)$ if and only if

$$\forall S \subseteq LA \ m_x(S) = \sum_{T:T \supseteq S} (-1)^{|T-S|} \wedge_t (\mu_L(x) : L \in T)$$

by Shafer's inversion formula (see [8]) as required.

We refer to appropriateness measures of the above form as being generated by a particular t-norm. An axiomatic definition is as follows:

Definition 9. *Appropriateness Measures Generated by a t-norm*
The appropriateness measure on $LE \times \Omega$ generated by t-norm $\wedge_t$ is the unique function $\mu : LE \times \Omega \to [0,1]$ such that $\forall x \in \Omega, \theta \in LE$ $\mu_\theta(x)$ satisfies:

AMT1 $\forall \theta \in LE$ *if* $\models \theta$ *then* $\forall x \in \Omega$ $\mu_\theta(x) = 1$
AMT2 $\forall \theta, \varphi \in LE$ *if* $\theta \equiv \varphi$ *then* $\forall x \in \Omega$ $\mu_\theta(x) - \mu_\varphi(x)$
AMT3 $\forall \theta, \varphi \in LE$ *if* $\models \neg(\theta \wedge \varphi)$ *then* $\forall x \in \Omega$ $\mu_{\theta \vee \varphi}(x) = \mu_\theta(x) + \mu_\varphi(x)$
AMT4 $\forall R \subseteq LA, \forall x \in \Omega$ $\mu_{\left(\bigwedge_{L \in R} L\right)}(x) = \wedge_t(\mu_L(x) : L \in R)$

Theorem 1 and Proposition 1 show that appropriateness measures generated by a t-norm are characterized by a particular form of mass selection function. In [6] and [7] we have shown that the appropriateness measures generated by minimum and product t-norms are based on the consonant and independent mass selection functions respectively.

It is important to note however, that not all t-norms, generate fully consistent appropriateness measures. Indeed several well known t-norms generate appropriateness measures that are only consistent assuming certain constraints on the appropriateness degrees over the labels. Intially, we formally define the notions of universal and local consistency for appropriateness measures.

Definition 10. *Universally Consistent Appropriateness Measures*
The appropriateness measure μ based on t-norm $\wedge_t$ is said to be univerally consistent if and only if for all values of $\mu_{L_i}(x) \in [0,1] : i = 1, \ldots, n$ it holds that

$$\forall S \subseteq LA \ m_x(S) = \sum_{T:T \supseteq S} (-1)^{|T-S|} \wedge_t (\mu_L(x) : L \in T) \geq 0$$

Both min and product generate universally consistent appropriateness measures (see [6] and [7]).

Definition 11. *Locally Consistent Appropriateness Measures*
The appropriateness measure μ generated by t-norm $\wedge_t$ is said to be locally consistent if and only if there exists a non-empty open subset $\mathcal{A} \subseteq [0,1]^n$ such that if $\langle \mu_{L_1}(x), \ldots, \mu_{L_n}(x) \rangle \in \mathcal{A}$ then

$$\forall S \subseteq LA \ m_x(S) = \sum_{T:T \supseteq S} (-1)^{|T-S|} \wedge_t (\mu_L(x) : L \in T) \geq 0$$

In [7] it is shown that the appropriateness measure generated by the t-norm $\wedge_t(y_1, y_2) = \max(0, y_1 + y_2 - 1)$ is only locally consistent on the subset

$$\{\langle \mu_{L_1}(x), \ldots, \mu_{L_n}(x) \rangle : \sum_{i=1}^{n} \mu_{L_i}(x) \leq 1 \text{ or } \sum_{i=1}^{n} (1 - \mu_{L_i}(x)) \leq 1\}$$

We now investigate what t-norms can generate universally consistent appropriateness measures. To do this we must first consider the relationship between conjunctions and disjunctions of fuzzy labels in the current framework.

Proposition 2. *If μ is an appropriateness measure generated by t-norm $\wedge_t$ then for $\{L_1, \ldots L_m\} \subseteq LA$*

$$\forall x \in \Omega \ \mu_{L_1 \vee \ldots \vee L_m}(x) = \vee_t(\mu_{L_1}(x), \ldots, \mu_{L_m}(x))$$

where

$$\forall y_i \in [0,1] : i = 1, \ldots, m \ \vee_t(y_1, \ldots, y_m) = \sum_{\emptyset \neq T \subseteq \{y_1, \ldots y_m\}} (-1)^{|T|-1} \wedge_t(y_i : y_i \in T)$$

Proof
Follows trivially from the fact that AM1-AM3 imply that μ is a probability measure for every $x \in \Omega$ and hence

$$\mu_{L_1 \vee \ldots \vee L_m}(x) = \sum_{\emptyset \neq T \subseteq \{L_1, \ldots L_m\}} (-1)^{|T|-1} \mu \left(\bigwedge_{L \in T} L \right)(x)$$

The special case of the disjunction given in Proposition 2 when $m = 2$ is

$$\forall y_1, y_2 \in [0,1] \ \vee_t(y_1, y_2) = y_1 + y_2 - \wedge_t(y_1, y_2)$$

This is Frank's equation [3] and if we further assume that $\vee_t$ is the dual t-conorm of $\wedge_t$ then $\wedge_t$ is restricted to the family of Frank's t-norms defined as follows:

Definition 12. *Frank's Family of t-norms*
For parameter $s \in [0, \infty)$

$$\wedge_s(y_1, y_2) = \begin{cases} \min(y_1, y_2) : s = 0 \\ \log_s \left(1 + \frac{(s^{y_1}-1)(s^{y_2}-1)}{s-1} \right) : s > 0, \ s \neq 1 \\ y_1 \times y_2 : s = 1 \end{cases}$$

Theorem 2. *There is no universally consistent appropriateness measure generated by a Frank's t-norm with $s \geq 2$*

Proof

Let $LA = \{L_1, L_2, L_3\}$ and let μ be the appropriateness measure generated by $\wedge_s$ for $s > 1$ such that for some $x \in \Omega$ $\mu_{L_1}(x) = \mu_{L_2}(x) = \mu_{L_3}(x) = y$ for some $y \in [0, 1]$. Then by Proposition 1 and Definition 12 it follows that

$$m_x(\emptyset) = 1 - 3y + 3 \wedge_s (y, y) - \wedge_s(y, y, y) = 1 - 3y + \log_s \left(\frac{\left[1 + \frac{(s^y-1)^2}{s-1} \right]^3}{1 + \frac{(s^y-1)^3}{(s-1)^2}} \right)$$

We now show that for $s \geq 2$ there exists a value of y for which

$$1 - 3y + \log_s \left(\frac{\left[1 + \frac{(s^y-1)^2}{s-1} \right]^3}{1 + \frac{(s^y-1)^3}{(s-1)^2}} \right) < 0$$

Putting $z = s^y - 1$ and $w = s - 1$ this corresponds to:

$$\frac{(w + z^2)^3}{w(w^2 + z^3)} < \frac{(z + 1)^3}{w + 1}$$

where $w \geq 0$ and $z \in [0, w]$
$\Rightarrow (w + z^2)(w + 1) < w(w^2 + z^3)(x + 1)^3$
$\Rightarrow z^6 - 3wz^5 + 3w^2 z^4 - (w^3 + w)z^3 + 3w^2 z^2 - 3w^3 z + z^4 < 0$
$\Rightarrow (z^3 - w)(z - w)^3 < 0$
$\Rightarrow$ since $z \in [0, w]$ that $(z^3 - w) > 0$ and $z < w$
$\Rightarrow z > \sqrt[3]{w}$ and $z < w \Rightarrow s^y - 1 > \sqrt[3]{s - 1}$ and $s^y - 1 < s - 1$
$\Rightarrow y > \log_s(1 + \sqrt[3]{s - 1})$ and $y < 1$
$\Rightarrow \log_s(1 + \sqrt[3]{s - 1}) < 1 \Rightarrow 1 + \sqrt[3]{s - 1} < s \Rightarrow \sqrt[3]{s - 1} < s - 1$
$\Rightarrow s - 1 > 1 \Rightarrow s > 2$

Figures 1 and 2 show plots of the values of $m_x(\emptyset)$ where y (as defined in Theorem 2) varies between $[0, 1]$ and $s = 0.5$ and $s = 40$ respectively.

Theorem 3. *If $|LA| \leq 3$ then the appropriateness measure generated by $\wedge_s$ is universally consistent for all $s \in [0, 1]$*

Proof

We first prove the result for $|LA| = 3$
For $x \in \Omega$ let $\mu_{L_1}(x) = y_1, \mu_{L_2}(x) = y_2, \mu_{L_3}(x) = y_3$. Without loss of generality we need only consider the following four subsets: $\{L_1, L_2, L_3\}, \{L_1, L_2\}, \{L_1\}, \emptyset$. The $s = 1$ and $s = 0$ cases are aready proved (see [6], [7]). Therefore, we assume $s \in (0, 1)$.
Now by Definitions 9 and 12 we have:

$$m_x(\{L_1, L_2, L_3\}) = \wedge_s(y_1, y_2, y_3) = \log_s \left(1 + \frac{(s^{y_1} - 1)(s^{y_2} - 1)(s^{y_3} - 1)}{(s - 1)^2} \right)$$

$$m_x(\{L_1, L_2\}) = \wedge_t(y_1, y_2) - \wedge_s(y_1, y_2, y_3) = \log_s \left(\frac{1 + \frac{(s^{y_1}-1)(s^{y_2}-1)}{s-1}}{1 + \frac{(s^{y_1}-1)(s^{y_2}-1)(s^{y_3}-1)}{(s-1)^2}} \right)$$

$$m_x(\{L_1\}) = y_1 - \wedge_s(y_1, y_2) - \wedge_s(y_1, y_3) + \wedge_s(y_1, y_2, y_3)$$

$$= \log_s \left(\frac{s^{y_1} \left(1 + \frac{(s^{y_1}-1)(s^{y_2}-1)(s^{y_3}-1)}{(s-1)^2} \right)}{\left(1 + \frac{(s^{y_1}-1)(s^{y_2}-1)}{s-1} \right) \left(1 + \frac{(s^{y_1}-1)(s^{y_3}-1)}{s-1} \right)} \right)$$

$$m_x(\emptyset) = 1 - y_1 - y_2 - y_3 + \wedge_s(y_1, y_2) + \wedge_s(y_1, y_3) + \wedge_s(y_2, y_3) - \wedge_s(y_1, y_2, y_3)$$

$$= \log_s \left(\frac{s \left(1 + \frac{(s^{y_1}-1)(s^{y_2}-1)}{s-1} \right) \left(1 + \frac{(s^{y_1}-1)(s^{y_3}-1)}{s-1} \right) \left(1 + \frac{(s^{y_2}-1)(s^{y_3}-1)}{s-1} \right)}{s^{y_1} s^{y_2} s^{y_3} \left(1 + \frac{(s^{y_1}-1)(s^{y_2}-1)(s^{y_3}-1)}{(s-1)^2} \right)} \right)$$

Now let $z_1 = s^{y_1} - 1, z_2 = s^{y_2} - 1$ *and* $z_3 = s^{y_3} - 1$ *and note that* $z_1, z_2, z_3 \in [s-1, 0]$:
Now $m_x(\{L_1, L_2, L_3\}) \geq 0$ *trivially since* $\wedge_s$ *is a t-norm.*
Since $s \in (0, 1)$ $m_x(\{L_1, L_2\}) \geq 0 \Leftrightarrow$

$$\frac{(s-1)(s-1+z_1 z_2)}{(s^2 - 2s + 1 + z_1 z_2 z_3)} \leq 1$$

$\Leftrightarrow$ *(since the denominator is* ≥ 0*)* $(s-1)(s-1+z_1 z_2) - s^2 + 2s - 1 - z_1 z_2 z_3 \leq 0 \Leftrightarrow$
$z_1 z_2 (s - 1 - z_3) \leq 0$ *This holds trivially since* $z_1 \leq 0$, $z_2 \leq 0$ *and* $(s - 1 - z_3) \leq 0$.
Since $s \in (0, 1)$ $m_x(\{L_1\}) \geq 0 \Leftrightarrow$

$$\frac{(s^2 - 2s + 1 + z_1 z_2 z_3)(z_1 + 1)}{(s - 1 + z_1 z_3)(s - 1 + z_1 z_2)} \leq 1$$

$\Leftrightarrow$ $(s^2 - 2s + 1 + z_1 z_2 z_3)(z_1 + 1) - (s - 1 + z_1 z_3)(s - 1 + z_1 z_2) \leq 0$
$\Leftrightarrow$ *(since the denominator is* ≥ 0*)* $z_1(1 - s + z_3)(1 - s + z_2) \leq 0$.
This holds trivially since $z_1 \leq 0$, $(1 - s + z_2) \leq 0$ *and* $(1 - s + z_3) \leq 0$. *Since*
$s \in (0, 1)$ $m_x(\emptyset) \geq 0 \Leftrightarrow$

$$\frac{s(s - 1 + z_1 z_2)(s - 1 + z_1 z_3)(s - 1 + z_2 z_3)}{(s - 1)(z_1 + 1)(z_2 + 1)(z_3 + 1)(s^2 - 2s + 1 + z_1 z_2 z_3)} \leq 1$$

$\Leftrightarrow$ *(since the denominator is* ≤ 0*)*
$s(s - 1 + z_1 z_2)(s - 1 + z_1 z_3)(s - 1 + z_2 z_3) - (s - 1)(z_1 + 1)(z_2 + 1)(z_3 + 1)(s^2 - 2s + 1 + z_1 z_2 z_3) \geq 0 \Leftrightarrow (1 - s + z_3)(1 - s + z_2)(1 - s + z_1)(1 - s + z_1 z_2 z_3) \geq 0$
This holds trivially since $(1 - s + z_1) \geq 0$, $(1 - s + z_2) \geq 0$, $(1 - s + z_3) \geq 0$ *and*
$(1 - s + z_1 z_2 z_3) \geq 0$.

Since the $|LA| = 3$ is universally consistent then it must follow that the $|LA| < 3$ case must also be universally consistent, otherwise we could extend any counter example where $|LA| < 3$ to the $|LA| = 3$ case by setting the remaining appropriateness degrees to zero.

Empirical studies suggest that this result can be extended to cases where $|LA| > 3$ however, no general result has yet been proven.

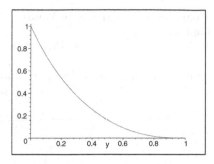

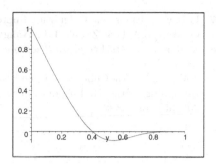

Fig. 1. Plot of values of $m_x(\emptyset)$ where $s = 0.5$ $\mu_{L_1}(x) = \mu_{L_2}(x) = \mu_{L_3}(x) = y$ and y varies between 0 and 1

Fig. 2. Plot of values of $m_x(\emptyset)$ where $s = 40$ $\mu_{L_1}(x) = \mu_{L_2}(x) = \mu_{L_3}(x) = y$ and y varies between 0 and 1

5   Conclusions

In this paper we have outlined a random set model of fuzzy labels defined on subsets of labels and for which functionality is maintained through theuse of mass selection functions. This model was shown to be characterised by a simple axiomization of appropriateness measures allowing for the functional representation of fuzzy concepts while preserving the law of the excluded middle and standard logical equivalence properties. It was, also, shown how t-norms can be used to generate appropriateness measures and we argued that in this context attention should be restricted to the family of Frank's t-norms. It was shown that no Frank t-norm with $s \geq 2$ can generate a universally consistent appropriateness measure and it was shown that for $|LA| \leq 3$ all Frank's t-norms with $s \in [0, 1]$ generate universally consistent appropriateness measures. Empirical tests suggest this latter result can be extended but further research is required.

References

1. Dubois D., Prade H.: An Introduction to Possibility and Fuzzy Logics, in Non-Standard Logics for Automated Reasoning (eds. P. Smets et al.), Academic Press (1988) pp. 742–755
2. Elkan C.: The paradoxical Success of Fuzzy Logic in Proceedings of the Eleventh National Conference on Artificial Intelligence MIT Press (1993) pp. 698–703
3. Frank M.J.: On the Simultaneous Associativity of $F(x, y)$ and $x + y - F(x, y)$, Aequationes Math 19 (1979)
4. Goodman I.R.: Fuzzy Sets as Equivalence Classes of Random Sets in Fuzzy Set and Possibility Theory (ed. R. Yager) (1982) pp. 327–342
5. Goodman I.R., Nguyen H.T.: *Uncertainty Models for Knowledge Based Systems* North Holland (1985)
6. Lawry J.: Label Semantics: A Formal Framework for Modelling with Words. Lecture Notes in Artificial Intelligence, **2143** (ed. S. Benferhat, P. Besnard), (2001) 374–384

7. Lawry J.: Emergent Calculi for Imprecise Concepts, Computing with Words – Semantics, (ed. L.A. Zadeh, P.P. Wang), (submitted) (2003)
8. Shafer G.: *A Mathematical Theory of Evidence* Princeton University Press, Princeton (1976)
9. Zadeh L.A.: The Concept of Linguistic Variable and its Application to Approximate Reasoning PartI-III, Information Sciences Vols. 8–9, (1975–76), pp. 119–429, pp. 301–357, pp. 43–80

On the Induction of Different Kinds of First-Order Fuzzy Rules

Henri Prade, Gilles Richard, and Mathieu Serrurier

IRIT - Université Paul Sabatier
118 route de Narbonne, 31062 Toulouse France
{henri.prade,serrurier}@irit.fr
grichard@ifi.edu.vn

Abstract. The paper describes a method for inducing first-order rules with fuzzy predicates from a database. First, the paper makes a distinction between fuzzy rules allowing for some tolerance with respect to the interpretative scope of the predicates, and fuzzy rules aiming at expressing a set of ordinary rules in a global way. Moreover the paper only considers the induction of Horn-like implicative-based fuzzy rules. Specific confidence degrees are associated with each kind of fuzzy rules in the inductive process. This technique is illustrated on an experimental application. The interest of learning various types of fuzzy first-order logic expressions is emphasized.

Keywords: inductive logic programming, fuzzy rule, confidence degree

1 Introduction

Inductive Logic Programming (ILP) [14] provides a general framework for learning classical first-order logic rules, for which reasonably efficient algorithms have been developed (Progol [11], FOIL [17]...). But, first-order logic cannot directly handle rules with exceptions, which are common in practice. This has been a motivation for introducing probabilities in ILP ([12]). In fact, probabilities, already implicitly appear the control procedure in FOIL. Indeed, during the gain computation, the value associated to a rule can be viewed as a confidence degree expressed in terms of "domain probabilities". Such probabilities, together with "world probabilities", are the basic notions of Halpern's first-order probabilistic logic [8]. Domain probabilities are used to capture statistical information for a fixed first-order logic interpretation. These probabilities are obtained by applying a probability measure to the set of valuations which make the rules true in the interpretation. So, there is no longer any genuine quantifier in a rule when there is a non-zero probability to encounter exceptions.

World probabilities are used in order to evaluate the set of interpretations where a rule is universally true. Bacchus [2] uses them for capturing degrees of belief, given a knowledge base KB, by computing the proportion of interpretations which are models of KB and of the target assertion, among the interpretations

T.D. Nielsen and N.L. Zhang (Eds.): ECSQARU 2003, LNAI 2711, pp. 370–381, 2003.

of KB. But the effective calculus is generally tricky. In a recent paper [15], it has been pointed out that these world probabilities could be also used for handling fuzzy predicates, modeled in terms of likelihood functions (this work only considers one kind of fuzzy rules). Halpern's framework has also been adapted for dealing with relational databases [7]. Then, world probabilities are interpreted as probabilistic dependencies of interpretations and are represented by Bayesian networks. Besides, Muggleton in [12] presents another approach to induction with probabilities. His goal is to learn Stochastic Logic Programs (SLP). In this latter framework, the probability associated to a formula is not a confidence degree, but it rather represents the potential of the rule for explaining examples. Koller [10] describes a method for computing the confidence degree of a rule from examples by using Bayesian networks. Confidence values are then computed independently from the learning process on the basis of other examples.

In the propositional framework, confidence degrees have been integrated in the induction process, together with the handling of fuzzy properties. At least three main trends of works can be distinguished w.r.t. this latter concern. First, neuro-fuzzy learning techniques have been developed for tuning fuzzy membership functions in fuzzy rules; see [13] for a survey. The fuzzy rules, which are produced in that way, are used for functions approximation in automatic control problems. Another research line has been investigated with a greater concern for the descriptive power of the fuzzy rules from the user's point of view, by extending Quinlan's [16] ID3 algorithm to fuzzy decision trees, involving a fuzzy descriptions of classes and making use of entropy measures (extended to fuzzy sets) for building the fuzzy rules; see [4] for a survey. More recently, the use of fuzzy membership functions has been advocated by several researches for providing association rules in data mining with a better representation power, e.g. [9]. In these different problems, fuzzy rules are derived, which involve *unary* fuzzy properties generally. Moreover, fuzzy association rules are completed with (usually scalar) confidence and support degrees.

However, fuzzy degrees [3] have been proposed for taking into account the possible variation of these degrees with the level cuts of the fuzzy sets. In the above mentioned works, fuzzy sets are introduced either for equipping rules with interpolative mechanism or for making them more robust. Indeed fuzzy sets can serve various purposes, and moreover there exist different types of fuzzy rules [6], modeling uncertainty or graduality in property satisfaction. Propositional-like rules having a limited expression power, the aim of this paper is to adapt the ILP approach (restricted here to non-recursive function-free Horn clauses) and the computation of confidence degrees in order to allow for the learning of various types of first-order rules which may involve fuzzy predicates. For this purpose, we use domain probabilities in order to describe the associated confidence degrees of each kind of rules. Moreover algorithms such as FOIL embed confidence degrees for controlling the learning process. This will enable us to handle the fuzziness of the predicates directly in the computation.

The paper is organized as follows. Sections 2 provides a brief background on ILP and probabilistic logic. Section 3 presents different types of fuzzy rules and an approach for computing the confidence degree associated to each type. Sections 4 and 5 describe our algorithm and illustrate the approach on an example.

2   Background

2.1   ILP

We first briefly recall the standard definitions and notations. Given a first-order language $\mathcal{L}$ with a set of variables Var, we build the set of terms $Term$, atoms $Atom$ and formulas as usual. The set of ground terms is the Herbrand universe $\mathcal{H}$ and the set of ground atoms or facts is the Herbrand base $\mathcal{B} \subset Atom$. A *literal* l is just an atom a (positive literal) or its negation $\neg a$ (negative literal). A (resp. ground) substitution σ is an application from Var to (resp. $\mathcal{H}$) $Term$ with inductive extension to $Atom$. We denote $Subst$ the set of ground substitutions. A *clause* is a finite disjunction of literals $l_1 \vee \ldots \vee l_n$ also denoted $\{l_1, \ldots, l_n\}$. A Horn clause is a clause with at most one positive literal. A Herbrand interpretation I is just a subset of $\mathcal{B}$: I is the set of true ground atomic formulas and its complementary denotes the set of false ground atomic formulas. Let us denote $\mathcal{I} = 2^{\mathcal{B}}$, the power set of $\mathcal{B}$ i.e. the set of all Herbrand interpretations. We can now proceed with the notion of logical consequence.

Definition 1. *Given A an atomic formula, $I, \sigma \models A$ means that $\sigma(A) \in I$. As usual, the extension to general formulas F uses compositionality.*
$I \models F$ means $\forall \sigma$, $I, \sigma \models F$ (we say I is a model of F).
$\models F$ means $\forall I \in \mathcal{I}$, $I \models F$.
$F \models G$ means that all models of F are models of G.

Stated in the general context of first-order logic, the task of *induction* is to find a set of formulas H such that:

$$B \cup H \models E \tag{1}$$

given a background theory B and a set of observations E (training set), where E, B and H here denote sets of clauses. A set of formulas is here, as usual, considered as the conjunction of its elements. Of course, one may add two natural restrictions:

- $B \not\models E$ since, in such a case, H would not be necessary to explain E.
- $B \cup H \not\models \perp$: this means $B \cup H$ is a consistent theory.

In the setting of relational databases, inductive logic programming is often restricted to Horn clauses and function-free formulas, E is just a set of ground facts. Moreover, the set E itself satisfies the previous requirement but it is generally not considered as an acceptable solution since it has no predictive ability. Usually, rules extraction fits with the idea of providing a compression of the information content of E.

There are two general types of algorithms, *top down* and *bottom up* algorithms. *Top down* ones start from the most general clause and specialize it step by step. *Bottom up* procedures start from a fact and generalize it. In our case, we will use the FOIL algorithm [17] which is of the *top down* type. The goal of FOIL is to produce rules until all the examples are covered. Rules with conclusion part C, the target predicate, are found in the following way:

1. take $A \rightarrow C$ as the most general clause with $A = \top$
2. choose the literal l such as the clause $l \wedge A \rightarrow C$ maximizes the gain function
3. $A = l \wedge A$
4. if confidence$(A \rightarrow C) <$ threshold goto 2
5. return $A \rightarrow C$

The gain function is computed by the formula:

$$gain(l \wedge A \rightarrow C, A \rightarrow C) = n * (log_2(cf(l \wedge A \rightarrow C)) - log_2(cf(A \rightarrow C)))$$

where n is the number of distinct examples covered by $l \wedge A \rightarrow C$. Given a Horn clause $A \rightarrow C$, the confidence $cf(A \rightarrow C) = \frac{P(A \wedge C)}{P(A)}$. The way for computing probabilities of first-order logic rules is presented in the next subsection.

2.2 Probabilistic Logic

We focus here on the logic of probability as developed by Halpern in [8]. The aim of Halpern's work, inspired by previous works of Bacchus [1], is to design a first-order logic for capturing reasoning about beliefs and statistical information. Here we restrict Halpern's framework to the usual logic programming setting. This means that the domain object is the Herbrand universe $\mathcal{H}$, an interpretation I is just a subset of $\mathcal{B}$. In fact, we just apply Halpern's definitions for attaching probabilities to Horn clauses, without using the associated notion of logical consequence.

Let us give a meaning to the probability of a non-closed first-order formula in a given interpretation. Halpern names type 1 structure the triple $M = \{I, \mathcal{H}, P\}$ where I is an Herbrand interpretation, $\mathcal{H}$ is the Herbrand universe, and P is a probabilistic measure over $\mathcal{H}$ (of course, the probability P^n is available over the product domain $\mathcal{H}^n$). Given a type 1 structure M and a non-closed formula F with the vector $\overrightarrow{t}$ of n free variables, the meaning of $P^I(F)$ (abbreviated in $P(F)$ when I is clear from the context) is the probability that a random vector $\overrightarrow{x}$ on $\mathcal{H}^n$ makes $\sigma[\overrightarrow{t}/\overrightarrow{x}](F)$ true in I, and so the formal definition:

Definition 2. *Given $M = \{I, \mathcal{H}, P\}$, F a formula with a vector $\overrightarrow{t}$ on n free variables, the probability of F is given by:*

$$P(F) = P^n\{\overrightarrow{x} \in \mathcal{H}^n \mid I \models \sigma[\overrightarrow{t}/\overrightarrow{x}](F)\} \tag{2}$$

If P is a uniform probability over $\mathcal{H}$, it is easy to see that $P(F)$ is a frequency.

Type 1 structures are useful for capturing statistical information but these structures are insufficient for describing probabilities on closed formulas. Indeed, a closed formula has no free variable. So the type 1 probability of a closed formula is 0 or 1 according as this formulas is true or false in I.

3   Various Types of Fuzzy Rules and Confidence Degrees

We consider a first-order logic database K with fuzzy predicates (e.g., comfortable, close_to) as a set of positive facts labeled by real numbers in $[0, 1]$. For instance in Sect. 4 we shall deal with a database containing facts such as $(comfortable(a), 0.5)$ and $(close\_to(a, sea), 0.4)$. Thus, K is made of pairs of the form $(A(\overrightarrow{x}), \mu(A(\overrightarrow{x})))$ for $\overrightarrow{x} \in \mathcal{H}^n$, where $A(\overrightarrow{x})$ is a fact, and $\mu(A(\overrightarrow{x}))$ is the satisfaction degree associated with the fuzzy property A for $\overrightarrow{x}$.

3.1   Different Types of Fuzzy Rules

There exist at least two reasons for introducing fuzzy predicates in universally quantified rules. This may be for making them either more flexible, or more expressive. Indeed, a fuzzy predicate can be viewed as a family of ordinary predicates whose characteristic functions are the level cut functions μ_{F_α} associated to the fuzzy set membership function μ_F, namely $\mu_{F_\alpha}(\overrightarrow{x}) = 1$ iff $\mu(F(\overrightarrow{x})) \geq \alpha$ and $\mu_{F_\alpha}(\overrightarrow{x}) = 0$ otherwise. Thus a rule "$A(\overrightarrow{t}) \to C(\overrightarrow{t})$" is naturally associated with the crisp rules "$A_\alpha(\overrightarrow{t}) \to C_\beta(\overrightarrow{t})$". Note that, if $A_\beta(\overrightarrow{t})$ holds then $A_\alpha(\overrightarrow{t})$ also holds for $\alpha \leq \beta$. So we may only consider the crisp approximations "$A_\alpha(\overrightarrow{t}) \to C_\alpha(\overrightarrow{t})$".

Then, if we are concerned by *flexibility*, a possible understanding of the fuzzy rule "$A(\overrightarrow{t}) \to C(\overrightarrow{t})$" can be

$$\forall \overrightarrow{x}, \exists \alpha \ A_\alpha(\overrightarrow{x}) \to C_\alpha(\overrightarrow{x}), \tag{3}$$

i.e. there exists a crisp understanding of the fuzzy rule which covers each example (but it is not necessary the same for each example since α depends on $\overrightarrow{x}$). This is a kind of rule already considered in [15]. By flexible rules, we mean here rule which are robust, since its predicates can be adapted to borderline situations.

If we are concerned by *expressivity*, we may look for fuzzy rules such that the rule holds for *each of* its level cut counterpart. This means that we have

$$\forall \overrightarrow{x}, \forall \alpha \ A_\alpha(\overrightarrow{x}) \to C_\alpha(\overrightarrow{x}). \tag{4}$$

This is clearly more restrictive than (3) since the fuzzy rule is equivalent to a set of ordinary rules with nested predicates and summarizes it into a unique fuzzy rule. In fact (4) is nothing but a gradual rule [6] expressing "The more $\overrightarrow{x}$ satisfies A, the more $\overrightarrow{x}$ satisfies C" (since they are modeled by a constraint of the form $\mu(A(\overrightarrow{x})) \geq \mu(C(\overrightarrow{x}))$).

Gradual rules are one of the four basic kinds of fuzzy rules [6]. Two of them, namely gradual rules and certainty rules, are based on implication connectives and express constraints on the possible models of the world. The two other types, named possibility rules and antigradual rules rather express that some values are guaranteed to be possible (i.e. that they exist in the base of examples). For instance, let us take possibility rules of the form "The more $\overrightarrow{x}$ is A, the more all the interpretations which makes C true (truth becomes a matter of degree when C is fuzzy) are guaranteed to be possible ". This means in practice that

"The more $\overrightarrow{x}$ is A, the more there are examples for any possible interpretation of C". Note that this rule cannot have any counter-example.

In the following, we only consider gradual and certainty rules. Certainty rules contrast with possibility rules, and express that "the more $\overrightarrow{x}$ is A, the more certain $\overrightarrow{x}$ is C". Let us first consider the case where "A" is a fuzzy predicate and "C" is an ordinary predicate. This expresses that "the more $\overrightarrow{x}$ is A, i.e. the greater α such that $A(\overrightarrow{x}) \geq \alpha$, the smaller the number of exceptions of the rule $A_\alpha(\overrightarrow{t}) \rightarrow C(\overrightarrow{t})$". Indeed when α decreases the number of exceptions cannot but increase since the scope of A_α is then enlarged. When C is also a fuzzy predicate, in order to preserve this understanding of the rule, we are led to look for rules of the form

$$\forall \overrightarrow{x}, \forall \alpha \ A_\alpha(\overrightarrow{x}) \rightarrow C_{1-\alpha}(\overrightarrow{x}),\tag{5}$$

since when α increases $C_{1-\alpha}$ cover more cases.

3.2 Confidence Degree in the Crisp Case

For computing confidence degrees, we must define probabilities on first-order logic formulas from ILP data. ILP data are supposed to describe one interpretation under Closed World Assumption, i.e. we use domain probabilities. We call I_{ILP} this interpretation. So, given a fact f:

$$I_{ILP} \models f \text{ iff } B \wedge E \models f.$$

The domain $\mathcal{H}$ is the Herbrand domain described by B and E. We take P as a uniform probability on $\mathcal{H}$. So it is easy to deduce that the confidence in a clause $A \rightarrow C$, with $\overrightarrow{t}$ as vector on the n free variables, is :

$$cf(A(\overrightarrow{t}) \rightarrow C(\overrightarrow{t}))_{I_{ILP}} = \frac{|\{\overrightarrow{x} \in \mathcal{H}^n \mid I_{ILP} \models \sigma[\overrightarrow{t}/\overrightarrow{x}](A(\overrightarrow{t}) \wedge C(\overrightarrow{t}))\}|}{|\{\overrightarrow{x} \in \mathcal{H}^n \mid I_{ILP} \models \sigma[\overrightarrow{t}/\overrightarrow{x}](A(\overrightarrow{t}))\}|}\tag{6}$$

where $| \ |$ denotes cardinality. Another possible definition of a confidence degree might be taken here as the proportion of the number of positive examples covered by the rule w.r.t. the number of total examples (positive and negative) covered by the rule. This confidence degree would represent the probability that a fact deduced from the rule is true. But this definition would not take into account the number of situations covered in the condition part of the rule, which is not always the total number of examples covered since we are in a first-order setting.

In ILP, the goal is to learn a concept represented by a predicate. E is the set of all facts pertaining to the target predicate. B is the set of facts pertaining to predicates other than the target one. So the learned rules are (in the non-recursive case) composed by predicates that appear in B for the condition part and by the target predicate in the consequence part.

3.3 Confidence Degree in the Fuzzy Case

Flexible Rules. This first type of meaning for a fuzzy rule "$A(\overrightarrow{t}) \rightarrow C(\overrightarrow{t})$" is close to the one of a classical rule. Of course, we are now expecting that the satisfaction degrees of $A(\vec{x})$ and $C(\vec{x})$ are as high as possible. So we can introduce classical interpretations associated with each α-cut.

Definition 3. *An α-interpretation I_α, given a fact f, is defined by:*

$$I_\alpha \models f \ \ iff \ \ B \wedge E \models f \ and \ \mu(f) \geq \alpha$$

In this type of interpretations, only facts that have a satisfaction degree greater than α are true. Of course we have $I_\alpha \subset I_{ILP}$. Now we have to compute the confidence degree of the rule in the classical way (using (6)) for each α-interpretation. According to the intended meaning of the fuzzy rule, we must favour the confidence degrees of the rule computed in high α-interpretations. Indeed, we prefer that the examples be covered at a high degree of satisfaction. The following definition, which is an adaptation in term of first-order logic of the one proposed by [5], takes this into account:

$$cf_{flex}(A(\vec{t}) \rightarrow C(\vec{t})) = \sum_{\alpha_i}(\alpha_i - \alpha_{i+1}) * cf(A(\vec{t}) \rightarrow C(\vec{t}))_{I_{\alpha_i}}$$

where $\alpha_1 = 1, ..., \alpha_t = 0$ is the less and less ordered list of the satisfaction degrees that appear in the database. This confidence degree corresponds to the discretization of a Choquet integral of the confidence degrees on α-interpretations.

Gradual Rules. In this case, the values of the satisfaction degrees are only useful for comparing satisfaction degrees in condition and conclusion parts. So, we do not priviledge the confidence degree in high α-interpretation as previously.

$$cf_{grad}(A(\vec{t}) \rightarrow C(\vec{t})) =$$
$$\frac{|\{\vec{x} \in \mathcal{H}^n \mid I_{ILP} \models \sigma[\vec{t}/\vec{x}](A \wedge C), \mu(\sigma[\vec{t}/\vec{x}]C) \geq \mu(\sigma[\vec{t}/\vec{x}]A)\}|}{|\{\vec{x} \in \mathcal{H}^n \mid I_{ILP} \models \sigma[\vec{t}/\vec{x}](A)\}|}$$

When the valuation of the condition part of the rule is a conjunction of grounds literals, the satisfaction degree of this conjunction is the minimum of the degree of each literal.

Certainty Rules with Fuzzy Conditions. The meaning of the fuzzy rule "$A(\vec{t}) \rightarrow C(\vec{t})$" is then "the more $\vec{x}$ is A, the more certain $\vec{x}$ is C". For these rules we are not interested in the satisfaction degrees of the consequence parts. This type of rule will be referred to as type 1 certainty rules in the following. The α-cut for these rules correspond to the following type of classical interpretation:

Definition 4. *An α-certainty interpretation, given a fact f, is defined by:*

$$I_{\alpha-cert} \models f \ \ iff \ \ (B \models f \ and \ \mu(f) \geq \alpha) \ or \ E \models f$$

Note that we cannot construct this type of interpretation in the recursive case, since $B \cap E \neq \emptyset$. With this kind of rules, confidence degrees are expected to be high for high α-certainty interpretation. The idea is that we can be more permissive with respect to exceptions for the classical counterparts of the rule

"$A(\overrightarrow{t}) \to C(\overrightarrow{t})$" corresponding small values of α. So, we are led to use the following Choquet integral.

$$cf_{cert1}(A(\overrightarrow{t}) \to C(\overrightarrow{t})) = \sum_{\alpha_i}^{t}(\alpha_i - \alpha_{i+1}) * cf(A(\overrightarrow{t}) \to C(\overrightarrow{t}))_{I_{\alpha_i - cert}}$$

Certainty Rules with Fuzzy Conditions and Conclusions. The above definition is modified in the following way for taking care of the satisfaction degree of the consequence of the rules. This type of rule will be referred to as type 2 certainty rules in the following
$cf_{cert2}(A(\overrightarrow{t}) \to C(\overrightarrow{t})) =$

$$\frac{|\{\overrightarrow{x} \in \mathcal{H}^n \mid I_{ILP} \models \sigma[\overrightarrow{t}/\overrightarrow{x}](A \wedge C), \mu(\sigma[\overrightarrow{t}/\overrightarrow{x}]C) > 1 - \mu(\sigma[\overrightarrow{t}/\overrightarrow{x}]A)\}|}{|\{\overrightarrow{x} \in \mathcal{H}^n \mid I_{ILP} \models \sigma[\overrightarrow{t}/\overrightarrow{x}](A)\}|}$$

Examples of Confidence Degree Computation: consider the following database with satisfaction degrees associated with fuzzy predicates A and C:
$B_1 = \{A(a,b), 1; A(a,c), 0.5; A(b,a), 0.7; A(c,b), 0.2\}$ $E_1 = \{C(a), 0.8; C(b), 0.4\}$.
Any other fact is assumed to be false.
$cf_{flex}(A(X,Y) \to C(X)) = 0.61; \; cf_{grad}(A(X,Y) \to C(X)) = 0.25$
$cf_{cert1}(A(X,Y) \to C(X)) = 0.95; \; cf_{cert2}(A(X,Y) \to C(X)) = 0.75$

$B_2 = \{A(a,b), 0.8; A(a,c), 0.1; A(b,a), 0.4; A(c,b), 0.3\}$
$E_2 = \{C(a), 0.9; C(b), 0.6\}$.
$cf_{flex}(A(X,Y) \to C(X)) = 0.70; \; cf_{grad}(A(X,Y) \to C(X)) = 0.75$
$cf_{cert1}(A(X,Y) \to C(X)) = 0.70; \; cf_{cert2}(A(X,Y) \to C(X)) = 0.25$

4   Algorithmic Issues

In the FOIL algorithm, the inductive process in a given state is guided by three things: the confidence degree, the stopping condition and the number of distinct examples that are covered by the rule. An example is an element of E, a counter-example is a fact pertaining to the target predicate which is false in the ILP interpretation. Confidence degrees for different kinds of fuzzy rules have been defined in the previous section, we have now to describe the halting condition and the counting of distinct examples covered by the rules.

In the crisp case, the FOIL algorithm stops if there are no counter-examples covered by the rule. In this case, the confidence degree is 1, i.e. the rule is totally certain. But, in the fuzzy case, a rule that covers only positive examples may have a low confidence degree. For example, given the fuzzy data $B = \{A(a,b), 0.2\}$ $E = \{C(a), 1\}$, the rule "$A(X,Y) \to C(X)$" covers the unique example, but we have $cf_{flex}(A(X,Y) \to C(X)) = 0.2$. This suggests the use of a threshold.

The number n of positive examples covered by the rule is needed for comparing rules which have similar confidence degrees. The counterpart of n in the fuzzy case is different according to the type of the fuzzy rule. In the case of gradual rules or of type 2 certainty rules, n is the number of examples covered by the crisp version of the rule and whose conditions and consequence obey the requirement about satisfaction degrees. Let us call $\overrightarrow{t_1}$ the q free variables that appear in the head of the rule and $\overrightarrow{t_2}$ be the other r variables that appear in the rule. Then we have:

$$n_{grad}(A(\overrightarrow{t}) \rightarrow C(\overrightarrow{t})) = |\{\overrightarrow{x_1} \in \mathcal{H}^q, \exists \overrightarrow{x_2} \in \mathcal{H}^r \mid$$
$$I_{ILP} \models \sigma[\overrightarrow{t_1}, \overrightarrow{t_2}/\overrightarrow{x_1}, \overrightarrow{x_2}](A \wedge C, \mu(\sigma[\overrightarrow{t_1}/\overrightarrow{x_1}]C) \geq \mu(\sigma[\overrightarrow{t_1}, \overrightarrow{t_2}/\overrightarrow{x_1}, \overrightarrow{x_2}]A)\}|$$

and

$$n_{cert2}(A(\overrightarrow{t}) \rightarrow C(\overrightarrow{t})) = |\{\overrightarrow{x_1} \in \mathcal{H}^q, \exists \overrightarrow{x_2} \in \mathcal{H}^r \mid$$
$$I_{ILP} \models \sigma[\overrightarrow{t_1}, \overrightarrow{t_2}/\overrightarrow{x_1}, \overrightarrow{x_2}](A \wedge C), \mu(\sigma[\overrightarrow{t_1}/\overrightarrow{x_1}]C) > 1 - \mu(\sigma[\overrightarrow{t_1}, \overrightarrow{t_2}/\overrightarrow{x_1}, \overrightarrow{x_2}]A)\}|$$

In the case of rules that handle flexibility, we are more interested in the examples covered by high α-interpretations. So, we compute a Choquet integral of the number of distinct examples covered in each α-interpretation.

$$n_{flex}(A(\overrightarrow{t}) \rightarrow C(\overrightarrow{t})) =$$
$$\sum_{\alpha_i}(\alpha_i - \alpha_{i+1}) * |\{\overrightarrow{x_1} \in \mathcal{H}^q, \exists \overrightarrow{x_2} \in \mathcal{H}^r \mid I_{\alpha_i} \models \sigma[\overrightarrow{t_1}, \overrightarrow{t_2}/\overrightarrow{x_1}, \overrightarrow{x_2}](A \wedge C)\}|$$

For the type 1 certainty rules, we are especially interested in the examples covered in the high α-cert interpretation, for which the confidence degree is high. Then we have:

$$n_{cert1}(A(\overrightarrow{t}) \rightarrow C(\overrightarrow{t})) =$$
$$\sum_{\alpha_i}(\alpha_i - \alpha_{i+1}) * |\{\overrightarrow{x_1} \in \mathcal{H}^q, \exists \overrightarrow{x_2} \in \mathcal{H}^r \mid I_{\alpha\ cert} \models \sigma[\overrightarrow{t_1}, \overrightarrow{t_2}/\overrightarrow{x_1}, \overrightarrow{x_2}](A \wedge C)\}|$$

Example of Computation of 'n':
with B_1, E_1 as in Sect. 3.3:
$n_{flex}(A(X,Y) \rightarrow C(X)) = 1.1$; $n_{grad}(A(X,Y) \rightarrow C(X)) = 1$
$n_{cert1}(A(X,Y) \rightarrow C(X)) = 1.5$; $n_{cert2}(A(X,Y) \rightarrow C(X)) = 2$

Thus, we can use the FOIL algorithm for inducing various kinds of first-order fuzzy rules by adapting confidence degree and cardinality with the type of rules that we want to learn.

5   Illustrative Example

As an illustration of our approach, we have explored a database that can be found on the PRETI platform (http://www.irit.fr/PRETI/). This database describes houses to let for vacations. There are more than 600 houses described in terms of about 25 attributes. A lot of these attributes are about distances between the house and another place (sea, fishing place, swimming pool, ...) or about prices at different periods in a year (June, weekend, scholar vacations ...). Typically, these attributes have a fuzzy interpretation. So, from our database, we build a fuzzy database by merely changing price, number of room, and distance information into fuzzy information such as "cheap", "expensive", "small_capacity", "high_capacity" (these two latter expressions refer to the size of the house), "far", "not_too_far", "not_far" together with a membership degree. For instance, "cheap" and "expensive" are represented by the following trapezoids (0, 0, 800, 2000) and (2500, 3800, 10000, 10000). "close_to", "not_too_far" and "far" are represented by the following trapezoids (0, 0, 5, 10), (5, 10, 30, 35) and (30, 35, 100, 100) respectively. For discrete attribute membership, degrees have to be directly associated which each possible values.

For example, the fact that the house x_1 lies at 5.5 km from sea, represented by the logical atomic formula $distance(x_1, sea, 5.5)$, becomes the fuzzy predicate $close\_to(x_1, sea)$ with 0.8 as satisfaction degree and $no\_too\_far(x_1, sea)$ with 0.2 as satisfaction degree. The tables below present some examples of first-order rules that have been found by the algorithm, for each type of fuzzy rule.

Flexible Rules	Confidence
$expensive(A, B), dishwasher(A), small\_capacity(A) \rightarrow comfortable(A)$	0.91
$very\_comfortable(A), expensive(A, B) \rightarrow close\_to(A, sea)$	0.86
$not\_comfortable(A), far(A, B) \rightarrow cheap(A, September)$	0.56
$expensive(A, C), B = shop, small\_capacity(A) \rightarrow close\_to(A, B)$	0.90
Gradual Rules	
$expensive(A, B), washingmachine(A) \rightarrow comfortable(A)$	0.96
$expensive(A, B) \rightarrow comfortable(A)$	0.90
$area(A, NARBONNAIS), high\_capacity(A) \rightarrow close\_to(A, sea)$	1
$not\_comfortable(A), far(A, B), small\_capacity(A) \rightarrow cheap(A, September)$	0.88
Type 1 Certainty Rules	
$area(A, LAURAGAIS), expensive(A, C) \rightarrow comfortable(A)$	0.92
$very\_comfortable(A) \rightarrow close\_to(A, sea)$	0.83
$area(A, LIMOUXIN) \rightarrow cheap(A, September)$	0.86
$expensive(A, B), phone(A), small\_capacity(A) \rightarrow television(A)$	0.91
Type 2 Certainty Rules	
$dishwasher(A), area(A, B), television(A) \rightarrow comfortable(A)$	0.93
$area(A, NARBONNAIS), high\_capacity(A) \rightarrow close\_to(A, sea)$	0.90
$number\_of\_chamber(A, 1), pet\_accepted(A), far(A, sea) \rightarrow not\_comfortable(A)$	0.93
$high\_capacity(A), area(A, NARBONNAIS), phone(A) \rightarrow very\_comfortable(A)$	1

Note that some rules could be expressed in propositional logic, but here the instantiations are automatically generated by the algorithm. As shown in some rules, the algorithm can mix fuzzy predicates and non-fuzzy predicates.

Since flexible rules have the same meaning as crisp ones, but just privilege the high α-cuts for the instantiation of the rule; the rules found remain quite similar to the ones that could be found in the non-fuzzy approach. For the gradual rules, what is learn is an original kind of rule. For example, the first rule in the gradual rules table means: "the more there exists a time period when the house is really expensive and if the house has a washingmachine, the more the house is comfortable". The fuzzy rules that handle certainty tend to favour the non-fuzzy predicates in condition part because they leave more freedom with respect to the satisfaction degree of covered examples.

6   Conclusion

This paper has described a formal framework and a procedure for learning various kinds of first-order rules involving fuzzy (or non-fuzzy) predicates. The definition of confidence degrees for rules with fuzzy predicates allows us to easily introduce them in any learning algorithm which uses confidence degrees as a basis for the guiding process. Since the confidence computation is a weigthed version of FOIL's one, it's easy to deduce that the complexity of the algorithm is the same as the FOIL's one. Learning rules with fuzzy predicates has some obvious advantages. A first one is that fuzzy rules can involve fuzzy categories as often used by people. Generally speaking, it is well known that fuzzy sets defined on subsets of the real line provide a flexible interface with precise numerical values. The use of fuzzy predicates also contributes to reduce the hypothesis space. Moreover, since it's also known that ILP has difficulties for handling real numbers, the use of fuzzy predicates for representing numerically valued predicates (as made with the PRETI database) can provide a valuable improvement. The different kinds of rules that can be learned increase the expressivity. Moreover, the paper proposes a method for learning gradual rules, a topic which has not been much considered until now.

The definition of confidence degrees for each kind of rules allows us to take into account the fuzzy predicates in the algorithms that use confidence degrees for guiding the learning process. But we also see that trying to learn rules which do not cover any counter-example, as in classical ILP, is not sufficient in case of fuzzy predicates. It is why, we need to formally describe the ILP setting for rules with fuzzy predicates by incorporating confidence degrees. However the proposed algorithm could still be improved. First, as in data mining, other degrees like support could be computed and used for controlling the learning process. Besides, our algorithm has the same limitations as FOIL and cannot find all the "interesting" rules ([18]). It is an open track to build an extraction algorithm by-passing classical ILP techniques. Finally, another line of research is to study the prediction capabilities of the induced rules.

References

1. F. Bacchus. *Representing and Reasoning With Probabilistic Knowledge*. MIT press, 1990.
2. F. Bacchus, A.J. Grove, J.Y. Halpern, and D. Koller. Generating degrees of belief from statistical information: an overview. In *13 th Conf. of Foundations of Software Technologie and Theorical Computer Science*, Bombay, 1993.
3. P. Bosc, D. Dubois, O. Pivert, H. Prade, and M. de Calmes. Fuzzy sumarisation of data using fuzzy cardinalities. In *Proc. Inter. Conf. Information Processing and Management of Uncertainty in Knowledge-based Systems (IPMU 2002)*, pages 1553–1559, Annecy-France, July 2002.
4. B. Bouchon-Meunier and C. Marsala. Learning fuzzy decision rules, in. *Fuzzy Sets in Approximate Reasoning and Information Systems*,(J.C. Bezdek, D. Dubois, H. Prade, eds.), The Handbooks of Fuzzy Sets Series. Kluwer Academic Publishers, 1999, 279–304.

5. M. Delgado, D. Sanchez, and M.A. Vila. Fuzzy cardinality based evaluation of quantified sentences. *Inter. J. of Approximate Reasoning*, pages 23:23–66, 2000.
6. D. Dubois and H. Prade. What are fuzzy rules and how to use them. *Fuzzy Sets and Systems*, 84(2):169–189, 1996.
7. L. Getoor, N. Friedman, and D. Koller. Learning structured statistical models from relational data. *Linköping Elec. Art. in Comp. and Inform. Sci.*, 7(13), 2002.
8. J. Halpern. An analysis of first-order logics of probability. *Artificial Intelligence*, 46:310–355, 1990.
9. E. Hüllermeier. Implication-based fuzzy association rules. In L. De Raedt and A. Siebes, editors, *Proc. PKDD-01, 5th Conf. on Principles and Pratice of Knowledge Discovery in Databases*, number 2168 in LNAI, pages 241–252, 2001.
10. D. Koller and A. Pfeffer. Learning probabilities for noisy first-order rules. In *Proc. of the 15th Int. Joint Conf. on Artif. Intellig. (IJCAI-97)*, pages 1316–1321, Nagoya, 1997.
11. S.H. Muggleton. Inverse entailment and Progol. *New Generation Computing*, 13:245–286, 1995.
12. S.H. Muggleton. Learning stochastic logic programs. *Electronic Transactions in Artificial Intelligence*, 5(041), 2000.
13. D. Nauck and R. Kruse. Neuro-fuzzy methods in fuzzy rule generation, in. *Fuzzy Sets in Approximate Reasoning and Information Systems*,(J.C. Bezdek, D. Dubois, H. Prade, eds.), The Handbooks of Fuzzy Sets Series. Kluwer Acad. Pub., 1999, 305–334.
14. S-H Nienhuys-Cheng and R. de Wolf. *Foundations of Inductive Logic Programming*. Number 1228 in LNAI series. Springer, 1997.
15. H. Prade, G. Richard, and M. Serrurier. Learning first order fuzzy rules. In *Proc. of 10 th Int. Fuzzy Systems Association (IFSA-03)*, Istanbul, 2003.
16. J. R. Quinlan. Induction of decision trees. *Machine Learning*, 1(1):81–106, 1986.
17. J. R. Quinlan. Learning logical definitions from relations. *Machine Learning*, 5:239–266, 1990.
18. B.L. Richards and R.J. Mooney. Learning relations by pathfinding. In *Proc. of the AAAI conference*, pages 50–55, San Jose, 1992. AAAI Press.

Reasoning under Vagueness Expressed by Nuanced Statements

Mazen El-Sayed and Daniel Pacholczyk

University of Angers, 2 Boulevard Lavoisier, 49045 Angers Cedex 01, France
{elsayed,pacho}@univ-angers.fr

Abstract. We study knowledge-based systems using symbolic many-valued logic and multiset theory. In previous papers we have proposed a symbolic representation of nuanced statements like "John is very tall". In this representation, we have interpreted some nuances of natural language as linguistic modifiers and we have defined them within a multiset context. In this paper, we continue the presentation of our symbolic model and we propose new deduction rules dealing with nuanced statements. More precisely, we present new Generalized Modus Ponens rules and we study the form of graduality verified by these rules.

Keywords: knowledge representation and reasoning, imprecision, vagueness, many-valued logic, multiset theory

1 Introduction

The development of knowledge-based systems is a rapidly expanding field in applied artificial intelligence. The knowledge base is comprised of a database and a rule base. We suppose that the database contains facts representing *nuanced statements*, like "Jo is very tall", to which one associates truth degrees. The *nuanced statements* can be represented more formally under the form "x is m_α A" where m_α and A are labels denoting respectively a nuance and a vague or imprecise term of natural language. The rule base contains rules of the form *"if x is m_α A then y is m_β B"* to which one associates truth degrees.

Our work presents a symbolic-based model which permits a qualitative management of vagueness in knowledge-based systems. In dealing with vagueness, there are two issues of importance: (1) how to represent vague data, and (2) how to draw inference using vague data.

When imprecise information is evaluated in a *numerical way*, fuzzy logic which is introduced by Zadeh [10], is recognized as a good tool for dealing with aforementioned issues and performing reasoning upon common sense and vague knowledge-bases. In this logic, "x is m_α A" is considered as a fuzzy proposition where A is modeled by a fuzzy set which is defined by a membership function. This one is generally defined upon a numerical scale. The nuance m_α is defined such as a *fuzzy modifier* [2,9,10] which represents, from the fuzzy set A, a new fuzzy set "m_α A". So, "x is m_α A" is interpreted by Zadeh as "x is (m_α A)" and is regarded as many-valued statement. A second formalism, refers to a symbolic

T.D. Nielsen and N.L. Zhang (Eds.): ECSQARU 2003, LNAI 2711, pp. 382–394, 2003.

many-valued logic [7,9], is used when imprecise information is evaluated in a *symbolic way*. This logic is the logical counterpart of a *multiset theory* introduced by De Glas [7]. In this theory, the term m_α linguistically expresses the degree to which the object x satisfies the term A. So, "x is m_α A" means "x (is m_α) A", and then is regarded as boolean statement. In other words, "m_α A" does not represent a new vague term obtained from A.

In previous papers [5,6], we have proposed a symbolic-based model to represent nuanced statements. This model is based on the many-valued logic proposed by Pacholczyk [9]. Our basic idea has been to consider that some nuances of natural language can not be interpreted as satisfaction degrees and must be instead defined such as *linguistic modifiers*. In Sect. 3, we present a short review of this model. In this paper, our basic contribution is to propose deduction rules dealing with nuanced information. For that purpose, we propose deduction rules generalizing the *Modus Ponens* rule in a many-valued logic proposed by Pacholczyk [9]. We notice that the first version of this rule has been proposed in a fuzzy context by Zadeh [10] and has been studied later by various authors [1,2,8].

In Sect. 2, we present briefly the basic concepts of the M-valued predicate logic which forms the backbone of our work. Section 3 introduces briefly the symbolic representation model previously proposed. In Sect. 4, we study various types of inference rules and we propose new *Generalized Modus Ponens* rules in which we use only simple statements. In Sect. 5, we propose a generalized production system in which we define more Generalized Modus Ponens rules in more complex situations. In Sect. 6, we study the problem of graduality of inference and we demonstrate the forms of graduality satisfied by our GMP rules.

2   M-Valued Predicate Logic

Within a multiset context, to a vague term A and a nuance m_α are associated respectively a multiset $\mathbb{A}$ and a symbolic degree τ_α. So, the statement "x is m_α A" means that x belongs to multiset $\mathbb{A}$ with a degree τ_α. The M-valued predicate logic [9] is the logical counterpart of the multiset theory. In this logic, to each multiset $\mathbb{A}$ and a membership degree τ_α are associated a M-valued predicate **A** and a truth degree τ_α−true. In this context, the following equivalence holds: x is m_α A $\Leftrightarrow x \in_\alpha \mathbb{A} \Leftrightarrow$ "x is m_α **A**" is true $\Leftrightarrow$ "x is **A**" is τ_α−true. One supposes that the membership degrees are symbolic degrees which form an ordered set $\mathcal{L}_M = \{\tau_\alpha, \alpha \in [1, M]\}$. We can then define in $\mathcal{L}_M$ two operators $\wedge$ and $\vee$ and a decreasing involution $\sim$ as follows: $\tau_\alpha \vee \tau_\beta = \tau_{max(\alpha,\beta)}, \tau_\alpha \wedge \tau_\beta = \tau_{min(\alpha,\beta)}$ and $\sim \tau_\alpha = \tau_{M+1-\alpha}$. One obtains then a chain $\{\mathcal{L}_M, \vee, \wedge, \leq\}$ having the structure of De Morgan lattice [9]. On this set, an implication $\rightarrow$ and a T-norm T can be defined respectively as follows: $\tau_\alpha \rightarrow \tau_\beta = \tau_{min(\beta-\alpha+M,M)}$ and $T(\tau_\alpha, \tau_\beta) = \tau_{max(\beta+\alpha-M,1)}$.

Example 1. For example, by choosing M=9, we can introduce: $\mathcal{L}_9$={*not at all, little, enough, fairly, moderately, quite, almost, nearly, completely*}.

3   Representation of Nuanced Statements

Let us suppose that our knowledge base is characterized by a finite number of concepts C_i. A set of terms P_{ik} is associated with each concept C_i, whose respective domain is denoted as X_i. The terms P_{ik} are said to be the *basic terms* connected with the concept C_i. A finite set of *linguistic modifiers* m_α allows us to define *nuanced terms*, denoted as $"m_\alpha P_{ik}"$.

In previous papers [5,6], we have proposed a symbolic-based model to represent nuanced statements of natural language. We have proposed firstly a new method to symbolically represent vague terms. In this method, we suppose that a domain of a vague term, denoted by X, is simulated by a *"rule"* (cf. Fig. 1) representing an arbitrary set of objects.

Our basic idea has been to associate with each multiset P_i a symbolic concept which represents an equivalent to the membership function in fuzzy set theory. For that, we have introduced a new concept, called "rule", which has a geometry similar to a membership L-R function and its role is to illustrate the membership graduality to the multisets. In order to define the geometry of this "rule", we use notions similar to those defined within a fuzzy context like the core, the support and the fuzzy part of a fuzzy set [10]. We define these notions within a multiset theory as follows: the core of a multiset P_i, denoted as $Core(P_i)$, represents the elements belonging to P_i with a τ_M degree, the support, denoted as $Sp(P_i)$, contains the elements belonging to P_i with at least τ_2 degree, and the fuzzy part, denoted as $F(P_i)$, contains the elements belonging to P_i with degrees varying from τ_2 to τ_{M-1}. We associate with each multiset a "rule" that contains the elements of its support (cf. Fig. 3). This "rule" is the union of three disjoint subsets: *the left fuzzy part, the right fuzzy part* and *the core*. For a multiset P_i, they are denoted respectively by L_i, R_i and C_i.

We suppose that the left (resp. right) fuzzy part L_i (resp. R_i) is the union of M-2 subsets, denoted as $[L_i]_\alpha$ (resp. $[R_i]_\alpha$), which partition it. $[L_i]_\alpha$ (resp.

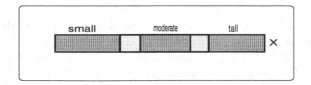

Fig. 1. Representation with *"rule"* of a domain X

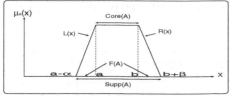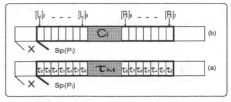

Fig. 2. A membership L-R function   **Fig. 3.** Representation with *"rule"*

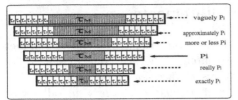

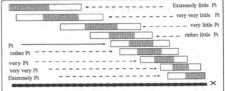

Fig. 4. Precision modifiers   **Fig. 5.** Translation modifiers

$[R_i]_\alpha$) contains the elements of L_i (resp. R_i) belonging to P_i with a τ_α degree. In order to keep a similarity with the fuzzy sets of type L-R, we choose to place, in a "rule" associated with a multiset, the subsets $[L_i]_\alpha$ and $[R_i]_\alpha$ so that the larger α is, the closer the $[L_i]_\alpha$ subsets and $[R_i]_\alpha$ are to the core C_i (cf. Fig. 3). That can be interpreted as follows: the elements of the core of a term represent the typical elements of this term, and the more one object moves away from the core, the less it satisfies the term. Finally, we have denoted a multiset P_i with which we associate a "rule" as $P_i = (L_i, C_i, R_i)$, and we have introduced symbolic parameters which enable us to describe the form of the "rule" and its position in the universe X. These parameters have a role similar to the role of numerical parameters which are used to define a fuzzy set within a fuzzy context.

3.1 Linguistic Modifiers

By using the "rule" concept we have defined the linguistic modifiers. We have used two types of linguistic modifiers.

- *Precision Modifiers*: The precision modifiers increase or decrease the precision of the basic term. We distinguish two types of precision modifiers: contraction modifiers and dilation modifiers. We use $\mathbb{M}_6 = \{m_k | k \in [1..6]\}$ ={*exactly, really, ∅, more or less, approximately, vaguely*} which is totally ordered by $j \le k \Leftrightarrow m_j \le m_k$ (Fig. 4).
- *Translation Modifiers*: The translation modifiers operate both a translation and precision variation (contraction or dilation) on the basic term. We use $\mathbb{T}_9 = \{t_k | k \in [1..9]\}$ ={*extremely little, very very little, very little, rather little, ∅, rather, very, very very, extremely*} totally ordered by $k \le l \Leftrightarrow t_k \le t_l$ (Fig. 5). The multisets $t_k P_i$ cover the domain X.

In this paper, we continue to propose our model for managing nuanced statements. In the following, we focus our intention to study the problem of exploitation of nuanced statements.

4   Exploitation of Nuanced Statements

In this section, we treat the exploitation of nuanced information. In particular, we are interested to propose some generalizations of the Modus Ponens rule within a many-valued context [9]. We notice that the classical Modus Ponens rule has the following form: If we know that {*If "x is A" then "y is B" is true and "x is A" is true*} we conclude that "y is B" is true. Within a many-valued context, a generalization of Modus Ponens rule has one of the following forms:

F1- If we know that {*If "x is A" then "y is B" is τ_β-true and "x is $A^{'}$" is τ_ϵ-true*} and that {$A^{'}$ *is more or less near to* A}, what can we conclude for "y is B", in other words, to what degree "y is B" is true?

F2- If we know that {*If "x is A" then "y is B" is τ_β-true and "x is $A^{'}$" is τ_ϵ-true*} and that {$A^{'}$ *is more or less near to* A}, can we find a $B^{'}$ such as {$B^{'}$ *is more or less near to* B} and to what degree "y is $B^{'}$" is true?

These forms of *Generalized Modus Ponens* (GMP) rule have been studied firstly by Pacholczyk in [9]. In this section, we propose new versions of GMP rule in which we use new relations of nearness.

4.1   First GMP Rule

In Pacholczyk's versions of GMP, the concept of nearness binding multisets A and $A^{'}$ is modeled by a similarity relation which is defined as follows:

Definition 1. *Let A and B be two multisets. A is said to be τ_α-similar to B, denoted as $A \approx_\alpha B$, if and only if: $\forall x | x \in_\gamma A$ and $x \in_\beta B \Rightarrow min\{\tau_\gamma \to \tau_\beta, \tau_\beta \to \tau_\gamma\} \geq \tau_\alpha$.*

This relation generalizes the equivalence relation in a many-valued context as the similarity relation of Zadeh [10] has been in a fuzzy context. It is (1) reflexive: $A \approx_M A$, (2) symmetrical: $A \approx_\alpha B \Leftrightarrow B \approx_\alpha A$, and (3) weakly transitive: $\{A \approx_\alpha B, B \approx_\beta C\} \Rightarrow A \approx_\gamma C$ with $\tau_\gamma \geq T(\tau_\alpha, \tau_\beta)$ where T is a T-norm.

By using the similarity relation to model the nearness binding between multisets, the inference rule can be interpreted as: {*more the rule and the fact are true*} and {*more $A^{'}$ and A are similar*}, *more the conclusion is true*. In particular, when $A^{'}$ is more precise than A ($A^{'} \subset A$) but they are very weakly similar, any conclusion can be deduced or the conclusion deduced isn't as precise as one can expect. This is due to the fact that the similarity relation isn't able alone to model in a satisfactory way the nearness between $A^{'}$ and A. For that, we add to the similarity relation a new relation called *nearness relation* whose role is to define the nearness of $A^{'}$ to A when $A^{'} \subset A$. In other words, it indicates the degree to which $A^{'}$ is included in A.

Definition 2. *Let A and B be two multisets such that $A \subset B$. A is said to be τ_α-near to B, denoted as $A \sqsubset_\alpha B$, if and only if {$\forall x \in F(B)$, $x \in_\beta A$ and $x \in_\gamma B \Rightarrow \tau_\alpha \to \tau_\beta \leq \tau_\gamma$}.*

The nearness relation satisfies the following properties: (1) Reflexivity: $A \sqsubset_M A$, and (2) Weak transitivity: $A \sqsubset_\alpha B$ and $B \sqsubset_\beta C \Rightarrow A \sqsubset_\gamma C$ with $\tau_\gamma \leq min(\tau_\alpha, \tau_\beta)$. In the relation $A \sqsubset_\alpha B$, the less the value of α is, the more A is included in B. Finally, by using similarity and nearness relations, we propose a first *Generalized Modus Ponens* rule.

Proposition 1. *Let A and A' be predicates associated with the concept C_i, B be predicate associated with the concept C_e. Given the following assumptions:*

1. it is τ_β-true that if "x is A" then "y is B"

2. "x is A'" is τ_ϵ-true with $A' \approx_\alpha A$.

Then, we conclude : "y is B" is τ_δ-true with $\tau_\delta = T(\tau_\beta, T(\tau_\alpha, \tau_\epsilon))$. If A' is such that $A' \sqsubset_{\alpha'} A$, we conclude: "y is B" is τ_δ-true with $\tau_\delta = T(\tau_\beta, \tau_{\alpha'} \longrightarrow \tau_\epsilon)$.

Example 2. Given that "really tall" $\approx_8$ "tall" and "really tall" $\sqsubset_8$ "tall", from the following rule and fact:
- if "x is tall" then "its weight is important" is true
- "Pascal is really tall" is quite-true,
we can deduce: "Pascal's weight is really important" is almost-true.

4.2   GMP Rules Using Precision Modifiers

In the previous paragraph we calculate the degree to which the conclusion of the rule is true. In the following, we present two new versions of GMP rule in which the predicate of the conclusion obtained by the deduction process is not B but a new predicate B' which is more or less near to B. More precisely, the new predicate is derived from B by using precision modifiers[1] ($B' = mB$). The first version assumes that the predicates A and A' are more or less similar. In other words, A' may be less precise or more precise than A. The second one assumes that A' is more precise than A.

Proposition 2. *Given the following assumptions:*

1. it is τ_β-true that if "x is A" then "y is B"

2. "x is A'" is τ_ϵ-true with $A' \approx_\alpha A$.

Let $\tau_\theta = T(\tau_\beta, T(\tau_\alpha, \tau_\epsilon))$. If $\tau_\theta > \tau_1$ then there exists a $\tau_{n(\delta)}-dilation$ modifier m, with $\tau_\delta \leq T(\tau_\alpha, \tau_\beta)$, such that: "$y$ is mB" is $\tau_{\epsilon'}$-true and $\tau_{\epsilon'} = \tau_\delta \longrightarrow \tau_\theta$. Moreover, we have: $B \subset mB$ and $mB \approx_\delta B$.

This proposition prove that if we know that A' is more or less similar to A, without any supplementary information concerning its precision compared to A, the predicate of the conclusion obtained by the deduction process (mB) is less precise than B (i.e. $B \subset mB$) and which is more or less similar to B. In the following proposition, we assume that A' is more precise than A.

Proposition 3. *Given the following assumptions:*

1. it is τ_β-true that if "x is A" then "y is B"

2. "x is A'" is τ_ϵ-true with $A' \sqsubset_\alpha A$.

---

[1] The definitions of these are presented in appendix A.

Let $\tau_\theta = T(\tau_\beta, \tau_\alpha \longrightarrow \tau_\epsilon)$. If $\tau_\theta > \tau_1$ then there exists a $\tau_{n(\delta)}$ – contraction modifier m, with $\tau_\delta \geq \tau_\beta \longrightarrow \tau_\alpha$, such that: "y is mB" is $\tau_{\epsilon'}$-true and $\tau_{\epsilon'} = T(\tau_\delta, \tau_\theta)$.
Moreover, we have: $mB \sqsubset_\delta B$.

This proposition prove that from a predicate A' which is more or less near to A we obtain a predicate mB which is more or less near to B. More precisely, if A' is more precise than A then mB is more precise than B. The previous propositions (2 and 3) present two general cases in which we consider arbitrary predicates A'. In the following, we present two corollaries representing special cases of propositions 2 and 3 in which we assume that the rule is completely true and that A' is obtained from A by using precision modifiers.

Corollary 1. *Let the following rule and fact:*

1. *it is true that if "x is A" then "y is B"*
2. *"x is $m_k A$" is τ_ϵ-true where m_k is a τ_{γ_k} – dilation modifier.*

If $T(\sim \tau_{\gamma_k}, \tau_\epsilon) > \tau_1$ then we conclude: "y is $m_k B$" is $\tau_{\epsilon'}$-true, with $\tau_{\epsilon'} = \sim \tau_{\gamma_k} \longrightarrow T(\sim \tau_{\gamma_k}, \tau_\epsilon)$.

Example 3. Given the following data:
- if "x is tall" then "its weight is important" is true,
- "Jo is more or less tall" is moderately-true.
Then, we can deduce: "Jo's weight is more or less important" is moderately-true.

Corollary 2. *Let the following rule and fact:*

1. *it is true that if "x is A" then "y is B"*
2. *"x is $m_k A$" is τ_ϵ-true where m_k is a τ_{γ_k} – contraction modifier.*

Then, we conclude that: "y is $m_k B$" is τ_ϵ-true.

Example 4. Given the following data:
- if "x is tall" then "its weight is important" is true,
- "Pascal is really tall" is moderately-true.
Then, we can deduce: "Pascal's weight is really important" is moderately-true.

These two corollaries present a particular form of graduality of inference. This form is known as graduality by means of linguistic modifiers [3]. It enables us to obtain, from a fact whose predicate A' is nuanced by linguistic modifiers, a conclusion whose predicate is also nuanced by linguistic modifiers.

4.3   Other Inference Rules

In the previous paragraphs, we presented GMP rules in which we can either (1) calculate the degree to which the conclusion of the rule is true, or (2) to obtain a new conclusion which is more or less near to the rule's one and to calculate the degree to which it is true. In this paragraph, we present new inference rules in which the predicate of the conclusion obtained by the deduction process is a new predicate B' which is more or less near to B. The new predicate is chosen from the set of nuanced predicates associated with a concept. The existence of such a predicate is not always sure and is depending on the predicate B and on the other predicates associated with the same concept. We notice that these forms of inference rules can be used to evaluate the truth of a statement by using rules and facts which are available in the knowledge-based system. In other words, if we know that $\{$If "x is A" then "y is B" is τ_β-true and "x is A'" is τ_ϵ-true$\}$ and that $\{A'$ and B' are respectively more or less near to A and $B\}$, can we calculate the degree to which "y is B'" is true?

We present below two inference rules. The first version assumes that the predicates A and A' are more or less similar. The second one assumes that A' is more precise than A.

Proposition 4. *Given the following assumptions:*

1. it is τ_β-true that if "x is A" then "y is B"

2. "x is A'" is τ_ϵ-true with $A' \approx_\alpha A$.

Let $\tau_\theta = T(\tau_\beta, T(\tau_\alpha, \tau_\epsilon))$. If $\tau_\theta > \tau_1$ and if there exists a predicate B' such that $B' \approx_\delta B$, then we can conclude that: "y is B'" is $\tau_{\epsilon'}$-true and $\tau_{\epsilon'} = T(\tau_\delta, \tau_\theta)$. If the predicate B' is such that $B \sqsubset_{\delta'} B'$, we conclude: "y is B'" is $\tau_{\epsilon'}$-true with $\tau_{\epsilon'} = \tau_{\delta'} \longrightarrow \tau_\theta$.

Proposition 5. *Given the following assumptions:*

1. it is τ_β-true that if "x is A" then "y is B"

2. "x is A'" is τ_ϵ-true with $A' \sqsubset_\alpha A$.

Let $\tau_\theta = T(\tau_\beta, \tau_\alpha \longrightarrow \tau_\epsilon)$. If $\tau_\theta > \tau_1$ and if there exists a predicate B' such that $B' \approx_\delta B$, then we can conclude that: "y is B'" is $\tau_{\epsilon'}$-true and $\tau_{\epsilon'} = T(\tau_\delta, \tau_\theta)$. If the predicate B' is such that $B \sqsubset_{\delta'} B'$, we conclude: "y is B'" is $\tau_{\epsilon'}$-true with $\tau_{\epsilon'} = \tau_{\delta'} \longrightarrow \tau_\theta$.

Example 5. Let "very important" $\sqsubset_6$ "important", "really tall" $\approx_8$ "tall" and "really tall" $\sqsubset_8$ "tall". Let our knowledge-based system contain:
- if "x is tall" then "its weight is important" is true,
- "Jo is really tall" is quite-true.
Then, we want to know the truth degree of the statement "Jo's weight is very important". By applying the proposition 5, we can deduce:
"Jo's weight is very important" is fairly-true.

5   Generalized Production System

In this section, we present some Generalized Modus Ponens rules in more complex situations. More precisely, we study the reasoning in 4 situations:

1. When the antecedent of the rule is a conjunction of statements.
2. When the antecedent is a disjunction of statements.
3. In presence of propagation of inferences. In other words, when the conclusion of the first rule is the antecedent of the second rule, and so on.
4. When a combination of imprecision is possible. In other words, when we have some rules which have the same statement in their conclusion parts.

So, we present the following 4 propositions representing inference rules in these situations.

Proposition 6 (Antecedent is a conjunction). *Given the following assumptions:*

1. *if "x_1 is A_1" and ... and "x_n is A_n" then "y is B" is τ_β-true,*
2. *for $i = 1..n$, "x_i is A_i'" is τ_{ϵ_i}-true,*
3. *for $i = 1..n$, $A_i \approx_{\alpha_i} A_i'$.*

Then, we can deduce: "y is B" is τ_δ-true with $\tau_\delta = T(\tau_\beta, T(\tau_{\alpha_1}, \tau_{\epsilon_1})) \wedge ... \wedge T(\tau_\beta, T(\tau_{\alpha_n}, \tau_{\epsilon_n}))$. If, for $i = j .. k$, the predicates A_i' are such that $A_i' \sqsubset_{\alpha_i'} A_i$, we can deduce: "$y$ is B" is τ_δ-true with $\tau_\delta = \tau_{\delta_1} \wedge ... \wedge \tau_{\delta_n}$ and $\tau_{\delta_i} = T(\tau_{\alpha_i'} \longrightarrow \tau_{\epsilon_i}, \tau_\beta)$ if $i \in [j, k]$ and $\tau_{\delta_i} = T(\tau_\beta, T(\tau_{\alpha_i}, \tau_{\epsilon_i}))$ if not.

Proposition 7 (Antecedent is a disjunction). *Given the following assumptions:*

1. *if "x_1 is A_1" or ... or "x_n is A_n" then "y is B" is τ_β-true,*
2. *for $i = 1..k$, "x_i is A_i'" is τ_{ϵ_i}-true,*
3. *for $i = 1..k$, $A_i \approx_{\alpha_i} A_i'$.*

Then, we can deduce: "y is B" is τ_δ-true with $\tau_\delta = T(\tau_\beta, T(\tau_{\alpha_1}, \tau_{\epsilon_1})) \vee ... \vee T(\tau_\beta, T(\tau_{\alpha_k}, \tau_{\epsilon_k}))$. If, for $i = j .. L$, the predicates A_i' are such that $A_i' \sqsubset_{\alpha_i'} A_i$, we can deduce: "$y$ is B" is τ_δ-true with $\tau_\delta = \tau_{\delta_1} \vee ... \vee \tau_{\delta_k}$ and $\tau_{\delta_i} = T(\tau_{\alpha_i'} \longrightarrow \tau_{\epsilon_i}, \tau_\beta)$ if $i \in [j, L]$ and $\tau_{\delta_i} = T(\tau_\beta, T(\tau_{\alpha_i}, \tau_{\epsilon_i}))$ if not.

Proposition 8 (Propagation of inference). *Given the following assumptions:*

1. *if "x is A" then "y is B" is τ_β-true,*
2. *if "y is B" then "z is C" is τ_γ-true,*
3. *there exists $\tau_\epsilon > \tau_1$ such that "x is A'" is τ_ϵ-true,*
4. *there exists τ_α such that $A \approx_\alpha A'$.*

Then, we can deduce: "z is C" is τ_δ-true, with $\tau_\delta = T(T(\tau_\beta, \tau_\gamma), T(\tau_\alpha, \tau_\epsilon))$. If the predicate A' is such that $A' \sqsubset_{\alpha'} A$, then we can deduce: "z is C" is τ_δ-true, with $\tau_\delta = T(T(\tau_\beta, \tau_\gamma), \tau_{\alpha'} \longrightarrow \tau_\epsilon)$.

Proposition 9 (Combination of imprecision). *Given the following assumptions:*

1. *for* $i = 1..n$, *if* *"x_i is A_i"* *then* *"y is B"* *is* τ_{β_i}*-true,*
2. *for* $i = 1..n$, *"x_i is A'_i"* *is* τ_{ϵ_i}*-true,*
3. *for* $i = 1..n$, $A_i \approx_{\alpha_i} A'_i$,

then we can deduce that: "y is B" is τ_δ-true with $\tau_\delta = T(\tau_{\beta_1}, T(\tau_{\alpha_1}, \tau_{\epsilon_1})) \vee ... \vee T(\tau_{\beta_n}, T(\tau_{\alpha_n}, \tau_{\epsilon_n}))$. If, for $i = j .. k$, the predicates A'_i are such that $A'_i \sqsubset_{\alpha'_i} A_i$, then we can deduce: "$y$ is B" is τ_δ-true with $\tau_\delta = \tau_{\delta_1} \vee ... \vee \tau_{\delta_n}$ and $\tau_{\delta_i} = T(\tau_{\alpha'_i} \longrightarrow \tau_{\epsilon_i}, \tau_{\beta_i})$ if $i \in [j, k]$ and $\tau_{\delta_i} = T(\tau_{\beta_i}, T(\tau_{\alpha_i}, \tau_{\epsilon_i}))$ if not.

We present below an example in which we use the GMP rules presented in this section. In this example, we use index cards written by a doctor after his consultations. From index cards (IC_i) and some rules ($\mathcal{R}_j$), we wish deduce a diagnosis.

Example 6. Let assume that we have the following rules in our base of rules.

$\mathcal{R}_1$– "If the temperature is high, the patient is ill" is almost true,
$\mathcal{R}_2$– "If the tension is always high, the patient is ill" is nearly true,
$\mathcal{R}_3$– "If the temperature is high and the eardrum color is very red, the disease is an otitis" is true,
$\mathcal{R}_4$– "If fat eating is high, the cholesterol risk is high" is true,
$\mathcal{R}_5$– "If the cholesterol risk is high, a diet with no fat is recommended" is true.

Let us assume now that we have an index card for a patient and we want to deduce a diagnosis.

$\mathcal{F}_1$– "the temperature is rather high" is nearly true,
$\mathcal{F}_2$– "the tension is always more or less high" is almost true,
$\mathcal{F}_3$– "the eardrum color is really very red" is quite true,
$\mathcal{F}_4$– "the fat eating is very very high" is moderately true.

Using the GMP rules previously presented, we deduce the following diagnosis:

$\mathcal{D}_1$– "the patient is ill" is almost true,
$\mathcal{D}_2$– "the disease is an otitis" is almost true,
$\mathcal{D}_3$– "the cholesterol risk is high" is true,
$\mathcal{D}_4$– "a diet with no fat is recommended" is true.

Let us assume that we have the following relations: "rather high" $\sqsubset_7$ "high", "more or less high" $\approx_8$ "high", "really very red" $\sqsubset_8$ "very red" and "very very high" $\sqsubset_2$ "high". Then, the diagnosis ($\mathcal{D}_1$ - $\mathcal{D}_4$) are obtained as follows.

  - $\mathcal{D}_1$ is obtained by applying proposition 9 to ($\mathcal{F}_1, \mathcal{F}_2$) and ($\mathcal{R}_1, \mathcal{R}_2$),
  - $\mathcal{D}_2$ is obtained by applying proposition 6 to ($\mathcal{F}_1, \mathcal{F}_3$) and $\mathcal{R}_3$,
  - $\mathcal{D}_3$ is obtained by applying proposition 1 to $\mathcal{F}_4$ and $\mathcal{R}_4$,
  - $\mathcal{D}_4$ is obtained by applying proposition 8 to F_4 and ($\mathcal{R}_4, \mathcal{R}_5$).

6   Graduality of Inference

In this section, we are interested to investigate the graduality of inference verified by our GMP rules. We distinguish mainly five forms of gradual rule involving graduality: (1) on the truth value, (2) on inclusion between multisets, (3) by means of linguistic modifiers, (4) or dealing with the degree of similarity or the proximity of multisets, (5) or graduality on terms associated with a concept. In this section, we are limited to study the graduality based on the truth value and on inclusion between multisets. Other forms of graduality will be investigated in next papers.

In the following, we study the graduality verified by the GMP rules proposed in paragraphs 4.1 and 4.2. The following proposition prove the form of graduality underlying by the first GMP rule (proposition 1).

Proposition 10. *Given the following assumptions:*

1. it is τ_β-true that if "x is A" then "y is B"

2. "x is $A^{'}$" is τ_{ϵ_1}-true,

then, we can conclude: "y is B" is $\tau_{\epsilon_1^{'}}$-true.

If we have the fact "x is $A^{''}$" is τ_{ϵ_2}-true such that $\{A^{''} \subset A^{'}$ and $\tau_{\epsilon_2} \geq \tau_{\epsilon_1}\}$, we can conclude: "y is B" is $\tau_{\epsilon_2^{'}}$-true with $\tau_{\epsilon_2^{'}} \geq \tau_{\epsilon_1^{'}}$.

In other words, the GMP rule in the proposition 1 satisfies the following gradual rule: *the more (the less) the proposition "x is $A^{'}$" is true and the more (the less) $A^{'}$ is included in A ($A^{'} \subset A$), the more (the less) the proposition "y is B" is true.*

The following proposition prove the graduality underlying by the GMP rules in the propositions 2 and 3.

Proposition 11. *Given the following assumptions:*

1. it is τ_β-true that if "x is A" then "y is B"

2. "x is $A^{'}$" is τ_{ϵ_1}-true,

then, there exists a precision modifier m_1 such that: "y is m_1B" is $\tau_{\epsilon_1^{'}}$-true.

If we have the fact "x is $A^{''}$" is τ_{ϵ_2}-true such that $\{A^{''} \subset A^{'}$ and $\tau_{\epsilon_2} \geq \tau_{\epsilon_1}\}$, then we can find a precision modifier m_2 such that: "y is m_2B" is $\tau_{\epsilon_2^{'}}$-true, with $\{m_2B \subset m_1B$ and $\tau_{\epsilon_2^{'}} \geq \tau_{\epsilon_1^{'}}\}$.

This proposition is valid if either $A \subset A^{''} \subset A^{'}$ or $A^{''} \subset A^{'} \subset A$. In the first case, we have the following form of gradual rule which is verified by the GMP rule in proposition 2: *the less the proposition "x is $A^{'}$" is true and the less $A^{'}$ is included in A (i.e. the more A is included in $A^{'}$), the less the proposition "y is mB" is true and the less mB is included in B.*

In the case of $A^{''} \subset A^{'} \subset A$, we have the following form of gradual rule which is verified by the GMP rule in proposition 3: *the more the proposition "x is $A^{'}$" is true and the more $A^{'}$ is included in A, the more the proposition "y is mB" is true and the more mB is included in B.*

7   Conclusion

In this paper, we have proposed a symbolic-based model dealing with nuanced information. This model is inspired from the representation method on fuzzy logic. In previous papers, we have proposed a new representation method of nuanced statements. In this paper, we proposed some deduction rules dealing with nuanced statements and we presented new *Generalized Modus Ponens* rules. In these rules we can use either simple statements or complex statements. Finally, we have studied the problem of graduality of inference and we have studied the forms of graduality satisfied by our GMP rules.

References

1. J. F. Baldwin. A new approach to approximate reasoning using fuzzy logic. *Fuzzy Sets and Systems*, 2:309 – 325, 1979.
2. B. Bouchon-Meunier and J. Yao. Linguistic modifiers and imprecise categories. *Int. J. of Intelligent Systems*, 7:25–36, 1992.
3. J. Delechamp and B. Bouchon-Meunier. Graduality by means of analogical reasoning. *Lecture notes in computer science*, 1244:210–222, 1997.
4. D. Dubois and H. Prade. Fuzzy sets in approximate reasoning, part 1: Inference with possibility distributions. *Fuzzy Sets and Systems*, 40:143–202, 1991.
5. M. El-Sayed and D. Pacholczyk. A qualitative reasoning with nuanced information. *8th European Conference on Logics in Artificial Intelligence (JELIA 02)*, 283–295, Italy, 2002.
6. M. El-Sayed and D. Pacholczyk. A symbolic approach for handling nuanced information. *IASTED International Conference on Artificial Intelligence and Applications (AIA 02), 285 - 290, Spain*, 2002.
7. M. De glas. Knoge representation in fuzzy setting. Technical Report 48, LAFORIA, 1989.
8. L. D. Lascio, A. Gisolfi, and U. C. Garcia. Linguistic hedges and the generalized modus ponens. *Int. Journal of Intelligent Systems*, 14:981–993, 1999.
9. D. Pacholczyk. *Contribution au traitement logico-symbolique de la connaissance*. PhD thesis, University of Paris VI, 1992.
10. L. A. Zadeh. A theory of approximate reasoning. *Int. J. Hayes, D. Michie and L. I. Mikulich (eds); Machine Intelligence*, 9:149–194, 1979.

Appendix A: Definitions of Precision Modifiers

We distinguish two types of precision modifiers: contraction modifiers and dilation modifiers. A contraction (resp. dilation) modifier m produces nuanced term mP_i more (resp. less) precise than the basic term P_i. In other words, the "rule" associated with mP_i is smaller (resp. bigger) than that associated with P_i. We define these modifiers in a way that the contraction modifiers contract simultaneously the core and the support of a multiset P_i, and the dilation modifiers dilate them. The amplitude of the modification (contraction or dilation) for a precision modifier m is given by a new parameter denoted as τ_γ. The higher τ_γ, the more important the modification is.

Definition 3. *m is said to be a τ_γ-contraction modifier if, and only if it is defined as follows:*

1. *if $P_i = (L_i, C_i, R_i)$ then $mP_i = (L_i', C_i', R_i')$ such that $L_i' \trianglelefteq_M L_i$ and $R_i' \trianglelefteq_M R_i$*
2. *$\forall x, x \in_\alpha P_i$ with $\tau_\alpha < \tau_M \Rightarrow x \in_\beta mP_i$ such that $\beta = max(1, \alpha - \gamma + 1)$.*

Definition 4. *m is said to be a τ_γ-dilation modifier if, and only if it is defined as follows:*

1. *if $P_i = (L_i, C_i, R_i)$ then $mP_i = (L_i', C_i', R_i')$ such that $L_i' \trianglelefteq_M L_i$ and $R_i' \trianglelefteq_M R_i$*
2. *$\forall x, x \in_\alpha P_i$ with $\tau_\alpha > \tau_1 \Rightarrow x \in_\beta mP_i$ such that $\beta = min(M, \gamma + \alpha - 1)$.*

Partial Lattice-Valued Possibilistic Measures and Some Relations Induced by Them

Ivan Kramosil

Institute of Computer Science
Academy of Sciences of the Czech Republic
Pod vodárenskou věží 2, 182 07 Prague 8, Czech Republic
kramosil@cs.cas.cz

Abstract. For a number of reasons rooted in our surrounding real world, the degrees of uncertainty and, in particular, the values of possibilistic measures related to various phenomena, need not be definable quantitatively, by real numbers from the unit interval, say, but rather only qualitatively and related to each other (greater than, not smaller than,...). Moreover, the values of possibilistic measures need not be known or even defined for every event from the field of events under consideration. Three extensions of partial lattice-valued possibilistic and necessity measures to the whole system of events under consideration are introduced and some assertions showing their various properties and mutual relations are presented and proved.

1   Introduction, Motivation, Preliminaries

Because of a very limited extend of this contribution we have to leave purposedly aside the history, motivation and intuition leading to and staying behind the notion of possibilistic measure and possibility theory, as well as the most elementary definitions and results concerning the classical possibilistic measures conceived as mappings which take the whole power-set of all subsets of a universe of discourse into the unit interval of real numbers and meet some well-known conditions. The reader is kindly asked to consult [3,4], or another appropriate source for these sakes, our more detailed reasonings will begin with the notion of partial (numerical) possibilistic measure with the aim to modify it, below, to the case of non-numerical possibilistic values, in particular to those taking their values in a complete lattice.

Definition 1.1. Let Ω be a nonempty set, let $\emptyset \neq \mathcal{R} \subset \mathcal{P}(\Omega)$ be a nonempty system of subsets of Ω. A mapping Π which takes $\mathcal{R}$ into $[0,1]$ ($\Pi : \mathcal{R} \to [0,1]$, in symbols) is called a *partial possibilistic measure* on $\mathcal{R}$, if

(i) $\Pi(\emptyset) = 0$ and /or $\Pi(\Omega) = 1$, if $\emptyset$ and/or Ω are in $\mathcal{R}$,
(ii) for each $\mathcal{R}_0 = \{A, B\} \subset \mathcal{R}$ such that $\cup \mathcal{R}_0 = \bigcup_{A \in \mathcal{R}_0} A$ is in $\mathcal{R}$, the equality $\Pi(\cup \mathcal{R}_0) = \vee \{\Pi(A) : A \in \mathcal{R}_0\}$ holds.

T.D. Nielsen and N.L. Zhang (Eds.): ECSQARU 2003, LNAI 2711, pp. 395–406, 2003.
© Springer-Verlag Berlin Heidelberg 2003

A partial possibilistic measure Π on $\mathcal{R}$ is called *finitely complete*, if (ii) holds for each finite nonempty $\mathcal{R}_0 \subset \mathcal{R}$ such that $\bigcup \mathcal{R}_0 \in \mathcal{R}$. A partial possibilistic measure Π on $\mathcal{R}$ is called *complete*, if (ii)holds for each nonempty $\mathcal{R}_0 \subset \mathcal{R}$ such that $\bigcup \mathcal{R}_0 \in \mathcal{R}$. □

The condition (ii) for $\mathcal{R} = \{A, B\}$ simply claims that $\Pi(A \cup B) = \Pi(A) \vee \Pi(B)$ for each A, $B \in \mathcal{R}$ such that $A \cup B \in \mathcal{R}$. In spite of the case of total possibilistic measures (when $\mathcal{R} = \mathcal{P}(\Omega)$), a partial possibilistic measure need not be finitely complete. Indeed, there may be A, B, $C \in \mathcal{R}$ such that $A \cup B \cup C \in \mathcal{R}$, but neither $A \cup B$, nor $A \cup C$, nor $B \cup C$ are in $\mathcal{R}$, so that $\Pi(A \cup B \cup C) = \Pi(A) \vee \Pi(B) \vee \Pi(C)$ need not hold for a partial possibilistic measure defined on $\mathcal{R}$. Each partial possibilistic measure on $\mathcal{R}$ is a special case of the so called *partial fuzzy measure*; it is a mapping $\Pi : \mathcal{R} \to [0, 1]$ such that (i) of Definition 1.1 holds and the inequality $\Pi(A) \leq \Pi(B)$ is valid for each A, $B \in \mathcal{R}$ such that $A \subset B$.

Partial lattice-valued possibilistic measures were investigated in detail by De Cooman [2] under the rather strong and simplifying assumption that the domain $\mathcal{R} \subset \mathcal{P}(\Omega)$ on which the possibilistic measure in question, say Π, is defined, is the so called ample field, i.e., that $\mathcal{R}$ is closed w.r.to all unions, intersections, and complements. Given $\omega \in \Omega$, the atom $[\omega]_{\mathcal{R}} = \cap\{A \in \mathcal{R} : \omega \in \mathcal{R}\}$ is defined, so yielding an equivalence relation $\approx_{\mathcal{R}}$ on Ω, according to which $\omega_1 \approx_{\mathcal{R}} \omega_2$ iff $[\omega_1]_{\mathcal{R}} = [\omega_2]_{\mathcal{R}}$ holds. As a matter of fact, a partial possibilistic measure on $\mathcal{R}$ can be replaced by a total possibilistic measure on the power-set of all subsets of the factor-space $\Omega / \approx_{\mathcal{R}}$, so that the greatest part of the notions, methods and results used in the case of total possibilistic measures (possibilitic distributions, e.g.) can be applied.

Nevertheless, in what follows, we intentionally aim to keep our reasoning at the level as general as possible, not introducing some specific assumptions as far as the structure of the system $\mathcal{R}$ is concerned. This approach is motivated by the idea to develop a tool enabling to process, to the degree as possible, collections of pieces of information concerning qualitative possibility preferences given to particular pairs of phenomena (events). A more detailed description and discussion on this motivation can be found in [8], but the limited extend of this contribution does not allow to introduce it here.

Applying the idea used in the standard measure theory, we arrive at the notion of inner and outer measure.

Definition 1.2. Let Ω and $\mathcal{R}$ be as in Definition 1.1, let Π be a mapping which takes $\mathcal{R}$ into $[0, 1]$. The *inner (lower) measure* Π_* and the *outer (upper) measure* Π^* induced on $\mathcal{P}(\Omega)$ by Π are defined, for each $A \subset \Omega$, by

$$\Pi_*(A) = \vee\{\Pi(B) : B \subset A, B \in \mathcal{R}\}, \tag{1.1}$$
$$\Pi^*(A) = \wedge\{\Pi(B) : B \supset A, B \in \mathcal{R}\}, \tag{1.2}$$

here $\vee$ and $\wedge$ denote the standard supremum and infimum in $[0, 1]$; for the empty subset of $[0, 1]$ the conventions $\vee \emptyset = 0$ and $\wedge \emptyset = 1$ apply (or we enrich $\mathcal{R}$ by $\emptyset$ and/or Ω). □

As can be easily seen, if Π is a partial fuzzy measure on $\mathcal{R}$, Π_* and Π^* are fuzzy measures on $\mathcal{P}(\Omega)$, both extending conservatively Π from $\mathcal{R}$ to $\mathcal{P}(\Omega)$, so that $\Pi_*(A) = \Pi(A) = \Pi^*(A)$ holds for each $A \in \mathcal{R}$ (only the inequality $\Pi_*(A) \leq \Pi^*(A)$ is valid in general for $A \subset \Omega$). On the other side, if Π is a partial possibilistic measure on $\mathcal{R}$, neither Π_* nor Π^* need be possibilistic measures on $\mathcal{P}(\Omega)$ unless some rather strong supplementary conditions are satisfied (cf. [7] for some results concerning inner and outer possibilistic measures).

An alternative way to extend Π from its domain $\mathcal{R} \subset \mathcal{P}(\Omega)$ to the whole power-set $\mathcal{P}(\Omega)$ reads as follows. Set, for every $\omega \in \Omega$,

$$\pi_0(\omega) = \wedge \{\Pi(R) : \omega \in R \in \mathcal{R}\}. \tag{1.3}$$

Hence, if the singleton $\{\omega\}$ is in $\mathcal{R}$, then obviously $\pi_0(\omega) = \Pi(\{\omega\})$. Supposing that π_0 is a possibilistic distribution on Ω, i.e., that $\vee_{\omega \in \Omega} \pi_0(\omega) = 1$, set for each $A \subset \Omega$

$$\Pi_0(A) = \vee_{\omega \in A} \pi_0(\omega), \tag{1.4}$$

so obtaining a complete and total possibilistic measure Π_0 on $\mathcal{P}(\Omega)$. The condition $\vee_{\omega \in \Omega} \pi_0(\omega) = 1$ need not hold in general, indeed, take an infinite set Ω, take $\mathcal{R}$ containing just the empty set, all singletons $\{\omega\}$, $\omega \in \Omega$, and all infinite subsets of Ω, and set $0 = \Pi(\{\omega\}) = \Pi(\emptyset)$ for each $\omega \in \Omega$, $\Pi(A) = 1$ for each infinite subset of Ω. Consequently, $\pi_0(\omega) = \Pi(\{\omega\}) = 0$ for each $\omega \in \Omega$, so that π_0 does not define a possibilistic distribution on Ω.

Finally, given a partial possibilistic measure Π defined on $\emptyset \neq \mathcal{R} \subset \mathcal{P}(\Omega)$, the induced *partial necessity measure* N_Π can be defined on the system $\mathcal{R}^- = \{A \subset \Omega : \Omega - A \in \mathcal{R}\}$ of all complements of sets from $\mathcal{R}$, setting $N_\Pi(A) = 1 - \Pi(\Omega - A)$ for each $A \in \mathcal{R}^-$.

The aim of this contribution will be to introduce non-numerical (in particular, lattice-valued) partial fuzzy and possibilistic measures and to modify the definitions of the induced mappings Π_*, Π^*, Π_0 and N_Π to this case.

2   Partial Lattice-Valued Possibilistic Measures

For partially ordered sets, lattices, Boolean algebras, and related structures the reader is kindly asked to consult [1,5,9], or some more recent source. The outgoing notion of our further reasoning will be that of partially ordered set.

Definition 2.1. Let T be a nonempty set. A binary relation $\leq$ on T (i.e., a subset of Cartesian product $T \times T$) is called a *partial ordering*, if it is reflexive, antisymmetric and transitive, i.e., if for each $x \in T$, $x \leq x$ holds, if for each $x, y \in T$ such that $x \leq y$ and $y \leq x$ hold simultaneously, the identity $x = y$ follows, and if, for each $x, y, z \in T$, if $x \leq y$ and $y \leq z$ hold simultaneously, then $x \leq z$ also holds. If $\leq$ is a partial ordering on T, then the pair $\mathcal{T} = \langle T, \leq \rangle$ is called a *partially ordered set* (p.o.set). $\qquad \square$

Given a p.o.set $\mathcal{T} = \langle T, \leq \rangle$ and a nonempty subset $S \subset T$, its *supremum* $\vee_{t \in S} t$ ($\vee S$, abbreviately) and *infimum* $\wedge_{t \in S} t$ ($\wedge S$, abbreviately) are defined in the standard way, of course, $\vee S$ and/or $\wedge S$ may be undefined for some $S \subset T$. A p.o.set $\mathcal{T} = \langle T, \le \rangle$ is called a *complete lattice*, if for each $\emptyset \ne S \subset T$ the supremum $\vee S$ and the infimum $\wedge S$ are defined. Hence, also the *minimum (element)* $\mathbf{0}_{\mathcal{T}} = \wedge T$ and the *maximum (element)* $\mathbf{1}_{\mathcal{T}} = \vee T$ are defined and we can set, for the empty subset of T, $\vee \emptyset = \mathbf{0}_{\mathcal{T}}$ and $\wedge \emptyset = \mathbf{1}_{\mathcal{T}}$.

Let us recall that the notion of complete lattice is still general enough to cover qualitatively different structures like, e. g., the unit interval of real numbers with their standard linear ordering, and a complete Boolean algebra, in particular, the power-set of all subsets of a given space, partially ordered by the relation of set-theoretic inclusion. The main difference between complete lattices in general and both the examples just mentioned consists in the fact that complete lattice lacks an operation of negation or complement, represented by the operation $1 - x$ in the first example, and by the set-theoretic complement $X - A$, X being the space in question, in the second example. A partial remedy may read as follows.

Definition 2.2. Let $\mathcal{T} = \langle T, \le \rangle$ be a complete lattice. For each $t \in T$, its *(pseudo-) complement* t^c is defined by

$$t^c = \vee \{ s \in T : s \wedge t = \mathbf{0}_{\mathcal{T}} \}. \tag{2.1}$$

$\square$

A dual approach according to which $t^c = \wedge \{ s \in T : s \vee t = \mathbf{1}_{\mathcal{T}} \}$ would be also possible, but we limit ourselves, in what follows, to (2.1). If $\mathcal{B} = \langle B, \vee, \wedge, \neg \rangle$ is a Boolean algebra and $\le$ is the standard partial ordering induced in $\mathcal{B}$, i. e., $x \le y$ iff $x \wedge y = x$ (iff $x \vee y = y$), then the pseudo-complement in $\langle B, \le \rangle$ agrees with the complement in $\mathcal{B}$, hence, $x^c = \neg x$ whenever x^c is defined. In particular, for $\mathcal{T} = \langle \mathcal{P}(X), \subset \rangle$, $A^c = X - A$ for each $A \subset X$.

Definition 2.3. Let $\mathcal{T} = \langle T, \le \rangle$ be a complete lattice, let Ω be a nonempty set, let $\mathcal{R}$ be a nonempty system of subsets of Ω. A mapping $\Pi : \mathcal{R} \to T$ is called a *partial $\mathcal{T}$-(valued) fuzzy measure* on $\mathcal{R}$, if $\Pi(\emptyset) = \mathbf{0}_{\mathcal{T}}$ and/or $\Pi(\Omega) = \mathbf{1}_{\mathcal{T}}$ supposing that $\emptyset \in \mathcal{R}$ and/or $\Omega \in \mathcal{R}$, and if the relation $\Pi(A) \le \Pi(B)$ holds for each $A, B \in \mathcal{R}$ such that $A \subset B$. A partial $\mathcal{T}$-fuzzy measure Π on $\mathcal{R}$ is called a *partial $\mathcal{T}$-possibilistic measure* on $\mathcal{R}$, if the relation $\Pi(A \cup B) = \Pi(A) \vee \Pi(B)$ holds for each $A, B \in \mathcal{R}$ such that $A \cup B \in \mathcal{R}$. A partial $\mathcal{T}$-possibilistic measure Π on $\mathcal{R}$ is called *finitely complete*, if $\Pi(\cup \mathcal{R}_0) = \vee_{R \in \mathcal{R}_0} \Pi(R)$ holds for each finite subsystem $\mathcal{R}_0 \subset \mathcal{R}$ such that $\cup \mathcal{R}_0 \in \mathcal{R}$, and it is called *complete*, if the same relation holds for each $\emptyset \ne \mathcal{R}_0 \subset \mathcal{R}$ such that $\cup \mathcal{R}_0 \in \mathcal{R}$, here $\cup \mathcal{R}_0$ stands for $\cup_{R \in \mathcal{R}_0} R$. $\square$

Also the definition of inner and outer measures copies the way applied in the case of numerical mappings.

Definition 2.4. Let $\mathcal{T}$, Ω, and $\mathcal{R}$ be as in Definition 2.3, let Π be any mapping which takes $\mathcal{R}$ into T. The *inner (or lower) measure* Π_* and the *outer (or upper)* *measure* Π^* induced by Π on $\mathcal{P}(\Omega)$ are defined, for any $A \subset \Omega$, by

$$\Pi_*(A) = \vee\{\Pi(B) : B \subset A, B \in \mathcal{R}\}, \qquad (2.2)$$

$$\Pi^*(A) = \wedge\{\Pi(B) : B \supset A, B \in \mathcal{R}\}, \qquad (2.3)$$

applying the conventions $\vee\emptyset = \mathbf{0}_{\mathcal{T}}$ and $\wedge\emptyset = \mathbf{1}_{\mathcal{T}}$, if necessary, or joining $\emptyset$ and Ω with $\mathcal{R}$ and ascribing them the requested values $\Pi(\emptyset) = \mathbf{0}_{\mathcal{T}}$ and $\Pi(\Omega) = \mathbf{1}_{\mathcal{T}}$.

$\square$

As in the case of numerical partial possibilistic measures, Definition 2.4 implies almost obviously, that if Π is a partial $\mathcal{T}$-fuzzy measure on $\mathcal{R}$, both Π_* and Π^* are $\mathcal{T}$-fuzzy measures on $\mathcal{P}(\Omega)$ extending conservatively Π, so that $\Pi_*(A) \leq \Pi^*(A)$ and $\Pi_*(B) = \Pi(B) = \Pi^*(B)$ holds for each $A \subset \Omega$ and each $B \in \mathcal{R}$.

Dual mappings to those introduced in Definition 2.3 can be defined in two ways which are equivalent provided that some rather general conditions are fulfilled.

Definition 2.5. Let $\mathcal{T}$, Ω, and $\mathcal{R}$ be as in Definition 2.3. A mapping $\Pi : \mathcal{R} \to T$ is called a *dual partial $\mathcal{T}$-(valued) possibilistic measure on* $\mathcal{R}$, if $\Pi(\emptyset) = \mathbf{0}_{\mathcal{T}}$ and/or $\Pi(\Omega) = \mathbf{1}_{\mathcal{T}}$ supposing that $\emptyset \in \mathcal{R}$ and/or $\Omega \in \mathcal{R}$ and if $\Pi(A \cap B) = \Pi(A) \wedge \Pi(B)$ for every A, $B \in \mathcal{R}$ such that $A \cap B$. A dual partial $\mathcal{T}$-possibilistic measure Π on $\mathcal{R}$ is called *(finitely) complete*, if $\Pi(\cap \mathcal{R}_0) = \wedge_{R \in \mathcal{R}_0} \Pi(R)$ holds for each (finite) $\emptyset \neq \mathcal{R}_0 \subset \mathcal{R}$ such that $\cap \mathcal{R}_0 = \cap_{R \in \mathcal{R}_0} R$ is in $\mathcal{R}$.

$\square$

Definition 2.6. Let $\mathcal{T}$, Ω, and $\mathcal{R}$ be as in Definition 2.3, let $\Pi : \mathcal{R} \to T$ be a partial $\mathcal{T}$-possibilistic measure on $\mathcal{R}$, let $\mathcal{R}^- = \{A \subset \Omega : \Omega - A \in \mathcal{R}\}$ be the system of all complements of subsets from $\mathcal{R}$. The mapping $N_{\Pi} : \mathcal{R}^- \to T$ defined by

$$N_{\Pi}(A) = (\Pi(\Omega - A))^c = \vee\{s \in T : s \wedge \Pi(\Omega - A) = \mathbf{0}_{\mathcal{T}}\} \qquad (2.4)$$

for every $A \in \mathcal{R}^-$ is called the *partial $\mathcal{T}$-(valued) necessity measure* induced by Π on $\mathcal{R}^-$.

$\square$

Each dual partial $\mathcal{T}$-possibilistic measure on $\mathcal{R}$ is obviously also a partial $\mathcal{T}$-fuzzy measure on $\mathcal{R}$. Also the fact that if Π is a partial $\mathcal{T}$-possibilistic measure on $\mathcal{R}$, the mapping N_{Π} is a dual partial $\mathcal{T}$-possibilistic measure on $\mathcal{R}^-$, is almost evident (cf. Lemma 5.1 in [8]). The converse implication to the last one does not hold in general, as the following assertion states (cf. Theorem 5.1 in [8] for the proof).

Theorem 2.1. Let $\mathcal{T}$, Ω, and $\mathcal{R}$ be as in Definition 2.3, let $(t^c)^c = t$ holds for each $t \in T$. Then there exists, for each dual partial $\mathcal{T}$-possibilistic measure $\Sigma : \mathcal{R} \to T$, a partial $\mathcal{T}$-possibilistic measure Π_{Σ} on $\mathcal{R}^-$ such that Σ is identical with N_{Π} on $\mathcal{R}$ (as a matter of fact, the only we have to do is to set $\Pi_{\Sigma}(A) = (\Sigma(\Omega - A))^c$ for each $A \in \mathcal{R}^-$).

$\square$

Let us recall that the relation $(t^c)^c = t$ does not hold in general. If $\mathcal{T} = \langle \mathcal{P}(X), \subset \rangle$ for some $X \neq \emptyset$, then this is the case, as $(A^c)^c = \Omega - (\Omega - A) = A$ trivially holds for each $A \subset \Omega$. However, if $\mathcal{T} = \langle [0, 1], \leq \rangle$, then for each $t \in (0, 1)$ we obtain that $t^c = \vee\{s \in [0, 1] : s \wedge t = 0\} = 0$, so that $(t^c)^c = 0^c = \vee\{s \in [0, 1] : s \wedge 0 = 0\} = 1 > t$ holds.

We have chosen complete lattices as the structures in which possibilistic measures take their values, as complete lattices are perhaps the most specific structures still general enough to cover the two most often used particular cases: set-valued (or, slightly generalizing, boolean-valued) possibilistic measures with values partially ordered by set inclusion, and real-valued possibilistic measures taking their values in the unit interval equipped by its standard linear ordering. For these reasons we prefer also to define the notion of (pseudo)-complement in a way general enough to need just the structure of complete lattice, even if the resulting operation is not compatible neither with the set-theoretic complement $X - \cdot$, if $\mathcal{T} = \langle \mathcal{P}(X), \subset \rangle$, nor with the standard abstraction $1 - \cdot$ in $\langle [0, 1], \leq \rangle$. An alternative approach would be to enrich the complete lattice $\mathcal{T} = \langle T, \leq \rangle$ by a new (and ontologically independent) operation of negation or complement meeting some reasonable conditions axiomatically imposed on it. However, let us postpone a more detailed development of this idea till another occasion.

3   Inner, Outer, and Necessity Measures Induced by a Partial $\mathcal{T}$-Possibilistic Measure

As a matter of fact, if Π is a $\mathcal{T}$-possibilistic measure on $\mathcal{R} \subset \mathcal{P}(\Omega)$, then neither Π_* nor Π^* need be a $\mathcal{T}$-possibilistic measure on $\mathcal{P}(\Omega)$. Indeed, take $\mathcal{R}_1 = \{\emptyset, \Omega\}$ and set $\Pi_1(\emptyset) = \mathbf{0}_\mathcal{T}$, $\Pi_1(\Omega) = \mathbf{1}_\mathcal{T}$, so that Π_1 is the most trivial partial $\mathcal{T}$-possibilistic measure. Given a nonempty proper subset A of Ω, we obtain that $\Pi_{1*}(A) = \Pi_{1*}(\Omega - A) = \mathbf{0}_\mathcal{T}$, so that $\Pi_{1*}(A \cup (\Omega - A)) = \Pi_{1*}(\Omega) = \mathbf{1}_\mathcal{T} > \mathbf{0}_\mathcal{T} = \Pi_{1*}(A) \vee \Pi_{1*}(\Omega - A)$ follows. Now, take $\mathcal{R}_2 = \{\emptyset, A, B, \Omega\}$, where A and B are mutually disjoint nonempty subsets of Ω such that $A \cup B \neq \Omega$, hence, $A \cup B \notin \mathcal{R}$, and set $\Pi_2(\emptyset) = \Pi_2(A) = \Pi_2(B) = \mathbf{0}_\mathcal{T}$, $\Pi_2(\Omega) = \mathbf{1}_\mathcal{T}$. So, Π_2 is a partial $\mathcal{T}$-possibilistic measure on $\mathcal{R}_2$ and we obtain that $\Pi_2^*(\Omega) = \Pi_2^*(A \cup B) = \mathbf{1}_\mathcal{T} > \Pi_2^*(A) \vee \Pi_2^*(B) = \mathbf{0}_\mathcal{T} \vee \mathbf{0}_\mathcal{T} = \mathbf{0}_\mathcal{T}$. Consequently, neither Π_{1*} nor Π_2^* are $\mathcal{T}$-possibilistic measures on $\mathcal{P}(\Omega)$.

The next statement introduces some sufficient conditions under which the inner measure Π_* induced by a partial $\mathcal{T}$-possibilistic measure Π on $\mathcal{R}$ is also a $\mathcal{T}$-possibilistic measure.

Theorem 3.1. Let $\mathcal{T}$, Ω, and $\mathcal{R}$ be as in Definition 3.2, let Π be a partial $\mathcal{T}$-possibilistic measure on $\mathcal{R}$. Set

$$\mathcal{R}_0 = \{A \subset \Omega : A \cap C \in \mathcal{R} \text{ for each } C \in \mathcal{R}\}. \tag{3.1}$$

Then Π_* is a partial $\mathcal{T}$-possibilistic measure on $\mathcal{R}_0$.   □

Proof. Cf. Theorem 6.1 in [8].

The three following remarks are worth being stated explicitly.

(i) If $\mathcal{R}$ is closed with respect to intersections, i.e., if $A \cap B \in \mathcal{R}$ holds for each $A, B \in \mathcal{R}$, then the inclusion $\mathcal{R} \subset \mathcal{R}_0$ easily follows, so that Π_* extends Π conservatively from $\mathcal{R}$ to $\mathcal{R}_0$.

(ii) If $\mathcal{R}$ is closed w.r.to subsets, i.e., if $C \in \mathcal{R}$ and $D \subset C$ implies that $D \in \mathcal{R}$, and if $\Omega \in \mathcal{R}$, then $\mathcal{R}_0 = \mathcal{P}(\Omega)$(such systems are called *hereditary* in [6]).

(iii) If Π is (finitely) complete partial $\mathcal{T}$-possibilistic measure on $\mathcal{R}$ and if the other conditions of Theorem 3.1 are satisfied, then Π_* is a (finitely) complete partial $\mathcal{T}$-possibilistic measure on $\mathcal{R}_0$.

A partially ordered set $\mathcal{T} = \langle T, \leq \rangle$ is called *continuous from above* ($\downarrow$-*continuous*, abbreviately), if for each $x \in T$ the infimum of all elements greater than x is defined and identical with x, in symbols, if $x = \wedge\{t \in T : t > x\}$ holds for each $x \in T$.

Theorem 3.2. Let Ω be a nonempty set, let $\mathcal{R}$ be a nonempty system of subsets of Ω closed w.r.to unions, i.e., $A \cup B \in \mathcal{R}$ for each $A, B \in \mathcal{R}$, let $\mathcal{T}$ be a $\downarrow$-continuous complete lower semilattice and (not necessarily complete) upper semilattice, let Π be a partial $\mathcal{T}$-possibilistic measure on $\mathcal{R}$. Then Π^* is a $\mathcal{T}$-possibilistic measure on $\mathcal{R}(\Omega)$. $\square$

Proof. Cf. Theorem 6.2 in [8].

Given a partial $\mathcal{T}$-fuzzy measure Π on a system $\mathcal{R}$ of subsets of a nonempty set Ω, and supposing, in order to simplify further considerations and reasonings, that $\{\emptyset, \Omega\} \subset \mathcal{R}$, we may either extend it to $\mathcal{P}(\Omega)$, defining Π_* and Π^* as above, or we may define the necessity measure N_Π on $\mathcal{R}^- = \{A \subset \Omega : \Omega - A \in \mathcal{R}\}$, setting $N_\Pi(A) = (\Pi(\Omega - A))^c$ for every $A \in \mathcal{R}^-$. These operations can be applied also sequentially, step by step, and in different order. So, we arrive at $N_{(\Pi_*)}$, if Π_* is defined first, or to $(N_\Pi)_*$, if N_Π on $\mathcal{R}^-$ is defined and then extended to $\mathcal{P}(\Omega)$. Also the dual cases $N_{(\Pi^*)}$ and $(N_\Pi)^*$ will be investigated.

Theorem 3.3. Under the notations and conditions introduced, the inequality

$$(N_\Pi)_*(A) \leq N_{(\Pi_*)}(A) \tag{3.2}$$

holds for each $A \subset \Omega$. $\square$

Proof. For each $A \subset \Omega$ we obtain that

$$(N_\Pi)_*(A) = \vee\{N_\Pi(B) : B \subset A, B \in \mathcal{R}^-\} = \tag{3.3}$$
$$= \vee\{(\Pi(\Omega - B))^c : \Omega - B \supset \Omega - A, \Omega - B \in \mathcal{R}\} =$$
$$= \vee\{\vee\{s \in T : s \wedge \Pi(\Omega - B) = 0_T\} : \Omega - B \supset \Omega - A, \Omega - B \in \mathcal{R}\}.$$

For each $B \subset \Omega$, if $\Omega - B \in \mathcal{R}$ and $\Omega - B \supset \Omega - A$ holds, then the inequality

$$\Pi(\Omega - B) \geq \Pi^*(\Omega - A) \geq \Pi_*(\Omega - A) \qquad (3.4)$$

follows. Consequently, for each $B \subset \Omega$, $\Omega - B \in \mathcal{R}$, and each $s \in T$, if $s \wedge \Pi(\Omega - B) = \mathbf{0}_T$, then also $s \wedge \Pi_*(\Omega - A) = \mathbf{0}_T$ holds. Hence, the inclusion

$$\cup \{\{s \in T : s \wedge \Pi(\Omega - B) = \mathbf{0}_T\} : B \subset \Omega,\ \Omega - B \in \mathcal{R},\ \Omega - B \supset \Omega - A\} \quad (3.5)$$
$$\subset \{s \in T : s \wedge \Pi_*(\Omega - A) = \mathbf{0}_T\}$$

is valid. Taking the suprema of both the sets in (3.5) and applying (3.3), we obtain that

$$(N_\Pi)_*(A) \leq \vee \{s \in T : s \wedge \Pi_*(\Omega - A) = \mathbf{0}_T\} = (\Pi_*(\Omega - A))^c = \quad (3.6)$$
$$= N_{(\Pi_*)}(A).$$

The assertion is proved. $\qquad\qquad\qquad\qquad\qquad\qquad\qquad\qquad\qquad\qquad\square$

The most trivial example illustrates that equality in (3.2) need not hold in general. Take $\mathcal{R} = \{\emptyset, \Omega\}$, $\Pi(\emptyset) = \mathbf{0}_T$, $\Pi(\Omega) = \mathbf{0}_T$. Then

$$N_\Pi(\emptyset) = (\Pi(\Omega - \emptyset))^c = (\Pi(\Omega))^c = \mathbf{1}_T^c = \mathbf{0}_T, \qquad (3.7)$$
$$N_\Pi(\Omega) = (\Pi(\Omega - \Omega))^c = (\Pi(\emptyset))^c = \mathbf{0}_T^c = \mathbf{1}_T. \qquad (3.8)$$

Hence, for each $\emptyset \neq A \neq \Omega$, $A \subset \Omega$, we obtain that

$$(N_\Pi)_*(A) = \vee \{N_\Pi(B) : B \subset A, B \in \mathcal{R}^-\} = N_\Pi(\emptyset) = \mathbf{0}_T, \qquad (3.9)$$

as $\emptyset$ is the only subset of A which is in $\mathcal{R}^-$. However,

$$N_{(\Pi_*)}(A) = (\Pi_*(\Omega - A))^c = (\vee \{\Pi(B) : B \subset \Omega - A, B \in \mathcal{R}\})^c = \quad (3.10)$$
$$= (\Pi(\emptyset))^c = \mathbf{0}_T^c = \mathbf{1}_T,$$

as $\emptyset$ is the only subset of $\Omega - A$ which is in $\mathcal{R}$, so that the inequality $(N_\Pi)_*(A) < N_{(\Pi_*)}(A)$ follows.

The assertion dual to Theorem 3.3 reads as follows.

Theorem 3.4. Under the notations and conditions introduced, the inequality

$$(N_\Pi)^*(A) \geq N_{(\Pi_*)}(A) \qquad (3.11)$$

holds for each $A \subset \Omega$. $\qquad\qquad\qquad\qquad\qquad\qquad\qquad\qquad\qquad\qquad\square$

Proof. Analyzing the definitions of $(N_\Pi)^*(A)$ and $N_{(\Pi_*)}(A)$, we obtain that

$$(N_\Pi)^*(A) = \wedge \{N_\Pi(B) : B \supset A, B \in \mathcal{R}^-\} = \qquad (3.12)$$
$$= \wedge \{(\Pi(\Omega - B))^c : B \supset A, B \in \mathcal{R}^-\} =$$
$$= \wedge \{[\vee \{s \in T : s \wedge \Pi(\Omega - B) = \mathbf{0}_T\}] : B \supset A, B \in \mathcal{R}^-\},$$

and

$$N_{(\Pi^*)}(A) = (\Pi^*(\Omega - A))^c = \vee \{s \in T : s \wedge \Pi^*(\Omega - A) = \mathbf{0}_T\}. \qquad (3.13)$$

Take $A \subset \Omega$, take $B \in \mathcal{R}^-$ such that $B \supset A$ holds, then $\Omega - B \in \mathcal{R}$, $\Omega - B \subset \Omega - A$ and, consequently, also

$$\Pi(\Omega - B) \leq \Pi_*(\Omega - A) = \vee \{\Pi(C) : C \subset \Omega - A, C \in \mathcal{R}\} \leq \Pi^*(\Omega - A) \quad (3.14)$$

follows. Hence, for each $s \in T$ such that $s \wedge \Pi^*(\Omega - A) = \mathbf{0}_T$, also $s \wedge \Pi(\Omega - B) = \mathbf{0}_T$ holds, so that the set inclusion

$$\{s \in T : s \wedge \Pi^*(\Omega - A) = \mathbf{0}_T\} \subset \{s \in T : s \wedge \Pi(\Omega - B) = \mathbf{0}_T\} \qquad (3.15)$$

is valid for each $B \in \mathcal{R}^-$, $B \supset A$. Consequently, for each such B we obtain that

$$\vee \{s \in T : s \wedge \Pi^*(\Omega - A) = \mathbf{0}_T\} \leq \vee \{s \in T : s \wedge \Pi(\Omega - B) = \mathbf{0}_T\}, \qquad (3.16)$$

so that the inequality

$$\vee \{s \in T : s \wedge \Pi^*(\Omega - A) = \mathbf{0}_T\} \leq \qquad (3.17)$$
$$\leq \wedge \{[\vee \{s \in T : s \wedge \Pi(\Omega - B) = \mathbf{0}_T\}] : B \in \mathcal{R}^-, B \supset A\}$$

follows. Due to (3.12) and (3.13) this inequality immediately implies (3.11), so that the assertion is proved. $\qquad\square$

The same most trivial example as above with $\mathcal{R} = \{\emptyset, \Omega\}$, $\Pi(\emptyset) = \mathbf{0}_T$, and $\Pi(\Omega) = \mathbf{1}_T$ demonstrates that also in (3.11) the equality need not hold in general. Again, taking $A \subset \Omega$, $\emptyset \neq A \neq \Omega$, we obtain that

$$(N_{\Pi})^*(A) = \wedge \{N_{\Pi}(B) : B \supset A, B \in \mathcal{R}^-\} = N_{\Pi}(\Omega) = \mathbf{1}_T, \qquad (3.18)$$

but

$$N_{(\Pi^*)}(A) = (\Pi^*(\Omega - A))^c = (\wedge \{\Pi(C) : C \supset \Omega - A, C \in \mathcal{R}\})^c = \quad (3.19)$$
$$= (\Pi(\Omega))^c = \mathbf{1}_T^c = \mathbf{0}_T,$$

so that the strict inequality $(N_{\Pi})^*(A) > N_{(\Pi^*)}(A)$ follows.

4   Possibilistic Completion of Partial $\mathcal{T}$-Possibilistic Measures

The next statement introduces the lattice-valued modifications of the mappings π_0 and Π_0, defined by (1.3) and (1.4) for the numerical case and proves, under which conditions the modified mappings define $\mathcal{T}$-possibilistic distribution of Ω and $\mathcal{T}$-possibilistic measure on $\mathcal{P}(\Omega)$.

Theorem 4.1. Let $\mathcal{T}$ be a complete lattice, let Ω be a nonempty set, let $\mathcal{R}$ be a system of subsets of Ω containing $\emptyset$ and Ω, let Π be a complete partial $\mathcal{T}$-possibilistic measure on $\mathcal{R}$. Set, for each $\omega \in \Omega$,

$$\pi_0(\omega) = \wedge\{\Pi(R) : \omega \in R \in \mathcal{R}\}. \tag{4.1}$$

Then $\pi_0(\omega) : \Omega \to T$ is a $\mathcal{T}$-possibilistic distribution on Ω, i.e., $\vee_{\omega \in \Omega}\pi_0(\omega) = 1_\mathcal{T}$. $\qquad\square$

Proof. Setting $\mathcal{R}_\omega = \{R \in \mathcal{R} : \omega \in R\}$ for each $\omega \in \Omega$, we have to prove that

$$\vee_{\omega \in \Omega}\left(\wedge\{\Pi(R) : R \in \mathcal{R}_\omega\}\right) = 1_\mathcal{T}. \tag{4.2}$$

First, suppose that $\vee\{t \in T : t < 1_\mathcal{T}\} = t_0 < 1$, and suppose that (4.2) does not hold. Hence, $\wedge\{\Pi(R) : R \in \mathcal{R}_\omega\} \le t_0$ for each $\omega \in \Omega$ follows. If $\Pi(R) > t_0$ holds for each $R \in \mathcal{R}_\omega$, then $\Pi(R) = 1_\mathcal{T}$ for each such R holds and $\wedge\{\Pi(R) : R \in \mathcal{R}_\omega\} = 1_\mathcal{T} > t_0$ follows. So, for each $\omega \in \Omega$ there exists $R_\omega \in \mathcal{R}_\omega$ such that $\Pi(R_\omega) \le t_0$ holds. However, $\omega \in R_\omega$, so that $\cup_{\omega \in \Omega} R_\omega = \Omega$ and $\Pi\left(\cup_{\omega \in \Omega} R_\omega\right) = \vee_{\omega \in \Omega}\Pi(R_\omega) = 1_\mathcal{T}$ follows due to the supposed completeness of Π on $\mathcal{R}$. On the other side, $\Pi(R_\omega) \le t_0$ for each $\omega \in \Omega$ yields that $\vee_{\omega \in \Omega}\Pi(R_\omega) \le t_0 < 1$ should be valid – a contradiction.

Hence, suppose that $\vee\{t \in T : t < 1_\mathcal{T}\} = 1_\mathcal{T}$ and suppose that, formally written,

$$(\exists t \in T, t < 1_\mathcal{T})\,(\forall \omega \in \Omega)\,(\exists R_\omega \in \mathcal{R}_\omega)\,(\Pi(R_\omega) \le t). \tag{4.3}$$

Using the same way of reasoning as above, we arrive, again, at the contradiction that $\cup_{\omega \in \Omega} R_\omega = \Omega$, but $\vee_{\omega \in \Omega}\Pi(R_\omega) \le t < 1_\mathcal{T}$ should hold. What remains reads that $\vee\{t \in T : t < 1_\mathcal{T}\} = 1_\mathcal{T}$ and the negation of (4.3), i.e.,

$$(\forall t \in T, t < 1)\,(\exists \omega \in \Omega)\,(\forall R_\omega \in \mathcal{R}_\omega)\,(\Pi(R_\omega) > t) \tag{4.4}$$

hold together. However, (4.4) implies that

$$(\forall t \in T, t < 1)\,(\exists \omega \in \Omega)\,(\pi_0(\omega) \ge t), \tag{4.5}$$

so that

$$\vee_{\omega \in \Omega}\pi_0(\omega) = \vee\{t \in T : t < 1_\mathcal{T}\} = 1_\mathcal{T} \tag{4.6}$$

follows. The assertion is proved. $\qquad\square$

Hence, supposing that π_0 is a $\mathcal{T}$-possibilistic distribution on Ω and setting $\Pi_0(A) = \vee\{\pi_0(\omega) : \omega \in A\}$ for every $A \subset \Omega$, we obtain that Π_0 is a complete $\mathcal{T}$-possibilistic measure on $\mathcal{P}(\Omega)$. The inequality $\Pi_0(A) \le \Pi(A)$ for every $A \in \mathcal{R}$ easily follows, as $A \in \mathcal{R}_\omega$ holds for each $\omega \in A$, so that $\pi_0(\omega) \le \Pi(A)$ is valid for every $\omega \in A$, hence, also for $\Pi_0(A)$. This inequality cannot be, in general, replaced by equality, as the following simple example demonstrates.

Let $\Omega = \{1, 2, 3, 4, 5\}$, let $A_1 = \{1, 2\}$, $A_2 = \{3, 4\}$, $A_3 = \{2, 3\}$, let $\mathcal{R} = \{\emptyset, A_1, A_2, A_3, \Omega\}$, let $\Pi : \mathcal{R} \to T$ be such that $\Pi(\emptyset) = \Pi(A_1) = \Pi(A_2) = 0_\mathcal{T}$,

$\Pi(A_3) = \Pi(\Omega) = 1_\mathcal{T}$. Π is a partial $\mathcal{T}$-possibilistic measure on $\mathcal{R}$ and π_0 is a $\mathcal{T}$-possibilistic distribution on Ω. Indeed, for each $i = 1, 2, 3, 4$,

$$\pi_0(i) = \wedge\{\Pi(R) : i \in R \in \mathcal{R}\} = \mathbf{0}_\mathcal{T}, \qquad (4.7)$$

but $\pi_0(5) = \Pi(\Omega) = 1_\mathcal{T}$. Consequently,

$$\Pi_0(A_3) = \Pi_0(\{2, 3\}) = \pi_0(2) \vee \pi_0(3) = \mathbf{0}_\mathcal{T} < 1_\mathcal{T} = \Pi(A_3). \qquad (4.8)$$

For singletons the identity $\Pi_0(\{\omega\}) = \pi_0(\omega) = \Pi(\{\omega\})$ obviously holds for each $\omega \in \Omega$ such that $\{\omega\} \in \mathcal{R}$. If $\mathcal{R}$ is closed with respect to intersections, i. e., if $A \cap B \in \mathcal{R}$ holds for each $A, B \in \mathcal{R}$, then $\Pi_0(A) = \Pi(A)$ for every $A \in \mathcal{R}$ supposing that Π is complete on $\mathcal{R}$ (cf. [8] for more detail).

As in the case of inner and outer measure, we can define the necessity measures N_Π, $(N_\Pi)_0$, and $N_{(\Pi_0)}$. The following inequalities between their values can be proved.

Theorem 4.2. Let $\Omega \neq \emptyset$, let $\{\emptyset, \Omega\} \subset \mathcal{R} \subset \mathcal{P}(\Omega)$, let $\mathcal{T} = \langle T, \leq \rangle$ be a complete lattice, let Π be a partial $\mathcal{T}$-possibilistic measure on $\mathcal{R}$. Then, for each $A \in \mathcal{R}^-$, the inequality

$$(N_\Pi)_0(A) \leq N_\Pi(A) \leq N_{(\Pi_0)}(A) \qquad (4.9)$$

holds.   □

Proof. Cf. Lemma 8.2 in [8].   □

No inequality relation valid in general binds the values of the mappings Π_0 and Π_*. Indeed, take $\mathcal{R} = \{\emptyset, \Omega\}$ with $\Pi(\emptyset) = \mathbf{0}_\mathcal{T}$ and $\Pi(\Omega) = 1_\mathcal{T}$. Then, for each $\omega \in \Omega$, $\pi_0(\omega) = \Pi(\Omega) = 1_\mathcal{T}$, so that $\Pi_0(A) = 1_\mathcal{T}$ for every $\emptyset \neq A \subset \Omega$. On the other side, $\Pi_*(A) = \Pi(\emptyset) = \mathbf{0}_\mathcal{T}$ for every $A \subset \Omega$, $A \neq \Omega$, so that the strict inequality $\Pi_*(A) < \Pi_0(A)$ for every $\emptyset \neq A \neq \Omega$ follows. However, recalling the example with $\Omega = \{1, 2, 3, 4, 5\}$ from above, we remember that $\Pi_0(A_3) = \mathbf{0}_\mathcal{T}$, but $\Pi_*(A_3) = \Pi(A_3) = 1_\mathcal{T}$, so that the inequality $\Pi_0(A_3) < \Pi_*(A_3)$ holds.

One of the reviewers of this contribution suggests still another interesting way how to extend a partial $\mathcal{T}$-possibilistic measure Π from its domain $\mathcal{R} \subset \mathcal{P}(\Omega)$ to the whole $\mathcal{P}(\Omega)$. Namely, denote by D_Π the set of all $\mathcal{T}$-possibilistic distributions $\pi : \Omega \to T$ such that $\vee_{\omega \in A} \pi(\omega) = \Pi(A)$ holds for each $A \in \mathcal{R}$, in other words, the total possibilistic measures defined by distributions from D_Π agree with Π on $\mathcal{R}$. Supposing that the set D_Π is nonempty and that it contains the maximum element in the pointwise sense, i. e., that there exists $\pi_0 \in D_\Pi$ such that the inequality $\pi_0(\omega) \geq \pi(\omega)$ holds for each $\omega \in \Omega$ and each $\pi \in D_\Pi$, the total possibilistic measure on $\mathcal{P}(\Omega)$ defined by π_0 is defined as the extension of Π from $\mathcal{R}$ to $\mathcal{P}(\Omega)$. The idea is certainly worth being investigated in more detail, but what would be necessary, first of all, is to find some nontrivial sufficient conditions under which the set D_Π is nonempty and dominated by a pointwise maximum element. As such investigations seem to be far from being trivial, let us postpone them till another occasion, as well as a more detailed analysis of possible relations between the approaches introduced above and the last one.

Acknowledgement. Support of COST Action 274 (TARSKI) is acknowledged.

References

1. Birkhoff, G.: Lattice Theory, 3rd edition. Providence, Rhode Island (1967)
2. De Cooman, G.: Possibility theory I, II, III. International Journal of General Systems 25 (1997), 4, pp. 291–323, 325–351, 353–371
3. Dubois, D., Prade, H.: Théorie des Possibilités – Applications à la Représentation des Connaissances en Informatique. Mason, Paris (1985)
4. Dubois, D., Nguyen, H., Prade, H.: Possibility theory, probability theory and fuzzy sets: misunderstandings, bridges and gaps. In: The Handbook of Fuzzy Sets Series (D. Dubois and H. Prade, Eds.), Kluwer Adacemic Publishers, Boston (2000)
5. Faure, R., Heurgon, E.: Structures Ordonnées et Algèbres de Boole. Gauthier-Villars, Paris (1971)
6. Halmos, P.R.: Measure Theory. D. van Nonstrand, New York, Toronto, London (1950)
7. Kramosil, I.: Almost-measurability induced by fuzzy and possibilistic measures. In: Proceedings of the IMPU 2002 International Conference, Annecy (2002), vol. I, 521–527
8. Kramosil, I.: Extensions of partial lattice-valued possibilistic and necessity measures. Submitted for publication
9. Sikorski, R.: Boolean Algebras, 2nd Edit., Springer-Verlag, Berlin, Göttingen, Heidelberg, New York (1964)

Coherent Conditional Probability as a Measure of Uncertainty of the Relevant Conditioning Events

Giulianella Coletti[1] and Romano Scozzafava[2]

[1] Dipartimento di Matematica, Università di Perugia
Via Vanvitelli, 1 – 06100 Perugia (Italy)
coletti@dipmat.unipg.it
[2] Dipartimento Metodi e Modelli Matematici, Università "La Sapienza"
Via Scarpa, 16 – 00161 Roma (Italy)
romscozz@dmmm.uniroma1.it

Abstract. In previous papers, by resorting to the most effective concept of conditional probability, we have been able not only to define fuzzy subsets, but also to introduce in a very natural way the basic continuous T-norms and the relevant dual T-conorms, bound to the former by *coherence*. Moreover, we have given, as an interesting and fundamental by-product of our approach, a natural interpretation of *possibility functions*, both from a semantic and a syntactic point of view. In this paper we study the properties of a coherent conditional probability looked on as a general *non-additive uncertainty measure* of the conditioning events, and we prove that this measure is a *capacity* if and only if it is a *possibility*.

1 Introduction

The starting point of our approach is a synthesis of the available information (and possibly also of the modalities of its acquisition), expressing it by one or more *events*: to this purpose, the concept of event must be given its more general meaning, *i.e.* it must not looked on just as a possible outcome (a subset of the so–called "sample space"), but expressed by a *proposition*.

Moreover, events play a two–fold role, since we must consider not only those events which are the direct object of study, but also those which represent the relevant "state of information": in fact *conditional* events and *conditional* probability are the tools that allow to manage specific (conditional) statements and to update degrees of belief on the basis of the evidence.

On the other hand, what is usually emphasized in the literature – when a conditional probability $P(E|H)$ is taken into account – is only the fact that $P(\cdot|H)$ *is a probability for any given H*: this is a very restrictive (and misleading) view of conditional probability, corresponding trivially to just a modification of the so-called "sample space" Ω.

It is instead essential – for a correct handling of the subtle and delicate problems concerning the use of conditional probability – to regard the conditioning

T.D. Nielsen and N.L. Zhang (Eds.): ECSQARU 2003, LNAI 2711, pp. 407–418, 2003.

event H as a "variable", *i.e.* the "status" of H in $E|H$ is not just that of some-thing representing a given *fact*, but that of an (uncertain) *event* (like E) for which the knowledge of its truth value is not required (this means, using a ter-minology due to Koopman [15], that H must be looked on – even if *asserted* – as being *contemplated*: similar terms are, respectively, *acquired* versus *assumed*).

The concepts of conditional event and conditional probability (as dealt with in this paper) play a central role for the probabilistic reasoning. In particular, here we study the properties of a coherent conditional probability looked on as a general non-additive uncertainty measure of the conditioning events, and we prove that this measure is a *capacity* if and only if it is a *possibility*.

2   Conditional Events and Coherent Conditional Probability

In a series of paper (see, e.g., [5] and [7], and the recent book [8]) we showed that, if we do not assign the same "third value" $t(E|H) = u$ (undetermined) to *all* conditional events, but make it suitably depend on $E|H$, it turns out that this function $t(E|H)$ can be taken as a general conditional *uncertainty measure* (for example, conditional *probability* and conditional *possibility* correspond to particular choices of the relevant operations between conditional events, looked on as particular random variables, as shown, respectively, in [5] and [1]).

By taking as *partial* operations the ordinary sum and product in a given family $\mathcal{C}$ of conditional events, with the only requirement that the resulting value of $t(E|H)$ be a *function* of (E, H), we proved in [5] that this function $t(\cdot|\cdot)$ satisfies "familiar" rules.

In particular, if the set $\mathcal{C} = \mathcal{G} \times \mathcal{B}$ of conditional events $E|H$ is such that $\mathcal{G}$ is a Boolean algebra and $\mathcal{B} \subseteq \mathcal{G}$ is closed with respect to (finite) logical sums, then, putting $t(\cdot|\cdot) = P(\cdot|\cdot)$, these rules can be expressed as follows, where $\mathcal{B}^o = \mathcal{B} \setminus \{\emptyset\}$:

  (i) $P(H|H) = 1$, for every $H \in \mathcal{B}^o$
  (ii) $P(\cdot|H)$ is a (finitely additive) probability on $\mathcal{A}$ for any given $H \in \mathcal{B}^o$
  (iii) $P((E \wedge A)|H) = P(E|H) \cdot P(A|(E \wedge H))$, for every $A \in \mathcal{A}$ and E, $H \in \mathcal{B}^o$, $E \wedge H \neq \emptyset$.

The function $P(\cdot|\cdot)$ is called a *conditional probability* on $\mathcal{G} \times \mathcal{B}^o$, and these rules *coincide with the usual axioms* due to de Finetti [12], Rényi [17], Krauss [16], Dubins [13].

And what about an assessment P on an *arbitrary* set $\mathcal{C}$ of conditional events? We will say that the assessment $P(\cdot|\cdot)$ on $\mathcal{C}$ is *coherent* if there exists $\mathcal{C}' \supset \mathcal{C}$, with $\mathcal{C}' = \mathcal{G} \times \mathcal{B}^o$ ($\mathcal{G}$ a Boolean algebra, $\mathcal{B}$ an additive set), such that $P(\cdot|\cdot)$ can be extended from $\mathcal{C}$ to $\mathcal{C}'$ as a *conditional probability*.

We list the peculiarities (which entail a large flexibility in the management of any kind of uncertainty) of this concept of *coherent* conditional probability versus the usual one:

- due to the *direct* assignment of $P(E|H)$ as a whole, the knowledge (or the assessment) of the "joint" and "marginal" unconditional probabilities $P(E \wedge H)$ and $P(H)$ is not required;

- the *conditioning* event H (which *must* be a *possible* one) may have *zero probability*, so that the class of admissible conditional probability assessments and that of possible extensions are larger (and the ensuing algorithms are more flexible);

- it allows a management of *stochastic* independence (see, e.g., [3]) (conditional or not) which avoids many of the usual inconsistencies related to *logical* dependence. In fact, the latter situation may arise in the usual probabilistic approach, for example when dealing with graphical models;

- a suitable interpretation of the extreme values 0 and 1 of $P(E|H)$ for situations which are different, respectively, from the trivial ones $E \wedge H = \emptyset$ and $H \subseteq E$, leads to a "natural" treatment of the default reasoning [11];

- it is possible to represent "vague" statements as those of fuzzy theory (as done in [4], [6], [9]).

The following characterization of coherence has been discussed in many previous papers: here we adopt the formulation essentially given in [2] (see also [8]).

Theorem 1. Let $\mathcal{C}$ be an *arbitrary* family of conditional events, and consider, for every $n \in \mathbb{N}$, any finite subfamily

$$\mathcal{F} = \{E_1|H_1, \ldots, E_n|H_n\} \subseteq \mathcal{C};$$

denote by $\mathcal{A}_o$ the set of atoms A_r generated by the (unconditional) events $E_1, H_1, \ldots, E_n, H_n$. For a real function P on $\mathcal{C}$ the following three statements are equivalent:

(a) P is a *coherent* conditional probability on $\mathcal{C}$;

(b) for every finite subset $\mathcal{F} \subseteq \mathcal{C}$, there exists a class of coherent (unconditional) probabilities $\{P_\alpha^\mathcal{F}\}$ (to avoid a cumbersome notation, in the sequel we put $P_\alpha^\mathcal{F} = P_\alpha$), each probability P_α being defined on a suitable subset $\mathcal{A}_\alpha \subseteq \mathcal{A}_o$, and for any $E_i|H_i \in \mathcal{C}$ there is a unique P_α satisfying

$$\sum_{\substack{r \\ A_r \subseteq H_i}} P_\alpha(A_r) > 0,$$ (1)

and

$$P(E_i|H_i) = \frac{\sum_{\substack{r \\ A_r \subseteq E_i \wedge H_i}} P_\alpha(A_r)}{\sum_{\substack{r \\ A_r \subseteq H_i}} P_\alpha(A_r)};$$ (2)

moreover $\mathcal{A}_{\alpha'} \subset \mathcal{A}_{\alpha''}$ for $\alpha' > \alpha''$ and $P_{\alpha''}(A_r) = 0$ if $A_r \in \mathcal{A}_{\alpha'}$;

(c) for every finite subset $\mathcal{F} \subseteq \mathcal{C}$, all systems of the following sequence, with unknowns $x_r^\alpha = P_\alpha(A_r) \geq 0$, $A_r \in \mathcal{A}_\alpha$, $\alpha = 0, 1, 2, \ldots, k \leq n$, are compatible:

$$(S_\alpha) \quad \begin{cases} \displaystyle\sum_{r \atop A_r \subseteq E_i \wedge H_i} x_r^\alpha = P(E_i|H_i) \sum_{r \atop A_r \subseteq H_i} x_r^\alpha, \\[2mm] \left[\text{for all } E_i|H_1 \in \mathcal{F} \text{ such that } \sum_{r \atop A_r \subseteq H_i} x_r^{\alpha-1} = 0 \,, \; \alpha \geq 1,\right] \\[2mm] \displaystyle\sum_{r \atop A_r \subseteq H_o^\alpha} x_r^\alpha = 1 \end{cases}$$

where $H_o^o = H_o = H_1 \vee \ldots \vee H_n$ and $\displaystyle\sum_{r \atop A_r \subseteq H_i} x_r^{-1} = 0$ for **all** H_i's, while H_o^α denotes, for $\alpha \geq 1$, the union of the H_i's such that $\displaystyle\sum_{r \atop A_r \subseteq H_i} x_r^{\alpha-1} = 0$. •

Any class $\{P_\alpha\}$ singled-out by the condition *(b)* is said *to agree* with the conditional probability P. Notice that in general there are infinite classes of probabilities $\{P_\alpha\}$; in particular we have *only one agreeing class* in the case that $\mathcal{C}$ is the product $\mathcal{G} \times \mathcal{G}^o$ (with $\mathcal{G}$ Boolean algebra).

3   Zero-Layers

We recall now the concept of *zero-layer* [3], which naturally arises from the nontrivial structure of conditional probability brought out by Theorem 1. (We refer, for simplicity, only to finite sets of conditional events).

Definition 1. Given a class $\mathcal{P} = \{P_\alpha\}$, agreeing with a conditional probability in the sense of the characterization Theorem 1, it *naturally induces* the *zero-layer* $\circ(H)$ of an event H, defined as

$$\circ(H) = \alpha \quad \text{if } P_\alpha(H) > 0 \,,$$

and the zero-layer of a conditional event $E|H$ as

$$\circ(E|H) = \circ(E \wedge H) - \circ(H).$$

The zero-layers single-out a partition of the family of the conditioning events: on the other hand we may have, if E is not one of them, $P_\alpha(E) = 0$ for every $\alpha = 0, 1, 2, \ldots, k$. Nevertheless, as shown in [5], it is possible to assign to it an arbitrary probability $P_{k+1}(E) > 0$, so that $\circ(E) = k + 1$.

Obviously, for the certain event Ω and for any event E with positive probability, we have $\circ(\Omega) = \circ(E) = 0$ (so that, if the class contains only an *everywhere positive* probability P_o, there is only one (trivial) zero-layer, *i.e.* $\alpha = 0$), while we put $\circ(\emptyset) = +\infty$. Clearly,

$$\circ(A \vee B) = \min\{\circ(A), \circ(B)\}.$$

Moreover, notice that $P(E|H) > 0$ if and only if $\circ(E \wedge H) = \circ(H)$, that is iff $\circ(E|H) = 0$.

Notice that the zero-layer (which is obviously significant mainly for events of zero probability) is a tool to detect "how much" a null event (conditional or not) is ... null.

For the connection of the concept of zero-layer to Spohn's ranking function, see the discussion in Sect. 12.3 of the book [8].

4   Coherent Extensions

A fundamental result is the following, essentially due (for unconditional events, and referring to an *equivalent* form of coherence in terms of betting scheme) to de Finetti [12].

Theorem 2. Let $\mathcal{C}$ be a family of conditional events and P a corresponding assessment; then there exists a (possibly not unique) coherent extension of P to an *arbitrary* family $\mathcal{K} \supseteq \mathcal{C}$, *if and only if* P is coherent on $\mathcal{C}$.

The following theorem (see [8]) shows that a coherent assignment of $P(\cdot|\cdot)$ to a family of conditional events whose conditioning ones are a *partition* of Ω is essentially unbound.

Theorem 3. Let $\mathcal{C}$ be a family of conditional events $\{E_i|H_i\}_{i \in I}$, where $card(I)$ is arbitrary and the events H_i's are a *partition* of Ω. Then *any* function $f : \mathcal{C} \to [0, 1]$ such that

$$f(E_i|H_i) = 0 \quad \text{if} \quad E_i \wedge H_i = \emptyset, \quad \text{and} \quad f(E_i|H_i) = 1 \quad \text{if} \quad H_i \subseteq E_i \quad (3)$$

is a coherent conditional probability.

Proof. Coherence follows easily from Theorem 1; in fact, for any finite subset $\mathcal{F} \subseteq \mathcal{C}$ we must consider the relevant systems (S_α): each equation is "independent" from the others, since the events H_i's have no atoms in common, and so for any choice of $P(E_i|H_i)$ each equation (and then the corresponding system) has trivially a solution (actually, many solutions).

Corollary 1. Let $\mathcal{C}$ be a family of conditional events $\{E|H_i\}_{i \in I}$, where $card(I)$ is arbitrary and the events H_i's are a *partition* of Ω, and let $P(\cdot|\cdot)$ be a coherent conditional probability such that $P(E|H_i) \in \{0, 1\}$. Then the following two statements are equivalent

(i) $P(\cdot|\cdot)$ is the *only* coherent assessment on $\mathcal{C}$;

(ii) $H_i \wedge E = \emptyset$ for every $H_i \in \mathcal{H}_o$ and $H_i \subseteq E$ for every $H_i \in \mathcal{H}_1$, where $\mathcal{H}_r = \{H_i : P(E|H_i) = r\}$, $r = 0, 1$.

The latter two theorems constitute the main basis for the aforementioned interpretation of a fuzzy subset (through the membership function) and of a possibility distribution in terms of coherent conditional probability.

5   Fuzzy Sets and Possibility

We recall from [9] the following two definitions (Definitions 2 and 3 below).

If X is a (not necessarily numerical) random quantity with range C_X, let A_x, for any $x \in C_X$, be the event $\{X = x\}$. The family $\{A_x\}_{x \in C_x}$ is obviously a *partition* of the certain event Ω.

Let φ be any *property* related to the random quantity X: notice that a *property*, even if expressed by a proposition, does not single–out an *event*, since the latter needs to be expressed by a *nonambiguous* statement that can be either *true* or *false*. Consider now the **event**

$$E_\varphi = \text{``You claim } \varphi\text{''}$$

and a coherent conditional probability $P(E_\varphi | A_x)$, looked on as a real function

$$\mu_{E_\varphi}(x) = P(E_\varphi | A_x)$$

defined on C_X.

Since the events A_x are incompatible, then (by Theorem 3) every $\mu_{E_\varphi}(x)$ with values in $[0, 1]$ is a coherent conditional probability.

Remark. Given $x_1, x_2 \in C_X$ and the corresponding conditional probabilities $\mu_{E_\varphi}(x_1)$ and $\mu_{E_\varphi}(x_2)$, a coherent extension of P to the conditional event $E_\varphi | (A_{x_1} \vee A_{x_2})$ is not necessarily additive with respect to the conditioning events (yet, see the Remark following Corollary 2).

Definition 2. Given a random quantity X with range C_X and a related property φ, a *fuzzy subset* E_φ^* of C_X is the pair

$$E_\varphi^* = \{E_\varphi \, , \, \mu_{E_\varphi}\},$$

with $\mu_{E_\varphi}(x) = P(E_\varphi | A_x)$ for every $x \in C_X$.

So a coherent conditional probability $P(E_\varphi | A_x)$ is a measure of how much You, given the event $A_x = \{X = x\}$, are willing to *claim* the property φ, and it plays the role of the membership function of the fuzzy subset E_φ^*.

In [6] we have been able not only to define fuzzy subsets, but also to introduce in a very natural way the basic continuous T-norms and the relevant dual T-conorms, bound to the former by *coherence*. In fact, given a T-norm (that in this framework singles-out the value $P(E_\varphi \wedge E_\psi | A_x \wedge A_y)$ of the conjunction), then the corresponding choice of the T-conorm (which determines the value of the disjunction) is *uniquely* driven by the coherence of the relevant conditional probability (and the dual operation is what is actually obtained).

Definition 3. Let E be an arbitrary event and P any coherent conditional probability on the family $\mathcal{G} = \{E\} \times \{A_x\}_{x \in C_X}$, admitting $P(E | \Omega) = 1$ as (coherent) extension. A *distribution of possibility* on C_X is the real function π defined by $\pi(x) = P(E | A_x)$.

6   Conditional Probability as a Nonadditive Uncertainty Measure

Actually, the previous definition can be used as well to introduce any general distribution φ, to be called just *uncertainty measure*.

Definition 4. Let E be an arbitrary event and P any coherent conditional probability on the family $\mathcal{G} = \{E\} \times \{A_x\}_{x \in C_X}$, admitting $P(E|\Omega) = 1$ as (coherent) extension. A *distribution of uncertainty measure* on C_X is the real function φ defined by $\varphi(x) = P(E|A_x)$.

Remark. When C_X is finite, since every extension of $P(E|\cdot)$ must satisfy axioms *(i)*, *(ii)* and *(iii)* of a conditional probability, condition $P(E|\Omega) = 1$ gives

$$P(E|\Omega) = \sum_{x \in C_x} P(A_x|\Omega)P(E|A_x) \qquad \text{and} \qquad \sum_{x \in C_x} P(A_x|\Omega) = 1 \,.$$

Then

$$1 = P(E|\Omega) \leq \max_{x \in C_x} P(E|A_x) \,;$$

therefore $P(E|A_x) = 1$ for at least one event A_x.

On the other hand, we notice that in our framework (where *null probabilities for possible conditioning events are allowed*) it does not necessarily follow that $P(E|A_x) = 1$ for every x; in fact we may will have $P(E|A_y) = 0$ (or else equal to any other number between 0 and 1) for some $y \in C_X$.

Obviously, the constraint $P(E|A_x) = 1$ for some x is not necessary when the cardinality of C_X is infinite.

We will study now the properties of coherent extensions of the function φ, seen as coherent conditional probability $P(E|\cdot)$, to the algebra spanned by the events A_x.

First of all we note that if $\mathcal{A}$ is an algebra, E an arbitrary event and $P(E|\cdot)$ a coherent conditional probability on $\{E\} \times \mathcal{A}^o$, then function $f(\cdot)$ defined on $\mathcal{A}$ by putting $f(\emptyset) = 0$ and $f(A) = P(E|A)$ *is not necessarily additive*. On the contrary (as we will see in the following Theorem 4) f is necessarily sub-additive (0-alternating).

Lemma 1. Let $\mathcal{C}$ be a family of conditional events $\{E|H_i\}_{i \in I}$, where $card(I)$ is arbitrary and the events H_i's are a *partition* of Ω, and let $P(E|\cdot)$ an arbitrary (coherent) conditional probability on $\mathcal{C}$. Then any coherent extension of P to $\mathcal{C}' = \{E|H : H \in \mathcal{H}^o\}$, where $\mathcal{H}$ is the algebra spanned by H_i, is such that, for every $H, K \in \mathcal{H}$, with $H \wedge K = \emptyset$

$$\min\{P(E|H), P(E|K)\} \leq P(E|H \vee K) \leq \max\{P(E|H), P(E|K)\} \,.$$

Proof. By Theorem 2, P can be extended to a coherent conditional probability on $\mathcal{C}'$, and the latter in turn can be extended to a coherent conditional probability on $\mathcal{C}'' = \mathcal{C}' \cup \{H|K : H, K \in \mathcal{H}\}$. This satisfies, by axiom *(iii)* of a conditional probability,

$$P(E|H \vee K) = P(E|H)P(H|H \vee K) + P(E|K)P(K|H \vee K) \,,$$

for every $H \wedge K = \emptyset$. The conclusion follows, since – by axioms *(i)* and *(ii)* – we have $P(H|H \vee K) + P(K|H \vee K) = 1$.

Corollary 2. Let $\mathcal{C}$ be a family of conditional events $\{E|H_i\}_{i \in I}$, where $card(I)$ is arbitrary and the events H_i's are a *partition* of Ω, and let $P(E|\cdot)$ an arbitrary (coherent) conditional probability on $\mathcal{C}$. Then any coherent extension of P to $\mathcal{C}' = \{E|H : H \in \mathcal{H}^o\}$, where $\mathcal{H}$ is the algebra spanned by H_i, is such that, for every $H, K \in \mathcal{H}$, with $II \wedge K = \emptyset$,

$$P(E|H \vee K) \leq P(E|H) + P(E|K).$$

Proof. The prof is a trivial consequence of Lemma 1.

Remark. Can equality hold in the previous relation? If this happens, it means (by Lemma 1) that either $P(E|H)$ or $P(E|K)$ is equal to zero, so that, if $P(E|\Omega) > 0$, an easy induction leads to the conclusion that for all elements of the partition *except one* we have $P(E|H_i) = 0$.

Recalling that a function f is 2-alternating if, for every H, K, we have

$$f(H \vee K) \leq f(H) + f(K) - f(H \wedge K),$$

the following example shows the existence of coherent extensions of the conditional probability P to $\mathcal{C}' = \{E|H : H \in \mathcal{H}^o\}$ which are *not* 2-alternating measures.

Example. Let H_1, H_2, H_3 be a partition of Ω and E an event logically independent of H_i. Consider the following assessment:

$$P(E|H_1) = 1/2, \ P(E|H_2) = 1/3, \ P(E|H_3) = 1,$$

$$P(E|H_1 \vee H_2) = 5/12, \ P(E|H_1 \vee H_3) = 1, \ P(E|H_1 \vee H_2 \vee H_3) = P(E|\Omega) = 1.$$
This assessment is not 2-alternating, in fact we have

$$1 = P(E|H_1 \vee H_2 \vee H_3) > P(E|H_1 \vee H_2) + P(E|H_1 \vee H_3) - P(E|H_1) = 11/12.$$

Nevertheless the assessment is a coherent conditional probability (and so admits a coherent extension to $\mathcal{C}'$). By condition (c) of Theorem 1, to prove coherence consider the probabilities of the relevant atoms $x_i = P_o(E \wedge H_i)$ and $x'_i = P_o(E^c \wedge H_i)$ as unknowns in the following system:

$$
\begin{cases}
x_1 = \frac{1}{2}(x_1 + x'_1) \\
x_2 = \frac{1}{3}(x_2 + x'_2) \\
x_3 = (x_3 + x'_3) \\
x_1 + x_2 = \frac{5}{12}(x_1 + x_2 + x'_1 + x'_2) \\
x_1 + x_3 = (x_1 + x_3 + x'_1 + x'_3) \\
x_1 + +x_2 + x_3 = (x_1 + x_2 + x_3 + x'_1 + x'_2 + x'_3) \\
\sum_{k=1}^{3}(x_k + x'_k) = 1 \\
x_k \geq 0
\end{cases}
$$

which has the solution $x_3 = 1$, $x_1 = x_2 = x'_i = 0 \ (i = 1, 2, 3)$.

Putting now $y_i = P_1(E \wedge H_i)$ and $y'_i = P_1(E^c \wedge H_i)$ $(i = 1,2)$, we need to consider the second system

$$\begin{cases} y_1 = \frac{1}{2}(y_1 + y'_1) \\ y_2 = \frac{1}{3}(y_2 + y'_2) \\ y_1 + y_2 = \frac{5}{12}(y_1 + y_2 + y'_1 + y'_2) \\ \sum_{k=1}^{2}(y_k + y'_k) = 1 \\ y_k \geq 0 \end{cases}$$

which has the solution $y_1 = y'_1 = \frac{1}{4}$, $y_2 = \frac{1}{6}$, $y'_2 = \frac{1}{3}$.

We note that this 0-alternating (but not 2-alternating) function $P(E|\cdot)$ is *not monotone* with respect to $\subseteq$, i.e. there exist $H, K \in \mathcal{H}$, with $H \subseteq K$, such that $P(E|H) > P(E|K)$: just take $H = H_1$ and $K = H_1 \vee H_2$. •

So the function $f(H) = P(E|H)$, with P a coherent conditional probability, in general *is not a capacity*.

The following theorem focuses the condition that assures the monotonicity of $P(E|\cdot)$.

Theorem 4. Let $\mathcal{C}$ be a family of conditional events $\{E|H_i\}_{i \in I}$, where $card(I)$ is arbitrary and the events H_i's are a *partition* of Ω, and let $P(E|\cdot)$ an arbitrary (coherent) conditional probability on $\mathcal{C}$. A coherent extension of P to $\mathcal{C}' = \{E|H : H \in \mathcal{H}^\circ\}$, where $\mathcal{H}$ is the algebra spanned by H_i, is monotone with respect to $\subseteq$ if and only if for every $H, K \in \mathcal{H}$

$$P(E|H \vee K) = \max\{P(E|H), P(E|K)\}.$$

Proof. The proof is a direct consequence of Lemma 1.

The question now is: are there coherent conditional probabilities $P(E|\cdot)$ monotone with respect to $\subseteq$?

We will reach a positive answer by means of the following theorem (given in [9]), which represents the main tool to introduce *possibility functions* in our context referring to coherent conditional probabilities.

Theorem 5. Let E be an arbitrary event and $\mathcal{C}$ be the family of conditional events $\{E|H_i\}_{i \in I}$, where $card(I)$ is arbitrary and the events H_i's are a *partition* of Ω. Denote by $\mathcal{H}$ the algebra spanned by the H_i's and let $f : \mathcal{C} \to [0,1]$ be *any* function such that (3) holds (with $E_i = E$ for every $i \in I$). Then any P extending f on $\mathcal{K} = \{E\} \times \mathcal{H}^\circ$ and such that

$$P(E|H \vee K) = \max\{P(E|H), P(E|K)\}, \quad \text{for every } H, K \in \mathcal{H}^\circ. \qquad (4)$$

is a coherent conditional probability.

Remark. If $card(I)$ is infinite, there exists a coherent extension of the function f as conditional probability on $\mathcal{K} = \{E\} \times \mathcal{H}^o$, satisfying (4), even if we put the further constraint $P(E|\Omega) = 1$. (Recall that the ensuing assessment $P(E) = 1$ by no means implies $E = \Omega$). On the other hand, when $card(I)$ is finite, this extension is possible only if $P(E|H_i) = 1$ for some i.

Remark. If $card(I)$ is finite, then for every $H \in \mathcal{H}^o$,

$$P(E|H) = \max_{H_i \subset H} P(E|H_i).$$

So the knowledge of the function P on the given partition is enough to determine the whole conditional probability on $\mathcal{H}^o$. On the other hand, in the general case, if the event H is an infinite disjunction of elements of $\mathcal{H}^o$, it is not necessarily true that the conditional probability $P(E|H)$ is the superior of the $P(E|H_i)$'s.

The above result allowed us to introduce a "convincing" (from our point of view) definition of possibility measure. On the other hand, for a classic approach, see the book [14].

Definition 5. Let $\mathcal{H}$ be an algebra of subsets of C_X (the range of a random quantity X) and E an arbitrary event. If P is any coherent conditional probability on $\mathcal{K} = \{E\} \times \mathcal{H}^o$, with $P(E|\Omega) = 1$ and such that

$$P(E|H \vee K) = \max\{P(E|H), P(E|K)\}, \quad \text{for every } H, K \in \mathcal{H}^o,$$

then a *possibility measure* on $\mathcal{H}$ is a real function Π defined by $\Pi(H) = P(E|H)$ for $H \in \mathcal{H}^o$ and $\Pi(\emptyset) = 0$.

Remark. Theorem 5 assures (in our context) that any possibility *measure* can be obtained as coherent extension (unique, in the finite case) of a possibility *distribution*. Vice versa, given any possibility measure Π on an algebra $\mathcal{H}$, there exists an event E and a coherent conditional probability P on $\mathcal{K} = \{E\} \times \mathcal{H}^o$ agreeing with Π, i.e. whose extension to $\{E\} \times \mathcal{H}$ (putting $P(E|\emptyset) = 0$) coincides with Π.

The following Theorem 6, which is an immediate consequence of Theorems 4 and 5, is the main result of this paper.

Theorem 6. Let E be an arbitrary event and $\mathcal{C}$ be the family of conditional events $\{E|H_i\}_{i \in I}$, where $card(I)$ is arbitrary and the events H_i's are a *partition* of Ω. Denote by $\mathcal{H}$ the algebra spanned by the H_i's and let $f : \mathcal{C} \to [0,1]$ be *any* function such that (3) holds (with $E_i = E$ for every $i \in I$). Then any coherent P extending f on $\mathcal{K} = \{E\} \times \mathcal{H}^o$ **is a capacity if and only if it is a possibility**.

7   Conclusions

Going back to our interpretation of a membership function $\mu(x)$ through a suitable coherent conditional probability (a measure of how much You, given the event $A_x = \{X = x\}$, are willing to *claim* the relevant property φ), and putting

$$H_o = \{x \in C_X : \mu(x) = 0\}, \ H_1 = \{x \in C_X : \mu(x) = 1\},$$

the conditional probability $P(E|H^c)$, with $H = H_o \vee H_1$, is *a measure of how much You are willing to claim property* φ if the only fact you know is that $x \in H$. And this will is "independent" of your beliefs corresponding to the single values x: in fact, even if "H false" corresponds to the truth of $\{\bigvee_x A_x : x \in H^c\}$, nevertheless there is no additivity requirement, since conditional probability is not additive with respect to the disjunction of conditioning events.

On the other hand, *every membership function can be regarded as a possibility distribution*. If $\mathcal{A}$ is an algebra of subsets of $\mathcal{C}_X$, the ensuing possibility *measure* can be interpreted in the following way: it is a sort of "global" membership (relative to each finite $A \in \mathcal{A}$) which takes, among all the possible choices for its value on A, *i.e.* among all possible extensions satisfying (4), the *maximum* of the membership in A. Moreover, we proved in [9] that we can regard every possibility measure Π as a decreasing function of the elements of the *zero-layer set* $\{0, 1, 2, \ldots, k\}$ generated by the coherent conditional probability P agreeing with Π (in the sense of the last Remark of Sect. 3). In conclusion, **the coherent extensions of a conditional probability** $P(E|A_x)$ **that satisfy (4)** *give rise to different zero-layers* for the *atoms* A_x corresponding to different $P(E|A_x)$, so that such a coherent conditional probability $P(E|\cdot)$ can be suitably associated to a measure of your "disbelief" in the events $A \in \mathcal{A}$.

Then some of the above conclusions may appear counterintuitive (for example, considering the statement "Mary is young", if you know that Mary's age is $x = 39$, you may be willing to put $\mu(x) = .2$, while if you know that her age is $y = 26$, you may be willing to put $\mu(y) = .9$; then, knowing instead that her age is between 26 and 39, the corresponding possibility is still .9): in fact, the "global" membership should possibly decrease when the information is not concentrated on a given x, but is "spread" over a larger set. So our results may suggest to take as such global measure a function which is **not** a capacity, yet satisfying the weaker conditions of Lemma 1.

In a forthcoming paper [10] we will deepen these aspects, looking on a coherent conditional probability as a suitable (anti–monotone) *information measure*.

References

1. Bouchon-Meunier, B., Coletti, G., Marsala, C.: Conditional Possibility and Necessity. In: Bouchon-Meunier, B., Gutiérrez-Rios, J., Magdalena, L., Yager, R.R. (eds.): Technologies for Constructing Intelligent Systems, Vol.2, Springer, Berlin (2001) 59–71.
2. Coletti, G., Scozzafava, R.: Characterization of Coherent Conditional Probabilities as a Tool for their Assessment and Extension. International Journal of Uncertainty, Fuzziness and Knowledge-Based System **4** (1996) 103–127.
3. Coletti, G., Scozzafava, R.: Zero probabilities in stochastic independence. In: Bouchon-Meunier, B., Yager, R.R., Zadeh, L.A. (eds.): Information, Uncertainty, Fusion. Kluwer, Dordrecht (2000) 185–196 (Selected papers from IPMU 1998).
4. Coletti, G., Scozzafava, R.: Conditional Subjective Probability and Fuzzy Theory. In: Proc. of 18th NAFIPS International Conference, IEEE, New York (1999) 77–80.
5. Coletti, G., Scozzafava, R.: Conditioning and Inference in Intelligent Systems. Soft Computing **3** (1999) 118–130.

6. Coletti, G., Scozzafava, R.: Fuzzy sets as conditional probabilities: which meaningful operations can be defined? In: Proc. of 20th NAFIPS International Conference, IEEE, Vancouver, Canada (2001) 1892–1895.
7. Coletti, G., Scozzafava, R.: From conditional events to conditional measures: a new axiomatic approach. Annals of Mathematics and Artificial Intelligence **32** (2001) 373–392.
8. Coletti, G., Scozzafava, R.: Probabilistic logic in a coherent setting. Trends in Logic, n.15, Kluwer, Dordrecht / Boston / London (2002).
9. Coletti, G., Scozzafava, R.: Conditional probability, fuzzy sets and possibility: a unifying view. Fuzzy Sets and Systems (2003), to appear.
10. Coletti, G., Scozzafava, R.: Coherent conditional probability as a measure of information of the relevant conditioning events. In: Lecture Notes in Computers Science (IDA-2003, Berlin), submitted.
11. Coletti, G., Scozzafava, R., Vantaggi, B.: Coherent Conditional Probability as a Tool for Default Reasoning. In: Proc. IPMU 2002, Annecy, France (2002) 1663–1670.
12. de Finetti, B.: Sull'impostazione assiomatica del calcolo delle probabilità. Annali Univ. Trieste **19** (1949) 3–55. (Engl. transl.: Ch.5 in: Probability, Induction, Statistics, Wiley, London, 1972)
13. Dubins, L.E.: Finitely Additive Conditional Probabilities, Conglomerability and Disintegration. Annals of Probability **3** (1975) 89–99.
14. Dubois, D., Prade, H.: Possibility Theory. Plenum Press, New York (1988)
15. Koopman, B.O.: The Bases of Probability. Bulletin A.M.S. **46** (1940) 763–774.
16. Krauss, P.H.: Representation of Conditional Probability Measures on Boolean Algebras. Acta Math. Acad. Scient. Hungar. **19** (1968) 229–241.
17. Rényi, A.: On Conditional Probability Spaces Generated by a Dimensionally Ordered Set of Measures. Theory of Probability and its Applications **1** (1956) 61–71.

Decision Trees and Qualitative Possibilistic Inference: Application to the Intrusion Detection Problem

Nahla Ben Amor[1], Salem Benferhat[2], Zied Elouedi[1], and Khaled Mellouli[1]

[1] Institut Supérieur de Gestion Tunis, 41 Avenue de la liberté
2000 Le Bardo, Tunisie
`nahla.benamor,zied.elouedi@gmx.fr`
`khaled.mellouli@ihec.rnu.tn`
[2] CRIL – CNRS, Université d'Artois, Rue Jean Souvraz SP 18
62307 Lens, Cedex, France
`benferhat@cril.univ-artois.fr`

Abstract. In this paper, we apply decision trees (DT) to intrusion detection problems. Experimentations are done on KDD'99 datasets. These data offer main features needed to evaluate intrusion detection systems. We consider three levels of attack granularities depending on whether dealing with all attacks, or grouping them in special categories or just focusing on normal and abnormal behaviours. We also extend the classification procedure to handle uncertain observations encountered in connection features. To this end, uncertainty is represented by possibility distributions and the inference in DT is based on the qualitative possibilistic logic.

1 Introduction

Decision trees [2,15,11,13] are one of the most commonly classification methods used in supervised learning approaches. Standard decision trees only allow to deal with instances where all attributes are precisely defined. They are thus inappropriate to classify instances with uncertain attributes. Ignoring this uncertainty can affect the efficiency of the obtained results.

This paper proposes an extension of the inference method for classifying new instances containing uncertain attributes. This uncertainty is handled in a possibilistic logic framework.

An application to the intrusion detection problem in the context of information systems using classical decision trees is detailed. Our aim is not only to evaluate the capacity of DT in the classification problem, but also to see how decision trees can be appropriate for a detection intrusion problem. Different experimentations are performed on the KDD'99 datasets. These data are appropriate to evaluate an intrusion detection system. Indeed, the set of different attack are not equitably represented. For instance, in the training set, there are only 0.01% of U2R attacks, while DOS attacks are represented by 79.24%.

T.D. Nielsen and N.L. Zhang (Eds.): ECSQARU 2003, LNAI 2711, pp. 419–431, 2003.

Moreover, there are attacks which are present in the testing test but not in the training set. Hence, these data can be used to check the capability of an intrusion detection system to detect new attacks. In this paper, experimentations are performed according to three levels of attack granularities depending on whether dealing with all attacks, or grouping them in special categories or just focusing on normal and abnormal behaviours. Then, an illustrative example of the use of qualitative decision trees in the intrusion detection problems is presented.

This paper is organized as follows: Sect. 2 provides a brief background on decision trees. Section 3 presents an extension of the classification procedure when testing instances contains uncertain attributes represented by qualitative possibility distributions. Section 4 presents intrusion detection problems. Then, Sect. 5 experiments the use of decision trees in intrusion detection with a deep analysis of the normal behaviour. Finally, Sect. 6 illustrates the use of qualitative decision trees in this field.

2   Basics of Decision Trees

Decision trees are especially used in artificial intelligence due to their ability to express classification knowledge in a formalism easy to interpret. Decision trees present a system using a top-down strategy based on the divide and conquer approach where the major aim is to partition the tree in many mutually exclusive subsets. Each subset partition corresponds to a classification sub-problem. A decision tree is composed of three basic elements:
− *decision nodes* specifying the test attribute,
− *edges* corresponding to one of the possible values of the test attribute outcomes,
− *leaves* including objects that, typically, belong to the same class.

Two major procedures should be ensured with decision trees:

1. Building the Tree. Based on a given training set, a decision tree is built. Under an attribute selection measure a test attribute should be chosen at each decision node allowing to diminish as much as possible the mixture of classes between each subset created by the test. In other words, the main idea is therefore to find the test attribute in order to get disjoint data facilitating the determination of objects' classes. This process will continue for each sub decision tree until reaching leaves and fixing their corresponding classes.

2. Classification. Once the tree is constructed, it is used in order to classify a new instance. We start at the root of the decision tree, we test the attribute specified by this node. The result of this test allows us to move down the tree branch according to the attribute value of the given instance. This process is repeated until a leaf is encountered, the instance is being then classified in the same class as the one characterizing the reached leaf.

A generic decision tree algorithm is characterized by the next properties:

− **The Attribute Selection Measure:** The idea is to use an attribute selection measure taking into account the discriminative power of each attribute over classes. The selection measure is generally based on the information theory, we can for instance mention those suggested by Quinlan: *the information gain* [11] and *the gain ratio* [13]. More details concerning the different attribute selection measures can be found in [14].

– **The Partitioning Strategy:** The current training set will be divided by taking into account the selected test attribute. When we deal with discrete attributes, it consists in testing all the possible attribute values. However, a discretization step is generally needed [16] in the case of numeric attributes.

– **The Stopping Criteria:** They determine whether or not a training subset will be further divided. It is generally fulfilled when all the remaining objects belong to only one class. Therefore, the part of the decision tree verifying this criterion will be declared as a leaf.

3 Qualitative Possibilistic Inference

Standard versions of decision trees are inadequate to ensure their role of classification in an uncertain environment. In such a case the correctness of classification results may be affected. Indeed, existing approaches [3,5,12], which to some extent allow to deal with missing or uncertain data, always classify an uncertain instance in a unique class. This can lead to an arbitrary choice in ignorance situations. Thus, the idea in this section is to develop a qualitative possibilistic inference procedure adapting decision trees to classify instances characterized by uncertain attributes. This uncertainty is represented by the means of qualitative possibility distributions.

3.1 A Brief Refresher on Qualitative Possibilistic Logic

This sub-section briefly introduces possibilistic logic (see [4] for more details) which is an extension of classical logic to deal with uncertain information. Uncertainty is here assumed to be represented qualitatively by a finite and totally ordered scale denoted by $L = \{1, \alpha_1, ..., \alpha_n, 0\}$ such that $1 > \alpha_1 > ... > \alpha_n > 0$. The basic concept of a qualitative possibilistic logic is the notion of Qualitative Possibility Distribution (QPD), denoted by π.

A QPD π is a function which associates to each element ω of the universe of discourse Ω, here a set of interpretations of a propositional language, an element from L, (π encodes our beliefs on a real world). By convention, $\pi(\omega) = 1$ means that it is completely possible that ω is the real world, $\pi(\omega) = 0$ means that ω cannot be the real world, and $\pi(\omega) \geq \pi(\omega')$ means that ω is as at least possible as ω' to be the real world. A QPD π is said to be normalized if there exists ω such that $\pi(\omega) = 1$.

At the *syntactic* level, uncertain information are represented by means of a qualitative knowledge possibilistic base. A qualitative possibilistic knowledge base (KB) Σ is a set of weighted formulas of the form (ϕ_i, α_i) where ϕ_i is a propositional formula and $\alpha_i \in L$ is its uncertainty degree which estimates to what extent it is certain that ϕ_i is true considering the available data. Each qualitative possibilistic knowledge base Σ induces a unique QPD π_Σ of the form:

$$\forall \omega \in \Omega, \pi_\Sigma(\omega) = \begin{cases} 1 & \text{if } \forall (\phi_i, \alpha_i) \in \Sigma, \omega \models \phi_i \\ \min\{Ne(\alpha_i) : (\phi_i, \alpha_i) \in \Sigma, \omega \not\models \phi_i\} & \text{otherwise.} \end{cases}$$

where Ne is a reversing scale function, namely:

$$Ne(\alpha_i) \in L, Ne(1) = 0, Ne(0) = 1, Ne(Ne(\alpha_i)) = \alpha_i \text{ and } Ne(\alpha_i) > Ne(\alpha_j) \text{ iff}$$
$$\alpha_i < \alpha_j.$$

The syntactic inference in possibilistic logic is achieved using the following resolution principle:

$$(p \vee q, \alpha_i)$$
$$(\neg q \vee r, \alpha_j)$$
$$\overline{}$$
$$(p \vee r, min(\alpha_i, \alpha_j))$$

Then to check if a conclusion ψ is a possibilistic consequence of a possibilistic knowledge base Σ, denoted by $\Sigma \models_\pi \psi$, we proceed by refutation in the following way. First, we add $(\neg\psi, 1)$ to the knowledge base Σ. Then we compute, using the possibilistic resolution rule above, the highest degree associated with contradiction $\bot$. Then this degree is the certainty degree associated with ψ from Σ [4].

3.2   Qualitative Decision Tree Inference for Uncertain Observations

This sub-section shows how qualitative possibilistic logic [4] can be used for the inference in decision trees in presence of uncertain observations.

Standard decision trees only deal with completely certain information. Namely, all attributes uniquely determine the class to which the instance belongs, since there exists exactly one path, from the root node to the leaf class, which is applicable.

Nevertheless, in practice, attributes are not always precisely defined. Let $A_1, ..., A_n$ be different attributes of the problem. The instance to classify is described by a vector of possibility distributions $\vec{v} = (\pi_{A_1}, ..., \pi_{A_n})$. An attribute A_i is precisely defined if there exists exactly one value $a \in D_{A_i}$ such that $\pi_{A_i}(a) = 1$, and for all other values $a' \neq a, \pi_{A_i}(a') = 0$. A missing data regarding an attribute A_i, is represented by a uniform possibility distribution π_A (i.e., $\forall a \in D_A, \pi_A(a) = 1$).

At the *semantic* level, handling uncertain observations in possibilistic logic is achieved by combining conjunctively (using the minimum operator) the possibility distributions π_{A_i}'s with the possibility distribution π_Σ associated with decision tree (which represents the knowledge base). The possibility distribution π_Σ is a two layers one i.e., each interpretation has either 0 or 1 value. Let $a_1 \wedge ... \wedge a_n \wedge c_i$ be a given interpretation, then:

$$\pi(a_1 \wedge ... \wedge a_n \wedge c_i) = \begin{cases} 1 & \text{if there exists a path from the root to } c_i \text{ using } \{a_1 \wedge ... \wedge a_n\} \\ 0 & \text{otherwise.} \end{cases}$$

Then, the selection of the class(es) to which the instance $\vec{v} = (\pi_{A_1}, ..., \pi_{A_n})$ belongs to is defined following two steps:

– Combine $\pi_{A_1}, ..., \pi_{A_n}$ and π_{Σ} in a conjunctive way, namely compute:

$$\pi_{Result} = min(\pi_{A_1}, ..., \pi_{A_n}, \pi_{\Sigma}).$$

– Select class(es) c_i having a highest possibility degree in π_{Result}.

At the *syntactic* level, the uncertainty regarding an attribute A_i can also be represented by a possibilistic knowledge base Σ_{A_i}. Of course, Σ_{A_i} should be associated with π_{A_i} using definition of Sect. 3.1. Note that standard possibilistic logic only deals with binary variables, while generally attributes used in decision trees are not necessarily binary. In this case, the introduction of domain exclusion domain constraints is necessary. For instance, let us assume that the domain associated with an attribute A_i is $\{b_1, b_2, b_3\}$. Assume that the available information about A_i is: the value of A_1 can be either b_1 or b_2 (namely, b_3 is excluded), and b_1 is more plausible (with a degree α). These pieces of information are represented by: $\Sigma_{A_i} = \{(\neg b_1 \vee \neg b_2, 1), (\neg b_1 \vee \neg b_3, 1), (\neg b_2 \vee \neg b_3, 1), (b_1 \vee b_2 \vee b_3, 1), (b_1 \vee b_2, 1), (b_1, \alpha)\}$.

The first 4 formulas represent the exclusion domain constraints while the last 2 formulas encode the available information on A_i. It can be checked that Σ_{A_i} can be equivalently rewritten as : $\Sigma_{A_i} = \{(\neg b_3, 1), (\neg b_2, \alpha), (b_1 \vee b_2, 1), (b_1, \alpha)\}$, and that π_{A_i} is $\pi_{A_i}(b_1) = 1, \pi_{A_i}(b_2) = 1 - \alpha, \pi_{A_i}(b_3) = 0$.

The decision tree can also be immediately represented in possibilistic logic base Σ in the following way: if $(a_1(root), ..., a_n, c)$ is a path, then we add to the knowledge base the rule: $(a_1 \wedge ... \wedge a_n \Rightarrow c, 1)$.

Now, we can check that, given $\Sigma_{A_1}, ..., \Sigma_{A_n}$ and Σ, the possibilistic knowledge base associated to $\pi_r es$ is simply the union of knowledge bases $\Sigma_{A_1} \cup ... \cup \Sigma_{A_n} \cup \Sigma$. Therefore, an instance $\vec{v} = (\pi_{A_1}, ..., \pi_{A_n})$ belongs to a class c if c is a possibilistic consequence of $\Sigma_{A_1} \cup ... \cup \Sigma_{A_n} \cup \Sigma$.

In almost all fields where decision trees are applied and whenever uncertainty happens, the qualitative decision tree inference will be useful. An illustrative example on intrusion detection systems will be presented in Sect. 6. But first we briefly present what is an intrusion detection system and how decision trees can be used.

4   Intrusion Detection Systems

Intrusion in the context of information systems is regarded as a set of attempts to compromise a computer network resource security. There are two general approaches to intrusion detection (for an introductory work on intrusion detection systems, see [1]):

– *Anomaly Detection:* based on the detection of an anomaly in a user behaviour. The idea is that each user has a certain profile within the system that will not be changed a lot in time. Then, this profile is expected to be 'normal' and consequently any significant deviation from it will be considered as an anomaly.

– *Misuse Detection:* also named signature detection since in this case any intrusion can be described by its signature characterized by the values of its features.

Detecting intrusions is generally ensured by using the audit data generated by the operating system. This paper is more oriented to the anomaly detection approach.

The data used here are those proposed in the KDD'99 for intrusion detection [9] which are generally used for benchmarking intrusion detection problems. They set up an environment to collect TCP/IP dump raws from a host located on a simulated military network. Each TCP/IP connection is described by 41 discrete and continuous features and labeled as either normal, or as an attack, with exactly one specific attack type. Attacks fall into four main categories:

- *Denial of Service Attacks (DOS)* in which an attacker overwhelms the victim host with a huge number of requests. Such attacks are easy to perform and can cause a shutdown of the host or a significant slow in its performance (e.g. Pod, Teardrop, Neptune, Smurf).
- *Probing* in which an attacker attempts to gather useful information about machines and services available on the network in order to look for exploits (e.g. Portsweep, Saint, Satan, Mscan).
- *User to Root Attacks (U2R)* in which an attacker or a hacker tries to get the access rights from a normal host in order, for instance, to gain the root access to the system (e.g. Ftp-write, Imap, Guess_passwd, Phf).
- *Remote to User Attacks (R2L)* in which the intruder tries to exploit the system vulnerabilities in order to control the remote machine through the network as a local user (e.g. Pearl, Xterm, Ps, Rootkit).

The 41 features characterizing each connection are divided into *basic features* of individual TCP connections, *content features* within a connection suggested by domain knowledge, *time based* traffic features computed using a two-second time window and *host based* traffic features computed using a window of 100 connections used to characterize attacks that scan the hosts (or ports) using much larger time interval than two seconds. Some of these features are listed in Table 1.

5   Decision Trees for Intrusion Detection Systems

This section presents results on intrusion detection using standard decision trees of Quinlan [13]. Several experimentations will be performed on KDD'99 dataset.

5.1   Different Case Studies

We handle 10% of this dataset corresponding to 494019 training connections and 311029 testing connections. There exist several recent works on using decision trees on KDD'99 dataset [10]. However, experimental results presented here give a new perspective, in particular different levels of classification's results are considered. Indeed, we perform several experimentations according to three levels of attack granularities:

Table 1. List of features

Feature name	Description
Basic features of individual TCP connections	
A1 duration	length (number of seconds) of the connection
A2 protocol_type	type of the protocol, e.g. tcp, udp, etc.
A3 service	network service on the destination, e.g., http, telnet, etc.
A4 flag	normal or error status of the connection
A5 src_bytes	number of data bytes from source to destination
A6 dst_bytes	number of data bytes from destination to source
A7 land	1 if connection is from/to the same host/port; 0 otherwise
A8 wrong_fragment	number of "wrong" fragments
Content features within a connection suggested by domain knowledge	
A9 hot	number of "hot" indicators
A10 num_failed_logins	number of failed login attempts
A11 logged_in	1 if successfully logged in; 0 otherwise
A12 num_compromised	number of "compromised" conditions
A13 num_file_creations	number of file creation operations
A14 num_shells	number of shell prompts
Time based traffic features computed using a two-second time window	
A15 count	number of connections to the *same host*
A16 same_srv_rate	% of connections to the *same host* using the *same service*
Host-based traffic features computed using a window of 100 connections	
A17 dst_host_count	number of connections to the *same host*
A18 dst_host_srv_count	number of connections to the *same host* using the *same service*
A19 dst_host_diff_srv_rate	% of connections to the *same host* using *different services*
A20 dst_host_same_src_port_rate	% of connections to the *same host* having the same src port
A21 dst_host_srv_diff_host_rate	% of connections to the *same host* and *same service* using *different hosts*
A22 dst_host_srv_serror_rate	% of connections to the *same host* and *same service* having "SYN" errors
A23 dst_host_rerror_rate	% of connections to the *same host* having "REJ" errors

– *Whole-Attacks*: all attack classes presented by KDD dataset in addition to the normal situation.

– *Five-Classes*: the four attack categories (i.e. DOS, R2L, U2R, Probing). Note that there are 19.69% (resp. 79.24%, 0.23%, 0.01%, 0.83%) of normal (resp. DOS, R2L, U2R,Probing) training connections and 19.48% (resp. 73.90%, 5.21%, 0.07%, 1.34%) of normal (resp. DOS, R2L, U2R, Probing) testing connections.

– *Two-Classes*: i.e. Normal and Abnormal by grouping all attacks in the same class (i.e. Abnormal).

In the five-class and two-class cases, there are two strategies to gather results either before or after classification.

The evaluation of classification efficiency is based on the *Percent of Correct Classification* (PCC) of the instances belonging to the testing set.

$$PCC = \frac{\text{number of well classified instances}}{\text{number of classified instances}}$$

5.2   Experimental Results

Table 2 gives the PCC of the testing set according to the three levels of attack
granularities where in the five-class and two-class cases gathering is done before
classification. More precisely, in the five-class case we slightly modify the dataset
by grouping attacks belonging to the same attack category (i.e. DOS, R2L,
U2R or Probing) and in the two-class case we group them in a unique class i.e.
abnormal.

It is clear that in the three experimentations the PCC is almost the same and
it presents a good rate. This means that dealing with all attacks, specific categories or only one class, namely the abnormal one, do not affect the classification
quality using the decision tree technique.

Table 2. PCC's of the testing set

Two-classes	Five-classes	Whole-attacks
92.42%	92.21%	91.73%

In order to analyze misclassified connections, we have studied confusion matrices by focusing on normal connections over the abnormal ones, namely in
the whole-attack and five-class cases, we gather results regarding attacks in a
unique abnormal class after the classification procedure[1]. Induced results are
summarized in Table 3.

Table 3. Confusion matrix relative to the normal and abnormal classes (values between
parentheses are relative to gathering whole-attacks and five classes results into two
classes after classification)

CLASSIFIED AS →	Normal	Abnormal
Normal	**98.24%**	1.76%
(60593)	**(99.42%, 98.28%)**	(0.58%, 1.72%)
Abnormal	8.98%	**91.02%**
(250436)	(9.02%, 9.00%)	**(90.98%, 91.00%)**
PCC	92.42%	
	(92.62%, 92.42%)	

This table shows that normal connections are usually very well classified. It
also shows that for classifying normal instances, it is better to gather different
attacks in abnormal ones after classification using the initial dataset (i.e. containing the whole attacks) rather than before learning it (two-class or five-class
cases). This behaviour can be explained by the fact that each leaf in the decision

---

[1] The confusion matrices also provide the recall criterion, which can be read from the
diagonal of the matrix

Table 4. Confusion matrices relative to five classes (values between parentheses are relative to gathering whole-attacks results into five classes after classification)

CLASSIFIED AS →	Normal	DOS	R2L	U2R	Probing
Normal (60593)	**98.28%**	1.33%	0.02%	0.01%	0.36%
	(99.42%)	(0.15%)	(0.03%)	(0.01%)	(0.40%)
DOS (229853)	2.72%	**97.28%**	0.00%	0.00%	0.00%
	(2.67%)	**(96.87%)**	(0.00%)	(0.00%)	(0.46%)
R2L (16189)	93.79%	0.01%	**3.40%**	0.67%	2.13%
	(96.80%)	(0.00%)	**(3.04%)**	(0.03%)	(0.13%)
U2R (228)	91.67%	0.44%	2.63%	**3.51%**	1.75%
	(58.33%)	(0.44%)	(7.46%)	**(5.26%)**	(28.51%)
Probing (4166)	21.22%	3.77%	0.24%	0.00%	**74.77%**
	(15.70%)	(5.42%)	(0.00%)	(0.00%)	**(78.88%)**
PCC	92.21%				
	(92.18%)				

tree is labeled by the more probable class. So, the larger number of attack classes is, the biggest chance to have leaves labeled as normal class, and consequently most normal testing connections will be well classified.

Contrary to normal connections, abnormal ones are not always well classified as confirmed by PCC of abnormal instances given in Table 3 (even if the global PCC is high). Indeed, a thorough analysis of misclassified abnormal connections (see Table 4) shows that the U2R and R2L attacks in the testing set are always misclassified (only 3.51% (resp. 3.40%) of U2R (resp. R2L) connections are well-classified when we gather attacks before classification). This behaviour does not reflect the optimistic results obtained on the training data where 82.69% (resp. 98.93%) of U2R (resp. R2L) connections are well-classified. This is due to the fact that the proportions, in the training set, of U2R and R2L attacks are very low (0.01% for U2R and 0.23% for R2L).

In fact, within decision trees, when a class is presented by a low number of training instances, then it leads to a weak learning regarding this class and consequently to a misclassification of testing connections really belonging to it. Hence, we can have new testing instances really belonging to U2R and R2L attacks, but characterized by attributes' values which deviate from those characterizing these two classes in the training set. These instances are not already learned in the construction phase and their resulting class when applying the induced tree are generally wrong. To illustrate this, let us analyze the rule base relative to U2R induced from the decision tree:

- **R1:** if $A15 \leq 64$, $A22 \leq 0.03$, $A12 \leq 0$, $A8 \leq 0$, $A21 \leq 0.48$, $A19 \leq 0.91$, $A9 \leq 0$, $A20 \leq 0.99$, $A16 > 0.32$, $A4 = SF$, $A5 > 6$, $A14 \leq 0$, $A6 > 6$, $A5 \leq 36530$, $A13 \leq 0$, $A18 \leq 4$, $A3 = telnet$, $A6 \leq 1342$, $A1 > 20$ **then** $U2R$
- **R2:** if $A15 \leq 64$, $A22 \leq 0.03$, $A12 \leq 0$, $A8 \leq 0$, $A21 \leq 0.48$, $A19 \leq 0.91$, $A9 \leq 0$, $A20 \leq 0.99$, $A16 > 0.32$, $A4 = SF$, $A5 > 6$, $A14 \leq 0$, $A6 > 6$, $A5 \leq 36530$, $A13 > 0$, $A18 \leq 3$ **then** $U2R$

- **R3:** if $A15 \leq 64$, $A22 \leq 0.82$, $A12 \leq 0$, $A8 \leq 0$, $A21 \leq 0.48$, $A19 \leq 0.91$, $A9 \leq 0$, $A20 \leq 0.99$, $A16 > 0.32$, $A4 = SF$, $A5 > 6$, $A14 > 0$, $A3 = telnet$ then $U2R$
- **R4:** if $A15 \leq 64$, $A22 \leq 0.82$, $A12 \leq 0$, $A8 \leq 0$, $A21 \leq 0.48$, $A19 \leq 0.91$, $A9 \leq 0$, $A20 > 0.99$, $A5 \leq 19$, $A17 \leq 1$, $A2 = tcp$, $A7 = 0$, $A3 = ftp\_data$, $A4 = SF$ then $U2R$
- **R5:** if $A15 \leq 64$, $A22 \leq 0.82$, $A12 \leq 0$, $A8 \leq 0$, $A21 \leq 0.48$, $A19 \leq 0.91$, $A9 \leq 0$, $A20 > 0.99$, $A5 \leq 19$, $A17 > 1$, $A6 > 1$, $A3 = ftp\_data$, $A11 = 1$ then $U2R$
- **R6:** if $A15 \leq 64$, $A22 \leq 0.82$, $A12 \leq 0$, $A8 \leq 0$, $A21 \leq 0.48$, $A19 \leq 0.91$, $A9 > 0$, $A4 = SF$, $A5 \leq 132$, $A21 > 0.01$ then $U2R$
- **R7:** if $A15 \leq 64$, $A22 \leq 0.82$, $A12 \leq 0$, $A8 \leq 0$, $A21 \leq 0.48$, $A19 \leq 0.91$, $A9 > 0$, $A4 = SF$, $A5 \leq 132$, $A1 \leq 140$, $A18 \leq 2$, $A13 > 2$ then $U2R$
- **R8:** if $A15 \leq 64$, $A22 \leq 0.82$, $A12 \leq 0$, $A8 \leq 0$, $A21 \leq 0.48$, $A6 > 6$, $A23 \leq 0.45$, $A10 \leq 0$, $A5 \leq 1$ then $U2R$
- **R9:** if $A15 \leq 64$, $A22 \leq 0.82$ $A12 > 0$, $A5 \leq 10073$, $A6 > 0.09$, $A12 \leq 13$, $A3 = telnet$, $A6 \leq 6223$ then $U2R$
- **R10:** if $A15 > 64$, $A6 > 1$, $A18 \leq 69$, $A13 > 0$ then $U2R$

When analyzing the testing subset relative to U2R attacks, we firstly note that for the attribute $A15$ which is the root of the tree, all its corresponding values are less or equal than 64 which excludes the use of **R10**. Continuing analyzing the U2R testing connections, we remark that the majority should follow rules from **R1** to **R5** (187 of them satisfy $A15 \leq 64$, $A22 \leq 0.82$, $A12 \leq 0$, $A8 \leq 0$, $A21 \leq 0.48$, $A19 \leq 0.91$, $A9 \leq 0$). However, in all of these rules $A4$ should be equal to SF which is not the case in the majority of testing connections which implies their miss-classification since they do not satisfy any of the rules **R1** to **R10**. This can be explained by the fact that in the learning phase $A4$ appears with the value SF while in the majority of testing connections it takes the value REJ which never appears in the learning set with U2R attacks.

6   Qualitative Decision Trees for Intrusion Detection Systems

Different experimentations performed above suppose that the connections to classify are certainly known which is not always the case in the real TCP/IP traffic. Indeed, the used testing set corresponds to an Off line traffic and a more interesting task will be to classify connections On line. This supposes that at an instant t we should be able to classify a connection even if some of its characteristic attributes are partially known. Of course, the partially specified attributes are not always the same, and are generally different from one connection to another.

In such a case the use of qualitative decision trees presented in Sect. 3 seems to be appropriate since it allows the classification of uncertain connections. So what we have proposed may not only classify connections having some missing values but also those characterized by possibility distributions on their values.

Let us illustrate this with the decision tree (representing four classes namely N, S, P and T) given in Fig. 1.

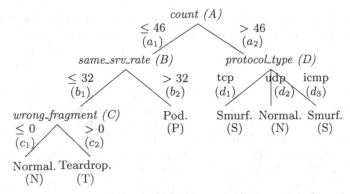

Fig. 1. A decision tree for intrusion detection

$$(a_1 \wedge b_1 \wedge c_1 \Rightarrow N, 1) \quad (a_1, 1)$$

$$(b_1 \wedge c_1 \Rightarrow N, 1) \quad (c_1, 1)$$

$$(b_1 \Rightarrow N, 1) \quad (b_1, Ne(\alpha))$$

$$(N, Ne(\alpha)) \quad (\neg N, 1)$$

$$(\bot, Ne(\alpha))$$

Fig. 2. Refutation proof for $(N, Ne(\alpha))$

Assume that the instance to classify is $\vec{v} = (\pi_A, \pi_B, \pi_C, \pi_D)$ with:

$$\pi_A = \begin{matrix} a_1 \\ a_2 \end{matrix} \begin{pmatrix} 1 \\ 0 \end{pmatrix}, \pi_B = \begin{matrix} b_1 \\ b_2 \end{matrix} \begin{pmatrix} 1 \\ \alpha_2 \end{pmatrix}, \pi_C = \begin{matrix} c_1 \\ c_2 \end{matrix} \begin{pmatrix} 1 \\ 0 \end{pmatrix}, \pi_D = \begin{matrix} d_1 \\ d_2 \\ d_3 \end{matrix} \begin{pmatrix} 1 \\ \alpha_2 \\ 0 \end{pmatrix}$$

Namely A and C are precisely described, while there are some uncertainty on B and D. The knowledge bases associated to $\pi_A, \pi_B, \pi_C, \pi_D$ and to the DT are: $\Sigma_A = \{(a_1, 1)\}, \Sigma_B = \{(b_1, Ne(\alpha_2))\}, \Sigma_C = \{(c_1, 1)\}, \Sigma_D = \{(d_1 \vee d_2, 1), (d_1, Ne(\alpha_2))\}, \Sigma = \{(a_1 \wedge b_1 \wedge c_1 \Rightarrow N, 1), (a_1 \wedge b_1 \wedge c_2 \Rightarrow T, 1), (a_1 \wedge b_2 \Rightarrow P, 1), (a_2 \wedge (d_1 \vee d_3) \Rightarrow S, 1), (a_2 \wedge d_2 \Rightarrow N, 1)\}$.

To these knowledge bases, we should add the following domain exclusion constraints: $(d_1 \vee d_2 \vee d_3, 1), (\neg d_1 \vee \neg d_2, 1), (\neg d_1 \vee \neg d_3, 1), (\neg d_2 \vee \neg d_3, 1)$.

From these knowledge bases, we can check that: $\Sigma \cup \Sigma_A \cup \Sigma_B \cup \Sigma_C \cup \Sigma_D \models_\pi$ $(N, Ne(\alpha_2))$, where $\models_\pi$ is the possibilistic logic inference. Indeed, let us add $(\neg N, 1)$ to the knowledge base, namely let us assume that the instance does not belong to the *normal* class. The following refutation shows that there is a contradiction and hence provides the certainty degree of N which is $Ne(\alpha)$.

No one of the other classes, i.e. (S, T, P) can be inferred with a weight greater than $Ne(\alpha_2)$. Hence, $\vec{v}$ will be classified as a normal connection. In this example, there was no problem in classifying the instance $\vec{v}$. Assume now that we have the following instance $\vec{v'} = (\pi_A, \pi_B, \pi_C, \pi_D)$ to classify, with:

$$\pi_A = \begin{matrix} a_1 \\ a_2 \end{matrix} \begin{pmatrix} 0 \\ 1 \end{pmatrix}, \pi_B = \begin{matrix} b_1 \\ b_2 \end{matrix} \begin{pmatrix} 1 \\ 0 \end{pmatrix}, \pi_C = \begin{matrix} c_1 \\ c_2 \end{matrix} \begin{pmatrix} 1 \\ 0 \end{pmatrix}, \pi_D = \begin{matrix} d_1 \\ d_2 \\ d_3 \end{matrix} \begin{pmatrix} 1 \\ 1 \\ 0 \end{pmatrix}$$

In this instance, all variables are precisely defined, except D where the only available information is that the protocol type is not an icmp.

The knowledge base associated to $\pi_A, ..., \pi_D$ and to the decision tree are:

$$\Sigma_A = \{(\neg a_1, 1)\}, \Sigma_B = \{(b_1, 1)\}, \Sigma_C = \{(c_1, 1)\} \Sigma_D = \{(d_1 \vee d_2, 1)\},$$
$$\Sigma = \{(a_1 \wedge b_1 \wedge c_1 \Rightarrow N, 1), (a_1 \wedge b_1 \wedge c_2 \Rightarrow T, 1), (a_1 \wedge b_2 \Rightarrow P, 1), (a_2 \wedge (d_1 \vee d_3) \Rightarrow S, 1), (a_2 \wedge d_2 \Rightarrow N, 1)\}.$$

Of course, we also add the domain exclusion constraints as above. From these knowledge bases, we can check that no class can be inferred with some certainty. The only thing that can be inferred is: $(S \vee N, 1)$, which expresses the fact that the instance $\overrightarrow{v}$ certainly belongs to either Normal class or Smurf class. This result is satisfactory. Possibilistic logic refuses to make arbitrary choices between these two classes, which is not the case when using standard decision trees. Another advantage of using possibilistic is the fact that it is incremental in the sense that the knowledge base can be easily updated upon the arrival of the new information. This is particularly useful since the value of several attributes becomes more and more precise with the time, and are only completely defined at the end of connections.

7   Conclusion

There are two main contributions in this paper. The first one is an extension of decision trees to classify instances with uncertain or missing attributes, in a possibilistic logic framework. This extension avoids arbitrary classifications of instances in partial ignorance situations. Handling uncertain observations is very important in intrusion detection systems. Indeed, a complete description of all attributes is only possible when connections end up. This can be too late to react, and hence it is very recommended to provide plausible classification from missing data. The second contribution concerns the use of decision trees in intrusion detection systems. The different experimental results presented in this paper are very encouraging. This is particularly true when only focusing on normal/abnormal connections. Indeed, a best strategy allows us to have until 99.42% of normal connections as well classified, and until 91.02% of abnormal connections as well classified. A further work will be to test experimentally qualitative decision trees on the intrusion detection problem and make comparisons with other algorithms.

References

1. Axelsson, S.: Intrusion detection systems: a survey and taxonomy, Technical report 99–15, March 2000.
2. Breiman, L., Friedman, J.H., Olshen, R.A., Stone, C.J.: Classification and regression trees, Monterey, CA: Wadsworth & Brooks, 1984.
3. Denoeux T., Skarstein-Bjanger M.: Induction of decision trees for partially classified data, Proceedings of the IEEE International Conference on Systems, Man, and Cybernetics, Nashville, USA, 2923–2928, 2000.
4. Dubois, D., Lang, J., Prade, H.: Possibilistic logic. In Handbook on Logic in Artificial Intelligence and Logic Programming, 3, 439–513, 1994.
5. Elouedi Z., Mellouli K., Smets P.: Belief decision trees: Theoretical foundations, International Journal of Approximate Reasoning 28, 91–124, 2001.
6. Hullermeier E., Possibilistic induction in decision-tree learning, ECML'02, 2002.
7. Michie, D., Spiegelhalter, D.J., Taylor, C.C.: Machine learning of rules and trees. In machine Learning. Neural and statistical Classification. Ellis Horwood, 1994.
8. Porras, P.A., Neumann., P.G.: EMERALD: Event monitoring enabling responses to anomalous live disturbances. In Proceedings of the 20th National Information Systems Security Conference, 353–365, 1997.
9. http://kdd.ccs.uci.edu/databases/kddcup99/task.html.
10. Portier, P., Froment-Curtil J.: Data mining techniques for intrusion detection, Technical report, University of Texas at Austin, Spring, 2000.
11. Quinlan, J.R.: Induction of decision trees, Machine Learning 1, 1–106, 1986.
12. Quinlan, J.R.: Probabilistic decision trees, Machine Learning, Vol. 3, Chap. 5, Morgan Kaufmann, 267–301, 1990.
13. Quinlan, J.R.: C4.5: Programs for machine learning. Morgan Kaufmann San Mateo Ca, 1993.
14. Mingers, J.: An empirical comparison of selection measures for decision tree induction. Machine learning, 4, 227–243, 1989.
15. Mitchell, T.M.: Decision tree learning. Chapter 3 of Machine Learning, Co-published by the MIT Press and the McGraw-Hill Compagnies, Inc., 1997.
16. Fayyad, U.M., Irani, K.B.: On the handling of continuous-valuues attributes in decision tree generation. Machine Learning, 8, 87–102, 1992

Multi-valued Conditional Events Avoid Lewis' Triviality Result

Tania Paneni and Romano Scozzafava*

Dipartimento Metodi e Modelli Matematici, Università "La Sapienza"
Via Scarpa, 16 – 00161 Roma (Italy)
{romscozz,paneni}@dmmm.uniroma1.it

Abstract. The concept of conditional event dealt with here is that given by Coletti and Scozzafava in a series of paper: a detailed account of the relevant theory is in their book *"Probabilistic Logic in a Coherent Setting"*, Kluwer (2002). In this paper, our aim is to show that **relying on this definition** many of the (putative) inconsistencies and flaws concerning this concept disappear. In particular, the well-known Lewis' triviality principles can be looked on, in this framework, under a different perspective, also due to the circumstance that the concept of "indicative conditionals" (as put by Lewis, and also by Adams) is **a very particular case** of this general concept of conditional event. A crucial role is played, in our approach, by conditional events of probability 0 and 1.

1 Introduction

Our aim is to show that, relying on the concept of *conditional event* as introduced by Coletti and Scozzafava in [2], many of the (putative) inconsistencies and flaws concerning this concept disappear.

In particular, the well-known Lewis' triviality principles (discussed in [12] and partly reshuffled in [13]) can be looked on, in our framework, under a different perspective, also due to the circumstance that the concept of "indicative conditionals" (as put by Lewis, and also by Adams [1]) is a very particular case of the concept of conditional event given in [2].

This concept plays a central role also for the probabilistic reasoning. It generalizes (or better, in a sense, it gives up) the idea of de Finetti [6] of looking at a conditional event $E|H$, with $H \neq \emptyset$ (the *impossible* event), as a three-valued logical entity (*true* when both E and H are true, *false* when H is true and E is false, "undetermined" when H is false) by letting the third value *suitably depend on the given ordered pair* (E, H) and not being just an undetermined *common value* for all pairs.

It turns out that this function can be seen as a measure of the degree of belief in the conditional event $E|H$, which under "natural" conditions reduces to the conditional probability $P(E|H)$, in its most general sense related to the concept of *coherence*, and satisfying the classic axioms as given by de Finetti in [7].

---

* Corresponding author

T.D. Nielsen and N.L. Zhang (Eds.): ECSQARU 2003, LNAI 2711, pp. 432–439, 2003.

We will refer to a suitable multi-valued logic (for an expository paper on this subject, see [14]) with *partial* (and truth–functional) connectives, where the truth-values have a "logical meaning" in terms of a betting interpretation. This approach is explained in detail in [3], while a formal axiomatic account will be given in a forthcoming paper [8].

We stress that this approach neither refers to Boolean-like structures, nor tries to define logical operations for *every* pair of conditional events. So it clearly differs from (and is much simpler than) other well-known interpretations existing in the relevant literature, such as, e.g., those of Dubois and Prade [9] and Goodman and Nguyen [10] (by the way, also these authors examine critically Lewis' results).

As a final comment, let us mention that, according to an anonymous referee, a "very similar solutions to Lewis' triviality results" appeared in "Reasoning over Impossible Worlds" by A. Lopez-Ortiz, Journal of Computing and Information, Vol 1, 1995 (and also in International Conference on Computing and Informatics, ICCI, 1994). We checked this issue (and **all** the others) of that Journal (and also the list of papers of 1994 ICCI Conference), and we were not able to find the aforementioned paper. Nevertheless we have found a working paper with the same title on the web site of the author: its content *has nothing to do* with our approach, in which conditioning with respect to $H = \emptyset$ (the impossible "world") *makes no sense*. We allow instead (as repeatedly explained in the paper) conditioning with respect to **not impossible** events of probability zero (see Sects. 4 and 5), which is definitely a quite different stuff. Last (but not least) in that paper Lewis' triviality principle is not challenged!

2   Events

An *event* can be singled-out by a (nonambiguous) statement E, that is a (Boolean) *proposition* that can be either *true* or *false* (corresponding to the two "values" 1 or 0 of the *indicator* I_E of E).

Two particular cases are the *certain* event Ω (that is always true) and the *impossible* event $\emptyset$ (that is always false): notice that Ω is the contrary of $\emptyset$, and vice versa. Notice that **only in these two particular cases the relevant propositions correspond to an *assertion***.

To make an assertion, we need to say something extra-logical or concerning the existence of some logical relation, such as "You know that E is false" (so that $E = \emptyset$).

The "logic of certainty" deals with TRUE and FALSE as final, and **not asserted**, possible answers, while *with respect to a given state of information* there exist, as alternatives concerning an event, besides that of being *possible*, also those of being *certain* or *impossible*.

Probability is a function (defined on a Boolean algebra of events) which satisfies **the usual and classic properties**, *i.e.*: its range is between zero and one (these two extreme values being assumed by – **but not kept only for** – the *impossible* and the *certain* event, respectively), and it is additive for mutually exclusive events.

Notice that (as it is well-known) an *impossible* event (that is, an event **known to be false**) has probability 0, but NOT conversely (so that we may have many **possible** events whose probability is zero). Analogous remarks can be stated for a *certain* event (that is, an event **known to be true**), which may not be the **only** one having probability 1.

3   Conditional Events

Are conditional events truth valued? If "truth valued" means **two-valued** (i.e., Boolean), the answer (in agreement with Lewis) is certainly "NO". But if we refer to a "multi-valued" logic, **conditional events** can be seen as truth valued, in the following sense (in terms of a betting scheme), which extends the well-known interpretation of the probability $P(E)$ of an **event** E as the amount paid to bet on E, with the proviso of receiving an amount 1 if E is true (the bet is won) or 0 if E is false (the bet is lost), so that

"the indicator I_E is just the amount got back by paying $P(E)$ in a bet on E"

Consider now a *conditional* bet on $E|H$: an amount $t(E, H)$ is paid to bet on $E|H$ getting, *when H is true*, either an amount 1 if also E is true (the bet is won) or an amount 0 if E is false (the bet is lost), and *getting back the amount $t(E, H)$ if H turns out to be false* (the bet is called off).

In short, the *truth-value $T(E|H)$* of a conditional event $E|H$ – that reduces, for an (unconditional) event E, to the *indicator $I_E = T(E|\Omega)$* – is introduced in the following way:

"the value of $T(E|H)$ is just the amount got back
by paying $t(E, H)$ in a bet on $E|H$",

so that it can be written (assuming, for any given H, that $t(\cdot, H)$ *is not identically equal to zero*),

$$T(E|H) = 1 \cdot I_{E \wedge H} + 0 \cdot I_{E^c \wedge H} + t(E, H) \cdot I_{H^c}.$$

In other words, a conditional event $E|H$ (or, better, its truth-value) can be seen as a *discrete random quantity*

$$T(E|H) = Y = \sum_{k=1}^{\nu} y_k I_{E_k},$$

taking $\nu = 3$, $E_1 = E \wedge H$, $E_2 = E^c \wedge H$, $E_3 = H^c$, and $y_1 = 1$, $y_2 = 0$, $y_3 = t(E, H)$.

The (ordered) pair (E, H) is called the *Boolean support* of the conditional event $E|H$.

More details are in the book [3], Chapter 10, where it is also shown that, if we have an *arbitrary* family $\mathcal{C}$ of conditional events $E|H$ and consider the relevant set $\mathcal{T}$ of random quantities $T(E|H)$, this can be endowed with two *partial* operations (sum and product) in such a way that, by requiring the closure of these operations inside this particular class $\mathcal{T}$, it turns out that the map $t(E, H)$ satisfies the classic de Finetti–Popper axioms of a *conditional probability*:

(i) $t(H, H) = 1$,

(ii) $t\Big((E \vee A), H\Big) = t(E, H) + t(A, H)$, for $E \wedge A \wedge H = \emptyset$,

(iii) $t\Big((E \wedge A), H\Big) = t(E, H) \cdot t\Big(A, (E \wedge H)\Big)$.

So the function $t(E, H)$ can be denoted also by the usual symbol $P(E|H)$.

The multi-valued logic associated with a given family $\mathcal{C} = \{E_i|H_i\}_{i \in I}$ of conditional events reduces to a two-valued one when $H_i = \Omega$ for all H_i, $i \in I$ (i.e. when all **conditional events** reduce to (Boolean) **events**).

It is important to stress that the latter condition is sufficient, but not necessary to have a family of *two-valued conditional events* (see the next section).

4   Conditional Probabilities Equal to 0 or 1

Consider a family $\mathcal{C}$ such that, for any $E_i|H_i \in \mathcal{C}$, either $t(E_i, H_i) = 1$ or $t(E_i, H_i) = 0$. In the first case a conditional event $E|H$ can be seen as the event $H^c \vee E$, and in the second case as the event $E \wedge H$ (as follows easily by checking the truth values of $E|H$ and of the aforementiond corresponding (Boolean) events).

In particular, if we **assert** $H^c \vee E = \Omega$, then $H \subseteq E$ (E logically implies H), so we certainly have $t(E, H) = 1$; if we **assert** $E \wedge H = \emptyset$, then we certainly have $t(E, H) = 0$ (in the latter two cases the conditional event $E|H$ is actually even **one-valued**).

Notice that for situations which are different, respectively, from the trivial ones $E \wedge H = \emptyset$ and $H \subseteq E$, the extreme values 0 and 1 admit suitable interpretations (for the connections with the concept of *coherence*, see the book [3]). In particular, a deepening of the case $P(E|H) = 1$ leads to a "natural" treatment of the *default reasoning*: see [4], [5].

Moreover, $P(E) = 1$ does not imply $P(E|H) = 1$, as in the usual framework, where $P(E) = 1$ and (the necessary assumption) $P(H) > 0$ imply $E \wedge H \neq \emptyset$. We can take instead $P(H) = 0$ (the *conditioning* event H - which *must* be a *possible* one - may in fact have *zero probability*, since in the assignment of $P(E|H)$ we are driven only by the relevant axioms); then we may have *logical relations between H and E* (in particular, $E \wedge H = \emptyset$, and so $P(E|H) = 0$).

On the other hand, it is clearly possible (as it can be seen by a simple application of Theorem 4 of [3], that characterizes coherent assignments of conditional probability) to assess *coherently* $P(E|H) = p$ for every value $p \in [0, 1]$. In conclusion, **a probability equal to 1 *can be, in our framework, updated*** (so that the same is true, obviously, for a probability equal to 0).

5   Lewis' Triviality Principles

The argument of Lewis to establish his triviality results is essentially based on proving that, if we apply to a conditional event $E|H$ the following classic probability formula

$$P(A) = P(E)P(A|E) + P(E^c)P(A|E^c)$$

(taking $A = E|H$ and assuming that both $P(H \wedge E)$ and $P(H \wedge E^c)$ are *positive*), we get $P(E|H) = P(E)$ for any such pairs of events (i.e., stochastic independence of H and E), since, denoting $P(A|B) = P_B(A)$, *closure under condizionalisation* requires $P_H(A|B) = P(A|B \wedge H)$.

Of course, these positivity assumptions are required by the fact that Lewis assumes the usual definition of conditional probability, in the sense that $E|H$ is looked on as an object such that, for any probability function P and for any events H and E, with $P(H) > 0$,

$$P(E|H) = \frac{P(E \wedge H)}{P(H)} \ . \tag{1}$$

Instead in our framework, due to the *direct* assignment of $P(E|H)$ as a whole, the knowledge (or the assessment) of the "joint" and "marginal" unconditional probabilities $P(E \wedge H)$ and $P(H)$ is not required (so that, as already observed at the end of Sect. 4, we may have $P(H) = 0$).

Then Lewis' interpretation of a conditional event (called by him "indicative conditional") is (in agreement with Adams) a very restrictive one. The (putative) lack of $E|H$ of being truth-valued (in fact they mean *non-Boolean*, due to the fact that multi-valued logics are not taken into consideration) leads Lewis and Adams *to deal with a conditional event* **only** *through its conditional probability* (in the classic sense) $P(E|H)$.

Their starting point is that *assertability* of an event E is associated to the requirement that $P(E)$ is "sufficiently close to 1" (since *the value 1 is kept only for the certain event*), so resorting to a kind of "probabilistic transform" of truth assignment (where "highly probable" is substituted throughout for the word "true").

For conditional events they adopt a similar interpretation, linked to the requirement of "high probability"; moreover they claim (as a soundness criterion for inferences) that it should not be possible for a premise H to be probable while the conclusion E is improbable.

The first requirement limits the consideration of conditional events only to situations corresponding to the so-called *default logic*, but with the second requirement what is considered is in fact a very particular case of this theory.

In this (very restrictive) framework, a *trivial language* is (using our notation and terminology) a family of events containing only Ω and $\emptyset$, and Lewis shows (*first triviality result*) that any language (i.e., family of events) equipped with a conditional event – i.e., an object satisfying (1) – is a *trivial* language.

The *second triviality result* (in Lewis's framework, but still using our terminology) is the following: if a class of probability assignments (on a given family of events) is closed under conditionalizing, then the family cannot be equipped with conditional events, unless the class consists entirely of trivial probability functions, i.e. those never assigning *positive* probability to more than two incompatible events.

6 A Counterexample

Given events E_1, H_1, E_2, H_2, with $E_2 \wedge H_1 = \emptyset$, $E_1 \wedge H_2 = \emptyset$ and

$$P(E_1 \wedge H_1) = P(E_2 \wedge H_2) = \frac{1}{4},$$

$$P(E_1 \wedge H_1^c \wedge E_2^c) = P(E_2 \wedge H_2^c \wedge E_1^c) = \frac{1}{6},$$

$$P(E_1 \wedge E_2) = P(E_1^c \wedge E_2^c \wedge H_1^c \wedge H_2^c) = \frac{1}{12},$$

consider the family of conditional events

$$\mathcal{C} = \{E_1|H_1 , E_2|H_2 , E_1^c|H_1 , E_2^c|H_2\}.$$

We have $t(E_1, H_1) = t(E_2, H_2) = 1$, $t(E_1^c, H_1) = t(E_2^c, H_2) = 0$.

Moreover, the five pairwise incompatible events of the family

$$\mathcal{E} = \{E_1 \wedge H_1 , E_2 \wedge H_2 , E_1 \wedge H_1^c \wedge E_2^c , E_1 \wedge E_2 , E_2 \wedge H_2^c \wedge E_1^c\}$$

have positive probability, and

$$t(E_i, H_i) = P(E_i|H_i) = 1 \neq P(E_i) = \frac{1}{2},$$

$$t(E_i^c, H_i) = P(E_i^c|H_i) = 0 \neq P(E_i^c) = \frac{1}{2}.$$

Notice that we can consider as "closed under conditionalising" (to use Lewis' terminology) the class made up by $\mathcal{E}$ and the initially given four events E_1, H_1, E_2, H_2, since all possible conditioning events have positive probability.

So in this framework **Lewis' first and second triviality results do not hold**.

In his second paper [13] Lewis modifies his interpretation of "closed under conditionalising", considering only conditioning with respect to a given finite partition: our example needs only a slight modification, by introducing the partition whose elements are those of $\mathcal{E}$ plus the contrary of their disjunction, and then allowing conditioning only with respect to these six events.

7 Further (and Final) Comments

A further specific features of our approach is that, contrary to what is usually emphasized in the literature when a conditional probability $P(E|H)$ is taken into account (i.e., that $P(\cdot|H)$ *is a probability for any given* H, a very restrictive – and misleading – view of conditional probability, corresponding trivially to just a modification of the so-called "sample space" Ω), the conditioning event H is instead regarded as a "variable", i.e. the "status" of H in $E|H$ is not just that of something representing a given *fact*, but that of an (uncertain) *event* (like E) for which the knowledge of its truth value is not required (so that H is always looked on as an *assumed* proposition).

Then, due to this general meaning and interpretation of conditioning, Jeffrey's generalized conditioning [11], introduced by Lewis in his second paper [13], is not needed.

We recall in fact that Jeffrey's conditioning is based on an argument (that *does not apply to our framework*) of this kind (again, our notation and terminology): the usual updating from $P(E)$ to $P(E|H)$ is limited to H *representing a set of certainties*, while in many situations you (the expert) may claim to be less than certain that H is actually true. Then Jeffrey's claim is to consider in turn H as an *information* (with respect to a suitable partition of Ω) *regarding its probability*: for details, see [11], but what should be clear is that in our framework we can challenge the above argument. For a deepening concerning *assumed* or *asserted* propositions, see Sect. 18.6 of [3].

References

1. Adams, E.: The Logic of Conditionals. Reidel, Dordrecht (1975).
2. Coletti, G., Scozzafava, R.: Conditioning and Inference in Intelligent Systems. Soft Computing **3** (1999) 118–130.
3. Coletti, G., Scozzafava, R.: Probabilistic logic in a coherent setting. Trends in Logic, n.15, Kluwer, Dordrecht (2002).
4. Coletti, G., Scozzafava, R., Vantaggi, B.: Coherent Conditional Probability as a Tool for Default Reasoning. In: Proc. IPMU 2002, Annecy, France (2002) 1663–1670.
5. Coletti, G., Scozzafava, R., Vantaggi, B.: Default Logic in a Coherent Setting. In: Benferhat, S., Giunchiglia, E. (eds.): Proc. 9th International Workshop on Non-Monotonic Reasoning, NMR'2002, Toulouse, France (2002) 275–282.
6. de Finetti, B.: La logique de la probabilité. In: Actes du Congrès International de Philosophie Scientifique, Paris 1935, Hermann **IV** (1936) 1–9.
7. de Finetti, B.: Sull'impostazione assiomatica del calcolo delle probabilità. Annali Univ. Trieste **19** (1949) 3–55. (Engl. transl.: Ch.5 in: Probability, Induction, Statistics, Wiley, London, 1972)
8. Di Nola, A., Scozzafava, R.: Partial Conditional Spaces (2003), to appear.
9. Dubois, D., Prade, H.: Conditional Objects as Nonmonotonic Consequence Relationships. IEEE Transactions on Systems, Man, and Cybernetics **24** (1994) 1724–1740.

10. Goodman, I. R., Nguyen, H. T.: Mathematical foundations of conditionals and their probabilistic assignments. International Journal of Uncertainty, Fuzziness and Knowledge-Based System **3** (1995) 247–339.
11. Jeffrey, R.C.: The logic of decision. McGraw-Hill, New York (1965).
12. Lewis, D.: Probability of conditionals and conditional probabilities. The Philosophical Review **85** (1976) 297–315.
13. Lewis, D.: Probability of conditionals and conditional probabilities II. The Philosophical Review **95** (1986) 581–589.
14. Panti, G.: Multi-valued Logics. In: Gabbay, D.M., Smets, Ph. (eds.): Handbook of Defeasible Reasoning and Uncertainty Management Systems, Vol.1, Kluwer, Dordrecht (1998) 25–74.

Solving Semantic Problems with Odd-Length Cycles in Argumentation

Pietro Baroni and Massimiliano Giacomin

Università di Brescia
Dipartimento di Elettronica per l'Automazione
Via Branze 38, I-25123 Brescia, Italy
{baroni,giacomin}@ing.unibs.it

Abstract. In the context of Dung's abstract framework for argumentation, two main semantics have been considered to assign a defeat status to arguments: the grounded semantics and the preferred semantics. While the two semantics agree in most situations, there are cases where the preferred semantics appears to be more powerful. However, we notice that the preferred semantics gives rise to counterintuitive results in some other cases, related to the presence of odd-length cycles in the attack relation between arguments. To solve these problems, we propose a new semantics which preserves the desirable properties of the preferred semantics, while correctly dealing with odd-length cycles. We check the behavior of the proposed semantics in a number of examples and discuss its relationships with both grounded and preferred semantics.

1 Introduction

Argumentation theory is a framework for practical and uncertain reasoning which has received a great deal of attention in several application areas, such as the realization of intelligent autonomous agents [1], automated negotiation in multi-agent systems [2] and defeasible reasoning [3]. In a nutshell, common-sense reasoning dealing with incomplete and uncertain information is modeled as the process of constructing and comparing arguments for propositions. The construction of arguments proceeds, from a given set of premises, by chaining rules of inference which may represent just provisional reasons for their conclusions. Due to the uncertainty affecting both premises and rules of inference, it may well be the case that different arguments support contradictory conclusions, therefore the core problem consists in computing the *defeat status* of the arguments, namely in determining which ones of them emerge undefeated from conflict: their conclusions are the most credible ones and are considered as justified, while other arguments, being defeated in the conflict, are rejected.

In order to analyze and compare different kinds of *semantics* underlying the defeat status computation, Dung [4] has proposed an abstract framework where arguments are simply conceived as the elements of a set, whose origin is not specified, and the interaction between them is represented by a binary relation of *attack*: this way, the current set of arguments can be represented by means of

T.D. Nielsen and N.L. Zhang (Eds.): ECSQARU 2003, LNAI 2711, pp. 440–451, 2003.

a directed graph, called *defeat graph* in [1]. Thus, an argumentation semantics can be introduced in a declarative way by defining what arguments are justified within a generic defeat graph. As pointed out in [5], this definition can follow two alternative approaches, namely a unique-status approach or a multiple-status approach. In the first approach, the defeat status of the arguments is defined in such a way that there is always exactly one possible way to assign them a status. This approach is adopted e.g. in the argumentation system introduced in [1], and is represented by the *grounded semantics* in Dung's framework. On the other hand, in a multiple-status approach several *extensions* are identified. Roughly, an extension is a set of arguments which do not conflict among them and which attack their attackers. An argument is considered as justified if it belongs to all extensions. This is the approach adopted e.g. in [6,7,3], and in Dung's framework is captured by the *preferred semantics*.

It has been proved in [4] that the preferred semantics "agrees" with the grounded semantics in those arguments that the latter considers as definitely justified or rejected. On the other hand, the preferred semantics appears to be more powerful with respect to the grounded semantics, in that it is sometimes able to discriminate some of the arguments that are left undecided by the grounded semantics [8].

After recalling concepts and definitions about argumentation semantics in Sect. 2, we point out in Sect. 3 that the preferred semantics improperly deals with odd-length cycles in the defeat graph and we identify some examples where this limitation gives rise to counter-intuitive defeat status assignments. To solve these problems, we propose in Sect. 4 a new semantics which preserves the desirable properties of the preferred semantics, while correctly dealing with odd-length cycles. In Sect. 5, the relationships with grounded and preferred semantics are investigated. Finally, Sect. 6 concludes the paper.

2   The Grounded and Preferred Semantics

In the abstract framework proposed by Dung [4], the primitive notion is that of *argumentation framework*:

Definition 1. *An argumentation framework is a pair* AF $=< \mathcal{A}, \rightarrow >$, *where* $\mathcal{A}$ *is a set of arguments and* $\rightarrow$ *is a binary relation of 'attack' between them.*

It should be noticed that this definition is generic with respect to the interpretation of $\mathcal{A}$, which is not specified. In any case, we assume $\mathcal{A}$ to be finite, as it is necessarily the case when considering a *real* reasoner.

In the following, nodes that attack a given $\alpha \in \mathcal{A}$ are called *defeaters* of α, and form a set denoted as parents(α). If parents(α) $= \emptyset$, then α is called an *initial* node. Following Pollock [1] we define the grounded semantics inductively (an alternative fixed-point definition is given and shown to be equivalent in [4]):

Definition 2. *Given an argumentation framework* AF $=< \mathcal{A}, \rightarrow>$, *we define for all* $i \geq 0$ *the sets* $\mathcal{A}_i \subseteq \mathcal{A}$ *as follows:*

$$\mathcal{A}_i = \begin{cases} \mathcal{A} & \text{if } i = 0 \\ \{\alpha \in \mathcal{A} \mid \nexists \beta \in \mathcal{A}_{i-1} : \beta \rightarrow \alpha\} & \text{if } i > 0 \end{cases}$$

Definition 3. *Given an argumentation framework* AF $=< \mathcal{A}, \rightarrow>$, *the set of* undefeated, defeated *and* provisionally defeated *arguments are respectively defined as follows:*

- $U_{\mathcal{G}}(\text{AF}) = \{\alpha \in \mathcal{A} \mid \exists m : \forall i \geq m \ \alpha \in \mathcal{A}_i\}$
- $D_{\mathcal{G}}(\text{AF}) = \{\alpha \in \mathcal{A} \mid \exists m : \forall i \geq m \ \alpha \notin \mathcal{A}_i\}$
- $P_{\mathcal{G}}(\text{AF}) = \{\alpha \in \mathcal{A} \mid \forall m \ \exists i \geq m : \alpha \in \mathcal{A}_i \wedge \exists j \geq m : \alpha \notin \mathcal{A}_j\}$

The idea is that an undefeated argument should be believed given the current set of arguments $\mathcal{A}$, a defeated argument should not be believed, while a provisionally defeated argument is controversial, thus it should not be believed but it should retain the potential to prevent other arguments to be justified. This is shown in the following examples.

Example 1. With reference to the argumentation framework AF$_1$ shown in Fig. 1, it is easy to see that α belongs to $\mathcal{A}_i$ for all $i \geq 0$, since it has no defeaters, therefore α is undefeated. As a consequence, $\forall i \geq 1 \ \beta \notin \mathcal{A}_i$, therefore β is defeated. This entails in turn that $\forall i \geq 2$, $\gamma \in \mathcal{A}_i$, therefore γ is undefeated.

Example 2. With reference to the argumentation framework AF$_2$ of Fig. 1, it is easy to see that, for all $k \geq 0$, both α and β belong to $\mathcal{A}_{2k}$ but don't belong to $\mathcal{A}_{2k+1}$, therefore they are provisionally defeated. This alternation of levels is inherited by γ, which turns out to be provisionally defeated as well.

$$\text{AF}_1 \qquad\qquad\qquad \text{AF}_2$$

Fig. 1. Two different chains

In the context of the preferred semantics, the notion of 'defence' is introduced by the following definitions:

Definition 4. *Given an argumentation framework* AF $=< \mathcal{A}, \rightarrow>$, *a set* $S \subseteq \mathcal{A}$ *is* conflict-free *if and only if* $\nexists \alpha, \beta \in S$ *such that* $\alpha \rightarrow \beta$.

Definition 5. *Given an argumentation framework* AF $=< \mathcal{A}, \rightarrow>$, *a set* $S \subseteq \mathcal{A}$ *is* admissible *if and only if* S *is conflict-free and* $\forall \alpha \in S$, *if* $\exists \beta \in \mathcal{A}$ *such that* $\beta \rightarrow \alpha$ *then* $\exists \gamma \in S$ *such that* $\gamma \rightarrow \beta$.

Accordingly, a preferred extension is defined as a maximal set which is able to defend all its elements:

Definition 6. *Given an argumentation framework* AF $=< \mathcal{A}, \rightarrow >$, *a preferred extension of* AF *is a maximal (with respect to set inclusion) admissible set* $S \subseteq \mathcal{A}$. *The set of preferred extensions will be denoted as* $\mathcal{FP}(\text{AF})$.

As shown in [4], $\mathcal{FP}(\text{AF})$ is never empty, though there are cases where $\mathcal{FP}(\text{AF}) = \{\emptyset\}$, e.g. $\mathcal{FP}(\text{AF}_5)$ in Example 4 below. Also in this semantics three sets of arguments are identified: undefeated arguments belong to all extensions, defeated arguments to none, while provisionally defeated only to some of them.

Definition 7. *Given an argumentation framework* AF $=< \mathcal{A}, \rightarrow >$, *we define the following three sets, forming a partition of* $\mathcal{A}$:

- $\text{U}_\mathcal{P}(\text{AF}) = \{\alpha \in \mathcal{A} \mid \forall P \in \mathcal{FP}(\text{AF}) \; \alpha \in P\}$
- $\text{D}_\mathcal{P}(\text{AF}) = \{\alpha \in \mathcal{A} \mid \forall P \in \mathcal{FP}(\text{AF}) \; \alpha \notin P\}$
- $\text{P}_\mathcal{P}(\text{AF}) = \{\alpha \in \mathcal{A} \mid \exists P_1, P_2 \in \mathcal{FP}(\text{AF}) : \alpha \in P_1 \wedge \alpha \notin P_2\}$

Turning to Example 1 and Example 2, it is easy to see that the preferred semantics gives the same outcome as the grounded semantics, since we have that $\mathcal{FP}(\text{AF}_1) = \{\{\alpha, \gamma\}\}$, while $\mathcal{FP}(\text{AF}_2) = \{\{\alpha, \gamma\}, \{\beta\}\}$. The relation between grounded and preferred semantics has been analyzed in [4]: in a nutshell, the grounded semantics is more cautious than preferred semantics, since for all argumentation frameworks it turns out that all the arguments undefeated and defeated according to the grounded semantics have the same status in the preferred semantics. On the other hand, there may be arguments provisionally defeated in the grounded semantics which are defeated or undefeated in the preferred semantics, as in the case of *floating arguments* [5] exemplified below.

Example 3. With reference to the argumentation framework AF$_3$ shown in Fig. 2, it is easy to see that, according to the grounded semantics, all arguments are provisionally defeated. On the other hand, it turns out that $\mathcal{FP}(\text{AF}_3) = \{\{\alpha, \delta\}, \{\beta, \delta\}\}$, therefore we have that $\text{P}_\mathcal{P}(\text{AF}_3) = \{\alpha, \beta\}$, $\text{D}_\mathcal{P}(\text{AF}_3) = \{\gamma\}$ and $\text{U}_\mathcal{P}(\text{AF}_3) = \{\delta\}$.

In the example above, every preferred extension includes an argument which attacks γ, while no argument attacking γ belongs to all extensions: this is a case of 'floating defeat', as it has been called in [8], which determines in turn the 'floating acceptance' of δ. The inability to discriminate floating arguments is not a specific disadvantage of grounded semantics, since Schlechta has proved in [9] that it affects any possible single-status approach.

3   Odd-Length Cycles: A Problem in Preferred Semantics

According to the definitions presented in the previous section, if the nodes of a defeat graph are arranged in a cycle of attack relationships, then they are not justified (i.e. they are provisionally defeated) according to both the grounded

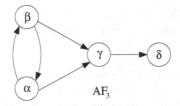

Fig. 2. Argumentation framework with a floating argument

and preferred semantics. This seems to be the intuitively right result, since all arguments in a cycle should be treated equally for obvious symmetry reasons and considering them all justified would yield a contradiction. However this result is obtained in rather different ways in the two semantics. In the context of the grounded semantics, all arguments forming a cycle simply turn out to belong to $\mathcal{A}_i$ if i is even and not to belong to $\mathcal{A}_i$ if i is odd (see Definitions 2 and 3).

On the other hand, the preferred semantics features a sort of asymmetry, since it treats odd-length cycles differently from the even-length ones.

Example 4. Considering the argumentation framework AF_4 of Fig. 3, we have that $\mathcal{FP}(AF_4) = \{\{\alpha\}, \{\beta\}\}$, therefore both arguments belong to $P_{\mathcal{P}}(AF_4)$. With reference to the argumentation framework AF_5, Definition 6 identifies the empty set as the unique preferred extension, therefore all the arguments belong to $D_{\mathcal{P}}(AF_5)$. More generally, with odd-length cycles there is a unique empty extension, while with even-length cycles non-empty extensions exist but their intersection is empty.

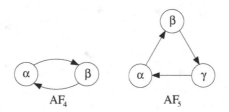

Fig. 3. Even-length and odd-length cycles

The peculiar way to assign a defeat status to odd-length cycles has recently been indicated as "puzzling" by Pollock [10]. As to our knowledge, however, this difference has been considered a mere question of symmetry and elegance in previous literature. We show in the following example that the different treatment of odd-length cycles is a real problem since it gives rise to counter-intuitive results.

Example 5. Considering the argumentation framework AF_6 shown in Fig. 4, it turns out that $\mathcal{FP}(AF_6) = \{\{\alpha, \delta\}\}$, therefore α and δ are justified according to the preferred semantics. By replacing the cycle (α, β, γ) with a two-length cycle, we obtain the argumentation framework AF_7 whose arguments all belong to $P_\mathcal{P}(AF_7)$ (and a similar result is obtained with any other even-length cycle).

In the example above α and δ emerge (unreasonably) undefeated, while all nodes would be provisionally defeated with a similar graph encompassing an even-length cycle. It does not seem acceptable that different results in conceptually similar situations depend on the cycle length: symmetry reasons suggest that all cycles should be treated equally. The difference arises because an odd-length cycle has no extensions besides the empty one: as a consequence, there is no extension where δ is out and γ is in (such an extension would instead exist with an even-length cycle). Since δ defeats γ, in this context also α survives. Notice that a similar situation arises by replacing the three-length cycles with any odd-length cycle: in a sense, odd-length cycles are in this case 'weaker' than even-length cycles, since they are not able to prevent δ from being justified. The opposite happens in the following example:

Example 6. With reference to the argumentation framework AF_8 shown in Fig. 4, it turns out that $\mathcal{FP}(AF_8) = \{\{\delta_2\}\}$, therefore δ_2 is undefeated while all the other arguments are not justified. On the other hand, by replacing the three-length cycle with an even-length cycle, we obtain an argumentation framework whose arguments are all provisionally defeated.

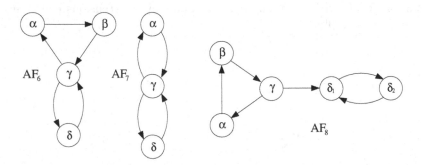

Fig. 4. Two problematic argumentation frameworks for preferred semantics

In the example above, the absence of non-empty extensions for the three-length cycle prevents the existence of extensions including δ_1, leaving δ_2 as the only accepted argument, while this would not happen with an even-length cycle. Notice that in this case odd-length cycles are 'stronger' than even-length cycles, since the status of δ_1 is the same as if it would be attacked by an initial node. In summary, we notice that besides being treated differently with respect to even-length cycles, odd-length cycles exhibit anomalous behaviors: they change their capability of defeating other arguments depending on the topology of the defeat graph.

4   Exploiting the Notion of Maximal Conflict-Free Set

The analysis carried out in previous sections shows that neither the grounded nor the preferred semantics are completely satisfactory and suggests the following requirements for the study of an improved semantics, able to preserve the advantages of both of them:

- it should discriminate floating arguments as the preferred semantics;
- it should handle odd-length cycles in the same way as even-length cycles, as the grounded semantics;
- it should correctly handle the problematic examples shown above;
- it should not be more skeptical than the grounded semantics, in particular, it should agree with it upon the status of undefeated and defeated arguments.

On the basis of the results provided by Schlechta [9], mentioned in Sect. 2, the first requirement can only be satisfied by a multiple-status approach. Thus, to satisfy the second requirement we look for a new notion of extension, able to remove the anomalous treatment of odd-length cycles. After identifying our candidate definition, we will check its properties concerning third and fourth requirement. To figure out a proper notion of extension, let us consider again Example 4, in which we have recognized as anomalous the fact that AF_5 admits the empty set as its unique extension. In order to reconcile the treatments of AF_4 and AF_5, we can look for the set $\mathcal{E}$ of non-empty extensions that can be admitted for AF_5. First of all, we cannot tolerate contradictions in any extension, therefore each extension has to include one node exactly. Moreover, all nodes should be treated equally, therefore the only possibility for $\mathcal{E}$ is the set $\{\{\alpha\}, \{\beta\}, \{\gamma\}\}$. We notice that $\mathcal{E}$ is made up of all conflict-free sets of AF_5 that are maximal, and this suggests to exploit this notion as a basis for a new definition of extension.

Definition 8. *Given an argumentation framework* AF $=< \mathcal{A}, \rightarrow >$*, we denote as* $\mathcal{FI}(AF)$ *the set made up of the maximal (with respect to set inclusion) conflict-free subsets of* $\mathcal{A}$*.*

The above intuition is confirmed by the fact that, by defining the set of justified arguments as the intersection of all maximal conflict-free sets, the problematic examples of the above section are handled correctly. In particular, with reference to the argumentation framework AF_6 of Example 5, we have that $\mathcal{FI}(AF_6) = \{\{\alpha, \delta\}, \{\gamma\}, \{\beta, \delta\}\}$, therefore all the arguments are provisionally defeated, as prescribed by the grounded semantics.

Notice that Definition 8 is strictly weaker than Definition 6, since the absence of conflicts is one of the conditions for admissibility. Actually, while this brings about a correct handling of Example 4 and Example 5, it does not represent a satisfactory solution, since due to the increased number of extensions, it would tend to assign the status of provisionally defeated to a large number of arguments (often all of them): this happens, for instance, even for the argumentation framework AF_1 of Example 1, where we have that $\mathcal{FI}(AF_1) = \{\{\alpha, \gamma\}, \{\beta\}\}$. Notice that, in this case, the requirement of admissibility would have excluded, among the elements of $\mathcal{FI}(\text{AF}_1)$, the set $\{\beta\}$, yielding the intuitively correct result. Thus, we are lead to add some further condition to the Definition 8, in order to capture only a subset of the maximal conflict-free sets. In order to do this, we draw inspiration from the way the defeat status can be computed according to the grounded semantics. Considering again Example 1 as a simple reference, basically, computation proceeds from the frontier of the defeat graph towards the inside: the initial node α is assigned the status of undefeated, causing β, which is attacked by α, to be assigned the status of defeated, and this in turn causes γ, whose unique defeater β is defeated, to be assigned the status of undefeated. Thus, the set $\{\beta\}$ is rejected in this computation schema, which is therefore a promising candidate as a way to identify the extensions among maximal conflict-free sets.

In order to refine this intuition, let us consider again Example 3: according to the first requirement stated above, our approach should capture exactly the preferred extensions $P_1 = \{\alpha, \delta\}$ and $P_2 = \{\beta, \delta\}$. Starting from the frontier of the graph, the construction of these extensions might proceed according to the following steps:

1. Consider the subgraph involving $\{\alpha, \beta\}$, and identify the relevant maximal conflict-free sets $\overline{P_1} = \{\alpha\}$ and $\overline{P_2} = \{\beta\}$;
2. Consider then node γ for possible additions to the sets identified in the previous step: notice that $\overline{P_1}$ includes the defeater α of γ, therefore γ cannot be added to $\overline{P_1}$. For the same reason, γ cannot be added to $\overline{P_2}$ as well;
3. Consider node δ: it can be added to $\overline{P_1}$ obtaining the extension P_1, since its unique defeater γ has not be added to $\overline{P_1}$. In the same way, we obtain P_2 as $\overline{P_2} \cup \{\delta\}$.

Notice that, in steps 1–3, we have considered the *strongly connected components* of the defeat graph, i.e. $\{\alpha, \beta\}$, $\{\gamma\}$ and $\{\delta\}$, respectively. In a sense, we have generalized the defeat status computation prescribed by the grounded semantics, by considering strongly connected components instead of single nodes. In particular, the extensions have been constructed by completing maximal conflict-free sets in an incremental way, starting from the frontier of the graph and proceeding towards the interior. In order to proceed with this analysis in more formal terms, let us introduce the following definitions.

Definition 9. *Given an argumentation framework* AF $=< \mathcal{A}, \rightarrow>$, *two nodes* $\alpha, \beta \in \mathcal{A}$ *are path-equivalent iff either* $\alpha = \beta$ *or there is a path from* α *to* β *and a path from* β *to* α. *The strongly connected components of* AF *are the equivalence classes of vertices under the relation of path-equivalence. The set of the strongly connected components of* AF *is denoted as* SCC(AF).

Definition 10. *Given an argumentation framework* AF $=< \mathcal{A}, \rightarrow>$ *and a strongly connected component* $S \in$ SCC(AF), parents$(S) = \{P \in$ SCC(AF) $\mid P \neq S \wedge \exists \alpha \in P, \beta \in S : \alpha \rightarrow \beta\}$, *and* parents$^*(S) = \{\alpha \in \mathcal{A} \mid \alpha \notin S \wedge \exists \beta \in S : \alpha \rightarrow \beta\}$.

Definition 11. *Let* AF $=< \mathcal{A}, \rightarrow >$ *be an argumentation framework, and let* S *be a set* $S \subseteq \mathcal{A}$. *The restriction of* AF *to* S *is the argumentation framework* AF$\downarrow_S =< S, \rightarrow \cap (S \times S) >$.

Let $\mathcal{SG}$ be the graph obtained by considering strongly connected components as single nodes, i.e. $\mathcal{SG} =< \text{SCC(AF)}, R^* >$ where $(S_i, S_j) \in R^*$ iff $S_i \in \text{parents}(S_j)$. It is easy to see that $\mathcal{SG}$ is acyclic: this justifies the idea of computing a particular extension E from the frontier towards the inside of the defeat graph. Basically, we start from the strongly connected components S_i that are initial in $\mathcal{SG}$, including in E a maximal conflict-free set of AF$\downarrow_{S_i}$ for each S_i. Then, we proceed by considering an $S \in \text{SCC(AF)}$ such that every $P \in \text{parents}(S)$ is initial. Of course, E should not include those nodes of S that are attacked by nodes previously included in E. The question is how to proceed with the set S^U made up of the other nodes of S. If there is just a single node in S^U, the indications provided by Example 1 suggest to include it in E. If, on the other hand, $|S^U| > 1$, a tentative solution would be to include in E a maximal independent set of S^U. However, a simple example reveals that this option does not constrain enough the set of the extensions that can be identified from maximal conflict-free sets.

Example 7. Considering the argumentation framework AF$_9$ shown Fig. 5, we have that $\text{SCC(AF}_9) = \{S_1, S_2\}$, where $S_1 = \{\alpha\}$ and $S_2 = \{\beta_1, \beta_2, \beta_3, \beta_4\}$. S_1 is initial, and its unique maximal conflict-free set is $\{\alpha\}$ itself. This in turn excludes β_1 from all the extensions, leading to select a maximal conflict-free set of the subgraph AF$_9\downarrow_{S_2 \setminus \{\beta_1\}}$. It turns out that $\mathcal{FI}(\text{AF}_9\downarrow_{S_2 \setminus \{\beta_1\}}) = \{\{\beta_2, \beta_4\}, \{\beta_3\}\}$, therefore we get the two extensions $E_1 = \{\alpha, \beta_2, \beta_4\}$ and $E_2 = \{\alpha, \beta_3\}$, yielding α undefeated, β_1 defeated and $\beta_2, \beta_3, \beta_4$ provisionally defeated. However, in order to get the same outcome as the grounded (and preferred) semantics, only E_1 should be identified as an extension, while E_2 should be excluded.

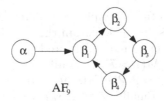

Fig. 5. An example supporting a recursive definition of extensions

In order to overcome this difficulty, in the example above $S_2 \setminus \{\beta_1\}$ should be treated in the same way as an ordinary graph, i.e. proceeding again from the frontier towards the inside. This suggests the alternative option that we choose, i.e. to define extensions recursively.

Definition 12. *Given an argumentation framework* AF $=< \mathcal{A}, \rightarrow >$, *a set* $E \subseteq \mathcal{A}$ *and a strongly connected component* $S \in \text{SCC(AF)}$, *we define:*

$-\ S^D(E) = \{\alpha \in S \mid \exists \beta \in \text{parents}^*(S) : \beta \in E \wedge \beta \to \alpha\}$

$-\ S^U(E) = S \setminus S^D(E)$

In our proposal, the set of extensions, denoted as $\mathcal{FM}(\text{AF})$, is defined as follows:

Definition 13. *Given an argumentation framework* $\text{AF} =< \mathcal{A}, \to >$ *and a set* $E \subseteq \mathcal{A}$*, we have that* $E \in \mathcal{FM}(\text{AF})$ *iff* $\forall S \in \text{SCC}(\text{AF})$

1. $S^D(E) \cap E = \emptyset$*; and*

2. $S^U(E) \cap E \begin{cases} \in \mathcal{FI}(\text{AF}\!\downarrow_{S^U(E)}) & \text{if } |\text{SCC}(\text{AF}\!\downarrow_{S^U(E)})| = 1 \\ \in \mathcal{FM}(\text{AF}\!\downarrow_{S^U(E)}) & \text{otherwise} \end{cases}$

Following the usual multiple-status approach, the defeat status of arguments is identified by the sets $\text{U}_{\mathcal{M}}(\text{AF})$, $\text{D}_{\mathcal{M}}(\text{AF})$, $\text{P}_{\mathcal{M}}(\text{AF})$, defined as in Definition 7 with reference to $\mathcal{FM}(\text{AF})$ instead of $\mathcal{FP}(\text{AF})$. In order to better understand Definition+13, let us show that, differently from the preferred semantics, it gives the right outcome to Example 6.

Example 8. We have that $\text{SCC}(\text{AF}_8) = \{S_1, S_2\}$, where $S_1 = \{\alpha, \beta, \gamma\}$ and $S_2 = \{\delta_1, \delta_2\}$. Taking into account Definition 12 and the fact that $\text{parents}(S_1) = \emptyset$, for any E $S_1^D(E) = \emptyset$ and $S_1^U(E) = S_1$. Thus, from Definition13 a generic extension E must satisfy $(S_1 \cap E) \in \mathcal{FI}(\text{AF}_8\!\downarrow_{S_1^U(E)})$, i.e. $(S_1 \cap E) \in \{\{\alpha\}, \{\beta\}, \{\gamma\}\}$. In case $(S_1 \cap E) = \{\alpha\}$, taking into account that $\text{parents}^*(S_2) = \{\gamma\}$ we get $S_2^D(E) = \emptyset$ and $(S_2 \cap E) \in \{\{\delta_1\}, \{\delta_2\}\}$: thus, we identify the extensions $E_1 = \{\alpha, \delta_1\}$ and $E_2 = \{\alpha, \delta_2\}$. Reasoning in a similar way in the case $(S_1 \cap E) = \{\beta\}$, we identify the extensions $E_3 = \{\beta, \delta_1\}$ and $E_4 = \{\beta, \delta_2\}$. Finally, if $(S_1 \cap E) = \{\gamma\}$ then $S_2^D(E) = \{\delta_1\}$, entailing by the first point of Definition 13 that $\delta_1 \notin E$. Moreover, $S_2^U(E) = \{\delta_2\}$, yielding $\delta_2 \in E$ and thus identifying the extension $E_5 = \{\gamma, \delta_2\}$. In sum, $\mathcal{FM}(\text{AF}_8) = \{E_1, E_2, E_3, E_4, E_5\}$, therefore all the arguments are provisionally defeated.

It can be seen that all other examples considered above are handled correctly by the proposed semantics. In particular, in the argumentation frameworks AF_1, AF_2, AF_7 and AF_9 where preferred and grounded semantics agree, our semantics gives the same results ($\mathcal{FM}() = \mathcal{FP}()$ in all cases). Also in the argumentation framework AF_3 $\mathcal{FM}(\text{AF}_3) = \mathcal{FP}(\text{AF}_3)$, therefore our semantics correctly agrees with preferred semantics. Finally, $\mathcal{FM}(\text{AF}_6) = \{\{\alpha, \delta\}, \{\beta, \delta\}, \{\gamma\}\}$, therefore our semantics agrees with grounded semantics as desired.

5   Relationships with Grounded and Preferred Semantics

After having validated our proposal by means of examples, in this section we show that it maintains some relationships with both the grounded and preferred semantics. First, we consider the fourth requirement stated in previous section, i.e. the agreement with the grounded semantics upon the status of undefeated and defeated arguments (proofs are not given due to space limitations). This result relies on two properties of the grounded semantics, which relate the defeat status assignment prescribed by the grounded semantics to the strongly connected components of the defeat graph. In particular, the first considers a non-trivial strongly connected component whose external attackers (if any) are all defeated or provisionally defeated, establishing that, in this case, all of its nodes are provisionally defeated.

Proposition 1. *Given* $\text{AF} =< \mathcal{A}, \rightarrow>$, *let* $S \in \text{SCC}(\text{AF})$ *be such that* $|S| > 1$ *and* $\forall \gamma \in \text{parents}^*(S)\ \gamma \in (\text{D}_{\mathcal{G}}(\text{AF}) \cup \text{P}_{\mathcal{G}}(\text{AF}))$. *Then,* $S \subseteq \text{P}_{\mathcal{G}}(\text{AF})$.

The subsequent property introduces two subsets related to $S^D(E)$ and $S^U(E)$ in Definition 12, and establishes some relationships between the status assigned by the grounded semantics to their nodes and the constraints on E stated in Definition 12.

Proposition 2. *Let us consider* $\text{AF} =< \mathcal{A}, \rightarrow>$ *and* $S \in \text{SCC}(\text{AF})$. *Let* $S^D \subseteq S$ *be a subset of* S *such that*

1. $S^D \supseteq \{\alpha \in S \mid \exists \beta \in \text{parents}^*(S), \beta \rightarrow \alpha, \beta \in \text{U}_{\mathcal{G}}(\text{AF})\}$; *and*
2. $S^D \subseteq \{\alpha \in S \mid \exists \beta \in \text{parents}^*(S), \beta \rightarrow \alpha, \beta \in (\text{U}_{\mathcal{G}}(\text{AF}) \cup \text{P}_{\mathcal{G}}(\text{AF}))\}$

and let $S^U = S \setminus S^D$. *Then, we have that* $\forall \alpha \in S^D\ \alpha \in (\text{D}_{\mathcal{G}}(\text{AF}) \cup \text{P}_{\mathcal{G}}(\text{AF}))$, *and* $\forall \gamma \in S^U$:

- *if* $\gamma \in \text{U}_{\mathcal{G}}(\text{AF})$, *then* $\gamma \in \text{U}_{\mathcal{G}}(\text{AF}\!\downarrow_{S^U})$;
- *if* $\gamma \in \text{D}_{\mathcal{G}}(\text{AF})$, *then* $\gamma \in \text{D}_{\mathcal{G}}(\text{AF}\!\downarrow_{S^U})$;

The following theorem, exploiting the above properties, proves the agreement with grounded semantics upon the status of defeated and undefeated arguments.

Theorem 1. *Given* $\text{AF} =< \mathcal{A}, \rightarrow>$, *we have that* $\forall E \in \mathcal{FM}(\text{AF})\ \text{U}_{\mathcal{G}}(\text{AF}) \subseteq E \wedge \text{D}_{\mathcal{G}}(\text{AF}) \subseteq (\mathcal{A} \setminus E)$.

Proof (Sketch). Referring to Definition 13, we consider a generic $E \in \mathcal{FM}(\text{AF})$, and we assume recursively that, $\forall S_i \in \text{SCC}(\text{AF})$,

- $\forall P \in \mathcal{FM}(\text{AF}\!\downarrow_{S_i^U(E)})\ \text{U}_{\mathcal{G}}(\text{AF}) \subseteq P$
- $\forall P \in \mathcal{FM}(\text{AF}\!\downarrow_{S_i^U(E)})\ \text{D}_{\mathcal{G}}(\text{AF}) \subseteq (\mathcal{A} \setminus P)$

Then, reasoning by induction on the strongly connected components of AF, we prove that $\text{U}_{\mathcal{G}}(\text{AF}) \subseteq E$ and that $\text{D}_{\mathcal{G}}(\text{AF}) \subseteq (\mathcal{A} \setminus E)$. In particular, Proposition 1 is exploited to show that, if $|\text{SCC}(\text{AF}\!\downarrow_{S^U(E)})| = 1$, then all the nodes of $S^U(E)$ are provisionally defeated, so that there is nothing to prove for them (this happens for instance for initial strongly connected components). On the other hand, the main roles of Proposition 2 concern the first point of Definition 13 and the case $|\text{SCC}(\text{AF}\!\downarrow_{S^U(E)})| > 1$, where it is exploited to prove that if $S^U(E) \cap E \in \mathcal{FM}(\text{AF}\!\downarrow_{S^U(E)})$, then the claim is satisfied for nodes of $S^U(E)$.

As far as preferred semantics is concerned, given a generic $\text{AF} =< \mathcal{A}, \rightarrow>$ it is possible to prove that any preferred extension is included in one of our extensions, i.e. $\forall P \in \mathcal{FP}(\text{AF})\ \exists E \in \mathcal{FM}(\text{AF}) : P \subseteq E$. This, in turn, entails that preferred semantics agrees upon the status of arguments that are defeated according to ours.

6   Conclusions

In this paper, we have proposed a novel argumentation semantics that, while maintaining the same capability of discriminating floating arguments as preferred semantics, correctly deals with the semantic problems arising from odd-length cycles and satisfies a set of requirements intuitively appealing. The symmetry assumptions that underly our work are related to an interpretation of argumentation as a framework for defeasible reasoning, following e.g. [1], while in other approaches that consider argumentation as a branch of dialogue [11] it may be the case that a different treatment of odd and even-length cycles is appropriate.

Our proposal builds on intuitions coming from both grounded and preferred semantics and, in a sense, combines the advantages of both of them, agreeing in several problematic examples with that among the two semantics which is closer to intuition. As for future work, we will investigate the relationship between our semantics and the notions of attack and defence lying at the heart of preferred semantics.

Acknowledgments. We thank the referees for their helpful comments.

References

1. Pollock, J.L.: How to reason defeasibly. Artificial Intelligence **57** (1992) 1–42
2. Parsons, S., Sierra, C., Jennings, N.: Agents that reason and negotiate by arguing. Journal of Logic and Computation **8** (1998) 261–292
3. Baroni, P., Giacomin, M., Guida, G.: Extending abstract argumentation systems theory. Artificial Intelligence **120** (2000) 251–270
4. Dung, P.M.: On the acceptability of arguments and its fundamental role in non-monotonic reasoning, logic programming, and n-person games. Artificial Intelligence **77** (1995) 321–357
5. Prakken, H., Vreeswijk, G.A.W.: Logics for defeasible argumentation. In Gabbay, D.M., Guenthner, F., eds.: Handbook of Philosophical Logic, Second Edition. Kluwer Academic Publishers, Dordrecht (2001)
6. Pollock, J.L.: Justification and defeat. Artificial Intelligence **67** (1994) 377–407
7. Vreeswijk, G.A.W.: Abstract argumentation systems. Artificial Intelligence **90** (1997) 225–279
8. Makinson, D., Sclechta, K.: Floating conclusions and zombie paths: Two deep difficulties in the 'directly skeptical' approach to defeasible inheritance networks. Artificial Intelligence **48** (1991) 199–209
9. Schlechta, K.: Directly sceptical inheritance cannot capture the intersection of extensions. Journal of Logic and Computation **3** (1993) 455–467
10. Pollock, J.L.: Defeasible reasoning with variable degrees of justification. Artificial Intelligence **133** (2001) 233–282
11. Walton, D., Krabbe, E.: Commitment in Dialogue: Basic concept of interpersonal reasoning. State University of New York Press, Albany NY (1995)

On the Relation between Reiter's Default Logic and Its (Major) Variants

James P. Delgrande[1] and Torsten Schaub[2]

[1] School of Computing Science, Simon Fraser University, Burnaby, B.C., Canada V5A 1S6
jim@cs.sfu.ca
[2] Institut für Informatik, Universität Potsdam, D–14415 Potsdam, Germany
torsten@cs.uni-potsdam.de

Abstract. Default logic is one of the best known and most studied of the approaches to nonmonotonic reasoning. Subsequently, several variants of default logic have been proposed to give systems with properties differing from the original. In this paper we show that these variants are in a sense superfluous, in that for any of these variants of default logic, we can exactly mimic the behaviour of a variant in standard default logic. We accomplish this by translating a default theory under a variant interpretation into a second default theory wherein the variant interpretation is respected.

1 Introduction

Default logic [17] is one of the best known approaches to nonmonotonic reasoning. In this approach, classical logic is augmented by *default rules* of the form $\frac{\alpha \,:\, \beta_1,\ldots,\beta_n}{\gamma}$. Such a rule is informally interpreted as "if α is true, and $\beta_1, \ldots, \beta_n$ are consistent with what is known, then conclude γ by default". The meaning of a rule then rests on notions of provability and consistency with respect to a given set of beliefs. A set of beliefs sanctioned by a set of default rules, with respect to an initial set of facts, is called an *extension* of this set of facts.

However, the very generality of default logic means that it lacks several important properties, including *existence of extensions* [17] and *cumulativity* [12]. In addition, differing intuitions concerning the role of default rules have led to differing opinions concerning other properties, including *semi-monotonicity* [17] and *commitment to assumptions* [16]. As a result, a number of modifications to the definition of a default extension have been proposed, resulting in a number of variants of default logic. Most notably these variants include *constrained default logic* [18,3], *cumulative default logic* [1], *justified default logic* [11], and *rational default logic* [15]. In each of these variants, the definition of an extension is modified, and a system with properties differing from the original is obtained.

In this paper we show that these variants are in a sense superfluous, in that each variant can be expressed within the framework of (the original) default logic. To accomplish this, we make use of translations mapping a default theory under a "'variant" interpretation onto a second theory under the interpretation of the original approach, such that the respectively resulting extensions are in a one-to-one correspondence. In the case of

T.D. Nielsen and N.L. Zhang (Eds.): ECSQARU 2003, LNAI 2711, pp. 452–463, 2003.

variant default logics that use the language of classical logic, we extend the language with labelled formulas. In the case of an *assertional default logic*, such as cumulative default logic, the situation is more complex since cumulative default logic makes use of "assertions," which extend the language of classical logic. Here we appeal to a quotation operator in which we can effectively name formulas; we then make assertions concerning quoted formulas by means of introduced predicates.

Hence we provide a unification of default logics, in that, we show that the original formulation of default logic is expressive enough to subsume its variants. The reverse relation does not to hold for constrained, justified, or cumulative default logic, in that one cannot express default logic in terms of these variants. However, rational default logic can be embedded in Reiter default logic, and vice versa. The translations that we provide show, in a precise sense, how each variant relates to standard default logic. As well, the approach lends some insight into characteristics of standard default theories. For example, our translations implicitly provide specific characterisations of default theories that are guaranteed to have extensions or are guaranteed to be semi-monotonic. That is, since we map variant default logics into default logic, the theories in the image of the mapping are guaranteed to retain properties of the original variant.

2   Default Logic and Its Variants

Default logic [17] augments classical logic by *default rules* of the form $\frac{\alpha \,:\, \beta_1, ..., \beta_n}{\gamma}$, where the constituent elements are formulas of classical propositional or first-order logic. Defaults with unbound variables are taken to stand for all corresponding instances. For simplicity, we deal just with *singular* defaults for which $n = 1$. A singular rule is *normal* if β is equivalent to γ; it is *semi-normal* if β implies γ. As regards standard default logic, [9] shows that any default rule can be transformed into a set of semi-normal defaults; similarly in constrained and rational default logic multiple justifications can be replaced by their conjunction. Moreover the great majority of applications use only semi-normal defaults, so the above assumption is a reasonable restriction. We denote the *prerequisite* α of a default $\delta = \frac{\alpha \,:\, \beta}{\gamma}$ by $Prereq(\delta)$, its *justification* β by $Justif(\delta)$ and its *consequent* γ by $Conseq(\delta)$. Conversely, to ease notation, in Sect. 3 we rely on a function δ to obtain the default rule in which a given prerequisite, justification, or consequent occurs, respectively. That is, for instance, $\delta(Prereq(\delta)) = \delta$. Moreover, for simplifying the technical results, we presuppose without loss of generality that default rules have unique components. To avoid confusion we will use the term *default logic* to refer solely to Reiter's original system. Variants will be referred to as constrained (cumulative, justified, etc.) default logic. Similar considerations apply to the notions of *default extension*.

A set of default rules D and a set of formulas W form a *default theory* (D, W) that may induce 0, 1, or multiple *extensions* in the following way.

Definition 1 ([17]). *Let (D, W) be a default theory. For any set S of formulas, let $\Gamma(S)$ be the smallest set of formulas such that*

1. $W \subseteq \Gamma(S)$,
2. $\Gamma(S) = Th(\Gamma(S))$,

3. if $\frac{\alpha\,:\,\beta}{\gamma} \in D$ and $\alpha \in \Gamma(S)$ and $S \cup \{\beta\} \not\vdash \bot$ then $\gamma \in \Gamma(S)$.

A set of formulas E is an extension of (D, W) iff $\Gamma(E) = E$.

That is, E is a fixed point of Γ. Any such extension represents a possible set of beliefs about the world at hand. For illustration, consider the default theories

$$(D_1, W_1) = (\{\tfrac{:B}{C}, \tfrac{:\neg B}{D}\}, \emptyset) \; ; \tag{1}$$

$$(D_2, W_2) = (\{\tfrac{:B}{C}, \tfrac{:\neg C}{D}\}, \emptyset) \; . \tag{2}$$

While (D_1, W_1) admits one extension, $Th(\{C, D\})$, the only extension of (D_2, W_2) is $Th(\{C\})$. In the literature (D_1, W_1) is often used as an illustrative example for what is sometimes referred to as *commitment to assumption* [16] (or: *regularity* [4]); similarly (D_2, W_2) illustrates *semi-monotonicity* [17].

Lukaszewicz [11] modifies default logic by attaching constraints to extensions in order to strengthen the applicability condition of default rules. A *justified extension* (called a *modified extension* in [11]) is defined as follows.

Definition 2 ([11]). *Let (D, W) be a default theory. For any pair of sets of formulas (S, T) let $\Gamma(S, T)$ be the pair of smallest sets of formulas S', T' such that*

1. $W \subseteq S'$,
2. $Th(S') = S'$,
3. for any $\frac{\alpha\,:\,\beta}{\gamma} \in D$, if $\alpha \in S'$ and $S \cup \{\gamma\} \cup \{\eta\} \not\vdash \bot$ for every $\eta \in T \cup \{\beta\}$ then $\gamma \in S'$ and $\beta \in T'$.

A set of formulas E is a justified extension of (D, W) for a set of formulas J iff $\Gamma(E, J) = (E, J)$.

So a default rule $\frac{\alpha\,:\,\beta}{\gamma}$ applies if all justifications of other applying default rules are consistent with the considered extension E and γ, and if additionally γ and β are consistent with E. The set of justifications J need not be deductively closed nor consistent.

In our examples, (D_1, W_1) has one justified extension, containing C and D. However, theory (D_2, W_2) has two justified extensions, one with C and one containing D.

In [18,3] *constrained default logic* is defined. The central idea is that the justifications and consequents of a default rule jointly provide a context or assumption set for default rule application. The definition of a *constrained extension* is as follows.

Definition 3 ([3]). *Let (D, W) be a default theory. For any set of formulas T, let $\Gamma(T)$ be the pair of smallest sets of formulas (S', T') such that*

1. $W \subseteq S' \subseteq T'$,
2. $S' = Th(S')$ and $T' = Th(T')$,
3. for any $\frac{\alpha\,:\,\beta}{\gamma} \in D$, if $\alpha \in S'$ and $T \cup \{\beta\} \cup \{\gamma\} \not\vdash \bot$ then $\gamma \in S'$ and $\beta \wedge \gamma \in T'$.

A pair of sets of formulas (E, C) is a constrained extension of (D, W) iff $\Gamma(C) = (E, C)$.

Unlike Lukaszewicz's approach, the contextual information is here a deductively closed superset of the actual extension.

In our example, (D_1, W_1) has two constrained extensions, one containing C and another including D. Also, theory (D_2, W_2) has two constrained extensions, one with C and one with D.

The following is an alternative characterisation of *rational extensions*, originally proposed in [14], given in [10]:

Definition 4 ([14]). *Let (D, W) be a default theory. For any set of formulas T let $\Gamma(T)$ be the pair of smallest sets of formulas (S', T') such that*

1. $W \subseteq S' \subseteq T'$,
2. $S' = Th(S')$ and $T' = Th(T')$,
3. *for any $\frac{\alpha : \beta}{\gamma} \in D$, if $\alpha \in S'$ and $T \cup \{\beta\} \not\vdash \bot$ then $\gamma \in S'$ and $\beta \wedge \gamma \in T'$.*

A pair of sets of formulas (E, C) is a rational extension of (D, W) iff $\Gamma(C) = (E, C)$.

This definition is the same as that of constrained default logic, except for the consistency check. As with constrained default logic, (D_1, W_1) has two rational extensions, one containing C and one including D. However, theory (D_2, W_2) has only one rational extension with C.

Brewka [1] describes a variant of default logic where the applicability condition for default rules is strengthened, and the justification for adopting a default conclusion is made explicit. In order to keep track of implicit assumptions, Brewka introduces *assertions*, or formulas labeled with the set of justifications and consequents of the default rules which were used for deriving them. Intuitively, assertions represent formulas along with the reasons for believing them.

Definition 5 ([1]). *Let $\alpha, \gamma_1, \ldots, \gamma_m$ be formulas. An assertion ξ is any expression of the form $\langle \alpha, \{\gamma_1, \ldots, \gamma_m\}\rangle$, where $\alpha = Form(\xi)$ is called the asserted formula and the set $\{\gamma_1, \ldots, \gamma_m\} = Supp(\xi)$ is called the support of α.[1]*

To correctly propagate the supports, the classical inference relation is extended as follows.

Definition 6 ([1]). *Let S be a set of assertions. Then $\widehat{Th}(S)$, the assertional consequence closure operator, is the smallest set of assertions such that*

1. $S \subseteq \widehat{Th}(S)$,
2. *if $\xi_1, \ldots, \xi_n \in \widehat{Th}(S)$ and $Form(\xi_1), \ldots, Form(\xi_n) \vdash \gamma$ then $\langle \gamma, Supp(\xi_1) \cup \cdots \cup Supp(\xi_n)\rangle \in \widehat{Th}(S)$.*

An *assertional default theory* is a pair $(D, \mathcal{W})$, where D is a set of default rules and $\mathcal{W}$ is a set of assertions. An *assertional extension* is defined as follows.

Definition 7 ([1]). *Let $(D, \mathcal{W})$ be an assertional default theory. For any set of assertions S let $\Gamma(S)$ be the smallest set of assertions S' such that*

---

[1] The two projections extend to sets of assertions in the obvious way. We sometimes misuse *Supp* for denoting the support of an asserted formula, e.g. $\langle \alpha, Supp(\alpha)\rangle$.

1. $W \subseteq S'$,
2. $\widehat{Th}(S') = S'$,
3. *for any* $\frac{\alpha : \beta}{\gamma} \in D$, *if* $\langle \alpha, Supp(\alpha) \rangle \in S'$ *and* $Form(S) \cup Supp(S) \cup \{\beta\} \cup \{\gamma\} \not\vdash \perp$
   then $\langle \gamma, Supp(\alpha) \cup \{\beta\} \cup \{\gamma\} \rangle \in S'$.

A set of assertions $\mathcal{E}$ is an assertional extension of (D, W) iff $\Gamma(\mathcal{E}) = \mathcal{E}$.

For illustration, consider the assertional default theory (often used for illustrating the failure of *cumulativity* [12])

$$(D_3, W_3) = (\{ \tfrac{:A}{A}, \tfrac{A \vee B : \neg A}{\neg A} \}, \emptyset). \tag{3}$$

This theory has one assertional extension, including $\langle A, \{A\} \rangle$ as well as $\langle A \vee B, \{A\} \rangle$. Adding the latter assertion to the set of assertional facts yields the assertional default theory

$$(D_4, W_4) = (\{ \tfrac{:A}{A}, \tfrac{A \vee B : \neg A}{\neg A} \}, \{ \langle A \vee B, \{A\} \rangle \}) \tag{4}$$

which has the same assertional extension. Note that without the support $\{A\}$ for $A \vee B$, one obtains a second assertional extension with $\langle \neg A, \{\neg A\} \rangle$. This is what happens in the previously-described default logics.

It is well-known that cumulative and constrained extensions are equivalent whenever the underlying facts contain no support. Similar relationships are given among original and Q-default logic [5], justified and affirmative [10], rational and CA-default logic [5], respectively (cf. [10]).

3   Correspondence with Constrained, Justified, and Rational Default Logic

This section presents encodings for representing major variant default logics in Reiter's default logic. For a default theory Δ, we produce a translated theory $\mathcal{T}_x \Delta$, such that there is a 1–1 correspondence between the extensions of Δ in x-default logic and (standard) extensions of $\mathcal{T}_x \Delta$. We begin with constrained and rational default logic, whose encoding is less involved, then consider that of justified default logic.

3.1   Correspondence with Constrained Default Logic

For a language $\mathcal{L}$ over alphabet $\mathcal{P}$, let $\mathcal{L}'$ be the language over $\mathcal{P}' = \{p' \mid p \in \mathcal{P}\}$. For a formula α, let α' be the formula obtained by replacing any symbol $p \in \mathcal{P}$ by p'; in addition define for a set W of formulas, $W' = \{\alpha' \mid \alpha \in W\}$.

Definition 8. *For default theory (D, W), define $\mathcal{T}_c(D, W) = (D_c, W_c)$ where*

$$W_c = W \cup W' \quad and \quad D_c = \left\{ \left. \tfrac{\alpha : \beta' \wedge \gamma'}{\gamma \wedge (\beta' \wedge \gamma')} \right| \tfrac{\alpha : \beta}{\gamma} \in D \right\}.$$

Informally, we retain the justification of an applied default rule in an extension, but as a primed formula; this set of primed formulas then corresponds to the set C in Definition 3. Thus we essentially encode Definition 3, but in a standard default theory. Other variants of default logic are similarly encoded, although sometimes in a somewhat more complex formulation. For our examples in (1) and (2), we obtain:

$$\mathcal{T}_c(D_1, W_1) = \left(\left\{ \frac{:B' \wedge C'}{C \wedge B' \wedge C'}, \frac{:\neg B' \wedge D'}{D \wedge \neg B' \wedge D'} \right\}, \emptyset \right)$$

$$\mathcal{T}_c(D_2, W_2) = \left(\left\{ \frac{:B' \wedge C'}{C \wedge B' \wedge C'}, \frac{:\neg C' \wedge D'}{D \wedge \neg C' \wedge D'} \right\}, \emptyset \right) .$$

Now, theory $\mathcal{T}_c(D_1, W_1)$ yields two extensions in standard default logic, one containing $C \wedge B' \wedge C'$ and the other including $D \wedge \neg B' \wedge D'$. Analogously, we obtain two extensions from $\mathcal{T}_c(D_2, W_2)$, one with $C \wedge B' \wedge C'$ and the other with $D \wedge \neg C' \wedge D'$. In general, we have the following result.

Theorem 1. *For a default theory* (D, W), *we have that*

1. *if* (E, C) *is a constrained extension of* (D, W) *then* $Th(E \cup C')$ *is an extension of* $\mathcal{T}_c(D, W)$;
2. *if* F *is an extension of* $\mathcal{T}_c(D, W)$ *then* $(F \cap \mathcal{L}, \{\varphi \mid \varphi' \in F \cap \mathcal{L}'\})$ *is a constrained extension of* (D, W).

Theorem 2. *The constrained extensions of a default theory* (D, W) *and the extensions of the translation* $\mathcal{T}_c(D, W)$ *are in a 1–1 correspondence.*

3.2 Correspondence with Rational Default Logic

As expected, the mapping of rational default logic into standard default logic is close to that of constrained default logic:

Definition 9. *For default theory* (D, W), *define* $\mathcal{T}_r(D, W) = (D_r, W_r)$ *where*

$$W_r = W \cup W' \quad and \quad D_r = \left\{ \frac{\alpha : \beta'}{\gamma \wedge (\beta' \wedge \gamma')} \mid \frac{\alpha : \beta}{\gamma} \in D \right\} .$$

As before, the consequent of rules in D_r encodes the formulas in a rational extension (Definition 4). For our examples in (1) and (2), we obtain:

$$\mathcal{T}_r(D_1, W_1) = \left(\left\{ \frac{:B'}{C \wedge B' \wedge C'}, \frac{:\neg B'}{D \wedge \neg B' \wedge D'} \right\}, \emptyset \right)$$

$$\mathcal{T}_r(D_2, W_2) = \left(\left\{ \frac{:B'}{C \wedge B' \wedge C'}, \frac{:\neg C'}{D \wedge \neg C' \wedge D'} \right\}, \emptyset \right) .$$

As with theory $\mathcal{T}_c(D_1, W_1)$, theory $\mathcal{T}_r(D_1, W_1)$ yields two extensions, one containing $C \wedge B' \wedge C'$ and $D \wedge \neg B' \wedge D'$, respectively. In contrast to $\mathcal{T}_c(D_2, W_2)$, however, we obtain one extension from $\mathcal{T}_r(D_2, W_2)$, containing $C \wedge B' \wedge C'$.

In general, we have the following result.

Theorem 3. *For a default theory* (D, W), *we have that*

1. *if* (E, C) *is a rational extension of* (D, W) *then* $Th(E \cup C')$ *is an extension of* $\mathcal{T}_r(D, W)$;
2. *if* F *is an extension of* $\mathcal{T}_r(D, W)$ *then* $(F \cap \mathcal{L}, \{\varphi \mid \varphi' \in F \cap \mathcal{L}'\})$ *is a rational extension of* (D, W).

As with Theorem 2, one can show that the extensions of a default theory (D, W) and the translation $\mathcal{T}_r(D, W)$ are in a 1–1 correspondence.

3.3 Correspondence with Justified Default Logic

Define for a language $\mathcal{L}$ over alphabet $\mathcal{P}$ and some set S, the family $(\mathcal{L}^s)_{s \in S}$ of languages over $\mathcal{P}^s = \{p^s \mid p \in \mathcal{P}\}$ for $s \in S$. For $\alpha \in \mathcal{L}$ and $s \in S$, let α^s be the formula obtained by replacing every symbol $p \in \mathcal{P}$ in α by p^s; in addition define for a set W of formulas, $W^s = \{\alpha^s \mid \alpha \in W\}$.

In what follows, we let the set of default rules D induce copies of the original language.

Definition 10. *For default theory* (D, W), *define* $\mathcal{T}_j(D, W) = (D_j, W_j)$ *where*

$$W_j = W \cup \bigcup_{\varsigma \in D} W^\varsigma \text{ and } D_j = \left\{ \frac{\alpha : (\beta^\delta \wedge \gamma^\delta) \wedge (\bigwedge_{\varsigma \in D} \gamma^\varsigma)}{\gamma \wedge (\beta^\delta \wedge \gamma^\delta) \wedge (\bigwedge_{\varsigma \in D} \gamma^\varsigma)} \;\middle|\; \delta = \frac{\alpha : \beta}{\gamma} \in D \right\}.$$

For simplicity, we write $\beta = Justif^\circ(\delta)$ whenever $Justif(\delta) = (\beta^\delta \wedge \gamma^\delta) \wedge (\bigwedge_{\varsigma \in D} \gamma^\varsigma)$.

Abbreviating the two default rules in both examples, (1) and (2), by $\delta 1, \delta 2$ and $\delta 1, \delta 4$, respectively, we get (after removing duplicates):

$$\mathcal{T}_j(D_1, W_1) = \left(\left\{ \frac{: B^{\delta 1} \wedge C^{\delta 1} \wedge C^{\delta 2}}{C \wedge B^{\delta 1} \wedge C^{\delta 1} \wedge C^{\delta 2}}, \frac{: \neg B^{\delta 2} \wedge D^{\delta 2} \wedge D^{\delta 1}}{D \wedge \neg B^{\delta 2} \wedge D^{\delta 2} \wedge D^{\delta 1}} \right\}, \emptyset \right)$$

$$\mathcal{T}_j(D_2, W_2) = \left(\left\{ \frac{: B^{\delta 1} \wedge C^{\delta 1} \wedge C^{\delta 4}}{C \wedge B^{\delta 1} \wedge C^{\delta 1} \wedge C^{\delta 4}}, \frac{: \neg C^{\delta 4} \wedge D^{\delta 4} \wedge D^{\delta 1}}{D \wedge \neg C^{\delta 4} \wedge D^{\delta 4} \wedge D^{\delta 1}} \right\}, \emptyset \right)$$

In standard default logic, theory $\mathcal{T}_j(D_1, W_1)$ results in one extension containing C, D, $B^{\delta 1}, C^{\delta 1}, D^{\delta 1}$, and $\neg B^{\delta 2}, C^{\delta 2}, D^{\delta 2}$. Unlike this, $\mathcal{T}_j(D_2, W_2)$ gives two extensions, one with $C \wedge B^{\delta 1} \wedge C^{\delta 1} \wedge C^{\delta 4}$ and another including $D \wedge \neg C^{\delta 4} \wedge D^{\delta 4} \wedge D^{\delta 1}$.

We have the following general result.

Theorem 4. *For a default theory* (D, W), *we have that*

1. *if* (E, J) *is a justified extension of* (D, W) *then*
   $$F = Th\left(E \cup \bigcup_{\varsigma \in D} E^\varsigma \cup \bigcup_{\beta \in J} \{\beta^{\delta(\beta)}\} \right) \text{ is an extension of } \mathcal{T}_j(D, W);$$
2. *if* F *is an extension of* $\mathcal{T}_j(D, W)$ *then* $(F \cap \mathcal{L}, J)$ *is a justified extension of* (D, W), *where* $J = \{\beta \mid \beta = Justif^\circ(\delta) \text{ and } \delta \in GD(\mathcal{T}_j(D, W), F)\}$.

$GD(\mathcal{T}_j(D, W), F)$ gives the set of default rules generating F; see the full version for a formal definition.

In analogy to Theorem 2, one can show that the extensions of a default theory (D, W) and the translation $\mathcal{T}_j(D, W)$ are in a 1–1 correspondence.

3.4   Correspondence with (Standard) Default Logic

We can show that there is a self-embedding for standard default logic to standard default logic, using the encoding of the previous subsection:

Definition 11. *For default theory* (D, W), *define* $\mathcal{T}_d(D, W) = (D_d, W_d)$ *where*

$$
W_d = W \cup \bigcup\nolimits_{\varsigma \in D} W^\varsigma \text{ and } D_d = \left\{ \frac{\alpha : \beta^\delta}{\gamma \wedge (\beta^\delta \wedge \gamma^\delta) \wedge (\bigwedge_{\varsigma \in D} \gamma^\varsigma)} \;\middle|\; \delta = \frac{\alpha : \beta}{\gamma} \in D \right\} .
$$

One can show that this mapping results in extensions that are in a 1–1 correspondence to those of the original theory. That is, one obtains a result similar to that in Theorem 4. This embedding also illustrates in a different fashion how default logic and justified default logic relate. As well, this translation allows for embedding standard default logic into rational default logic, as made precise next.

Theorem 5. *For a default theory* (D, W), *we have that*

1. *if* E *is an extension of* (D, W) *then* (F, F) *is a rational extension of* $\mathcal{T}_d(D, W)$,

   where $F = Th\left(E \cup \bigcup_{\varsigma \in D} E^\varsigma \cup \bigcup_{\delta \in GD((D,W),E)} \{Justif(\delta)^\delta\} \right)$;
2. *if* (F, F) *is a rational extension of* $\mathcal{T}_d(D, W)$ *then* $F \cap \mathcal{L}$ *is an extension of* (D, W).

As before, one can show that the extensions of a default theory (D, W) and the translation $\mathcal{T}_d(D, W)$ are in a 1–1 correspondance.

For our examples in (1) and (2), we get:

$$
\mathcal{T}_d(D_1, W_1) = \left(\left\{ \frac{: B^{\delta 1}}{C \wedge B^{\delta 1} \wedge C^{\delta 1} \wedge C^{\delta 2}}, \frac{: \neg B^{\delta 2}}{D \wedge \neg B^{\delta 2} \wedge D^{\delta 2} \wedge D^{\delta 1}} \right\}, \emptyset \right)
$$

$$
\mathcal{T}_d(D_2, W_2) = \left(\left\{ \frac{: B^{\delta 1}}{C \wedge B^{\delta 1} \wedge C^{\delta 1} \wedge C^{\delta 4}}, \frac{: \neg C^{\delta 4}}{D \wedge \neg C^{\delta 4} \wedge D^{\delta 4} \wedge D^{\delta 1}} \right\}, \emptyset \right) .
$$

In contrast to the two rational extensions obtained from (D_1, W_1), theory $\mathcal{T}_d(D_1, W_1)$ results in one rational extension containing $C, D, B^{\delta 1}, C^{\delta 1}, D^{\delta 1}$, and $\neg B^{\delta 2}, C^{\delta 2}, D^{\delta 2}$. As well, $\mathcal{T}_d(D_2, W_2)$ gives one rational extension with $C \wedge B^{\delta 1} \wedge C^{\delta 1} \wedge C^{\delta 4}$.

Note that a corresponding mapping into justified or constrained default logic is impossible; this is not a matter of the specific translation but rather a principal impossibility.

Theorem 6. *There is no mapping* $\mathcal{T}$ *such that for any default theory* (D, W), *we have that the extensions of* (D, W) *are in a 1–1 correspondance with the constrained/justified extensions of* $\mathcal{T}(D, W)$.

To see this, consider theory $\left(\left\{ \frac{: B}{\neg B} \right\}, \emptyset \right)$, having *no* extension. On the other hand, it is well known that every default theory has at least *one* justified and constrained extension [11, 3].

Finally, we note that a correspondence, as expressed in Theorem 5, can be established between justified and constrained extensions; we omit the details.

4   Correspondence with Cumulative Default Logic

This section presents an encoding for representing cumulative default logic and cumulative extensions in default logic. In order to be able to talk about an assertion $\langle\alpha,\{\beta_1,\ldots,\beta_n\}\rangle$ within a (classical, logical) theory, an assertion is *reified* as an atomic formula $\langle\cdot,\cdot\rangle^{re}$, where each argument is a reified formula that does not contain an instance of $\langle\cdot,\cdot\rangle^{re}$. Thus $\langle\alpha,\{\beta_1,\ldots,\beta_n\}\rangle$ is represented in the object language as $\langle\alpha,\beta_1\wedge\cdots\wedge\beta_n\rangle^{re}$. So that translated assertions have appropriate properties, we employ a set of formulas Ax_{re} axiomatising the reified formulas:

Definition 12. *Ax_{re} is the least set containing instances of the following schemata:*

1. *If $\vdash\alpha$ then $\langle\alpha,\emptyset\rangle^{re}\in Ax_{re}$.*
2. *$(\beta_1\equiv\beta_2)\supset(\langle\alpha,\beta_1\rangle^{re}\equiv\langle\alpha,\beta_2\rangle^{re})$.*
3. *$\langle\alpha,\gamma\rangle^{re}\wedge\langle\alpha\supset\beta,\psi\rangle^{re}\supset\langle\beta,\psi\wedge\gamma\rangle^{re}$.*

We have the following analogue of Definition 6:

Theorem 7. *If $\langle\alpha_1,\beta_1\rangle^{re},\langle\alpha_2,\beta_2\rangle^{re}\in\Gamma$ and $\{\alpha_1,\alpha_2\}\vdash\gamma$ then $\Gamma\vdash\langle\gamma,\beta_1\wedge\beta_2\rangle^{re}$.*

From this we establish a correspondence between extensions of cumulative default logic and default logic. We first define correspondences between assertions and formulas of classical logic.

Definition 13.
   For Γ a set of assertions, define $Re\,(\Gamma)=\{\langle\alpha,\beta\rangle^{re}\mid\langle\alpha,\beta\rangle\in\Gamma\}$.
   For Γ a set of formulas of classical logic, define $Re^{-1}(\Gamma)=\{\langle\alpha,\beta\rangle\mid\langle\alpha,\beta\rangle^{re}\in\Gamma\}$.
   For Γ a set of assertions, define $Re^{+}(\Gamma)=Re\,(\Gamma)\cup Form(\Gamma)\cup Supp(\Gamma)\cup Ax_{re}$.

Definition 14. *For assertional default theory $(D,\mathcal{W})$, define $\mathcal{T}_a(D,\mathcal{W})=(D_a,W_a)$ where*

$$W_a=Re^{+}(\mathcal{W})\qquad and\qquad D_a=\left\{\frac{\langle\alpha,\psi\rangle^{re}:\beta\wedge\gamma}{\langle\gamma,\psi\wedge\beta\wedge\gamma\rangle^{re}\wedge\beta\wedge\gamma}\;\middle|\;\frac{\alpha:\beta}{\gamma}\in D,\;\psi\in\mathcal{L}\right\}.$$

The superscript *re* on formulas or sets of formulas indicates that these (sets of) formulas are in the image of our mapping, and are intended to be components satisfying a definition of a (Reiter) default extension.

This translation nicely shows that the support of (reified) assertions is only needed for keeping track of underlying assumptions when adding default conclusions to the set of facts; the consistency check remains unaffected. In fact, the treatment of $\beta\wedge\gamma$ in Definition 14 is identical to that of $\beta'\wedge\gamma'$ in Definition 8.

Consider our examples in (1) and (2):

$$\mathcal{T}_a(D_3,W_3)=\left(\left\{\frac{\langle\top,\psi\rangle^{re}:A}{\langle A,\psi\wedge A\rangle^{re}\wedge A},\;\frac{\langle A\vee B,\psi\rangle^{re}:\neg A}{\langle\neg A,\psi\wedge\neg A\rangle^{re}\wedge\neg A}\;\middle|\;\psi\in\mathcal{L}\right\},Ax_{re}\right)$$

$$\mathcal{T}_a(D_4,W_4)=\left(\left\{\frac{\langle\top,\psi\rangle^{re}:A}{\langle A,\psi\wedge A\rangle^{re}\wedge A},\;\frac{\langle A\vee B,\psi\rangle^{re}:\neg A}{\langle\neg A,\psi\wedge\neg A\rangle^{re}\wedge\neg A}\;\middle|\;\psi\in\mathcal{L}\right\},Ax_{re}\cup\right.$$
$$\left.\{\langle A\vee B,\{A\}\rangle^{re}\}\cup\{A\vee B\}\cup\{A\}\right)$$

Both theories $T_a(D_3, W_3)$ and $T_a(D_4, W_4)$ yield one extension in standard default logic, containing $\langle A, \{A\} \rangle^{re}$.

We have the following general result.

Theorem 8. *For an assertional default theory* (D, W), *we have that*

1. *if* $\mathcal{E}$ *is an assertional extension of* (D, W), *then* $Th(Re^+(\mathcal{E}))$ *is an extension of* $T_a(D, W)$;
2. *if* E *is an extension of* $T_a(D, W)$, *then* $Re^{-1}(E)$ *is an assertional extension of* (D, W).

Similar to the previous results, we also have a 1-1 correspondence between the extensions of a default theory and the extensions of the translation.

The translation given here for cumulative default logic is different from the previous translations, which clearly yielded a polynomial increase in size of the translated over the original theory. In the present case, Definition 14 gives an infinite number of defaults (due to the presence of ψ in the formula schemata). However, in practice we can nonetheless work with a translated theory that is only a polynomial increase over the original. First, for an assertional extension $\mathcal{E}$ and its translated counterpart $Th(Re^+(\mathcal{E}))$, we clearly have a 1-1 mapping between the respective sets of generating defaults. Second, any instantiation of ψ in Definition 14 (corresponding to the support of the prerequisite) can only draw upon elements of W or consequents of members of D; hence the size of any translated rule will be bounded by $|W| \times |D|$. As a result, an intelligent default prover can be restricted to a subset of the translated theory that is at worst a polynomial increase in size over the original.

5 Concluding Remarks

We have shown how variants of default logic can be expressed in Reiter's original approach. Similarly, we have shown that rational default logic and default logic may be encoded, one into the other. This work then complements previous work in nonmonotonic reasoning which has shown links between (seeming) disparate approaches. Here we show links between (seemingly) disparate variants of default logic. As well, the translations clearly illustrate the relationships between alternative approaches to default logic. In fact, there is a division between default logic and rational default logic on the one hand, and the remaining variants on the other, manifesting itself through the property of semi-monotonicity. Although it has often been informally argued that the computational advantages[2] of semi-monotonicity are offset by a loss of representational power, this claim has up to now not been formally sustained. The results reported in [9] provide another indication of the relation between semi-monotonicity and expressiveness: normal default logic is a semi-monotonic fragment of Reiter's default logic and strictly less expressive than default logic. The same can be stated about cumulativity, as prerequisite-free, normal default logic (which corresponds to parallel circumscription) is strictly less expressive than normal default logic.

---

[2] Semi-monotonicity allows for incremental constructions, also guaranteeing the existence of extensions.

Our contributions can also be seen as a refinement of the investigations of complexity and/or expressiveness conducted in [7,19,13,8,6,9]. From the perspective of complexity, there were of course hints that such mappings are possible. First, it is well-known that the reasoning problems of all considered variants are at the second level of the polynomial hierarchy [7,19]. The same is true for the "existence of extensions" problem in default logic and rational default logic, while it is trivial in justified and constrained default logic (and analogously for the respective assertional counterparts). In view of the same complexity of reasoning tasks, observe that our impossibility claim expressed in Theorem 6 is about the non-existence of corresponding sets of extensions. This does not exclude the possibility of an encoding of incoherent Reiter or rational default theories in a semi-monotonic variant that, for instance, indicates incoherence through a special-purpose symbol. However, there would be no 1–1 mapping here, since for any justified or constrained extension containing this special-purpose symbol, there would be no corresponding standard or rational extension.

The most closely related work to our own is that of Tomi Janhunen [9], who has investigated translations among specific subclasses of Reiter's default logic. For instance, he gives a translation mapping arbitrary default theories into semi-normal theories, showing that semi-normal default theories are as expressive as general ones. Other translation schemes can be found in [13], where among others the notion of semi-representability is introduced. This concept deals with the representation of default theories within restricted subclasses of default theories over an extended language. Although semi-representability adheres to a fixed interpretation of default logic, one can view our results as semi-representation results among different interpretations of default theories. As regards future research, it would be interesting to see whether the results presented here lead to new relationships in the hierarchy of non-monotonic logics established in [9]. Also, a more detailed analysis of time and space complexity is an issue of future research.

The present work may also, in fact, lend insight into computational characteristics of default logic. For example, our mappings provide specific syntactic characterisations of default theories that are guaranteed to have extensions. That is, for example, constrained default theories are guaranteed to have extensions; hence default theories appearing in the image of our mapping (Definition 8) are guaranteed to have extensions.

Apart from the theoretical insights, the great advantage of mappings such as we have given, is that it suffices to have one general implementation of default logic for capturing a whole variety of different approaches. In this respect, our results allow us to handle all sorts of default logics by standard default logic implementations, such as DeReS [2].

Acknowledgements. We would like to thank Tomi Janhunen for many helpful remarks on earlier drafts of this paper. Also, we are grateful to the anonymous referees for their constructive remarks, although we were not able to take all of them into account in this abridged report. The first author was partially supported by a Canadian NSERC Research Grant; the second author was partially supported by the German DFG grant FOR 375/1-1, TP C.

References

1. G. Brewka. Cumulative default logic: In defense of nonmonotonic inference rules. *Artificial Intelligence*, 50(2):183–205, 1991.
2. P. Cholewiński, V. Marek, and M. Truszczyński. Default reasoning system DeReS. In *Proceedings of the Fifth International Conference on the Principles of Knowledge Representation and Reasoning*, pages 518–528. Morgan Kaufmann Publishers, 1996.
3. J.P. Delgrande, T. Schaub, and K. Jackson. Alternative approaches to default logic. *Artificial Intelligence*, 70(1-2):167–237, October 1995.
4. C. Froidevaux and J. Mengin. Default logic: A unified view. *Computational Intelligence*, 10(3):331–369, 1994.
5. L. Giordano and A. Martinelli. On cumulative default logics. *Artificial Intelligence*, 66(1):161–179, 1994.
6. G. Gogic, H. Kautz, C. Papadimitriou, and B. Selman. The comparative linguistics of knowledge representation. In C. Mellish, editor, *Proceedings of the International Joint Conference on Artificial Intelligence*, pages 862–869. Morgan Kaufmann Publishers, 1995.
7. G. Gottlob. Complexity results for nonmonotonic logics. *Journal of Logic and Computation*, 2(3):397–425, June 1992.
8. G. Gottlob and Z. Mingyi. Cumulative default logic: Finite characterization, algorithms, and complexity. *Artificial Intelligence*, 69(1-2):329–345, 1994.
9. T. Janhunen. Classifying semi-normal default logic on the basis of its expressive power. In M. Gelfond, N. Leone, and G. Pfeifer, editors, *Proceedings of the Fifth International Conference on Logic Programming and Nonmonotonic Reasoning (LPNMR'99)*, volume 1730 of *Lecture Notes in Artificial Intelligence*, pages 19–33. Springer Verlag, 1999.
10. T. Linke and T. Schaub. Towards a classification of default logics. *Journal of Applied Non-Classical Logics*, 7(4):397–451, 1997.
11. W. Lukaszewicz. Considerations on default logic: An alternative approach. *Computational Intelligence*, 4(1):1–16, Jan. 1988.
12. D. Makinson. General theory of cumulative inference. In M. Reinfrank, editor, *Proc. of the Second International Workshop on Non-Monotonic Reasoning*, volume 346 of *Lecture Notes in Artificial Intelligence*, pages 1–18. Springer Verlag, 1989.
13. V. Marek and M. Truszczyński. *Nonmonotonic logic: context-dependent reasoning*. Artifical Intelligence. Springer-Verlag, 1993.
14. A. Mikitiuk and M. Truszczyński. Rational default logic and disjunctive logic programming. In A. Nerode and L. Pereira, editors, *Proceedings of the Second International Workshop on logic Programming and Non-monotonic Reasoning.*, pages 283–299. The MIT Press, 1993.
15. A. Mikitiuk and M. Truszczyński. Constrained and rational default logics. In *Proceedings of the International Joint Conference on Artificial Intelligence*, pages 1509–1515, Montréal, 1995. Morgan Kaufmann Publishers.
16. D.L. Poole. What the lottery paradox tells us about default reasoning (extended abstract). In *Proceedings of the First International Conference on the Principles of Knowledge Representation and Reasoning*, Toronto, Ont., 1989.
17. R. Reiter. A logic for default reasoning. *Artificial Intelligence*, 13:81–132, 1980.
18. T. Schaub. *Considerations on Default Logic*. PhD thesis, Technische Hochschule Darmstadt, FB Informatik, FG Intellektik, Alexanderstr. 10, nov 1992.
19. J. Stillman. It's not my default: The complexity of membership problems in restricted propositional default logics. In *Proceedings of the Second International Conference on the Principles of Knowledge Representation and Reasoning*, pages 571–578, 1991.

Probable Consistency Checking for Sets of Propositional Clauses

Anthony Hunter

Department of Computer Science
University College London
Gower Street, London WC1E 6BT, UK

Abstract. Inconsistencies inevitably arise in knowledge during practical reasoning. In a logic-based approach, this gives rise to the need for consistency checking. Unfortunately, this can be difficult. In classical propositional logic, this is intractable. However, there is a useful alternative to the notion of consistency called probable consistency. This offers a weakening of classical consistency checking where polynomial time tests are done on a set of formulae to determine the probability that the set of formulae is consistent. In this paper, we present a framework for probable consistency checking for sets of clauses, and analyse some classes of polynomial time tests.

1 Introduction

In order to manage inconsistency in knowledge, we need to undertake consistency checking. However, consistency checking is inherently intractable in the case of propositional classical logic. To address this problem, we can consider using (A) tractable subsets of classical logic (for example binary disjunctions of literals [3]), (B) heuristics to direct the search for a model[1] (for example in semantic tableau [7], GSAT [10], and constraint satisfaction [2]), (C) some form of knowledge compilation (for example [6,1]), and (D) formalization of approximate consistency checking based on notions described below, such as approximate entailment, and partial and probable consistency.

Approximate Entailment. Proposed in [5], and developed in [9,4], classical entailment is approximated by two sequences of entailment relations. The first is sound but not complete, and the second is complete but not sound. Both sequences converge to classical entailment. For a set of propositional formulae Δ, a formula α, and an approximate entailment relation $\models_i$, the decision of whether $\Delta \models_i \alpha$ holds or $\Delta \not\models_i \alpha$ holds can be computed in polynomial time.

Partial Consistency. Consistency checking does not necessarily involve an exponential search space. Furthermore, consistency checking for a set of formulae Δ can be

---

[1] Heuristic approaches can be either complete such as semantic tableau or incomplete such as in the GSAT system. Whilst in general, using heuristics to direct search has the same worst-case computational properties as undirected search, it can offer better performance in practice for some classes of theories. Note, heuristic approaches do not tend to be oriented to offering any analysis of theories beyond a decision on consistency.

T.D. Nielsen and N.L. Zhang (Eds.): ECSQARU 2003, LNAI 2711, pp. 464–476, 2003.

prematurely terminated when the search space exceeds some threshold. When the checking of Δ is prematurely terminated, partial consistency is the degree to which Δ is consistent. This can be measured in a number of ways including the proportion of formulae from Δ that can be shown to form a consistent subset of Δ. Maximum generalized satisfiability [8] may be viewed as an example of this.

Probable Consistency. Determining the probability that a set of formulae is consistent on the basis of polynomial time classifications of those formulae. Classifications for the propositional case can be based on tests including counting the number of different propositional letters, counting the multiple occurrences of each propositional letter, and determining the degree of nesting for each logical symbol. The more a set of formulae is tested, the greater the confidence in the probability value for consistency/inconsistency, but this is at the cost of undertaking the tests.

Identifying approximate consistency for a set of formulae Δ is obviously not a guarantee that Δ is consistent. However, approximate consistency checking is useful because it helps focus where problems possibly lie in Δ, and so prioritize resolution tasks. For example, if Δ and Γ are two parts of a larger knowledgebase that is thought to be inconsistent, and the probability of consistency is much greater for Δ than Γ, then Γ is more likely to be problematical and so should be examined more closely. Similarly, if Δ and Γ are two parts of a larger knowledgebase that is thought to be inconsistent, and a partial consistency identified for Δ is greater than for Γ, then Γ seems to contain more problematical data and so should be examined more closely by the user.

The notions of probable consistency and partial consistency provide complementary means for reasoning with knowledge. For a set of formulae Δ, with partial consistency, we may identify subsets of Δ that are consistent, but have no certainty on whether Δ is consistent, whereas with probable consistency, we can obtain a view on the whole of Δ, but cannot guarantee to find consistent subsets even if they exist.

In this paper, we explore probable consistency checking in more detail. In the next section, we provide some basic definitions, then in the following sections we formalize probable consistency, and give an example in detail.

2 Basic Definitions for Syntax

In this section, we recall some of the usual definitions for classical logic, and then provide some additional definitions for analysing the syntax of formulae that will be used in the rest of the paper.

Definition 1. *Let $\mathcal{L}_{atoms}$ be a set of **atoms** and let $\mathcal{L}$ be the set of **classical propositional formulae** formed from $\mathcal{L}_{atoms}$, and the $\wedge, \vee, \rightarrow$ and $\neg$ connectives. For each atom $\alpha \in \mathcal{L}_{atoms}$, α is a **positive literal** and $\neg\alpha$ is a **negative literal**. Let $\mathcal{L}_{literals}$ be the set of literals in $\mathcal{L}$.*

Example 1. From the propositional atoms α, β and γ, members of $\mathcal{L}$ include $\alpha, \beta \wedge \gamma$, $\neg\alpha \wedge \alpha$ and $(\alpha \wedge \beta) \rightarrow \neg\neg\gamma$.

Definition 2. *For $\alpha_1 \vee .. \vee \alpha_n \in \mathcal{L}$, $\alpha_1 \vee .. \vee \alpha_n$ is a **clause** iff each of $\alpha_1, .., \alpha_n$ is a literal. Let $\mathcal{C} \subset \mathcal{L}$ be the set of clauses. Let $\mathcal{C}_i \subset \mathcal{C}$ be the set of clauses of arity i (i.e. the clauses that are a disjunction of i literals).*

So, $\mathcal{C}_1$ is the set of literals, $\mathcal{C}_2$ is the set of binary clauses, and $\mathcal{C}_3$ is the set of ternary clauses.

Definition 3. *Let α be a literal, then α^* is the complementary literal. So if β is an atom, then β^* is $\neg\beta$, and $(\neg\beta)^*$ is β.*

Definition 4. *For clauses, $\alpha \vee \beta$, $\neg\beta \vee \gamma$, $\alpha \vee \gamma \in \mathcal{L}$, $\alpha \vee \gamma$ is a **resolvent** of $\alpha \vee \beta$ and $\neg\beta \vee \gamma$.*

Definition 5. *Let the **atoms function**, denoted Atoms, be a function from $\wp(\mathcal{L})$ into $\mathcal{L}_{atoms}$ such that $\mathsf{Atoms}(\Gamma)$ gives the set of atoms used in Γ.*

Example 2. For $\alpha, \beta, \gamma \in \mathcal{L}_{atoms}$, $\mathsf{Atoms}(\{\alpha \wedge \beta\}) = \{\alpha, \beta\}$, and $\mathsf{Atoms}(\{\alpha \wedge \alpha, (\neg\alpha \wedge \beta \wedge \gamma) \rightarrow \alpha\}) = \{\alpha, \beta, \gamma\}$.

Definition 6. *Let $\mathcal{A}$ be a finite subset of $\mathcal{L}_{atoms}$. Let $\mathcal{L}^{\mathcal{A}}$ be the subset of $\mathcal{L}$ where*

$$\mathcal{L}^{\mathcal{A}} = \{\alpha \in \mathcal{L} \mid \mathsf{Atoms}(\{\alpha\}) \subseteq \mathcal{A}\}$$

So, $\mathcal{L}^{\mathcal{A}}_{atoms} = \mathcal{A}$, and $\mathcal{L}^{\mathcal{A}}_{literals} = \mathcal{A} \cup \{\neg\alpha \mid \alpha \in \mathcal{A}\} = \mathcal{C}^{\mathcal{A}}_1$, and $\mathcal{C}^{\mathcal{A}}_i = \mathcal{C}_i \cap \mathcal{L}^{\mathcal{A}}$.

3 Probable Consistency for Sets of Clauses

Suppose a set of formulae Γ is either $\{\alpha \vee \alpha, \neg\alpha \vee \neg\alpha\}$ or $\{\alpha \vee \neg\alpha, \beta \vee \gamma\}$, and it is equally likely that it is either of them, then the probability of Γ being consistent is $1/2$. Using this idea, if we can determine whether a given set of formulae Γ is in a particular class of sets of formulae where the probability of consistency is known, then we have a probability of consistency for Γ. To do this, we need polynomial time tests to analyse each set of formulae. These tests may include a count of the number of propositional letters used in the formulae in the set, a count of the number of formulae in the set, and a count of the number of types of logical symbols used in the formulae in the set. These polynomial time tests delineate classes of sets of formulae. To support this, we need to determine, in advance, the proportion of inconsistent formulae for these classes.

Example 3. Let $\Gamma \in \wp(\mathcal{C})$. If $\mathsf{Atoms}(\Gamma) = \{\alpha\}$, and $|\Gamma| = 2$, where one formula is a positive literal and the other is a negative literal, then the sample space containing Γ has just one element, which is $\{\alpha, \neg\alpha\}$. So the probability that Γ is inconsistent is 1.

Example 4. Let $\Gamma \in \wp(\mathcal{C})$. If $\mathsf{Atoms}(\Gamma) = \{\alpha, \beta\}$, and $|\Gamma| = 2$, where one is a positive literal and the other is a negative literal, then the sample space containing Γ has 2 elements $\{\alpha, \neg\beta\}$ and $\{\beta, \neg\alpha\}$. So the probability that Γ is inconsistent is 0.

In this paper, we restrict consideration to sets of clauses. Informally, given some set of clauses Γ, and the results of some tests on Γ, we want to determine the conditional probability that Γ is inconsistent. For this paper, we will assume a uniform distribution over the sample space containing Γ. Assuming a uniform distribution may be too restrictive for some applications. Alternatives include giving a weighted distribution that is determined by either past usage, or predicted usage, of the formulae, or the propositional letters used in the language. Using the uniform distribution, if $\Theta \subseteq \wp(\mathcal{C})$, and m elements of Θ are inconsistent, and $|\Theta| = n$, then the probability of inconsistency of a randomly selected member Γ of Θ is m/n. Also, the probability of consistency of a randomly selected member Γ of Θ is $1 - m/n$.

Example 5. Consider $\Delta = \{\alpha, \neg\alpha, \beta, \neg\beta\}$. Here the probability of a randomly selected element of $\wp(\Delta)$ being inconsistent is $7/16$.

Definition 7. *Let $\mathcal{Q} = \wp(\mathcal{C})$. Let $\mathcal{Q}_{incon}$ be the class of inconsistent sets in $\mathcal{Q}$ and let $\mathcal{Q}_{mis}$ be the class of minimal inconsistent sets in $\mathcal{Q}$.*

$$\mathcal{Q}_{incon} = \{\Gamma \in \mathcal{Q} \mid \Gamma \vdash \bot\}$$
$$\mathcal{Q}_{mis} = \{\Gamma \in \mathcal{Q}_{incon} \mid \neg\exists\Gamma' \in \mathcal{Q}_{incon} \ s.t. \ \Gamma' \subset \Gamma\}$$

Suppose $\mathcal{Q}_t \subseteq \mathcal{Q}$. So if by some test t, we show a set Γ is a member of $\mathcal{Q}_t$, then we use the conditional probability statement $P(\mathcal{Q}_{incon} \mid \mathcal{Q}_t)$ to get a valuation of probable consistency/inconsistency for Γ.

Example 6. Let $\mathcal{Q}_{t_1} = \wp(\{\alpha, \neg\alpha, \beta, \neg\beta\})$. So $P(\mathcal{Q}_{incon} \mid \mathcal{Q}_{t_1}) = 7/16$. If we know by test $t1$, $\Gamma \in \mathcal{Q}_{t_1}$, then according to this, the probability of inconsistency for Γ is $7/16$.

Example 7. Let $\mathcal{Q}_{t_2} = \wp(\{\alpha, \neg\alpha\})$. So $P(\mathcal{Q}_{incon} \mid \mathcal{Q}_{t_2}) = 1/4$. If we know by test t_2, $\Gamma \in \mathcal{Q}_{t_2}$, then according to this, the probability of inconsistency for Γ is $1/4$.

Clearly, if $\Gamma \in \mathcal{Q}_t$ and $P(\mathcal{Q}_{incon} \mid \mathcal{Q}_t) = 1$ then $\Gamma \vdash \bot$ holds. Similarly, if for all $\Gamma \in \mathcal{Q}_t$, $\Gamma \vdash \bot$ holds, then $P(\mathcal{Q}_{incon} \mid \mathcal{Q}_t) = 1$.

Definition 8. *Let $\mathcal{Q}_{t_1} \subseteq \mathcal{Q}$ and ... and $\mathcal{Q}_{t_n} \subseteq \mathcal{Q}$. A* **probable consistency system** *is a set Π of conditional probability statements defined as follows, where $p_1, .., p_n \in [0, 1]$.*

$$\Pi = \{P(\mathcal{Q}_{incon} \mid \mathcal{Q}_{t_1}) = p_1, .., P(\mathcal{Q}_{incon} \mid \mathcal{Q}_{t_n}) = p_n\}.$$

The **universe** *for Π is $\mathcal{Q}_{t_1} \cup ... \cup \mathcal{Q}_{t_n}$.*

In general, we may find by using a battery of test functions that a set of clauses Γ is a member of a number of delineated subsets of $\mathcal{Q}$. If we denoted these subsets $\mathcal{Q}_{t_1}, ..., \mathcal{Q}_{t_n}$, then this can be captured by a conditional probability of the form:

$$P(\mathcal{Q}_{incon} \mid \mathcal{Q}_{t_1} \cap ... \cap \mathcal{Q}_{t_n})$$

Couching test functions in terms of observations means that we can undertake a series of tests on a set of clauses, and that the net result is independent of the order in which the tests are done. In other words, we can easily show that all sequences of a set of tests give the same result.

For a probable consistency system Π, and a set of clauses Γ, the conditional probability chosen is the conditional probability with the most specific reference class for the test results.

Definition 9. *If Π is a probable consistency system, then Π_Γ and Π_Γ^{min} are subsets defined as follows, where $\Gamma \in \mathcal{Q}$ and $\mathcal{Q}_{t_i} \subseteq \mathcal{Q}$.*

$$\Pi_\Gamma = \{P(\mathcal{Q}_{incon} \mid \mathcal{Q}_{t_i}) \in \Pi \mid \Gamma \in \mathcal{Q}_{t_i}\}$$

$$\Pi_\Gamma^{min} = \{P(\mathcal{Q}_{incon} \mid \mathcal{Q}_{t_i}) \in \Pi_\Gamma \mid$$
$$\text{there is no } P(\mathcal{Q}_{incon} \mid \mathcal{Q}_{t_j}) \in \Pi_\Gamma \text{ such that } \mathcal{Q}_{t_j} \subset \mathcal{Q}_{t_i}\}$$

This is used in the following classification, where τ is a fixed threshold such as 0.5.

If for all $P(\mathcal{Q}_{incon} \mid \mathcal{Q}_{t_i}) \in \Pi_\Gamma^{min}, P(\mathcal{Q}_{incon} \mid \mathcal{Q}_{t_i}) < \tau$ holds,
*then Γ is **probably consistent** according to Π.*

In the same way, for $\Gamma' \in \mathcal{Q}_t$, we can have analogous definitions for Γ is probably inconsistent according to Π, and for Γ is probably minimally inconsistent according to Π. The later definition is potentially important in finding faults in knowledgebases and in finding arguments from knowledgebases.

Whilst for small examples, the total cost of using test functions may be greater than undertaking a classical consistency check, in general, they can be cost-effective when used for larger sets of formulae and/or used for more expensive tasks such as searching for minimal inconsistent sets.

4   Case Study with Binary Clauses

Whilst consistency checking for sets of binary clauses is tractable, we will use them to illustrate the probable consistency checking approach. It is simple to check whether a set of formulae is a set of binary clauses. We can define a polynomial test in terms of a small finite state machine. Further simple tests can determine the number of atom symbols used and the number of clauses in a set. The focus of this case study is therefore on various classes of sets of binary clauses to determine the proportion of inconsistent sets within each class, and in particular, the probability that a set of binary clauses is a minimal inconsistent set.

Obviously, if $\Gamma \in \wp(\mathcal{C}_2^{\mathcal{A}})$ is a singleton a set, then the probability that Γ is an minimal inconsistent set is 0. For sets of binary clauses of cardinality greater than 1, we need to consider the nature of minimal inconsistent subsets in a little more detail. In particular, we need to consider the different ways that we can construct conflicting arguments from sets of binary clauses.

4.1   Types of Inconsistency in Sets of Binary Clauses

First we consider the types of contradictory arguments that can be constructed from a set of binary clauses.

Definition 10. *A resolution se uence $\Gamma \in \wp(\mathcal{C}_2^{\mathcal{A}})$ is a sequence of clauses $(\phi_1, ..., \phi_n)$, where $n \geq 1$, such that for each clause ϕ_i (except ϕ_1 and ϕ_n) in the sequence, one of the disjuncts in ϕ_i resolves with one of the disjuncts in the immediate predecessor clause ϕ_{i-1} in the sequence, and the other disjuncts in ϕ_i resolves with one of the disjuncts in the immediate successor clause ϕ_{i+1} in the sequence. The literal in ϕ_1 that does not resolve with a literal in ϕ_2 is a* **tail***. The literal in ϕ_n that does not resolve with a literal in ϕ_{n-1} is also a* **tail***.*

A resolution sequence $(\phi_1, ..., \phi_n)$ gives a proof of a clause $\alpha \vee \beta$ where α is the tail of ϕ_1 and β is the tail of ϕ_n.

Definition 11. *A* **chain** *Γ is a resolution sequence with tails α and β and there is no subset of $\Delta \subset \Gamma$ such that Δ is a resolution sequence with tails α and β*

Example 8. $(\delta \vee \alpha, \neg\delta \vee \gamma, \beta \vee \neg\gamma)$ is a chain.

A chain $(\phi_1, ..., \phi_n)$ gives a minimal proof of a clause $\alpha \vee \beta$ where α is the tail of ϕ_1 and β is the tail of ϕ_n.

Proposition 1. *Let $\vdash$ be the classical consequence relation. For any $\Gamma \in \wp(\mathcal{C}_2^{\mathcal{A}})$, $\phi \in \mathcal{C}_2^{\mathcal{A}}$, if $\Gamma \vdash \phi$, and $\Gamma \not\vdash \bot$, and there is no $\Gamma' \subset \Gamma$ such that $\Gamma' \vdash \phi$, then Γ is a chain.*

Clearly, $(\phi_1, ..., \phi_n)$ is a chain iff $(\phi_n, ..., \phi_1)$ is a chain.

Definition 12. *An* **isochain** *is a chain $(\phi_1, ..., \phi_n)$ where for ϕ_1 and ϕ_n, there is a disjunct in common. This disjunct is called the* **head** *of the isochain. The other disjunct in ϕ_1 resolves with one of the disjuncts in ϕ_2. The other disjunct in ϕ_n resolves with one of the disjuncts in ϕ_{n-1}.*

An isochain gives a minimal proof of a literal. So for each isochain $(\phi_1, .., \phi_n)$ there is a literal α such that $\{\phi_1, .., \phi_n\} \vdash \alpha$, where α is the head of the isochain.

Example 9. The following are two examples of an isochain. Both have α as head.

$$(\alpha \vee \beta, \neg\beta \vee \gamma, \neg\gamma \vee \delta, \neg\delta \vee \alpha)$$
$$(\beta \vee \alpha, \neg\beta \vee \gamma, \alpha \vee \neg\gamma)$$

Example 10. An isochain can use one or more of the same clauses at the start and end of the chain. In the following the first two clauses and the last two clauses are the same.

$$(\alpha \vee \beta, \neg\beta \vee \gamma, \neg\gamma \vee \delta, \neg\delta \vee \neg\gamma, \neg\beta \vee \gamma, \alpha \vee \beta)$$

Definition 13. *A* **superchain** *is a chain* $(\phi_1, ..., \phi_n)$ *such that for some* i, $(\phi_1, ..., \phi_i)$ *is an isochain and* $(\phi_{i+1}, ..., \phi_n)$ *is a chain and so* ϕ_i *has a disjunct that resolves with* ϕ_{i+1}.

The isochain gives a minimal proof of a literal β, and the chain gives a minimal proof of a binary clause $\neg\beta \vee \alpha$, and so the superchain gives a minimal proof of α.

Example 11. The following are two examples of a superchain

$$(\beta \vee \beta, \alpha \vee \neg\beta)$$
$$(\neg\delta \vee \neg\delta, \delta \vee \neg\gamma, \neg\beta \vee \gamma, \beta \vee \alpha)$$

Example 12. A superchain can use one or more of the same clauses in the isochain and chain parts of the sequence. Consider the superchain

$$(\alpha \vee \beta, \neg\beta \vee \gamma, \neg\gamma \vee \alpha, \neg\alpha \vee \beta, \neg\beta \vee \gamma, \neg\gamma \vee \delta)$$

which is composed from the isochain $(\alpha \vee \beta, \neg\beta \vee \gamma, \neg\gamma \vee \alpha)$ and the chain $(\neg\alpha \vee \beta, \neg\beta \vee \gamma, \neg\gamma \vee \delta)$ and have the chain $(\neg\beta \vee \gamma)$ in common.

Proposition 2. *Let* $(\phi_1, ..., \phi_n)$ *be a superchain. If* $(\phi_1, ..., \phi_i)$ *is an isochain, then* $(\phi_{i+1}, ..., \phi_n)$ *is not an isochain.*

Proposition 3. *Let* $(\phi_1, ..., \phi_n)$ *be a chain. If* $(\phi_1, ..., \phi_n)$ *is an isochain, then* $(\phi_1, ..., \phi_n)$ *is not a superchain.*

Proof: Let $(\phi_1, ..., \phi_n)$ be an isochain with head α. So α is a tail in ϕ_1 and α is a tail in ϕ_n. Now suppose, $(\phi_1, ..., \phi_n)$ is also a superchain. Then this superchain incorporates an isochain with head α. So, there is a subset of $\{\phi_1, .., \phi_n\}$ that has the same tails as $(\phi_1, .., \phi_n)$. Therefore, $(\phi_1, ..., \phi_n)$ is not a chain. This contradiction means that it cannot be a superchain.$\square$

Definition 14. *For any* $\Gamma \in \wp(\mathcal{C}_2^{\mathcal{A}})$, Γ *is an* **argument** *for the literal* α *iff* $\Gamma \vdash \alpha$, *and there is no* $\Gamma' \subset \Gamma$ *such that* $\Gamma' \vdash \alpha$, *and* Γ *is an isochain or a superchain.*

Definition 15. *Let* α *be a literal. A* **chainconflict** *is a pair of chains*

$$((\phi_1, ..., \phi_n), (\psi_1, ..., \psi_m))$$

such that $(\phi_1, ..., \phi_n)$ *is an argument for* α *and* $(\psi_1, ..., \psi_m)$ *is an argument for* α^*.

Proposition 4. *For any* $\Delta \in \wp(\mathcal{C}_2^{\mathcal{A}})$, *if* Δ *is a minimal inconsistent set then there is a chainconflict* $((\phi_1, .., \phi_n), (\psi_1, .., \psi_m))$ *such that* $\Delta = \{\phi_1, .., \phi_n\} \cup \{\psi_1, .., \psi_m\}$.

The converse does not hold as illustrated below.

Example 13. Let $(\gamma \vee \gamma, \neg\gamma \vee \alpha)$ be an argument for α, and let $(\neg\gamma \vee \neg\gamma, \gamma \vee \neg\alpha)$ be an argument for $\neg\alpha$. But there is subset of $\{\gamma \vee \gamma, \neg\gamma \vee \alpha\} \cup \{\neg\gamma \vee \neg\gamma, \gamma \vee \neg\alpha\}$ that is inconsistent.

Definition 16. *Let* $((\phi_1, ..., \phi_n), (\psi_1, ..., \psi_m))$ *be a chainconflict. It is a* **disjoint chainconflict***, if* $\{\phi_1, ..., \phi_n\} \cap \{\psi_1, ..., \psi_m\} = \emptyset$*, otherwise it is a* **joint chainconflict***.*

Example 14. The following is a disjoint chainconflict with the first item being an argument for α and the second being an argument for $\neg\alpha$.

$$((\alpha \vee \beta, \neg\beta \vee \gamma, \neg\gamma \vee \alpha), (\delta \vee \delta, \neg\delta \vee \neg\alpha))$$

Example 15. The following is a joint chainconflict, with the first item being an argument for α and the second being an argument for $\neg\alpha$, and $(\gamma \vee \beta, \neg\beta \vee \gamma)$ is a subsequence in common with both superchains.

$$((\gamma \vee \beta, \neg\beta \vee \gamma, \neg\gamma \vee \delta, \neg\delta \vee \alpha), (\gamma \vee \beta, \neg\beta \vee \gamma, \neg\gamma \vee \neg\epsilon, \epsilon \vee \neg\alpha))$$

Example 16. The pair $((\alpha \vee \beta, \neg\beta \vee \neg\delta, \delta \vee \alpha), (\neg\alpha \vee \beta, \neg\beta \vee \neg\delta, \delta \vee \neg\alpha)$ is a joint chainconflict. So we have the isochain $(\alpha \vee \beta, \neg\beta \vee \neg\delta, \delta \vee \alpha)$ and the isochain $(\neg\alpha \vee \beta, \neg\beta \vee \neg\delta, \delta \vee \neg\alpha)$. Together they conflict on α with $(\neg\beta \vee \neg\delta)$ being the chain in common.

We will use this characterization of isochains and superchains in joint and disjoint chainconflicts to enumerate the possible minimal inconsistent sets of binary clauses.

4.2   Combinatorics of Sets of Binary Clauses

We now consider the combinatorics for constructing chainconflicts, and thereby gain the proportion of sets of binary clauses that are minimal inconsistent sets. Our approach here is to consider the formats for minimal inconsistent sets of binary clauses of various cardinalities.

Definition 17. *A* **clause scheme** *is one of the following, where* $i, j \in \mathbb{N}$*, and* X_i *and* X_j *are meta-variables symbols (place holders for literals), and* X_i^* *(respectively* X_j^**) has to be instantiated with the complement of* X_i *(respectively* X_j*).*

$$X_i \vee X_j \qquad X_i \vee X_j^* \qquad X_i^* \vee X_j \qquad X_i^* \vee X_j^*$$

Definition 18. *A* **grounding** *is an assignment of a literal to a meta-variable where the meta-variable is given on the left-hand-side of the* $=$ *symbol and the literal is in the right-hand-side. A* **grounding set** *is a set of groundings where each meta-variable occurs at most once, and each meta-variable is ground with a different atom symbol in the literal (i.e. for all grounding sets if* $X_i = \alpha_i$ *and* $X_j = \alpha_j$ *and* $i \neq j$*, then* $\text{Atoms}(\{\alpha_i\}) \neq \text{Atoms}(\{\alpha_j\})$*).*

Definition 19. *Let Φ be a clause scheme, and G be a grounding. The* Instantiate(Φ, G) *function uses the groundings in G to instantiate the meta-variables in Φ. The result is an* **instantiation** *of Φ.*

When a set of clause schema is instantiated, we obtain a clause from each clause scheme.

Example 17. Let $\{X_1 \vee X_2, X_2^* \vee X_3, X_2 \vee X_4^*\}$ be a set of clause schema, and let $\{X_1 = \neg\alpha, X_2 = \neg\beta, X_3 = \delta, X_4 = \gamma\}$ be a grounding set. Then we obtain the set of clauses $\{\neg\alpha \vee \neg\beta, \beta \vee \delta, \neg\beta \vee \neg\gamma\}$ which is an instantiation.

Clause schema are used to define a set of chainconflicts.

Definition 20. *A* **conflict scheme** *is a set of clause schema $\{\Phi_1, .., \Phi_n\}$, such that if there is a grounding set G that can instantiate each of these clause schema, then* Instantiate$(\Phi_1, G) \cup .. \cup$ Instantiate(Φ_n, G) *is a minimal inconsistent set.*

Example 18. The set $\{X_1 \vee X_1, X_1^* \vee X_1^*\}$ is a conflict scheme. If we let $X_1 = \alpha$, where $\alpha \in \mathcal{A}$, then we obtain $\{\alpha \vee \alpha, \neg\alpha \vee \neg\alpha\}$, which is a minimal inconsistent set.

We also require some subsidiary definitions.

Definition 21. *Let Φ be a set of clause schema. The function* Letters(Φ) *gives the number of different meta-variable symbols used in Φ.*

Example 19. Let $\Phi = \{X_1 \vee X_2, X_2^* \vee X_3, X_2 \vee X_4^*\}$. Then Letters$(\Phi) = 4$.

Definition 22. *Let Φ be a set of clause schema. The function* Heteroclauses(Φ) *gives the* **number of schema** *in Φ where the first disjunct has a different meta-variable symbol to the second disjunct.*

Example 20. Let $\Phi = \{X_1 \vee X_2, X_2^* \vee X_3, X_2 \vee X_2^*\}$. Then Heteroclauses$(\Phi) = 2$. Here the first and second disjuncts of $X_2 \vee X_2^*$ have the same meta-variable symbol.

Some conflict schema are symmetrical in the sense that there are n different grounding sets for each instantiation. For instance, for $\{X_1 \vee X_1, X_1^* \vee X_1^*\}$, there are two groundings for the each instantiation. So for the instantiation $\{\alpha \vee \alpha, \neg\alpha \vee \neg\alpha\}$, we have $G_1 = \{X_1 = \alpha\}$ and $G_2 = \{X_1 = \neg\alpha\}$.

Definition 23. *Let Φ be a set of clause schema. The function* Symmetry *is defined as follows: If there are n different grounding sets $G_1, .., G_n$ such that* Instantiate$(\Phi, G_1) = .. =$ Instantiate(Φ, G_n), *for each instantiation of Φ, then* Symmetry$(\Phi) = 1/n$.

Example 21. To illustrate the Symmetry function, consider the following:

$$\text{Symmetry}(\{X_1 \vee X_2, X_2^* \vee X_3, X_2 \vee X_4^*\}) = 1$$
$$\text{Symmetry}(\{X_1^* \vee X_1, X_1 \vee X_1^*\}) = 1/2$$
$$\text{Symmetry}(\{X_1 \vee X_2, X_2^* \vee X_1, X_1^* \vee X_2, X_2^* \vee X_1^*\}) = 1/2$$

Now we consider how we get the number of chainconflicts from a conflict scheme and a set of atoms.

Definition 24. *For a conflict scheme Φ, the* **number of chainconflicts** *that can be obtained with a set of atoms $\mathcal{A}$ is determined by the function* $\mathsf{Conflictcount}(\Phi, \mathcal{A})$. *We assume a chainconflict* $((\phi_1, .., \phi_n), (\psi_1, .., \psi_m))$ *is the same as* $((\psi_1, .., \psi_m), (\phi_1, .., \phi_n))$ *and so would count them only once.*

Proposition 5. *Let $f = \mathsf{Heteroclauses}(\Phi) - 1$, if $\mathsf{Heteroclauses}(\Phi) \neq 0$, and $f = 0$ otherwise, $g = \mathsf{Symmetry}(\Phi)$, $h = \mathsf{Letters}(\Phi)$, and $a = |\mathcal{A}|$. Hence*

$$\mathsf{Conflictcount}(\Phi, \mathcal{A}) = \frac{a!}{(a-h)!} \times 2^h \times 2^f \times g \text{ if } a \geq h$$

$$\mathsf{Conflictcount}(\Phi, \mathcal{A}) = 0 \text{ if } a < h$$

Proof: For $a < h$, there are insufficient atom symbols in $\mathcal{A}$ to form a grounding set, and so there are 0 instantiations. For $a \geq h$, we need to justify the four terms as follows. The first term gives all permutations of the a atom symbols in $|\mathcal{A}|$ used to instantiate the sequence of h atomic meta-variable symbols in Φ. The second term gives the number of choices of positive and negative literals for the sequence of h atomic meta-variable symbols in Φ. The third term gives the permutations for each disjunct in each clause being the first or second disjunct in the heterogeneous clauses except for the first heterogeneous clause. The fourth term eliminates the duplicate counts obtained in the second and third terms in cases of symmetry. $\square$

Definition 25. *A* **conflict profile**, *denoted Ψ, of degree k is a set of conflict schema where for all $\Phi \in \Psi$, $|\Phi| = k$, and for each minimal inconsistent set $\Gamma \in \wp(C_2^\mathcal{A})$, if $|\Gamma| = k$, then there is exactly one conflict scheme $\Phi' \in \Psi$ such that an instantiation of Φ' is Γ.*

Conflict profiles for degrees 2 to 4, are given in Tables 1 to 3.

Proposition 6. *The number of minimal inconsistent sets of cardinality k in $\wp(C_2^\mathcal{A})$ is calculated as follows, where $\Psi = \{\Phi_1, .., \Phi_n\}$ is a conflict profile of degree k:*

$$\sum_{i=1}^{n} \mathsf{Conflictcount}(\Phi_i, \mathcal{A})$$

Proof: Each chainconflict corresponds to a minimal inconsistent set. According to Definition 25, the set of minimal inconsistent sets generated by each conflict scheme is disjoint from those generated by the other conflict schema. Therefore, the number of minimal inconsistent sets of cardinality k is the sum of the minimal inconsistent sets generated by each conflict scheme. $\square$

Example 22. Let Φ_{2a} be defined by 2a in Table 1. Let $|\mathcal{A}| = 5$. Since $a = 5$, $f = 0$, $g = 1/2$, and $h = 1$, we have the following, and hence the number of minimal inconsistent sets of cardinality 5 in $\wp(C_2^\mathcal{A})$ is 5.

$$\mathsf{Conflictcount}(\Phi_{2a}, \mathcal{A}) = \frac{5!}{(5-1)!} \times 2^1 \times 2^0 \times 1/2 = 5$$

Example 23. Let $\Phi_{3a}, .., \Phi_{3c}$ be defined by 3a,..,3c in Table 2. Let $|\mathcal{A}| = 2$. The number of minimal inconsistent sets of cardinality 3 in $\wp(\mathcal{C}_2^{\mathcal{A}})$ is 40, as follows.

> For $\Phi_{3a}, f = 1, g = 1$, and $h = 2$, so Conflictcount$(\Phi_{3a}, \mathcal{A}) = 16$
> For $\Phi_{3b}, f = 0, g = 1$, and $h = 2$, so Conflictcount$(\Phi_{3b}, \mathcal{A}) = 8$
> For $\Phi_{3c}, f = 1, g = 1$, and $h = 2$, so Conflictcount$(\Phi_{3c}, \mathcal{A}) = 16$

It is straightforward to obtain conditional probabilities of inconsistency using the count of minimal inconsistent sets.

Proposition 7. *Let $a = |\mathcal{A}|$. The number of sets of cardinality k in $\wp(\mathcal{C}_2^{\mathcal{A}})$ is the following number of combinations of sets of size k, where $n = (2a)^2$ is the number of binary clauses that can be formed from the $2a$ literals obtained from $\mathcal{A}$.*

$$\frac{n!}{k!(n-k)!}$$

Proposition 8. *The probability that any set of cardinality k is a minimal inconsistent set given by the following ratio, where the numerator is obtained from Proposition 6 and the denominator is obtained from Proposition 7.*

$$\frac{number\ of\ min\ inconsistent\ sets\ of\ cardinality\ k\ in\ \wp(\mathcal{C}_2^{\mathcal{A}})}{number\ of\ sets\ of\ cardinality\ k\ in\ \wp(\mathcal{C}_2^{\mathcal{A}})}$$

This case study is intended to indicate the promise of probable consistency checking. In order to count larger minimal inconsistent sets in $\wp(\mathcal{C}_2^{\mathcal{A}})$, we need to generate conflict profiles of degree greater than 4. In order to render this viable, we are currently exploring the development of an algorithm to generate conflict profiles. In parallel, we are seeking more general results that would enable the counting of minimal inconsistent sets in $\wp(\mathcal{C}_2^{\mathcal{A}})$, and in $\wp(\mathcal{C}_i^{\mathcal{A}})$ for $i > 2$, more directly.

5   Discussion

Consistency checking is increasingly important in artificial intelligence, data and knowledge engineering, and software engineering. In approaches to knowledge representation and reasoning such as truth maintenance systems, argumentation systems based on identifying consistent subsets, and default reasoning systems, consistency checking is an integral part of inferencing. Probable consistency checking potentially offers more efficient inferencing, either by directing conflict resolution to the more problematical areas of the data, or by allowing inferences before eliminating all possibilities of an inconsistency.

More generally, probable consistency checking is potentially important in information integration, requirements engineering, negotiation, and multi-agent interaction. It seems that the real advantage with probable consistency checking in all these activities is the relative ordering we can obtain rather than the absolute probability values. The relative ordering helps prioritize search or further analysis.

Table 1. A conflict profile of degree 2 is composed of conflict scheme 2a. The first line is for the first argument and the second line is for the second argument

	Conflict scheme	Type
2a	$X_1 \vee X_1$	disjoint
	$X_1^* \vee X_1^*$	isochains

Table 2. A conflict profile of degree 3 is composed of conflict schema 3a–3c

	Conflict scheme	Type
3a	$X_1 \vee X_2, X_2^* \vee X_1$	disjoint
	$X_1^* \vee X_1^*$	isochains
3b	$X_1 \vee X_1, X_1^* \vee X_2$	disjoint isochain
	$X_2^* \vee X_2^*$	+ superchain
3c	$X_1 \vee X_1, X_1^* \vee X_2$	joint
	$X_1 \vee X_1, X_1^* \vee X_2^*$	superchains

Table 3. A conflict profile of degree 4 is composed of conflict schema 4a–4f

	Conflict scheme	Type
4a	$X_1 \vee X_2, X_2^* \vee X_3, X_3^* \vee X_1$	disjoint
	$X_1^* \vee X_1^*$	isochains
4b	$X_1 \vee X_2, X_2^* \vee X_1, X_1^* \vee X_3$	disjoint isochain
	$X_3^* \vee X_3^*$	+ superchain
4c	$X_1 \vee X_2, X_2^* \vee X_1$	disjoint
	$X_1^* \vee X_3^*, X_3 \vee X_1^*$	isochains
4d	$X_1 \vee X_2, X_2^* \vee X_1$	disjoint
	$X_1^* \vee X_2^*, X_2 \vee X_1^*$	isochains
4e	$X_1 \vee X_1, X_1^* \vee X_2$	disjoint
	$X_3 \vee X_3, X_3^* \vee X_2^*$	superchains
4f	$X_1 \vee X_1, X_1^* \vee X_2, X_2^* \vee X_3$	joint
	$X_1 \vee X_1, X_1^* \vee X_3^*$	superchains

Of course, none of these probabilities take into account psychological or cognitive factors in developing or handling knowledgebases. For example, psychological observations may reveal an increased error resulting from an increased complexity of a specification. If such an observation were sufficiently precise, then perhaps there should be some weighting applied to the probability of inconsistency of formulae so that larger formulae are more likely *a priori* to be inconsistent.

References

1. A. Darwiche. Compiling knowledge into decomposible negation normal form. In *Proceedings of the International Joint Conference on Artificial Intelligence (IJCAI'99)*, pages 284–289, 1999.
2. R. Dechter and J. Pearl. Network-based heuristics for constraint-satisfaction problems. *Artificial Intelligence*, 34:1–38, 1987.

3. M. Garey and D. Johnson. *Computers and Intractability: A Guide to the Theory of NP-Completeness*. Freeman, 1979.
4. F. Koriche. On anytime coherence-based reasoning. In *Symbolic and Quantitative Approaches to Reasoning with Uncertainty (Ecsqaru'01)*, volume 2143 of *Lecture Notes in Computer Science*, pages 556–567. Springer, 2001.
5. H. Levesque. A logic of implicit and explicit belief. In *Proceedings of the National Conference on Artificial Intelligence (AAAI'84)*, pages 198–202, 1984.
6. P. Marquis. Knowledge compilation using prime implicates. In *Proceedings of the International Joint Conference on Artificial Intelligence (IJCAI'95)*, pages 837–843, 1995.
7. F. Oppacher and E. Suen. HARP: A tableau-based theorem prover. *Journal of Automated Reasoning*, 4:69–100, 1988.
8. C. Papadimitriou. *Computational Complexity*. Addison-Wesley, 1994.
9. M. Schaerf and M. Cadoli. Tractable reasoning via approximation. *Artificial Intelligence*, 74:249–310, 1995.
10. B. Selman, H. Levesque, and D. Mitchell. A new method for solving hard satisfiability problems. In *Proceedings of the Tenth National Conference on Artificial Intelligence (AAAI'92)*, pages 440–446, 1992.

On Iterated Revision in the AGM Framework

A. Herzig, S. Konieczny. and L. Perrussel

Institut de Recherche en Informatique de Toulouse
118 route de Narbonne, 31062 Toulouse, France
{herzig,konieczny,perrussel}@irit.fr

Abstract. While AGM belief revision identifies belief states with sets of
formulas, proposals for iterated revision are usually based on more complex belief states. In this paper we investigate within the AGM framework
several postulates embodying some aspects of iterated revision. Our main
results are negative: when added to the AGM postulates, our postulates
force revision to be maxichoice (whenever the new piece of information is
inconsistent with the current beliefs the resulting belief set is maximal).
We also compare our results to revision operators with memory and we
investigate some postulates proposed in this framework.

1   Introduction

While AGM belief revision identifies belief states with sets of formulas, proposals
for iterated revision are usually based on more complex belief states. Following
the work of [7], they are usually represented by total pre-orders on interpretations. In fact in [6], Darwiche and Pearl first stated their postulates (C1-C4) in
the classical AGM framework. But it has been shown in [8,15] that (C2) is inconsistent with AGM, and that under the AGM postulates (C1) implies (C3) and
(C4). To remove these contradictions, Darwiche and Pearl rephrased their and
the AGM postulates in terms of epistemic states [7]. This has lead to a widely
accepted framework for iterated revision, and most of the work on iterated belief
revision now uses this more complex framework.

So an interesting question investigated in this paper is which requirements
on iteration one can consistently add to the usual AGM framework. We focus
on the status of old information, and formulate several postulates embodying
that aspect of iterated revision. They all express that old information about A
determine in some way the current status of A.

In particular, the first postulate says that if the agent was informed about A
before revision (in the sense that either A or $\neg A$ was accepted) then the agent
should remain informed about A after revision.

Our second postulate is motivated by the following basic algorithm for the
revision of a belief set B by a new piece of information A [11,19]: first put A
in the new belief set, then add as many old beliefs from B as possible. So the
second postulate expresses that the corresponding operator is idempotent with
respect to B. We also study a family of postulates that generalizes this idea.

We also review other postulates coming from the iterated revision literature,
in the classical belief set framework.

T.D. Nielsen and N.L. Zhang (Eds.): ECSQARU 2003, LNAI 2711, pp. 477–488, 2003.

Our results are mainly negative: when added to the AGM postulates, our postulates lead to extreme revision operators. In particular the first two postulates force revision to be maxichoice: whenever the new piece of information is inconsistent with the current beliefs then the resulting belief set is maximal.

These "impossibility results" about iterated revision in the usual AGM framework can be seen as a justification for the increase in representational complexity that shows up when one goes from AGM to iterated belief revision frameworks (see e.g. [7,15,18,13,17,4]). Instead of "flat" belief sets (alias sets of interpretations), the latter work with epistemic states, that can be represented by pre-orders on interpretations.

The paper is organized as follows. In Sect. 2 we give some definitions and notations. In Sect. 3 we consider the Darwiche and Pearl postulates in the AGM framework. More specifically, we focus on their first postulate. In Sect. 4 we investigate the implications of trying to retain old information as much as possible. In Sect. 5 we explore a family of postulates, saying that re-introducing old pieces of information is harmless. In Sect. 6 we compare our results to revision operators with memory [13,14] and we investigate the implications of some postulates coming from this work. We conclude in Sect. 7.

2   Preliminaries

We work with a propositional language built from a set of atomic variables, denoted by $p, q, \ldots$ Formulas are denoted by $A, B, C, \ldots$ We identify finite sets of formulas (that we call belief sets) with the conjunction of their elements. A belief set B is *informed about* a formula C if $B \vdash C$ or $B \vdash \neg C$. A belief set B is *maximal* (or complete) if B is informed about every C.

The set of all interpretations is denoted $\mathcal{W}$, and the set of all belief sets is denoted $\mathcal{B}$. For a formula B, $Mod(B)$ denotes the set of models of B, i.e. $Mod(B) = \{\omega \in \mathcal{W} : \omega \models B\}$. For a set of interpretations $M \subseteq \mathcal{W}$, $Form(W)$ denotes the formula (up to logical equivalence) whose set of models is M, i.e. $Form(W) = \{B : \omega \models B \text{ iff } \omega \in M\}$.

A pre-order $\leq$ is a reflexive and transitive relation. $<$ is its strict counterpart: $\omega < \omega'$ if and only if $\omega \leq \omega'$ and $\omega' \not\leq \omega$. And $\simeq$ is defined by $\omega \simeq \omega'$ iff $\omega \leq \omega'$ and $\omega' \leq \omega$. A pre-order is total is for all ω, ω' we have $\omega \leq \omega'$ or $\omega' \leq \omega$. $\min(M, \leq)$ denotes the set $\{\omega \in M | \nexists \omega' \in M : \omega' < \omega\}$.

Definition 1 (AGM belief revision). *An AGM belief revision operator $\star$ is a function that maps a belief set B and a formula A to a belief set $B \star A$ such that :*

(R1) $B \star A \vdash A$
(R2) *If* $B \wedge A \nvdash \bot$, *then* $B \star A \equiv B \wedge A$
(R3) *If* $A \nvdash \bot$, *then* $B \star A \nvdash \bot$
(R4) *If* $B_1 \equiv B_2$ *and* $A_1 \equiv A_2$, *then* $B_1 \star A_1 \equiv B_2 \star A_2$
(R5) $(B \star A) \wedge C \vdash B \star (A \wedge C)$
(R6) *If* $(B \star A) \wedge C \nvdash \bot$, *then* $B \star (A \wedge C) \vdash (B \star A) \wedge C$

The postulates (R1-R4) are often called the *basic* AGM postulates, and the set (R1-R6) the *extended* AGM postulates, indicating that people consider the former to be more fundamental. Notice however that they do not put very hard constraints on $\star$. It is the two last ones (R5) and (R6) that allow to state the below representation theorem, which says that a revision operator corresponds to a family of pre-orders on interpretations. (The theorem is due to Katsuno and Mendelzon, but the idea can be directly traced back to Grove [10].) But first we need the following:

Definition 2 (faithful assignment). *A function that maps each belief set B to a pre-order $\leq_B$ on interpretations is called a* faithful assignment *if and only if the following holds:*

1. *If $\omega \models B$ and $\omega' \models B$, then $\omega \simeq_B \omega'$*
2. *If $\omega \models B$ and $\omega' \not\models B$, then $\omega <_B \omega'$*
3. *If $B_1 = B_2$, then $\leq_{B_1} = \leq_{B_2}$*

Theorem 1. *A revision operator $\star$ satisfies postulates (R1-R6) if and only if there exists a faithful assignment that maps each belief set B to a total pre-order $\leq_B$ such that:*

$$Mod(B \star A) = \min(Mod(A), \leq_B)$$

We say that the assignment is the faithful assignment *corresponding to* the revision operator.

Let us now introduce a special family of revision operators, called maxichoice revision operators [1,9].

Definition 3 (maxichoice revision). *A belief revision operator $\star$ is a* maxichoice *revision operator if for every B and A, if $B \vdash \neg A$ then $B \star A$ is maximal.*

Maxichoice revision operators are not very satisfactory, since they are too precise and have a too drastic behaviour. In fact, with those operators, learning any piece of information that conflicts with the current beliefs, however incomplete they are, causes the agent to have beliefs on any formula: for any formula A, either the agent believes that A holds or he believes that $\neg A$ holds. They are considered as an upper-bound for revision operators (the lower-bound being full-meet revision operators [1,9]).

We will use a characterization of maxichoice operators on the semantical level. First we define:

Definition 4. *A linear faithful assignment is a faithful assignment that satisfies*

4. *If $\omega \not\models B$ and $\omega' \not\models B$, then $\omega <_B \omega'$ or $\omega' <_B \omega$*

The following result is is part of the folklore in the literature on revision:

Theorem 2. *A revision operator $\star$ is a maxichoice operator if and only if its corresponding assignment is a linear faithful assignment.*

The proof is straightforward.

3   Darwiche and Pearl Postulates in the AGM Framework

In [6], Darwiche and Pearl first stated their well-known postulates (C1-C4) in the classical AGM framework.

(C1) If $A \vdash C$, then $(B \star C) \star A \equiv B \star A$
(C2) If $A \vdash \neg C$, then $(B \star C) \star A \equiv B \star A$
(C3) If $B \star A \vdash C$, then $(B \star C) \star A \vdash C$
(C4) If $B \star A \nvdash \neg C$, then $(B \star C) \star A \nvdash \neg C$

But it has been shown in [8,15] that (C2) is inconsistent with AGM, and that under the AGM postulates (C1) implies (C3) and (C4). To remove these contradictions, Darwiche and Pearl rephrased their and the AGM postulates in terms of epistemic states [7].

As (C1) is consistent with the AGM postulates, one might wonder what the constraints imposed by this postulate on the revision operators are like. This question has not been investigated as far as we know. The consistency of (C1) with AGM is easily established by noticing that the full meet revision operator satisfies (C1) [15]. But is this the only AGM operator satisfying (C1), or do we face a wider family?

Let us define another particular family of revision operators.

Definition 5. *Let $\leq$ be a total pre-order on interpretations. A revision operator $\star$ is said to be imposed by $\leq$ if its corresponding faithful assignment satisfies the following property:*

  i. *If $\omega \not\models B$ and $\omega' \not\models B$, then $(\omega \leq_B \omega'$ iff $\omega \leq \omega')$.*

As far as we know, this family of operators has not been studied yet. Such operators are not satisfactory since the result of a revision does not depend of the belief set, but merely of the new piece of information (see theorem 3). This seems to be counter-intuitive and to go against the basic ideas behind revision. Nevertheless, such operators fulfill all AGM postulates, and the full meet revision operator is a particular case (when $\leq$ is a flat pre-order, i.e. $\omega \simeq \omega', \forall \omega, \omega' \in \mathcal{W}$).

Theorem 3. *Let $\star$ be an AGM revision operator, and let f be any function mapping formulas to formulas such that $f(A) \vdash A$ and if $A_1 \equiv A_2$ then $f(A_1) \equiv f(A_2)$. $\star$ is imposed if and only if for any belief set B and formula A, the following holds:*

(IMP) *If $B \vdash \neg A$ then $B \star A \equiv f(A)$.*

Proof. The only if part is straightforward: define $f(A)$ as $\min(Mod(A), \leq)$.

For the if part we need to build the imposed pre-order $\leq$ from $f(A)$. This can be established by noting that if we take a formula A that has exactly two (distinct) models ω and ω', then by (IMP) for every B such that $A \wedge B \vdash \bot$, we have $B \star A \equiv f(A)$. By (R1) and (R3), $Mod(f(A)) = \{\omega\}$ or $Mod(f(A)) = \{\omega'\}$ or $Mod(f(A)) = \{\omega, \omega'\}$. Since $\star$ is an AGM operator, the faithful assignment gives us, for *every* B inconsistent with A, that $\omega <_B \omega'$ whenever $Mod(f(A)) = \{\omega\}$, $\omega' <_B \omega$ whenever $Mod(f(A)) = \{\omega'\}$, and $\omega \simeq_B \omega'$ whenever $Mod(f(A)) = \{\omega, \omega'\}$. That means that there exists a pre-order $\leq$ defined as $\omega \leq \omega'$ iff $\omega \in Mod(f(Form(\omega, \omega')))$ and such that for all B such that $\omega, \omega' \not\models B$, $\omega \leq_B \omega'$ iff $\omega \leq \omega'$.

This result states that for any revision that is not an expansion the old belief set is not taken into account in the result of the revision.

Now let us return to the case of the (C1) postulate and state the following result:

Theorem 4. *An AGM revision operator satisfies (C1) if and only if it is imposed.*

Proof. The if part is straighforward, since either $B \wedge A$ is consistent and then (C1) is a consequence of (R2), or $B \wedge A$ is not consistent, and then (C1) is a consequence of theorem 3.

For the only if part, suppose that the operator $\star$ satisfies (R1-R6) and (C1). We will show that the operator is imposed and there exists an f such that (IMP) is satisfied. If $\star$ satisfies (C1) then (IMP) holds, since for every A and B such that $A \wedge B$ is not consistent, by (R2) we have that $B \star A \equiv (\neg A \star (A \vee B)) \star A$. Thus by (C1) we get that $(\neg A \star (A \vee B)) \star A = \neg A \star A$, consequently we get $B \star A \equiv \neg A \star A$. Thus f can be defined by stipulating that $f(A) = \neg A \star A$. This means that the result of the revision depends only on the input A.

This result casts serious doubts on the (C1) postulate in the AGM framework.

4   "Keep On Being Informed about A"

When an agent receives new information she has to modify her current set of beliefs B in order to take it into account. One major requirement of AGM theory is the principle of *minimal change*, that means that when one revises a belief set by a new piece of information, one has to keep *"as much as possible"* of the old belief set.

The following property tries to capture this intuition, by saying that revising by A can not induce a loss of information: if B is informed about C, then learning A can not lead to loose this information.

(Compl) If $B \vdash C$ then $B \star A \vdash C$ or $B \star A \vdash \neg C$

Unfortunately it can be proved that :

Theorem 5. *If $\star$ satisfies (R1-R6) and (Compl), then $\star$ is a maxichoice revision operator.*

Proof. This can be proved straightforwardly: suppose $B \vdash A$. If $\vdash A$ then the theorem holds. Else we have $B \vdash A \vee C$ and $B \vdash A \vee \neg C$. By (Compl), $B \star \neg A \vdash$

$A \vee C$ or $B \star \neg A \vdash \neg A \wedge \neg C$, and $B \star \neg A \vdash A \vee \neg C$ or $B \star \neg A \vdash \neg A \wedge C$. Among the four cases, the one where $B \star \neg A \vdash (A \vee C) \wedge (A \vee \neg C)$ is impossible because $B \star \neg A \vdash A$ by (R4) and $\nvdash A$. The one where $B \star \neg A \vdash (\neg A \wedge \neg C) \wedge (\neg A \wedge C)$ is impossible because $B \star \neg A \vdash \bot$. It follows that $B \star \neg A \vdash \neg C$ or $B \star \neg A \vdash C$.

It is straightforward to show that every maxichoice revision operator satisfies (Compl). Together with the preceding theorem it follows that (Compl) characterizes maxichoice revision.

Remark 1. Formula (3.17) in [9] is just (COMPL) (modulo a typo). There, proposition (3.19) says that "$B \star A$ is maximal for any sentence A such that $\neg A \in B$", i.e. (3.17) entails maxichoice revision. The proof refers to observation 3.2 of [2], but the latter presupposes already that $\star$ is a maxichoice operator, and establishes that this entails maximality.

So this postulate puts too strong a requirement on classical AGM revision operators.

In the next section we will investigate another requirement also based on the assumption that we can keep as much as possible of the old information.

5   "Re-introducing Old Information Doesn't Harm"

Another way of ensuring that one does not forget previous information is to suppose that we can re-introduce the old belief set without changing the current one. It can be seen as some kind of left-idempotency of the revision operator. This idea is very close to the one used for defining revision with memory operators [14,13,3].

First we need the following abbreviations.

Definition 6. *Given a set of beliefs B and pieces of information A_i, then for $1 \leq i \leq n$ we define B_i by:*

$$B_i = (...((B \star A_1) \star A_2) \star ...) \star A_i$$

Thus $B_0 = B$, $B_1 = B \star A_1$, and $B_2 = (B \star A_1) \star A_2$.

Our abbreviation enables us to concisely formulate the following family of postulates:

(**Mem**$_i$) $B_i \equiv B \star B_i$, for $i \geq 0$

Hence:

(**Mem**$_0$) says $B_0 \equiv B \star B_0$, i.e. $B \equiv B \star B$,
(**Mem**$_1$) says $B_1 \equiv B \star B_1$, i.e. $B \star A_1 \equiv B \star (B \star A_1)$, and
(**Mem**$_2$) says $B_2 \equiv B \star B_2$, i.e. $(B \star A_1) \star A_2 \equiv B \star ((B \star A_1) \star A_2)$.

$\vdots$

Let us see now what is the relation of the postulates (Mem$_i$) with the AGM postulates.

Theorem 6. *(Mem$_0$) is derivable from the basic AGM postulates.*

The proof only uses the postulate (R2).

Theorem 7. *(Mem$_1$) is derivable from the extended AGM postulates.*

Proof. From (R1) we know that $(B \star A) \wedge A \equiv B \star A$. Now using (R5) and (R6) with $C = B \star A$, we have $B \star (A \wedge (B \star A)) \equiv (B \star A) \wedge (B \star A)$. That is directly $B \star (B \star A) \equiv B \star A$.

Theorem 8. *(Mem$_2$), (Mem$_3$), etc. cannot be derived from the AGM postulates.*

Proof. This can be established e.g. by considering Dalal's revision operator [5], which is known to satisfy the AGM postulates [12] and showing that is does not satisfy the (Mem$_i$) postulates. Indeed, consider $B = \neg p$, $A_1 = \neg q$, $A_2 = p \vee q$. Then $B_2 = (\neg p \star \neg q) \star (p \vee q) = (\neg p \wedge \neg q) \star (p \vee q) = p \oplus q$ where $\oplus$ is the exclusive or. But this is different from $B \star B_2 = \neg p \star ((\neg p \star \neg q) \star (p \vee q))$ $= \neg p \star ((\neg p \wedge \neg q) \star (p \vee q)) = \neg p \star (p \oplus q) = \neg p \wedge q$.

We can easily find revision operators satisfying these additional postulates :

Theorem 9. *If $\star$ is a maxichoice revision operator then $\star$ satisfies every postulate (Mem$_i$).*

The postulates of this family are ordered by strength, as shows the following result:

Theorem 10. *If $\star$ satisfies postulate (Mem$_{i+1}$) then $\star$ satisfies postulate (Mem$_i$).*

The other way round, (Mem$_i$) does not always imply (Mem$_{i+1}$): this is immediate for $i = 0$.

So is those families of operators, defined from the (Mem$_i$) postulates, are wide ones ? It is not the case. We show that, once again, only maxichoice revision operators satisfy our postulates.

Theorem 11. *If $\star$ satisfies (R1-R6) and (Mem$_2$), then $\star$ is a maxichoice revision operator.*

Proof. Suppose that A is consistent and that $B \vdash \neg A$. We want to show that $B \star A$ is maximal, i.e. for an arbitrary C we have that either $B \star A \vdash C$, or $B \star A \vdash \neg C$.

First, (Mem$_2$) tells us that $(\neg A \vee C) \star B \star A = (\neg A \vee C) \star ((\neg A \vee C) \star B \star A)$, and similarly $(\neg A \vee \neg C) \star B \star A = (\neg A \vee \neg C) \star ((\neg A \vee \neg C) \star B \star A)$. As $B \vdash \neg A$ we have $B = (\neg A \vee C) \star B$ by (R2), and similarly $B = (\neg A \vee \neg C) \star B$. Hence $(\neg A \vee C) \star B \star A = (\neg A \vee C) \star ((\neg A \vee C) \star B \star A) = (\neg A \vee C) \star (B \star A)$, and similarly

$(\neg A \vee \neg C) \star B \star A = (\neg A \vee \neg C) \star ((\neg A \vee \neg C) \star B \star A) = (\neg A \vee \neg C) \star (B \star A)$.
Now suppose that not(either $B \star A \vdash C$, or $B \star A \vdash \neg C$), i.e. $B \star A$ is consistent with C, and $B \star A$ consistent with $\neg C$. Then we must have $(\neg A \vee C) \star B \star A = (\neg A \vee C) \star ((\neg A \vee C) \star B \star A) = (\neg A \vee C) \star (B \star A) = (\neg A \vee C) \wedge (B \star A)$, and $(\neg A \vee \neg C) \star B \star A = (\neg A \vee \neg C) \star ((\neg A \vee \neg C) \star B \star A) = (\neg A \vee \neg C) \star (B \star A) = (\neg A \vee \neg C) \wedge (B \star A)$. As $B \star A \vdash A$, we would have that $(\neg A \vee C) \wedge (B \star A) \vdash C$, and $(\neg A \vee \neg C) \wedge (B \star A) \vdash \neg C$. But by AGM $(\neg A \vee C) \star (B \star A)$ must be consistent.

A corollary of the theorems 10 and 11 is that a revision operator satisfies a (Mem_i) postulate if and only if it is a maxichoice revision operator. So each postulate of this family is a characterisation of maxichoice operators.

As explained at the beginning of this section, the idea of this family of postulates seems very close to the one behind the definition of revision with memory operators. In the next section we will investigate more deeply the links between revision with memory operators and the requirements on classical AGM revision operators.

6   The Relation with Revision with Memory Operators

Belief revision operators with memory [14,13] keep trace of the history of beliefs in order to be able to use them whenever further revisions make this possible. They are based on a notion of belief state that is more complex than the flat set of beliefs of the AGM framework.

Basically, if we represent epistemic states Φ by a pre-order on interpretations, noted $\leq_\Phi$, we can extract the associated belief set with the projection operator $Bel(\Phi) = \min(\mathcal{W}, \leq_\Phi)$. The pre-order $\leq_\Phi$ represents the agent's relative confidence in interpretations. For example $\omega <_\Phi \omega'$ means that for the agent in the epistemic state Φ the interpretation ω seems (strictly) more plausible than the interpretation ω'.

The usual logical notations extend straightforwardly to epistemic states (they in fact denote conditions on the associated belief sets). For example $\Phi \vdash C$, $\Phi \wedge C$ and $\omega \models \Phi$ respectively mean $Bel(\Phi) \vdash C$, $Bel(\Phi) \wedge C$ and $\omega \models Bel(\Phi)$.

Now let us define revision with memory operators. This family of operators is parametrized by a classical AGM operator. It can be seen as a tool to change a classical AGM operator with bad iteration properties into an operator that has good ones.

Definition 7 (revision with memory). *Suppose that we dispose of a classical AGM operator $\star$. (We will use its corresponding faithful assignment $C \rightarrow \leq_C$.) Then we define the epistemic state (the pre-order) $\Phi \circ C$ that results from the revision with memory of Φ by the new information C as:*

$$\omega \leq_{\Phi \circ C} \omega' \text{ iff } \omega <_C \omega' \text{ or}$$
$$\omega \simeq_C \omega' \text{ and } \omega \leq_\Phi \omega'$$

This definition means that each incoming piece of information induces some credibility ordering. (The exact ordering induced depends on the classical AGM operator that has been chosen.[1]) And the new epistemic state is built by listening first to this incoming piece of information, and then to the old epistemic state (this is the well known *primacy of update* principle).

In fact, it is shown in [13], that an epistemic state for revision with memory operators can be encoded as the history of the new pieces of information acquired by the agent since its "birth". So we can suppose that the agent starts from an "empty" epistemic state Ξ, that is represented by a flat pre-order[2], and successively accommodates all the pieces of information. So if we suppose that all revision sequences start from Ξ, it can be shown that all revision with memory operators satisfy the (Mem$_i$) postulates, since they all take the history of the revisions into account.

Theorem 12. *A revision operator with memory satisfies (Mem$_i$), $\forall i$.*

In fact, a logical characterization for revision with memory operators has been given in [13]. Most of the postulates are generalizations of AGM postulates in the epistemic states framework, but there are also some specific postulates characterizing revision with memory. We will examine now their status in the classical belief set framework. Those postulates have been written for epistemic states, but we can translate them for belief sets (with some simplifications) as follows :

(Hist1) $(B \star A) \star C \equiv B \star (A \star C)$
(Hist2) If $C \star A \equiv A$, then $(B \star C) \star A \equiv B \star A$
(Hist3) If $C \star A \vdash D$, then $(B \star C) \star A \vdash D$

The first postulate expresses some kind of associativity and aims at expressing the strong influence of the new piece of information. The second one says that if a formula C does not distinguish between the models of A, then learning C before A is without effect on the resulting belief set. The third one says that the consequences of a revision also holds if we first learn another piece of information.

The counterpart of (Hist1), (Hist2) and (Hist3) for epistemic states are respectively named (H7), (H'7) and (H'8) in [13]. It is shown there that in the presence of the other postulates (H1-H6) (that are mainly a generalisation of AGM postulates in the epistemic state framework), (H7) is equivalent to (H'7-H'8).

This equivalence no longer holds in the belief set framework. Let us see now the implications of these three postulates in this framework.

Theorem 13. *There is no operator that satisfies (R1-R6) and (Hist1).*

---

[1] Note that one of the possibilities is a two level pre-order with the models of the formula at the lowest level, and the counter-models at the top level. That gives the more "classical" operator of the family [18,16,20,3].

[2] that is $\forall \omega, \omega' \ \omega \simeq_{\Xi} \omega'$

Proof. Let $\omega_0, \omega_1, \omega_2, \omega_3$ be 4 distinct interpretations. Now take four formulas A, B, C, D such that $Mod(A) = \{\omega_1, \omega_2\}$, $Mod(B) = \{\omega_0, \omega_1\}$, $Mod(C) = \{\omega_2, \omega_3\}$ and $Mod(D) = \{\omega_1, \omega_3\}$. From (Hist1) we have that $(B \star A) \star C = B \star (A \star C)$, that is from (R2) $(B \wedge A) \star C = B \star (A \wedge C)$. As $Mod(A \wedge C) = \{\omega_2\}$, from (R1) and (R3) it follows that $Mod(B \star (A \wedge C)) = \{\omega_2\}$, hence $Mod((B \wedge A) \star C) = \{\omega_2\}$. On the other side, starting from (Hist1) with $(B \star D) \star C = B \star (D \star C)$, we obtain similarly $Mod(B \star (D \wedge C)) = Mod((B \wedge D) \star C) = \{\omega_3\}$. Now notice that $B \wedge D \equiv B \wedge A$, so (R4) says that $(B \wedge A) \star C \equiv (B \wedge D) \star C$. Contradiction.

Note that (Hist2) is stronger that the postulate (C1) proposed by Darwiche and Pearl. As (C1) is consistent with the AGM postulates we will consider a weakening of the (Hist2) postulate, that accounts for the case when $A \not\vdash C$:

(StrictHist2) If $C \star A \equiv A$ and $A \not\vdash C$, then $(B \star C) \star A \equiv B \star A$

Theorem 14. *If an operator $\star$ satisfies (R1-R6) and (StrictHist2), then $\star$ is a maxichoice revision operator.*

Proof. We show that if $\star$ satisfies (StrictHist2), then $\star$ is maxichoice. If $\star$ is not maxichoice, then there exists a formula C such that $\leq_C$ is not linear, that means that we can find a formula A and two distinct interpretations ω, ω', with $Mod(A) = \{\omega, \omega'\}$ (with $\omega \neq \omega'$) such that $C \wedge A$ is not consistent[3] and $\omega \simeq_C \omega'$, ie $C \star A = A$. (StrictHist2) then says that for all B $(B \star C) \star A = B \star A$. In particular if we take B such that $Mod(B) = Mod(C) \cup \{\omega\}$, that means that $C \star A = B \star A = A$. But from (R2) we get that $B \star A = B \wedge A$, so $Mod(B \star A) = \{\omega\}$. Contradiction.

So, as a corollary of theorems 14 et 4, every operator satisfying (R1-R6) and (Hist2) must be an imposed maxichoice operator.

Theorem 15. *There is no operator that satisfies (R1-R6) and (Hist3).*

Proof. Let $\omega_0, \omega_1, \omega_2$ be 3 distinct interpretations. Now take four formulas A, B, C, D such that $Mod(A) = \{\omega_1, \omega_2\}$, $Mod(B) = \{\omega_0\}$, $Mod(C) = \{\omega_0, \omega_1\}$, and $Mod(D) = \{\omega_0, \omega_2\}$. As from (R2) $C \star A = C \wedge A$, then $Mod(C \star A) = \{\omega_1\}$, so from (Hist3) and (R3), that means that $Mod((B \star C) \star A) = \{\omega_1\}$. On the other side, starting from $D \star A$, we find similarly that $Mod((B \star D) \star A) = \{\omega_2\}$. Finally, as from (R2) we find easily that $(B \star C) \equiv (B \star D)$, from (R4) we have that $(B \star C) \star A \equiv (B \star D) \star A$. Contradiction.

These three results show, once again, that it is hard to try to formulate iteration postulates in the AGM framework. Whereas those properties are meaningful in the epistemic state framework, two of them, (Hist1) and (Hist3), are not consistent with AGM postulates for belief set revision, and the last one, (StrictHist2), implies the maxichoice property.

---

[3] When $\star$ is an AGM revision operator and $C \star A \equiv A$, then $C \wedge A \not\vdash \bot$ is equivalent to $A \vdash C$.

7 Conclusion

Studies in iterated belief revision have been stated in the epistemic state framework mainly because of the influence of Darwiche and Pearl's proposal [6,7] and its incompatibility with the AGM belief set framework. But since, few work has been done to see if some properties on iteration can be stated in the classical framework.

We have addressed this issue in this paper by looking at some candidates postulates. In different ways, all of them express that the result of a revision must keep as much as possible of the old information.

Our results are mainly negative. When the proposed postulates are not inconsistent with classical AGM ones, they inexorably lead to the maxichoice property, which is far from satisfactory for a sensible revision operator. So the results obtained in this paper can be seen as "impossibility results" about iteration in the classical AGM framework.

This study is then important to justify the gap, both in terms of knowledge representation and in terms of computational complexity, induced by all the iterated revision approaches that abandon the classical framework and work with more complex objects, viz. epistemic states.

References

1. C. E. Alchourrón, P. Gärdenfors, and D. Makinson. On the logic of theory change: Partial meet contraction and revision functions. *Journal of Symbolic Logic*, 50:510–530, 1985.
2. C. E. Alchourrón and D. Makinson. The logic of theory change: Contraction functions and their associated revision functions. *Theoria*, 48:14–37, 1982.
3. S. Benferhat, D. Dubois, and O. Papini. A sequential reversible belief revision method based on polynomials. In *Proceedings of the Sixteenth National Conference on Artificial Intelligence (AAAI'99)*, pages 733–738, 1999.
4. R. Booth. On the logic of iterated non-prioritised revision. In *Workshop on Conditionals, Information and Inference. Hagen, Germany*, 2002.
5. M. Dalal. Investigations into a theory of knowledge base revision: preliminary report. In *Proceedings of the National Conference on Artificial Intelligence (AAAI'88)*, pages 475–479, 1988.
6. A. Darwiche and J. Pearl. On the logic of iterated belief revision. In Morgan Kaufmann, editor, *Theoretical Aspects of Reasoning about Knowledge: Proceedings of the 1994 Conference (TARK'94)*, pages 5–23, 1994.
7. A. Darwiche and J. Pearl. On the logic of iterated belief revision. *Artificial Intelligence*, 89:1–29, 1997.
8. M. Freund and D. Lehmann. Belief revision and rational inference. Technical Report TR-94-16, Institute of Computer Science, The Hebrew University of Jerusalem, 1994.
9. P. Gärdenfors. *Knowledge in flux*. MIT Press, 1988.
10. A. Grove. Two modellings for theory change. *Journal of Philosophical Logic*, 17(157-180), 1988.
11. Sven Ove Hansson. *A textbook of belief dynamics*. Kluwer Academic Press, 1999.

12. H. Katsuno and A. O. Mendelzon. Propositional knowledge base revision and minimal change. *Artificial Intelligence*, 52:263–294, 1991.
13. S. Konieczny and R. Pino Pérez. A framework for iterated revision. *Journal of Applied Non-Classical Logics*, 10(3-4):339–367, 2000.
14. S. Konieczny and R. Pino Pérez. Some operators for iterated revision. In *Proceedings of the Sixth European Conference on Symbolic and Quantitative Approaches to Reasoning with Uncertainty (ECSQARU'01)*, pages 498–509, 2001.
15. D. Lehmann. Belief revision, revised. In *Proceedings of the Fourteenth International Joint Conference on Artificial Intelligence (IJCAI'95)*, pages 1534–1540, 1995.
16. P. Liberatore. The complexity of iterated belief revision. In *Proccedings of the Sixth International Conference on Database Theory (ICDT'97)*, pages 276–290, 1997.
17. T. Meyer. Basic infobase change. *Studia Logica*, 67:215–242, 2001.
18. A. C. Nayak. Iterated belief change based on epistemic entrenchment. *Erkenntnis*, 41:353–390, 1994.
19. B. Nebel. Syntax-based approaches to belief revision. In P. Gärdenfors, editor, *Belief revision*, volume 29 of *Journal of Cambridge Tracts in Theoretical Computer Science*, pages 52–88. Cambridge University Press, 1992.
20. O. Papini. Iterated revision operations stemming from the history of an agent's observations. In H. Rott and M. A. Williams, editors, *Frontiers in Belief revision*, pages 279–301. Kluwer, 1999.

Epistemic Logics for Information Fusion

Churn-Jung Liau

Institute of Information Science
Academia Sinica, Taipei, 115, Taiwan
liaucj@iis.sinica.edu.tw

Abstract. In this paper, we propose some extensions of epistemic logic for reasoning about information fusion. The fusion operators considered in this paper include majority merging, arbitration, and general merging. Some modalities corresponding to these fusion operators are added to epistemic logics and the Kripke semantics of these extended logics are presented. While most existing approaches treat information fusion operators as meta-level constructs, these operators are directly incorporated into our object logic language. Thus it is possible to reason about not only the merged results but also the fusion process in our logics.

Keywords: epistemic logic, database merging, belief fusion, majority merging, arbitration, general merging, belief revision, multi-agent systems

1 Introduction

The philosophical analysis of knowledge and belief has stimulated the development of the so-called epistemic logic [21]. This kind of logic has attracted the attention of researchers from diverse fields such as artificial intelligence(AI), economics, linguistics, and theoretical computer science. Among them, the AI researchers and computer scientists develop some technically sophisticated formalisms and apply them to the analysis of distributed and multi-agent systems [20,36].

The application of epistemic logic to AI and computer science puts its emphasis on the interaction of agents, so multi-agent epistemic logic is urgently needed. One representative example of such logic is proposed by Fagin et al. [20]. The term "knowledge" is used in a broad sense in [20] to cover cases of belief and information.[1] The most novel feature of their logic is the consideration of common knowledge and distributed knowledge among a group of agents. Distributed knowledge is that which can be deduced by pooling together everyone's knowledge. While it is required that proper knowledge must be true, the belief of an agent may be wrong. Therefore, in general, there will be conflict

---

[1] More precisely, the logic for belief is called doxastic logic. However, here we will use the three terms knowledge, belief, and information interchangeably, so epistemic logic is assumed to cover all these notions.

T.D. Nielsen and N.L. Zhang (Eds.): ECSQARU 2003, LNAI 2711, pp. 489–501, 2003.
© Springer-Verlag Berlin Heidelberg 2003

in the beliefs to be merged. In this case, everything can be deduced from the distributed beliefs due to the notorious omniscience property of epistemic logic, so the merged result will be useless for further reasoning.

Instead of directly putting all beliefs of the agents together, there are other sophisticated techniques for knowledge base merging [12,15,25,26,27,33,34,35]. Most of the approaches treat belief fusion operators as meta-level constructs, so given a set of knowledge bases, these fusion operators will return the merged results. More precisely, a fusion operator is used to combine a set of knowledge bases $T_1, T_2, \cdots, T_k$, where each knowledge base is a theory in some logical langauge.

Some of the above-mentioned works present concrete operators that can be used directly in the fusion process, while others stipulate the desirable properties of reasonable belief fusion operators by postulates. However, few of the approaches provide the capability of reasoning about the fusion process. In this paper, we propose that belief fusion operators can be incorporated into the object language of the multi-agent epistemic logic, so we can reason not only with the merged results but also about the fusion process.

1.1   Preliminary

Let $\mathcal{L}$ denote the language of epistemic logic. The alphabet of $\mathcal{L}$ contains the following symbols: a countable set $\Phi_0 = \{p, q, r, \ldots\}$ of atomic propositions; the propositional constants $\perp$ (falsum or falsity constant) and $\top$ (verum or truth constant); the binary Boolean operator $\vee$ (or), and unary Boolean operator $\neg$ (not); a set $Ag = \{1, 2, \ldots, n\}$ of agents; the modal operator-forming symbols "[" and "]"; and the left and right parentheses "(" and ")".

The set of well-formed formulas(wffs)is defined as the smallest set containing $\Phi_0 \cup \{\perp, \top\}$ and closed under Boolean operators and the following rule:

if φ is a wff, then $[G]\varphi$ is a wff for any nonempty $G \subseteq Ag$.

The intuitive meaning of $[G]\varphi$ is "The group of agents G has distributed belief φ"

As usual, other classical Boolean connectives $\wedge$ (and), $\supset$ (implication), and $\equiv$ (equivalence) can be defined as abbreviations. Also, we will write $\langle G \rangle \varphi$ as an abbreviation of $\neg[G]\neg\varphi$. When G is a singleton $\{i\}$, we will write $[i]\varphi$ instead of $[\{i\}]\varphi$, so $[i]\varphi$ means that agent i knows φ.

For the semantics, a possible world model for $\mathcal{L}$ is a structure

$$(W, (\mathcal{R}_i)_{1 \leq i \leq n}, V),$$

where

- W is a set of possible worlds,
- $\mathcal{R}_i \subseteq W \times W$ is a serial binary relation[2] over W for $1 \leq i \leq n$,

---

[2] A binary relation $\mathcal{R}$ is serial if $\forall w \exists u. \mathcal{R}(w, u)$.

– $V : \Phi_0 \to 2^W$ is a truth assignment mapping each atomic proposition to the set of worlds in which it is true.

From the binary relations $\mathcal{R}_i$'s, we can define a derived relation $\mathcal{R}_G$ for each nonempty $G \subseteq Ag$:

$$\mathcal{R}_G = \cap_{i \in G} \mathcal{R}_i.$$

Informally, $\mathcal{R}_i(w)$ is the set of worlds that agent i considers possible under w according to his belief, so $\mathcal{R}_G(w)$ is the set of worlds that are considered possible under w according to the direct fusion of agents' beliefs. The informal intuition is reflected in the definition of the satisfaction relation. Let $M = (W, (\mathcal{R}_i)_{1 \leq i \leq n}, V)$ be a model and Φ be the set of wffs for $\mathcal{L}$, then the satisfaction relation $\models_M \subseteq W \times \Phi$ is defined by the following inductive rules(we will use the infix notation for the relation and omit the subscript M for convenience):

1. $w \models p$ iff $w \in V(p)$, for each $p \in \Phi_0$,
2. $w \not\models_M \perp$ and $w \models_M \top$,
3. $w \models \neg\varphi$ iff $w \not\models \varphi$,
4. $w \models \varphi \lor \psi$ iff $w \models \varphi$ or $w \models \psi$,
5. $w \models [G]\varphi$ iff for all $u \in \mathcal{R}_G(w)$, $u \models \varphi$.

In the presentation below, we will extensively use the notions of pre-order. Let S be a set, then a pre-order over S is a reflexive and transitive binary relation $\leq$ on S. A pre-order over S is called total (or connected) if for all $x, y \in S$, either $x \leq y$ or $y \leq x$ holds. We will write $x < y$ as the abbreviation of $x \leq y$ and $y \not\leq x$. For a subset S' of S, $\min(S', \leq)$ is defined as the set $\{x \in S' \mid \forall y \in S', y \not< x\}$.

2 Merging by Majority

Majority voting is a method to resolve conflict between agents. For example, if three knowledge bases $T_1 = \{\varphi\}, T_2 = \{\varphi\}$, and $T_3 = \{\neg\varphi\}$ are combined, then the result would be $\{\varphi\}$, since two vote for φ, whereas only one votes against it.

One of the most general merging functions based on majority is defined in [34]. A function $Merge$ is applied to weighted knowledge bases. Let $wt : \{T_1, T_2, \cdots, T_k\} \to R^+$ be a weight function which assigns a positive real number to each component knowledge base, then a total pre-order over the set of propositional interpretations is defined as:

$$w \preceq_{(\{T_1, T_2, \cdots, T_k\}, wt)} w' \text{ iff } \sum_{i=1}^{k} dist(w, T_i) \cdot wt(T_i) \leq \sum_{i=1}^{k} dist(w', T_i) \cdot wt(T_i),$$

where $dist$ is a function denoting the distance between a propositional interpretation and a knowledge base. When the propositional language is finite, the so-called Dalal distance (or Hamming distance) between two interpretations of the language is used [16]. It is defined as the number of atoms whose valuations differs in the two interpretations. Let $dist(w, w')$ denote the Dalal distance between two interpretations w and w', then the distance from w to a theory T, denoted by $dist(w, T)$, is defined as:

$$dist(w, T) = \min\{dist(w, w') \mid w' \models T\}.$$

The merged result $Merge(T_1, T_2, \cdots, T_k, wt)$ is defined as:

$$\{\varphi \mid \forall w \in min(\Omega, \preceq), w \models \varphi\},$$

where Ω is the set of all propositional interpretations and $\preceq$ is $\preceq_{(\{T_1, T_2, \cdots, T_k\}, wt)}$.

This kind of weighted merging operator can be incorporated into epistemic logic in the following way. Syntactically, a new class of modal operators $[M(G, wt)]$ for any nonempty $G \subseteq \{1, 2, \cdots, n\}$ and weight function $wt : Ag \to R^+$ is added to our logic language. Then the semantics for the new modal operators is defined by extending a possible world model to $(W, (\mathcal{R}_i)_{1 \leq i \leq n}, V, \mu)$, where $(W, (\mathcal{R}_i)_{1 \leq i \leq n}, V)$ is an $\mathcal{L}$ model, whereas $\mu : W \times W \to R^+ \cup \{0\}$ is a distance metric function between possible worlds satisfying $\mu(w, w) = 0$ and $\mu(w, w') = \mu(w', w)$.

The distance metric between possible worlds is defined as in the semantics of conditional logic [37,40]. The distance from a possible world w to the belief state of an agent i in the possible world u is defined by:

$$dist_u(w, i) = \inf\{\mu(w, w') \mid (u, w') \in \mathcal{R}_i\}.$$

Then a total pre-order $\preceq^u_{(G, wt)}$ over the possible worlds is defined for each possible world u and modal operator $[M(G, wt)]$:

$$w \preceq^u_{(G, wt)} w' \text{ iff } \sum_{i \in G} dist_u(w, i) \cdot wt(i) \leq \sum_{i \in G} dist_u(w', i) \cdot wt(i).$$

The most straightforward definition for the satisfaction of the wff $[M(G, wt)]\varphi$ is:

$$u \models [M(G, wt)]\varphi \text{ iff for all } w \in min(W, \preceq^u_{(G, wt)}), w \models \varphi.$$

However, since for infinite W, the set $min(W, \preceq^u_{(G, wt)})$ may be empty, the definition may result in $u \models [M(G, wt)]\bot$ in some cases. Alternatively, since $\preceq^u_{(G, wt)}$ is a total pre-order, it is simply a system-of-spheres in the semantics of conditional logic [37], so we can define the satisfaction of the wff $[M(G, wt)]\varphi$ by

$$u \models [M(G, wt)]\varphi \text{ iff there exists } w_0 \text{ such that for all } w \preceq^u_{(G, wt)} w_0, w \models \varphi.$$

Note that the function wt is used only for encoding the reliability of agents. It is tempting to propagate the weights into a group of agents so that we have a weight $wt(G)$ for each group G. This weight may be useful in the belief fusion of two groups of agents. However, we do not really need this because if we want to merge the beliefs of two groups G_1 and G_2, we can simply merge the beliefs of agents in $G_1 \cup G_2$.

3   Arbitration

The notion of distance measure between possible worlds is also used in arbitration, another type of merging operator [32,38,39].

A semantic characterization for arbitration is given in [32]. A knowledge base in [32] is identified with a set of propositional models, thus the semantic characterization for this kind of arbitration is given by assigning to each subset of models A a binary relation $\leq_A$ over the set of model sets satisfying the following conditions (the subscript is omitted when it means all binary relations of the form $\leq_A$):

1. transitivity: if $A \leq B$ and $B \leq C$ then $A \leq C$,
2. if $A \subseteq B$ then $B \leq A$,
3. $A \leq A \cup B$ or $B \leq A \cup B$,
4. $B \leq_A C$ for every C iff $A \cap C \neq \emptyset$,
5. $A \leq_{C \cup D} B \Leftrightarrow \begin{cases} C \leq_{A \cup B} D \text{ and } A \leq_C B \text{ or} \\ D \leq_{A \cup B} C \text{ and } A \leq_D B. \end{cases}$

By slightly abusing the notation, $\leq_A$ may also denote binary relations between models in the sense that $w \leq_A w'$ iff $\{w\} \leq_A \{w'\}$. The arbitration between two sets of models A and B is then defined as:

$$A \triangle B = \min(A, \leq_B) \cup \min(B, \leq_A). \tag{1}$$

To incorporate the arbitration operator of [32] into epistemic logic, we first note that according to (1), the arbitration is commutative but not necessarily associative. Thus, the arbitration operator should be a binary operator between two agents. We can add a class of modal operators for arbitration into our logic just as in the case of majority merging. However, to be more expressive, we will also consider the interaction between arbitration and other epistemic operators, so we define the set of *arbitration expressions* over Ag recursively as the smallest set containing Ag and closed under the binary operators $+, \cdot$, and $\triangle$. Here $+$ and $\cdot$ correspond respectively to the distributed belief and the so-called "everybody knows" operators in multi-agent epistemic logic [20]. Then the operator $[G]$ in epistemic logic can be replaced with a new class of modal operators $[a]$ where a is an arbitration expression.

For the semantics, a model is extended to $(W, (\mathcal{R}_i)_{1 \leq i \leq n}, V, \leq)$, where $\leq$ is a function assigning to each subset of possible worlds A a binary relation $\leq_A \subseteq 2^W \times 2^W$ satisfying the above-mentioned five conditions. Note that the first two conditions imply that $\leq_A$ is a pre-order over 2^W. Then for each arbitration expression, we can define the binary relations $\mathcal{R}_{a \triangle b}, \mathcal{R}_{a \cdot b}$ and $\mathcal{R}_{a+b}$ over W recursively by:

$$\mathcal{R}_{a \triangle b}(w) = \min(\mathcal{R}_a(w), \leq_{\mathcal{R}_b(w)}) \cup \min(\mathcal{R}_b(w), \leq_{\mathcal{R}_a(w)})$$

$$\mathcal{R}_{a+b} = \mathcal{R}_a \cap \mathcal{R}_b$$

$$\mathcal{R}_{a \cdot b} = \mathcal{R}_a \cup \mathcal{R}_b$$

Thus the satisfaction for the wff $[a]\varphi$ is defined as:

$$u \models [a]\varphi \text{ iff for all } w \in \mathcal{R}_a(u), w \models \varphi.$$

Note that the original distributed belief operator $[G]$ is equivalent to $[i_1 + (i_2 + \cdots (i_{k-1} + i_k))]$ if $G = \{i_1, i_2, \cdots, i_k\}$. Furthermore, it has been shown that the only associative arbitration satisfying postulates 7 and 8 of [32] is $A \triangle B = A \cup B$, so if $\triangle$ is an associative arbitration satisfying those postulates, then $[a \triangle b]\varphi$ is reduced to $[a \cdot b]\varphi$, which is in turn equivalent to $[a]\varphi \wedge [b]\varphi$.

By this kind of modal operators, the postulates 2-8 of [32] can be translated into the following axioms:

1. $[a \triangle b]\varphi \equiv [b \triangle a]\varphi$,
2. $[a \triangle b]\varphi \supset [a + b]\varphi$,
3. $\neg[a + b]\bot \supset ([a + b]\varphi \supset [a \triangle b]\varphi)$,
4. $[a \triangle b]\bot \supset [a]\bot \wedge [b]\bot$,
5. $([a \triangle (b \cdot c)]\varphi \equiv [a \triangle b]\varphi) \vee ([a \triangle (b \cdot c)]\varphi \equiv [a \triangle c]\varphi) \vee ([a \triangle (b \cdot c)]\varphi \equiv [(a \triangle b) \cdot (a \triangle c)]\varphi)$,
6. $[a]\varphi \wedge [b]\varphi \supset [a \triangle b]\varphi$,
7. $\neg[a]\bot \supset \neg[a + (a \triangle b)]\bot$.

However, since the set of possible worlds W may be infinite in our logic, the minimal models in (3) may not exist, so the axioms 4 and 7 are not sound with respect to the semantics. To make them sound, we must add the following limit assumption [2] to the binary relations $\leq_A$ for any $A \subseteq W$:

$$\text{for any nonempty } U \subseteq W, \min(U, \leq_A) \text{ is nonempty.}$$

4   General Merging

In [26], an axiomatic framework unifying the majority merging and arbitration operators is presented. A set of postulates common to majority and arbitration operators is first proposed to characterize the general merging operators and then additional postulates for differentiating them are considered respectively. In that framework, a knowledge base is also a finite set of propositional sentences. The general merging operator is defined as a mapping from a multi-set[3] of knowledge base, called a *knowledge set*, to a knowledge base. Therefore, the arbitration operator defined via this approach can merge more than two knowledge bases, whereas the definition of arbitration operator in [32] is limited to two knowledge bases. The merging operator is denoted by $\triangle$, so for each knowledge set E, $\triangle(E)$ is a knowledge base. Two equivalent semantic characterizations are also given for the merging operators. One is based on the so-called *syncretic assignment*. A syncretic assignment maps each knowledge set E to a pre-order $\leq_E$ over interpretations such that some conditions reflecting the postulated properties

---

[3] A multi-set, also called a bag, is a collection of elements over some domain which allows multiple occurrences of elements.

of the merging operators must be satisfied. Then $\triangle(E)$ is the knowledge base whose models are the minimal interpretations according to $\leq_E$.

This logical framework is further extended to dealing with integrity constraints in [27]. Let E be a knowledge set and φ be a propositional sentence denoting the integrity constraints, then the merging of knowledge bases in E with integrity constraint φ, $\triangle_\varphi(E)$, is a knowledge base which implies φ. The models of $\triangle_\varphi(E)$ are characterized by $\min(Mod(\varphi), \leq_E)$, i.e., the minimal models of φ with respect to the ordering $\leq_E$. $\triangle_\varphi(E)$ is called an IC merging operator. According to the semantics, it is obvious that $\triangle(E)$ is a special case of IC merging operator $\triangle_\top(E)$. It is also shown that when E contains exactly one knowledge base, the operator is reduced to the AGM revision operator proposed in [1]. Therefore, IC merging is general enough to cover majority merging, arbitration, and AGM revision operator.

To incorporate IC merging operators into epistemic logic, we will extend its syntax with the following formation rule:

– if φ and ψ are wffs, then for any nonempty $G \subseteq \{1, 2, \ldots, n\}$, $[\triangle_\varphi(G)]\psi$ is also a wff.

For the convenience of naming, we will call a subset of possible worlds a belief state. Let $\mathcal{U} = \{U_1, U_2, \ldots, U_k\}$ denote a multi-set of belief states, then $\bigcap \mathcal{U} = U_1 \cap \cdots U_k$. For the semantics, a possible world model is extended to $(W, (\mathcal{R}_i)_{1 \leq i \leq n}, V, \leq)$, where $\leq$ is an assignment mapping each multi-set of belief states $\mathcal{U}$ to a total pre-order $\leq_\mathcal{U}$ over W satisfying the following conditions:

1. If $w, w' \in \bigcap \mathcal{U}$, then $w \leq_\mathcal{U} w'$,
2. If $w \in \bigcap \mathcal{U}$ and $w' \notin \bigcap \mathcal{U}$ then $w <_\mathcal{U} w'$,
3. For any $w \in U_1$, there exists $w' \in U_2$, such that $w' \leq_{\{U_1, U_2\}} w$, where U_1 and U_2 are two belief states,
4. If $w \leq_{\mathcal{U}_1} w'$ and $w \leq_{\mathcal{U}_2} w'$, then $w \leq_{\mathcal{U}_1 \sqcup \mathcal{U}_2} w'$, where $\sqcup$ denotes the union of two multi-sets,
5. If $w <_{\mathcal{U}_1} w'$ and $w \leq_{\mathcal{U}_2} w'$, then $w <_{\mathcal{U}_1 \sqcup \mathcal{U}_2} w'$.

These conditions are model-theoretic correspondences of those for syncretic assignments in [26,27]. Condition 1 says that possible worlds appearing in the belief states of all agents are equally plausible. Condition 2 asserts that a possible worlds appearing in the belief states of all agents is more plausible than those not. Condition 3 requires that all agents are treated fairly. Therefore, if agent 1 considers w possible, then w is not more plausible than all worlds in the belief state of agent 2. Conditions 4 and 5 essentially require that if two groups of agents agree on the ordering between w and w', then the united group of these two groups does not reverse the ordering.

For a group of agents G and a possible world u, let us define a total pre-order $\leq_G^u$ over W as follows:

$$w \leq_G^u w' \text{ iff } w \leq_{\{\mathcal{R}_i(u) | i \in G\}} w'.$$

The truth condition of $[\triangle_\varphi(G)]\psi$ is defined as that for conditional logic [10,9]. Formally, $u \models [\triangle_\varphi(G)]\psi$ iff

(i) there are no possible worlds in W satisfying φ, or

(ii) there exists $w_0 \in W$ such that $w_0 \models \varphi$ and for any $w \leq^u_G w_0$, $w \models \varphi \supset \psi$.

Note that in IC merging, a knowledge set consists of a multi-set of objective sentences, whereas for the modal operator $[\triangle_\varphi(G)]$, G is a set of agents whose beliefs may contain subjective sentences or beliefs of other agents. Also, an integrity constraint in [27] must be an objective sentence, whereas φ may be arbitrary complex wffs of our extended language. Furthermore, instead of selecting minimal models of φ, since the set of possible worlds may be infinite in our case, we adopt the system-of-spheres semantics as in Sect. 2 for the epistemic operator $[\triangle_\varphi(G)]$.

5   Belief Change

Unlike knowledge merging, where the component knowledge bases are equally important, belief change is a kind of asymmetry operator, where new information always outweighs the old. The main belief change operators are belief revision and update. They are characterized by different postulates [1,23,24]. In [23], a uniform model-theoretic framework is provided for the semantic characterization of the revision and update operators. In that context, a knowledge base is a finite set of propositional sentences, so it can also be represented by a single sentence(i.e., the conjunction of all sentences in the knowledge base).

For the revision operator, it is assumed that there is a total pre-order $\leq_\psi$ over the propositional interpretations for each knowledge base ψ. The revision operators satisfying the AGM postulates in [1] are exactly those that select from the models of the new information φ the minimal ones with respect to the ordering $\leq_\psi$. More precisely, let ψ be a knowledge base and φ denote the new information, then the result of revising ψ by φ, denoted by $\psi \circ \varphi$, will have the set of models

$$Mod(\psi \circ \varphi) = \min(Mod(\varphi), \leq_\psi).$$

As for the update operator, assume for each propositional interpretation w, there exists some partial pre-order $\leq_w$ over the interpretations for closeness to w, then update operators select for each model w in $Mod(\psi)$ the set of models from $Mod(\varphi)$ that are closest to w. The updated theory is characterized by the union of all such models. That is,

$$Mod(\psi \diamond \varphi) = \bigcup_{w \in Mod(\psi)} \min(Mod(\varphi), \leq_w),$$

where $\psi \diamond \varphi$ is the result of updating the knowledge base ψ by φ.

Both belief revision and update may occur in the observation of new information φ. For belief revision, it is assumed that the world is static, so if the new information is incompatible with the agent's original beliefs, then the agent may have an incorrect belief about the world. Thus he will try to accommodate the new information by minimally changing his original beliefs. However, for the belief update, it is assumed that the observation may be due to dynamic changes of the outside world, so the agent's belief may be out-of-date, though it may be totally correct for the original world. Thus the agent will assume the possible worlds are those resulting from the minimal change of the original world. In [11], a generalized update model is proposed which combines aspects of both revision and update. It is shown that a belief update model will be inadequate without modelling the dynamic aspect (i.e. the events causing the update) in the same time. Since the dynamic change of the external worlds does not play a role in the belief fusion process, we will not model belief update in our logic. Therefore, in what follows, we will concentrate on the belief revision operator.

Let us now consider the possibility of incorporating the belief revision operator into epistemic logic. In addition to the original meaning of revising a knowledge base ψ by new information φ, there is an alternative reading for the revision operator. That is, we can consider $\circ$ as a prioritized belief fusion operator that gives priority to its second argument [22]. In the context of knowledge base revision, these two interpretations are essentially equivalent. However, from the perspective of our logic in multi-agents systems, they may be quite different. Roughly speaking, $i \circ \varphi$ will denote the result of revising the beliefs of agent i by new information φ, whereas $i \circ j$ is the result of merging the beliefs of agents i and j by giving priority to j. More formally, a *revision expression* will be defined inductively as follows:

- If $1 \leq i, j \leq n$ and φ is a wff, then $i \circ j$ and $i \circ \varphi$ are revision expressions.
- If r is a revision expression, $1 \leq i \leq n$ and φ is a wff, then $r \circ i$ and $r \circ \varphi$ are revision expressions.

The syntactic rule is extended to include the modal operators $[r]$ for any revision expression r, so $[r]\varphi$ would be a wff if φ is. Note that a revision expression allows us to represent a revision sequence, which is directly related to iterated revision in [8,17].

To interpret the modal operator in our semantic framework, a possible world model is extended to $(W, (\mathcal{R}_i)_{1 \leq i \leq n}, V, \leq)$, where $\leq$ is an assignment mapping each belief state (i.e. subset of possible worlds) U to a total pre-order $\leq_U$ over W such that (i) if $w, w' \in U$, then $w \leq_U w'$ and (ii) if $w \in U$ and $w' \notin U$, then $w <_U w'$. Let $S \cdot U$ denote the sequence $(U_1, U_2, \cdots, U_k, U)$ if $S = (U_1, U_2, \cdots, U_k)$ is a sequence of belief state, then the assignment $\leq$ is extended to sequences of belief states in the following way (we assume $\leq_{(U)} = \leq_U$):

1. $w <_{S \cdot U} w'$ if $w \in U$ and $w' \notin U$,
2. $w \leq_{S \cdot U} w'$ iff $w \leq_S w'$ when both $w, w' \in U$ or both $w, w' \notin U$.

For each wff φ, let the truth set of φ, denoted by $|\varphi|$, be defined as $\{w \in W \mid w \models \varphi\}$. For each possible world u, define a function mapping any agent i and revision expression r into a sequence of belief states $u(i)$ and $u(r)$ as follows:

1. $u(i) = (\mathcal{R}_i(u))$,
2. $u(r \circ i) = u(r) \cdot \mathcal{R}_i(u)$,
3. $u(r \circ \varphi) = u(r) \cdot |\varphi|$.

Then the truth condition for the wff $[r \circ \varphi]\psi$ is $u \models [r \circ \varphi]\psi$ iff

(i) there are no possible worlds in W satisfying φ, or
(ii) there exists $w_0 \in W$ such that $w_0 \models \varphi$ and for any $w \leq_{u(r)} w_0$, $w \models \varphi \supset \psi$.

Analogously, the truth condition for the wff $[r \circ i]\psi$ is

$u \models [r \circ i]\psi$ iff there exists $w_0 \in \mathcal{R}_i(u)$ such that for any $w \leq_{u(r)} w_0$, if $w \in \mathcal{R}_i(u)$, then $w \models \psi$.

It can be seen that $[i \circ \varphi]\psi$ is equivalent to $[\triangle_\varphi(\{i\})]\psi$ in Sect. 4 according to the semantics.

6   Concluding Remarks

In preceding sections, we assume an agent's belief states are represented as a subset of possible worlds, i.e. $\mathcal{R}_i(w)$ is the belief state of agent i in world w. However, some more fine-grained representations have been also proposed, such as total pre-orders over the set of possible worlds [8,17,28,41], ordinal conditional functions [11,43,44], possibility distributions [3,18,19], belief functions [42] and pedigreed belief states [22]. Further development of logical systems that incorporate fusion operators based on more fine-grained representations of belief states should be a very interesting research direction.

We mainly present the semantics of epistemic logics for information fusion in this paper. However, to do practical reasoning, we must develop proof methods for these logics. There have been some previous works on the development of axiomatic or Gentzen-style calculi for information fusion. For example, in [4,5, 6,7], logics for information fusion based on possibility theory are proposed. The Hilbert-style or Gentzen-style proof systems of those logics are also presented. In particular, the logic $\mathbf{PL}_n^\otimes$ in [4] is an extension of QML in [29,30,31] with distributed belief operator, so the fusion operator in $\mathbf{PL}_n^\otimes$ is different than the merging operators used in this paper. The axiomatic system and theorem prover for a majority fusion logic MF have also been developed in [13,14]. The belief bases in MF are sets of literals, so it does not allow nested modalities as in our logics. In spite of these differences, the further development of proof theory for logics proposed in this paper could take these previous works as good starting points.

References

1. C.E. Alchourrón, Gärdenfors, and D. Makinson. "On the logic of theory change: Partial meet contraction and revision functions". *Journal of Symbolic Logic*, 50:510–530, 1985.
2. H.L. Arlo-Costa and S.J. Shapiro. "Maps between nonmonotonic and conditional logic". In B. Nebel, C. Rich, and W. Swartout, editors, *Proceedings of the 3rd International Conference on Principle of Knowledge Representation and Reasoning*, pages 553–564. Morgan Kaufmann, 1992.

3. S. Benferhat, D. Dubois, and H. Prade. "From semantic to syntactic approaches to information combination in possibilistic logic". In B. Bouchon-Meunier, editor, *Aggregation and Fusion of Imperfect Information*, pages 141–161. Physica-Verlag, 1997.
4. L. Boldrin and A. Saffiotti. "A modal logic for merging partial belief of multiple reasoners". *Journal of Logic and Computation*, 9(1):81–103, 1999.
5. L. Boldrin and C. Sossai. "An algebraic semantics for possibilistic logic". In *Proceedings of the 11th International Conference on Uncertainty in ArtiOcial Intelligence*, pages 24–37, 1995.
6. L. Boldrin and C. Sossai. "Partial information and necessity-valued logic". In *Proceedings of the 6th International Conference on Information Processing and Management of Uncertainty in Knowledge-Based Systems*, pages 941–946, 1996.
7. L. Boldrin and C. Sossai. "Local possibilistic logic". *Journal of Applied Non-Classical Logic*, 7(3):309–333, 1997.
8. C. Boutilier. "Revision sequences and nested conditionals". In *Proceedings of the 13th International Joint Conference on Artificial Intelligence*, pages 519–525, 1993.
9. C. Boutilier. "Conditional logics of normality : a modal approach". *Artificial Intelligence*, 68:87–154, 1994.
10. C. Boutilier. "Toward a logic for qualitative decision theory". In *Proceedings of the Fourth International Conference on Principles of Knowledge Representation and Reasoning*, pages 75–86, 1994.
11. C. Boutilier. "Generalized update: Belief change in dynamic settings". In *Proceedings of the 14th International Joint Conference on Artificial Intelligence*, pages 1550–1556, 1995.
12. L. Cholvy. "A logiccal approach to multi-souces reasoning". In M. Masuch and L. Pólos, editors, *Knowledge Representation and Reasoning under Uncertainty*, LNCS 808, pages 183–196. Springer-Verlag, 1994.
13. L. Cholvy and Ch. Garion. "A logic to reason with contradictory beliefs with a majority approach". In *Proceedings of the IJCAI Workshop on Inconsistency in Data and Knowledge*, 2001.
14. L. Cholvy and Ch. Garion. "Answering queries addressed to several databases: a query evaluator which implements a majority merging approach". In M.-S. Hacid, Z.W. Ra, and D.A. Zighed andY. Kodratoff, editors, *Proc of 13th International Symposium on Methodologies for Intelligent Systems*, LNAI 2366, pages 131–139. Springer-Verlag, 2002.
15. L. Cholvy and A. Hunter. "Information fusion in logic: A brief overview". In *Qualitative and Quantitative Practical Reasoning(ECSQARU'97/FAPR'97)*, LNAI 1244, pages 86–95. Springer-Verlag, 1997.
16. M. Dalal. "Investigations into a theory of knowledge base revision: Preliminary report". In *Proceedings of the 7th National Conference on Artificial Intelligence*, pages 475–479. AAAI Press, 1988.
17. A. Darwiche and J. Pearl. "On the logic of iterated belief revision". *Artificial Intelligence*, 89(1):1–29, 1997.
18. D. Dubois and H. Prade. "Belief change and possibility theory". In P. Gärdenfors, editor, *Belief Revision*, pages 142–182. Cambridge University Press, 1992.
19. D. Dubois and H. Prade. "Possibility theory in information fusion". In *Proc. of the Third International Conference on Information Fusion*, pages TuA-1, 2000.
20. R. Fagin, J.Y. Halpern, Y. Moses, and M.Y. Vardi. *Reasoning about Knowledge*. MIT Press, 1996.
21. J. Hintikka. *Knowledge and Belief.* Cornell University Press, 1962.

22. P. Maynard-Reid II and Y. Shoham. "Belief fusion: Aggregating pedigreed belief states". *Journal of Logic, Language and Information,* 10(2):183–209, 2001.
23. H. Katsuno and A. Medelzon. "On the difference between updating a knowledge base and revising it". In *Proceedings of the Second International Conference on Principles of Knowledge Representation and Reasoning (KR'91),* pages 387–394. Morgan Kaufmann Publisher, 1991.
24. H. Katsuno and A. Medelzon. "Propositional knowledge base revision and minimal change". *Artificial Intelligence,* 52:263–294, 1991.
25. S. Konieczny. "On the difference between merging knowledge bases and combining them". In *Proceedings of the Seventh International Conference on Principles of Knowledge Representation and Reasoning (KR'00).,* pages 135–144. Morgan Kaufmann Publisher, 2000.
26. S. Konieczny and R. Pino Pérez. "On the logic of merging". In *Proceedings of the Sixth International Conference on Principles of Knowledge Representation and Reasoning (KR'98),* pages 488–498. Morgan Kaufmann Publisher, 1998.
27. S. Konieczny and R. Pino Pérez. "Merging with integrity constraints". In A. Hunter and S. Parsons, editors, *Proceedings of the Fifth European Conference on Symbolic and Quantitative Approaches to Reasoning with Uncertainty (ECSQARU'99),* LNAI 1638, pages 233–244. Springer-Verlag, 1999.
28. D. Lehmann. "Belief revision, revised". In *Proceedings of the 14th International Joint Conference on Artificial Intelligence,* pages 1534–1540, 1995.
29. C.J. Liau and I.P. Lin. "Quantitative modal logic and possibilistic reasoning". In B. Neumann, editor, *Proceedings of the 10th ECAI,* pages 43–47. John Wiley & Sons. Ltd, 1992.
30. C.J. Liau and I.P. Lin. "Proof methods for reasoning about possibility and necessity". *International Journal of Approximate Reasoning,* 9(4):327–364, 1993.
31. C.J. Liau and I.P. Lin. "Possibilistic Reasoning—A Mini-survey and Uniform Semantics". *Artificial Intelligence,* 88:163 193, 1996.
32. P. Liberatore and M. Schaerf. "Arbitration: A commutative operator for belief revision". In *Proceedings of the Second World Conference on the Fundamentals of Artificial Intelligence (WOCFAI '95),* pages 217–228, 1995.
33. J. Lin. "Information sharing and knowledge merging in cooperative information systems". In *Proceedings of the Fourth Workshop on Information Technologies and Systems,* pages 58–66, 1994.
34. J. Lin. "Integration of weighted knowledge bases". *Artificial Intelligence,* 83(2):363–378, 1996.
35. J. Lin and A.O. Mendelzon. "Knowledge base merging by majority". In R. Pareschi and B. Fronhoefer, editors, *Dynamic Worlds: From the Frame Problem to Knowledge Management.* Kluwer Academic Publisher, 1999.
36. J.-J.Ch. Meyer and W. van der Hoek. *Epistemic Logic for AI and Computer Science.* Cambridge University Press, 1995.
37. D. Nute. "Conditional logic". In D.M. Gabbay and F. Guenthner, editors, *Handbook of Philosophical Logic, Vol II: Extensions of Classical Logic,* pages 387–439. D. Reidel Publishing Company, 1984.
38. P.Z. Revesz. "On the semantics of theory change: Arbitration between old and new information". In *Proceedings of the Twelfth ACM SIGACT-SIGMOD-SIGART Symposium on Principles of Database Systems,* pages 71–82, 1993.
39. P.Z. Revesz. "On the semantics of arbitration". *International Journal of Algebra and Computation,* 7(2):133–160, 1997.

40. K. Schlechta and D. Makinson. "Local and global metrics for the semantics of counterfactual conditionals". *Journal of Applied Non-Classical Logics*, 4(2):129–140, 1994.
41. K. Segerberg. "Belief revision from the point of view of doxastic logic". *Bull. of the IGPL*, 3(4):535–553, 1995.
42. P. Smets. " Data fusion in the transferable belief model". In *Proc. of the Third International Conference on Information Fusion*, pages WeA–1, 2000.
43. W. Spohn. "Ordinal conditional functions: a dynamic theory of epistemic states". In W.L. Harper and B. Skyrms, editors, *Causation in Decision, Belief Change, and Statistics, II*, pages 105–134. Kluwer Academic Publishers, 1988.
44. M.A. Williams. "Transmutations of knowledge systems". In J. Doyle, E. Sande-wall, and P. Torasso, editors, *Proceedings of the 4th International Conference on Principle of Knowledge Representation and Reasoning*, pages 619–629. Morgan Kaufmann Publishers, 1994.

Propositional Fusion Rules

Anthony Hunter and Rupert Summerton

Department of Computer Science
University College London
Gower Street, London WC1E 6BT, UK

Abstract. In previous papers, we have presented a logic-based framework for merging structured news reports [14,16,15]. Structured news reports are XML documents, where the text entries are restricted to individual words or simple phrases, such as names and domain-specific terminology, and numbers and units. We assume structured news reports do not require natural language processing. In this paper, we present propositional fusion rules as a way of implementing logic-based fusion for structured news reports. Fusion rules are a form of scripting language that define how structured news reports should be merged. The antecedent of a fusion rule is a call to investigate the information in the structured news reports and the background knowledge, and the consequent of a fusion rule is a formula specifying an action to be undertaken to form a merged report. It is expected that a set of fusion rules is defined for any given application. We give the syntax and mode of execution for fusion rules, and explain how the resulting actions give a merged report.

1 Introduction

Structured news reports are XML documents, where the text entries are restricted to individual words or simple phrases (such as names and domain-specific terminology), dates, numbers and units. We assume that strucutured news reports do not require natural language processing. In addition, each tag provides semantic information about the textentries, and a structured news report is intended to have some semantic coherence. To illustrate, news reports on corporate acquisitions can be represented as structured news reports using tags including `buyer`, `seller`, `acquisition`, `value`, and `date`. Structured news reportscan be obtained from information extraction systems (e.g. [8]).

In order to merge structured news reports, we need to take account of the contents. Different kinds of content need to be merged in different ways as illustrated in Example 1. There are many further examples we could consider, each with particular features that indicate how the merged report should be formed.

Example 1. Consider the following two conflicting weather reports which are for the same day and same country.

T.D. Nielsen and N.L. Zhang (Eds.): ECSQARU 2003, LNAI 2711, pp. 502–514, 2003.

```
⟨report⟩                              ⟨report⟩
   ⟨source⟩ TV1 ⟨/source⟩               ⟨source⟩ TV3 ⟨/source⟩
   ⟨date⟩ 19/3/02 ⟨/date⟩               ⟨date⟩ 19 March 2002 ⟨/date⟩
   ⟨country⟩ UK ⟨/country⟩              ⟨country⟩ UK ⟨/country⟩
   ⟨today⟩ showers ⟨/today⟩            ⟨today⟩ inclement ⟨/today⟩
   ⟨windspeed⟩ 10 kph ⟨/windspeed⟩     ⟨windspeed⟩ 15 kph ⟨/windspeed⟩
   ⟨tomorrow⟩ sun ⟨/tomorrow⟩          ⟨tomorrow⟩ rain ⟨/tomorrow⟩
   ⟨regionalreport⟩                    ⟨regionalreport⟩
      ⟨region⟩ South East ⟨/region⟩       ⟨region⟩ North West ⟨/region⟩
      ⟨maxtemp⟩ 20C ⟨/maxtemp⟩            ⟨maxtemp⟩ 18C ⟨/maxtemp⟩
   ⟨/regionalreport⟩                   ⟨/regionalreport⟩
⟨/report⟩                             ⟨/report⟩
```

We can merge them so the source is TV1 and TV3, and the weather for today is showers and inclement, and the weather for tomorrow is sun or rain. Also we may wish to take each subtree that is rooted at regionalreport in the input, and put them both in the merged report.

```
⟨report⟩
        ⟨source⟩ TV1 and TV3 ⟨/source⟩
        ⟨date⟩ 19.03.02 ⟨/date⟩
        ⟨country⟩ UK ⟨/country⟩
        ⟨today⟩ showers and inclement ⟨/today⟩
        ⟨windspeed⟩ 10 − 15 kph ⟨/windspeed⟩
        ⟨tomorrow⟩ sun or rain ⟨/tomorrow⟩
        ⟨regionalreport⟩
                ⟨region⟩ South East ⟨/region⟩
                ⟨maxtemp⟩ 20C ⟨/maxtemp⟩
        ⟨/regionalreport⟩
        ⟨regionalreport⟩
                ⟨region⟩ North West ⟨/region⟩
                ⟨maxtemp⟩ 18C ⟨/maxtemp⟩
        ⟨/regionalreport⟩
⟨/report⟩
```

An alternative way of merging these reports may be possible if we have a preference for one source over the other. Suppose we have a preference for TV3 in the case of conflict, then we may prefer the textentry rain for the tag tomorrow.

In our approach to merging structured news reports, we draw on domain knowledge to help produce merged reports. The approach is based on fusion rules defined in a logical meta-language. These rules are of the form $\alpha \Rightarrow \beta$, expressing that if α holds, then β is made to hold. So we consider α as a condition to check the information in the structured reports and in the background information, and we consider β as an action to undertake to construct the merged report.

To merge a set of structured news reports, we start with the background knowledge and the information in the news reports to be merged, and attempt to apply all the fusion rules to this information. The application of the fusion rules is then a monotonic process that builds up a set of actions that define how the merged structured news report to be output should be constructed.

2 Structured News Reports

We use XML to represent structured news reports. So each structured news report is an XML document, but not vice versa, as defined below. This restriction means that we can easily represent each structured news report by a ground term in classical logic.

Definition 1. Structured news report: *If ϕ is a tagname (i.e an element name), and ψ is a textentry, then $\langle\phi\rangle\psi\langle/\phi\rangle$ is a structured news report. If ϕ is a tagname and $\sigma_1, ..., \sigma_n$ are structured news reports, then $\langle\phi\rangle\sigma_1...\sigma_n\langle/\phi\rangle$ is a structured news report.*

Clearly each structured news report is isomorphic to a tree with the non-leaf nodes being the tagnames and the leaf nodes being the textentries.

Definition 2. Tree: *If $\langle\phi\rangle\psi\langle/\phi\rangle$ is a structured news report, then there is an isomorphic tree that has the root ϕ and a child ψ where ψ is a leaf. If $\langle\phi\rangle\sigma_1...\sigma_n\langle/\phi\rangle$ is a structured news report, then there is an isomorphic tree where (1) the root is ϕ and (2) by recursion there is an isomorphic tree ρ_i for each $\sigma_i \in \{\sigma_1, .., \sigma_n\}$ where the root of ρ_i is a child of ϕ.*

This isomorphism allows us to give a definition for a branch of a structured news report.

Definition 3. Branch: *Let σ be a structured news report and let ρ be a tree that is isomorphic to σ. A sequence of tagnames $\phi_1/../\phi_n$ is a branch of ρ iff (1) ϕ_1 is the root of ρ and (2) for each i, if $1 \leq i < n$, then ϕ_i is the parent of ϕ_{i+1}. Note, the child of ϕ_n is not necessarily a leaf node. By extension, $\phi_1/../\phi_n$ is a branch of σ iff $\phi_1/../\phi_n$ is a branch of ρ*

When we refer to a subtree (of a structured news report), we mean a subtree formed from the tree representation of the structured news report, where the root of the subtree is a tagname and the leaves are textentries. We formalize this as follows.

Definition 4. Subtree: *Let σ be a structured news report and let ρ be a tree that is isomorphic to σ. A tree ρ' is a subtree of ρ iff (1) the set of nodes in ρ' is a subset of the set of nodes in ρ, and (2) for each node ϕ_i in ρ', if ϕ_i is the parent of ϕ_j in ρ, then ϕ_j is in ρ' and ϕ_i is the parent of ϕ_j in ρ'. By extension, if σ' is a structured news report, and ρ' is isomorphic to σ', then we describe σ' as a subtree of σ.*

Each structured news report is also isomorphic with a ground term (of classical logic) where each tagname is a function symbol and each textentry is a constant symbol.

Definition 5. News term: *Each structured news report is isomorphic with a ground term (of classical logic) called a news term. This isomorphism is defined inductively as follows: (1) If $\langle\phi\rangle\psi\langle/\phi\rangle$ is a structured news report, where ψ is a textentry, then $\phi(\psi)$ is* *a news term that is isomorphic with* $\langle\phi\rangle\psi\langle/\phi\rangle$; *and (2) If* $\langle\phi\rangle\psi_1..\psi_n\langle/\phi\rangle$ *is a structured news report, and* ψ_1' *is a news term that is isomorphic with* ψ_1, ..., *and* ψ_n' *is a news term that is isomorphic with* ψ_n, *then* $\phi(\psi_1',..,\psi_n')$ *is a news term that is isomorphic with* $\langle\phi\rangle\psi_1..\psi_n\langle/\phi\rangle$.

Via this isomorphic relationship, we can refer to a branch of a news term by using the branch of the isomorphic structured news report, and we can refer to a subtree of a news term by using the subtree of the isomorphic structured news report.

Definition 6. *Let* σ *be a structured news report and let* π *be a news term that is isomorphic to* σ. *By extending Definition 3,* $\phi_1/../\phi_n$ *is a branch of* π *iff* $\phi_1/../\phi_n$ *is a branch of* σ. *Let* σ' *be a structured news report and let* π' *be a news term such that* π' *is isomorphic to* σ'. *By extending Definition 4,* π' *is a subtree of* π *iff* σ' *is a subtree of* σ.

We now define two functions that allow us to obtain subtrees and textentries from news terms.

Definition 7. *Let* π *be a news term, let* π' *be a subtree of* π, *and let* ψ *be a textentry. If* $\phi_1/../\phi_n$ *is a branch of* π, *and the root of* π' *is* ϕ_n, *then let* $\mathsf{Subtree}(\phi_1/../\phi_n, \pi) = \pi'$, *otherwise let* $\mathsf{Subtree}(\phi_1/../\phi_n, \pi) = \mathsf{null}$. *If* $\phi_1/../\phi_n$ *is a branch of* π, *and* ψ *is the child of* ϕ_n, *then let* $\mathsf{Textentry}(\phi_1/../\phi_n, \pi) = \psi$, *otherwise* $\mathsf{Textentry}(\phi_1/../\phi_n, \pi) = \mathsf{null}$.

Example 2. Consider the following structured news report.

```
⟨auctionreport⟩
    ⟨buyer⟩⟨firstname⟩John⟨/firstname⟩⟨surname⟩Smith⟨/surname⟩⟨/buyer⟩
    ⟨property⟩Lot37⟨/property⟩
⟨/auctionreport⟩
```

This can be represented by the following news term:

```
auctionreport(buyer(firstname(John), surname(Smith)), property(Lot37))
```

In this news term, `auctionreport/buyer/firstname` is a branch. If the news term is denoted by π, we have

$$\mathsf{Subtree}(\mathtt{auctionreport/buyer}, \pi) = \mathtt{buyer(firstname(John), surname(Smith))}$$
$$\mathsf{Subtree}(\mathtt{auctionreport/buyer/firstname}, \pi) = \mathtt{firstname(John)}$$
$$\mathsf{Textentry}(\mathtt{auctionreport/buyer/firstname}, \pi) = \mathtt{John}$$

Definition 8. *A* **skeleton** *is of the form* $\phi(\psi_1,..,\psi_n)$ *where* ϕ *is a tagname and* $\psi_1,..,\psi_n$ *are skeletons. If* ψ_i *is a tagname, then it is a skeleton. A skeleton* $\phi(\psi_1,..,\psi_n)$ *can be regarded as a tree.*

A skeleton is a equivalent to a structured news report without text entries. It is the underlying structure without the content.

3   Fusion Rules

In this paper, we restrict consideration to merging sets of structured news reports of a fixed cardinality. So a set of fusion rules is specified for an application to take exactly n structured news reports as input to produce a merged report as output.

Definition 9. *We assume an arbitrary naming of the input reports with names from a set of report names* $\{\text{in}_1, .., \text{in}_n\}$. *The set of* **report names** *is denoted* $\mathcal{N}$.

Definition 10. *Let* $\phi_1/../\phi_n$ *be a branch, and let* $\mu \in \mathcal{N}$ *be a report name. A* **subtree variable** *is denoted* $\mu//\phi_1/.../\phi_n$, *and a* **textentry variable** *is denoted* $\mu//\phi_1/.../\phi_n\#$. *A* **schema variable** *is either a subtree variable or a textentry variable. Let the set of schema variables be denoted* $\mathcal{S}$.

In the following definition, we augment a definition for a classical logic language (where function symbols are not nested) with notation for schema variables which are just placeholders to be instantiated with news terms before logical reasoning.

Definition 11. *Let* $\mathcal{C}$ *be a set of constant symbols, let* $\mathcal{S}$ *be a set of schema variables, and* $\mathcal{F}$ *be a set of function symbols. The set of ground terms* $\mathcal{G}$ *is* $\mathcal{C} \cup \{f(c_1, .., c_k) \mid f \in \mathcal{F}$ *and* $c_1, .., c_k \in \mathcal{C}\}$. *The set of terms* $\mathcal{T}$ *is* $\mathcal{C} \cup \{f(d_1, .., d_k) \mid f \in \mathcal{F}$ *and* $d_1, .., d_k \in \mathcal{C} \cup \mathcal{S}\}$. *Let* $\mathcal{P}$ *be a set of predicate symbols. The set of atoms* $\mathcal{A}$ *is* $\{p(t_1, .., t_k) \mid p \in \mathcal{P}$ *and* $t_1, .., t_k \in \mathcal{T}\}$. *The set of literals* $\mathcal{L}$ *is* $\mathcal{A} \cup \{\neg\gamma \mid \gamma \in \mathcal{A}\}$. *The set of ground atoms* $\mathcal{B}$ *is* $\{p(g_1, .., g_k) \mid p \in \mathcal{P}$ *and* $g_1, .., g_k \in \mathcal{G}\}$. *The set of ground literals* $\mathcal{M}$ *is* $\mathcal{B} \cup \{\neg\gamma \mid \gamma \in \mathcal{B}\}$.

Definition 12. *Let* $\phi(\psi_1, ..\psi_n)$ *be a news term. The* **subterms** *of this news term are given by the function* Subterms *as follows.*

$$\text{Subterms}(\phi(\psi_1, .., \psi_n)) = \{\phi(\psi_1, .., \psi_n)\} \cup \text{Subterms}(\psi_1) \cup .. \cup \text{Subterms}(\psi_n)$$

For a set of news terms Φ, *let* $\text{Subterms}(\Phi) = \bigcup_{\phi(\psi_1, .., \psi_n) \in \Phi} \text{Subterms}(\phi(\psi_1, .., \psi_n))$

We assume that for all possible news terms π, we have $\text{Subterms}(\pi) \subset \mathcal{G}$. We also assume that if $\phi_1/../\phi_n$ is a branch, then it is a constant symbol, called a **branch constant**, and it is in $\mathcal{G}$. Similarly, if $\phi(\psi_1, .., \psi_n)$ is a skeleton, then it is a constant symbol, called a **skeleton constant**, and it is in $\mathcal{G}$.

Definition 13. *A* **propositional fusion rule** *is of the following form where* $\alpha_1, .., \alpha_n \in \mathcal{L}$ *and* $\beta \in \mathcal{A}$.

$$\alpha_1 \wedge .. \wedge \alpha_n \Rightarrow \beta$$

We call $\alpha_1, .., \alpha_n$ *the condition literals and* β *the action atom.*

We regard a fusion rule that incorporates schema variables, as a scheme for one or more classical propositional formulae. These propositional formulae are obtained by grounding schema variables as we explain below. We discuss condition literals in Sect. 3.1 and action literals in Sect. 3.2.

Example 3. The following is a propositional fusion rule for Example 1.

¬Synonymous(in₁//report/today#, in₂//report/today#)
∧ Coherent(in₁//report/today#, in₂//report/today#)
⇒ AddText(Conjunction(in₁//report/today#,
                                    in₂//report/today#), report/today)

Definition 14. *Let Φ be a set of structured news reports to be merged. Let λ be an assignment (bijection) from the report names $\mathcal{N}$ to Φ. τ is a* **valid grounding for a subtree variable** $\mu//\phi_1/.../\phi_k$ *iff $\tau \in$ Subterms($\lambda(\mu)$) and Subtree($\phi_1/.../\phi_k, \lambda(\mu)$) = τ. τ is a* **valid grounding for a textentry variable** $\mu//\phi_1/.../\phi_k\#$ *iff $\tau \in$ Subterms($\lambda(\mu)$) and Textentry($\phi_1/.../\phi_k, \lambda(\mu)$) = τ.*

Example 4. Consider the rule in Example 3. For in₁//report/today#, the valid grounding is Textentry(report/today, λ(in₁)). This is evaluated to showers if we let λ(in₁) refer to the top left structured news report in Example 1. Similarly, the valid grounding for variable in₂//report/today# is Textentry(report/today, λ(in₂)), which is evaluated to inclement if we let λ(in₂) refer to the top right structured news report in Example 1.

Definition 15. *A* **ground fusion rule** *is a propositional fusion rule with every schema variable replaced by a valid grounding. Let* Ground(δ, Φ) *be the set of all ground fusion rules formed from the propositional fusion rule δ where each schema variable in δ is systematically replaced by a valid grounding from* Subterms(Φ).

Example 5. The ground fusion rule obtained with the fusion rule given in Example 3 with the news reports in Example 1 is the following:

¬Synonymous(showers, inclement)
∧ Coherent(showers, inclement)
⇒ AddText(Conjunction(showers, inclement), report/today)

Proposition 1. *If γ is a ground fusion rule, then γ is a formula of propositional classical logic.*

This result means that we have a clear and simple characterization of propositional fusion rules as schema for classical propositional formulae such that once we have the grounded versions of them, reasoning with them is straightforward. As we discuss next, fusion rules provide a bridge between structured news reports and logical reasoning with background knowledge.

3.1   Condition Literals

The condition literals in fusion rules relate the contents of structured news reports to the background knowledge. There are many possible condition literals that we could define that relate one or more features from one or more structured news reports to the background knowledge. To illustrate, these literals may include the following kinds: SameDate(T, T′) where T and T′ are news terms with equal date; SameSource(T, T′) where T and T′ are news terms that refer to the same source; SameCity(T, T′) where T and T′ are news terms that refer to the same city; Synonymous(T, T′) where T and T′ are news terms that are synonyms; and Coherent(T, T′) where T and T′ are news terms that are coherent.

Example 6. Some examples of condition literals (when ground) may include the following.

$$\text{SameDate}(\text{date}(14\text{Nov}01), \text{date}(14.11.01))$$
$$\text{SameDate}(\text{date}(\text{day}(14), \text{month}(11), \text{year}(01)), \text{date}(14.11.01))$$
$$\text{SameCity}(\text{city}(\text{Mumbai}), \text{city}(\text{Bombay}))$$
$$\text{Coherent}(\text{snow}, \text{sleet})$$
$$\text{Coherent}(\text{sun}, \text{sunny})$$
$$\text{Coherent}(\text{showers}, \text{inclement})$$
$$\neg\text{Coherent}(\text{sun}, \text{rain})$$
$$\neg\text{Coherent}(\text{sun}, \text{snow})$$
$$\neg\text{Synonymous}(\text{showers}, \text{rain})$$

The condition literals are evaluated by querying background knowledge. In the simplest case, the background knowledge may be just a set of ground atoms that hold. However, we would expect the background knowledge would include classical quantified formulae that can be handled using automated reasoning. In any case, the background knowledge is defined by a knowledge engineer building a fusion system for an application.

3.2   Action Atoms

Action atoms specify the structure and content for a merged report. In a ground fusion rule $\alpha' \Rightarrow \beta'$, if the ground literals in the antecedent α' hold, then the merged report should meet the specification represented by the ground atom β'. We look at this in more detail in the next section. Here we consider the syntax for action literals.

Each action atom is a member of $\mathcal{A}$. These incorporate terms based on action functions that take one or more news terms as arguments and return a news term. There are many possiblities for action functions including the following where X and Y are grounded with textentries: Interval(X, Y) returns an interval X − Y as a textentry; Conjunction(X, Y) returns a textentry X and Y; and Disjunction(X, Y) returns a textentry X or Y. We assume action functions are interpreted in the underlying implementation and return the appropriate textentries for evaluating the action atom.

Example 7. The following ground function, on the left of the = symbol, are rewritten to the news terms on the right:

$$\texttt{Interval(18C, 25C)} = \texttt{18} - \texttt{25C}$$
$$\texttt{Conjunction(TV1, TV3)} = \texttt{TV1 and TV3}$$
$$\texttt{Disjunction(sun, rain)} = \texttt{sun or rain}$$

We now define a basic set of action atoms. A number of further definitions for action atoms are possible.

Definition 16. *The* **action atoms** *are literals that include the following specifying how the merged report should be constructed.*

1. $\texttt{Initialize}(\phi(\psi_1, .., \psi_n))$ *where* $\phi(\psi_1, .., \psi_n)$ *is a skeleton constant. The intended action is to start the construction of the merged structured news report with the basic structure being defined by* $\phi(\psi_1, .., \psi_n)$ *. The root of the merged report is* ϕ.
2. $\texttt{AddText}(\texttt{T}, \phi_1/../\phi_n)$ *where* $\texttt{T}$ *is a textentry, and* $\phi_1/../\phi_n$ *is a branch constant. The intended action is to add the textentry* $\texttt{T}$ *as the child to the tagname* ϕ_n *in the merged report on the branch* $\phi_1/../\phi_n$.
3. $\texttt{AddTree}(\texttt{T}, \phi_1/../\phi_n)$ *where* $\texttt{T}$ *is a news term, and* $\phi_1/../\phi_n$ *is a branch constant. The intended action is to add* $\texttt{T}$ *to the merged report so that the tagname for the root of* $\texttt{T}$ *has the parent* ϕ_n *on the branch* $\phi_1/../\phi_n$.

The action atoms are specifications that are intended to be made to hold by producing a merged report that satisfies the specification.

Example 8. Consider the action literal in the consequent of Example 3.

$$\texttt{AddText(Conjunction(showers, inclement), report/today)}$$

The term $\texttt{Conjunction(showers, inclement)}$ is rewritten by the system to the term $\texttt{showers and inclement}$, and so the action literal is now the following:

$$\texttt{AddText(showers and inclement, report/today)}$$

This specifies that the textentry should be $\texttt{showers and inclement}$ in the merged report for tagname $\texttt{today}$ on the branch $\texttt{report/today}$, as obtained in Example 1

4 Rule Execution

In order to use a set of fusion rules, we need to be able to execute them with background knowledge and a set of structured news reports.

Definition 17. *A* **fusion call** *is a triple* (Δ, Γ, Φ) *where* Γ *is a set of fusion rules,* Δ *is a background knowledgebase (a set of classical first-order formulae), and* Φ *is a set of structured news reports.*

To merge some reports, the fusion rules are ground with the structured news reports, and then a form of modus ponens is exhaustively applied together with the background knowledge.

Definition 18. *Let* (Δ, Γ, Φ) *be a fusion call.*

$$\text{Actions}(\Delta, \Gamma, \Phi) = \{\beta' \mid \alpha' \Rightarrow \beta' \in \text{Ground}(\delta, \Phi) \text{ and } \delta \in \Gamma \text{ and } \Delta \vdash \alpha'\}$$

where $\vdash$ *is the classical consequence relation.*

Example 9. A fusion call with an appropriate set of fusion rules and the pair of news reports given in the top of Example 1 together with appropriate background knowledge can give the following action atoms:

```
Initialize(report(source, date, country, today, windspeed, tomorrow))
AddText(Conjunction(TV1, TV3), report/source)
AddText(19.03.02, report/date)
AddText(UK, report/country)
AddText(Conjunction(showers, inclement), report/today)
AddText(Interval(18Kph, 15Kph), report/windspeed)
AddText(Disjunction(sun, rain), report/tomorrow)
AddTree(regionalreport(region(SouthEast), maxtemp(20C)), report)
AddTree(regionalreport(region(NorthWest), maxtemp(18C)), report)
```

These action atoms specify the merged report given in the bottom of Example 1.

Proposition 2. *Let* (Δ, Γ, Φ) *be a fusion call.* Actions(Δ, Γ, Φ) *is a finite set iff* Γ *is a finite set of fusion rules.*

Given a fusion call (Δ, Γ, Φ), the set Actions(Δ, Γ, Φ) is input to an algorithm for constructing a merged report. The minimum we expect of a set of action atoms is that a merged report can be produced that meets the specification. We formalize this as follows.

Definition 19. *Let* (Δ, Γ, Φ) *be a fusion call and let* σ *be a structured news report.*

$$\sigma \text{ meets Actions}(\Delta, \Gamma, \Phi) \text{ iff } \forall \beta \in \text{Actions}(\Delta, \Gamma, \Phi) \ \sigma \text{ meets } \beta$$

where σ *is isomorphic with a news term* π *such that*

σ *meets* Initialize$(\phi(\psi_1, .., \psi_n))$
  iff each branch of $\sigma(\psi_1, .., \psi_n)$ *is a branch of* π

σ *meets* AddText$(T, \phi_1/../\phi_n)$
  iff Textentry$(\phi_1/../\phi_n, \pi) = T$

σ *meets* AddTree$(T, \phi_1/../\phi_n)$
  iff Subtree$(\phi_1/../\phi_n/\phi_{n+1}, \pi) = T$ *and the root of* T *is* ϕ_{n+1}

However, the meets relation is a little too relaxed in the sense that a report may meet an action sequence but may also include extra information that has not been specified.

Definition 20. *The* **matches** *relation is defined as follows where* σ *is a structured news report and* (Δ, Γ, Φ) *is a fusion call:* σ *matches* Actions(Δ, Γ, Φ) *iff* σ *meets* Actions(Δ, Γ, Φ) *and there is no* σ' *s.t.* $(\sigma'$ *meets* Actions(Δ, Γ, Φ) *and* Subterms$(\sigma') \subset$ Subterms$(\sigma))$.

The matches relation identifies the minimal structured news report(s) that meet(s) the action sequence. In other words, it identifies the news reports that do not include any superfluous information.

Definition 21. *A fusion call* (Δ, Γ, Φ) *is* **complete** *iff there is a* ψ *for which* Initialize(ψ) *atom is in* Actions(Δ, Γ, Φ) *and for all branches* $\phi_1/../\phi_n$ *of* ψ *there is an action atom* AddText$(T, \phi_1/../\phi_n)$ *in* Actions(Δ, Γ, Φ) *for some* T.

In other words, an action sequence is complete if it is not the case that the structured news report that results has missing textentries.

Definition 22. *A fusion call* (Δ, Γ, Φ) *is* **consistent** *iff (1) there is exactly one* Initialize(ψ) *atom in* Actions(Δ, Γ, Φ); *and (2) if* AddText$(T, \phi_1/../\phi_n)$ *is in* Actions(Δ, Γ, Φ), *then for all* AddText$(T', \phi_1/../\phi_n)$ *in* Actions(Δ, Γ, Φ) $T = T'$;

Proposition 3. *A fusion call* (Δ, Γ, Φ) *is complete and consistent iff there is a structured news report* π *such that* π *meets* Actions(Δ, Γ, Φ).

Definition 23. *A fusion system* (Δ, Γ) *is* **well-behaved** *iff for all* Φ *either* (Δ, Γ, Φ) *is a complete and consistent fusion call or there is no* ψ *such that the* Initialize(ψ) *atom is in* Actions(Δ, Γ, Φ).

This means the fusion rules in a fusion system need to be engineered so that exactly one Initialize atom is obtained for any set of structured news reports Φ that are to be covered by the fusion system, and no Initialize atom is to be obtained for any set of structured news reports Φ that are not to be covered by the fusion system.

The set of action atoms that we have defined in this paper is only part of the range of possible action atoms. We have implemented others including ExtendTree$(T, \phi_1/../\phi_n)$ where T is a news term, and $\phi_1/../\phi_n$ is a branch constant, and the intended action is to extend the merged report with T so that the tagname for the root of T is ϕ_n on the branch $\phi_1/../\phi_n$. We intend to extend the range of implemented functions to include functions based on voting strategies so that for example if the majority of news reports input have a particular textentry on a particular branch, then the merged report will have that textentry on that branch.

5   Discussion

The definition for a fusion call suggests an implementation based on existing automated reasoning technology and on XML programming technology. Once information is in the form of XML documents, a number of technologies for managing and manipulating information in XML are available. We have developed a prototype implementation in

Java for executing executing fusion rules that are marked up in FusionRuleML and constructing the merged reports [17]. Background knowledge is handled in a Prolog system and this is queried by the Java implementation.

Our logic-based approach differs from other logic-based approaches for handling inconsistent information such as belief revision theory (e.g. [11,9,18,20]) and knowledgebase merging (e.g. [19,1]). These proposals are too simplistic in certain respects for handling news reports. Each of them has one or more of the following weaknesses: (1) One-dimensional preference ordering over sources of information — for news reports we require finer-grained preference orderings; (2) Primacy of updates in belief revision — for news reports, the newest reports are not necessarily the best reports; and (3) Weak merging based on a meet operator — this causes unnecessary loss of information. Furthermore, none of these proposals incorporate actions on inconsistency or context-dependent rules specifying the information that is to be incorporated in the merged information, nor do they offer a route for specifying how merged reports should be composed.

Merging information is also an important topic in database systems. A number of proposals have been made for approaches based in schema integration (e.g. [24]), the use of global schema (e.g. [12]), and conceptual modelling for information integration based on description logics [4,3,10,23,2]. These differ from our approach in that they do not seek an automated approach that uses domain knowledge for identifying and acting on inconsistencies. Heterogeneous and federated database systems are relevant, but they do not identify and act on inconsistency in a context-sensitive way [26,22,6], though there is increasing interest in bringing domain knowledge into the process (e.g. [5,27]). Also relevant is revision programming, a logic-based framework for describing and enforcing database constraints [21].

Our approach also goes beyond other technologies for handling news reports. The approach of wrappers offers a practical way of defining how heterogeneous information can be merged (see for example [13,7,25]). However, there is little consideration of problems of conflicts arising between sources. Our approach therefore goes beyond these in terms of formalizing reasoning with inconsistent information and using this to analyse the nature of the news report and for formalizing how we can act on inconsistency.

Acknowledgements. The authors wish to thank Weiru Liu and the referees for helpful feedback on the paper.

References

1. C. Baral, S. Kraus, J. Minker, and V. Subrahmanian. Combining knowledgebases consisting of first-order theories. *Computational Intelligence*, 8:45–71, 1992.
2. S. Bergamaschi, S. Castano, M. Vincini, and D. Beneventano. Semantic integration of heterogeneous information sources. *Data and Knowledge Engineering*, 36:215–249, 2001.
3. D. Calvanese, G. De Giacomo, M. Lenzerini, D. Nardi, and R. Rosati. Description logic framework for information integration. In *Proceedings of the 6th Conference on the Principles of Knowledge Representation and Reasoning (KR'98)*, pages 2–13. Morgan Kaufmann, 1998.

4. D. Calvanese, G. De Giacomo, M. Lenzerini, D. Nardi, and R. Rosati. Source integration in data warehousing. In *Proceedings of the 9th International Workshop on Database and Expert Systems (DEXA'98)*, pages 192–197. IEEE Computer Society Press, 1998.
5. L. Cholvy. Reasoning with data provided by federated databases. *Journal of Intelligent Information Systems*, 10:49–80, 1998.
6. L. Cholvy and S. Moral. Merging databases: Problems and examples. *International Journal of Intelligent Systems*, 10:1193–1221, 2001.
7. W. Cohen. A web-based information system that reasons with structured collections of text. In *Proceedings of Autonomous Agents'98*, 1998.
8. J. Cowie and W. Lehnert. Information extraction. *Communications of the ACM*, 39:81–91, 1996.
9. D. Dubois and H. Prade, editors. *Handbook of Defeasible Resoning and Uncertainty Management Systems*, volume 3. Kluwer, 1998.
10. E. Franconi and U. Sattler. A data warehouse conceptual data model for multidimensional aggregation. In S. Gatziu, M. Jeusfeld, M. Staudt, and Y. Vassiliou, editors, *Proceedings of the Workshop in Design and Management of Data Warehouses*, 1999.
11. P. Gardenfors. *Knowledge in Flux*. MIT Press, 1988.
12. G. Grahne and A. Mendelzon. Tableau techniques for querying information sources through global schemas. In *Proceedings of the 7th International Conference on Database Theory (ICDT'99)*, Lecture Notes in Computer Science. Springer, 1999.
13. J. Hammer, H. Garcia-Molina, S. Nestorov, and R. Yerneni. Template-based wrappers in the TSIMMIS system. In *Proceedings of ACM SIGMOD'97*. ACM, 1997.
14. A. Hunter. Merging potentially inconsistent items of structured text. *Data and Knowledge Engineering*, 34:305–332, 2000.
15. A. Hunter. Logical fusion rules for merging structured news reports. *Data and Knowledge Engineering*, 42:23–56, 2002.
16. A. Hunter. Merging structured text using temporal knowledge. *Data and Knowledge Engineering*, 41:29–66, 2002.
17. A. Hunter and R. Summerton. FusionRuleML: Representing and executing fusion rules. Technical report, UCL Department of Computer Science, 2002.
18. H. Katsuno and A. Mendelzon. On the difference between updating a knowledgebase and revising it. In *Principles of Knowledge Representation and Reasoning: Proceedings of the Second International Conference (KR'91)*, pages 387–394. Morgan Kaufmann, 1991.
19. S. Konieczny and R. Pino Perez. On the logic of merging. In *Proceedings of the Sixth International Conference on Principles of Knowledge Representation and Reasoning (KR'98)*, pages 488–498. Morgan Kaufmann, 1998.
20. P. Liberatore and M. Schaerf. Arbitration (or how to merge knowledgebases). *IEEE Transactions on Knowledge and Data Engineering*, 10:76–90, 1998.
21. V. Marek and M. Truszczynski. Revision programming. *Theoretical Computer Science*, 190:241–277, 1998.
22. A. Motro. Cooperative database systems. *International Journal of Intelligent Systems*, 11:717–732, 1996.
23. N. Paton, R. Stevens, P. Baker, C. Goble, S. Bechhofer, and A. Brass. Query processing in the TAMBIS bioinformatics source integration system. In *Proceedings of the 11th International Conference on Scientific and Statistical Databases*, 1999.
24. A. Poulovassilis and P. McBrien. A general formal framework for schema transformation. *Data and Knowledge Engineering*, 28:47–71, 1998.
25. A. Sahuguet and F. Azavant. Building light-weight wrappers for legacy web data-sources using W4F. In *Proceedings of the International Conference on Very Large Databases (VLDB'99)*, 1999.

26. A. Sheth and J. Larson. Federated database systems for managing distributed, heterogeneous, and autonomous databases. *ACM Computing Surveys*, 22:183–236, 1990.
27. K. Smith and L. Obrst. Unpacking the semantics of source and usage to perform semantic reconciliation in large-scale information systems. In *ACM SIGMOD RECORD*, volume 28, pages 26–31, 1999.

Preferential Logics for Reasoning with Graded Uncertainty

Ofer Arieli

Department of Computer Science, The Academic College of Tel-Aviv
4 Antokolski street, Tel-Aviv 61161, Israel
`oarieli@mta.ac.il`

Abstract. We introduce a family of preferential logics that are useful for handling information with different levels of uncertainty. The corresponding consequence relations are non-monotonic, paraconsistent, adaptive, and rational. It is also shown that any formalism in this family that is based on a well-founded ordering of the different types of uncertainty, can be embedded in a corresponding four-valued logic with at most three uncertainty levels.

1 Motivation

The ability to reason in a 'rational' way with incomplete or inconsistent information is a major challenge, and its significance should be obvious. It is well-known that classical logic is not suitable for this task, thus non-classical formalisms are usually used for handling uncertainty.[1] Such formalisms should be able, moreover, to distinguish among different types of uncertainty in the underlying data, since each kind of uncertainty may require a different treatment. The following example demonstrates such a case:

Example 1. Let $\mathcal{P} = \{p \leftarrow \text{true} , \neg p \leftarrow \text{true} , q \leftarrow \text{not } \neg r , \neg q \leftarrow \text{not } r\}$. This is a 'prolog-like' program, with two kinds of negation operators: one, $\neg$, intuitively represents explicit negation, and the other, **not**, represents implicit negative information, and may be intuitively understood as a 'negation-as-failure' (to prove or verify the corresponding assertion on the basis of the available information). The meaning of the last two clauses of $\mathcal{P}$ is, therefore, that q (respectively, $\neg q$) holds provided that $\neg r$ (respectively, r) cannot be verified.

The theory above depicts several types of uncertainty: the information about r is *incomplete*, since r does not appear in a head of any clause in $\mathcal{P}$, and so no *explicit* data about it (nor about its negation) is available. This implies, in particular, that one cannot conclude that either r or $\neg r$ holds, and so, by the last two clauses, the data about q is *inconsistent*. Clearly, by the first two clauses, the information about p is inconsistent as well. Note, however, that there is a difference between the inconsistent information about p and about q: while the contradiction regarding p is based on *explicit data*, the evidence about q is

---

[1] See, e.g., [12,15,18,23] for some recent collections of papers on this topic.

T.D. Nielsen and N.L. Zhang (Eds.): ECSQARU 2003, LNAI 2711, pp. 515–527, 2003.

less 'stable', since it relies on the (possibly temporary) fact that neither r nor $\neg r$ holds. In particular, once r is validated or falsified, the information about q would not remain contradictory anymore! One may also argue that although the information about r is incomplete, there is still more knowledge about r (e.g., that it determines the validity of q) than about, say, s (about which we don't know anything whatsoever). Here, again, we have two different degrees of uncertainty.

The example above demonstrates one case in which it is natural to attach different levels of uncertainty to different assertions. This kind of information may be used, for instance, by algorithms for consistency restoration, since data with higher degree of inconsistency may be treated (i.e., eliminated) first.

In this paper we consider a framework that supports this type of considerations, and provides means to reason with different levels of uncertain information. We show that the logics that are obtained are nonmonotonic, paraconsistent [19], adaptive in the sense of Batens [10,11], and rational in the sense of Lehmann and Magidor [28]. It is also shown that under a certain assumption on the grading relations, for each one of these formalisms there is a logically equivalent four-valued logic with at most three different levels of uncertainty.

2   The Framework

2.1   Logical Lattices and Their Consequence Relations

In order to overcome the shortcomings of classical logic in properly handling uncertainty, we turn to multiple-valued logics. This is a common approach that is the basis of many formal systems (see [9] for a recent survey), including systems that are based on fuzzy logic [22], probabilistic reasoning [33], possibilistic logics [21], annotated logics [26,37], and fixpoint semantics for extended/disjunctive logic programs (see, e.g., [3,29], and a survey in [20]).

In most of the approaches mentioned above, as in the present one, the truth-values are arranged in a lattice structure. In what follows we denote by $\mathcal{L} = (L, \leq)$ a bounded lattice that has at least four elements: a $\leq$-maximal element and a $\leq$-minimal element that correspond to the classical values (denoted, respectively, by t and f), and two intermediate elements (denoted by $\top$ and $\bot$) that may intuitively be understood as representing the two basic types of uncertainty: inconsistency and incompleteness (respectively). As usual, the meet and the join operations on $\mathcal{L}$ are denoted by $\wedge$ and $\vee$. In addition, we assume that $\mathcal{L}$ has an involution operator $\neg$ (a "negation") s.t. $\neg t = f$, $\neg f = t$, $\neg\top = \top$, $\neg\bot = \bot$. We denote by $\mathcal{D}$ the set of the *designated values* of L (i.e., the set of the truth values in L that represent true assertions). We shall assume that $\mathcal{D}$ is a prime filter in $\mathcal{L}$,[2] s.t. $\top \in \mathcal{D}$ and $\bot \notin \mathcal{D}$. The pair $(\mathcal{L}, \mathcal{D})$ is called a *logical lattice* [6].

---

[2] In particular, $t \in \mathcal{D}$ and $f \notin \mathcal{D}$.

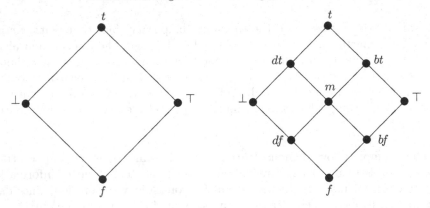

Fig. 1. $\mathcal{FOUR}$ and $\mathcal{NINE}$

Example 2. The smallest logical lattice is shown in Fig. 1 (left). We denote it by $\mathcal{FOUR}$. This lattice, together with the set $\mathcal{D} = \{t, \top\}$ of designated values, is the algebraic structure behind Belnap's well-known four-valued logic [13,14], and it will play an important role here as well (see Sect. 3). $\mathcal{NINE}$ (Fig. 1, right), may be viewed as an extended version of $\mathcal{FOUR}$ for default reasoning (dt = true by default, bt = 'biased' for t, etc.). This lattice depicts three main levels of uncertainty: incomplete data ($\bot$), inconsistent data ($\top$), and a middle level of uncertainty (m). The latter kind of uncertainty sometimes follows from contradictory default assumptions, so it may be retracted when further information arrives. The decision whether to view m as designated is one of the differences between the two logical lattices that $\mathcal{NINE}$ induces, namely ($\mathcal{NINE}, \{t, bt, \top\}$) and ($\mathcal{NINE}, \{t, dt, bt, bf, m, \top\}$).

The set $\mathcal{U} = \{(x, y) \mid 0 \leq x \leq 1, \ 0 \leq y \leq 1\}$ with $(x_1, y_1) \vee (x_2, y_2) = (\max(x_1, x_2), \min(y_1, y_2))$ and $(x_1, y_1) \wedge (x_2, y_2) = (\min(x_1, x_2), \max(y_1, y_2))$ is an infinite lattice, and $(\mathcal{U}, \{(1, x) \mid 0 \leq x \leq 1\})$ is a logical lattice with $t = (1, 0)$, $f = (0, 1)$, $\top = (1, 1)$, and $\bot = (0, 0)$. One way to intuitively understand the meaning of an element $(x, y) \in \mathcal{U}$ is such that x represents the amount of belief for the underlying assertion, and y represents the amount of belief against it. Following this intuition, every element $(x, x) \in \mathcal{U}$ may be associated with a different degree of inconsistency.

Given a logical lattice $(\mathcal{L}, \mathcal{D})$, the standard semantical notions are natural generalizations of the classical ones: a (multiple-valued) *valuation* ν is a function that assigns an element of L to each atomic formula. The set of valuations onto L is denoted by $\mathcal{V}^L$. Extension to complex formulae is done in the usual way. A valuation is a *model* of a set of assertions Γ if it assigns a designated value to every formula in Γ. The set of all the models of Γ is denoted by $mod(\Gamma)$.

The language considered here is a propositional one. Note that there are no tautologies in the language of $\{\neg, \vee, \wedge\}$, since if all the atomic formulae that appear in a formula ψ are assigned $\bot$ by a valuation ν, then $\nu(\psi) = \bot$ as well. It follows that the definition of the material implication $p \rightsquigarrow q$ as $\neg p \vee q$ is not adequate for representing entailments in our semantics. Instead, we use another connective, which does function as an implication in our setting:

Definition 1. [4,8] Let $(\mathcal{L}, \mathcal{D})$ be a logical lattice. Define: $x \to y = y$ if $x \in \mathcal{D}$, and $x \to y = t$ otherwise.[3]

The language of $\{\neg, \vee, \wedge, \to\}$ together with the propositional constants $t, f, \top$ and $\bot$, will be denoted by Σ. Given a set of formulae Γ in Σ, we shall denote by $\mathcal{A}(\Gamma)$ the set of the atomic formulae that appear in some formula of Γ.

Now, a natural definition of a lattice-based consequence relation is the following:

Definition 2. Let $(\mathcal{L}, \mathcal{D})$ be a logical lattice, Γ a set of formulae, and ψ a formula. Denote $\Gamma \models^{\mathcal{L}, \mathcal{D}} \psi$ if every model of Γ is a model of ψ.

The relation $\models^{\mathcal{L}, \mathcal{D}}$ of Definition 2 is a consequence relation in the standard sense of Tarski [38]. In [4] it is shown that this relation is monotonic, compact, paraconsistent [19], and has a corresponding sound and complete cut-free Gentzen-type system. The major drawbacks of $\models^{\mathcal{L}, \mathcal{D}}$ are that it is strictly weaker than classical logic even for consistent theories (e.g., $\psi \not\models^{\mathcal{L}, \mathcal{D}} \neg\phi \vee \phi$), and that it always invalidates some intuitively justified inference rules, like the Disjunctive Syllogism (that is, $\psi, \neg\psi \vee \phi \not\models^{\mathcal{L}, \mathcal{D}} \phi$). In the next section we consider a family of logics that overcome these drawbacks.

2.2   Preferential Reasoning and the Consequence Relation $\models_c^{\mathcal{L}, \mathcal{D}}$

In order to recapture within our many-valued framework classical reasoning (where its use is appropriate), as well as standard non-monotonic and paraconsistent methods, we incorporate a concept first introduced by McCarthy [32] and later considered by Shoham [36], according to which inferences from a given theory are made w.r.t. a subset of the models of that theory (and not w.r.t. every model of the theory; see also [24,27,30,31,35]). This set of *preferential models* is determined according to some conditions that can be specified by a set of (usually second-order) propositions [7], or by some order relation on the models of the theory [4,5]. This relation should reflect some kind of preference criterion on the models of the set of premises. In our case the idea is to give precedence to those valuations that minimize the amount of uncertain information in the set of premises. The truth values are therefore arranged according to an order relation that reflects differences in the amount of uncertainty that each one of them exhibits. Then we choose those valuations that minimize the amount of uncertainty w.r.t. this order. The intuition behind this approach is that incomplete or contradictory data corresponds to inadequate information about the real world, and therefore it should be minimized. Next we formalize this idea.

---

[3] Note that on $\{t, f\}$ the material implication ($\rightsquigarrow$) and the new implication ($\to$) are identical, and both of them are generalizations of the classical implication.

Definition 3. A partial order $<$ on a set L is called *modular* if $y < x_2$ for every $x_1, x_2, y \in L$ s.t. $x_1 \not< x_2$, $x_2 \not< x_1$, and $y < x_1$.

Proposition 1. [28] *Let $<$ be a partial order on L. The following conditions are equivalent:*
a) $<$ *is modular.*
b) *For every $x_1, x_2, y \in L$, if $x_1 < x_2$ then either $y < x_2$ or $x_1 < y$.*
c) *There is a totally ordered set L' with a strict order $\prec$ and a function $g : L \to L'$ s.t. $x_1 < x_2$ iff $g(x_1) \prec g(x_2)$.*

Definition 4. An *inconsistency order* $<_c^{\mathcal{L}, \mathcal{D}}$ on a logical lattice $(\mathcal{L}, \mathcal{D})$ is a well-founded modular order on L, with the following properties:
a) t and f are minimal and $\top$ is maximal w.r.t. $<_c^{\mathcal{L}, \mathcal{D}}$,
b) if $\{x, \neg x\} \subseteq \mathcal{D}$ while $\{y, \neg y\} \not\subseteq \mathcal{D}$, then $x \not<_c^{\mathcal{L}, \mathcal{D}} y$,
c) x and $\neg x$ are either equal or $<_c^{\mathcal{L}, \mathcal{D}}$-incomparable.

Inconsistency orders are used here for grading uncertainty in general, and inconsistency in particular. Intuitively, the meaning of $x <_c^{\mathcal{L}, \mathcal{D}} y$ is that formulae that are assigned x are more definite than formulae with a truth value y. Modularity is needed for assuring a proper grading of the truth values.[4] Condition (b) in Definition 4 assures that truth values that intuitively represent inconsistent data will not be considered as more consistent than those ones that correspond to consistent data. The last condition makes sure that any truth value and its negation have the same degree of (in)consistency.

Example 3. $\mathcal{FOUR}$ has four inconsistency orders:
a) The degenerated order, $<_{c_0}^4$, in which $t, f, \bot, \top$ are all incomparable.
b) $<_{c_1}^4$, in which $\bot$ is considered as minimally inconsistent: $\{t, f, \bot\} <_{c_1}^4 \top$.
c) $<_{c_2}^4$, in which $\bot$ is maximally inconsistent: $\{t, f\} <_{c_2}^4 \{\top, \bot\}$.
d) $<_{c_3}^4$, in which $\bot$ is an intermediate level of inconsistency: $\{t, f\} <_{c_3}^4 \bot <_{c_3}^4 \top$.

In the rest of the paper we shall continue to use the notations of Example 3 for denoting the inconsistency orders in $\mathcal{FOUR}$.

Given an inconsistency order $<_c^{\mathcal{L}, \mathcal{D}}$ on a logical lattice $(\mathcal{L}, \mathcal{D})$, it induces an equivalence relation on L, in which two elements in L are equivalent iff they are equal or $<_c^{\mathcal{L}, \mathcal{D}}$-incomparable. For every $x \in \mathcal{L}$, we denote by $[x]$ the equivalence class of x with respect to this equivalence relation. I.e.,

$$[x] = \{y \mid y = x, \text{ or } x \text{ and } y \text{ are } <_c^{\mathcal{L}, \mathcal{D}}\text{-incomparable}\}.$$

The order relation on these classes is defined as usual by representatives: we denote $[x] \leq_c^{\mathcal{L}, \mathcal{D}} [y]$ iff either $x <_c^{\mathcal{L}, \mathcal{D}} y$, or x and y are $<_c^{\mathcal{L}, \mathcal{D}}$-incomparable.[5] It is

---

[4] That is, to eliminate orders such as $\{\{t\}, \{f \prec \bot \prec \top\}\}$, in which $\top$ and $\bot$ are not comparable with t, while they are comparable with $\neg t$.

[5] As usual, we use the same notation to denote the order relation among equivalence classes and the order relation among their elements.

easy to verify that this definition is proper, i.e. it does not depend on the choice of the representatives.

An inconsistency order on $(\mathcal{L}, \mathcal{D})$ induces the following pre-order on $\mathcal{V}^L$:

Definition 5. Let $<_c^{\mathcal{L},\mathcal{D}}$ be an inconsistency order on $(\mathcal{L}, \mathcal{D})$, and let $\nu_1, \nu_2 \in \mathcal{V}^L$.
a) $\nu_1 \leq_c^{\mathcal{L},\mathcal{D}} \nu_2$ iff for every atom p, $[\nu_1(p)] \leq_c^{\mathcal{L},\mathcal{D}} [\nu_2(p)]$.
b) $\nu_1 <_c^{\mathcal{L},\mathcal{D}} \nu_2$ if $\nu_1 \leq_c^{\mathcal{L},\mathcal{D}} \nu_2$ and there is an atom q s.t. $[\nu_1(q)] <_c^{\mathcal{L},\mathcal{D}} [\nu_2(q)]$.

Definition 6. Let $<_c^{\mathcal{L},\mathcal{D}}$ be an inconsistency order in a logical lattice $(\mathcal{L}, \mathcal{D})$. The set of the *c-most consistent models* of a set Γ of formulae in Σ (abbreviation: the *c-mcms* of Γ) are the minimal inconsistent models of Γ, i.e.:

$$!(\Gamma, \leq_c^{\mathcal{L},\mathcal{D}}) = \{\nu \in mod(\Gamma) \mid \neg \exists \mu \in mod(\Gamma) \text{ s.t. } \mu <_c^{\mathcal{L},\mathcal{D}} \nu\}.$$

Now we can refine the inference process, defined by the lattice-based consequence relation $\models^{\mathcal{L},\mathcal{D}}$ (Definition 2). Instead of considering every possible model of the premises, we take into account only the c-most consistent ones.

Definition 7. Let $<_c^{\mathcal{L},\mathcal{D}}$ be an inconsistency order on a logical lattice $(\mathcal{L}, \mathcal{D})$. Denote: $\Gamma \models_c^{\mathcal{L},\mathcal{D}} \psi$ if every c-mcm of Γ is a model of ψ.

Example 4. Consider one direction of the barber paradox:[6]

$$\Gamma = \{\neg \text{shaves}(\text{x}, \text{x}) \rightarrow \text{shaves}(\text{Barber}, \text{x})\}.$$

Denote by ν_1, ν_2, and ν_3 the valuations that assign t, $\perp$, and $\top$ (respectively) to the assertion $\text{shaves}(\text{Barber}, \text{Barber})$. Using $\mathcal{FOUR}$ as the underlying logical lattice, we have that $!(\Gamma, \leq_{c_2}^4) = !(\Gamma, \leq_{c_3}^4) = \{\nu_1\}$, $!(\Gamma, \leq_{c_1}^4) = \{\nu_1, \nu_2\}$, and $!(\Gamma, \leq_{c_0}^4) = \{\nu_1, \nu_2, \nu_3\}$. Thus, $\Gamma \not\models_{c_i}^4 \text{shaves}(\text{Barber}, \text{Barber})$ when $i = 0, 1$, while $\Gamma \models_{c_i}^4 \text{shaves}(\text{Barber}, \text{Barber})$ when $i = 2, 3$.

3   Embedding in Four-Valued Logics

Four-valued reasoning may be traced back to the 1950's, where is has been investigated by a number of people, including Bialynicki-Birula [16], Rasiowa [17], and Kalman [25]. Later, Belnap [13,14] introduced a corresponding four-valued algebraic structure (denoted here by $\mathcal{FOUR}$) for paraconsistent reasoning. Theorem 1 below, which is our main result here, shows that this structure is canonical for reasoning with graded uncertainty. Following [5], this is another evidence for the robustness of four-valued logics as representing commonsense reasoning.

---

[6] Here we assume that formulae with variables are universally quantified. Consequently, a set of assertions Γ, containing a non-grounded formula, ψ, is viewed as representing the corresponding set of ground formulae, formed by substituting for each variable that appears in ψ, every element in the relevant Herbrand universe.

Definition 8. $\mathcal{V}^L$ is *stoppered* w.r.t. $\leq_c^{\mathcal{L},\mathcal{D}}$ if for every Γ and every $\nu \in mod(\Gamma)$, either $\nu \in \;!(\Gamma, \leq_c^{\mathcal{L},\mathcal{D}})$, or there is an $\nu' \in \;!(\Gamma, \leq_c^{\mathcal{L},\mathcal{D}})$ s.t. $\nu' <_c^{\mathcal{L},\mathcal{D}} \nu$.[7]

Note that in case that $\mathcal{V}^L$ is well-founded w.r.t. $\leq_c^{\mathcal{L},\mathcal{D}}$ (i.e., $\mathcal{V}^L$ does not have an infinitely descending chain w.r.t. $\leq_c^{\mathcal{L},\mathcal{D}}$), then it is in particular stoppered.

Theorem 1. *Let $\leq_c^{\mathcal{L},\mathcal{D}}$ be an inconsistency order on a logical lattice $(\mathcal{L}, \mathcal{D})$ such that $\mathcal{V}^L$ is stoppered (with respect to the induced order on valuations). Then $\Gamma \models_c^{\mathcal{L},\mathcal{D}} \psi$ iff $\Gamma \models_{c_i}^4 \psi$ for some $0 \leq i \leq 3$.*

In the rest of this section we prove Theorem 1. First, we consider some notations and definitions.

Definition 9. Given a logical lattice $(\mathcal{L}, \mathcal{D})$, its elements may be divided into the following four sets:

$$\mathcal{T}_t^{\mathcal{L},\mathcal{D}} = \{x \in L \mid x \in \mathcal{D}, \neg x \notin \mathcal{D}\}, \qquad \mathcal{T}_f^{\mathcal{L},\mathcal{D}} = \{x \in L \mid x \notin \mathcal{D}, \neg x \in \mathcal{D}\},$$

$$\mathcal{T}_\top^{\mathcal{L},\mathcal{D}} = \{x \in L \mid x \in \mathcal{D}, \neg x \in \mathcal{D}\}, \qquad \mathcal{T}_\perp^{\mathcal{L},\mathcal{D}} = \{x \in L \mid x \notin \mathcal{D}, \neg x \notin \mathcal{D}\}.$$

Henceforth we shall usually omit the superscripts, and write $\mathcal{T}_t, \mathcal{T}_f, \mathcal{T}_\top, \mathcal{T}_\perp$.

Definition 10. Let $(\mathcal{L}, \mathcal{D})$ be a logical lattice. Denote:

$$\min_{\leq_c^{\mathcal{L},\mathcal{D}}} \mathcal{T}_x = \{y \in \mathcal{T}_x \mid \neg \exists y' \in \mathcal{T}_x \text{ s.t. } y' <_c^{\mathcal{L},\mathcal{D}} y\} \quad (x \in \{t, f, \top, \perp\})$$

$$\Omega_{\leq_c^{\mathcal{L},\mathcal{D}}} = \min_{\leq_c^{\mathcal{L},\mathcal{D}}} \mathcal{T}_t \cup \min_{\leq_c^{\mathcal{L},\mathcal{D}}} \mathcal{T}_f \cup \min_{\leq_c^{\mathcal{L},\mathcal{D}}} \mathcal{T}_\perp \cup \min_{\leq_c^{\mathcal{L},\mathcal{D}}} \mathcal{T}_\top$$

Definition 11. Let $(\mathcal{L}_1, \mathcal{D}_1)$ and $(\mathcal{L}_2, \mathcal{D}_2)$ be two logical lattices. Suppose that x_i is some element in L_i and ν_i is a valuation onto L_i $(i = 1, 2)$.
a) x_1 and x_2 are *similar* if $x_1 \in \mathcal{T}_y^{\mathcal{L}_1, \mathcal{D}_1}$ implies that $x_2 \in \mathcal{T}_y^{\mathcal{L}_2, \mathcal{D}_2}$ $(y \in \{t, f, \top, \perp\})$.
b) ν_1 and ν_2 are *similar* if for every atom p, $\nu_1(p)$ and $\nu_2(p)$ are similar.

Proposition 2. *Let $(\mathcal{L}_1, \mathcal{D}_1)$ and $(\mathcal{L}_2, \mathcal{D}_2)$ be two logical lattices and suppose that ν_1 and ν_2 are two similar valuations on L_1 and L_2 (respectively). Then for every formula ψ, $\nu_1(\psi)$ and $\nu_2(\psi)$ are similar.*

Proof. By an induction on the structure of ψ.[8]

Proof (of Theorem 1). We shall denote by m_x some element in $\min_{\leq_c^{\mathcal{L},\mathcal{D}}} \mathcal{T}_x^{\mathcal{L},\mathcal{D}}$ $(x \in \{t, f, \top, \perp\})$, and by $\omega : L \to \{t, f, \top, \perp\}$ the "categorization" function: $\omega(y) = x$ iff $y \in \mathcal{T}_x$. Also, in the rest of this proof we shall abbreviate $[y] \cap \Omega_{\leq_c^{\mathcal{L},\mathcal{D}}}$ by $[y]$ (thus we shall refer here to classes that consist only of elements in $\Omega_{\leq_c^{\mathcal{L},\mathcal{D}}}$).

Lemma 1. *If $M \in \;!(\Gamma, \leq_c^{\mathcal{L},\mathcal{D}})$ then for every atom p, $M(p) \in \Omega_{\leq_c^{\mathcal{L},\mathcal{D}}}$.*

---

[7] The notion "stopperdness" is due to Mackinson [31]. In [27] the same property is called *smoothness*.
[8] Note that the fact that $\mathcal{D}$ is a *prime filter* is crucial here.

Proof. Suppose that there is some atom p_0 s.t. $M(p_0) \notin \Omega_{\leq_c^{\mathcal{L},\mathcal{D}}}$. Then, assuming that $M(p_0) \in \mathcal{T}_x$, there is an element $m_x \in \min_{\leq_c^{\mathcal{L},\mathcal{D}}} \mathcal{T}_x$ s.t. $m_x <_c^{\mathcal{L},\mathcal{D}} M(p_0)$. Consider the following valuation:

$$N(p) = \begin{cases} m_x & \text{if } p = p_0 \\ M(p) & \text{if } p \neq p_0 \end{cases}$$

N is similar to M, and so, by Proposition 2, N is also a model of Γ. Moreover, $N <_c^{\mathcal{L},\mathcal{D}} M$, thus $M \notin \,!(\Gamma, \leq_c^{\mathcal{L},\mathcal{D}})$. $\square$

Now, since $\leq_c^{\mathcal{L},\mathcal{D}}$ is well-founded and since $\mathcal{T}_x$ is nonempty for every $x \in \{t, f, \top, \bot\}$, $\min_{\leq_c^{\mathcal{L},\mathcal{D}}} \mathcal{T}_x$ is nonempty as well, and so there is at least one element of the form m_x for every $x \in \{t, f, \top, \bot\}$. Also, it is clear that for every $m_x, m_x' \in \min_{\leq_c^{\mathcal{L},\mathcal{D}}} \mathcal{T}_x$, $[m_x] = [m_x']$ (otherwise either $m_x <_c^{\mathcal{L},\mathcal{D}} m_x'$ or $m_x >_c^{\mathcal{L},\mathcal{D}} m_x'$, and so either $m_x' \notin \min_{\leq_c^{\mathcal{L},\mathcal{D}}} \mathcal{T}_x$ or $m_x \notin \min_{\leq_c^{\mathcal{L},\mathcal{D}}} \mathcal{T}_x$). It follows, therefore, that there are no more than three equivalence classes in $\Omega_{\leq_c^{\mathcal{L},\mathcal{D}}}$:

$$\min_{\leq_c^{\mathcal{L},\mathcal{D}}} \mathcal{T}_t \cup \min_{\leq_c^{\mathcal{L},\mathcal{D}}} \mathcal{T}_f \subseteq [t], \quad \min_{\leq_c^{\mathcal{L},\mathcal{D}}} \mathcal{T}_\bot \subseteq [m_\bot], \quad \min_{\leq_c^{\mathcal{L},\mathcal{D}}} \mathcal{T}_\top \subseteq [m_\top],$$

where $m_\bot$ is some element of $\min_{\leq_c^{\mathcal{L},\mathcal{D}}} \mathcal{T}_\bot$, and $m_\top$ is some element of $\min_{\leq_c^{\mathcal{L},\mathcal{D}}} \mathcal{T}_\top$. By Definition 4, $[t]$ must be a minimal inconsistency class among those in $\Omega_{\leq_c^{\mathcal{L},\mathcal{D}}}$, and $[m_\top]$ must be a maximal one. It follows, then, that the inconsistency classes in $\Omega_{\leq_c^{\mathcal{L},\mathcal{D}}}$ are arranged in one of the following orders:

0. $[t] = [m_\bot] = [m_\top]$,   2. $[t] <_c^{\mathcal{L},\mathcal{D}} [m_\bot] = [m_\top]$,

1. $[t] = [m_\bot] <_c^{\mathcal{L},\mathcal{D}} [m_\top]$,   3. $[t] <_c^{\mathcal{L},\mathcal{D}} [m_\bot] <_c^{\mathcal{L},\mathcal{D}} [m_\top]$.

If the order relation among the inconsistency classes in $\Omega_{\leq_c^{\mathcal{L},\mathcal{D}}}$ corresponds to case i above ($0 \leq i \leq 3$) we say that the inconsistency order $\leq_c^{\mathcal{L},\mathcal{D}}$ is *of type i.*[9]

Lemma 2. *If $\leq_c^{\mathcal{L},\mathcal{D}}$ is an inconsistency order of type i, then for every $m, m' \in \Omega_{\leq_c^{\mathcal{L},\mathcal{D}}}$, $[m] <_c^{\mathcal{L},\mathcal{D}} [m']$ iff $[\omega(m)] <_{c_i}^4 [\omega(m')]$.*

Proof. Immediate from the definition of inconsistency order of type i, and the definition of $\leq_{c_i}^4$. $\square$

Lemma 3. *If $\leq_c^{\mathcal{L},\mathcal{D}}$ is an inconsistency order of type i in $(\mathcal{L},\mathcal{D})$, then $\models_c^{\mathcal{L},\mathcal{D}}$ is the same as $\models_{c_i}^4$.*

Proof. Suppose that $\Gamma \models_c^{\mathcal{L},\mathcal{D}} \psi$ but $\Gamma \not\models_{c_i}^4 \psi$. Then there is a c_i^4-mcm M^4 of Γ s.t. $M^4(\psi) \notin \{t, \top\}$. Now, for every atom p let $M^L(p)$ be some element in $\min_{\leq_c^{\mathcal{L},\mathcal{D}}} \mathcal{T}_{M^4(p)}$. Thus $\omega \circ M^L = M^4$, and M^L is similar to M^4. By Proposition 2, M^L is a model of Γ and it is not a model of ψ. To get a contradiction to $\Gamma \models_c^{\mathcal{L},\mathcal{D}} \psi$, it remains to show, then, that M^L is a c-mcm of Γ in $(\mathcal{L},\mathcal{D})$. Indeed, otherwise by stopperdness there is a c-mcm N^L of Γ s.t. $N^L <_c^{\mathcal{L},\mathcal{D}} M^L$. So for every atom

---

[9] In particular, for every $0 \leq i \leq 3$, the inconsistency order $\leq_{c_i}^4$ in $\mathcal{FOUR}$ is of type i.

p, $[N^L(p)] \leq_c^{\mathcal{L},\mathcal{D}} [M^L(p)]$, and there is an atom p_0 s.t. $[N^L(p_0)] <_c^{\mathcal{L},\mathcal{D}} [M^L(p_0)]$. Let $N^4 = \omega \circ N^L$. Again, N^4 is similar to N^L, therefore it is a (four-valued) model of Γ. Also, by the definition of M, for every atom p, $M^L(p) \in \Omega_{\leq_c^{\mathcal{L},\mathcal{D}}}$ and by Lemma 1, $\forall p \ N^L(p) \in \Omega_{\leq_c^{\mathcal{L},\mathcal{D}}}$. Thus, by Lemma 2,

$$[N^4(p)] = [\omega \circ N^L(p)] \leq_{c_i}^4 [\omega \circ M^L(p)] = [M^4(p)].$$

Also, by the same lemma,

$$[N^4(p_0)] = [\omega \circ N^L(p_0)] <_{c_i}^4 [\omega \circ M^L(p_0)] = [M^4(p_0)].$$

It follows that $N^4 <_{c_i}^4 M^4$, but this contradicts the assumption that M^4 is a c_i^4-mcm of Γ.

For the converse, suppose that $\Gamma \models_{c_i}^4 \psi$, but $\Gamma \not\models_c^{\mathcal{L},\mathcal{D}} \psi$. Then there is a c-mcm M^L of Γ in $(\mathcal{L},\mathcal{D})$ s.t. $M^L(\psi) \notin \mathcal{D}$. Define, for every atom p, $M^4(p) = \omega \circ M^L(p)$. By the definition of ω, M^4 is similar to M^L and so M^4 is a model of Γ in $\mathcal{FOUR}$, but it is not a model of ψ. It remains to show, then, that M^4 is a c_i^4-mcm of Γ. Indeed, otherwise there is a model N^4 of Γ s.t. $N^4 <_{c_i}^4 M^4$, that is, for every atom p $[N^4(p)] \leq_{c_i}^4 [M^4(p)]$, and there is an atom p_0 for which this inequality is strict: $[N^4(p_0)] <_{c_i}^4 [M^4(p_0)]$. Now, for every atom p, let $N^L(p)$ be some element in $\min_{\leq_c^{\mathcal{L},\mathcal{D}}} \mathcal{T}_{N^4(p)}$. Thus $\omega \circ N^L = N^4$, and N^L is similar to N^4. By Proposition 2, N^L is in particular a model of Γ in $(\mathcal{L},\mathcal{D})$. Moreover, for every atom p,

$$[\omega \circ N^L(p)] = [N^4(p)] \leq_{c_i}^4 [M^4(p)] = [\omega \circ M^L(p)].$$

Now, by the definition of N^L we have that for every atom p, $N^L(p) \in \Omega_{\leq_c^{\mathcal{L},\mathcal{D}}}$, and by Lemma 1, $M^L(p) \in \Omega_{\leq_c^{\mathcal{L},\mathcal{D}}}$ as well. Hence, by Lemma 2, $[N^L(p)] \leq_c^{\mathcal{L},\mathcal{D}} [M^L(p)]$. Similarly,

$$[\omega \circ N^L(p_0)] = [N^4(p_0)] <_{c_i}^4 [M^4(p_0)] = [\omega \circ M^L(p_0)]$$

and again this entails that $[N^L(p_0)] <_c^{\mathcal{L},\mathcal{D}} [M^L(p_0)]$. It follows that $N^L <_c^{\mathcal{L},\mathcal{D}} M^L$, but this contradicts the assumption that M^L is a c-mcm of Γ in $(\mathcal{L},\mathcal{D})$. This concludes the proof of Lemma 3 and Theorem 1.   □

Note 1. The proof of Theorem 1 also induces a simple algorithm for determining which one of the four-valued consequence relations is the same as a given consequence relation of the form $\models_c^{\mathcal{L},\mathcal{D}}$: given an inconsistency order $\leq_c^{\mathcal{L},\mathcal{D}}$ in $(\mathcal{L},\mathcal{D})$, choose some $m_\perp \in \min_{\leq_c^{\mathcal{L},\mathcal{D}}} \mathcal{T}_\perp$ and $m_\top \in \min_{\leq_c^{\mathcal{L},\mathcal{D}}} \mathcal{T}_\top$. If $[m_\top] = [t]$ then $\models_c^{\mathcal{L},\mathcal{D}} = \models_{c_0}^4$. Otherwise, if $[m_\perp] = [t]$, then $\models_c^{\mathcal{L},\mathcal{D}} = \models_{c_1}^4$. Otherwise, if $[m_\top] = [m_\perp]$, then $\models_c^{\mathcal{L},\mathcal{D}} = \models_{c_2}^4$. Otherwise, $\models_c^{\mathcal{L},\mathcal{D}} = \models_{c_3}^4$.

4   Reasoning with $\models_c^{\mathcal{L},\mathcal{D}}$

We conclude by briefly considering some basic properties of $\models_c^{\mathcal{L},\mathcal{D}}$.[10] In what follows we assume stopperdness, and so, by Theorem 1, it is sufficient to consider

---

[10] Most of the propositions in this section easily follow from similar results concerning modular preferential relations, considered in [1]. Due to space limitations, corresponding proofs are omitted.

$\mathcal{FOUR}$ and the four corresponding consequence relations $\models^4_{c_i}$ ($i=0,\ldots,3$). First, we consider the relative strength of these logics:

Proposition 3. *Let Γ be a set of formulae and ψ a formula in Σ.*
a) *The consequence relations $\models^4_{c_i}$, $0\leq i\leq 3$, are all different.*
b) *For every $1\leq i\leq 3$, if $\Gamma\models^4_{c_0}\psi$ then $\Gamma\models^4_{c_i}\psi$.*
c) *No one of $\models^4_{c_1}$, $\models^4_{c_2}$, and $\models^4_{c_3}$, is stronger than the other.*

In what follows we shall write $\models^2$ for the classical consequence relation, and $\models^4_c$ for any one of $\models^4_{c_i}$, $0\leq i\leq 3$. As the next proposition shows, reasoning with $\models^4_c$ does not reduce to triviality when the set of premises is not consistent.

Proposition 4. $\models^4_c$ *is paraconsistent.*

Proposition 5. *If $\Gamma\models^4_c\psi$ then $\Gamma\models^2\psi$.*

The converse of Proposition 5 is not true in general. For instance, excluded middle is not valid w.r.t. $\models^4_{c_0}$ and $\models^4_{c_1}$. However, with respect to the other basic four-valued consequence relations, the converse of Proposition 5 does hold.

Proposition 6. *Let Γ be a classically consistent theory. Then for every formula ψ in Σ we have that $\Gamma\models^2\psi$ iff $\Gamma\models^4_{c_2}\psi$ iff $\Gamma\models^4_{c_3}\psi$.*

By Propositions 4 and 6, it follows that with (any consequence relation of the form $\models^{\mathcal{L},\mathcal{D}}_c$ that is equivalent to) $\models^4_{c_2}$ and $\models^4_{c_3}$ one can draw classical conclusions from (classically) consistent theories, while the set of conclusions is not "exploded" when the theory becomes inconsistent. Batens [10] describes this property as an "oscillation" between some lower limit (paraconsistent) logic and an upper limit (classical) logic.

Proposition 7. $\models^4_{c_0}$ *is a monotonic consequence relation, while $\models^4_{c_i}$, $i=1,2,3$, are nonmonotonic relations.*

The last proposition implies that unless the inconsistency order is degenerated, $\models^{\mathcal{L},\mathcal{D}}_c$ is not monotonic, thus it is not a consequence relation in the sense of Tarski [38]. In such cases it is usual to require a weaker condition:

Proposition 8. [24,27] $\models^4_c$ *satisfies cautious left monotonicity: if $\Gamma\models^4_c\psi$ and $\Gamma\models^4_c\phi$, then $\Gamma,\psi\models^4_c\phi$.*

A desirable property of non-monotonic consequence relations is the ability to preserve any conclusion when learning about a new fact that has no influence on the set of premises. Consequence relations that satisfy this property are called *rational* [28]. The next proposition shows that $\models^4_{c_i}$ ($i=0,\ldots,3$) are rational.

Proposition 9. *If $\Gamma\models^4_c\psi$ and $\mathcal{A}(\Gamma\cup\{\psi\})\cap\mathcal{A}(\phi)=\emptyset$, then $\Gamma,\phi\models^4_c\psi$.*[11]

---

[11] Recall that $\mathcal{A}(\Gamma)$ is the set of atomic formulae that appear in some formula of Γ.

Intuitively, the second condition in Proposition 9 guarantees that ϕ is 'irrelevant' for Γ and ψ. The intuitive meaning of Proposition 9 is, therefore, that the reasoner does not have to retract ψ when learning that ϕ holds.

Note 2. In order to assure rationality, Lehmann and Magidor [28] introduced the rule of *rational monotonicity:* if $\Gamma \mathrel{|\!\sim} \psi$ then $\Gamma, \phi \mathrel{|\!\sim} \psi$, unless $\Gamma \mathrel{|\!\sim} \neg\phi$.

Rational monotonicity may be considered as too strong for assuring rationality, and many general patterns of nonmonotonic reasoning do not satisfy this rule. For instance, $\models^4_{c_1}$ is rational (Proposition 9), but it does not satisfy rational monotonicity (consider, e.g., $\Gamma = \{p, \ q \rightarrow \neg p\}$, $\psi = \neg p \rightarrow \neg q$, and $\phi = q$).

In terms of Batens [10,11], $\models^4_{c_2}$ and $\models^4_{c_3}$ are also *adaptive*, i.e.: if it is possible to distinguish between a consistent part and an inconsistent part of a given theory, then every assertion that classically follows from the consistent part, and is not related to the inconsistent part, is also a $\models^4_{c_i}$-consequence ($i = 2, 3$) of the whole theory. Thus, as the following proposition shows, $\models^4_{c_2}$ and $\models^4_{c_3}$ presuppose a consistency of all the assertions 'unless and until proven otherwise'.

Proposition 10. *Let* $\Gamma = \Gamma' \cup \Gamma''$ *be a set of formulae in* Σ *s.t.* Γ' *is classically consistent and* $\mathcal{A}(\Gamma') \cap \mathcal{A}(\Gamma'') = \emptyset$. *Then for every* ψ *s.t.* $\mathcal{A}(\psi) \cap \mathcal{A}(\Gamma'') = \emptyset$, *the fact that* $\Gamma' \models^2 \psi$ *entails that* $\Gamma \models^4_{c_2} \psi$ *and* $\Gamma \models^4_{c_3} \psi$.

We conclude by noting that consequence relations of the form $\models^{\mathcal{L}, \mathcal{D}}_c$ naturally generalize some related formalisms such as the consequence relations $\models^{\mathcal{L}, \mathcal{D}}_{\mathcal{I}_1}$, $\models^{\mathcal{L}, \mathcal{D}}_{\mathcal{I}_2}$, introduced in [5,6], and the logic LPm of Priest [34].[12]

References

1. O. Arieli. Reasoning with modularly pointwise preferential relations. *Proc. BNAIC'00*, A. van den Bosch and H. Weigand, editors, BNVKI, pp. 61–68, 2000.
2. O. Arieli. Useful adaptive logics for rational and paraconsistent reasoning. *Technical Report CW286*, Depatrment of Computer Science, University of Leuven, 2001.
3. O. Arieli. Paraconsistent declarative semantics for extended logic programs. *Annals of Mathematics and Artificial Intelligence* 36(4), pp. 381–417, 2002.
4. O. Arieli, A. Avron. Reasoning with logical bilattices. *Journal of Logic, Language, and Information* 5(1), pp. 25–63, 1996.
5. O. Arieli, A. Avron. The logical role of the four-valued bilattice. *Proc. LICS'98*, IEEE Press, pp.218–226, 1998.
6. O. Arieli, A. Avron. Nonmonotonic and paraconsistent reasoning: From basic entailments to plausible relations. *Proc. ECSQARU'99*, LNAI 1638, A.Hunter and S.Parsons, editors, Springer, pp. 11–22, 1999.
7. O. Arieli, M.Denecker. Modeling paraconsistent reasoning by classical logic. *Proc. FoIKS'02*, LNCS 2284, T. Eiter and K.D. Schewe, editors, Springer, pp. 1–14, 2002.
8. A. Avron. Simple consequence relations. *Journal of Information and Computation* 92, pp. 105–139, 1991.

---

[12] See [2] for a proof of this claim.

9. A.Avron. Classical Gentzen-type methods in propositional many-valued logics. *Theory and Applications in Multiple-Valued Logics*, M.Fitting and E.Orlowska, editors, Springer, pp. 113–151, 2002.

10. D. Batens. Inconsistency-adaptive logics. *Logic at Work*, E. Orlowska, editor, Physica Verlag, pp. 445–472, 1998.

11. D. Batens. On a partial decision method for dynamic proofs. *Proc. PCL'02, ICLP'02 Workshop on Paraconsistent Computational Logic*, H. Decker, J. Villadsen, and T. Waragai, editors, pp. 91–108, 2002.

12. D. Batens, C. Mortensen, G. Priest, J. Van Bendegem. *Frontiers of Paraconsistent Logic*, Studies in Logic and Computation 8, Research Studies Press, 2000.

13. N.D. Belnap. A useful four-valued logic. *Modern Uses of Multiple-Valued Logic*, G. Epstein and J.M. Dunn, editors, Reidel Publishing Company, pp. 7–37, 1977.

14. N.D. Belnap. How a computer should think. *Contemporary Aspects of Philosophy*, G. Ryle, editor, Oriel Press, pp. 30–56, 1977.

15. S. Benferhat, Ph. Besnard. *Proc. ECSQARU'01*, LNAI 2143, Springer, 2001.

16. A. Bialynicki-Birula. Remarks on quasi-boolean algebras. *Bull. Acad. Polonaise des Sciences Cl. III* V(6), pp. 615–619, 1957.

17. A. Bialynicki-Birula, H. Rasiowa. On the representation of quasi-boolean algebras. *Bull. Acad. Polonaise des Sciences Cl. III* V(3), pp. 259–261, 1957.

18. W. Carnielli, M.E. Coniglio, I.M.L. D'Ottaviano. Paraconsistency: The logical way to the inconsistent. *Lecture Notes in Pure and Applied Mathematics* 228, Marcel Dekker, 2002.

19. N.C. A.da-Costa. On the theory of inconsistent formal systems. *Notre Dam Journal of Formal Logic* 15, pp. 497–510, 1974.

20. C.M. Damasio, L.M. Pereira. A survey on paraconsistent semantics for extended logic programs. *Handbook of Defeasible Reasoning and Uncertainty Management Systems* Vol. 2, D.M. Gabbay and Ph.Smets, editors, Kluwer, pp. 241–320, 1998.

21. D. Dubois, J. Lang, H. Prade. Possibilistic logic. *Handbook of Logic in Artificial Intelligence and Logic Programming*, D. Gabbay, C. Hogger, and J. Robinson, editors, Oxford Science Publications, pp. 439–513, 1994.

22. P. Hajek. *Metamathematics of Fuzzy Logic*. Kluwer Academic Publishers, 1998.

23. A. Hunter, S. Parsons. *Proc. ECSQARU'99*, LNAI 1638, Springer, 1999.

24. D.M. Gabbay. Theoretical foundation for non-monotonic reasoning in expert systems. *Proc. of the NATO Advanced Study Inst. on Logic and Models of Concurrent Systems*, K.P. Apt, editor, Springer, pp. 439–457, 1985.

25. J.A. Kalman. Lattices with involution. *Trans. of the American Mathematical Society* 87, pp. 485–491, 1958.

26. M. Kifer, E.L. Lozinskii. A logic for reasoning with inconsistency. *Automated Reasoning* 9(2), pp. 179-215, 1992.

27. S. Kraus, D. Lehmann, M. Magidor. Nonmonotonic reasoning, preferential models and cumulative logics. *Artificial Intelligence* 44(1–2), pp. 167–207, 1990.

28. D. Lehmann, M. Magidor. What does a conditional knowledge base entail? *Artificial Intelligence* 55, pp. 1–60, 1992.

29. Th. Lukasiewicz. Fixpoint characterizations for many-valued disjunctive logic programs with probabilistic semantics. *Proc. LPNMR'01*, LNAI 2173, Springer, pp. 336–350, 2001.

30. D. Makinson. General theory of cumulative inference. *Non-Monotonic Reasoning*, LNAI 346, M.Reinfrank, editor, Springer, pp. 1–18, 1989.

31. D. Makinson. General patterns in nonmonotonic reasoning. *Handbook of Logic in Artificial Intelligence and Logic Programming* 3, D. Gabbay, C. Hogger, and J. Robinson, editors, Oxford Science Publications, pp. 35–110, 1994.

32. J. McCarthy. Circumscription – A form of non monotonic reasoning. *Artificial Intelligence* 13(1–2), pp. 27–39, 1980.
33. J. Pearl. Reasoning under uncertainty. *Annual Review of Computer Science* 4, pp. 37–72, 1989.
34. G. Priest. *Minimally inconsistent LP*. Studia Logica 50, pp. 321–331, 1991.
35. K. Schlechta. Unrestricted preferential structures. *Journal of Logic and Computation* 10(4), pp. 573–581, 2000.
36. Y. Shoham. *Reasoning about change*, MIT Press, 1988.
37. V.S. Subrahmanian. Mechanical proof procedures for many-valued lattice-based logic programming. *Journal of Non-Classical Logic* 7, pp. 7–41, 1990.
38. A. Tarski. *Introduction to logic*, Oxford University Press, 1941.

Paraconsistent Reasoning via Quantified Boolean Formulas, II: Circumscribing Inconsistent Theories*

Philippe Besnard[1], Torsten Schaub[2]**, Hans Tompits[3], and Stefan Woltran[3]

[1] IRIT-CNRS,
118, route de Narbonne, F–31062 Toulouse Cedex, France
besnard@irit.fr
[2] Institut für Informatik, Universität Potsdam,
Postfach 90 03 27, D–14439 Potsdam, Germany
torsten@cs.uni-potsdam.de
[3] Institut für Informationssysteme 184/3, Technische Universität Wien
Favoritenstraße 9–11, A–1040 Vienna, Austria
[tompits,stefan]@kr.tuwien.ac.at

Abstract. Through minimal-model semantics, three-valued logics provide an interesting formalism for capturing reasoning from inconsistent information. However, the resulting paraconsistent logics lack so far a uniform implementation platform. Here, we address this and specifically provide a translation of two such paraconsistent logics into the language of quantified Boolean formulas (QBFs). These formulas can then be evaluated by off-the-shelf QBF solvers. In this way, we benefit from the following advantages: First, our approach allows us to harness the performance of existing QBF solvers. Second, different paraconsistent logics can be compared with in a unified setting via the translations used. We alternatively provide a translation of these two paraconsistent logics into quantified Boolean formulas representing circumscription, the well-known system for logical minimization. All this forms a case study inasmuch as the other existing minimization-based many-valued paraconsistent logics can be dealt with in a similar fashion.

1 Introduction

The capability of reasoning in the presence of inconsistencies constitutes a major challenge for any intelligent system because in practical settings it is common to have contradictory information. In fact, despite its many appealing features for knowledge representation and reasoning, classical logic falls in a trap: A single contradiction may wreck an entire reasoning system, since it allows for deriving any proposition. This comportment is due to the fact that a contradiction denies any classical two-valued model, since a proposition must be either true or false. We thus aim at providing formal reasoning systems satisfying the *principle of paraconsistency*: $\{\alpha, \neg\alpha\} \not\vdash \beta$ for some α, β. In other words, given a contradictory set of premises, this should not necessarily lead to concluding all formulas.

---

* This work was partially supported by the Austrian Science Foundation under grant P15068.
** Affiliated with the School of Computing Science at Simon Fraser University, Burnaby, Canada.

The idea underlying the approaches elaborated upon in this paper is to counterbalance the effect of contradictions by providing a third truth value that accounts for contradictory propositions. As already put forth in [27], this provides us with inconsistency-tolerating three-valued models. However, this approach turns out to be rather weak in that it invalidates certain classical inferences, even if there is no contradiction. Intuitively, this is because there are too many three-valued models, in particular those assigning the inconsistency-tolerating truth-value to propositions that are unaffected by contradictions. For instance, the three-valued logic LP [27] denies inference by disjunctive syllogism. That is, β is not derivable from the (consistent!) premise $(\alpha \lor \beta) \land \neg\alpha$. As pointed out in [15], this deficiency also applies to the closely related paraconsistent systems J_3 [17], L [22], and RP [19]. As a consequence, none of the aforementioned systems coincides with classical logic when reasoning from consistent premises.

The pioneering work to overcome this deficiency was done by Priest in [28]. The key idea is to restrict the set of three-valued models by taking advantage of some preference criterion that aims at "minimizing inconsistency". In this way, a "maximum" of a classically inconsistent knowledge base should be recovered. While minimization is understood in Priest's seminal work [28], proposing his logic LP_m, as preferring three-valued models as close as possible to two-valued interpretations, the overall approach leaves room for different preference criteria. Another criterion is put forth in [9] by giving more importance to the given knowledge base. In this approach, one prefers three-valued models that are as similar as possible to two-valued models of the knowledge base in the sense that those models assign *true* to as many items of the knowledge base as possible. Furthermore, [21] considers cardinality-based versions of the last two preference criteria. Even more criteria are conceivable by distinguishing symbols having different importance.

However, up to know, all these advanced approaches lack effectively implementable inference methods. While Priest defines LP_m in purely semantical terms, a Hilbert calculus comprising 26 axiom schemata is proposed by Besnard and Schaub [9] for axiomatizing their approach. Also, inference is not at issue in [21]. This shortcoming is addressed in this paper. To wit, we develop translations for the three-valued paraconsistent logics defined in [28] and [9]. More precisely, our translations allow for mapping the respective entailment problems into the satisfiability problem for *quantified Boolean formulas* (QBFs). These formulas can then be evaluated by off-the-shelf QBF solvers. The motivation of this particular approach to implementing these logics (as opposed to more direct calculizations) stems from its unique uniformity, even beyond the framework of three-valued logics. In fact, we have already developed in a companion paper [11] similar translations for a rather different family of paraconsistent logics, called *signed systems* [10]; a forthcoming paper deals with approaches to paraconsistency based on the selection of maximally consistent subsets [24,8].

Our general methodology offers several benefits: First, we obtain uniform axiomatizations of rather different approaches. This allows us to compare different paraconsistent logics in a unified setting. Second, once such an axiomatization is available, existing QBF solvers can be used for implementation in a uniform manner. The availability of efficient QBF solvers, like the systems described in [12,20,6], makes such a rapid prototyping approach practically applicable. Third, these axiomatizations provide a direct access to the complexity of the original approach. Conversely, we can exploit existing complexity results for ensuring the adequateness of our axiomatizations. Finally, we remark that this approach allows us, in some sense, to express paraconsistent reasoning in (higher order) classical propositional logic and so to harness classical reasoning mechanisms from (a conservative extension of) propositional logic.

2   Paraconsistent Three-Valued Logics

We deal with a language $\mathcal{L}$ over a set $\mathcal{P}$ of propositional variables and use the logical symbols $\top, \bot, \neg, \vee, \wedge$, and $\rightarrow$ to construct formulas in the standard way. Formulas are denoted by Greek lower-case letters (possibly with subscripts).

An interpretation is a function $v : \mathcal{P} \rightarrow \{t, f, o\}$ extending to $\overline{v} : \mathcal{L} \rightarrow \{t, f, o\}$ according to the truth tables below.

$$
\begin{array}{cccccccc}
\bot & \top & \neg &
\begin{array}{c|ccc} \wedge & t & f & o \\ \hline t & t & f & o \\ f & f & f & f \\ o & o & f & o \end{array} &
\begin{array}{c|ccc} \vee & t & f & o \\ \hline t & t & t & t \\ f & t & f & o \\ o & t & o & o \end{array} &
\begin{array}{c|ccc} \rightarrow & t & f & o \\ \hline t & t & f & o \\ f & t & t & t \\ o & t & f & o \end{array}
\end{array}
\tag{1}
$$

$$
\begin{array}{cc} \bot \\ \hline f \end{array} \quad
\begin{array}{cc} \top \\ \hline t \end{array} \quad
\begin{array}{c|c} \neg \\ \hline t & f \\ f & t \\ o & o \end{array}
$$

We sometimes leave an interpretation v implicit and write $p : x$ instead of $v(p) = x$, for $x \in \{t, f, o\}$. An interpretation v is said to be *two-valued* whenever $v(p) \in \{t, f\}$ for all $p \in \mathcal{P}$; otherwise, it is *three-valued*. A *three-valued model* of a formula α is an interpretation that assigns either t or o to α. Modelhood extends to sets of formulas in the standard way. As usual, given a set S of formulas and a formula ϕ, we define $S \models \phi$ if each model of S is a model of ϕ. Whenever necessary, we write $\models_3$ and $\models_2$ to distinguish three-valued from two-valued entailment.

Note that the truth value of $\alpha \rightarrow \beta$ differs from that of $\neg \alpha \vee \beta$ only in the case of $v = \{\alpha : o, \beta : f\}$ resulting in $\overline{v}(\alpha \rightarrow \beta) = f$ and $\overline{v}(\neg \alpha \vee \beta) = o$. This difference is prompted by the fact that t and o indicate modelhood, which motivates the assignment of the same truth values to $\alpha \rightarrow \beta$ no matter whether we have $\alpha : t$ or $\alpha : o$. This has actually to do with the difference between *modus ponens* and *disjunctive syllogism*: The latter yields β from $\alpha \wedge \neg \alpha \wedge \neg \beta$ because $\alpha \vee \beta$ follows from α. The overall inference seems wrong because in the presence of $\alpha \wedge \neg \alpha$, $\alpha \vee \beta$ is satisfied (by $\alpha : o$) with no need for β to be t. As pointed out in [21], one may actually view $\rightarrow$ as *"the 'right' generalization of classical implication because $\rightarrow$ is the internal implication connective [5] for the defined inference relation in the sense that a deduction (meta)theorem holds for it: $\Sigma \wedge \alpha \models_3 \beta$ iff $\Sigma \models_3 \alpha \rightarrow \beta$."* On the other hand, a formula composed of the connectives $\neg, \vee$, and $\wedge$ can never be inconsistent; that is, each such formula has at least one three-valued model [13]. Finally, we mention that the entailment problem for $\models_3$ is *coNP*-complete, no matter whether $\rightarrow$ is included or not [26,13,15].

As mentioned in the introductory section, Priest's logic LP_m [28] was conceived to overcome the failure of disjunctive syllogism in LP [27]. LP amounts to the three-valued logic obtained by restricting $\mathcal{L}$ to connectives $\neg, \vee$ and $\wedge$ (and defining $\alpha \rightarrow \beta$ as $\neg \alpha \vee \beta$). In LP_m, modelhood is then limited to models containing a minimal number of *propositional variables* being assigned o. This allows for drawing *"all classical inferences except where inconsistency makes them doubtful anyway"* [28]. Formally, the consequence relation of LP_m can be defined as follows. For three-valued interpretations v, w, define the partial ordering

$$v \leq_m w \quad \text{iff} \quad \{p \in \mathcal{P} \mid v(p) = o\} \subseteq \{p \in \mathcal{P} \mid w(p) = o\} .$$

Then, $T \models_m \phi$ iff every three-valued model of T that is minimal with respect to $\leq_m$ is a three-valued model of ϕ.

Unlike this, the approach of Besnard and Schaub [9] prefers three-valued models that assign *true* to as many items of the knowledge base T as possible: For three-valued interpretations v, w, define the partial ordering

$$v \leq_n w \quad \text{iff} \quad \{\phi \in T \mid \overline{v}(\phi) = o\} \subseteq \{\phi \in T \mid \overline{w}(\phi) = o\} .$$

Then, $T \models_n \phi$ iff each three-valued model of T which is $\leq_n$-minimal is a three-valued model of ϕ.

The major difference between the last two approaches is that the restriction of modelhood in LP_m focuses on models as close as possible to two-valued *interpretations*, while the one in the last approach aims at models next to two-valued *models* of the considered premises. According to [9], the effects of making the formula select its preferred models can be seen by looking at $T = \{p, \neg p, (\neg p \vee q)\}$: While LP_m yields two $\leq_m$-preferred models, $\{p : o, q : t\}$ and $\{p : o, q : f\}$, from which one obtains $p \wedge \neg p$, the second approach yields q as additional conclusion. In fact, $\{p : o, q : t\}$ is the only $\leq_n$-preferred model of the premises $\{p, \neg p, (\neg p \vee q)\}$; it assigns t to $(\neg p \vee q)$, while this premise is attributed o by the second $\leq_m$-preferred model $\{p : o, q : f\}$; hence the latter is not $\leq_n$-preferred. So, while $T \not\models_m q$ and $T \models_n q$, we note that $T \cup \{(p \vee \neg q)\} \not\models_l q$ for $l = m, n$. On the other hand, $\models_n$ is clearly more syntax-dependent than $\models_m$ since the items within the knowledge base are used for distinguishing $\leq_n$-preferred models.

In fact, both inference relations $\models_m$ and $\models_n$ amount to their classical (two-valued) counterpart whenever the set of premises is classically consistent. Also, it is shown in [15] that deciding entailment for $\models_m$ and $\models_n$ is Π_2^p-complete, no matter whether $\rightarrow$ is included or not. A logical analysis of both relations can be found in [21] and in the original literature [28,9].

3 Axiomatizing Three-Valued Paraconsistent Logics

In what follows, we provide axiomatizations of the three-valued paraconsistent logics introduced in the last section in terms of QBFs.

Quantified Boolean Formulas. As a conservative extension of classical propositional logic, *quantified Boolean formulas* (QBFs) generalize ordinary propositional formulas by the admission of quantifications over propositional variables (QBFs are denoted by Greek upper-case letters). Informally, a QBF of form $\forall p \exists q \, \Phi$ means that for all truth assignments of p there is a truth assignment of q such that Φ is true. Given that $\mathcal{K}$ is the language of QBFs over a set $\mathcal{P}$ of propositional variables, the semantical meaning of QBFs can be defined as follows: An interpretation is a function $v : \mathcal{P} \to \{t, f\}$ extending to $\hat{v} : \mathcal{K} \to \{t, f\}$ according to the truth tables in (1) and the following two conditions, for every $\Phi \in \mathcal{K}$,

$$\hat{v}(\forall p\, \Phi) = \hat{v}(\Phi[p/\top] \wedge \Phi[p/\bot]) \quad \text{and} \quad \hat{v}(\exists p\, \Phi) = \hat{v}(\Phi[p/\top] \vee \Phi[p/\bot]) .$$

We write $\Phi[p_1/\phi_1, \dots, p_n/\phi_n]$ to denote the result of uniformly substituting each free occurrence[1] of a variable p_i in Φ by a formula ϕ_i, for $1 \le i \le n$. If Φ contains no free variable occurrences, then Φ is *closed*. Closed QBFs are either true under every interpretation or false under every interpretation. Hence, for closed QBFs there is no need to refer to particular interpretations.

In the sequel, we use the following abbreviations: The set of all atoms occurring in a formula ϕ is denoted by $var(\phi)$. Similarly, for a set S of formulas, $var(S) = \bigcup_{\phi \in S} var(\phi)$. For a set $P = \{p_1, \dots, p_n\}$ of propositional variables and a quantifier $Q \in \{\forall, \exists\}$, we let $QP\, \Phi$ stand for the formula $Qp_1 Qp_2 \cdots Qp_n\, \Phi$. Furthermore, for indexed sets $S = \{\phi_1, \dots, \phi_n\}$ and $T = \{\psi_1, \dots, \psi_n\}$ of formulas, $S \le T$ abbreviates $\bigwedge_{i=1}^{n}(\phi_i \to \psi_i)$, and $S < T$ stands for $S \le T \wedge \neg(T \le S)$.

Encoding Three-Valued Logic. We start with encoding the truth evaluation of the three-valued logic given in Sect. 2 by means of classical propositional logic.

To this end, we introduce for each atom p a globally new atom p' and define $\mathcal{P}' = \{p' \mid p \in \mathcal{P}\}$ for a given alphabet $\mathcal{P}$.

Let v be a three-valued interpretation over alphabet $\mathcal{P}$. We define the *associated two-valued interpretation* v_2 by setting

$$
\begin{aligned}
v_2(p) = v_2(p') = t \quad &\text{if } v(p) = t; \\
v_2(p) = v_2(p') = f \quad &\text{if } v(p) = f; \\
v_2(p) = f \text{ and } v_2(p') = t \quad &\text{if } v(p) = o,
\end{aligned}
$$

for any $p \in \mathcal{P}$ and any $p' \in \mathcal{P}'$. Conversely, for a given two-valued interpretation v over alphabet $\mathcal{P} \cup \mathcal{P}'$ such that $\overline{v}(p \to p') = t$, we define the *associated three-valued interpretation* v_3 by setting

$$
v_3(p) = \begin{cases} v(p) & \text{if } v(p) = v(p') \\ o & \text{if } v(p) = f \text{ and } v(p') = t \end{cases}
$$

for any $p \in \mathcal{P}$.

Moreover, we need the following parameterized translation:

Definition 1. *For $p \in \mathcal{P}$ and $\phi, \psi \in \mathcal{L}$, we define*

1. (a) $\tau(p, t) = p$;
   (b) $\tau(p, f) = \neg p'$;
   (c) $\tau(p, o) = \neg p \wedge p'$;
2. (a) $\tau(\neg\phi, t) = \tau(\phi, f)$;

---

[1] An occurrence of a propositional variable p in a QBF Φ is *free* if it does not appear in the scope of a quantifier Qp ($Q \in \{\forall, \exists\}$).

(b) $\tau(\neg\phi, f) = \tau(\phi, t)$;
(c) $\tau(\neg\phi, o) = \tau(\phi, o)$;
3. (a) $\tau(\phi \land \psi, t) = \tau(\phi, t) \land \tau(\psi, t)$;
   (b) $\tau(\phi \land \psi, f) = \tau(\phi, f) \lor \tau(\psi, f)$;
   (c) $\tau(\phi \land \psi, o) = \neg\tau(\phi \land \psi, f) \land \neg\tau(\phi \land \psi, t)$;
4. (a) $\tau(\phi \lor \psi, t) = \tau(\phi, t) \lor \tau(\psi, t)$;
   (b) $\tau(\phi \lor \psi, f) = \tau(\phi, f) \land \tau(\psi, f)$;
   (c) $\tau(\phi \lor \psi, o) = \neg\tau(\phi \lor \psi, t) \land \neg\tau(\phi \lor \psi, f)$;
5. (a) $\tau(\phi \to \psi, t) = \tau(\phi, f) \lor \tau(\psi, t)$;
   (b) $\tau(\phi \to \psi, f) = \neg\tau(\phi, f) \land \tau(\psi, f)$;
   (c) $\tau(\phi \to \psi, o) = \neg\tau(\phi, f) \land \tau(\psi, o)$.

For computing the three-valued models of a set $T = \{\phi_1, \ldots, \phi_n\}$ of formulas, we use $\bigwedge_{\phi \in T} \neg\tau(\phi, f)$ and abbreviate the latter by $\neg\tau(T, f)$.[2]
For example, consider $T = \{p, \neg p, (\neg p \lor q)\}$. We get:

$$
\begin{aligned}
\neg\tau(T, f) &= \neg\tau(p, f) \land \neg\tau(\neg p, f) \land \neg\tau((\neg p \lor q), f) \\
&= \neg\neg p' \land \neg\tau(p, t) \land \neg(\tau(\neg p, f) \land \tau(q, f)) \\
&= p' \land \neg p \land \neg(\tau(p, t) \land \neg q') \\
&= p' \land \neg p \land (\neg p \lor \neg\neg q') \\
&= p' \land \neg p .
\end{aligned}
$$

The resulting formula possesses four two-valued models, all of which assign $p : f$ and $p' : t$ while varying on q and q'. In order to establish a correspondence among the four two-models of $\neg\tau(T, f)$ and the three three-valued models of T, assigning o to p and varying on q, the relation between the two alphabets $\mathcal{P}$ and $\mathcal{P}'$ must be fixed. In fact, this is accomplished by adding $r \to r'$ for every $r \in \mathcal{P}$.

In this way, we obtain the following result.

Theorem 1. *Let ϕ be a formula with $P = var(\phi)$, let $P' = \{p' \mid p \in P\}$, and let $x \in \{t, f, o\}$.*

Then, the following conditions hold:

1. *For any three-valued interpretation v over $\mathcal{P}$, if $\bar{v}(\phi) = x$, then $\bar{v}_2((P \leq P') \land \tau(\phi, x)) = t$, where v_2 is the associated two-valued interpretation of v.*
2. *For any two-valued interpretation v over $\mathcal{P} \cup \mathcal{P}'$, if $\bar{v}((P \leq P') \land \tau(\phi, x)) = t$, then $\bar{v}_3(\phi) = x$, where $\bar{v}_3$ is the associated three-valued interpretation of v.*

Since the formula $\tau(\phi, t) \lor \tau(\phi, f) \lor \tau(\phi, o)$ is clearly a tautology of classical logic, we immediately get the following relation between the three-valued models of a theory and the two-valued models of the corresponding encoding:

Corollary 1. *Let T be a finite set of formulas with $P = var(T)$ and let $P' = \{p' \mid p \in P\}$.*

Then, there is a one-to-one correspondence between the three-valued models of T and the two-valued models of the formula

$$(P \leq P') \land \neg\tau(T, f). \tag{2}$$

---

[2] Note that generally $\bigwedge_{\phi \in T} \tau(\phi, x) \neq \tau(\bigwedge_{\phi \in T} \phi, x)$.

In particular, the three-valued model of T corresponding to a two-valued model v of (2) is given by the associated three-valued interpretation v_3 of v.

For illustration, consider $T = \{p, \neg p, (\neg p \vee q)\}$ along with

$$(\{p, q\} \leq \{p', q'\}) \wedge \neg\tau(T, f) \quad = \quad (p \rightarrow p') \wedge (q \rightarrow q') \wedge (p' \wedge \neg p) .$$

Unlike above, we obtain now three two-valued models, $\{p : f, p' : t, q : t, q' : t\}$, $\{p : f, p' : t, q : f, q' : t\}$, and $\{p : f, p' : t, q : f, q' : f\}$, being in a one-to-one correspondence with the three three-valued models, $\{p : o, q : t\}$, $\{p : o, q : o\}$, and $\{p : o, q : f\}$, of T, respectively.

The role of the implications $\{p, q\} \leq \{p', q'\}$ can be further illustrated by looking at the following translation:

$$\begin{aligned}
\tau(T, t) &= \tau(p, t) \wedge \tau(\neg p, t) \wedge \tau((\neg p \vee q), t) \\
&= p \wedge \tau(p, f) \wedge (\tau(\neg p, t) \vee \tau(q, t)) \\
&= p \wedge \neg p' \wedge (\tau(p, f) \vee q) \\
&= p \wedge \neg p' \wedge (\neg p' \vee q) \\
&= p \wedge \neg p' .
\end{aligned}$$

While the last formula admits four two-valued models, the formula $(\{p, q\} \leq \{p', q'\}) \wedge \tau(T, t)$ has no two-valued model, which corresponds to the fact that T has no three-valued model assigning t to all members of T.

Consequently, since there are no three-valued models assigning t "to" T, the formulas $\neg\tau(T, f)$ and $\tau(T, o)$ must be equivalent; this can be verified as follows:

$$\begin{aligned}
\tau(T, o) &= \neg\tau(T, f) \wedge \neg\tau(T, t) \\
&= \neg\big(\tau(p, f) \vee \tau(\neg p, f) \vee \tau(\neg p \vee q, f)\big) \wedge \neg(p \wedge \neg p') \\
&= \neg\big(\neg p' \vee p \vee (\tau(\neg p, f) \wedge \tau(q, f))\big) \wedge (\neg p \vee p') \\
&= \neg\big(\neg p' \vee p \vee (p \wedge \neg q')\big) \wedge (\neg p \vee p') \\
&= p' \wedge \neg p \wedge (\neg p \vee q') \wedge (\neg p \vee p') \\
&= p' \wedge \neg p .
\end{aligned}$$

Encoding Three-Valued Paraconsistent Logics. To begin with, it is instructive to see that the previous elaboration already allows for a straightforward encoding of three-valued entailment, and, in particular, inference in the logic *LP* [27]:

Definition 2. *Let T be a set formulas and ϕ a formula.*
For $P = var(T \cup \{\phi\})$, we define

$$\mathcal{T}_3(T, \phi) = \forall P, P'\Big(\big((P \leq P') \wedge \neg\tau(T, f)\big) \rightarrow \neg\tau(\phi, f)\Big) .$$

Then, we have the following result.

Theorem 2. $T \models_3 \phi$ *iff $\mathcal{T}_3(T, \phi)$ is true.*

To be precise, we obtain (original) inference in *LP* [27] when restricting T and ϕ to formulas whose connectives are among $\neg$, $\wedge$, and $\vee$ only.

Let us now turn to Priest's logic LP_m [28]. For this, we must, roughly speaking, enhance the encoding of *LP* in order to account for the principle of "minimizing inconsistency" used in LP_m. This is accomplished in the next definition by means of the QBF named $Min_m(T)$.

Definition 3. *Let T be a set formulas with $P = var(T)$, V an indexed set of globally new atoms corresponding to P, and ϕ a formula. Moreover, let $O_P = \{\tau(p,o) \mid p \in P\}$ and $O_V = \{\tau(v,o) \mid v \in V\}$.*

We define

$$Min_m(T) = (P \leq P') \wedge \neg \exists V, V'\Big((O_V < O_P) \wedge (V \leq V') \wedge \neg\tau(T[P/V], f)\Big)$$

and, for $R = P \cup var(\phi)$,

$$\mathcal{T}_m(T, \phi) = \forall R, R'\Big((Min_m(T) \wedge \neg\tau(T, f)) \to \neg\tau(\phi, f)\Big).$$

For illustration, let us return to $T = \{p, \neg p, (\neg p \vee q)\}$. We have $P = \{p, q\}$ and correspondingly $V = \{u, v\}$. We start our analysis on the subformula

$$(O_V < O_P) \wedge (V \leq V') \wedge \neg\tau(T[P/V], f), \tag{3}$$

having

$$O_V < O_P = \quad (\tau(u,o) \to \tau(p,o)) \wedge (\tau(v,o) \to \tau(q,o)) \wedge$$
$$\neg((\tau(p,o) \to \tau(u,o)) \wedge (\tau(q,o) \to \tau(v,o))).$$

From the definition of $\leq$ and $<$, one can see that $(O_V < O_P) \wedge (V \leq V')$ is true under a two-valued interpretation v iff

- for any variable from V assigned o under the associated interpretation v_3, the corresponding variable from P is also assigned o under v_3; and
- there exists at least one variable from V which is not assigned o under v_3, although the corresponding variable from P is assigned o under v_3.

Additionally, v has to be a two-valued model of $\neg\tau(f, T[P/V])$. By Corollary 1, v_3 then has to be a three-valued model of $T[P/V]$. From our previous discussion and by renaming, we know that $T[P/V]$ possesses three three-valued models, viz. $\{u : o, v : t\}$, $\{u : o, v : o\}$, and $\{u : o, v : f\}$. In the case of model $\{u : o, v : o\}$, we cannot find an assignment to p, q which has more variables being assigned o. The other two cases extend to two two-valued models, v' and v'', of (3) with their associated three-valued interpretations v_3' and v_3'' given by $\{p : o, q : o, u : o, v : t\}$ and $\{p : o, q : o, u : o, v : f\}$, respectively. Now, one can check that the only three-valued interpretation w such that $Min_m(T)$ is false under w_2 is $\{p : o, q : o\}$. Recalling the three-valued models of T, we have that the two-valued models of $Min_m(T) \wedge \neg\tau(T, f)$ yield two three-valued models, $\{p : o, q : t\}$ and $\{p : o, q : f\}$.

In general, we have the following result.

Theorem 3. $T \models_m \phi$ *iff* $\mathcal{T}_m(T, \phi)$ *is true.*

To be precise, we obtain (original) inference in LP_m [28] when restricting T and ϕ to formulas whose connectives are among $\neg$, $\wedge$, and $\vee$ only.

Analogously, we can now give an axiomatization of Besnard and Schaub's approach [9].

Definition 4. *Let T be a set formulas with $P = var(T)$, Q an indexed set of globally new atoms corresponding to P, and ϕ a formula. Moreover, let $O_T = \{\tau(\phi, o) \mid \phi \in T\}$ and $O_{T[P/Q]} = \{\tau(\phi, o) \mid \phi \in T[P/Q]\}$.*
We define

$$Min_n(T) = (P \leq P') \wedge \neg \exists Q, Q' \Big((O_{T[P/Q]} < O_T) \wedge (Q \leq Q') \Big)$$

and, for $R = P \cup var(\phi)$,

$$\mathcal{T}_n(T, \phi) = \forall R, R' \Big(\big(Min_n(T) \wedge \neg \tau(T, f) \big) \rightarrow \neg \tau(\phi, f) \Big).$$

The salient difference between the previous definition and the one given in Definition 3 manifests itself in the sets O_P, O_V and $O_T, O_{T[P/Q]}$, respectively. Note that the latter take the original set of premises T into account so that the translation formula $\neg \tau(T[P/V], f)$ can be dropped.

Theorem 4. $T \models_n \phi$ *iff* $\mathcal{T}_n(T, \phi)$ *is true.*

Alternative Encodings. In view of the discussion given below, we may alternatively capture both approaches as follows.

To begin with, concerning LP_m, we introduce additional new variables $S = \{s_p \mid p \in var(T)\}$ and $S' = \{s'_p \mid p \in var(T)\}$, and define

$$Min_{m'}(T) = (P \leq P') \wedge (S \leq O_P) \wedge$$
$$\neg \exists S', Q, Q' \Big((S' < S) \wedge (Q \leq Q') \wedge (S' \leq O_Q) \wedge \neg \tau(T[P/Q], f) \Big)$$

and

$$\mathcal{T}_{m'}(T, \phi) = \forall S, P, P' \Big(\big(Min_{m'}(T) \wedge \neg \tau(T, f) \big) \rightarrow \neg \tau(\phi, f) \Big).$$

For Besnard and Schaub's approach [9], on the other hand, we similarly introduce additional new variables according to the elements of T, viz. $S = \{s_\phi \mid \phi \in T\}$ and $S' = \{s'_\phi \mid \phi \in T\}$, and define

$$Min_{n'}(T) = (P \leq P') \wedge (S \leq O_P) \wedge$$
$$\neg \exists S', Q, Q' \Big((S' < S) \wedge (Q \leq Q') \wedge (S' \leq O_Q) \Big)$$

and

$$\mathcal{T}_{n'}(T, \phi) = \forall S, P, P' \Big(\big(Min_{n'}(T) \wedge \neg \tau(T, f) \big) \rightarrow \neg \tau(\phi, f) \Big).$$

In analogy to Theorems 3 and 4, we then obtain the following result:

Theorem 5. $T \models_\nu \phi$ *iff* $\mathcal{T}_{\nu'}(T, \phi)$ *is true, for both $\nu \in \{m, n\}$.*

Employing Circumscription. In order to shed some more light on the two paraconsistent logics discussed above, let us slightly reformulate their minimization axiom in terms of circumscription [25]: Let T be a propositional theory and (P, Q, Z) a partition of $var(T)$. Assume two (two-valued) models v, v' of T, and define $v \leq_{P;Z} v'$ iff the following conditions are satisfied:

1. $\{q \in Q \mid v(q) = t\} = \{q \in Q \mid v'(q) = t\}$;
2. $\{p \in P \mid v(p) = t\} \subseteq \{p \in P \mid v'(p) = t\}$.

A model v of T is called $(P; Z)$-*minimal* if no model v' of T with $v' \neq v$ satisfies $v' \leq_{P;Z} v$.

Informally, the partition (P, Q, Z) can be interpreted as follows: The set P contains the variables to be minimized, Z are those variables that can vary in minimizing P, and the remaining variables Q are fixed in minimizing P.

Let T be a theory and (P, Q, Z) a partition of $var(T)$, where $P = \{p_1, \ldots, p_n\}$ and $Z = \{z_1, \ldots, z_m\}$. The set of $(P; Z)$-minimal models of T is given by the truth assignments to the QBF

$$Circ(T; P; Z) = T \wedge \neg \exists \tilde{P}, \tilde{Z}\Big((\tilde{P} < P) \wedge T[P/\tilde{P}, Z/\tilde{Z}] \Big),$$

where $\tilde{P} = \{\tilde{p}_1, \ldots, \tilde{p}_n\}$ and $\tilde{Z} = \{\tilde{z}_1, \ldots, \tilde{z}_m\}$ are sets of new variables corresponding to P and Z, respectively.

Then, for $P = var(T)$, we have that $Min_{m'}(T) \wedge \neg\tau(T, f)$ can be written as

$$\mathcal{C}_m(T) = Circ((P \leq P') \wedge (S \leq \{\tau(p, o) \mid p \in P\}) \wedge \neg\tau(T, f); S; P \cup P'),$$

where $S = \{s_p \mid p \in var(T)\}$, and, analogously, $Min_{n'}(T)$ can be written as

$$\mathcal{C}_n(T) = Circ((P \leq P') \wedge (S \leq \{\tau(\phi, o) \mid \phi \in T\}); S; P \cup P')$$

where $S = \{s_\phi \mid \phi \in T\}$.

Summarizing, we have[3]

1. $T \models_m \phi$ iff $\big(\mathcal{C}_m(T) \wedge \neg\tau(T, f)\big) \to \neg\tau(\phi, f)$ is true;
2. $T \models_n \phi$ iff $\big(\mathcal{C}_n(T) \wedge \neg\tau(T, f)\big) \to \neg\tau(\phi, f)$ is true.

This demonstrates how the principle of circumscription can be exploited for characterizing the minimization process in the two considered paraconsistent logics.

4 Related Work

A whole variety of approaches uses lattices for dealing with inconsistency, e.g., [1, 7,29]. For instance, [1,2] describes a system based on four-valued logic that allows for constraining "the most consistent" models in the meta-level by a user-given set of propositions taking classical truth-values only. In fact, in [3] the preference relation $\leq_m$ is generalized to four-valued logics, giving rise to two distinct orderings: Given two four-valued interpretations over truth values $\{t, f, o, o'\}$[4], define

---

[3] In fact, $(\mathcal{C}_m(T) \wedge \neg\tau(T, f)) \to \neg\tau(\phi, f)$ is true iff $\mathcal{C}_m(T) \to \neg\tau(\phi, f)$ is true.

[4] In a four-valued setting, o, o' are usually denoted by $\bot, \top$.

- $v \leq_1 w$ iff $\{p \in \mathcal{P} \mid v(p) = o\} \subseteq \{p \in \mathcal{P} \mid w(p) = o\}$; and
- $v \leq_2 w$ iff $\{p \in \mathcal{P} \mid v(p) \in \{o, o'\}\} \subseteq \{p \in \mathcal{P} \mid w(p) \in \{o, o'\}\}$.

As with $\models_m$, the models minimal with respect to these orderings are then used to define two distinct four-valued consequence relations. Although we do not detail it here, we mention that an appropriate encoding of the underlying four-valued logic (similar to the one given in Definition 1), along with a slightly generalized QBF encoding (similar to the one given in Definition 3), allows for a straightforward encoding of the two four-valued consequence relations by means of QBFs. Interestingly, both four-valued paraconsistent logics have recently been implemented in [4] by appeal to special-purpose circumscription solvers [16]. Furthermore, [14] proposes a translation-based approach to reasoning in the presence of contradictions that translates a logic into a family of other logics, e.g., classical logic into three-valued logics.

Among the existing inference methods for three-valued paraconsistent logics, we mention the following ones. A resolution-based system close to LP yet with a stronger disjunction is described in [23]. In fact, there is an indirect way of implementing LP_m because its consequence relation has recently been shown in [15] to be equivalent to a particular relation within the family of signed systems [10], whose inference can also be mapped onto QBFs, as shown in [11]. The resulting encoding is, however, of little interest since it lacks the spirit of "minimizing inconsistency" and thus fails to provide insight into LP_m; also, it is not extendible with the genuine implication $\rightarrow$ or even to alternative approaches such as [9]. We recall from the introductory section that the latter approach was originally axiomatized in [9] by means of a Hilbert system comprising 26 axiom schemata.

5   Conclusion

Considering two paraconsistent logics based on a minimization principle applied to a three-valued logic, we have shown how a translation into the language of quantified Boolean formulas is possible. The translations obtained clearly fall under the same umbrella, giving rise to a uniform setting for the axiomatization of such logics. (In particular, we have provided translations explicitly displaying the connection with circumscription, the classical proof theory for logical minimization.) Moreover, once such an axiomatization is available, existing QBF solvers can be used for implementation without further ado. Having efficient QBF solvers, like the systems described in [12,20,6], makes such a rapid prototyping approach practicably applicable. Finally, we remark that what we did allows us, in some sense, to express this kind of paraconsistent reasoning in (higher order) classical propositional logic and so to harness classical reasoning mechanisms from (a conservative extension of) propositional logic.

References

1. O. Arieli and A. Avron. Logical bilattices and inconsistent data. In *Proc. LICS*, pages 468–476, 1994.
2. O. Arieli and A. Avron. Automatic diagnoses for properly stratified knowledge-bases. In *Proc. ICTAI'96*, pages 392–399. IEEE Computer Society Press, 1996.

3. O. Arieli and A. Avron. The value of four values. *Artificial Intelligence*, 102(1):97–141, 1998.
4. O. Arieli and M. Denecker. Modeling paraconsistent reasoning by classical logic. In *Proc. FOIKS'02*, number 2284 in LNCS, pages 1–14. Springer-Verlag, 2002.
5. A. Avron. Simple consequence relations. *Information and Computation*, 92:105–139, 1991.
6. A. Ayari and D. Basin. QUBOS: Deciding quantified Boolean logic using propositional satisfiability solvers. In *Proc. FMCAD 2002*, volume 2517 of *LNCS*, pages 187–201. Springer-Verlag, 2002.
7. N. Belnap. A useful four-valued logic. In J. Dunn and G. Epstein, editors, *Modern Uses of Multiple-Valued Logic*. Reidel, 1977.
8. S. Benferhat, C. Cayrol, D. Dubois, J. Lang, and H. Prade. Inconsistency management and prioritized syntax-based entailment. In *Proc. IJCAI'93*, pages 640–647, 1993.
9. P. Besnard and T. Schaub. Circumscribing inconsistency. In *Proc. IJCAI'97*, pages 150–155, 1997.
10. P. Besnard and T. Schaub. Signed systems for paraconsistent reasoning. *Journal of Automated Reasoning*, 20(1-2):191–213, 1998.
11. P. Besnard, T. Schaub, H. Tompits, and S. Woltran. Paraconsistent reasoning via quantified Boolean formulas, I: Axiomatising signed systems. In *Proc. JELIA'02*, volume 2424 of *LNCS*, pages 320–331. Springer-Verlag, 2002.
12. M. Cadoli, A. Giovanardi, and M. Schaerf. An algorithm to evaluate quantified Boolean formulae. In *Proc. AAAI-98*, pages 262–267. AAAI Press, 1998.
13. M. Cadoli and M. Schaerf. On the complexity of entailment in propositional multivalued logics. *Annals of Mathematics and Artificial Intelligence*, 18:29–50, 1996.
14. W. Carnielli, L. Fariñas del Cerro, and M. Lima Marques. Contextual negations and reasoning with contradictions. In *Proc. IJCAI'91*, pages 532–537, 1991.
15. S. Coste-Marquis and P. Marquis. Complexity results for paraconsistent inference relations. In *Proc. KR'02*, pages 61–72, 2002.
16. P. Doherty, W. Lukaszewicz, and A. Szalas. Computing circumscription revisited: A reduction algorithm. *Journal of Automated Reasoning*, 18:297–334, 1997.
17. I. D'Ottaviano and N. da Costa. Sur un problème de Jaśkowski. In *Comptes Rendus de l'Académie des Sciences de Paris*, volume 270, pages 1349–1353, 1970.
18. R. Feldmann, B. Monien, and S. Schamberger. A distributed algorithm to evaluate quantified Boolean formulas. In *Proc. AAAI-00*, pages 285–290. AAAI Press, 2000.
19. A. Frisch. Inference without chaining. In *Proc. IJCAI'87*, pages 515–519, 1987.
20. E. Giunchiglia, M. Narizzano, and A. Tacchella. QuBE: A system for deciding quantified Boolean formulas satisfiability. In *Proc. IJCAR'01*, pages 364–369. Springer-Verlag, 2001.
21. S. Konieczny and P. Marquis. Three-valued logics for inconsistency handling. In *Proc. JELIA'02*, volume 2424 of *LNCS*, pages 332–344. Springer-Verlag, 2002.
22. H. Levesque. A knowledge-level account of abduction. In *Proc. IJCAI'89*, pages 1061–1067, 1989.
23. F. Lin. Reasoning in the presence of inconsistency. In *Proc. AAAI'87*, pages 139–143, 1987.
24. R. Manor and N. Rescher. On inferences from inconsistent information. *Theory and Decision*, 1:179–219, 1970.
25. J. McCarthy. Applications of circumscription to formalizing common-sense knowledge. *Artificial Intelligence*, 28:89–116, 1986.
26. D. Mundici. Satisfiability in many-valued sentential logic is NP-complete. *Theoretical Computer Science*, 52(1-2):145–153, 1987.
27. G. Priest. Logic of paradox. *Journal of Philosophical Logic*, 8:219–241, 1979.
28. G. Priest. Reasoning about truth. *Artificial Intelligence*, 39:231–244, 1989.
29. E. Sandewall. A functional approach to non-monotonic logic. *Computational Intelligence*, 1:80–87, 1985.

Modal (Logic) Paraconsistency

Philippe Besnard[1] and Paul Wong[2]

[1] IRIT, CNRS, Université Paul Sabatier
118 route de Narbonne, 31062 Toulouse cedex, France
besnard@irit.fr
[2] SITACS, University of Wollongong
NSW 2522 Australia
paul_wong@uow.edu.au

Abstract. According to the standard definition, a logic is said to be paraconsistent if it fails the (so-called) rule of ex falso: i.e., $\alpha, \neg\alpha \nvdash \beta$. Thus, paraconsistency captures an important sense in which a logic is inconsistency-tolerant, namely when arbitrary inference is prohibited in the presence of inconsistencies. We investigate a family of notions of paraconsistency within the context of modal logics.
An illustration comes from an epistemic version of the lottery paradox showing how important it sometimes is to distinguish between ordinary and higher order beliefs: A logic may fail to tolerate inconsistent beliefs at a given level while tolerating inconsistent beliefs across different levels. We identify a few properties arising from some well-known modal theorems and inference rules in order to classify modal logics according to their capacity to tolerate modalized inconsistencies. In doing so, we show various relationships among these logics.

1 Introduction

In the extensional case, paraconsistency is a feature of logics that do not identify inconsistent theories with trivial theories (those that consist of all formulae of the logical language under consideration). Notably, the inadequacy of classical logic[1] in this respect is illustrated by the so-called *ex falso* which is the following tautologous schema:

$$\models \alpha \wedge \neg\alpha \rightarrow \beta$$

Indeed, the ex falso can be understood as specifying conditions of *deductive breakdown* – when inference can go in any direction. As intensionality enters the picture through modal operators, more notions of deductive breakdown and triggering conditions arise. In an extension of classical logic such as the standard modal logic K (we are to follow the naming convention adopted in [Chellas 1980]) for example, the following holds:

$$\vdash_K \Box\alpha \wedge \Box\neg\alpha \rightarrow \Box\beta$$

---

[1] Throughout the text, the symbol $\models$ is strictly reserved for classical logic whereas $\vdash$ (whether subscripted or not) is used for other logics.

T.D. Nielsen and N.L. Zhang (Eds.): ECSQARU 2003, LNAI 2711, pp. 540–551, 2003.
© Springer-Verlag Berlin Heidelberg 2003

Thus, the conclusion set $\{\Box\beta \mid \beta \in \mathcal{L}\}$ (where $\mathcal{L}$ denotes the set of all formulas of the language, whether they are modal or not) can be seen as a modal kind of deductive breakdown of the logic. Note that a related version of such a modal ex falso is *not* provable in K:

$$\nvdash_K \Box\Box\alpha \wedge \Box\Box\neg\alpha \to \Box\beta$$

More generally, the modal logic K enforces that inconsistencies split over identical modalities

$$\vdash_K \Box\Box\alpha \wedge \Box\Box\neg\alpha \to \Box\Box\beta$$
$$\vdash_K \Box\Box\Box\alpha \wedge \Box\Box\Box\neg\alpha \to \Box\Box\Box\beta$$

$$\vdots$$

are contrasted with inconsistencies defined accross distinct modalities

$$\nvdash_K \Box\alpha \wedge \Box\Box\neg\alpha \to \Box\beta$$
$$\nvdash_K \Box\Box\alpha \wedge \Box\neg\alpha \to \Box\Box\beta$$

$$\vdots$$

This indicates that modalized inconsistencies of a certain modal depth may give arbitrary conclusions of the *same* modal depth but need not give arbitrary conclusions of any modal depth.

Presumably the most striking example is an epistemic counterpart of the lottery paradox ([Kyburg 1997]). Consider for instance an agent who has the capacity to form (ordinary) beliefs (e.g., George is bald) as well as *higher order* beliefs about her own beliefs. If holding a large collection of beliefs, she may have grounds to believe that at least one of her ordinary beliefs is mistaken. But of each of her ordinary belief, she has no grounds to believe that this particular one is mistaken and so she does believe in each of her ordinary beliefs after all. Interpreting $\Box$ as the belief operator, we may write:

$$\Box\neg\Box(\alpha_1 \wedge \ldots \wedge \alpha_n) \tag{1}$$
$$\Box\alpha_1 \wedge \ldots \wedge \Box\alpha_n \tag{2}$$

where each α_i stands for an ordinary belief and so contains no occurrence of $\Box$. As (2) above is equivalent to

$$\Box(\alpha_1 \wedge \ldots \wedge \alpha_n) \tag{3}$$

in standard epistemic logic, the nature of the conflict between (1) and (3) should clearly be distinguished from believing contradictory claims:

$$\Box\alpha \wedge \Box\neg\alpha \tag{4}$$

Interpreting $\Box$ as the knowledge operator, (1) and (3) are actually inconsistent in view of the famous principle $\Box\alpha \to \alpha$. And a stronger modal logic can generate even more inconsistencies – modalities interacting awkwardly with each other (see [Meyer and van der Hoek 1998] [Priest 2002] [Wansing 2002] for discussions of epistemic inconsistencies).

These considerations provide the impetus to develop a principled method to make finer distinctions than the original ex falso. In particular, we need at least to distinguish between extensional inconsistency and intensional inconsistency. As a logic may have more operators, for instance two negations, one being extensional but not necessarily the other, the interaction of operators also raises the issue of corresponding forms of the ex falso (see [Carnielli & Marcos 1999, 2002]).

Even though some paraconsistent logics have been defined from modal logics [Perzanowski 1975] [Blaszczuk 1984] and [Béziau 2002], the idea here is a more general investigation of paraconsistency in a pure modal setting.

2   Modal Paraconsistency Based on Conditional Formulae

We consider modal logics over a propositional language involving the unary operator $\Box$. They may have none, some or all of the modal inference rules below:

$$[RE] \ \frac{\alpha \to \beta \qquad \beta \to \alpha}{\Box\alpha \to \Box\beta}$$

$$[RM] \ \frac{\alpha \to \beta}{\Box\alpha \to \Box\beta}$$

$$[RT] \ \frac{\Box\alpha}{\alpha}$$

$$[R4] \ \frac{\Box\alpha}{\Box\Box\alpha}$$

Of special interest are the following non-modal rules:

$$modus\ ponens \ \frac{\alpha \qquad \alpha \to \beta}{\beta}$$

$$the\ transitivity\ rule \ \frac{\alpha \to \beta \qquad \beta \to \gamma}{\alpha \to \gamma}$$

The starting analysis involves the presence of an inconsistency symbol $\bot$ in the language so that it is possible to rewrite the ex falso as:

$$\models \bot \to \beta$$

Of course, β stands for all formulae of the language and these include the modal ones when it comes to a logic which is a modal extension of classical logic. Incidentally, this shows that modal paraconsistency requires the ex falso to be modified so as to have modalities occurring in the resulting schema:

Modal paraconsistency is essentially modal.

Accordingly, the simplest modal counterpart of the ex falso is:

$$\Box\bot \to \Box\beta$$

Thus, $\Box\bot$ is the simplest modal inconsistency. Generalization is straightforward, with $\Box^n$-inconsistency being $\Box^n\bot$ and the ex falso taking the form:

$$\Box^n\bot \to \Box^n\beta$$

Although not all the logics we will consider are extensions of classical logic, our analysis is based on classical antinomies: Letting $\mathcal{T}$ denote the class of all non-modal tautologous schemata, define $\mathcal{A} = \{\alpha \mid \alpha \to \bot \in \mathcal{T}\}$.

We are now in the position to specify a generic notion of modal paraconsistency via conditional formulae:

Definition 1. *Let $\varphi \in \mathcal{A}$. For $n \geq 1$, a logic is $\Box^n\varphi$-paraconsistent iff it fails to have $\Box^n\varphi \to \Box^n\beta$ as a theorem.*

Note that this definition is parameterized to both φ and n. For different choices of φ and n, a logic need not behave the same with respect to those different cases for $\Box^n\varphi$-paraconsistency. Definition 1 also relies on theoremhood being non-empty in the modal logic under consideration and another approach is needed when it comes to logics without any theorems. This will be discussed in the next section about a rule-based formulation of modal paraconsistency.

Example 1. Take φ to be $\neg(\alpha \to (\beta \to \alpha))$. Consider the modal logic $S0.9$ that can be axiomatized by the tautologous schemata and $\Box(\alpha \to \beta) \to (\Box\alpha \to \Box\beta)$ and $\Box\alpha \to \alpha$ (as well as $\Box\alpha$ if α is in any of these three categories) together with the rule: from $\Box(\alpha \to \beta)$ and $\Box(\beta \to \alpha)$, infer $\Box(\Box\alpha \to \Box\beta)$. For every $n \geq 1$, it fails to be $\Box^n\varphi$-paraconsistent. Many well-known modal logics (KT, $S4$, ...) accordingly fail to be $\Box^n\neg(\alpha \to (\beta \to \alpha))$-paraconsistent.

Example 2. Take φ to be $\alpha \wedge \neg\alpha$ and ψ to be $\neg(\alpha \vee \neg\alpha)$. Consider a (non-modal) strongly paracomplete logic (in symbols, $\nvdash \neg(\alpha \vee \neg\alpha) \to \beta$) which happens to fail paraconsistency (in symbols, $\vdash \alpha \wedge \neg\alpha \to \beta$) and define a minimal extension of it closed under the rule $[RM]$. Such a modal logic tolerates the necessary rejection of the excluded middle (i.e., it is $\Box^n\psi$-paraconsistent: $\nvdash \Box^n\neg(\alpha \vee \neg\alpha) \to \Box^n\beta$) without also tolerating the necessity of a "blatant contradiction" (i.e., it fails to be $\Box^n\varphi$-paraconsistent: $\vdash \Box^n(\alpha \wedge \neg\alpha) \to \Box^n\beta$).

The first question is: In what sense are some of these notions of paraconsistency weaker than one another?

Property 1. *Let $n \geq 1$. If a logic admitting $[RM]$ is $\Box^n\varphi$-paraconsistent then it also is $\Box^m\varphi$-paraconsistent for all $m < n$.*

Property 2. *Let $n \geq 1$. If a logic admitting the transitivity rule and the well-known axiom schema*

$$T : \Box\alpha \to \alpha$$

is $\Box^n\varphi$-paraconsistent then it also is $\Box^m\varphi$-paraconsistent for all $m < n$.

Of course, T is needlessly strong. It could be replaced by the less familiar[2] schema $4_c : \Box\Box\alpha \to \Box\alpha$.

While each of these two properties gives a sufficient condition for one level (modal depth) of paraconsistency to spread to some others (it spreads downwards from n), there is a limit where one level spreads to all others:

Property 3. *Let $\varphi \in \mathcal{A}$. Consider a logic admitting the transitivity rule and the well-known axiom schemata*

$$T : \Box\alpha \to \alpha$$
$$4 : \Box\alpha \to \Box\Box\alpha$$

It is $\Box^m\varphi$-paraconsistent in some $m \geq 1$ iff it is $\Box^n\varphi$-paraconsistent in all $n \geq 1$.

Again, T is needlessly strong. T and 4 could be replaced by just 4! which is 4 augmented with its own converse, 4_c (see above).

In a sense, Property 3 is actually a degenerate case because T and 4 together (or equivalently 4!) shrink all $\Box^n$ ($n \geq 1$) prefix to $\Box$. In less degenerate cases, $\Box^n$ may shrink to $\Box^i$ for some arbitrary but fixed limit $i < n$. For instance, 4! may be weakened so as to give a family of modal logics with the following versions of 4 and 4_c:

$$4^i : \Box^i\alpha \to \Box^{i+1}\alpha \qquad 4_c^i : \Box^{i+1}\alpha \to \Box^i\alpha$$

In any of these logics, there is an exact counterpart to Property 3. The only change required is that $m \geq i$ and $n \geq i$ for the arbitrary but fixed limit i.

Turning to the question of the relationship between $\Box^n\varphi$-paraconsistency and $\Box^n\psi$-paraconsistency, consider now a logic which satisfies the principle of uniform substitution. For all $n \geq 1$, if such a logic is $\Box^n\varphi$-paraconsistent then it is $\Box^n\psi$-paraconsistent provided that $\varphi \in \mathcal{A}$ can be obtained from $\psi \in \mathcal{A}$ by uniform substitution. There are of course other possibilities, for instance:

Property 4. *Consider a logic which admits both [RM] and the transitivity rule. For $n \geq 1$, if it is a $\Box^n\varphi$-paraconsistent logic then it also is $\Box^n\psi$-paraconsistent for all $\psi \in \mathcal{A}$ such that $\varphi \to \psi$ is a theorem of the logic.*

Weaker conditions are possible when considering the equivalence between $\Box^n\varphi$-paraconsistency and $\Box^n\psi$-paraconsistency. Stating that φ and ψ are equivalent iff both $\varphi \to \psi$ and $\psi \to \varphi$ are theorems of the logic, it is enough to consider a modal rule of which [RM] is a special case:

---

[2] However, a temporal interpretation of modality identifies $\Box\Box\alpha \to \Box\alpha$ with density.

Property 5. *Let $n \geq 1$. Consider a logic having $[RE]$ and the transitivity rule. Whenever φ and ψ are equivalent in that logic, it is $\square^n\varphi$-paraconsistent iff it is $\square^n\psi$-paraconsistent.*

What does it take for a logic to have all the variations of $\square^n\psi$-paraconsistency (for n fixed) to collapse into one and only $\square^n\varphi$-paraconsistency as all $\varphi \in \mathcal{A}$ are equivalent under deduction in classical logic? From Property 5, an answer is:

Property 6. *For every $n \geq 1$, a logic which is an extension of classical logic admitting $[RE]$ is $\square^n\varphi$-paraconsistent iff it is $\square^n\psi$-paraconsistent.*

Presenting sufficient conditions for a logic to fail to be $\square^n\varphi$-paraconsistent in all parameters (φ and n) is worthwhile although this should *not* (unless $n = 1$) be taken to mean that all modal formulae are inferred from $\square^n\varphi$ where $\varphi \in \mathcal{A}$, regardless of whether the logic admits modus ponens. Here is a class of logics that enjoy no $\square^n\varphi$-paraconsistent at all:

Property 7. *A logic which is an extension of classical logic and admits $[RM]$ fails to be $\square^n\varphi$-paraconsistent for all $n \geq 1$ and for all $\varphi \in \mathcal{A}$.*

Note that Property 7 does not say that all logic admitting $[RM]$ would fail to be $\square^n\varphi$-paraconsistent. That systematically fails only for those which are extensions of classical logic. Other logics might still enjoy $\square^n\varphi$-paraconsistency (even if they admit principles such as $\vdash \bot \rightarrow \beta$ and $[RM]$) but there are certain necessary conditions.

Interestingly enough, $\square^n\varphi$-paraconsistency is not a notion arising only from (classical) antinomies governed by a $\square^n$ modality. A modal ex falso can follow from the equivalence of all contradictions in the form:

$$(\alpha \wedge \neg\alpha) \rightarrow (\beta \wedge \neg\beta)$$

Property 8. *Consider a logic admitting $[RE]$ and the well-known schemata:*

$$M : \square(\alpha \wedge \beta) \rightarrow \square\alpha \wedge \square\beta$$

$$C : \square\alpha \wedge \square\beta \rightarrow \square(\alpha \wedge \beta)$$

as well as the non-modal principles:

$$\frac{\alpha \rightarrow \beta \quad \beta \rightarrow \gamma}{\alpha \rightarrow \gamma} \qquad\qquad \alpha \wedge \beta \rightarrow \alpha \qquad\qquad (\alpha \wedge \neg\alpha) \rightarrow (\beta \wedge \neg\beta)$$

For $n \geq 1$ and all non-modal α, the logic fails to be $\square^n(\alpha \wedge \neg\alpha)$-paraconsistent.

In general, a modal logic can have the ex falso as a theorem and still be $\square^n(\alpha \wedge \neg\alpha)$-paraconsistent for any $n \geq 1$ but it is obvious that a logic which has the ex falso as a theorem and $[RM]$ as an admissible rule fails, for all $n \geq 1$ and for all non-modal α, to be $\square^n(\alpha \wedge \neg\alpha)$-paraconsistent. A variation is:

Property 9. *Consider a logic L whose non-modal inference within modality $\Box^n$ for some fixed $n \geq 1$ is given by an explosive non-modal logic L' as follows:*

$$\vdash_{L'} \alpha \rightarrow \beta \quad \Rightarrow \quad \vdash_L \Box^n \alpha \rightarrow \Box^n \beta \quad \text{for all non-modal } \alpha \text{ and } \beta$$

where explosive means that the ex falso is a theorem of the logic (L' here). Then, L fails to be $\Box^n(\alpha \wedge \neg\alpha)$-paraconsistent.

In classical logic, trivialization is an immediate consequence of the ex falso: From a contradiction, every formula is deduced. Even if considering only modal logics that admit modus ponens, the situation is different here because modal depth makes room for levels upon which modal paraconsistency need not impose a uniform effect to take place: Specific trivialization answers the failure of $\Box^n \varphi$-paraconsistency, depending on n. By $\Box^n$-*trivialization*, we mean that all formulae of the form $\Box^n \beta$ are inferred. If $n \neq m$, $\Box^n$-trivialization is in general independent from $\Box^m$-trivialization unless the logic is too strong to exhibit any kind of paraconsistency at all:

Property 10. *Consider a logic such as in Property 3, additionally admitting modus ponens. In the event that it fails to be $\Box^n \bot$-paraconsistent in all $n \geq 1$, any $\Box^m$-inconsistency for some $m \geq 1$ entails $\Box^n$-trivialization for all $n \geq 1$.*

Property 11. *A logic such as in Property 9 for $n = 1$, that additionally admits modus ponens and enjoys the well-know schema:*

$$C : \Box\alpha \wedge \Box\beta \rightarrow \Box(\alpha \wedge \beta)$$

is such that $\Box(\alpha \wedge \neg\alpha)$ yields $\Box$-trivialization for all non-modal α.

There exists a violation of the independence between $\Box^n$-trivialization and $\Box^m$-trivialization that is of utmost importance: For any logic which admits modus ponens, even being $\Box^n \varphi$-paraconsistent in *every* $\varphi \in \mathcal{A}$ does not prevent $\Box^n$-trivialization to occur when there is a $\Box^m$-inconsistency for some $m < n$ such that the logic fails to be $\Box^m \bot$-paraconsistent. More generally:

Property 12. *Consider a logic admitting modus ponens. For all $n \geq 1$ and all φ such that the logic fails to be $\Box^n \varphi$-paraconsistent, $\Box^n \varphi$ yields $\Box^m$-trivialization for all $m > n$.*

In a nutshell, this is the reason why logics such that $\Box^n \varphi$-paraconsistency implies $\Box^m \varphi$-paraconsistency for all $m < n$ should be preferred.

Another way to look at the same phenomenon consists of switching to a rule-based formulation, as is done in the next section. Still another option would be to adopt an amended definition of $\Box^n \varphi$-paraconsistency (with the immediate but important consequence that being $\Box^n \varphi$-paraconsistent unconditionally implies being $\Box^m \varphi$-paraconsistent for all $m < n$) as follows:

Definition 2. *Let $\varphi \in \mathcal{A}$. For $n \geq 1$, a logic is $\Box^n \varphi$-paraconsistent iff there exists no $u \geq 1$ such that $\Box^u \varphi \rightarrow \Box^n \beta$ is a theorem of the logic.*

In order to obtain a generalization (here given from Definition 1 but a formulation for Definition 2 is unproblematic) of $\Box^n\varphi$-paraconsistency, consider the class of all non-modal tautologous schemata $\alpha_1 \to (\alpha_2 \to (\ldots \to (\alpha_p \to \bot)\ldots))$ for all $p \geq 1$.

Definition 3. *Let $F \in \mathcal{T}$ be $\alpha_1 \to (\alpha_2 \to (\ldots \to (\alpha_p \to \bot)\ldots))$. For all $n \geq 1$, a logic is $\Box^n F$-paraconsistent iff $\Box^n\alpha_1 \to (\Box^n\alpha_2 \to (\ldots \to (\Box^n\alpha_p \to \Box^n\beta)\ldots))$ fails to be a theorem.*

All previous properties have counterparts here, provided that a few things are taken care of. For example, either $[RM]$ is generalized to

$$[RM^p] \quad \frac{\alpha_1 \to (\alpha_2 \to (\ldots \to (\alpha_p \to \beta)\ldots))}{\Box\alpha_1 \to (\Box\alpha_2 \to (\ldots \to (\Box\alpha_p \to \Box\beta)\ldots))}$$

or the following modal and non-modal principles apply:

$$\Box(\alpha \to \beta) \to (\Box\alpha \to \Box\beta) \qquad\qquad \frac{\alpha}{\Box\alpha} \qquad\qquad \frac{\alpha \quad \alpha \to \beta}{\beta}$$
$$(\alpha \to \beta) \to ((\beta \to \gamma) \to (\alpha \to \gamma))$$

3   Modal Paraconsistency in Rule-Based Formulation

Further generalization arises from weakening the principles at stake by rewriting schemata as rules. Definition 3 becomes:

Definition 4. *Let $p \geq 1$ and $S = \{\alpha_1, \ldots, \alpha_p\}$ (all α_i's are non-modal schemata) be such that*
$$\frac{\alpha_1 \quad \cdots \quad \alpha_p}{\bot} \text{ is admissible in classical logic}$$
For $n \geq 1$, a logic is $[\Box^n S]$-paraconsistent iff it fails to have

$$[\Box^n S] \quad \frac{\Box^n\alpha_1 \quad \cdots \quad \Box^n\alpha_p}{\Box^n\beta}$$

as an admissible rule.

Abbreviations. Let $\mathcal{I}$ denote the set of all (non-modal) admissible rules in classical logic that have the form:

$$\frac{\alpha_1 \quad \cdots \quad \alpha_p}{\bot}$$

Also, $\mathcal{C}$ will be taken to denote the set of all finite sets of non-modal schemata $S = \{\alpha_1, \ldots, \alpha_p\}$ such that

$$\frac{\alpha_1 \quad \cdots \quad \alpha_p}{\bot} \in \mathcal{I}$$

There is an obvious connection between modal paraconsistency in rule-based formulation and modal paraconsistency based on conditional formulae:

Property 13. *Let $\alpha_1, \ldots, \alpha_p$ be finitely many formulae obeying $\alpha_1 \wedge \ldots \wedge \alpha_p \in \mathcal{A}$. If a logic which admits modus ponens and*

$$the\ rule\ of\ adjunction\quad \frac{\alpha \qquad \beta}{\alpha \wedge \beta}$$

is $[\Box^n\{\alpha_1, \ldots, \alpha_p\}]$-paraconsistent then it is $\Box^n(\alpha_1 \wedge \ldots \wedge \alpha_p)$-paraconsistent.

In view of Property 13, the comment at the end of Example 1 extends to modal paraconsistency in rule-based formulation: Many well-known modal logics fail to be $[\Box^n S]$-paraconsistent for $S = \{\neg(\alpha \to (\beta \to \alpha))\}$, or $S = \{\alpha, \neg\alpha\}$, ...

Property 14. *Let $n \geq 1$. If a logic which admits $[RT]$ is $[\Box^n S]$-paraconsistent then it also is $[\Box^m S]$-paraconsistent for all $m < n$.*

The sufficient condition (in Property 14) for $[\Box^n S]$-paraconsistency to be stronger than $[\Box^m S]$-paraconsistency has a special case which is a sufficient condition for $[\Box^n S]$-paraconsistency to be unique whatever n:

Property 15. *A logic which admits both $[RT]$ and $[R4]$ is $[\Box^m S]$-paraconsistent in some $m \geq 1$ iff it is $[\Box^n S]$-paraconsistent in all $n \geq 1$.*

Indeed, Property 14 is the counterpart of Property 2 and Property 15 is the counterpart of Property 3.

Notation. From now on, we write S_Φ and S_Ψ to denote two sets in $\mathcal{C}$ which consist of exactly the same schemata except for some $\{\phi_1, \ldots, \phi_k\}$ and $\{\psi_1, \ldots, \psi_k\}$. I.e., there exists some (possibly empty) S' such that $S_\Phi = S' \cup \{\phi_1, \ldots, \phi_k\}$ and $S_\Psi = S' \cup \{\psi_1, \ldots, \psi_k\}$.

Property 16. *Let $n \geq 1$. Consider a logic admitting the rule:*

$$\frac{\Box\alpha}{\Box\beta}\qquad provided\ that\ \frac{\alpha}{\beta}\ is\ admissible$$

For all $i = 1..k$, let the logic further admit the family of rules: from ϕ_i, infer ψ_i. If it is $[\Box^n S_\Phi]$-paraconsistent then it also is $[\Box^n S_\Psi]$-paraconsistent.

In contradistinction with Property 4, Property 16 shows that the conditions for $[\Box^n S_\Phi]$-paraconsistency to be stronger than $[\Box^n S_\Psi]$-paraconsistency do not resort to a common rule with the conditions for $[\Box^n S]$-paraconsistency to be stronger than $[\Box^m S]$-paraconsistency (cf $[RM]$ in Property 1 and Property 4).

Property 17. *Let $n \geq 1$. Consider a logic admitting the rule:*

$$\frac{\Box\alpha}{\Box\beta}\qquad provided\ that\ \frac{\alpha}{\beta}\ and\ \frac{\beta}{\alpha}\ are\ both\ admissible$$

Whenever the logic also admits the rules:

$$\frac{\phi_i}{\psi_i}\qquad and\qquad \frac{\psi_i}{\phi_i}\qquad 1 \leq i \leq k$$

it is $[\Box^n S_\Phi]$-paraconsistent iff it is $[\Box^n S_\Psi]$-paraconsistent.

The previous property can easily be expressed for classical equivalence:

Property 18. *Consider a logic that is an extension of classical logic and admits the rule:*

$$\frac{\Box\alpha}{\Box\beta} \quad provided\ that\ \frac{\alpha}{\beta}\ and\ \frac{\beta}{\alpha}\ are\ both\ admissible$$

For every $n \geq 1$, for every Φ and Ψ such that ϕ_i and ψ_i are classically equivalent when $i = 1..k$, the logic is $[\Box^n S_\Phi]$-paraconsistent iff it is $[\Box^n S_\Psi]$-paraconsistent.

Lastly, here is a condition which makes $[\Box^n S]$-paraconsistency to be unique:

Property 19. *A logic that is an extension of classical logic and admits the rule:*

$$\frac{\Box\alpha}{\Box\beta} \quad provided\ that\ \frac{\alpha}{\beta}\ is\ admissible$$

fails to be $[\Box^n S]$-paraconsistent for all $n \geq 1$ and for all $S \in \mathcal{C}$.

There are no counterparts to Property 10 (or Property 12) because the rule-based formulation adopted now makes $[\Box^n S]$-paraconsistency to capture most of the notion of $\Box^n$-trivialization, which can then be dispensed with.

4 Arbitrary Modal Paraconsistency

A further step can be taken against generalization, by considering distinct modalities to be mixed in the formulation of modal paraconsistency. We must introduce a convenient way of describing the modalities we are to deal with:

$$\mathcal{W} = \neg^*(\Box\neg^*)^+$$

Definition 4 becomes:

Definition 5. *For $p \geq 1$, let $S = \{\alpha_1, \ldots, \alpha_p\}$ (all α_i's are non-modal schemata) be such that*

$$\frac{\alpha_1 \quad \cdots \quad \alpha_p}{\bot}\ is\ admissible\ in\ classical\ logic$$

For $\omega_i \in \mathcal{W} \cup \{\epsilon\}$ (ϵ denotes the empty string) where $1 \leq i \leq p$, for $\omega_{p+1} \in \mathcal{W}$, a logic is $[\{\omega_j\}_j S]$-paraconsistent ($1 \leq j \leq p+1$) iff it fails to have

$$[\{\omega_i\}_i S]\ \frac{\omega_1\alpha_1 \quad \cdots \quad \omega_p\alpha_p}{\omega_{p+1}\beta}$$

as an admissible rule.

Example 3. The example in the introduction about the modal logic K can now be captured through expressing that it is a $[\{\Box\Box, \Box\Box, \Box\}\{\alpha, \neg\alpha\}]$-paraconsistent logic while it is not $[\{\Box, \Box, \Box\}\{\alpha, \neg\alpha\}]$-paraconsistent.

To illustrate that there is no special problem in this generalization, we may consider how Property 14 can be reformulated accordingly. Let S be just as in Definition 5, taking $\{\omega_i\}_i$ and $\{\omega_i'\}_i$ to be two indexed families of modalities. Then, for each i, $1 \leq i \leq p$, the corresponding $[RT]$ rule would be:

$$[RT_i] \ \frac{\omega_i \alpha_i}{\omega_i' \alpha_i}$$

Define

$$W = \{\omega_i\}_i \cup \{\omega_{p+1}\} \qquad W' = \{\omega_i'\}_i \cup \{\omega_{p+1}\}$$

Now the corresponding property says that if a logic is $[WS]$-paraconsistent then it is also $[W'S]$-paraconsistent.

Example 4. As to the epistemic version of the lottery paradox, a logic tolerating it would be paraconsistent with respect to the following expression:

$$\nvdash \frac{\alpha \qquad \Box \neg \alpha}{\Box \beta}$$

Example 5. All sensible modal logics are $[\{\neg\Box, \neg\Box, M\}\{\alpha, \neg\alpha\}]$-paraconsistent where M is any modality (it can even be empty). This simply reflects

$$\nvdash \frac{\Diamond \neg \alpha \qquad \Diamond \alpha}{M \beta}$$

which is certainly an indispensable feature of modal logics. The moral here is that the expressiveness of Definition 5 requires to pay some attention to what cases induce a meaningful instance of modal paraconsistency (even though technically no problem arises at all).

Summing up, a special form of paraconsistency can arise in modal logics – even some of those that would not be paraconsistent if it were not from the presence of modalities. Although investigating the ex falso in the form of a schema is enough for logics that admit modus ponens and the deduction theorem, Sect. 4 indicates how to take care of other logics. Among them are logics with connectives different than classical ones. It is unproblematic as long as they conform to a truth-functional many-valued system: It suffices to restrict the range of these truth-functional connectives to the classical truth-values to obtain connectives of classical logic (e.g., Sheffer's stroke, ...) and form any classical antinomies using these connectives.

5   Concluding Remarks

Although no brevity or minimality requirement is imposed on $\mathcal{A}$ (or similarly $\mathcal{T}$ or $\mathcal{C}$ or $\mathcal{I}$), it should be clear that any item in these sets which is more complex than necessary fails to induce any interesting kind of modal paraconsistency:

Regarding the schemata in $\mathcal{A}$ for instance, $\alpha \wedge \neg \alpha \wedge \beta \wedge \neg \beta$ is not worth considering due to $\alpha \wedge \neg \alpha \in \mathcal{A}$ or $\beta \wedge \neg \beta \in \mathcal{A}$.

At no point did we consider that modal paraconsistency might be based on schemata of the form $\Box^n(\varphi \to \beta)$ as opposed to $\Box^n \varphi \to \Box^n \beta$. Why? If modal contexts are to be of any use with respect to paraconsistency, modalities such as $\Box^n$ are expected to isolate (so to speak) a class of conclusions from others. Thus, the class should be immune from inconsistencies spreading but such is not the case with $\Box^n(\varphi \to \beta)$: The non-modal logic must already be paraconsistent or the modal context $\Box^n$ is not to govern a class of conclusions resisting deductive breakdown.

An implicit assumption throughout the text is that whenever the modal logic under consideration has its language which is not a classical one extended by a modal operator, the obvious adjustements are taken: E.g., replacing $\mathcal{A}$ by its intersection with the modal language when disjunction or some other usual connective is missing. Similarly if there is more than one negation ...

References

1. Béziau J. Y. Paraconsistent Logics from a Modal Viewpoint. *Proceedings of the Workshop on Paraconsistent Logic (WoPaLo): 14th European Summer School in Logic, Language and Information*, Trento, Italy, 2002.

2. Blaszczuk J. J. Some Paraconsistent Sentential Calculi. *Studia Logica*, 43 (1-2):51–61, 1984.

3. Carnielli W. A., and Marcos J. Limits for Paraconsistent Calculi. *Notre Dame Journal of Formal Logic*, 40 (3):375–390, 1999.

4. Carnielli W. A., and Marcos J. A Taxonomy of C–systems. *Paraconsistency – The Logical Way to the Inconsistent, Lecture Notes in Pure and Applied Mathematics* W. A. Carnielli, M. E. Coniglio, I. M. L. D'Ottaviano (eds). Volume 228, pp. 1–94. Marcel Dekker Pub., 2002.

5. Chellas B. F. *Modal Logic*. Cambridge University Press, 1980.

6. Hughes G. E., and Cresswell M. J. *A New Introduction to Modal Logic*. Routledge Press, 1996.

7. Kyburg H. E. The Rule of Adjunction and Reasonable Inference. *The Journal of Philosophy*, 94(3):109–125, 1997.

8. Meyer J.-J. Ch., and van der Hoek W. Modal Logics for Representing Incoherent Knowledge. *Handbook of Defeasible Reasoning and Uncertainty Management Systems*. D. Gabbay and Ph. Smets (eds). *Volume 2: Reasoning with Actual and Potential Contradictions*. Ph. Besnard and A. Hunter (eds). Kluwer Academic Pub., 1998.

9. Perzanowski J. On M-fragments and L-fragments of normal propositional logics. *Reports on Mathematical Logic* 5:63–72, 1975.

10. Priest G. Paraconsistent Logic. *Handbook of Philosophical Logic, Second Edition, Volume 6*. D. M. Gabbay (ed). Kluwer Academic Pub., 2002.

11. Wansing H. Diamonds are a Philosopher's Best Friends: The Knowability Paradox and Modal Epistemic Relevance Logic. *Journal of Philosophical Logic*, 31:591–612, 2002.

A Formal Framework for Handling Conflicting Desires

Leila Amgoud

Institut de Recherche en Informatique de Toulouse (IRIT)
118, route de Narbonne, 31062 Toulouse, France
amgoud@irit.fr
http://www.irit.fr/recherches/RPDMP/persos/Leila/index.html

Abstract. This paper combines ideas from argumentation [1,8] with desires and planning rules, in order to give a formal account of how consistent sets of intentions can be obtained from a conflicting set of desires. We show how conflicts may arise between desires and we resolve them. We argue that the set of desires can be clustered in three categories: i) the *intentions* of the agent, ii) the *rejected desires* and iii) the *desires in abeyance*. Finally, we show that the use of argumentation with desires is different from the usual kind of argumentation with default rules.

1 Introduction

An increasing number of software applications are being conceived, designed, and implemented using the notion of autonomous agents. These applications vary from email filtering, through electronic commerce, to large industrial applications. In all of these disparate cases, however, the notion of autonomy is used to denote the fact that the software has the ability to decide for itself which goals it should adopt and how these goals should be achieved.

Different architectures have emerged as candidates for studying these agent-based systems [2,3,4,6,12,10,11]. One of these architectures regards the system as a rational agent adopting certain *mental* attitudes: the beliefs (B), the desires (D) and the intentions (I). An agent can have contradictory desires. However, its intentions are a coherent subset of desires which the agent is committed to achieve.

In [5], the authors explored principles governing rational balance among an agent's beliefs, goals, actions and intentions. In [10] Rao and Georgeff showed how different rational agents can be modeled by imposing certain conditions on the persistence of an agent's beliefs, desires or intentions (the BDI model). In decision theory, Pearl [9] illustrated how planning agents are provided with goals – defined as desires together with commitments – and charged with the task of discovering (or performing) some sequence of actions to achieve those goals.

Most of formalizations are sophisticated enough to handle many aspects of BDI agents. However, they do not show how agent's intentions are calculated from the whole set of its desires. In other words, it is not clear how an agent chooses a subset of its possibly contradictory desires.

T.D. Nielsen and N.L. Zhang (Eds.): ECSQARU 2003, LNAI 2711, pp. 552–563, 2003.

Inspired from work on argumentation theory, we present in this paper a framework for handling contradictory desires. We will show that the problem can be formulated exactly as in argumentation theory and then we show that we can use all the techniques of argumentation to resolve it.

We suppose that an agent is equipped with a base of desires, a base of plans to carry out in order to achieve the desires (we are not interested in the way in which these plans are generated), and finally a knowledge base. Then we show how conflicts can emerge between desires, how to formalize these conflicts and finally how to solve them to obtain the intentions of the agent. Let's illustrate our purposes by the following example.

Example 1. *X is an agent who has the two following desires:*

1. *To go on a journey to central Africa. (jca)*
2. *To finish a publication before going on a journey. (fp)*

Let's suppose that the following plans to achieve the above desires are generated:

$$\begin{cases} t \wedge vac \rightarrow jca \\ w \quad \rightarrow fp \\ ag \quad \rightarrow t \\ fr \quad \rightarrow t \\ hop \quad \rightarrow vac \\ dr \quad \rightarrow vac \end{cases}$$

with: t = "to get the tickets", vac = "to be vaccinated", w = "to work", ag = "to pass to the agency", fr = "to have a friend who may bring the tickets", hop = "to go to a hospital", dr = "to go to a doctor".

For example, the rule $t \wedge vac \rightarrow jca$ means that to go on a journey in central Africa, the agent X should get tickets and should be vaccinated. The rule $w \rightarrow fp$ expresses that the agent should work in order to finish his paper. To get tickets, the agent can either pass to an agency or ask a friend of him to get them. Similarly, to be vaccinated, the agent has the choice between going to a doctor or going to a hospital. In these two last cases, the agent has two plans for each action.

Note that getting tickets *and* being vaccinated *become two* sub-desires *of the agent with each one having its own plans.*

In addition to the set of plans and the set of desires, the agent may have also another base containing its knowlege and some integrity constraints. In our example, we have:

$$\begin{cases} w \rightarrow \neg ag \\ w \rightarrow \neg dr \end{cases}$$

These two rules means that if the agent works, he can neither pass to an agency nor go to a doctor. Consequently, the plans of its two initial desires are conflicting.

Of course, it would be ideal if all the desires can become intentions. As our example illustrates, this is not always the case. In this paper we will answer to the following questions: which desire will become an intention of the agent, and with which plan?

2   Argumentation Frameworks

Argumentation is a reasoning model based on the construction of arguments and counter-arguments (or defeaters) followed by the selection of the most acceptable of them.

In Dung's work [7,8], an argumentation framework is defined as a pair consisting of a set of arguments and a binary relation representing the defeasibility relation between arguments. Here, an argument is an abstract entity whose role is only determined by its relation to other arguments. Then its structure and its origin are not known.

Definition 1 ([8]). *An argumentation framework is a pair $< \mathcal{A}, \mathcal{R} >$ where $\mathcal{A}$ is a set of arguments and $\mathcal{R}$ is a binary relation representing a defeasibility relationship between arguments, i.e. $\mathcal{R} \subseteq \mathcal{A} \times \mathcal{A}$. $(A, B) \in \mathcal{R}$ or equivalently "$A \mathcal{R} B$" means that the argument A defeats the argument B. We also say that A and B are in conflict.*
An argumentation framework is finitary *iff for each argument A there are finitely many arguments which defeat A.*

Definition 2. *Let $< \mathcal{A}, \mathcal{R} >$ be an argumentation framework, and $S \subseteq \mathcal{A}$.*

- *S is* conflict-free *iff $\nexists\ A, B \in S$ such that $A \mathcal{R} B$.*
- *S defends A iff $\forall\ B \in \mathcal{A}$, if $B \mathcal{R} A$ then $\exists\ C \in S$ such that $C \mathcal{R} B$.*

Each defeasibility relation leads to an argumentation framework. Defeating arguments can in turn be defeated by other arguments so we need to define a notion of the *status* of arguments. This notion of *status* is the central element of any argumentation framework. Its definition takes as input the set of all possible arguments and their mutual relations of defeat, and produces as output a division of arguments into three classes of arguments:

- The class of *acceptable arguments*. They represent the "good" arguments. In the case of handling inconsistency in knowledge bases, for example, the formulas supported by such arguments will be inferred from the base.
- The class of *rejected arguments*. They are those arguments defeated by acceptable arguments. Such arguments would not be considered in the process of inference from a knowledge base, for example.
- The arguments which are neither acceptable nor rejected are gathered in the so-called class of *arguments in abeyance*.

Note that to define the rejected arguments and the arguments in abeyance of a given argumentation framework, we first need to determine the set of acceptable arguments of that framework. For that purpose Dung suggested several semantics: *basic semantics* and *preferred semantics*.

Definition 3. *Let* $< \mathcal{A}, \mathcal{R} >$ *be an argumentation framework, and* $S \subseteq \mathcal{A}$.

- *S is a* preferred extension *iff S is maximal (for set inclusion), conflict-free and it defends all its elements.*
- *S is a* basic extension *iff S is the least fixpoint of the function* $\mathcal{F}(S) = \{A \in \mathcal{A} - A$ *is defended by* $S\}$.

3   Basic Definitions

In this section, we present the basic notions of a framework for handling an agent's desires: a logical language, a desire, an action, a realization tree of a desire and finally defeasibility between actions.

3.1   Logical Language

Let $\mathcal{L}$ be a propositional language. $\vdash$ denotes classical inference and $\equiv$ denotes logical equivalence. Each agent is equipped with three bases $<\mathcal{D}, \mathcal{P}, \Sigma>$ such that:

- $\mathcal{D}$ contains formulas of $\mathcal{L}$. The elements of $\mathcal{D}$ represent the initial desires of the agent. For example, an agent may have the following desires: *to finish a publication, to go to a dentist,* etc... Note that the set $\mathcal{D}$ may be inconsistent. This means that an agent is allowed to have contradictory desires.
- $\mathcal{P}$ is considered as a base of plans. It contains formulas having the form $\varphi_1 \wedge \ldots \wedge \varphi_n \to h$ where $\varphi_1, \ldots, \varphi_n, h$ are literals of $\mathcal{L}$. Such a formula means that to achieve h, the agent should realize $\varphi_1, \ldots, \varphi_n$.
- Σ contains formulas of $\mathcal{L}$. They represent the knowledge of the agent and some integrity constraints.

Example 2. *In example 1, the agent has the following bases:*

$$\mathcal{D} = \{jca, fp\}, \mathcal{P} = \begin{cases} t \wedge vac \to jca \\ w \quad \to fa \\ ag \quad \to t \\ fr \quad \to t \\ hop \to vac \\ dr \quad \to vac \end{cases}$$

and $\Sigma = \begin{cases} w \to \neg ag \\ w \to \neg dr \end{cases}$

3.2   The Notion of Desire

A desire is either an element h of $\mathcal{D}$ or a sub-desire of h. In example 1, the desire of going on a journey to central Africa has two sub-desires which are:

- getting the tickets
- being vaccinated

Let's note that the sub-desires are not in the base $\mathcal{D}$. Formally:

Definition 4 (Desire). *A desire is:*

- *a formulae $h \in \mathcal{D}$.*
- *a formulae h such that $\exists \varphi_1 \ldots \wedge \varphi_n \rightarrow h \in \mathcal{P} \cup \Sigma$*
- *a formulae h such that $\exists \varphi_1 \wedge h \ldots \wedge \varphi_n \rightarrow h' \in \mathcal{P}$. In this case, h is called a sub-desire of h'. The function Subdesire(h') returns the set $\{h', \varphi_1, \ldots \varphi_n\}$ of the sub-desires of h'. Note that each desire is a sub-desire of itself.*

Example 3. *In example 1, the agent has two desires (jca, fa) and several sub-desires like: w, tb, vac, ag, fr, hop and dr.*

3.3   The Notion of Action

As noted above, a desire may have a plan to achieve it. We bring the two notions together in a new notion of *action*.

Definition 5 (Action). *An action is a pair $a = < h, H >$ such that:*

- *h is a desire.*
- *If $\exists \varphi_1 \wedge \ldots \wedge \varphi_n \rightarrow h \in \mathcal{P} \cup \Sigma$ then $H = \{\varphi_1, \ldots, \varphi_n\}$ else $H = \emptyset$.*

The function Desire(a) = h returns the desire of an action a and the function Plan(a) = H returns its plan.
We denote by $\aleph$ the set of all actions which may be constructed from the triple $<\mathcal{D}, \mathcal{P}, \Sigma>$.

Remark 1. –
- *If the set H (the plan) is empty, this means that the desire has not yet gotten a plan to achieve it or the desire is atomic which means that it does not need any plan to be achieved.*
- *A desire may have several plans to be achieved. In this case, we have as many actions for that desire as plans.*

Example 4. *In example 1, we have the following actions: $a_1 = <jca, \{t, vac\}>$, $a_2 = <fa, \{w\}>$ and $a_3 = <w, \emptyset>$. Action a_3 means that:*

1. *The desire of working is atomic or,*
2. *The plan of working is not given yet.*

The realization of an action, *ie* the execution of its plan, requires in certain situations the decomposition of this plan. Each element of the initial plan gives place to a new action with a new plan. We call this kind of actions *sub-actions*. Formally:

Definition 6 (Sub-action). *Let a_1 and a_2 be two actions of $\aleph$. a_1 is a sub-action of a_2 iff Desire(a_1) $\in$ Plan(a_2). In other words, Desire(a_1) is a sub-desire of Desire(a_2).*

Example 5. *In example 1, the action $a_1 = <jca, \{t, vac\}>$ has the following sub-actions: $a_{11a} = <t, \{ag\}>$, $a_{11b} = <t, \{fr\}>$, $a_{12a} = <vac, \{dr\}>$, and $a_{12b} = <vac, \{hop\}>$*

An action may have consequences.

Definition 7 (Action's consequences). *Let $a \in \aleph$.*

$$Consequence(a) = \{\phi_i : such\,that\,Desire(a) \cup Plan(a) \cup \Sigma \vdash \phi_i\}.$$

Example 6. *In example 1, the action $a_2 = <fp, \{w\}>$ has the following consequences: $\{\neg ag, \neg dr, fp, w\}$*

3.4 Conflicting Actions

After a small study undertaken on the various conflicts which may exist between actions (desires), we think that there are four great families of conflicts. In fact, two actions a_1 and a_2 may be conflicting for one of the following reasons:

- *desire-desire* conflict, ie $Desire(a_1) \cup Desire(a_2) \cup \Sigma \vdash \bot$
- *plan-plan* conflict, ie $Plan(a_1) \cup Plan(a_2) \cup \Sigma \vdash \bot$.
- *consequence-consequence* conflict, ie $Consequence(a_1) \cup Consequence(a_2) \vdash \bot$.
- *plan-consequence* conflict, ie $Plan(a_1) \cup Consequence(a_2) \vdash \bot$ or $Plan(a_2) \cup Consequence(a_1) \vdash \bot$.

Example 7. *Let's consider an agent equipped with the following bases: $\mathcal{D} = \{fp, b, s\}$, $\Sigma = \{b \rightarrow \neg ws\}$ and*

$$\mathcal{P} = \begin{cases} ws \wedge wd \rightarrow fp \\ c \quad\;\; \rightarrow b \\ \neg c \quad\; \rightarrow s \end{cases}$$

with:
 ws = *"to work Saturday"*
 wd = *"to work Sunday"*
 fp = *"to finish the paper"*
 c = *"to take the car"*
 b = *"to go to the beach Saturday"*
 s = *"to make savings"*
 $\aleph$ *contains the following actions:*

- $a_1 = <fp, \{ws, wd\}>$.
- $a_2 = <b, \{c\}>$.
- $a_3 = <s, \{\neg c\}>$.

There exists a plan-plan conflict between a_2 and a_3. The two actions have contradictory plans here.

The consequences of action a_2 are $(Consequence(a_2) = \{ps, \neg ws\})$. There exists a plan-consequence conflict between a_2 and a_1. There exists also a consequence-consequence conflict between a_1 and a_2. Contrary to the conflict between a_2 and a_3, the plans of a_1 and a_2 seemed compatible, the conflict emerges from the consequences of the plans.

These different kinds of conflicts between actions are brought together in a unique relation of *conflict* defined as follows:

Definition 8 (Conflict). *Let a_1 and a_2 be two actions of $\aleph$. a_1 conflicts* with *a_2 iff:* $\{Desire(a_1), Desire(a_2)\} \cup Plan(a_1) \cup Plan(a_2) \cup \Sigma \vdash \bot$.

Example 8. *In example 1, $a_{11a} = <t, \{ag\}>$ conflicts with $a_2 = <fp, \{w\}>$. Indeed, $Plan(a_{11a}) \cup \Sigma \vdash \{\neg w\}$ and $Plan(a_2) = \{w\}$, thus a_{11a} and a_2 are incompatible.*

Property 1. The *conflicts* relation is symmetrical. However, it is neither *reflexive* nor *transitive*.

Example 9. *Let's consider an agent with a base of desires $\mathcal{D} = \{h_1, h_2, h_3\}$ and a base of plans:*

$$\mathcal{P} = \left\{ \begin{array}{ll} a & \rightarrow h_1 \\ b & \rightarrow h_2 \\ \neg a \wedge \neg b & \rightarrow h_3 \end{array} \right.$$

Let's suppose that $\Sigma = \emptyset$. a_1, a_2 and a_3 are actions such that: $a_1 = <h_1, \{a\}>$, $a_2 = <h_2, \{b\}>$ and $a_3 = <h_3, \{\neg a, \neg b\}>$.

a_1 conflicts with a_3 and a_3 conflicts a_2. However, a_1 does not conflicts with a_2.

Remark 2. *An action may conflict with itself.*

Let's consider the following example:

Example 10. *Let $\mathcal{D} = \{\neg a'\}$, $\mathcal{P} = \{a \wedge b \wedge c \rightarrow \neg a'\}$ and $\Sigma = \{a \rightarrow a'\}$. The action $< \neg a', \{a, b, c\} >$ conflicts with itself.*

3.5   Tree of Realization

In example 1, the action a_2 does not attack action a_1. However, it attacks one of its sub-actions such as a_{11a}. In this case, we cannot say that the two desires $Desire(a_1)$ and $Desire(a_2)$ are realizable in the the same time.

Thus, to check if a given desire is realizable, the corresponding action and all its sub-actions must be taken into account. It is then necessary to introduce a new notion of a *tree of realization* of a given desire.

A *tree of realization* of a given desire d is an *AND* tree. Its nodes are actions and its arcs represent the sub-action relationship. The root of the tree is an action for the desire d.

It is an AND tree because all the sub-actions of a given action must be carried out. When for the same desire, there are several plans to carry it out, only one plan is considered. Formally:

Definition 9. *A tree of realization g of a desire h is a finite tree such that:*

$-\ < h, H >$ *is the root of the tree.*

- A node $< h', \{\varphi_1, \ldots, \varphi_n\} >$ has exactly n children [1] $< \varphi_1, H'_1 >, \ldots, <$ $\varphi_n, H'_n >$.
- The leaves of the tree are atomic actions.

The function $Root(g) = h$ returns the desire of the root. The function $Nodes(g)$ returns the set of all the actions of the tree g.
$\mathcal{G}(\aleph)$ denotes the set of all the trees of realization that we can build from the set $\aleph$.

Remark 3. By analogy with argumentation theory, a realization tree can compared to an argument. A realization tree is built to achieve a given desire whereas an argument is built to support a given conclusion. A conclusion may be supported by several arguments and similarly, a desire can have several trees of realization. This case arises when one of its sub-desires has several plans.

Example 11. In example 1, the desire "jca" whose action is $a_1 = <jca, \{t,$ $vac\}>$ has four trees of realization as shown in Fig. 1.

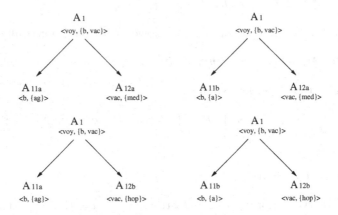

Fig. 1. Trees of realization

Since the actions may be conflicting, two realization trees may then be conflicting too. That relation between realization trees will be called "Attack" relation.

Definition 10 (Attack). Let $g_1, g_2 \in \mathcal{G}(\aleph)$. g_1 attacks g_2 iff $\exists a_1 \in Nodes(g_1)$ and $\exists a_2 \in Nodes(g_2)$ such that a_1 conflicts a_2.

Property 2. The relation attack is symmetrical.

Let's now consider the following example:

---

[1] If a desire has several plans to carry it out, only one is considered in a tree.

Example 12. *Let's suppose an agent equipped with the following bases:* $\mathcal{D} = \{c\}$, $\Sigma = \emptyset$ *and* $\mathcal{P} = \{a \wedge b \rightarrow c, e \rightarrow a, d \wedge g \rightarrow b, \neg e \rightarrow g, x \rightarrow d\}$.
The realization tree of the desire c *contains the following actions:* $< c, \{a, b\} >$, $< a, \{e\} >$, $< b, \{d, g\} >$, $< g, \{\neg e\} >$, $< d, \{x\} >$, $< e, \emptyset >$, $< \neg e, \emptyset >$ *and* $< x, \emptyset >$.
It is clear that $< a, \{e\} >$ *conflicts* $< g, \{\neg e\} >$.

This example shows clearly that a realization tree of a desire can attack itself. Such trees are said *self-attacked realization trees*.

They can be compared to self-defeating arguments. Like conclusions supported only by self-defeating arguments cannot be inferred from a knowledge base (for example), it is obvious that a desire whose trees of realization are all inconsistent is a *rejected* one. This means it is impossible to carry out such desire.

4   A Formal System for Handling Desires

From the preceding definitions, we can now introduce a formal system for handling conflicting desires of an agent.

Definition 11 (System for handling desires). *Let's consider a triple* $<\mathcal{D}$, $\mathcal{P}$, $\Sigma>$.
A system for handling desires (SHD) is a pair $< \mathcal{G}(\aleph), Attack >$ *such that* $\mathcal{G}(\aleph)$ *is a set of realization trees and Attack is a binary relation representing the defeasibility relation between the realization trees (Attack* $\subseteq \mathcal{G}(\aleph) \times \mathcal{G}(\aleph)$).

As in argumentation theory, we partition the set $\mathcal{G}(\aleph)$ into three cateories of realizations trees:

- The class of *acceptable realization trees*. They represent the *good plans* to achieve their corresponding desires. That desires will become the intentions of the agent.
- The class of *rejected realization trees*. They are those attacked by acceptable realization trees.
- The class of *realization trees in abeyance* which gathers the realization trees which are neither acceptable nor rejected.

In what follows we give the different semantics of "acceptable realization trees". We first start by giving new definitions of *conflict-free* and *defence* in the context of conflicting desires.

Definition 12 (Conflict-free). *Let* $< \mathcal{G}(\aleph), Attack >$ *be a SHD and* $S \subseteq \mathcal{G}(\aleph)$. *$S$ is conflict-free iff:* $\nexists\ g_1$ *and* g_2 *in S such that g_1 attacks g_2. It follows that if S is conflict-free then* $\forall g_i \in S$, g_i *is not self-attacked.*

As we can see, the notion of conflict-free is very similar to the one in argumentation theory. However, it is not the case for the notion of defence. The semantics of a realization tree is a complete plan to achieve a desire and our aim is to achieve a maximum of desires. The idea is if a given desire d_1 can be achieved with a plan g_1 then if another plan g_2 for the same desire attacks a plan g_3 of another desire d_2, we will accept g_3 to enable the agent to achieve its two desires. Formally:

Definition 13 (Defence). *Let $< \mathcal{G}(\aleph), Attack >$ be a SHD, $S \subseteq \mathcal{G}(\aleph)$ and $g \in \mathcal{G}(\aleph)$. S defends g iff $\forall g' \in \mathcal{G}(\aleph)$ s.t g' attacks g $\exists g" \in S$ s.t Desire(g") = Desire(g').*

Preferred Extensions

Using the new definition of defence, we show the following property:

Property 3. Each SHD has at least one preferred extension.

Let S_1, ..., S_n be the different preferred extensions of a SHD. For a given set of trees, the function $Desires(S_i) = \{h \in \mathcal{D}$ such that $\exists g \in S_i$ and $Root(g) = h\}$ returns the different desires of these trees.

Property 4. Let $< \mathcal{G}(\aleph), Attack >$ be a SHD and S_1, ..., S_n the corresponding extensions. The sets $Desires(S_1)$, ..., $Desires(S_n)$ are not always maximal (for set inclusion).

Let's consider the follwing example:

Example 13. *In example 1, we can construct 5 realization trees. Four of them correspond to the desire jca. Let's note them g_1, g_2, g_3, g_4. The fifth one corresponds to the desire fp and it is denoted by g_5.*
In this case, we have exactly two extensions:

- $S_1 = \{g_1, g_2, g_3, g_4\}$ *with* $Desires(S_1) = \{jca\}$
- $S_2 = \{g_4, g_5\}$ *with* $Desires(S_2) = \{jca, fp\}$

Note that $Desires(S_1) \subseteq Desirs(S_2)$.

The goal is to carry out the maximum of desires of the agent. In the preceding example, the agent can carry out its two desires in extension S_2. Thus among all the preferred extensions, we keep only those which carry out a maximum of desires (for set inclusion). Let denote them by S_i, ..., S_j.

Example 14. *In example 1, the two desires of the agent become intentions. However, to achieve these intentions, the agent should use the plans of the trees $\{g_4, g_5\}$.*

Preferred extensions give us different sets of desires which may be achieved together. There is no preference between the extensions.

Basic Extension

The basic extension characterises the set of acceptable realization trees by a function $\mathcal{F}$ that returns for each set of realization trees the ones that are defended by that set.

Theorem 1. –
- Let $< \mathcal{G}(\aleph), Attack >$ be a SHD. The function $\mathcal{F}$ is monotonic (for set inclusion). In other terms, if $S, S' \subseteq \mathcal{G}(\aleph)$ such that $S \subseteq S'$ then $\mathcal{F}(S) \subseteq \mathcal{F}(S')$.
- The function $\mathcal{F}$ has a least fixpoint: $\mathcal{S}$
- $\mathcal{S}$ is the basic extension of the SHD.

When the system SHD is finitary (each realization tree is attacked by a finite number of realization trees), the function $\mathcal{F}$ is *continuous*. In that case, the least fixpoint of $\mathcal{F}$ can be obtained by iterative applications of the function $\mathcal{F}$ to the emptyset.

Theorem 2. Let $< \mathcal{G}(\aleph), Attack >$ be a SHD.

- $< \mathcal{G}(\aleph), Attack >$ is finitary.
- $\mathcal{F}$ is continuous.
- The least fixpoint of $\mathcal{F}$ is: $\mathcal{S} = \bigcup_{i \geq 1} F^i(\emptyset) = \mathcal{C} \cup \bigcup_{i \geq 1} F^i(\mathcal{C}))$. $\mathcal{C}$ denotes the set of non-attacked realization trees.

Unlike in argumentation theory, the function $\mathcal{F}$ does not preserve the conflict-free property. In other words, if S is conflict-free, it is not always the case for $\mathcal{F}(S)$. This phenomenon occurs in a very particular case when the two defeasible trees, let's say g_1 and g_2, are both other alternatives of their corrsponding desires. In this case, the second alternatives are both in the set S.

Theorem 3. –
- The set $\mathcal{S}* = \mathcal{S} \setminus \{g, g' \in \mathcal{S} \text{ s.t } g \text{ attacks } g'\}$ is conflict-free.
- The intentions of the agent are gathered in the set $\mathcal{I} = \{Root(g_i) - g_i \in \mathcal{S}*\}$

5   Conclusion

This paper introduces a formal model for computing the intentions of an agent from its set of possibly contradictory desires. We showed how and when desires can conflict. We formalized this concept of conflicts and then we showed how to solve them inspired from work on argumentation theory.

More work, of course, remains to be done in this area. Particularly, we shall study the meaning of other semantics in argumentation like stable extension and complete extensions in our context. In [1], the authors have proposed a proof theory testing whether a given argument is acceptable (using the basic semantics). We shall use those results to test if a given realization tree is acceptable and consequently its desire is an intention.

We shall also enrich the model by introducing preferences between the desires. This will help to refine the classification of the desires by leaving less desires in abeyance. We can imagine two sources of preferences. The first one is the agent itself. This means that an agent can have preferences over its set of desires $\mathcal{D}$. In this case, if there is a conflict between two actions, we keep the one whose desire is mostly preferred by the agent. The second source of preferences is *argumentation*. In this case, two actions a_1 and a_2 can be in conflict but one of them can have a good reason (*argument*) to be carried out. We are currently investigating these matters.

References

1. L. Amgoud and C. Cayrol. A reasoning model based on the production of acceptable arguments. 34:197–216, 2002.
2. M. Bratman. *Intentions, plans, and practical reason.* Harvard University Press, Massachusetts., 1987.
3. M. Bratman, D. Israel, and M. Pollack. *Plans and resource bounded reasoning.*, volume 4. Computational Intelligence., 1988.
4. P.R. Cohen and H.J. Levesque. Intention is choice with commitment. In *Artificial Intelligence*, volume 42, 1990.
5. P.R. Cohen and H.J. Levesque. Rational interaction as the basis for communication. In *In P. R. Cohen, J. Morgan and M. E. Pollack, eds. Intentions in communication*, pages 221–256, 1990.
6. J. Doyle. *Rationality and its role in reasoning.*, volume 8. Computational Intelligence., 1992.
7. P.M. Dung. On the acceptability of arguments and its fundamental role in nonmonotonic reasoning and logic programming. In *Proceedings of the 13th International Joint Conference on Artificial Intelligence, IJCAI'93*, pages 852–857, 1993.
8. P.M. Dung. On the acceptability of arguments and its fundamental role in nonmonotonic reasoning, logic programming and n-person games. *Artificial Intelligence*, 77:321–357, 1995.
9. J. Pearl. From conditional ought to qualitative decision theory. In *Proceedings of UAI'93*, pages 12–20, 1993.
10. A.S. Rao and M.P. Georgeff. Modeling rational agents within a bdi architecture. In *Proceedings of KR'91*, 1991.
11. A.S. Rao and M.P. Georgeff. An abstract architecture for rational agents. In *Proceedings of KR'92*, 1992.
12. A.S. Rao and M.P. Georgeff. Bdi agents: from theory to practice. In *Proceedings of the 1st International Conference on Multi Agent Systems*, pages 312–319, 1995.

A Sequent Calculus for Skeptical Reasoning in Predicate Default Logic

(Extended Abstract)*

Robert Saxon Milnikel

Kenyon College, Gambier, OH 43022, USA
milnikelr@kenyon.edu

Abstract. A sound and complete sequent calculus for skeptical consequence in predicate default logic is presented. While skeptical consequence is decidable in the finite propositional case, the move to predicate or infinite theories increases the complexity of skeptical reasoning to being Π_1^1-complete. This implies the need for sequent rules with countably many premises, and such rules are employed.

1 Introduction

Skeptical consequence is a notion common to all forms of nonmonotonic reasoning. Every nonmonotonic formalism permits different world views to be justified using the same set of facts and principles; the skeptical consequences of a framework are the notions common to all world views associated with that framework. Our purpose in this paper is to present a Gentzen-style sequent calculus (incorporating some infinitary rules) which will allow us to deduce the skeptical consequences of a given framework. Such sequent calculi (with purely finite rules) were defined for several types of nonmonotonic systems by Bonatti and Olivetti in [1], but they restricted their attention to finite propositional systems for which skeptical consequence is decidable. We will adapt and extend their systems to accommodate infinite predicate systems.

We will focus on default logic (Reiter, [2]) in this extended abstract, but there are also versions for stable model logic programming (Gelfond and Lifschitz, [3]), and autoepistemic logic (Moore, [4]) in the full version of this paper. In all three cases, when one steps from the finite and propositional to the predicate and potentially infinite, finding the set of skeptical consequences of a framework goes from being decidable to being Π_1^1-complete, at the same level of the computability hierarchy as true arithmetic. This result was proved for stable model logic programming by Marek, Nerode, and Remmel in [5], but it translates to the other systems quite easily.

Members of Π_1^1 sets correspond to finite-path computable (or Π_1^0) subtrees of $\omega^{<\omega}$ in a very natural way. See [6] for an excellent exposition. This makes

---

* This paper grew out of the author's dissertation, written under the direction of Anil Nerode.

T.D. Nielsen and N.L. Zhang (Eds.): ECSQARU 2003, LNAI 2711, pp. 564–575, 2003.

skeptical consequence a natural fit for sequent calculi with infinitary rules, since a sequent proof is, at its core, a finite-path tree. Bonatti and Olivetti also addressed credulous consequence ("Can this notion be a part of *some* world view?") in their paper, but in the cases they were interested in, this question was also decidable. In our more general context, credulous reasoning is Σ_1^1-complete, not a natural type of question to address with trees-as-proofs. (One could write a sequent calculus for credulous reasoning in Π_2^1 logic, but this would take us too far afield.)

In default logic, there has been debate since Reiter first defined the framework in 1980 about how to treat unbounded variables in the rules. Reiter ([2]) advocated treating open variables (at least in the negative premises of a default rule) in the same way that they are treated in logic programs: as abbreviations for the same rule with each possible ground term of the language substituted. This has the result of turning a finite default theory into an infinite grounded theory; this is the definition we will use in this paper. However, there is some quite justified criticism of this approach. Under these definitions, the default theory $(\dfrac{\;:MP(x)}{P(x)}, \neg P(a))$ does not imply $(\forall x)[P(x) \leftrightarrow x \neq a]$. Lifschitz, in [7], defines extensions (the possible world views associated with default logic) relative to fixed domains. For finite theories and finite domains, everything is decidable, but over infinite domains this is no longer the case. In [8], it is shown that skeptical reasoning over countable domains using Lifschitz' definition of extension is Π_2^1-complete, the same level as for predicate circumscription and thus beyond the scope of this paper.

Because nonmonotonic logics deal not only with proof but with lack of proof, we will need not only standard monotone sequent calculi, but also rule systems for showing a lack of proof. We will call these antisequent calculi, using the terminology of Bonatti from [9]. While propositional provability and lack of provability are decidable, predicate provability is recursively enumerable, and hence predicate nonprovability is co-r.e. Just as Σ_1^1 sets do not lend themselves naturally to tree-based proofs, neither do co-r.e. sets. However, while Σ_1^1 sets required a jump to Π_2^1 logic, co-r.e. sets are easily accommodated in the Π_1^1 framework within which we will already be working. Bringing such enormously powerful logical machinery to bear on such a relatively simple problem may seem like overkill, but it works out quite naturally. The reader is thus warned that infinitary proofs will appear throughout the paper, even when talking about something as simple as lack of a standard predicate logic proof.

2   Default Logic Preliminaries

We will assume that the reader has some familiarity with classical propositional and predicate logic, including the notion of a Herbrand base for a given predicate language and the standard sequent calculus **LK** for predicate logic.

Default logic is one of the most intuitive and widely-studied nonmonotonic formalisms. Default logics are built upon classical propositional or predicate logic, and we will assume the reader is familiar with the languages and the basics of axiomatic treatments of these logics.

Definition 1 (Default).

Let $\mathcal{L}$ be a predicate language. A default is a triple $\langle \varphi, \Psi, \theta \rangle$ where φ and θ are formulas from $\mathcal{L}$ and $\Psi = \{\psi_1, \ldots, \psi_n\}$ is a finite set of formulas from $\mathcal{L}$. A default is usually written

$$\frac{\varphi \; : \; M\psi_1, \ldots, M\psi_m}{\theta},$$

with the intended interpretation "if φ is true and each ψ_i is possible, conclude θ."

The formula φ will be called the prerequisite of the default, Ψ the justifications, and θ the conclusion. If a default contains formulas with unbounded variables, we will refer to the default as open. A default that is not open is closed.

A default theory is a pair (D, W), where D is a set of defaults and W is a set of formulas of $\mathcal{L}$. Note that we do not restrict D or W to being finite. If both D and W are finite, we will refer to (D, W) as a finite default theory. If D contains open defaults, we will call (D, W) an open default theory. If D consists entirely of closed defaults, we will call (D, W) closed.

We will not want to work directly with default rules containing open formulas, but will look at a default which includes an open formula among its prerequisite, justifications, and conclusion as an abbreviation for the set of groundings of that formula.

Let $d = \dfrac{\varphi; M\psi_1, \ldots, M\psi_n}{\theta}$ be an open default. The *grounding of d*, denoted ground(d), will be the set of closed defaults obtained by replacing each unbounded variable x occurring in d by some ground term t of $\mathcal{L}$, and doing so uniformly throughout the default. (If d is not open, let ground(d) = $\{d\}$.) Let us define the grounding of a set D of defaults to be the set of all defaults occurring in the grounding of some default in D. (So ground(D) = $\bigcup\{$ground(d)$|d \in D\}$.) We will occasionally abuse notation by writing ground((D, W)) for (ground(D), W). Note that D = ground(D) if D is closed. One effect of grounding is that if $\mathcal{L}$ contains an infinite number of ground terms, then even when D is finite, ground(D) might be infinite.

It will simplify work we will do later to look at sets which contain both defaults and formulas. We can define the language $\mathcal{L}^{def}$ as the union of all formulas in $\mathcal{L}$ with the collection of all defaults constructed from formulas of $\mathcal{L}$. This will allow us to express the default theory (D, W) as the single set $D \cup W$ in $\mathcal{L}^{def}$.

Example 1. Let $\mathcal{L}$ be a language with equality, one constant 0, one unary function S, and a unary relation A. Let us examine the default theory (D, W) where W is a classical theory with axioms for equality and the sentences $\forall x, y(A(x) \wedge A(y) \rightarrow x = y)$ and $\forall x(x \neq Sx)$. Let $D = \{\dfrac{: MA(x)}{A(x)}\}$. The

classical part insists upon an infinite domain and says "$A(x)$ holds of at most one x," while the open default chooses an x at random for which $A(x)$ will hold. The grounding of D is, of course, $\{\dfrac{:MA(0)}{A(0)}, \dfrac{:MA(S0)}{A(S0)}, \dfrac{:MA(SS0)}{A(SS0)},$
$\dfrac{:MA(SSS0)}{A(SSS0)}, \ldots\}.$

Default rules without justifications ($\dfrac{\varphi:}{\theta}$) are monotonic and classical in nature. It should not cause confusion if we conflate these with classical rules of inference of the form $\dfrac{\varphi}{\theta}$. When such rules arise from considering a default $\dfrac{\varphi:M\psi_1,\ldots,M\psi_n}{\theta}$ in a context in which the ψ_i's are guaranteed to be possible, we will call them *residues*. We will define $\mathcal{L}^{res}$ analogously to $\mathcal{L}^{def}$, as the formulas of $\mathcal{L}$ taken together with residues built from $\mathcal{L}$.

We will say that the *closure* of a set $\Gamma \subseteq \mathcal{L}^{res}$, denoted $\mathrm{Cl}(\Gamma)$, is the least set T of formulas of $\mathcal{L}$ which is deductively closed, $\Gamma \cap \mathcal{L} \subseteq T$, and has the additional property that if $\dfrac{\varphi}{\theta} \in \Gamma$ and $\varphi \in T$ then $\theta \in T$. We are now in a position to define reducts of default theories and extensions for default theories.

Definition 2 (Reduct of a Default Theory).
Let S be a set of formulas of $\mathcal{L}$.

1. *A default*
$$\frac{\varphi:M\psi_1,\ldots,M\psi_n}{\theta}$$
   is irrelevant with respect to S if $\neg\psi_j \in S$ for at least one ψ_j.
2. *Let Γ be a closed default theory (in $\mathcal{L}^{def}$). The reduct of Γ with respect to S, denoted by Γ_S, is obtained from Γ by:*
   a) *Removing all defaults that are irrelevant with respect to S.*
   b) *Replacing each remaining default*
$$\frac{\varphi:M\psi_1,\ldots,M\psi_n}{\theta}$$
   with its residue $\dfrac{\varphi}{\theta}$.

What remains after taking the reduct Γ_S of a default theory Γ is a residue theory.

Definition 3 (Default Extension).
Let $\Gamma = D \cup W$ be a closed default theory. We say that a set of formulas S of $\mathcal{L}$ is a default extension for Γ if $S = \mathrm{Cl}(\Gamma_S)$. We will say that S is an extension of open default theory Γ if S is an extension of ground(Γ).

Example 2. Let us reexamine Example 1 in light of these two definitions. Let us choose a fixed n and let $S = Th(W \cup \{A(\underline{n})\})$. (We use the convention that $\underline{n}$ is

n S's followed by a 0.) From W and $A(\underline{n})$, we can prove $\neg A(\underline{m})$ for all $m \neq n$, so the only default which is relevant in context S is $\dfrac{: MA(\underline{n})}{A(\underline{n})}$. Its residue is $\overline{A(\underline{n})}$, and clearly $Th(W \cup \{A(\underline{n})\}) = \mathrm{Cl}(W \cup \{\overline{A(\underline{n})}\})$. Thus, we see that the extensions of (D, W) will be $\{Th(W \cup \{A(\underline{n})\}) | n \in \omega\}$. (If A fails for all x, then all defaults would be relevant, and $A(x)$ would be derivable for all x, leading to a contradiction.)

Definition 4 (Skeptical Consequence).
A formula φ in predicate language $\mathcal{L}$ is in the set of skeptical consequences *of a default theory (D, W) if for every extension S of (D, W), $\varphi \in S$.*

Example 3. We will continue to exploit Example 1. We saw in Example 2 that extensions of (D, W) are $\{Th(W \cup \{A(\underline{n})\}) | n \in \omega\}$. The only items common to all of these are the consequences of W along with the sentence $\exists x A(x)$, making $Th(W \cup \{\exists x A(x)\})$ the set of skeptical consequences of (D, W). There is no compactness theorem for skeptical consequence. By that we mean that although in each particular extension S of (D, W), some finite portion of the reduct of the theory was used to prove $\exists x A(x)$, there is no finite portion of ground(D) which is responsible for $\exists x A(x)$ being present in all extensions.

3   Skeptical Sequent Calculus for Default Logic

Throughout this section, we will be working in a predicate language $\mathcal{L}$ without equality. (Our running example uses equality, but our use of equality is quite limited and could be accommodated by a defined equivalence relation.)

The definition of an extension insists that certain formulas be derivable and that others not be derivable (to keep the defaults used in the derivations relevant). Thus, as we accumulate information about potential extensions by backtracking through a sequent proof, we will find that we need to establish, at various points, both derivability and non-derivability. Because of the compactness of classical logic, establishing derivability will be straightforward. Establishing non-derivability, on the other hand, will be quite complicated. However, when we limit ourselves to finite sets of premises, non-derivability is fairly straightforward to establish.

3.1   An Antisequent Calculus for Predicate Logic

Bonatti in [9] presented an antisequent calculus for propositional logic, and our antisequent calculus will be the one of that paper extended by four rules. The four rules we add to Bonatti's formulation are counterparts of the four rules for quantifiers from Gentzen's **LK**. We assume that the reader is familiar with Gentzen's sequent calculus **LK**, and will here list only the rules pertaining to quantifiers. In the rules $\vdash \forall$ and $\exists \vdash$, we must insist that x not appear as a free variable in Γ or in Δ. (This formulation is drawn from [10].)

Table 1. Quantifier Rules from the Sequent Calculus LK

$$(\forall \vdash) \ \frac{\Gamma, \varphi(t) \vdash \Delta}{\Gamma, (\forall x)\varphi(x) \vdash \Delta} \quad (\vdash \forall) \ \frac{\Gamma \vdash \Delta, \varphi(x)}{\Gamma \vdash \Delta, (\forall x)\varphi(x)}$$

$$(\exists \vdash) \ \frac{\Gamma, \varphi(x) \vdash \Delta}{\Gamma, (\exists x)\varphi(x) \vdash \Delta} \quad (\vdash \exists) \ \frac{\Gamma \vdash \Delta, \varphi(t)}{\Gamma \vdash \Delta, (\exists x)\varphi(x)}$$

Because of the way extensions of open default theories are defined, the general case of skeptical default reasoning for even finite predicate default theories will necessitate infinitary sequent rules. For this reason, we will not hesitate to bring the enormous Π_1^1 power of infinitary sequent rules to bear on our comparatively simple Π_1^0 problem of showing that there is no proof in the sequent calculus **LK** of the sequent $\Gamma \vdash \Delta$.

An *antisequent* is a pair $\langle \Gamma, \Delta \rangle$ of finite sets of formulas, denoted $\Gamma \nvdash \Delta$. We will call $\Gamma \nvdash \Delta$ *true* if there is a model of Γ in which all of the formulas of Δ are false. We have the benefit of the Soundness and Completeness Theorems for **LK**, which tells us that $\Gamma \nvdash \Delta$ is true if and only if $\Gamma \vdash \Delta$ is false if and only if $\Gamma \vdash \Delta$ is not derivable in **LK**.

An antisequent $\Gamma \nvdash \Delta$ will be considered an *axiom* of our antisequent calculus if $\Gamma \cup \Delta$ consists entirely of atomic formulas and $\Gamma \cap \Delta = \emptyset$. The rules for the antisequent calculus can be found in Table 2.

The usual proviso that x may not be free in $\Gamma \cup \Delta$ applies to $\nvdash \forall$ and $\exists \nvdash$.

Showing that the antisequent calculus is sound is the counterpart to showing the classical sequent calculus **LK** complete, and vice versa. The classical theorems are relied on heavily in the proof of the following theorem:

Theorem 1. *Antisequent $\Gamma \nvdash \Delta$ is provable if and only if it is true.*

Example 4. Let us show that $(\forall x)(P(x) \vee Q(x)) \nvdash (\forall y)(P(y)) \vee (\forall z)(Q(z))$ for unary relations P and Q. The following is a partial proof, with an infinite number of premises remaining at the top.

$$\frac{\{P(t) \vee Q(t) \nvdash P(y), Q(z) | t \text{ is a term of } \mathcal{L}\}}{\dfrac{(\forall x)(P(x) \vee Q(x)) \nvdash P(y), Q(z)}{\dfrac{(\forall x)(P(x) \vee Q(x)) \nvdash P(y), (\forall z)(Q(z))}{\dfrac{(\forall x)(P(x) \vee Q(x)) \nvdash (\forall y)(P(y)), (\forall z)(Q(z))}{(\forall x)(P(x) \vee Q(x)) \nvdash (\forall y)(P(y)) \vee (\forall z)(Q(z))}}}}$$

We are left with an infinite number of premises of the form $P(t) \vee Q(t) \nvdash P(y), Q(z)$ to prove. By rules ($\bullet \vee \nvdash$) and ($\vee \bullet \nvdash$), we need to be able to show only either $P(t) \nvdash P(y), Q(z)$ or $Q(t) \nvdash P(y), Q(z)$. As long as $t \neq y$, $P(t) \nvdash P(y), Q(z)$ is an axiom. If $t = y$, $Q(t) \nvdash P(y), Q(z)$ is an axiom. This provides us with proofs of all of the infinitely many premises of the form $P(t) \vee Q(t) \nvdash P(y), Q(z)$ and completes the proof.

Table 2. Rules of the Antisequent Calculus

$$
(\neg \nvdash) \quad \frac{\Gamma \nvdash \Delta, \varphi}{\Gamma, \neg\varphi \nvdash \Delta}
\qquad\qquad
(\nvdash \neg) \quad \frac{\Gamma, \varphi \nvdash \Delta}{\Gamma \nvdash \Delta, \neg\varphi}
$$

$$
(\wedge \nvdash) \quad \frac{\Gamma, \varphi, \psi \nvdash \Delta}{\Gamma, \varphi \wedge \psi \nvdash \Delta}
\qquad\qquad
(\nvdash \bullet\wedge) \quad \frac{\Gamma \nvdash \Delta, \varphi}{\Gamma \nvdash \Delta, \varphi \wedge \psi}
$$

$$
(\nvdash \wedge\bullet) \quad \frac{\Gamma \nvdash \Delta, \psi}{\Gamma \nvdash \Delta, \varphi \wedge \psi}
$$

$$
(\bullet\vee \nvdash) \quad \frac{\Gamma, \varphi \nvdash \Delta}{\Gamma, \varphi \vee \psi \nvdash \Delta}
\qquad\qquad
(\nvdash \vee) \quad \frac{\Gamma \nvdash \Delta, \varphi, \psi}{\Gamma \nvdash \Delta, \varphi \vee \psi}
$$

$$
(\vee\bullet \nvdash) \quad \frac{\Gamma, \psi \nvdash \Delta}{\Gamma, \varphi \vee \psi \nvdash \Delta}
$$

$$
(\bullet \to \nvdash) \quad \frac{\Gamma \nvdash \Delta, \varphi}{\Gamma, \varphi \to \psi \nvdash \Delta}
\qquad\qquad
(\nvdash \to) \quad \frac{\Gamma, \varphi \nvdash \Delta, \psi}{\Gamma \nvdash \Delta, \varphi \to \psi}
$$

$$
(\bullet \to \nvdash) \quad \frac{\Gamma, \psi \nvdash \Delta}{\Gamma, \varphi \to \psi \nvdash \Delta}
$$

$$
(\forall \nvdash) \quad \frac{\{\Gamma, \varphi(t) \nvdash \Delta \mid t \text{ is a term in } \mathcal{L}\}}{\Gamma, (\forall x)\varphi(x) \nvdash \Delta}
\qquad
(\nvdash \forall) \quad \frac{\Gamma \nvdash \Delta, \varphi(x)}{\Gamma \nvdash \Delta, (\forall x)\varphi(x)}
$$

$$
(\exists \nvdash) \quad \frac{\Gamma, \varphi(x) \nvdash \Delta}{\Gamma, (\exists x)\varphi(x) \nvdash \Delta}
\qquad
(\nvdash \exists) \quad \frac{\{\Gamma \nvdash \Delta, \varphi(t) \mid t \text{ is a term in } \mathcal{L}\}}{\Gamma \nvdash \Delta, (\exists x)\varphi(x)}
$$

3.2 A Sequent Calculus and an Antisequent Calculus for Residues

The sequent calculus for monotone proofs based on predicate logic will be the standard propositional sequent calculus **LK** extended by two rules for dealing with residues, very closely related to our one-rule sequent calculus for Horn programs.

A *residue sequent* is a pair $\langle \Gamma, \Delta \rangle$ where both $\Gamma \subseteq \mathcal{L}^{res}$ and $\Delta \subseteq \mathcal{L}$ are finite, and is usually written $\Gamma \vdash \Delta$. We say that $\Gamma \vdash \Delta$ is *true* if $\bigvee \Delta \in \mathrm{Cl}(\Gamma)$.

If we extend the classical predicate sequent calculus **LK** (restricted to $\mathcal{L}$) by the following two rules about residues, we obtain a sequent calculus for residues.

$$
\frac{\Gamma \vdash \Delta}{\Gamma, \frac{\varphi}{\theta} \vdash \Delta}
\qquad\qquad
\frac{\Gamma \vdash \varphi \quad \Gamma, \theta \vdash \Delta}{\Gamma, \frac{\varphi}{\theta} \vdash \Delta}
$$

This sequent calculus for residues was defined by Bonatti and Olivetti in [1], and they proved this theorem about it:

Theorem 2. $\Gamma \vdash \Delta$ *is derivable in the sequent calculus for residues if and only if it is true.*

Their proof was based on the soundness and completeness of propositional rather than predicate logic, but the proof in either case is identical.

We can also extend antisequents to deductions from residues. A *residue antisequent* will be a pair of finite sets $\Gamma \subseteq \mathcal{L}^{res}$ and $\Delta \subseteq \mathcal{L}$ written $\Gamma \nvdash \Delta$. And just as the residue sequent $\Gamma \vdash \Delta$ was considered true if $\bigvee \Delta \in \mathrm{Cl}(\Gamma)$, we will consider the residue antisequent $\Gamma \nvdash \Delta$ to be *true* if $\bigvee \Delta \notin \mathrm{Cl}(\Gamma)$. Just as we extended the classical sequent calculus (limited to $\mathcal{L}$) by two rules to produce a sound and complete residue sequent calculus, we will also extend the predicate antisequent calculus (again limited to $\mathcal{L}$) by the two rules below to produce a sound and complete residue antisequent calculus.

$$\frac{\Gamma \nvdash \Delta \quad \Gamma \nvdash \varphi}{\Gamma, \frac{\varphi}{\theta} \nvdash \Delta} \qquad \frac{\Gamma, \theta \nvdash \Delta}{\Gamma, \frac{\varphi}{\theta} \nvdash \Delta}$$

Bonatti and Olivetti proved the following in [1]:

Theorem 3. *Antisequent* $\Gamma \nvdash \Delta$ *is derivable in the antisequent calculus of residues if and only if it is true.*

Again, their proof was for a residue antisequent calculus built over propositional rather than predicate logic, but the same proof works here.

3.3   Skeptical Sequent Calculus

One can think of Gentzen proof systems as failed exhaustive searches for countermodels. Thus, what we will want to do as we search for a countermodel to the claim "All extensions of default theory (D, W) must contain φ" is keep track of which formulas are in and out of our potential countermodel to the claim. We will want to make sure that all formulas we would like to see in our potential countermodel do, in fact, have proofs; and we want also to make sure that all formulas we plan to exclude do not have proofs. Finally, we will use our increasing information about the potential countermodel to determine which defaults will be dismissed as irrelevant and which will be retained as residues.

The sequents for skeptical reasoning for default logic will be triples $\langle \Sigma, \Gamma, \Delta \rangle$, usually notated $\Sigma; \Gamma \mathrel{|\!\sim} \Delta$. This notation is drawn directly from [1]. The sets Γ and Δ are relatively straightforward. Γ is a closed predicate default theory, and Δ is a set of formulas of $\mathcal{L}$, neither necessarily finite. The set Σ is more complicated. In Bonatti and Olivetti's formulation, it was a finite collection of *provability constraints* of the form $L\varphi$ or $\neg L\varphi$ where $\phi \in \mathcal{L}$. The intention was to suggest the modal operator L, and indicate whether φ was in or out of the potential countermodel, as it exists so far. We will need to extend the notion of a provability constraint to be more explicit than "φ can be proved." We will need to be able to say "φ can be proved from these specific rules." Thus, in addition to provability constraints of the form $L\varphi$ and $\neg L\varphi$ (which we will call *implicit provability constraints*), we will also include *explicit provability constraints* $L_\Gamma \varphi$ where Γ is a finite set of formulas from $\mathcal{L}$. The intended meaning of $L_\Gamma \varphi$ is "$\Gamma \vdash \varphi$." Together, explicit and implicit provability constraints will be known as *general provability constraints.* We can now finally describe Σ as a set of general provability constraints.

We will say that a theory $T \subseteq \mathcal{L}$ satisfies $L\varphi$ if $\varphi \in T$ and satisfies $\neg L\varphi$ if $\varphi \notin T$. We will say that T satisfies $L_\Gamma \varphi$ if $\varphi \in T$ and in addition $\Gamma \vdash \varphi$.

The reader may wonder why we do not need explicit provability constraints of the form $\neg L_\Gamma \varphi$. We will be making claims both of the form "φ has a proof" and of the form "φ has no proof". To contradict a claim of the form "φ has no proof," it is necessary simply to exhibit a single proof of φ. On the other hand, to contradict a claim of the form "φ has a proof," we must look at all possible proofs of φ, that is all (relevant) explicit proof constraints.

We will say that $\Sigma; \Gamma \! \sim \! \Delta$ is *true* if every extension S of $\Gamma \subseteq \mathcal{L}^{def}$ which satisfies all constraints in Σ includes at least one member of Δ. Thus, φ is a skeptical consequence of the default theory (D, W) if $\emptyset; \text{ground}((D, W)) \! \sim \! \varphi$ is a true sequent.

This calculus incorporates three sorts of sequents: residue sequents, residue antisequents, and the skeptical reasoning sequents just defined. The sequent calculus for skeptical reasoning will include all axioms and rules of the residue sequent and antisequent calculi, plus five new rules. (No additional axioms will be necessary. The leaves of every proof tree will be classical predicate sequent and antisequent axioms.)

Definition 5 (Skeptical Sequent Calculus – Default Logic).

The axioms of the skeptical sequent calculus are classical predicate sequents $\Gamma \vdash \Delta$ with $\Gamma \cap \Delta \neq \emptyset$; and predicate antisequents $\Gamma \nvdash \Delta$ with $\Gamma \cup \Delta$ all atomic formulas and $\Gamma \cap \Delta = \emptyset$. The rules are:

0. *The rules of **LK** and the antisequent rules from Table 2, all limited to sequents and antisequents in $\mathcal{L}$; plus the two pairs of additional rules for residue sequents and antisequents.*

1. $\dfrac{\Sigma', \Gamma' \vdash \Delta'}{\Sigma; \Gamma \! \sim \! \Delta}$ *where $\Gamma' \subseteq \Gamma \cap \mathcal{L}^{res}$ is finite, $\Sigma' \subseteq (\{\varphi | L\varphi \in \Sigma\} \cup \{\varphi | L_{\Gamma''}\varphi \in \Sigma$ for some $\Gamma''\})$, and $\Delta' \subseteq \Delta$ is finite.*

2. $\dfrac{\Sigma', \Gamma' \vdash \varphi}{\neg L\varphi, \Sigma; \Gamma \! \sim \! \Delta}$ *where $\Gamma' \subseteq \Gamma \cap \mathcal{L}^{res}$ is finite, $\Sigma' \subseteq (\{\varphi | L\varphi \in \Sigma\} \cup \{\varphi | L_{\Gamma''}\varphi \in \Sigma$ for some $\Gamma''\})$.*

3. $\dfrac{\Gamma_0 \nvdash \varphi}{L_{\Gamma_0}\varphi, \Sigma; \Gamma \! \sim \! \Delta}$ *where $\Gamma_0 \subseteq \mathcal{L}^{res}$ is finite.*

4. $\dfrac{\{L_{\Gamma_0'}\varphi, \Sigma, \Sigma_0'; \Gamma_0', (\Gamma \setminus \Gamma') \! \sim \! \Delta | \Gamma' \subseteq \Gamma \text{ is finite}\}}{L\varphi, \Sigma; \Gamma \! \sim \! \Delta}$ *where*

   $\Gamma_0' = \{\dfrac{\varphi}{\theta} | \dfrac{\varphi; M\psi_1, \ldots, M\psi_n}{\theta} \in \Gamma'\}$ *and $\Sigma_0' = \{\neg L \neg \psi | \psi = \psi_j$ for some $\dfrac{\varphi; M\psi_1, \ldots, M\psi_n}{\theta} \in \Gamma'$ and some $1 \leq j \leq n\}$.*

5. $\dfrac{\neg L\neg\psi_1, \ldots, \neg L\neg\psi_n, \Sigma; \Gamma, \dfrac{\varphi}{\theta} \! \sim \! \Delta \quad L\neg\psi_1, \Sigma; \Gamma \! \sim \! \Delta \quad \cdots \quad L\neg\psi_n, \Sigma; \Gamma \! \sim \! \Delta}{\Sigma; \Gamma, \dfrac{\varphi; M\psi_1, \ldots, M\psi_n}{\theta} \! \sim \! \Delta}$

The reader may recall from the introduction that we noted that infinitary rules of inference would be necessary in some cases. When applied to a sequent with infinite Γ, rule 4 has infinitely many premises.

Let us examine what each of these rules accomplishes, thinking of ourselves as traversing a completed proof backwards, from conclusions to premises, examining each branch as a failed attempt to find a counterexample to the assertion made at the root of the tree. Just as we are moving backwards through the proof, let us also move backwards through the rules.

Rule 5 says: "Either default $\dfrac{\varphi; M\psi_1, \ldots, M\psi_n}{\theta}$ is relevant or it is not. If it is relevant, make sure that the context reflects that, and put the residue $\dfrac{\varphi}{\theta}$ into our list of usable rules. If it is not relevant, it must be because $\neg\psi_j$ is in the context for some ψ_j."

Rule 4 says: "If we are asserting that φ is in the extension we are trying to build, it must have a proof from the available clauses. Because in different extensions, it might have different proofs, we will need to examine each possible proof independently. If defaults from Γ are used, update the context to reflect their usability and replace them in Γ with their residues."

Rule 3 says: "If we have said that $\Gamma_0 \vdash \varphi$ and yet we can show that $\Gamma_0 \nvdash \varphi$, show this and stop."

Rule 2 says: "If we have said that φ has no proof, and yet from what we already know about the potential extension we are building we can show that that extension must contain φ, show this and stop."

Rule 1 says: "If from what we already know about the potential extension we are building, we can show that a member of Δ must be in that extension, show this and stop."

Example 5. We stated in Example 3 that $\exists x A(x)$ is in the set of skeptical consequences of default theory (D, W) from Example 1. Let us now show how our skeptical sequent calculus would prove this. The sequent we want to prove, then is:

$$; W, \frac{: MA(0)}{A(0)}, \frac{: MA(S0)}{A(S0)}, \frac{: MA(SS0)}{A(SS0)}, \ldots \mathrel{|\!\!\sim} \exists x A(x).$$

We will prove this sequent by rule 5. The two premises we will need are:

$$\neg L \neg A(0); W, \frac{}{A(0)}, \frac{: MA(S0)}{A(S0)}, \frac{: MA(SS0)}{A(SS0)}, \ldots \mathrel{|\!\!\sim} \exists x A(x)$$

and

$$L \neg A(0); W \frac{: MA(S0)}{A(S0)}, \frac{: MA(SS0)}{A(SS0)}, \ldots \mathrel{|\!\!\sim} \exists x A(x).$$

These sequents will have very different proofs. We can prove the former by means of rule 2, since $\dfrac{}{A(0)}$ is among the residue clauses in the Γ of the sequent, and a residue proof of $\exists x A(x)$ from $\dfrac{}{A(0)}$ is trivial. The latter we will prove by means of rule 4, which will have infinitely many premises, each of the form

$$L_{\Gamma_0'}, \Sigma_0'; \Gamma_0', (\Gamma \setminus \Gamma') \hspace{-0.3em}\sim\hspace{-0.3em} \exists x A(x)$$

where

$$\Gamma = W \cup \{ \frac{: MA(S0)}{A(S0)}, \frac{: MA(SS0)}{A(SS0)}, \frac{: MA(SSS0)}{A(SSS0)}, \dots \}.$$

We will look at a few representative premises. In each case, writing out the sequent with Γ_0 and the other terms expanded to fit the particular case would be unwieldy, so we will simply use the template above and refer to Γ_0' and so forth by name.

- In the case that Γ' consists of $\dfrac{: MA(SS0)}{A(SS0)}$ and $\forall x, y(A(x) \wedge A(y) \to x = y)$ plus enough of W to prove $SS0 \neq 0$, Γ_0' will consist of $\dfrac{}{A(SS0)}$ and $\forall x, y(A(x) \wedge A(y) \to x = y)$ together with the rest of the portions of Γ' drawn from W. Σ_0' will consist of $\neg L \neg A(SS0)$.

  In this case, the premise can be proved using rule 1, since $\dfrac{}{A(SS0)} \in \Gamma_0'$ and $\dfrac{}{A(SS0)} \vdash \exists x A(x)$.

- In the case that Γ' consists of $\dfrac{: MA(SS0)}{A(SS0)}$, $\forall x, y(A(x) \wedge A(y) \to x = y)$, and $\dfrac{: MA(SSS0)}{A(SSS0)}$, plus enough of W to prove $SS0 \neq 0$, we could proceed just as in the above case. We do have another option open to us in this case, though, which will illustrate the use of rule 2. Γ_0' will include both $\dfrac{}{A(SS0)}$ and $\dfrac{}{A(SSS0)}$, while Σ_0' will consist of both $\neg L \neg A(SS0)$ and $\neg L \neg A(SSS0)$. By taking $\dfrac{}{A(SS0)}$ from Γ_0' and the relevant portions of W from $\Gamma \setminus \Gamma'$, we can show that

$$\frac{}{A(SS0)}, \forall x, y(A(x) \wedge A(y) \to x = y), SS0 \neq SSS0, \vdash \neg A(SSS0)$$

  and use rule 2 to prove the desired sequent.

- In the case that Γ' is drawn entirely from W, it is not hard to show that $\Gamma_0' = \Gamma'$, and we can show $\Gamma_0' \nvdash \neg A(0)$. We can then use rule 3 to prove our sequent.

We have seen that we can derive at least some of the sequents which are rule 4 premises using rules 1, 2, and 3. In fact, all of the infinite set of premises of our particular application of rule 4 can be proved using these three rules. One application of rule 4 gets us one of our two premises of our desired case of rule 5, and the other was proved directly by rule 2. With one application of rule 5, our deduction is complete.

We conclude with the expected soundness and completeness theorem.

Theorem 4. *A default logic skeptical reasoning sequent* $\Sigma; \Gamma \mid\!\sim \Delta$ *is true if and only if it is provable.*

Proof. Due to limitations of space, only the barest sketch of a proof may be presented here. Proofs of the soundness of each of the five rules are straightforward and independent of each other. To prove the adequacy of the rules listed to generate all true sequents, we show that any sequent which has no deduction is false. If we let $\Sigma; \Gamma \mid\!\sim \Delta$ be a non-deducible sequent, we can build a failed attempt at a deduction which is guaranteed to have at least one branch not terminating in an axiom. Because of the nature of the five rules, only rules 4 and 5 will be used along this non-terminating branch. The context developed along this branch expanding by those two rules will be a witness to the falsehood of $\Sigma; \Gamma \mid\!\sim \Delta$.

We have now seen a sequent calculus for skeptical reasoning in default logic; versions exist for stable model logic programming and autoepistemic logic. One obvious direction in which to extend this work would be to do the same for predicate circumscription, which would require a Π_2^1 sequent calculus. One important feature of the calculus presented above is that the assertion that φ simply *has* a proof is not enough. We must look at all possible proofs of φ. This necessity to take an assertion of the existence of a proof and explicate it with an actual proof strongly suggests a connection with Artemov's logic of proofs (see [11]).

References

1. Bonatti, P., Olivetti, N.: Sequent calculi for propositional nonmonotonic logics. ACM Trans. Comput. Log. **3** (2002) 226–278
2. Reiter, R.: A logic for default reasoning. Art. Int. **13** (1980) 81–132
3. Gelfond, M., Lifschitz, V.: The stable semantics for logic programs. In Kowalski, R.A., Bowen, K.A., eds.: Proceedings of the 5th Annual Symposium on Logic Programming, MIT Press (1988) 1070–1080
4. Moore, R.C.: Possible-world semantics for the autoepistemic logic. In Reiter, R., ed.: Proceedings of the Workshop on Non-Monotonic Reasoning. (1984) 344–354
5. Marek, V.W., Nerode, A., Remmel, J.B.: The stable models of a predicate logic program. J. Log. Prog. **21** (1994) 129–154
6. Cenzer, D., Remmel, J.B.: π_1^0 classes in mathematics. In Ershov, Y.L., Goncharov, S.S., Marek, V.W., Nerode, A., Remmel, J.B., eds.: Handbook of Recursive Mathematics. Volume 2. North-Holland, Amsterdam (1998) 623–821
7. Lifschitz, V.: On open defaults. In Lloyd, J.W., ed.: Computational Logic. Symposium Proceedings, Springer-Verlag (1990) 80–95
8. Milnikel, R.S.: The complexity of predicate default logic over a countable domain. Ann. Pure Appl. Log. **120** (2003) 151–163
9. Bonatti, P.: A gentzen system for non-theorems. Technical Report CD-TR 93/52, Christian Doppler Labor für Expertensysteme (1993)
10. Barwise, J.: An introduction to first-order logic. In Barwise, J., ed.: Handbook of Mathematical Logic. North-Holland, Amsterdam (1977) 5–46
11. Artemov, S.N.: Explicit provability and constructive semantics. Bull. Symbolic Logic **7** (2001) 1–36

Probabilistic Lexicographic Entailment under Variable-Strength Inheritance with Overriding

Thomas Lukasiewicz*

Dipartimento di Informatica e Sistemistica, Università di Roma "La Sapienza"
Via Salaria 113, I-00198 Rome, Italy
lukasiewicz@dis.uniroma1.it

Abstract. In previous work, I have presented approaches to *nonmonotonic probabilistic reasoning*, which is a probabilistic generalization of default reasoning from conditional knowledge bases. In this paper, I continue this exciting line of research. I present a new probabilistic generalization of Lehmann's lexicographic entailment, called lex_λ-entailment, which is parameterized through a value $\lambda \in [0, 1]$ that describes the strength of the inheritance of purely probabilistic knowledge. Roughly, the new notion of entailment is obtained from logical entailment in model-theoretic probabilistic logic by adding (i) the inheritance of purely probabilistic knowledge of strength λ, and (ii) a mechanism for resolving inconsistencies due to the inheritance of logical and purely probabilistic knowledge. I also explore the semantic properties of lex_λ-entailment.

1 Introduction

During the recent decades, there has been a significant amount of research in AI that concentrates on probabilistic reasoning with interval restrictions for conditional probabilities, also called *conditional constraints* [26]. The main focus of this research was especially on the computational aspects of probabilistic reasoning in model-theoretic probabilistic logic, which is a major approach for handling conditional constraints that can be traced back to Boole [8]. A wide spectrum of formal languages has been explored in model-theoretic probabilistic logic, ranging from constraints for unconditional and conditional events (e.g., [1,14,25,26,28,32]) to linear inequalities over events [12]. Probabilistic reasoning in model-theoretic probabilistic logic, however, is not the only way of handling conditional constraints. An alternative approach to probabilistic reasoning with conditional constraints is based on the coherence principle of de Finetti (e.g., [5, 16,17]) and has been extensively explored especially in the field of statistics.

Example 1.1. Suppose we have the knowledge "ostriches are birds", "birds have legs", "birds fly with a probability of at least 0.95", and "ostriches fly with a probability of at most 0.05". In model-theoretic probabilistic logic, we then conclude that both birds and ostriches have legs, and that birds (resp., ostriches) fly with a probability of at least 0.95 (resp., at most 0.05). In coherence-based probabilistic logic, in contrast, we conclude that birds (resp., ostriches) have (resp., do not have) legs, and that they fly with a probability of at least 0.95 (resp., at most 0.05). □

---

* Alternate address: Institut für Informationssysteme, Technische Universität Wien, Favoritenstraße 9-11, A-1040 Vienna, Austria; e-mail: lukasiewicz@kr.tuwien.ac.at.

T.D. Nielsen and N.L. Zhang (Eds.): ECSQARU 2003, LNAI 2711, pp. 576–587, 2003.
© Springer-Verlag Berlin Heidelberg 2003

The relationship between model-theoretic and coherence-based probabilistic logic has recently been explored in [7]. In particular, it turned out that model-theoretic entailment is strictly stronger that entailment under coherence, while satisfiability in model-theoretic probabilistic logic is strictly weaker than consistency in probabilistic logic under coherence. Furthermore, model-theoretic probabilistic entailment is well-known to be a generalization of model-theoretic entailment in classical propositional logics, while probabilistic entailment under coherence is a generalization of classical default entailment from conditional knowledge bases in System P.

Hence, it is natural to wonder whether there are probabilistic generalizations of other formalisms for default reasoning from conditional knowledge bases.

The literature contains several different proposals for default reasoning from conditional knowledge bases and extensive work on its desired properties. The core of these properties are the rationality postulates of System P proposed by Kraus et al. [19]. It turned out that these rationality postulates constitute a sound and complete axiom system for several classical model-theoretic entailment relations under uncertainty measures on worlds. In detail, they characterize classical model-theoretic entailment under preferential structures, infinitesimal probabilities, possibility measures, and world rankings. They also characterize an entailment relation based on conditional objects. A survey of the above relationships is given in [4].

Mainly to solve problems with irrelevant information, rational closure as a more adventurous entailment relation was proposed by Lehmann [23]. It is equivalent to entailment in System Z by Pearl [33], to the least specific possibility entailment by Benferhat et al. [3], and to a conditional (modal) logic-based entailment by Lamarre [22]. Finally, mainly to solve problems with property inheritance from classes to exceptional subclasses, further formalisms were proposed, in particular, lexicographic entailment by Lehmann [24] and Benferhat et al. [2] and conditional entailment by Geffner [15].

Indeed, such formalisms for default reasoning from conditional knowledge bases can be generalized to the probabilistic framework of conditional constraints [29,30] (see Section 5 for more details on these formalisms and some of their applications):

- In [29], I introduce probabilistic generalizations of Pearl's entailment in System Z and Lehmann's lexicographic entailment, which lie between model-theoretic and coherence-based probabilistic entailment. Roughly, the main difference between model-theoretic and coherence-based probabilistic entailment is that the former realizes an inheritance of logical knowledge, while the latter does not. Intuitively, the new formalisms now add a strategy for resolving inconsistencies to model-theoretic entailment, and a restricted form of inheritance of logical knowledge to entailment under coherence. This is why they are weaker than model-theoretic probabilistic entailment and stronger than coherence-based probabilistic entailment.

- In [30], I introduce similar probabilistic generalizations of Pearl's entailment in System Z, Lehmann's lexicographic entailment, and Geffner's conditional entailment. They, however, behave quite differently from the ones in [29]. Roughly, model-theoretic probabilistic entailment realizes an inheritance of logical knowledge, but no inheritance of purely probabilistic knowledge. The formalisms in [30] now add an inheritance of purely probabilistic knowledge and a strategy for resolving inconsistencies (due to the inheritance of logical and purely probabilistic knowledge) to entailment in model-theoretic probabilistic logic. This is why they are generally much stronger than entailment in model-theoretic probabilistic logic.

In the present paper, I define a general approach to nonmonotonic probabilistic reasoning, which subsumes the above two approaches [29] and [30] as special cases, and which also allows for nonmonotonic probabilistic reasoning between them. Roughly, the main idea behind this new approach is to add to model-theoretic probabilistic entailment (i) some inheritance of purely probabilistic knowledge that is controlled by a strength $\lambda \in [0, 1]$, and (ii) a mechanism for resolving inconsistencies due to the inheritance of logical and purely probabilistic knowledge. Based on this idea, I define a new probabilistic generalization of Lehmann's lexicographic entailment. Other formalisms for default reasoning from conditional knowledge bases can be extended in quite much the same way (such an extension of Pearl's entailment in System Z is included in [31]). The main contributions of this paper can be summarized as follows:

- I present a new probabilistic generalization of Lehmann's lexicographic entailment, which is parameterized through a value $\lambda \in [0, 1]$ that describes the strength of the inheritance of purely probabilistic knowledge. For $\lambda = 0$ (resp., $\lambda = 1$), it coincides with probabilistic lexicographic entailment introduced in [29] (resp., [30]).
- I show that probabilistic lexicographic entailment of strength λ has similar properties as its classical counterpart. In particular, it satisfies the rationality postulates of System P and the property of Rational Monotonicity.
- I also show that probabilistic lexicographic entailment of strength λ is a proper generalization of its classical counterpart. Furthermore, it is weaker than some notion of logical entailment in model-theoretic probabilistic logic, and under certain conditions it coincides with this notion of entailment.

Note that detailed proofs of all results are given in [31].

2   Preliminaries

In this section, I define probabilistic knowledge bases. I then recall the notions of satisfiability and logical entailment from model-theoretic probabilistic logic, and the notions of g-coherence and g-coherent entailment from probabilistic logic under coherence.

2.1   Probabilistic Knowledge Bases

I assume a set of *basic events* $\Phi = \{p_1, \ldots, p_n\}$ with $n \geq 1$. I use $\perp$ and $\top$ to denote *false* and *true*, respectively. I define *events* by induction as follows. Every element of $\Phi \cup \{\perp, \top\}$ is an event. If ϕ and ψ are events, then also $\neg\phi$ and $(\phi \wedge \psi)$. A *conditional event* is an expression of the form $\psi|\phi$ with events ψ and ϕ. A *conditional constraint* is an expression $(\psi|\phi)[l, u]$ with events ψ, ϕ, and real numbers $l, u \in [0, 1]$. I define *probabilistic formulas* by induction as follows. Every conditional constraint is a probabilistic formula. If F and G are probabilistic formulas, then also $\neg F$ and $(F \wedge G)$. I use $(F \vee G)$ and $(F \Leftarrow G)$ to abbreviate $\neg(\neg F \wedge \neg G)$ and $\neg(\neg F \wedge G)$, respectively, where F and G are either two events or two probabilistic formulas, and adopt the usual conventions to eliminate parentheses. A *logical constraint* is an event of the form $\psi \Leftarrow \phi$. A *probabilistic knowledge base* $KB = (L, P)$ consists of a finite set of logical constraints L and a finite set of conditional constraints P.

Example 2.1. The knowledge "eagles are birds", "birds have legs", and "birds fly with a probability of at least 0.95" can be expressed by the probabilistic knowledge base $KB = (L, P) = (\{bird \Leftarrow eagle\}, \{(legs|bird)[1, 1], (fly|bird)[0.95, 1]\})$. Note that in model-theoretic probabilistic logic, $\psi \Leftarrow \phi \in L$ means the same as $(\psi|\phi)[1, 1] \in P$, whereas in probabilistic logic under coherence and in probabilistic lexicographic entailment, $\psi \Leftarrow \phi \in L$ is strict, while $(\psi|\phi)[1, 1] \in P$ may have exceptions. $\square$

Example 2.2. The knowledge "ostriches are birds", "birds have wings with a probability between 0.65 and 0.75", "birds fly with a probability of at least 0.95", and "ostriches fly with a probability of at most 0.05" can be expressed by the probabilistic knowledge base $KB = (L, P)$, where $L = \{bird \Leftarrow ostrich\}$ and $P = \{(wings|bird)[0.65, 0.75], (fly|bird)[0.95, 1], (fly|ostrich)[0, 0.05]\}$. $\square$

A *world* I is a truth assignment to the basic events in Φ (that is, a mapping $I : \Phi \to \{$**true, false**$\}$), which is inductively extended to all events by $I(\bot) = $ **false**, $I(\top) = $ **true**, $I(\neg\phi) = $ **true** iff $I(\phi) = $ **false**, and $I((\phi\wedge\psi)) = $ **true** iff $I(\phi) = I(\psi) = $ **true**. I use $\mathcal{I}_\Phi$ to denote the set of all worlds for Φ. A world I *satisfies* an event ϕ, or I is a *model* of ϕ, denoted $I \models \phi$, iff $I(\phi) = $ **true**. I extend worlds I to conditional events $\psi|\phi$ by $I(\psi|\phi) = $ **true** iff $I \models \psi \wedge \phi$, $I(\psi|\phi) = $ **false** iff $I \models \neg\psi \wedge \phi$, and $I(\psi|\phi) = $ **indeterminate** iff $I \models \neg\phi$. A *probabilistic interpretation* Pr is a probability function on $\mathcal{I}_\Phi$ (that is, a mapping $Pr : \mathcal{I}_\Phi \to [0, 1]$ such that all $Pr(I)$ with $I \in \mathcal{I}_\Phi$ sum up to 1). The *probability* of an event ϕ in Pr, denoted $Pr(\phi)$, is the sum of all $Pr(I)$ such that $I \in \mathcal{I}_\Phi$ and $I \models \phi$. For events ϕ and ψ with $Pr(\phi) > 0$, I write $Pr(\psi|\phi)$ to abbreviate $Pr(\psi \wedge \phi) / Pr(\phi)$. The *truth* of logical constraints and probabilistic formulas F in a probabilistic interpretation Pr, denoted $Pr \models F$, is defined as follows:

- $Pr \models \psi \Leftarrow \phi$ iff $Pr(\psi \wedge \phi) = Pr(\phi)$;
- $Pr \models (\psi|\phi)[l, u]$ iff $Pr(\phi) = 0$ or $Pr(\psi|\phi) \in [l, u]$;
- $Pr \models \neg F$ iff not $Pr \models F$;
- $Pr \models (F \wedge G)$ iff $Pr \models F$ and $Pr \models G$.

I say Pr *satisfies* F, or Pr is a *model* of F, iff $Pr \models F$. Moreover, Pr *satisfies* a set of logical constraints and probabilistic formulas $\mathcal{F}$, or Pr is a *model* of $\mathcal{F}$, denoted $Pr \models \mathcal{F}$, iff Pr is a model of all $F \in \mathcal{F}$.

2.2 Model-Theoretic Probabilistic Logic

I now recall the model-theoretic notions of satisfiability and logical entailment.

A set of logical constraints and probabilistic formulas $\mathcal{F}$ is *satisfiable* iff a model of $\mathcal{F}$ exists. A conditional constraint $(\psi|\phi)[l, u]$ is a *logical consequence* of $\mathcal{F}$, denoted $\mathcal{F} \parallel= (\psi|\phi)[l, u]$, iff each model of $\mathcal{F}$ is also a model of $(\psi|\phi)[l, u]$. It is a *tight logical consequence* of $\mathcal{F}$, denoted $\mathcal{F} \parallel=_{tight} (\psi|\phi)[l, u]$, iff $l = \inf Pr(\psi|\phi)$ (resp., $u = \sup Pr(\psi|\phi)$) subject to all models Pr of $\mathcal{F}$ with $Pr(\phi) > 0$. Here, I define $l = 1$ and $u = 0$, when $\mathcal{F} \parallel= (\phi|\top)[0, 0]$. A probabilistic knowledge base $KB = (L, P)$ is *satisfiable* iff $L \cup P$ is satisfiable. A conditional constraint $(\psi|\phi)[l, u]$ is a *logical consequence* of KB, denoted $KB \parallel= (\psi|\phi)[l, u]$, iff $L \cup P \parallel= (\psi|\phi)[l, u]$. It is a *tight logical consequence* of KB, denoted $KB \parallel=_{tight} (\psi|\phi)[l, u]$, iff $L \cup P \parallel=_{tight} (\psi|\phi)[l, u]$.

Table 1 Tight intervals under logical and g-coherent entailment from KB in Example 2.1

Conditional Event	$\models_{tight}$	$\mathrel{\mid\!\sim}^{g}_{tight}$	Conditional Event	$\models_{tight}$	$\mathrel{\mid\!\sim}^{g}_{tight}$
$legs\mid bird$	$[1,1]$	$[1,1]$	$fly\mid bird$	$[0.95,1]$	$[0.95,1]$
$legs\mid eagle$	$[1,1]$	$[0,1]$	$fly\mid eagle$	$[0,1]$	$[0,1]$

Example 2.3. Let $KB = (L, P)$ be as in Example 2.1. In model-theoretic probabilistic logic, KB represents the *logical knowledge* "all eagles are birds" and "all birds have legs", and the *probabilistic knowledge* "birds fly with a probability of at least 0.95". It is not difficult to see that KB is satisfiable. Some tight logical consequences of KB are shown in Table 1, left sides. For example, $(fly\mid eagle)[0, 1]$ is a tight logical consequence of KB. Observe that the logical property of having legs is inherited from birds down to the subclass of eagles, while the purely probabilistic property of being able to fly with a probability of at least 0.95 is not inherited. □

2.3 Probabilistic Logic under Coherence

I now recall the notions of g-coherence and g-coherent entailment. I define them by using some characterizations through concepts from default reasoning [7].

A probabilistic interpretation Pr *verifies* a conditional constraint $(\psi\mid\phi)[l, u]$ iff $Pr(\phi) > 0$ and $Pr \models (\psi\mid\phi)[l, u]$. A set of conditional constraints P is *under* a set of logical constraints L *in conflict* with $(\psi\mid\phi)[l, u]$ iff no model of $L \cup P$ verifies $(\psi\mid\phi)[l, u]$. A *conditional constraint ranking* σ on a probabilistic knowledge base $KB = (L, P)$ maps each element of P to a nonnegative integer. It is *admissible* with KB iff every $P' \subseteq P$ that is under L in conflict with some $C \in P$ contains a conditional constraint C' such that $\sigma(C') < \sigma(C)$. A probabilistic knowledge base KB is *g-coherent* iff there exists a conditional constraint ranking on KB that is admissible with KB.

Let $KB = (L, P)$ be a g-coherent probabilistic knowledge base, and let $(\psi\mid\phi)[l, u]$ be a conditional constraint. Then, $(\psi\mid\phi)[l, u]$ is a *g-coherent consequence* of KB, denoted $KB \mathrel{\mid\!\sim}^{g} (\psi\mid\phi)[l, u]$, iff $(L, P \cup \{(\psi\mid\phi)[p, p]\})$ is not g-coherent for all $p \in [0, l) \cup (u, 1]$. It is a *tight g-coherent consequence* of KB, denoted $KB \mathrel{\mid\!\sim}^{g}_{tight} (\psi\mid\phi)[l, u]$, iff $l = \inf p$ (resp., $u = \sup p$) subject to all g-coherent $(L, P \cup \{(\psi\mid\phi)[p, p]\})$.

Example 2.4. Let $KB = (L, P)$ be as in Example 2.1. In probabilistic logic under coherence, KB represents the *logical knowledge* "all eagles are birds", the *default logical knowledge* "generally, birds have legs", and the *default probabilistic knowledge* "generally, birds fly with a probability of at least 0.95". It is not difficult to see that KB is g-coherent. Some tight g-coherent consequences of KB are shown in Table 1, right sides. Observe that under g-coherent entailment, neither the logical property of having legs nor the purely probabilistic one of being able to fly with a probability of at least 0.95 is inherited from the class of birds down to the subclass of eagles. □

3   Probabilistic Lexicographic Entailment of Strength λ

I now introduce a new probabilistic generalization of Lehmann's lexicographic entailment, called lex_{λ}-entailment, which is parameterized through a value $\lambda \in [0, 1]$ that describes the *strength* of the inheritance of purely probabilistic knowledge. I first describe the main ideas behind the new formalism, I then define the concept of λ-consistency for probabilistic knowledge bases, and I finally define the notion of lex_λ-entailment.

3.1 Key Ideas

The *inheritance of logical knowledge* along subclass relationships is the following property (for all events ψ, ϕ, ϕ^*, probabilistic knowledge bases KB, and $c \in \{0, 1\}$):

L-INH. If $KB \hspace{1pt}\|\!\sim (\psi|\phi)[c, c]$ and $\phi \Leftarrow \phi^*$ is valid, then $KB \hspace{1pt}\|\!\sim (\psi|\phi^*)[c, c]$.

The *inheritance of purely probabilistic knowledge* along subclass relationships is defined as follows (for all events ψ, ϕ, ϕ^*, probabilistic knowledge bases KB, and intervals $[l, u] \subseteq [0, 1]$ different from $[0, 0]$, $[1, 1]$, and $[1, 0]$):

P-INH. If $KB \hspace{1pt}\|\!\sim (\psi|\phi)[l, u]$ and $\phi \Leftarrow \phi^*$ is valid, then $KB \hspace{1pt}\|\!\sim (\psi|\phi^*)[l, u]$.

It is not difficult to verify that logical entailment satisfies (*L-INH*), but does not satisfy (*P-INH*), while g-coherent entailment satisfies neither (*L-INH*) nor (*P-INH*).

The basic idea behind the new probabilistic generalization of Lehmann's lexicographic entailment in this paper is that it adds to the notion of logical (resp., g-coherent) entailment (i) some inheritance of purely probabilistic (resp., logical and purely probabilistic) knowledge, where the inheritance of purely probabilistic knowledge depends on a strength $\lambda \in [0, 1]$, and (ii) a mechanism for resolving inconsistencies due to the inheritance of logical and purely probabilistic knowledge.

The strength $\lambda \in [0, 1]$ determines to which extent purely probabilistic knowledge is inherited from classes down to subclasses. In the extreme cases of $\lambda = 0$ and $\lambda = 1$, purely probabilistic knowledge is not inherited at all [29] and completely inherited [30], respectively, while for $0 < \lambda < 1$, given the interval $[l, u]$ for the property of a class, some interval $[r, s] \supseteq [l, u]$ is inherited down to all subclasses, where the tightness of $[r, s]$ depends on the strength λ (roughly, the higher is λ, the tighter is $[r, s]$).

3.2 λ-Consistency

I now introduce the notion of λ-consistency for probabilistic knowledge bases.

A probabilistic interpretation Pr λ-*verifies* a conditional constraint $(\psi|\phi)[l, u]$ iff Pr verifies $(\psi|\phi)[l, u]$ and $Pr(\phi) \geq \lambda$. A set of conditional constraints P λ-*tolerates* a conditional constraint C under a set of logical constraints L iff $L \cup P$ has a model that λ-verifies C. I say P is under L in λ-*conflict* with C iff no model of $L \cup P$ λ-verifies C. A conditional constraint ranking σ on a probabilistic knowledge base $KB = (L, P)$ is λ-*admissible* with KB iff every $P' \subseteq P$ that is under L in λ-conflict with some $C \in P$ contains some C' such that $\sigma(C') < \sigma(C)$.

I say KB is λ-*consistent* iff there exists a conditional constraint ranking σ on KB that is λ-admissible with KB. Note that the notion of 0-consistency coincides with the notion of g-coherence. The following theorem characterizes the λ-consistency of $KB = (L, P)$ through the existence of an ordered partition of P.

Theorem 3.1. *A probabilistic knowledge base* $KB = (L, P)$ *is* λ-*consistent iff there exists an ordered partition* $(P_0, \ldots, P_k)$ *of* P *such that every* P_i, $0 \le i \le k$, *is the set of all* $C \in \bigcup_{j=i}^{k} P_j$ *that are* λ-*tolerated under* L *by* $\bigcup_{j=i}^{k} P_j$.

I call this ordered partition $(P_0, \ldots, P_k)$ of P the z_λ-*partition* of $KB = (L, P)$. The following two examples show some z_λ-partitions.

Example 3.1. Consider the probabilistic knowledge base $KB = (L, P)$ given in Example 2.1. For every $\lambda \in [0, 1]$, the z_λ-partition of KB is given by $(P_0) = (P)$. $\square$

Example 3.2. Let $KB = (L, P)$ be as in Example 2.2. For all $\lambda \in [0, \frac{1}{19}]$, the z_λ-partition of $KB = (L, P)$ is $(P_0) = (P)$, as $KB \models_{tight} (ostrich|\top)[0, \frac{1}{19}]$. For all $\lambda \in (\frac{1}{19}, 1]$, it is $(P_0, P_1) = (\{(wings|bird)[0.65, 0.75], (fly|bird)[0.95, 1]\}, \{(fly|ostrich)[0, 0.05]\})$. $\square$

3.3 Probabilistic Lexicographic Entailment of Strength λ

I now define a probabilistic generalization of Lehmann's lexicographic entailment [24] of strength $\lambda \in [0, 1]$ for λ-consistent probabilistic knowledge bases $KB = (L, P)$.

I use the z_λ-partition $(P_0, \ldots, P_k)$ of KB to define a lexicographic preference relation on probabilistic interpretations as follows. For probabilistic interpretations Pr and Pr', I say Pr is lex_λ-*preferable* to Pr' iff some $i \in \{0, \ldots, k\}$ exists such that $|\{C \in P_i | Pr \models C\}| > |\{C \in P_i \mid Pr' \models C\}|$ and $|\{C \in P_j \mid Pr \models C\}| = |\{C \in P_j \mid Pr' \models C\}|$ for all $i < j \le k$. A model Pr of a set of logical constraints and probabilistic formulas $\mathcal{F}$ is a lex_λ-*minimal model* of $\mathcal{F}$ iff no model of $\mathcal{F}$ is lex_λ-preferable to Pr. I use the expression $\phi \succeq \lambda$ to abbreviate the probabilistic formula $\neg(\phi|\top)[0, 0] \wedge (\phi|\top)[\lambda, 1]$.

I now define the notion of lex_λ-*entailment* as follows. A conditional constraint $(\psi|\phi)[l, u]$ is a lex_λ-*consequence* of KB, denoted $KB \hspace{0.5em}\mid\hspace{-0.9em}\sim^{lex_\lambda} (\psi|\phi)[l,u]$, iff every lex_λ-minimal model of $L \cup \{\phi \succeq \lambda\}$ satisfies $(\psi|\phi)[l, u]$. It is a *tight* lex_λ-*consequence* of KB, denoted $KB \hspace{0.5em}\mid\hspace{-0.9em}\sim^{lex_\lambda}_{tight} (\psi|\phi)[l,u]$, iff l (resp., u) is the infimum (resp., supremum) of $Pr(\psi|\phi)$ subject to all lex_λ-minimal models Pr of $L \cup \{\phi \succeq \lambda\}$.

The following example shows some tight conclusions under lex_λ-entailment. Similar to its classical counterpart, lex_λ-entailment realizes some subclass inheritance, without showing the problem of *inheritance blocking*, that is, properties are also inherited to subclasses that are exceptional relative to other properties. Observe also that *logical* properties are completely inherited along subclass relationships, while the inheritance of *purely probabilistic* properties depends on the strength λ.

Example 3.3. Some tight intervals under lex_λ-entailment from $KB = (L, P)$ of Example 2.1 (resp., 2.2) are shown in Table 2 (resp., 3). For example, $[l, u]$ with $KB \hspace{0.5em}\mid\hspace{-0.9em}\sim^{lex_\lambda}_{tight} (fly|eagle)[l, u]$ is given by $L \cup P \cup \{(eagle|\top)[\lambda, 1]\} \models_{tight} (fly|eagle)[l, u]$. $\square$

4   Semantic Properties

In this section, I explore the semantic properties of lex_λ-entailment. I first study some general nonmonotonic properties. I then explore the relationship to logical entailment and to Lehmann's lexicographic entailment.

Table 2 Tight intervals under lex_λ-entailment from KB in Example 2.1

Conditional Event	$\lambda = 0$	$\lambda = 0.2$	$\lambda = 0.4$	$\lambda = 0.6$	$\lambda = 0.8$	$\lambda = 1$
$legs\,\vert\,bird$	$[1,1]$	$[1,1]$	$[1,1]$	$[1,1]$	$[1,1]$	$[1,1]$
$legs\,\vert\,eagle$	$[1,1]$	$[1,1]$	$[1,1]$	$[1,1]$	$[1,1]$	$[1,1]$
$fly\,\vert\,bird$	$[0.95,1]$	$[0.95,1]$	$[0.95,1]$	$[0.95,1]$	$[0.95,1]$	$[0.95,1]$
$fly\,\vert\,eagle$	$[0,1]$	$\mathbf{[0.75,1]}$	$\mathbf{[0.88,1]}$	$\mathbf{[0.92,1]}$	$\mathbf{[0.94,1]}$	$\mathbf{[0.95,1]}$

Table 3 Tight intervals under lex_λ-entailment from KB in Example 2.2

Conditional Event	$\lambda = 0$	$\lambda = 0.2$	$\lambda = 0.4$	$\lambda = 0.6$	$\lambda = 0.8$	$\lambda = 1$
$wings\,\vert\,bird$	$[0.65,0.75]$	$[0.65,0.75]$	$[0.65,0.75]$	$[0.65,0.75]$	$[0.65,0.75]$	$[0.65,0.75]$
$wings\,\vert\,ostrich$	$[0,1]$	$[0,1]$	$\mathbf{[0.13,1]}$	$\mathbf{[0.42,1]}$	$\mathbf{[0.56,0.94]}$	$\mathbf{[0.65,0.75]}$
$fly\,\vert\,bird$	$[0.95,1]$	$[0.95,1]$	$[0.95,1]$	$[0.95,1]$	$[0.95,1]$	$[0.95,1]$
$fly\,\vert\,ostrich$	$[0,0.05]$	$[0,0.05]$	$[0,0.05]$	$[0,0.05]$	$[0,0.05]$	$[0,0.05]$

I first consider the postulates *Right Weakening (RW)*, *Reflexivity (Ref)*, *Left Logical Equivalence (LLE)*, *Cut*, *Cautious Monotonicity (CM)*, and *Or* by Kraus et al. [19], which are commonly regarded as being particularly desirable for any reasonable notion of nonmonotonic entailment. The following result shows that lex_λ-entailment satisfies (probabilistic versions of) these postulates. Here, $KB \mathrel{\|\!\sim}^{lex_\lambda} (\phi|\varepsilon \vee \varepsilon')[l, u]$ denotes that $Pr \models (\phi|\varepsilon)[l, u] \vee (\phi|\varepsilon')[l, u]$ for all lex_λ-minimal models Pr of $L \cup \{\varepsilon \succeq \lambda \vee \varepsilon' \succeq \lambda\}$.

Theorem 4.1. *Let $KB = (L, P)$ be a λ-consistent probabilistic knowledge base, let $\varepsilon, \varepsilon', \phi, \psi$ be events, and let $l, l', u, u' \in [0,1]$. Then,*

RW. If $(\phi|\top)[l, u] \Rightarrow (\psi|\top)[l', u']$ is logically valid and $KB \mathrel{\|\!\sim}^{lex_\lambda} (\phi|\varepsilon)[l, u]$, then $KB \mathrel{\|\!\sim}^{lex_\lambda} (\psi|\varepsilon)[l', u']$.

Ref. $KB \mathrel{\|\!\sim}^{lex_\lambda} (\varepsilon|\varepsilon)[1,1]$.

LLE. If $\varepsilon \Leftrightarrow \varepsilon'$ is logically valid, then $KB \mathrel{\|\!\sim}^{lex_\lambda} (\phi|\varepsilon)[l, u]$ iff $KB \mathrel{\|\!\sim}^{lex_\lambda} (\phi|\varepsilon')[l, u]$.

Cut. If $KB \mathrel{\|\!\sim}^{lex_\lambda} (\varepsilon|\varepsilon')[1,1]$ and $KB \mathrel{\|\!\sim}^{lex_\lambda} (\phi|\varepsilon\wedge\varepsilon')[l, u]$, then $KB \mathrel{\|\!\sim}^{lex_\lambda} (\phi|\varepsilon')[l, u]$.

CM. If $KB \mathrel{\|\!\sim}^{lex_\lambda} (\varepsilon|\varepsilon')[1,1]$ and $KB \mathrel{\|\!\sim}^{lex_\lambda} (\phi|\varepsilon')[l, u]$, then $KB \mathrel{\|\!\sim}^{lex_\lambda} (\phi|\varepsilon\wedge\varepsilon')[l, u]$.

Or. If $KB \mathrel{\|\!\sim}^{lex_\lambda} (\phi|\varepsilon)[l, u]$ and $KB \mathrel{\|\!\sim}^{lex_\lambda} (\phi|\varepsilon')[l, u]$, then $KB \mathrel{\|\!\sim}^{lex_\lambda} (\phi|\varepsilon\vee\varepsilon')[l, u]$.

Another desirable property is *Rational Monotonicity (RM)* [19], which describes a restricted monotony and allows to ignore some irrelevant knowledge. The next theorem shows that lex_λ-entailment satisfies (a weak form of) *RM*. Here, $KB \mathrel{\|\!\not\sim}^{lex_\lambda} \neg(\varepsilon'|\varepsilon)[1,1]$ denotes that $Pr \models (\varepsilon'|\varepsilon)[1,1]$ for some lex_λ-minimal model Pr of $L \cup \{\varepsilon \succeq \lambda\}$.

Theorem 4.2. *Let $KB = (L, P)$ be a λ-consistent probabilistic knowledge base, and let $\varepsilon, \varepsilon', \psi$ be events. Then,*

RM. If $KB \mathrel{\|\!\sim}^{lex_\lambda} (\psi|\varepsilon)[1,1]$ and $KB \mathrel{\|\!\not\sim}^{lex_\lambda} \neg(\varepsilon'|\varepsilon)[1,1]$, then $KB \mathrel{\|\!\sim}^{lex_\lambda} (\psi|\varepsilon\wedge\varepsilon')[1,1]$.

I next explore the relationship to logical entailment with conditional constraints. The following theorem shows that lex_λ-entailment of $(\psi|\phi)[l, u]$ from $KB = (L, P)$ is weaker than logical entailment of $(\psi|\phi)[l, u]$ from $L \cup P \cup \{\phi \succeq \lambda\}$.

Theorem 4.3. *Let $KB = (L, P)$ be a λ-consistent probabilistic knowledge base, and let $(\psi|\phi)[l, u]$ be a conditional constraint. Then, $KB \parallel\!\sim^{lex_\lambda}(\psi|\phi)[l, u]$ implies $L \cup P \cup \{\phi \succeq \lambda\} \models (\psi|\phi)[l, u].$*

In general, the converse does not hold. But, in the special case when $L \cup P \cup \{\phi \succeq \lambda\}$ is satisfiable, lex_λ-entailment of $(\psi|\phi)[l, u]$ from $KB = (L, P)$ coincides with logical entailment of $(\psi|\phi)[l, u]$ from $L \cup P \cup \{\phi \succeq \lambda\}$, as the following theorem shows.

Theorem 4.4. *Let $KB = (L, P)$ be a λ-consistent probabilistic knowledge base, and let $(\psi|\phi)[l, u]$ be a conditional constraint such that $L \cup P \cup \{\phi \succeq \lambda\}$ is satisfiable. Then, $KB \parallel\!\sim^{lex_\lambda}(\psi|\phi)[l, u]$ iff $L \cup P \cup \{\phi \succeq \lambda\} \models (\psi|\phi)[l, u].$*

I finally study the relationship to Lehmann's lexicographic entailment. The following result shows that the new notion of lex_λ-entailment for λ-consistent probabilistic knowledge bases generalizes Lehmann's lexicographic entailment for ε-consistent conditional knowledge bases, denoted $\parallel\!\sim^{lex}$ below.

Theorem 4.5. *Let $KB = (L, P)$ be a λ-consistent probabilistic knowledge base, where $P = \{(\psi_i|\phi_i)[1, 1] \mid i \in \{1, \ldots, n\}\}$, and let $(\beta|\alpha)[1, 1]$ be a conditional constraint. Then, $KB \parallel\!\sim^{lex_\lambda}(\beta|\alpha)[1, 1]$ iff $(L, \{\psi_i \leftarrow \phi_i \mid i \in \{1, \ldots, n\}\}) \parallel\!\sim^{lex} \beta \leftarrow \alpha.$*

5 Special Cases

The notion of lex_λ-entailment of strength $\lambda = 0$ (resp., $\lambda = 1$) coincides with the notion of probabilistic lexicographic entailment introduced in [29] (resp., [30]). I now briefly review these formalisms along with some of their applications.

5.1 Probabilistic Lexicographic Entailment of Strength   0

The notion of lex_0-entailment adds to logical (resp., g-coherent) entailment a strategy for resolving inconsistencies due to the inheritance of logical knowledge (resp., a restricted form of inheritance of logical knowledge). This is why lex_0-entailment is weaker than logical entailment and stronger than g-coherent entailment. Hence, lex_0-entailment is a refinement of both logical and g-coherent entailment. It can be used in place of logical entailment, when we want to resolve inconsistencies related to conditioning on zero events. Here, it is especially well-suited as it coincides with logical entailment as long as we condition on non-zero events [29]. Moreover, lex_0-entailment can be used in place of g-coherent entailment, when we also want to have a restricted form of inheritance of logical knowledge. The following example illustrates the use of lex_0-entailment to resolve inconsistencies related to conditioning on zero events.

Example 5.1. Consider the probabilistic knowledge base $KB = (L, P)$ given by $L = \{bird \Leftarrow penguin\}$ and $P = \{(legs|bird)[1, 1], (fly|bird)[1, 1], (fly|penguin)[0, 0.05]\}$. It is not difficult to see that KB is satisfiable, g-coherent, and 0-consistent. Moreover, it holds that $KB \models_{tight} (legs|penguin)[1, 0]$ and $KB \models_{tight} (fly|penguin)[1, 0]$.

Here, the empty interval is due to the fact that the logical property of being able to fly is inherited from birds to penguins, and is incompatible there with penguins being able to fly with a probability of at most 0.05. That is, there exists no model Pr of $L \cup P$ such that $Pr(penguin) > 0$, and thus we are conditioning on the zero event $penguin$.

Hence, logical entailment does not provide the desired tight conclusions about penguins from KB: Rather than $(legs|penguin)[1,0]$ and $(fly|penguin)[1,0]$, we would like to conclude $(legs|penguin)[1,1]$ and $(fly|penguin)[0,0.05]$, respectively. These are exactly the tight conclusions about penguins obtained under lex_0-entailment:

$$KB \parallel\!\sim^{lex_0}_{tight} (legs|penguin)[1,1], \ KB \parallel\!\sim^{lex_0}_{tight} (fly|penguin)[0,0.05].$$

Note that the tight intervals under g-coherent entailment from KB are as follows:

$$KB \parallel\!\sim^{g}_{tight} (legs|penguin)[0,1], \ KB \parallel\!\sim^{g}_{tight} (fly|penguin)[0,0.05].$$

Hence, also g-coherent entailment resolves inconsistencies related to conditioning on zero events. However, g-coherent entailment is strictly weaker than lex_0-entailment, and thus does not always produce the desired tight conclusions. □

5.2 Probabilistic Lexicographic Entailment of Strength   1

The notion of lex_1-entailment adds to logical entailment (i) some inheritance of purely probabilistic knowledge, and (ii) a strategy for resolving inconsistencies due to the inheritance of logical and purely probabilistic knowledge. For this reason, lex_1-entailment is generally much stronger than logical entailment. Thus, it is especially useful where logical entailment is too weak, for example, in probabilistic logic programming [28,27] and probabilistic ontology reasoning in the semantic web [18]. Other applications are deriving degrees of belief from statistical knowledge and degrees of belief, handling inconsistencies in probabilistic knowledge bases, and probabilistic belief revision.

In particular, in reasoning from statistical knowledge and degrees of belief, lex_1-entailment shows a similar behavior as reference-class reasoning [35,20,21,34] in a number of uncontroversial examples. But it also avoids many drawbacks of reference-class reasoning [30]: It can handle complex scenarios and even purely probabilistic subjective knowledge as input. Moreover, conclusions are drawn in a global way from all the available knowledge as a whole. The following example illustrates the use of lex_1-entailment for reasoning from statistical knowledge and degrees of belief.

Example 5.2. Suppose that we have the statistical knowledge "all penguins are birds", "between 90% and 95% of all birds fly", "at most 5% of all penguins fly", and "at least 95% of all yellow objects are easy to see". Moreover, assume that we believe "Sam is a yellow penguin". What do we then conclude about Sam's property of being easy to see? Under reference-class reasoning, which is a machinery for dealing with such statistical knowledge and degrees of belief, we conclude "Sam is easy to see with a probability of at least 0.95". This is also what we obtain using the notion of lex_1-entailment:

More precisely, the above statistical knowledge can be represented by the probabilistic knowledge base $KB = (L, P) = (\{bird \Leftarrow penguin\}, \{(fly|bird)[0.9, 0.95],$ $(fly|penguin)[0, 0.05], (easy\_to\_see|yellow)[0.95, 1]\})$. It is then not difficult to verify that KB is 1-consistent, and that under lex_1-entailment from KB, we obtain the tight conclusion $(easy\_to\_see|yellow \wedge penguin)[0.95, 1]$, as desired.

Note that KB is also satisfiable and g-coherent. However, under both logical and g-coherent entailment from KB, we obtain the tight conclusion $(easy\_to\_see|yellow \wedge penguin)[0, 1]$, rather than the above desired one. $\square$

6   Summary and Outlook

I have presented the notion of lex_λ-entailment, which is a probabilistic generalization of Lehmann's lexicographic entailment that is parameterized through a value $\lambda \in [0, 1]$, which describes the strength of the inheritance of purely probabilistic knowledge. In the special case of $\lambda = 0$ (resp., $\lambda = 1$), the new probabilistic formalism coincides with probabilistic lexicographic entailment in [29] (resp., [30]). I have shown that lex_λ-entailment has similar properties as its classical counterpart. In particular, it satisfies the rationality postulates of System P and the property of Rational Monotonicity. Furthermore, lex_λ-entailment has a proper embedding of its classical counterpart.

An interesting topic of future research is to develop algorithms for probabilistic reasoning under lex_λ-entailment and to analyze its computational complexity (e.g., along the lines of [29,30]). Another exciting topic of future research is to develop and explore further formalisms for nonmonotonic probabilistic reasoning.

Acknowledgments. This work has been supported by a Marie Curie Individual Fellowship of the European Community programme "Human Potential" under contract number HPMF-CT-2001-001286 (Disclaimer: The author is solely responsible for information communicated and the European Commission is not responsible for any views or results expressed) and by the Austrian Science Fund under project N Z29-INF.

References

1. S. Amarger, D. Dubois, and H. Prade. Constraint propagation with imprecise conditional probabilities. In *Proceedings UAI-91*, pp. 26–34. Morgan Kaufmann, 1991.
2. S. Benferhat, C. Cayrol, D. Dubois, J. Lang, and H. Prade. Inconsistency management and prioritized syntax-based entailment. In *Proceedings IJCAI-93*, pp. 640–645, 1993.
3. S. Benferhat, D. Dubois, and H. Prade. Representing default rules in possibilistic logic. In *Proceedings KR-92*, pp. 673–684. Morgan Kaufmann, 1992.
4. S. Benferhat, D. Dubois, and H. Prade. Nonmonotonic reasoning, conditional objects and possibility theory. *Artif. Intell.*, 92(1-2):259–276, 1997.
5. V. Biazzo and A. Gilio. A generalization of the fundamental theorem of de Finetti for imprecise conditional probability assessments. *Int. J. Approx. Reasoning*, 24:251–272, 2000.
6. V. Biazzo, A. Gilio, T. Lukasiewicz, and G. Sanfilippo. Probabilistic logic under coherence: Complexity and algorithms. In *Proceedings ISIPTA-01*, pp. 51–61, 2001.
7. V. Biazzo, A. Gilio, T. Lukasiewicz, and G. Sanfilippo. Probabilistic logic under coherence, model-theoretic probabilistic logic, and default reasoning in System P. *Journal of Applied Non-Classical Logics*, 12(2):189–213, 2002.
8. G. Boole. *An Investigation of the Laws of Thought, on which are Founded the Mathematical Theories of Logic and Probabilities*. Walton and Maberley, London, 1854. (Reprint: Dover Publications, New York, 1958).

9. D. Dubois and H. Prade. Possibilistic logic, preferential models, non-monotonicity and related issues. In *Proceedings IJCAI-91*, pp. 419–424. Morgan Kaufmann, 1991.
10. D. Dubois and H. Prade. Conditional objects as nonmonotonic consequence relationships. *IEEE Trans. Syst. Man Cybern.*, 24(12):1724–1740, 1994.
11. T. Eiter and T. Lukasiewicz. Default reasoning from conditional knowledge bases: Complexity and tractable cases. *Artif. Intell.*, 124(2):169–241, 2000.
12. R. Fagin, J. Y. Halpern, and N. Megiddo. A logic for reasoning about probabilities. *Inf. Comput.*, 87:78–128, 1990.
13. N. Friedman and J. Y. Halpern. Plausibility measures and default reasoning. *J. ACM*, 48(4):648–685, 2001.
14. A. M. Frisch and P. Haddawy. Anytime deduction for probabilistic logic. *Artif. Intell.*, 69:93–122, 1994.
15. H. Geffner. *Default Reasoning: Causal and Conditional Theories*. MIT Press, 1992.
16. A. Gilio. Probabilistic consistency of conditional probability bounds. In *Advances in Intelligent Computing*, LNCS 945, pp. 200–209. Springer, 1995.
17. A. Gilio. Probabilistic reasoning under coherence in System P. *Ann. Math. Artif. Intell.*, 34(1-3):5–34, 2002.
18. R. Giugno and T. Lukasiewicz. P-$\mathcal{SHOQ}$(**D**): A probabilistic extension of $\mathcal{SHOQ}$(**D**) for probabilistic ontologies in the semantic web. In *Proceedings JELIA-02*, LNCS 2424, pp. 86–97. Springer, 2002.
19. S. Kraus, D. Lehmann, and M. Magidor. Nonmonotonic reasoning, preferential models and cumulative logics. *Artif. Intell.*, 14(1):167–207, 1990.
20. H. E. Kyburg, Jr. *The Logical Foundations of Statistical Inference*. D. Reidel, 1974.
21. H. E. Kyburg, Jr. The reference class. *Philos. Sci.*, 50:374–397, 1983.
22. P. Lamarre. A promenade from monotonicity to non-monotonicity following a theorem prover. In *Proceedings KR-92*, pp. 572–580. Morgan Kaufmann, 1992.
23. D. Lehmann. What does a conditional knowledge base entail? In *Proceedings KR-89*, pp. 212–222. Morgan Kaufmann, 1989.
24. D. Lehmann. Another perspective on default reasoning. *Ann. Math. Artif. Intell.*, 15(1):61–82, 1995.
25. T. Lukasiewicz. Local probabilistic deduction from taxonomic and probabilistic knowledge-bases over conjunctive events. *Int. J. Approx. Reasoning*, 21(1):23–61, 1999.
26. T. Lukasiewicz. Probabilistic deduction with conditional constraints over basic events. *J. Artif. Intell. Res.*, 10:199–241, 1999.
27. T. Lukasiewicz. Probabilistic logic programming under inheritance with overriding. In *Proceedings UAI-01*, pp. 329–336. Morgan Kaufmann, 2001.
28. T. Lukasiewicz. Probabilistic logic programming with conditional constraints. *ACM Trans. on Computational Logic (TOCL)*, 2(3):289–339, 2001.
29. T. Lukasiewicz. Nonmonotonic probabilistic logics between model-theoretic probabilistic logic and probabilistic logic under coherence. In *Proceedings NMR-02*, pp. 265–274, 2002.
30. T. Lukasiewicz. Probabilistic default reasoning with conditional constraints. *Ann. Math. Artif. Intell.*, 34(1-3):35–88, 2002.
31. T. Lukasiewicz. Nonmonotonic probabilistic reasoning under variable-strength inheritance with overriding. Technical Report INFSYS RR-1843-03-02, Institut für Informationssysteme, TU Wien, 2003.
32. N. J. Nilsson. Probabilistic logic. *Artif. Intell.*, 28(1):71–88, 1986.
33. J. Pearl. System Z: A natural ordering of defaults with tractable applications to default reasoning. In *Proceedings TARK-90*, pp. 121–135. Morgan Kaufmann, 1990.
34. J. L. Pollock. *Nomic Probabilities and the Foundations of Induction*. Oxford University Press, Oxford, 1990.
35. H. Reichenbach. *Theory of Probability*. University of California Press, Berkeley, CA, 1949.

ABEL: An Interactive Tool for Probabilistic Argumentative Reasoning

Rolf Haenni[1] and Norbert Lehmann[2]

[1] University of Konstanz, Center for Junior Research Fellows
D-78457 Konstanz, Germany
`rolf.haenni@uni-konstanz.de`
[2] University of Fribourg, Department of Informatics
CH-1700 Fribourg, Switzerland
`norbert.lehmann@unifr.ch`

Abstract. Most formal approaches to argumentative reasoning under uncertainty focus on the analysis of qualitative aspects. An exception is the framework of probabilistic argumentation systems. Its philosophy is to include both qualitative and quantitative aspects through a simple way of combining logic and probability theory. Probabilities are used to weigh arguments for and against particular hypotheses. ABEL is a language that allows to describe probabilistic argumentation systems and corresponding queries about hypotheses. It then returns arguments and counter-arguments with corresponding numerical weights.

1 Introduction

In the last couple of years, *argumentation* has gained growing recognition as a new and promising research direction in artificial intelligence. As a consequence of this increasing interest, different authors have investigated argumentation and its applications in various domains. By looking at today's literature on this subject, one realizes that argumentation is understood in fairly different ways. The common feature of most approaches is their restriction to particular types of logic. As a consequence, they are all limited in the way they combine arguments for and against a particular hypothesis.

The approach we present in this paper is known as *probabilistic argumentation systems* (PAS) [9]. The idea of the PAS framework goes back to the concept of *assumption-based truth maintenance systems* (ATMS) [6]. It is also closely related to *abduction* [4,11]. The idea is to understand argumentation as a deductive tool that helps to judge *hypotheses*, that is open questions about the unknown or future world, in the light of the given uncertain and partial background knowledge.

The principal PAS problem is to derive *arguments* in favor and *counter-arguments* against the hypothesis of interest. There are efficient anytime algorithms in which the search is focussed on the most relevant arguments [7,8]. The strength of the arguments is then measured by underlying probabilities. This leads to *degree of support* and *degree of possibility*, which corresponds to *belief*

T.D. Nielsen and N.L. Zhang (Eds.): ECSQARU 2003, LNAI 2711, pp. 588–593, 2003.

and *plausibility*, respectively, in the Dempster-Shafer theory of evidence [10,13, 14]. Such a quantitative judgement is often required to decide whether a hypothesis can be accepted, rejected, or whether the available knowledge does not permit to decide.

A system called ABEL [2,3] is an implementation of probabilistic argumentation systems (check out `http://www2-iiuf.unifr.ch/tcs/ABEL`). It includes an appropriate modeling and query language, as well as corresponding inference mechanisms. ABEL is an interactive system in which queries are answered immediately. Problems from a broad spectrum of application domains show that the ABEL system is very general and powerful [1]. It has an open architecture that permits the later inclusion of further or more advanced deduction techniques.

The aim of this paper is to provide a short introduction to probabilistic argumentation and ABEL. Our hope is to increase the recognition of PAS as a legitimate formal model and ABEL as powerful tool for reasoning under uncertainty.

2 Probabilistic Argumentation Systems

The basic ingredients for probabilistic argumentation systems (PAS) are *propositional logic* and *probability theory*. More formally, we require two disjoint sets $P = \{p_1, \ldots, p_n\}$ and $A = \{a_1, \ldots, a_m\}$ of propositional symbols. The elements of P are called *propositions* and the elements of A *assumptions*. With $\mathcal{L}_{A \cup P}$ we denote the corresponding propositional language that consist of elements of $A \cup P$ only. Furthermore, we require a propositional sentence $\xi \in \mathcal{L}_{A \cup P}$ that expresses the qualitative part of the given knowledge. The formula ξ is called *knowledge base*. Finally, a set $\Pi = \{p(a_i) : a_i \in A\}$ of independent probabilities is required to express the quantitative knowledge. Note how the connection between propositional logic and probability theory is established through the assumptions. A quadruple (P, A, ξ, Π) is called *probabilistic argumentation system* (PAS).

Example 1. Let $P = \{X, Y, Z\}$ and $A = \{a_1, a_2, a_3, a_4, a_5\}$ be the sets of propositions and assumptions, respectively. Furthermore, suppose that

$$\Pi = \{p(a_1) = 0.2,\ p(a_2) = 0.4,\ p(a_3) = 0.8,\ p(a_4) = 0.3,\ p(a_5) = 0.3\}$$

are the probabilities of the assumptions and

$$\xi = (a_1 \rightarrow X) \wedge ((a_2 \vee \neg a_3) \rightarrow Y) \wedge ((X \wedge Y) \rightarrow Z) \wedge (\neg a_4 \rightarrow Z)$$
$$\wedge ((a_5 \wedge Y) \rightarrow \neg Z)$$

the given knowledge base. This forms a probabilistic argumentation system (P, A, ξ, Π). Note that the knowledge base ξ is a conjunction that can be represented more easily as a conjunctive set

$$\Sigma = \{a_1 \rightarrow X,\ (a_2 \vee \neg a_3) \rightarrow Y,\ (X \wedge Y) \rightarrow Z,\ \neg a_4 \rightarrow Z,\ (a_5 \wedge Y) \rightarrow \neg Z\}$$

of five individual formulas.

The question now is how to use a PAS for the purpose of analyzing and answering queries about *hypotheses*. A hypothesis h is usually expressed by a simple expression that includes symbols of $A \cup P$. To be most general, we consider arbitrary propositional formulas $h \in \mathcal{L}_{A \cup P}$.

The approach we promote is to construct *arguments* and *counter-arguments* based on the set of assumptions A and to weigh them with the aid of the given probabilities Π. An argument can be regarded as a defeasible proof. In other words, arguments are combinations of true or false assumptions that permit to infer the truth of the hypothesis h from the given knowledge base. Every argument provides thus a sufficient reason that proves the hypothesis in the light of the available knowledge. And it finally contributes to the possibility of believing or accepting the hypothesis. In other words, arguments *support* and counter-arguments *defeat* the hypothesis h. Note that counter-arguments can be regarded as arguments in favor of the negated hypothesis $\neg h$ and vice versa. The sets of all arguments and counter-arguments are denoted by $sp(h, \xi)$ and $sp(\neg h, \xi)$, respectively. For corresponding formal definitions and descriptions of appropriate inference techniques we refer to the literature [8,7,9].

Example 2. Consider the same PAS as in Example 1 and let $h = Z$ be the hypothesis of interest. There are four (minimal) arguments, namely:

$a_1 \wedge a_2 \wedge \neg a_5$	because a_1 implies X, a_2 implies Y, X and Y imply Z, and $\neg a_5$ disallows the conflict $Z \wedge \neg Z$
$a_1 \wedge \neg a_3 \wedge \neg a_5$	because a_1 implies X, $\neg a_3$ implies Y, X and Y imply Z, and $\neg a_5$ disallows the conflict $Z \wedge \neg Z$
$\neg a_4 \wedge \neg a_5$	because $\neg a_4$ implies Z and $\neg a_5$ disallows the conflict $Z \wedge \neg Z$
$\neg a_2 \wedge a_3 \wedge \neg a_4$	because $\neg a_4$ implies Z and $\neg a_2 \wedge a_3$ disallows the conflict $Z \wedge \neg Z$

Similarly, there are two counter-arguments, namely:

$\neg a_1 \wedge a_2 \wedge a_4 \wedge a_5$	because a_2 implies Y, $a_5 \wedge Y$ implies $\neg Z$, and $\neg a_1 \wedge a_4$ disallows the conflict $Z \wedge \neg Z$
$\neg a_1 \wedge \neg a_3 \wedge a_4 \wedge a_5$	because $\neg a_3$ implies Y, $a_5 \wedge Y$ implies $\neg Z$, and $\neg a_1 \wedge a_4$ disallows the conflict $Z \wedge \neg Z$

Note that $a_1 \wedge a_2 \wedge a_5$, $a_1 \wedge \neg a_3 \wedge a_5$, and $\neg a_4 \wedge a_5$ are not compatible with the knowledge base ξ. Such incompatible terms are called *conflicts*.

A quantitative judgement of the situation is obtained by considering the probabilities that the arguments and counter-arguments are valid. The *credibility* of a hypothesis is measured by the probabilities that it is supported or defeated by at least one argument or one counter-argument, respectively. Conflicts are handled through conditioning. The resulting *degree of support* $dsp(h, \xi)$ and *degree of possibility* $dps(h, \xi) = 1 - dsp(h, \xi)$ correspond to *belief* and *plausibility*, respectively, in the Dempster-Shafer theory of evidence [13,14].

Example 3. Consider the arguments, counter-arguments, and conflicts shown in the previous example. The probabilities that at least one argument, counter-argument, or conflict holds correspond to the probabilities of the disjunctive normal forms (DNF)

$$\Phi_Z = (a_1 \wedge a_2 \wedge \neg a_5) \vee (a_1 \wedge \neg a_3 \wedge \neg a_5) \vee (\neg a_4 \wedge \neg a_5) \vee (\neg a_2 \wedge a_3 \wedge \neg a_4),$$

$$\Phi_{\neg Z} = (\neg a_1 \wedge a_2 \wedge a_4 \wedge a_5) \vee (\neg a_1 \wedge \neg a_3 \wedge a_4 \wedge a_5),$$

$$\Phi_\perp = (a_1 \wedge a_2 \wedge a_5) \vee (a_1 \wedge \neg a_3 \wedge a_5) \vee (\neg a_4 \wedge a_5),$$

respectively. Using the probabilities $p(a_i)$ as specified in Example 1, we get $p(\Phi_Z) = 0.612$, $p(\Phi_{\neg Z}) = 0.037$, and $p(\Phi_\perp) = 0.119$. For information about how to compute probabilities of DNF's we refer to the corresponding literature, in particular to Darwiche's d-DNNF compiler [5]. Finally, we get the following degree of support and degree of possibility, respectively:

$$dsp(Z, \xi) = \frac{p(\Phi_Z)}{1 - p(\Phi_\perp)} = 0.695, \qquad dps(Z, \xi) = 1 - \frac{p(\Phi_{\neg Z})}{1 - p(\Phi_\perp)} = 0.958.$$

These results tell us that the hypothesis Z is supported by a relatively high degree. At the same time, there are only few reasons against Z which leads to a degree of possibility close to 1.

3   ABEL

ABEL stands for *"Assumption-Based Evidential Language"*. Working with ABEL typically involves two sequential steps. First, the given information is *modeled* using the command `tell`. This command is used to define the two sets A and P, the probabilities Π, and the knowledge base ξ. Second, queries about the knowledge base are expressed using the command `ask`.

The ABEL language is based on three other computer languages: (1) from *Common Lisp* [16] it adopts *prefix notation*; (2) from *Pulcinella* [12] it takes the idea of the commands `tell`, `ask`, and `empty`; and (3) from a former ABEL prototype it inherits the concept of *modules* and the syntax of the queries. Consider former publications on ABEL for a detailed language specification [3,1]. The ABEL interface is interactive and behaves like a Common Lisp environment. The current version is based on the platform independent XEmacs environment [15].

An ABEL model usually starts with the declaration of the sets P, A, and Π. The distinction between the elements of P and A is made by using two distinct commands `var` and `ass`. Look below how it's done for the example introduced in the previous section. Assumptions with different probabilities must be defined on different lines. The keyword `binary` means that only two values are allowed (*true* and *false*). Note that ABEL also supports discrete variables with more than two values [1,2,3] as well as integers and reals (with some restrictions) [3].

```
(tell
  (var X Y Z binary)
```

```
(ass a1 binary 0.2)
(ass a2 binary 0.4)
(ass a3 binary 0.8)
(ass a4 a5 binary 0.3))
```

The knowledge base ξ is then described using a LISP-like prefixed language. If ξ is given as a set Σ of statements ξ_i, then every individual statement is written on a separate line. Again, consider the example of the previous section and look how it's done.

```
(tell
  (-> a1 X)
  (-> (or a2 (not a3)) Y)
  (-> (and X Y) Z)
  (-> (not a4) Z)
  (-> (and a5 Y) (not Z)))
```

Statements can also be distributed among different **tell**-commands. Furthermore, it is also possible to mix variable declarations and statements about the knowledge base. The only rule is that every variable must be declared before it is first used.

ABEL supports different types of queries. In the context of argumentative reasoning, the most important commands are **sp** (support), **dsp** (degree of support), and **dps** (degree of possibility). Let Z be the hypothesis of interest as in Example 2. Observe how **sp** can be used to compute arguments and counterarguments for Z (the percentages indicated left to the arguments show the relative weights of their probabilities).

```
? (ask (sp Z))
  53.3% : (NOT A4) (NOT A5)
  24.0% : A1 A2 (NOT A5)
  18.7% : A1 (NOT A3) (NOT A5)
   4.0% : A3 (NOT A2) (NOT A4)

? (ask (sp (not Z)))
  56.3% : A2 A4 A5 (NOT A1)
  43.7% : A4 A5 (NOT A1) (NOT A3)
```

This corresponds to the results shown in Example 2. Note that $\neg a_4$ alone is not an argument for Z, because $\neg a_4$ together with a_5 produces a conflict. To get a quantitative evaluation of the hypothesis, we can compute corresponding degrees of support and possibility.

```
? (ask (dsp Z))
  0.695

? (ask (dps Z))
  0.958
```

These results correspond to the ones shown in Example 3.

Acknowledgements. Research supported by (1) Alexander von Humboldt Foundation, (2) German Federal Ministry of Education and Research, (3) German Program for the Investment in the Future, (4) Swiss National Science Foundation

References

1. B. Anrig, R. Bissig, R. Haenni, J. Kohlas, and N. Lehmann. Probabilistic argumentation systems: Introduction to assumption-based modeling with ABEL. Technical Report 99-1, Institute of Informatics, University of Fribourg, 1999.
2. B. Anrig, R. Haenni, J. Kohlas, and N. Lehmann. Assumption-based modeling using ABEL. In D. Gabbay, R. Kruse, A. Nonnengart, and H. J. Ohlbach, editors, *Proceedings of the First International Joint Conference on Qualitative and Quantitative Practical Reasoning ECSQARU/FAPR'97*, LNCS 1146, pages 171–182. Springer, 1997.
3. B. Anrig, R. Haenni, and N. Lehmann. ABEL – a new language for assumption-based evidential reasoning under uncertainty. Technical Report 97-01, Institute of Informatics, University of Fribourg, 1997.
4. D. Berzati, R. Haenni, and J. Kohlas. Probabilistic argumentation systems and abduction. *Annals of Mathematics and Artificial Intelligence*, 34(1–3):177–195, 2002.
5. A. Darwiche. A compiler for deterministic, decomposable negation normal form. In *Proceedings of the 18th National Conference on Artificial Intelligence*, pages 627–634. AAAI Press, 2002.
6. J. de Kleer. An assumption-based TMS. *Artificial Intelligence*, 28:127–162, 1986.
7. R. Haenni. Cost-bounded argumentation. *International Journal of Approximate Reasoning*, 26(2):101–127, 2001.
8. R. Haenni. A query-driven anytime algorithm for argumentative and abductive reasoning. In D. Bustard, W. Liu, and R. Sterrit, editors, *Soft-Ware 2002, 1st International Conference on Computing in an Imperfect World*, LNCS 2311, pages 114–127. Springer-Verlag, 2002.
9. R. Haenni, J. Kohlas, and N. Lehmann. Probabilistic argumentation systems. In J. Kohlas and S. Moral, editors, *Handbook of Defeasible Reasoning and Uncertainty Management Systems, Volume 5: Algorithms for Uncertainty and Defeasible Reasoning*, pages 221–288. Kluwer, Dordrecht, 2000.
10. R. Haenni and N. Lehmann. Probabilistic argumentation systems: a new perspective on Dempster-Shafer theory. *International Journal of Intelligent Systems (Special Issue: the Dempster-Shafer Theory of Evidence)*, 18(1):93–106, 2003.
11. D. Poole. Probabilistic Horn abduction and Bayesian networks. *Artificial Intelligence*, 64:81–129, 1993.
12. A. Saffiotti and E. Umkehrer. PULCINELLA: A general tool for propagating uncertainty in valuation networks. Technical report, IRIDIA, Université de Bruxelles, 1991.
13. G. Shafer. *The Mathematical Theory of Evidence*. Princeton University Press, 1976.
14. Ph. Smets and R. Kennes. The transferable belief model. *Artificial Intelligence*, 66:191–234, 1994.
15. R. Stallman and B. Wing. *XEmacs User's Manual*, 1994.
16. G.L. Steele. *Common Lisp – the Language*. Digital Press, 1990.

The Hugin Tool for Learning Bayesian Networks

Anders L. Madsen, Michael Lang, Uffe B. Kjærulff, and Frank Jensen

Hugin Expert A/S
Niels Jernes Vej 10
DK-9220 Aalborg Ø
Denmark
{Anders.L.Madsen,Michael.Lang,Uffe.Kjaerulff,Frank.Jensen}@hugin.com

Abstract. In this paper, we describe the Hugin Tool as an efficient tool for knowledge discovery through construction of Bayesian networks by fusion of data and domain expert knowledge. The Hugin Tool supports structural learning, parameter estimation, and adaptation of parameters in Bayesian networks. The performance of the Hugin Tool is illustrated using real-world Bayesian networks, commonly used examples from the literature, and randomly generated Bayesian networks.

1   Introduction

Probabilistic graphical models such as Bayesian networks [9,3] are efficient models for (automated) reasoning under uncertainty. A Bayesian network can be used as an efficient tool for knowledge representation and inference. Unfortunately, the construction of a Bayesian network can be a quite labor intensive task to perform. For this reason, automated construction of Bayesian networks have in recent years received a lot of attention. This attention has focused on the automated construction of models from a combination of data and domain expert knowledge. In this paper, we consider the model construction task as a task of fusing observational data and domain expert knowledge. Through automated construction, Bayesian networks can be used as efficient tools for knowledge discovery and data mining [5].

The Hugin Tool [1,6] is a general purpose tool for probabilistic graphical models such as Bayesian networks and influence diagrams. In this paper, we describe the knowledge discovery functionality of the Hugin Tool related to (automated) construction of Bayesian networks through learning. That is, we describe the capabilities of the Hugin Tool for learning the structure and parameters of a Bayesian network. In [6] a recent survey of the general functionality of the Hugin Tool is given. The present paper extends and details the description of the learning functionality of the Hugin Tool given in [6].

2   Preliminaries and Notation

A Bayesian network $\mathcal{N} = (G = (V, E), \mathcal{P})$ consists of an acyclic, directed graph (DAG) G and a set of probability distributions $\mathcal{P}$. Each node $X \in V$ represents a

T.D. Nielsen and N.L. Zhang (Eds.): ECSQARU 2003, LNAI 2711, pp. 594–605, 2003.

unique random variable. (We use the terms "node" and "variable" interchangeably and consider only discrete variables.) For each variable $X \in V$ there is a conditional probability distribution $P(X \mid pa(X)) \in \mathcal{P}$.

A Bayesian network $\mathcal{N} = (G, \mathcal{P})$ is an efficient representation of a joint probability distribution $P(V)$ over V when $G = (V, E)$ is not dense. $P(V)$ factorizes according to the structure of G as:

$$P(V) = \prod_{X \in V} P(X \mid pa(X)).$$

We denote variables by uppercase letters $X, Y, \ldots$, sets of variables by uppercase letters $S, S_{XY}, \ldots$, and states of variables by lowercase letters $x, y, \ldots$. Through the parameters, it is possible to specify unconstrained probabilistic dependence relations between a node and its parents.

The graph G of $\mathcal{N}$ induces a set of (conditional) dependence and independence relations (CIDRs) $\mathcal{M}_G$, which can be read off G using the d-separation criteria [4]. The relation $X \perp_P Y \mid S$ states conditional independence between X and Y given S under the probability distribution P whereas $X \perp_G Y \mid S$ states conditional independence between X and Y given S in the DAG G (i.e. d-separation). When no confusion is possible, subscripts are omitted. The faithfulness assumption [13] (a.k.a. stability [10]) says that the distribution P over V induced by (G, Θ) satisfies no independence relations beyond those implied by the structure of G.

A DAG represents a set of CIDRs and two DAGs may represent the same set of CIDRs. Two DAGs representing the same set of CIDRs are equivalent. A DAG is an acyclic, directed graph whereas a PDAG is an acyclic, partially directed graph, i.e. an acyclic graph with some edges undirected (a.k.a. a pattern [10]). A PDAG can be used to represent the equivalence class of a DAG. The equivalence class of a DAG G is the set of DAGs with the same set of d-separation relations as G. Two DAGs G_1 and G_2 are equivalent if they have the same skeleton and the same set of colliders (i.e. $X \to Y \leftarrow Z$-structures), see e.g. [10].

Example 2.1 [Chest Clinic]
Dyspnoea(D) may be due to tuberculosis(T), lung cancer(L), or bronchitis(B), or none of them, or more than one of them. A recent visit to Asia(A) increases the chances of tuberculosis, while smoking(S) is known to be a risk factor for both lung cancer and bronchitis. The result of a single chest X-ray(X) does not discriminate between lung cancer and tuberculosis, as neither does the presence or absence of dyspnoea, see e.g.[3].

The qualitative knowledge of this diagnostic problem can be captured by the DAG shown in Fig. 1(a) with a mediating variable E representing the disjunction of tuberculosis and lung cancer.

3   Learning a Bayesian Network

In the remainder of this paper, we will assume that P_0 is a DAG faithful probability distribution with underlying DAG G_0. We consider learning a Bayesian

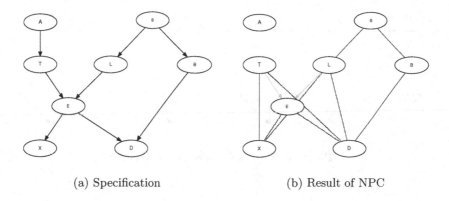

(a) Specification   (b) Result of NPC

Fig. 1. The Chest Clinic example

network as the task of identifying a DAG structure G and a set of corresponding parameters Θ from a sample of data cases $D = \{c_1, \ldots, c_N\}$ drawn at random from P_0 and possibly some domain expert background knowledge.

3.1 Structural Learning

Structural learning is supported through a constraint-based approach [16,15, 13]. In the constraint-based approach, the graph G of a Bayesian network $\mathcal{N}$ is considered as an encoding of a set of CIDRs $\mathcal{M}$. Structural learning is then the task of identifying a DAG structure from a set of CIDRs derived from the data by statistical tests.

Two algorithms for structural learning are supported. The PC algorithm [12, 13] (which is similar to the IC algorithm [15,10]) and its extension, the NPC algorithm [14]. The main steps of the PC algorithm are:

1. Test for (conditional) independence between each pair of variables.
2. Identify the skeleton of the graph induced by the derived CIDRs.
3. Identify colliders.
4. Identify derived directions.

The PC algorithm produces a PDAG. In step 1, the hypothesis is that X and Y are independent given S_{XY}. This hypothesis is tested by statistical tests using conditioning sets S_{XY} of size 0, 1, 2, 3. If $X \perp Y \mid S_{XY}$ is found to be satisfied with some significance level α, the search for independence between X and Y is terminated.

Various improvements of the straightforward incremental testing scheme have been implemented. These improvements are related to maintaining an undirected graph describing the current set of neighbors of each node and only performing independence tests conditional on subsets of the neighbors of X and Y. The order in which we try out the possible conditioning sets of a fixed size is according to how likely they are to cause independence for the edge under consideration. We

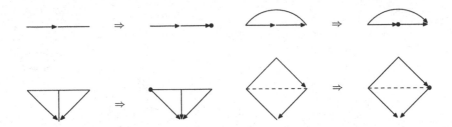

Fig. 2. Four rules for orientation of edges

use the heuristic rule that the variables of the conditioning set should be strongly correlated with both endpoints of the edge being tested. The neighbor graph is updated after each independence test accepting the hypothesis.

Due to the nature of the testing scheme, the conditioning set S_{XY} for an identified independence relation $X \perp Y \mid S_{XY}$ is minimal in the sense that no proper subset of S_{XY} and no set of cardinality less than the cardinality of S_{XY} produce independence. An undirected edge is added between each pair of variables X, Y whenever no conditional independence relation has been found between X and Y. This produces the skeleton of the graph.

Once the skeleton has been identified, colliders are identified. If X and Y are neighbors, Z and Y are neighbors, X and Z are not neighbors, and $Y \notin S_{XZ}$ for any S_{XZ} satisfying $X \perp Z \mid S_{XZ}$, then a collider is created at Y.

Starting with any PDAG G, a maximally directed PDAG can be obtained following four necessary [15] and sufficient [8] rules, see Fig. 2. That is, by repeated application of these four rules all edges common to the equivalence class of G are identified. The fourth rule is unnecessary, if the orientation of the initial PDAG is limited to colliders (i.e. no background knowledge). The four rules are necessary and sufficient for achieving maximal orientation (up to equivalence) of the PDAG returned by the PC algorithm. The first rule follows from the fact that no collider was identified, the remaining rules ensure that no directed cycle is created.

Correctness of the PC algorithm has been proved under the assumption of infinite data sets. In real-life, data sets are finite. When dealing with finite data sets, the faithfulness assumption is often violated. Hence, when the derived set of CIDRs is induced by statistical tests on finite data sets, we cannot in general expect that there exists a DAG (or PDAG) which represents all CIDRs. Often too many conditional independence relations are derived due to the limited data set. This suggests to represent all conditional dependence relations, but not all conditional independence relations in the induced DAGs. Applying the principle of Occam's Razor, we will choose the simplest model among equally good models.

As mentioned above, the NPC algorithm is an extension of the PC algorithm. The new feature of the NPC learning algorithm is the introduction of the notion of a *Necessary Path Condition* [14]. Informally, the necessary path condition says that in order for two variables X and Y to be independent (in a DAG faithful data set) conditional on a set S and no subset $S' \subset S$, there must exist a path between X and every $Z \in S$ (not crossing Y) and between Y and every $Z \in S$ (not crossing X). Otherwise, the inclusion of each Z in S is unexplained. Thus, in order for an independence relation to be valid, a number of edges are required to be present in the graph.

An edge (X, Y) is an uncertain edge, if the absence of (X, Y) depends on the presence of an edge (X', Y'), and vice versa. A maximal set of interdependent uncertain edges is an ambiguous region. An uncertain edge indicates inconsistency in the set of independence relations derived by the statistical tests.

In order to increase reliability and stability of the NPC algorithm, the iteration step for a fixed size of the conditioning set is completed even if an independence statement is found. Thus, multiple independence relations may be found for a pair of variables. If one of these independence relations satisfy the necessary path condition, then it is accepted.

Prior to the testing phase, background knowledge in the form of constraints on the structure of the DAG can be specified. It is possible to specify the presence and absence of edges, the orientation of edges, and a combination. At the moment, user specified constraints are not tested. In practice, this has produced some unwanted behavior of the edge orientation algorithm.

Example 3.1 [Structural learning in Chest Clinic]
Figure 1(b) shows the PDAG generated by the NPC algorithm applied on a random sample of $10,000$ cases drawn from the Chest Clinic network with a significance level of $\alpha = 0.05$.

The sets of edges $\{(T, X), (E, X), (L, X)\}$ and $\{(T, D), (E, D), (L, D)\}$ are the two ambiguous regions of Fig. 1(b). The two ambiguous regions are due to the deterministic relation between E and L, T (i.e. $E = L \vee T$). This produces, for instance, $\{(X \perp E \mid T, L), (X \perp T \mid E), (X \perp L \mid E)\}$, which is impossible according to the necessary path condition. The simplest resolution is to include the edge (E, X). Notice that some certain edges are directed and some are undirected.

3.2   Parameter Estimation

The task of parameter estimation is to estimate the values of the parameters Θ corresponding to a given DAG structure G. Parameter estimation is supported through the EM algorithm [7]. The EM algorithm is well-suited for calculating maximum likelihood and maximum a posteriori estimates in the case of missing data.

Let $\mathcal{N} = (G, \mathcal{P})$ be a Bayesian network with parameters Θ such that $\theta_{ijk} = P(X_i = k \mid \mathrm{pa}(X_i) = j)$ for each i, j, k. Following [7] the EM algorithm is based on computing the expected value of the log-likelihood function:

$$Q(\Theta^* \mid \Theta) = \mathbb{E}_\Theta \{\log P(X \mid \Theta^*) \mid D\},$$

where P is the density function for X, and D is the observed data $D = g(X)$. Given an initial value of the parameters Θ, the E-step is to compute the current expected value of Q with respect to Θ while the subsequent M-step is to maximize Q in Θ^*. These two steps are alternated iteratively until a stopping criterion is satisfied. In the case of missing data, the log-likelihood function is a linear function in the sufficient marginals [7]. The log-likelihood function $l(\Theta \mid D)$ of the parameters Θ given the data D and DAG G is:

$$l(\Theta \mid D) = \sum_{i=1}^{N} \log P(c_i \mid \Theta).$$

In the case of Bayesian networks, the E-step of the EM algorithm is to compute expected counts for each family $\mathrm{fa}(X_i)$ and parent $\mathrm{pa}(X_i)$ configuration of each node X_i under Θ:

$$n^*(Y) = \mathbb{E}_\Theta \{n(Y) \mid D\},$$

where Y is either $\mathrm{pa}(X_i) = j$ or $X_i = k, \mathrm{pa}(X_i) = j$. The M-step computes new estimates of θ_{ijk}^* from the expected counts under θ_{ijk}:

$$\theta_{ijk}^* = \frac{n^*(X_i = k, \mathrm{pa}(X_i) = j)}{n^*(\mathrm{pa}(X_i) = j)}.$$

The E-step and M-step are iterated until convergence of $l(\Theta)$ (or until a limit on the number of iterations is reached). In the Hugin Tool convergence is achieved when the difference between the log-likelihoods of two consecutive iterations is less than or equal to the numerical value of a log-likelihood threshold times the log-likelihood. Alternatively, the user can specify an upper limit on the number of iterations to ensure that the procedure terminates.

When both data and domain expert knowledge is available, these two sources of knowledge can be fused. In [11] the notion of experience is introduced. Experience is the quantitative knowledge related to a probability distribution based on quantitative expert knowledge. Expert knowledge on the parameters is specified as Dirichlet distributions. For each variable X_i, the distribution $P(X_i \mid \mathrm{pa}(X_i)) = \{p_{ijk}\}$ and the experience counts $\alpha_{i1}, \ldots, \alpha_{i \mid \mathrm{pa}(X_i) \mid}$ associated with X_i are used to specify the prior expert knowledge. Hence, the experience table of a variable X_i indicates the experience related to the child distribution for each configuration of the parents. In the case of expert knowledge, the E-step does not change whereas the M-step becomes:

$$\theta_{ijk}^* = \frac{n^*(X_i = k, \mathrm{pa}(X) = j) + p_{ijk}\alpha_{ij}}{n^*(\mathrm{pa}(X) = j) + \alpha_{ij}}.$$

The quality of the model is expressed in the value of $l(\Theta \mid D)$ computed after each iteration. It should be noticed that $l(\Theta \mid D)$ as a quality measure does not incorporate the complexity of the model. For comparison of models with different complexity other measures such as BIC or AIC should be used.

The experience counts for the prior beliefs in the conditional probability distribution of variable X_i given its parents $\mathrm{pa}(X_i)$ are specified in a separate table including one experience count for each configuration of $\text{pa}(X_i)$. After the termination of the EM algorithm the expected counts are stored as the experience counts.

Example 3.2 [Parameter estimation in Chest Clinic]
Assume that the qualitative knowledge of the Chest Clinic example is as shown in Fig. 1 and that a database $D = \{c_1, \dots, c_N\}$ with $N = 10,000$ is available. From the qualitative knowledge, we know $E = L \vee T$. This is specified in $P(E \mid L, T)$ and no experience table is allocated to E in order to avoid estimation of this table from the data whereas all other variables have an experience consisting of zeros indicating no expert knowledge on the distributions.

The EM algorithm will produce a maximum likelihood estimate of the parameters of the model under the constraint that $P(E \mid L, T)$ encodes disjunction. If we had expert knowledge on $P(S)$, for instance, we would specify this in $P(S)$ and encode the second order uncertainty in the experience table of S.

3.3   Sequential Updating

Sequential updating or adaptation [11,3] is the task of sequentially updating the conditional probability distributions of a Bayesian network when the structure and an initial specification of the conditional probability distributions are given in advance. In sequential learning, experience is extended to include both quantitative expert knowledge and past cases (e.g. from EM learning). Thus, the result of EM learning could be used as the input for sequential learning.

Let X_i be a variable with n states, then the prior belief in the parameter vector $\theta_{ij} = (\theta_{ij1}, \dots, \theta_{ijn})$, i.e. the conditional probability distribution of a variable X_i given its parents $\text{pa}(X_i) = j$, is specified as an n-dimensional Dirichlet distribution $\mathcal{D}(\alpha_{ij1}, \dots, \alpha_{ijn})$. This distribution is represented using a single experience count α_{ij} (equivalent sample size) and the initial content of $P(X_i \mid \text{pa}(X_i) = j)$. The experience count α_{ijk} for a particular state k of X_i given $\text{pa}(X_i) = j$ is $\alpha_{ijk} = \alpha_{ij} p_{ijk}$.

After a complete observation on $(X_i = k, \text{pa}(X_i) = j)$, the posterior belief in the distribution is updated as $\alpha_{ijk}^* = \alpha_{ijk} + 1$ and $\alpha_{ijl}^* = \alpha_{ijl}$ for $l \neq k$. After an incomplete observation, the posterior belief in θ_{ij} is a Dirichlet mixture, which is approximated by a single Dirichlet distribution having the same means and sum of variances as the mixture. The approximation is used in order to avoid the combinatorial explosion, which would otherwise occur when subsequent incomplete observations are made. The updated mean and variance are computed as:

$$m_{ijk}^* = \frac{\alpha_{ijk} + p_{ijk} + m_{ijk}(1 - p_{ijk})}{\alpha_{ij} + 1},$$

$$v_{ijk}^* = \frac{m_{ijk}(1 - m_{ijk})}{\alpha_{ij} + 1}.$$

The updated experience count is computed from the mean and variance.

This process is referred to as retrieval of experience. Dissemination of experience is the process of calculating prior conditional probability distributions for the variables in the Bayesian network given the experience, and it proceeds by setting the value of each parameter equal to the mean of the corresponding updated Dirichlet distribution, i.e. $\theta_{ijk} = m_{ijk}^*$.

In order to reduce the influence of the past and possibly outdated information, an optional feature of fading is provided. Fading proceeds by reducing the experience count before the retrieval of experience takes place. The experience count α_{ij} is faded by a factor of $0 < \lambda_{ij} \leq 1$ typically close to 1 according to $p_{ij} = P(\text{pa}(X_i) = j)$ such that $\alpha_{ij}^* = \alpha_{ij}((1 - p_{ij}) + \lambda_{ij}p_{ij})$. Notice, that experience counts corresponding to parent configurations, which are inconsistent with the evidence are unchanged. The fading factors of a variable X_i are specified in a separate table including one fading factor for each configuration of $\text{pa}(X_i)$.

Example 3.3 [Adaptation in Chest Clinic]
Assume we have evidence $\epsilon = \{S = n, A = y, D = y\}$ on a patient, i.e. a non-smoking patient with dyspnoea who has recently been to Asia. The evidence is entered and propagated followed by an adaptation of parameters. Table 1 shows the experience counts for L, B, and S before (i.e. after EM learning using $10,000$ randomly generated cases) and after the adaptation with fading factor of 0.999 for each distribution. Notice, that since S is an observed variable without parents, the experience count α_S for $P(S)$ will converge to $\frac{1}{\lambda} = 1001$ if $S = n$ is observed multiple times.

Table 1. Experience counts for B, L, and S before and after adaptation

	α_S	$\alpha_{L\mid S=no}$	$\alpha_{L\mid S=yes}$	$\alpha_{B\mid S=no}$	$\alpha_{B\mid S=yes}$
Before	$10,000$	4970.88	5029.12	4970.88	5029.12
After	$9,001$	4472.71	5029.12	4473.73	5029.12

4 Learning Wizard

The learning functionality of the Hugin Tool is supported through a Learning Wizard. A full learning cycle, as performed by the Learning Wizard consists of three main steps: Data acquisition, structural learning, and parameter estimation. Each of these consists of a number of sub-steps, which guide the user in the process of learning the Bayesian network from data and possibly expert knowledge. The user has the option of performing only one of the steps, but in both cases, the data acquisition step is required.

4.1 Data Acquisition

The data acquisition step serves two purposes: Read data from a data source and preprocess the data. In the first step, the user can read in data from various data sources, including data bases and data files. In the second step, the user can preprocess the data, e.g. discretize a variable. It is also possible for the user to use his own preprocessor, if the existing preprocessor does not suffice.

4.2 Structural Learning and Parameter Estimation

The structural learning step contains two sub-steps: Structural learning and data analysis. In the structural learning phase, the user can choose from two algorithms for performing the learning (PC and NPC). Common for these algorithms are, that the user can control the result to some extent by specifying a significance-level parameter and by adding structural constraints on the structure of the DAG before the learning takes place. These structural constraints provide a way for the user to force known dependences/independences onto the learning algorithm. As it can be a tiresome task to specify these constraints for complex networks, the wizard facilitates the saving and loading of network information, including constraints, node positions, node labels, etc.

If the user chooses NPC for the learning algorithm, he will also have the possibility of resolving ambiguous regions or unresolved directions found during the learning process, see e.g. Fig. 1. In the data analysis phase, the strength of both the marginal dependences and the found data dependences can be examined and the complexity of the learned network is indicated.

The parameter estimation phase gives the user the possibility of specifying the initial value of the parameters and the parameters for the EM-algorithm. The initial distribution is determined by any prior possibilities and experience counts specified by the user. To examine if the algorithm may have found a local maximum, it is possible to randomize the prior probabilities, so that the initial distribution can be different for subsequent runs.

5 Performance Evaluation

In the performance evaluation we have used the ALARM network [2], which has become a standard benchmark for structural learning. The ALARM network consists of 37 variables and 46 edges. Each variable has between two and four states with an average of 1.2 parents of each variable.

The PDAG shown in Fig. 3, which is the result of NPC learning on a sample of 10,000 cases generated from the ALARM [2] network with a significance level $\alpha = 0.01$, contains three ambiguous regions. The three ambiguous regions will be resolved by selecting the *correct* edges ((ArtCO2,Catechol), (VentLung,KinkedTube), and (LVFailure,LVEDVolume)) and adjacent edges are directed correctly. A few edges cannot be directed based on the data alone, a wrong collider is present at Intubation, no other edge is directed incorrectly, no

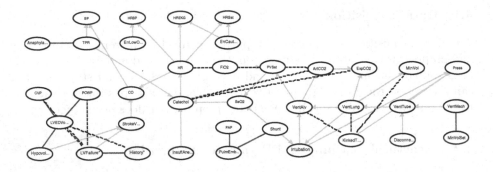

Fig. 3. NPC learning on a sample from ALARM with $\alpha = 0.01$

extra edges are present, and one edge (MinVol,Intubation) is missing. The result of applying the PC algorithm to the same set of data produced a DAG with two incorrect colliders, the two edges (TPR,Anaphylaxis) and (LVFailure,History) missing, and a few incorrect directions on edges. At the moment, the PC algorithm generates a DAG structure where some edges have been given direction at random. Using the NPC algorithm with $\alpha = 0.05$ produce no missing edges, but an additional collider at Intubation.

To evaluate the performance of the PC and NPC algorithms as a function of the significance level α we have performed tests with values of α equal to 0.001, 0.01, 0.05, and 0.1. The results are shown in Table 2. The tests have been performed using samples generated from the ALARM network.

The table shows the number of edges found including neighbors with the number of incorrect edges found in parentheses, the number of edges with correct orientation, the time to perform the learning in milliseconds for both algorithms. Furthermore, for the NPC algorithm the number of ambiguous regions and the number of uncertain edges in each region with the number of missing edges which are represented as an uncertain edge in parentheses. The values are average values over 25 samples of 10, 000 cases with 5% missing values (MCAR).

Table 2. Results from using different values of α

Algorithm	α	Edges	Direction	Time (ms)	Regions	Uncertain edges
PC	0.001	45.25(0.5)	44.75	419		
PC	0.01	45.5(0.25)	42.5	426		
PC	0.05	44.25(0)	41.75	415		
PC	0.1	45.25(0.25)	44	434		
NPC	0.001	43.75(0)	39	4, 015	1.5	5(1.25)
NPC	0.01	44(0.25)	34.5	4, 152	2	7(2)
NPC	0.05	43(0)	36.25	3, 805	2.25	9.25(2.75)
NPC	0.1	44.25(0)	38.75	4, 125	1	4(1)

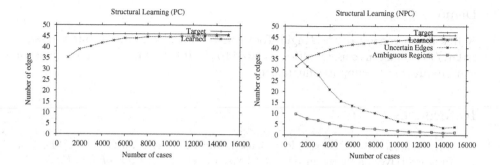

Fig. 4. Results of structural learning as a function of N

Table 3. Average run-time in seconds as a function of number of nodes

	25	50	75	100	150	200
PC	0.2	0.8	2	5	16	29
NPC	2	11	30	71	204	330

The results show that the average run-time of the PC algorithm is lower than that of the NPC algorithm. The PC algorithm is faster since fever tests are performed and since there is no notion of ambiguous regions requiring additional computations. The PC algorithm is able to direct more edges then the NPC algorithm, but some of these are directed at random in order to obtain a DAG.

Some of the differences between the NPC and PC algorithm, which seems to be shortcomings of the NPC algorithm can be remedied by improving the implementation. For instance, the principle of Occam's Razor has not been applied to the ambiguous regions to reduce the number of uncertain edges in each region. On the ALARM network, this led to ambiguous regions containing a single edge, which is present in the ALARM network.

The performances of the PC and NPC algorithms on large networks have been evaluated using randomly generated networks. For a fix size in terms of the number of variables, 10 networks with random topology (zero to five parents) and distribution have been generated. Each variable has from two to five states. The results are shown in Table 3. The time performance tests have been performed using 10,000 cases with 5% missing cases (MCAR) drawn at random from the distribution of the network.

All tests have been performed on a HP Omnibook xe4500 with a 1700 MHz Pentium 4 processor and 256MB of RAM running Linux Redhat 8.

Demo

A free demo-version of the Hugin Tool can be downloaded from our web-site: http://www.hugin.com. Questions related to the functionality of the Hugin Tool can be directed to support@hugin.com.

References

1. S.K. Andersen, K.G. Olesen, F.V. Jensen, and F. Jensen. HUGIN — a Shell for Building Bayesian Belief Universes for Expert Systems. In *Proc. of the 11th IJCAI*, pages 1080–1085, 1989.
2. I.A. Beinlich, H.J. Suermondt, R.M. Chavez, and G.F. Cooper. The ALARM monitoring system: A case study with two probabilistic inference techniques for belief networks. In *Proc. of the Second European Conference on Artificial Intelligence in Medicine*, pages 247–256, 1989.
3. R.G. Cowell, A.P. Dawid, S.L. Lauritzen, and D.J. Spiegelhalter. *Probabilistic Networks and Expert Systems*. Springer-Verlag, 1999.
4. D. Geiger, T. Verma, and J. Pearl. Identifying independence in Bayesian networks. *Networks*, 20(5):507–534, 1990. Special Issue on Influence Diagrams.
5. D. Heckerman. A tutorial on learning Bayesian networks. In *Learning in Graphical Models*, 1999.
6. F. Jensen, U.B. Kjærulff, M. Lang, and A.L. Madsen. HUGIN - The Tool for Bayesian Networks and Influence Diagrams. In *First European Workshop on Probabilistic Graphical Models*, pages 212–221, 2002.
7. S.L. Lauritzen. The EM algorithm for graphical association models with missing data. *Computational Statistics & Analysis*, 19:191–201, 1995.
8. C. Meek. Causal inference and causal explanation with background knowledge. In *Proc. of the 11th UAI*, pages 403–410, 1995.
9. J. Pearl. *Probabilistic Reasoning in Intelligence Systems*. Series in Representation and Reasoning. Morgan Kaufmann Publishers, 1988.
10. J. Pearl. *Causality. Models, Reasoning, and Inference*. Cambridge University Press, 2000.
11. D. Spiegelhalter and S.L. Lauritzen. Sequential updating of conditional probabilities on directed graphical structures. *Networks*, 20:579–605, 1990.
12. P. Spirtes and C. Glymour. An algorithm for fast recovery of sparse causal graphs. *Social Science Computing Review*, 9(1):62–72, 1991.
13. P. Spirtes, C. Glymour, and R. Scheines. *Causation, Prediction, and Search*. Adaptive Computation and Machine Learning. MIT Press, Cambridge, Massachusetts, second edition, 2000.
14. H. Steck and V. Tresp. Bayesian belief networks for data mining. Proc. 2nd Workshop "Data Mining und Data Warehousing als Grundlage moderner entscheidungsunterstuetzender Systeme", 1999.
15. T. Verma and J. Pearl. An Algorithm for Deciding if a Set of Observed Independencies Has a Causal Explanation. In *Proc. of the 8th UAI*, pages 323–330, 1992.
16. N. Wermuth and S.L. Lauritzen. Graphical and recursive models for contingency tables. *Biometrika*, 70:537–552, 1983.

Author Index